LITERATURE and OURSELVES

A Thematic Introduction for Readers and Writers

GLORIA HENDERSON
Gordon College

WILLIAM DAY
Gordon College

SANDRA WALLER
DeKalb College

HarperCollinsCollegePublishers

Acquisitions Editor: Lisa Moore
Developmental Editor: Randee Falk
Project Coordination, Text and Cover Design: A-R Editions, Inc.
Cover Illustration: *Clown* 1929 by Paul Klee. Oil on canvas,
    26⅜ × 19⅝ in. Private collection, St. Louis.
Photo Researcher: Leslie Coopersmith
Production: Jeffrey Taub
Compositor: A-R Editions, Inc.
Printer and Binder: Courier Companies, Inc.
Cover Printer: The Lehigh Press, Inc.

Literature and Ourselves: A Thematic Introduction for Readers and Writers

Library of Congress Cataloging-in-Publication Data

Henderson, Gloria, 1936–
    Literature and ourselves : a thematic introduction for readers and writers / Gloria Henderson, William Day, Sandra Waller.
        p. cm.
    Includes bibliographical references and index.
    ISBN 0–06–501538–X (student edition)
    ISBN 0–06–501938–5 (instructor's edition)
    1. Literature—Collections. I. Day, William, 1944–
II. Waller, Sandra. III. Title.
PN6014.H455 1993
808.8--dc20   93–28199
                                                                              CIP

93 94 95 96 9 8 7 6 5 4 3 2 1

BRIEF CONTENTS

DETAILED CONTENTS

INTRODUCTION

LITERATURE   1

ESSAYS   4

FICTION   8

POETRY   14

HUMAN VULNERABILITY

ESSAYS   408

FREEDOM AND RESPONSIBILITY

QUEST

PREFACE

Literature and Ourselves treats literature as a continually expanding commentary on people's infinitely varied lives, a commentary intimately related to the lives of the students who read it. The book has been designed to enable an instructor to use it in both introduction to literature and composition courses. *Literature and Ourselves* opens with an introduction that does the following:

- gives an overview of text-, author-, and reader-oriented approaches to literature
- discusses the elements of all four genres
- provides guidance on writing about literature and the research paper (including MLA documentation guidelines)

Themes were chosen to engage students in exploration of their own lives through literature. Each thematic section includes literature from all four genres—essays, fiction, poetry, and drama—and balances traditional with contemporary selections. We have made a special effort to include selections from women and people of color. Casebooks on selected authors provide a context for writing short research papers about literature from each genre and build toward the full-length research paper for instructors who cover the research paper in their second-semester composition courses. Additional writing suggestions for each section further emphasize the link between reading and writing about literature. A glossary defines all literary terms mentioned in both the introductions and the questions.

The six thematic sections are arranged so that they progress outward from the self to concerns beyond the self. Since they also move from the concrete to the abstract, they become progressively more challenging. The sections are designed to form a coherent whole whose selections constitute a rich and varied commentary on the theme, and each section begins with a brief introduction. Within thematic sections, selections are ordered by genre; within genres, they are ordered chronologically. An instructor may choose to concentrate on one or two themes or assign the entire book in a semester-long course in introduction to literature or across a two-semester composition course.

We think we have packed an extraordinary variety of works into a relatively small anthology. The traditional works allow teachers to assign what they are familiar and comfortable with, and the new works allow them to share with their students the joy of discovery. The selections also represent a variety of cultures, including works by Third World writers, several of whom (among them the African writers Wole Soyinka, Chinua Achebe, and Bessie Head) write in English, and a larger percentage of selections by women and ethnic minorities than are available elsewhere. Our text contains an unusual number and variety of questions for discussion and suggestions for writing. Questions follow every work, and suggestions for writing follow most with some works having as many as six or seven of each. This feature evolved as we worked on the text and as we came to see that, at least in our departments, of all the pedagogical aids in textbooks, teachers use the questions most. The questions and suggestions encourage students to think critically not only about literature but also about their own experiences. Our approach, then, is inductive, encouraging students to learn and develop their own ideas as they read.

Unlike many freshman literature anthologies, which emphasize text over author and reader, our book includes many author-oriented and reader-oriented questions as well as text-oriented ones. We have encouraged students to see the works as commentaries on their own lives and to bring their own experience to bear on what they read and write. We have also encouraged them to analyze and evaluate their own experience based on what they read. We hope that, as a result, students will develop a lifelong appreciation of literature as intimately connected to their lives.

Literature and Ourselves includes casebooks on five authors: James Baldwin, Henrik Ibsen, Robert Frost, Alice Walker, and Flannery O'Connor. Some of the casebooks contain two, three, or more works by an author, including the author's statements about writing; all include critical essays. These casebooks can be very useful for teaching research papers, as teachers can base controlled practice papers and/or finished research papers on one or more of them. The primary works as well as the critical essays in these casebooks have been carefully selected and excerpted so that students can readily see relationships between them and can compare differing critical approaches to literature. The suggestions for research and writing, some designed to be quite challenging for freshmen, invite students to see such relationships and draw conclusions leading to thesis statements. Such features encourage students to study the author in some depth.

Believing that students need to read excellent nonfiction as well as fiction, drama, and poetry, we have included essays. We believe that these essays not only are works of art but also can serve as models of good prose style. Since their statements of theme are often more explicit than those of other genres, they begin each thematic section and should initiate thoughtful exploration of each theme.

Our preparation of this text would not have been possible without the invaluable help of a number of people. We are indebted to Matt Harr for believing that our text was a valuable idea and for taking it to Harper-Collins. Our debt to Lisa Moore, our Acquisitions Editor, is immeasurable; she has encouraged us at each step in the production of this book, sharing with us her enthusiasm and her knowledge of the market and of literature, sometimes pushing us beyond our own expectations, and never letting us give up. We were also fortunate in our Development Editor, for

Randee Falk, with her infinite patience and wonderful talent with language, helped us to gain a new perspective on both the content and writing in our text. Betty Slack, Director of Development for the Humanities, encouraged and reassured us when questions arose. Alison Griffiths, our Permissions Editor, was diligent, persistent, and unfailingly cheerful as we asked her to perform the impossible. Barbra Guerra, our Project Editor, was a wonderful guide for neophyte authors; and our Copyeditor, Jane Crouse, gave us many valuable suggestions for improving our text.

We are also deeply indebted to many colleagues at Gordon College and DeKalb College. The administration at Gordon, Dr. Jerry Williamson and Dr. James O. Richards, supported us in our project and allowed us to use equipment and supplies to prepare the book. The knowledgeable and cooperative library staff at both Gordon and DeKalb rescued us numerous times by helping us to locate materials and making valuable suggestions. In the Gordon College Word Processing Department, Marianne King, Betty Niblett, and Cindy Green were extremely cooperative and supportive in helping us to prepare materials for the book. Our colleagues in the English Departments have also added suggestions about the contents of the text and about classroom techniques which resulted in stimulating discussions and well written papers. At Gordon, Drs. Susan Ellzey, Mary Alice Money, Michael Montgomery, and Rhonda Wilcox shared their innovative ideas with us. At DeKalb, Dr. Faye Tate was most generous in allowing us to use the workroom and equipment; Landon Coleman shared with us his expertise in drama and helped with the selection of plays; Dr. Maxine Sample offered helpful recommendations and constructive advice; and Drs. Grace McNamara, Harris Green, Steven Beauchamp, Susan Thomas, and Tim Tarkington offered valuable suggestions for selections.

We are deeply indebted to the reviewers of our book for their astute observations, constructive criticism, and valuable suggestions for added selections: Kirk D. Adams, Tarrant City Junior College; Edith Blicksilver, Georgia Tech; Thomas Dukes, University of Akron; Elinor Flewellen, Santa Barbara City College; Katherine Griffin, Tuskeegee University; Brian Keener, New York Technical College; Mary Klayder, University of Kansas; Loise Marchino, University of Texas–El Paso; John O'Connor, George Mason University; Esther Panitz, William Paterson College of New Jersey; Glenn Sadler, Bloomsburg State University; Al Sawyer, Richard J. Daly College; Kay Smith, Valencia Community College West; Rita Sturm, Santa Fe Community College; Gladys Willis, Lincoln University.

Finally, we would like to thank the members of our families for their patience in allowing us to persevere in our work even though this perseverance often meant that they saw much less of us than they wished.

Gloria Henderson   William Day   Sandra Waller

INTRODUCTION

Literature

LITERATURE IS AN ART FORM WHOSE medium is language, oral and written. It differs from ordinary spoken or written language primarily in three ways: (1) it is concentrated and meaningful (even sometimes when it denies meaning); (2) its purpose is not simply to explain, argue, or make a point but rather to give a sense of pleasure in the discovery of a new experience; (3) it demands intense concentration from readers. Literature, as defined and included in this text, falls into four large classes or **genres: essays, fiction, poetry,** and **drama.**

Literature is not only about ideas but also about experiences. It communicates what it feels like to undergo an experience, whether physical or emotional. A psychiatrist, in writing a case study of a patient, concentrates strictly on the facts. Though the doctor may give readers an understanding of the patient, he or she does not attempt to make readers feel what it is like to be that patient. In fact, the psychiatrist must strive to remain strictly objective, as should the readers. Writers of essays, fiction, drama, and poetry, however, may try to put their readers inside the mind of such a character, making readers intimately share the patient's experience and feel what it is like to be the patient. In interpreting literature, readers may adopt one or more of three basic approaches: text-oriented approaches, artist-oriented approaches, and reader-oriented approaches.

TEXT-ORIENTED APPROACHES

Adopting a text-oriented approach, a reader may analyze a work of literature as complete in itself without relating it to the outside world. This approach, which was fashionable from about 1920 to 1950, dominates many freshman literature anthologies. It finds expression in the line "a poem should not mean but be" from Archibald MacLeish's poem "Ars poetica." In its extreme form this approach insists that the author's life and time as well as readers' responses to his or her work are not only unnecessary, but irrelevant. The kind of close analysis and attention to words and their contexts that this method requires can be very useful, both in illuminating a literary work and in teaching students to read carefully and critically. Consequently, this book emphasizes a text-oriented approach in the introductions to the four genres and in many of the questions for discussion and suggestions for exploration and writing that follow anthologized works.

Writing suggestions that require analysis of **tone, theme, plot,** or **character** are text-oriented. For example, one question about William Faulkner's "Barn Burning" asks how poverty and illiteracy affect the Snopes' behavior. In asking about character the question requires only an analysis of various passages in the story. A text-oriented question about Wilfred Owen's "Dulce et Decorum Est" requires the reader to contrast the patriotic last line to the first stanza. This question requires only a close examination of the poem itself.

AUTHOR-ORIENTED APPROACHES

Adopting an author-oriented approach, a reader may study an author's life, time, and culture to better understand the author's work. This approach requires research. A reader might, for example, in studying *Othello,* research the roles of women in Renaissance Venice and Elizabethan England in order to understand Othello's expectations of Desdemona. In addition to historical and biographical research, research on other literature, myths, rituals, and art forms can illuminate a work. For example, a reader might choose to research Nigerian tribal dances to illuminate the long elaborate dances in Wole Soyinka's *The Lion and the Jewel.* Another reader might simply choose to read Mark 4:10–20 in order to understand Robert Frost's allusion to Mark in the poem "Directive." Other works by the author being studied, including letters, statements of artistic purpose, and reviews, can also enhance a reader's understanding of a work. For example, Flannery O'Connor's essay "The Catholic Novelist in the Protestant South" in the casebook on O'Connor reveals how her devout Christianity shaped her stories. Many of the questions and suggestions in the casebooks require an author-oriented approach. Chinua Achebe's essay "Africa and Her Writers" applies a variation of an author-oriented approach in an especially interesting way to the Yoruban art festival called *mbari.*

READER-ORIENTED APPROACHES

Each reader brings a unique set of experiences and expectations to literature. In its extreme form, the reader-oriented approach argues that a work of literature is recreated each time it is read; that it is produced by the reading, perceiving, imagining mind of the reader; and that, consequently, any reading of a work is valid. Certainly a range of interpretation, some of it conditioned by the reader's particular expectations, is not only valid, but desirable. Men and women, for example, are likely to react differently to such works as *The Lion and the Jewel, Othello,* and Bessie Head's "Snapshots of a Wedding." Similarly, atheists, Jews, evangelical Christians, and persons of other religious perspectives will react differently to the stories of Flannery O'Connor; the poems of Judith Ortiz Cofer, Gerard Manley Hopkins, and William Butler Yeats; and the plays of August Wilson and Harvey Fierstein. Quite fashionable today, reader-oriented interpretation is far from new. The writers of the New Testament, for example, read and reinterpreted Old Testament scripture in the light of Jesus' life and ministry. Among contemporary writers included in this anthology, Barry Lopez's essay "Language and Narrative" presents a particularly interesting reader-oriented theory.

Some of the questions for discussion and suggestions for exploration and writing in this text require a reader-oriented approach in conjunction with a text-oriented approach. For example, a text-oriented question on Ursula LeGuin's "The Ones Who Walk Away from Omelas," which asks about the details that make Omelas a Utopia, is immediately followed by the reader-oriented question "How does LeGuin involve the reader in making her description of Omelas believable?" The latter question requires readers to examine their own response, then return to the text to analyze the sources of that response. Similarly, the questions "How would you ordinarily feel about a sow? How does the poem make you feel about one?" require readers first to articulate an emotional response to Galway Kinnell's "Saint Francis and the Sow," and then to analyze how the poem produces such a response.

Since one function of literature is to expose us to other people's experience, we should be open to others' interpretations as well as our own. This is not to say, however, that all interpretations are equal in value or even that all are valid. The most satisfying readings of literature may incorporate all three approaches, and all three apply equally to the four genres of literature included in this anthology.

Essays

The word **essay** as used in this text refers to a short, unified work of nonfiction prose. Included in this anthology are many kinds of essays, such as **expository essays, argumentative essays, sermons, epistolary essays, biographical essays, critical essays, personal essays,** and even essays excerpted from books. These categories are not mutually exclusive, and a single essay may fit more than one category. The most common are expository essays, argumentative essays, and personal essays. The primary purpose of an **expository essay** is to inform or explain; examples of such essays include Guan Keguang's "A Chinese Reporter on Cape Cod" and Mark Mathabane's "The Road to Alexandria," an excerpt from a book which might also be called a biographical essay. In an **argumentative essay**, the writer tries to convince an audience to agree with his or her position on an issue; the Declaration of Independence and Martin Luther King, Jr.'s "Letter from Birmingham City Jail" are argumentative essays. The vast majority of essays in this anthology are **personal essays,** which, as their name implies, reveal much about their authors. Examples of personal essays include Joan Didion's "On Going Home," James Agee's "Knoxville: Summer 1915," and Annie Dillard's "Heaven and Earth in Jest."

Perhaps because they do not present fictional, imagined worlds but explore facts and ideas, essays are often neglected in literature textbooks. Unlike stories and plays, essays do not ordinarily develop characters or plots. They may contain well-developed portraits of actual human beings and may even tell stories, but these portraits and stories usually develop and are subordinate to an idea.

THEME

The reader of an essay must understand its **theme,** or main idea, and the various subpoints and examples that develop the theme. In expository and argumentative essays, theme is usually quite clear. There is little question about the main idea of the Declaration of Independence or of King's "Letter from Birmingham City Jail." In personal essays like most of the ones in this anthology, the theme may be more subtly and obliquely stated, hence more difficult to comprehend. Often, a reader can find no **thesis,** no single sentence or group of sentences that fairly summarize the author's theme. James Agee, for example, in "Knoxville: Summer 1915," gives us no thesis saying that he remembers fondly childhood evenings in Knoxville where a loving and nurturing family gave him a sense of security, peace, and even melancholy. A reader must abstract that theme from the essay's details.

In addition to understanding an essayist's theme, a reader must understand how an essay is **unified,** how every part of the essay develops its theme. Chinua Achebe, for example, in "Africa and Her Writers" describes *mbari,* a festival practiced by the Igbo people of Nigeria in which selected members of the tribe work with skilled artists to fill a house with art. Achebe uses *mbari* to exemplify the interdependence of art and the people who produce it. In the Declaration of Independence, Thomas Jefferson lists the colonists' many grievances against the English king. This list has a purpose in Jefferson's argument: to demonstrate that the king has violated the unwritten contract between governments and the people they govern. In "Heaven and Earth in Jest," Annie Dillard's many precisely observed details illustrate her point: that nature is governed by a powerful unseen spirit, one that violently "pummels us," but that also delights us with moments of extraordinary grace and beauty. Thus, a good essay is unified; all its details and ideas develop its theme.

TONE

Tone may be defined as an author's attitude toward his or her subject. In some essays, the tone may be so personal that readers come to feel they know the author intimately. Anne Tyler's personal tone in "Still Just Writing" as well as the content of her essay make her real to readers and make them want to meet her. Among the essays on family included in this text, Agee's tone in "Knoxville: Summer 1915" is nostalgic, warm, and gentle, whereas Didion's in "On Going Home" is regretful over lost intimacy with her family. Even in Martin Luther King, Jr.'s "Letter from Birmingham City Jail," the carefully measured, calmly reasoning tone becomes an integral part of the argument.

In reading or writing about an essay, then, a reader must consider not only the author's main idea but also his or her distinctive tone. Is he or she gently humorous or bitingly satiric, nostalgic or regretful, angry or forgiving, calmly controlled or awestruck? Like theme, tone helps to unify an essay. A reader should see how particular details form a pattern, thereby developing the theme and creating a tone appropriate to it.

IMAGERY

Essayists frequently use **images,** combinations of words which create pictures. In Garrison Keillor's "Attitudes," for example, the image of physically inept middle-aged men behaving as if they were major league baseball players is hilarious. They spit, rub dirt between their hands, and tap the bat on their sneakers, imitating professional players. Keillor's image enables a reader to see, simultaneously, their physical awkwardness and their ritualistic imitation of star players, thus rendering them ridiculous. The image develops both the tone of amused self-mockery and the theme that middle-aged men will go to absurd lengths to assert their masculinity. In "Heaven and Earth in Jest," Annie Dillard's gruesome image of a frog, its body sucked dry by a giant water bug, its "skin, formless as a pricked balloon," develops her idea of the extraordinary violence of nature and suggests her wonder at that violence. Anne Tyler opens her essay "Still Just Writing" with the sentence "While I was painting in the downstairs hall I thought of a novel to write." The image of a novelist performing such a humble, ordinary act immediately begins to create in the reader's mind a sense of a unique personality, a writer who is modest, slightly amused by life's quirks and ironies, and quite ordinarily human.

DICTION

A good essayist chooses words very carefully, paying particular attention to their **connotations,** their suggested or implied meanings, as opposed to their **denotations,** or explicit meanings. Consider for example the word *delicate* in the following passage from Annie Dillard's "Heaven and Earth in Jest": "When I cross again the bridge . . . , the wind has thinned to the delicate air of twilight." The word *delicate* refers to something very fine and pleasing, fragile, or sensitive; none of these denotations seems to cover Dillard's meaning. As Dillard uses it, the word seems to connote air more than usually transparent, a breeze whose touch is so soft and gentle as to be barely felt.

An essayist's **level of diction,** his or her choice of words that are slangy or formal, unfamiliar or common, should also be appropriate to his or her theme and tone. Anne Tyler's diction in the passage quoted about her painting the hall, for example, is quite simple: none of the fourteen words contains more than two syllables and eleven are monosyllables. This simplicity of diction reinforces the quiet, modest tone created by the image of a novelist painting a room. Similarly, the more elevated diction of the Declaration of Independence and of Martin Luther King's "Letter from Birmingham City Jail" reinforces the seriousness of those documents.

SYNTAX

Finally, **syntax,** the patterns of an author's sentences, may develop his or her theme and tone. An author's sentences may be predominantly short and simple, even abrupt; or they may be predominantly long, ornate, and complex. Keillor, for example, ends "Attitude," his humorous essay about the middle-aged softball team, with the sentences "This is *ball,* ladies and gentlemen. This is what it's about." The short, even abrupt sentences contribute in their businesslike terseness, their intentional understatement and muting of emotion, to Keillor's gentle mockery of both his own and others' ineptitude. By contrast, the long, complex sentences of the Declaration of Independence suggest the logical relationships between ideas in a serious and carefully reasoned document. The long opening sentence is an example:

> When in the course of human events, it becomes necessary for one people to dissolve the political bands which have connected them with another, and to assume among the powers of the earth, the separate and equal station to which the Laws of Nature and Nature's God entitle them, a decent respect to the opinions of mankind requires that they should declare the causes which impel them to the separation.

Here the many subordinate clauses and phrases, including the long opening clause beginning with *when,* precisely define the logical dependence of one idea on another. Every part of the very long sentence is logically related to every other part.

Tone, imagery, diction, and syntax, then, develop the theme of an essay. In the following passage from James Agee's "Knoxville: Summer 1915," all four work together:

> All my people are larger bodies than mine, quiet, with voices gentle and meaningless like the voices of sleeping birds. One is an artist, he is living at home. One is a musician, she is living at home. One is my mother who is good to me. One is my father who is good to me. By some chance, here they are, all on this earth; and who shall ever tell the sorrow of being on this earth, lying, on quilts, in the grass, in a summer evening, among the sounds of the night.

The simple, almost childlike diction and syntax of this passage combine with the image of the loving family clustered together on a quilt under the vast summer night to produce a unified tone of nostalgia, of warm security, of ineffable sadness and wonder. This tone fits perfectly Agee's theme that he remembers fondly the peace and security of summer evenings in Knoxville with his loving family.

The following questions are a brief guide to reading and analyzing an essay.

Theme

1. What is the author's theme? Is it simple enough to summarize in a sentence or will it require several sentences?

2. How do the author's subpoints and examples develop his or her theme?

Tone

1. How would you describe the essay's tone?

2. How does the essay's tone help develop its theme?

Imagery

1. How does the writer's use of imagery contribute to the theme and tone of the essay?

2. What kinds of images does the essay contain? Are there images of animals? of violence? of religion?

3. How do the various images relate to one another?

Diction

1. What highly connotative words does the writer choose?

2. Is the essay's diction elevated, vulgar, simple, obscure?

3. How does the writer's diction contribute to the theme and tone of the essay?

Syntax

1. Is the writer's syntax complex and elaborate, simple, precise?

2. How does the writer's syntax contribute to the theme and tone of the essay?

Fiction

The short story is a relatively new form, although short fiction has long been a source of enjoyment and instruction in such forms as **parables, fables,** and **anecdotes** or **jokes. Fiction** is often thought of as the opposite of fact, but it may be based on facts and certainly includes factual material. A work described as fiction should be a **narrative;** that is, it should tell about a sequence of events. In addition, calling a work fiction denotes that it has **unity,** that all of its parts cohere. Short stories differ from other forms of short fiction in purpose. Parables and fables teach a lesson or a moral; anecdotes generally illustrate a point; and jokes entertain through humor. Furthermore, anecdotes and jokes, and even parables and fables, usually lack the complicated plots or the structure of most short stories. The longest form of fiction, the **novel,** is not included in this text precisely because of its prohibitive length; but most novels are made up of the same elements as short stories. The primary difference is length. In fact, readers sometimes disagree about whether a piece of fiction is a long short story, a **novella** or **novelette** (both terms used for short novels), or a novel. Because of the brevity of the short story, the writer should make every word and every scene an integral part of the creation.

Reading short stories with real understanding and appreciation is demanding. This kind of appreciation often requires at least three readings: a first reading of the story to enjoy the plot; a second reading to analyze its individual elements; and a third reading to see how those elements work together to create a cohesive, integrated whole. These elements include **point of view, setting, style, character, plot,** and **theme.**

Point of View

Point of view, the focus from which the story is told, is a crucial element; for it determines what we know about the characters and the action. The **omniscient,** all-knowing, point of view allows the author, writing in third person, to tell readers what any or all of the characters think or do.

The **first person** point of view allows readers to see the action through the eyes of one character and to know only that character's thoughts. That character may be the main character or a minor character. When the author uses first person point of view, readers must decide whether the narrator is reliable or unreliable, whether the reader can trust him or her to tell the truth or even to understand the truth. An unreliable narrator may be too young or too slow-witted to perceive the truth, or he or she may select or alter details in order to present a biased account. For example, by using a biased and unreliable narrator, an author may effectively create irony or humor, as in Eudora Welty's "Why I Live at the P.O." One very popular first person point of view in modern literature is that of a child whose innocence and lack of knowledge allow readers to draw their own conclusions or that of an adult remembering his or her childhood experiences and drawing adult conclusions, as in Truman Capote's "A Christmas Memory." William Faulkner uses a variation of the first person point of view in "A Rose for Emily," which is told from the point of view of the townspeople using the pronoun *we* instead of *I.*

In the **third-person-limited** point of view, the author tells readers the thoughts of only one character and follows that character throughout the action. Carson McCullers uses this point of view when she follows Martin throughout "A Domestic Dilemma," telling only his thoughts and his theories about the causes of Emily's behavior rather than letting readers into her mind. When using third-person-limited point of view, as in first person, authors select the character who can reveal the information they want told in the story but who will not know the information which they want withheld from readers.

SETTING

The **setting** of a story—the time, place, and culture in which the action occurs—may be extremely significant. Time, place, and culture are integral elements in Alice Walker's "Nineteen Fifty-five," for neither the music nor the racial relationships would be the same in another setting. Kurt Vonnegut's "Harrison Bergeron" takes place in the United States in 2081, a setting which is essential because the story depicts the ultimate fulfillment of the constitutional guarantee of equality. Ursula LeGuin's "The Ones Who Walk Away from Omelas" gains universality by taking place in some unknown mythic time and place.

STYLE

Style—the selection of words (**diction**); sentence structure (**syntax**); figurative devices, such as **simile** and **metaphor**; and **symbolism**—sets the **tone** and reflects the individuality of each author. Some writers use fairly simple straightforward sentences, especially if they are using a first-person narrator who is unsophisticated. In "A Christmas Memory," Capote's adult narrator, remembering his childhood friendship and writing in present tense as if he were still a child, uses simple sentences like "Imagine a morning in late November" and "Queenie [the dog] tries to eat an angel." However, he combines childhood delight with adult perception and style when he vividly describes shelling pecans: "A cheery crunch, scraps of miniature thunder sound as the shells collapse and the golden mound of sweet oily ivory meat mounts in the milk-glass bowl." Some writers, like William Faulkner, use styles which are extremely complex and often almost poetic. They employ many of the metaphorical devices and sometimes even the rhythmical effects which readers expect from poetry. In "A Rose for Emily" Faulkner's narrators describe:

> the very old men—some in their brushed Confederate uniforms— on the porch and the lawn, talking of Miss Emily as if she had been a contemporary of theirs, believing that they had danced with her and courted her perhaps, confusing time with its mathematical progression, as the old do, to whom all the past is not a diminishing road, but instead, a huge meadow which no winter ever quite touches, divided from them now by the narrow bottleneck of the most recent decade of years.

The author's selection of descriptive details or his or her inclusion of a scene in a story may seem casual but seldom is. For example, in "A Good Man Is Hard to Find," Flannery O'Connor's vivid description of the grandmother's apparel as the family leaves home subtly reveals character and foreshadows the end of the story. While the other members of the family dress comfortably, the grandmother wears a "navy blue straw sailor hat with a bunch of white violets on the brim and a navy blue dress with a small white dot in the print," believing that "anyone seeing her dead on the highway would know at once that she was a lady." Similarly, the scene at Red Sammy's Barbecue, which at first glance may seem unimportant, further reveals the grandmother's character as she describes the cheating Red Sammy as a "good man." The scene also prepares readers for her reaction to the Misfit in the conclusion.

Similes and **metaphors** are elements of style which can make description more vivid and aid in interpretation. In William Faulkner's "Barn Burning," the "stiff foot" of Sarty's father which "came down on the boards with clocklike finality" reveals the father's unyielding nature; and the strong ties to family which influence Sarty and fill him with "despair and grief" are vividly expressed in the metaphor "the old fierce pull of blood." In O'Connor's "A Good Man Is Hard to Find," the simile describing the forest "like a dark open mouth" foreshadows the death of the family in the woods.

A **symbol** stands for both the thing it names and something else. Some symbols are almost universal: light is often used to symbolize a growth in knowledge, a realization, or enlightenment. Other symbols are symbolic only in the particular context of the story and may be interpreted differently by different readers. For example, the open window in Kate Chopin's "The Story of an Hour" may symbolize Mrs. Mallard's desire for freedom, especially because her name also suggests the possibility of flight.

All elements of style help the author create the tone of the story, the author's attitude toward the work, or the mood. The ominous and foreboding atmosphere of Charlotte Perkins Gilman's "The Yellow Wallpaper," for example, is emphasized by the unusual alliterative sounds with which the narrator describes her perceptions: "The color is repellent, almost revolting: a smouldering unclean yellow, strangely faded by the slow-turning sunlight. It is a dull yet lurid orange in some places, a sickly sulphur tint in others." The description seems to be hissing at the reader. Similarly, the short, choppy paragraphs reflect the narrator's thought patterns as she approaches insanity.

CHARACTER

Character refers to the people authors create to inhabit their stories. Characters should be believable and consistent. Being believable means not that all characters be like people we have known, but that they be believable in the context of the story. Consistency requires not that the characters remain exactly the same, but that any changes in character be sufficiently motivated by what happens to them in the story. Authors may reveal characters in a variety of ways: by telling about them directly, by letting their actions and speech reveal their personalities, or by having other characters tell about them.

The major characters are usually **round characters;** that is, their personalities are well developed and believable. These characters frequently change as the story progresses; if they do, they are also described as **dynamic.** Minor characters often are **flat characters:** we see only one aspect of their personalities, presumably because the author does not need to reveal more about them for the purposes of the story. Flat characters are usually **static** characters; that is, they do not change. In Faulkner's "Barn Burning," Major de Spain is a flat character; he is not fully developed. On the other hand, Sarty is both a round and a dynamic character, for readers learn many facets of his personality, and he faces a crisis which causes him to change dramatically.

PLOT

The most apparent element of most short stories is the **plot,** the pattern of the action. A story has a beginning, a middle, and an end. The beginning of the story may not be the beginning of the action, for the story may begin at some high point in the action and use **flashback** or some other technique to fill in the information necessary for an understanding of the situation. Faulkner's "A Rose for Emily" begins just before the end of the action and then works back in time to inform readers about Miss Emily's life and her relationship to the other characters and to the town. If readers are to comprehend the plot of a story, the beginning must include **exposition,** information about the setting and the characters. The middle of the story presents a complication or conflict— within the main character, between the character and some force in nature, or between characters. This conflict builds until the story reaches a **climax,** a peak of action or suspense. The end presents the **resolution,** a solution or unraveling of the conflict, sometimes called the **denouement.** In modern stories, the ending seldom resolves all of the problems faced by the characters; however, the ending should include a sense of completion and an increase in the characters' or at least the readers' knowledge. In James Baldwin's "Sonny Blues," the exposition begins simultaneously with the complication when the narrator reads in a newspaper article that his brother Sonny has been arrested on a drug charge. This shock triggers a flashback: the narrator's memory of the first time Sonny tried heroin. The complication continues with Sonny's release and return to Harlem and with further flashbacks describing their mother's advice and her account of a parallel situation faced by their father and uncle. The death of the narrator's little girl marks a turning point in the narrator's understanding of human suffering. The climax and resolution occur at the nightclub when the narrator sees Sonny in his element and, for the first time, really listens to Sonny's music.

THEME

Perhaps surprisingly, theme may be the most difficult aspect of a short story to identify. The **theme** is the major idea of the story. Readers often disagree about a story's theme: One reader may believe the theme of Carson McCullers' "A Domestic Dilemma" is the ways in which the complexities of love can serve as traps; another reader may say that the theme is that modern mobility may cause insecurity; a third reader might say that the theme is the conflict between love for a spouse and love for one's children.

While we may disagree about themes, a story without a theme usually seems trivial. We expect the author of a short story to use style, plot, and character to offer us insight into human behavior, to leave us feeling as if we have learned something about our world and about ourselves. This new insight may be repugnant or inspirational, sad or delightful: it may make us aware of human bestiality or nobility, of the wonders of friendship, or of the complexities of love. Whatever it says to readers and however they respond, the theme is the heart of the short story, its reason for being.

The following questions provide a general guide to reading and writing about short stories. Specific guidance follows each short story in the anthology.

Point of View

1. What is the point of view in the story?

2. If it is first person or third person limited, through which character do readers see the story? Is the character a reliable or an unreliable narrator? How does his or her personality affect the perception of other characters and of the action?

3. Could the story be written just as effectively or more effectively from another point of view? If so, how and why? If not, why not?

Setting

1. Where and when does the story take place?

2. How does the author let readers know the time and place?

3. Could the story take place in any other time or place?

Style

1. What kind of sentence structure does the author seem to prefer in this story? Could the sentences be described as simple or complex? Are the language and sentence structure dictated by the point of view? If so, how?

2. What kind of imagery does the author use? Does the language seem poetic? Examine any examples of similes, metaphors, or personifi-

cation to see if they give clues about characters or foreshadow something in the plot.

3. Look for any symbols in the story, both symbols which are universally accepted, and symbols which are particular to the story. What do they represent in the story and how do they enrich its meaning?

4. What is the tone of the story? How is it accomplished?

Character

1. Are the characters in the story believable? Why or why not?

2. How are the characters revealed: through what the author says about them, through what the other characters say about them, and/or through what they say and do?

3. Which characters are round characters?

4. Which characters are flat characters? Does their lack of development affect the success of the story? If so, in what way?

5. Do any of the characters develop or change in the story? Is this change one of the major points of the story?

Plot

1. What is the conflict in the story? Where do you first realize that there is a conflict?

2. List the steps in the development of the conflict.

3. Where does the conflict reach a climax?

4. What is the resolution of the conflict?

Theme

1. What is the theme of the story? If possible, state it in a sentence.

2. How do the elements of the story work together to convey the theme?

3. Did the theme provide an insight or understanding which you had not previously had? Did the theme relate to insights you have had?

4. Could the author have conveyed the same idea just as effectively in an essay? Why or why not?

Poetry

Unlike essays and short stories, poems are written in verse. Their primary units are lines and stanzas rather than sentences and paragraphs. Lyric poems, the kind included in this anthology, differ from narrative poems, which tell a story, and epic poems, which are very long and heroic narrative poems. Usually short and often songlike in their rhythms, lyric poems lack plots. They focus not on a sequence of related events leading from conflict to climax but on a speaker's response to a single event, object, situation, or person.

SPEAKER AND SITUATION

In most poems the **speaker** is a character created by the author. For example, in T. S. Eliot's "The Love Song of J. Alfred Prufrock," Prufrock speaks and in Robert Browning's "My Last Duchess" the Duke of Ferrara speaks. In Eliot's poem, Prufrock reveals himself to be a very timid man who has "measured out [his] life with coffee spoons" and who cannot generate enough assertiveness even to ask a question. Browning's Ferrara, on the other hand, shows himself to be a callous and egotistical murderer. Neither Prufrock nor Ferrara bears a clear resemblance to his creator.

Occasionally, if they have compelling reasons for doing so, readers may identify the speaker of a poem with the author. Sylvia Plath's "Daddy," for example, is clearly autobiographical. Like the speaker, Plath lost her father to suicide when she was quite young and had difficulty coping with that loss. Also like her speaker, Plath had tried to kill herself. It is reasonable, then, to identify the speaker of "Daddy" with Plath.

Some poems, too, seem to arise out of a clearly defined **situation** in which the speaker is addressing a particular person for a particular purpose. In "My Last Duchess," for example, the Duke of Ferrara addresses the agent of a count in order to arrange a marriage to the count's daughter. Plath in "Daddy" clearly is addressing her dead father, hoping through the ritual of the poem to exorcise from her memory his oppressive presence. In such poems as Andrew Marvell's "To His Coy Mistress" and Robert Herrick's "Corinna's Going A-Maying," the speakers address women they love, trying to get those women to realize their mortality and enjoy their youth and beauty while they can. Finally, in Dwight Okita's "In Response to Executive Order 9066," a teenage girl addresses the impersonal U.S. government that has consigned her to an internment camp. In each of these cases, understanding the speaker and the speaker's situation is essential to understanding the poem.

THEME

Though not all poems have a recognizable and paraphrasable **theme**, or major idea, many do. William Shakespeare's Sonnet 18, for example, clearly states that the beloved is "more lovely" than a beautiful day in summer and that the sonnet itself will ensure her immortality. Similarly, Mary TallMountain's "There Is No Word for Goodbye" clearly states the theme in its title, and Dylan Thomas' "Do Not Go Gentle into That Good Night" insistently repeats its theme that we should fight death with every ounce of will and energy we can muster. Other poems seem to have no readily paraphrasable theme, so subtle and complex is their meaning. For example, though we may understand them, it would be difficult to state the theme of Li-Young Lee's "Persimmons," of T. S. Eliot's "The Love Song of J. Alfred Prufrock," or of Sylvia Plath's "Daddy."

TONE

Whatever its apparent subject, the true subject of a lyric is a state of mind or attitude, known by the technical term **tone.** It may be defined as a complex of interrelated attitudes, those of the speaker, writer, and reader toward the poem's situation. A lyric, then, communicates a tone or attitude, the essence of what it feels like to be in a particular situation. Li-Young Lee's poem "Persimmons," for example, is not simply about persimmons. Rather, it is about a whole range of intense and complex emotions, attitudes, and relationships associated with persimmons in the speaker's and the author's minds.

The tone of a poem may be quite complex, expressing feeling which cannot even be suggested by such general words as *love, joy,* and *pain.* Anne Sexton's apparently simple poem "Ringing the Bells," for example, not only communicates the mind-numbing boredom of therapy in a mental institution, but simultaneously communicates the speaker's mounting hysteria.

> And this is the way they ring
> the bells in Bedlam
> and this is the bell-lady
> who comes each Tuesday morning
> to give us a music lesson
> and because the attendants make you go
> and because we mind by instinct
> like bees caught in the wrong hive,
> we are the circle of the crazy ladies
> who sit in the lounge of the mental house

As a poem's situation changes, its tone may change as well. In Wilfred Owen's "Dulce et Decorum Est," the first stanza graphically communicates the pain and exhaustion of World War I soldiers moving from trenches on the front lines to a place of rest behind the lines.

> Men marched asleep. Many had lost their boots
> But limped on, bloodshod. All went lame; all blind.

In the second stanza, as gas bombs drop among the soldiers and one soldier, unable to don his gas mask in time, dies a gruesome death, the tone changes to panic and horror.

> Gas! Gas! Quick boys!—An ecstasy of fumbling,
> Fitting the clumsy helmets just in time;
> But someone still was yelling out and stumbling
> And flound'ring like a man in fire or lime . . .

Though "Dulce et Decorum Est" is charged with overwhelming emotion which the speaker seems unable to control, in many poems the emotion seems much more subdued. In Emily Dickinson's "I Heard a Fly Buzz," for example, the speaker is clearly in control of her emotion.

> I willed my Keepsakes—Signed away
> What portion of me be
> Assignable—and then it was
> There interposed a Fly—

The death she foresees does not scare her or even sadden her; rather she sees her death as the most ordinary of events. Similarly, the urbane speaker of Andrew Marvell's "To His Coy Mistress" declares his love in a carefully measured, precise, and witty compliment.

> Had we but world enough, and time,
> This coyness, lady, were no crime.
> We would sit down, and think which way
> To walk, and pass our long love's day.

Various elements of a poem work together to create its tone. The main elements are diction, syntax, imagery, and sound.

DICTION

In creating **tone**, a poet uses language which communicates emotion. Curses, groans, and common adjectives such as *beautiful, wonderful,* and *marvelous* express emotion; but they do not often communicate so that the listener shares the speaker's feeling. Successful poets use language not merely to express but also to communicate emotion precisely. Their choice of words is called **diction.**

The **level of diction** in a poem may range from the very polite, complex, and formal to the very simple, slangy, even vulgar or profane. In Anne Sexton's "Ringing the Bells," for example, the very simple, ordinary, flat diction suggests the boredom of the music therapy session in which the speaker is trapped. In Robert Browning's "My Last Duchess," the Duke of Ferrara is speaking to a count's agent about marrying the count's daughter. As the Duke subtly recalls how he had his first duchess murdered, his precise, formal diction reveals his extraordinary self-control and frightening callousness.

> That's my last Duchess painted on the wall,
> Looking as if she were alive. I call
> That piece a wonder, now; Fra Pandolf's hands
> Worked busily a day, and there she stands.

A poet may choose to use many verbs to emphasize action as in the following lines from John Donne's "Batter My Heart Three-Personed God."

> Batter my heart, three-person'd God; for, you
> As yet but knocke, breathe, shine, and seeke to mend.

On the other hand, a poet may use nonsense words like John Hollander in "Adam's Task."

> Thou, paw-paw-paw; thou glurd; thou, spotted
>   Glurd; thou, whitestap, lurching through
> The high-grown brush; thou, pliant-footed,
>   Implex; thou, awagabu.

Here Hollander's nonsense names for animals help create a sense of joy in playing with language and a delight in its power.

A poet's **diction,** his or her choice of words, may create paradox or verbal irony. A paradox is an apparent contradiction. For example, in "Batter My Heart," John Donne addresses God with the paradoxes:

> Except You'enthrall mee, never shall be free,
> Nor ever chast, except you ravish mee.

Since *enthrall* literally means to enslave or imprison, *chaste* means sexually pure, and *ravish* means rape, the two statements appear contradictory. For Donne, however, the ultimate freedom is service to God, and being overpowered by God is the ultimate purity. **Verbal irony** is simply saying the opposite of what one means. Owen's title "Dulce et Decorum Est," meaning "It is sweet and proper," is bitterly ironic since the entire poem emphatically demonstrates that dying in war is neither sweet nor proper.

SYNTAX

A poem's **syntax**—the structure of its phrases, clauses, and sentences—may also contribute to its tone. For example, though it is one very long sentence throughout most of its length, Sexton's "Ringing the Bells" is syntactically simple. The long sentence is almost childlike in its compounding of clauses, not complex like most adult writing and speech. Coordinating conjunctions like *and,* used frequently in Sexton's poem, merely connect phrases and clauses without emphasizing one over the other.

> And this is the way they ring
> the bells in Bedlam
> and this is the bell-lady
> . . . .
> and this is the gray dress next to me
> . . . .
> and this is the small hunched squirrel-girl
> . . . .
> and this is how the bells really sound

Like the poem's very ordinary diction, the dull, repetitious compounding of clauses contributes to the sense of stifling boredom in the mental institution.

On the other hand, in Browning's "My Last Duchess," the sentences are long, formal, and complex with many subordinate clauses. The speaker uses perfect parallelism; similar forms in phrases and clauses joined by *and*. This parallelism, followed by a brutally short, blunt, and unemotional recounting of his command to have his wife murdered, contributes to a reader's sense of the Duke's self-control and monstrous callousness.

> Who'd stoop to blame
> This sort of trifling? Even had you skill
> In speech—(which I have not)—to make your will
> Quite clear to such a one, and say, "Just this
> Or that in you disgusts me; here you miss,
> Or there exceed the mark"—and if she let
> Herself be lessoned so, nor plainly set
> Her wits to yours, forsooth, and made excuse
> —E'en then would be some stooping; and I choose
> Never to stoop. Oh sir, she smiled, no doubt,
> Whene'er I passed her; but who passed without
> Much the same smile? This grew; I gave commands;
> Then all smiles stopped together. . . .

Who among us could speak so well in recalling a murder we had ordered? The perfect and precise control of the long second sentence and the short, matter-of-fact, almost smirking last sentence seem to reveal a mind incapable of guilt.

IMAGERY

Probably a poet's most powerful tool for creating tone is **imagery.** An image is a word picture; the phrase "neatly trimmed lawn," for example, is an image. In analyzing images in a poem, readers should look for patterns, for the kinds of images that predominate. In stanza three of Owen's "Dulce et Decorum Est," images such as the following powerfully convey the horror of war:

> If in some smothering dreams you too could pace
> Behind the wagon that we flung him in,
> And watch the white eyes writhing in his face
> . . . .
> If you could hear, at every jolt, the blood
> Come gargling from the froth-corrupted lungs.

Similes, explicit comparisons between unlike things using such indicators of comparison as *like* and *as,* and **metaphors,** implicit comparisons between unlike things lacking such indicators, create images. In Sexton's "Ringing the Bells," there are several images of animals; the simile "like bees caught in the wrong hive" and the metaphor "the small hunched squirrel girl" suggest that the institution in which the speaker finds herself reduces its inmates to a subhuman state.

A **symbol** is an image used in such a way that it comes to mean more than it would ordinarily mean. A symbol, however, must be distinguished from a sign. A sign is a word or image that exactly corresponds to a particular meaning beyond itself. The meaning of a symbol is far less definite. For example, a stop sign signifies a particular command universally agreed upon throughout our culture. On the other hand, a stop sign removed from its normal setting, mangled into a heap of barely recognizable metal and placed in an art museum, may symbolize far more: perhaps the brutality of our culture, perhaps the degree to which machines dominate and even destroy lives, perhaps our sheer wastefulness and carelessness. Similarly, the word *bell* signifies a kind of musical instrument. In Sexton's "Ringing the Bells," however, bells take on far more meaning: they symbolize the dull, mechanical lives of the women in the mental hospital.

SOUND

Finally, in poetry, as in music, **sound** is important. Poems create patterns in sound as they do in diction, imagery, and syntax. **Onomatopoeia** is the use of words which imitate the sounds they stand for, such as the word *buzz*. Words need not be onomatopoeic, however, for their sounds to affect a poem. At the most basic level, the sounds of words themselves may have emotional overtones apart from the meanings of those words. Such nonsense syllables as *hey diddle diddle* and *heigh ho* suggest joy, while *ugh* suggests pain or disgust. In the first stanza of Wilfred Owen's "Dulce et Decorum Est" such words as *trudge, sludge,* and *hags* have harsh, unpleasant sounds appropriate to the tone of the stanza. On the other hand, such names for animals as *kabasch, implex,* and *awagabu* in John Hollander's "Adam's Task" suggest joy in their rich and tongue-twisting variety, and the smooth vowels and soft consonants in Marvell's "To His Coy Mistress" are pleasantly mellifluous.

> Had we but world enough, and time,
> This coyness, lady, were no crime.
> We would sit down, and think which way
> To walk, and pass our long love's day.

The movement or flow of a poem's sound may be fast or slow, smooth or rough, steady or broken and disjointed. For example, in the lines quoted above from the first stanza of "To His Coy Mistress," the movement is very smooth, stately, and unhurried. The frequent commas slow the passage to the pace of pleasant conversation and prevent the lines from becoming monotonous. On the other hand, the first stanza of Owen's "Dulce et Decorum Est" moves slowly and unsteadily with frequent stops and starts.

> Bent double, like old beggars under sacks,
> Knock-kneed, coughing like hags, we cursed through sludge.

Here the frequent commas and the difficulty of pronouncing hard consonants slow down the line so that it moves in fits and starts, seeming to imitate the movement of the soldiers as they stagger forward, hurting and exhausted.

Meter, an important element in a poem's sound, refers to the regular pattern of accented and unaccented syllables in a poetic line. There are five basic metrical patterns in English: **iambic, trochaic, anapestic, dactylic,** and **spondaic.** An **iambic foot,** or metrical unit, consists of an unaccented syllable followed by an accented one. In the following line from Marvell's "To His Coy Mistress," accented syllables have been marked by ´, unaccented ones by ˘, and metrical feet separated by /.

> Nŏr wóuld / Ĭ lóve / ăt lów / ĕr ráte.

A **trochaic foot** consists of an accented foot followed by an unaccented foot. An **anapestic foot,** consisting of three syllables, accents the third syllable, and a **dactylic foot,** also containing three syllables, accents the first. A **spondaic foot** consists of two consecutive accented syllables.

Trimeter, tetrameter, pentameter, and **hexameter** refer to the number of feet in a line. Thus, **iambic trimeter** refers to a poetic line of three iambic feet; **trochaic tetrameter** to a line of four trochaic feet; **pentameter** to a line of five feet; and **hexameter** to a line of six feet.

Iambic is by far the most natural and common metrical pattern in English. In fact, the rhythms of English prose are often iambic. Departures from the natural **iambs** of English often call attention to themselves. John Donne uses a strong trochaic foot to emphasize the word *batter* in the opening line of his Holy Sonnet.

> Báttĕr / m̆y heárt, / thr̆ee-pér / sŏñed Gód.

In the following lines from the second stanza of "To His Coy Mistress," the fourth line begins with a strong trochaic foot.

> Bŭt át / m̆y báck / Ĭ ál / wăys heár,
> Tiḿe's wíng / ĕd chár / iŏt húr / ry̆ng néar.
> Añd yónd / ĕr áll / bĕfóre / ŭs líe
> Dĕsĕrts / ŏf vást / ĕtér / nĭtý.

The inverted accent emphasizes the word *deserts*. This accent and the metaphor "deserts of vast eternity" increase the poem's urgency.

In spite of such departures from the basic meter, "To His Coy Mistress" is a very regular poem, using one of the most regular, tightly controlled verse forms in English poetry, the **couplet,** a pair of metrically regular, rhymed lines. This regularity of meter suggests that the speaker is very much in control of his emotion. Often, regularity suggests control as it does in Marvell's poem. In Browning's "My Last Duchess," also written in couplets, the regularity suggests the wife-murdering Duke of Ferrara's inappropriate, even pathological control. Sometimes metrical regularity may be comic, as in nursery rhymes. Lack of regularity, on the other hand, may suggest a speaker's lack of emotional control, as in Sexton's "Ringing the Bells" and Owen's "Dulce et Decorum Est." Poetry is so rich and diverse, however, that it is dangerous to generalize.

Alliteration and **rhyme** repeat certain sounds, thereby emphasizing them and helping to unify the poem. Alliteration, the repetition of consonants at the beginning of words or syllables, may enhance the effect of the repeated sounds. In the following lines from John Donne's "Batter My Heart," the hard alliterative *b*s reinforce the violence of the strong verbs.

> That I may rise, and stand, o'erthrow mee,'and bend
> Your force, to breake, blowe, burn, and make me new.

When words rhyme, their final accented syllables sound alike, as in *bestow* and *below* or *career* and *fear*. Rhymes usually occur at the end of poetic lines and are designated by letters so that the first sound is designated *a* and each new sound gets the next letter in the alphabet. In the following example from John Donne's "A Valediction: Forbidding Mourning," the rhyme scheme is *abab*.

> As virtuous men pass mildly away   *a*
> And whisper to their souls to go   *b*
> Whilst some of their sad friends do say   *a*
> The breath goes now, and some say no   *b*

Common rhyme patterns in English poetry include *abab, abba, abcb,* and couplets, in which successive lines rhyme.

Together, meter and rhyme define the stanza patterns of poems. The most common patterns in English include the quatrain, the couplet, and the sonnet. The **quatrain,** a stanza of four lines using any one of various rhyme schemes and metrical patterns, is the most often used stanza in English poetry. William Blake's "The Lamb" and "The Tyger" and John Hollander's "Adam's Task" are written in quatrains. Quatrains are the loosest and most flexible of the three stanza forms defined here. A **couplet** is simply a pair of metrically regular, rhymed lines. Couplets are tightly controlled and difficult to write because of the difficulty of finding rhymes in English. A **sonnet** is a tightly controlled poem of fourteen lines written in iambic pentameter. The **Italian sonnet** consists of two parts, an eight-line octave rhyming *abbaabba* and a six-line sestet often rhyming *cdecde* or *cdcdcd*. The **English** or **Shakespearean sonnet** consists of three quatrains followed by a couplet. The most common rhyme scheme is *abab cdcd efef gg*. Because of its precise rhyme scheme and meter, the sonnet is a demanding form. William Shakespeare, John Donne, William Wordsworth, Edna St. Vincent Millay, and Gerard Manley Hopkins are among the writers of sonnets included in this text.

The following questions provide a general guide to reading and writing about poems.

Speaker, Situation, and Theme

1. What kind of person is speaking in the poem?

2. Is there reason to equate the speaker with the poet?

3. To whom is the poem addressed?

4. What is the situation of the poem?

5. Does the poem have a paraphrasable theme? If so, what is it?

6. Do tone, diction, syntax, imagery, and sound develop the theme of the poem?

Tone

1. How would you describe the tone of the poem?

2. Does the tone change over the course of the poem?

3. Do diction, syntax, imagery, and sound develop the tone of the poem?

Diction

1. What is the level of the poem's diction? Is it formal, informal, colloquial? Is it simple, difficult, elegant, profane, coarse?

2. Does the poem use paradox or verbal irony?

Syntax

1. How difficult are the sentences? Are they short and simple, or are they long and complex?

2. Are there any departures from standard grammar or syntax such as fragmented elliptical passages (incomplete due to words left out)?

3. Does the syntax change over the course of the poem?

Imagery

1. What patterns does the imagery suggest?

2. What colors predominate?

3. To what senses does the imagery appeal?

4. What similes, metaphors, and symbols does the poet use?

5. Are there contrasting images?

6. Does the imagery change through the course of the poem?

Sound

1. What effects are created by the sounds and location of particular words?

2. Does the poem move fast or slow? Does it flow smoothly, or does it contain abrupt shifts, stops, and starts?

3. How regular is the meter of the poem? If the poem uses a regular metrical pattern, what is that pattern? What meter does it use?

4. Does the poem use rhyme or alliteration? If so, what effects are created?

5. Does the sound of the poem change?

Drama

When people first looked at the sunset or the mating games of animals and birds, they saw drama unfolding. Imitating nature became an inevitable step. Whereas nature's dramas are not orchestrated for human entertainment, on a stage actors can orchestrate nature's rituals and embellish scenes for human amusement and diversion. People can change the locales, shift words in the mouths of participants, add or subtract colorful costumes, and tell the story realistically, abstractly, surrealistically, or absurdly. The playwright can also combine creation's dramas with critical or sometimes solemn discussions of issues pertinent to his or her agenda; thus, the playwright blends the uncomplicated with the complicated. For example, Wole Soyinka, a modern Nigerian writer, successfully combines the ritual of the snake dance, the devil-horse dance, and the jungle dance with the eternal problem of tradition versus innovation in *The Lion and the Jewel*. Thus, directly or indirectly, in drama humans fulfill their desire to be entertained and to entertain, to watch and to be watched, and to see and to be seen.

PERFORMANCE VERSUS READING: STAGE DIRECTIONS

A play is meant to be performed and to be watched; therefore, the substance of a play can best be conveyed before an audience. Spectators are able to notice the actor's body language, to inspect the set, and to scrutinize the interplay between the people on the stage. The playwright may give elaborate instructions to the stage manager, the director, the actors, and all others involved in the production. These instructions are called **stage directions.**

Included in the stage directions are references to the set and props, which, along with the curtain, may be among the first items the audience sees. In some plays, the stage directions may be vague or unspecified, leaving the set, movement, and gestures entirely or partially dependent upon the director. In other plays, the stage directions may allow the actors and actresses to improvise. The opening and closing of a curtain and the dimming of lights in some productions indicate changes in dramatic time while **props** and **set** help to define the **setting,** the cultural and physical environment as well as the time when the action takes place.

Another element of a play, technically known as blocking, is readily apparent only in performance. **Blocking** includes the gestures and body language of characters as well as their interactions and movements on stage. Again, many times the stage directions may be explicit; at other times they may be implied and, therefore, open to interpretation. Blocking enhances performance. Even Shakespeare's great play *Othello* would be dull if the actors simply stood on stage and mechanically recited their lines. Iago's facial expressions and movement can reveal much about him, and an actor portraying Iago has much room for interpretation. In his soliloquy in act I, scene 3, ll. 366–377, beginning "Thus do I ever make my fool my purse," one actor may portray Iago with a snarling smile; another may assume a dark and deadly serious facial expression. In Susan Glaspell's *Trifles,* the gestures and facial expressions of the women reveal that they know why Mrs. Wright killed her husband and that they do not intend to divulge their knowledge to their husbands.

Unfortunately, not everyone can see a particular play. The written words of the play then become the primary vehicle by which the playwright offers readers his or her version of truth. Nor does the playwright have the option, as does the fiction writer, of using **narrative point of view** to reveal necessary background information or a character's innermost thoughts. Rather, the playwright must rely almost exclusively on **dialogue,** the conversations the characters have with each other, to develop character and to handle **exposition,** or background information necessary to the readers' understanding.

SETTING

Setting encompasses both the physical location and the cultural background associated with that location. For example, in Henrik Ibsen's *A Doll's House,* set in 1870s Norway, the Victorian attitude toward women is crucial to our understanding of the play. Similarly, the deserted disorderly farmhouse in Susan Glaspell's *Trifles* is important to the revelation of character and the unfolding of plot. Props and set also help to define the play's setting. By describing set and props as "the kitchen in [a] now abandoned farmhouse," a "disordered" and "gloomy kitchen" with "unwashed pans under the sink" and "other signs of incomplete work," Glaspell enhances a setting and sets the tone of the play. The cultural environment of the African-American family struggling with racial problems clarifies family relationships and deepens the understanding of August Wilson's *Fences.*

STYLE

Style, the manner in which the playwright expresses himself or herself, also encompasses imagery, symbolism, diction, sentence structure. When a playwright must reveal to the audience information about a character and the playwright wants to conceal the details from other characters, he or she relies on the **soliloquy,** a stylistic technique in which a character voices thoughts aloud to the audience. In Shakespeare's *Othello,* for example, Iago reveals to the audience through soliloquies motives he wants to conceal from other characters. Iago's deception is revealed in part by his variations in style. To those around him he appears the blunt, direct military man unable to embellish a compliment to women. But the complexity of imagery in his soliloquies and in some of his dialogues with Othello reveals a far more facile and manipulative command of language. His use of coarse sexual and animal imagery, too, helps to reveal his malignity. On the other hand, in Fierstein's *On Tidy Endings,* Arthur's use of one-liners and humor reveal the hidden pain and suffering caused by the death of his lover. Even the verbal sparring between Marion and Arthur underlines the reality of loss and underscores the author's style.

Another stylistic device used to impart characters' thoughts is the **aside,** a passage or remark the characters speak to the audience or to themselves, giving the illusion that, while the audience hears them, other characters on stage do not.

Finally, playwrights may use their unique style to reveal much about a character's concealed attitudes and motivation by having him or her voice opposing opinions in different scenes with different characters present. As a simple hypothetical example, the playwright might imagine two consecutive scenes in a comedy: in the first, a woman laughingly rejects her would-be lover's advances; in the next, she tells her friend how much she loves that would-be lover. A series of scenes which effectively reveal concealed motives occurs in the first act of *Othello.* In one scene Iago promises loyalty to Roderigo in the latter's efforts to destroy Othello; then in the next scene Iago appears loyal to Othello.

CHARACTER

The term **character** refers, of course, to the people created by the playwright and actors and imagined by the readers or spectators. The main character in a play is the **protagonist;** his or her opponent or opposing force is the **antagonist.** Minor characters can also play a role in establishing meaning in any given situation. John Wright in *Trifles* is dead when the play begins. He is a minor character, yet his function is to initiate the investigation of his death and of the killer's motivation. Although he does not speak, the women deduce, as readers and spectators eventually do, what type of person he was and what conditions his wife was forced to endure.

Another element of character is **motivation,** the driving force or incentive for an action or actions. Sometimes the motivation is determined by a character flaw or defect, called **hamartia** by the ancient Greek philosopher Aristotle. In classical Greek tragedy this hamartia often leads to the downfall of the protagonist. Thus, in Sophocles' *Oedipus the King,* readers and spectators are acutely aware of how Oedipus' quick temper or lack of foresight (his hamartia) contributes to his fall from nobility to lonely exile. At other times, social conditions combine with personal attributes to motivate a person to act or react certain ways. In *Fences,* Troy Maxson, a responsible worker who hands over his paycheck every Friday night, minus his "allowance" for the week, is driven to act irresponsibly by the fences that restrict his life and by his desire to escape the boundaries of his marriage. These acts seem to be contradictory in nature but reflect the complexity of reality.

Another element of characterization is the protagonist's or antagonist's **anagnorisis,** Aristotle's term for recognition or discovery of some important truth. This discovery leads to the protagonist's self-awareness, a very important part of character development. For example, anagnorisis or, to use a modern term, **epiphany,** a manifestation or revelation, occurs in *Oedipus the King.* Oedipus, in discovering the truth about his origins, realizes that what Tiresias said has come true: those who have eyes (Oedipus) sometimes cannot "see"; those who do not have eyes (Tiresias) can "see" the truth. Oedipus' self-awareness, his "seeing" or anagnorisis, is his understanding of his inability to escape his fate and his knowledge that he has polluted the city by killing his father and marrying his mother. Similarly, in *Trifles,* Mrs. Hale and Mrs. Peters recognize the motivation of Mrs. Wright: the horror of her marriage and John Wright's killing of the bird. Nora, in *A Doll's House,* comes to realize that Helmer, her husband, has responded to the threat of exposure only as a father or authoritarian figure, demanding and controlling her life. This epiphany or anagnorisis leads to her bold decision at the end. Whether a character comprehends or discovers truth is a distinguishing trait in his or her temperament.

Dramatic characters may be classified as dynamic or static. If a character changes or grows during the course of the play, he or she is **dynamic.** If, on the other hand, the character is stereotyped and simplified and fails to change or grow, he or she is **static.** In Soyinka's *The Lion and the Jewel,* for example, Sidi is a dynamic character: she grows throughout the course of the play as she comes to appreciate the role of the Bale and agrees to marry him. The men in Susan Glaspell's *Trifles,* on the other hand, are static characters. Throughout the play, they remain condescending toward the women's preoccupation with apparent "trifles" and unaware of the women's discoveries about the murder of John Wright.

PLOT

In his *Poetics,* Aristotle claims that the most important element of a play is its plot. Most dramatists rely on **plot** as a framework, using a pattern of exposition, conflict, complication, climax, and resolution. As in fiction, a playwright may also use the **flashback** technique to convey missing information: he or she breaks into the chronology of the play to return to a previous time. Sometimes flashbacks allow readers to connect past events with present situations in order to understand personalities, the playwright's purpose, and/or theme. As a plot approaches its **climax,** the high point of the action, **dramatic tension,** the audience's desire to see the conflict resolved, increases. In Sophocles' *Oedipus the King,* for instance, attentive readers and spectators learn immediately through the priest that the city is suffering a plague, then begin to sense the conflict in Oedipus' insistence that he will save the city from the plague. As Oedipus tries without success to get information from Tiresias and Creon, the conflict between Oedipus and the gods who have decreed his fate becomes more apparent and more complicated. Dramatic tension increases markedly at the climax as Oedipus finds out the truth; tension decreases at the resolution as he accepts banishment as his fate.

Dramatic irony, which may increase the dramatic tension of the plot, occurs when an important character, lacking information the audience knows, behaves in a way that is diametrically opposed to his or her own best interest or unknowingly says something that has a double meaning. A famous example occurs in Sophocles' *Oedipus the King.* The audience knows that Oedipus murdered his father and married his mother and that his deed has brought a plague on his kingdom of Thebes. Oedipus, who fled Corinth as a young man to avoid fulfillment of a prophecy that he would kill his father and marry his mother, is completely unaware that he has fulfilled the prophecy. As a consequence, his actions throughout the play are dramatically ironic as he first condemns to banishment the person responsible for the plague, unaware that he is condemning himself, then repeatedly acts in a manner contrary to his own interest. Similarly, in Susan Glaspell's *Trifles,* the men's dismissal of the women's detailed knowledge of housekeeping as "trifles" is dramatically ironic since the audience shares the women's knowledge of Mrs. Wright's motivation for killing her husband and sees the men's search for evidence as misguided.

Though most of the plays in this anthology follow traditional patterns of plot, some modern and contemporary playwrights have experimented with plot: sometimes eliminating one or more of its traditional parts, sometimes deliberately avoiding a chronological sequence, and sometimes obscuring altogether any sense that one event necessarily follows or causes another. **Theater of the absurd,** in which both the form and the content of the play reflect the playwright's view of the absurdity of the human condition, exemplifies this experimentation with plot.

THEME

Theme refers to the major ideas or moral precepts in a particular work. Sometimes it is impossible for any two people to agree upon the wording of the theme or themes because moral positions and abstract principles are, naturally, more difficult to express than concrete facts. Even when theme is expressed, often the tendency is to simplify a sometimes complex idea. In many cases, themes can also be related to social problems. For instance, when Susan Glaspell in *Trifles* confronts the different gender perceptions of a crime, she is also discussing the women's disillusionment in marriages. In order to understand the murder of John Wright, readers or audiences must understand his wife's disillusionment. Only then can they arrive at a statement of theme.

Though drama may elucidate problems, it seldom advocates solutions to them. Sophocles' *Oedipus the King,* for example, raises questions about the origins of evil and suffering as well as questions about the proper limits of human power and authority. Though Oedipus has committed grievous evils, readers and spectators may wonder whether he merits his suffering, having sinned in ignorance. Tragic as *Oedipus the King* is, however, it also affirms the dignity of suffering humanity. To understand the theme of the play, an audience or reader must consider all of these questions and ideas.

Harvey Fierstein's short play *On Tidy Endings* is also thematically complex in its exploration of the relationships between the dead man Collin and the other characters: his wife, his lover, and his son. These relationships are further complicated by the reality of AIDS, society's attitude toward gay relationships, and family values.

The following questions are intended as a general guide to reading and writing about a play. Specific guidance is provided by the questions following each of the plays in this anthology.

Stage Directions

1. Have the stage directions helped you to envision the play? If so, how? Have the directions transmitted any of the author's meaning? If so, how? What are some of the unusual features concerning the stage in this particular play?

2. What are some of the explicit descriptions of the set? How does the set help develop character, plot, theme, and setting?

3. What objects or props have contributed the most to the understanding of the story? How?

Setting

1. How does the playwright use the setting to convey character traits, theme, conflict, or irony?

2. How or why is the cultural or physical environment important to the readers' understanding of the play?

3. How important is the setting to the play as a whole?

Style

1. Are characters distinguished from each other by their style—their use of imagery, diction, and sentence structure?

2. How does the playwright use language to develop characters or to convey them?

3. Does the playwright use structural devices to convey meaning? How?

Character

1. What types of characters are presented on the stage? Are they stereotypes or individuals?

2. Are the characters dynamic or static? If dynamic, how do they change or grow? How does the author reveal their depth and complexity?

3. How does the playwright develop character? What does the dialogue tell about characters? Does he or she also use stage movements, gestures, or facial expressions?

4. How does the playwright impart to the audience the thoughts, feelings, and ideas a character wants to conceal from other characters?

5. What motivates the protagonist, antagonist, and/or minor characters?

6. Does the protagonist experience anagnorisis? If so, precisely when does it occur and what does the character discover?

7. Does the protagonist have a tragic flaw (hamartia)? If so, how does this defect in character lead to his or her downfall?

8. What actions reveal qualities of character or personality?

Plot

1. Is the plot the traditional Aristotelian plot of beginning, middle, and end? If it is not traditional, what structure does the playwright use? How do the acts and/or scenes contribute to the overall understanding of the play?

2. What is the basic conflict in the play? Is it between two characters, within a character, or between a character and some large force such as fate, the environment, or an institution?

3. How does the author reveal the conflict? How does he or she create and sustain dramatic tension?

4. Is dramatic irony used to reinforce dramatic tension? If so, how does the playwright overcome the problem of revealing to the audience what he or she does not want a character to know?

Theme

1. What, in your opinion, is the main idea or theme in the play? Is there more than one theme?

2. What questions does the play raise or illuminate? Does it attempt to answer the questions or to solve a problem?

3. How do the plot, character, setting, style, and conflict develop the play's theme?

Writing

Writing a paper is a process like building a house or baking bread; you should not try doing everything at once. A competent builder will not lay a foundation without a plan or frame the walls before he or she has laid a foundation and floor. Similarly, in writing, you should not try to plan, write, edit, and proofread all at the same time. Rather, you should write one step at a time.

Some papers may require more steps than others. A short, timed, in-class writing assignment may allow time for only three steps: planning, writing, and proofreading. A simple plan for such an assignment need answer only two questions: What am I going to say? How am I going to develop my idea convincingly? Suppose, in an essay test covering Alice Walker's "Nineteen Fifty-five," you had thirty minutes to write a paragraph answering the question "Why does Traynor not understand the significance of Gracie Mae's song?" You might decide, in a brief plan, to say "Traynor does not understand Gracie Mae's song because he has not lived it" and to develop this idea by contrasting Traynor's protected life with Gracie Mae's rich and tumultuous one. In writing the paragraph, you might double space to allow room for corrections. Even in a short assignment, correcting errors or checking the spelling of words as you write might distract you from efficiently developing your ideas. Instead of correcting as you write, you should save a few minutes to proofread after you have finished writing.

On the other hand, a long, out-of-class research paper will probably require seven steps: brainstorming, researching, organizing, drafting, editing, rewriting, and proofreading. Suppose, for example, that your teacher asks you to write a research paper based on one of the casebooks in this anthology. You decide to write about Alice Walker's "Everyday Use" and "Nineteen Fifty-five," using the critical essays in the casebook as well as Walker's own essay, "In Search of Our Mother's Gardens." After reading the suggestions for exploration, research, and writing in the Walker casebook, you decide to write on number four:

> In a researched essay, contrast the conception of heritage exempli-
> fied by Dee and Traynor with that exemplified by Maggie and
> Gracie Mae Still. Is a heritage best preserved by protecting it or by
> living it?

If you have not read the stories recently, you should begin by rereading them. Once you have read the stories, you should brainstorm.

Brainstorming is simply a way of generating observations and ideas. You list ideas as they come to mind without paying attention to sentence structure, spelling, order, or even relevance. The purpose is to produce ideas, not to criticize or edit them. You may brainstorm for a few minutes or several hours alone or in a study group; your teacher may even have you do some brainstorming in class, either in groups or in whole-class discussion. Twenty minutes of brainstorming might produce the following list of ideas:

- Dee-Wangero—display hang churn quilt
- Maggie and mother use quilt churn "everyday use"
- Traynor buys what's not his
- Gracie Mae's songs her life, experience, emotion
- Singing naturally—shower, driving—natural choice suits mood
- Songs on radio artificial, not natural choice, mood
- Traynor packages song mass appeal
- Social too—Gracie Mae's song her people's
- Common experience—expression of a people
- Square dance, jam session, hymn sing
- Quilts, garden too, part of life in "In Search"
- Grandfather's Bible
- Walker likes "everyday use," art expressing people
- But is art ok only among producers? Can heritage only be lived?
- Questions classical music, jazz in white clubs
- Also plays, opera—what about Walker's fiction?

Note that this list has no apparent order or consistent form. Brainstorming may take fifteen minutes, an hour, or even longer; you should brainstorm until you have a wealth of specific ideas about your topic.

Once brainstorming has produced a good list of ideas, you need to begin researching them. Begin by rereading the stories, marking passages that relate to your ideas. Then, skim the critical essays for useful ideas. Make a bibliography card for each essay and story you will use; a bibliography card is simply a three-inch by five-inch card listing information you will need on your works cited page. See section on MLA documentation. Your card may be similar to this:

> Byerman, Keith E. <u>Fingering the Jagged Grain.</u> Athens: University of Georgia Press, 1985.

The cards allow you to add sources and arrange them alphabetically without having to rewrite as you would with a list.

Take notes on three-inch by five-inch cards, listing author and page at the top and only one piece of information, either quoted or carefully paraphrased on each card.

> Byerman 161
> "Gracie Mae cannot tell Traynor what the song absolutely means because the meaning changes."

You may also find it helpful to copy onto cards passages from the stories that you want to quote. Then you can draft the paper without repeatedly referring to the textbook. Once you have planned the organization of your paper, you should add a topic heading in the upper right corner of each note card. One alternative to note cards uses xeroxed copies with the appropriate passages highlighted and named by topic. Another alternative is to download data from a CD ROM onto your own computer disk.

You might think of your paper, or any piece of writing, as a kind of contract. If it is properly organized, it will first create an expectation in its **thesis**, a brief statement of the main point contained in the introduction to the paper; then it will fulfill that expectation in the body that follows. A thesis like "Alice Walker wrote about art in her stories" or "Alice Walker's stories and theories about art are interesting" creates no clear expectation. A better thesis might be "Alice Walker's 'Everyday Use' and 'Nineteen Fifty-five' suggest that art loses its meaning and its power when it is separated from the culture that produced it." This thesis constitutes an informal contract with readers that what follows, the body of the paper, will discuss Walker's stories, showing that art separated from its history loses meaning. The thesis will probably change, however, becoming clearer and more precise as the research paper evolves.

Although your teacher may require a formal outline, you may also find other methods of organization helpful. One such method is blocking, the arranging and rearranging of ideas in blocks or groups. Blocking produces not a finished order, but a series of starting points from which to work. You might begin simply by blocking information by characters, grouping ideas related to each, or you might simply block information by its source, the particular work from which it comes. Approaching the material story by story or character by character, however, might seem rather mechanical, so you might rearrange blocks until you arrive at a pattern that seems promising, perhaps something like this:

- Art
  - Quilts, churn, song, my singing in car, in shower
  - Grandfather' Bible in attic
- Producers of art
  - Gracie Mae, Maggie, Mother, Aunt, Grandfather, me
  - Natural part of life
  - Group expression: square dance, jam session, hymn sing
- Consumers/protectors of art
  - Traynor, Dee, me
  - Commercial media
  - Packaged, lowest common denominator

Such a plan might well be sufficient to guide you through a draft of your paper.

Another way of organizing your writing is to follow models of different ways to organize information. Among the most useful of these models are description, exemplification, enumeration, analysis, classification, comparison contrast, and cause effect. These models represent choices; you may choose to use one, two, or even more simultaneously. The models may help organize writing of any length, whether a single paragraph or a book. Also like blocks, models are not finished products but changeable patterns.

Description is usually based on observation and is often organized spacially. It may be ordered from top to bottom or bottom to top. In describing a person, for example, you might begin at his or her feet and move progressively to his or her head, or in describing a face you might begin at the hair and move down to the chin. You might also order description from left to right or right to left, from near to far or far or near, or clockwise or counterclockwise. Finally, you may organize a description to emphasize a mood or dominant impression. For example, in describing a dancer to emphasize grace, you may choose details that contribute to an impression of grace and order them from least important to most important.

Exemplification and **enumeration** are common methods of illustrating ideas. The former uses specific examples to develop a point. If, for example, you cite hymns sung at a revival to illustrate art that naturally expresses both communal emotions and values and a natural, living heritage, you are exemplifying. In fact, the preceding sentence exemplifies. Enumeration is a list of examples, usually in brief form with little detail. As examples of living art, you might list Gracie Mae's songs, fraternity drinking songs, music at a community celebration, music sung at a protest march, and jazz at a jam session.

Analysis examines the relationships between parts or characteristics of a subject. In analyzing Dee-Wangero in "Everyday Use," for example, you might say that she is self-confident and successful, well educated, and condescending toward her less successful and uneducated family. In analyzing Gracie Mae Still, you might point out that she lives simply, that the songs she writes and sings express her experience, and that she understands and enjoys those songs because she has lived them.

Classification requires the division into categories of a large group of people, ideas, or objects. Classification follows a consistent principle. You would not, for example, classify new cars as inexpensive, expensive, and fast; to do so would be to mix two inconsistent principles, cost and speed. The opening part of the introduction in this anthology classifies approaches to literature according to their orientation as text-oriented, author-oriented, and reader-oriented. You could classify the characters in Walker's two stories as insiders, those who are part of a cultural tradition, and outsiders, those who are outside that tradition. The blocks labeled "Producers of art" and "Consumers of art" classify and, in fact, correspond precisely to the insiders and outsiders.

Two common methods of organizing comparisons and contrasts are the block method and the alternating method. The first method devotes a separate block of writing—a sentence, series of sentences, paragraph, or series of paragraphs—to each of the two subjects being compared. If, for example, you were comparing the costs of owning a Ford Taurus and a Honda Accord, you would first discuss the Ford, then discuss the Honda. The alternating method focuses on one common characteristic at a time, referring alternately to one subject, then to another. Using an alternating method to compare costs of the Ford and Honda, you might first focus on initial cost, second focus on the costs of gas and maintenance, and finally focus on resale value. If you were comparing Maggie to her sister Dee, either you could write a block on one followed by a block on the other, or you could compare first their sophistication and level of education, second their attitudes toward family, and finally their attitudes toward family heirlooms like the churn and quilt.

Causal analysis examines the relationships between causes and effects. Such analysis can trace the various causes of a particular effect or the various effects of a particular cause. You might, for example, discuss causes of Traynor's failure to understand Gracie Mae's song, his lack of close relationships, his immersion in luxury, and his insulation from meaningful experience. On the other hand, you might examine the effects of his first encounter with Gracie Mae: his returning to her house and showering her with gifts, his futile efforts to learn the meaning of her song, and his realization that his life is sterile and empty. It is important to realize that most causes have multiple effects and that most effects have multiple causes.

You should not think of your draft as a finished product. At this stage neither neatness nor correctness is important. Your primary goal in drafting should be to get your ideas down in a reasonable order. If you stop to concern yourself with spelling, sentence structure, grammar, and neatness, you may lose your train of thought. If you cannot continue with one paragraph, begin another and return later to the difficult one.

You may want to leave gaps or write marginal notes in your manuscript to indicate omissions or changes you want to make later. Note the markings and marginal notations in the following introductory paragraph:

write out

~~In Alice Walker's "Everyday Use" and "1955," she~~ In "Everyday Use" and "1955," Alice Walker shows the close relationship between art and the people and culture that produced it. When art is taken out of its cultural (word?), it loses its vitality and meaning⊠. When I was ten years old, my ~~mother's~~ maternal grandfather died. ~~I did not find out~~ Not until I got into high school did I find out that he had left me <u>in his will his personal Bible,</u> which was full of his own notes in the margin, comments, and even drawings stuck between the pages. For five years that Bible, from which he had read to me often, sat ~~carefully wrapped~~unused and carefully wrapped in our attic. Is a work of art like my grandfather's Bible best left wrapped and protected and unused or even

rephrase

change of ¶ order of

write out

displayed in some museum, or is it best used and enjoyed by those to whom it is a vital and meaningful part of their heritage? This is one question raised by Alice Walker's short stories "Everyday Use" and "1955."

As this introduction indicates, when you draft a paper, you are likely to begin one way, change your mind, then begin another way. While this introduction is neither well organized nor economically written, it is a promising draft.

Once you have drafted a paper and, if possible, spent several hours or even a day away from it, you should begin editing and rewriting it. To edit your paper, read it closely, marking in the margin passages you need to change. Look for phrases, sentences, and paragraphs that seem out of place; passages that lack adequate support and detail; and sentences that seem awkward, wordy, or unclear. Mark these passages as in the following example:

In Alice Walker's "Everyday Use" and "1955," she In "Everyday Use" and "1955," Alice Walker shows the close relationship between art and the people and culture that produced it. When art is taken out of its cultural (word?), it loses its vitality and meaningful. When I was ten years old, my mother's maternal grandfather died. I did not find out Not until I got into high school did I find out that he had left me in his will his personal Bible, which was full of his own notes in the margin, comments, and even drawings stuck between the pages. For five years that Bible, from which he had read to me often, sat carefully wrappedunused and carefully wrapped in our attic. Is a work of art like my grandfather's Bible best left wrapped and protected and unused or even displayed in some museum, or is it best used and enjoyed by those to whom it is a vital and meaningful part of their heritage? This is one question raised by Alice Walker's short stories "Everyday Use" and "1955."

Begin rewriting the passages you have marked. You may wish to try several different versions of sentences and paragraphs to see which you like best. Experiment with different combinations; you have much to gain and nothing to lose by playing with your sentences at this stage. You might, for example, try several possibilities for improving the opening of the introduction:

Do you like to see art kept wrapped up in an attic or storage place of a museum for protection?

What happens to art when it is packaged, taken from its producers, and boxed for everyone?

Does art belong to the artist, to those who show it and display it, or to those who use it? That is the question raised by Alice Walker's stories "Everyday Use" and "Nineteen Fifty-five."

> When I was ten, my maternal grandfather, to whom I was very close, died.

After much rewriting, the introduction above might read as follows:

> When I was ten, my maternal grandfather died. My grandfather and I had spent countless hours on his big porch swing reading together from his old leather Bible with his personal notes, his comments, and even his own drawings stuck between its pages. Not until I entered high school did I learn that he willed that Bible to me. For five years that Bible had lain carefully wrapped in our attic because my parents were afraid I might damage this precious heirloom. Was I right to be angry at my parents for withholding the Bible? Is such art as my grandfather's Bible best left in protective storage, or is it best used and enjoyed by those for whom it is a vital part of their heritage? This is one question raised by Alice Walker's short stories "Everyday Use" and "Nineteen Fifty-five." Walker's stories reveal how art is intimately connected to the people and culture that produced it. When such art is removed from its cultural context, it loses vitality and meaning.

The final step in preparing a paper is proofreading, the process of reading your paper to correct errors. You will probably be more successful in proofreading if you wait until you are fresh to do it; proofreading a paper at 3:00 A.M. immediately after finishing it is not a good idea. You should break proofreading into two steps: reading and correcting. To proofread effectively, you must read slowly and carefully. One careful, slow, attentive proofreading is better than six careless ones. Look for and mark the following: errors in spelling and usage, sentence fragments and comma splices, inconsistencies in number between nouns and pronouns and between subjects and verbs, faulty parallelism, any other errors in grammar, unintentional repetitions, and omissions. Some students find it helpful to place a blank sheet of paper under each line as they read to slow them down, correcting obvious errors as they go but marking with a check errors they must look up in a dictionary or a grammar handbook. If the paper is handwritten, correct the errors *even if doing so will detract from the neatness of your paper.* Most teachers prefer a slightly messy but correct paper to a neat, incorrect one. If your paper is typewritten, make neat corrections with a fine point pen. If you type your paper on a computer, you should be able to make corrections easily and print another copy.

Documenting a Researched Paper: MLA Style Sheet

When assigned a research paper, ask your instructor what style sheet you should use to document your paper. Many excellent style sheets are available, some designed for particular disciplines. Two of the most often used for papers in the humanities are *The MLA [Modern Language Association] Handbook for Writers of Research Papers* and *The Chicago Manual of Style.* In this text, the *MLA Handbook* will be the basis for documentation in the sample essays. This study is briefly summarized in this section. You might want to consult the *MLA Handbook* for further information and examples.

Documentation of Quotations, Paraphrases, and Summaries

Unless the information is common knowledge, you *must* document any information borrowed from other sources, whether quoted, paraphrased, or summarized. **Paraphrasing** is retelling the original material *in your own words;* if your paraphrase includes any of the original wording, those words must be put in quotation marks. In paraphrasing, be careful not to alter the author's tone or meaning. A paraphrase differs from a summary primarily in length: a paraphrase is about the same length as the original source, but a summary is a concise overview. Because paraphrases and summaries are based on ideas that are not your own, you must document them even though you are not quoting the author directly. Failure to do so is **plagiarism,** the academic equivalent of stealing. Any material quoted must be put in quotation marks and documented. Use quotations judiciously, and avoid back-to-back quotations. Most teachers prefer that no more than one-fifth of your paper be in quotation marks. To prevent your paper from becoming a string of quotations, you should develop the technique of blending paraphrase with short quotations.

Parenthetical Citations

You should always introduce your quotations, making sure that they connect with your sentences grammatically. One method of introducing quotations is simply to mention the speaker or writer:

> Prufrock repeats, "In the room the women come and go / Talking of Michelangelo" (Eliot 4).

You may also use a whole sentence followed by a colon to introduce a quotation:

> Then Mrs. Turpin notices Mary Grace: "Next to her was a fat girl of eighteen or nineteen, scowling into a thick blue book which Mrs. Turpin saw was entitled *Human Development*" (O'Connor 318).

If the material quoted is already in quotation marks, put a single quotation inside the double quotation marks:

> In "The Portable Phonograph," Doctor Jenkins shows the other men the books he selected to save: " 'Shakespeare, the Bible, *Moby Dick,* the *Divine Comedy,*' one of them said softly. 'You might have done worse, much worse' " (Clark 777).

As these examples show, the *MLA Handbook* requires parenthetical citation immediately following a quotation, paraphrase, or summary. The citations correspond to titles listed on the Works Cited page at the end of the paper. After a paraphrase, the documentation precedes the punctuation, if any punctuation is appropriate at that point in the sentence. After quotations, the parenthetical documentation usually follows quotation marks and precedes terminal punctuation. If the final punctuation is a question mark or an exclamation point, the parenthetical documentation may be included earlier in the sentence:

> The grandmother (O'Connor 367) asks, "'You wouldn't shoot a lady, would you?'"

Your parenthetical citation must give the reader (1) enough information to locate the complete bibliographical information on the Works Cited page and (2) the exact page where the cited material appears. If the Works Cited page lists only one source by an author and the author's name has not already been mentioned in the sentence, your citation will consist of the author's last name and the page number. If the author's name has been given in the sentence, you need give only the page number. Notice that no comma appears before the page number. In paraphrases, an effective technique is to introduce the borrowed material with the author's name and to add the page number at the end of the borrowed material. This method lets the reader know exactly where the paraphrase begins. The following examples illustrate correct documentation where a paraphrase or quotation is introduced with the author's name:

> In Gilman's "The Yellow Wallpaper," the narrator implies that, although her husband loves her, he wants to tell her exactly what to do (253).

> Didion says, "Marriage is the classic betrayal" (167).

If the Works Cited page includes two or more works by the same author, your parenthetical citation must include a title. Long titles may be shortened. In the following examples, the full title is "A Good Man Is Hard to Find."

> O'Connor describes the Misfit: "He was an older man than the other two. His hair was just beginning to gray and he wore silver-rimmed spectacles that gave him a scholarly look" ("A Good Man" 146).

> The grandmother says, " 'If you would pray, . . . Jesus would help you' " (O'Connor, "A Good Man" 150).

If you want to use information that is already quoted, you should first try to find the original source. If you cannot find the original, however, you may use the material by giving credit to both sources, as in the following example:

James Russell Lowell decided to omit Thoreau's last sentence in *The Maine Woods,* which says, " 'It [the pine tree] is as immortal as I am, and perchance will go to as high a heaven, there to tower above me still' " (Thoreau as cited by Matthews 251).

The complete bibliographical material on the Works Cited page would be listed under Matthews, not under Thoreau.

If your source has two or three authors, all last names are listed in the parenthetical citation; if there are more than three authors, the first author is listed followed by "et al.," meaning "and others."

If the source has no author, use its title. Thus, the citation should be as follows: ("Wife Is Not Convicted of Murder" 20).

If the work referred to has more than one volume, its number must be included as in the following (Graves 1: 256).

If several works provide the same information that is being paraphrased, the documentation should give credit to all: (Graves 1: 256; Campbell 112; Hamilton 29). If more than three authors give the same information and it is not considered general knowledge, content notes are effective (see below).

LONG QUOTATIONS AND POETRY

If your quotation is long, over four lines, you must indent it on the left. The indentation indicates that the information is quoted. Therefore, quotation marks are not needed unless the material quoted was already in quotation marks, as in the second example below. Note that in an indented quotation final punctuation precedes the parenthetical citation.

> Capote's narrator says,
> > This is our last Christmas together.
> > Life separates us. Those who Know Best decide that I belong in a military school. . . . I have a new home too. But it doesn't count. Home is where my friend is, and there I never go. (48–49)

> Ozzie recounts to his friend Itzie the rabbi's extreme reaction:
> > "Finally, he starts screaming that I was deliberately simpleminded and a wise guy, and that my mother had to come, and this was the last time. And that I'd never get bar-mitzvahed if he could help it." (Roth 456)

Quotation marks are necessary here because the passage is quoted in the source.

When you are quoting poetry, if you cite one or two lines, include the quotation in the text, using a slash to show where the line ended:

> In "A Prayer for My Daughter," Yeats wishes, "And may her bridegroom bring her to a house / Where all's accustomed . . . " (ll. 74–75).

If you quote more than two lines of poetry, indent the quotation and set the lines as the poet does:

> Yeats prays that his daughter have beauty but know how to value it:
> > May she be granted beauty and yet not
> > Beauty to make a stranger's eye distraught,
> > Or hers before a looking glass . . . . (ll. 17–19)

Notice that citations to poetry list line rather than page numbers.

You must reproduce quotations *exactly* unless you indicate that changes have been made. Changes may be indicated by using ellipses or brackets.

If you omit something from a quotation, let the reader know by using ellipses, three spaced dots. If you omit a whole sentence, use four dots (three ellipses and a period). If you omit a line or more of poetry or a whole paragraph include a whole line of spaced dots. Most teachers prefer that if you quote only a few words and make them a grammatical part of your sentence, you omit the ellipses.

> Greiner describes Frost's "An Old Man's Winter Night" as "nothing if not a poem of despair, and . . . a companion piece . . . to T. S. Eliot's equally fine 'Gerontion' " (231).

> Frost, in his poem " 'Out, Out—,' " personifies the saw, saying,
> > . . . At the word, the saw,
> > As if to prove saws knew what supper meant,
> > Leaped out at the boy's hand, . . .
> > . . . .
> > Neither refused the meeting. . . . (ll. 13–17)

> Gerber believes that Frost's "Home Burial" is "modern in theme" (229).

Brackets are used to add information inside a quotation for clarification or grammatical correctness or to indicate that the original material contains an error:

> When Kugelmass visits Persky the Great, Persky "[removes] some old silk handkerchiefs that were lying on [the cabinet's] top" (Allen 341).

The Latin word *sic* is used to indicate an error in a quotation:

> The reporter accused the senator of "having forgotten his principals [sic]" (Johnson A1).

Works Cited Page

On the Works Cited page, list alphabetically *all* sources for your paper.

BOOKS

Basic citations for books include the following information if it is available or applicable: author, title, editor, edition, place, publisher, publication date, and volume. Examples of some book citations follow:

Book with one author:

Keillor, Garrison. *Happy to Be Here: Stories and Comic Pieces.* New York: Atheneum, 1982.

Two or more works by the same author:

O'Connor, Flannery. *The Violent Bear It Away.* New York: Farrar, Straus & Cudahy, 1960.

———. *Wise Blood.* 2nd ed. New York: Farrar, Straus & Cudahy, 1962.

Work with two authors or editors:

Andrew, Malcolm, and Ronald Waldron, eds. *The Poems of the Pearl Manuscript: Pearl, Cleanness, Patience, Sir Gawain and the Green Knight.* Berkeley: University of California Press, 1979.

Work with more than two authors:

Tucker, Susan Martin, et al. *Patient Care Standards: Nursing Process, Diagnosis, and Outcome.* 5th ed. St. Louis: Mosby Year Book, 1992.

Work with both author and editor:

Webster, John. *The White Devil.* Ed. John Russell Brown. Oxford: Manchester University Press, 1968.

Work with a translator:

Mann, Thomas. *The Magic Mountain.* Trans. H. T. Lowe-Porter. New York: Knopf, 1953.

An introduction or preface:

Woollcott, Alexander. Introduction. *The Complete Works of Lewis Carroll.* New York: Modern Library, n.d.

(Notice the use of n.d. when the book does not include a publication date. Similarly n.p. means no publisher is given in the book.)

Article or story printed as a part of a book:

Hemingway, Ernest. "The Snows of Kilimanjaro." *The Short Stories of Ernest Hemingway.* New York: Charles Scribner's Sons, 1966. 52–77.

Poem, story, or article reprinted in a book:

Kenny, Maurice. "Wild Strawberry." *Dancing Back Strong the Nation.* Fredonia, New York: White Pine Press, 1981. Rpt. in *Harper's Anthology of 20th Century Native American Poetry.* Ed. Duane Niatum. New York: Harper and Row, 1988. 37–38.

Notice that when a work is published or reprinted as a part of a book, as illustrated in the two entries above, specific pages are given.

Work of several volumes:

Bullough, Geoffrey, ed. *Narrative and Dramatic Sources of Shakespeare.* 8 vols. London: Routledge and Kegan Paul, 1966–1975.

One volume of a multiple volume set:

Bullough, Geoffrey, ed. *The Comedies: 1597–1603.* 1968. Vol. 3 of *Narrative and Dramatic Sources of Shakespeare.* 8 vols. London: Routledge and Kegan Paul, 1966–1975.

PERIODICALS

Basic citations for periodicals include the following information: author, article title, periodical name, series number or name, volume number (for a scholarly journal), publication date, and page numbers.

Article in a scholarly journal:

Licala, Elizabeth. "Charles Clough's Dreampix." *Art in America* 80 (July 1992): 94–97.

Article from a monthly magazine:

Barrett, Michael J. "The Case for More School Days." *The Atlantic Monthly* Nov. 1990: 78, 80–81.

Article in a weekly magazine:

McCallister, J. F. O. "The Other Player." *Time* 10 August 1992: 30.

Article from a journal found on microfilm:

Marston, Jane. "Epistemology and the Solipsistic Consciousness in Flannery O'Connor's 'Greenleaf.' " Microfilm. *Studies in Short Fiction* 21 (Fall 1984): 375–82.

Newspaper article:

Mydans, Seth. "In an Assault on Tradition, More Schools Last All Year." *New York Times* 18 Aug. 1991: A1, A22.

OTHER SOURCES

There are many other sources of information including computer software, television and radio programs, recordings, performances, works of art, letters, interviews, and films. Consult the *MLA Handbook* for complete details. Representative samples are shown here:

Personal interview:

Lindbergh, Marsha. Orchestra Director, Jonesboro (GA) Middle School. Interview. 25 June 1992.

Film:

Bram Stoker's Dracula. Dir. Francis Ford Coppola. Columbia, 1992.

Videotape:

Barnburning. Videocassette. Dir. Peter Werner. Prod. Calvin Scaggs. American Short Story Series. Monterey Home Video, 1980. 40 minutes. Based on William Faulkner's "Barnburning."

CONTENT NOTES

You may use content notes to add information that you would like the reader to know but that would interfere with the flow or organization of your paper. Content notes do not, as a rule, give documentation; but if you are citing so many sources that listing them in the text would be awkward, you could list them in content notes instead. Also if the content note itself includes a quotation, give the citation and list the source in the Works Cited page. Include the notes on a separate page before the Works Cited page. Indicate notes in the text with consecutive numbers one-half space above the line like this: [1] On the Content Notes page indent the first line of each note and precede it with a raised number corresponding to the number in the text.

Some examples of content notes follow:

Acknowledgments

[1]The author would like to thank Maxine Sample for lending her essential materials on Alice Walker.

Comparison

[2]Cf. [Compare] Carlos Baker's comment on Hemingway's return (121–22). [Note: Baker must be listed on Works Cited page]

[3]Similar opinions are expressed by Marcus (123–27), Johnston (14–19), and Wilcox (211–21).

Exceptions to prevailing point of view

[4]Wilson disagrees with this interpretation (198–203).

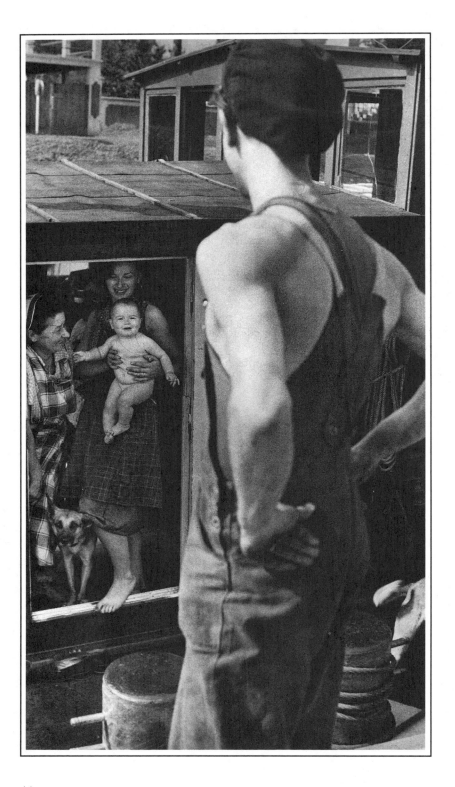

FAMILY

THE EARLIEST AND USUALLY THE STRONGEST influence on each of us is the family. Throughout history, individuals from every walk of life have accused or thanked, bemoaned or celebrated members of their own families. As a result, family relationships have provided the subject matter for a wide variety of themes from the destructive to the productive: from the strangling, inhibiting, and sometimes abusive behavior possible in families to the loving and supportive security offered by parents, grandparents, and siblings; from the lack of communication between generations to the values of family traditions. As readers, we can sympathize with, perhaps even identify with, authors as they share their own family experiences and characters, and as they cope with problems involving parents, siblings, and other family members.

Through the characters in the stories or poems or the real people in the essays, we can vicariously experience family life in a variety of times, economic levels, and cultures. We can reminisce with Agee about the peace of a summer evening in Knoxville in 1915. With the help of writers like Agueros and Liang and Shapiro, we can compare or contrast our experiences of growing up with those of children from other cultural backgrounds. Writers as diverse as Yeats and Hongo share with us the depth of a parent's love for a child. Plath, on the other hand, describes the bitterness of a daughter toward her father. In *On Tidy Endings*, Fierstein explores the complexities of changing family relationships as they affect individual identity and as they are intensified by presently incurable diseases. By allowing us to participate in the hardships and confusion of a modern dysfunctional family, Carson McCullers helps us to understand that the "immense complexity of love" sometimes causes problems which have no easy solutions.

Authors teach us the value of learning to laugh at our problems within our families. They also share with us the realization that even the most disparate family members can work through problems to reach solutions and an even greater depth of love. We can laugh with Frank O'Connor and Eudora Welty at the perceptions and misperceptions of their narrators and wonder if we have similar misperceptions. In "Sonny's Blues," James Baldwin lets us share in the stories of two generations of brothers and participate in the reconciliation of these two very different brothers. Truman Capote, drawing from his real-life experiences, tells us of the beautiful friendship between a little boy and an older woman in "A Christmas Memory." Through the enjoyment of this literature—the tears, the curses, the prayers, and the laughter—we can deepen our own understanding of others and of ourselves.

ESSAYS

JAMES AGEE (1909–1955)

James Agee is known primarily for two books, A Death in the Family, *a posthumously published novel which is preceded by "Knoxville: Summer 1915," and* Let Us Now Praise Famous Men *(1941), a moving journalistic examination of sharecroppers in the South on which Agee collaborated with photographer Walker Evans. Multitalented, Agee also wrote other pieces of journalism, poetry, film scripts, and criticism.*

Knoxville: Summer 1915

1   We are talking now of summer evenings in Knoxville, Tennessee in the time that I lived there so successfully disguised to myself as a child. It was a little bit mixed sort of block, fairly solidly lower middle class, with one or two juts apiece on either side of that. The houses corresponded: middle-sized gracefully fretted wood houses built in the late nineties and early nineteen hundreds, with small front and side and more spacious back yards, and trees in the yards, and porches. These were softwooded trees, poplars, tulip trees, cottonwoods. There were fences around one or two of the houses, but mainly the yards ran into each other with only now and then a low hedge that wasn't doing very well. There were few good friends among the grown people, and they were not poor enough for the other sort of intimate acquaintance, but everyone nodded and spoke, and even might talk short times, trivially, and at the two extremes of the general or the particular, and ordinarily nextdoor neighbors talked quite a bit when they happened to run into each other, and never paid calls. The men were mostly small businessmen, one or two very modestly executives, one or two worked with their hands, most of them clerical, and most of them between thirty and forty-five.

2   But it is of these evenings, I speak.

3   Supper was at six and was over by half past. There was still daylight, shining softly and with a tarnish, like the lining of a shell; and the carbon lamps lifted at the corners were on in the light, and the locusts were started, and the fire flies were out, and a few frogs were flopping in the dewy grass, by the time the fathers and the children came out. The children ran out first hell bent and yelling those names by which they were known; then the fathers sank out leisurely in crossed suspenders,

their collars removed and their necks looking tall and shy. The mothers
stayed back in the kitchen washing and drying, putting things away,
recrossing their traceless footsteps like the lifetime journeys of bees,
measuring out the dry cocoa for breakfast. When they came out they had
taken off their aprons and their skirts were dampened and they sat in
rockers on their porches quietly.

It is not of the games children play in the evening that I want to speak   4
now, it is of a contemporaneous atmosphere that has little to do with
them: that of the fathers of families, each in his space of lawn, his shirt
fishlike pale in the unnatural light and his face nearly anonymous, hosing
their lawns. The hoses were attached at spiggots that stood out of the
brick foundations of the houses. The nozzles were variously set but
usually so there was a long sweet stream of spray, the nozzle wet in the
hand, the water trickling the right forearm and the peeled-back cuff, and
the water whishing out a long loose and low-curved cone, and so gentle
a sound. First an insane noise of violence in the nozzle, then the still
irregular sound of adjustment, then the smoothing into steadiness and a
pitch as accurately tuned to the size and style of stream as any violin. So
many qualities of sound out of one hose: so many choral differences out
of those several hoses that were in earshot. Out of any one hose, the
almost dead silence of the release, and the short still arch of the separate
big drops, silent as a held breath, and the only noise the flattering noise
on leaves and the slapped grass at the fall of each big drop. That, and the
intense hiss with the intense stream; that, and that same intensity not
growing less but growing more quiet and delicate with the turn of the
nozzle, up to that extreme tender whisper when the water was just a wide
bell of film. Chiefly, though, the hoses were set much alike, in a compromise between distance and tenderness of spray (and quite surely a
sense of art behind this compromise, and a quiet deep joy, too real to
recognize itself), and the sounds therefore were pitched much alike;
pointed by the snorting start of a new hose; decorated by some man
playful with the nozzle; left empty, like God by the sparrow's fall, when
any single one of them desists: and all, though near alike, of various
pitch; and in this unison. These sweet pale streamings in the light lift out
their pallors and their voices all together, mothers hushing their children,
the hushing unnaturally prolonged, the men gentle and silent and each
snail-like withdrawn into the quietude of what he singly is doing, the
urination of huge children stood loosely military against an invisible wall,
and gentle happy and peaceful, tasting the mean goodness of their living
like the last of their suppers in their mouths; while the locusts carry on
this noise of hoses on their much higher and sharper key. The noise of the
locust is dry, and it seems not to be rasped or vibrated but urged from
him as if through a small orifice by a breath that can never give out. Also
there is never one locust but an illusion of at least a thousand. The noise
of each locust is pitched in some classic locust range out of which none
of them varies more than two full tones: and yet you seem to hear each
locust discrete from all the rest, and there is a long, slow, pulse in their

noise, like the scarcely defined arch of a long and high set bridge. They are all around in every tree, so that the noise seems to come from nowhere and everywhere at once, from the whole shell heaven, shivering in your flesh and teasing your eardrums, the boldest of all the sounds of night. And yet it is habitual to summer nights, and is of the great order of noises, like the noises of the sea and of the blood her precocious grandchild, which you realize you are hearing only when you catch yourself listening. Meantime from low in the dark, just outside the swaying horizons of the hoses, conveying always grass in the damp of dew and its strong green-black smear of smell, the regular yet spaced noises of the crickets, each a sweet cold silver noise threenoted, like the slipping each time of three matched links of a small chain.

5   But the men by now, one by one, have silenced their hoses and drained and coiled them. Now only two, and now only one, is left, and you see only ghostlike shirt with the sleeve garters, and sober mystery of his mild face like the lifted face of large cattle enquiring of your presence in a pitchdark pool of meadow; and now he too is gone; and it has become that time of evening when people sit on their porches, rocking gently and talking gently and watching the street and the standing up into their sphere of possession of the trees, of birds hung havens, hangars. People go by; things go by. A horse, drawing a buggy, breaking his hollow iron music on the asphalt; a loud auto; a quiet auto; people in pairs, not in a hurry, scuffling, switching their weight of aestival body, talking casually, the taste hovering over them of vanilla, strawberry, pasteboard and starched milk, the image upon them of lovers and horsemen, squared with clowns in hueless amber. A street car raising its iron moan; stopping, belling and starting; stertorous; rousing and raising again its iron increasing moan and swimming its gold windows and straw seats on past and past and past, the bleak spark crackling and cursing above it like a small malignant spirit set to dog its tracks; the iron whine rises on rising speed; still risen, faints; halts; the faint stinging bell; rises again, still fainter; fainter, lifting, lifts, faints foregone: forgotten. Now is the night one blue dew.

6   Now is the night one blue dew, my father has drained, he has coiled the hose.

7   Low on the length of lawns, a frailing of fire who breathes.

8   Content, silver, like peeps of light, each cricket makes his comment over and over in the drowned grass.

9   A cold toad thumpily flounders.

10   Within the edges of damp shadows of side yards are hovering children nearly sick with joy of fear, who watch the unguarding of a telephone pole.

11   Around white carbon corner lamps bugs of all sizes are lifted elliptic, solar systems. Big hardshells bruise themselves, assailant: he is fallen on his back, legs squiggling.

Parents on porches: rock and rock: From damp strings morning glories: 12
hang their ancient faces.

The dry and exalted noise of the locusts from all the air at once enchants   13
my eardrums.

On the rough wet grass of the back yard my father and mother have   14
spread quilts. We all lie there, my mother, my father, my uncle, my aunt,
and I too am lying there. First we were sitting up, then one of us lay
down, and then we all lay down, on our stomachs, or on our sides, or on
our backs, and they have kept on talking. They are not talking much, and
the talk is quiet, of nothing in particular, of nothing at all in particular,
of nothing at all. The stars are wide and alive, they seem each like a smile
of great sweetness, and they seem very near. All my people are larger
bodies than mine, quiet, with voices gentle and meaningless like the
voices of sleeping birds. One is an artist, he is living at home. One is a
musician, she is living at home. One is my mother who is good to me.
One is my father who is good to me. By some chance, here they are, all
on this earth; and who shall ever tell the sorrow of being on this earth,
lying, on quilts, on the grass, in a summer evening, among the sounds of
the night. May God bless my people, my uncle, my aunt, my mother, my
good father, oh, remember them kindly in their time of trouble; and in
the hour of their taking away.

After a little I am taken in and put to bed. Sleep, soft smiling, draws me   15
unto her: and those receive me, who quietly treat me, as one familiar and
well-beloved in that home: but will not, oh, will not, not now, not ever;
but will not ever tell me who I am.

❏ Questions for Discussion

1. What is the effect created by Agee's long description of the
   men watering the lawn and of the various sounds that harmo-
   nize with the water's spray? Why does Agee dwell on a very
   ordinary act? To what does Agee compare the sounds of the
   hoses, locusts, and crickets in an extended analogy?

2. In his description of Knoxville during the summer of 1915,
   Agee uses many devices—**alliteration, onomatopoeia, simile, metaphor, personification,** and **oxymoron**—to create a mood of
   peace in this beautifully descriptive passage. Point out at least
   one example of each device.

3. Agee says, "People go by; things go by." Is he speaking generally or only about the specific setting of the essay? If generally,
   what does he mean?

4. What emotions dominate the final image of the family sitting
   together on the lawn? What emotions do you suppose the
   adult writer felt upon recalling the rituals of summer evenings
   at home?

❏ **Suggestions for Exploration and Writing**

1. The **narrator** says in the first sentence that he lived in Knoxville "so successfully disguised to myself as a child" and in the last sentence that "those who receive me" in sleep "will not ever tell me who I am." In relationship to the whole essay, discuss what the author means by these phrases.

2. Write a description of an evening in your childhood which has special meaning for you. If possible, make the mood of your passage appropriate to its meaning as Agee does.

JACK AGUEROS (1934–   )

Agueros was born in Harlem in New York City. His parents, Puerto Rican immigrants, wanted their son to become a doctor. Instead, Agueros, who always loved to read, chose a writing career. He often writes about his experiences growing up Puerto Rican in New York. Agueros has always been active in social causes, fighting poverty and helping young people. "Halfway to Dick and Jane" reveals his concern for the youth of cities and for the preservation of cultural diversity.

from *Halfway to Dick and Jane*

1   My mother kept an immaculate household. Bedspreads (chenille seemed to be very in) and lace curtains, washed at home like everything else, were hung up on huge racks with rows of tight nails. The racks were assembled in the living room, and the moisture from the wet bedspreads would fill the apartment. In a sense, that seems to be the lasting image of that period of my life. The house was clean. The neighbors were clean. The streets, with few cars, were clean. The buildings were clean and uncluttered with people on the stoops. The park was clean. The visitors to my house were clean and the relationships that my family had with other Puerto Rican families, and the Italian families that my father had met through baseball and my mother through the garment center, were clean. Second Avenue was clean and most of the apartment windows had awnings. There was always music, there seemed to be no rain, and snow did not become slush. School was fun, we wrote essays about how grand America was, we put up hunchbacked cats at Halloween, we believed Santa Claus visited everyone. I believed everyone was Catholic. I grew up with dogs, nightingales, my godmother's guitar, rocking chair, cat, guppies, my father's occasional roosters, kept in a cage on the fire escape. Laundry delivered and collected by horse and wagon, fruits and vegetables sold the same way, windowsill refrigeration in winter, iceman and box in summer. The police my friends, likewise the teachers.

2   In short, the first seven or so years of my life were not too great a variation on Dick and Jane, the school book figures who, if my memory

serves me correctly, were blond Anglo-Saxons, not immigrants, not migrants like the Puerto Ricans, and not the children of either immigrants or migrants.

My family moved in 1941 to Lexington Avenue into a larger apart- 3 ment where I could have my own room. It was a light, sunny, railroad flat on the top floor of a well-kept building. I transferred to a new school, and whereas before my classmates had been mostly black, the new school had few blacks. The classes were made up of Italians, Irish, Jews, and a sprinkling of Puerto Ricans. My block was populated by Jews, Italians, and Puerto Ricans.

And then a whole series of different events began. I went to junior 4 high school. We played in the backyards, where we tore down fences to build fires to cook stolen potatoes. We tore up whole hedges, because the green tender limbs would not burn when they were peeled, and thus made perfect skewers for our stolen "mickies." We played tag in the abandoned buildings, tearing the plaster off the walls, tearing the wire lath off the wooden slats, tearing the wooden slats themselves, good for fires, for kites, for sword fighting. We ran up and down the fire escapes playing tag and over and across many rooftops. The war ended and the heavy Puerto Rican migration began. The Irish and the Jews disappeared from the neighborhood. The Italians tried to consolidate east of Third Avenue.

What caused the clean and open world to end? Many things. Into an 5 ancient neighborhood came pouring four to five times more people than it had been designed to hold. Men who came running at the promise of jobs were jobless as the war ended. They were confused. They could not see the economic forces that ruled their lives as they drank beer on the corners, reassuring themselves of good times to come while they were hell-bent toward alcoholism. The sudden surge in numbers caused new resentments, and prejudice was intensified. Some were forced to live in cellars, and were then characterized as cave dwellers. Kids came who were confused by the new surroundings; their Puerto Ricanness forced us against a mirror asking, "If they are Puerto Ricans, what are we?" and thus they confused us. In our confusion we were sometimes pathetically reaching out, sometimes pathologically striking out. Gangs. Drugs. Wine. Smoking. Girls. Dances and slow-drag music. Mambo. Spics, Spooks, and Wops. Territories, brother gangs, and war councils establishing rules for right of way on blocks and avenues and for seating in the local theater. Pegged pants and zip guns. Slang.

Dick and Jane were dead, man. Education collapsed. Every classroom 6 had ten kids who spoke no English. Black, Italian, Puerto Rican relations in the classroom were good, but we all knew we couldn't visit one another's neighborhoods. Sometimes we could not move too freely within our own blocks. On 109th, from the lamp post west, the Latin Aces, and from the lamp post east, the Senecas, the "club" I belonged to. The kids who spoke no English became known as Marine Tigers, picked up from a popular Spanish song. (The *Marine Tiger* and the *Marine Shark* were two ships that sailed from San Juan to New York and brought over many, many migrants from the island.)

7   The neighborhood had its boundaries. Third Avenue and east, Italian. Fifth Avenue and west, black. South, there was a hill on 103rd Street known locally as Cooney's Hill. When you got to the top of the hill, something strange happened: America began, because from the hill south was where the "Americans" lived. Dick and Jane were not dead; they were alive and well in a better neighborhood.

8   When, as a group of Puerto Rican kids, we decided to go swimming to Jefferson Park Pool, we knew we risked a fight and a beating from the Italians. And when we went to La Milagrosa Church in Harlem, we knew we risked a fight and a beating from the blacks. But when we went over Cooney's Hill, we risked dirty looks, disapproving looks, and questions from the police like, "What are you doing in this neighborhood?" and "Why don't you kids go back where you belong?"

9   Where we belonged! Man, I had written compositions about America. Didn't I belong on the Central Park tennis courts, even if I didn't know how to play? Couldn't I watch Dick play? Weren't these policemen working for me too?

❏ Questions for Discussion

1. How does Agueros change when he enters junior high school in a new neighborhood? How is his new neighborhood different from his old one? How does he use Dick and Jane to measure the changes in his neighborhood as he grew up? Why "halfway"?

2. Who are the Americans over Cooney's Hill if they are not the Italians, Blacks, and Puerto Ricans? Why do the various ethnic groups suddenly become very territorial, very protective of their home turf?

3. What does Agueros' final series of questions suggest about equal opportunity in America? From a minority's point of view, what are some negatives about the neighborhood?

4. What is suggested by the question, "Couldn't I watch Dick play [on the Central Park tennis courts]?"

❏ Suggestion for Exploration and Writing

1. Agueros says that the students got along well and relationships were good in the classroom, but "we all knew we couldn't visit one another's neighborhoods." Is this statement true today? Write an essay that discusses barriers to multicultural friendships.

JOAN DIDION (1934–   )

Didion, an American novelist and journalist, grew up in California. In essays such as those collected in Slouching Toward Bethlehem *(1968), from which "On Going Home" comes, she examines contemporary Americans' loss of communal values and direction.*

On Going Home

I am home for my daughter's first birthday. By "home" I do not mean 1
the house in Los Angeles where my husband and I and the baby live, but the place where my family is, in the Central Valley of California. It is a vital although troublesome distinction. My husband likes my family but is uneasy in their house, because once there I fall into their ways, which are difficult, oblique, deliberately inarticulate, not my husband's ways. We live in dusty houses ("D-U-S-T," he once wrote with his finger on surfaces all over the house, but no one noticed it) filled with mementos quite without value to him (what could the Canton dessert plates mean to him? how could he have known about the assay scales, why should he care if he did know?), and we appear to talk exclusively about people we know who have been committed to mental hospitals, about people we know who have been booked on drunk-driving charges, and about property, particularly about property, land, price per acre and C-2 zoning and assessments and freeway access. My brother does not understand my husband's inability to perceive the advantage in the rather common real-estate transaction known as "sale-leaseback," and my husband in turn does not understand why so many of the people he hears about in my father's house have recently been committed to mental hospitals or booked on drunk-driving charges. Nor does he understand that when we talk about sale-leasebacks and right-of-way condemnations we are talking in code about things we like best, the yellow fields and the cottonwoods and the rivers rising and falling and the mountain roads closing when the heavy snow comes in. We miss each other's points, have another drink and regard the fire. My brother refers to my husband, in his presence, as "Joan's husband." Marriage is the classic betrayal.

Or perhaps it is not any more. Sometimes, I think that those of us who 2
are now in our thirties were born into the last generation to carry the burden of "home," to find in family life the source of all tension and drama. I had by all objective accounts a "normal" and a "happy" family situation, and yet I was almost thirty years old before I could talk to my family on the telephone without crying after I had hung up. We did not fight. Nothing was wrong. And yet some nameless anxiety colored the emotional charges between me and the place that I came from. The question of whether or not you could go home again was a very real part of the sentimental and largely literary baggage with which we left home in the fifties; I suspect that it is irrelevant to the children born of the fragmentation after World War II. A few weeks ago in a San Francisco

bar I saw a pretty young girl on crystal take off her clothes and dance for the cash prize in an "amateur-topless" contest. There was no particular sense of moment about this, none of the effect of romantic degradation, of "dark journey," for which my generation strived so assiduously. What sense could that girl possibly make of, say, *Long Day's Journey into Night?* Who is beside the point?

3   That I am trapped in this particular irrelevancy is never more apparent to me than when I am home. Paralyzed by the neurotic lassitude engendered by meeting one's past at every turn, around every corner, inside every cupboard, I go aimlessly from room to room. I decide to meet it head-on and clear out a drawer, and I spread the contents on the bed. A bathing suit I wore the summer I was seventeen. A letter of rejection from *The Nation,* an aerial photograph of the site for a shopping center my father did not build in 1954. Three teacups hand-painted with cabbage roses and signed "E.M.," my grandmother's initials. There is no final solution for letters of rejection from *The Nation* and teacups hand-painted in 1900. Nor is there any answer to snapshots of one's grandfather as a young man on skis, surveying around Donner Pass in the year 1910. I smooth out the snapshot and look into his face, and do and do not see my own. I close the drawer, and have another cup of coffee with my mother. We get along very well, veterans of a guerilla war we never understood.

4   Days pass. I see no one. I come to dread my husband's evening call, not only because he is full of news of what by now seems to me our remote life in Los Angeles, people he has seen, letters which require attention, but because he asks what I have been doing, suggests uneasily that I get out, drive to San Francisco or Berkeley. Instead I drive across the river to a family graveyard. It has been vandalized since my last visit and the monuments are broken, overturned in the dry grass. Because I once saw a rattlesnake in the grass I stay in the car and listen to a country-and-Western station. Later I drive with my father to a ranch he has in the foothills. The man who runs his cattle on it asks us to the round-up, a week from Sunday, and although I know that I will be in Los Angeles I say, in the oblique way my family talks, that I will come. Once home I mention the broken monuments in the graveyard. My mother shrugs.

5   I go to visit my great-aunts. A few of them think now that I am my cousin, or their daughter who died young. We recall an anecdote about a relative last seen in 1948, and they ask if I still like living in New York City. I have lived in Los Angeles for three years, but I say that I do. The baby is offered a horehound drop, and I am slipped a dollar bill "to buy a treat." Questions trail off, answers are abandoned, the baby plays with the dust motes in a shaft of the afternoon sun.

6   It is time for the baby's birthday party: a white cake, strawberry-marshmallow ice cream, a bottle of champagne saved from another party. In the evening, after she has gone to sleep, I kneel beside the crib and touch her face, where it is pressed against the slats, with mine. She is an open and trusting child, unprepared for and unaccustomed to the

ambushes of family life, and perhaps it is just as well that I can offer her little of that life. I would like to give her more. I would like to promise her that she will grow up with a sense of her cousins and of rivers and her great-grandmother's teacups, would like to pledge her a picnic on a river with fried chicken and her hair uncombed, would like to give her *home* for her birthday, but we live differently now and I can promise her nothing like that. I give her a xylophone and a sundress from Madeira, and promise to tell her a funny story.

❏ Questions for Discussion

1. What does Didion mean when she says, "Marriage is the classic betrayal"? What is the source of tension between Didion's family and her husband?

2. Didion says that until she was "almost thirty," she would cry after calling her family. Why do you think she cried?

3. What is Didion's definition of home? What does she mean when she says, "I would like to give her [her daughter] *home,* but we live differently now"? How does the **symbolism** of the graveyard develop Didion's feeling of rootlessness?

4. Why, in an essay about going home, does Didion begin and end with her daughter's first birthday?

5. Why does Didion say that she and her mother are "veterans of a guerilla war we never understood"?

❏ Suggestions for Exploration and Writing

1. Discuss in detail how your relationship to your family has changed since you began college. How does your experience compare with Didion's?

2. Nuclear families often develop private rituals, in-jokes, and special word usages which only they understand. Such rituals, jokes, and usages are one source of conflict between the writer's family and her husband. Write an essay in which you examine the private rituals and language of your own family.

3. Write an essay agreeing with or attacking Didion's belief that today's generation is unlikely to know the kind of home she describes.

LIANG HENG (1954–   ) AND JUDITH SHAPIRO (1953–   )

Liang Heng was born in China and grew up as a Red Guard, a loyal supporter of Mao Zedong. Gradually, however, he rejected Chinese communism. In 1979, as a student at Hunan Teachers' College, he met Judith Shapiro, a graduate student in Asian Studies at the University of California, Berkeley. Shapiro had been hired by the Chinese government to teach English. Liang and Shapiro met secretly to translate an article into Chinese, and their clandestine translation project blossomed into a secret romance. Currently, they are married and live in New York.

Chairman Mao's Good Little Boy

1   Once when I was nearly four, I decided to escape from the child-care center. The idea of waiting through another Saturday afternoon was unbearable. I would stand with the other children in the office doorway, yelling out the names of those whose relatives we spotted coming to rescue them. I would become frantic and miserable as the possibility that I had been forgotten seemed more and more real. Then at last the frail figure of my beloved Waipo, my maternal grandmother, would appear to take me away. But this week I wouldn't have to wait. I had just discovered a doorway leading from the kitchen directly on to the Changsha streets, left ajar, perhaps, by the cooks now that the bitter winter weather had passed. So, during after-lunch nap, I crawled over the green bars of my crib and stole softly out, past the sleeping rows of my fellow inmates, past Nurse Nie dozing in her chair. I crept into the coal-dark kitchen with its silent black works. Then I exploded out the door into the dazzling light of freedom.

2   The child-care center was hateful. You couldn't eat sweets when you wanted to, and you had to fold your hands behind your back and sing a song before the nurses would let you eat your meals. Then, if you ate too fast, they hit you over the head with a fly swatter. The songs and dances—like "Sweeping the Floor," "Working in the Factory," and "Planting Trees in the Countryside"—were fun, but I was constantly in trouble for wanting to dance the army dance when it was time for the hoeing dance or for refusing to take the part of the landlord, the wolf, or the lazybones. I also had problems with the interminable rest periods. We weren't allowed to get up even if we weren't tired, so I had nothing to do but stare at a small mole on my leg for hours at a time.

3   At the time, such early education was a privilege for which only the children of cadres were eligible. Although neither of my parents' ranks was high, my father's position as reporter, editor, and founding member of the Party newspaper the *Hunan Daily,* and my mother's as a promising cadre in the Changsha Public Security Bureau were enough to qualify me. My parents were deeply involved in all the excitement of working to transform China into a great Socialist country, eager to sacrifice themselves for others. They dreamed passionately of the day when they would be deemed pure and devoted enough to be accepted into the Party. It was only natural that the family come second; Father's duties at the newspaper often kept him away for several months at a time, and my mother came home only on Sundays, if at all, for she had a room in her own unit and stayed there to attend evening meetings. So at the age of three I was

sent off to the child-care center for early training in Socialist thought through collective living, far from the potentially corrupting influence of family life. My departure may have been harder for my two grandmothers, of course. They had had the major responsibility of raising the three of us children; I was the last child to go and they would miss me very much.

I had lived first with my paternal grandmother, my Nai Nai, a tall, 4 stern, bony woman who always wore traditional black. She lived in the apartment the *Hunan Daily* had allotted to Father, two rooms on the second floor of a cadres' dormitory, spacious enough but with a shared kitchen and an outhouse some distance away. She was a pious Buddhist and a vegetarian, strict with herself and everyone else but her own grandchildren.

At ten pounds, I had been the biggest baby ever recorded at Changsha's 5 No. 1 Hospital, and Nai Nai had hired a series of seven wet nurses before she found one who could satisfy my appetite. She was a nineteen-year-old peasant girl from a town beyond the city whose own baby had died. Nai Nai told me later that she was the only one who had enough milk so that I could suck her breasts dry without throwing a tantrum immediately afterwards; I have always given credit to her for my unusual height—I am 6'1". Then after she left because she had no Changsha city residence card, Nai Nai sent me to live with my maternal grandmother, my Waipo, who lived off a winding little alleyway not far away.

It was much more crowded there, since Waipo, my Uncle Yan, and his 6 wife and their small children made three generations in a single dark room. But I liked the place for its liveliness and because I was Waipo's favorite. She gave me candies and took me everywhere with her, even to the free market to buy from the peasants who had carried in their vegetables from the suburbs. Waipo was a tiny woman with big twisted teeth and little wrinkled hands, talkative and lively and very different from Nai Nai. Her husband had died when she was young, after only two children, whereas Nai Nai's husband had given her nine before he slipped and fell on the icy road in front of the old City Gate. In the old society, a woman couldn't remarry and remain respectable, so Waipo had supported herself and her children by making shoe soles at home. She continued to do this even after Mother and Uncle Yan were grown and had jobs, and the cloth patches she used were among my first toys.

Another reason I liked living with Waipo was that Mother often 7 preferred to go there on Sundays rather than to our own home, where Nai Nai was, because she didn't get along well with her mother-in-law. Nai Nai sometimes carried her concern for others so far that she became a busybody. She was always the first to sweep the public stairwell or volunteer to lead neighborhood hygiene movements, and she was constantly scolding Mother for not dressing us warmly enough or not buying us more milk to drink. She was so tall that she must have been imposing for Mother to deal with, and tradition demanded that Mother obey her. So although Mother was a feisty woman, she was supposed to look on silently as Nai Nai spoiled us with candy and, in later years, did my second sister's homework for her. Father was no help, because he was bound by the same filial laws as she.

8   In any case, Mother's ties to her new home could not have been strong ones, for she had hardly known Father before they married. Someone had introduced them as prospective mates; they had exchanged a few letters (Father was working in Guilin at the time) and decided the question soon after on the basis of their common political enthusiasm. Father was far more intellectual than she, for he had been trained by the Party as a reporter, had a wide range of literary interests, and was an accomplished poet as well as an amateur composer and conductor. Mother was capable too, of course, a strong-willed person who liked to express her opinions, and a loving mother when she had the time. Still, as I thought back on it in later years, I realized my parents were so rarely together that it was almost a marriage of convenience.

9   So it was Waipo's home that was my early emotional center, and it was there that I went on the fresh spring day of my flight. I had to cross a large street, but fortunately I made it from one side to the other without mishap, and ran the remaining few hundred yards to the narrow room off the little gray alley.

10   To my utter dismay, Waipo didn't look at all glad to see me. "Little Fatso, what are you doing here?" she cried, and with scarcely a pause grabbed my hand and pulled me the few blocks to Nai Nai's home in *Hunan Daily* compound. From there the two old ladies half lifted, half dragged me back to my confinement, ignoring my screams and tears.

11   The nurses had discovered my absence. Without any show of the politeness they usually maintained before their charges' relatives, they cursed and scolded me as if they would never stop. When my grand-mothers had left, they locked me up in a room with two other offenders, saying, "You are not Chairman Mao's good little boy; you haven't upheld Revolutionary discipline. You can stay in there until you think things over."

12   My fellow captives were as miserable as I. One had stolen some candy, and the other, having graduated proudly from wearing slit pants, had promptly soiled his new ones. Although it was certainly convenient to be able to squat down anywhere and do one's business, among us children the slit was an embarrassing symbol of immaturity. It had another drawback too: Nai Nai's blows still stung on my bottom. I looked at the unlucky boy with pity. He would now be doomed to at least another year of babyhood and easy spankings.

13   The nurses' words had another kind of sting for me, since I had been taught Chairman Mao was like the sun itself. At home, "Mao" had been my first word after "Mama," "Baba," and "Nai Nai," for I had been held up to the large framed picture Father had hung over the doorway and instructed in the sound. Later I had learned how to say "I love Chairman Mao" and "Long Live Chairman Mao." But it wasn't until I got to the

child-care center that I really began to understand. He presided over our rest and play like a benevolent god, and I believed that apples, grapes, everything had been given to us because he loved us. When the nurses told me the next day that Chairman Mao had forgiven me, I was the happiest child in the world.

During the next year, my second at the child-care center, I learned how to write my first characters. The first word was made up of the four strokes in the Chairman's name. Next I learned to write the characters in my own name, and I discovered that I was not called "Little Fatso," as Waipo had proudly nicknamed me, but something quite different, with a political story behind it: 14

On the morning of May 2, 1954, the Vietnamese won a decisive victory over the French at Dien Bien Phu. That very afternoon my mother gave birth to me, a ten-pound baby boy, the distant sounds of drums and cymbals an accompaniment to her labors. My father, reporting the Vietnam story for the *Hunan Daily,* thought it only natural to name me Liang Dian-jie, "Liang Good News from Dien Bien Phu." He was flushed with a double victory, for at last he had a son to carry on the family line.   15

It wasn't the first time he had chosen a significant name for a child. My eldest sister was born in 1949, so she joined the ranks of thousands of children named for the birth of New China with the name Liang Fang, "Liang Liberation." My second sister, born in 1952 when the Chinese armies were marching across the Yalu River to defend Korea against the Americans, was called Liang Wei-ping, "Liang Defender of Peace." As we grew up we discovered that you could often guess someone's age by his name, and that at times, if someone had been named at the height of some movement that was later discredited, a name could become an embarrassment, a burden, or even a reason for being attacked. My parents' own names reflected an earlier, less politicized time; my mother Yan Zhi-de was "Yan the Moral," and my father Liang Ying-qiu was "Liang Whose Requests Will Be Answered," although he usually went by his literary name, Liang Shan.   16

I came gradually to recognize all of these characters and more, for during the third year and final fourth year at the child-care center we began our study properly, writing "Chairman Mao is our Great Saving Star," "We are all Chairman Mao's good little children," "The Communist Party is like the sun," "When I am big I will be a worker" (or peasant or soldier). We also learned simple arithmetic, paper folding and paper cutting, and were given small responsibilities like watering the plants or cleaning the classroom.   17

Meanwhile, whenever I went home to Waipo's, I hoped Mother would be there, for I loved her very much despite our limited time together. But when I was about four, I began to sense there was something wrong. She would come home looking worried and she never played with me, just talked on and on with Uncle Yan in a hushed Liuyang County dialect   18 which I couldn't understand. Finally, one Saturday afternoon it was Nai Nai who came to get me, and I was told Mother had gone away and I shouldn't go to Waipo's house anymore.

19   Only years later was I old enough to understand what had happened, and more than twenty years passed before anyone, including Mother herself, got the full picture. In early 1957 the "Hundred Flowers Movement" had been launched. Its official purpose was to give the Party a chance to correct its shortcomings by listening to the masses' criticisms. Father was away in the countryside reporting on something, but in the Changsha Public Security Building, meetings were held and everyone was urged to express his or her opinions freely.

20   Mother didn't know what to do. She really loved the Party and didn't have any criticisms to make; the Party had given her a job and saved her from the most abject poverty. Still, her leaders said that everyone should participate actively in the movement, especially those who hoped someday to join the Party. Mother was already in favor; she had been given the important job of validating arrest warrants for the whole city. So, regarding it her duty to come up with something, she finally thought of three points she could make. She said that her Section Head sometimes used crude language and liked to criticize people, that he should give his housekeeper a bed to sleep on instead of making her sleep on the floor, and that sometimes when it came time to give raises, the leaders didn't listen to the masses' opinions.

21   But then, with utterly confusing rapidity, the "Hundred Flowers Movement" changed into the "Anti-Rightist Movement." Perhaps the Party was caught off guard by the amount of opposition and felt compelled to crack down. Or maybe, as I've heard said, the "Hundred Flowers Movement" had been a trap designed from the beginning to uncover Rightist elements. Anyway, every unit was given a quota of Rightists, and Mother's name was among those at the Public Security Bureau.

22   It was disastrous. When she was allowed to see her file in 1978, she found out that she had been given a Rightist's "cap" solely because of those three criticisms she had made. Perhaps her Section Head was angry at her; perhaps her unit was having trouble filling its quota. At the time she had no idea what the verdict was based on, she only knew that a terrible wrong had been done. But there was no court of appeal. Mother was sent away to the suburb of Yuan Jia Ling for labor reform. She lost her cadre's rank and her salary was cut from fifty-five to fifteen *yuan* a month. (A *yuan* is one hundred Chinese cents. . . .). My naive and trusting mother went to work as a peasant.

23   Just as his wife was being declared an enemy of the Party, Father was actively participating in the Anti-Rightist Movement in his own unit. Father believed in the Party with his whole heart, believed that the Party could never make a mistake or hand down a wrong verdict. It was a tortuous dilemma; Father's traditional Confucian sense of family obli-

gation told him to support Mother while his political allegiance told him to condemn her. In the end, his commitment to the Party won out, and he denounced her. He believed that was the only course that could save the family from ruin.

I still remember the first time Mother came home for a visit. It was a   24
rainy Sunday in late autumn, and Father and Nai Nai were both out. There were footsteps on the stairs and in the corridor, but it was almost a minute before the knock came, timidly. Liang Fang opened the door.

Mother was almost unrecognizable. She was in patched blue peasant   25
clothing, muddy up to the knees. The skin on her kind round face looked thick, leathery, and not too clean, and someone had chopped her hair off short and uneven. There was something both broader and thinner about her. "Mama!" cried Liang Fang.

Liang Wei-ping and I ran up to her too, and she was hugging us all at   26
once, weeping, forgetting to put down her oilpaper umbrella. Then as my sisters rushed to pour tea and bring a basin of hot water for her to wash her face, she sat on the bed and held me tightly for a long time. After she had rested, she busied herself with all the housework Nai Nai couldn't do alone, sweeping, dusting, and sharpening our pencils for us, scrubbing our clothes, and cleaning the windows. She wouldn't speak of where she'd been, just asked us about our schoolwork, our health, Father's health. We were so happy. We thought Mother had come home.

She was tying bows on Liang Fang's braids when Father came back. He   27
was astounded to see her, and not very warm. "What are you doing here?" he demanded. "Did you ask for leave?"

Mother lowered her head at his harshness. "Of course I asked for   28
leave," she said defensively. "I can come home once a month."

This silenced Father for a few minutes, and he paced meditatively   29
around the room, his tall thin frame overpowering hers as Nai Nai's used to do. Then he poured out a stream of words, political words—on the meaning of the Anti-Rightist Movement, on her obligation to recognize her faults and reform herself. It was as if he had turned into a propaganda machine. I suppose he thought it was his duty to help reeducate her.

For a while she listened in silence, her head bowed, but at last she   30
protested. "All right, I'm a Rightist, it's all my fault. You don't have to say anything else, my head is bursting. I hear this kind of thing all day long, write self-criticisms every week, and now I come home and I have to hear it all over again."

"I don't think you recognize what you've done. You're just wasting   31
your labor reform," he said.

"What makes you so sure?" Mother's face was white and defiant.   32

Father exploded: "Rightist element! Have some thought for your   33
influence on the children."

It was Mother's turn to lose control. "What did I ever do wrong? The   34
Party asked me to make suggestions, so I did. You give me one

example—" But Mother stopped midsentence, for Father had struck her a ringing blow across the face.

35   She fell back on the bed, weeping; Father strode into the other room and slammed the door. Then slowly, painfully, she picked up her dirty jacket and umbrella as we sobbed miserably. When she was halfway out the door, Father emerged and shouted after her, "Don't come back until you've reformed yourself. The children in this house need a Revolutionary mother, not a Rightist mother." When she paused and turned her tear-streaked face to him, his voice became gentler. "It doesn't matter what you say here, I won't tell anyone. But please watch what you say at the labor camp."

36   Despite Father's cruelty, Mother came back every month to see us. She must have missed us very much to endure Father's lectures and the inevitable fights. Sometimes she slept in Father's bed and I slept with them; she never lay still and her pillow was always wet in the morning. On other occasions the quarrel was so fierce that she left again almost as soon as she arrived. Father often warned us against her, and if we defended her he became furious, calling us ignorant children who understood nothing.

37   We didn't know that Father had already raised the question of divorce. He must have reasoned that all of us were doomed unless he broke off with Mother completely, for the custom in such instances was that the whole family would be considered as guilty as the single member who had committed the crime. If there were no legal separation, Father would never be allowed to join the Party, and the files that would be opened on us when we came of age for middle school would say that we came from a Rightist background. We would be branded forever as people with "questions," and it would be difficult for us to go to middle school and college, get decent jobs, or find husbands and wives. Mother's misfortune might mean the end of all of Father's dreams for himself and for his children; he must have hated her for what she had done.

38   Mother was a proud woman. She believed so deeply she had been wrongly accused that she told him she would divorce him only after her Rightist label was removed. Her stubbornness enraged Father, particularly because there was a secondary movement to criticize those with Rightist tendencies, and with his Rightist wife, Father was a natural target. He had to criticize Mother publicly, write reports confessing his innermost thoughts. And the pressure became even greater after what happened to Uncle Yan.

39   When Mother first came under attack, her older brother had been as outraged as she. He went to the Public Security Bureau to argue in her defense, and spoke for her at his own unit, the No. 1 Hospital, where he worked with the Communist Youth League. He even came to our house to urge Father to try to help her, although Father thought he was crazy to stick out his neck like that. Sure enough, Uncle Yan was punished for

his family loyalties and given a Rightist "cap" of his own to wear, bringing a second black cloud to rest over Waipo's home. His experience proved that Father's sad choice had been a practical one in view of the harsh political realities; when we were old enough to understand, we could hardly blame Father for what he and done.

Nai Nai was frightened to see how easily the Rightist label could spread from one member of the family to another. She had been an enthusiastic supporter of the "Get Rid of the Four Evils" hygiene movement, but where cartoons had once shown housewives sweeping away rats, flies, mosquitoes, and fleas, now they had added a fifth evil, Rightists. Nai Nai could no longer face lecturing lazy neighbors on the dangers of letting water stagnate; she could imagine what they might be saying behind her back about how she ought to get rid of that evil in her own house. When, with traditional filial deference, Father asked for her opinion on the divorce question, she agreed with relief. The family burden was too heavy for her. 40

Meanwhile, Mother was working hard to rid herself of her "cap." The calluses on her hands were thicker and sharper every time she came home, and her shoulders were rough where the shoulder pole rested. Her skin toasted to a rich yellow-brown. It was a hard life for a young woman who had lived between the protection of her mother's home and her Public Security Bureau office. 41

The Rightists at Yuan Jia Ling were all trying to prove to the political officials in charge that they had reformed themselves and were ready to leave. There were all types of people, intellectuals, high-ranking cadres, and ordinary workers, but friendships were impossible because the best strategy for gaining the officials' confidence was to report on others. Thus everyone was always watching everyone else, and a grain of rice dropped on the floor could mean an afternoon of criticism for disrespecting the labors of the peasants. Everything was fair game, even what people said in their sleep. 42

The second essential strategy was to write constant Thought Reports about oneself. Few of the people in the camp felt they were really Rightists, but the only thing to do was confess one's crimes penitently, record one's lapses, and invent things to repent. Writing these reports eventually became a kind of habit, and Mother almost believed what she was saying about herself. 43

The last important route to freedom was hard work. One had to add deliberately to one's misery in small ways, like going without a hat under the hot summer sun or continuing to work in the rain after everyone else had quit. Generally the Rightists did ordinary peasants' work, like digging fish-breeding ponds and planting fruit trees, but sometimes they were taken in trucks to special laboring areas to break and carry stones. Then they were put together with ordinary thieves, hoodlums, and Kuomintang (KMT) spies. The people whose arrest warrants Mother had once been in charge of validating were now her equals; it was almost 44 more than she could bear. Still, bear it she did, and all the rest of it, and after three long years, when she could carry more than a hundred pounds of rocks on her back with ease, a bored-looking official summoned her and told her she was no longer a Rightist. She could go home.

45   She came to the house late at night, looking like a beggar traveling with her ragged belongings. But when she spoke, her voice was clear and proud. "Old Liang," she announced to Father, "I'm a person again." She told us she had been assigned to the headlight-manufacturing plant on May First Road as an ordinary worker. Her salary would be much lower than it had been at the Public Security Bureau and the loss of her cadre status would be permanent, but she was free, a normal member of society. My sisters and I thought all the trouble was over, but that night as I lay in bed with them I heard talk not of the beginning of a new family life but of how to institute divorce proceedings.

46   The difficulty lay in what to do with us. We were fought over like basketballs that winter, for Mother insisted that she wanted at least one of us, preferably Liang Fang, who was already eleven and understood life better than Liang Wei-ping and I. Mother was staying at Waipo's, but she came every day to the house. When I got home from the *Hunan Daily*'s Attached Primary School, she was always there, waiting.

47   One bitterly cold Sunday she took the three of us out to the Martyr's Park so we could talk alone. No one else was out in that weather; they were all at home huddled under their blankets or warming themselves by coal burners. We were bundled up in everything we had, and I felt as though I could have been rolled down a hill, but I was still cold. The park was desolate and beautiful, the huge monument to the dead martyrs a lonely pinnacle over the city, the pavilions gray and defenseless against the wind. We walked to the large manmade lake, the park's main attraction, and sat by the water, usually filled with rowboats but now covered with a thin layer of ice. I crawled between Mother's knees and Liang Fang and Liang Wei-ping pressed up on each side of her. She spoke to us with great emotion and tenderness.

48   "Your mother is an unlucky woman. When you're older, you'll understand how I've wept for all of us these three years. Now I won't be able to come see you anymore, but you can visit me at Waipo's house. Liang Fang will live with me, but I don't have enough money for all of you. . . ."

49   Liang Wei-ping and I were in tears, saying that we wanted to go with her too. Soon everyone was crying, Mother held us so tightly that I could hardly believe it was true that she would go away.

50   We stayed in the park for a long time, but when Mother noticed that my cheeks were chapped red, she took us home. She brought us to the stairwell and refused to come up. Her parting words were "Remember, Liang Fang, you'll come with me."

51   That evening Father called us into the inner room. "Children, you're still small and there are many things you don't understand," he said sadly. "If you went with your mother, your life with her would be

unhappy. Look at the way your father has to criticize himself because of her. Stay here with me and Nai Nai and we'll take care of you."

Liang Fang wouldn't listen. "Mama isn't a Rightist anymore," she 52 said. "What difference does it make who I go with? Isn't it glorious to be a worker?"

"Your mother's political life is over," said Father with annoyance. 53 "Her file will always have a black mark, and the Party will never trust her again. Don't you know that if you want to go to middle school you'll be asked if your parents have made any political mistakes? If you stay with me, you won't even have to mention your mother, because there will be a legal separation. But if you go with her, you might not even get to go to middle school, to say nothing of joining the Communist Youth League or the Party. And you," he said angrily, turning to me and Liang Wei-ping. "Can't you guess why you haven't been allowed to join the Young Pioneers? Isn't it because of your mother?"

Nai Nai rushed into the room to urge him to control his temper, then 54 she turned to us. "Children your father is good to you, he understands the situation. Don't I wish I had a good daughter-in-law? Don't I know you need a good mother? But Fate is inevitable. Stay with us, children. It's the only way."

Ultimately, the question was decided in court. Father came home one 55 afternoon looking exhausted and said, "It's settled, you'll all stay with me. Mother is coming in a little while to say good-bye."

We had dinner with her that night, and even Nai Nai's eyes were wet. 56 No one said anything, and no one had any appetite for the fish or the tofu soup. As Nai Nai took the dishes away and washed up, Mother went through her possessions, leaving almost everything for us. Father sat smoking furiously, as he did whenever he was upset. Finally she stood up to leave.

Then the three of us broke out of our numbness and ran to her, begging 57 her not to go, pulling her back, wrapping ourselves around her legs so she couldn't walk. Father didn't interfere; he just let her embrace us again and again and at last shake us off and close the door firmly behind herself. We ran to the balcony and called after her until her broad square figure turned the corner and she was gone.

In fact, Father had been much too optimistic, and the divorce did 58 nothing to rid us of having a Rightist in the family. He even forbade our having the slightest contact with Mother, thinking that if we drew a clear line of separation, things might be better. But there wasn't the slightest change in our status: in the eyes of the Party, my sisters and I were the children of a Rightist and Father had a Rightist wife. Liang Fang still had to say she had a Rightist mother on her application to go to middle school, Liang Wei-ping still found "Rightist child" written on her desk in chalk when she went to class, and I was still turned down when I asked to be allowed to join the Young Pioneers.

When I first went to the Attached Primary School in the *Hunan Daily* 59 compound at age six, my classmates had often teased me about Mother.

I had always shrugged off their taunts because I did well and achieved more than enough recognition to offset a few minor slights. I remember how pleased Father was when I started to take prizes for my paintings; my drawing of a morning glory was first in the whole primary school.

60   But as I got older, more and more stress was placed on the three stages of Revolutionary glory: the Young Pioneers, the Communist Youth League and the Party itself. It became clear to me that success in the political arena was a prerequisite for success in anything else, and if I had the slightest ambitions for myself I had to achieve these basic signs of social recognition. Those students who had the right to wear the Pioneer's triangular red scarf received much more praise than those who didn't, no matter what their grades; and at home Father and Nai Nai were constantly asking me if my application had been approved. But it was no use. I was rejected year after year, until I found myself in a tiny minority of outsiders whose "political performances" were the very worst in the class.

61   One day I was given a clue to the trouble when our teacher gave us a lecture. "We all have to join forces to oppose Capitalist thought," Teacher Luo said. "Some students want to eat well and dress well from the time they are small. This is Capitalist thought. Some students are from good worker or Revolutionary cadre backgrounds; they should be careful not to be proud of themselves. And those students from families with questions—they must be more careful to draw a clear line of separation." He looked meaningfully at me and at the other boy with a Rightist in his family. And all the students in the classroom turned to stare at us too.

62   In fact, after the divorce I had continued to go secretly to see my mother despite Father's warnings that doing so would harm my future. She was always overjoyed to see me, and, even during China's hard years, just after the breakup, she always found a way to give me a few *fen* (a *fen* is a Chinese cent . . .) or a roasted sweet potato. But after Teacher Luo's lecture, it really began to bother me when other students mocked me as a Rightist's son. And they became bolder in their mockery, as well. They would slap me, or kick me when I wasn't looking, and then pretend not to have done anything. Sometimes I would get into real fights, and then there were reprimands from Father and the teachers. The other Rightist's son was as lonely as I, but we never spoke much, for that might have made things even worse.

63   So perhaps inevitably, over the years, I came to resent my mother for making my life so miserable. I began to believe that she really had done something wrong. My father and teachers said so, and my classmates hated me for her supposed crimes. At last I no longer wished to visit her despite my loneliness, and when I saw her at a distance I didn't even call out to her. I cut her out of my life just as I had been told to do, and became solitary and self-reliant. But that was when I was much older, and many things happened before then.

❏ Questions for Discussion

1. In what ways was Liang Chairman Mao's Bad Little Boy?

2. What is the purpose of the child care center and the reason for its severity? What is the significance of training Chinese children so young? Why does the party deprive children of parental love and care?

3. Why do you think the "Hundred Flowers Movement" changed very quickly to the "Anti-Rightist campaign"? Discuss the appropriateness of these terms—not only their literal significance, but also their connotations.

4. Why is loyalty to Mao so strong that it even divides families? Why does Father turn against Mother so harshly? What is the ultimate effect on young Liang of repeated unjustified attacks on his mother?

❏ Suggestions for Exploration and Writing

1. This autobiographical essay vividly depicts the early life of a young boy who must have been very confused by a culture which pulled him in two different directions. What evidence of the older Chinese culture is given in the essay? How does the new culture conflict with the old?

2. Write an essay attacking or defending the following statement: Nothing like the "Anti-Rightist campaign" could happen in the United States.

3. Many American parents send their children to day-care centers while the parents work. After reading this essay, do you see any dangers in this practice?

4. Write an essay attacking or defending the following statement: Loyalty to the family is more important than loyalty to the government or loyalty to ideology.

FICTION

LUKE

Although few facts about the life of Luke are positively known, scholars believe that Luke, "the beloved physician," wrote the New Testament books Luke and Acts. They believe that Luke was a

*Gentile from Antioch in Syria and that he was a close companion of
Paul. Although the exact date is unknown, the book of Luke was
written after AD70.*

The Parable of the Prodigal Son
Luke 15:11–32

11 And he said, A certain man had two sons:

12 And the younger of them said to *his* father, Father, give me the
portion of goods that falleth to *me*. And he divided unto them *his* living.

13 And not many days after the younger son gathered all together, and
took his journey into a far country, and there wasted his substance with
riotous living.

14 And when he had spent all, there arose a mighty famine in that
land; and he began to be in want.

15 And he went and joined himself to a citizen of that country; and he
sent him into his fields to feed swine.

16 And he would fain have filled his belly with the husks that the
swine did eat: and no man gave unto him.

17 And when he came to himself, he said, How many hired servants
of my father's have bread enough and to spare, and I perish with hunger!

18 I will arise and go to my father, and will say unto him, Father, I
have sinned against heaven, and before thee.

19 And am no more worthy to be called thy son: make me as one of
thy hired servants.

20 And he arose, and came to his father. But when he was yet a great
way off, his father saw him, and had compassion, and ran, and fell on his
neck, and kissed him.

21 And the son said unto him, Father, I have sinned against heaven,
and in thy sight, and am no more worthy to be called thy son.

22 But the father said to his servants, Bring forth the best robe, and
put *it* on him; and put a ring on his hand, and shoes on *his* feet:

23 And bring hither the fatted calf, and kill *it;* and let us eat, and be
merry:

24 For this my son was dead, and is alive again; he was lost, and is
found. And they began to be merry.

25 Now his elder son was in the field: and as he came and drew nigh
to the house, he heard musick and dancing.

26 And he called one of the servants, and asked what these things
meant.

27 And he said unto him, Thy brother is come; and thy father hath
killed the fatted calf, because he hath received him safe and sound.

28 And he was angry, and would not go in: therefore came his father
out, and intreated him.

29 And he answering said to *his* father, Lo, these many years do I serve
thee, neither transgressed I at any time thy commandment: and yet thou
never gavest me a kid, that I might make merry with my friends:

30 But as soon as this thy son was come, which hath devoured thy living with harlots, thou hast killed for him the fatted calf.

31 And he said unto him, Son, thou art ever with me, and all that I have is thine.

32 It was meet that we should make merry, and be glad: for this thy brother was dead, and is alive again; and was lost, and is found.

❏ Questions for Discussion

1. Why would the son choose to give up the security of home and family for "riotous living" in a "far country"? Is it realistic for him to do so?

2. The father, upon seeing his son's return, prepares a rich feast and gives the returning son the "best robe" and a ring. Is such behavior fair or just? Why does the father greet the wasteful son so warmly? Why is the oldest son so angry? Is his reaction an expected one? Explain.

3. What does the father mean by the following words to the oldest son: "Son, thou art ever with me, and all that I have is thine"?

❏ Suggestions for Exploration and Writing

1. Examine an act of unconditional love from several points of view.

2. Write an essay discussing a modern-day conflict between two siblings and discuss ways in which they might solve this conflict. For example, one brother might have fought in a war while the other marched for peace, or one sister might be pro-choice and the other pro-life.

FRANK O'CONNOR (1903–1966)

Frank O'Connor, born Michael John O'Donovan, is known primarily as a short story writer but also wrote novels and literary criticism and translated Irish works from the Gaelic into English. In addition, O'Connor was active in Irish politics as a member of the Irish Republican Army (IRA) and participated in the Irish literary revival. O'Connor's stories are characterized by humor and great insight into human behavior. The material for "My Oedipus Complex" is rooted in O'Connor's own life: his deep love for his mother, intensified by his father's periodic violent drunken sprees.

My Oedipus Complex

1   Father was in the army all through the war—the first war, I mean—so, up to the age of five, I never saw much of him, and what I saw did not worry me. Sometimes I woke and there was a big figure in khaki peering down at me in the candlelight. Sometimes in the early morning I heard the slamming of the front door and the clatter of nailed boots down the cobbles of the lane. These were Father's entrances and exits. Like Santa Claus he came and went mysteriously.

2   In fact, I rather liked his visits, though it was an uncomfortable squeeze between Mother and him when I got into the big bed in the early morning. He smoked, which gave him a pleasant musty smell, and shaved, an operation of astounding interest. Each time he left a trail of souvenirs—model tanks and Gurkha knives with handles made of bullet cases, and German helmets and cap badges and button-sticks, and all sorts of military equipment—carefully stowed away in a long box on top of the wardrobe, in case they ever came in handy. There was a bit of the magpie about Father; he expected everything to come in handy. When his back was turned, Mother let me get a chair and rummage through his treasures. She didn't seem to think so highly of them as he did.

3   The war was the most peaceful period of my life. The window of my attic faced southeast. My mother had curtained it, but that had small effect. I always woke with the first light and, with all the responsibilities of the previous day melted, feeling myself rather like the sun, ready to illumine and rejoice. Life never seemed so simple and clear and full of possibilities as then. I put my feet out from under the clothes—I called them Mrs. Left and Mrs. Right—and invented dramatic situations for them in which they discussed the problems of the day. At least Mrs. Right did; she was very demonstrative, but I hadn't the same control of Mrs. Left, so she mostly contented herself with nodding agreement.

4   They discussed what Mother and I should do during the day, what Santa Claus should give a fellow for Christmas, and what steps should be taken to brighten the home. There was that little matter of the baby, for instance. Mother and I could never agree about that. Ours was the only house in the terrace without a new baby, and Mother said we couldn't afford one till Father came back from the war because they cost seventeen and six. That showed how simple she was. The Geneys up the road had a baby, and everyone knew they couldn't afford seventeen and six. It was probably a cheap baby, and Mother wanted something really good, but I felt she was too exclusive. The Geneys' baby would have done us fine.

5   Having settled my plans for the day, I got up, put a chair under the attic window, and lifted the frame high enough to stick out my head. The window overlooked the front gardens of the terrace behind ours, and beyond these it looked over a deep valley to the tall, red-brick houses

terraced up the opposite hillside, which were all still in shadow, while those at our side of the valley were all lit up, though with long strange shadows that made them seem unfamiliar; rigid and painted.

After that I went into Mother's room and climbed into the big bed. She 6
woke and I began to tell her of my schemes. By this time, though I never seem to have noticed it, I was petrified in my nightshirt, and I thawed as I talked until, the last frost melted, I fell asleep beside her and woke again only when I heard her below in the kitchen, making the breakfast.

After breakfast we went into town; heard Mass at St. Augustine's and 7
said a prayer for Father, and did the shopping. If the afternoon was fine we either went for a walk in the country or a visit to Mother's great friend in the convent, Mother St. Dominic. Mother had them all praying for Father, and every night, going to bed, I asked God to send him back safe from the war to us. Little, indeed, did I know what I was praying for!

One morning, I got into the big bed, and there, sure enough, was 8
Father in his usual Santa Claus manner, but later, instead of uniform, he put on his best blue suit, and Mother was as pleased as anything. I saw nothing to be pleased about, because, out of uniform, Father was altogether less interesting, but she only beamed, and explained that our prayers had been answered, and off we went to Mass to thank God for having brought Father safely home.

The irony of it! That very day when he came in to dinner he took off 9
his boots and put on his slippers, donned the dirty old cap he wore about the house to save him from colds, crossed his legs, and began to talk gravely to Mother, who looked anxious. Naturally, I disliked her looking anxious, because it destroyed her good looks, so I interrupted him.

"Just a moment, Larry!" she said gently. 10

This was only what she said when we had boring visitors, so I attached 11
no importance to it and went on talking.

"Do be quiet, Larry!" she said impatiently. "Don't you hear me talking 12
to Daddy?"

This was the first time I had heard those ominous words, "talking to 13
Daddy," and I couldn't help feeling that if this was how God answered prayers, he couldn't listen to them very attentively.

"Why are you talking to Daddy?" I asked with as great a show of 14
indifference as I could muster.

"Because Daddy and I have business to discuss. Now, don't interrupt 15
again!"

In the afternoon, at Mother's request, Father took me for a walk. This 16
time we went into town instead of out the country, and I thought at first, in my usual optimistic way, that it might be an improvement. It was nothing of the sort. Father and I had quite different notions of a walk in town. He had no proper interest in trams, ships, and horses, and the only thing that seemed to divert him was talking to fellows as old as himself. When I wanted to stop he simply went on, dragging me behind him by

the hand; when he wanted to stop I had no alternative but to do the same. I noticed that it seemed to be a sign that he wanted to stop for a long time whenever he leaned against a wall. The second time I saw him do it I got wild. He seemed to be settling himself forever. I pulled him by the coat and trousers, but, unlike Mother who, if you were too persistent, got into a wax and said: "Larry, if you don't behave yourself, I'll give you a good slap," Father had an extraordinary capacity for amiable inattention. I sized him up and wondered would I cry, but he seemed to be too remote to be annoyed even by that. Really, it was like going for a walk with a mountain! He either ignored the wrenching and pummelling entirely, or else glanced down with a grin of amusement from his peak. I had never met anyone so absorbed in himself as he seemed.

17   At teatime, "talking to Daddy" began again, complicated this time by the fact that he had an evening paper, and every few minutes he put it down and told Mother something new out of it. I felt this was foul play. Man for man, I was prepared to compete with him anytime for Mother's attention, but when he had it all made up for him by other people it left me no chance. Several times I tried to change the subject without success.

18   "You must be quiet while Daddy is reading, Larry," Mother said impatiently.

19   It was clear that she either genuinely liked talking to Father better than talking to me, or else that he had some terrible hold on her which made her afraid to admit the truth.

20   "Mummy," I said that night when she was tucking me up, "do you think if I prayed hard God would send Daddy back to the war?"

21   She seemed to think about that for a moment.

22   "No, dear," she said with a smile. "I don't think he would."

23   "Why wouldn't he, Mummy?"

24   "Because there isn't a war any longer, dear."

25   "But, Mummy, couldn't God make another war, if He liked?"

26   "He wouldn't like to, dear. It's not God who makes wars, but bad people."

27   "Oh!" I said.

28   I was disappointed about that. I began to think that God wasn't quite what he was cracked up to be.

29   Next morning I woke at my usual hour, feeling like a bottle of champagne. I put out my feet and invented a long conversation in which Mrs. Right talked of the trouble she had with her own father till she put him in the Home. I didn't quite know what the Home was but it sounded the right place for Father. Then I got my chair and stuck my head out of the attic window. Dawn was just breaking, with a guilty air that made me feel I had caught it in the act. My head bursting with stories and schemes, I stumbled in next door, and in the half-darkness scrambled into the big bed. There was no room at Mother's side so I had to get between her and Father. For the time being I had forgotten about him, and for several minutes I sat bolt upright, racking my brains to know what I could do

with him. He was taking up more than his fair share of the bed, and I couldn't get comfortable, so I gave him several kicks that made him grunt and stretch. He made room all right, though. Mother waked and felt for me. I settled back comfortably in the warmth of the bed with my thumb in my mouth.

"Mummy!" I hummed, loudly and contentedly. "Sssh! dear," she whispered. "Don't wake Daddy!" 30

This was a new development, which threatened to be even more serious than "talking to Daddy." Life without my early-morning conferences was unthinkable. 31

"Why?" I asked severely. 32

"Because poor Daddy is tired." 33

This seemed to me a quite inadequate reason, and I was sickened by the sentimentality of her "poor Daddy." I never liked that sort of gush; it always struck me as insincere. 34

"Oh!" I said lightly. Then in my most winning tone: "Do you know where I want to go with you today, Mummy?" 35

"No, dear," she sighed. 36

"I want to go down the Glen and fish for thornybacks with my new net, and then I want to go out to the Fox and Hounds, and—" 37

"Don't-wake-Daddy!" she hissed angrily, clapping her hand across my mouth. 38

But it was too late. He was awake, or nearly so. He grunted and reached for the matches. Then he stared incredulously at his watch. 39

"Like a cup of tea, dear?" asked Mother in a meek, hushed voice I had never heard her use before. It sounded almost as though she were afraid. 40

"Tea?" he exclaimed indignantly. "Do you know what the time is?" 41

"And after that I want to go up the Rathcooney Road," I said loudly, afraid I'd forget something in all those interruptions. 42

"Go to sleep at once, Larry!" she said sharply. 43

I began to snivel. I couldn't concentrate, the way that pair went on, and smothering my early-morning schemes was like burying a family from the cradle. 44

Father said nothing, but lit his pipe and sucked it, looking out into the shadows without minding Mother or me. I knew he was mad. Every time I made a remark Mother hushed me irritably. I was mortified. I felt it wasn't fair; there was even something sinister in it. Every time I had pointed out to her the waste of making two beds when we could both sleep in one, she had told me it was healthier like that, and now here was this man, this stranger, sleeping with her without the least regard for her health! 45

He got up early and made tea, but though he brought Mother a cup he brought none for me. 46

"Mummy," I shouted, "I want a cup of tea, too." 47

"Yes, dear," she said patiently. "You can drink from Mummy's saucer." 48

49   That settled it. Either Father or I would have to leave the house. I didn't want to drink from Mother's saucer; I wanted to be treated as an equal in my own home, so, just to spite her, I drank it all and left none for her. She took that quietly, too.

50   But that night when she was putting me to bed she said gently:

51   "Larry, I want you to promise me something."

52   "What is it?" I asked.

53   "Not to come in and disturb poor Daddy in the morning. Promise?"

54   "Poor Daddy" again! I was becoming suspicious of everything involving that quite impossible man.

55   "Why?" I asked.

56   "Because poor Daddy is worried and tired and he doesn't sleep well."

57   "Why doesn't he, Mummy?"

58   "Well, you know, don't you, that while he was at the war Mummy got the pennies from the Post Office?"

59   "From Miss MacCarthy?"

60   "That's right. But now, you see, Miss MacCarthy hasn't any more pennies, so Daddy must go out and find us some. You know what would happen if he couldn't?"

61   "No," I said, "tell us."

62   "Well, I think we might have to go out and beg for them like the poor old woman on Fridays. We wouldn't like that, would we?"

63   "No," I agreed. "We wouldn't."

64   "So you'll promise not to come in and wake him?"

65   "Promise."

66   Mind you, I meant that. I knew pennies were a serious matter, and I was all against having to go out and beg like the old woman on Fridays. Mother laid out all my toys in a complete ring around the bed so that, whatever way I got out, I was bound to fall over one of them.

67   When I woke I remembered my promise all right. I got up and sat on the floor and played—for hours, it seemed to me. Then I got my chair and looked out the attic window for more hours. I wished it was time for Father to wake; I wished someone would make me a cup of tea. I didn't feel in the least like the sun; instead, I was bored and so very, very cold! I simply longed for the warmth and depth of the big featherbed.

68   At last I could stand it no longer. I went into the next room. As there was still no room at Mother's side I climbed over her and she woke with a start.

69   "Larry," she whispered, gripping my arm very tightly, "what did you promise?"

70   "But I did Mummy," I wailed, caught in the very act. "I was quiet for ever so long."

71   "Oh, dear, and you're perished!" she said sadly, feeling me all over. "Now, if I let you stay will you promise not to talk?"

72   "But I want to talk, Mummy," I wailed.

"That has nothing to do with it," she said with a firmness that was new
to me. "Daddy wants to sleep. Now, do you understand that?" 73

I understood it only too well. I wanted to talk, he wanted to sleep—
whose house was it, anyway? 74

"Mummy," I said with equal firmness, "I think it would be healthier
for Daddy to sleep in his own bed." 75

That seemed to stagger her, because she said nothing for a while. 76

"Now, once for all," she went on, "you're to be perfectly quiet or go
back to your own bed. Which is it to be?" 77

The injustice of it got me down. I had convicted her out of her own
mouth of inconsistency and unreasonableness, and she hadn't even attempted to reply. Full of spite, I gave Father a kick, which she didn't
notice but which made him grunt and open his eyes in alarm. 78

"What time is it?" he asked in a panic-stricken voice, not looking at
Mother but at the door, as if he saw someone there. 79

"It's early yet," she replied soothingly. "It's only the child. Go to sleep
again. . . . Now, Larry," she added, getting out of bed, "you've wakened
Daddy and you must go back." 80

This time, for all her quiet air, I knew she meant it, and knew that my
principal rights and privileges were as good as lost unless I asserted them
at once. As she lifted me, I gave a screech, enough to wake the dead, not
to mind Father. He groaned. 81

"That damn child! Doesn't he ever sleep?" 82

"It's only a habit, dear," she said quietly, though I could see she was
vexed. 83

"Well, it's time he got out of it," shouted Father, beginning to heave in
the bed. He suddenly gathered all the bedclothes about him, turned to the
wall, and then looked back over his shoulder with nothing showing only
two small, spiteful, dark eyes. The man looked very wicked. 84

To open the bedroom door, Mother had to let me down, and I broke
free and dashed for the farthest corner, screeching. Father sat bolt upright
in bed. 85

"Shut up, you little puppy!" he said in a choking voice. 86

I was so astonished that I stopped screeching. Never, never had anyone
spoken to me in that tone before. I looked at him incredulously and saw
his face convulsed with rage. It was only then that I fully realized how
God had codded me, listening to my prayers for the safe return of this
monster. 87

"Shut up, you!" I bawled, beside myself. 88

"What's that you said?" shouted Father, making a wild leap out of the
bed. 89

"Mick, Mick!" cried Mother. "Don't you see the child isn't used to
you?" 90

"I see he's better fed than taught," snarled Father, waving his arms
wildly. "He wants his bottom smacked." 91

92   All his previous shouting was as nothing to these obscene words referring to my person. They really made my blood boil.

93   "Smack your own!" I screamed hysterically. "Smack your own! Shut up! Shut up!"

94   At this he lost his patience and let fly at me. He did it with the lack of conviction you'd expect of a man under Mother's horrified eyes, and it ended up as a mere tap, but the sheer indignity of being struck at all by a stranger, a total stranger who had cajoled his way back from the war into our big bed as a result of my innocent intercession, made me completely dotty. I shrieked and shrieked, and danced in my bare feet, and Father, looking awkward and hairy in nothing but a short gray army shirt, glared down at me like a mountain out for murder. I think it must have been then that I realized he was jealous too. And there stood Mother in her nightdress, looking as if her heart was broken between us. I hoped she felt as she looked. It seemed to me that she deserved it all.

95   From that morning out my life was a hell. Father and I were enemies, open and avowed. We conducted a series of skirmishes against one another, he trying to steal my time with Mother and I his. When she was sitting on my bed, telling me a story, he took to looking for some pair of old boots which he alleged he had left behind him at the beginning of the war. While he talked to Mother I played loudly with my toys to show my total lack of concern. He created a terrible scene one evening when he came in from work and found me at his box, playing with his regimental badges, Gurkha knives and button-sticks. Mother got up and took the box from me.

96   "You mustn't play with Daddy's toys unless he lets you, Larry," she said severely. "Daddy doesn't play with yours."

97   For some reason Father looked at her as if she had struck him and then turned away with a scowl.

98   "Those are not toys," he growled, taking down the box again to see had I lifted anything. "Some of those curios are very rare and valuable."

99   But as time went on I saw more and more how he managed to alienate Mother and me. What made it worse was that I couldn't grasp his method or see what attraction he had for Mother. In every possible way he was less winning than I. He had a common accent and made noises at his tea. I thought for a while that it might be the newspapers she was interested in, so I made up bits of news on my own to read to her. Then I thought it might be the smoking, which I personally thought attractive, and took his pipes and went round the house dribbling into them till he caught me. I even made noises at my tea, but Mother only told me I was disgusting. It all seemed to hinge round that unhealthy habit of sleeping together, so I made a point of dropping into their bedroom and nosing round, talking to myself, so that they wouldn't know I was watching them, but they were never up to anything that I could see. In the end it beat me. It seemed to depend on being grown-up and giving people rings, and I realized I'd have to wait.

But at the same time I wanted him to see that I was only waiting, not giving up the fight. One evening when he was being particularly obnoxious, chattering away well above my head, I let him have it.

"Mummy," I said, "do you know what I'm going to do when I grow up?"

"No, dear," she replied. "What?"

"I'm going to marry you," I said quietly.

Father gave a great guffaw out of him, but he didn't take me in. I knew it must only be pretense. And Mother, in spite of everything, was pleased. I felt she was probably relieved to know that one day Father's hold on her would be broken.

"Won't that be nice?" she said with a smile.

"It'll be very nice," I said confidently. "Because we're going to have lots and lots of babies."

"That's right, dear," she said placidly. "I think we'll have one soon, and then you'll have plenty of company."

I was no end pleased about that because it showed that in spite of the way she gave in to Father she still considered my wishes. Besides, it would put the Geneys in their place.

It didn't turn out like that, though. To begin with, she was very preoccupied—I supposed about where she would get the seventeen and six—and though Father took to staying out late in the evenings it did me no particular good. She stopped taking me for walks, became as touchy as blazes, and smacked me for nothing at all. Sometimes I wished I'd never mentioned the confounded baby—I seemed to have a genius for bringing calamity on myself.

And calamity it was! Sonny arrived in the most appalling hullabaloo—even that much he couldn't do without a fuss—and from the first moment I disliked him. He was a difficult child—so far as I was concerned he was always difficult—and demanded far too much attention. Mother was simply silly about him, and couldn't see when he was only showing off. As company he was worse than useless. He slept all day, and I had to go round the house on tiptoe to avoid waking him. It wasn't any longer a question of not waking Father. The slogan now was "Don't-wake-Sonny!" I couldn't understand why the child wouldn't sleep at the proper time, so whenever Mother's back was turned I woke him. Sometimes to keep him awake I pinched him as well. Mother caught me at it one day and gave me a most unmerciful flaking.

One evening, when Father was coming in from work, I was playing trains in the front garden. I let on not to notice him; instead, I pretended to be talking to myself, and said in a loud voice: "If another bloody baby comes into this house, I'm going out."

Father stopped dead and looked at me over his shoulder.

"What's that you said?" he asked sternly.

"I was only talking to myself," I replied, trying to conceal my panic. "It's private."

115   He turned and went in without a word. Mind you, I intended it as a solemn warning, but its effect was quite different. Father started being quite nice to me. I could understand that, of course. Mother was quite sickening about Sonny. Even at mealtimes she'd get up and gawk at him in the cradle with an idiotic smile, and tell Father to do the same. He was always polite about it, but he looked so puzzled you could see he didn't know what she was talking about. He complained of the way Sonny cried at night, but she only got cross and said that Sonny never cried except when there was something up with him—which was a flaming lie, because Sonny never had anything up with him, and only cried for attention. It was really painful to see how simpleminded she was. Father wasn't attractive, but he had a fine intelligence. He saw through Sonny, and now he knew that I saw through him as well.

116   One night I woke with a start. There was someone beside me in the bed. For one wild moment I felt sure it must be Mother, having come to her senses and left Father for good, but then I heard Sonny in convulsions in the next room, and Mother saying: "There! There! There!" and I knew it wasn't she. It was Father. He was lying beside me, wide awake, breathing hard and apparently as mad as hell.

117   After awhile it came to me what he was mad about. It was his turn now. After turning me out of the big bed, he had been turned out himself. Mother had no consideration now for anyone but that poisonous pup, Sonny. I couldn't help feeling sorry for Father. I had been through it all myself, and even at that age I was magnanimous. I began to stroke him down and say: "There! There!" He wasn't exactly responsive.

118   "Aren't you asleep either?" he snarled.

119   "Ah, come on and put your arm around us, can't you?" I said, and he did, in a sort of way. Gingerly, I suppose, is how you'd describe it. He was very bony but better than nothing.

120   At Christmas he went out of his way to buy me a really nice model railway.

❏ Questions for Discussion

1. One of the major sources of humor in this story is the **irony**. Point out examples in which Larry's prayers or behavior have ironic results. Also point out examples of humor which stem directly from Larry's misconceptions.

2. Why is the narrator's **point of view** effective in this story? What does the narrator tell you about himself as an adult?

❏ Suggestions for Exploration and Writing

1. Write an essay tracing the changes in the relationship between Larry and his father and clarifying the reasons for each change.

2. Using this story as background, write an essay discussing the compromises family members make to survive in a household.

EUDORA WELTY (1909–)

Eudora Welty was born in Jackson, Mississippi, attended Mississippi State College for Women, and received her B.A. from the University of Wisconsin. She has written many collections of short stories, among them The Collected Stories of Eudora Welty *(1980); several novels, such as* The Robber Bridegroom *(1942) and* The Optimist's Daughter *(1972); and an autobiography,* One Writer's Beginnings *(1984). Among her many awards are two Guggenheim Fellowships, three O. Henry awards, the Pulitzer prize, the National Medal for Literature, and the Presidential Medal of Freedom. Welty writes of Southern rural or small town life and portrays lower-middle-class characters. Her favorite themes include the mystery of human life and human relationships, people and nature, and the power of love to restore.*

Why I Live at the P.O.

I was getting along fine with Mama, Papa-Daddy and Uncle Rondo   1
until my sister Stella-Rondo just separated from her husband and came back home again. Mr. Whitaker! Of course I went with Mr. Whitaker first, when he first appeared here in China Grove, taking "Pose Yourself" photos, and Stella-Rondo broke us up. Told him I was one-sided. Bigger on one side than the other, which is a deliberate, calculated falsehood: I'm the same. Stella-Rondo is exactly twelve months to the day younger than I am and for that reason she's spoiled.

She's always had anything in the world she wanted and then she'd   2
throw it away. Papa-Daddy gave her this gorgeous Add-a-Pearl necklace when she was eight years old and she threw it away playing baseball when she was nine, with only two pearls.

So as soon as she got married and moved away from home the first   3
thing she did was separate! From Mr. Whitaker! This photographer with the popeyes she said she trusted. Came home from one of those towns up in Illinois and to our complete surprise brought this child of two.

Mama said she like to made her drop dead for a second. "Here you had   4
this marvelous blonde child and never so much as wrote your mother a word about it," says Mama. "I'm thoroughly ashamed of you." But of course she wasn't.

Stella-Rondo just calmly takes off this *hat,* I wish you could see it. She   5
says, "Why, Mama, Shirley-T.'s adopted, I can prove it."

"How?" says Mama, but all I says was, "H'm!" There I was over the   6
hot stove, trying to stretch two chickens over five people and a completely unexpected child into the bargain, without one moment's notice.

"What do you mean—'H'm!'?" says Stella-Rondo, and Mama says, "I   7
heard that, Sister."

I said that oh, I didn't mean a thing, only that whoever Shirley-T. was,   8
she was the spit-image of Papa-Daddy if he'd cut off his beard, which of course he'd never do in the world. Papa-Daddy's Mama's papa and sulks.

9   Stella-Rondo got furious! She said, "Sister, I don't need to tell you you got a lot of nerve and always did have and I'll thank you to make no future reference to my adopted child whatsoever."

10   "Very well," I said. "Very well, very well. Of course I noticed at once she looks like Mr. Whitaker's side too. That frown. She looks like a cross between Mr. Whitaker and Papa-Daddy."

11   "Well, all I can say is she isn't."

12   "She looks exactly like Shirley Temple to me," says Mama, but Shirley-T. just ran away from her. So the first thing Stella-Rondo did at the table was turn Papa-Daddy against me.

13   "Papa-Daddy," she says. He was trying to cut up his meat. "Papa-Daddy!" I was taken completely by surprise. Papa-Daddy is about a million years old and's got this long-long beard. "Papa-Daddy, Sister says she fails to understand why you don't cut off your beard."

14   So Papa-Daddy l-a-y-s down his knife and fork! He's real rich. Mama says he is, he says he isn't. So he says, "Have I heard correctly? You don't understand why I don't cut off my beard?"

15   "Why," I says, "Papa-Daddy, of course I understand, I did not say any such of a thing, the idea!"

16   He says, "Hussy!"

17   I says, "Papa-Daddy, you know I wouldn't any more want you to cut off your beard than the man in the moon. It was the farthest thing from my mind! Stella-Rondo sat there and made that up while she was eating breast of chicken."

18   But he says, "So the postmistress fails to understand why I don't cut off my beard. Which job I got you through my influence with the government. 'Bird's nest'—is that what you call it?"

19   Not that it isn't the next to smallest P.O. in the entire state of Mississippi.

20   I says, "Oh, Papa-Daddy," I says, "I didn't say any such of a thing, I never dreamed it was a bird's nest, I have always been grateful though this is the next to smallest P.O. in the state of Mississippi, and I do not enjoy being referred to as a hussy by my own grandfather."

21   But Stella-Rondo says, "Yes, you did say it too. Anybody in the world could of heard you, that had ears."

22   "Stop right there," says Mama, looking at *me*.

23   So I pulled my napkin straight back through the napkin ring and left the table.

24   As soon as I was out of the room Mama says, "Call her back, or she'll starve to death," but Papa-Daddy says, "This is the beard I started growing on the Coast when I was fifteen years old." He would of gone on till nightfall if Shirley-T. hadn't lost the Milky Way she ate in Cairo.

25   So Papa-Daddy says, "I am going out and lie in the hammock, and you can all sit here and remember my words: I'll never cut off my beard as long as I live, even one inch, and I don't appreciate it in you at all." Passed right by me in the hall and went straight out and got in the hammock.

It would be a holiday. It wasn't five minutes before Uncle Rondo   26
suddenly appeared in the hall in one of Stella-Rondo's flesh-colored
kimonos, all cut on the bias, like something Mr. Whitaker probably
thought was gorgeous.

"Uncle Rondo!" I says. "I didn't know who that was! Where are you   27
going?"

"Sister," he says, "get out of my way, I'm poisoned."   28

"If you're poisoned stay away from Papa-Daddy," I says. "Keep out of   29
the hammock. Papa-Daddy will certainly beat you on the head if you
come within forty miles of him. He thinks I deliberately said he ought to
cut off his beard after he got me the P.O., and I've told him and told him
and told him, and he acts like he just don't hear me. Papa-Daddy must of
gone stone deaf."

"He picked a fine day to do it then," says Uncle Rondo, and before you   30
could say "Jack Robinson" flew out in the yard.

What he'd really done, he'd drunk another bottle of that prescription.   31
He does it every single Fourth of July as sure as shooting, and it's horribly
expensive. Then he falls over in the hammock and snores. So he insisted
on zigzagging right on out to the hammock, looking like a half-wit.

Papa-Daddy woke up with this horrible yell and right there without   32
moving an inch he tried to turn Uncle Rondo against me. I heard every
word he said. Oh, he told Uncle Rondo I didn't learn to read till I was
eight years old and he didn't see how in the world I ever got the mail put
up at the P.O., much less read it all, and he said if Uncle Rondo could
only fathom the lengths he had gone to get me that job! And he said on
the other hand he thought Stella-Rondo had a brilliant mind and deserved credit for getting out of town. All the time he was just lying there
swinging as pretty as you please and looping out his beard, and poor
Uncle Rondo was *pleading* with him to slow down the hammock, it was
making him as dizzy as a witch to watch it. But that's what Papa-Daddy
likes about a hammock. So Uncle Rondo was too dizzy to get turned
against me for the time being. He's Mama's only brother and is a good
case of a one-track mind. Ask anybody. A certified pharmacist.

Just then I heard Stella-Rondo raising the upstairs window. While she   33
was married she got this peculiar idea that it's cooler with the windows
shut and locked. So she has to raise the window before she can make a
soul hear her outdoors.

So she raises the window and says, *"Oh!"* You would have thought she   34
was mortally wounded.

Uncle Rondo and Papa-Daddy didn't even look up, but kept right on   35
with what they were doing. I had to laugh.

I flew up the stairs and threw the door open! I says, "What in the wide   36
world's the matter, Stella-Rondo? You mortally wounded?"

"No," she says, "I am not mortally wounded but I wish you would do   37
me the favor of looking out that window there and telling me what you
see."

So I shade my eyes and look out the window.   38

39   "I see the front yard," I says.

40   "Don't you see any human beings?" she says.

41   "I see Uncle Rondo trying to run Papa-Daddy out of the hammock," I says. "Nothing more. Naturally, it's so suffocating-hot in the house, with all the windows shut and locked, everybody who cares to stay in their right mind will have to go out and get in the hammock before the Fourth of July is over."

42   "Don't you notice anything different about Uncle Rondo?" asks Stella-Rondo.

43   "Why, no, except he's got on some terrible-looking flesh-colored contraption I wouldn't be found dead in, is all I can see," I says.

44   "Never mind, you won't be found dead in it, because it happens to be part of my trousseau, and Mr. Whitaker took several dozen photographs of me in it," says Stella-Rondo. "What on earth could Uncle Rondo *mean* by wearing part of my trousseau out in the broad open daylight without saying so much as 'Kiss my foot,' *knowing* I only got home this morning after my separation and hung my negligee up on the bathroom door just as nervous as I could be?"

45   "I'm sure I don't know, and what do you expect me to do about it?" I says. "Jump out the window?"

46   "No, I expect nothing of the kind. I simply declare that Uncle Rondo looks like a fool in it, that's all," she says. "It makes me sick to my stomach."

47   "Well, he looks as good as he can," I says. "As good as anybody in reason could." I stood up for Uncle Rondo, please remember. And I said to Stella-Rondo, "I think I would do well not to criticize so freely if I were you and came home with a two-year-old child I had never said a word about, and no explanation whatever about my separation."

48   "I asked you the instant I entered this house not to refer one more time to my adopted child, and you gave me your word of honor you would not," was all Stella-Rondo would say and started pulling out every one of her eyebrows with some cheap Kress tweezers.

49   So I merely slammed the door behind me and went down and made some green-tomato pickle. Somebody had to do it. Of course Mama had turned both the niggers loose; she always said no earthly power could hold one anyway on the Fourth of July, so she wouldn't even try. It turned out that Jaypan fell in the lake and came within a very narrow limit of drowning.

50   So Mama trots in. Lifts up the lid and says, "H'm! Not very good for your Uncle Rondo in his precarious condition, I must say. Or poor little adopted Shirley-T. Shame on you!"

51   That made me tired. I says, "Well, Stella-Rondo had better thank her lucky stars it was her instead of me came trotting in with that very peculiar-looking child. Now if it had been me that trotted in from Illinois and brought a peculiar-looking child of two, I shudder to think of the reception I'd of got, much less controlled the diet of an entire family."

"But you must remember, Sister, that you were never married to Mr. 52
Whitaker in the first place and didn't go up to Illinois to live," says
Mama, shaking a spoon in my face. "If you had I would of been just as
overjoyed to see you and your little adopted girl as I was to see Stella-
Rondo, when you wound up with your separation and came on back
home."

"You would not," I says. 53

"Don't contradict me, I would," says Mama. 54

But I said she couldn't convince me though she talked till she was blue 55
in the face. Then I said, "Besides, you know as well as I do that that child
is not adopted."

"She most certainly is adopted," says Mama, stiff as a poker. 56

I says, "Why, Mama, Stella-Rondo had her just as sure as anything in 57
this world, and just too stuck up to admit it."

"Why, Sister," said Mama. "Here I thought we were going to have a 58
pleasant Fourth of July, and you start right out not believing a word your
own baby sister tells you!"

"Just like Cousin Annie Flo. Went to her grave denying the facts of 59
life," I remind Mama.

"I told you if you ever mentioned Annie Flo's name I'd slap your face," 60
says Mama, and slaps my face.

"All right, you wait and see," I says. 61

"I," says Mama, "I prefer to take my children's word for anything 62
when it's humanly possible." You ought to see Mama, she weighs two
hundred pounds and has real tiny feet.

Just then something perfectly horrible occurred to me. 63

"Mama," I says, "can that child talk?" I simply had to whisper! 64
"Mama, I wonder if that child can be—you know—in any way? Do you
realize," I says, "that she hasn't spoken one single, solitary word to a
human being up to this minute? This is the way she looks," I says, and
I looked like this.

Well, Mama and I just stood there and stared at each other. It was 65
horrible!

"I remember well that Joe Whitaker frequently drank like a fish," says 66
Mama. "I believed to my soul he drank *chemicals*." And without another
word she marches to the foot of the stairs and calls Stella-Rondo.

"Stella-Rondo? O-o-o-o-o! Stella-Rondo!" 67

"What?" says Stella-Rondo from upstairs. Not even the grace to get up 68
off the bed.

"Can that child of yours talk?" asks Mama. 69

Stella-Rondo says, "Can she what?" 70

"Talk! Talk!" says Mama. "Burdyburdyburdyburdy!" 71

So Stella-Rondo yells back, "Who says she can't talk?" 72

"Sister says so," says Mama. 73

"You didn't have to tell me, I know whose word of honor don't mean 74
a thing in this house," says Stella-Rondo.

75   And in a minute the loudest Yankee voice I ever heard in my life yells out, "OE'm Pop-OE the Sail-or-r-r Ma-a-an!" and then somebody jumps up and down in the upstairs hall. In another second the house would of fallen down.

76   "Not only talks, she can tap-dance!" calls Stella-Rondo. "Which is more than some people I won't name can do."

77   "Why, the little precious darling thing!" Mama says, so surprised. "Just as smart as she can be!" Starts talking baby talk right there. Then she turns on me. "Sister, you ought to be thoroughly ashamed! Run upstairs this instant and apologize to Stella-Rondo and Shirley-T."

78   "Apologize for what?" I says. "I merely wondered if the child was normal, that's all. Now that she's proved she is, why, I have nothing further to say."

79   But Mama just turned on her heel and flew out, furious. She ran right upstairs and hugged the baby. She believed it was adopted. Stella-Rondo hadn't done a thing but turn her against me from upstairs while I stood there helpless over the hot stove. So that made Mama, Papa-Daddy and the baby all on Stella-Rondo's side.

80   Next, Uncle Rondo.

81   I must say that Uncle Rondo has been marvelous to me at various times in the past and I was completely unprepared to be made to jump out of my skin, the way it turned out. Once Stella-Rondo did something perfectly horrible to him—broke a chain letter from Flanders field—and he took the radio back he had given her and gave it to me. Stella-Rondo was furious! For six months we all had to call her Stella instead of Stella-Rondo, or she wouldn't answer. I always thought Uncle Rondo had all the brains of the entire family. Another time he sent me to Mammoth Cave, with all expenses paid.

82   But this would be the day he was drinking that prescription, the Fourth of July.

83   So at supper Stella-Rondo speaks up and says she thinks Uncle Rondo ought to try to eat a little something. So finally Uncle Rondo said he would try a little cold biscuits and ketchup, but that was all. So *she* brought it to him.

84   "Do you think it wise to disport with ketchup in Stella-Rondo's flesh-colored kimono?" I says. Trying to be considerate! If Stella-Rondo couldn't watch out for her trousseau, somebody had to.

85   "Any objections?" asks Uncle Rondo, just about to pour out all the ketchup.

86   "Don't mind what she says, Uncle Rondo," says Stella-Rondo. "Sister has been devoting this solid afternoon to sneering out my bedroom window at the way you look."

87   "What's that?" says Uncle Rondo. Uncle Rondo has got the most terrible temper in the world. Anything is liable to make him tear the house down if it comes at the wrong time.

So Stella-Rondo says, "Sister says, 'Uncle Rondo certainly does look like a fool in that pink kimono!'"

Do you remember who it was really said that?

Uncle Rondo spills out all the ketchup and jumps out of his chair and tears off the kimono and throws it down on the dirty floor and puts his foot on it. It had to be sent all the way to Jackson to the cleaners and repleated.

"So that's your opinion of your Uncle Rondo, is it?" he says. "I look like a fool, do I? Well, that's the last straw. A whole day in this house with nothing to do, and then to hear you come out with a remark like that behind my back!"

"I didn't say any such of a thing, Uncle Rondo," I says, "and I'm not saying who did, either. Why, I think you look all right. Just try to take care of yourself and not talk and eat at the same time," I says. "I think you better go lie down."

"Lie down my foot," says Uncle Rondo. I ought to of known by that he was fixing to do something perfectly horrible.

So he didn't do anything that night in the precarious state he was in— just played Casino with Mama and Stella-Rondo and Shirley-T. and gave Shirley-T. a nickel with a head on both sides. It tickled her nearly to death, and she called him "Papa." But at 6:30 A.M. the next morning, he threw a whole five-cent package of some unsold one-inch firecrackers from the store as hard as he could into my bedroom and they every one went off. Not one bad one in the string. Anybody else, there'd be one that wouldn't go off.

Well, I'm just terribly susceptible to noise of any kind, the doctor has always told me I was the most sensitive person he had ever seen in his whole life, and I was simply prostrated. I couldn't eat! People tell me they heard it as far as the cemetery, and old Aunt Jep Patterson, that had been holding her own so good, thought it was Judgment Day and she was going to meet her whole family. It's usually so quiet here.

And I'll tell you it didn't take me any longer than a minute to make up my mind what to do. There I was with the whole entire house on Stella-Rondo's side and turned against me. If I have anything at all I have pride.

So I just decided I'd go straight down to the P.O. There's plenty of room there in the back, I says to myself.

Well! I made no bones about letting the family catch on to what I was up to. I didn't try to conceal it.

The first thing they knew, I marched in where they were all playing Old Maid and pulled the electric oscillating fan out by the plug, and everything got real hot. Next I snatched the pillow I'd done the needlepoint on right off the davenport from behind Papa-Daddy. He went "Ugh!" I beat Stella-Rondo up the stairs and finally found my charm bracelet in her bureau drawer under a picture of Nelson Eddy.

100   "So that's the way the land lies," says Uncle Rondo. There he was, piecing on the ham. "Well, Sister, I'll be glad to donate my army cot if you got any place to set it up, providing you'll leave right this minute and let me get some peace." Uncle Rondo was in France.

101   "Thank you kindly for the cot and 'peace' is hardly the word I would select if I had to resort to firecrackers at 6:30 A.M. in a young girl's bedroom," I says back to him. "And as to where I intend to go, you seem to forget my position as postmistress of China Grove, Mississippi," I says, "I've always got the P.O."

102   Well, that made them all sit up and take notice.

103   I went out front and started digging up some four o'clocks to plant around the P.O.

104   "Ah-ah-ah!" says Mama, raising the window. "Those happen to be my four-o'clocks. Everything planted in that star is mine. I've never known you to make anything grow in your life."

105   "Very well," I says. "But I take the fern. Even you, Mama, can't stand there and deny that I'm the one watered that fern. And I happen to know where I can send in a box top and get a packet of one thousand mixed seeds, no two the same kind, free."

106   "Oh, where?" Mama wants to know.

107   But I says, "Too late. You 'tend to your house, and I'll 'tend to mine. You hear things like that all the time if you know how to listen to the radio. Perfectly marvelous offers. Get anything you want free."

108   So I hope to tell you I marched in and got that radio, and they could of all bit a nail in two, especially Stella-Rondo, that it used to belong to, and she well knew she couldn't get it back, I'd sue for it like a shot. And I very politely took the sewing-machine motor I helped pay the most on to give Mama for Christmas back in 1929, and a good big calendar, with the first-aid remedies on it. The thermometer and the Hawaiian ukulele certainly were rightfully mine, and I stood on the step-ladder and got all my watermelon-rind preserves and every fruit and vegetable I'd put up, every jar. Then I began to pull the tacks out of the bluebird wall vases on the archway to the dining room.

109   "Who told you you could have those, Miss Priss?" says Mama, fanning as hard as she could.

110   "I bought 'em and I'll keep track of 'em," I says. "I'll tack 'em up one on each side the post-office window, and you can see 'em when you come to ask me for your mail, if you're so dead to see 'em."

111   "Not I! I'll never darken the door to that post office again if I live to be a hundred," Mama says. "Ungrateful child! After all the money we spent on you at the Normal."

112   "Me either," says Stella-Rondo. "You can just let my mail lie there and *rot*, for all I care. I'll never come and relieve you of a single, solitary piece."

113   "I should worry," I says. "And who you think's going to sit down and write you all those big fat letters and postcards, by the way? Mr.

Whitaker? Just because he was the only man ever dropped down in China Grove and you got him—unfairly—is he going to sit down and write you a lengthy correspondence after you come home giving no rhyme nor reason whatsoever for your separation and no explanation for the presence of that child? I may not have your brilliant mind, but I fail to see it."

So Mama says, "Sister, I've told you a thousand times that Stella- 114
Rondo simply got homesick and this child is far too big to be hers," and she says, "Now, why don't you all just sit down and play Casino?"

Then Shirley-T. sticks out her tongue at me in this perfectly horrible 115
way. She has no more manners than the man in the moon. I told her she was going to cross her eyes like that some day and they'd stick.

"It's too late to stop me now," I says. "You should have tried that 116
yesterday. I'm going to the P.O. and the only way you can possibly see me is to visit me there."

So Papa-Daddy says, "You'll never catch me setting foot in that post 117
office, even if I should take a notion into my head to write a letter some place." He says, "I won't have you reachin' out of that little old window with a pair of shears and cuttin' off any beard of mine. I'm too smart for you!"

"We all are," says Stella-Rondo. 118
But I said, "If you're so smart, where's Mr. Whitaker?" 119
So then Uncle Rondo says, "I'll thank you from now on to stop reading 120
all the orders I get on postcards and telling everybody in China Grove what you think is the matter with them," but I says, "I draw my own conclusions and will continue in the future to draw them." I says, "If people want to write their inmost secrets on penny postcards, there's nothing in the wide world you can do about it, Uncle Rondo."

"And if you think we'll ever *write* another postcard you're sadly 121
mistaken," says Mama.

"Cutting off your nose to spite your face then," I says. "But if you're 122
all determined to have no more to do with the U.S. mail, think of this: What will Stella-Rondo do now, if she wants to tell Mr. Whitaker to come after her?"

"Wah!" says Stella-Rondo. I knew she'd cry. She had a conniption fit 123
right there in the kitchen.

"It will be interesting to see how long she holds out," I says. "And 124
now—I am leaving."

"Good-bye," says Uncle Rondo. 125
"Oh, I declare," says Mama, "to think that a family of mine should 126
quarrel on the Fourth of July, or the day after, over Stella-Rondo leaving old Mr. Whitaker and having the sweetest little adopted child! It looks like we'd all be glad!"

"Wah!" says Stella-Rondo, and has a fresh conniption fit. 127
"*He* left *her*—you mark my words," I says. "That's Mr. Whitaker. I 128
know Mr. Whitaker. After all, I knew him first. I said from the beginning he'd up and leave her. I foretold every single thing that's happened."

129   "Where did he go?" asks Mama.

130   "Probably to the North Pole, if he knows what's good for him," I says.

131   But Stella-Rondo just bawled and wouldn't say another word. She flew to her room and slammed the door.

132   "Now look what you've gone and done, Sister," says Mama. "You go apologize."

133   "I haven't got time, I'm leaving," I says.

134   "Well, what are you waiting around for?" asks Uncle Rondo.

135   So I just picked up the kitchen clock and marched off, without saying "Kiss my foot" or anything, and never did tell Stella-Rondo good-bye.

136   There was a nigger girl going along on a little wagon right in front.

137   "Nigger girl," I says, "come help me haul these things down the hill, I'm going to live in the post office."

138   Took her nine trips in her express wagon. Uncle Rondo came out on the porch and threw her a nickel.

139   And that's the last time I've laid eyes on any of my family or my family laid eyes on me for five solid days and nights. Stella-Rondo may be telling the most horrible tales in the world about Mr. Whitaker, but I haven't heard them. As I tell everybody, I draw my own conclusions.

140   But oh, I like it here. It's ideal, as I've been saying. You see, I've got everything cater-cornered, the way I like it. Hear the radio? All the war news. Radio, sewing machine, book ends, ironing board and that great big piano lamp—peace, that's what I like. Butter-bean vines planted all along the front where the strings are.

141   Of course, there's not much mail. My family are naturally the main people in China Grove, and if they prefer to vanish from the face of the earth, for all the mail they get or the mail they write, why, I'm not going to open my mouth. Some of the folks here in town are taking up for me and some turned against me. I know which is which. There are always people who will quit buying stamps just to get on the right side of Papa-Daddy.

142   But here I am, and here I'll stay. I want the world to know I'm happy.

143   And if Stella-Rondo should come to me this minute, on bended knees, and *attempt* to explain the incidents of her life with Mr. Whitaker, I'd simply put my fingers in both my ears and refuse to listen.

❏ Questions for Discussion

1. Why do Mama and Stella-Rondo seem so sensitive about Shirley-T and so insistent that she is adopted? Does Mama really think Shirley-T is adopted? Explain.

2. Why do you think there is so much rivalry between Stella-Rondo and the narrator, her sister? What does Sister do that is irritating?

3. Sister's apparent purpose in the story is to blame Stella-Rondo for forcing Sister to leave the house. What does Sister inadvertently reveal about herself in telling the story? In what ways is the story Sister tells inappropriate as self-justification?

4. Do the family members seem eccentric? normal? typical?

❏ **Suggestions for Exploration and Writing**

1. The key to the story's theme is found in the narrator's character. Write a **character analysis** of the narrator or of any other character.

2. Show how a knowledge of "The Prodigal Son" deepens and enriches your understanding of this story. How has Welty elaborated on and changed the parable and what are the implications of these changes?

3. Write an essay examining sibling rivalry in your family.

CARSON MCCULLERS (1917–1967)

Born in Columbus, Georgia, Carson Smith McCullers is famous for her portrayal of lonely and insecure people. Some of her short stories and novels are described as modern **Gothic.** *Her most famous novels include* The Heart Is a Lonely Hunter *(1940),* The Ballad of the Sad Cafe *(1951), and* The Member of the Wedding *(1946), which was made into an award-winning play and into a movie starring Julie Harris and Ethel Waters. McCullers learned about suffering first-hand: her health began to deteriorate because of a misdiagnosis of rheumatic fever while she was still in high school; and her marriage to Reeves McCullers was marked by many separations.*

A Domestic Dilemma

On Thursday Martin Meadows left the office early enough to make the first express bus home. It was the hour when the evening lilac glow was fading in the slushy streets, but by the time the bus had left the Mid-town terminal the bright city night had come. On Thursdays the maid had a half-day off and Martin liked to get home as soon as possible, since for the past year his wife had not been—well. This Thursday he was very tired and, hoping that no regular commuter would single him out for conversation, he fastened his attention to the newspaper until the bus had crossed the George Washington Bridge. Once on 9-W Highway Martin always felt that the trip was halfway done, he breathed deeply, even in cold weather when only ribbons of draught cut through the smoky air of the bus, confident that he was breathing country air. It used to be that at this point he would relax and begin to think with pleasure of his home. But in this last year nearness brought only a sense of tension and he did not anticipate the journey's end. This evening Martin kept his face close to the window and watched the barren fields and lonely lights of passing townships. There was a moon, pale on the dark earth and areas of late, porous snow; to Martin the countryside seemed vast and somehow desolate that evening. He took his hat from the rack and put his folded newspaper in the pocket of his overcoat a few minutes before time to pull the cord.

2   The cottage was a block from the bus stop, near the river but not directly on the shore; from the living-room window you could look across the street and opposite yard and see the Hudson. The cottage was modern, almost too white and new on the narrow plot of yard. In summer the grass was soft and bright and Martin carefully tended a flower border and a rose trellis. But during the cold, fallow months the yard was bleak and the cottage seemed naked. Lights were on that evening in all the rooms in the little house and Martin hurried up the front walk. Before the steps he stopped to move a wagon out of the way.

3   The children were in the living room, so intent on play that the opening of the front door was at first unnoticed. Martin stood looking at his safe, lovely children. They had opened the bottom drawer of the secretary and taken out the Christmas decorations. Andy had managed to plug in the Christmas tree lights and the green and red bulbs glowed with out-of-season festivity on the rug of the living room. At the moment he was trying to trail the bright cord over Marianne's rocking horse. Marianne sat on the floor pulling off an angel's wings. The children wailed a startling welcome. Martin swung the fat little baby girl up to his shoulder and Andy threw himself against his father's legs.

4   "Daddy, Daddy, Daddy!"

5   Martin set down the little girl carefully and swung Andy a few times like a pendulum. Then he picked up the Christmas tree cord.

6   "What's all this stuff doing out? Help me put it back in the drawer. You're not to fool with the light socket. Remember I told you that before. I mean it, Andy."

7   The six-year-old child nodded and shut the secretary drawer. Martin stroked his fair soft hair and his hand lingered tenderly on the nape of the child's frail neck.

8   "Had supper yet, Bumpkin?"

9   "It hurt. The toast was hot."

10   The baby girl stumbled on the rug and, after the first surprise of the fall, began to cry; Martin picked her up and carried her in his arms back to the kitchen.

11   "See, Daddy," said Andy. "The toast——"

12   Emily had laid the childrens' supper on the uncovered porcelain table. There were two plates with the remains of cream-of-wheat and eggs and

silver mugs that had held milk. There was also a platter of cinnamon toast, untouched except for one tooth-marked bite. Martin sniffed the bitten piece and nibbled gingerly. Then he put the toast into the garbage pail.

"Hoo—phui—What on earth!"   13

Emily had mistaken the tin of cayenne for the cinnamon.   14

"I like to have burnt up," Andy said. "Drank water and ran outdoors   15
and opened my mouth. Marianne didn't eat none."

"Any," corrected Martin. He stood helpless, looking around the walls   16
of the kitchen. "Well, that's that, I guess," he said finally. "Where is your mother now?"

"She's up in you alls' room."   17

Martin left the children in the kitchen and went up to his wife. Outside   18
the door he waited for a moment to still his anger. He did not knock and once inside the room he closed the door behind him.

Emily sat in the rocking chair by the window of the pleasant room. She   19
had been drinking something from a tumbler and as he entered she put the glass hurriedly on the floor behind the chair. In her attitude there was confusion and guilt which she tried to hide by a show of spurious vivacity.

"Oh, Marty! You home already? The time slipped up on me. I was just   20
going down——" She lurched to him and her kiss was strong with sherry. When he stood unresponsive she stepped back a pace and giggled nervously.

"What's the matter with you? Standing there like a barber pole. Is   21
anything wrong with you?"

"Wrong with *me?*" Martin bent over the rocking chair and picked up   22
the tumbler from the floor. "If you could only realize how sick I am— how bad it is for all of us."

Emily spoke in a false, airy voice that had become too familiar to him.   23
Often at such times she affected a slight English accent, copying perhaps some actress she admired. "I haven't the vaguest idea what you mean. Unless you are referring to the glass I used for a spot of sherry. I had a finger of sherry—maybe two. But what is the crime in that, pray tell me? I'm quite all right. Quite all right."

"So anyone can see."   24

As she went into the bathroom Emily walked with careful gravity. She   25
turned on the cold water and dashed some on her face with her cupped hands, then patted herself dry with the corner of a bath towel. Her face was delicately featured and young, unblemished.

"I was just going down to make dinner." She tottered and balanced   26
herself by holding to the door frame.

"I'll take care of dinner. You stay up here. I'll bring it up."   27

"I'll do nothing of the sort. Why, whoever heard of such a thing?"   28

"Please," Martin said.   29

30   "Leave me alone. I'm quite all right. I was just on the way down——"

31   "Mind what I say."

32   "Mind your grandmother."

33   She lurched toward the door, but Martin caught her by the arm. "I don't want the children to see you in this condition. Be reasonable."

34   "Condition!" Emily jerked her arm. Her voice rose angrily. "Why, because I drink a couple of sherries in the afternoon you're trying to make me out a drunkard. Condition! Why, I don't even touch whiskey. As well you know. *I* don't swill liquor at bars. And that's more than you can say. I don't even have a cocktail at dinnertime. I only sometimes have a glass of sherry. What, I ask you, is the disgrace of that? Condition!"

35   Martin sought words to calm his wife. "We'll have a quiet supper by ourselves up here. That's a good girl." Emily sat on the side of the bed and he opened the door for a quick departure.

36   "I'll be back in a jiffy."

37   As he busied himself with the dinner downstairs he was lost in the familiar question as to how this problem had come upon his home. He himself had always enjoyed a good drink. When they were still in Alabama they had served long drinks or cocktails as a matter of course. For years they had drunk one or two—possibly three drinks before dinner, and at bedtime a long nightcap. Evenings before holidays they might get a buzz on, might even become a little tight. But alcohol had never seemed a problem to him, only a bothersome expense that with the increase in the family they could scarcely afford. It was only after his company had transferred him to New York that Martin was aware that certainly his wife was drinking too much. She was tippling, he noticed, during the day.

38   The problem acknowledged, he tried to analyze the source. The change from Alabama to New York had somehow disturbed her; accustomed to the idle warmth of a small Southern town, the matrix of the family and cousinship and childhood friends, she had failed to accommodate herself to the stricter, lonelier mores of the North. The duties of motherhood and housekeeping were onerous to her. Homesick for Paris City, she had made no friends in the suburban town. She read only magazines and murder books. Her interior life was insufficient without the artifice of alcohol.

39   The revelations of incontinence insidiously undermined his previous conceptions of his wife. There were times of unexplainable malevolence, times when the alcoholic fuse caused an explosion of unseemly anger. He encountered a latent coarseness in Emily, inconsistent with her natural simplicity. She lied about drinking and deceived him with unsuspected strategems.

40   Then there was an accident. Coming home from work one evening about a year ago, he was greeted with screams from the childrens' room. He found Emily holding the baby, wet and naked from her bath. The

baby had been dropped, her frail, frail skull striking the table edge, so that a thread of blood was soaking into the gossamer hair. Emily was sobbing and intoxicated. As Martin cradled the hurt child, so infinitely precious at that moment, he had an affrighted vision of the future.

The next day Marianne was all right. Emily vowed that never again   41 would she touch liquor, and for a few weeks she was sober, cold and downcast. Then gradually she began—not whiskey or gin—but quantities of beer, or sherry, or outlandish liqueurs; once he had come across a hatbox of empty crème de menthe bottles. Martin found a dependable maid who managed the household competently. Virgie was also from Alabama and Martin had never dared tell Emily the wage scale customary in New York. Emily's drinking was entirely secret now, done before he reached the house. Usually the effects were almost imperceptible—a looseness of movement or the heavy-lidded eyes. The times of irresponsibilities, such as the cayenne-pepper toast were rare, and Martin could dismiss his worries when Virgie was at the house. But, nevertheless, anxiety was always latent, a threat of undefined disaster that underlaid his days.

"Marianne!" Martin called, for even the recollection of that time   42 brought the need for reassurance. The baby girl, no longer hurt, but no less precious to her father, came into the kitchen with her brother. Martin went on with the preparations for the meal. He opened a can of soup and put two chops in the frying pan. Then he sat down by the table and took his Marianne on his knees for a pony ride. Andy watched them, his fingers wobbling the tooth that had been loose all that week.

"Andy-the-candyman!" Martin said. "Is that old critter still in your   43 mouth? Come closer, let Daddy have a look."

"I got a string to pull it with." The child brought from his pocket a   44 tangled thread. "Virgie said to tie it to the tooth and tie the other end to the doorknob and shut the door real suddenly."

Martin took out a clean handkerchief and felt the loose tooth carefully.   45 "That tooth is coming out of my Andy's mouth tonight. Otherwise I'm awfully afraid we'll have a tooth tree in the family."

"A what?"   46

"A tooth tree," Martin said. "You'll bite into something and swallow   47 that tooth. And the tooth will take root in poor Andy's stomach and grow into a tooth tree with sharp little teeth instead of leaves."

"Shoo, Daddy," Andy said. But he held the tooth firmly between his   48 grimy little thumb and forefinger. "There ain't any tree like that. I never seen one."

"There *isn't* any tree like that and I never *saw* one."   49

Martin tensed suddenly. Emily was coming down the stairs. He lis-   50 tened to her fumbling footsteps, his arm embracing the little boy with dread. When Emily came into the room he saw from her movements and her sullen face that she had again been at the sherry bottle. She began to yank open drawers and set the table.

51   "Condition!" she said in a furry voice. "You talk to me like that. Don't think I'll forget. I remember every dirty lie you say to me. Don't you think for a minute that I forget."

52   "Emily!" he begged. "The children——"

53   "The children—yes! Don't think I don't see through your dirty plots and schemes. Down here trying to turn my own children against me. Don't think I don't see and understand."

54   "Emily! I beg you—please go upstairs."

55   "So you can turn my children—my very own children——" Two large tears coursed rapidly down her cheeks. "Trying to turn my little boy, my Andy, against his own mother."

56   With drunken impulsiveness Emily knelt on the floor before the startled child. Her hands on his shoulders balanced her. "Listen, my Andy— you wouldn't listen to any lies your father tells you? You wouldn't believe what he says? Listen, Andy, what was your father telling you before I came downstairs?" Uncertain, the child sought his father's face. "Tell me. Mama wants to know."

57   "About the tooth tree."

58   "What?"

59   The child repeated the words and she echoed them with unbelieving terror. "The tooth tree!" She swayed and renewed her grasp on the child's shoulder. "I don't know what you're talking about. But listen, Andy, Mama is all right, isn't she?" The tears were spilling down her face and Andy drew back from her, for he was afraid. Grasping the table edge, Emily stood up.

60   "See! You have turned my child against me."

61   Marianne began to cry, and Martin took her in his arms.

62   "That's all right, you can take *your* child. You have always shown partiality from the very first. I don't mind, but at least you can leave me my little boy."

63   Andy edged close to his father and touched his leg. "Daddy," he wailed.

64   Martin took the children to the foot of the stairs. "Andy, you take up Marianne and Daddy will follow you in a minute."

65   "But Mama?" the child asked, whispering.

66   "Mama will be all right. Don't worry."

67   Emily was sobbing at the kitchen table, her face buried in the crook of her arm. Martin poured a cup of soup and set it before her. Her rasping sobs unnerved him; the vehemence of her emotion, irrespective of the source, touched in him a strain of tenderness. Unwillingly he laid his hand on her dark hair. "Sit up and drink the soup." Her face as she looked up at him was chastened and imploring. The boy's withdrawal or the touch of Martin's hand had turned the tenor of her mood.

68   "Ma-Martin," she sobbed. "I'm so ashamed."

69   "Drink the soup."

70   Obeying him, she drank between gasping breaths. After a second cup she allowed him to lead her up to their room. She was docile now and

more restrained. He laid her nightgown on the bed and was about to leave when a fresh round of grief, the alcoholic tumult, came again.

"He turned away. My Andy looked at me and turned away."   71

Impatience and fatigue hardened his voice, but he spoke warily. "You   72 forget that Andy is still a little child—he can't comprehend the meaning of such scenes."

"Did I make a scene? Oh, Martin, did I make a scene before the   73 children?"

Her horrified face touched and amused him against his will. "Forget it.   74 Put on your nightgown and go to sleep."

"My child turned away from me. Andy looked at his mother and   75 turned away. The children——"

She was caught in the rhythmic sorrow of alcohol. Martin withdrew   76 from the room saying: "For God's sake go to sleep. The children will forget by tomorrow."

As he said this he wondered if it was true. Would the scene glide so   77 easily from memory—or would it root in the unconscious to fester in the after-years? Martin did not know, and the last alternative sickened him. He thought of Emily, foresaw the morning-after humiliation: the shards of memory, the lucidities that glared from the obliterating darkness of shame. She would call the New York office twice—possibly three or four times. Martin anticipated his own embarrassment, wondering if the others at the office could possibly suspect. He felt that his secretary had divined the trouble long ago and that she pitied him. He suffered a moment of rebellion against his fate; he hated his wife.

Once in the childrens' room he closed the door and felt secure for the   78 first time that evening. Marianne fell down on the floor, picked herself up and calling: "Daddy, watch me," fell again, got up, and continued the falling-calling routine. Andy sat in the child's low chair, wobbling the tooth. Martin ran the water in the tub, washed his own hands in the lavatory, and called the boy into the bathroom.

"Let's have another look at that tooth." Martin sat on the toilet, hold-   79 ing Andy between his knees. The child's mouth gaped and Martin grasped the tooth. A wobble, a quick twist and the nacreous milk tooth was free. Andy's face was for the first moment split between terror, astonishment, and delight. He mouthed a swallow of water and spat into the lavatory.

"Look, Daddy! It's blood. Marianne!"   80

Martin loved to bathe his children, loved inexpressibly the tender,   81 naked bodies as they stood in the water so exposed. It was not fair of Emily to say that he showed partiality. As Martin soaped the delicate boy-body of his son he felt that further love would be impossible. Yet he admitted the difference in the quality of his emotions for the two children. His love for his daughter was graver, touched with a strain of melancholy, a gentleness that was akin to pain. His pet names for the little boy were the absurdities of daily inspiration—he called the little girl always Marianne, and his voice as he spoke it was a caress. Martin patted dry the fat baby stomach and the sweet little genital fold. The washed child faces were radiant as flower petals, equally loved.

82 "I'm putting the tooth under my pillow. I'm supposed to get a quarter."

83 "What for?"

84 "*You* know, Daddy. Johnny got a quarter for his tooth."

85 "Who puts the quarter there?" asked Martin. "I used to think the fairies left it in the night. It was a dime in my day, though."

86 "That's what they say in kindergarden."

87 "Who does put it there?"

88 "Your parents," Andy said. "You!"

89 Martin was pinning the cover on Marianne's bed. His daughter was already asleep. Scarcely breathing, Martin bent over and kissed her forehead, kissed again the tiny hand that lay palm-upward, flung in slumber beside her head.

90 "Good night, Andy-man."

91 The answer was only a drowsy murmur. After a minute Martin took out his change and slid a quarter underneath the pillow. He left a night light in the room.

92 As Martin prowled about the kitchen making a late meal, it occurred to him that the children had not once mentioned their mother or the scene that must have seemed to them incomprehensible. Absorbed in the instant—the tooth, the bath, the quarter—the fluid passage of child-time had borne these weightless episodes like leaves in the swift current of a shallow stream while the adult enigma was beached and forgotten on the shore. Martin thanked the Lord for that.

93 But his own anger, repressed and lurking, arose again. His youth was being frittered by a drunkard's waste, his very manhood subtly undermined. And the children, once the immunity of incomprehension passed—what would it be like in a year or so? With his elbows on the table he ate his food brutishly, untasting. There was no hiding the truth—soon there would be gossip in the office and in the town; his wife was a dissolute woman. Dissolute. And he and his children were bound to a future of degradation and slow ruin.

94 Martin pushed away from the table and stalked into the living room. He followed the lines of a book with his eyes but his mind conjured miserable images: he saw his children drowned in the river, his wife a disgrace on the public street. By bedtime the dull, hard anger was like a weight upon his chest and his feet dragged as he climbed the stairs.

95 The room was dark except for the shafting light from the half-opened bathroom door. Martin undressed quietly. Little by little, mysteriously, there came in him a change. His wife was asleep, her peaceful respiration sounding gently in the room. Her high-heeled shoes with the carelessly dropped stockings made to him a mute appeal. Her underclothes were flung in disorder on the chair. Martin picked up the girdle and the soft, silk brassière and stood for a moment with them in his hands. For the first time that evening he looked at his wife. His eyes rested on the sweet forehead, the arch of the fine brow. The brow had descended to Mari-

anne, and the tilt at the end of the delicate nose. In his son he could trace the high cheekbones and pointed chin. Her body was full-bosomed, slender and undulant. As Martin watched the tranquil slumber of his wife the ghost of the old anger vanished. All thoughts of blame or blemish were distant from him now. Martin put out the bathroom light and raised the window. Careful not to awaken Emily he slid into the bed. By moonlight he watched his wife for the last time. His hand sought the adjacent flesh and sorrow paralleled desire in the immense complexity of love.

❏ Questions for Discussion

1. What clues does McCullers give early in the story that **fore-shadow** the problem in this family?

2. How would you describe the scene to which Martin returns home? If you were in Martin's position, how would you react to this scene?

3. What particular scenes and actions affect your judgment of Martin as a father? How does he show tenderness toward his children?

4. Martin feels anger at Emily's drunkenness and fear for the children under her care. Yet only a few minutes later, Martin feels tenderness and love for Emily. How can his feelings change so drastically in a few minutes? How is the **theme** of the story summed up in the phrase "the immense complexity of love"?

5. Explain what you think Martin should do in this situation.

❏ Suggestions for Exploration and Writing

1. Write a character sketch of either Martin or Emily.

2. Examine a disturbing problem in your life that you refused to confront. Why did you fail to confront the problem? What were the consequences of this failure?

3. In the second half of the twentieth century, families often move several times during their lifetime, yet most cope with the move better than Emily does. Write either a personal narrative about a relocation of your family or a cause-and-effect essay about relocation and its effect on family members.

TRUMAN CAPOTE (1924–1984)

Truman Capote, born Truman Streckfus Persons in New Orleans, spent much of his childhood in Alabama, the background for "A Christmas Memory." He took the surname of his stepfather and during his adolescence lived in Greenwich, Connecticut, and New York City. Capote began to write as a copy boy for The New Yorker. *His first short story, "Miriam" was published in 1946 and* Other Voices, Other Rooms, *a novel, was published in 1948. From that point he became what he called a media presence; moving to Hollywood, he wrote the script for* Breakfast at Tiffany's. *The publication of* In Cold Blood: A True Account of a Multiple Murder and its Consequences *in 1965 marked the beginning of a new genre called the nonfiction novel. A collection of short essays,* Music for Chameleon, *was published in 1980. His unfinished novel,* Answered Prayers, *was published after his death.*

A Christmas Memory

1   Imagine a morning in late November. A coming of winter morning more than twenty years ago. Consider the kitchen of a spreading old house in a country town. A great black stove is its main feature; but there is also a big round table and a fireplace with two rocking chairs placed in front of it. Just today the fireplace commenced its seasonal roar.

2   A woman with shorn white hair is standing at the kitchen window. She is wearing tennis shoes and a shapeless gray sweater over a summery calico dress. She is small and sprightly, like a bantam hen; but, due to a long youthful illness, her shoulders are pitifully hunched. Her face is remarkable—not unlike Lincoln's, craggy like that, and tinted by sun and wind; but it is delicate too, finely boned, and her eyes are sherry-colored and timid. "Oh my," she exclaims, her breath smoking the windowpane, "it's fruitcake weather!"

3   The person to whom she is speaking is myself. I am seven; she is sixty-something. We are cousins, very distant ones, and we have lived together—well, as long as I can remember. Other people inhabit the house, relatives; and though they have power over us, and frequently make us cry, we are not, on the whole, too much aware of them. We are each other's best friend. She calls me Buddy, in memory of a boy who was formerly her best friend. The other Buddy died in the 1880's, when she was still a child. She is still a child.

4   "I knew it before I got out of bed," she says, turning away from the window with a purposeful excitement in her eyes. "The courthouse bell sounded so cold and clear. And there were no birds singing; they've gone to warmer country, yes indeed. Oh, Buddy, stop stuffing biscuit and fetch our buggy. Help me find my hat. We've thirty cakes to bake."

5   It's always the same: a morning arrives in November, and my friend, as though officially inaugurating the Christmas time of year that exhilarates her imagination and fuels the blaze of her heart, announces: "It's fruitcake weather! Fetch our buggy. Help me find my hat."

6   The hat is found, a straw cartwheel corsaged with velvet roses out-of-doors has faded: it once belonged to a more fashionable relative. Together, we guide our buggy, a dilapidated baby carriage, out to the

garden and into a grove of pecan trees. The buggy is mine; that is, it was bought for me when I was born. It is made of wicker, rather unraveled, and the wheels wobble like a drunkard's legs. But it is a faithful object; springtimes, we take it to the woods and fill it with flowers, herbs, wild fern for our porch pots; in the summer we pile it with picnic parapher- nalia and sugar-cane fishing poles and roll it down to the edge of a creek; it has its winter uses, too: as a truck for hauling firewood from the yard to the kitchen, as a warm bed for Queenie, our tough little orange and white rat terrier who has survived distemper and two rattlesnake bites. Queenie is trotting beside it now.

Three hours later we are back in the kitchen hulling a heaping buggy-   7 load of windfall pecans. Our backs hurt from gathering them: how hard they were to find (the main crop having been shaken off the trees and sold by the orchard's owners, who are not us) among the concealing leaves, the frosted, deceiving grass. Caarackle! A cheery crunch, scraps of min- iature thunder sound as the shells collapse and the golden mound of sweet oily ivory meat mounts in the milk-glass bowl. Queenie begs to taste, and now and again my friend sneaks her a mite, though insisting we deprive ourselves. "We mustn't, Buddy. If we start, we won't stop. And there's scarcely enough as there is. For thirty cakes." The kitchen is growing dark. Dusk turns the window into a mirror: our reflections mingle with the rising moon as we work by the fireside in the firelight. At last, when the moon is quite high, we toss the final hull into the fire and, with joined sighs, watch it catch flame. The buggy is empty, the bowl is brimful.

We eat our supper (cold biscuits, bacon, blackberry jam) and discuss   8 tomorrow. Tomorrow the kind of work I like best begins: buying. Cherries and citron, ginger and vanilla and canned Hawaiian pineapple, rinds and raisins and walnuts and whiskey and oh, so much flour, butter, so many eggs, spices, flavorings: why, we'll need a pony to pull the buggy home.

But before these purchases can be made, there is the question of   9 money. Neither of us has any. Except for skinflint sums persons in the house occasionally provide (a dime is considered very big money); or what we earn ourselves from various activities: holding rummage sales, selling buckets of hand-picked blackberries, jars of homemade jam and apple jelly and peach preserves, rounding up flowers for funerals and weddings. Once we won seventy-ninth prize, five dollars, in a national football contest. Not that we know a fool thing about football. It's just that we enter any contest we hear about: at the moment our hopes are centered on the fifty-thousand-dollar Grand Prize being offered to name a new brand of coffee (we suggested "A.M."; and, after some hesitation, for my friend thought it perhaps sacrilegious, the slogan "A.M.! Amen!"). To tell the truth, our only *really* profitable enterprise was the Fun and Freak Museum we conducted in a back-yard woodshed two summers ago. The Fun was a stereopticon with slide views of Washington and

New York lent us by a relative who had been to those places (she was furious when she discovered why we'd borrowed it); the Freak was a three-legged biddy chicken hatched by one of our own hens. Everybody hereabouts wanted to see that biddy: we charged grownups a nickel, kids two cents. And took in a good twenty dollars before the museum shut down due to the decease of the main attraction.

10   But one way and another we do each year accumulate Christmas savings, a Fruitcake Fund. These moneys we keep hidden in an ancient bead purse under a loose board under the floor under a chamber pot under my friend's bed. The purse is seldom removed from this safe location except to make a deposit, or, as happens every Saturday, a withdrawal; for on Saturdays I am allowed ten cents to go the picture show. My friend has never been to a picture show, nor does she intend to: "I'd rather hear you tell the story, Buddy. That way I can imagine it more. Besides, a person my age shouldn't squander their eyes. When the Lord comes, let me see Him clear." In addition to never having seen a movie, she has never: eaten in a restaurant, traveled more than five miles from home, received or sent a telegram, read anything except funny papers and the Bible, worn cosmetics, cursed, wished someone harm, told a lie on purpose, let a hungry dog go hungry. Here are the few things she has done, does do: killed with a hoe the biggest rattlesnake ever seen in this county (sixteen rattles), dip snuff (secretly), tame hummingbirds (just try it) till they balance on her finger, tell ghost stories (we both believe in ghosts) so tingling they chill you in July, talk to herself, take walks in the rain, grow the prettiest japonicas in town, know the recipe for every sort of old-time Indian cure, including a magical wart-remover.

11   Now, with supper finished, we retire to the room in a faraway part of the house where my friend sleeps in a scrap-quilt-covered iron bed painted rose pink, her favorite color. Silently, wallowing in the pleasures of conspiracy, we take the bead purse from its secret place and spill its contents on the scrap quilt. Dollar bills, tightly rolled and green as May buds. Somber fifty-cent pieces, heavy enough to weight a dead man's eyes. Lovely dimes, the liveliest coin, the one that really jingles. Nickels and quarters, worn smooth as creek pebbles. But mostly a hateful heap of bitter-odored pennies. Last summer others in the house contracted to pay us a penny for every twenty-five flies we killed. Oh, the carnage of August: the flies that flew to heaven! Yet it was not work in which we took pride. And, as we sit counting pennies, it is as though we were back tabulating dead flies. Neither of us has a head for figures; we count slowly, lose track, start again. According to her calculations, we have $12.73. According to mine, exactly $13. "I do hope you're wrong, Buddy. We can't mess around with thirteen. The cakes will fall. Or put somebody in the cemetery. Why, I wouldn't dream of getting out of bed on the thirteenth." This is true: she always spends thirteenths in bed. So, to be on the safe side, we subtract a penny and toss it out the window.

Of the ingredients that go into our fruitcakes, whiskey is the most 12
expensive, as well as the hardest to obtain: State laws forbid its sale. But
everybody knows you can buy a bottle from Mr. Haha Jones. And the
next day, having completed our more prosaic shopping, we set out for
Mr. Haha's business address, a "sinful" (to quote public opinion) fish-fry
and dancing café down by the river. We've been there before, and on the
same errand; but in previous years our dealings have been with Haha's
wife, an iodine-dark Indian woman with brassy peroxided hair and a
dead-tired disposition. Actually, we've never laid eyes on her husband,
though we've heard that he's an Indian too. A giant with razor scars
across his cheeks. They call him Haha because he's so gloomy, a man
who never laughs. As we approach his café (a large log cabin festooned
inside and out with chains of garish-gay naked light bulbs and standing
by the river's muddy edge under the shade of river trees where moss drifts
through the branches like gray mist) our steps slow down. Even Queenie
stops prancing and sticks close by. People have been murdered in Haha's
café. Cut to pieces. Hit on the head. There's a case coming up in court
next month. Naturally these goings-on happen at night when the colored
lights cast crazy patterns and the victrola wails. In the daytime Haha's is
shabby and deserted. I knock at the door, Queenie barks, my friend calls:
"Mrs. Haha, ma'am? Anyone to home?"

Footsteps. The door opens. Our hearts overturn. It's Mr. Haha Jones 13
himself! And he *is* a giant; he *does* have scars; he *doesn't* smile. No, he
glowers at us through Satan-tilted eyes and demands to know: "What
you want with Haha?"

For a moment we are too paralyzed to tell. Presently my friend 14
half-finds her voice, a whispery voice at best: "If you please, Mr. Haha,
we'd like a quart of your finest whiskey."

His eyes tilt more. Would you believe it? Haha is smiling! Laughing, 15
too. "Which one of you is a drinkin' man?"

"It's for making fruitcakes, Mr. Haha. Cooking." 16

This sobers him. He frowns. "That's no way to waste good whiskey." 17
Nevertheless, he retreats into the shadowed café and seconds later appears carrying a bottle of daisy-yellow unlabeled liquor. He demonstrates
its sparkle in the sunlight and says: "Two dollars."

We pay him with nickels and dimes and pennies. Suddenly, as he 18
jangles the coins in his hand like a fistful of dice, his face softens. "Tell
you what," he proposed, pouring the money back into our bead purse,
"just send me one of them fruitcakes instead."

"Well," my friend remarks on our way home, "there's a lovely man. 19
We'll put an extra cup of raisins in *his* cake."

The black stove, stoked with coal and firewood, glows like a lighted 20
pumpkin. Eggbeaters whirl, spoons spin round in bowls of butter and
sugar, vanilla sweetens the air, ginger spices it; melting, nose-tingling
odors saturate the kitchen, suffuse the house, drift out to the world on

puffs of chimney smoke. In four days our work is done. Thirty-one cakes, dampened with whiskey, bask on window sills and shelves.

21   Who are they for?

22   Friends. Not necessarily neighbor friends: indeed, the larger share is intended for persons we've met maybe once, perhaps not at all. People who've struck our fancy. Like President Roosevelt. Like the Reverend and Mrs. J. C. Lucey, Baptist missionaries to Borneo who lectured here last winter. Or the little knife grinder who comes through town twice a year. Or Abner Packer, the driver of the six o'clock bus from Mobile, who exchanges waves with us every day as he passes in a dust-cloud whoosh. Or the young Wistons, a California couple whose car one afternoon broke down outside the house and who spent a pleasant hour chatting with us on the porch (young Mr. Wiston snapped our picture, the only one we've ever had taken). Is it because my friend is shy with everyone *except* strangers that these strangers, and merest acquaintances, seem to us our truest friends? I think yes. Also the scrapbooks we keep of thank-you's on White House stationery, time-to-time communications from California and Borneo, the knife grinder's penny post cards, make us feel connected to eventful worlds beyond the kitchen with its view of a sky that stops.

23   Now a nude December fig branch grates against the window. The kitchen is empty, the cakes are gone; yesterday we carted the last of them to the post office, where the cost of stamps turned our purse inside out. We're broke. That rather depresses me, but my friend insists on celebrating—with two inches of whiskey left in Haha's bottle. Queenie has a spoonful in a bowl of coffee (she likes her coffee chicory-flavored and strong). The rest we divide between a pair of jelly glasses. We're both quite awed at the prospect of drinking straight whiskey; the taste of it brings screwed-up expressions and sour shudders. But by and by we begin to sing, the two of us singing different songs simultaneously. I don't know the words to mine, just: *Come on along, come on along, to the dark-town strutters' ball.* But I can dance: that's what I mean to be, a tap-dancer in the movies. My dancing shadow rollicks on the walls; our voices rock the chinaware; we giggle: as if unseen hands were tickling us. Queenie rolls on her back, her paws plow the air, something like a grin stretches her black lips. Inside myself, I feel warm and sparky as those crumbling logs, carefree as the wind in the chimney. My friend waltzes round the stove, the hem of her poor calico skirt pinched between her fingers as though it were a party dress: *Show me the way to go home,* she sings, her tennis shoes squeaking on the floor. *Show me the way to go home.*

24   Enter: two relatives. Very angry. Potent with eyes that scold, tongues that scald. Listen to what they have to say, the words tumbling together into a wrathful tune: "A child of seven! whiskey on his breath! are you out of your mind? feeding a child of seven! must be loony! road to

ruination! remember Cousin Kate? Uncle Charlie? Uncle Charlie's brother-in-law? shame! scandal! humiliation! kneel, pray, beg the Lord!"

Queenie sneaks under the stove. My friend gazes at her shoes, her chin quivers, she lifts her skirt and blows her nose and runs to her room. Long after the town has gone to sleep and the house is silent except for the chimings of clocks and the sputter of fading fires, she is weeping into a pillow already as wet as a widow's handkerchief.

"Don't cry," I say, sitting at the bottom of her bed and shivering despite my flannel nightgown that smells of last winter's cough syrup, "don't cry," I beg, teasing her toes, tickling her feet, "you're too old for that."

"It's because," she hiccups, "I *am* too old. Old and funny."

"Not funny. Fun. More fun than anybody. Listen. If you don't stop crying you'll be so tired tomorrow we can't go cut a tree."

She straightens up. Queenie jumps on the bed (where Queenie is not allowed) to lick her cheeks. "I know where we'll find real pretty trees, Buddy. And holly, too. With berries big as your eyes. It's way off in the woods. Farther than we've ever been. Papa used to bring us Christmas trees from there: carry them on his shoulder. That's fifty years ago. Well, now: I can't wait for morning."

Morning. Frozen rime lusters the grass; the sun, round as an orange and orange as hot-weather moons, balances on the horizon, burnishes the silvered winter woods. A wild turkey calls. A renegade hog grunts in the undergrowth. Soon, by the edge of knee-deep, rapid-running water we have to abandon the buggy. Queenie wades the stream first, paddles across barking complaints at the swiftness of the current, the pneumonia-making coldness of it. We follow, holding our shoes and equipment (a hatchet, a burlap sack) above our heads. A mile more: of chastising thorns, burs and briers that catch at our clothes; of rusty pine needles brilliant with gaudy fungus and molted feathers. Here, there, a flash, a flutter, an ecstasy of shrillings remind us that not all the birds have flown south. Always, the path unwinds through lemony sun pools and pitch-black vine tunnels. Another creek to cross: a disturbed armada of speck-led trout froths the water round us, and frogs the size of plates practice belly flops; beaver workmen are building a dam. On the farther shore, Queenie shakes herself and trembles. My friend shivers, too: not with cold but enthusiasm. One of her hat's ragged roses sheds a petal as she lifts her head and inhales the pine-heavy air. "We're almost there; can you smell it, Buddy?" she says, as though we were approaching an ocean.

And, indeed, it is a kind of ocean. Scented acres of holiday trees, prickly-leafed holly. Red berries shiny as Chinese bells: black crows swoop upon them screaming. Having stuffed our burlap sacks with enough greenery and crimson to garland a dozen windows, we set about choosing a tree. "It should be," muses my friend, "twice as tall as a boy. So a boy can't steal the star." The one we pick is twice as tall as me. A brave handsome brute that survives thirty hatchet stokes before it keels with a creaking rending cry. Lugging it like a kill, we commence the long trek out. Every few yards we abandon the struggle, sit down and pant. But we have the strength of triumphant huntsmen; that and the tree's virile, icy perfume revive us, goad us on. Many compliments accompany our sunset return along the red clay road to town; but my friend is sly and noncommittal when passersby praise the treasure perched in our buggy: what a fine tree and where did it come from? "Yonderways," she murmurs vaguely. Once a car stops and the rich mill owner's lazy wife leans out and whines: "Giveya two-bits cash for that ol tree." Ordinarily my friend is afraid of saying no; but on this occasion she promptly shakes her head: "We wouldn't take a dollar." The mill owner's wife persists. "A dollar, my foot! Fifty cents. That's my last offer. Goodness, woman, you can get another one." In answer, my friend gently reflects: "I doubt it. There's never two of anything."

32   Home: Queenie slumps by the fire and sleeps till tomorrow, snoring loud as a human.

33   A trunk in the attic contains: a shoebox of ermine tails (off the opera cape of a curious lady who once rented a room in the house), coils of frazzled tinsel gone gold with age, one silver star, a brief rope of dilapidated, undoubtedly dangerous candy-like light bulbs. Excellent decorations, as far as they go, which isn't far enough: my friend wants our tree to blaze "like a Baptist window," droop with weighty snows of ornament. But we can't afford the made-in-Japan splendors at the five-and-dime. So we do what we've always done: sit for days at the kitchen table with scissors and crayons and stacks of colored paper. I make sketches and my friend cuts them out: lots of cats, fish too (because they're easy to draw), some apples, some watermelons, a few winged angels devised from saved-up sheets of Hershey-bar tin foil. We use safety pins to attach these creations to the tree; as a final touch, we sprinkle the branches with shredded cotton (picked in August for this purpose). My friend, surveying the effect, clasps her hands together. "Now honest, Buddy. Doesn't it look good enough to eat?" Queenie tries to eat an angel.

34   After weaving and ribboning holly wreaths for all the front windows, our next project is the fashioning of family gifts. Tie-dye scarves for the ladies, for the men a home-brewed lemon and licorice and aspirin syrup to be taken "at the first Symptoms of a Cold and after Hunting." But when it comes time for making each other's gift, my friend and I separate to work secretly. I would like to buy her a pearl-handled knife, a radio, a whole pound of chocolate-covered cherries (we tasted some once, and she always swears: "I could live on them, Buddy, Lord yes I could— and that's not taking His name in vain"). Instead, I am building her a kite. She would like to give me a bicycle (she's said so on several million occasions: "If only I could, Buddy. It's bad enough in life to do without something *you* want; but confound it, what gets my goat is not being able to give somebody something you want *them* to have. Only one of these days I

will, Buddy. Locate you a bike. Don't ask how. Steal it, maybe"). Instead, I'm fairly certain that she is building me a kite—the same as last year, and the year before: the year before that we exchanged slingshots. All of which is fine by me. For we are champion kite-fliers who study the wind like sailors; my friend, more accomplished than I, can get a kite aloft when there isn't enough breeze to carry clouds.

Christmas Eve afternoon we scrape together a nickel and go to the butcher's to buy Queenie's traditional gift, a good gnawable beef bone. The bone, wrapped in funny paper, is placed high in the tree near the silver star. Queenie knows it's there. She squats at the foot of the tree staring up in a trance of greed: when bedtime arrives she refuses to budge. Her excitement is equaled by my own. I kick the covers and turn my pillow as though it were a scorching summer's night. Somewhere a rooster crows: falsely, for the sun is still on the other side of the world. 35

"Buddy, are you awake?" It is my friend, calling from her room, which is next to mine; and an instant later she is sitting on my bed holding a candle. "Well, I can't sleep a hoot," she declares. "My mind's jumping like a jack rabbit. Buddy, do you think Mrs. Roosevelt will serve our cake at dinner?" We huddle in the bed, and she squeezes my hand I-love-you. "Seems like your hand used to be so much smaller. I guess I hate to see you grow up. When you're grown up, will we still be friends?" I say always. "But I feel so bad, Buddy. I wanted so bad to give you a bike. I tried to sell my cameo Papa gave me. Buddy"—she hesitates, as though embarrassed—"I made you another kite." Then I confess that I made her one, too; and we laugh. The candle burns too short to hold. Out it goes, exposing the starlight, the stars spinning at the window like a visible caroling that slowly, slowly daybreak silences. Possibly we doze; but the beginnings of dawn splash us like cold water: we're up, wide-eyed and wandering while we wait for others to waken. Quite deliberately my friend drops a kettle on the kitchen floor. I tap-dance in front of closed doors. One by one the household emerges, looking as though they'd like to kill us both; but it's Christmas so they can't. First, a gorgeous breakfast: just everything you can imagine—from flapjacks and fried squirrel to hominy grits and honey-in-the-comb. Which puts everyone in a good humor except my friend and me. Frankly, we're so impatient to get at the presents we can't eat a mouthful. 36

Well, I'm disappointed. Who wouldn't be? With socks, a Sunday school shirt, some handkerchiefs, a hand-me-down sweater and a year's subscription to a religious magazine for children. *The Little Shepherd*. It makes me boil. It really does. 37

My friend has a better haul. A sack of Satsumas, that's her best present. She is proudest, however, of a white wool shawl knitted by her married sister. But she *says* her favorite gift is the kite I built her. And it *is* very beautiful; though not as beautiful as the one she made me, which is blue and scattered with gold and green Good Conduct stars; moreover, my name is painted on it, "Buddy." 38

39   "Buddy, the wind is blowing."

40   The wind is blowing, and nothing will do till we've run to a pasture below the house where Queenie has scooted to bury her bone (and where, a winter hence, Queenie will be buried, too). There, plunging through the healthy waist-high grass, we unreel our kites, feel them twitching at the string like sky fish as they swim into the wind. Satisfied, sun-warmed, we sprawl in the grass and peel Satsumas and watch our kites cavort. Soon I forget the socks and hand-me-down sweater. I'm as happy as if we'd already won the fifty-thousand-dollar Grand Prize in the coffee-naming contest.

41   "My, how foolish I am!" my friend cries, suddenly alert, like a woman remembering too late she has biscuits in the oven. "You know what I've always thought?" she asks in a tone of discovery, and not smiling at me but a point beyond. "I've always thought a body would have to be sick and dying before they saw the Lord. And I imagined that when He came it would be like looking at the Baptist window: pretty as colored glass with the sun pouring through, such a shine you don't know it's getting dark. And it's been a comfort: to think of that shine taking away all the spooky feeling. But I'll wager it never happens. I'll wager at the very end a body realizes the Lord has already shown Himself. That things as they are"—her hand circles in a gesture that gathers clouds and kites and grass and Queenie pawing earth over her bone—"just what they've always seen, was seeing Him. As for me, I could leave the world with today in my eyes."

42   This is our last Christmas together.

43   Life separates us. Those who Know Best decide that I belong in a military school. And so follows a miserable succession of bugle-blowing prisons, grim reveille-ridden summer camps. I have a new home too. But it doesn't count. Home is where my friend is, and there I never go.

44   And there she remains, puttering around the kitchen. Alone with Queenie. Then alone. ("Buddy dear," she writes in her wild hard-to-read script, "yesterday Jim Macy's horse kicked Queenie bad. Be thankful she didn't feel much. I wrapped her in a Fine Linen sheet and rode her in the buggy down to Simpson's pasture where she can be with all her Bones . . ."). For a few Novembers she continues to bake her fruitcakes single-handed; not as many, but some: and, of course, she always sends me "the best of the batch." Also, in every letter she encloses a dime wadded in toilet paper: "See a picture show and write me the story." But gradually in her letters she tends to confuse me with her other friend, the Buddy who died in the 1880's; more and more thirteenths are not the only days she stays in bed: a morning arrives in November, a leafless birdless coming of winter morning, when she cannot rouse herself to exclaim: "Oh my, it's fruitcake weather!"

45   And when that happens, I know it. A message saying so merely confirms a piece of news some secret vein had already received, severing from me an irreplaceable part of myself, letting loose like a kite on a

broken string. That is why, walking across a school campus on this particular December morning, I keep searching the sky. As if I expected to see, rather like hearts, a lost pair of kites hurrying toward heaven.

❏ Questions for Discussion

1. The boy says of his friend, "She is still a child." Is this statement a compliment or an insult? What are her childlike qualities? In what ways are the boy and the woman alike?

2. What does "she" mean by " 'As for me, I could leave the world with today in my eyes' "?

3. How would you describe the rest of the family's relationship to Buddy and his friend? Discuss the pattern of nurturing in which someone who is not a member of the immediate family nurtures the child.

4. In this story the **point of view** is that of an adult remembering his childhood. Why is this point of view essential to the creation of the story? Why is it written in present tense?

5. Why do the two friends go to the great trouble and expense of making and mailing fruitcakes every Christmas?

6. Explain the **symbolism** of the kites.

❏ Suggestions for Exploration and Writing

1. At the end of Capote's story, Buddy is sent off to military school. How does the child rearing in a military school compare to the day-care in "Chairman Mao's Good Little Boy"?

2. Write an essay describing your most memorable holiday.

3. In an age of dysfunctional families, discuss how this short story exemplifies a truly functional family.

4. One of the strengths of the story is the vivid sensory detail given in the descriptions. Discuss Capote's use of such details, concentrating on at least three senses.

POETRY

WILLIAM BUTLER YEATS (1865–1939)

An Irish poet and playwright, William Butler Yeats is regarded by many as one of the greatest twentieth-century poets. Yeats' first poems were published in 1885. Active in the Irish National Theatre,

he became a leader in the Irish literary revival. His Collected Poems
*(1933), spanning fifty years, shows his extraordinary range and his
growth as a poet. Much of Yeats' poetry is powerfully and elaborately symbolic, referring to his vision of a spiritual world and his
cyclical theory of history.*

A Prayer for my Daughter

Once more the storm is howling, and half hid
Under this cradle-hood and coverlid
My child sleeps on. There is no obstacle
But Gregory's wood and one bare hill
5   Whereby the haystack- and roof-levelling wind,
Bred on the Atlantic, can be stayed;
And for an hour I have walked and prayed
Because of the great gloom that is in my mind.

I have walked and prayed for this young child an hour
10   And heard the sea-wind scream upon the tower,
And under the arches of the bridge, and scream
In the elms above the flooded stream;
Imagining in excited reverie
That the future years had come,
15   Dancing to a frenzied drum,
Out of the murderous innocence of the sea.

May she be granted beauty and yet not
Beauty to make a stranger's eye distraught,
Or hers before a looking-glass, for such,
20   Being made beautiful overmuch,
Consider beauty a sufficient end,
Lose natural kindness and maybe
The heart-revealing intimacy
That chooses right, and never find a friend.

25   Helen being chosen found life flat and dull
And later had much trouble from a fool,
While that great Queen, that rose out of the spray,
Being fatherless could have her way
Yet chose a bandy-leggèd smith for man.
30   It's certain that fine women eat
A crazy salad with their meat
Whereby the Horn of Plenty is undone.

In courtesy I'd have her chiefly learned;
Hearts are not had as a gift but hearts are earned
35   By those that are not entirely beautiful;
Yet many, that have played the fool
For beauty's very self, has charm made wise,

And many a poor man that has roved,
Loved and thought himself beloved,
From a glad kindness cannot take his eyes.   40

May she become a flourishing hidden tree
That all her thoughts may like the linnet be,
And have no business but dispensing round
Their magnanimities of sound,
Nor but in merriment begin a chase,   45
Nor but in merriment a quarrel.
O may she live like some green laurel
Rooted in one dear perpetual place.

My mind, because the minds that I have loved,
The sort of beauty that I have approved,   50
Prosper but little, has dried up of late,
Yet knows that to be choked with hate
May well be of all evil chances chief.
If there's no hatred in a mind
Assault and battery of the wind   55
Can never tear the linnet from the leaf.

An intellectual hatred is the worst,
So let her think opinions are accursed.
Have I not seen the loveliest woman born
Out of the mouth of Plenty's horn,   60
Because of her opinionated mind
Barter that horn and every good
By quiet natures understood
For an old bellows full of angry wind?

Considering that, all hatred driven hence,   65
The soul recovers radical innocence
And learns at last that it is self-delighting,
Self-appeasing, self-affrighting,
And that its own sweet will is Heaven's will;
She can, though every face should scowl   70
And every windy quarter howl
Or every bellows burst, be happy still.

And may her bridegroom bring her to a house
Where all's accustomed, ceremonious;
For arrogance and hatred are the wares   75
Peddled in the thoroughfares.
How but in custom and in ceremony
Are innocence and beauty born?
Ceremony's a name for the rich horn,
And custom for the spreading laurel tree.   80

❏ **Questions for Discussion**

1. The speaker of the poem has been praying silently for an entire hour. What is he so concerned about that he prays at such length? Why does he pray that his daughter not be "beautiful overmuch"?

2. Why does Yeats declare "opinions accursed"?

3. Throughout the poem Yeats uses the **images** of the Horn of Plenty and "a flourishing hidden" laurel tree, and he returns to these in the last two lines of the poem. What do these images suggest that the narrator wants for his daughter as a result of his own experiences?

4. In light of the women's movement, do you think any of Yeats' comments are sexist? If so, which ones and why?

❏ **Suggestions for Exploration and Writing**

1. Yeats does not pray for control of his daughter; rather he prays that she may grow into a resilient, joyous woman who can protect herself psychologically from the perils of a hostile world. To what degree have your parents tried to control you and to what degree have they encouraged you to grow?

2. Yeats clearly regards custom and ceremony as important elements in a family's life. Discuss the importance of custom and ceremony in your own family or in two or more works in this section.

3. Choosing one of Yeats' abstract words such as *innocence, kindness,* or *beauty,* write an essay explaining why you think this quality is important.

THEODORE ROETHKE (1908–1963)

Theodore Roethke was both an acclaimed poet and an exuberant and popular professor of poetry. Partly because he threw himself wholeheartedly into both professions, he often suffered from exhaustion and mental breakdowns. Roethke's relationship with his own father, a German-American who combined authoritarianism with sensitivity, seems to have been ambivalent. His father died when Roethke was fourteen. Roethke received many awards during his long literary career, including two Guggenheim Fellowships, two Ford Foundation Grants, and a Pulitzer Prize in poetry in 1954 for The Waking: Poems 1933–53.

My Papa's Waltz

The whiskey on your breath
Could make a small boy dizzy;
But I hung on like death:
Such waltzing was not easy.

We romped until the pans   5
Slid from the kitchen shelf;
My mother's countenance
Could not unfrown itself.

The hand that held my wrist
Was battered on one knuckle;   10
At every step you missed
My right ear scraped a buckle.

You beat time on my head
With a palm caked hard by dirt,
Then waltzed me off to bed   15
Still clinging to your shirt.

❏ Questions for Discussion

1. In spite of the drunken waltz, what evidence in the poem indicates that there is a deep love within the family?

2. To what does the word *waltz* in the title refer? As he is "waltzed" to bed, the boy is "still clinging" to his father. What does this reaction indicate about the boy's feelings for his father? What attracts the boy to his father?

3. What details does Roethke use to describe the father, and what do they indicate?

4. Roethke uses the three-beat line which reflects the three beats of the waltz, yet the poem's effect is far from the smooth gliding motion of the dance. Would a smooth **rhythm** be appropriate for the subject? Why or why not?

❏ Suggestions for Exploration or Writing

1. Using your imagination and the details given in the poem, describe this family.

2. Write an essay analyzing why memories which may be negative to some adults are not so to children. Also see Nikki Giovanni's poem "Nikki-Rosa" and Frank O'Connor's "My Oedipus Complex."

MARY TALLMOUNTAIN (1918–　)

Mary TallMountain is from Alaska. Part Athabaskan, she has written several books of poems, including Nine Poems *(1979) and* There Is No Word for Goodbye *(1981). She celebrates in this poem a unique feature of her native American language and culture.*

There Is No Word for Goodbye

Sokoya, I said, looking through
　　the net of wrinkles into
　　wise black pools
　　of her eyes.

5　What do you say in Athabaskan
　　when you leave each other?
　　What is the word
　　for goodbye?

A shade of feeling rippled
10　　the wind-tanned skin.
　　Ah, nothing, she said,
　　watching the river flash.

She looked at me close.
　　We just say, Tlaa. That means,
15　See you.
　　We never leave each other.
　　When does your mouth
　　say goodbye to your heart?

She touched me light
20　　as a bluebell.
　　You forget when you leave us;
　　you're so small then.
　　We don't use that word.

We always think you're coming back,
25　　but if you don't,
　　we'll see you someplace else.
　　You understand.
　　There is no word for goodbye.

❏ **Questions for Discussion**

1. The speaker's *sokoya*, or aunt, is described with natural **images,** particularly water. What do these images suggest about her character? What do they say about the sources of her wisdom?

2. Why is there no Athabaskan word for goodbye? What does the absence of such a word suggest about Athabaskans?

3. Explain the meaning of the question "When does your mouth say goodbye to your heart?" What does this question reveal about the relationship between the speaker and her aunt?

4. The speaker says, "we'll see you someplace else." Where might they see each other? Does the poem's imagery give any clue?

Maxine Kumin (1925–   )

Maxine Kumin is a poet, essayist, and writer of fiction and children's books. A poet of middle-class exurbia, Kumin often expresses in her poetry a fascination with nature—with its rhythms and its survival in the face of brutal human manipulation.

Nurture

From a documentary on marsupials I learn
that a pillowcase makes a fine
substitute pouch for an orphaned kangaroo.

I am drawn to such dramas of animal rescue.
They are warm in the throat. I suffer, the critic proclaims,   5
from an overabundance of maternal genes.

Bring me your fallen fledgling, your bummer lamb,
lead the abused, the starvelings, into my barn.
Advise the hunted deer to leap into my corn.

And had there been a wild child—   10
filthy and fierce as a ferret, he is called
in one nineteenth-century account—

a wild child to love, it is safe to assume,
given my fireside inked with paw prints,
there would have been room.   15

Think of the language we two, same, and not-same,
might have constructed from sign,
scratch, grimace, grunt, vowel:

Laughter our first noun, and our long verb, howl.

❏ Questions for Discussion

1. How does the opening reference to "a documentary on marsupials" relate to the speaker's "maternal genes"?

2. In what ways do the speaker and the "wild child" she imagines taking in constitute a family?

3. What does the "fireside inked with paw prints" reveal about the speaker?

4. Why might the speaker and the "wild child" she imagines construct a language from gestures and inarticulate sounds? How does the speaker feel about creating such a language? What does she mean by "Laughter our first noun, and our long verb, howl"?

❏ **Suggestions for Exploration and Writing**

1. Write an essay discussing how your pet or pets are a part of your family. How do they communicate with you and the rest of the family? How do you communicate with them?

2. Develop a lexicon of noises, idioms, and signs that the narrator and her wild child might use to communicate.

SYLVIA PLATH (1932–1963)

Sylvia Plath is often admired for her powerful, intensely personal poetry. Her father, Otto Plath, died when she was only eight years old. In 1956, she married Ted Hughes, Poet Laureate of England. After writing about her emotional turmoil and her suicidal tendencies in The Bell Jar, *Plath killed herself shortly after its publication in 1963. In her posthumously published* Ariel, *she reveals an inner turmoil and fascination with death that to some readers are almost unbearable.*

Daddy

You do not do, you do not do
Any more, black shoe
In which I have lived like a foot
For thirty years, poor and white,
5   Barely daring to breathe or Achoo.

Daddy, I have had to kill you.
You died before I had time—
Marble-heavy, a bag full of God,
Ghastly statue with one grey toe
10   Big as a Frisco seal

And a head in the freakish Atlantic
Where it pours bean green over blue
In the waters off beautiful Nauset.
I used to pray to recover you.
15   Ach, du.

In the German tongue, in the Polish town
Scraped flat by the roller
Of wars, wars, wars.
But the name of the town is common.
My Polack friend   20

Says there are a dozen or two.
So I never could tell where you
Put your foot, your root,
I never could talk to you.
The tongue stuck in my jaw.   25

It stuck in a barb wire snare.
Ich, ich, ich, ich,
I could hardly speak.
I thought every German was you.
And the language obscene   30

An engine, an engine
Chuffing me off like a Jew.
A Jew to Dachau, Auschwitz, Belsen.
I began to talk like a Jew.
I think I may well be a Jew.   35

The snows of the Tyrol, the clear beer of Vienna
Are not very pure or true.
With my gypsy ancestress and my weird luck
And my Taroc pack and my Taroc pack
I may be a bit of a Jew.   40

I have always been scared of *you*,
With your Luftwaffe, your gobbledygoo.
And your neat moustache
And your Aryan eye, bright blue.
Panzer-man, panzer-man, O You——   45

Not God but a swastika
So black no sky could squeak through.
Every woman adores a Fascist,
The boot in the face, the brute
Brute heart of a brute like you.   50

You stand at the blackboard, daddy,
In the picture I have of you,
A cleft in your chin instead of your foot
But no less a devil for that, no not
Any less the black man who   55

Bit my pretty red heart in two.
I was ten when they buried you.
At twenty I tried to die

And get back, back, back to you.
60 I thought even the bones would do.

But they pulled me out of the sack.
And they stuck me together with glue.
And then I knew what to do.
I made a model of you,
65 A man in black with a Meinkampf look

And a love of the rack and the screw.
And I said I do, I do.
So daddy, I'm finally through.
The black telephone's off at the root,
70 The voices just can't worm through.

If I've killed one man, I've killed two—
The vampire who said he was you
And drank my blood for a year,
Seven years, if you want to know.
75 Daddy, you can lie back now.

There's a stake in your fat black heart
And the villagers never liked you.
They are dancing and stamping on you.
They always *knew* it was you.
80 Daddy, daddy, you bastard, I'm through.

❑ Questions for Discussion

1. The speaker remembers her father as a "black shoe," "a bag full of God," a huge and ghastly statue, a devil, a Nazi, and a vampire. Collectively, what do these **images** suggest to you about the father?

2. List and examine the various references to death and to killing in the poem. If the father is dead, how can he be such a threat to his daughter that she fears his "chuffing [her] off like a Jew . . . to Dachau, Auschwitz, Belsen"? In what sense must the speaker kill her father? Why?

3. If the speaker still feels love for her father, why does she repeatedly refer to destroying him and her memory of him?

4. Many readers find this poem powerful and disturbing, even frightening. What elements contribute to its fearsome power?

5. Why do you think the speaker and her father have never been able to communicate? Is the speaker necessarily Plath? Explain.

Suggestion for Exploration and Writing

1. Write a character sketch of Daddy as he is depicted by Plath, using quotations from the poem to support your characterizations.

ALICIA OSTRIKER (1937–   )

Alicia Ostriker is a contemporary American poet who is especially noted for her ability to portray the wide range of emotions shared by women of all ages. A professor of English, mother of two daughters, and wife of an astrophysicist, she lives in New Jersey.

First Love

When the child begins to suffer, the mother
Finds in her mouth those burning coals
You can neither spit out nor swallow—

It tells you about this in Zen, you know
You're illuminated when   5
The coals dissolve and your mouth is cool—

The child's lost boyfriend permeates the home
Like hyacinth perfume,
Nothing can escape it, it is too much,

It is maddening, like the insane yellow   10
Of the first blooming forsythia, like a missing
Limb that goes on hurting the survivor.

Whatever doesn't suffer isn't alive,
You know your daughter's pain is perfectly normal.
Nevertheless you imagine   15

Rinsing all grief from the child's tender face
The way a sculptor might peel the damp dropcloths
Off the clay figure she's been working on

So she can add fresh clay, play
With some details, pat it, bring it closer   20
To completion, and so people can see

How good and beautiful it already is.

Questions for Discussion

1. Why does the speaker use the Zen image of burning coals in her mouth?

2. Why is a fragrance appropriate to describe the way "the child's lost boyfriend permeates the house"?

3. Explain the double meaning of the poem's title.

4. In describing her empathy for her daughter, the mother uses a series of **similes** and **metaphors**. Identify each of these devices. Why do you think the mother uses metaphors rather than direct statements? What is particularly appropriate about the simile of the sculpture to describe the child?

❏ **Suggestion for Exploration and Writing**

1. Using two of the following works, explain how the mother or father conveys a daughter's specialness: Yeats, "A Prayer for My Daughter"; McCullers, "A Domestic Dilemma"; Ostriker, "First Love."

RAYMOND CARVER (1939–1988)

A highly regarded contemporary writer of short stories and poems, Raymond Carver won many awards, including the National Book Award, the National Book Critics Circle Award, and the Pulitzer Prize. Carver writes in a plain, very spare style about blue-collar Americans. He is admired for his unadorned style and moving portraits of plain, inarticulate, suffering people.

Photograph of My Father in His Twenty-second Year

October. Here in this dank, unfamiliar kitchen
I study my father's embarrassed young man's face.
Sheepish grin, he holds in one hand a string
of spiny yellow perch, in the other
5   a bottle of Carlsbad beer.

In jeans and denim shirt, he leans
against the front fender of a 1934 Ford.
He would like to pose bluff and hearty for his posterity,
wear his old hat cocked over his ear.
10   All his life my father wanted to be bold.

But the eyes give him away, and the hands
that limply offer the string of dead perch
and the bottle of beer. Father, I love you,
yet how can I say thank you, I who can't hold my liquor either,
15   and don't even know the places to fish?

❏ **Questions for Discussion**

1. What is significant about the time of year and the setting of the poem?

2. The father has obviously posed for the picture. What impression has he tried to give by his manner of posing? What does the speaker mean by "the eyes give him away, and the hands"? What do they give away?

3. Although both Carver and Plath write from the **point of view** of an adult remembering the past, the **tone** of Carver's poem contrasts sharply with that of Plath's "Daddy." What is the **tone** of Carver's poem?

4. What does Carver say about the power of memory? the power of heredity?

❏ **Suggestion for Exploration and Writing**

1. Write a **comparison-contrast essay** using at least two of the poems about fathers. As you write, consider such elements as **point of view, tone,** and use of specific detail.

Nikki Giovanni (1943–)

Yolande Cornelia Giovanni, Jr., was born in Knoxville, Tennessee. She received her B.A. from Fisk University in 1967. Giovanni has published many poems and articles, notably Black Feeling Black Talk *(1968),* Spin a Soft Black Song: Poems for Children *(1971), and* My House: Poems *(1972), a collection of poems about being Black in America.* James Baldwin and Nikki Giovanni: A Dialogue *was published in 1975, and* Cotton Candy on a Rainy Day *in 1980. Known as a militant African-American poet, Giovanni also writes very personal poetry.*

Nikki-Rosa

childhood remembrances are always a drag
if you're Black
you always remember things like living in Woodlawn
with no inside toilet
and if you become famous or something   5
they never talk about how happy you were to have your
    mother
all to yourself and

how good the water felt when you got your bath from one of
   those
big tubs that folk in chicago barbecue in
and somehow when you talk about home
it never gets across how much you
understood their feelings
as the whole family attended meetings about Hollydale
and even though you remember
your biographers never understand
your father's pain as he sells his stock
and another dream goes
and though you're poor it isn't poverty that
concerns you
and though they fought a lot
it isn't your father's drinking that makes any difference
but only that everybody is together and you
and your sister have happy birthdays and very good
   christmasses
and I really hope no white person ever has cause to write
   about me
because they never understand Black love is Black wealth and
   they'll
probably talk about my hard childhood and never understand
   that
all the while I was quite happy

❏ Questions for Discussion

1. What stereotype does Giovanni attack in this poem? Why does Giovanni not want a white biographer?

2. What attitude does this poem take toward poverty? What matters most to Giovanni about her childhood?

3. What does Giovanni mean by "Black love is Black wealth"? What are the qualities of "Black love" that Giovanni speaks of?

4. Why, in the opening line, does Giovanni say that "childhood remembrances"—not childhood—"are always a drag"?

❏ Suggestions for Exploration and Writing

1. Discuss ways in which outsiders may misunderstand events, relationships, or traditions that occur within your family.

2. Discuss some differences between private, ordinary families and public, famous families.

GARRETT HONGO (1951–)
Born in Hawaii of Japanese descent, Garrett Hongo grew up in California. His two books of poems, Yellow Light *(1982) and* The River of Heaven *(1988), often reveal Asian Americans in search of their ancestral roots in a modern society which emphasizes other cultures.*

The Hongo Store
29 Miles Volcano
Hilo, Hawaii   *1982*

From a photograph

My parents felt those rumblings
Coming deep from the earth's belly,
Thudding like the bell of the Buddhist Church.
Tremors in the ground swayed the bathinette
Where I lay squalling in soapy water.   5

My mother carried me around the house,
Back through the orchids, ferns, and plumeria
Of that greenhouse world behind the store,
And jumped between gas pumps into the car.

My father gave it the gun   10
And said, "Be quiet," as he searched
The frequencies, flipping for the right station
(The radio squealing more loudly than I could cry).

And then even the echoes stopped—
The only sound the Edsel's grinding   15
And the bark and crackle of radio news
Saying stay home or go to church.

"Dees time she no blow!"
My father said, driving back
Over the red ash covering the road.   20
"I worried she went go for broke already!"

So in this print the size of a matchbook,
The dark skinny man, shirtless and grinning,
A toothpick in the corner of his smile,
Lifts a naked baby above his head—   25
Behind him the plate glass of the store only cracked.

❏ Questions for Discussion

1. This brief narrative, according to the author, is reconstructed from a photograph. What details in the photograph give clues about the situation?

2. How do the family members appear to feel about the situation at the beginning? How do their feelings change?

3. Like "Photograph of My Father in His Twenty-second Year," this poem is written from the **point of view** of a son looking at a picture of his father. In Hongo's poem, however, the narrator also appears in the picture. What is the significance of the father's holding of "the naked baby above his head" in front of the cracked plate glass of the store?

4. What details in the poem reveal the Hawaiian culture? the economic level of the family? the father's pride?

DRAMA

AUGUST WILSON (1945–   )

August Wilson grew up in a Pittsburgh, Pennsylvania, ghetto probably much like the neighborhood in which Fences *is set. Wilson's mother so strongly encouraged his learning that he was reading by age four. Nevertheless, he dropped out before finishing high school. While working at various blue-collar jobs, Wilson developed an interest in poetry and drama and in 1968 founded the Black Horizons Theater Company. Besides his Pulitzer prize-winning* Fences, *which was first produced by the Yale Repertory Theater in 1985, his plays include* Ma Rainey's Black Bottom *(1984) and* Joe Turner's Come and Gone *(1986).*

Fences

List of Characters

TROY MAXSON
JIM BONO,   *Troy's friend*
ROSE,   *Troy's wife*
LYONS,   *Troy's oldest son by previous marriage*
GABRIEL,   *Troy's brother*
CORY,   *Troy and Rose's son*
RAYNELL,   *Troy's daughter*

Setting

The setting is the yard which fronts the only entrance to the Maxson house-hold, an ancient two-story brick house set back off a small alley in a big-city neighborhood. The entrance to the house is gained by two or three steps leading to a wooden porch badly in need of paint.

A relatively recent addition to the house and running its full width, the porch lacks congruence. It is a sturdy porch with a flat roof. One or two chairs of dubious value sit at one end where the kitchen window opens onto the porch. An old-fashioned icebox stands silent guard at the opposite end.

The yard is a small dirt yard, partially fenced, except for the last scene, with a wooden sawhorse, a pile of lumber, and other fence-building equipment set off to the side. Opposite is a tree from which hangs a ball made of rags. A baseball bat leans against the tree. Two oil drums serve as garbage receptacles and sit near the house at right to complete the setting.

The Play

Near the turn of the century, the destitute of Europe sprang on the city with tenacious claws and an honest and solid dream. The city devoured them. They swelled its belly until it burst into a thousand furnaces and sewing machines, a thousand butcher shops and bakers' ovens, a thousand churches and hospitals and funeral parlors and moneylenders. The city grew. It nourished itself and offered each man a partnership limited only by his talent, his guile, and his willingness and capacity for hard work. For the immigrants of Europe, a dream dared and won true.

The descendants of African slaves were offered no such welcome or participa-tion. They came from places called the Carolinas and the Virginias, Georgia, Alabama, Mississippi, and Tennessee. They came strong, eager, searching. The city rejected them and they fled and settled along the riverbanks and under bridges in shallow, ramshackle houses made of sticks and tar-paper. They col-lected rags and wood. They sold the use of their muscles and their bodies. They cleaned houses and washed clothes, they shined shoes, and in quiet desperation and vengeful pride, they stole, and lived in pursuit of their own dream. That they could breathe free, finally, and stand to meet life with the force of dignity and whatever eloquence the heart could call upon.

By 1957, the hard-won victories of the European immigrants had solidified the industrial might of America. War had been confronted and won with new energies that used loyalty and patriotism as its fuel. Life was rich, full, and flourishing. The Milwaukee Braves won the World Series, and the hot winds of change that would make the sixties a turbulent, racing, dangerous, and provoc-ative decade had not yet begun to blow full.

ACT 1

SCENE I

It is 1957, Troy and Bono enter the yard, engaged in conversation. Troy is fifty-three years old, a large man with thick, heavy hands; it is this largeness that he strives to fill out and make an accommodation with. Together with his blackness, his largeness informs his sensibilities and the choices he has made in his life.

Of the two men, Bono is obviously the follower. His commitment to their friendship of thirty-odd years is rooted in his admiration of Troy's honesty, capacity for hard work, and his strength, which Bono seeks to emulate.

It is Friday night, payday, and the one night of the week the two men engage in a ritual of talk and drink. Troy is usually the most talkative and at times he can be crude and almost vulgar, though he is capable of rising to profound heights of expression. The men carry lunch buckets and wear or carry burlap aprons and are dressed in clothes suitable to their jobs as garbage collectors.

BONO. Troy, you ought to stop that lying!

TROY. I ain't lying! The nigger had a watermelon this big. (*He indicates with his hands.*) Talking about . . . "What watermelon, Mr. Rand?" I liked to fell out! "What watermelon, Mr. Rand?" . . . And it sitting there big as life.

BONO. What did Mr. Rand say?

TROY. Ain't said nothing. Figure if the nigger too dumb to know he carrying a watermelon, he wasn't gonna get much sense out of him. Trying to hide that great big old watermelon under his coat. Afraid
10   to let the white man see him carry it home.

BONO. I'm like you . . . I ain't got no time for them kind of people.

TROY. Now what he look like getting mad cause he see the man from the union talking to Mr. Rand?

BONO. He come to me talking about . . . "Maxson gonna get us fired." I told him to get away from me with that. He walked away from me calling you a trouble maker. What Mr. Rand say?

TROY. Ain't said nothing. He told me to go down the Commissioner's office next Friday. They called me down there to see them.

BONO. Well, as long as you got your complaint filed, they can't fire
20   you. That's what one of them white fellows tell me.

TROY. I ain't worried about them firing me. They gonna fire me cause I asked a question? That's all I did. I went to Mr. Rand and asked him, "Why? Why you got the white mens driving and the colored lifting?" Told him, "what's the matter, don't I count? You think only white fellows got sense enough to drive a truck. That ain't no paper job! Hell, anybody can drive a truck. How come you got all white driving and the colored lifting?" He told me "take it to the union." Well, hell that's what I done! Now they wanna come up with this pack of lies.

30   BONO. I told Brownie if the man come and ask him any questions . . . just tell the truth! It ain't nothing but something they done trumped up on you cause you filed a complaint on them.

TROY. Brownie don't understand nothing. All I want them to do is change the job description. Give everybody a chance to drive the truck. Brownie can't see that. He ain't got that much sense.

BONO. How you figure he be making out with that gal be up at Taylors' all the time . . . that Alberta gal?

TROY. Same as you and me. Getting just as much as we is. Which is to say nothing.

BONO. It is, huh? I figure you doing a little better than me . . . and I ain't saying what I'm doing. 40

TROY. Aw, nigger, look here . . . I know you. If you had got anywhere near that gal, twenty minutes later you be looking to tell somebody. And the first one you gonna tell . . . that you gonna want to brag to . . . is gonna be me.

BONO. I ain't saying that. I see where you be eyeing her.

TROY. I eye all the women. I don't miss nothing. Don't never let nobody tell you Troy Maxson don't eye the women.

BONO. You been doing more than eyeing her. You done bought her a drink or two. 50

TROY. Hell yeah, I bought her a drink! What that mean? I bought you one, too. What that mean cause I buy her a drink? I'm just being polite.

BONO. It's all right to buy her one drink. That's what you call being polite. But when you wanna be buying two or three . . . that's what you call eyeing her.

TROY. Look here, as long as you known me . . . you ever known me to chase after women?

BONO. Hell yeah! Long as I done known you. You forgetting I knew you when. 60

TROY. Naw, I'm talking about since I been married to Rose?

BONO. Oh, not since you been married to Rose. Now, that's the truth, there. I can say that.

TROY. All right then! Case closed.

BONO. I see you be walking up around Alberta's house. You supposed to be at Taylors' and you be walking up around there.

TROY. What you watching where I'm walking for? I ain't watching after you.

BONO. I seen you walking around there more than once.

TROY. Hell, you liable to see me walking anywhere! That don't mean 70 nothing cause you see me walking around there.

BONO. Where she come from anyway? She just kinda showed up one day.

TROY. Tallahassee. You can look at her and tell she one of them Florida gals. They got some big healthy women down there. Grow them right up out the ground. Got a little bit of Indian in her. Most of them niggers down in Florida got some Indian in them.

BONO. I don't know about that Indian part. But she damn sure big and healthy. Woman wear some big stockings. Got them great big old legs and hips as wide as the Mississippi River. 80

TROY. Legs don't mean nothing. You don't do nothing but push them out of the way. But them hips cushion the ride!

BONO. Troy, you ain't got no sense.

TROY. It's the truth! Like you riding on Goodyears!

(*Rose enters from the house. She is ten years younger than Troy, her devotion to him stems from her recognition of the possibilities of her life without him: a succession of abusive men and their babies, a life of partying and running the streets, the Church, or aloneness with its attendant pain and frustration. She recognizes Troy's spirit as a fine and illuminating one and she either ignores or forgives his faults, only some of which she recognizes. Though she doesn't drink, her presence is an integral part of the Friday night rituals. She alternates between the porch and the kitchen, where supper preparations are under way.*)

ROSE. What you all out here getting into?

TROY. What you worried about what we getting into for? This is men talk, woman.

ROSE. What I care what you all talking about? Bono, you gonna stay for supper?

90 BONO. No, I thank you, Rose. But Lucille say she cooking up a pot of pigfeet.

TROY. Pigfeet! Hell, I'm going home with you! Might even stay the night if you got some pigfeet. You got something in there to top them pigfeet, Rose?

ROSE. I'm cooking up some chicken. I got some chicken and collard greens.

TROY. Well, go on back in the house and let me and Bono finish what we was talking about. This is men talk. I got some talk for you later. You know what kind of talk I mean. You go on and powder it up.

100 ROSE. Troy Maxson, don't you start that now!

TROY (*puts his arm around her*). Aw, woman . . . come here. Look here, Bono . . . when I met this woman . . . I got out that place, say, "Hitch up my pony, saddle up my mare . . . there's a woman out there for me somewhere. I looked here. Looked there. Saw Rose and latched on to her." I latched on to her and told her—I'm gonna tell you the truth—I told her, "Baby, I don't wanna marry, I just wanna be your man." Rose told me . . . tell him what you told me, Rose.

ROSE. I told him if he wasn't the marrying kind, then move out the way so the marrying kind could find me.

110 TROY. That's what she told me. "Nigger, you in my way. You blocking the view! Move out the way so I can find me a husband." I thought it over two or three days. Come back—

ROSE. Ain't no two or three days nothing. You was back the same night.

TROY. Come back, told her . . . "Okay, baby . . . but I'm gonna buy me a banty rooster and put him out there in the backyard . . . and when he sees a stranger come, he'll flap his wings and crow . . ."

Look here, Bono, I could watch the front door by myself . . . it was
that back door I was worried about.

ROSE. Troy, you ought not talk like that. Troy ain't doing nothing but   120
telling a lie.

TROY. Only thing is . . . when we first got married . . . forget the
rooster . . . we ain't had no yard!

BONO. I hear you tell it. Me and Lucille was staying down there on
Logan Street. Had two rooms with the outhouse in the back. I ain't
mind the outhouse none. But when the goddamn wind blow
through there in the winter . . . that's what I'm talking about! To
this day I wonder why in the hell I ever stayed down there for six
long years. But see, I didn't know I could do no better. I thought
only white folks had inside toilets and things.   130

ROSE. There's a lot of people don't know they can do no better than
they doing now. That's just something you got to learn. A lot of
folks still shop at Bella's.

TROY. Ain't nothing wrong with shopping at Bella's. She got fresh food.

ROSE. I ain't said nothing about if she got fresh food. I'm talking
about what she charge. She charge ten cents more than the A&P.

TROY. The A&P ain't never done nothing for me. I spends my money
where I'm treated right. I go down to Bella, say, "I need a loaf of
bread, I'll pay you Friday." She give it to me. What sense that make
when I got money to go and spend it somewhere else and ignore the   140
person who done right by me? That ain't in the Bible.

ROSE. We ain't talking about what's in the Bible. What sense it make
to shop there when she overcharge?

TROY. You shop where you want to. I'll do my shopping where the
people been good to me.

ROSE. Well, I don't think it's right for her to overcharge. That's all I
was saying.

BONO. Look here . . . I got to get on. Lucille going be raising all kind
of hell.

TROY. Where you going, nigger? We ain't finished this pint. Come   150
here, finish this pint.

BONO. Well, hell, I am . . . if you ever turn the bottle loose.

TROY (*hands him the bottle*). The only thing I say about the A&P is
I'm glad Cory got that job down there. Help him take care of his
school clothes and things. Gabe done moved out and things getting
tight around here. He got that job. . . . He can start to look out for
himself.

ROSE. Cory done went and got recruited by a college football team.

TROY. I told that boy about that football stuff. The white man ain't
gonna let him get nowhere with that football. I told him when he   160
first come to me with it. Now you come telling me he done went
and got more tied up in it. He ought to go and get recruited in how
to fix cars or something where he can make a living.

ROSE. He ain't talking about making no living playing football. It's just something the boys in school do. They gonna send a recruiter by to talk to you. He'll tell you he ain't talking about making no living playing football. It's a honor to be recruited.

TROY. It ain't gonna get him nowhere. Bono'll tell you that.

BONO. If he be like you in the sports . . . he's gonna be all right. Ain't but two men ever played baseball as good as you. That's Babe Ruth and Josh Gibson. Them's the only two men ever hit more home runs than you.

TROY. What it ever get me? Ain't got a pot to piss in or a window to throw it out of.

ROSE. Times have changed since you was playing baseball, Troy. That was before the war. Times have changed a lot since then.

TROY. How in hell they done changed?

ROSE. They got lots of colored boys playing ball now. Baseball and football.

BONO. You right about that, Rose. Times have changed, Troy. You just come along too early.

TROY. There ought not never have been no time called too early! Now you take that fellow . . . what's that fellow they had playing right field for the Yankees back then? You know who I'm talking about Bono. Used to play right field for the Yankees.

ROSE. Selkirk?

TROY. Selkirk! That's it! Man batting .269, understand? .269. What kind of sense that make? I was hitting .432 with thirty-seven home runs! Man batting .269 and playing right field for the Yankees! I saw Josh Gibson's daughter yesterday. She walking around with raggedy shoes on her feet. Now I bet you Selkirk's daughter ain't walking around with raggedy shoes on her feet! I bet you that!

ROSE. They got a lot of colored baseball players now. Jackie Robinson was the first. Folks had to wait for Jackie Robinson.

TROY. I done seen a hundred niggers play baseball better than Jackie Robinson. Hell, I know some teams Jackie Robinson couldn't even make! What you talking about Jackie Robinson. Jackie Robinson wasn't nobody. I'm talking about if you could play ball then they ought to have let you play. Don't care what color you were. Come telling me I come along too early. If you could play . . . then they ought to have let you play.

(Troy takes a long drink from the bottle.)

ROSE. You gonna drink yourself to death. You don't need to be drinking like that.

TROY. Death ain't nothing. I done seen him. Done wrassled with him. You can't tell me nothing about death. Death ain't nothing but a fastball on the outside corner. And you know what I'll do to that!

Lookee here, Bono . . . am I lying? You get one of them fastballs, about waist high, over the outside corner of the plate where you can get the meat of the bat on it . . and good god! You can kiss it good- 210
bye. Now, am I lying?

BONO. Naw, you telling the truth there. I seen you do it.

TROY. If I'm lying . . . that 450 feet worth of lying! (*Pause.*) That's all death is to me. A fastball on the outside corner.

ROSE. I don't know why you want to get on talking about death.

TROY. Ain't nothing wrong with talking about death. That's part of life. Everybody gonna die. You gonna die, I'm gonna die. Bono's gonna die. Hell, we all gonna die.

ROSE. But you ain't got to talk about it. I don't like to talk about it.

TROY. You the one brought it up. Me and Bono was talking about 220
baseball . . . you tell me I'm gonna drink myself to death. Ain't that right, Bono? You know I don't drink this but one night out of the week. That's Friday night. I'm gonna drink just enough to where I can handle it. Then I cuts it loose. I leave it alone. So don't you worry about me drinking myself to death. 'Cause I ain't worried about Death. I done seen him. I done wrestled with him.

Look here, Bono . . . I looked up one day and Death was march-ing straight at me. Like Soldiers on Parade! The Army of Death was marching straight at me. The middle of July, 1941. It got real cold 230
just like it be winter. It seem like Death himself reached out and touched me on the shoulder. He touch me just like I touch you. I got cold as ice and Death standing there grinning at me.

ROSE. Troy, why don't you hush that talk.

TROY. I say . . . What you want, Mr. Death? You be wanting me? You done brought your army to be getting me? I looked him dead in the eye. I wasn't fearing nothing. I was ready to tangle. Just like I'm ready to tangle now. The Bible say be ever vigilant. That's why I don't get but so drunk. I got to keep watch.

ROSE. Troy was right down there in Mercy Hospital. You remember he had pneumonia? Laying there with a fever talking plumb out of 240
his head.

TROY. Death standing there staring at me . . . carrying that sickle in his hand. Finally he say, "You want bound over for another year?" See, just like that . . . "You want bound over for another year?" I told him, "Bound over hell! Let's settle this now!"

It seem like he kinda fell back when I said that, and all the cold went out of me. I reached down and grabbed that sickle and threw it just as far as I could throw it . . . and me and him commenced to wrestling.

We wrestled for three days and three nights. I can't say where I 250
found the strength from. Every time it seemed like he was gonna get the best of me, I'd reach way down deep inside myself and find the strength to do him one better.

ROSE. Every time Troy tell the story he find different ways to tell it. Different things to make up about it.

TROY. I ain't making up nothing. I'm telling you the facts of what happened. I wrestled with Death for three days and three nights and I'm standing here to tell you about it. (*Pause.*) All right. At the end of the third night we done weakened each other to where we can't hardly move. Death stood up, throwed on his robe . . . had him a white robe with a hood on it. He threwed on that robe and went off to look for his sickle. Say, "I'll be back." Just like that. "I'll be back." I told him, say, "Yeah, but . . . you gonna have to find me!" I wasn't no fool. I wasn't going looking for him. Death ain't nothing to play with. And I know he's gonna get me. I know I got to join his army . . . his camp followers. But as long as I keep my strength and see him coming . . . as long as I keep up my vigilance . . . he's gonna have to fight to get me. I ain't going easy.

BONO. Well, look here, since you got to keep up your vigilance . . . let me have the bottle.

TROY. Aw hell, I shouldn't have told you that part. I should have left out that part.

ROSE. Troy be talking that stuff and half the time don't even know what he be talking about.

TROY. Bono know me better than that.

BONO. That's right, I know you. I know you got some Uncle Remus in your blood. You got more stories than the devil got sinners.

TROY. Aw hell, I done seen him too! Done talked with the devil.

ROSE. Troy, don't nobody wanna be hearing all that stuff.

(*Lyons enters the yard from the street. Thirty-four years old, Troy's son by a previous marriage, he sports a neatly trimmed goatee, sport coat, white shirt, tieless and buttoned at the collar. Though he fancies himself a musician, he is more caught up in the rituals and "idea" of being a musician than in the actual practice of the music. He has come to borrow money from Troy, and while he knows he will be successful, he is uncertain as to what extent his lifestyle will be held up to scrutiny and ridicule.*)

LYONS. Hey, Pop.

TROY. What you come "Hey, Popping" me for?

LYONS. How you doing, Rose? (*He kisses her.*) Mr. Bono. How you doing?

BONO. Hey, Lyons . . . how you been?

TROY. He must have been doing all right. I ain't seen him around here last week.

ROSE. Troy, leave your boy alone. He come by to see you and you wanna start all that nonsense.

TROY. I ain't bothering Lyons. (*Offers him the bottle.*) Here . . . get

you a drink. We got an understanding. I know why he come by to 290
see me and he know I know.

LYONS. Come on, Pop . . . I just stopped by to say hi . . . see how you
was doing.

TROY. You ain't stopped by yesterday.

ROSE. You gonna stay for supper, Lyons? I got some chicken cooking
in the oven.

LYONS. No, Rose . . . thanks. I was just in the neighborhood and
thought I'd stop by for a minute.

TROY. You was in the neighborhood alright, nigger. You telling the
truth there. You was in the neighborhood cause it's my payday. 300

LYONS. Well, hell, since you mentioned it . . . let me have ten dollars.

TROY. I'll be damned! I'll die and go to hell and play blackjack with
the devil before I give you ten dollars.

BONO. That's what I wanna know about . . . that devil you done seen.

LYONS. What . . . Pop done seen the devil? You too much, Pops.

TROY. Yeah, I done seen him. Talked to him too!

ROSE. You ain't seen no devil. I done told you that man ain't had
nothing to do with the devil. Anything you can't understand, you
want to call it the devil.

TROY. Look here, Bono . . . I went down to see Hertzberger about 310
some furniture. Got three rooms for two-ninety-eight. That what it
say on the radio. "Three rooms . . . two-ninety-eight." Even made
up a little song about it. Go down there . . . man tell me I can't get
no credit. I'm working every day and can't get no credit. What to
do? I got an empty house with some raggedy furniture in it. Cory
ain't got no bed. He's sleeping on a pile of rags on the floor. Working every day and can't get no credit. Come back here—Rose'll tell
you—madder than hell. Sit down . . . try to figure what I'm gonna
do. Come a knock on the door. Ain't been living here but three
days. Who know I'm here? Open the door . . . devil standing there 320
bigger than life. White fellow . . . got on good clothes and everything. Standing there with a clipboard in his hand. I ain't had to say
nothing. First words come out of his mouth was . . . "I understand
you need some furniture and can't get no credit." I liked to fell
over. He say, "I'll give you all the credit you want, but you got to
pay the interest on it." I told him, "Give me three rooms worth and
charge whatever you want." Next day a truck pulled up here and
two men unloaded them three rooms. Man what drove the truck
give me a book. Say send ten dollars, first of every month to the
address in the book and everything will be alright. Say if I miss a 330
payment the devil was coming back and it'll be hell to pay. That
was fifteen years ago. To this day . . . the first of the month I send
my ten dollars, Rose'll tell you.

ROSE. Troy lying.

TROY. I ain't never seen that man since. Now you tell me who else that could have been but the devil? I ain't sold my soul or nothing like that, you understand. Naw, I wouldn't have truck with the devil about nothing like that. I got my furniture and pays my ten dollars the first of the month just like clockwork.

340 BONO. How long you say you been paying this ten dollars a month?

TROY. Fifteen years!

BONO. Hell, ain't you finished paying for it yet? How much the man done charged you.

TROY. Aw hell, I done paid for it. I done paid for it ten times over! The fact is I'm scared to stop paying it.

ROSE. Troy lying. He got that furniture from Mr. Glickman. He ain't paying no ten dollars a month to nobody.

TROY. Aw hell, woman. Bono know I ain't that big a fool.

LYONS. I was just getting ready to say . . . I know where there's a
350 bridge for sale.

TROY. Look here, I'll tell you this . . . it don't matter to me if he was the devil. It don't matter if the devil give credit. Somebody had got to give it.

ROSE. It ought to matter. You going around talking about having truck with the devil . . . God's the one you gonna have to answer to. He's the one gonna be at the Judgment.

LYONS. Yeah, well, look here, Pop . . . let me have that ten dollars. I'll give it back to you. Bonnie got a job working at the hospital.

TROY. What I tell you, Bono? The only time I see this nigger is when
360 he wants something. That's the only time I see him.

LYONS. Come on, Pop, Mr. Bono don't want to hear all that. Let me have the ten dollars. I told you Bonnie working.

TROY. What that mean to me? "Bonnie working." I don't care if she working. Go ask her for the ten dollars if she working. Talking about "Bonnie working." Why ain't you working?

LYONS. Aw, Pop, you know I can't find no decent job. Where am I gonna get a job at? You know I can't get no job.

TROY. I told you I know some people down there. I can get you on the rubbish if you want to work. I told you that the last time you came
370 by here asking me for something.

LYONS. Naw, Pop . . . thanks. That ain't for me. I don't wanna be carrying nobody's rubbish. I don't wanna be punching nobody's time clock.

TROY. What's the matter, you too good to carry people's rubbish? Where you think that ten dollars you talking about come from? I'm just supposed to haul people's rubbish and give my money to you cause you too lazy to work. You too lazy to work and wanna know why you ain't got what I got.

ROSE. What hospital Bonnie working at? Mercy?

380 LYONS. She's down at Passavant working in the laundry.

TROY. I ain't got nothing as it is. I give you that ten dollars and I got to eat beans the rest of the week. Naw . . . you ain't getting no ten dollars here.

LYONS. You ain't got to be eating no beans. I don't know why you wanna say that.

TROY. I ain't got no extra money. Gabe done moved over to Miss Pearl's paying her the rent and things done got tight around here. I can't afford to be giving you every payday.

LYONS. I ain't asked you to give me nothing. I asked you to loan me ten dollars. I know you got ten dollars.

TROY. Yeah. I got it. You know why I got it? Cause I don't throw my money away out there in the streets. You living the fast life . . . wanna be a musician . . . running around in them clubs and things . . . then, you learn to take care of yourself. You ain't gonna find me going and asking nobody for nothing. I done spent too many years without.

LYONS. You and me is two different people, Pop.

TROY. I done learned my mistake and learned to do what's right by it. You still trying to get something for nothing. Life don't owe you nothing. You owe it to yourself. Ask Bono. He'll tell you I'm right.

LYONS. You got your way of dealing with the world . . . I got mine. The only thing that matters to me is the music.

TROY. Yeah, I can see that! It don't matter how you gonna eat . . . where your next dollar is coming from. You telling the truth there.

LYONS. I know I got to eat. But I got to live too. I need something that gonna help me to get out of the bed in the morning. Make me feel like I belong in the world. I don't bother nobody. Just stay with my music cause that's the only way I can find to live in the world. Otherwise there ain't no telling what I might do. Now I don't come criticizing you and how you live. I just come by to ask you for ten dollars. I don't wanna hear all that about how I live.

TROY. Boy, your mama did a hell of a job raising you.

LYONS. You can't change me, Pop. I'm thirty-four years old. If you wanted to change me, you should have been there when I was growing up. I come by to see you . . . ask for ten dollars and you want to talk about how I was raised. You don't know nothing about how I was raised.

ROSE. Let the boy have ten dollars, Troy.

TROY (*To Lyons*). What the hell you looking at me for? I ain't got no ten dollars. You know what I do with my money. (*To Rose*) Give him ten dollars if you want him to have it.

ROSE. I will. Just as soon as you turn it loose.

TROY (*handing Rose the money*). There it is. Seventy-six dollars and forty-two cents. You see this, Bono? Now, I ain't gonna get but six of that back.

ROSE. You ought to stop telling that lie. Here, Lyons. (*She hands him the money.*)

LYONS. Thanks, Rose. Look . . . I got to run . . I'll see you later.

TROY. Wait a minute. You gonna say, "thanks, Rose" and ain't gonna look to see where she got that ten dollars from? See how they do me, Bono?

430 LYONS. I know she got it from you, Pop. Thanks. I'll give it back to you.

TROY. There he go telling another lie. Time I see that ten dollars . . . he'll be owing me thirty more.

LYONS. See you, Mr. Bono.

BONO. Take care, Lyons!

LYONS. Thanks, Pop. I'll see you again.

(Lyons exits the yard.)

TROY. I don't know why he don't go and get him a decent job and take care of that woman he got.

BONO. He'll be alright, Troy. The boy is still young.

440 TROY. The *boy* is thirty-four years old.

BONO. Let's not get off into all that.

BONO. Look here . . . I got to be going. I got to be getting on. Lucille gonna be waiting.

TROY *(puts his arm round Rose)*. See this woman, Bono? I love this woman. I love this woman so much it hurts. I love her so much . . . I done run out of ways of loving her. So I got to go back to basics. Don't you come by my house Monday morning talking about time to go to work . . . 'cause I'm still gonna be stroking!

ROSE. Troy! Stop it now!

450 BONO. I ain't paying him no mind. Rose. That ain't nothing but gin-talk. Go on, Troy. I'll see you Monday.

TROY. Don't you come by my house, nigger! I done told you what I'm gonna be doing.

(The lights go down to black.)

SCENE 2

The lights come up on Rose hanging up clothes. She hums and sings softly to herself. It is the following morning.

ROSE *(Sings)*.
Jesus, be a fence all around me every day
Jesus, I want you to protect me as I travel on my way
Jesus, be a fence all around me every day.

(Troy enters from the house.)

ROSE *(continues)*.
Jesus, I want you to protect me
As I travel on my way.

(To Troy) 'Morning. You ready for breakfast? I can fix it soon as I
460 finish hanging up these clothes?

TROY. I got the coffee on. That'll be all right. I'll just drink some of that this morning.

ROSE. That 651 hit yesterday. That's the second time this month. Miss Pearl hit for a dollar . . . seem like those that need the least always get lucky. Poor folks can't get nothing.

TROY. Them numbers don't know nobody. I don't know why you fool with them. You and Lyons both.

ROSE. It's something to do.

TROY. You ain't doing nothing but throwing your money away.

ROSE. Troy, you know I don't play foolishly. I just play a nickel here and a nickel there. 470

TROY. That's two nickels you done thrown away.

ROSE. Now I hit sometimes . . . that makes up for it. It always comes in handy when I do hit. I don't hear you complaining then.

TROY. I ain't complaining now. I just say it's foolish. Trying to guess out of six hundred ways which way the number gonna come. If I had all the money niggers, these Negroes, throw away on numbers for one week—just one week—I'd be a rich man.

ROSE. Well, you wishing and calling it foolish ain't gonna stop folks from playing numbers. That's one thing for sure. Besides . . . some good things come from playing numbers. Look where Pope done bought him that restaurant off of numbers. 480

TROY. I can't stand niggers like that. Man ain't had two dimes to rub together. He walking around with his shoes all run over bumming money for cigarettes. All right. Got lucky there and hit the numbers . . .

ROSE. Troy, I know all about it.

TROY. Had good sense, I'll say that for him. He ain't throwed his money away. I seen niggers hit the numbers and go through two thousand dollars in four days. Man bought him that restaurant down there . . . fixed it up real nice . . . and then didn't want nobody to come in it! A Negro go in there and can't get no kind of service. I seen a white fellow come in there and order a bowl of stew. Pope picked all the meat out the pot for him. Man ain't had nothing but a bowl of meat! Negro come behind him and ain't got nothing but the potatoes and carrots. Talking about what numbers do for people, you picked a wrong example. Ain't done nothing but make a worser fool out of him than he was before. 490

ROSE. Troy, you ought to stop worrying about what happened at work yesterday. 500

TROY. I ain't worried. Just told me to be down there at the Commissioner's office on Friday. Everybody think they gonna fire me. I ain't worried about them firing me. You ain't got to worry about that. (*Pause.*) Where's Cory? Cory in the house? (*Calls*) Cory?

ROSE. He gone out.

TROY. Out, huh? He gone out 'cause he know I want him to help me with this fence. I know how he is. That boy scared of work.

(*Gabriel enters. He comes halfway down the alley and, hearing Troy's voice, stops.*)

TROY (*continues*). He ain't done a lick of work in his life.

510   ROSE. He had to go to football practice. Coach wanted them to get in a little extra practice before the season start.

TROY. I got his practice . . . running out of here before he get his chores done.

ROSE. Troy, what is wrong with you this morning? Don't nothing set right with you. Go on back in there and go to bed . . . get up on the other side.

TROY. Why something got to be wrong with me? I ain't said nothing wrong with me.

ROSE. You got something to say about everything. First it's the num-
520   bers . . . then it's the way the man runs his restaurant . . . then you done got on Cory. What's it gonna be next? Take a look up there and see if the weather suits you . . . or is it gonna be how you gonna put up the fence with the clothes hanging in the yard.

TROY. You hit the nail on the head then.

ROSE. I know you like I know the back of my hand. Go on in there and get you some coffee . . . see if that straighten you up. 'Cause you ain't right this morning.

(*Troy starts into the house and sees Gabriel. Gabriel starts singing. Troy's brother, he is seven years younger than Troy. Injured in World War II, he has a metal plate in his head. He carries an old trumpet tied around his waist and believes with every fiber of his being that he is the Archangel Gabriel. He carries a chipped basket with an assortment of discarded fruits and vegetables he has picked up in the strip district and which he attempts to sell.*)

GABRIEL (*singing*).
  Yes, ma'am, I got plums
  You ask me how I sell them
530   Oh ten cents apiece
  Three for a quarter
  Come and buy now
  'Cause I'm here today
  And tomorrow I'll be gone

(*Gabriel enters.*)

  Hey, Rose!

ROSE. How you doing, Gabe?

GABRIEL. There's Troy . . . Hey, Troy!

TROY. Hey, Gabe. (*Exits into kitchen.*)

ROSE (*to Gabriel*). What you got there?

GABRIEL. You know what I got, Rose. I got fruits and vegetables.   540
ROSE (*looking in basket*). Where's all these plums you talking about?
GABRIEL. I ain't got no plums today, Rose. I was just singing that.
Have some tomorrow. Put me in a big order for plums. Have
enough plums tomorrow for St. Peter and everybody.

(*Troy re-enters from kitchen, crosses to steps.*)

(*To Rose*) Troy's mad at me.
TROY. I ain't mad at you. What I got to be mad at you about? You
ain't done nothing to me.
GABRIEL. I just moved over to Miss Pearl's to keep out from in your
way. I ain't mean no harm by it.
TROY. Who said anything about that? I ain't said anything about that.   550
GABRIEL. You ain't mad at me, is you?
TROY. Naw . . . I ain't mad at you, Gabe. If I was mad at you I'd tell
you about it.
GABRIEL. Got me two rooms. In the basement. Got my own door, too.
Wanna see my key? (*He holds up a key.*) That's my own key! Ain't
nobody else got a key like that. That's my key! My two rooms!
TROY. Well, that's good, Gabe. You got your own key . . . that's good.
ROSE. You hungry, Gabe? I was just fixing to cook Troy his breakfast.
GABRIEL. I'll take some biscuits. You got some biscuits? Did you know
when I was in heaven . . . every morning me and St. Peter would sit   560
down by the gate and eat some big fat biscuits? Oh, yeah! We had
us a good time. We'd sit there and eat us them biscuits and then St.
Peter would go off to sleep and tell me to wake him up when it's
time to open the gates for the judgment.
ROSE. Well, come on . . . I'll make up a batch of biscuits.

(*Rose exits into the house.*)

GABRIEL. Troy . . . St. Peter got your name in the book. I seen it. It say
. . . Troy Maxson. I say . . . I know him! He got the same name like
what I got. That's my brother!
TROY. How many times you gonna tell me that, Gabe?
GABRIEL. Ain't got my name in the book. Don't have to have my   570
name. I done died and went to heaven. He got your name though.
One morning St. Peter was looking at his book . . . marking it up
for the judgment . . . and he let me see your name. Got it in there
under M. Got Rose's name . . . I ain't seen it like I seen yours . . .
but I know it's in there. He got a great big book. Got everybody's
name what was ever been born. That's what he told me. But I seen
your name. Seen it with my own eyes.
TROY. Go on in the house there. Rose going to fix you something to
eat.
GABRIEL. Oh, I ain't hungry. I done had breakfast with Aunt Jemimah.   580
She come by and cooked me up a whole mess of flapjacks. Remember how we used to eat them flapjacks?

TROY. Go on in the house and get you something to eat now.

GABRIEL. I got to sell my plums. I done sold some tomatoes. Got me two quarters. Wanna see? (*He shows Troy his quarters.*) I'm gonna save them and buy me a new horn so St. Peter can hear me when it's time to open the gates. (*Gabriel stops suddenly. Listens.*) Hear that? That's the hellhounds. I got to chase them out of here . . . Go on get out of here! Get out! (*Gabriel exits singing.*)

590   Better get ready for the judgment
Better get ready for the judgment
My Lord is coming down

(*Rose enters from the house.*)

TROY. He gone off somewhere.

GABRIEL (*offstage*).
Better get ready for the judgment
Better get ready for the judgment morning
Better get ready for the judgment
My God is coming down

ROSE. He ain't eating right. Miss Pearl say she can't get him to eat nothing.

600   TROY. What you want me to do about it, Rose? I done did everything I can for the man. I can't make him get well. Man got half his head blown away . . . what you expect?

ROSE. Seem like something ought to be done to help him.

TROY. Man don't bother nobody. He just mixed up from that metal plate he got in his head. Ain't no sense for him to go back into the hospital.

ROSE. Least he be eating right. They can help him take care of himself.

TROY. Don't nobody wanna be locked up, Rose. What you wanna lock him up for? Man go over there and fight the war . . . messin'

610   around with them Japs . . . get half his head blown off . . and they give him a lousy three thousand dollars. And I had to swoop down on that.

ROSE. Is you fixing to go into that again?

TROY. That's the only way I got a roof over my head . . . cause of that metal plate.

ROSE. Ain't no sense you blaming yourself for nothing. Gabe wasn't in no condition to manage that money. You done what was right by him. Can't nobody say you ain't done what was right by him. Look how long you took care of him . . . till he wanted to have his own

620   place and moved over there with Miss Pearl.

TROY. That ain't what I'm saying, woman! I'm just stating the facts. If my brother didn't have that metal plate in his head . . . I wouldn't have a pot to piss in or a window to throw it out of. And I'm fifty-three years old. Now see if you can understand that!

(*Troy gets up from the porch and starts to exit the yard.*)

ROSE. Where you going off to? You been running out of here every
Saturday for weeks. I thought you was gonna work on this fence?

TROY. I'm gonna walk down to Taylors'. Listen to the ball game. I'll
be back in a bit. I'll work on it when I get back.

(*He exits the yard. The lights go to black.*)

SCENE 3

*The lights come up on the yard. It is four hours later. Rose is taking
down the clothes from the line. Cory enters carrying his football
equipment.*

ROSE. Your daddy like to had a fit with you running out of here without doing your chores. 630

CORY. I told you I had to go to practice.

ROSE. He say you were supposed to help him with this fence.

CORY. He been saying that the last four or five Saturdays, and then he
don't never do nothing, but go down to Taylors'. Did you tell him
about the recruiter?

ROSE. Yeah, I told him.

CORY. What he say?

ROSE. He ain't said nothing too much. You get in there and get started
on your chores before he gets back. Go on and scrub down them
steps before he gets back here hollering and carrying on. 640

CORY. I'm hungry. What you got to eat, Mama?

ROSE. Go on and get started on your chores. I got some meat loaf in
there. Go on and make you a sandwich . . . and don't leave no mess
in there. (*Cory exists into the house. Rose continues to take down
the clothes. Troy enters the yard and sneaks up and grabs her from
behind.*) Troy! Go on, now. You liked to scared me to death. What
was the score of the game? Lucille had me on the phone and I
couldn't keep up with it.

TROY. What I care about the game? Come here, woman. (*He tries to
kiss her.*)

ROSE. I thought you went down Taylors' to listen to the game. Go on,
Troy! You supposed to be putting up this fence. 650

TROY (*attempting to kiss her again*). I'll put it up when I finish with
what is at hand.

ROSE. Go on, Troy. I ain't studying you.

TROY (*chasing after her*). I'm studying you . . . fixing to do my homework!

ROSE. Troy, you better leave me alone.

TROY. Where's Cory? That boy brought his butt home yet?

ROSE. He's in the house doing his chores.

TROY (*calling*). Cory! Get your butt out here, boy!

(*Rose exits into the house with the laundry. Troy goes over to the
pile of wood, picks up a board, and starts sawing. Cory enters from
the house.*)

660   TROY. You just now coming in here from leaving this morning?

CORY. Yeah, I had to go to football practice.

TROY. Yeah, what?

CORY. Yessir.

TROY. I ain't but two seconds off you noway. The garbage sitting in there overflowing . . . you ain't done none of your chores . . . and you come in here talking about "Yeah."

CORY. I was just getting ready to do my chores now, Pop . . .

TROY. Your first chore is to help me with this fence on Saturday. Everything else come after that. Now get that saw and cut them
670   boards.

(*Cory takes the saw and begins cutting the boards. Troy continues working. There is a long pause.*)

CORY. Hey, Pop . . . why don't you buy a TV?

TROY. What I want with a TV? What I want one of them for?

CORY. Everybody got one. Earl, Ba Bra . . . Jesse!

TROY. I ain't asked you who had one. I say what I want with one?

CORY. So you can watch it. They got lots of things on TV. Baseball games and everything. We could watch the World Series.

TROY. Yeah . . . and how much this TV cost?

CORY. I don't know. They got them on sale for around two hundred dollars.

680   TROY. Two hundred dollars, huh?

CORY. That ain't that much, Pop.

TROY. Naw, it's just two hundred dollars. See that roof you got over your head at night? Let me tell you something about that roof. It's been over ten years since that roof was last tarred. See now . . . the snow come this winter and sit up there on that roof like it is . . . and it's gonna seep inside. It's just gonna be a little bit . . . ain't gonna hardly notice it. Then the next thing you know, it's gonna be leaking all over the house. Then the wood rot from all that water and you gonna need a whole new roof. Now, how much you think
690   it cost to get that roof tarred?

CORY. I don't know.

TROY. Two hundred and sixty-four dollars . . . cash money. While you thinking about a TV, I got to be thinking about the roof . . . and whatever else go wrong around here. Now if you had two hundred dollars, what would you do . . . fix the roof or buy a TV?

CORY. I'd buy a TV. Then when the roof started to leak . . . when it needed fixing . . . I'd fix it.

TROY. Where you gonna get the money from? You done spent it for a TV. You gonna sit up and watch the water run all over your brand
700   new TV.

CORY. Aw, Pop. You got money. I know you do.

TROY. Where I got it at, huh?

CORY. You got it in the bank.

TROY. You wanna see my bankbook? You wanna see that seventy-three dollars and twenty-two cents I got sitting up in there?

CORY. You ain't got to pay for it all at one time. You can put a down payment on it and carry it on home with you.

TROY. Not me. I ain't gonna owe nobody nothing if I can help it. Miss a payment and they come and snatch it right out of your house. Then what you got? Now, soon as I get two hundred dollars clear, then I'll buy a TV. Right now, as soon as I get two hundred and sixty-four dollars, I'm gonna have this roof tarred. 710

CORY. Aw . . . Pop!

TROY. You go on and get your two hundred dollars and buy one if ya want it. I got better things to do with my money.

CORY. I can't get no two hundred dollars. I ain't never seen two hundred dollars.

TROY. I'll tell you what . . . you get a hundred dollars and I'll put the other hundred with it.

CORY. All right, I'm gonna show you. 720

TROY. You gonna show me how you can cut them boards right now.

(Cory begins to cut the boards. There is a long pause.)

CORY. The Pirates won today. That make five in a row.

TROY. I ain't thinking about the Pirates. Got an all-white team. Got that boy . . . that Puerto Rican boy . . . Clemente. Don't even half-play him. That boy could be something if they give him a chance. Play him one day and sit him on the bench the next.

CORY. He gets a lot of chances to play.

TROY. I'm talking about playing regular. Playing every day so you can get your timing. That's what I'm talking about.

CORY. They got some white guys on the team that don't play every day. You can't play everybody at the same time. 730

TROY. If they got a white fellow sitting on the bench . . . you can bet your last dollar he can't play! The colored guy got to be twice as good before he get on the team. That's why I don't want you to get all tied up in them sports. Man on the team and what it get him? They got colored on the team and don't use them. Same as not having them. All them teams the same.

CORY. The Braves got Hank Aaron and Wes Covington. Hank Aaron hit two home runs today. That makes forty-three.

TROY. Hank Aaron ain't nobody. That's what you supposed to do. That's how you supposed to play the game. Ain't nothing to it. It's just a matter of timing . . . getting the right follow-through. Hell, I can hit forty-three home runs right now! 740

CORY. Not off no major-league pitching, you couldn't.

TROY. We had better pitching in the Negro leagues. I hit seven home runs off of Satchel Paige. You can't get no better than that!

CORY. Sandy Koufax. He's leading the league in strike-outs.

TROY. I ain't thinking of no Sandy Koufax.

CORY. You got Warren Spahn and Lew Burdette. I bet you couldn't hit
750   no home runs off of Warren Spahn.

TROY. I'm through with it now. You go on and cut them boards.
(*Pause.*) Your mama tell me you done got recruited by a college
football team? Is that right?

CORY. Yeah. Coach Zellman say the recruiter gonna be coming by to
talk to you. Get you to sign the permission papers.

TROY. I thought you supposed to be working down there at the A&P.
Ain't you suppose to be working down there after school?

CORY. Mr. Stawicki say he gonna hold my job for me until after the
football season. Say starting next week I can work weekends.

760   TROY. I thought we had an understanding about this football stuff?
You suppose to keep up with your chores and hold that job down
at the A&P. Ain't been around here all day on a Saturday. Ain't
none of your chores done . . . and now you telling me you done quit
your job.

CORY. I'm gonna be working weekends.

TROY. You damn right you are! And ain't no need for nobody coming
around here to talk to me about signing nothing.

CORY. Hey, Pop . . . you can't do that. He's coming all the way from
North Carolina.

770   TROY. I don't care where he coming from. The white man ain't gonna
let you get nowhere with that football noway. You go on and get
your book-learning so you can work yourself up in that A&P or
learn how to fix cars or build houses or something, get you a trade.
That way you have something can't nobody take away from you.
You go on and learn how to put your hands to some good use. Besides hauling people's garbage.

CORY. I get good grades, Pop. That's why the recruiter wants to talk
with you. You got to keep up your grades to get recruited. This way
I'll be going to college. I'll get a chance . . .

780   TROY. First you gonna get your butt down there to the A&P and get
your job back.

CORY. Mr. Stawicki done already hired somebody else 'cause I told
him I was playing football.

TROY. You a bigger fool than I thought . . . to let somebody take away
your job so you can play some football. Where you gonna get your
money to take out your girlfriend and whatnot? What kind of foolishness is that to let somebody take away your job?

CORY. I'm still gonna be working weekends.

TROY. Naw . . . naw. You getting your butt out of here and finding
790   you another job.

CORY. Come on, Pop! I got to practice. I can't work after school and
play football, too. The team needs me. That's what Coach Zellman
say . . .

TROY. I don't care what nobody else say. I'm the boss . . . you understand? I'm the boss around here. I do the only saying what counts.

CORY. Come on, Pop!

TROY. I asked you . . . did you understand?

CORY. Yeah . . .

TROY. What?!

CORY. Yessir.   800

TROY. You go on down there to that A&P and see if you can get your job back. If you can't do both . . . then you quit the football team. You've got to take the crookeds with the straights.

CORY. Yessir. (*Pause.*) Can I ask you a question?

TROY. What the hell you wanna ask me? Mr. Stawicki the one you got the questions for.

CORY. How come you ain't never liked me?

TROY. Liked you? Who the hell say I got to like you? What law is there say I got to like you? Wanna stand up in my face and ask a damn fool-ass question like that. Talking about liking somebody.   810 Come here, boy, when I talk to you.

(*Cory comes over to where Troy is working. He stands slouched over and Troy shoves him on his shoulder.*)

Straighten up, goddammit! I asked you a question . . . what law is there say I got to like you?

CORY. None.

TROY. Well, all right then! Don't you eat every day? (*Pause*) Answer me when I talk to you! Don't you eat every day?

CORY. Yeah.

TROY. Nigger, as long as you in my house, you put that sir on the end of it when you talk to me!

CORY. Yes . . . sir.   820

TROY. You eat every day.

CORY. Yessir!

TROY. Got a roof over your head.

CORY. Yessir!

TROY. Got clothes on your back.

CORY. Yessir.

TROY. Why you think that is?

CORY. Cause of you.

TROY. Aw, hell I know it's 'cause of me . . . but why to you think that is?   830

CORY (*hesitant*). Cause you like me.

TROY. Like you? I go out of here every morning . . . bust my butt . . . putting up with them crackers every day . . . cause I like you? You about the biggest fool I ever saw. (*Pause.*) It's my job. It's my responsibility! You understand that? A man got to take care of his family. You live in my house . . . sleep you behind on my bedclothes . . . fill you belly up with my food . . . cause you my son. You my flesh and blood. Not 'cause I like you! Cause it's my duty to take care of you. I owe a responsibility to you!

840   Let's get this straight right here . . . before it go along any further . . . I ain't got to like you. Mr. Rand don't give me money come payday cause he likes me. He gives me cause he owe me. I done give you everything I had to give you. I gave you your life! Me and your mama worked that out between us. And liking your black ass wasn't part of the bargain. Don't you try and go through life worrying about if somebody like you or not. You best be making sure they doing right by you. You understand what I'm saying, boy?

CORY. Yessir.

TROY. Then get the hell out of my face, and get on down to that A&P.

(Rose has been standing behind the screen door for much of the scene. She enters as Cory exits.)

850 ROSE. Why don't you let the boy go ahead and play football, Troy? Ain't no harm in that. He's just trying to be like you with the sports.

TROY. I don't want him to be like me! I want him to move as far away from my life as he can get. You the only decent thing that ever happened to me. I wish him that. But I don't wish him a thing else from my life. I decided seventeen years ago that boy wasn't getting involved in no sports. Not after what they did to me in the sports.

ROSE. Troy, why don't you admit you was too old to play in the major leagues? For once . . . why don't you admit that?

TROY. What do you mean too old? Don't come telling me I was too

860 old. I just wasn't the right color. Hell, I'm fifty-three years old and can do better then Selkirk's .269 right now!

ROSE. How's was you gonna play ball when you were over forty? Sometimes I can't get no sense out of you.

TROY. I got good sense, woman. I got sense enough not to let my boy get hurt over playing no sports. You been mothering that boy too much. Worried about if people like him.

ROSE. Everything that boy do . . . he do for you. He wants you to say "Good job, son." That's all.

TROY. Rose, I ain't got time for that. He's alive. He's healthy. He's got

870 to make his own way. I made mine. Ain't nobody gonna hold his hand when he get out there in that world.

ROSE. Times have changed from when you was young, Troy. People change. The world's changing around you and you can't even see it.

TROY *(slow, methodical)*. Woman . . . I do the best I can do. I come in here every Friday. I carry a sack of potatoes and a bucket of lard. You all line up at the door with your hand out. I give you the lint from my pockets. I give you my sweat and my blood. I ain't got no tears. I done spent them. We go upstairs in that room at night . . . and I fall down on you and try to blast a hole into forever. I get up

Monday morning . . . find my lunch on the table. I go out. Make   880
my way. Find my strength to carry me through to the next Friday.
(*Pause.*) That's all I got, Rose. That's all I got to give. I can't give
nothing else.

(*Troy exits into the house. The lights go down to black.*)

SCENE 4

*It is Friday. Two weeks later. Cory starts out of the house with his
football equipment. The phone rings.*

CORY (*calling*). I got it!

(*He answers the phone and stands in the screen door talking.*)

Hello? Hey, Jesse. Naw . . . I was just getting ready to leave now.

ROSE (*calling*). Cory!

CORY. I told you, man, them spikes is all tore up. You can use them if
you want, but they ain't no good. Earl got some spikes.

ROSE (*calling*). Cory!

CORY (*calling to Rose*). Mam? I'm talking to Jesse. (*Into phone*) When   890
she say that? (*Pause.*) Aw, you lying, man. I'm gonna tell her you
said that.

ROSE (*calling*). Cory, don't you go nowhere!

CORY. I got to go to the game, Ma! (*Into the phone*) Yeah, hey, look,
I'll talk to you later. Yeah, I'll meet you over Earl's house. Later.
Bye, Ma.

(*Cory exits the house and starts out the yard.*)

ROSE. Cory, where you going off to? You got that stuff all pulled out
and thrown all over your room.

CORY (*in the yard*). I was looking for my spikes. Jesse wanted to borrow my spikes.   900

ROSE. Get up there and get that cleaned up before your daddy get
back in here.

CORY. I got to go to the game! I'll clean it up when I get back.

(*Cory exits.*)

ROSE. That's all he need to do is see that room all messed up.

(*Rose exits into the house. Troy and Bono enter the yard. Troy is
dressed in clothes other than his work clothes.*)

BONO. He told him the same thing he told you. Take it to the union.

TROY. Brownie ain't got that much sense. Man wasn't thinking about
nothing. He wait until I confront them on it . . . then he wanna
come crying seniority. (*Calls*) Hey Rose!

BONO. I wish I could have seen Mr. Rand's face when he told you.

TROY. He couldn't get it out of his mouth! Liked to bit his tongue!   910
When they called me down there to the Commissioner's office . . .
he thought they was gonna fire me. Like everybody else.

BONO. I didn't think they was gonna fire you. I thought they was gonna put you on the warning paper.

TROY. Hey, Rose! (*To Bono*). Yeah, Mr. Rand like to bit his tongue.

(*Troy breaks the seal on the bottle, takes a drink, and hands it to Bono.*)

BONO. I see you run right down to Taylors' and told that Alberta gal.

TROY (*calling*). Hey Rose! (*To Bono*) I told everybody. Hey, Rose! I went down there to cash my check.

ROSE (*entering from the house*). Hush all that hollering, man! I know
920   you out here. What they say down there at the Commissioner's office?

TROY. You supposed to come when I call you, woman. Bono'll tell you that. (*To Bono*). Don't Lucille come when you call her?

ROSE. Man, hush your mouth. I ain't no dog . . . talk about "come when you call me."

TROY (*puts his arm around Rose*). You hear this Bono? I had me an old dog used to get uppity like that. You say, "C'mere, Blue!" . . . and he just lay there and look at you. End up getting a stick and chasing him away trying to make him come.

ROSE. I ain't studying you and your dog. I remember you used to sing
930   that old song.

TROY (*he sings*).
Hear it ring! Hear it ring!
I had a dog and his name was Blue.

ROSE. Don't nobody wanna hear you sing that old song.

TROY (*sings*).
You know Blue was mighty true.

ROSE. Used to have Cory running around here singing that song.

BONO. Hell, I remember that song myself.

TROY (*sings*).
You know Blue was a good old dog
Blue treed a possum in a hollow log.
That was my daddy's song. My daddy made up that song.

940   ROSE. I don't care who made it up. Don't nobody wanna hear you sing it.

TROY (*makes a song like calling a dog*). Come here, woman.

ROSE. You come in here carrying on, I reckon they ain't fired you. What they say down there at the Commissioner's office?

TROY. Look here, Rose . . . Mr. Rand called me into his office today when I got back from talking to them people down there . . . it come from up top . . . he called me in and told me they was making me a driver.

ROSE. Troy, you kidding!

950   TROY. No I ain't. Ask Bono.

ROSE. Well, that's great, Troy. Now you don't have to hassle them people no more.

(Lyons enters from the street.)

TROY. Aw hell, I wasn't looking to see you today. I thought you was in jail. Got it all over the front page of the *Courier* about them raiding Sefus' place . . . where you be hanging out with all them thugs.

LYONS. Hey, Pop . . . that ain't got nothing to do with me. I don't go down there gambling. I go down there to sit in with the band. I ain't got nothing to do with the gambling part. They got some good music down there.

TROY. They got some rogues . . . is what they got.   960

LYONS. How you been, Mr. Bono? Hi, Rose.

BONO. I see where you playing down at the Crawford Grill tonight.

ROSE. How come you ain't brought Bonnie like I told you. You should have brought Bonnie with you, she ain't been over in a month of Sundays.

LYONS. I was just in the neighborhood . . . thought I'd stop by.

TROY. Here he come . . .

BONO. Your daddy got a promotion on the rubbish. He's gonna be the first colored driver. Ain't got to do nothing but sit up there and read the paper like them white fellows.   970

LYONS. Hey, Pop . . . if you knew how to read you'd be all right.

BONO. Naw . . . naw . . . you mean if the nigger knew how to drive he'd be all right. Been fighting with them people about driving and ain't even got a license. Mr. Rand know you ain't got no driver's license?

TROY. Driving ain't nothing. All you do is point the truck where you want it to go. Driving ain't nothing.

BONO. Do Mr. Rand know you ain't got no driver's license? That's what I'm talking about. I ain't asked if driving was easy. I asked if Mr. Rand know you ain't got no driver's license.

TROY. He ain't got to know. The man ain't got to know my business.   980
Time he find out, I have two or three driver's licenses.

LYONS *(going into his pocket)*. Say look here, Pop . . .

TROY. I knew it was coming. Didn't I tell you, Bono? I know what kind of "Look here, Pop" that was. The nigger fixing to ask me for some money. It's Friday night. It's my payday. All them rogues down there on the avenue . . . the ones that ain't in jail . . . and Lyons is hopping in his shoes to get down there with them.

LYONS. See, Pop . . . if you give somebody else a chance to talk sometime, you'd see that I was fixing to pay you back your ten dollars like I told you. Here . . . I told you I'd pay you when Bonnie got   990
paid.

TROY. Naw . . . you go ahead and keep that ten dollars. Put it in the bank. The next time you feel like you wanna come by here and ask me for something . . . you go on down there and get that.

LYONS. Here's your ten dollars, Pop. I told you I don't want you to give me nothing. I just wanted to borrow ten dollars.

TROY. Naw . . . you go on and keep that for the next time you want to ask me.

LYONS. Come on, Pop . . . here go your ten dollars.

1000   ROSE. Why don't you go on and let the boy pay you back, Troy?

LYONS. Here you go, Rose. If you don't take it I'm gonna have to hear about it for the next six months. (*He hands her the money.*)

ROSE. You can hand yours over here too, Troy.

TROY. You see this, Bono. You see how they do me.

BONO. Yeah, Lucille do me the same way.

(*Gabriel is heard singing offstage. He enters.*)

GABRIEL. Better get ready for the Judgment! Better get ready for . . . Hey! . . . Hey! . . . There's Troy's boy!

LYONS. How you doing, Uncle Gabe?

1010   GABRIEL. Lyons . . . The King of the Jungle! Rose . . . hey, Rose. Got a flower for you. (*He takes a rose from his pocket.*) Picked it myself. That's the same rose like you is!

ROSE. That's right nice of you, Gabe.

LYONS. What you been doing, Uncle Gabe?

GABRIEL. Oh, I been chasing hellhounds and waiting on the time to tell St. Peter to open the gates.

LYONS. You been chasing hellhounds, huh? Well . . . you doing the right thing, Uncle Gabe. Somebody got to chase them.

GABRIEL. Oh, yeah . . . I know it. The devil's strong. The devil ain't no pushover. Hellhounds snipping at everybody's heels. But I got my

1020   trumpet waiting on the judgment time.

LYONS. Waiting on the Battle of Armageddon, huh?

GABRIEL. Ain't gonna be too much of a battle when God get to waving that Judgment sword. But the people's gonna have a hell of a time trying to get into heaven if them gates ain't open.

LYONS (*putting his arm around Gabriel*). You hear this, Pop. Uncle Gabe, you all right!

GABRIEL (*laughing with Lyons*). Lyons! King of the Jungle.

ROSE. You gonna stay for supper, Gabe. Want me to fix you a plate?

GABRIEL. I'll take a sandwich, Rose. Don't want no plate. Just wanna

1030   eat with my hands. I'll take a sandwich.

ROSE. How about you, Lyons? You staying? Got some short ribs cooking.

LYONS. Naw, I won't eat nothing till after we finished playing. (*Pause.*) You ought to come down and listen to me play, Pop.

TROY. I don't like that Chinese music. All that noise.

ROSE. Go on in the house and wash up, Gabe . . . I'll fix you a sandwich.

GABRIEL (*to Lyons, as he exits*). Troy's mad at me.

LYONS. What you mad at Uncle Gabe for, Pop?

ROSE. He thinks Troy's mad at him cause he moved over to Miss 1040
Pearl's.

TROY. I ain't mad at the man. He can live where he want to live at.

LYONS. What he move over there for? Miss Pearl don't like nobody.

ROSE. She don't mind him none. She treats him real nice. She just
don't allow all that singing.

TROY. She don't mind that rent he be paying . . . that's what she don't
mind.

ROSE. Troy, I ain't going through that with you no more. He's over
there cause he want to have his own place. He can come and go as
he please. 1050

TROY. Hell, he could come and go as he please here. I wasn't stopping
him. I ain't put no rules on him.

ROSE. It ain't the same thing, Troy. And you know it. (*Gabriel comes
to the door*). Now that's the last I wanna hear about that. I don't
wanna hear nothing else about Gabe and Miss Pearl. And next
week . . .

GABRIEL. I'm ready for my sandwich, Rose.

ROSE. And next week when that recruiter come from that school . . . I
want you to sign that paper and go on and let Cory play football.
Then that'll be the last I have to hear about that. 1060

TROY (*to Rose as she exits into the house*). I ain't thinking about Cory
nothing.

LYONS. What . . . Cory got recruited? What school he going to?

TROY. That boy walking around here smelling his piss . . . thinking
he's grown. Thinking he's gonna do what he want, irrespective of
what I say. Look here, Bono . . . I left the Commissioner's office and
went down to the A&P . . . that boy ain't working down there. He
lying to me. Telling me he got his job back . . . telling me he working weekends . . . telling me he working after school . . . Mr. Stawicki tell me he ain't working down there at all! 1070

LYONS. Cory just growing up. He's just busting at the seams trying to
fill out your shoes.

TROY. I don't care what he's doing. When he get to the point where he
wanna disobey me . . . then it's time for him to move on. Bono'll
tell you that. I bet he ain't never disobeyed his daddy without paying the consequences.

BONO. I ain't never had a chance. My daddy came on through . . . but
I ain't never knew him to see him . . . or what he had on his mind
or where he went. Just moving on through. Searching out the New
Land. That's what the old folks used to call it. See a fellow moving 1080
around from place to place . . . woman to woman . . . called it
searching out the New Land. I can't say if he ever found it. I come
along, didn't want no kids. Didn't know if I was gonna be in one
place long enough to fix on them right as their daddy. I figured I

was going searching, too. As it turned out I been hooked up with Lucille near about as long as your daddy been with Rose. Going on sixteen years.

TROY. Sometimes I wish I hadn't known my daddy. He ain't cared nothing about no kids. A kid to him wasn't nothing. All he wanted was for you to learn how to walk so he could start you to working. When it come time for eating . . . he ate first. If there was anything left over, that's what you got. Man would sit down and eat two chickens and give you the wing.

LYONS. You ought to stop that, Pop. Everybody feed their kids. No matter how hard times is . . . everybody care about their kids. Make sure they have something to eat.

TROY. The only thing my daddy cared about was getting them bales of cotton in to Mr. Lubin. That's the only thing that mattered to him. Sometimes I used to wonder why he was living. Wonder why the devil hadn't come and got him "Get them bales of cotton in to Mr. Lubin" and find out he owe him money . . .

LYONS. He should have just went on and left when he saw he couldn't get nowhere. That's what I would have done.

TROY. How he gonna leave with eleven kids? And where he gonna go? He ain't knew how to do nothing but farm. No, he was trapped and I think he knew it. But I'll say this for him . . . he felt a responsibility toward us. Maybe he ain't treated us the way I felt he should have . . . but without that responsibility he could have walked off and left us . . . made his own way.

BONO. A lot of them did. Back in those days what you talking about . . . they walk out their front door and just take on down one road or another and keep on walking.

LYONS. There you go! That's what I'm talking about.

BONO. Just keep on walking till you come to something else. Ain't you never heard of nobody having the walking blues? Well, that's what you call it when you just take off like that.

TROY. My daddy ain't had them walking blues! What you talking about? He stayed right there with his family. But he was just as evil as he could be. My mama couldn't stand him. Couldn't stand that evilness. She run off when I was about eight. She sneaked off one night after he had gone to sleep. Told me she was coming back for me. I ain't never seen her no more. All his women run off and left him. He wasn't good for nobody.

When my turn come to head out, I was fourteen and got to sniffing around Joe Canewell's daughter. Had us an old mule we called Greyboy. My daddy sent me out to do some plowing and I tied Greyboy and went to fooling around with Joe Canewell's daughter. We done found us a nice little spot, got real cozy with each other. She about thirteen and we done figured we was grown anyway . . . so we down there enjoying ourselves . . . ain't thinking about nothing. We didn't know Greyboy had got loose and wandered back to the house and my daddy was looking for me. We down there by the creek enjoying ourselves when my daddy come up on us. Surprised us. He had them leather straps off the mule and commenced to whupping me like there was no tomorrow. I jumped up, mad and embarrassed. I was scared of my daddy. When he commenced to whupping on me . . . quite naturally I run to get out of the way. (*Pause.*)

Now I thought he was mad cause I ain't done my work. But I see where he was chasing me off so he could have the gal for himself. When I see what the matter of it was, I lost all fear of my daddy. Right there is where I become a man . . . at fourteen years of age. (*Pause.*)

Now it was my turn to run him off. I picked up them same reins that he had used on me. I picked up them reins and commenced to whupping on him. The gal jumped up and run off . . . and when my daddy turned to face me, I could see why the devil had never come to get him . . . cause he was the devil himself. I don't know what happened. When I woke up, I was laying right there by the creek, and Blue . . . this old dog we had . . . was licking my face. I thought I was blind. I couldn't see nothing. Both my eyes were swollen shut. I layed there and cried. I didn't know what I was gonna do. The only thing I knew was the time had come for me to leave my daddy's house. And right there the world suddenly got big. And it was a long time before I could cut it down to where I could handle it.

Part of that cutting down was when I got to the place where I could feel him kicking in my blood and knew that the only thing that separated us was the matter of a few years.

(*Gabriel enters from the house with a sandwich.*)

LYONS. What you got there, Uncle Gabe?
GABRIEL. Got me a ham sandwich. Rose gave me a ham sandwich.
TROY. I don't know what happened to him. I done lost touch with everybody except Gabriel. But I hope he's dead. I hope he found some peace.
LYONS. That's a heavy story, Pop. I didn't know you left home when you was fourteen.
TROY. And didn't know nothing. The only part of the world I knew was the forty-two acres of Mr. Lubin's land. That's all I knew about life.
LYONS. Fourteen's kinda young to be out on your own. (*Phone rings.*) I don't even think I was ready to be out on my own at fourteen. I don't know what I would have done.
TROY. I got up from the creek and walked on down to Mobile. I was through with farming. Figured I could do better in the city. So I walked the two hundred miles to Mobile.

LYONS. Wait a minute . . . you ain't walked no two hundred miles, Pop. Ain't nobody gonna walk no two hundred miles. You talking about some walking there.

BONO. That's the only way you got anywhere back in them days.

LYONS. Shhh. Damn if I wouldn't have hitched a ride with somebody!

TROY. Who you gonna hitch it with? They ain't had no cars and things like they got now. We talking about 1918.

1180   ROSE (*entering*). What you all out here getting into?

TROY (*to Rose*). I'm telling Lyons how good he got it. He don't know nothing about this I'm talking.

ROSE. Lyons, that was Bonnie on the phone. She say you supposed to pick her up.

LYONS. Yeah, okay, Rose.

TROY. I walked on down to Mobile and hitched up with some of them fellows that was heading this way. Got up here and found out . . . not only couldn't you get a job . . . you couldn't find no place to live. I thought I was in freedom. Shhh. Colored folks living down

1190   there on the riverbanks in whatever kind of shelter they could find for themselves. Right down there under the Brady Street Bridge. Living in shacks made of sticks and tarpaper. Messed around there and went from bad to worse. Started stealing. First it was food. Then I figure, hell, if I steal money I can buy me some food. Buy me some shoes, too! One thing led to another. Met your mama and had you. What I do that for? Now I got to worry about feeding you and her. Got to steal three times as much. Went out one day looking for somebody to rob . . . that's what I was, a robber. I'll tell you the truth. I'm ashamed of it today. But it's the truth. Went to rob this

1200   fellow . . . pulled out my knife . . . and he pulled out a gun. Shot me in the chest. It felt just like somebody had taken a hot branding iron and laid it on me. When he shot me I jumped at him with my knife. They told me I killed him and they put me in the penitentiary and locked me up for fifteen years. That's where I met Bono. That's where I learned how to play baseball. Got out that place and your mama had taken you and went on to make life without me. Fifteen years was a long time for her to wait. But that fifteen years cured me of that robbing stuff. Rose'll tell you. She asked me when I met her if I had gotten all that foolishness out of my system. And I told

1210   her "Baby, it's you and baseball all what count with me." You hear me, Bono? I meant it, too. She say, "Which one comes first?" I told her, "Baby, ain't no doubt it's baseball . . . but you stick and get old with me and we'll both outlive this baseball." Am I right, Rose? And it's true.

ROSE. Man, hush your mouth. You ain't said no such thing. Talking about "Baby, you know you'll always be number one with me." That's what you was talking.

TROY. You hear that, Bono. That's why I love her.

BONO. Rose'll keep you straight. You get off the track, she'll straighten you up. 1220

ROSE. Lyons, you better get on up and get Bonnie. She waiting on you.

LYONS (*gets up to go*). Hey, Pop, why don't you come on down to the Grill and hear me play?

TROY. I ain't going down there. I'm too old to be sitting around in them clubs.

BONO. You got to be good to play down at the Grill.

LYONS. Come on, Pop . . .

TROY. I got to get up in the morning.

LYONS. You ain't got to stay long.

TROY. Naw, I'm gonna get my supper and go on to bed. 1230

LYONS. Well, I got to go. I'll see you again.

TROY. Don't you come around my house on my payday.

ROSE. Pick up the phone and let somebody know you coming. And bring Bonnie with you. You know I'm always glad to see her.

LYONS. Yeah, I'll do that, Rose. You take care now. See you, Pop. See you, Mr. Bono. See you, Uncle Gabe.

GABRIEL. Lyons! King of the Jungle!

(*Lyons exits.*)

TROY. Is supper ready, woman? Me and you got some business to take care of. I'm gonna tear it up, too.

ROSE. Troy, I done told you now! 1240

TROY (*puts his arm around Bono*). Aw hell, woman . . . this is Bono. Bono like family. I done known this nigger since . . . how long I done know you?

BONO. It's been a long time.

TROY. I done known this nigger since Skippy was a pup. Me and him done been through some times.

BONO. You sure right about that.

TROY. Hell, I done know him longer than I known you. And we still standing shoulder to shoulder. Hey, look here, Bono . . . a man can't ask for no more than that. (*Drinks to him.*) I love you, nigger. 1250

BONO. Hell, I love you too . . . but I got to get home see my woman. You got yours in hand. I got to go get mine.

(*Bono starts to exit as Cory enters the yard, dressed in his football uniform. He gives Troy a hard, uncompromising look.*)

CORY. What you do that for, Pop? (*He throws his helmet down in the direction of Troy.*)

ROSE. What's the matter? Cory . . . what's the matter?

CORY. Papa done went up to the school and told Coach Zellman I can't play football no more. Wouldn't even let me play the game. Told him to tell the recruiter not to come.

ROSE. Troy . . .

1260

TROY. What you Troying me for. Yeah, I did it. And the boy know why I did it.

CORY. Why you wanna do that to me? That was the one chance I had.

ROSE. Ain't nothing wrong with Cory playing football, Troy.

TROY. The boy lied to me. I told the nigger if he wanna play football . . . to keep up his chores and hold down that job at the A&P. That was the conditions. Stopped down there to see Mr. Stawicki . . .

CORY. I can't work after school during the football season, Pop! I tried to tell you that Mr. Stawicki's holding my job for me. You don't never want to listen to nobody. And then you wanna go and do this to me!

1270

TROY. I ain't done nothing to you. You done it to yourself.

CORY. Just became you didn't have a chance! You just scared I'm gonna be better than you, that's all.

TROY. Come here.

ROSE. Troy . . .

(Cory reluctantly crosses over to Troy.)

TROY. All right! See. You done made a mistake.

CORY. I didn't even do nothing!

TROY. I'm gonna tell you what your mistake was. See . . . you swung at the ball and didn't hit it. That's strike one. See, you in the batter's box now. You swung and you missed. That's strike one. Don't

1280

you strike out!

(Lights fade to black.)

ACT 2

SCENE I

The following morning. Cory is at the tree hitting the ball with the bat. He tries to mimic Troy, but his swing is awkward, less sure. Rose enters from the house.

ROSE. Cory, I want you to help me with this cupboard.

CORY. I ain't quitting the team. I don't care what Poppa say.

ROSE. I'll talk to him when he gets back. He had to go see about your Uncle Gabe. The police done arrested him. Say he was disturbing the peace. He'll be back directly. Come on in here and help me clean out the top of this cupboard.

(Cory exits into the house. Rose sees Troy and Bono coming down the alley.)

Troy . . . what they say down there?

TROY. Ain't said nothing. I give them fifty dollars and they let him go. I'll talk to you about it. Where's Cory?

1290

ROSE. He's in there helping me clean out these cupboards.

TROY. Tell him to get his butt out here.

(*Troy and Bono go over to the pile of wood. Bono picks up the saw and begins sawing.*)

TROY (*to Bono*). All they want is the money. That makes six or seven times I done went down there and got him. See me coming they stick out their *hands*.

BONO. Yeah. I know what you mean. That's all they care about . . . that money. They don't care about what's right. (*Pause.*) Nigger, why you got to go and get some hard wood? You ain't doing nothing but building a little old fence. Get you some soft pine wood. That's all you need.

TROY. I know what I'm doing. This is outside wood. You put pine   1300
wood inside the house. Pine wood is inside wood. This here is outside wood. Now you tell me where the fence is gonna be?

BONO. You don't need this wood. You can put it up with pine wood and it'll stand as long as you gonna be here looking at it.

TROY. How you know how long I'm gonna be here, nigger? Hell, I might just live forever. Live longer than old man Horsely.

BONO. That's what Magee used to say.

TROY. Magee's a damn fool. Now you tell me who you ever heard of gonna pull their own teeth with a pair of rusty pliers.

BONO. The old folks . . . my granddaddy used to pull his teeth with   1310
pliers. They ain't had no dentists for the colored folks back then.

TROY. Get clean pliers! You understand? Clean pliers! Sterilize them! Besides we ain't living back then. All Magee had to do was walk over to Doc Goldblum's.

BONO. I see where you and that Tallahassee gal . . . that Alberta . . . I see where you all done got tight.

TROY. What do you mean "got tight?"

BONO. I see where you be laughing and joking with her all the time.

TROY. I laughs and jokes with all of them, Bono. You know me.

BONO. That ain't the kind of laughing and joking I'm talking about.   1320

(*Cory enters from the house.*)

CORY. How you doing, Mr. Bono?

TROY. Cory? Get that saw from Bono and cut some wood. He talking about the wood's too hard to cut. Stand back there, Jim, and let that young boy show you how it's done.

BONO. He's sure welcome to it.

(*Cory takes the saw and begins to cut the wood.*)

Whew-e-e! Look at that. Big old strong boy. Look like Joe Louis. Hell, must be getting old the way I'm watching that boy whip through that wood.

CORY. I don't see why Mama want a fence around the yard noways.

TROY. Damn if I know either. What the hell she keeping out with it?   1330
She ain't got nothing nobody want.

BONO. Some people build fences to keep people out . . . and other people build fences to keep people in. Rose wants to hold on to you all. She loves you.

TROY. Hell, nigger, I don't need nobody to tell me my wife loves me. Cory . . . go on in the house and see if you can find that other saw.

CORY. Where's it at?

TROY. I said find it! Look for it till you find it!

(*Cory exits into the house.*)

What's that supposed to mean? Wanna keep us in?

1340 BONO. Troy . . . I done known you seem like damn near my whole life. You and Rose both. I done know both of you all for a long time. I remember when you met Rose. When you was hitting them baseball out the park. A lot of them old gals was after you then. You had the pick of the litter. When you picked Rose, I was happy for you. That was the first time I knew you had any sense. I said . . . My man Troy knows what he's doing . . . I'm gonna follow this nigger . . . he might take me somewhere. I been following you, too. I done learned a whole heap of things about life watching you. I done

1350 learned how to tell where the shit lies. How to tell it from the alfalfa. You done learned me a lot of things. You showed me how to not make the same mistakes . . . to take life as it comes along and keep putting one foot in front of the other. (*Pause.*) Rose a good woman, Troy.

TROY. Hell, nigger, I know she a good woman. I been married to her for eighteen years. What you got on your mind, Bono?

BONO. I just say she a good woman. Just like I say anything. I ain't got to have nothing on my mind.

TROY. You just gonna say she a good woman and leave it hanging out there like that? Why you telling me she a good woman?

1360 BONO. She loves you, Troy. Rose loves you.

TROY. You saying I don't measure up. That's what you trying to say. I don't measure up cause I'm seeing this other gal. I know what you trying to say.

BONO. I know what Rose means to you, Troy. I'm just trying to say I don't want to see you mess up.

TROY. Yeah, I appreciate that, Bono. If you was messing around on Lucille I'd be telling you the same thing.

BONO. Well that's all I got to say. I just say that because I love you both.

1370 TROY. Hell, you know me . . . I wasn't out there looking for nothing. You can't find a better woman than Rose. I know that. But seems like this woman just stuck onto me where I can't shake her loose. I done wrestled with it, tried to throw her off me . . . but she just stuck on tighter. Now she's stuck on for good.

BONO. You's in control . . . that's what you tell me all the time. You responsible for what you do.

TROY. I ain't ducking the responsibility of it. As long as it sets right in my heart . . . then I'm okay. Cause that's all I listen to. It'll tell me right from wrong every time. And I ain't talking about doing Rose no bad turn. I love Rose. She done carried me a long ways and I love and respect her for that. 1380

BONO. I know you do. That's why I don't want to see you hurt her. But what you gonna do when she find out? What you got then? If you try to juggle both of them . . . sooner or later you gonna drop one of them. That's common sense.

TROY. Yeah, I hear what you saying, Bono. I been trying to figure a way to work it out.

BONO. Work it out right, Troy. I don't want to be getting all up between you and Rose's business . . . but work it so it come out right.

TROY. Aw hell, I get all up between you and Lucille's business. When 1390 you gonna get that woman that refrigerator she been wanting? Don't tell me you ain't got no money now. I know who your banker is. Mellon don't need that money bad as Lucille want that refrigerator. I'll tell you that.

BONO. Tell you what I'll do . . . when you finish building this fence for Rose . . . I'll buy Lucille that refrigerator.

TROY. You done stuck your foot in your mouth now! (*Troy grabs up a board and begins to saw. Bono starts to walk out the yard.*) Hey, nigger . . . where you going?

BONO. I'm going home. I know you don't expect me to help you now. 1400 I'm protecting my money. I wanna see you put that fence up by yourself. That's what I want to see. You'll be here another six months without me.

TROY. Nigger, you ain't right.

BONO. When it comes to my money . . . I'm right as fireworks on the Fourth of July.

TROY. All right, we gonna see now. You better get out your bankbook.

(*Bono exits, and Troy continues to work. Rose enters from the house.*)

ROSE. What they say down there? What's happening with Gabe?

TROY. I went down there and got him out. Cost me fifty dollars. Say 1410 he was disturbing the peace. Judge set up a hearing for him in three weeks. Say to show cause why he shouldn't be recommitted.

ROSE. What was he doing that cause them to arrest him?

TROY. Some kids was teasing him and he run them off home. Say he was howling and carrying on. Some folks seen him and called the police. That's all it was.

ROSE. Well, what's you say? What'd you tell the Judge?

TROY. Told him I'd look after him. It didn't make no sense to recommit the man. He stuck out his big greasy palm and told me to give him fifty dollars and take him on home. 1420

ROSE. Where's he at now? Where'd he go off to?

TROY. He's gone on about his business. He don't need nobody to hold his hand.

ROSE. Well, I don't know. Seem like that would be the best place for him if they did put him into the hospital. I know what you're gonna say. But that's what I think would be best.

TROY. The man done had his life ruined fighting for what? And they wanna take and lock him up. Let him be free. He don't bother nobody.

1430 ROSE. Well, everybody got their own way of looking at it I guess. Come on and get your lunch. I got a bowl of lima beans and some cornbread in the oven. Come on get something to eat. Ain't no sense you fretting over Gabe.

(Rose turns to go into the house.)

TROY. Rose . . . got something to tell you.

ROSE. Well, come on . . . wait till I get this food on the table.

TROY. Rose! *(She stops and turns around.)* I don't know how to say this. *(Pause.)* I can't explain it none. It just sort of grows on you till it gets out of hand. It starts out like a little bush . . . and the next thing you know it's a whole forest.

1440 ROSE. Troy . . . what is you talking about?

TROY. I'm talking, woman, let me talk. I'm trying to find a way to tell you . . . I'm gonna be a daddy. I'm gonna be somebody's daddy.

ROSE. Troy . . . you're not telling me this? You're gonna be . . . what?

TROY. Rose . . . now . . . see . . .

ROSE. You telling me you gonna be somebody's daddy? You telling your *wife* this?

(Gabriel enters from the street. He carries a rose in his hand.)

GABRIEL. Hey, Troy! Hey, Rose!

ROSE. I have to wait eighteen years to hear something like this.

GABRIEL. Hey, Rose . . . I got a flower for you. *(He hands it to her.)*
1450   That's a rose. Same rose like you is.

ROSE. Thanks, Gabe.

GABRIEL. Troy, you ain't mad at me is you? Them bad mens come and put me away. You ain't mad at me is you?

TROY. Naw, Gabe, I ain't mad at you.

ROSE. Eighteen years and you wanna come with this.

GABRIEL *(takes a quarter out of his pocket)*. See what I got? Got a brand new quarter.

TROY. Rose . . . it's just . . .

ROSE. Ain't nothing you can say, Troy. Ain't no way of explaining
1460   that.

GABRIEL. Fellow that give me this quarter had a whole mess of them. I'm gonna keep this quarter till it stop shining.

ROSE. Gabe, go on in the house there. I got some watermelon in the frigidaire. Go on and get you a piece.

GABRIEL. Say, Rose . . . you know I was chasing hellhounds and them bad mens come and get me and take me away. Troy helped me. He come down there and told them they better let me go before he beat them up. Yeah, he did!

ROSE. You go on and get you a piece of watermelon, Gabe. Them bad mens is gone now.   1470

GABRIEL. Okay, Rose . . . gonna get me some watermelon. The kind with the stripes on it.

(Gabriel exits into the house.)

ROSE. Why, Troy? Why? After all these years to come dragging this in to me now. It don't make no sense at your age. I could have expected this ten or fifteen years ago, but not now.

TROY. Age ain't got nothing to do with it, Rose.

ROSE. I done tried to be everything a wife should be. Everything a wife could be. Been married eighteen years and I got to live to see the day you tell me you been seeing another woman and done fathered a child by her. And you know I ain't never wanted no half nothing   1480 in my family. My whole family is half. Everybody got different fathers and mothers . . . my two sisters and my brother. Can't hardly tell who's who. Can't never sit down and talk about Papa and Mama. It's your papa and your mama and my papa and my mama . . .

TROY. Rose . . . stop it now.

ROSE. I ain't never wanted that for none of my children. And now you wanna drag your behind in here and tell me something like this.

TROY. You ought to know. It's time for you to know.

ROSE. Well, I don't want to know, goddamn it!

TROY. I can't just make it go away. It's done now. I can't wish the cir-   1490 cumstance of the thing away.

ROSE. And you don't want to either. Maybe you want to wish me and my boy away. Maybe that's what you want? Well, you can't wish us away. I've got eighteen years of my life invested in you. You ought to have stayed upstairs in my bed where you belong.

TROY. Rose . . . now listen to me . . . we can get a handle on this thing. We can talk this out . . . come to an understanding.

ROSE. All of a sudden it's "we." Where was "we" at when you was down there rolling around with some god-forsaken woman? "We" should have come to an understanding before you started making a   1500 damn fool of yourself. You're a day late and a dollar short when it comes to an understanding with me.

TROY. It's just . . . She gives me a different idea . . . a different understanding about myself. I can step out of this house and get away from the pressures and problems . . . be a different man. I ain't got to wonder how I'm gonna pay the bills or get the roof fixed. I can just be a part of myself that ain't never been.

ROSE. What I want to know . . . is do you plan to continue seeing her. That's all you can say to me.

1510   TROY. I can sit up in her house and laugh. Do you understand what I'm saying. I can laugh out loud . . . and it feels good. It reaches all the way down to the bottom of my shoes. (*Pause.*) Rose, I can't give that up.

ROSE. Maybe you ought to go on and stay down there with her . . . if she a better woman than me.

TROY. It ain't about nobody being a better woman or nothing. Rose, you ain't the blame. A man couldn't ask for no woman to be a better wife than you've been. I'm responsible for it. I done locked my-self into a pattern trying to take care of you all that I forget about

1520   myself.

ROSE. What the hell was I there for? That was my job, not somebody else's.

TROY. Rose, I done tried all my life to live decent . . . to live a clean . . . hard . . . useful life. I tried to be a good husband to you. In every way I knew how. Maybe I come into the world backwards, I don't know. But . . . you born with two strikes on you before you come to the plate. You got to guard it closely . . . always looking for the curve-ball on the inside corner. You can't afford to let none get past you. You can't afford a call strike. If you going down . . .

1530   you going down swinging. Everything lined up against you. What you gonna do. I fooled them, Rose. I bunted. When I found you and Cory and a halfway decent job . . . I was safe. Couldn't nothing touch me. I wasn't gonna strike out no more. I wasn't going back to the penitentiary. I wasn't gonna lay in the streets with a bottle of wine. I was safe. I had me a family. A job. I wasn't gonna get that last strike. I was on first looking for one of them boys to knock me in. To get me home.

ROSE. You should have stayed in my bed, Troy.

TROY. Then when I saw that gal . . . she firmed up my backbone. And

1540   I got to thinking that if I tried . . . I just might be able to steal second. Do you understand after eighteen years I wanted to steal second.

ROSE. You should have held me tight. You should have grabbed me and held on.

TROY. I stood on first base for eighteen years and I thought . . . well, goddamn it . . . go on for it!

ROSE. We're not talking about baseball! We're talking about you going off to lay in bed with another woman . . . and then bring it home to me. That's what we're talking about. We ain't talking about no

1550   baseball.

TROY. Rose, you're not listening to me. I'm trying the best I can to explain it to you. It's not easy for me to admit that I been standing in the same place for eighteen years.

ROSE. I been standing with you! I been right here with you, Troy. I got a life too. I gave eighteen years of my life to stand in the same spot with you. Don't you think I ever wanted other things? Don't you

think I had dreams and hopes? What about my life? What about
me? Don't you think it ever crossed my mind to want to know
other men? That I wanted to lay up somewhere and forget about
my responsibilities? That I wanted someone to make me laugh so I   1560
could feel good? You not the only one who's got wants and needs.
But I held on to you, Troy. I took all my feelings, my wants and
needs, my dreams . . . and I buried them inside you. I planted a seed
and watched and prayed over it. I planted myself inside you and
waited to bloom. And it didn't take me no eighteen years to find out
the soil was hard and rocky and it wasn't never gonna bloom.

But I held on to you, Troy. I held on tighter. You was my husband. I owed you everything I had. Every part of me I could find to
give you. And upstairs in that room . . . with the darkness falling in
on me . . . I gave everything I had to try and erase the doubt that   1570
you wasn't the finest man in the world. And wherever you was going . . . I wanted to be there with you. Cause you was my husband.
Cause that's the only way I was gonna survive as your wife. You
always talking about what you give . . . and what you don't have to
give. But you take, too. You take . . . and don't even know nobody's giving!

(Rose turns to exit into the house; Troy grabs her arm.)

TROY You say I take and don't give!
ROSE. Troy! You're hurting me!
TROY. You say I take and don't give.
ROSE. Troy . . . you're hurting my arm! Let go!   1580
TROY. I done give you everything I got. Don't you tell that lie on me.
ROSE. Troy!
TROY. Don't you tell that lie on me!

(Cory enters from the house.)

CORY. Mama!
ROSE. Troy. You're hurting me.
TROY. Don't you tell me about no taking and giving.

*(Cory comes up behind Troy and grabs him. Troy, surprised, is
thrown off balance just as Cory throws a glancing blow that catches
him on the chest and knocks him down. Troy is stunned, as is Cory.)*

ROSE. Troy. Troy. No!

(Troy gets to his feet and starts at Cory.)

Troy . . . no. Please! Troy!

(Rose pulls on Troy to hold him back. Troy stops himself.)

TROY *(to Cory)*. All right. That's strike two. You stay away from
around me, boy. Don't you strike out. You living with a full count.   1590
Don't you strike out.

(Troy exits out the yard as the lights go down.)

It is six months later, early afternoon. Troy enters from the house and starts to exit the yard. Rose enters from the house.

ROSE. Troy, I want to talk to you.

TROY. All of a sudden, after all this time, you want to talk to me, huh? You ain't wanted to talk to me for months. You ain't wanted to talk to me last night. You ain't wanted no part of me then. What you wanna talk to me about now?

ROSE. Tomorrow's Friday.

TROY. I know what day tomorrow is. You think I don't know tomorrow's Friday? My whole life I ain't done nothing but look to see Friday coming and you got to tell me it's Friday.

ROSE. I want to know if you're coming home.

TROY. I always come home, Rose. You know that. There ain't never been a night I ain't come home.

ROSE. That ain't what I mean . . . and you know it. I want to know if you're coming straight home after work.

TROY. I figure I'd cash my check . . . hang out at Taylors' with the boys . . . maybe play a game of checkers . . .

ROSE. Troy, I can't live like this. I won't live like this. You livin' on borrowed time with me. It's been going on six months now you ain't been coming home.

TROY. I be here every night. Every night of the year. That's 365 days.

ROSE. I want you to come home tomorrow after work.

TROY. Rose . . . I don't mess up my pay. You know that now. I take my pay and I give it to you. I don't have no money but what you give me back. I just want to have a little time to myself . . . a little time to enjoy life.

ROSE. What about me? When's my time to enjoy life?

TROY. I don't know what to tell you, Rose. I'm doing the best I can.

ROSE. You ain't been home from work but time enough to change your clothes and run out . . . and you wanna call that the best you can do?

TROY. I'm going over to the hospital to see Alberta. She went into the hospital this afternoon. Look like she might have the baby early. I won't be gone long.

ROSE. Well, you ought to know. They went over to Miss Pearl's and got Gabe today. She said you told them to go ahead and lock him up.

TROY. I ain't said no such thing. Whoever told you that is telling a lie. Pearl ain't doing nothing but telling a big fat lie.

ROSE. She ain't had to tell me. I read it on the papers.

TROY. I ain't told them nothing of the kind.

ROSE. I saw it right there on the papers.

TROY. What it say, huh?

ROSE. It said you told them to take him.

TROY. Then they screwed that up, just the way they screw up everything. I ain't worried about what they got on the paper.

ROSE. Say the government send part of his check to the hospital and the other part to you.

TROY. I ain't got nothing to do with that if that's the way it works. I ain't made up the rules about how it work.　　　　　1640

ROSE. You did Gabe just like you did Cory. You wouldn't sign the paper for Cory . . . but you signed for Gabe. You signed that paper.

(The telephone is heard ringing inside the house.)

TROY. I told you I ain't signed nothing, woman! The only thing I signed was the release form. Hell, I can't read, I don't know what they had on that paper! I ain't signed nothing about sending Gabe away.

ROSE. I said send him to the hospital . . . you said let him be free . . . now you done went down there and signed him to the hospital for half his money. You went back on yourself, Troy. You gonna have to answer for that.　　　　　1650

TROY. See now . . . you been over there talking to Miss Pearl. She done got mad cause she ain't getting Gabe's rent money. That's all it is. She's liable to say anything.

ROSE. Troy, I seen where you signed the paper.

TROY. You ain't seen nothing I signed. What she doing got papers on my brother anyway? Miss Pearl telling a big fat lie. And I'm gonna tell her about it too! You ain't seen nothing I signed. Say . . . you ain't seen nothing I signed.

(Rose exits into the house to answer the telephone. Presently she returns.)

ROSE. Troy . . . that was the hospital. Alberta had the baby.

TROY. What she have? What is it?　　　　　1660

ROSE. It's a girl.

TROY. I better get on down to the hospital to see her.

ROSE. Troy.

TROY. Rose . . . I got to see her now. That's only right . . . what's the matter . . . the baby's all right, ain't it?

ROSE. Alberta died having the baby.

TROY. Died . . . you say she's dead? Alberta's dead?

ROSE. They said they done all they could. They couldn't do nothing for her.

TROY. The baby? How's the baby?　　　　　1670

ROSE. They say it's healthy. I wonder who's gonna bury her.

TROY. She had family, Rose. She wasn't living in the world by herself.

ROSE. I know she wasn't living in the world by herself.

TROY. Next thing you gonna want to know if she had any insurance.

ROSE. Troy, you ain't got to talk like that.

TROY. That's the first thing that jumped out your mouth. "Who's gonna bury her?" Like I'm fixing to take on that task for myself.

ROSE. I am your wife. Don't push me away.

TROY. I ain't pushing nobody away. Just give me some space. That's all. Just give me some room to breathe.

1680

(*Rose exits into the house. Troy walks about the yard.*)

TROY (*with a quiet rage that threatens to consume him*). All right . . . Mr. Death. See now . . . I'm gonna tell you what I'm gonna do. I'm gonna take and build me a fence around this yard. See? I'm gonna build me a fence around what belongs to me. And then I want you to stay on the other side. See? You stay over there until you're ready for me. Then you come on. Bring your army. Bring your sickle. Bring your wrestling clothes. I ain't gonna fall down on my vigilance this time. You ain't gonna sneak up on me no more. When you ready for me . . . when the top of your list say Troy Maxson

1690

. . . that's when you come around here. You come up and knock on the front door. Ain't nobody else got nothing to do with this. This is between you and me. Man to man. You stay on the other side of that fence until you ready for me. Then you come up and knock on the front door. Anytime you want. I'll be ready for you.

(*The lights go down to black.*)

SCENE 3

The lights come up on the porch. It is late evening three days later. Rose sits listening to the ball game waiting for Troy. The final out of the game is made and Rose switches off the radio. Troy enters the yard carrying an infant wrapped in blankets. He stands back from the house and calls.

Rose enters and stands on the porch. There is a long, awkward silence, the weight of which grows heavier with each passing second.

TROY. Rose . . . I'm standing here with my daughter in my arms. She ain't but a wee bittie little old thing. She don't know nothing about grownups' business. She innocent . . . and she ain't got no mama.

ROSE. What you telling me for, Troy?

(*She turns and exits into the house.*)

TROY Well . . . I guess we'll just sit out here on the porch.

(*He sits down on the porch. There is an awkward indelicateness about the way he handles the baby. His largeness engulfs and seems to swallow it. He speaks loud enough for Rose to hear.*)

1700

A man's got to do what's right for him. I ain't sorry for nothing I done. It felt right in my heart. (*To the baby*) What you smiling at? Your daddy's a big man. Got these great big old hands. But sometimes he's scared. And right now your daddy's scared cause we sitting out here and ain't got no home. Oh, I been homeless before. I

ain't had no little baby with me. But I been homeless. You just be out on the road by your lonesome and you see one of them trains coming and you just kinda go like this . . . (*He sings as a lullaby*)
Please, Mr. Engineer let a man ride the line
Please, Mr. Engineer let a man ride the line
I ain't got no ticket please let me ride the blinds   1710

(*Rose enters from the house. Troy hearing her steps behind him, stands and faces her.*)

She's my daughter, Rose. My own flesh and blood. I can't deny her no more than I can deny them boys. (*Pause.*) You and them boys is my family. You and them and this child is all I got in the world. So I guess what I'm saying is . . . I'd appreciate it if you'd help me take care of her.

ROSE. Okay, Troy . . . you're right. I'll take care of your baby for you . . . cause . . . like you say . . . she's innocent . . . and you can't visit the sins of the father upon the child. A motherless child has got a hard time. (*She takes the baby from him.*) From right now . . . this child got a mother. But you a womanless man.   1720

(*Rose turns and exits into the house with the baby. Lights go down to black.*)

SCENE 4

It is two months later. Lyons enters from the street. He knocks on the door and calls.

LYONS. Hey, Rose! (*Pause.*) Rose!
ROSE (*from inside the house*). Stop that yelling. You gonna wake up Raynell. I just got her to sleep.
LYONS. I just stopped by to pay Papa this twenty dollars I owe him. Where's Papa at?
ROSE. He should be here in a minute. I'm getting ready to go down to the church. Sit down and wait on him.
LYONS. I got to go pick up Bonnie over her mother's house.
ROSE. Well, sit it down there on the table. He'll get it.
LYONS (*enters the house and sets the money on the table*). Tell Papa I said thanks. I'll see you again.   1730
ROSE. All right, Lyons. We'll see you.

(*Lyons starts to exit as Cory enters.*)

CORY. Hey, Lyons.
LYONS. What's happening, Cory. Say man, I'm sorry I missed your graduation. You know I had a gig and couldn't get away. Otherwise, I would have been there, man. So what you doing?
CORY. I'm trying to find a job.
LYONS. Yeah I know how that go, man. It's rough out here. Jobs are scarce.

1740 CORY. Yeah, I know.

LYONS. Look here, I got to run. Talk to Papa . . . he know some people. He'll be able to help get you a job. Talk to him . . . see what he say.

CORY. Yeah . . . all right, Lyons.

LYONS. You take care. I'll talk to you soon. We'll find some time to talk.

(Lyons exits the yard. Cory wanders over to the tree, picks up the bat and assumes a batting stance. He studies an imaginary pitcher and swings. Dissatisfied with the result, he tries again. Troy enters. They eye each other for a beat. Cory puts the bat down and exits the yard. Troy starts into the house as Rose exits with Raynell. She is carrying a cake.)

TROY. I'm coming in and everybody's going out.

ROSE. I'm taking this cake down to the church for the bake sale. Lyons was by to see you. He stopped by to pay you your twenty dollars. It's laying in there on the table.

TROY *(going into his pocket)*. Well . . . here go this money.

1750 ROSE. Put it in there on the table, Troy. I'll get it.

TROY. What time you coming back?

ROSE. Ain't no use you studying me. It don't matter what time I come back.

TROY. I just asked you a question, woman. What's the matter . . . can't I ask you a question?

ROSE. Troy, I don't want to go into it. Your dinner's in there on the stove. All you got to do is heat it up. And don't you be eating the rest of them cakes in there. I'm coming back for them. We having a bake sale at the church tomorrow.

(Rose exits the yard. Troy sits down on the steps, takes a pint bottle from his pocket, opens it and drinks. He begins to sing.)

TROY.

1760   Hear it ring! Hear it ring!
   Had an old dog his name was Blue
   You know Blue was mighty true
   You know Blue was a good old dog
   Blue treed a possum in a hollow log
   You know from that he was a good old dog

(Bono enters the yard.)

BONO. Hey, Troy.

TROY. Hey, what's happening, Bono?

BONO. I just thought I'd stop by to see you.

TROY. What you stop by and see me for? You ain't stopped by in a month of Sundays. Hell, I must owe you money or something.

1770 BONO. Since you got your promotion I can't keep up with you. Used to see you every day. Now I don't even know what route you working.

TROY. They keep switching me around. Got me out in Greentree now . . . hauling white folks' garbage.

BONO. Greentree, huh? You lucky, at least you ain't got to be lifting them barrels. Damn if they ain't getting heavier. I'm gonna put in my two years and call it quits.

TROY. I'm thinking about retiring myself.

BONO. You got it easy. You can *drive* for another five years.

TROY. It ain't the same, Bono. It ain't like working the back of the 1780 truck. Ain't got nobody to talk to . . . feel like you working by yourself. Naw, I'm thinking about retiring. How's Lucille?

BONO. She all right. Her arthritis get to acting up on her sometime. Saw Rose on my way in. She going down to the church, huh?

TROY. Yeah, she took up going down there. All them preachers looking for somebody to fatten their pockets. (*Pause.*) Got some gin here.

BONO. Naw, thanks. I just stopped by to say hello.

TROY. Hell, nigger . . . you can take a drink. I ain't never known you to say no to a drink. You ain't got to work tomorrow.

BONO. I just stopped by. I'm fixing to go over to Skinner's. We got us 1790 a domino game going over his house every Friday.

TROY. Nigger, you can't play no dominoes. I used to whup you four games out of five.

BONO. Well, that learned me. I'm getting better.

TROY. Yeah? Well, that's all right.

BONO. Look here . . . I got to be getting on. Stop by sometime, huh?

TROY. Yeah, I'll do that, Bono. Lucille told Rose you bought her a new refrigerator.

BONO. Yeah, Rose told Lucille you had finally built your fence . . . so I figured we'd call it even. 1800

TROY. I knew you would.

BONO. Yeah . . . okay. I'll be talking to you.

TROY. Yeah, take care, Bono. Good to see you. I'm gonna stop over.

BONO. Yeah. Okay, Troy.

(*Bono exits. Troy drinks from the bottle.*)

TROY.

Old Blue died and I dig his grave
Let him down with a golden chain
Every night when I hear old Blue bark
I know Blue treed a possum in Noah's Ark.
Hear it ring! Hear it ring!

(*Cory enters the yard. They eye each other for a beat. Troy is sitting in the middle of the steps. Cory walks over.*)

CORY. I got to get by. 1810

TROY. Say what? What's you say?

CORY. You in my way. I got to get by.

TROY. You got to get by where? This is my house. Bought and paid for. Took me fifteen years. And if you wanna go in my house and I'm sitting on the steps . . . you say excuse me. Like your mama taught you.

CORY. Come on, Pop . . . I got to get by.

(*Cory starts to maneuver his way past Troy. Troy grabs his leg and shoves him back.*)

TROY. You just gonna walk over top of me?

CORY. I live here, too!

1820 TROY (*advancing toward him*). You just gonna walk over top of me in my own house?

CORY. I ain't scared of you.

TROY. I ain't asked if you was scared of me. I asked you if you was fixing to walk over top of me in my own house? That's the question. You ain't gonna say excuse me? You just gonna walk over top of me?

CORY. If you wanna put it like that.

TROY. How else am I gonna put it?

CORY. I was walking by you to go into the house cause you sitting on the steps drunk, singing to yourself. You can put it like that.

1830 TROY. Without saying excuse me???

(*Cory doesn't respond.*)

I asked you a question. Without saying excuse me???

CORY. I ain't got to say excuse me to you. You don't count around here no more.

TROY. Oh, I see . . . I don't count around here no more. You ain't got to say excuse me to your daddy. All of a sudden you done got so grown that your daddy don't count around here no more . . . Around here in his own house and yard that he done paid for with the sweat of his brow. You done got so grown to where you gonna take over. You gonna take over my house. Is that right? You gonna

1840 wear my pants. You gonna go in there and stretch out on my bed. You ain't got to say excuse me cause I don't count around here no more. Is that right?

CORY. That's right. You always talking this dumb stuff. Now, why don't you just get out my way.

TROY. I guess you got someplace to sleep and something to put in your belly. You got that, huh? You got that? That's what you need. You got that, huh?

CORY. You don't know what I got. You ain't got to worry about what I got.

1850 TROY. You right! You one hundred percent right! I done spent the last seventeen years worrying about what you got. Now it's your turn, see? I'll tell you what to do. You grown . . . we done established that. You a man. Now, let's see you act like one. Turn your behind around and walk out this yard. And when you get out there in the alley . . . you can forget about this house. See? 'Cause this is my house. You go on and be a man and get your own house. You can forget about this. 'Cause this is mine. You go on and get yours 'cause I'm through with doing for you.

CORY. You talking about what you did for me . . . what'd you ever give me?   1860

TROY. Them feet and bones! That pumping heart, nigger! I give you more than anybody else is ever gonna give you.

CORY. You ain't never gave me nothing! You ain't never done nothing but hold me back. Afraid I was gonna be better than you. All you ever did was try and make me scared of you. I used to tremble every time you called my name. Every time I heard your footsteps in the house. Wondering all the time . . . what's Papa gonna say if I do this? . . . What's he gonna say if I do that? . . . What's Papa gonna say if I turn on the radio? And Mama, too . . . she tries . . . but she's scared of you.   1870

TROY. You leave your mama out of this. She ain't got nothing to do with this.

CORY. I don't know how she stands you . . . after what you did to her.

TROY. I told you to leave your mama out of this!

(He advances toward Cory.)

CORY. What you gonna do . . . give me a whupping? You can't whup me no more. You're too old. You just an old man.

TROY *(shoves him on his shoulder)*. Nigger! That's what you are. You just another nigger on the street to me!

CORY. You crazy! You know that?

TROY. Go on now! You got the devil in you. Get on away from me!   1880

CORY. You just a crazy old man . . . talking about I got the devil in me.

TROY. Yeah, I'm crazy! If you don't get on the other side of that yard . . . I'm gonna show you how crazy I am! Go on . . . get the hell out of my yard.

CORY. It ain't your yard. You took Uncle Gabe's money he got from the army to buy this house and then you put him out.

TROY *(advances on Cory)*. Get your black ass out of my yard!

(Troy's advance backs Cory up against the tree. Cory grabs up the bat.)

CORY. I ain't going nowhere! Come on . . . put me out! I ain't scared of you.

TROY. That's my bat!   1890

CORY. Come on!

TROY. Put my bat down!

CORY. Come on, put me out.

(Cory swings at Troy, who backs across the yard.)

What's the matter? You so bad . . . put me out!

(Troy advances toward Cory.)

CORY *(backing up)*. Come on! Come on!

TROY. You're gonna have to use it! You wanna draw that bat back on me . . . you're gonna have to use it.

CORY. Come on! . . . Come on!

(*Cory swings the bat at Troy a second time. He misses. Troy continues to advance toward him.*)

TROY. You're gonna have to kill me! You wanna draw that bat back on me. You're gonna have to kill me.

(*Cory, backed up against the tree, can go no farther. Troy taunts him. He sticks out his head and offers him a target.*)

Come on! Come on!

(*Cory is unable to swing the bat. Troy grabs it.*)

TROY. Then I'll show you.

(*Cory and Troy struggle over the bat. The struggle is fierce and fully engaged. Troy ultimately is the stronger, and takes the bat from Cory and stands over him ready to swing. He stops himself.*)

Go on and get away from around my house.

(*Cory, stung by his defeat, picks himself up, walks slowly out of the yard and up the alley.*)

CORY. Tell Mama I'll be back for my things.

TROY. They'll be on the other side of that fence.

(*Cory exits.*)

TROY. I can't taste nothing. Helluljah! I can't taste nothing no more.
(*Troy assumes a batting posture and begins to taunt Death, the fastball in the outside corner.*) Come on! It's between you and me now! Come on! Anytime you want! Come on! I be ready for you . . . but I ain't gonna be easy.

(*The lights go down on the scene.*)

SCENE 5

The time is 1965. The lights come up in the yard. It is the morning of Troy's funeral. A funeral plaque with a light hangs beside the door. There is a small garden plot off to the side. There is noise and activity in the house as Rose, Lyons, and Bono have gathered. The door opens and Raynell, seven years old, enters dressed in a flannel nightgown. She crosses to the garden and pokes around with a stick. Rose calls from the house.

ROSE. Raynell!

RAYNELL. Mam?

ROSE. What you doing out there?

RAYNELL. Nothing.

(*Rose comes to the door.*)

ROSE. Girl, get in here and get dressed. What you doing?

RAYNELL. Seeing if my garden growed.

ROSE. I told you it ain't gonna grow overnight. You got to wait.

RAYNELL. It don't look like it never gonna grow. Dag!

ROSE. I told you a watched pot never boils. Get in here and get dressed.

RAYNELL. This ain't even no pot, Mama. 1920

ROSE. You just have to give it a chance. It'll grow. Now you come on and do what I told you. We got to be getting ready. This ain't no morning to be playing around. You hear me?

RAYNELL. Yes, mam.

(Rose exits into the house. Raynell continues to poke at her garden with a stick. Cory enters. He is dressed in a Marine corporal's uniform, and carries a duffel bag. His posture is that of a military man, and his speech has a clipped sternness.)

CORY *(to Raynell)*. Hi. *(Pause.)* I bet your name is Raynell.

RAYNELL. Uh huh.

CORY. Is your mama home?

(Raynell runs up on the porch and calls through the screen door.)

RAYNELL. Mama . . . there's some man out here. Mama?

(Rose comes to the door.)

ROSE. Cory? Lord have mercy! Look here, you all!

(Rose and Cory embrace in a tearful reunion as Bono and Lyons enter from the house dressed in funeral clothes.)

BONO. Aw, looka here . . . 1930

ROSE. Done got all grown up!

CORY. Don't cry, Mama. What you crying about?

ROSE. I'm just so glad you made it.

CORY. Hey Lyons. How you doing, Mr. Bono.

(Lyons goes to embrace Cory.)

LYONS. Look at you, man. Look at you. Don't he look good, Rose? Got them Corporal stripes.

ROSE. What took you so long?

CORY. You know how the Marines are, Mama. They got to get all their paperwork straight before they let you do anything.

ROSE. Well, I'm sure glad you made it. They let Lyons come. Your 1940 Uncle Gabe's still in the hospital. They don't know if they gonna let him out or not. I just talked to them a little while ago.

LYONS. A Corporal in the United States Marines.

BONO. Your daddy knew you had it in you. He used to tell me all the time.

LYONS. Don't he look good, Mr. Bono?

BONO. Yeah, he remind me of Troy when I first met him. *(Pause.)* Say, Rose, Lucille's down at the church with the choir. I'm gonna go down and get the pallbearers lined up. I'll be back to get you all.

ROSE. Thanks, Jim. 1950

CORY. See you, Mr. Bono.

LYONS (*with his arm around Raynell*). Cory . . . look at Raynell. Ain't she precious? She gonna break a whole lot of hearts.

ROSE. Raynell, come and say hello to your brother. This is your brother, Cory. You remember Cory.

RAYNELL. No, Mam.

CORY. She don't remember me, Mama.

ROSE. Well, we talk about you. She heard us talk about you. (*To Raynell*) This is your brother, Cory. Come on and say hello.

1960   RAYNELL. Hi.

CORY. Hi. So you're Raynell. Mama told me a lot about you.

ROSE. You all come on into the house and let me fix you some breakfast. Keep up your strength.

CORY. I ain't hungry, Mama.

LYONS. You can fix me something, Rose. I'll be in there in a minute.

ROSE. Cory, you sure you don't want nothing? I know they ain't feeding you right.

CORY. No, Mama . . . thanks. I don't feel like eating. I'll get something later.

1970   ROSE. Raynell . . . get on upstairs and get that dress on like I told you.

(*Rose and Raynell exit into the house.*)

LYONS. So . . . I hear you thinking about getting married.

CORY. Yeah, I done found the right one, Lyons. It's about time.

LYONS. Me and Bonnie been split up about four years now. About the time Papa retired. I guess she just got tired of all them changes I was putting her through. (*Pause.*) I always knew you was gonna make something out yourself. Your head was always in the right direction. So . . . you gonna stay in . . . make it a career . . . put in your twenty years?

CORY. I don't know. I got six already. I think that's enough.

1980   LYONS. Stick with Uncle Sam and retire early. Ain't nothing out here. I guess Rose told you what happened with me. They got me down the workhouse. I thought I was being slick cashing other people's checks.

CORY. How much time you doing?

LYONS. They give me three years. I got that beat now. I ain't got but nine more months. It ain't so bad. You learn to deal with it like anything else. You got to take the crookeds with the straights. That's what Papa used to say. He used to say that when he struck out. I seen him strike out three times in a row . . . and the next time

1990   up he hit the ball over the grandstand. Right out there in Homestead Field. He wasn't satisfied hitting in the seats . . . he want to hit it over everything! After the game he had two hundred people standing around waiting to shake his hand. You got to take the crookeds with the straights. Yeah, Papa was something else.

CORY. You still playing?

LYONS. Cory . . . you know I'm gonna do that. There's some fellows down there we got us a band . . . we gonna try and stay together when we get out . . . but yeah, I'm still playing. It still helps me to get out of bed in the morning. As long as it do that I'm gonna be right there playing and trying to make some sense out of it.

ROSE (*calling*). Lyons, I got these eggs in the pan.

LYONS. Let me go on and get these eggs, man. Get ready to go bury Papa. (*Pause.*) How you doing? You doing all right?

(*Cory nods. Lyons touches him on the shoulder and they share a moment of silent grief. Lyons exits into the house. Cory wanders about the yard. Raynell enters.*)

RAYNELL. Hi.

CORY. Hi.

RAYNELL. Did you used to sleep in my room?

CORY. Yeah . . . that used to be my room.

RAYNELL. That's what Papa call it. "Cory's room." It got your football in the closet.

(*Rose comes to the door.*)

ROSE. Raynell, get in there and get them good shoes on.

RAYNELL. Mama, can't I wear these? Them other one hurt my feet.

ROSE. Well, they just gonna have to hurt your feet for a while. You ain't said they hurt your feet when you went down to the store and got them.

RAYNELL. They didn't hurt then. My feet done got bigger.

ROSE. Don't you give me no backtalk now. You get in there and get them shoes on. (*Raynell exits into the house.*) Ain't too much changed. He still got that piece of rag tied to that tree. He was out here swinging that bat. I was just ready to go back in the house. He swung that bat and then he just fell over. Seem like he swung it and stood there with this grin on his face . . . and then he just fell over. They carried him on down to the hospital, but I knew there wasn't no need . . . why don't you come on in the house?

CORY. Mama . . I got something to tell you. I don't know how to tell you this . . . but I've got to tell you . . . I'm not going to Papa's funeral.

ROSE. Boy, hush your mouth. That's your daddy you talking about. I don't want hear that kind of talk this morning. I done raised you to come to this? You standing there all healthy and grown talking about you ain't going to your daddy's funeral?

CORY. Mama . . . listen . . .

ROSE. I don't want to hear it, Cory. You just get that thought out of your head.

CORY. I can't drag Papa with me everywhere I go. I've got to say no to him. One time in my life I've got to say no.

ROSE. Don't nobody have to listen to nothing like that. I know you
and your daddy ain't seen eye to eye, but I ain't got to listen to that
kind of talk this morning. Whatever was between you and your
daddy . . . the time has come to put it aside. Just take it and set it
over there on the shelf and forget about it. Disrespecting your daddy
ain't gonna make you a man, Cory. You got to find a way to come
to that on your own. Not going to your daddy's funeral ain't gonna
make you a man.
CORY. The whole time I was growing up . . . living in his house . . .
Papa was like a shadow that followed you everywhere. It weighed
on you and sunk into your flesh. It would wrap around you and lay
there until you couldn't tell which one was you anymore. That
shadow digging in your flesh. Trying to crawl in. Trying to live
through you. Everywhere I looked, Troy Maxson was staring back
at me . . . hiding under the bed . . . in the closet. I'm just saying I've
got to find a way to get rid of that shadow, Mama.
ROSE. You just like him. You got him in you good.
CORY. Don't tell me that, Mama.
ROSE. You Troy Maxson all over again.
CORY. I don't want to be Troy Maxson. I want to be me.
ROSE. You can't be nobody but who you are, Cory. That shadow
wasn't nothing but you growing into yourself. You either got to
grow into it or cut it down to fit you. But that's all you got to make
life with. That's all you got to measure yourself against that world
out there. Your daddy wanted you to be everything he wasn't . . .
and at the same time he tried to make you into everything he was. I
don't know if he was right or wrong . . . but I do know he meant to
do more good than he meant to do harm. He wasn't always right.
Sometimes when he touched he bruised. And sometimes when he
took me in his arms he cut.
   When I first met your daddy I thought . . . Here is a man I can
lay down with and make a baby. That's the first thing I thought
when I seen him. I was thirty years old and had done seen my share
of men. But when he walked up to me and said, "I can dance a
waltz that'll make you dizzy," I thought, Rose Lee, here is a man
that you can open yourself up to and be filled to bursting. Here is a
man that can fill all them empty spaces you been tipping around the
edges of. One of them empty spaces was being somebody's mother.
   I married your daddy and settled down to cooking his supper and
keeping clean sheets on the bed. When your daddy walked through
the house he was so big he filled it up. That was my first mistake.
Not to make him leave some room for me. For my part in the matter. But at that time I wanted that. I wanted a house that I could
sing in. And that's what your daddy gave me. I didn't know to keep
up his strength I had to give up little pieces of mine. I did that. I
took on his life as mine and mixed up the pieces so that you

couldn't hardly tell which was which anymore. It was my choice. It was my life and I didn't have to live it like that. But that's what life offered me in the way of being a woman and I took it. I grabbed hold of it with both hands.

By the time Raynell came into the house, me and your daddy had done lost touch with one another. I didn't want to make my blessing off of nobody's misfortune . . . but I took on to Raynell like she was all them babies I had wanted and never had. (*The phone rings.*) Like I'd been blessed to relive a part of my life. And 2090 if the Lord see fit to keep up my strength . . . I'm gonna do her just like your daddy did you . . . I'm gonna give her the best of what's in me.

RAYNELL (*entering, still with her old shoes*). Mama . . . Reverend Tollivier on the phone.

(*Rose exits into the house.*)

RAYNELL. Hi.
CORY. Hi.
RAYNELL. You in the Army or the Marines?
CORY. Marines.
RAYNELL. Papa said it was the Army. Did you know Blue?   2100
CORY. Blue? Who's Blue?
RAYNELL. Papa's dog what he sing about all the time.
CORY (*singing*).
    Hear it ring! Hear it ring!
    I had a dog his name was Blue
    You know Blue was mighty true
    You know Blue was a good old dog
    Blue treed a possum in a hollow log
    You know from that he was a good old dog.
    Hear it ring! Hear it ring!

(*Raynell joins in singing*)

CORY AND RAYNELL.
    Blue treed a possum out on a limb   2110
    Blue looked at me and I looked at him
    Grabbed that possum and put him in a sack
    Blue stayed there till I came back
    Old Blue's feets was big and round
    Never allowed a possum to touch the ground.

    Old Blue died and I dug his grave
    I dug his grave with a silver spade
    Let him down with a golden chain
    And every night I call his name
    Go on Blue, you good dog you   2120
    Go on Blue, you good dog you.

RAYNELL.
> Blue laid down and died like a man
> Blue laid down and died . . .

BOTH.
> Blue laid down and died like a man
> Now he's treeing possums in the Promised Land
> I'm gonna tell you this to let you know
> Blue's gone where the good dogs go
> When I hear old Blue bark
> When I hear old Blue bark
> Blue treed a possum in Noah's Ark
> Blue treed a possum in Noah's Ark

2130

(Rose comes to the screendoor.)

ROSE. Cory, we gonna be ready to go in a minute.

CORY *(to Raynell)*. You go on in the house and change them shoes like Mama told you so we can go to Papa's funeral.

RAYNELL. Okay, I'll be back.

(Raynell exits into the house. Cory gets up and crosses over to the tree. Rose stands in the screendoor watching him. Gabriel enters from the alley.)

GABRIEL *(calling)*. Hey, Rose!

ROSE. Gabe?

GABRIEL. I'm here, Rose. Hey Rose, I'm here!

(Rose enters from the house.)

ROSE. Lord . . . Look here, Lyons!

2140

LYONS. See, I told you, Rose . . . I told you they'd let him come.

CORY. How you doing, Uncle Gabe?

LYONS. How you doing, Uncle Gabe?

GABRIEL. Hey, Rose. It's time. It's time to tell St. Peter to open the gates. Troy, you ready? You ready, Troy. I'm gonna tell St. Peter to open the gates. You get ready now.

(Gabriel, with great fanfare, braces himself to blow. The trumpet is without a mouthpiece. He puts the end of it into his mouth and blows with great force, like a man who has been waiting some twenty-odd years for this single moment. No sound comes out of the trumpet. He braces himself and blows again with the same result. A third time he blows. There is a weight of impossible description that falls away and leaves him bare and exposed to a frightful realization. It is a trauma that a sane and normal mind would be unable to withstand. He begins to dance. A slow, strange dance, eerie and life-giving. A dance of atavistic signature and ritual. Lyons attempts to embrace him. Gabriel pushes Lyons away. He begins to howl in what is an attempt at song, or perhaps a song turning back

into itself in an attempt at speech. He finishes his dance and the
gates of heaven stand open as wide as God's closet.)

That's the way that go!

BLACKOUT

❑ Questions for Discussion

1. Why is Troy so bitter? What are some of the things he is bitter about?

2. In act 1, Troy says, "Death ain't nothing but a fastball on the outside corner." Explain what he means by this baseball imagery.

3. Explain what Troy means when he says, "What law is there I got to like you?" Do you agree with his answer?

4. Why does Troy sabotage Cory's chances to play football?

5. Why is Troy unfaithful to Rose? Why does his unfaithfulness upset her so much?

6. Troy sings a favorite song, "Old Blue," when he is drinking; and the whole family sings "Old Blue" at the end of the play. What is the significance of this song?

7. Why does Cory threaten Troy with a baseball bat? Why does Troy drive Cory, his own son, away from home?

❑ Suggestions for Exploration and Writing

1. Explain the symbolism of fences in this play. Why is Troy building a fence? Why does it take him so long to finish it?

2. Before his father drives him away from home, Cory says, "You ain't never gave me nothing! You ain't never done nothing but hold me back." What has Troy given Cory? What has he failed to give that Cory needs?

3. Lyons says of his father as the family prepares for Troy's funeral, "He wasn't satisfied hitting it in the seats . . . he want to hit it over everything!" How does this description of Troy apply to his life apart from baseball?

4. Troy says to Rose, "Woman . . . I do the best I can do. I come in here every Friday. I carry a sack of potatoes and a bucket of lard. You all line up at the door with your hands out. I give you the lint from my pockets. I give you my sweat and my blood." What is Troy's conception of a father and husband's responsibilities? What does he lack as father and husband? Why?

5. Troy tells Rose that at Alberta's house he can "laugh out loud." Beginning with this idea, contrast Troy's relationship with Rose to his relationship with Alberta.

HARVEY FIERSTEIN (1954–)

Born and raised in New York City, Harvey Fierstein has won awards as both playwright and actor. His Torch Song Trilogy *(1976–1979), winner of the Tony, Theatre World, and Drama Desk awards, was one of the first plays about homosexuality to receive critical acclaim.* On Tidy Endings *was first produced in New York City in 1987.*

On Tidy Endings

The curtain rises on a deserted, modern Upper West Side apartment. In the bright daylight that pours in through the windows we can see the living room of the apartment. Far Stage Right is the galley kitchen, next to it the multilocked front door with intercom. Stage Left reveals a hallway that leads to the two bedrooms and baths.

Though the room is still fully furnished (couch, coffee table, etc.), there are boxes stacked against the wall and several photographs and paintings are on the floor leaving shadows on the wall where they once hung. Obviously someone is moving out. From the way the boxes are neatly labeled and stacked, we know that this is an organized person.

From the hallway just outside the door we hear the rattling of keys and two arguing voices:.

JIM (*Offstage*). I've got to be home by four. I've got practice.

MARION (*Offstage*). I'll get you to practice, don't worry.

JIM (*Offstage*). I don't want to go in there.

MARION (*Offstage*). Jimmy, don't make Mommy crazy, alright? We'll go inside, I'll call Aunt Helen and see if you can go down and play with Robbie. (*The door opens. Marion is a handsome woman of forty. Dressed in a business suit, her hair conservatively combed, she appears to be going to a business meeting. Jim is a boy of eleven. His playclothes are typical, but someone has obviously just combed his hair. Marion recovers the key from the lock.*)

JIM. Why can't I just go down and ring the bell?

MARION. Because I said so.

(*As Marion steps into the room she is struck by some unexpected emotion. She freezes in her path and stares at the empty apartment. Jim lingers by the door.*)

JIM. I'm going downstairs.

10 MARION. Jimmy, please.

JIM. This place gives me the creeps.

MARION. This was your father's apartment. There's nothing creepy about it.

JIM. Says you.

MARION. You want to close the door, please?

(*Jim reluctantly obeys.*)

MARION. Now, why don't you go check your room and make sure you didn't leave anything.

JIM. It's empty.

MARION. Go look.

JIM. I looked last time.   20

MARION (*Trying to be patient*). Honey, we sold the apartment. We're never going to be here again. Go make sure you have everything you want.

JIM. But Uncle Arthur packed everything.

MARION (*Less patiently*). Go make sure.

JIM. There's nothing in there.

MARION (*Exploding*). I said make sure!

(*Jim jumps, then realizing that she's not kidding, obeys.*)

MARION. Everything's an argument with that one. (*She looks around the room and breathes deeply. There is sadness here. Under her breath:*) I can still smell you. (*Suddenly not wanting to be alone*) Jimmy? Are you okay?   30

JIM (*Returning*). Nothing. Told you so.

MARION. Uncle Arthur must have worked very hard.

JIM. What for? Robbie says (*Fey mannerisms*) "They love to clean up things!"

MARION. Sometimes you can be a real joy.

JIM. Did you call Aunt Helen?

MARION. Do I get a break here? (*Approaching the boy understandingly*) Wouldn't you like to say goodbye?

JIM. To who?

MARION. To the apartment. You and your daddy spent a lot of time   40
here together. Don't you want to take one last look around?

JIM. Ma, get a real life.

MARION. "Get a real life!" (*Going for the phone*) Nice. Very nice.

JIM. Could you call already?

MARION (*Dialing*). Jimmy, what does this look like I'm doing?

(*Jim kicks at the floor impatiently. Someone answers the phone at the other end*)

MARION (*Into the phone*). Helen? Hi, we're upstairs. . . . No, we just walked in the door. Jimmy wants to know if he can come down. . . . Oh, thanks.

(*Hearing that, Jim breaks for the door*)

MARION (*Yelling after him*). Don't run in the halls! And don't play
with the elevator buttons!

(The door slams shut behind him)

MARION (*Back to the phone*). Hi. . . . No, I'm okay. It's a little weird
being here. . . . No. Not since the funeral, and then there were so
many people. Jimmy told me to get "a real life." I don't think I
could handle anything realer. . . . No, please. Stay where you are.
I'm fine. The doorman said Arthur would be right back and my
lawyer should have been here already. . . . Well, we've got the papers to sign and a few other odds and ends to clean up. Shouldn't
take long.

(The intercom buzzer rings)

MARION. Hang on, that must be her. (*Marion goes to the intercom and
speaks*) Yes? . . . Thank you. (*Back to the phone*) Helen? Yeah, it's
the lawyer. I'd better go. . . . Well, I could use a stiff drink, but I
drove down. Listen, I'll stop by on my way out. Okay? Okay. 'Bye.

*(She hangs up the phone, looks around the room. That uncomfort-
able feeling returns to her quickly. She gets up and goes to the front
door, opens it and looks out. No one there yet. She closes the door,
shakes her head knowing that she's being silly and starts back into
the room. She looks around, can't make it and retreats to the door.
She opens it, looks out, closes it, but stays right there, her hand on
the doorknob. The bell rings. She throws open the door)*

MARION. That was quick.

*(June Lowell still has her finger on the bell. Her arms are loaded
with contracts. Marion's contemporary, June is less formal in appearance and more hyper in her manner)*

JUNE. *That* was quicker. What, were you waiting by the door?
MARION (*Embarrassed*). No. I was just passing it. Come on in.
JUNE. Have you got your notary seal?
MARION. I think so.
JUNE. Great. Then you can witness. I left mine at the office and thanks
to gentrification I'm double-parked downstairs. (*Looking for a place
to dump her load*) Where?
MARION (*Definitely pointing to the coffee table*). Anywhere. You mean
you're not staying?
JUNE. If you really think you need me I can go down and find a parking lot. I think there's one over on Columbus. So, I can go down,
park the car in the lot and take a cab back if you really think you
need me.
MARION. Well . . . ?
JUNE. But you shouldn't have any problems. The papers are about as
straightforward as papers get. Arthur is giving you power of attorney to sell the apartment and you're giving him a check for half the

purchase price. Everything else is just signing papers that state that you know that you signed the other papers. Anyway, he knows the deal, his lawyers have been over it all with him, it's just a matter of signatures.

MARION (*Not fine*). Oh, fine.

JUNE. Unless you just don't want to be alone with him . . . ?

MARION. With Arthur? Don't be silly.

JUNE (*Laying out the papers*). Then you'll handle it solo? Great. My car thanks you, the parking lot thanks you, and the cab driver that wouldn't have gotten a tip thanks you. Come have a quick look-see.   90

MARION (*Joining her on the couch*). There are a lot of papers here.

JUNE. Copies. Not to worry. Start here.

(*Marion starts to read*)

JUNE. I ran into Jimmy playing Elevator Operator.

(*Marion jumps*)

JUNE. I got him off at the sixth floor. Read on.

MARION. This is definitely not my day for dealing with him. (*June gets up and has a look around*)

JUNE. I don't believe what's happening to this neighborhood. You made quite an investment when you bought this place.

MARION. Collin was always very good at figuring out those things.

JUNE. Well, he sure figured this place right. What, have you tripled your money in ten years?   100

MARION. More.

JUNE. It's a shame to let it go.

MARION. We're not ready to be a two-dwelling family.

JUNE. So, sublet it again.

MARION. Arthur needs the money from the sale.

JUNE. Arthur got plenty already. I'm not crying for Arthur.

MARION. I don't hear you starting in again, do I?

JUNE. Your interests and your wishes are my only concern.

MARION. Fine.

JUNE. I still say we should contest Collin's will.   110

MARION. June . . . !

JUNE. You've got a child to support.

MARION. And a great job, and a husband with a great job. Tell me what Arthur's got.

JUNE. To my thinking, half of everything that should have gone to you. And more. All of Collin's personal effects, his record collection . . .

MARION. And I suppose their three years together meant nothing.

JUNE. When you compare them to your sixteen-year marriage? Not nothing, but not half of everything.

MARION (*Trying to change the subject*). June, who gets which copies?   120

JUNE. Two of each to Arthur. One you keep. The originals and everything else come back to me. (*Looking around*) I still say you should've sublet the apartment for a year and then sold it. You would've gotten an even better price. Who wants to buy a apartment when they know someone died in it. No one. And certainly no one wants to buy a apartment when they know the person died of AIDS.

MARION (*Snapping*). June. Enough!

JUNE (*Catching herself*). Sorry. That was out of line. Sometimes my
130   mouth does that to me. Hey, that's why I'm a lawyer. If my brain worked as fast as my mouth I would have gotten a real job.

MARION (*Holding out a stray paper*). What's this?

JUNE. I forgot. Arthur's lawyer sent that over yesterday. He found it in Collin's safety-deposit box. It's an insurance policy that came along with some consulting job he did in Japan. He either forgot about it when he made out his will or else he wanted you to get the full payment. Either way, it's yours.

MARION. Are you sure we don't split this?

JUNE. Positive.

140   MARION. But everything else . . . ?

JUNE. Hey, Arthur found it, his lawyer sent it to me. Relax, it's all yours. Minus my commission, of course. Go out and buy yourself something. Anything else before I have to use my cut to pay the towing bill?

MARION. I guess not.

JUNE (*Starting to leave*). Great. Call me when you get home. (*Stopping at the door and looking back*) Look, I know that I'm attacking this a little coldly. I am aware that someone you loved has just died. But there's a time and place for everything. This is about tidying up
150   loose ends, not holding hands. I hope you'll remember that when Arthur gets here. Call me.

(*And she's gone*)

(*Marion looks ill at ease to be alone again. She nervously straightens the papers into neat little piles, looks at them and then remembers:*)

MARION. Pens. We're going to need pens.

(*As a last chore to be done. She looks in her purse and finds only one. She goes to the kitchen and opens a drawer where she finds two more. She starts back to the table with them but suddenly remembers something else. She returns to the kitchen and begins going through the cabinets until she finds what she's looking for: a blue Art Deco teapot. Excited to find it, she takes it back to the couch. Guilt strikes. She stops, considers putting it back, wavers, then:*)

MARION (*To herself*). Oh, he won't care. One less thing to pack.

(*She takes the teapot and places it on the couch next to her purse. She is happier. Now she searches the room with her eyes for any other treasures she may have overlooked. Nothing here. She wanders off into the bedroom.*

We hear keys outside the front door. Arthur lets himself into the apartment carrying a load of empty cartons and a large shopping bag.

Arthur is in his mid-thirties, pleasant looking though sloppily dressed in work clothes and slightly overweight.

Arthur enters the apartment just as Marion comes out of the bedroom carrying a framed watercolor painting. They jump at the sight of each other.)

MARION. Oh, hi, Arthur. I didn't hear the door.

ARTHUR (*Staring at the painting*). Well hello, Marion.

MARION (*Guiltily*). I was going to ask you if you were thinking of taking this painting because if you're not going to then I'll take it. Unless, of course, you want it.

ARTHUR. No. You can have it.

MARION. I never really liked it, actually. I hate cats. I didn't even like the show. I needed something for my college dorm room. I was never the rock star poster type. I kept it in the back of a closet for years till Collin moved in here and took it. He said he liked it. 160

ARTHUR. I do too.

MARION. Well, then you keep it.

ARTHUR. No. Take it.

MARION. I've really got no room for it. You keep it.

ARTHUR. I don't want it.

MARION. Well, if you're sure.

ARTHUR (*Seeing the teapot*) You want the teapot? 170

MARION. If you don't mind.

ARTHUR. One less thing to pack.

MARION. Funny, but that's exactly what I thought. One less thing to pack. You know, my mother gave it to Collin and me when we moved in to our first apartment. Silly sentimental piece of junk, but you know.

ARTHUR. That's not the one.

MARION. Sure it is. Hall used to make them for Westinghouse back in the thirties. I see them all the time at antiques shows and I always wanted to buy another, but they ask such a fortune for them. 180

ARTHUR. We broke the one your mother gave you a couple of years ago. That's a reproduction. You can get them almost anywhere in the Village for eighteen bucks.

MARION. Really? I'll have to pick one up.

ARTHUR. Take this one. I'll get another.

MARION. No, it's yours. You bought it.

ARTHUR. One less thing to pack.

MARION. Don't be silly. I didn't come here to raid the place.

ARTHUR. Well, was there anything else of Collin's that you thought
190   you might like to have?

MARION. Now I feel so stupid, but actually I made a list. Not for me.
But I started thinking about different people; friends, relatives, you
know, that might want to have something of Collin's to remember
him by. I wasn't sure just what you were taking and what you were
throwing out. Anyway, I brought the list. (*Gets it from her purse*)
Of course these are only suggestions. You probably thought of a
few of these people yourself. But I figured it couldn't hurt to write
it all down. Like I said, I don't know what you are planning on
keeping.

200   ARTHUR (*Taking the list*). I was planning on keeping it all.

MARION. Oh, I know. But most of these things are silly. Like his high
school yearbooks. What would you want with them?

ARTHUR. Sure. I'm only interested in his Gay period.

MARION. I didn't mean it that way. Anyway, you look it over. They're
only suggestions. Whatever you decide to do is fine with me.

ARTHUR (*Folding the list*). It would have to be, wouldn't it. I mean, it's
all mine now. He did leave this all to me.

(*Marion is becoming increasingly nervous, but tries to keep a light
approach as she takes a small bundle of papers from her bag*)

MARION. While we're on the subject of what's yours. I brought a
bunch of condolence cards that were sent to you care of me. Rela-
210   tives mostly.

ARTHUR (*Taking them*). More cards? I'm going to have to have another printing of thank-you notes done.

MARION. I answered these last week, so you don't have to bother. Unless you want to.

ARTHUR. Forge my signature?

MARION. Of course not. They were addressed to both of us and they're
mostly distant relatives or friends we haven't seen in years. No one
important.

ARTHUR. If they've got my name on them, then I'll answer them
220   myself.

MARION. I wasn't telling you not to, I was only saying that you don't
have to.

ARTHUR. I understand.

(*Marion picks up the teapot and brings it to the kitchen*)

MARION. Let me put this back.

ARTHUR. I ran into Jimmy in the lobby.

MARION. Tell me you're joking.

ARTHUR. I got him to Helen's.

MARION. He's really racking up the points today.

ARTHUR. You know, he still can't look me in the face.

MARION. He's reacting to all of this in strange ways. Give him time. 230
He'll come around. He's really very fond of you.

ARTHUR. I know. But he's at that awkward age: under thirty. I'm sure
in twenty years we'll be the best of friends.

MARION. It's not what you think.

ARTHUR. What do you mean?

MARION. Well, you know.

ARTHUR. No I don't know. Tell me.

MARION. I thought that you were intimating something about his
blaming you for Collin's illness and I was just letting you know that
it's not true. (*Foot in mouth, she braves on*) We discussed it a lot 240
and . . . uh . . . he understands that his father was sick before you
two ever met.

ARTHUR. I don't believe this.

MARION. I'm just trying to say that he doesn't blame you.

ARTHUR. First of all, who asked you? Second of all, that's between him
and me. And third and most importantly, of course he blames me.
Marion, he's eleven years old. You can discuss all you want, but the
fact is that his father died of a "fag" disease and I'm the only fag
around to finger.

MARION. My son doesn't use that kind of language. 250

ARTHUR. Forget the language. I'm talking about what he's been
through. Can you imagine the kind of crap he's taken from his
friends? That poor kid's been chased and chastised from one end
of town to the other. He's got to have someone to blame just to
survive. He can't blame you, you're all he's got. He can't blame
his father; he's dead. So, Uncle Arthur gets the shaft. Fine, I can
handle it.

MARION. You are so wrong, Arthur. I know my son and that is not
the way his mind works.

ARTHUR. I don't know what you know. I only know what I know. 260
And all I know is what I hear and see. The snide remarks, the little
smirks . . . And it's not just the illness. He's been looking for a
scape goat since the day you and Collin first split up. Finally he has
one.

MARION (*Getting very angry now*). Wait. Are you saying that if he's
going to blame someone it should be me?

ARTHUR. I think you should try to see things from his point of view.

MARION. Where do you get off thinking you're privy to my son's point
of view?

ARTHUR. It's not that hard to imagine. Life's rolling right along, he's 270
having a happy little childhood, when suddenly one day his father's
moving out. No explanations, no reasons, none of the fights that
usually accompany such things. Divorce is hard enough for a kid to
understand when he's listened to years of battles, but yours?

MARION. So what should we have done? Faked a few months' worth of fights before Collin moved out?

ARTHUR. You could have told him the truth plain and simple.

MARION. He was seven years old at the time. How the hell do you tell a seven-year-old that his father is leaving his mother to go sleep with other men?

280

ARTHUR. Well, not like that.

MARION. You know, Arthur, I'm going to say this as nicely as I can: Butt out. You're not his mother and you're not his father.

ARTHUR. Thank you. I wasn't acutely aware of that fact. I will certainly keep that in mind from now on.

MARION. There's only so much information a child that age can handle.

ARTHUR. So it's best that he reach his capacity on the street.

MARION. He knew about the two of you. We talked about it.

290

ARTHUR. Believe me, he knew before you talked about it. He's young, not stupid.

MARION. It's very easy for you to stand here and criticize, but there are aspects that you will just never be able to understand. You weren't there. You have no idea what it was like for me. You're talking to someone who thought that a girl went to college to meet a husband. I went to protest rallies because I liked the music. I bought a guitar because I thought it looked good on the bed! This lifestyle, this knowledge that you take for granted, was all a little out of left field for me.

300

ARTHUR. I can imagine.

MARION. No, I don't think you can. I met Collin in college, married him right after graduation and settled down for a nice quiet life of Kids and Careers. You think I had any idea about this? Talk about life's little surprises. You live with someone for sixteen years, you share your life, your bed, you have a child together, and then you wake up one day and he tells you that to him it's all been a lie. A lie. Try that on for size. Here you are the happiest couple you know, fulfilling your every life fantasy and he tells you he's living a lie.

310

ARTHUR. I'm sure he never said that.

MARION. Don't be so sure. There was a lot of new ground being broken back then and plenty of it was muddy.

ARTHUR. You know that he loved you.

MARION. What's that supposed to do, make things easier? It doesn't. I was brought up to believe, among other things, that if you had love that was enough. So what if I wasn't everything he wanted. Maybe he wasn't exactly everything I wanted either. So, you know what? You count your blessings and you settle.

ARTHUR. No one has to settle. Not him. Not you.

MARION. Of course not. You can say, "Up yours!" to everything and 320
everyone who depends and needs you, and go off to make yourself
happy.

ARTHUR. It's not that simple.

MARION. No. This is simpler. Death is simpler. (*Yelling, out*) Happy
now?

(*They stare at each other. Marion calms the rage and catches her
breath. Arthur holds his emotions in check*)

ARTHUR. How about a nice hot cup of coffee? Tea with lemon? Hot
cocoa with a marshmallow floating in it?

MARION (*laughs*). I was wrong. You *are* a mother.

(*Arthur goes into the kitchen and starts preparing things. Marion
loafs by the doorway.*)

MARION. I lied before. He *was* everything I ever wanted.

(*Arthur stops, looks at her, and then changes the subject as he goes
on with his work.*)

ARTHUR. When I came into the building and saw Jimmy in the lobby I 330
absolutely freaked for a second. It's amazing how much they look
alike. It was like seeing a little miniature Collin standing there.

MARION. I know. He's like Collin's clone. There's nothing of me in him.

ARTHUR. I always kinda hoped that when he grew up he'd take after
me. Not much chance, I guess.

MARION. Don't do anything fancy in there.

ARTHUR. Please. Anything we can consume is one less thing to pack.

MARION. So you've said.

ARTHUR. So *we've* said.

MARION. I want to keep seeing you and I want you to see Jim. You're 340
still part of this family. No one's looking to cut you out.

ARTHUR. Ah, who'd want a kid to grow up looking like me anyway. I
had enough trouble looking like this. Why pass on the misery?

MARION. You're adorable.

ARTHUR. Is that like saying I have a good personality?

MARION. I think you are one of the most naturally handsome men I
know.

ARTHUR. Natural is right, and the bloom is fading.

MARION. All you need is a few good nights' sleep to kill those rings
under your eyes. 350

ARTHUR. Forget the rings under my eyes, (*Grabbing his middle*) . . .
how about the rings around my moon?

MARION. I like you like this.

ARTHUR. From the time that Collin started using the wheelchair until
he died, about six months, I lost twenty-three pounds. No gym, no
diet. In the last seven weeks I've gained close to fifty.

MARION. You're exaggerating.

ARTHUR. I'd prove it on the bathroom scale, but I sold it in working order.

360 MARION. You'd never know.

ARTHUR. Marion, *you'd* never know, but ask my belt. Ask my pants. Ask my underwear. Even my stretch socks have stretch marks. I called the ambulance at five A.M., he was gone at nine and by nine-thirty, I was on a first-name basis with Sara Lee. I can quote the business hours of every ice-cream parlor, pizzeria and bakery on the island of Manhattan. I know the location of every twenty-four-hour grocery in the greater New York area, and I have memorized the phone numbers of every Mandarin, Szechuan and Hunan restaurant with free delivery.

370 MARION. At least you haven't wasted your time on useless hobbies.

ARTHUR. Are you kidding? I'm opening my own Overeater's Hotline. We'll have to start small, but expansion is guaranteed.

MARION. You're the best, you know that? If I couldn't be everything that Collin wanted then I'm grateful that he found someone like you.

ARTHUR (*Turning on her without missing a beat*). Keep your god-damned gratitude to yourself. I didn't go through any of this for you. So your thanks are out of line. And he didn't find "someone like" me. It was me.

380 MARION (*Frightened*). I didn't mean . . .

ARTHUR. And I wish you'd remember one thing more: He died in my arms, not yours.

(*Marion is totally caught off guard. She stares disbelieving, open-mouthed. Arthur walks past her as he leaves the kitchen with place mats. He puts them on the coffee table. As he arranges the papers, and place mats, he speaks, never looking at her.*)

ARTHUR. Look, I know you were trying to say something supportive. Don't waste your breath. There's nothing you can say that will make any of this easier for me. There's no way for you to help me get through this. And that's your fault. After three years you still have no idea or understanding of who I am. Or maybe you do know but refuse to accept it. I don't know and I don't care. But at least understand, from my point of view, who you are: You are my

390 husband's *ex*-wife. If you like, the mother of *my* stepson. Don't flatter yourself into thinking you were any more than that. And whatever you are, you're certainly not my friend.

(*He stops, looks up at her, then passes her again as he goes back to the kitchen. Marion is shaken, working hard to control herself. She moves toward the couch.*)

MARION. Why don't we just sign these papers and I'll be out of your way.

ARTHUR. Shouldn't you say *I'll* be out of *your* way? After all, I'm not just signing papers. I'm signing away my home.

MARION (*Resolved not to fight, she gets her purse*). I'll leave the papers here. Please have them notarized and returned to my lawyer.

ARTHUR. Don't forget my painting.

MARION (*Exploding*). What do you want from me, Arthur?　　　　400

ARTHUR (*Yelling back*). I want you the hell out of my apartment! I want you out of my life! And I want you to leave Collin alone!

MARION. The man's dead. I don't know how much more alone I can leave him.

(Arthur laughs at the irony, but behind the laughter is something much more desperate.)

ARTHUR. Lots more, Marion. You've got to let him go.

MARION. For the life of me, I don't know what I did or what you think I did, for you to treat me like this. But you're not going to get away with it. You will not take your anger out on me. I will not stand here and be badgered and insulted by you. I know you've been hurt and I know you're hurting but you're not the only one　　410 who lost someone here.

ARTHUR (*Topping her*). Yes I am! You didn't just lose him. I did! You lost him five years ago when he divorced you. This is not your moment of grief and loss, it's mine! (*Picking up the bundle of cards and throwing it toward her*) These condolences do not belong to you, they're mine. (*Tossing her list back to her*) His things are not yours to give away, they're mine! This death does not belong to you, it's mine! Bought and paid for outright. I suffered for it, I bled for it.

I was the one who cooked his meals. I was the one who spoon-fed them. I pushed his wheelchair. I carried and bathed him. I wiped　　420 his backside and changed his diapers. I breathed life into and wrestled fear out of his heart. I kept him alive for two years longer than any doctor thought possible and when it was time I was the one who prepared him for death.

I paid in full for my place in his life and I will *not* share it with you. We are not the two widows of Collin Redding. Your life was not here. Your husband didn't just die. You've got a son and a life somewhere else. Your husband's sitting, waiting for you at home, wondering, as I am, what the hell you're doing here and why you　　430 can't let go.

(Marion leans back against the couch. She's blown away. Arthur stands staring at her)

ARTHUR (*Quietly*). Let him go, Marion. He's mine. Dead or alive; mine.

(The teakettle whistles. Arthur leaves the room, goes to the kitchen and pours the water as Marion pulls herself together. Arthur carries

the loaded tray back into the living room and sets it down on the coffee table. He sits and pours a cup)

ARTHUR. One marshmallow or two?

(Marion stares, unsure as to whether the attack is really over or not)

ARTHUR *(Placing them in her cup)*. Take three, they're small.

(Marion smiles and takes the offered cup)

ARTHUR *(Campily)*. Now let me tell you how I *really* feel.

(Marion jumps slightly, then they share a small laugh. Silence as they each gather themselves and sip their refreshments)

MARION *(Calmly)*. Do you think that I sold the apartment just to throw you out?

ARTHUR. I don't care about the apartment . . .

MARION. . . . Because I really didn't. Believe me.

440   ARTHUR. I know.

MARION. I knew the expenses here were too much for you, and I knew you couldn't afford to buy out my half . . . I figured if we sold it, that you'd at least have a nice chunk of money to start over with.

ARTHUR. You could've given me a little more time.

MARION. Maybe. But I thought the sooner you were out of here, the sooner you could go on with your life.

ARTHUR. Or the sooner you could to on with yours.

MARION. Maybe. *(Pause to gather her thoughts)* Anyway, I'm not go-
450   ing to tell you that I have no idea what you're talking about. I'd have to be worse than deaf and blind not to have seen the way you've been treated. Or mistreated. When I read Collin's obituary in the newspaper and saw my name and Jimmy's name and no mention of you . . . *(Shakes her head, not knowing what to say)* You know that his secretary was the one who wrote that up and sent it in. Not me. But I should have done something about it and I didn't. I know.

ARTHUR. Wouldn't have made a difference. I wrote my own obituary for him and sent it to the smaller papers. They edited me out.

MARION. I'm sorry. I remember, at the funeral, I was surrounded by
460   all of Collin's family and business associates while you were left with your friends. I knew it was wrong. I knew I should have said something but it felt good to have them around me and you looked like you were holding up . . . Wrong. But saying that it's all my fault for not letting go . . . ? There were other people involved.

ARTHUR. Who took their cue from you.

MARION. Arthur, you don't understand. Most people that we knew as a couple had no idea that Collin was gay right up to his death. And even those that did know only found out when he got sick and the word leaked out that it was AIDS. I don't think I have to tell you
470   how stupid and ill-informed most people are about homosexuality. And AIDS . . . ? The kinds of insane behavior that word inspires . . .?

Those people at the funeral, how many times did they call to see how he was doing over these years? How many of them ever went to see him in the hospital? Did any of them even come here? So, why would you expect them to act any differently after his death?

So, maybe that helps to explain their behavior, but what about mine, right? Well, maybe there is no explanation. Only excuses. And excuse number one is that you're right, I have never really let go of him. And I am jealous of you. Hell, I was jealous of anyone that Collin ever talked to, let alone slept with . . . let alone loved.

The first year, after he moved out, we talked all the time about the different men he was seeing. And I always listened and advised. It was kind of fun. It kept us close. It kept me a part of his intimate life. And the bottom line was always that he wasn't happy with the men he was meeting. So, I was always allowed to hang on to the hope that one day he'd give it all up and come home. Then he got sick.

He called me, told me he was in the hospital and asked if I'd come see him. I ran. When I got to his door there was a sign, IN-STRUCTIONS FOR VISITORS OF AN AIDS PATIENT. I nearly died.

ARTHUR. He hadn't told you?

MARION. No. And believe me, a sign is not the way to find these things out. I was so angry . . . And he was so sick . . . I was sure that he'd die right then. If not from the illness then from the hospital staff's neglect. No one wanted to go near him and I didn't bother fighting with them because I understood that they were scared. I was scared. That whole month in the hospital I didn't let Jimmy visit him once.

You learn.

Well, as you know, he didn't die. And he asked if he could come stay with me until he was well. And I said yes. Of course, yes. Now, here's something I never thought I'd ever admit to anyone: had he asked to stay with me for a few weeks I would have said no. But he asked to stay with me until he was well and knowing there was no cure I said yes. In my craziness I said yes because to me that meant forever. That he was coming back to me forever. Not that I wanted him to die, but I assumed from everything I'd read . . . And we'd be back together for whatever time he had left. Can you understand that?

(Arthur nods.)

MARION *(Gathers her thoughts again)*. Two weeks later he left. He moved in here. Into this apartment that we had bought as an invest-ment. Never to live in. Certainly never to live apart in. Next thing I knew, the name Arthur starts appearing in every phone call, every dinner conversation.

"Did you see the doctor?"

"Yes. Arthur made sure I kept the appointment."

"Are you going to your folks for Thanksgiving?"

"No. Arthur and I are having some friends over."

I don't know which one of us was more of a coward, he for not telling or me for not asking about you. But eventually you became a given. Then, of course, we met and became what I had always thought of as friends.

(Arthur winces in guilt)

MARION. I don't care what you say, how could we not be friends with someone so great in common: love for one of the most special human beings there ever was. And don't try and tell me there weren't times when you enjoyed me being around as an ally. I can think of a dozen occasions when we ganged up on him, teasing him with our intimate knowledge of his personal habits.

(Arthur has to laugh)

MARION. Blanket stealing? Snoring? Excess gas, no less? *(Takes a moment to enjoy this truce)* I don't think that my loving him threatened your relationship. Maybe I'm not being truthful with myself. But I don't. I never tried to step between you. Not that I ever had the opportunity. Talk about being joined at the hip! And that's not to say I wasn't jealous. I was. Terribly. Hatefully. But always lovingly. I was happy for Collin because there was no way to deny that he was happy. With everything he was facing, he was happy. Love did that. You did that.

He lit up with you. He came to life. I envied that and all the time you spent together, but more, I watched you care for him (sometimes *overcare* for him), and I was in awe. I could never have done what you did. I never would have survived. I really don't know how you did.

ARTHUR. Who said I survived?

MARION. Don't tease. You did an absolutely incredible thing. It's not as if you met him before he got sick. You entered a relationship that you knew in all probability would end this way and you never wavered.

ARTHUR. Of course I did. Don't have me sainted, Marion. But sometimes you have no choice. Believe me, if I could've gotten away from him I would've. But I was a prisoner of love.

(He makes a campy gesture and pose)

MARION. Stop.

ARTHUR. And there were lots of pluses. I got to quit a job I hated, stay home all day and watch game shows. I met a lot of doctors and learned a lot of big words. *(Arthur jumps up and goes to the pile of boxes where he extracts one and brings it back to the couch.)*

And then there was all the exciting traveling I got to do. This box has a souvenir from each one of our trips. Wanna see? *(Marion nods. He opens the box and pulls things out one by one. Holding up an old bottle)*

This is from the house we rented in Reno when we went to clear out his lungs. (*Holding handmade potholders)*

This is from the hospital in Reno. Collin made them. They had a great arts and crafts program. (*Copper bracelets)* 560

These are from a faith healer in Philly. They don't do much for fever, but they look great with a green sweater. (*Glass ashtrays)*

These are from our first visit to the clinic in France. Such lovely people. (*A Bible)*

This is from our second visit to the clinic in France. (*A lead necklace)*

A Voodoo doctor in New Orleans. Next time we'll have to get there earlier in the year. I think he sold all the pretty ones at Mardi Gras. (*A tiny piñata)*

Then there was Mexico. Black market drugs and empty wallets. (*Now pulling things out at random)*

L.A., San Francisco, Houston, Boston . . . We traveled everywhere 570
they offered hope for sale and came home with souvenirs. (*Arthur quietly pulls a few more things out and then begins to put them all back into the box slowly. Softly as he works:)* Marion, I would have done anything, traveled anywhere to avoid . . . or delay . . . Not just because I loved him so desperately, but when you've lived the way we did for three years . . . the battle becomes your life. (*He looks at her and then away)* His last few hours were beyond any scenario I had imagined. He hadn't walked in nearly six months. He was totally incontinent. If he spoke two words in a week I was thankful. Days went by without his eyes ever focusing on me. He just stared out at I don't know what. Not the meals as I fed him. Not the TV 580
I played constantly for company. Just out. Or maybe in.

It was the middle of the night when I heard his breathing become labored. His lungs were filling with fluid again. I knew the sound. I'd heard it a hundred times before. So, I called the ambulance and got him to the hospital.

They hooked him up to the machines, the oxygen, shot him with morphine and told me that they would do what they could to keep him alive.

But, Marion, it wasn't the machines that kept him breathing. He 590
did it himself. It was that incredible will and strength inside him. Whether it came from his love of life or fear of death, who knows. But he'd been counted out a hundred times and a hundred times he fought his way back.

I got a magazine to read him, pulled a chair up to the side of his bed and holding his hand, I wondered whether I should call Helen to let the cleaning lady in or if he'd fall asleep and I could sneak home for an hour. I looked up from the page and he was looking at me. Really looking right into my eyes. I patted his cheek and said, "Don't worry, honey, you're going to be fine."

600　　　But there was something else in his eyes. He wasn't satisfied with that. And I don't know why, I have no idea where it came from, I just heard the words coming out of my mouth, "Collin, do you want to die?"

His eyes filled and closed, he nodded his head.

I can't tell you what I was thinking, I'm not sure I was. I slipped off my shoes, lifted his blanket and climbed into bed next to him. I helped him to put his arms around me, and mine around him, and whispered as gently as I could into his ear, "It's alright to let go now. It's time to go on." And he did.

610　　　Marion, you've got your life and your son. All I have is an intangible place in a man's history. Leave me that. Respect that.

MARION. I understand.

(Arthur suddenly comes to life, running to get the shopping bag that he'd left at the front door)

ARTHUR. Jeez! With all the screamin' and sad storytelling I forgot something. *(He extracts a bouquet of flowers from the bag)* I brung you flowers and everything.

MARION. You brought me flowers?

ARTHUR. Well, I knew you'd never think to bring me flowers and I felt that on an occasion such as this somebody oughta get flowers from somebody.

620　　MARION. You know, Arthur, you're really making me feel like a worthless piece of garbage.

ARTHUR. So what else is new? *(He presents the flowers)* Just promise me one thing. Don't press one in a book. Just stick them in a vase and when they fade just throw them out. No more memorabilia.

MARION. Arthur, I want to do something for you and I don't know what. Tell me what you want.

ARTHUR. I want little things. Not much. I want to be remembered. If you get a Christmas card from Collin's mother make sure she sent me one too. If his friends call to see how you are, ask if they've

630　　called me. Have me to dinner so I can see Jimmy. Let me take him out now and then. Invite me to his wedding. *(They both laugh)*

MARION. You've got it.

ARTHUR *(Clearing the table)*. Let me get all this cold cocoa out of the way. You still have the deed to do.

MARION *(Checking her watch)*. And I've got to get Jimmy home in time for practice.

ARTHUR. Band practice?

MARION. Baseball. *(Picking her list off the floor)* About this list, you do what you want.

640　　ARTHUR. Believe me, I will. But I promise to consider your suggestions. Just don't rush me. I'm not ready to give it all away. *(Arthur is off to the kitchen with his tray and the phone rings. He answers in the kitchen)* "Hello? . . . Just a minute. (*Calling out*) It's your eager Little Leaguer.

(Marion picks up the living room extension and Arthur hangs his up)

MARION (*Into phone*). Hello, honey . . . I'll be down in five minutes. No. You know what? You come up here and get me. . . . No, I said you should come up here. . . . I said I want you to come up here. . . . Because I said so. . . . Thank you. (*She hangs up the receiver*)

ARTHUR (*Rushing to the papers*). Alright, where do we start on these?

MARION (*Getting out her seal*). I guess you should just start signing everything and I'll stamp along with you. Keep one of everything on the side for you.   650

ARTHUR. Now I feel so rushed. What am I signing?

MARION. You want to do this another time?

ARTHUR. No. Let's get it over with. I wouldn't survive another session like this.

(He starts to sign and she starts her job)

MARION. I keep meaning to ask you; how are you?

ARTHUR (*At first puzzled and then:*) Oh, you mean my health? Fine. No. I'm fine. I've been tested, and nothing. We were very careful. We took many precautions. Collin used to make jokes about how we should invest in rubber futures.   660

MARION. I'll bet.

ARTHUR (*Stops what he's doing*). It never occurred to me until now. How about you?

MARION (*Not stopping*). Well, we never had sex after he got sick.

ARTHUR. But before?

MARION (*Stopping but not looking up*). I have the antibodies in my blood. No signs that it will ever develop into anything else. And it's been five years so my chances are pretty good that I'm just a carrier.

ARTHUR. I'm so sorry. Collin never told me.

MARION. He didn't know. In fact, other than my husband and the doctors, you're the only one I've told.   670

ARTHUR. You and your husband . . . ?

MARION. Have invested in rubber futures. There'd only be a problem if we wanted to have a child. Which we do. But we'll wait. Miracles happen every day.

ARTHUR. I don't know what to say.

MARION. Tell me you'll be there if I ever need you.

(Arthur gets up, goes to her and puts his arm around her. They hold each other. He gently pushes her away to make a joke.)

ARTHUR. Sure! Take something else that should have been mine.

MARION. Don't even joke about things like that.

(The doorbell rings. They pull themselves together)

ARTHUR. You know we'll never get these done today.   680

MARION. So, tomorrow.

(*Arthur goes to open the door as Marion gathers her things. He opens the doors and Jimmy is standing in the hall*)

JIM. C'mon, Ma. I'm gonna be late.

ARTHUR. Would you like to come inside?

JIM. We've gotta go.

MARION. Jimmy, come on.

JIM. Ma!

(*She glares. He comes in. Arthur closes the door*)

MARION (*Holding out the flowers*). Take these for Mommy.

JIM (*Taking them*). Can we go?

MARION (*Picking up the painting*). Say good-bye to your Uncle Arthur.

690   JIM. 'Bye, Arthur. Come on.

MARION. Give him a kiss.

ARTHUR. Marion don't.

MARION. Give your uncle a kiss good-bye.

JIM. He's not my uncle.

MARION. No. He's a hell of a lot more than your uncle.

ARTHUR (*Offering his hand*). A handshake will do.

MARION. Tell Uncle Arthur what your daddy told you.

JIM. About what?

MARION. Stop playing dumb. You know.

700   ARTHUR. Don't embarrass him.

MARION. Jimmy, please.

JIM (*He regards his mother's softer tone and then speaks*). He said that after me and Mommy he loved you the most.

MARION (*Standing behind him*). Go on.

JIM. And that I should love you too. And make sure that you're not lonely or very sad.

ARTHUR. Thank you.

(*Arthur reaches down to the boy and they hug. Jim gives him a little peck on the cheek and then breaks away*)

MARION (*Going to open the door*). Alright, kid, you done good. Now let's blow this joint before you muck it up.

(*Jim rushes out the door. Marion turns to Arthur*)

710   MARION. A child's kiss is magic. Why else would they be so stingy with them. I'll call you.

(*Arthur nods understanding. Marion pulls the door closed behind her. Arthur stands quietly as the lights fade to black*)

THE END

Note: If being performed on film, the final image should be of Arthur leaning his back against the closed door on the inside of the apartment and Marion leaning on the outside of the door. A moment of thought and then they both move on.

❏ Questions for Discussion

1. What are the advantages of setting the play in Collin and Arthur's empty apartment?

2. In what ways were Marion's expectations for her marriage realistic or unrealistic?

3. Marion and Arthur feel anger and jealousy toward one another. Who is the more angry? Why?

4. Explain the **irony** of Marion's revelation about the state of her health at the conclusion of the play.

5. Arthur began his relationship with Collin knowing that Collin already had AIDS. What does Arthur's willingness to begin such a risky relationship suggest about him?

6. What about Collin's death has been hardest for Arthur? How does the play help you to sympathize with him?

7. What are the dramatic and thematic functions of the minor characters June and Jim?

8. In what ways does Collin's leaving home affect his family?

❏ Suggestions for Exploration and Writing

1. What is the effect of the comedy in the play? To what degree does the comedy enhance or detract from the seriousness of AIDS and the dignity of its sufferers? Some politicians have denounced gays as a threat to the family. In what ways does this play foster that view? What positive family values does the play uphold?

2. Write an essay from Jimmy's point of view, describing what you believe would be the reactions of an eleven-year-old boy to the changes in his life.

CASEBOOK
on James Baldwin

JAMES BALDWIN (1924–1987)

James Baldwin knew firsthand the rigors of poverty in Harlem, for he grew up there along with eight half-brothers and sisters. His mother worked as a domestic; his stepfather, a laborer and part-time preacher, seemed to resent his small, unattractive stepson. Thus Baldwin learned early the importance of family and the need for love, both themes which appear in "Sonny's Blues" and in his other works. Baldwin's novels, essays, and stories reveal both his talent as a writer and his intolerance of bigotry. To escape American racial prejudice, he spent much of his life in France. His most famous novels are Go Tell It on the Mountain *(1953) and* Giovanni's Room *(1956). Baldwin's essays collected in* Notes of a Native Son *(1955),* Nobody Knows My Name *(1961), and* The Fire Next Time *(1963) strongly influenced his contemporaries.*

Sonny's Blues

1   I heard about it in the paper, in the subway, on my way to work. I read it, and I couldn't believe it, and I read it again. Then perhaps I just stared at it, at the newsprint spelling out his name, spelling out the story. I stared at it in the swinging lights of the subway car, and in the faces and bodies of the people, and in my own face, trapped in the darkness which roared outside.

2   It was not to be believed and I kept telling myself that, as I walked from the subway station to the high school. And at the same time I couldn't doubt it. I was scared, scared for Sonny. He became real to me again. A great block of ice got settled in my belly and kept melting there slowly all day long, while I taught my classes algebra. It was a special kind of ice. It kept melting, sending trickles of ice water all up and down my veins, but it never got less. Sometimes it hardened and seemed to expand until I felt my guts were going to come spilling out or that I was going to choke or scream. This would always be at a moment when I was remembering some specific thing Sonny had done said or done.

3   When he was about as old as the boys in my classes his face had been bright and open, there was a lot of copper in it; and he'd had wonderfully direct brown eyes, and great gentleness and privacy. I wondered what he looked like now. He had been picked up, the evening before, in a raid on an apartment downtown, for peddling and using heroin.

4   I couldn't believe it: but what I mean by that is that I couldn't find any room for it anywhere inside me. I had kept it outside me for a long time.

I hadn't wanted to know. I had had suspicions, but I didn't name them, I kept putting them away. I told myself that Sonny was wild, but he wasn't crazy. And he'd always been a good boy, he hadn't ever turned hard or evil or disrespectful, the way kids can, so quick, so quick, especially in Harlem, I didn't want to believe that I'd ever see my brother going down, coming to nothing, all that light in his face gone out, in the condition I'd already seen so many others. Yet it had happened and here I was, talking about algebra to a lot of boys who might, every one of them for all I knew, be popping off needles every time they went to the head. Maybe it did more for them than algebra could.

I was sure that the first time Sonny had ever had horse, he couldn't $\quad$ 5 have been much older than these boys were now. These boys, now, were living as we'd been living then, they were growing up with a rush and their heads bumped abruptly against the low ceiling of their actual possibilities. They were filled with rage. All they really knew were two darknesses, the darkness of their lives, which was now closing in on them and the darkness of the movies, which had blinded them to that other darkness, and in which they now, vindictively, dreamed, at once more together than they were at any other time, and more alone.

When the last bell rang, the class ended, I let out my breath. It seemed $\quad$ 6 I'd been holding it for all that time. My clothes were wet—I may have looked as though I'd been sitting in a steam bath, all dressed up, all afternoon. I sat alone in the classroom a long time. I listened to the boys outside, downstairs, shouting and cursing and laughing. Their laughter struck me for perhaps the first time. It was not the joyous laughter which—God knows why—one associates with children. It was mocking and insular, its intent was to denigrate. It was disenchanted, and in this, also, lay the authority of their curses. Perhaps I was listening to them because I was thinking about my brother and in them I heard my brother. And myself.

One boy was whistling a tune, at once very complicated and very $\quad$ 7 simple, it seemed to be pouring out of him as though he were a bird, and it sounded very cool and moving through all that harsh, bright air, only just holding its own through all those other sounds.

I stood up and walked over to the window and looked down into the $\quad$ 8 courtyard. It was the beginning of the spring and the sap was rising in the boys. A teacher passed through them every now and again, quickly, as though he or she couldn't wait to get out of that courtyard, to get those boys out of their sight and off their minds. I started collecting my stuff. I thought I'd better get home and talk to Isabel.

The courtyard was almost deserted by the time I got downstairs. I saw $\quad$ 9 this boy standing in the shadow of a doorway, looking just like Sonny. I almost called his name. Then I saw that it wasn't Sonny, but somebody we used to know, a boy from around our block. He'd been Sonny's friend. He'd never been mine, having been too young for me, and anyway, I'd never liked him. And now, even though he was a grown-up man, he still hung around that block, still spent hours on the street corners, was always high and raggy. I used to run into him from time to time and he'd often work around to asking me for a quarter or fifty cents. He always had some real good excuse, too, and I always gave it to him. I don't know why.

10   But now, abruptly, I hated him. I couldn't stand the way he looked at me, partly like a dog, partly like a cunning child. I wanted to ask him what the hell he was doing in the school courtyard.

11   He sort of shuffled over to me, and he said, "I see you got the papers. So you already know about it."

12   "You mean about Sonny? Yes, I already know about it. How come they didn't get you?"

13   He grinned. It made him repulsive and it also brought to mind what he'd looked like as a kid. "I wasn't there. I stay away from them people."

14   "Good for you." I offered him a cigarette and I watched him through the smoke. "You come all the way down here just to tell me about Sonny?"

15   "That's right." He was sort of shaking his head and his eyes looked strange, as though they were about to cross. The bright sun deadened his damp dark brown skin and it made his eyes look yellow and showed up the dirt in his kinked hair. He smelled funky. I moved a little away from him and I said, "Well, thanks. But I already know about it and I got to get home."

16   "I'll walk you a little ways," he said. We started walking. There were a couple of kids still loitering in the courtyard and one of them said goodnight to me and looked strangely at the boy beside me.

17   "What're you going to do?" he asked me. "I mean, about Sonny?"

18   "Look. I haven't seen Sonny for over a year, I'm not sure I'm going to do anything. Anyway, what the hell *can* I do?"

19   "That's right," he said quickly, "ain't nothing you can do. Can't much help old Sonny no more, I guess."

20   It was what I was thinking and so it seemed to me he had no right to say it.

21   "I'm surprised at Sonny, though," he went on—he had a funny way of talking, he looked straight ahead as though he were talking to himself— "I thought Sonny was a smart boy, I thought he was too smart to get hung."

22   "I guess he thought so too," I said sharply, "and that's how he got hung. And now about you? You're pretty goddamn smart, I bet."

23   Then he looked directly at me, just for a minute. "I ain't smart," he said. "If I was smart, I'd have reached for a pistol a long time ago."

24   "Look. Don't tell *me* your sad story, if it was up to me, I'd give you one." Then I felt guilty—guilty, probably, for never having supposed that the poor bastard *had* a story of his own, much less a sad one, and I asked, quickly, "What's going to happen to him now?"

25   He didn't answer this. He was off by himself some place. "Funny

thing," he said, and from his tone we might have been discussing the quickest way to get to Brooklyn, "when I saw the papers this morning, the first thing I asked myself was if I had anything to do with it. I felt sort of responsible."

I began to listen more carefully. The subway station was on the corner, just before us, and I stopped. He stopped, too. We were in front of a bar and he ducked slightly, peering in, but whoever he was looking for didn't seem to be there. The juke box was blasting away with something black and bouncy and I half watched the barmaid as she danced her way from the juke box to her place behind the bar. And I watched her face as she laughingly responded to something someone said to her, still keeping time to the music. When she smiled one saw the little girl, one sensed the doomed, still-struggling woman beneath the battered face of the semi-whore.   26

"I never *give* Sonny nothing," the boy said finally, "but a long time ago I come to school high and Sonny asked me how it felt." He paused, I couldn't bear to watch him, I watched the barmaid, and I listened to the music which seemed to be causing the pavement to shake. "I told him it felt great." The music stopped, the barmaid paused and watched the juke box until the music began again. "It did."   27

All this was carrying me some place I didn't want to go. I certainly didn't want to know how it felt. It filled everything, the people, the houses, the music, the dark, quicksilver barmaid, with menace; and this menace was their reality.   28

"What's going to happen to him now?" I asked again.   29

"They'll send him away some place and they'll try to cure him." He shook his head. "Maybe he'll even think he's kicked the habit. Then they'll let him loose" — he gestured, throwing his cigarette into the gutter. "That's all."   30

"What do you mean, that's *all?*"   31

But I knew what he meant.   32

"I *mean*, that's *all*." He turned his head and looked at me, pulling down the corners of his mouth. "Don't you know what I mean?" he asked, softly.   33

"How the hell *would* I know what you mean?" I almost whispered it, I don't know why.   34

"That's right," he said to the air, "how would *he* know what I mean?" He turned toward me again, patient and calm, and yet I somehow felt him shaking, shaking as though he were going to fall apart. I felt that ice in my guts again, the dread I'd felt all afternoon; and again I watched the barmaid, moving about the bar, washing glasses, and singing. "Listen. They'll let him out and then it'll just start all over again. That's what I mean."   35

"You mean — they'll let him out. And then he'll just start working his way back in again. You mean he'll never kick the habit. Is that what you mean?"   36

37   "That's right," he said, cheerfully. "*You* see what I mean."

38   "Tell me," I said it last, "why does he want to die? He must want to die, he's killing himself, why does he want to die?"

39   He looked at me in surprise. He licked his lips. "He don't want to die. He wants to live. Don't nobody want to die, ever."

40   Then I wanted to ask him—too many things. He could not have answered, or if he had, I could not have borne the answers. I started walking. "Well, I guess it's none of my business."

41   "It's going to be rough on old Sonny," he said. We reached the subway station. "This is your station?" he asked. I nodded. I took one step down. "Damn!" he said, suddenly. I looked up at him. He grinned again. "Damn it if I didn't leave all my money home. You ain't got a dollar on you, have you? Just for a couple of days, is all."

42   All at once something inside gave and threatened to come pouring out of me. I didn't hate him any more. I felt that in another moment I'd start crying like a child.

43   "Sure," I said, "Don't sweat." I looked in my wallet and didn't have a dollar, I only had a five. "Here," I said. "That hold you?"

44   He didn't look at it—he didn't want to look at it. A terrible, closed look come over his face, as though he were keeping the number on the bill a secret from him and me. "Thanks," he said, and now he was dying to see me go. "Don't worry about Sonny. Maybe I'll write him or something."

45   "Sure," I said. "You do that. So long."

46   "Be seeing you," he said. I went on down the steps.

47   And I didn't write Sonny or send him anything for a long time. When I finally did, it was just after my little girl died, he wrote me back a letter which made me feel like a bastard.

48   Here's what he said:

49   Dear brother,

50   You don't know how much I needed to hear from you. I wanted to write you many a time but I dug how much I must have hurt you and so I didn't write. But now I feel like a man who's been trying to climb up out of some deep, real deep and funky hole and just saw the sun up there, outside. I got to get outside.

51   I can't tell you much about how I got here. I mean I don't know how to tell you. I guess I was afraid of something or I was trying to escape from something and you know I have never been very strong in the head (smile). I'm glad Mama and Daddy are dead and can't see what's happened to their son and I swear if I'd known what I was doing I would never have hurt you so, you and a lot of other fine people who were nice to me and who believed in me.

52   I don't want you to think it had anything to do with me being a musician. It's more than that. Or maybe less than that. I can't get anything straight in my head down here and I try not to think about what's going to happen to me when I get outside again. Sometime

I think I'm going to flip and *never* get outside and sometime I think I'll come straight back. I tell you one thing, though, I'd rather blow my brains out than go through this again. But that's what they all say, so they tell me. If I tell you when I'm coming to New York and if you could meet me, I sure would appreciate it. Give my love to Isabel and the kids and I was sure sorry to hear about little Gracie. I wish I could be like Mama and say the Lord's will be done, but I don't know it seems to me that trouble is the one thing that never does get stopped and I don't know what good it does to blame it on the Lord. But maybe it does some good if you believe it.

Your brother, 53

Sonny 54

Then I kept in constant touch with him and I sent him whatever I could 55 and I went to meet him when he came back to New York. When I saw him many things I thought I had forgotten came flooding back to me. This was because I had begun, finally, to wonder about Sonny, about the life that Sonny lived inside. This life, whatever it was, had made him older and thinner and it had deepened the distant stillness in which he had always moved. He looked very unlike my baby brother. Yet, when he smiled, when we shook hands, the baby brother I'd never known looked out from the depths of his private life, like an animal waiting to be coaxed into the light.

"How you been keeping?" he asked me. 56

"All right. And you?" 57

"Just fine." He was smiling all over his face. "It's good to see you 58 again."

"It's good to see you." 59

The seven years' difference in our ages lay between us like a chasm: I 60 wondered if these years would ever operate between us as a bridge. I was remembering, and it made it hard to catch my breath, that I had been there when he was born; and I had heard the first words he had ever spoken. When he started to walk, he walked from our mother straight to me. I caught him just before he fell when he took the first steps he ever took in this world.

"How's Isabel?" 61

"Just fine. She's dying to see you." 62

"And the boys?" 63

"They're fine, too. They're anxious to see their uncle." 64

"Oh, come on. You know they don't remember me." 65

"Are you kidding? Of course they remember you." 66

He grinned again. We got into a taxi. We had a lot to say to each other, 67 far too much to know how to begin.

As the taxi began to move, I asked, "You still want to go to India?" 68

He laughed. "You still remember that. Hell, no. This place is Indian 69 enough to me."

"It used to belong to them," I said. 70

71   And he laughed again. "They damn sure knew what they were doing when they got rid of it."

72   Years ago, when he was around fourteen, he'd been all hipped up on the idea of going to India. He read books about people sitting on rocks, naked, in all kinds of weather, but mostly bad, naturally, and walking barefoot through hot coals and arriving at wisdom. I used to say that it sounded to me as though they were getting away from wisdom as fast as they could. I think he sort of looked down on me for that.

73   "Do you mind," he asked "if we have the driver drive alongside the park? On the west side—I haven't seen the city in so long."

74   "Of course not," I said. I was afraid that I might sound as though I were humoring him, but I hoped he wouldn't take it that way.

75   So we drove along, between the green of the park and the stony, lifeless elegance of hotels and apartment buildings, toward the vivid, killing streets of our childhood. These streets hadn't changed, though housing projects jutted up out of them now like rocks in the middle of a boiling sea. Most of the houses in which we had grown up had vanished, as had the stores from which we had stolen, the basements in which we had first tried sex, the rooftops from which we had hurled tin cans and bricks. But houses exactly like the houses of our past yet dominated the landscape, boys exactly like the boys we once had been found themselves smothering in these houses, came down into the streets for light and air and found themselves encircled by disaster. Some escaped the trap, most didn't. Those who got out always left something of themselves behind, as some animals amputate a leg and leave it in the trap. It might be said, perhaps, that I had escaped, after all, I was a school teacher; or that Sonny had, he hadn't lived in Harlem for years. Yet, as the cab moved uptown through streets which seemed, with a rush, to darken with dark people, and as I covertly studied Sonny's face, it came to me that what we both were seeking through our separate cab windows was that part of ourselves which had been left behind. It's always at the hour of trouble and confrontation that the missing member aches.

76   We hit 110th Street and started rolling up Lenox Avenue. And I'd known this avenue all my life, but it seemed to me again, as it had seemed on the day I'd first heard about Sonny's trouble, filled with a hidden menace which was its very breath of life.

77   "We almost there," said Sonny,

78   "Almost." We were both too nervous to say anything more.

79   We live in a housing project. It hasn't been up long. A few days after it was up it seemed uninhabitably new, now, of course, it's already rundown. It looks like a parody of the good, clean, faceless life—God knows the people who live in it do their best to make it a parody. The beat-looking grass lying around isn't enough to make their lives green, the hedges will never hold out the streets, and they know it. The big windows fool no one, they aren't big enough to make space out of no space. They don't bother with the windows, they watch the TV screen

instead. The playground is most popular with the children who don't play at jacks, or skip rope, or roller skate, or swing, and they can be found in it after dark. We moved in partly because it's not too far from where I teach, and partly for the kids; but it's really just like the houses in which Sonny and I grew up. The same things happen, they'll have the same things to remember. The moment Sonny and I started into the house I had the feeling that I was simply bringing him back into the danger he had almost died trying to escape.

Sonny has never been talkative. So I don't know why I was sure he'd be dying to talk to me when supper was over the first night. Everything went fine, the oldest boy remembered him, and the youngest boy liked him, and Sonny had remembered to bring something for each of them; and Isabel, who is really much nicer than I am, more open and giving, had gone to a lot of trouble about dinner and was genuinely glad to see him. And she's always been able to tease Sonny in a way that I haven't. It was nice to see her face so vivid again and to hear her laugh and watch her make Sonny laugh. She wasn't, or, anyway, she didn't seem to be, at all uneasy or embarrassed. She chatted as though there were no subject which had to be avoided and she got Sonny past his first, faint stiffness. And thank God she was there, for I was filled with that icy dread again. Everything I did seemed awkward to me, and everything I said sounded freighted with hidden meaning. I was trying to remember everything I'd heard about dope addiction and I couldn't help watching Sonny for signs. I wasn't doing it out of malice. I was trying to find out something about my brother. I was dying to hear him tell me he was safe.   80

"Safe!" my father grunted, whenever Mama suggested trying to move to a neighborhood which might be safer for children. "Safe, hell! Ain't no place safe for kids, nor nobody."   81

He always went on like this, but he wasn't, ever, really as bad as he sounded, not even on weekends, when he got drunk. As a matter of fact, he was always on the lookout for "something a little better," but he died before he found it. He died suddenly, during a drunken weekend in the middle of the war, when Sonny was fifteen. He and Sonny hadn't ever got on too well. And this was partly because Sonny was the apple of his father's eye. It was because he loved Sonny so much and was frightened for him, that he was always fighting with him. It doesn't do any good to fight with Sonny. Sonny just moves back, inside himself, where he can't be reached. But the principal reason that they never hit it off is that they were so much alike. Daddy was big and rough and loud-talking, just the opposite of Sonny, but they both had—that same privacy.   82

Mama tried to tell me something about this, just after Daddy died. I was home on leave from the army.   83

This was the last time I ever saw my mother alive. Just the same, this picture gets all mixed up in my mind with pictures I had of her when she was younger. The way I always see her is the way she used to be on Sunday afternoon, say, when the old folks were talking after the big   84

Sunday dinner. I always see her wearing pale blue. She'd be sitting on the sofa. And my father would be sitting in the easy chair, not far from her. And the living room would be full of church folks and relatives. There they sit, on chairs all around the living room, and the night is creeping up outside, but nobody knows it yet. You can see the darkness growing against the windowpanes and you hear the street noises every now and again, or maybe the jangling beat of a tambourine from one of the churches close by, but it's real quiet in the room. For a moment nobody's talking, but every face looks darkening, like the sky outside. And my mother rocks a little from the waist, and my father's eyes are closed. Everyone is looking at something a child can't see. For a minute they've forgotten the children. Maybe a kid is lying on the rug, half asleep. Maybe somebody's got a kid in his lap and is absent-mindedly stroking the kid's head. Maybe there's a kid, quiet and big-eyed, curled up in a big chair in the corner. The silence, the darkness coming, and the darkness in the faces frightens the child obscurely. He hopes that the hand which strokes his forehead will never stop—will never die. He hopes that there will never come a time when the old folks won't be sitting around the living room, talking about where they've come from, and what they've seen, and what's happened to them and their kinfolk.

85   But something deep and watchful in the child knows that this is bound to end, is already ending. In a moment someone will get up and turn on the light. Then the old folks will remember the children and they won't talk any more that day. And when light fills the room, the child is filled with darkness. He knows that every time this happens he's moved just a little closer to that darkness outside. The darkness outside is what the old folks have been talking about. It's what they've come from. It's what they endure. The child knows that they won't talk any more because if he knows too much about what's happened to *them,* he'll know too much too soon, about what's going to happen to *him.*

86   The last time I talked to my mother, I remember I was restless. I wanted to get out and see Isabel. We weren't married then and we had a lot to straighten out between us.

87   There Mama sat, in black, by the window. She was humming an old church song, *Lord, you brought me from a long ways off.* Sonny was out somewhere. Mama kept watching the streets.

88   "I don't know," she said, "if I'll ever see you again, after you go off from here. But I hope you'll remember the things I tried to teach you."

89   "Don't talk like that," I said, and smiled. "You'll be here a long time yet."

90   She smiled, too, but she said nothing. She was quiet for a long time. And I said, "Mama, don't you worry about nothing. I'll be writing all the time, and you be getting the checks. . . ."

91   "I want to talk to you about your brother," she said, suddenly. "If anything happens to me he ain't going to have nobody to look out for him."

"Mama," I said, "ain't nothing going to happen to you *or* Sonny. 92
Sonny's all right. He's a good boy and he's got good sense."

"It ain't a question of his being a good boy," Mama said, "nor of his 93
having good sense. It ain't only the bad ones, nor yet the dumb ones that
gets sucked under." She stopped, looking at me. "Your Daddy once had
a brother," she said, and she smiled in a way that made me feel she was
in pain. "You didn't never know that, did you?"

"No," I said, "I never knew that," and I watched her face. 94

"Oh, yes," she said, "your Daddy had a brother." She looked out of 95
the window again. "I know you never saw your Daddy cry. But *I*
did—many a time, through all these years."

I asked her, "What happened to his brother? How come nobody's ever 96
talked about him?"

This was the first time I ever saw my mother look old. 97

"His brother got killed," she said, "when he was just a little younger 98
than you are now. I knew him. He was a fine boy. He was maybe a little
full of the devil, but he didn't mean nobody no harm."

Then she stopped and the room was silent, exactly as it had sometimes 99
been on those Sunday afternoons. Mama kept looking out into the
streets.

"He used to have a job in the mill," she said, "and, like all young folks, 100
he just liked to perform on Saturday nights. Saturday nights, him and
your father would drift around to different place, go to dances and things
like that, or just sit around with people they knew, and your father's
brother would sing, he had a fine voice, and play along with himself on
his guitar. Well, this particular Saturday night him and your father was
coming home from some place, and they were both a little drunk and
there was a moon that night, it was bright like day. Your father's brother
was feeling kind of good, and he was whistling to himself, and he had his
guitar slung over his shoulder. They was coming down a hill and beneath
them was a road that turned off from the highway. Well, your father's
brother, being always kind of frisky, decided to run down this hill, and
he did, with that guitar banging and clanging behind him, and he ran
across the road, and he was making water behind a tree. And your father
was sort of amused at him and he was still coming down the hill, kind of
slow. Then he heard a car motor and that same minute his brother
stepped from behind the tree, into the road, in the moonlight. And he
started to cross the road. And your father started to run down the hill, he
says he don't know why. This car was full of white men. They was all
drunk, and when they seen your father's brother they let out a great
whoop and holler and they aimed the car straight at him. They was
having fun, they just wanted to scare him, the way they do sometimes,
you know. But they was drunk. And I guess the boy, being drunk, too,
and scared, kind of lost his head. By the time he jumped it was too late.
Your father says he heard his brother scream when the car rolled over
him, and he heard the wood of that guitar when it give, and he heard

them strings go flying, and he heard them white men shouting and the car kept on a-going and it ain't stopped till this day. And, time your father got down the hill, his brother weren't nothing but blood and pulp."

101   Tears were gleaming on my mother's face. There wasn't anything I could say.

102   "He never mentioned it," she said, "because I never let him mention it before you children. Your Daddy was like a crazy man that night and for many a night thereafter. He says he never in his life seen anything as dark as that road after the lights of that car had gone away. Weren't nothing, weren't nobody on that road, just your Daddy and his brother and that busted guitar. Oh, yes. Your Daddy never did really get right again. Till the day he died he weren't sure but that every white man he saw was the man that killed his brother."

103   She stopped and took out her handkerchief and dried her eyes and looked at me.

104   "I ain't telling you all this," she said, "to make you scared or bitter or to make you hate nobody. I'm telling you this because you got a brother. And the world ain't changed."

105   I guess I didn't want to believe this. I guess she saw this in my face. She turned away from me, toward the window again, searching those streets.

106   "But I praise my Redeemer," she said at last, "that He called your Daddy home before me. I ain't saying it to throw no flowers at myself, but, I declare, it keeps me from feeling too cast down to know I helped your father get safely through this world. Your father always acted like he was the roughest, strongest man on earth. And everybody took him to be like that. But if he hadn't had *me* there—to see his tears!"

107   She was crying again. Still I couldn't move. I said, "Lord, Lord, Mama, I didn't know it was like that."

108   "Oh, honey," she said, "there's a lot that you don't know. But you are going to find it out." She stood up from the window and came over to me. "You got to hold on to your brother," she said, "and don't let him fall, no matter what it looks like is happening to him and no matter how evil you gets with him. You going to be evil with him many a time. But don't you forget what I told you, you hear?"

109   "I won't forget," I said. "Don't you worry, I won't forget. I won't let nothing happen to Sonny."

110   My mother smiled as though she were amused at something she saw in my face. Then, "You may not be able to stop nothing from happening. But you got to let him know you's *there*."

111   Two days later I was married, and then I was gone. And I had a lot of things on my mind and I pretty well forgot my promise to Mama until I got shipped home on a special furlough for her funeral.

112   And, after the funeral, with just Sonny and me alone in the empty kitchen, I tried to find out something about him.

113   "What do you want to do?" I asked him.

"I'm going to be a musician," he said.   114

For he had graduated, in the time I had been away, from dancing to the   115
juke box to finding out who was playing what, and what they were doing
with it, and he had bought himself a set of drums.

"You mean, you want to be a drummer?" I somehow had the feeling   116
that being a drummer might be all right for other people but not for my
brother Sonny.

"I don't think," he said, looking at me very gravely, "that I'll ever be 117
a good drummer. But I think I can play a piano."

I frowned. I'd never played the role of the older brother quite so   118
seriously before, had scarcely ever, in fact, *asked* Sonny a damn thing. I
sensed myself in the presence of something I didn't really know how to
handle, didn't understand. So I made my frown a little deeper as I asked:
"What kind of musician do you want to be?"

He grinned. "How many kinds do you think there are?"   119

"Be *serious,*" I said.   120

He laughed, throwing his head back, and then looked at me. "I *am*   121
serious."

"Well, then, for Christ's sake, stop kidding around and answer a   122
serious question. I mean, do you want to be a concert pianist, you want
to play classical music and all that, or—or what?" Long before I finished
he was laughing again. "For Christ's *sake,* Sonny!"

He sobered, but with difficulty. "I'm sorry. But you sound so—   123
scared!" and he was off again.

"Well, you may think it's funny now, baby, but it's not going to be so   124
funny when you have to make your living at it, let me tell you *that.*" I was
furious because I knew he was laughing at me and I didn't know why.

"No," he said, very sober now, and afraid, perhaps, that he'd hurt me,   125
"I don't want to be a classical pianist. That isn't what interests me. I
mean"—he paused, looking hard at me, as though his eyes would help
me to understand, and then gestured helplessly, as though perhaps his
hand would help—"I mean, I'll have a lot of studying to do, and I'll have
to study *everything,* but, I mean, I want to play *with*—jazz musicians."
He stopped. "I want to play jazz," he said.

Well, the word had never before sounded as heavy, as real, as it   126
sounded that afternoon in Sonny's mouth. I just looked at him and I was
probably frowning a real frown by this time. I simply couldn't see why on
earth he'd want to spend his time hanging around nightclubs, clowning
around on bandstands, while people pushed each other around a dance
floor. It seemed—beneath him, somehow. I had never thought about it
before, had never been forced to, but I suppose I had always put jazz
musicians in a class with what Daddy called "good-time people."

"Are you *serious?*"   127

"Hell, *yes,* I'm serious."   128

He looked more helpless than ever, and annoyed, and deeply hurt.   129

I suggested, helpfully: "You mean—like Louis Armstrong?"   130

131   His face closed as though I'd struck him. "No. I'm not talking about none of that old-time, down home crap."

132   "Well, look, Sonny, I'm sorry, don't get mad. I just don't altogether get it, that's all. Name somebody—you know a jazz musician you admire."

133   "Bird."

134   "Who?"

135   "Bird! Charlie Parker! Don't they teach you nothing in the goddamn army?"

136   I lit a cigarette. I was surprised and then a little amused to discover that I was trembling. "I've been out of touch," I said. "You'll have to be patient with me. Now. Who's this Parker character?"

137   "He's just one of the greatest jazz musicians alive," said Sonny, sullenly, his hands in his pockets, his back to me. "Maybe *the* greatest," he added, bitterly, "that's probably why *you* never heard of him."

138   "All right," I said, "I'm ignorant. I'm sorry. I'll go out and buy all the cat's records right away, all right?"

139   "It don't" said Sonny, with dignity, "make any difference to me. I don't care what you listen to. Don't do me no favors."

140   I was beginning to realize that I'd never seen him so upset before. With another part of my mind I was thinking that this would probably turn out to be one of those things kids go through and that I shouldn't make it seem important by pushing it too hard. Still, I didn't think it would do any harm to ask: "Doesn't all this take a lot of time? Can you make a living at it?"

141   He turned back to me and half leaned, half sat, on the kitchen table. "Everything takes time," he said, "and—well, yes, sure, I can make a living at it. But what I don't seem to be able to make you understand is that it's the only thing I want to do."

142   "Well, Sonny," I said, gently, "you know people can't always do exactly what they *want* to do—"

143   "*No,* I don't know that," said Sonny, surprising me. "I think people *ought* to do what they want to do, what else are they alive for?"

144   "You getting to be a big boy," I said desperately, "it's time you started thinking about your future."

145   "I'm thinking about my future," said Sonny, grimly. "I think about it all the time."

146   I gave up. I decided, if he didn't change his mind, that we could always talk about it later. "In the meantime," I said, "you got to finish school." We had already decided that he'd have to move in with Isabel and her folks. I knew this wasn't the ideal arrangement because Isabel's folks are inclined to be dicty and they hadn't especially wanted Isabel to marry me. But I didn't know what else to do. "And we have to get you fixed up at Isabel's."

147   There was a long silence. He moved from the kitchen table to the window. "That's a terrible idea. You know it yourself."

148   "Do you have a *better* idea?"

He just walked up and down the kitchen for a minute. He was as tall 149
as I was. He had started to shave. I suddenly had the feeling that I didn't
know him at all.

He stopped at the kitchen table and picked up my cigarettes. Looking 150
at me with a kind of mocking, amused defiance, he put one between his
lips. "You mind?"

"You smoking already?" 151

He lit the cigarette and nodded, watching me though the smoke. "I just 152
wanted to see if I'd have the courage to smoke in front of you." He
grinned and blew a great cloud of smoke to the ceiling. "It was easy." He
looked at my face. "Come on, now. I bet you was smoking at my age, tell
the truth."

I didn't say anything but the truth was on my face, and he laughed. But 153
now there was something very strained in his laugh. "Sure. And I bet that
ain't all you was doing."

He was frightening me a little. "Cut the crap," I said. "We already 154
decided that you was going to go and live at Isabel's. Now what's got into
you all of a sudden?"

"*You* decided it," he pointed out. "*I* didn't decide nothing." He 155
stopped in front of me, leaning against the stove, arms loosely folded.
"Look, brother. I don't want to stay in Harlem no more, I really don't."
He was very earnest. He looked at me, then over toward the kitchen
window. There was something in his eyes I'd never seen before, some
thoughtfulness, some worry all his own. He rubbed the muscle of one
arm. "It's time I was getting out of here."

"Where do you want to go, Sonny?" 156

"I want to join the army. Or the navy, I don't care. If I say I'm old 157
enough, they'll believe me."

Then I got mad. It was because I was so scared. "You must be crazy. 158
You goddamn fool, what the hell do you want to go and join the *army*
for?"

"I just told you. To get out of Harlem." 159

"Sonny, you haven't even finished *school*. And if you really want to be 160
a musician, how do you expect to study if you're in the *army?*"

He looked at me, trapped, and in anguish. "There's ways. I might be 161
able to work out some kind of deal. Anyway, I'll have the G.I. Bill when
I come out."

"*If* you come out." We stared at each other. "Sonny, please. Be 162
reasonable. I know the setup is far from perfect. But we got to do the best
we can."

"I ain't learning nothing in school," he said. "Even when I go." He 163
turned away from me and opened the window and threw his cigarette out
into the narrow alley. I watched his back. "At least, I ain't learning
nothing you'd want me to learn." He slammed the window so hard I
thought the glass would fly out, and turned back to me. "And I'm sick of
the stink of these garbage cans!"

164   "Sonny," I said, "I know how you feel. But if you don't finish school now, you're going to be sorry later that you didn't." I grabbed him by the shoulders. "And you only got another year. It ain't so bad. And I'll come back and I swear I'll help you do *whatever* you want to do. Just try to put up with it till I come back. Will you please do that? For me?"

165   He didn't answer and he wouldn't look at me.

166   "Sonny. You hear me?"

167   He pulled away. "I hear you. But you never hear anything I say."

168   I didn't know what to say to that. He looked out of the window and then back at me. "OK," he said, and sighed. "I'll try."

169   Then I said, trying to cheer him up a little, "They got a piano at Isabel's. You can practice on it."

170   And as a matter of fact, it did cheer him up for a minute. "That's right," he said to himself. "I forgot that." His face relaxed a little. But the worry, the thoughtfulness, played on it still, the way shadows play on a face which is staring into the fire.

171   But I thought I'd never hear the end of that piano. At first, Isabel would write me, saying how nice it was that Sonny was so serious about his music and how, as soon as he came in from school, or wherever he had been when he was supposed to be at school, he went straight to that piano and stayed there until suppertime. And, after supper, he went back to that piano and stayed there until everybody went to bed. He was at the piano all day Saturday and all day Sunday. Then he bought a record player and started playing records. He'd play one record over and over again, all day long sometimes, and he'd improvise along with it on the piano. Or he'd play one section of the record, one chord, one change, one progression, then he'd do it on the piano. Then back to the record. Then back to the piano.

172   Well, I really don't know how they stood it. Isabel finally confessed that it wasn't like living with a person at all, it was like living with sound. And the sound didn't make any sense to her, didn't make any sense to any of them—naturally. They began, in a way, to be afflicted by this presence that was living in their home. It was as though Sonny were some sort of god, or monster. He moved in an atmosphere which wasn't like theirs at all. They fed him and he ate, he washed himself, he walked in and out of their door; he certainly wasn't nasty or unpleasant or rude, Sonny isn't any of those things; but it was as though he were all wrapped up in some cloud, some fire, some vision all his own; and there wasn't any way to reach him.

173   At the same time, he wasn't really a man yet, he was still a child, and they had to watch out for him in all kinds of ways. They certainly couldn't throw him out. Neither did they dare to make a great scene about that piano because even they dimly sensed, as I sensed, from so many thousands of miles away, that Sonny was at that piano playing for his life.

But he hadn't been going to school. One day a letter came from the   174
school board and Isabel's mother got it—there had apparently, been
other letters but Sonny had torn them up. This day, when Sonny came in,
Isabel's mother showed him the letter and asked where he'd been spending his time. And she finally got it out of him that he'd been down in
Greenwich Village, with musicians and other characters, in a white girl's
apartment. And this scared her and she started to scream at him and what
came up, once she began—though she denies it to this day—was what
sacrifices they were making to give Sonny a decent home and how little
he appreciated it.

Sonny didn't play the piano that day. By evening, Isabel's mother had   175
calmed down but then there was the old man to deal with, and Isabel
herself. Isabel says she did her best to be calm but she broke down and
started crying. She says she just watched Sonny's face. She could tell, by
watching him, what was happening with him. And what was happening
was that they penetrated his cloud, they had reached him. Even if their
fingers had been a thousand times more gentle than human fingers ever
are, he could hardly help feeling that they had stripped him naked and
were spitting on that nakedness. For he also had to see that his presence,
that music, which was life or death to him, had been torture for them,
and that they had endured it, not at all for his sake, but only for mine.
And Sonny couldn't take that. He can take it a little better today than he
could then but he's still not very good at it and, frankly, I don't know
anybody who is.

The silence of the next few days must have been louder than the sound   176
of all the music ever played since time began. One morning, before she
went to work, Isabel was in his room for something and she suddenly
realized that all of his records were gone. And she knew for certain that
he was gone. And he was. He went as far as the navy would carry him.
He finally sent me a postcard from some place in Greece and that was the
first I knew that Sonny was still alive. I didn't see him any more until we
were both back in New York and the war had long been over.

He was a man by then, of course, but I wasn't willing to see it. He came   177
by the house from time to time, but we fought almost every time we met.
I didn't like the way he carried himself, loose and dreamlike all the time,
and I didn't like his friends, and his music seemed to be merely an excuse
for the life he led. It sounded just that weird and disordered.

Then we had a fight, a pretty awful fight, and I didn't see him for   178
months. By and by I looked him up, where he was living, in a furnished
room in the Village, and I tried to make it up. But there were lots of other
people in the room and Sonny just lay on his bed, and he wouldn't come
downstairs with me, and he treated these other people as though they
were his family and I weren't. So I got mad and then he got mad, and then
I told him that he might just as well be dead as live the way he was living.
Then he stood up and he told me not to worry about him any more in life,
that he *was* dead as far as I was concerned. Then he pushed me to the

door and the other people looked on as though nothing were happening, and he slammed the door behind me. I stood in the hallway, staring at the door. I heard somebody laugh in the room and then the tears came to my eyes. I started down the steps, whistling to keep from crying, I kept whistling to myself, *You going to need me, baby, one of these cold, rainy days.*

179   I read about Sonny's trouble in the spring. Little Grace died in the fall. She was a beautiful little girl. But she only lived a little over two years. She died of polio and she suffered. She had a slight fever for a couple of days, but it didn't seem like anything and we just kept her in bed. And we would certainly have called the doctor, but the fever dropped, she seemed to be all right. So we thought it had just been a cold. Then, one day, she was up, playing, Isabel was in the kitchen fixing lunch for the two boys when they'd come in from school, and she heard Grace fall down in the living room. When you have a lot of children you don't always start running when one of them falls, unless they start screaming or something. And, this time, Grace was quiet. Yet, Isabel says that when she heard that *thump* and then that silence, something happened in her to make her afraid. And she ran to the living room and there was little Grace on the floor, all twisted up, and the reason she hadn't screamed was that she couldn't get her breath. And when she did scream, it was the worst sound, Isabel says, that she'd ever heard in all her life, and she still hears it sometimes in her dreams. Isabel will sometimes wake me up with a low, moaning, strangled sound and I have to be quick to awaken her and hold her to me and where Isabel is weeping against me seems a mortal wound.

180   I think I may have written Sonny the very day that little Grace was buried. I was sitting in the living room in the dark, by myself, and I suddenly thought of Sonny. My trouble made his real.

181   One Saturday afternoon, when Sonny had been living with us, or, anyway, been in our house, for nearly two weeks, I found myself wandering aimlessly about the living room, drinking from a can of beer, and trying to work up the courage to search Sonny's room. He was out, he was usually out whenever I was home, and Isabel had taken the children to see their grandparents. Suddenly I was standing still in front of the living room window, watching Seventh Avenue. The idea of searching Sonny's room made me still. I scarcely dared to admit to myself what I'd be searching for. I didn't know what I'd do if I found it. Or if I didn't.

182   On the sidewalk across from me, near the entrance to a barbecue joint, some people were holding an old-fashioned revival meeting. The barbecue cook, wearing a dirty white apron, his conked hair reddish and metallic in the pale sun, and a cigarette between his lips, stood in the doorway, watching them. Kids and older people paused in their errands and stood there, along with some older men and a couple of very tough-looking women who watched everything that happened on the

avenue, as though they owned it, or were maybe owned by it. Well, they were watching this, too. The revival was being carried on by three sisters in black, and a brother. All they had were their voices and their Bibles and a tambourine. The brother was testifying and while he testified two of the sisters stood together, seeming to say, amen, and the third sister walked around with the tambourine outstretched and a couple of people dropped coins into it. Then the brother's testimony ended and the sister who had been taking up the collection dumped the coins into her palm and transferred them to the pocket of her long black robe. Then she raised both hands, striking the tambourine against the air, and then against one hand, and she started to sing. And the two other sisters and the brother joined in.

It was strange, suddenly, to watch, though I had been seeing these 183
street meetings all my life. So, of course, had everybody else down there. Yet, they paused and watched and listened and I stood still at the window. *"Tis the old ship of Zion,"* they sang and the sister with the tambourine kept a steady, jangling beat, *"it has rescued many a thousand!"* Not a soul under the sound of their voices was hearing this song for the first time, not one of them had been rescued. Nor had they seen much in the way of rescue work being done around them. Neither did they especially believe in the holiness of the three sisters and the brother, they knew too much about them, knew where they lived, and how. The woman with the tambourine, whose voice dominated the air, whose face was bright with joy, was divided by very little from the woman who stood watching her, a cigarette between her heavy, chapped lips, her hair a cuckoo's nest, her face scarred and swollen from many beatings, and her black eyes glittering like coal. Perhaps they both knew this, which was why, when, as rarely, they addressed each other, they addressed each other as Sister. As the singing filled the air the watching, listening faces underwent a change, the eyes focusing on something within; the music seemed to soothe a poison out of them; and time seemed, nearly, to fall away from the sullen, belligerent, battered faces, as though they were fleeing back to their first condition, while dreaming of their last. The barbecue cook half shook his head and smiled, and dropped his cigarette and disappeared into his joint. A man fumbled in his pockets for change and stood holding it in his hand impatiently, as though he had just remembered a pressing appointment further up the avenue. He looked furious. Then I saw Sonny, standing on the edge of the crowd. He was carrying a wide, flat notebook with a green cover, and it made him look, from where I was standing, almost like a schoolboy. The coppery sun brought out the copper in his skin, he was very faintly smiling, standing very still. Then the singing stopped, the tambourine turned into a collection plate again. The furious man dropped in his coins and vanished, so did a couple of the women, and Sonny dropped some change in the plate, looking directly at the woman with a little smile. He started across the

avenue, toward the house. He has a slow, loping walk, something like the way Harlem hipsters walk, only he's imposed on this his own half-beat. I had never really noticed it before.

184   I stayed at the window, both relieved and apprehensive. As Sonny disappeared from my sight, they began singing again. And they were still singing when his key turned in the lock.

185   "Hey," he said.

186   "Hey, yourself. You want some beer?"

187   "No. Well, maybe." But he came up to the window and stood beside me, looking out. "What a warm voice," he said.

188   They were singing *If I could only hear my mother pray again!*

189   "Yes," I said, "and she can sure beat that tambourine."

190   "But what a terrible song," he said, and laughed. He dropped his notebook on the sofa and disappeared into the kitchen. "Where's Isabel and the kids?"

191   "I think they went to see their grandparents. You hungry?"

192   "No." He came back into the living room with his can of beer. "You want to come some place with me tonight?"

193   I sensed, I don't know how, that I couldn't possibly say no. "Sure. Where?"

194   He sat down on the sofa and picked up his notebook and started leafing through it. "I'm going to sit in with some fellows in a joint in the Village."

195   "You mean, you're going to play, tonight?"

196   "That's right." He took a swallow of his beer and moved back to the window. He gave me a sidelong look. "If you can stand it."

197   "I'll try," I said.

198   He smiled to himself and we both watched as the meeting across the way broke up. The three sisters and their brother, heads bowed, were singing *God be with you till we meet again.* The faces around them were very quiet. Then the song ended. The small crowd dispersed. We watched the three women and the lone man walk slowly up the avenue.

199   "When she was singing before," said Sonny, abruptly, "her voice reminded me for a minute of what heroin feels like sometimes—when it's in your veins. It makes you feel sort of warm and cool at the same time. And distant. And—and sure." He sipped his beer, very deliberately not looking at me. I watched his face. "It makes you feel—in control. Sometimes you've got to have that feeling."

200   "Do you?" I sat down slowly in the easy chair.

201   "Sometimes." He went to the sofa and picked up his notebook again. "Some people do."

202   "In order," I asked, "to play?" And my voice was very ugly, full of contempt and anger.

203   "Well"—he looked at me with great, troubled eyes, as though, in fact, he hoped his eyes would tell me things he could never otherwise say— "they *think* so. And *if* they think so—!"

"And what do *you* think?" I asked. 204

He sat on the sofa and put his can of beer on the floor. "I don't know," 205
he said, and I couldn't be sure if he was answering my question or
pursuing his thoughts. His face didn't tell me. "It's not so much to *play*.
It's to *stand* it, to be able to make it at all. On any level." He frowned and
smiled: "In order to keep from shaking to pieces."

"But these friends of yours," I said, "they seem to shake themselves to 206
pieces pretty goddamn fast."

"Maybe." He played with the notebook. And something told me that 207
I should curb my tongue, that Sonny was doing his best to talk, that I
should listen. "But of course you only know the ones that've gone to
pieces. Some don't— or at least they haven't *yet* and that's just about all
any of us can say." He paused. "And then there are some who just live,
really, in hell, and they know it and they see what's happening and they
go right on. I don't know." He sighed, dropped the notebook, folded his
arms. "Some guys, you can tell from the way they play, they on something *all* the time. And you can see that, well, it makes something real for
them. But of course," he picked up his beer from the floor and sipped it
and put the can down again, "they *want* to, too, you've got to see that.
Even some of them that say they don't—*some*, not all."

"And what about you?" I asked—I couldn't help it. "What about you? 208
Do *you* want to?"

He stood up and walked to the window and remained silent for a long 209
time. Then he sighed. "Me," he said. Then: "While I was downstairs
before, on my way here, listening to that woman sing, it struck me all of
a sudden how much suffering she must have had to go through—to sing
like that. It's *repulsive* to think you have to suffer that much."

I said: "But there's no way not to suffer—is there, Sonny?" 210

"I believe not," he said and smiled, "but that's never stopped anyone 211
from trying." He looked at me. "Has it?" I realized, with this mocking
look, that there stood between us, forever, beyond the power of time or
forgiveness, the fact that I had held silence—so long!—when he needed
human speech to help him. He turned back to the window. "No, there's
no way not to suffer. But you try all kinds of ways to keep from drowning
in it, to keep on top of it, and to make it seem—well, like *you*. Like you
did something, all right, and now you're suffering for it. You know?" I
said nothing. "Well you know," he said, impatiently, "why *do* people
suffer? Maybe it's better to do something to give it a reason, *any* reason."

"But we just agreed," I said, "that there's no way not to suffer. Isn't it 212
better, then, just to—take it?"

"But nobody just takes it," Sonny cried, "that's what I'm telling you! 213
Everybody tries not to. You're just hung up on the *way* some people
try—it's not *your* way!"

The hair on my face began to itch, my face felt wet. "That's not true," 214
I said, "that's not true. I don't give a damn what other people do, I don't
even care how they suffer. I just care how *you* suffer." And he looked at

me. "Please believe me," I said, "I don't want to see you—die—trying not to suffer."

215   "I won't," he said, flatly, "die trying not to suffer. At least, not any faster than anybody else."

216   "But there's no need," I said, trying to laugh, "is there? in killing yourself."

217   I wanted to say more, but I couldn't. I wanted to talk about will power and how life could be—well, beautiful. I wanted to say that it was all within; but was it? or, rather, wasn't that exactly the trouble? And I wanted to promise that I would never fail him again. But it would all have sounded—empty words and lies.

218   So I made the promise to myself and prayed that I would keep it.

219   "It's terrible sometimes, inside," he said, "that's what's the trouble. You walk these streets, black and funky and cold, and there's not really a living ass to talk to, and there's nothing shaking, and there's no way of getting it out—that storm inside. You can't talk it and you can't make love with it, and when you finally try to get with it and play it, you realize *nobody's* listening. So *you've* got to listen. You got to find a way to listen."

220   And then he walked away from the window and sat on the sofa again, as though all the wind had suddenly been knocked out of him. "Sometimes you'll do *anything* to play, even cut your mother's throat." He laughed and looked at me. "Or your brother's." Then he sobered. "Or your own." Then: "Don't worry. I'm all right now and I think I'll *be* all right. But I can't forget—where I've been. I don't mean just the physical place I've been, I mean where I've *been*. And *what* I've been."

221   "What have you been, Sonny?" I asked.

222   He smiled—but sat sideways on the sofa, his elbow resting on the back, his fingers playing with his mouth and chin, not looking at me. "I've been something I didn't recognize, didn't know I could be. Didn't know anybody could be." He stopped, looking inward, looking helplessly young, looking old. "I'm not talking about it now because I feel *guilty* or anything like that—maybe it would be better if I did, I don't know. Anyway, I can't really talk about it. Not to you, not to anybody," and now he turned and faced me. "Sometimes, you know, and it was actually when I was most *out* of the world, I felt that I was in it, that I was *with* it, really, and I could play or I didn't really have to *play*, it just came out of me, it was there. And I don't know how I played, thinking about it now, but I know I did awful things, those times, sometimes, to people. Or it wasn't that I *did* anything to them—it was that they weren't real." He picked up the beer can; it was empty; he rolled it between his palms: "And other times—well, I needed a fix, I needed to find a place to lean, I needed to clear a space to *listen*—and I couldn't find it, and I—went crazy, I did terrible things to *me*, I was terrible *for* me." He began pressing the beer can between his hands, I watched the metal begin to give. It glittered, as he played with it, like a knife, and I was afraid he

would cut himself, but I said nothing. "Oh well. I can never tell you. I was all by myself at the bottom of something, stinking and sweating and crying and shaking, and I smelled it, you know? *my* stink, and I thought I'd die if I couldn't get away from it and yet, all the same, I knew that everything I was doing was just locking me in with it. And I didn't know," he paused, still flattening the beer can, "I didn't know, I still *don't* know, something kept telling me that maybe it was good to smell your own stink, but I didn't think that *that* was what I'd been trying to do—and—who can stand it?" and he abruptly dropped the ruined beer can, looking at me with a small, still smile, and then rose, walking to the window as though it were the lodestone rock. I watched his face, he watched the avenue. "I couldn't tell you when Mama died—but the reason I wanted to leave Harlem so bad was to get away from drugs. And then, when I ran away, that's what I was running from—really. When I came back, nothing had change, *I* hadn't changed, I was just—older." And he stopped, drumming with his fingers on the windowpane. The sun had vanished, soon darkness would fall. I watched his face. "It can come again," he said, almost as though speaking to himself. Then he turned to me. "It can come again," he repeated. "I just want you to know that."

"All right," I said, at last. "So it can come again. All right." 223

He smiled, but the smile was sorrowful. "I had to try to tell you," he 224
said.

"Yes," I said. "I understand that." 225

"You're my brother," he said, looking straight at me, and not smiling 226
at all.

"Yes," I repeated, "yes. I understand that." 227

He turned back to the window, looking out. "All that hatred down 228
there," he said, "all that hatred and misery and love. It's a wonder it
doesn't blow the avenue apart."

We went to the only nightclub on a short, dark street, downtown. We 229
squeezed through the narrow, chattering, jam-packed bar to the entrance
of the big room, where the bandstand was. And we stood there for a
moment, for the lights were very dim in this room and we couldn't see.
Then, "Hello, boy," said a voice and an enormous black man, much
older than Sonny or myself, erupted out of all that atmospheric lighting
and put an arm around Sonny's shoulder. "I been sitting right here," he
said, "waiting for you."

He had a big voice, too, and heads in the darkness turned toward us. 230

Sonny grinned and pulled a little away, and said, "Creole, this is my 231
brother. I told you about him."

Creole shook my hand. "I'm glad to meet you, son," he said, and it was 232
clear that he was glad to meet me *there*, for Sonny's sake. And he smiled,
"You got a real musician in *your* family," and he took his arm from
Sonny's shoulder and slapped him, lightly, affectionately, with the back
of his hand.

233   "Well. Now I've heard it all," said a voice behind us. This was another musician, a friend of Sonny's, a coal-black, cheerful-looking man, built close to the ground. He immediately began confiding to me, at the top of his lungs, the most terrible things about Sonny, his teeth gleaming like a lighthouse and his laugh coming up out of him like the beginning of an earthquake. And it turned out that everyone at the bar knew Sonny, or almost everyone; some were musicians, working there, or nearby, or not working, some were simply hangers-on, and some were there to hear Sonny play. I was introduced to all of them and they were all very polite to me. Yet, it was clear that, for them, I was only Sonny's brother. Here, I was in Sonny's world. Or, rather: his kingdom. Here, it was not even a question that his veins bore royal blood.

234   They were going to play soon and Creole installed me, by myself, at a table in a dark corner. Then I watched them, Creole, and the little black man, and Sonny, and the others, while they horsed around, standing just below the bandstand. The light from the bandstand spilled just a little short of them and, watching them laughing and gesturing and moving about, I had the feeling that they, nevertheless, were being most careful not to step into that circle of light too suddenly: that if they moved into the light too suddenly, without thinking, they would perish in flame. Then, while I watched, one of them, the small, black man, moved into the light and crossed the bandstand and started fooling around with his drums. Then—being funny and being, also, extremely ceremonious— Creole took Sonny by the arm and led him to the piano. A woman's voice called Sonny's name and a few hands started clapping. And Sonny, also being funny and being ceremonious, and so touched, I think, that he could have cried, but neither hiding it nor showing it, riding it like a man, grinned, and put both hands to his heart and bowed from the waist.

235   Creole then went to the bass fiddle and a lean, very bright-skinned brown man jumped up on the bandstand and picked up his horn. So there they were, and the atmosphere on the bandstand and in the room began to change and tighten. Someone stepped up to the microphone and announced them. Then there were all kinds of murmurs. Some people at the bar shushed others. The waitress ran around, frantically getting in the last orders, guys and chicks got closer to each other, and the lights on the bandstand, on the quartet, turned to a kind of indigo. Then they all looked different there. Creole looked about him for the last time, as though he were making certain that all his chickens were in the coop, and then he—jumped and struck the fiddle. And there they were.

236   All I know about music is that not many people ever really hear it. And even then, on the rare occasions when something opens within, and the music enters, what we mainly hear, or hear corroborated, are personal, private, vanishing evocations. But the man who creates the music is hearing something else, is dealing with the roar rising from the void and imposing order on it as it hits the air. What is evoked in him, then, is of another order, more terrible because it has no words, and triumphant, too, for that same reason. And his triumph, when he triumphs, is ours. I

just watched Sonny's face. His face was troubled, he was working hard, but he wasn't with it. And I had the feeling that, in a way, everyone on the bandstand was waiting for him, both waiting for him and pushing him along. But as I began to watch Creole, I realized that it was Creole who held them all back. He had them on a short rein. Up there, keeping the beat with his whole body, wailing on the fiddle, with his eyes half closed, he was listening to everything, but he was listening to Sonny. He was having a dialogue with Sonny. He wanted Sonny to leave the shoreline and strike out for the deep water. He was Sonny's witness that deep water and drowning were not the same thing—he had been there, and he knew. And he wanted Sonny to know. He was waiting for Sonny to do the thing on the keys which would let Creole know that Sonny was in the water.

And, while Creole listened, Sonny moved, deep within, exactly like someone in torment. I had never before thought of how awful the relationship must be between the musician and his instrument. He has to fill it, this instrument, with the breath of life, his own. He has to make it do what he wants it to do. And a piano is just a piano. It's made out of so much wood and wires and little hammers and big ones, and ivory. While there's only so much you can do with it, the only way to find this out is to try; to try and make it do everything.

And Sonny hadn't been near a piano for over a year. And he wasn't on much better terms with his life, not the life that stretched before him now. He and the piano stammered, started one way, got scared, stopped; started another way, panicked, marked time, started again; then seemed to have found a direction, panicked again, got stuck. And the face I saw on Sonny I'd never seen before. Everything had been burned out of it, and, at the same time, things usually hidden were being burned in, by the fire and fury of the battle which was occurring in him up there.

Yet, watching Creole's face as they neared the end of the first set, I had the feeling that something had happened, something I hadn't heard. Then they finished, there was scattered applause, and then, without an instant's warning, Creole started into something else, it was almost sardonic, it was *Am I Blue*. And, as though he commanded, Sonny began to play. Something began to happen. And Creole let out the reins. The dry, low, black man said something awful on the drums, Creole answered, and the drums talked back. Then the horn insisted, sweet and high, slightly detached perhaps, and Creole listened, commenting now and then, dry, and driving, beautiful and calm and old. Then they all came together again, and Sonny was part of the family again. I could tell this from his face. He seemed to have found, right there beneath his fingers, a damn brand-new piano. It seemed that he couldn't get over it. Then, for awhile, just being happy with Sonny, they seemed to be agreeing with him that brand-new pianos certainly were a gas.

Then Creole stepped forward to remind them that what they were playing was the blues. He hit something in all of them, he hit something in me, myself, and the music tightened and deepened, apprehension

237

238

239

240

began to beat the air. Creole began to tell us what the blues were all about. They were not about anything very new. He and his boys up there were keeping it new, at the risk of ruin, destruction, madness, and death, in order to find new ways to make us listen. For, while the tale of how we suffer, and how we are delighted, and how we may triumph is never new, it always must be heard. There isn't any other tale to tell, it's the only light we've got in all this darkness.

241   And this tale, according to that face, that body, those strong hands on those strings, has another aspect in every country, and a new depth in every generation. Listen, Creole seemed to be saying listen. Now these are Sonny's blues. He made the little black man on the drums know it, and the bright, brown man on the horn. Creole wasn't trying any longer to get Sonny in the water. He was wishing him Godspeed. Then he stepped back, very slowly, filling the air with the immense suggestion that Sonny speak for himself.

242   Then they all gathered around Sonny and Sonny played. Every now and again one of them seemed to say, amen. Sonny's fingers filled the air with life, his life. But that life contained so many others. And Sonny went all the way back, he really began with the spare, flat statement of the opening phrase of the song. Then he began to make it his. It was very beautiful because it wasn't hurried and it was no longer a lament. I seemed to hear with what burning he had made it his, with what burning we had yet to make it ours, how we could cease lamenting. Freedom lurked around us and I understood, at last, that he could help us to be free if we would listen, that he would never be free until we did. Yet, there was no battle in his face now. I heard what he had gone through, and would continue to go through until he came to rest in earth. He had made it his: that long line, of which we knew only Mama and Daddy. And he was giving it back, as everything must be given back, so that, passing through death, it can live forever. I saw my mother's face again, and felt, for the first time, how the stones of the road she had walked on must have bruised her feet. I saw the moonlit road where my father's brother died. And it brought something else back to me, and carried me past it, I saw my little girl again and felt Isabel's tears again, and I felt my own tears begin to rise. And I was yet aware that this was only a moment, that the world waited outside, as hungry as a tiger, and that trouble stretched above us, longer than the sky.

243   Then it was over. Creole and Sonny let out their breath, both soaking wet, and grinning. There was a lot of applause and some of it was real. In the dark, the girl came by and I asked her to take drinks to the bandstand. There was a long pause, while they talked up there in the indigo light and after awhile I saw the girl put a Scotch and milk on top of the piano for Sonny. He didn't seem to notice it, but just before they started playing again, he sipped from it and looked toward me, and nodded. Then he put it back on top of the piano. For me, then, as they began to play again, it glowed and shook above my brother's head like the very cup of trembling.

❏ **Questions for Discussion**

1. Why do you think the **narrator,** after his daughter dies, chooses to write to Sonny, whom he has ignored for years?

2. Why does Sonny's letter make the narrator feel guilty?

3. Why do Isabel and her family seem to disapprove of Sonny? Does the narrator also disapprove of his brother? Why would Sonny give up his "future" for music?

4. What does the narrator mean when he says of his students, "All they really knew were two darknesses, the darkness of their lives . . . and the darkness of the movies"? What is suggested by these and other references to darkness?

5. "Sonny's Blues" contains a story within a story, the mother's tale of the narrator's father and his father's brother. What is the significance of this story?

6. Explain the importance of the sidewalk revival and of the location from which each brother views it.

7. In the last scene, the narrator enters Sonny's world for the first time. Explain the symbolism of the location, the jazz, and the drink.

James Baldwin's "Sonny's Blues": Complicated and Simple[1]

by Donald C. Murray

"One boy was whistling a tune, at once very complicated and very simple, it seemed to be pouring out of him as though he were a bird, and it sounded very cool and moving through all that harsh, bright air, only just holding its own through all those other sounds."[2]

In the world of "Sonny's Blues," the short story by James Baldwin, the author deals with man's need to find his identity in a hostile society and, in a social situation which invites fatalistic compliance, his ability to understand himself through artistic creation which is both individual and communal. "Sonny's Blues" is the story of a boy's growth to adulthood at a place, the Harlem ghetto, where it's easier to remain a "cunning child," and at a time when black is not beautiful because it's simpler to submerge oneself in middle-class conformity, the modish antics of the hipster set, or else, at the most dismal level, the limbo of drug addition, rather than to truly find oneself. Sonny's brother, the narrator of the

[1] Donald C. Murray, "James Baldwin's 'Sonny's Blues': Complicated and Simple," *Studies in Short Fiction* (1977): 355–57.

[2] James Baldwin, "Sonny's Blues," *Partisan Review*, 24, No. 3 (Summer 1957), 327–358. Further quotations will be from this text and will be indicated by the page number in parentheses.

story, opts for the comforts of a respectable profession and his specialty, the teaching of algebra, suggests his desire for standard procedures and elegant, clear-cut solutions. On the other hand, Sonny at first traffics with the hipster world; yet not without imposing "his own halfbeat" on "the way the Harlem hipsters walk" (p. 349). Eventually, however, as if no longer able to hold his own through all those other sounds of enticement and derision, Sonny is sentenced to a government institution due to his selling and using heroin.

With his brother in a penal establishment and himself a member of the educational establishment, it's fitting that the narrator would learn of Sonny's imprisonment while reading the newspaper, probably an establishment press, and while riding in a subway, an appropriate vehicle for someone who hasn't risen above his origins so far as he hopes. The subway world of roaring darkness is both the outside world of hostile forces and the inner heart of darkness which we encounter at our peril, yet encounter we must. The narrator at first cannot believe that Sonny has gone "down" ("I had kept it outside me for a long time."), but he is forced to realize that it has happened, and, thinking of heroin, he suspects that perhaps "it did more for [Black boys like Sonny] than algebra could" (p. 328). Playing upon the homonym of Sonny, Baldwin writes that, for the narrator's brother, "all the light in [Sonny's] face" had gone out.

Images of light and darkness are used by Baldwin to illustrate his theme of man's painful quest for an identity. Light can represent the harsh glare of reality, the bitter conditions of ghetto existence which harden and brutalize the young. Early in the story the narrator comes upon a boy in the shadow of a doorway, a psychologically stunted creature "looking just like Sonny," "partly like a dog, partly like a cunning child" (p. 329). Shortly thereafter he watches a barmaid in a dingy pub and notes that, "When she smiled one saw the little girl, one sensed the doomed, still-struggling woman beneath the battered face of the semi-whore" (p. 330). Both figures will appear again, in other forms, during the revival meeting later in the story. At this point, however, the narrator turns away and goes on "down the steps" into the subway. He retreats from the light, however dim.

Another kind of light is that of the movie theater, the light which casts celluloid illusions on the screen. It is this light, shrouded in darkness, which allows the ghetto-dwellers' temporary relief from their condition. "All they really knew were two darknesses," Baldwin writes, "the darkness of their lives, which was now closing in on them, and the darkness of the movies, which had blinded them to that other darkness" (p. 328). This image of the movie theater neatly represents the state of people who are at once together and alone, seated side-by-side yet without communication. Baldwin deftly fuses the theater and subway images: "They were growing up with a rush and their heads bumped abruptly against the low ceiling of their actual possibilities" (p. 328). The realities are far different from the idealistic dreams of the cinema; as outside the subway window, so behind the cinema screen there is nothing but roaring darkness.

There is no escape from the darkness for Sonny and his family. Dreams and aspirations are always dispelled, the narrator comments, because someone will always "get up and turn on the light." "And when light fills the room," he continues, "the child is filled with darkness" (p. 337). Grieved by the death of his child, fortuitously named Grace, and aware of the age difference between himself and Sonny, the narrator seems unconsciously to seek out the childlike qualities of everyone he meets. He is not quite the self-satisfied conformist which some critics have made him out to be.[3] He looks back toward a period in the lives of others when they presumably were not tormented by the need to choose between modes of living and to assert themselves. To the extent that he is given to this psychological penchant, the narrator is close in age to Sonny and "Sonny's Blues" is the story of the narrator's dawning self-awareness. The revelation of his father's brother's murder and the fact of Grace's death make Sonny's troubles real for the narrator and prompt the latter's growth in awareness.

To be aware of oneself, Baldwin believes, is to feel a sense of loss, to know where we are and what we've left behind: Sonny's presence forces the narrator to examine his own past; that is, the past which he left behind in the ghetto ("the vivid, killing streets of our childhood") and, before that, in the South. "Some escaped the trap," the narrator notes, "most didn't." "Those who got out always left something of themselves behind," he continues, "as some animals amputate a leg and leave it in the trap" (p. 334). The image is violent and is in keeping with the narrator's tendency to see people "encircled by disaster." The violence reminds us of the fate of the narrator's uncle, a kind of black Orpheus who, carrying his guitar, was deliberately run-down by a group of drunken whites. The narrator's father, we are told, was permanently disturbed by the slaughter of his brother. The age difference between the narrator and Sonny, like that between the narrator and his uncle and that between Sonny and his fellow musician Creole, all suggest that the fates of the generations are similar, linked by influences and effects. "The same things happen," the narrator reflects, "[our children will] have the same things to remember" (p. 335).

So, too, the story is cyclical. We begin in the present, move into the immediate past, then into the more remote past of the narrator's family, then forward to the time of the narrator's marriage and his early conversations with Sonny about his proposed career as a musician, thereafter to Sonny's release from prison and his most recent discussion of music ("It makes you feel—in control," p. 350), and finally to the night club episode in the immediate present. Similarities in the characters and events link the various sections of the story. The barmaid in the opening section, who was "still keeping time to the music," and the boy whose birdlike

[3] For additional observations see Elaine R. Ognibene, "Black Literature Revisited: 'Sonny's Blues,'" *English Journal*, 60 (1971), 36–37; and John M. Reilly, "'Sonny's Blues': James Baldwin's Image of Black Community," *Negro American Literature Forum for School and University Teachers*, 3 (1969), 56–60.

whistling just holds its own amid the noise, are linked to the revivalists, whose "singing filled the air," and to Sonny whose culture hero is "Bird" Parker and whose role is to create music rather than merely keep time. The revivalists are singing near the housing project whose "beat-looking grass lying around isn't enough to make [the inhabitants'] lives green" (p. 335). Looking like one of the narrator's schoolboys, Sonny watches the three sisters and brother in black and carries a notebook "with a green cover," emblematic of the creative life he hopes to lead. Unlike his brother's forced payment to the indigent, childlike man, Sonny drops change into the revivalist's tambourine and the instrument, with this gratuitous gift, turns into a "collection plate." The group has been playing *"If I could only hear my mother play again!"* and Sonny, after "faintly smiling," returns to this brother's home, as if in response to the latter's promise to their mother that he will safeguard Sonny. Recognizing Sonny as both a creative individual and a brother, the narrator is "both relieved and apprehensive" (p. 349).

The narrator's apprehension is justified in that he is about to witness Sonny's torturous rebirth as a creative artist. "But I can't forget—where I've been." Sonny remarks to his brother and then adds: " 'I don't mean just the physical place I've been, I mean where I've *been.* And *what* I've been' " (p. 353). In terms which might recall Gerard Manley Hopkins' anguished sonnet "I wake and feel the fell of darkness," Sonny goes on to describe his own dark night of the soul: " 'I was all by myself at the bottom of something, stinking and sweating and crying and shaking, and I smelled it, you know? *my* stink, and I thought I'd die' " (p. 353). Because of the enormous energy and dedication involved in his role as Blues musician, Sonny is virtually described as a sacrificial victim as well as an initiate into the mysteries of creativity. Somewhat like the Christ of *noli me tangere,* Sonny's smile is "sorrowful" and he finds it hard to describe his own terrible anguish because he knows that it can come again and he almost wonders whether it's worth it. Yet his anguish is not only personal but representative, for as he looks down from the window of his brother's apartment he sees " 'all that hatred and misery and love,' " and he notes that, " 'It's a wonder it doesn't blow the avenue apart' " (p. 354). As the pressure mounts within Sonny, the author sets the scene for the final episode of the story.

Befitting the special evening which ends "Sonny's Blues," the locale shifts to the "only night club" on a dark downtown street. Sonny and the narrator pass through the narrow bar and enter a large, womblike room where Sonny is greeted with " 'Hello boy' " by a voice which "erupted out of all that atmospheric lighting" (p. 354). Indeed the atmosphere is almost grandly operatic in its stage quality. The booming voice belongs to the quasi-midwife, Creole, who slaps Sonny "lightly, affectionately," as if performing the birth rite. Creole is assisted by a "coal-black" demiurge, "built close to the ground," with laughter "coming up out of him like the beginning of an earthquake" (p. 355). As if to underscore the portentiousness of this evening in Sonny's "kingdom," the narrator thinks that, "Here it was not even a question that [Sonny's] veins bore royal blood" (p. 355). The imagery of light now blends with that of water as the narrator, describing the light which "spilled" from the bandstand and the way in which Sonny seems to be "riding" the waves of applause, relates how Sonny and the other musicians prepare to play. It is as if Sonny were about to undergo another stage in his initiation into mature musicianship, this time a trial by fire. "I had the feeling that they, nevertheless, were being most careful not to step into that circle of light too suddenly," the narrator continues, "that if they moved into the light too suddenly, without thinking, they would perish in flame" (p. 355). Next the imagery suggests that Sonny is embarking upon a sacred and perilous voyage, an approach to the wholly other in the biblical sense of the phrase; for the man who creates music, the narrator observes, is "hearing something else, is dealing with the roar rising from the void and imposing order on it as it hits the air" (p. 356). The roaring darkness of the subway is transformed into something luminous. Appropriately, the lighting turns to indigo and Sonny is transfigured.

Now the focus again shifts to Creole, who seems to hold the musicians on a "short rein": "He wanted Sonny to leave the shore line and strike out for the deep water. He was Sonny's witness that deep water and drowning were not the same thing—he had been there, and he knew" (p. 356). Creole now takes on the dimensions of the traditional father-figure. He is a better teacher than the narrator because he has been in the deep water of life; he is a better witness than Sonny's father because he has not been "burned out" by his experiences in life. Creole's function in the story, to put it prosaically, is to show that only through determination and perseverance, through the taking of a risk, can one find a proper role in life. To fail does not mean to be lost irretrievably, for one can always start again. To go forward, as Sonny did when Creole "let out the reins," is to escape the cycle which, in the ghetto of the mind, stifles so many lives, resulting in mean expectations and stunted aspirations. The narrator makes the point that the essence of Sonny's blues is not new; rather, it's the age-old story of triumph, suffering, and failure. But there is no other tale to tell, he adds, "it's the only light we've got in all this darkness" (p. 357).

Baldwin is no facile optimist. The meaning of "Sonny's Blues" is not, to use the glib phrase, the transcendence of the human condition through art. Baldwin is talking about love and joy, tears of joy because of love. As the narrator listens to his brother's blues, he recalls his mother, the moonlit road on which his uncle died, his wife Isabel's tears, and he again sees the face of his dead child, Grace. Love is what life should be about, he realizes; love which is all the more poignant because involved with pain, separation, and death. Nor is the meaning of "Sonny's Blues" the belief that music touches the heart without words; or at least the meaning of the story is not just that. His brother responds deeply to Sonny's music because he knows that he is with his black brothers and is watching his own brother, grinning and "soaking wet." This last physiological detail is important, not just imagistically, because Baldwin is not sentimentalizing his case in "Sonny's Blues." The narrator is well aware, for example, that his profound response to the blues is a matter of "only a moment, that the world waited outside, as hungry as tiger" — a great cat ready to destroy the birdlike whistling — "and that trouble stretched above us, longer than the sky" (p. 358). The final point of the story is that the narrator, through his own suffering and the example of Sonny, is at last able to find himself in the brotherhood of man. Such an identification is an act of communion and "Sonny's Blues" ends, significantly, with the image of the homely Scotch-and-milk glass transformed into "the very cup of trembling," the Grail, the goal of the quest and the emblem of initiation.[4]

"Sonny's Blues"
James Baldwin's Image of Black Community[1]

by John M. Reilly

A critical commonplace holds that James Baldwin writes better essays than he does fiction or drama; nevertheless, his leading theme — the discovery of identity — is nowhere presented more successfully than in the short story "Sonny's Blues." Originally published in *Partisan Review*, in 1957, and reprinted in the collection of stories *Going to Meet the Man*, in 1965, "Sonny's Blues" not only states dramatically the motive for Baldwin's famous polemics in the cause of black freedom but also provides an aesthetic linking for his work in all literary genres, with the cultures of the black ghetto.[2]

The fundamental movement of "Sonny's Blues" represents the slow accommodation of a first-person narrator's consciousness to the meaning of his younger brother's way of life. The process leads Baldwin's readers to a sympathetic engagement with the young man by providing a knowledge of the human motives of the youths, whose lives normally are reported to others only by their inclusion in statistics of school dropout rates, drug usage, and unemployment.

The basis of the story, however, and its relationship to the purpose of Baldwin's writing generally lies in his use of the blues as a key metaphor. The unique quality of the blues is its combination of personal and social significance in a lyric encounter with history. "The Blues-singer describes first-person experiences, but only such as are typical of the community and such as each individual in the community might have. The singer

[4] Baldwin transforms the wrath-bearing cup of *Isaiah* 51:17–22 through Sonny's victorious affirmation of the Blues.

[1] John M. Reilly, " 'Sonny's Blues": James Baldwin's Image of Black Community," *American Negro Literature Forum* (4) 1079: 56–60; rpt. in *James Baldwin: A Critical Evaluation*, ed. Therman B. O'Daniel (Washington D.C.: Howard UP, 1977): 161–69.

[2] James Baldwin, "Sonny's Blues," *Going to Meet the Man* (New York: Dial Press, 1965), 103–41.

never sets himself against the community or raises himself above it."[3] Thus, in the story of Sonny and his brother an intuition of the meaning of the blues repairs the relationship between the two men who have chosen different ways to cope with the menacing ghetto environment, and their reconciliation through the medium of this Afro-American musical form extends the meaning of the individual's blues until it becomes a metaphor for black community.

Sonny's life explodes into his older brother's awareness when the story of his arrest for peddling and using heroin is reported in the newspaper. Significantly, the mass medium of the newspaper with the impersonal story in it of a police bust is the only way the brothers have of communicating at the opening of the story. While the narrator says that because of the newspaper report Sonny "became real to me again," their relationship is only vestigially personal, for he "couldn't find any room" for the news "anywhere inside. . . ." (P. 103)

While he had had his suspicions about how Sonny was spending his life, the narrator had put them aside with rationalizations about how Sonny was, after all, a good kid. Nothing to worry about. In short, the storyteller reveals that along with his respectable job as an algebra teacher he had assumed a conventional way of thinking as a defense against recognizing that his own brother ran the risk of "coming to nothing." Provoked by the facts of Sonny's arrest to observe his students, since they are the same age as Sonny must have been when he first had heroin, he notices for the first time that their laughter is disenchanted rather than good-humored. In it he hears his brother, and perhaps himself. At this point in the story his opinion is evidently that Sonny and many of the young students are beaten and that he, fortunately, is not.

The conventionality of the narrator's attitude becomes clearer when he encounters a nameless friend of Sonny's, a boy from the block who fears he may have touted Sonny onto heroin by telling him, truthfully, how great it made him feel to be high. This man who "still spent hours on the street corner . . . high and raggy" explains what will happen to Sonny because of his arrest. After they send him someplace and try to cure him, they'll let Sonny loose, that's all. Trying to grasp the implication, the narrator asks: "You mean he'll never kick the habit. Is that what you mean?" He feels there should be some kind of renewal, some hope. A man should be able to bring himself up by his will, convention says. Convention also says that behavior like Sonny's is deliberately self-destructive. "Tell me," he asks the friend, "why does he want to die?" Wrong again. "Don't nobody want to die," says the friend, "ever." (P. 108)

Agitated though he is about Sonny's fate, the narrator doesn't want to feel himself involved. His own position on the middle-class ladder of success is not secure, and the supporting patterns of thought in his mind

---

[3] Janheinz Jahn, *Neo-African Literature: A History of Black Writing,* trans. Oliver Coburn and Ursula Lehrburger (New York: Grove Press, 1968), 166.

are actually rather weak. Listening to the nameless friend explain about Sonny while they stand together in front of a bar blasting "black and bouncy" music from its door, he senses something that frightens him. "All this was carrying me some place I didn't want to go. I certainly didn't want to know how it felt. It filled everything, the people, the houses, the music, the dark, quicksilver barmaid, with menace; and this menace was their reality." (P. 107)

Eventually a great personal pain—the loss of a young daughter—breaks through the narrator's defenses and makes him seek out his brother, more for his own comfort than for Sonny's. "My trouble made his real," he says. In that remark is a prefiguring of the meaning the blues will develop.

It is only a prefiguring, however, for by the time Sonny is released from the state institution where he has been confined, the narrator's immediate need for comfort has passed. When he meets Sonny, he is in control of himself, but very shortly he is flooded with complex feelings that make him feel again the menace of the 110th Street bar where he stood with Sonny's friend. There is no escaping a feeling of icy dread, so he must try to understand.

As the narrator casts his mind back over his and Sonny's past, he gradually identifies sources of his feelings. First he recalls their parents, especially concentrating on an image of his family on a typical Sunday. The scene is one of security amidst portentousness. The adults sit without talking, but every face looks darkening, like the sky outside. The children sit about, maybe one half-asleep and another being stroked on the head by an adult. The darkness frightens a child and he hopes "that the hand which strokes his forehead will never stop." The child knows, however, that it will end, and, now grown up, he recalls one of the meanings of the darkness in the story his mother told him of the death of his uncle, run over on a dark country road by a car full of drunken white men. Never had his companion, the boy's father, "seen anything as dark as that road after the lights of the car had gone away." The narrator's mother had attempted to apply her tale of his father's grief at the death of his own brother to the needs of their sons. They can't protect each other, she knows, "but," she says to the narrator about Sonny, "you got to let him know you's *there*." (P. 119)

Thus, guilt for not fulfilling their mother's request and a sense of shared loneliness partially explain the older brother's feeling toward Sonny. Once again, however, Baldwin stresses the place of the conventional set of the narrator's mind in the complex of feelings as he has him recall scenes from the time when Sonny started to become a jazz musician. The possibility of Sonny's being a jazz rather than a classical musician "seemed—beneath him, somehow." Trying to understand the ambition, the narrator asked if Sonny meant to play like Louis Armstrong, only to be told that Charlie Parker was the model. Hard as it is to believe, he had never heard of Bird until Sonny mentioned him. This ignorance reveals more than a gap between fraternal generations. It represents a cultural chasm. The narrator's inability to understand Sonny's choice of a musical leader shows his alienation from the mood of the postwar bebop subculture. In its hip style of dress, its repudiation of middlebrow norms, and its celebration of esoteric manner, the bebop subculture makes overtly evident its underlying significance as an assertion of black identity. Building upon a restatement of Afro-American music, bebop became an expression of a new self-awareness in the ghettos by a strategy of elaborate nonconformity. In committing himself to the bebop subculture Sonny attempted to make a virtue of the necessity of the isolation imposed upon him by his color. In contrast, the narrator's failure to understand what Sonny was doing indicates that his response to the conditions imposed upon him by racial status was to try to assimilate himself as well as he could into the mainstream American culture. For the one, heroin addiction sealed his membership in the exclusive group; for the other, adoption of individualistic attitudes marked his allegiance to the historically familiar ideal of transcending caste distinctions by entering into the middle class.

Following his way, Sonny became wrapped in the vision that rose from his piano, stopped attending school, and hung around with a group of musicians in Greenwich Village. His musical friends became Sonny's family, replacing the brother who had felt that Sonny's choice of his style of life was the same thing as dying, and for all practical purposes the brothers were dead to each other in the extended separation before Sonny's arrest on narcotics charges.

The thoughts revealing the brothers' family history and locating the sources of the narrator's complex feelings about Sonny all occur in the period after Sonny is released from the state institution. Though he has ceased to evade thoughts of their relationship, as he did in the years when they were separated and partially continued to do after Sonny's arrest, the narrator has a way to go before he can become reconciled to Sonny. His recollections of the past only provide his consciousness with raw feeling.

The next development—perception—begins with a scene of a revival meeting conducted on the sidewalk of Seventh Avenue, beneath the narrator's window. Everyone on the street has been watching such meetings all his life, but the narrator from his window, passersby on the street, and Sonny from the edge of the crowd all watch again. It isn't because they expect something different this time. Rather it is a familiar moment of communion for them. In basic humanity one of the sanctified sisters resembles the down-and-outer watching her, "a cigarette between her heavy, chapped lips, her hair a cuckoo's nest, her face scarred and swollen from many beatings. . . . Perhaps," the narrator thinks, "they both knew this, which was why when, as rarely, they addressed each other, they addressed each other as Sister." (P. 129) The point impresses both the narrator and Sonny, men who should call one another "brother," for the music of the revivalists seems to "soothe a poison" out of them.

The perception of this moment extends nearly to conception in the conversation between the narrator and Sonny that follows it. It isn't a comfortable discussion. The narrator still is inclined to voice moral judgments of the experiences and people Sonny tries to talk about, but he is making an honest effort to relate to his brother now and reminds himself to be quiet and listen. What he hears is that Sonny equates the feeling of hearing the revivalist sister sing with the sensation of heroin in the veins. "It makes you feel—in control. Sometimes you got to have that feeling." (P. 131) It isn't primarily drugs that Sonny is talking about, though, and when the narrator curbs his tongue to let him go on, Sonny explains the real subject of his thoughts.

Again, the facts of Sonny's experience contradict the opinion of "respectable" people. He did not use drugs to escape from suffering, he says. He knows as well as anyone that there's no way to avoid suffering, but what you can do is "try all kinds of ways to keep from drowning in it, to keep on top of it, and to make it seem . . . like *you*.." That is, Sonny explains, you can earn your suffering, make it seem "like you did something . . . and now you're suffering for it." (P. 132)

The idea of meriting your suffering is a staggering one. In the face of it the narrator's inclination to talk about "will power and how life could be—well, beautiful" is blunted, because he senses that by directly confronting degradation Sonny has asserted what degree of will was possible to him, and perhaps that kept him alive.

At this point in the story it is clear that there are two themes emerging. The first is the theme of the individualistic narrator's gradual discovery of the significance of his brother's life. This theme moves to a climax in the final scene of the story when Sonny's music impresses the narrator with a sense of the profound feeling it contains. From the perspective of that final scene, however, the significance of the blues itself becomes a powerful theme.

The insight into the suffering that Sonny displays establishes his priority in knowledge. Thus, he reverses the original relationship between the brothers, assumes the role of the elder, and proceeds to lead his brother, by means of the blues, to a discovery of self in community.

As the brothers enter the jazz club where Sonny is to play, he becomes special. Everyone has been waiting for him, and each greets him familiarly. Equally special is the setting—dark except for a spotlight, which the musicians approach as if it were a circle of flame. This is a sanctified spot, where Sonny is to testify to the power of souls to commune in the blues.

Baldwin explicates the formula of the blues by tracing the narrator's thoughts while Sonny plays. Many people, he thinks, don't really hear music being played except insofar as they invest it with "personal, private, vanishing evocation." He might be thinking of himself, referring to his having come to think of Sonny through the suffering of his own personal loss. The man who makes the music engages in a spiritual creation, and when he succeeds, the creation belongs to all present; "his triumph, when he triumphs, is ours." (P. 137)

In the first set, Sonny doesn't triumph, but in the second, appropriately begun by "Am I Blue," he takes the lead and begins to form a musical creation. He becomes, in the narrator's words, "part of the family again." (P. 139) What family? First of all, that of his fellow musicians. Then, of course, the narrator means to say that their fraternal relationship is at last fulfilled as their mother hoped it would be. But there is yet a broader meaning, too. Like the sisters at the Seventh Avenue revival meeting, Sonny and the band are not saying anything new. Still they are keeping the blues alive by expanding it beyond the personal lyric into a statement of the glorious capacity of human beings to take the worst and give it a form of their own choosing.

At this point the narrator synthesizes feelings and perception into a conception of the blues. He realizes Sonny's blues can help everyone who listens be free, in his own case free of the conventions that had alienated him from Sonny and that dimension of black culture represented in Sonny's style of living. Yet at the same time he knows the world outside of the blues moment remains hostile.

The implicit statement of the aesthetics of the blues in this story throws light upon much of Baldwin's writing. The first proposition of the aesthetics that we can infer from "Sonny's Blues" is that suffering is the prior necessity. Integrity of expression comes from "paying your dues." This is a point Baldwin previously made in *Giovanni's Room* (1956) and which he elaborated in the novel *Another Century* (1962).

The second implicit proposition of the blues aesthetics is that while the form is what it's all about, the form is transitory. The blues is an art in process and in that respect alien from any conception of fixed and ideal forms. This will not justify weaknesses in an artist's work, but insofar as Baldwin identifies his writing with the art of the singers of blues, it suggests why he is devoted to representation, in whatever genre, of successive moments of expressive feeling, and comparatively less concerned with achieving a consistent overall structure.

The final proposition of the aesthetics in the story "Sonny's Blues" is that the blues functions as an art of communion. It is popular rather than elite, worldly rather than otherwise. The blues is expression in which one uses the skill one has achieved by practice and experience in order to reach toward others. It is this proposition that gives the blues its metaphoric significance. The fraternal reconciliation brought about through Sonny's music is emblematic of a group's coming together, because the narrator learns to love his brother freely while he discovers the value of a characteristically Afro-American assertion of life-force. Taking Sonny on his own terms, he must also abandon the ways of thought identified with middle-class position, which historically has signified for black people the adoption of "white" ways.

An outstanding quality of the black literary tradition in America is its attention to the interdependence of personal and social experience. Obviously, necessity has fostered this virtue. Black authors cannot luxuriate in the assumption that there is such a thing as a purely private life. James Baldwin significantly adds to this aspect of the tradition in "Sonny's Blues" by showing that artful expression of personal yet typical experience is one way to freedom.

"Sonny's Blues": A Tale of Two Brothers

Deborah M. Simmons

English 101

Comparison/Contrast

James Baldwin's "Sonny's Blues" provides the reader with glimpses inside the hearts and minds of two brothers. The story is one from which each reader can learn. The reader can use the story to relate to his own familial brothers and sisters; or on a wider scale, the reader can use the story to relate to his other brothers and sisters, namely mankind. Although a wide societal gap seems to separate the brothers, on closer inspection the reader will find that Sonny and the narrator are very much alike.

First, Sonny and the narrator both come from the same economical background. They are young black men raised in the pre-civil rights era. Social injustice and prejudice are realities of life for them. Sonny and the narrator both try to escape the environment for their childhood—the narrator by climbing "... the middle class ladder of success..." (Reilly 164) and Sonny by engulfing himself in the false security of a clean, white powder—heroin.

In addition, the reader realizes that both brothers reach for the security and comfort that the other can provide, and yet, each one feels repulsed by the other because of his different lifestyle. After his parents die, Sonny needs the encouragement that the narrator can provide to further his musical interest. However, the narrator feels that this new form of music, jazz, is "... beneath him [Sonny] somehow" (Baldwin 602). Later, the narrator's daughter—Gracie—dies as a result of polio, and "... the loss of a young daughter ... makes him seek out his brother, more for his own comfort than for Sonny's" (Reilly 165). However, Sonny is imprisoned by this time for selling and using heroin, and "... by the time Sonny is released ... the narrator's immediate need for comfort has passed" (Reilly 165).

Furthermore, throughout the story the narrator is seen by the reader to be the teacher, leader, and elder of the brothers. In fact, his occupation is teaching high school algebra. Sonny, it seems, contributes nothing to the relationship. However, at the end of the story Sonny "... reverses the original relationship between the brothers, assumes the role of the elder, and proceeds to lead his brother, by means of the blues, to a discovery of self in community" (Reilly 167).

In conclusion, James Baldwin's "Sonny's Blues" is a tale of two brothers' efforts to evade the injustices of society. Although they choose two different avenues of escape, each one, in the end, finds his own peace of mind. Even though they lead very different lifestyles, the brothers choose to accept each other and not to conform to the other. Truly, Sonny has learned a great deal from the narrator; but the elder, the teacher, has learned more about life from his "uneducated" sibling. The knowledge that Sonny possesses is not learned in any classroom, but it is acquired in the myriad of flop houses and opium dens that abound in any city where people are oppressed in the darkness of prejudice, bigotry, and poverty and cannot see the light of hope shining through.

Works Cited

Baldwin, James. "Sonny's Blues." The Heath Introduction to Fiction. Ed. John J. Clayton. Lexington, Mass.: D.C. Heath and Co., 1977. 590–617.

Reilly, John M. " 'Sonny's Blues': James Baldwin's Image of Black Community." James Baldwin: A Critical Evaluation. Ed. Therman B. O'Daniel. Washington, D.C.: Howard Univ. Press, 1977. 163–69.

❏ **Suggestions for Exploration and Writing**

1. In "Sonny's Blues," Baldwin's **symbolism** enriches his story. Write an essay exploring the use of one or more of these **symbols:** light and darkness, windows, music.

2. Compare and contrast the story of the father and his brother with the story of Sonny and the narrator. Explain what the story within the story adds to the understanding of both the narrator and the reader.

3. What special claims does this story make for music as an art form? How can the blues played on instruments in a nightclub bring to mind for the narrator not only his own past but that of his whole family?

4. A key to an understanding of this story is an understanding of the character of the **narrator** since we see Sonny only through his eyes. How does the narrator perceive himself? How does this perception affect his opinion of Sonny?

5. Write an essay illustrating the ways in which the narrator changes in the story and the causes for these changes.

6. In an essay, explain the influence of Harlem on each of the brothers.

7. One of the major **themes** in literature is that we learn wisdom through suffering. Discuss the wisdom that the brothers learn through suffering.

❏ **Suggestions for Writing**

1. We often tend to think of families as consisting of a mother, a father, and one or more children who relate to each other in various conventional ways. Many of the families in this section are unconventional. Discuss unconventional families in one of the following pairs:

   • *Fences* and "Nikki Rosa"
   • *Fences* and "Daddy"
   • *On Tidy Endings* and "A Christmas Memory"
   • "My Oedipus Complex" and "Daddy"

2. Discuss the ways in which Welty and O'Connor use their narrators to make family situations humorous in "Why I Live at the P.O." and "My Oedipus Complex."

3. Use at least two of the poems in this unit as a basis for an essay about a parent's feelings for a child or about a child's perception of a parent.

4. Use one or two of the short stories in this unit to discuss problems faced by members of dysfunctional families.

5. Using two works from this unit, write an essay exploring the ways in which family problems vary in different cultures, or discuss similarities of family situations between two cultures.

6. Write an essay describing the ways in which your own identity has been shaped by your family.

7. In the four essays in this unit, all of the authors return to the past: a particular time or place, such as their childhood or their home. Using one of the essays as a guide, write an essay that describes a particular time in your past.

238

MEN AND WOMEN

THROUGH THE AGES, MEN AND WOMEN have treated each other respectfully and disrespectfully, trustfully and distrustfully; they have loved and hated each other, fought and made up, understood and misunderstood each other. In literature we can examine these complex relationships with an objectivity often impossible in real-life relationships. The attitudes of men and women toward each other portrayed in this anthology range from humorous to serious and from lightly sarcastic to bitter.

We can also examine the parameters of being a woman or of being a man. For example, Kincaid's "Girl" focuses on the restrictions placed on girls. Adrienne Rich's poem "Living in Sin" shows how differently men and women see the same room: the male presents a convenient fantasy; the female perceives a sordid reality. Both Gretel Ehrlich and David Osborne in their essays discuss men who break the stereotypes associated with virility. In *A Doll's House* and in *Trifles*, the authors explore the problems faced by women in the past—problems similar to those which women today confront.

Another part of learning to be a man or woman is learning to live in the generation to which we belong and to deal effectively with members of other generations. Janice Mirikitani in "Breaking Traditions" explores three generations of women and applauds their differences.

The **tone** of the selections also suggests attitudes toward gender. Dorothy Parker's "One Perfect Rose" lampoons all the old poems that imply that a rose is the way to a woman's heart. In her witty and sarcastic "When Grateful Begins to Grate," Ellen Goodman expresses the frustration many women feel toward men who fail to understand them. Millay shows the sometimes transitory nature of love in "What lips my lips have kissed, and where, and why." In contrast, Shakespeare's Sonnet 116 lauds the permanence of love. Similarly, the joy made possible when two people love unselfishly is celebrated in Elizabeth Barrett Browning's Sonnet 43 when she answers the question "How do I love thee?"

Literary treatment of relationships is not always humorous or light. The disasters that result from the failure of a man and a woman to understand one another are vividly portrayed by Ernest Hemingway in "Hills Like White Elephants," by Charlotte Perkins Gilman in "The Yellow Wallpaper," and by Robert Browning in "Porphyria's Lover" and "My Last Duchess."

In literature as in life, the roles of men and women are not always precisely defined. Perhaps the lesson most clearly revealed is that men and women are individuals who face insecurities, share romance, and struggle to understand themselves as well as members of the opposite sex.

ESSAYS

VIRGINIA WOOLF (1882–1941)

Though plagued throughout her lifetime by nervous breakdowns, Virginia Stephen Woolf became a major influence on English literature during her life. Today she is considered to be one of the most significant writers in the field of women's literature. Woolf was a member of the famous Bloomsbury circle, a group that stressed culture and opposed many restrictive Victorian standards. She excelled as a novelist with such works as Mrs. Dalloway *(1925) and* To the Lighthouse *(1927); as a critic; and as an essayist with* A Room of One's Own *(1929) and* Three Guineas *(1938). This speech was presented to The Women's Service League, a group of career women, in 1936.*

Professions for Women

1   When your secretary invited me to come here, she told me that your Society is concerned with the employment of women and she suggested that I might tell you something about my own professional experiences. It is true I am a woman; it is true I am employed; but what professional experiences have I had? It is difficult to say. My profession is literature; and in that profession there are fewer experiences for women than in any other, with the exception of the stage—fewer, I mean, that are peculiar to women. For the road was cut many years ago—by Fanny Burney, by Aphra Behn, by Harriet Martineau, by Jane Austen, by George Eliot— many famous women, and many more unknown and forgotten, have been before me, making the path smooth, and regulating my steps. Thus, when I came to write, there were very few material obstacles in my way. Writing was a reputable and harmless occupation. The family peace was not broken by the scratching of a pen. No demand was made upon the family purse. For ten and sixpence one can buy paper enough to write all the plays of Shakespeare—if one has a mind that way. Pianos and models, Paris, Vienna and Berlin, masters and mistresses, are not needed by a writer. The cheapness of writing paper is, of course, the reason why women have succeeded as writers before they have succeeded in the other professions.

But to tell you my story—it is a simple one. You have only got to figure 2 to yourselves a girl in a bedroom with a pen in her hand. She had only to move that pen from left to right—from ten o'clock to one. Then it occurred to her to do what is simple and cheap enough after all—to slip a few of those pages into an envelope, fix a penny stamp in the corner, and drop the envelope in the red box at the corner. It was thus that I became a journalist; and my effort was rewarded on the first day of the following month—a very glorious day it was for me—by a letter from an editor containing a cheque for one pound ten shillings and sixpence. But to show you how little I deserve to be called a professional woman, how little I know of the struggles and difficulties of such lives, I have to admit that instead of spending that sum upon bread and butter, rent, shoes and stockings, or butcher's bills, I went out and bought a cat—a beautiful cat, a Persian cat, which very soon involved me in bitter disputes with my neighbours.

What could be easier than to write articles and to buy Persian cats with 3 the profits? But wait a moment. Articles have to be about something. Mine, I seem to remember, was about a novel by a famous man. And while I was writing this review, I discovered that if I were going to review books I should need to do battle with a certain phantom. And the phantom was a woman, and when I came to know her better I called her after the heroine of a famous poem, The Angel in the House. It was she who used to come between me and my paper when I was writing reviews. It was she who bothered me and wasted my time and so tormented me that at last I killed her. You who come of a younger and happier generation may not have heard of her—you may not know what I mean by the Angel in the House. I will describe her as shortly as I can. She was intensely sympathetic. She was immensely charming. She was utterly unselfish. She excelled in the difficult arts of family life. She sacrificed herself daily. If there was chicken, she took the leg; if there was a draught she sat in it—in short she was so constituted that she never had a mind or a wish of her own, but preferred to sympathize always with the minds and wishes of others. Above all—I need not say it—she was pure. Her purity was supposed to be her chief beauty—her blushes, her great grace. In those days—the last of Queen Victoria—every house had its Angel. And when I came to write I encountered her with the very first words. The shadow of her wings fell on my page; I heard the rustling of her skirts in the room. Directly, that is to say, I took my pen in hand to review that novel by a famous man, she slipped behind me and whispered: "My dear, you are a young woman. You are writing about a book that has been written by a man. Be sympathetic; be tender; flatter; deceive; use all the arts and wiles of our sex. Never let anybody guess that you have a mind of your own. Above all, be pure." And she made as if to guide my pen. I now record the one act for which I take some credit to myself, though the credit rightly belongs to some excellent ancestors of mine who left me a certain sum of money—shall we say five hundred pounds a year?—so that it was not necessary for me to depend solely on charm for my living. I turned upon her and caught her by the throat. I did my best to kill her. My excuse, if I were to be had up in a court of law, would be that I acted in self-defence. Had I not killed her she would have killed me. She would have plucked the heart out of my writing. For, as I found, directly I put pen to paper, you cannot review even a novel without having a mind of your own, without expressing what you think to be the truth about human relations, morality, sex. And all these questions, according to the Angel in the House, cannot be dealt with freely and openly by women; they must charm, they must conciliate, they must—to put it bluntly—tell lies if they are to succeed. Thus, whenever I felt the shadow of her wing or the radiance of her halo upon my page, I took up the inkpot and flung it at her. She died hard. Her fictitious nature was of great assistance to her. It is far harder to kill a phantom than a reality. She was always creeping back when I thought I had despatched her. Though I flatter myself that I killed her in the end, the struggle was severe; it took much time that had better have been spent upon learning Greek grammar; or in roaming the world in search of adventures. But it was a real experience; it was an experience that was bound to befall all women writers at that time. Killing the Angel in the House was part of the occupation of a woman writer.

4   But to continue my story. The Angel was dead; what then remained? You may say that what remained was a simple and common object—a young woman in a bedroom with an inkpot. In other words, now that she had rid herself of falsehood, that young woman had only to be herself. Ah, but what is "herself"? I mean, what is a woman? I assure you, I do not know. I do not believe that you know. I do not believe that anybody can know until she has expressed herself in all the arts and professions open to human skill. That indeed is one of the reasons why I have come here—out of respect for you, who are in process of showing us by your experiments what a woman is, who are in process of providing us, by your failures and successes, with that extremely important piece of information.

5   But to continue the story of my professional experiences. I made one pound ten and six by my first review; and I bought a Persian cat with the proceeds. Then I grew ambitious. A Persian cat is all very well, I said; but a Persian cat is not enough. I must have a motor car. And it was thus that I became a novelist—for it is a very strange thing that people will give you a motor car if you will tell them a story. It is a still stranger thing that there is nothing so delightful in the world as telling stories. It is far pleasanter than writing reviews of famous novels. And yet, if I am to obey your secretary and tell you my professional experiences as a novelist, I must tell you about a very strange experience that befell me as a novelist. And to understand it you must try first to imagine a novelist's state of mind. I hope I am not giving away professional secrets if I say that a

novelist's chief desire is to be as unconscious as possible. He has to induce in himself a state of perpetual lethargy. He wants life to proceed with the utmost quiet and regularity. He wants to see the same faces, to read the same books, to do the same things day after day, month after month, while he is writing, so that nothing may break the illusion in which he is living—so that nothing may disturb or disquiet the mysterious nosings about, feelings round, darts, dashes and sudden discoveries of that very shy and illusive spirit, the imagination. I suspect that this state is the same both for men and women. Be that as it may, I want you to imagine me writing a novel in a state of trance. I want you to figure to yourselves a girl sitting with a pen in her hand, which for minutes, and indeed for hours, she never dips into the inkpot. The image that comes to my mind when I think of this girl is the image of a fisherman lying sunk in dreams on the verge of a deep lake with a rod held out over the water. She was letting her imagination sweep unchecked round every rock and cranny of the world that lies submerged in the depths of our unconscious being. Now came the experience, the experience that I believe to be far commoner with women writers than with men. The line raced through the girl's fingers. Her imagination had rushed away. It had sought the pools, the depths, the dark places where the largest fish slumber. And then there was a smash. There was an explosion. There was foam and confusion. The imagination had dashed itself against something hard. The girl was roused from her dream. She was indeed in a state of the most acute and difficult distress. To speak without figure she had thought of something, something about the body, about the passions which it was unfitting for her as a woman to say. Men, her reason told her, would be shocked. The consciousness of what men will say of a woman who speaks the truth about her passions had roused her from her artist's state of unconsciousness. She could write no more. The trance was over. Her imagination could work no longer. This I believe to be a very common experience with women writers—they are impeded by the extreme conventionality of the other sex. For though men sensibly allow themselves great freedom in these respects, I doubt that they realize or can control the extreme severity with which they condemn such freedom in women.

These then were two very genuine experiences of my own. These were two of the adventures of my professional life. The first—killing the Angel in the House—I think I solved. She died. But the second, telling the truth about my own experiences as a body, I do not think I solved. I doubt that any woman has solved it yet. The obstacles against her are still immensely powerful—and yet they are very difficult to define. Outwardly, what is simpler than to write books? Outwardly, what obstacles are there for a woman rather than for a man? Inwardly, I think, the case is very different; she has still many ghosts to fight, many prejudices to overcome. Indeed it will be a long time still, I think, before a woman can sit down to write a book without finding a phantom to be slain, a rock to be dashed against. And if this is so in literature, the freest of all professions for women, how is it in the new professions which you are now for the first time entering?

7   Those are the questions that I should like, had I time, to ask you. And indeed, if I have laid stress upon these professional experiences of mine, it is because I believe that they are, though in different forms, yours also. Even when the path is nominally open—when there is nothing to prevent a woman from being a doctor, a lawyer, a civil servant—there are many phantoms and obstacles, as I believe, looming in her way. To discuss and define them is I think of great value and importance; for thus only can the labour be shared, the difficulties be solved. But besides this, it is necessary also to discuss the ends and the aims for which we are fighting, for which we are doing battle with these formidable obstacles. Those aims cannot be taken for granted; they must be perpetually questioned and examined. The whole position, as I see it—here in this hall surrounded by women practicing for the first time in history I know not how many different professions—is one of extraordinary interest and importance. You have won rooms of your own in the house hitherto exclusively owned by men. You are able, though not without great labour and effort, to pay the rent. You are earning your five hundred pounds a year. But this freedom is only a beginning; the room is your own, but it is still bare. It has to be furnished; it has to be decorated; it has to be shared. How are you going to furnish it, how are you going to decorate it? With whom are you going to share it, and upon what terms? These, I think are questions of the utmost importance and interest. For the first time in history you are able to ask them; for the first time you are able to decide for yourselves what the answers should be. Willingly would I stay and discuss those questions and answers—but not tonight. My time is up; and I must cease.

❏ Questions for Discussion

1. According to Woolf, why have women "succeeded as writers before they have succeeded in the other professions"?

2. Who is the "Angel in the House," and what did she have to do with Woolf's writing? Why did the author have to kill the "Angel"?

3. What obstacle other than the "Angel in the House" did Woolf face? Why has she not overcome the obstacle?

4. What does Woolf mean when, after killing the "Angel," she asks herself "What is a woman?" and reports that she does not know?

5. What, according to Woolf, can a man talk about or write about that a woman cannot? What limits on free expression do women today face?

6. Explain Woolf's analogy between women pioneering in professions and an unfurnished room.

❏ Suggestions for Exploration and Writing

1. In an essay, discuss the degree to which the "Angel in the House" haunts women you know.

2. Argue for or against the following statement from Woolf's essay: "Even when the path is nominally open—when there is nothing to prevent a woman from being a doctor, a lawyer, a civil servant—there are many phantoms and obstacles, as I believe, looming in her way."

ELLEN GOODMAN (1941–)

Ellen Goodman is an award-winning journalist, radio and television commentator, and columnist for the Boston Globe. *Her columns have been sold in syndication to over 250 newspapers, and she won the Pulitzer Prize for commentary in 1980. Witty and sometimes pointedly satiric, Goodman often writes on family, children, and women's issues.*

When Grateful Begins to Grate

I know a woman who is a grateful wife. She has been one for years. In fact, her gratitude has been as deep and constant as her affection. And together they have traveled a long, complicated road.

In the beginning, this young wife was grateful to find herself married to a man who let her work. That was in 1964, when even her college professor said without a hint of irony that the young wife was "lucky to be married to a man who let her work." People talked like that then.

Later, the wife looked around her at the men her classmates and friends had married and was grateful that her husband wasn't threatened, hurt, neglected, insulted—the multiple choice of the mid-sixties—by her job.

He was proud. And her cup overran with gratitude. That was the way it was.

In the late sixties when other, younger women were having consciousness-raising groups, she was having babies and more gratitude.

You see, she discovered that she had a Helpful Husband. Nothing in her experience had led her to expect this. Her mother was not married to one; her sister was not married to one; her brother was not one.

But at four o'clock in the morning, when the baby cried and she was exhausted, sometimes she would nudge her husband awake (wondering only vaguely how he could sleep) and ask him to feed the boy. He would say sure. And she would say thank-you.

8   The Grateful Wife and the Helpful Husband danced this same pas de deux for a decade. When the children were small and she was sick, he would take charge. When it was their turn to carpool and she had to be at work early, he would drive. If she was coming home late, he would make dinner.

9   All you have to do is ask, he would say with a smile.

10   And so she asked. The woman who had minded her Ps and Qs as a child minded her pleases and thank yous as a wife. Would you please put the baby on the potty? Would you please stop at the store tonight for milk? Would you please pick up Joel at soccer practice? Thank you. Thank you. Thank you.

11   It is hard to know when gratitude first began to grate on my friend. Or when she began saying please and thank you dutifully rather than genuinely.

12   But it probably began when she was tired one day or night. In any case, during the car-time between one job and the other, when she would run lists through her head, she began feeling less thankful for her moonlighting job as household manager.

13   She began to realize that all the items of their shared life were stored in her exclusive computer. She began to realize that her queue was so full of minutia that she had no room for anything else.

14   The Grateful Wife began to wonder why she should say thank you when a father took care of his children and why she should say please when a husband took care of his house.

15   She began to realize that being grateful meant being responsible. Being grateful meant assuming that you were in charge of children and laundry and running out of toilet paper. Being grateful meant having to ask. And ask. And ask.

16   Her husband was not an oppressive or even thoughtless man. He was helpful. But helpful doesn't have to remember vacuum cleaner bags. And helpful doesn't keep track of early dismissal days.

17   Helpful doesn't keep a Christmas-present list in his mind. Helpful doesn't have to know who wears what size and colors. Helpful is reminded; helpful is asked. Anything you ask. Please and thank you.

18   The wife feels, she says, vaguely frightened to find herself angry at saying please and thank you. She wonders if she is, indeed, an ingrate. But her wondering doesn't change how she feels or what she wants.

19   The wife would like to take just half the details that clog her mind like grit in a pore, and hand them over to another manager. The wife would like someone who would be grateful when she volunteered to take *his* turn at the market, or *his* week at the laundry.

20   The truth is that after all those years when she danced her part perfectly, she wants something else. She doesn't want a helpful husband. She wants one who will share. For that, she would be truly grateful.

❏ **Questions for Discussion**

1. For what was the wife grateful?

2. Why is a "helpful husband" not enough? What does this essay reveal about the shared responsibilities of parenthood?

3. The wife's attitude changes even though her husband is helpful. How has he influenced this change?

4. Does the sarcastic **tone** enhance the points made by Goodman? Why does she use that **tone?**

5. What is the difference between being helpful and sharing?

❏ **Suggestions for Exploration and Writing**

1. Write an essay explaining both the advantages and disadvantages of being an employed mother.

2. Reverse your role. If you are a female, write about what you feel your role as a husband is. If you are a male, explain what you see as a wife's role.

3. Why were some men "threatened, hurt, neglected, insulted" in 1964 by wives who worked outside the home? To what extent are husbands still that way today? To what extent are the roles of husband and wife dictated by society?

GRETEL EHRLICH (1946–   )

Gretel Ehrlich is a contemporary poet and essayist. Born in New York, she went to the mountains of Wyoming on a film assignment for PBS. When her beloved co-worker died, she wandered about the West for two years trying to cope with the loss; and, after returning to Wyoming to stay on a friend's ranch, she adopted the rough, hard life-style of a ranch hand. The Solace of Open Spaces (1985), from which "About Men" is taken, records Ehrlich's odyssey in the American West.

About Men

When I'm in New York but feeling lonely for Wyoming I look for the   1
Marlboro ads in the subway. What I'm aching to see is horseflesh, the glint of a spur, a line of distant mountains, brimming creeks, and a reminder of the ranchers and cowboys I've ridden with for the last eight years. But the men I see in those posters with their stern, humorless looks remind me of no one I know here. In our hellbent earnestness to romanticize the cowboy we've ironically disesteemed his true character. If he's

"strong and silent" it's because there's probably no one to talk to. If he "rides away into the sunset" it's because he's been on horseback since four in the morning moving cattle and he's trying, fifteen hours later, to get home to his family. If he's "a rugged individualist" he's also part of a team: ranch work is teamwork and even the glorified open-range cowboys of the 1880s rode up and down the Chisholm Trail in the company of twenty or thirty other riders. Instead of the macho, trigger-happy man our culture has perversely wanted him to be, the cowboy is more apt to be convivial, quirky, and softhearted. To be "tough" on a ranch has nothing to do with conquests and displays of power. More often than not, circumstances—like the colt he's riding or an unexpected blizzard—are overpowering him. It's not toughness but "toughing it out" that counts. In other words, this macho, cultural artifact the cowboy has become is simply a man who possesses resilience, patience, and an instinct for survival. "Cowboys are just like a pile of rocks—everything happens to them. They get climbed on, kicked, rained and snowed on, scuffed up by wind. Their job is 'just to take it,'" one old-timer told me.

2   A cowboy is someone who loves his work. Since the hours are long—ten to fifteen hours a day—the pay is $30 he has to. What's required of him is an odd mixture of physical vigor and maternalism. His part of the beef-raising industry is to birth and nurture calves and take care of their mothers. For the most part his work is done on horseback and in a lifetime he sees and comes to know more animals than people. The iconic myth surrounding him is built on American notions of heroism: the index of a man's value as measured in physical courage. Such ideas have perverted manliness into a self-absorbed race for cheap thrills. In a rancher's world, courage has less to do with facing danger than with acting spontaneously—usually on behalf of an animal or another rider. If a cow is stuck in a boghole he throws a loop around her neck, takes his dally (a half hitch around the saddle horn), and pulls her out with horsepower. If a calf is born sick, he may take her home, warm her in front of the kitchen fire, and massage her legs until dawn. One friend, whose favorite horse was trying to swim a lake with hobbles on, dove under water and cut her legs loose with a knife, then swam her to shore, his arm around her neck lifeguard-style, and saved her from drowning. Because these incidents are usually linked to someone or something outside himself, the westerner's courage is selfless, a form of compassion.

3   The physical punishment that goes with cowboying is greatly under-played. Once fear is dispensed with, the threshold of pain rises to meet the demands of the job. When Jane Fonda asked Robert Redford (in the film *Electric Horseman*) if he was sick as he struggled to his feet one morning, he replied, "No, just bent." For once the movies had it right. The cowboys I was sitting with laughed in agreement. Cowboys are rarely complainers; they show their stoicism by laughing at themselves.

If a rancher or cowboy has been thought of as a "man's man"— 4
laconic, hard-drinking, inscrutable—there's almost no place in which the
balancing act between male and female, manliness and femininity, can be
more natural. If he's gruff, handsome, and physically fit on the outside,
he's androgynous at the core. Ranchers are midwives, hunters, nurturers,
providers, and conservationists all at once. What we've interpreted as
toughness—weathered skin, calloused hands, a squint in the eye and a
growl in the voice—only masks the tenderness inside. "Now don't go
telling me these lambs are cute," one rancher warned me the first day I
walked into the football-field-sized lambing sheds. The next thing I knew
he was holding a black lamb. "Ain't this little rat good-lookin'?"

So many of the men who came to the West were southerners—men 5
looking for work and a new life after the Civil War—that chivalrousness
and strict codes of honor were soon thought of as western traits. There
were very few women in Wyoming during territorial days, so when they
did arrive (some as mail-order brides from places like Philadelphia) there
was a stand-offishness between the sexes and a formality that persists
now. Ranchers still tip their hats and say, "Howdy, ma'am" instead of
shaking hands with me.

Even young cowboys are often evasive with women. It's not that 6
they're Jekyll and Hyde creatures—gentle with animals and rough on
women—but rather, that they don't know how to bring their tenderness
into the house and lack the vocabulary to express the complexity of what
they feel. Dancing wildly all night becomes a metaphor for the explosive
emotions pent up inside, and when these are, on occasion, released,
they're so battery-charged and potent that one caress of the face or one
"I love you" will peal for a long while.

The geographical vastness and the social isolation here make emo- 7
tional evolution seem impossible. Those contradictions of heart between
respectability, logic, and convention on the one hand, and impulse,
passion, and intuition on the other, played out wordlessly against the
paradisical beauty of the West, give cowboys a wide-eyed but drawn
look. Their lips pucker up, not with kisses but with immutability. They
may want to break out, staying up all night with a lover just to talk, but
they don't know how and can't imagine what the consequences will be.
Those rare occasions when they do bare themselves result in confusion.
"I feel as if I'd sprained my heart," one friend told me a month after such
a meeting.

My friend Ted Hoagland wrote, "No one is as fragile as a woman but 8
no one is as fragile as a man." For all the women here who use "frag-
ileness" to avoid work or as a sexual ploy, there are men who try to hide
theirs, all the while clinging to an adolescent dependency on women to
cook their meals, wash their clothes, and keep the ranch house warm in
winter. But there is true vulnerability in evidence here. Because these men
work with animals, not machines or numbers, because they live outside

in landscapes of torrential beauty, because they are confined to a place and a routine embellished with awesome variables, because calves die in the arms that pulled others into life, because they go to the mountains as if on a pilgrimage to find out what makes a herd of elk tick, their strength is also a softness, their toughness, a rare delicacy.

❑ Questions for Discussion

1. What does the "Marlboro man" represent? What about the ad, and the **stereotype** it represents, is Ehrlich attacking?

2. What unexpected qualities does Ehrlich see in cowboys? Through what specific actions do cowboys reveal these qualities?

3. Explain Ehrlich's concluding **paradox:** "Their strength is also a softness, their toughness, a rare delicacy."

❑ Suggestion for Exploration and Writing

1. Apply what Ehrlich says about cowboys to other groups of men in American life. Write an essay showing the underlying gentleness or femininity in a group of men often stereotyped as macho (e.g., truck drivers, construction workers, or professional athletes).

DAVID OSBORNE (1951–)

David Osborne, a political journalist and a consultant of the Clinton presidential campaign in 1992, has published articles in many prestigious magazines. His book, Reinventing Government *(1992), co-authored with Ted Gaebler, presents guidelines and suggestions for change in government. Osborne and his wife Rose, an obstetrician and gynecologist, and their four children live in Dedham, Massachusetts.*

Beyond the Cult of Fatherhood

1   If I ever finish this article, it will be a miracle. Nicholas woke up this morning with an earache and a temperature, and I spent half the day at the doctor's office and pharmacy. Another ear infection.

2   Nicholas is my son. Twenty months old, a stout little bundle of energy and affection.

3   I will never forget the moment when I realized how completely Nick would change my life. My wife is a resident in obstetrics and gynecology, which means, among other things, that she works 100 hours a week, leaves the house every day by six and works all night several times a week, and often all weekend too. I'm not a househusband; I take Nick to day care five days a week. But I come about as close to house-husbandry as I care to. I am what you might call a "nontraditional" father.

Nick was three weeks old when I learned what that actually meant. Rose had just gone back to work, and Nick and I were learning about bottles. I don't remember if it was Rose's first night back or her second, but she wasn't home.

I stayed up too late; I had not yet learned that, with a baby in the house, you grab sleep whenever you can—even if it means going to bed at nine. Just as I drifted off, about 11:30, Nick woke up. I fed him and rocked him and put him back to sleep. About 2 A.M. he woke again, crying, and I rocked him for 45 minutes before he quieted down.

When he started screaming at four, I was in the kitchen by the time I woke up. As every parent knows, the sound of an infant—your infant—screaming sends lightning bolts up the spine. Bells ring in the head; nerves jangle. Racing against my son's hunger, I boiled water, poured it into the little plastic sack, slipped the sack into the plastic bottle, put on the top, and plunged the bottle into a bowl of cold water to cool it. I had not yet learned that in Connecticut, where I live, the water need not be sterilized. (Fathers are the last to know.)

It takes a long time to boil water and cool it back to body temperature, and I was dead on my feet even before the screams rearranged my vertebrae. By the time the water had cooled, I was half-crazed, my motions rapid and jerky. I mixed in the powdered formula and slipped the nipple back on. I ran toward Nick's room, shaking the bottle as hard as I could to make sure it was thoroughly mixed. As I reached his crib, the top flew off—and the contents sprayed all over the room.

At that point, I lost it. I swore at the top of my lungs, I stomped around the room, I slammed the changing table, and I swore some more. That was when I realized what I had gotten myself into—and how much I had to learn.

With baby boomers well ensconced in the nation's newsrooms, fatherhood is sweeping American journalism. You can pick up the *New York Times Magazine,* or *Esquire,* or Bob Greene's best-seller, *Good Morning, Merry Sunshine: A Father's Journal of His Child's First Year* (Penguin), and read all about the wonders of being a father.

By all accounts, today's fathers are more involved and more sensitive than their own fathers were. But as warm and tender as their writing may be, it rings false. Rosalie Ziomek, a mother in Evanston, Illinois, said it perfectly in a letter to the *New Republic,* after it printed a scathing review of Bob Greene's book. "I was enraged by Greene's book," Ziomek wrote. "Anyone taking care of a newborn infant doesn't have time to write about it. Greene was cashing in on the experiences that most women have quietly and painfully lived without the glorification of fame and money. Meanwhile, because of the structure of his work/social life, which he is unwilling to alter, he avoids the thing that is the hardest part of new motherhood: the moment-to-moment dependency of a tiny, helpless, and demanding human being. I have more to say on the subject, but I have three children to take care of and writing is a luxury I can't afford right now."

11   Ziomek is right. I've been trying to keep a journal as Greene did, and it's impossible. There's no time. And how do you capture the essence of an exhausting, never-ending 24-hour day in a few paragraphs? Snapshots work if you spend an hour or two with a child, but if you spend days, everything dissolves in a blur.

12   My experience is different from that of the fathers I read about. Certainly I am not fulfilling the role of a traditional mother, and certainly no child could ask for a more loving mother than Nick has. But I do fix most of the meals and do most of the laundry and change a lot of the diapers and get Nick up and dressed in the morning and shuttle him back and forth to day care and cart him to the grocery store and sing him to sleep and clean up his toys and wipe his nose and deal with his tantrums and cuddle with him and tickle him and all the other wonderful and exhausting things mothers do. If you ask me what it all means, I can't say. After 20 months, I'm still dizzy, still desperate for a free hour or two, and still hopelessly in love with my little boy. All I have to offer are fragments; profound thoughts are for people who have more time. But if you want to go beyond the cult of fatherhood, I think I've been there.

13   My day starts about 6:30 or 7 A.M., when Nick stands up in his crib and calls out for me. I stumble into his room, pick him up, give him a kiss and a "Good morning, Pumpkin," and carry him back to bed. I lay him down on his mother's empty pillow, lie down beside him, and sometimes I drowse again before it's really time to get up. But most mornings Nick is ready to start his day, and he gradually drags me up toward consciousness. He smiles at me, climbs up on me, and rests his head against my cheek—even kisses me if I'm really lucky, or sits on my bladder and bounces, if I'm not. I tickle him, and he laughs and squirms and shrieks for more.

14   Sometimes he lies there for a few minutes, thinking his little boy thoughts, before sliding himself backward off the bed and going in search of something to do. Often he arrives back with a toy or two and asks to be picked "Up! Up!" Then he plays for a few minutes, making sure to keep an eye on my progress toward wakefulness. When he has waited long enough, he hands me my glasses, takes my hand, and pulls me out of bed.

15   While I shower, Nick plays in the bathroom, sitting on the floor with his toys. By the time I'm dressed, the kettle is whistling, and he's ready for breakfast. We always eat together, he has hot cereal, I have cold cereal, and often we share a bagel. I wish you could hear him say "cream cheese."

16   The rough times come on weekends. After 24 hours, I'm ready to be hung out on the line to dry. After 48 hours, I'm ready to pin medals on women who stay home every day with their kids. For single mothers, I'm ready to build monuments.

Don't let anyone tell you otherwise: traditional mothers work harder 17
than anyone else can even imagine. They are on duty 24 hours a day, 365
days a year. I remember wondering, as a youth, why my own mother
always rushed around with such urgency when she was cooking or
cleaning. To me, she was like a woman possessed. Now I do the same
thing. When you have a young child (or two, or three), you have very
little time to get the dishes done, or cook dinner, or vacuum, or do the
laundry so when you get a moment, you proceed with all possible haste.
If your children are asleep, they might wake up. If they're playing, they
might get bored and demand your attention.

Friends who visit me nowadays probably think I'm crazy, the way I 18
rush compulsively to get dinner ready or mow the lawn or finish the
laundry. I do feel somewhat self-conscious about it. But the fact is, if I'm
cooking, Nick is going to start demanding his meal soon, and if it's not
ready, he's going to get very cranky. And with all the chores that pile up
on a weekend — the lawn, the laundry, the groceries, and so on — I have to
seize every possible instant. If he naps, that may give me an hour and a
half. If he wakes up before I'm done, whatever I'm doing will never get
finished.

In any case, it is on weekends alone with Nick that I feel the full brunt 19
of child-rearing. Consider a typical weekend: Nick wakes at 7:00, and we
lie in bed and play for half an hour before getting up. But this morning
he feels feverish, so I take his temperature. It is 101.6 — not high for a
young child, but a fever nonetheless.

The first thing I do is call Maureen, who takes care of him during the 20
week. Both of her kids have a bug, and I want to find out what the
symptoms are, to see if Nick has the same thing. From what we can tell,
he does. On that basis, I decide to give him Tylenol for the fever, rather
than taking him in to the pediatrician to see if he's got an ear infection.
Besides, he wants to lie down for a nap at 10:00, before I have decided,
and doesn't wake until 1:00. By then the office is closed.

After lunch he feels much better — cool, happy, and bubbling. We play 21
with his lock-blocks for a while, then watch a basketball game. He's very
cuddly, because he's not feeling well. After the game it's off to the bank
and grocery store. He falls asleep on the way home, at 5:45. It's an
awkward time for a nap, but he only sleeps until 6:30. He wakes up
crying, with a high fever, feeling miserable.

To get him to swallow more Tylenol, which he hates, I promise him ice 22
cream. I give him half an ice-cream sandwich while I rush around the
kitchen cooking dinner, and when he finishes it, he cries for the other
half. I tell him he can have it after he eats his dinner. But when dinner is
ready, he won't eat; he just sits there pointing at the freezer, where the ice
cream is, and wailing. This is a major tantrum — hot tears, red face. I can't
help but sympathize, though, because it's born of feeling absolutely
wretched. How should I respond? I don't want to give in and teach him
he can get his way by screaming. I try to comfort him by holding him in

my lap, but he just sobs. Finally I take him into his room and rock him, holding him close. Gradually the sobs subside, and after 10 minutes I take him back into the kitchen, hold him on my lap, and feed him myself. He doesn't eat much, but enough to deserve his ice cream.

23   Though Nick gets over the incident in no time, I am traumatized. The fever is frightening—it has hit 102 by dinnertime, and it only drops to 101.4 by 8 p.m. Should I have taken him to the doctor? Will he spike a really high fever tonight? Am I being too relaxed? And what will Rose say? I cannot stop worrying; I feel heartsick as I read him his bedtime stories, though he cools down as he drifts to sleep in my arms. Would a mother feel so uncertain, I wonder? Do mothers feel adequate at moments like this? Or am I in a father's territory here?

24   Sunday morning Nick wakes at 6:30 and devours his breakfast, but pretty soon his temperature begins to rise. I call our pediatrician, who reassures me that it doesn't sound like an ear infection, and that I'm doing the right thing. Still, Nick isn't feeling well, and it makes him more demanding. He wants to be held; he wants me with him constantly; he insists that I do what he wants me to do and cries if I balk. It is a wearing day. He naps late, and when I wake him at seven, he is again miserable— temperature at 102.4, crying, refusing to let me change his diaper. But after more Tylenol and a good dinner he feels better.

25   I haven't heard from Rose all weekend, so I decide to call her at the hospital. She is furious that I haven't taken Nick to the doctor. A child who gets ear infections as often as he does has to be checked, she yells at me. He could blow out an eardrum! And why haven't I called her—she's his mother, for God's sake! I'm exhausted, I've been busting my hump all weekend, alone, doing the best I can, and now I'm being abused. I don't like it. My first impulse is to hang up on her, but instead I hand the phone to Nicholas, who has a long talk with her. He says "Mommy!" she says "Nicholas!" and he laughs and laughs.

26   Rose may be right, I know, but that doesn't help my anger. We part tersely, and I promise to take him to the pediatrician the next morning before I leave for California on an article assignment. After that's out of the way, Nick and I have a good evening. We read books, and several times he leads me into his room to get another handful. A short bath, more books, then off to bed. He wants to take two of his trucks to bed with him—a new wrinkle—but I finally convince him to say "night-night" to his trucks and turn out the lights.

27   I have several hours of work to do before I leave, so I don't get to bed until after midnight. I'm absolutely shot. When the alarm rings at 6:00, I haul myself out of bed, shower, get dressed, and get Nick up and fed and dressed. We speed down to the library to return several books, then to the doctor's office. No ear infection; it's just a bug, says the doc, and he should be over it by nightfall. I drop Nick off at Maureen's by 9:30, race home, and spend the next hour packing, vacuuming, cleaning up the

dishes and defrosting something for Rose and Nick's dinner. When I get to the airport, I realize I've misread my ticket and I'm half an hour early. I'm exhausted, and the trip has yet to begin.

Two nights later I call Rose. When I ask how she is, she bursts into tears. Nicholas has fallen at Maureen's and cut his forehead on a metal toy. Rose was caught in an ice storm between the hospital and home, so Maureen had to take her own kids to a neighbor's and rush Nick to the pediatrician's office for stitches. They gave him a local anesthetic, but he screamed the whole time. 28

"I feel so awful," Rose sobs, over and over. "I should have been there. I just feel awful." Guilt floods in, but it is nothing to match Rose's guilt. This is one of the differences I have discovered between mothers and fathers. 29

Rose has felt guilty since the day she went back to work—the hardest single thing I've ever watched her do. Deep inside her psyche lies a powerful message that she belongs at home, that if she is not with her child she is terribly irresponsible. 30

I feel guilty only occasionally. When I dropped Nick off at day care the first day after returning from California, and he sobbed because he thought I was leaving him again, the guilt just about killed me. I turned into a classic mother: as soon as I got home, I called to see if he was still crying. (He was.) Two guilt-ridden hours later I called again, desperate to hear that everything was fine. (It was.) 31

Deep within my psyche, however, the most powerful message is that I belong at work, that if I am not out making my mark on the world I am worth nothing. 32

The contradiction between family and career is nothing new; it is perhaps the central unresolved conflict in the lives of American women today. What I did not expect was the force with which that conflict would erupt in my life. 33

Like an addict, I now find myself squeezing in every last minute of work that I can. I wait until the last possible instant before rushing out the door to pick Nick up in the afternoon. I dart out to my study while he naps on weekends, using a portable intercom to listen for his cries. At night I compulsively page through old newspapers that pile up because I can no longer read them over breakfast, afraid I've missed something important. As I hit deadline time, I pray that Nicholas doesn't get sick. I have even tried writing on a Saturday afternoon, with Nick playing in my studio. That experiment lasted half an hour, at which point he hit the reset button on the back of my computer and my prose was lost to the ages. 34

This frantic effort to keep up is clearly not good for me, but I cannot seem to abandon it. I constantly feel as if I live in a pressure cooker. I long for a free day, even a free hour. But my career has taken off just as my 35 responsibilities as a father have hit their peak, and I cannot seem to scale down my commitment to either.

36   When Nick was four months old, I took him to a Christmas party, one Saturday when Rose was working. After an hour or so he got cranky, so I took him upstairs with a bottle. A little girl followed, and soon her brother and sister—equally bored by the goings-on downstairs—had joined us. It wasn't long before Dad came looking for them.

37   We introduced ourselves and talked for a bit. His wife, it turned out, was also a doctor. The curious part came when I asked what he did. First he told me all the things he had done in the past: carpentry, business, you name it. Then he said he'd done enough—he was about 40—and felt no need to prove himself any more. Finally he told me he stayed at home with the kids. And frankly, he pulled it off with far more dignity and less stammering than I would have, had our places been reversed.

38   I don't think I could do what he does. If I were to stay home full-time with Nick, I would quickly lose my self-esteem, and within months I would be deep into an identity crisis. Part of the reason I love my role as a father is that I am secure in my role as a writer. Without that, I would not feel good enough about myself to be the kind of father I am.

39   This is not simply a problem inside male heads. How many women would be content with men who stayed home with the kids? Not many, I'll wager. And not my wife, I know. From my experience, modern women want a man who will share the responsibilities at home but still be John Wayne in the outside world. They don't want any wimps wearing aprons. And men know it.

40   We are in a Burger King, in Fall River, Massachusetts. We are not having a good day. We drove two hours to shop in the factory outlets here, and all but a handful are closed because it's Sunday.

41   Nick likes Burger King, but he's not having a great day either. He has recently learned about tantrums, and as we get ready to leave, he decides to throw one. He doesn't want to leave; he doesn't want to put on his coat; he just doesn't want to be hauled around any more. So he stands up and wails.

42   Rose is mortified; she takes any misbehavior in public as an advertisement of her failings as a mother. It triggers all her guilt about working. This time, the timing couldn't be worse, because she is already on edge.

43   Our tantrum strategy is generally to let him yell, to ignore him, and thus to teach him that it does no good. But in a public restaurant, I don't have the stamina to ignore him, so I cross the room to pick him up.

44   Rose orders me away from him, in no uncertain terms. There are no negotiations, no consultations. We are going to do this her way or no way.

45   That lights my fuse, of course, and after simmering for 10 minutes, I bring it up. "Let it go," she tells me, almost in tears over Nicholas. "It's not important."

It's not important.   46

Ah, the double bind. You're in charge one day, playing mother and   47
father all wrapped into one, depended upon to feed him and clothe him
and change him and bathe him and rock him and meet his every need.
And the next day you're a third wheel, because Mom is around. You are
expected to put in the long hours, but to pretend in public that you don't,
for fear of undercutting your wife's sense of self-worth as a mother. How
could she be doing her job, her psyche seems to whisper, if she's letting
someone else make half the decisions and give half the care? There are
many double binds in modern relationships, and this is the one I like the
least.

I didn't let it drop that day, of course. At home, when Rose asserts the   48
traditional mother's prerogative to make decisions and handle problems
alone, on her terms, I often let it go. But when it happens in public, or in
front of family, it is too much. It is as if my entire contribution to raising
Nicholas is being denied, as if the world is being told that I am nothing
more than a spectator. Luckily, as Nick grows older, and it becomes clear
to Rose that she will always be number one in his heart, she has begun
to relax her public vigilance, and this problem seems to have abated.

This is the first time I've ever been part of a woman's world. I'm not   49
really a part of it, of course; the chasm between the sexes is too wide to
step across so lightly. But when it comes to children, I have instant
rapport with most mothers. We talk about the same things, think about
the same things, joke about the same things. With men, it is almost never
that way, even when the men are fathers and the subject is kids. We can
share enthusiasms, but the sense of being there, on the inside—the
unspoken understanding that comes out of shared experience—that is
missing.

In fact, most men don't have the slightest idea what my life with Nick   50
is like. When I tell colleagues—even those with children—that I have no
time to read, or to watch television, I get blank stares. (I never tell
mothers that; they already know. Who has time to read?) One friend,
also a writer, stopped in the middle of a recent conversation and said,
"You have Nick at home while you're working, don't you? What do you
do with him?" No such thought could pass a mother's lips.

None of this would have been possible had I not been forced into   51
taking care of Nick on my own much of the time. In fact, my entire
relationship with Nick would have been different had I not been forced
off the sidelines. I am convinced that in our society, when Mom is home
with the kids, it is almost impossible for Dad to be an equal partner in
their upbringing, even if he wants to be.

I believe this because for three weeks, while Rose was home after   52
Nick's birth, it felt impossible to me. Rose had carried Nick for nine
months; Rose had been through labor; and Rose was nursing him. For
nine months he had listened to her heartbeat, felt her pulse, been a part

of her being. Now he hunted her scent and drank from her body, and the bond between them was awesome. I was like some voyeur, peeking through the window at an ancient and sacred rite.

53   Then Rose went back to work, and I had no choice but to get off the sidelines. I *had* to get Nick dressed in the morning. I *had* to feed him. I *had* to burp him and rock him and change him and get up with him in the night. He may have wanted his mother, but she wasn't there.

54   Gradually, it all began to come naturally. I learned to carry him on my (nonexistent) hip and do anything—or any combination of things—with one hand. I learned to whip up a bottle in no time, to change a diaper and treat diaper rash and calm his tears.

55   Even on vacation, it is remarkably easy to slip back into a traditional role—for both Rose and me. But the day Rose goes back to work, I am always yanked back to reality. I complain a lot, but in truth, this is my great good fortune.

56   Last night Nick asked to go to the beach—"Go? Beach? Go? Beach?" I walked him the two blocks down, one of his hands firmly in mine, the other proudly holding the leash for Sam, our dog. We played on the swings for a long time, then strolled along the beach while Sam went swimming. It was that very still hour before dark, when the world slows to a hush, and little boys and girls slowly wind down. It was almost dark when we returned. Nick asked his daddy to give him his bath, then his mommy to put him to bed.

57   This morning when I woke he was lying beside me, on his mother's empty pillow. I looked over and he gave me a big smile, his eyes shining with that special, undiluted joy one sees only in children. Then he propped himself up on his elbows, leaned over and kissed me. If there are any better moments in life, I've never found them.

❏ Questions for Discussion

1. To what does Osborne's title refer?

2. Osborne's staying home with his son defies traditional family roles. What difficulties does this defiance create?

3. Osborne quotes a letter by Rosalie Ziomek to the *New Republic* as describing " 'the hardest part of new motherhood: the moment-to-moment dependency of a tiny, helpless, and demanding human being.' " Precisely what does that dependency entail for the mother? How does Osborne's essay convincingly develop the consequences of that dependency?

4. Certainly, Osborne's role as father differs from that of other, traditional fathers. It also, however, as he says, differs from that of traditional mothers. How?

5. Osborne spends much more time with Nicholas than does his wife, yet Rose feels greater guilt than Osborne when Nicholas is hurt or sick or when he throws a tantrum. Why?

❑ **Suggestions for Exploration and Writing**

1. Osborne calls the "contradiction between family and career . . . the central unresolved conflict in the lives of American women today." In an essay drawn from your experience or observation, develop this assertion.

2. Osborne declares that he could not stay at home full time: "Part of the reason I love my role as a father is that I am secure in my role as a writer. Without that, I would not feel good enough about myself to be the kind of father I am." Why must he prove himself in ways other than fatherhood? Do men share the "unresolved conflict" Osborne attributes to women?

FICTION

KATE CHOPIN (1850–1904)

Katherine O'Flaherty was born in St. Louis, Missouri, but moved to Louisiana when she married Oscar Chopin in 1870. New Orleans and the Grande Isle are the setting for most of her stories and for her novel The Awakening (1899), *which shocked readers because of her treatment of adultery and suicide. Her stories deal with marriages that are failing, women in the process of achieving independence, or subjects such as miscegenation and integration. Both "Désirée's Baby" and "The Story of an Hour" deal honestly with women's emotions.*

Désirée's Baby

As the day was pleasant, Madame Valmondé drove over to L'Abri to see Désirée and the baby.

It made her laugh to think of Désirée with a baby. Why, it seemed but yesterday that Désirée was little more than a baby herself; when Monsieur in riding through the gateway of Valmondé had found her lying asleep in the shadow of the big stone pillar.

The little one awoke in his arms and began to cry for "Dada." That was as much as she could do or say. Some people thought she might have strayed there of her own accord, for she was of the toddling age. The prevailing belief was that she had been purposely left by a party of

Texans, whose canvas-covered wagon, late in the day, had crossed the ferry that Coton Maïs kept, just below the plantation. In time Madame Valmondé abandoned every speculation but the one that Désirée had been sent to her by a beneficent Providence to be the child of her affection, seeing that she was without child of the flesh. For the girl grew to be beautiful and gentle, affectionate and sincere,—the idol of Valmondé.

4   It was no wonder, when she stood one day against the stone pillar in whose shadow she had lain asleep, eighteen years before, that Armand Aubigny riding by and seeing her there, had fallen in love with her. That was the way all the Aubignys fell in love, as if struck by a pistol shot. The wonder was that he had not loved her before; for he had known her since his father brought him home from Paris, a boy of eight, after his mother died there. The passion that awoke in him that day, when he saw her at the gate, swept along like an avalanche, or like a prairie fire, or like anything that drives headlong over all obstacles.

5   Monsieur Valmondé grew practical and wanted things well considered: that is, the girl's obscure origin. Armand looked into her eyes and did not care. He was reminded that she was nameless. What did it matter about a name when he could give her one of the oldest and proudest in Louisiana? He ordered the *corbeille* from Paris, and contained himself with what patience he could until it arrived; then they were married.

6   Madame Valmondé had not seen Désirée and the baby for four weeks. When she reached L'Abri she shuddered at the first sight of it, as she always did. It was a sad looking place, which for many years had not known the gentle presence of a mistress, old Monsieur Aubigny having married and buried his wife in France, and she having loved her own land too well ever to leave it. The roof came down steep and black like a cowl, reaching out beyond the wide galleries that encircled the yellow stuccoed house. Big, solemn oaks grew close to it, and their thick-leaved, far-reaching branches shadowed it like a pall. Young Aubigny's rule was a strict one, too, and under it his negroes had forgotten how to be gay, as they had been during the old master's easy-going and indulgent lifetime.

7   The young mother was recovering slowly, and lay full length, in her soft white muslins and laces, upon a couch. The baby was beside her, upon her arm, where he had fallen asleep, at her breast. The yellow nurse woman sat beside a window fanning herself.

8   Madame Valmondé bent her portly figure over Désirée and kissed her, holding her an instant tenderly in her arms. Then she turned to the child.

9   "This is not the baby!" she exclaimed, in startled tones. French was the language spoken at Valmondé in those days.

10   "I knew you would be astonished," laughed Désirée, "at the way he has grown. The little *cochon de lait!* Look at his legs, mamma, and his hands and fingernails,—real finger-nails. Zandrine had to cut them this morning. Isn't it true, Zandrine?"

The woman bowed her turbaned head majestically, "Mais si, 11
Madame."

"And the way he cries," went on Désirée, "is deafening. Armand heard 12
him the other day as far away as La Blanche's cabin."

Madame Valmondé had never removed her eyes from the child. She 13
lifted it and walked with it over to the window that was lightest. She
scanned the baby narrowly, then looked as searchingly at Zandrine,
whose face was turned to gaze across the fields.

"Yes, the child has grown, has changed;" said Madame Valmondé, 14
slowly, as she replaced it beside its mother. "What does Armand say?"

Désirée's face became suffused with a glow that was happiness itself. 15

"Oh, Armand is the proudest father in the parish, I believe, chiefly 16
because it is a boy, to bear his name; though he says not,—that he would
have loved a girl as well. But I know it isn't true. I know he says that to
please me. And mamma," she added, drawing Madame Valmondé's head
down to her, and speaking in a whisper, "he hasn't punished one of
them—not one of them—since baby is born. Even Négrillon, who pretended to have burnt his leg that he might rest from work—he only
laughed, and said Négrillon was a great scamp. Oh, mamma, I'm so
happy; it frightens me."

What Désirée said was true. Marriage, and later the birth of his son, 17
had softened Armand Aubigny's imperious and exacting nature greatly.
This was what made the gentle Désirée so happy, for she loved him
desperately. When he frowned she trembled, but loved him. When he
smiled, she asked no greater blessing of God. But Armand's dark, handsome face had not often been disfigured by frowns since the day he fell in
love with her.

When the baby was about three months old, Désirée awoke one day to 18
the conviction that there was something in the air menacing her peace. It
was at first too subtle to grasp. It had only been a disquieting suggestion;
an air of mystery among the blacks; unexpected visits from far-off
neighbors who could hardly account for their coming. Then a strange, an
awful change in her husband's manner, which she dared not ask him to
explain. When he spoke to her, it was with averted eyes, from which the
old love-light seemed to have gone out. He absented himself from home;
and when there, avoided her presence and that of her child, without
excuse. And the very spirit of Satan seemed suddenly to take hold of him
in his dealings with the slaves. Désirée was miserable enough to die.

She sat in her room, one hot afternoon, in her *peignoir*, listlessly 19
drawing through her fingers the strands of her long, silky brown hair that
hung about her shoulders. The baby, half naked, lay asleep upon her own
great mahogany bed, that was like a sumptuous throne, with its satin-
lined half-canopy. One of La Blanche's little quadroon boys—half naked
too—stood fanning the child slowly with a fan of peacock feathers.
Désirée's eyes had been fixed absently and sadly upon the baby, while she

was striving to penetrate the threatening mist that she felt closing about her. She looked from her child to the boy who stood beside him, and back again; over and over. "Ah!" It was a cry that she could not help which she was not conscious of having uttered. The blood turned like ice in her veins, and a clammy moisture gathered upon her face.

20   She tried to speak to the little quadroon boy; but no sound would come, at first. When he heard his name uttered, he looked up, and his mistress was pointing to the door. He laid aside the great, soft fan, and obediently stole away, over the polished floor, on his bare tiptoes.

21   She stayed motionless, with gaze riveted upon her child, and her face the picture of fright.

22   Presently her husband entered the room, and without noticing her, went to a table and began to search among some papers which covered it.

23   "Armand," she called to him, in a voice which must have stabbed him, if he was human. But he did not notice. "Armand," she said again. Then she rose and tottered toward him. "Armand," she panted once more, clutching his arm, "look at our child. What does it mean? tell me."

24   He coldly but gently loosened her fingers from about his arm and thrust the hand away from him. "Tell me what it means!" she cried despairingly.

25   "It means," he answered lightly, "that the child is not white; it means that you are not white."

26   A quick conception of all that this accusation meant for her nerved her with unwonted courage to deny it. "It is a lie; it is not true, I am white! Look at my hair, it is brown; and my eyes are gray, Armand, you know they are gray. And my skin is fair," seizing his wrist. "Look at my hand; whiter than yours, Armand," she laughed hysterically.

27   "As white as La Blanche's," he returned cruelly; and went away leaving her alone with their child.

28   When she could hold a pen in her hand, she sent a despairing letter to Madame Valmondé.

29   "My mother, they tell me I am not white. Armand has told me I am not white. For God's sake tell them it is not true. You must know it is not true. I shall die. I must die. I cannot be so unhappy, and live."

30   The answer that came was as brief:

31   "My own Désirée: Come home to Valmondé; back to your mother who loves you. Come with your child."

32   When the letter reached Désirée she went with it to her husband's study, and laid it open upon the desk before which he sat. She was like a stone image: silent, white, motionless after she placed it there.

33   In silence he ran his cold eyes over the written words. He said nothing. "Shall I go, Armand?" she asked in tones sharp with agonized suspense.

34   "Yes, go."

35   "Do you want me to go?"

"Yes, I want you to go."   36

He thought Almighty God had dealt cruelly and unjustly with him; and   37
felt, somehow, that he was paying Him back in kind when he stabbed
thus into his wife's soul. Moreover he no longer loved her, because of the
unconscious injury she had brought upon his home and his name.

She turned away like one stunned by a blow, and walked slowly   38
towards the door, hoping he would call her back.

"Good-by, Armand," she moaned.   39

He did not answer her. That was his last blow at fate.   40

Désirée went in search of her child. Zandrine was pacing the sombre   41
gallery with it. She took the little one from the nurse's arms with no word
of explanation, and descending the steps, walked away, under the live-
oak branches.

It was an October afternoon; the sun was just sinking. Out in the still   42
fields the negroes were picking cotton.

Désirée had not changed the thin white garment nor the slippers which   43
she wore. Her hair was uncovered and the sun's rays brought a golden
gleam from its brown meshes. She did not take the broad, beaten road
which led to the far-off plantation of Valmondé. She walked across a
deserted field, where the stubble bruised her tender feet, so delicately
shod, and tore her thin gown to shreds.

She disappeared among the reeds and willows that grew thick along   44
the banks of the deep, sluggish bayou; and she did not come back again.

* * * * *

Some weeks later there was a curious scene enacted at L'Abri. In the   45
centre of the smoothly swept back yard was a great bonfire. Armand
Aubigny sat in the wide hallway that commanded a view of the spectacle;
and it was he who dealt out to a half dozen negroes the material which
kept this fire ablaze.

A graceful cradle of willow, with all its dainty furbishings, was laid   46
upon the pyre, which had already been fed with the richness of a priceless
layette. Then there were silk gowns, and velvet and satin ones added to
these; laces, too, and embroideries; bonnets and gloves; for the *corbeille*
had been of rare quality.

The last thing to go was a tiny bundle of letters; innocent little   47
scribblings that Désirée had sent to him during the days of their espousal.
There was the remnant of one back in the drawer from which he took
them. But it was not Désirée's; it was part of an old letter from his mother
to his father. He read it. She was thanking God for the blessing of her
husband's love: —

"But, above all," she wrote, "night and day, I thank the good God for   48
having so arranged our lives that our dear Armand will never know that
his mother, who adores him, belongs to the race that is cursed with the
brand of slavery."

❏ Questions for Discussion

1. This story takes place in Louisiana in the latter part of the nineteenth century. Would the results of such a discovery about the baby be the same today? Why or why not?

2. Explain the **irony** of the phrase "cursed with the brand of slavery."

3. Define *white* and *quadroon*.

4. This story has a surprise ending. For such an ending to be artistically effective, the author should give readers clues that such an eventuality is possible. Were you sufficiently prepared for the end of the story? Explain your answer.

❏ Suggestions for Exploration and Writing

1. Write an essay either on the social acceptability of interracial marriages or on your personal feelings toward them.

2. Go beyond the story to speculate on what happens to Désirée and her baby.

The Story of an Hour

1   Knowing that Mrs. Mallard was afflicted with a heart trouble, great care was taken to break to her as gently as possible the news of her husband's death.

2   It was her sister Josephine who told her, in broken sentences; veiled hints that revealed in half concealing. Her husband's friend Richards was there, too, near her. It was he who had been in the newspaper office when intelligence of the railroad disaster was received, with Brently Mallard's name leading the list of "killed." He had only taken the time to assure himself of its truth by a second telegram, and had hastened to forestall any less careful, less tender friend in bearing the sad message.

3   She did not hear the story as many women have heard the same, with a paralyzed inability to accept its significance. She wept at once, with sudden, wild abandonment, in her sister's arms. When the storm of grief had spent itself she went away to her room alone. She would have no one follow her.

4   There stood, facing the open window, a comfortable, roomy armchair. Into this she sank, pressed down by a physical exhaustion that haunted her body and seemed to reach into her soul.

5   She could see in the open square before her house the tops of trees that were all aquiver with the new spring life. The delicious breath of rain was in the air. In the street below a peddler was crying his wares. The notes of a distant song which some one was singing reached her faintly, and countless sparrows were twittering in the eaves.

There were patches of blue sky showing here and there through the clouds that had met and piled one above the other in the west facing her window. 6

She sat with her head thrown back upon the cushion of the chair, quite motionless, except when a sob came up into her throat and shook her, as a child who has cried itself to sleep continues to sob in its dreams. 7

She was young, with a fair, calm face, whose lines bespoke repression and even a certain strength. But now there was a dull stare in her eyes, whose gaze was fixed away off yonder on one of those patches of blue sky. It was not a glance of reflection, but rather indicated a suspension of intelligent thought. 8

There was something coming to her and she was waiting for it, fearfully. What was it? She did not know; it was too subtle and elusive to name. But she felt it, creeping out of the sky, reaching toward her through the sounds, the scents, the color that filled the air. 9

Now her bosom rose and fell tumultuously. She was beginning to recognize this thing that was approaching to possess her, and she was striving to beat it back with her will—as powerless as her two white slender hands would have been. 10

When she abandoned herself a little whispered word escaped her slightly parted lips. She said it over and over under her breath: "free, free, free!" The vacant stare and the look of terror that had followed it went from her eyes. They stayed keen and bright. Her pulses beat fast and the coursing blood warmed and relaxed every inch of her body. 11

She did not stop to ask if it were or were not a monstrous joy that held her. A clear and exalted perception enabled her to dismiss the suggestion as trivial. 12

She knew that she would weep again when she saw the kind, tender hands folded in death; the face that had never looked save with love upon her, fixed and gray and dead. But she saw beyond that bitter moment a long procession of years to come that would belong to her absolutely. And she opened and spread her arms out to them in welcome. 13

There would be no one to live for her during those coming years; she would live for herself. There would be no powerful will bending hers in that blind persistence with which men and women believe they have a right to impose a private will upon a fellow-creature. A kind intention or a cruel intention made the act seem no less a crime as she looked upon it in that brief moment of illumination. 14

And yet she had loved him—sometimes. Often she had not. What did it matter! What could love, the unsolved mystery, count for in face of this possession of self-assertion which she suddenly recognized as the strongest impulse of her being! 15

"Free! Body and soul free!" she kept whispering. 16

Josephine was kneeling before the closed door with her lips to the keyhole, imploring for admission. "Louise, open the door! I beg; open 17 the door—you will make yourself ill. What are you doing, Louise? For heaven's sake open the door."

18   "Go away. I am not making myself ill." No; she was drinking in a very elixir of life through that open window.

19   Her fancy was running riot along those days ahead of her. Spring days, and summer days, and all sorts of days that would be her own. She breathed a quick prayer that life might be long. It was only yesterday she had thought with a shudder that life might be long.

20   She arose at length and opened the door to her sister's importunities. There was a feverish triumph in her eyes, and she carried herself unwittingly like a goddess of Victory. She clasped her sister's waist, and together they descended the stairs. Richards stood waiting for them at the bottom.

21   Some one was opening the front door with a latchkey. It was Brently Mallard who entered, a little travel-stained, composedly carrying his grip-sack and umbrella. He had been far from the scene of accident, and did not even know there had been one. He stood amazed at Josephine's piercing cry; at Richards' quick motion to screen him from the view of his wife.

22   But Richards was too late.

23   When the doctors came they said she had died of heart disease—of joy that kills.

❏ Questions for Discussion

1. Is Louise Mallard's initial response to the death of her husband normal? What is she waiting for? Why does she want to "beat it back with her will"?

2. Why does Mrs. Mallard feel joy and freedom at her husband's death? Is there any evidence that he mistreated her? Is his love for her in any sense deficient?

3. From whose point of view is the last phrase—"of joy that kills"—written? Explain the **irony** of this diagnosis.

4. Explain the **symbolism** of the open window and of Louise Mallard's last name.

❏ Suggestions for Exploration and Writing

1. Compare the attitudes of the husbands toward the wives in this story and in "The Yellow Wallpaper."

2. What do you discover about Brently Mallard from his wife? Write a character analysis of Brently Mallard.

3. Most of Kate Chopin's stories have some kind of **epiphany** or awakening. Discuss the awakening in this story.

CHARLOTTE PERKINS GILMAN (1860–1935)

Charlotte Perkins Gilman was best known during her lifetime as a lecturer and author of books on the rights of women and on socialism. Yet today she is most famous for what is generally acknowledged as her best short story, "The Yellow Wallpaper." According to Gilman, the story was written after she had suffered a nervous breakdown. A specialist in nervous diseases, consulted as a result of Gilman's depression, advised her first husband to allow her to participate only in domestic life and to terminate her painting and writing. After three months of this treatment, she was near a mental breakdown. Unlike the narrator of "The Yellow Wallpaper," Gilman went on to a successful second marriage and a career. She continued to suffer from depression at times and committed suicide in 1935 as a result of severe pain caused by cancer.

The Yellow Wallpaper

It is very seldom that mere ordinary people like John and myself secure ancestral halls for the summer. 1

A colonial mansion, a hereditary estate, I would say a haunted house and reach the height of romantic felicity—but that would be asking too much of fate! 2

Still I will proudly declare that there is something queer about it. 3

Else, why should it be let so cheaply? And why have stood so long untenanted? 4

John laughs at me, of course, but one expects that. 5

John is practical in the extreme. He has no patience with faith, an intense horror of superstition, and he scoffs openly at any talk of things not to be felt and seen and put down in figures. 6

John is a physician, and *perhaps*—(I would not say it to a living soul, of course, but this is dead paper and a great relief to my mind)—*perhaps* that is one reason I do not get well faster. 7

You see, he does not believe I am sick! And what can one do? 8

If a physician of high standing, and one's own husband, assures friends and relatives that there is really nothing the matter with one but temporary nervous depression—a slight hysterical tendency—what is one to do? 9

My brother is also a physician, and also of high standing, and he says the same thing. 10

So I take phosphates or phosphites—whichever it is—and tonics, and air and exercise, and journeys, and am absolutely forbidden to "work" until I am well again. 11

Personally, I disagree with their ideas. 12

Personally, I believe that congenial work, with excitement and change, would do me good. 13

But what is one to do? 14

I did write for a while in spite of them; but it *does* exhaust me a good deal—having to be so sly about it, or else meet with heavy opposition. 15

16   I sometimes fancy that in my condition, if I had less opposition and more society and stimulus—but John says the very worst thing I can do is to think about my condition, and I confess it always makes me feel bad.

17   So I will let it alone and talk about the house.

18   The most beautiful place! It is quite alone, standing well back from the road, quite three miles from the village. It makes me think of English places that you read about, for there are hedges and walls and gates that lock, and lots of separate little houses for the gardeners and people.

19   There is a *delicious* garden! I never saw such a garden—large and shady, full of box-bordered paths, and lined with long grape-covered arbors with seats under them.

20   There were greenhouses, but they are all broken now.

21   There was some legal trouble, I believe, something about the heirs and co-heirs; anyhow, the place has been empty for years.

22   That spoils my ghostliness, I am afraid, but I don't care—there is something strange about the house—I can feel it.

23   I even said so to John one moonlight evening, but he said what I felt was a draught, and shut the window.

24   I get unreasonably angry with John sometimes. I'm sure I never used to be so sensitive. I think it is due to this nervous condition.

25   But John says if I feel so I shall neglect proper self-control; so I take pains to control myself—before him, at least, and that makes me very tired.

26   I don't like our room a bit. I wanted one downstairs that opened onto the piazza and had roses all over the window, and such pretty old-fashioned chintz hangings! But John would not hear of it.

27   He said there was only one window and not room for two beds, and no near room for him if he took another.

28   He is very careful and loving, and hardly lets me stir without special direction.

29   I have a schedule prescription for each hour in the day; he takes all care from me, and so I feel basely ungrateful not to value it more.

30   He said he came here solely on my account, that I was to have perfect rest and all the air I could get. "Your exercise depends on your strength, my dear," said he, "and your food somewhat on your appetite; but air you can absorb all the time." So we took the nursery at the top of the house.

31   It is a big, airy room, the whole floor nearly, with windows that look all ways, and air and sunshine galore. It was nursery first, and then playroom and gymnasium, I should judge, for the windows are barred for little children, and there are rings and things in the walls.

32   The paint and paper look as if a boys' school had used it. It is stripped off—the paper—in great patches all around the head of my bed, about as far as I can reach, and in a great place on the other side of the room low down. I never saw a worse paper in my life. One of those sprawling, flamboyant patterns committing every artistic sin.

It is dull enough to confuse the eye in following, pronounced enough   33
constantly to irritate and provoke study, and when you follow the lame
uncertain curves for a little distance they suddenly commit suicide—
plunge off at outrageous angles, destroy themselves in unheard-of contradictions.

The color is repellent, almost revolting: a smouldering unclean yellow,   34
strangely faded by the slow-turning sunlight. It is a dull yet lurid orange
in some places, a sickly sulphur tint in others.

No wonder the children hated it! I should hate it myself if I had to live   35
in this room long.

There comes John, and I must put this away—he hates to have me   36
write a word.

We have been here two weeks, and I haven't felt like writing before,   37
since that first day.

I am sitting by the window now, up in this atrocious nursery, and there   38
is nothing to hinder my writing as much as I please, save lack of strength.

John is away all day, and even some nights when his cases are serious.   39

I am glad my case is not serious!   40

But these nervous troubles are dreadfully depressing.   41

John does not know how much I really suffer. He knows there is no   42
reason to suffer, and that satisfies him.

Of course it is only nervousness. It does weigh on me so not to do my   43
duty in any way!

I meant to be such a help to John, such a real rest and comfort, and   44
here I am a comparative burden already!

Nobody would believe what an effort it is to do what little I am able—   45
to dress and entertain, and order things.

It is fortunate Mary is so good with the baby. Such a dear baby!   46

And yet I *cannot* be with him, it makes me so nervous.   47

I suppose John never was nervous in his life. He laughs at me so about   48
this wallpaper!

At first he meant to repaper the room, but afterward he said that I was   49
letting it get the better of me, and that nothing was worse for a nervous
patient than to give way to such fancies.

He said that after the wallpaper was changed it would be the heavy   50
bedstead, and then the barred windows, and then the gate at the head of
the stairs, and so on.

"You know the place is doing you good," he said, "and really, dear, I   51
don't care to renovate the house just for a three months' rental."

"Then do let us go downstairs," I said. "There are such pretty rooms   52
there."

Then he took me in his arms and called me a blessed little goose, and   53
said he would go down cellar, if I wished, and have it whitewashed into
the bargain.

But he is right enough about the beds and windows and things.   54

55   It is as as airy and comfortable a room as anyone need wish, and, of course, I would not be so silly as to make him uncomfortable just for a whim.

56   I'm really getting quite fond of the big room, all but that horrid paper.

57   Out of one window I can see the garden—those mysterious deep-shaded arbors, the riotous old-fashioned flowers, and bushes and gnarly trees.

58   Out of another I get a lovely view of the bay and a little private wharf belonging to the estate. There is a beautiful shaded lane that runs down there from the house. I always fancy I see people walking in these numerous paths and arbors, but John has cautioned me not to give way to fancy in the least. He says that with my imaginative power and habit of story-making, a nervous weakness like mine is sure to lead to all manner of excited fancies, and that I ought to use my will and good sense to check the tendency. So I try.

59   I think sometimes that if I were only well enough to write a little it would relieve the press of ideas and rest me.

60   But I find I get pretty tired when I try.

61   It is so discouraging not to have any advice and companionship about my work. When I get really well, John says we will ask Cousin Henry and Julia down for a long visit; but he says he would as soon put fireworks in my pillow-case as to let me have those stimulating people about now.

62   I wish I could get well faster.

63   But I must not think about that. This paper looks to me as if it *knew* what a vicious influence it had!

64   There is a recurrent spot where the pattern lolls like a broken neck and two bulbous eyes stare at you upside down.

65   I get positively angry with the impertinence of it and the everlasting-ness. Up and down and sideways they crawl, and those absurd unblink-ing eyes are everywhere. There is one place where two breadths didn't match, and the eyes go all up and down the line, one a little higher than the other.

66   I never saw so much expression in an inanimate thing before, and we all know how much expression they have! I used to lie awake as a child and get more entertainment and terror out of blank walls and plain furniture than most children could find in a toy-store.

67   I remember what a kindly wink the knobs of our big old bureau used to have, and there was one chair that always seemed like a strong friend.

68   I used to feel that if any of the other things looked too fierce I could always hop into that chair and be safe.

69   The furniture in this room is no worse than inharmonious, however, for we had to bring it all from downstairs. I suppose when this was used as a playroom they had to take the nursery things out, and no wonder! I never saw such ravages as the children have made here.

70   The wallpaper, as I said before, is torn off in spots, and it sticketh closer than a brother—they must have had perseverance as well as hatred.

Then the floor is scratched and gouged and splintered, the plaster itself 71
is dug out here and there, and this great heavy bed, which is all we found
in the room, looks as if it had been through the wars.

But I don't mind it a bit—only the paper. 72

There comes John's sister. Such a dear girl as she is, and so careful of 73
me! I must not let her find me writing.

She is a perfect and enthusiastic housekeeper, and hopes for no better 74
profession. I verily believe she thinks it is the writing which made me
sick!

But I can write when she is out, and see her a long way off from these 75
windows.

There is one that commands the road, a lovely shaded winding road, 76
and one that just looks off over the country. A lovely country, too, full
of great elms and velvet meadows.

This wallpaper has a kind of sub-pattern in a different shade, a 77
particularly irritating one, for you can only see it in certain lights, and not
clearly then.

But in the places where it isn't faded and where the sun is just so—I can 78
see a strange, provoking, formless sort of figure that seems to skulk about
behind that silly and conspicuous front design.

There's sister on the stairs! 79

Well, the Fourth of July is over! The people are all gone, and I am tired 80
out. John thought it might do me good to see a little company, so we just
had Mother and Nellie and the children down for a week.

Of course I didn't do a thing. Jennie sees to everything now. 81

But it tired me all the same. 82

John says if I don't pick up faster he shall send me to Weir Mitchell in 83
the fall.

But I don't want to go there at all. I had a friend who was in his hands 84
once, and she says he is just like John and my brother, only more so!

Besides, it is such an undertaking to go so far. 85

I don't feel as if it was worthwhile to turn my hand over for anything, 86
and I'm getting dreadfully fretful and querulous.

I cry at nothing, and cry most of the time. 87

Of course I don't when John is here, or anybody else, but when I am 88
alone.

And I am alone a good deal just now. John is kept in town very often 89
by serious cases, and Jennie is good and lets me alone when I want her to.

So I walk a little in the garden or down that lovely lane, sit on the 90
porch under the roses, and lie down up here a good deal.

I'm getting really fond of the room in spite of the wallpaper. Perhaps 91
because of the wallpaper.

It dwells in my mind so! 92

I lie here on this great immovable bed—it is nailed down, I believe— 93
and follow that pattern about by the hour. It is as good as gymnastics, I
assure you. I start, we'll say, at the bottom, down in the corner over there

where it has not been touched, and I determine for the thousandth time that I *will* follow that pointless pattern to some sort of a conclusion.

94   I know a little of the principle of design, and I know this thing was not arranged on any laws of radiation, or alternation, or repetition, or symmetry, or anything else that I ever heard of.

95   It is repeated, of course, by the breadths, but not otherwise.

96   Looked at in one way, each breadth stands alone; the bloated curves and flourishes—a kind of "debased Romanesque" with delirium tremens go waddling up and down in isolated columns of fatuity.

97   But, on the other hand, they connect diagonally, and the sprawling outlines run off in great slanting waves of optic horror, like a lot of wallowing sea-weeds in full chase.

98   The whole thing goes horizontally, too, at least it seems so, and I exhaust myself trying to distinguish the order of its going in that direction.

99   They have used a horizontal breadth for a frieze, and that adds wonderfully to the confusion.

100   There is one end of the room where it is almost intact, and there, when the crosslights fade and the low sun shines directly upon it, I can almost fancy radiation after all—the interminable grotesque seems to form around a common center and rush off in headlong plunges of equal distraction.

101   It makes me tired to follow it. I will take a nap, I guess.

102   I don't know why I should write this.

103   I don't want to.

104   I don't feel able.

105   And I know John would think it absurd. But I *must* say what I feel and think in some way—it is such a relief!

106   But the effort is getting to be greater than the relief.

107   Half the time now I am awfully lazy, and lie down ever so much. John says I mustn't lose my strength, and has me take cod liver oil and lots of tonics and things, to say nothing of ale and wine and rare meat.

108   Dear John! He loves me very dearly, and hates to have me sick. I tried to have a real earnest reasonable talk with him the other day, and tell him how I wish he would let me go and make a visit to Cousin Henry and Julia.

109   But he said I wasn't able to go, nor able to stand it after I got there; and I did not make out a very good case for myself, for I was crying before I had finished.

110   It is getting to be a great effort for me to think straight. Just this nervous weakness, I suppose.

111   And dear John gathered me up in his arms, and just carried me upstairs and laid me on the bed, and sat by me and read to me till it tired my head.

112   He said I was his darling and his comfort and all he had, and that I must take care of myself for his sake, and keep well.

113   He says no one but myself can help me out of it, that I must use my will and self-control and not let any silly fancies run away with me.

There's one comfort—the baby is well and happy, and does not have 114
to occupy this nursery with the horrid wallpaper.

If we had not used it, that blessed child would have! What a fortunate 115
escape! Why, I wouldn't have a child of mine, an impressionable little
thing, live in such a room for worlds.

I never thought of it before, but it is lucky that John kept me here after 116
all; I can stand it so much easier than a baby, you see.

Of course I never mention it to them any more—I am too wise—but I 117
keep watch for it all the same.

There are things in that wallpaper that nobody knows about but me, 118
or ever will.

Behind that outside pattern the dim shapes get clearer every day. 119

It is always the same shape, only very numerous. 120

And it is like a woman stooping down and creeping about behind that 121
pattern. I don't like it a bit. I wonder—I begin to think—I wish John
would take me away from here!

It is so hard to talk with John about my case, because he is so wise, and 122
because he loves me so.

But I tried it last night. 123

It was moonlight. The moon shines in all around just as the sun does. 124

I hate to see it sometimes, it creeps so slowly, and always comes in by 125
one window or another.

John was asleep and I hated to waken him, so I kept still and watched 126
the moonlight on that undulating wallpaper till I felt creepy.

The faint figure behind seemed to shake the pattern, just as if she 127
wanted to get out.

I got up softly and went to feel and see if the paper *did* move, and when 128
I came back John was awake.

"What is it, little girl?" he said. "Don't go walking about like that— 129
you'll get cold."

I thought it was a good time to talk, so I told him that I really was not 130
gaining here, and that I wished he would take me away.

"Why, darling!" said he. "Our lease will be up in three weeks, and I 131
can't see how to leave before.

"The repairs aren't done at home, and I cannot possibly leave town 132
just now. Of course, if you were in any danger, I could and would, but
you really are better, dear, whether you can see it or not. I am a doctor,
dear, and I know. You are gaining flesh and color, your appetite is better,
I feel really much easier about you."

"I don't weigh a bit more," said I, "not as much; and my appetite may 133
be better in the evening when you are here but it is worse in the morning
when you are away!"

"Bless her little heart!" said he with a big hug. "She shall be as sick as 134
she pleases! But now let's improve the shining hours by going to sleep,
and talk about it in the morning!"

"And you won't go away?" I asked gloomily. 135

"Why, how can I, dear? It is only three weeks more and then we will 136 take a nice little trip of a few days while Jennie is getting the house ready. Really, dear, you are better!"

137 "Better in body perhaps—" I began, and stopped short, for he sat up straight and looked at me with such a stern, reproachful look that I could not say another word.

138 "My darling," said he, "I beg of you, for my sake and for our child's sake, as well as for your own, that you will never for one instant let that idea enter your mind! There is nothing so dangerous, so fascinating, to a temperament like yours. It is a false and foolish fancy. Can you not trust me as a physician when I tell you so?"

139 So of course I said no more on that score, and we went to sleep before long. He thought I was asleep first, but I wasn't, and lay there for hours trying to decide whether that front pattern and the back pattern really did move together or separately.

140 On a pattern like this, by daylight, there is a lack of sequence, a defiance of law, that is a constant irritant to a normal mind.

141 The color is hideous enough, and unreliable enough, and infuriating enough, but the pattern is torturing.

142 You think you have mastered it, but just as you get well under way in following, it turns a back-somersault and there you are. It slaps you in the face, knocks you down, and tramples upon you. It is like a bad dream.

143 The outside pattern is a florid arabesque, reminding one of a fungus. If you can imagine a toadstool in joints, an interminable string of toadstools, budding and sprouting in endless convolutions—why, that is something like it.

144 That is, sometimes!

145 There is one marked peculiarity about this paper, a thing nobody seems to notice but myself, and that is that it changes as the light changes.

146 When the sun shoots in through the east window—I always watch for that first long, straight ray—it changes so quickly that I never can quite believe it.

147 That is why I watch it always.

148 By moonlight—the moon shines in all night when there is a moon—I wouldn't know it was the same paper.

149 At night in any kind of light, in twilight, candlelight, lamplight, and worst of all by moonlight, it becomes bars! The outside pattern, I mean, and the woman behind it is as plain as can be.

150 I didn't realize for a long time what the thing was that showed behind, that dim sub-pattern, but now I am quite sure it is a woman.

151 By daylight she is subdued, quiet. I fancy it is the pattern that keeps her so still. It is so puzzling. It keeps me quiet by the hour.

152 I lie down ever so much now. John says it is good for me, and to sleep all I can.

153 Indeed he started the habit by making me lie down for an hour after each meal.

154 It is a very bad habit, I am convinced, for you see, I don't sleep.

155 And that cultivates deceit, for I don't tell them I'm awake—oh, no!

The fact is I am getting a little afraid of John. 156

He seems very queer sometimes, and even Jennie has an inexplicable 157
look.

It strikes me occasionally, just as a scientific hypothesis, that perhaps 158
it is the paper!

I have watched John when he did not know I was looking, and come 159
into the room suddenly on the most innocent excuses, and I've caught
him several times *looking at the paper!* And Jennie too. I caught Jennie
with her hand on it once.

She didn't know I was in the room, and when I asked her in a quiet, a 160
very quiet voice, with the most restrained manner possible, what she was
doing with the paper, she turned around as if she had been caught
stealing, and looked quite angry—asked me why I should frighten her so!

Then she said that the paper stained everything it touched, that she had 161
found yellow smooches on all my clothes and John's and she wished we
would be more careful!

Did not that sound innocent? But I know she was studying that 162
pattern, and I am determined that nobody shall find it out but myself!

Life is very much more exciting now than it used to be. You see, I have 163
something more to expect, to look forward to, to watch. I really do eat
better, and am more quiet than I was.

John is so pleased to see me improve! He laughed a little the other day, 164
and said I seemed to be flourishing in spite of my wallpaper.

I turned it off with a laugh. I had no intention of telling him it was 165
because of the wallpaper—he would make fun of me. He might even
want to take me away.

I don't want to leave now until I have found it out. There is a week 166
more, and I think that will be enough.

I'm feeling so much better! 167

I don't sleep much at night, for it is so interesting to watch develop- 168
ments; but I sleep a good deal during the daytime.

In the daytime it is tiresome and perplexing. 169

There are always new shoots on the fungus, and new shades of yellow 170
all over it. I cannot keep count of them, though I have tried conscien-
tiously.

It is the strangest yellow, the wallpaper! It makes me think of all the 171
yellow things I ever saw—not beautiful ones like buttercups, but old,
foul, bad yellow things.

But there is something else about that paper—the smell! I noticed it the 172
moment we came into the room, but with so much air and sun it was not
bad. Now we have had a week of fog and rain, and whether the windows
are open or not, the smell is here.

It creeps all over the house. 173

I find it hovering in the dining-room, skulking in the parlor, hiding in 174
the hall, lying in wait for me on the stairs.

It gets into my hair. 175

176   Even when I go to ride, if I turn my head suddenly and surprise it—there is that smell!

177   Such a peculiar odor, too! I have spent hours in trying to analyze it, to find what it smelled like.

178   It is not bad—at first—and very gentle, but quite the subtlest, most enduring odor I ever met.

179   In this damp weather it is awful. I wake up in the night and find it hanging over me.

180   It used to disturb me at first. I thought seriously of burning the house—to reach the smell.

181   But now I am used to it. The only thing I can think of that it is like is the *color* of the paper! A yellow smell.

182   There is a very funny mark on this wall, low down, near the mopboard. A streak that runs round the room. It goes behind every piece of furniture, except the bed, a long, straight, even *smooch,* as if it had been rubbed over and over.

183   I wonder how it was done and who did it, and what they did it for. Round and round and round—round and round and round—it makes me dizzy!

184   I really have discovered something at last.

185   Through watching so much at night, when it changes so, I have finally found out.

186   The front pattern *does* move—and no wonder! The woman behind shakes it!

187   Sometimes I think there are a great many women behind, and sometimes only one, and she crawls around fast, and her crawling shakes it all over.

188   Then in the very bright spots she keeps still, and in the very shady spots she just takes hold of the bars and shakes them hard.

189   And she is all the time trying to climb through. But nobody could climb through that pattern—it strangles so; I think that is why it has so many heads.

190   They get through and then the pattern strangles them off and turns them upside down, and makes their eyes white!

191   If those heads were covered or taken off it would not be half so bad.

192   I think that woman gets out in the daytime!

193   And I'll tell you why—privately—I've seen her!

194   I can see her out of every one of my windows!

195   It is the same woman, I know, for she is always creeping, and most women do not creep by daylight.

196   I see her in that long shaded lane, creeping up and down. I see her in those dark grape arbors, creeping all around the garden.

197   I see her on that long road under the trees, creeping along, and when a carriage comes she hides under the blackberry vines.

198   I don't blame her a bit. It must be very humiliating to be caught creeping by daylight!

I always lock the door when I creep by daylight. I can't do it at night, 199
for I know John would suspect something at once.

And John is so queer now that I don't want to irritate him. I wish he 200
would take another room! Besides, I don't want anybody to get that
woman out at night but myself.

I often wonder if I could see her out of all the windows at once. 201

But, turn as fast as I can, I can only see out of one at one time. 202

And though I always see her, she *may* be able to creep faster than I can 203
turn! I have watched her sometimes away off in the open country,
creeping as fast as a cloud shadow in a wind.

If only that top pattern could be gotten off from the under one! I mean 204
to try it, little by little.

I have found out another funny thing, but I shan't tell it this time! It 205
does not do to trust people too much.

There are only two more days to get this paper off, and I believe John 206
is beginning to notice. I don't like the look in his eyes.

And I heard him ask Jennie a lot of professional questions about me. 207
She had a very good report to give.

She said I slept a good deal in the daytime. 208

John knows I don't sleep very well at night, for all I'm so quiet! 209

He asked me all sorts of questions, too, and pretended to be very loving 210
and kind.

As if I couldn't see through him! 211

Still, I don't wonder he acts so, sleeping under this paper for three 212
months.

It only interests me, but I feel sure John and Jennie are affected by it. 213

Hurrah! This is the last day, but it is enough. John is to stay in town 214
over night, and won't be out until this evening.

Jennie wanted to sleep with me—the sly thing; but I told her I should 215
undoubtedly rest better for a night all alone.

That was clever, for really I wasn't alone a bit! As soon as it was 216
moonlight and that poor thing began to crawl and shake the pattern, I
got up and ran to help her.

I pulled and she shook. I shook and she pulled, and before morning we 217
had peeled off yards of that paper.

A strip about as high as my head and half around the room. 218

And then when the sun came and that awful pattern began to laugh at 219
me, I declared I would finish it today!

We go away tomorrow, and they are moving all my furniture down 220
again to leave things as they were before.

Jennie looked at the wall in amazement, but I told her merrily that I did 221
it out of pure spite at the vicious thing.

She laughed and said she wouldn't mind doing it herself, but I must not 222
get tired.

How she betrayed herself that time! 223

But I am here, and no person touches this paper but Me—not *alive!* 224

225   She tried to get me out of the room—it was too patent! But I said it was so quiet and empty and clean now that I believed I would lie down again and sleep all I could, and not to wake me even for dinner—I would call when I woke.

226   So now she is gone, and the servants are gone, and the things are gone, and there is nothing left but that great bedstead nailed down, with the canvas mattress we found on it.

227   We shall sleep downstairs tonight, and take the boat home tomorrow.

228   I quite enjoy the room, now it is bare again.

229   How those children did tear about here!

230   This bedstead is fairly gnawed!

231   But I must get to work.

232   I have locked the door and thrown the key down into the front path.

233   I don't want to go out, and I don't want to have anybody come in, till John comes.

234   I want to astonish him.

235   I've got a rope up here that even Jennie did not find. If that woman does get out, and tries to get away, I can tie her!

236   But I forgot I could not reach far without anything to stand on!

237   This bed will *not* move!

238   I tried to lift and push it until I was lame, and then I got so angry I bit off a little piece at one corner—but it hurt my teeth.

239   Then I peeled off all the paper I could reach standing on the floor. It sticks horribly and the pattern just enjoys it! All those strangled heads and bulbous eyes and waddling fungus growths just shriek with derision!

240   I am getting angry enough to do something desperate. To jump out of the window would be admirable exercise, but the bars are too strong even to try.

241   Besides I wouldn't do it. Of course not. I know well enough that a step like that is improper and might be misconstrued.

242   I don't like to *look* out of the windows even—there are so many of those creeping women and they creep so fast.

243   I wonder if they all come out of that wallpaper as I did?

244   But I am securely fastened now by my well-hidden rope—you don't get *me* out in the road there!

245   I suppose I shall have to get back behind the pattern when it comes night, and that is hard!

246   It is so pleasant to be out in this great room and creep around as I please!

247   I don't want to go outside. I won't, even if Jennie asks me to.

248   For outside you have to creep on the ground, and everything is green instead of yellow.

249   But here I can creep smoothly on the floor, and my shoulder just fits in that long smooch around the wall, so I cannot lose my way.

250   Why, there's John at the door!

It is no use, young man, you can't open it! 251

How he does call and pound! 252

Now he's crying to Jennie for an axe. 253

It would be a shame to break down that beautiful door! 254

"John, dear!" said I in the gentlest voice. "The key is down by the front 255
steps, under a plantain leaf!"

That silenced him for a few moments. 256

Then he said, very quietly indeed, "Open the door, my darling!" 257

"I can't," said I. "The key is down by the front door under a plantain 258
leaf!" And then I said it again, several times, very gently and slowly, and
said it so often that he had to go and see, and he got it of course, and
came in. He stopped short by the door.

"What is the matter?" he cried. "For God's sake, what are you doing!" 259

I kept on creeping just the same, but I looked at him over my shoulder. 260

"I've got out at last," said I, "in spite of you and Jane. And I've pulled 261
off most of the paper, so you can't put me back!"

Now why should that man have fainted? But he did, and right across 262
my path by the wall, so that I had to creep over him every time!

❏ Questions for Discussion

1. What kind of relationship does the **narrator** have with her husband John? How does he treat her? List the times that the narrator, after having given her opinion, adds "but John says" or a similar phrase.

2. What is the **point of view** of this story? Why is it crucial to the effectiveness of the story? How does the point of view create an **ironic** tone?

3. What is the role of John's sister in the story?

4. What is the significance of the narrator's not being allowed to see her baby?

5. What is the significance of the wallpaper's appeal to four of the five senses (touch, smell, sound, and sight)?

6. Why is the narrator unnamed for much of the story while John and Jennie have names? What is the significance of the name Jane?

❏ Suggestions for Exploration and Writing

1. In what ways is John's attitude toward his wife typical of the attitude of men toward women in the late nineteenth and early twentieth centuries in the United States? Does John love his wife? Support your answer.

2. Gilman's narrator says she feels "basely ungrateful" for not appreciating John's regulation of her days by the hour or his choice of their bedroom. Compare her feelings with those expressed in "When Grateful Begins to Grate" by Ellen Goodman.

3. Discuss the wallpaper. Why does it have an "everlastingness" about it? Why does the narrator's husband choose the nursery with the bars on the window and the ugly wallpaper rather than the first floor room with the view?

ERNEST HEMINGWAY (1899–1961)

Hemingway began his literary career as a cub reporter for the Kansas City Star. *There he learned a style of writing that many critics believe to have had a lasting influence on his fiction: his frequent use of short, simple or compound sentences. Hemingway continued his newspaper writing as a foreign correspondent throughout much of his life. As his works became famous, Hemingway also became a celebrity, often living the kind of adventures he wrote about: he fought in World War I, supported the Spanish Civil War, hunted in Africa, and married four times. His most famous novels include* The Sun Also Rises *(1926),* A Farewell to Arms *(1929),* For Whom the Bell Tolls *(1940), and* The Old Man and the Sea *(1952). In 1954, Hemingway was awarded the Nobel Prize for Literature.*

Hills Like White Elephants

1   The hills across the valley of the Ebro were long and white. On this side there was no shade and no trees and the station was between two lines of rails in the sun. Close against the side of the station there was the warm shadow of the building and a curtain, made of strings of bamboo beads, hung across the open door into the bar, to keep out flies. The American and the girl with him sat at a table in the shade, outside the building. It was very hot and the express from Barcelona would come in forty minutes. It stopped at this junction for two minutes and went on to Madrid.

2   "What should we drink?" the girl asked. She had taken off her hat and put it on the table.

3   "It's pretty hot," the man said.

4   "Let's drink beer."

5   "Dos cervezas," the man said into the curtain.

6   "Big ones?" a woman asked from the doorway.

7   "Yes. Two big ones."

8   The woman brought two glasses of beer and two felt pads. She put the felt pads and the beer glasses on the table and looked at the man and the

girl. The girl was looking off at the line of hills. They were white in the sun and the country was brown and dry.

"They look like white elephants," she said. 9

"I've never seen one," the man drank his beer. 10

"No, you wouldn't have." 11

"I might have," the man said. "Just because you say I wouldn't have doesn't prove anything." 12

The girl looked at the bead curtain. "They've painted something on it," she said. "What does it say?" 13

"Anis del Toro. It's a drink." 14

"Could we try it?" 15

The man called "Listen" through the curtain. The woman came out from the bar. 16

"Four reales." 17

"We want two Anis del Toro." 18

"With water?" 19

"Do you want it with water?" 20

"I don't know," the girl said. "Is it good with water?" 21

"It's all right." 22

"You want them with water?" asked the woman. 23

"Yes, with water." 24

"It tastes like licorice," the girl said and put the glass down. 25

"That's the way with everything." 26

"Yes," said the girl. "Everything tastes of licorice. Especially all the things you've waited so long for, like absinthe." 27

"Oh, cut it out." 28

"You started it," the girl said. "I was being amused. I was having a fine time." 29

"Well, let's try and have a fine time." 30

"All right. I was trying. I said the mountains looked like white elephants. Wasn't that bright?" 31

"That was bright." 32

"I wanted to try this new drink. That's all we do, isn't it—look at things and try new drinks?" 33

"I guess so." 34

The girl looked across at the hills. 35

"They're lovely hills," she said. "They don't really look like white elephants. I just meant the coloring of their skin through the trees." 36

"Should we have another drink?" 37

"All right." 38

The warm wind blew the bead curtain against the table. 39

"The beer's nice and cool," the man said. 40

"It's lovely," the girl said. 41

"It's really an awfully simple operation, Jig," the man said. "It's not really an operation at all." 42

The girl looked at the ground the table legs rested on. 43

44   "I know you wouldn't mind it, Jig. It's really not anything. It's just to let the air in."

45   The girl did not say anything.

46   "I'll go with you and I'll stay with you all the time. They just let the air in and then it's all perfectly natural."

47   "Then what will we do afterward?"

48   "We'll be fine afterward. Just like we were before."

49   "What makes you think so?"

50   "That's the only thing that bothers us. It's the only thing that's made us unhappy."

51   The girl looked at the bead curtain, put her hand out and took hold of two of the strings of beads.

52   "And you think then we'll be all right and be happy."

53   "I know we will. You don't have to be afraid. I've known lots of people that have done it."

54   "So have I," said the girl. "And afterward they were all so happy."

55   "Well," the man said, "if you don't want to you don't have to. I wouldn't have you do it if you didn't want to. But I know it's perfectly simple."

56   "And you really want to?"

57   "I think it's the best thing to do. But I don't want you to do if it you don't really want to."

58   "And if I do it you'll be happy and things will be like they were and you'll love me?"

59   "I love you now. You know I love you."

60   "I know. But if I do it, then it will be nice again if I say things are like white elephants, and you'll like it?"

61   "I'll love it. I love it now but I just can't think about it. You know how I get when I worry."

62   "If I do it you won't ever worry?"

63   "I won't worry about that because it's perfectly simple."

64   "Then I'll do it. Because I don't care about me."

65   "What do you mean?"

66   "I don't care about me."

67   "Well, I care about you."

68   "Oh, yes. But I don't care about me. And I'll do it and then everything will be fine."

69   "I don't want you to do it if you feel that way."

70   The girl stood up and walked to the end of the station. Across, on the other side, were fields of grain and trees along the banks of the Ebro. Far away, beyond the river, were mountains. The shadow of a cloud moved across the field of grain and she saw the river through the trees.

71   "And we could have all this," she said. "And we could have everything and every day we make it more impossible."

72   "What did you say?"

"I said we could have everything." 73

"We can have everything." 74

"No, we can't." 75

"We can have the whole world." 76

"No, we can't." 77

"We can go everywhere." 78

"No, we can't. It isn't ours any more." 79

"It's ours." 80

"No, it isn't. And once they take it away, you never get it back." 81

"But they haven't taken it away." 82

"We'll wait and see." 83

"Come on back in the shade," he said. "You mustn't feel that way." 84

"I don't feel any way," the girl said. "I just know things." 85

"I don't want you to do anything that you don't want to do —" 86

"Nor that isn't good for me," she said. "I know. Could we have another beer?" 87

"All right. But you've got to realize —" 88

"I realize," the girl said. "Can't we maybe stop talking?" 89

They sat down at the table and the girl looked across at the hills on the dry side of the valley and the man looked at her and at the table. 90

"You've got to realize," he said, "that I don't want you to do it if you don't want to. I'm perfectly willing to go through with it if it means anything to you." 91

"Doesn't it mean anything to you? We could get along." 92

"Of course it does. But I don't want anybody but you. I don't want any one else. And I know it's perfectly simple." 93

"Yes, you know it's perfectly simple." 94

"It's all right for you to say that, but I do know it." 95

"Would you do something for me now?" 96

"I'd do anything for you." 97

"Would you please please please please please please please stop talking?" 98

He did not say anything but looked at the bags against the wall of the station. There were labels on them from all the hotels where they had spent nights. 99

"But I don't want you to," he said, "I don't care anything about it." 100

"I'll scream," the girl said. 101

The woman came out through the curtains with two glasses of beer and put them down on the damp felt pads. "The train comes in five minutes," she said. 102

"What did she say?" asked the girl. 103

"That the train is coming in five minutes." 104

The girl smiled brightly at the woman, to thank her. 105

"I'd better take the bags over to the other side of the station," the man said. She smiled at him. 106

107 "All right. Then come back and we'll finish the beer."

108 He picked up the two heavy bags and carried them around the station to the other tracks. He looked up the tracks but could not see the train. Coming back, he walked through the barroom, where people waiting for the train were drinking. He drank an Anis at the bar and looked at the people. They were all waiting reasonably for the train. He went out through the bead curtain. She was sitting at the table and smiled at him.

109 "Do you feel better?" he asked.

110 "I feel fine," she said. "There's nothing wrong with me. I feel fine."

❏ Questions for Discussion

1. What is the couple's relationship like at the beginning of the story? How has that relationship recently changed? Who dominates the relationship?

2. How does the man attempt to manipulate the woman into having a "simple operation"? How responsible does he seem? What does he mean by " 'We'll be fine afterward. Just like we were before' "?

3. How do the landscapes on either side of the river differ? What might these contrasting landscapes suggest about the woman's state of mind?

4. How would you describe the woman's tone in talking about a "simple operation"?

5. Considering the symbolism of the landscapes, the man's references to the "simple operation," the recent changes in the couple's relationship, and the expected effect of the "operation" on the couple's relationship, what kind of operation do you think the couple are talking about? Why do the couple never openly name the operation?

6. How and when in the course of the conversation does the relationship between the two seem to change?

7. How do you interpret the woman's final words?

❏ Suggestions for Exploration and Writing

1. In an essay discuss how the relationship between the man and woman changes through the course of this very short story.

2. Clearly in this story the man tries to manipulate the woman into doing what he wants done without himself taking any re-

sponsibility for her action. In an essay discuss how a family member, friend, or acquaintance has similarly attempted to manipulate you.

JOHN STEINBECK (1902–1968)

Born in the Salinas Valley of California, John Steinbeck attended Stanford University and worked at odd jobs among the laborers he admired. He often felt indignant at the injustice, self-righteousness, and corruption of the economic system; as a result, many of these subjects appear in his novels and short stories. Some of his novels are The Grapes of Wrath *(1938),* Of Mice and Men *(1940),* East of Eden *(1952), and* The Winter of Our Discontent *(1961). In 1962 Steinbeck won the Nobel Prize for Literature.*

The Chrysanthemums

The high grey-flannel fog of winter closed off the Salinas Valley from   1
the sky and from all the rest of the world. On every side it sat like a lid on the mountains and made of the great valley a closed pot. On the broad, level land floor the gang plows bit deep and left the black earth shining like metal where the shares had cut. On the foothill ranches across the Salinas River, the yellow stubble fields seemed to be bathed in pale cold sunshine, but there was no sunshine in the valley now in December. The thick willow scrub along the river flamed with sharp and positive yellow leaves.

It was a time of quiet and of waiting. The air was cold and tender. A   2
light wind blew up from the southwest so that the farmers were mildly hopeful of a good rain before long; but fog and rain do not go together.

Across the river, on Henry Allen's foothill ranch there was little work   3
to be done, for the hay was cut and stored and the orchards were plowed up to receive the rain deeply when it should come. The cattle on the higher slopes were becoming shaggy and rough-coated.

Elisa Allen, working in her flower garden, looked down across the yard   4
and saw Henry, her husband, talking to two men in business suits. The three of them stood by the tractor shed, each man with one foot on the side of the little Fordson. They smoked cigarettes and studied the machine as they talked.

Elisa watched them for a moment and then went back to her work. She   5
was thirty-five. Her face was lean and strong and her eyes were as clear as water. Her figure looked blocked and heavy in her gardening costume, a man's black hat pulled low down over her eyes, clod-hopper shoes, a figured print dress almost completely covered by a big corduroy apron with four big pockets to hold the snips, the trowel and scratcher, the

seeds and the knife she worked with. She wore heavy leather gloves to protect her hands while she worked.

6   She was cutting down the old year's chrysanthemum stalks with a pair of short and powerful scissors. She looked down toward the men by the tractor shed now and then. Her face was eager and mature and handsome; even her work with the scissors was over-eager, over-powerful. The chrysanthemum stems seemed too small and easy for her energy.

7   She brushed a cloud of hair out of her eyes with the back of her glove, and left a smudge of earth on her cheek in doing it. Behind her stood the neat white farm house with red geraniums close-banked around it as high as the windows. It was a hard-swept looking little house with hard-polished windows, and a clean mud-mat on the front steps.

8   Elisa cast another glance toward the tractor shed. The strangers were getting into their Ford coupe. She took off a glove and put her strong fingers down into the forest of new green chrysanthemum sprouts that were growing around the old roots. She spread the leaves and looked down among the close-growing stems. No aphids were there, no sowbugs or snails or cutworms. Her terrier fingers destroyed such pests before they could get started.

9   Elisa started at the sound of her husband's voice. He had come near quietly, and he leaned over the wire fence that protected her flower garden from cattle and dogs and chickens.

10   "At it again" he said. "You've got a strong new crop coming."

11   Elisa straightened her back and pulled on the gardening glove again. "Yes. They'll be strong this coming year." In her tone and on her face there was a little smugness.

12   "You've got a gift with things," Henry observed. "Some of those yellow chrysanthemums you had this year were ten inches across. I wish you'd work out in the orchard and raise some apples that big."

13   Her eyes sharpened. "Maybe I could do it, too. I've a gift with things, all right. My mother had it. She could stick anything in the ground and make it grow. She said it was having planters' hands that knew how to do it."

14   "Well, it sure works with flowers," he said.

15   "Henry, who were those men you were talking to?"

16   "Why, sure, that's what I came to tell you. They were from the Western Meat Company. I sold those thirty head of three-year-old steers. Got nearly my own price, too."

17   "Good," she said. "Good for you."

18   "And I thought," he continued, "I thought how it's Saturday afternoon, and we might go into Salinas for dinner at a restaurant, and then to a picture show—to celebrate, you see."

19   "Good," she repeated. "Oh, yes. That will be good."

20   Henry put on his joking tone. "There's fights tonight. How'd you like to go to the fights?"

"Oh, no," she said breathlessly. "No, I wouldn't like fights." 21

"Just fooling, Elisa. We'll go to a movie. Let's see. It's two now. I'm 22
going to take Scotty and bring down those steers from the hill. It'll take
us maybe two hours. We'll go in town about five and have dinner at the
Cominos Hotel. Like that?"

"Of course I'll like it. It's good to eat away from home." 23

"All right, then. I'll go get up a couple of horses." 24

She said, "I'll have plenty of time to transplant some of these sets, I 25
guess."

She heard her husband calling Scotty down by the barn. And a little 26
later she saw the two men ride up the pale yellow hillside in search of the
steers.

There was a little square sandy bed kept for rooting the chrysanthe- 27
mums. With her trowel she turned the soil over and over, and smoothed
it and patted it firm. Then she dug ten parallel trenches to receive the sets.
Back at the chrysanthemum bed she pulled out the little crisp shoots,
trimmed off the leaves of each one with her scissors and laid it on a small
orderly pile.

A squeak of wheels and plod of hoofs came from the road. Elisa looked 28
up. The country road ran along the dense bank of willows and cottonwoods that bordered the river, and up this road came a curious vehicle,
curiously drawn. It was an old spring-wagon, with a round canvas top on
it like the cover of a prairie schooner. It was drawn by an old bay horse
and a little grey-and-white burro. A big stubble-bearded man sat between
the cover flaps and drove the crawling team. Underneath the wagon,
between the hind wheels, a lean and rangy mongrel dog walked sedately.
Words were painted on the canvas, in clumsy, crooked letters. "Pots,
pans, knives, sisors, lawn mores, Fixed." Two rows of articles, and the
triumphantly definitive "Fixed" below. The black paint had run down in
little sharp points beneath each letter.

Elisa, squatting on the ground, watched to see the crazy, loose-jointed 29
wagon pass by. But it didn't pass. It turned into the farm road in front of
her house, crooked old wheels skirling and squeaking. The rangy dog
darted from between the wheels and ran ahead. Instantly the two ranch
shepherds flew out at him. Then all three stopped, and with stiff and
quivering tails, with taut straight legs, with ambassadorial dignity, they
slowly circled, sniffing daintily. The caravan pulled up to Elisa's wire
fence and stopped. Now the newcomer dog, feeling out-numbered, lowered his tail and retired under the wagon with raised hackles and bared
teeth.

The man on the wagon seat called out, "That's a bad dog in a fight 30
when he gets started."

Elisa laughed. "I see he is. How soon does he generally get started?" 31

The man caught up her laughter and echoed it heartily. "Sometimes 32
not for weeks and weeks," he said. He climbed stiffly down, over the
wheel. The horse and the donkey drooped like unwatered flowers.

33   Elisa saw that he was a very big man. Although his hair and beard were greying, he did not look old. His worn black suit was wrinkled and spotted with grease. The laughter had disappeared from his face and eyes the moment his laughing voice ceased. His eyes were dark, and they were full of the brooding that gets in the eyes of teamsters and of sailors. The calloused hands he rested on the wire fence were cracked, and every crack was a black line. He took off his battered hat.

34   "I'm off my general road, ma'am," he said. "Does this dirt road cut over across the river to the Los Angeles highway?"

35   Elisa stood up and shoved the thick scissors in her apron pocket. "Well, yes, it does, but it winds around and then fords the river. I don't think your team could pull through the sand."

36   He replied with some asperity. "It might surprise you what them beasts can pull through."

37   "When they get started?" she asked.

38   He smiled for a second. "Yes. When they get started."

39   "Well," said Elisa, "I think you'll save time if you go back to the Salinas road and pick up the highway there."

40   He drew a big finger down the chicken wire and made it sing. "I ain't in any hurry, ma'am. I go from Seattle to San Diego and back every year. Takes all my time. About six months each way. I aim to follow nice weather."

41   Elisa took off her gloves and stuffed them in the apron pocket with the scissors. She touched the under edge of her man's hat, searching for fugitive hairs. "That sounds like a nice kind of a way to live," she said.

42   He leaned confidentially over the fence. "Maybe you noticed the writing on my wagon. I mend pots and sharpen knives and scissors. You got any of them things to do?"

43   "Oh, no," she said quickly. "Nothing like that." Her eyes hardened with resistance.

44   "Scissors is the worst thing," he explained. "Most people just ruin scissors trying to sharpen 'em, but I know how. I got a special tool. It's a little bobbit kind of thing, and patented. But it sure does the trick."

45   "No. My scissors are all sharp."

46   "All right, then. Take a pot," he continued earnestly, "a bent pot, or a pot with a hole. I can make it like new so you don't have to buy no new ones. That's a saving for you."

47   "No," she said shortly. "I tell you I have nothing like that for you to do."

48   His face fell to an exaggerated sadness. His voice took on a whining undertone. "I ain't had a thing to do today. Maybe I won't have no supper tonight. You see I'm off my regular road. I know folks on the highway clear from Seattle to San Diego. They save their things for me to sharpen up because they know I do it so good and save them money."

49   "I'm sorry," Elisa said irritably. "I haven't anything for you to do."

His eyes left her face and fell to searching the ground. They roamed 50 about until they came to the chrysanthemum bed where she had been working. "What's them plants, ma'am?"

The irritation and resistance melted from Elisa's face. "Oh, those are 51 chrysanthemums, giant whites and yellows. I raise them every year, bigger than anybody around here."

"Kind of a long-stemmed flower? Looks like a quick puff of colored 52 smoke?" he asked.

"That's it. What a nice way to describe them." 53

"They smell kind of nasty till you get used to them," he said. 54

"It's a good bitter smell," she retorted, "not nasty at all." 55

He changed his tone quickly. "I like the smell myself." 56

"I had ten-inch blooms this year," she said. 57

The man leaned farther over the fence. "Look. I know a lady down the 58 road a piece, has got the nicest garden you ever seen. Got nearly every kind of flower but no chrysanthemums. Last time I was mending a copper-bottom washtub for her (that's a hard job but I do it good), she said to me, 'If you ever run acrost some nice chrysanthemums I wish you'd try to get me a few seeds.' That's what she told me."

Elisa's eyes grew alert and eager. "She couldn't have known much 59 about chrysanthemums. You *can* raise them from seed, but it's much easier to root the little sprouts you see there."

"Oh," he said. "I s'pose I can't take none to her, then." 60

"Why yes you can," Elisa cried. "I can put some in damp sand, and 61 you can carry them right along with you. They'll take root in the pot if you keep them damp. And then she can transplant them."

"She'd sure like to have some, ma'am. You say they're nice ones?" 62

"Beautiful," she said. "Oh, beautiful." Her eyes shone. She tore off the 63 battered hat and shook out her dark pretty hair. "I'll put them in a flower pot, and you can take them right with you. Come into the yard."

While the man came through the picket gate Elisa ran excitedly along 64 the geranium-bordered path to the back of the house. And she returned carrying a big red flower pot. The gloves were forgotten now. She kneeled on the ground by the starting bed and dug up the sandy soil with her fingers and scooped it into the bright new flower pot. Then she picked up the little pile of shoots she had prepared. With her strong fingers she pressed them in the sand and tamped around them with her knuckles. The man stood over her. "I'll tell you what to do," she said. "You remember so you can tell the lady."

"Yes, I'll try to remember." 65

"Well, look. These will take root in about a month. Then she must set 66 them out, about a foot apart in good rich earth like this, see?" She lifted a handful of dark soil for him to look at. "They'll grow fast and tall. Now remember this: In July tell her to cut them down, about eight inches from the ground."

67   "Before they bloom?" he asked.

68   "Yes, before they bloom." Her face was tight with eagerness. "They'll grow right up again. About the last of September the buds will start."

69   She stopped and seemed perplexed. "It's the budding that takes the most care," she said hesitantly. "I don't know how to tell you." She looked deep into his eyes, searchingly. Her mouth opened a little, and she seemed to be listening. "I'll try to tell you," she said. "Did you ever hear of planting hands?"

70   "Can't say I have, ma'am."

71   "Well, I can only tell you what it feels like. It's when you're picking off the buds you don't want. Everything goes right down into your fingertips. You watch your fingers work. They do it themselves. You can feel how it is. They pick and pick the buds. They never make a mistake. They're with the plant. Do you see? Your fingers and the plant. You can feel that, right up your arm. They know. They never make a mistake. You can feel it. When you're like that you can't do anything wrong. Do you see that? Can you understand that?"

72   She was kneeling on the ground looking up at him. Her breast swelled passionately.

73   The man's eyes narrowed. He looked away self-consciously. "Maybe I know," he said. "Sometimes in the night in the wagon there—"

74   Elisa's voice grew husky. She broke in on him, "I've never lived as you do, but I know what you mean. When the night is dark—why, the stars are sharp-pointed, and there's quiet. Why, you rise up and up! Every pointed star gets driven into your body. It's like that. Hot and sharp and—lovely."

75   Kneeling there, her hand went out toward his legs in the greasy black trousers. Her hesitant fingers almost touched the cloth. Then her hand dropped to the ground. She crouched low like a fawning dog.

76   He said, "It's nice, just like you say. Only when you don't have no dinner it ain't."

77   She stood up then, very straight, and her face was ashamed. She held the flower pot out to him and placed it gently in his arms. "Here. Put it in your wagon, on the seat, where you can watch it. Maybe I can find something for you to do."

78   At the back of the house she dug in the can pile and found two old and battered aluminum saucepans. She carried them back and gave them to him. "Here, maybe you can fix these."

79   His manner changed. He became professional. "Good as new I can fix them." At the back of his wagon he set a little anvil, and out of an oily tool box dug a small machine hammer. Elisa came through the gate to watch him while he pounded out the dents in the kettles. His mouth grew sure and knowing. At a difficult part of the work he sucked his under-lip.

80   "You sleep right in the wagon?" Elisa asked.

81   "Right in the wagon, ma'am. Rain or shine I'm dry as a cow in there."

"It must be nice," she said. "It must be very nice. I wish women could 82
do such things."

"It ain't the right kind of a life for a woman." 83

Her upper lip raised a little, showing her teeth. "How do you know? 84
How can you tell?" she said.

"I don't know, ma'am," he protested. "Of course I don't know. Now 85
here's your kettles, done. You don't have to buy no new ones."

"How much?" 86

"Oh, fifty cents'll do. I keep my prices down and my work good. That's 87
why I have all them satisfied customers up and down the highway."

Elisa brought him a fifty-cent piece from the house and dropped it in 88
his hand. "You might be surprised to have a rival some time. I can
sharpen scissors, too. And I can beat the dents out of little pots. I could
show you what a woman might do."

He put his hammer back in the oily box and shoved the little anvil out 89
of sight. "It would be a lonely life for a woman, ma'am, and a scarey life,
too, with animals creeping under the wagon all night." He climbed over
the single-tree, steadying himself with a hand on the burro's white rump.
He settled himself in the seat, picked up the lines. "Thank you kindly,
ma'am," he said. "I'll do like you told me; I'll go back and catch the
Salinas road."

"Mind," she called, "if you're long in getting there, keep the sand damp." 90

"Sand, ma'am? . . . Sand? Oh, sure. You mean around the chrysan- 91
themums. Sure I will." He clucked his tongue. The beasts leaned luxu-
riously into their collars. The mongrel dog took his place between the
back wheels. The wagon turned and crawled out the entrance road and
back the way it had come, along the river.

Elisa stood in front of her wire fence watching the slow progress of the 92
caravan. Her shoulders were straight, her head thrown back, her eyes
half-closed, so that the scene came vaguely into them. Her lips moved
silently, forming the words "Good-bye—good-bye." Then she whispered, "That's a bright direction. There's a glowing there." The sound of
her whisper startled her. She shook herself free and looked about to see
whether anyone had been listening. Only the dogs had heard. They lifted
their heads toward her from their sleeping in the dust, and then stretched
out their chins and settled asleep again. Elisa turned and ran hurriedly
into the house.

In the kitchen she reached behind the stove and felt the water tank. It 93
was full of hot water from the noonday cooking. In the bathroom she
tore off her soiled clothes and flung them into the corner. And then she
scrubbed herself with a little block of pumice, legs and thighs, loins and
chest and arms, until her skin was scratched and red. When she had dried
herself she stood in front of a mirror in her bedroom and looked at her
body. She tightened her stomach and threw out her chest. She turned and
looked over her shoulder at her back.

94   After a while she began to dress, slowly. She put on her newest under-clothing and her nicest stockings and the dress which was the symbol of her prettiness. She worked carefully on her hair, penciled her eyebrows and rouged her lips.

95   Before she was finished she heard the little thunder of hoofs and the shouts of Henry and his helper as they drove the red steers into the corral. She heard the gate bang shut and set herself for Henry's arrival.

96   His step sounded on the porch. He entered the house calling, "Elisa, where are you?"

97   "In my room, dressing. I'm not ready. There's hot water for your bath. Hurry up. It's getting late."

98   When she heard him splashing in the tub, Elisa laid his dark suit on the bed, and shirt and socks and tie beside it. She stood his polished shoes on the floor beside the bed. Then she went to the porch and sat primly and stiffly down. She looked toward the river road where the willow-line was still yellow with frosted leaves so that under the high grey fog they seemed a thin band of sunshine. This was the only color in the grey afternoon. She sat unmoving for a long time. Her eyes blinked rarely.

99   Henry came banging out of the door, shoving his tie inside his vest as he came. Elisa stiffened and her face grew tight. Henry stopped short and looked at her. "Why—why, Elisa. You look so nice!"

100   "Nice? You think I look nice? What do you mean by 'nice'?"

101   Henry blundered on. "I don't know. I mean you look different, strong and happy."

102   "I am strong? Yes, strong. What do you mean 'strong'?"

103   He looked bewildered. "You're playing some kind of a game," he said helplessly. "It's a kind of a play. You look strong enough to break a calf over your knee, happy enough to eat it like a watermelon."

104   For a second she lost her rigidity. "Henry! Don't talk like that. You didn't know what you said." She grew complete again. "I'm strong," she boasted. "I never knew before how strong."

105   Henry looked down toward the tractor shed, and when he brought his eyes back to her, they were his own again. "I'll get out the car. You can put on your coat while I'm starting."

106   Elisa went into the house. She heard him drive to the gate and idle down his motor, and then she took a long time to put on her hat. She pulled it here and pressed it there. When Henry turned the motor off she slipped into her coat and went out.

107   The little roadster bounced along on the dirt road by the river, raising the birds and driving the rabbits into the brush. Two cranes flapped heavily over the willow-lane and dropped into the river-bed.

108   Far ahead on the road Elisa saw a dark speck. She knew.

109   She tried not to look as they passed it, but her eyes would not obey. She whispered to herself sadly, "He might have thrown them off the road. That wouldn't have been much trouble, not very much. But he kept the

pot," she explained. "He had to keep the pot. That's why he couldn't get them off the road."

The roadster turned a bend and she saw the caravan ahead. She swung 110 full around toward her husband so she could not see the little covered wagon and the mismatched team as the car passed them.

In a moment it was over. The thing was done. She did not look back. 111

She said loudly, to be heard above the motor, "It will be good, tonight, 112 a good dinner."

"Now you're changed again," Henry complained. He took one hand 113 from the wheel and patted her knee. "I ought to take you in to dinner oftener. It would be good for both of us. We get so heavy out on the ranch."

"Henry," she asked, "could we have wine at dinner?" 114

"Sure we could. Say! That will be fine." 115

She was silent for a while; then she said, "Henry, at those prize fights, 116 do the men hurt each other very much?"

"Sometimes a little, not often. Why?" 117

"Well, I've read how they break noses, and blood runs down their 118 chests. I've read how the fighting gloves get heavy and soggy with blood."

He looked around at her. "What's the matter, Elisa? I didn't know you 119 read things like that." He brought the car to a stop, then turned to the right over the Salinas River bridge.

"Do any women ever go the fights?" she asked. 120

"Oh, sure, some. What's the matter, Elisa? Do you want to go? I don't 121 think you'd like it, but I'll take you if you really want to go."

She relaxed limply in the seat. "Oh, no. No. I don't want to go. I'm 122 sure I don't." Her face was turned away from him. "It will be enough if we can have wine. It will be plenty." She turned up her coat collar so he could not see that she was crying weakly—like an old woman.

❏ Questions for Discussion

1. Steinbeck describes Elisa's cutting of the chrysanthemums as "over-eager, over-powerful." Why does she put so much strength and energy into growing chrysanthemums? What do they symbolize to her? Why is sharing her chrysanthemums so important to Elisa?

2. What does Elisa mean when she says to the traveling repair-man, " 'You might be surprised to have a rival some time. . . . I would show you what a woman might do' "? Why might she be attracted to the repairman's life of travel?

3. What happens to the chrysanthemums Elisa has given the re-pairman? How is she affected by what happens to them?

4. Why does this simple woman prepare herself so elaborately for a night out?

5. What is the significance of the boxing match and of Elisa's comments about the blood?

❏ **Suggestions for Exploration and Writing**

1. How does Elisa change during the course of the story? Write an essay describing Elisa at the beginning, at the peak of her happiness and assurance, and at the end of the story.

2. Although the husband and the itinerant peddler seem very dissimilar, they may have some characteristics in common. Discuss their common characteristics.

3. Show how the **setting** and the sense of isolation have influenced what Elisa has become.

4. Sometimes stories contain the age-old theme of victim/victimizer. Explain the victim/victimizer theme in this story.

BESSIE HEAD (1937–1986)

Bessie Head was born in a mental hospital, the daughter of a white South African woman and her black groom. After a white Afrikaner family adopted her, then rejected her because of her race, she was put into an orphanage. Head subsequently earned a primary school teaching certificate, married, and joined the Pan Africanist Congress. She later fled to Botswana but was refused citizenship there because of her political views. While writing the novel A Question of Power *(1973), Head suffered a nervous breakdown. Some of the concerns in Head's writing are human injustice, the abuse of authority, alienation and exile, and communal values. "Snapshots of a Wedding" portrays the customs and mores of village life.*

Snapshots of a Wedding

1   Wedding days always started at the haunting, magical hour of early dawn when there was only a pale crack of light on the horizon. For those who were awake, it took the earth hours to adjust to daylight. The cool and damp of the night slowly arose in shimmering waves like water and even the forms of the people who bestirred themselves at this unearthly hour were distorted in the haze; they appeared to be dancers in slow motion, with fluid, watery forms. In the dim light, four men, the relatives of the bridegroom, Kegoletile, slowly herded an ox before them towards the yard of MmaKhudu, where the bride, Neo, lived. People were already astir in MmaKhudu's yard, yet for a while they all came and peered closely at the distorted fluid forms that approached, to ascertain if it were indeed the relatives of the bridegroom. Then the ox, who was a rather stupid fellow and unaware of his sudden and impending end as meat for

the wedding feast, bellowed casually his early morning yawn. At this the beautiful ululating of the women rose and swelled over the air like water bubbling rapidly and melodiously over the stones of a clear, sparkling stream. In between ululating all the while, the women began to weave about the yard in the wedding dance; now and then they bent over and shook their buttocks in the air. As they handed over the ox, one of the bridegroom's relatives joked:

"This is going to be a modern wedding." He meant that a lot of the traditional courtesies had been left out of the planning for the wedding day; no one had been awake all night preparing diphiri or the traditional wedding breakfast of pounded meat and samp; the bridegroom said he had no church and did not care about such things; the bride was six months pregnant and showing it, so there was just going to be a quick marriage ceremony at the police camp.

"Oh, we all have our own ways," one of the bride's relatives joked back. "If the times are changing, we keep up with them," And she weaved away ululating joyously.

Whenever there was a wedding the talk and gossip that preceded it were appalling, except that this time the relatives of the bride, Neo, kept their talk a strict secret among themselves. They were anxious to be rid of her; she was an impossible girl with haughty, arrogant ways. Of all her family and relatives, she was the only one who had completed her "O" levels and she never failed to rub in this fact. She walked around with her nose in the air; illiterate relatives were beneath her greeting—it was done in a clever way, she just turned her head to one side and smiled to herself or when she greeted it was like an insult; she stretched her hand out, palm outspread, swung it down laughing with a gesture that plainly said: "Oh, that's you!" Only her mother seemed bemused by her education. At her own home Neo was waited on hand and foot. Outside her home nasty remarks were passed. People bitterly disliked conceit and pride.

"That girl has no manners!" the relatives would remark. "What's the good of education if it goes to someone's head so badly they have no respect for the people? Oh, she is not a person."

Then they would nod their heads in that fatal way, with predictions that one day life would bring her down. Actually, life had treated Neo rather nicely. Two months after completing her "O" levels she became pregnant by Kegoletile with their first child. It soon became known that another girl, Mathata, was also pregnant by Kegoletile. The difference between the two girls was that Mathata was completely uneducated; the only work she would ever do was that of a housemaid, while Neo had endless opportunities before her—typist, bookkeeper, or secretary. So Neo merely smiled; Mathata was no rival. It was as though the decision had been worked out by circumstance because when the families converged on Kegoletile at the birth of the children—he was rich in cattle and they wanted to see what they could get—he of course immediately proposed marriage to Neo; and for Mathata, he agreed to a court order to pay a maintenance of R10.00 a month until the child was twenty years old. Mathata merely smiled too. Girls like her offered no resistance to the approaches of men; when they lost them, they just let things ride.

7   "He is of course just running after the education and not the manners," Neo's relatives commented, to show they were not fooled by human nature. "He thinks that since she is as educated as he is they will both get good jobs and be rich in no time . . ."

8   Educated as he was, Kegoletile seemed to go through a secret conflict during the year he prepared a yard for his future married life with Neo. He spent most of his free time in the yard of Mathata. His behaviour there wasn't too alarming but he showered Mathata with gifts of all kinds—food, fancy dresses, shoes and underwear. Each time he came, he brought a gift and each time Mathata would burst out laughing and comment: "Ow, Kegoletile, how can I wear all these dresses? It's just a waste of money! Besides, I manage quite well with the R10.00 you give every month for the child . . ."

9   She was a very pretty girl with black eyes like stars; she was always smiling and happy; immediately and always her own natural self. He knew what he was marrying—something quite the opposite, a new kind of girl with false postures and acquired, grand-madame ways. And yet, it didn't pay a man these days to look too closely into his heart. They all wanted as wives, women who were big money-earners and they were so ruthless about it! And yet it was as though the society itself stamped each of its individuals with its own particular brand of wealth and Kegoletile had not yet escaped it; he had about him an engaging humility and eagerness to help and please that made him loved and respected by all who knew him. During those times he sat in Mathata's yard, he communicated nothing of the conflict he felt but he would sit on a chair with his arms spread out across its back, turn his head sideways and stare at what seemed to be an empty space beside him. Then he would smile, stand up and walk away. Nothing dramatic. During the year he prepared the huts in his new yard, he frequently slept at the home of Neo.

10   Relatives on both sides watched this division of interest between the two yards and one day when Neo walked patronisingly into the yard of an aunt, the aunt decided to frighten her a little.

11   "Well aunt," she said, with the familiar careless disrespect which went with her so-called, educated, status. "Will you make me some tea? And how's things?"

12   The aunt spoke very quietly.

13   "You may not know it, my girl, but you are hated by everyone around here. The debate we have going is whether a nice young man like Kegoletile should marry bad-mannered rubbish like you. He would be far better off if he married a girl like Mathata, who though uneducated, still treats people with respect."

14   The shock the silly girl received made her stare for a terrified moment at her aunt. Then she stood up and ran out of the house. It wiped the

superior smile off her face and brought her down a little. She developed
an anxiety to greet people and also an anxiety about securing Kegoletile
as a husband—that was why she became pregnant six months before the
marriage could take place. In spite of this, her own relatives still disliked
her and right up to the day of the wedding they were still debating
whether Neo was a suitable wife for any man. No one would have
guessed it though with all the dancing, ululating and happiness expressed
in the yard and streams of guests gaily ululated themselves along the
pathways with wedding gifts precariously balanced on their heads. Neo's
maternal aunts, all sedately decked up in shawls, sat in a select group by
themselves in a corner of the yard. They sat on the bare ground with their
legs stretched out before them but they were served like queens the whole
day long. Trays of tea, dry white bread, plates of meat, rice, and salad
were constantly placed before them. Their important task was to formally hand over the bride to Kegoletile's maternal aunts when they
approached the yard at sunset. So they sat the whole day with still,
expressionless faces, waiting to fulfill this ancient rite.

Equally still and expressionless were the faces of the long column of   15
women, Kegoletile's maternal aunts, who appeared outside the yard just
as the sun sank low. They walked slowly into the yard indifferent to the
ululating that greeted them and seated themselves in a group opposite
Neo's maternal aunts. The yard became very silent while each group
made its report. Kegoletile had provided all the food for the wedding
feast and a maternal aunt from his side first asked:

"Is there any complaint? Has all gone well?"   16

"We have no complaint," the opposite party replied.   17

"We have come to ask for water," Kegoletile's side said, meaning that   18
from times past the bride was supposed to carry water in her in-law's
home.

"It is agreed to," the opposite party replied.   19

Neo's maternal aunts then turned to the bridegroom and counselled   20
him: "Son, you must plough and supply us with corn each year."

Then Kegoletile's maternal aunts turned to the bride and counselled   21
her: "Daughter, you must carry water for your husband. Beware, that at
all times, he is the owner of the house and must be obeyed. Do not mind
if he stops now and then and talks to other ladies. Let him feel free to
come and go as he likes . . ."

The formalities over, it was now time for Kegoletile's maternal aunts   22
to get up, ululate and weave and dance about the yard. Then, still
dancing and ululating, accompanied by the bride and groom they slowly
wound their way to the yard of Kegoletile where another feast had been
prepared. As they approached his yard, an old woman suddenly dashed
out and chipped at the ground with a hoe. It was all only a formality. Neo
would never be the kind of wife who went to the lands to plough. She
already had a well-paid job in an office as a secretary. Following on this
another old woman took the bride by the hand and led her to a smeared

and decorated courtyard wherein had been placed a traditional animal-skin Tswana mat. She was made to sit on the mat and a shawl and kerchief were placed before her. The shawl was ceremonially wrapped around her shoulders; the kerchief tied around her head—the symbols that she was now a married woman.

23   Guests quietly moved forward to greet the bride. Then two girls started to ululate and dance in front of the bride. As they both turned and bent over to shake their buttocks in the air, they bumped into each other and toppled over. The wedding guests roared with laughter. Neo, who had all this time been stiff, immobile, and rigid, bent forward and her shoulders shook with laughter.

24   The hoe, the mat, the shawl, the kerchief, the beautiful flute-like ululating of the women seemed in itself a blessing on the marriage but all the guests were deeply moved when out of the crowd, a woman of majestic, regal bearing slowly approached the bride. It was the aunt who had scolded Neo for her bad manners and modern ways. She dropped to her knees before the bride, clenched her fists together and pounded the ground hard with each clenched fist on either side of the bride's legs. As she pounded her fists she said loudly:

25   "Be a good wife! Be a good wife!"

❏ Questions for Discussion

1. The wedding is described as " 'modern,' " not " 'traditional.' " What traditional elements have been left out? What elements about the wedding seem to be traditional and what elements seem modern?

2. How meaningful are the ancient rituals?

3. What does the word *ululate* mean? How do you imagine the women sound?

4. Why is the action of the regal and scolding aunt "deeply" moving to the guests? What does Neo's laughter at the wedding signify?

❏ Suggestions for Exploration and Writing

1. Although Head says that the marriage is a "modern" one, she is clearly referring to an African wedding. Compare and contrast her modern African wedding to a modern American wedding.

2. Agree or disagree with this statement: Neo would be better off without an education.

3. Discuss the choices men and women make in a marriage. Also examine "The Yellow Wallpaper" and "The Story of an Hour."

JAMAICA KINCAID (1949–)

Jamaica Kincaid was born on St. John's Island, Antigua, and attended college in the United States. She soon tired of college, however, and began to write. Many of her short stories have appeared in The New Yorker *and* Rolling Stone *magazines. Her love of family and country and her sense of independence permeate her stories. Kincaid is distinctive for her unconventional style and unusual dialogue, plot, and characters, as in "Girl."*

Girl

Wash the white clothes on Monday and put them on the stone heap; wash the color clothes on Tuesday and put them on the clothes-line to dry; don't walk barehead in the hot sun; cook pumpkin fritters in very hot sweet oil; soak your little cloths right after you take them off; when buying cotton to make yourself a nice blouse, be sure that it doesn't have gum on it, because that way it won't hold up well after a wash; soak salt fish overnight before you cook it; is it true that you sing benna in Sunday school?; always eat your food in such a way that it won't turn someone else's stomach; on Sundays try to walk like a lady and not like the slut you are so bent on becoming; don't sing benna in Sunday school; you mustn't speak to wharf-rat boys, not even to give directions; don't eat fruits on the street—flies will follow you; *but I don't sing benna on Sundays at all and never in Sunday school;* this is how to sew on a button; this is how to make a buttonhole for the button you have just sewed on; this is how to hem a dress when you see the hem coming down and so to prevent yourself from looking like the slut I know you are so bent on becoming; this is how you iron your father's khaki shirt so that it doesn't have a crease; this is how you iron your father's khaki pants so that they don't have a crease; this is how you grow okra—far from the house, because okra tree harbors red ants; when you are growing dasheen, make sure it gets plenty of water or else it makes your throat itch when you are eating it; this is how you sweep a corner; this is how you sweep a whole house; this is how you sweep a yard; this is how you smile to someone you don't like too much; this is how you smile to someone you don't like at all; this is how you smile to someone you like completely; this is how you set a table for tea; this is how you set a table for dinner; this is how you set a table for dinner with an important guest; this is how you set a table for lunch; this is how you set a table for breakfast; this is how to behave in the presence of men who don't know you very well, and this way they won't recognize immediately the slut I have warned you against becoming; be sure to wash every day, even if it is with your own spit; don't squat down to play marbles—you are not a boy, you know; don't pick people's flowers—you might catch something; don't throw stones at blackbirds, because it might not be a blackbird at all; this is how to make a bread pudding; this is how to make doukona;

this is how to make pepper pot; this is how to make a good medicine for a cold; this is how to make a good medicine to throw away a child before it even becomes a child; this is how to catch a fish; this is how to throw back a fish you don't like, and that way something bad won't fall on you; this is how to bully a man; this is how a man bullies you; this is how to love a man, and if this doesn't work there are other ways, and if they don't work don't feel too bad about giving up; this is how to spit up in the air if you feel like it, and this is how to move quick so that it doesn't fall on you; this is how to make ends meet; always squeeze bread to make sure it's fresh; *but what if the baker won't let me feel the bread?*; you mean to say that after all you are really going to be the kind of woman who the baker won't let near the bread?

❑ Questions for Discussion

1. What other words or phrases are repeated besides "This is how"? How do these repeated phrases define the girl's role?

2. What do you know about the relationship of the two people?

❑ Suggestions for Exploration and Writing

1. Using a favorite, oft repeated parental phrase, write an essay explaining why you resented, welcomed, or now understand this phrase.

2. Are men less frequently told what to do than women? As a male, write about what has been told to you. As a female, write about what should have been told to a boy and why.

POETRY

WILLIAM SHAKESPEARE (1564–1616)
The biography of William Shakespeare precedes Othello.

Sonnet 116

Let me not to the marriage of true minds
Admit impediments. Love is not love
Which alters when it alteration finds,
Or bends with the remover to remove:
5   O, no! it is an ever-fixed mark,
That looks on tempests and is never shaken;
It is the star to every wandering bark,

Whose worth's unknown, although his height be taken.
Love's not Time's fool, though rosy lips and cheeks
Within his bending sickle's compass come;   10
Love alters not with his brief hours and weeks,
But bears it out even to the edge of doom.
    If this be error, and upon me prov'd,
    I never writ, nor no man ever lov'd.

Sonnet 130

My mistress' eyes are nothing like the sun;
Coral is far more red than her lips' red:
If snow be white, why then her breasts are dun;
If hairs be wires, black wires grow on her head.
I have seen roses damask'd, red and white,   5
But no such roses see I in her cheeks;
And in some perfumes is there more delight
Than in the breath that from my mistress reeks.
I love to hear her speak, yet well I know
That music hath a far more pleasing sound: 10
I grant I never saw a goddess go;
My mistress, when she walks, treads on the ground:
    And yet, by heaven, I think my love as rare
    As any she belied with false compare.

Sonnet 138

When my love swears that she is made of truth,
I do believe her, though I know she lies,
That she might think me some untutor'd youth,
Unlearned in the world's false subtleties.
Thus vainly thinking that she thinks me young,   5
Although she knows my days are past the best,
Simply I credit her false-speaking tongue:
On both sides thus is simple truth supprest.
But wherefore says she not she is unjust?
And wherefore say not I that I am old?   10
O, love's best habit is in seeming trust,
And age in love loves not to have years told:
    Therefore I lie with her, and she with me,
    And in our faults by lies we flatter'd be.

❏ Questions for Discussion

1. In Sonnet 116, what claims does the speaker make for love?
   What cannot change it? What can?

2. Sonnet 130 differs from most love poetry of Shakespeare's day in its unflattering description of the loved woman's appearance. What does the speaker claim for his love?

3. Why do the speaker and his beloved lie to each other in Sonnet 138? What do you think of their behavior?

❏ Suggestions for Exploration and Writing

1. Examine one or more pairs of lovers in this section in the light of Shakespeare's definition of love in Sonnet 116.

2. Do you agree that the "marriage of true minds" is unaffected by change or time? Discuss some of the pressures that are put on a man and/or a woman in a seemingly "good" marriage or in "true love."

3. Explain why marriage is or is not an "ever-fixed mark."

4. Explain the qualities, other than physical appearance, that attract members of the opposite sex to each other.

JOHN DONNE (1572–1631)

John Donne, an Anglican priest highly regarded for his sermons, wrote conversational, sometimes tortuous, but carefully controlled poetry. His works include cynical court poetry such as the Satires, *strikingly sensual love poems in* Songs and Sonnets, *and powerful, often anguished religious poems such as the* Holy Sonnets. *Foremost among those poets later called* **metaphysical** *by Samuel Johnson, Donne often joins quite disparate concepts in elaborate images or conceits. The speaker's comparison of himself and his beloved to a compass in "A Valediction: forbidding Mourning" is among the most famous of Donne's conceits.*

A Valediction: forbidding Mourning

As virtuous men passe mildly'away,
  And whisper to their soules, to goe,
Whilst some of their sad friends doe say,
  The breath goes now, and some say, no:

5 So let us melt, and make no noise,
  No teare-floods, nor sigh-tempests move,
'Twere prophanation of our joyes
  To tell the layetie our love.

Moving of th'earth brings harmes and feares,
10 Men reckon what it did and meant,

But trepidation of the spheares,
　　Though greater farre, is innocent.

Dull sublunary lovers love
　　(Whose soule is sense) cannot admit
Absence, because it doth remove　　　　　　　　　　　15
　　Those things which elemented it.

But we by'a love, so much refin'd,
　　That our selves know not what it is,
Inter-assured of the mind,
　　Care lesse, eyes, lips, and hands to misse.　　　　　20

Our two soules therefore, which are one,
　　Though I must goe, endure not yet
A breach, but an expansion,
　　Like gold to ayery thinnesse beate.

If they be two, they are two so　　　　　　　　　　　25
　　As stiffe twin compasses are two,
Thy soule the fixt foot, makes no show
　　To move, but doth, if the'other doe.

And though it in the center sit,
　　Yet when the other far doth rome,　　　　　　　　　30
It leanes, and hearkens after it,
　　And growes erect, as it comes home.

Such wilt thou be to mee, who must
　　Like th'other foot, obliquely runne;
Thy firmnes makes my circle just,　　　　　　　　　　35
　　And makes me end, where I begunne.

❏ Questions for Discussion

1. What is the occasion for the poem?

2. How does the woman whom the speaker is addressing seem to feel about his impending departure? What, then, is the purpose of the poem?

3. How do the various images which define the couple's love help to fulfill the poem's purpose?

4. According to the speaker, how does this couple's love differ from that of other couples?

❏ Suggestion for Exploration and Writing

1. Carefully analyze Donne's poem, showing how **diction, imagery,** sound, and **syntax** all contribute to the soothing, reassuring **tone** of the poem.

ROBERT HERRICK (1591–1674)

An English poet and churchman, Robert Herrick wrote both secular and religious verse. His simple, jewel-like, exquisitely controlled poems praise the beauty of women and the richness of the English countryside while lamenting the evanescence of beauty and the imminence of death. In many of his most famous poems, Herrick develops the theme of carpe diem, *the idea that we must "seize the day," common in English poetry of his time. Poems like "Corinna's going a Maying" celebrate the joy of English rural life and of such simple traditions and rituals as the gathering of flowers on May Day.*

Corinna's *going a Maying*

Get up, get up for shame, the Blooming Morne
Upon her wings presents the god unshorne.
   See how *Aurora* throwes her faire
   Fresh-quilted colours through the aire:
5   Get up, sweet-Slug-a-bed, and see
   The Dew-bespangling Herbe and Tree.
Each Flower has wept, and bow'd toward the East,
Above an houre since; yet you not drest,
   Nay! not so much as out of bed?
10   When all the Birds have Mattens seyd,
   And sung their thankfull Hymnes: 'tis sin,
   Nay, profanation to keep in,
When as a thousand Virgins on this day,
Spring, sooner then the Lark, to fetch in May.

15 Rise; and put on your Foliage, and be seene
To come forth, like the Spring-time, fresh and greene;
   And sweet as *Flora*. Take no care
   For Jewels for your Gowne, or Haire:
   Feare not; the leaves will strew
20   Gemms in abundance upon you:
Besides, the childhood of the Day has kept,
Against you come, some *Orient Pearls* unwept:
   Come, and receive them while the light
   Hangs on the Dew-locks of the night:
25   And *Titan* on the Eastern hill
   Retires himselfe, or else stands still
Till you come forth. Wash, dresse, be briefe in praying:
Few Beads are best, when once we goe a Maying.

Come, my *Corinna*, come; and comming, marke
30 How each field turns a street; each street a Parke
   Made green, and trimm'd with trees: see how
   Devotion gives each House a Bough,

Or Branch: Each Porch, each doore, ere this,
    An Arke a Tabernacle is
Made up of white-thorn neatly enterwove;   35
As if here were those cooler shades of love.
    Can such delights be in the street,
    And open fields, and we not see't?
    Come, we'll abroad; and let's obay
    The Proclamation made for May: 40
And sin no more, as we have done, by staying;
But my *Corinna,* come, let's goe a Maying.

There's not a budding Boy, or Girle, this day,
But is got up, and gone to bring in May.
    A deale of Youth, ere this, is come   45
    Back, and with *White-thorn* laden home.
    Some have dispatcht their Cakes and Creame,
    Before that we have left to dreame:
And some have wept, and woo'd, and plighted Troth,
And chose their Priest, ere we can cast off sloth: 50
    Many a green-gown has been given;
    Many a kisse, both odde and even:
    Many a glance too has been sent
    From out the eye, Loves Firmament:
Many a jest told of the Keyes betraying   55
This night, and Locks pickt, yet w'are not a Maying.

Come, let us goe, while we are in our prime;
And take the harmlesse follie of the time.
    We shall grow old apace, and die
    Before we know our liberty.   60
    Our life is short; and our dayes run
    As fast away as do's the Sunne:
And as a vapour, or a drop of raine
Once lost, can ne'r be found againe:
    So when or you or I are made   65
    A fable, song, or fleeting shade;
    All love, all liking, all delight
    Lies drown'd with us in endlesse night.
Then while time serves, and we are but decaying;
Come, my *Corinna,* come, let's goe a Maying.   70

❏ Questions for Discussion

1. What is the function of Greek gods and goddesses Apollo, Aurora, and Titan in the poem?

2. Although Herrick was a Christian churchman, he wrote about Greek gods and goddesses and a celebration of a May Day

ritual—all considered idolatrous by the Puritans of his day. How can these inclusions be reconciled with Herrick's Christianity?

3. The last stanza is more serious than the rest of the poem. How does it effectively communicate the fragility and brevity of life?

4. The speaker implies that he is calling Corinna to join in celebrating a religious ritual. How do the language and **imagery** of the poem effectively relate nature to worship and worship to the listener?

5. How does the poem succeed in communicating the excitement and joy of the occasion?

❑ **Suggestion for Exploration and Writing**

1. Write an essay describing the things that young people cannot wait to do since "life is short and our days run / As fast away as does the sun."

ANDREW MARVELL (1621–1678)

*Andrew Marvell was a Puritan, a vocal advocate of personal freedom, and a member of the British Parliament. He, like John Donne, was one of the poets whom Samuel Johnson later called **metaphysical**. Marvell is known today for the exquisite craftsmanship of such poems as "The Garden," "To His Coy Mistress," and "An Horatian Ode upon Cromwell's Return from Ireland."*

To His Coy Mistress

Had we but world enough, and time,
This coyness, Lady, were no crime.
We would sit down, and think which way
To walk, and pass our long love's day.
5 Thou by the Indian Ganges' side
Shouldst rubies find: I by the tide
Of Humber would complain. I would
Love you ten years before the flood:
And you should, if you please, refuse
10 Till the conversion of the Jews.
My vegetable love should grow
Vaster than empires, and more slow.
An hundred years should go to praise
Thine eyes, and on thy forehead gaze.
15 Two hundred to adore each breast:

But thirty thousand to the rest.
An age at least to every part,
And the last age should show your heart:
For, Lady, you deserve this state;
Nor would I love at lower rate.   20
    But at my back I always hear
Time's wingèd chariot hurrying near:
And yonder all before us lie
Deserts of vast eternity.
Thy beauty shall no more be found;   25
Nor, in thy marble vault, shall sound
My echoing song: then worms shall try
That long-preserved virginity:
And your quaint honour turn to dust;
And into ashes all my lust.   30
The grave's a fine and private place,
But none, I think, do there embrace.
    Now, therefore, while the youthful hew
Sits on thy skin like morning dew,
And while thy willing soul transpires   35
At every pore with instant fires,
Now let us sport us while we may;
And now, like amorous birds of prey,
Rather at once our time devour,
Than languish in his slow-chapped power.   40
Let us roll all our strength, and all
Our sweetness, up into one ball:
And tear our pleasures with rough strife,
Thorough the iron grates of life.
Thus, though we cannot make our sun   45
Stand still, yet we will make him run.

❏ Questions for Discussion

1. How does the **tone** of the poem change from the first stanza to the second to the last?

2. Do you think the speaker genuinely loves his listener, or is he just feeding her a line? Defend your answer.

❏ Suggestions for Exploration and Writing

1. Like Herrick's "*Corinna's* going a Maying," this is a *carpe diem* poem. How does it differ in tone from Herrick's poem? Contrast the poems by Herrick and Marvell, looking at significant differences in **tone** between two poems of similar theme and subject.

2. Analyze some techniques that men or women use to be "coy"
   or to play "hard to get."

ELIZABETH BARRETT BROWNING (1806–1861)

*Elizabeth Barrett was famous as a well-educated and precocious
poet. By the time Robert Browning fell in love with her, she had
become a semi-invalid forbidden by her tyrannical father to marry.
After Elizabeth and Robert eloped to Italy, her health improved. The
depth of her love for her husband is beautifully illustrated by the
Sonnets from the Portuguese (1850), forty-four verses tracing the
progress of her love for Robert, who called her his little Portuguese.
"How Do I Love Thee?" is the most famous of these sonnets.*

Sonnet 43

How do I love thee? Let me count the ways.
I love thee to the depth and breadth and height
My soul can reach, when feeling out of sight
For the ends of Being and ideal Grace.
I love thee to the level of everyday's
Most quiet need, by sun and candlelight.
I love thee freely, as men strive for Right;
I love thee purely, as they turn from Praise.
I love thee with the passion put to use
In my old griefs, and with my childhood's faith.
I love thee with a love I seemed to lose
With my lost saints—I love thee with the breath,
Smiles, tears, of all my life!—and, if God choose,
I shall but love thee better after death.

❏ **Questions for Discussion**

1. Is this an English or Italian **sonnet**?

2. According to this sonnet, what are the different types of love
   necessary for a marriage to last?

❏ **Suggestions for Exploration and Writing**

1. Browning uses a series of **metaphorical** devices—**personification,
   metonymy,** and **synecdoche**—to describe her love. These are
   combined with poetic sound devices such as **anaphora, alliteration, assonance,** and **caesura.** Write an essay explaining how
   these devices, as well as the **sonnet** form, enable Browning to
   express great depths of feeling in the confined space of a
   sonnet.

2. Compare and contrast the depth of love described in this sonnet with the depth of love in Shakespeare's Sonnet 130.

ROBERT BROWNING (1812–1889)

*The English poet Robert Browning is famous for his perfection of the **dramatic monologue**, for the depth and breadth of knowledge displayed in his poetry, for his ideas, and for his role in one of the most famous love stories of the nineteenth century. His wife, Elizabeth Barrett Browning, immortalized their love in her* Sonnets from the Portuguese. *Robert Browning's most admired books,* Men and Women *(1855) and* Dramatis Personae *(1864), contain many of his frequently read poems. His book-length poem* The Ring and the Book *(1868), an account of a murder trial in seventeenth-century Rome, experiments with multiple **points of view** and is a precursor of the **nonfiction novel**.*

Porphyria's Lover

The rain set early in tonight,
   The sullen wind was soon awake,
It tore the elm-tops down for spite,
   And did its worst to vex the lake:
   I listened with heart fit to break.   5
When glided in Porphyria; straight
   She shut the cold out and the storm,
And kneeled and made the cheerless grate
   Blaze up, and all the cottage warm;
   Which done, she rose, and from her form   10
Withdrew the dripping cloak and shawl,
   And laid her soiled gloves by, untied
Her hat and let the damp hair fall,
   And, last, she sat down by my side
   And called me. When no voice replied,   15
She put my arm about her waist,
   And made her smooth white shoulder bare,
And all her yellow hair displaced,
   And, stooping, made my cheek lie there,
   And spread, o'er all, her yellow hair,   20
Murmuring how she loved me—she
   Too weak, for all her heart's endeavor,
To set its struggling passion free
   From pride, and vainer ties dissever,
   And give herself to me forever.   25
But passion sometimes would prevail,
   Nor could tonight's gay feast restrain

A sudden thought of one so pale
   For love of her, and all in vain:
30   So, she was come through wind and rain.
Be sure I looked up at her eyes
   Happy and proud; at last I knew
Porphyria worshiped me: surprise
   Made my heart swell, and still it grew
35   While I debated what to do.
That moment she was mine, mine, fair,
   Perfectly pure and good: I found
A thing to do, and all her hair
   In one long yellow string I wound
40   Three times her little throat around,
And strangled her. No pain felt she;
   I am quite sure she felt no pain.
As a shut bud that holds a bee,
   I warily oped her lids: again
45   Laughed the blue eyes without a stain.
And I untightened next the tress
   About her neck; her cheek once more
Blushed bright beneath my burning kiss:
   I propped her head up as before,
50   Only, this time my shoulder bore
Her head, which droops upon it still:
   The smiling rosy little head,
So glad it has its utmost will,
   That all it scorned at once is fled,
55   And I, its love, am gained instead!
Porphyria's love: she guessed not how
   Her darling one wish would be heard.
And thus we sit together now,
   And all night long we have not stirred,
60   And yet God has not said a word!

❏ Questions for Discussion

1. To whom is the narrator speaking? In what tone of voice? What does the tone reveal about the speaker?

2. What, according to the **narrator,** is Porphyria's "darling one wish"? How has the narrator granted it?

❏ Suggestion for Exploration and Writing

1. Contrast Porphyria with the Duchess.

My Last Duchess

FERRARA

That's my last Duchess painted on the wall,
Looking as if she were alive. I call
That piece a wonder, now: Frà Pandolf's hands
Worked busily a day, and there she stands.
Will 't please you sit and look at her? I said   5
"Frà Pandolf" by design, for never read
Strangers like you that pictured countenance,
The depth and passion of its earnest glance,
But to myself they turned (since none puts by
The curtain I have drawn for you, but I)   10
And seemed as they would ask me, if they durst,
How such a glance came there; so, not the first
Are you to turn and ask thus. Sir, 'twas not
Her husband's presence only, called that spot
Of joy into the Duchess' cheek: perhaps   15
Frà Pandolf chanced to say "Her mantle laps
Over my lady's wrist too much," or "Paint
Must never hope to reproduce the faint
Half-flush that dies along her throat": such stuff
Was courtesy, she thought, and cause enough   20
For calling up that spot of joy. She had
A heart—how shall I say?—too soon made glad,
Too easily impressed; she liked whate'er
She looked on, and her looks went everywhere.
Sir, 'twas all one! My favor at her breast,   25
The dropping of the daylight in the West,
The bough of cherries some officious fool
Broke in the orchard for her, the white mule
She rode with round the terrace—all and each
Would draw from her alike the approving speech,   30
Or blush, at least. She thanked men—good! but thanked
Somehow—I know not how—as if she ranked
My gift of a nine-hundred-years-old name
With anybody's gift. Who'd stoop to blame
This sort of trifling? Even had you skill   35
In speech—(which I have not)—to make your will
Quite clear to such an one, and say, "Just this
Or that in you disgusts me; here you miss,
Or there exceed the mark"—and if she let
Herself be lessoned so, nor plainly set   40
Her wits to yours, forsooth, and made excuse

—E'en then would be some stooping; and I choose
Never to stoop. Oh sir, she smiled, no doubt,
Whene'er I passed her; but who passed without
45   Much the same smile? This grew; I gave commands;
Then all smiles stopped together. There she stands
As if alive. Will 't please you rise? We'll meet
The company below, then. I repeat,
The Count your master's known munificence
50   Is ample warrant that no just pretense
Of mine for dowry will be disallowed;
Though his fair daughter's self, as I avowed
At starting, is my object. Nay, we'll go
Together down, sir. Notice Neptune, though,
55   Taming a sea horse, thought a rarity,
Which Claus of Innsbruck cast in bronze for me!

❏ Questions for Discussion

1. What qualities of the deceased Duchess annoyed the Duke? Why?

2. Why does the Duke want to make plain to this particular listener what he disliked about his deceased wife?

3. How do Ferrara's **diction** and sentence structure suggest his callous egotism?

❏ Suggestion for Exploration and Writing

1. This **dramatic monologue** in which the Duke describes his deceased wife reveals more about him than about her. Write a **character sketch** of the Duke.

EDNA ST. VINCENT MILLAY (1892–1950)

Edna St. Vincent Millay, winner of the 1923 Pulitzer Prize for Poetry, was talented as an actress, a musician, and a poet. After graduation from Vassar College, she moved to Greenwich Village, where she lived a bohemian life. Her poetry reflects both this life and her later devotion to her husband, her zest for life, her sense of humor, her capability for great depths of feeling, and her love of beauty.

Sonnet 42

What lips my lips have kissed, and where, and why,
I have forgotten, and what arms have lain
Under my head till morning; but the rain

Is full of ghosts tonight, that tap and sigh
Upon the glass and listen for reply,   5
And in my heart there stirs a quiet pain
For unremembered lads that not again
Will turn to me at midnight with a cry.
Thus in the winter stands the lonely tree,
Nor knows what birds have vanished one by one,   10
Yet knows its boughs more silent than before:
I cannot say what loves have come and gone,
I only know that summer sang in me
A little while, that in me sings no more.

❏ **Questions for Discussion**

1. In the **octave,** the poet describes her feelings. What is her mood?

2. In the **sestet,** rather than give an answer to her problem as is traditional in the Italian **sonnet,** Millay uses a **metaphor** to repeat the same mood. What is the metaphor, and how does it apply to her?

3. What does the speaker regret the most about those lost "summers"?

❏ **Suggestions for Exploration and Writing**

1. Write about a relationship that failed and explain the reasons for its failure.

2. Explain why remembered friendships or relationships seem so much sweeter than real, present ones.

DOROTHY PARKER (1893–1967)

Born in West End, New Jersey, to a Jewish father and a Scottish mother, Dorothy Parker became a minor editor at Vogue *and a drama critic for* Vanity Fair. *Especially remembered for her clever repartee, Parker excelled in essays, poetry, stories, and reviews; and she collaborated with others on novels and plays. Her poems and short fiction reflect a conversational style with* **epigrams, puns,** *and ironic, sarcastic* **tone.**

One Perfect Rose

A single flow'r he sent me, since we met.
    All tenderly his messenger he chose;
Deep-hearted, pure, with scented dew still wet—
    One perfect rose.

5   I knew the language of the floweret;
           "My fragile leaves," it said, "his heart enclose."
       Love long has taken for his amulet
           One perfect rose.

       Why is it no one ever sent me yet
10   One perfect limousine, do you suppose?
       Ah no, it's always just my luck to get
           One perfect rose.

❑ **Questions for Discussion**

1. Why, even though the speaker understands the **symbolism** of
   "one perfect rose," does she prefer "one perfect limousine"?
   Does this preference suggest something about the depth of
   her love for the gift-giver?

2. If the poem is a **parody**, what is Parker ridiculing?

3. What does Parker mean by "Love long has taken for his amulet / one perfect rose"? How is the word *amulet* used?

❑ **Suggestion for Exploration and Writing**

1. In Chaucer's *Canterbury Tales,* Queen Guinivere in "The Wife
   of Bath's Tale" tells the knight that he can save his life if he
   can find the answer to the question, "What do women want
   the most?" The answer is that women want power and control
   over their husbands. Write an essay that proposes what a modern woman or man wants the most from a mate.

ADRIENNE RICH (1929–   )

Adrienne Rich has won a Guggenheim fellowship and a National
Book Award for her highly regarded poems, which often advocate
the liberation of oppressed groups, especially women. From the clear
and traditional A Change of Worlds *(1951) to the highly polemical*
An Atlas of What's Difficult *(1992), her poems have become more*
difficult and more aggressively feminist.

Living in Sin

       She had thought the studio would keep itself;
       no dust upon the furniture of love.
       Half heresy, to wish the taps less vocal,
       the panes relieved of grime. A plate of pears,
5   a piano with a Persian shawl, a cat

stalking the picturesque amusing mouse
had risen at his urging.
Not that at five each separate stair would writhe
under the milkman's tramp; that morning light
so coldly would delineate the scraps   10
of last night's cheese and three sepulchral bottles;
that on the kitchen shelf among the saucers
a pair of beetle-eyes would fix her own —
envoy from some village in the moldings . . .
Meanwhile, he, with a yawn,   15
sounded a dozen notes upon the keyboard,
declared it out of tune, shrugged at the mirror,
rubbed at his beard, went out for cigarettes;
while she, jeered by the minor demons,
pulled back the sheets and made the bed and found   20
a towel to dust the table-top,
and let the coffee-pot boil over on the stove.
By evening she was back in love again,
though not so wholly but throughout the night
she woke sometimes to feel the daylight coming   25
like a relentless milkman up the stairs.

❏ Questions for Discussion

1. What illusion about romantic love did the woman have? How
   does the **image** "no dust upon the furniture of love" develop
   that illusion? Who appears to be assembling and arranging
   "the furniture of love," thereby helping to create the illusion?

2. What images are particularly effective in developing the rather
   sordid reality of this love?

3. Why is the speaker "back in love again" by evening?

❏ Suggestions for Exploration and Writing

1. Discuss the different ways that men and women have of looking at the same physical surroundings. Use the poem to support your analysis.

2. What is the significance of the title? Does the word *sin* add
   richness to the illusion? One myth of a married woman portrays her as trapped by children and housework, whereas the
   adulterous woman is free to indulge her sexual fantasies. How
   does this poem comment on such a myth?

3. Should couples live together without marriage? Discuss.

Sylvia Plath (1932–1963)

Metaphors

I'm a riddle in nine syllables,
An elephant, a ponderous house,
A melon strolling on two tendrils.
O red fruit, ivory, fine timbers!
This loaf's big with its yeasty rising.
Money's new-minted in this fat purse.
I'm a means, a stage, a cow in calf.
I've eaten a bag of green apples,
Boarded the train there's no getting off.

❑ Questions for Discussion

1. As the title suggests, this poem is a series of **metaphors.** What condition do the metaphors describe?
2. The poem has nine lines. Why is this significant?
3. How does the speaker feel about her condition in the first three lines? How does that feeling change in the middle three lines? In the last three lines?
4. What sensations appropriate to the speaker's condition does the last line suggest?

❑ Suggestion for Exploration and Writing

1. Using this poem as an example, discuss how speaking in metaphors can sometimes clarify and enrich concepts.

Janice Mirikitani (1942–)

Janice Mirikitani, a third-generation Japanese American who was interned during World War II, lives and works in the San Francisco area. Writing from a political point of view, Mirikitani expresses her outrage against racism, sexism, and oppression of any kind. Much of her work shows a dichotomy between traditional Japanese customs and beliefs and a newer Japanese-American or American identity.

Breaking Tradition

for my Daughter

My daughter denies she is like me,
Her secretive eyes avoid mine.

She reveals the hatreds of womanhood
already veiled behind music and smoke and telephones.
I want to tell her about the empty room 5
of myself.
This room we lock ourselves in
where whispers live like fungus,
giggles about small breasts and cellulite,
where we confine ourselves to jealousies, 10
bedridden by menstruation.
This waiting room where we feel our hands
are useless, dead speechless clamps
that need hospitals and forceps and kitchens
and plugs and ironing boards to make them useful. 15
I deny I am like my mother. I remember why:
She kept her room neat with silence,
defiance smothered in requirements to be otonashii,
passion and loudness wrapped in an obi,
her steps confined to ceremony, 20
the weight of her sacrifice she carried like
a foetus. Guilt passed on in our bones.
I want to break tradition—unlock this room
where women dress in the dark.
Discover the lies my mother told me. 25
The lies that we are small and powerless
that our possibilities must be compressed
to the size of pearls, displayed only as
passive chokers, charms around our neck.
Break Tradition. 30
I want to tell my daughter of this room
of myself
filled with tears of violins,
the light in my hands,
poems about madness, 35
the music of yellow guitars—
sounds shaken from barbed wire and
goodbyes and miracles of survival.
This room of open window where daring ones escape.
My daughter denies she is like me 40
her secretive eyes are walls of smoke
and music and telephones,
her pouting ruby lips, her skirts
swaying to salsa, teena marie and the stones,
her thighs displayed in carnavals of color. 45
I do not know the contents of her room.
She mirrors my aging.
She is breaking tradition.

❏ **Questions for Discussion**

1. To what is the speaker referring by "this room we lock ourselves in," and "she kept her room neat with silence"? Why
   does she want to "unlock this room / where women dress in
   the dark"?

2. What are "the hatreds of womanhood" that the daughter expresses? What is the poem about other than the generation gap?

3. What does the speaker mean by "she mirrors my aging"?

4. What is the speaker's **tone?** Explain your answer.

❏ **Suggestions for Exploration and Writing**

1. Three generations are pictured in the poem. Discuss why each
   daughter denies being like her mother.

2. In some families the parents are such high achievers that the
   children find it difficult to live up to their parents' standards.
   In other families the children are encouraged not to emulate
   their parents. Discuss the importance of family role models for
   sons or daughters, or discuss the need for sons or daughters
   to be distinct individuals.

DRAMA

SUSAN GLASPELL (1882–1948)

*Susan Glaspell, a feminist author, wrote many plays for the Province-
town Players in Cape Cod, Massachusetts. She won a Pulitzer Prize
for* Alison's House *(1931), a play based loosely on the family and
life-style of Emily Dickinson.* Trifles *(1916), written in ten days for
the Provincetown Players, was inspired by a murder trial that
Glaspell encountered while she was a reporter for a Des Moines
newspaper. One year later she wrote the short story version, "A Jury
of Her Peers."*

Trifles
Characters

GEORGE HENDERSON: *county attorney*
HENRY PETERS: *sheriff*
LEWIS HALE: *a neighboring farmer*
MRS. PETERS
MRS. HALE

Scene

The kitchen in the now abandoned farmhouse of John Wright, a gloomy kitchen, and left without having been put in order—unwashed pans under the sink, a loaf of bread outside the breadbox, a dish towel on the table—other signs of incompleted work. At the rear the outer door opens and the Sheriff comes in followed by the County Attorney and Hale. The Sheriff and Hale are men in middle life, the County Attorney is a young man; all are much bundled up and go at once to the stove. They are followed by two women—the Sheriff's wife first; she is a slight wiry woman, a thin nervous face. Mrs. Hale is larger and would ordinarily be called more comfortable looking, but she is disturbed now and looks fearfully about as she enters. The women have come in slowly, and stand close together near the door.

COUNTY ATTORNEY *(Rubbing his hands.)*: This feels good. Come up to the fire, ladies.

MRS. PETERS *(After taking a step forward.)*: I'm not—cold.

SHERIFF *(Unbuttoning his overcoat and stepping away from the stove as if to mark the beginning of official business.)*: Now, Mr. Hale, before we move things about, you explain to Mr. Henderson just what you saw when you came here yesterday morning.

COUNTY ATTORNEY: By the way, has anything been moved? Are things just as you left them yesterday?

SHERIFF *(Looking about.)*: It's just the same. When it dropped below zero last night I thought I'd better send Frank out this morning to   10
make a fire for us—no use getting pneumonia with a big case on, but I told him not to touch anything except the stove—and you know Frank.

COUNTY ATTORNEY: Somebody should have been left here yesterday.

SHERIFF: Oh—yesterday. When I had to send Frank to Morris Center for that man who went crazy—I want you to know I had my hands full yesterday, I knew you could get back from Omaha by today and as long as I went over everything here myself—

COUNTY ATTORNEY: Well, Mr. Hale, tell just what happened when you came here yesterday morning.   20

HALE: Harry and I had started to town with a load of potatoes. We came along the road from my place and as I got here I said, "I'm going to see if I can't get John Wright to go in with me on a party telephone." I spoke to Wright about it once before and he put me off, saying folks talked too much anyway, and all he asked was peace and quiet—I guess you know about how much he talked himself; but I thought maybe if I went to the house and talked about it before his wife, though I said to Harry that I didn't know as what his wife wanted made much difference to John—

COUNTY ATTORNEY: Let's talk about that later, Mr. Hale. I do want to   30
talk about that, but tell now just what happened when you got to the house.

HALE: I didn't hear or see anything; I knocked at the door, and still it

was all quiet inside. I knew they must be up, it was past eight
o'clock. So I knocked again, and I thought I heard somebody say,
"Come in." I wasn't sure, I'm not sure yet, but I opened the door—
this door *(Indicating the door by which the two women are still
standing)* and there in that rocker—*(Pointing to it)* sat Mrs. Wright.
(They all look at the rocker.)

COUNTY ATTORNEY: What—was she doing?

40 HALE: She was rockin' back and forth. She had her apron in her hand
and was kind of—pleating it.

COUNTY ATTORNEY: And how did she—look?

HALE: Well, she looked queer.

COUNTY ATTORNEY: How do you mean—queer?

HALE: Well, as if she didn't know what she was going to do next. And
kind of done up.

COUNTY ATTORNEY: How did she seem to feel about your coming?

HALE: Why, I don't think she minded—one way or other. She didn't
pay much attention. I said, "How do, Mrs. Wright, it's cold, ain't
50 it?" and she said, "Is it?"—and went on kind of pleating at her
apron. Well, I was surprised; she didn't ask me to come up to the
stove, or to set down, but just sat there, not even looking at me, so
I said, "I want to see John." And then she—laughed. I guess you
would call it a laugh. I thought of Harry and the team outside, so I
said a little sharp: "Can't I see John?" "No," she says, kind o' dull
like. "Ain't he home?" says I. "Yes," says she, "He's home." "Then
why can't I see him?" I asked her, out of patience. " 'Cause he's
dead," says she. "*Dead?*" says I. She just nodded her head, not getting a bit excited, but rockin' back and forth. "Why—where is he?"
60 says I, not knowing what to say. She just pointed upstairs—like that
(Himself pointing to the room above.) I got up, with the idea of going up there. I walked from there to here—then I says, "Why, what
did he die of?" "He died of a rope round his neck," says she, and
just went on pleatin' at her apron. Well, I went out and called
Harry. I thought I might—need help. We went upstairs and there he
was lyin'—

COUNTY ATTORNEY: I think I'd rather have you go into that upstairs,
where you can point it all out. Just go on now with the rest of the
story.

70 HALE: Well, my first thought was to get that rope off. It looked . . .
(Stops, his face twitches) . . . but Harry, he went up to him, and he
said, "No, he's dead all right, and we'd better not touch anything."
So we went back down stairs. She was still sitting that same way.
"Has anybody been notified?" I asked. "No," says she, uncon-
cerned. "Who did this, Mrs. Wright?" said Harry. He said it businesslike—and she stopped pleatin' of her apron. "I don't know,"
she says. "You don't *know?*" says Harry. "No," says she. "Weren't

you sleepin' in the bed with him?" says Harry. "Yes," says she, "but I was on the inside." "Somebody slipped a rope around his neck and strangled him and you didn't wake up?" says Harry. "I didn't wake up," she said after him. We must 'a looked as if we didn't see how that could be, for after a minute she said, "I sleep sound." Harry was going to ask her more questions but I said maybe we ought to let her tell her story first to the coroner, or the sheriff, so Harry went fast as he could to Rivers' place, where there's a telephone.

COUNTY ATTORNEY: And what did Mrs. Wright do when she knew that you had gone for the coroner?

HALE: She moved from that chair to this one over here *(Pointing to a small chair in the corner)* and just sat there with her hands held together and looking down. I got a feeling that I ought to make some conversation, so I said I had come in to see if John wanted to put in a telephone, and at that she started to laugh, and then she stopped and looked at me—scared. *(The County Attorney, who has had his notebook out, makes a note.)* I dunno, maybe it wasn't scared. I wouldn't like to say it was. Soon Harry got back, and then Dr. Lloyd came, and you, Mr. Peters, and so I guess that's all I know that you don't.

COUNTY ATTORNEY *(Looking around.)*: I guess we'll go upstairs first— and then out to the barn and around there. *(To the Sheriff)* You're convinced that there was nothing important here—nothing that would point to any motive.

SHERIFF: Nothing here but kitchen things.

(The County Attorney, after again looking around the kitchen, opens the door of a cupboard closet. He gets up on a chair and looks on a shelf. Pulls his hand away, sticky.)

COUNTY ATTORNEY: Here's a nice mess.

(The women draw nearer.)

MRS. PETERS *(To the other woman.)*: Oh, her fruit; it did freeze. *(To the County Attorney)* She worried about that when it turned so cold. She said the fire'd go out and her jars would break.

SHERIFF: Well, can you beat the women! Held for murder and worryin' about her preserves.

COUNTY ATTORNEY: I guess before we're through she may have something more serious than preserves to worry about.

HALE: Well, women are used to worrying over trifles.

(The two women move a little closer together.)

COUNTY ATTORNEY *(With the gallantry of a young politician.)*: And yet, for all their worries, what would we do without the ladies? *(The women do not unbend. He goes to the sink, takes a dipperful of water from the pail and pouring it into a basin, washes his* hands. *Starts to wipe them on the roller towel, turns it for a cleaner place.*) Dirty towels! (*Kicks his foot against the pans under the sink.*) Not much of a housekeeper, would you say, ladies?

MRS. HALE (*Stiffly.*): There's a great deal of work to be done on a farm.

COUNTY ATTORNEY: To be sure. And yet (*With a little bow to her*) I
120   know there are some Dickson county farmhouses which do not have such roller towels.

(*He gives it a pull to expose its full length again.*)

MRS. HALE: Those towels get dirty awful quick. Men's hands aren't always as clean as they might be.

COUNTY ATTORNEY: Ah, loyal to your sex, I see. But you and Mrs. Wright were neighbors. I suppose you were friends, too.

MRS. HALE (*Shaking her head.*): I've not seen much of her of late years. I've not been in this house—it's more than a year.

COUNTY ATTORNEY: And why was that? You didn't like her?

MRS. HALE: I liked her all well enough. Farmers' wives have their
130   hands full, Mr. Henderson. And then—

COUNTY ATTORNEY: Yes—?

MRS. HALE (*Looking about.*): It never seemed a very cheerful place.

COUNTY ATTORNEY: No—it's not cheerful. I shouldn't say she had the homemaking instinct.

MRS. HALE: Well, I don't know as Wright had, either.

COUNTY ATTORNEY: You mean that they didn't get on very well?

MRS. HALE: No, I don't mean anything. But I don't think a place'd be any cheerfuller for John Wright's being in it.

COUNTY ATTORNEY: I'd like to talk more of that a little later. I want to
140   get the lay of things upstairs now.

(*He goes to the left, where three steps lead to a stair door.*)

SHERIFF: I suppose anything Mrs. Peters does'll be all right. She was to take in some clothes for her, you know, and a few little things. We left in such a hurry yesterday.

COUNTY ATTORNEY: Yes, but I would like to see what you take, Mrs. Peters, and keep an eye out for anything that might be of use to us.

MRS. PETERS: Yes, Mr. Henderson.

(*The women listen to the men's steps on the stairs, then look about the kitchen.*)

MRS. HALE: I'd hate to have men coming into my kitchen, snooping around and criticizing.

(*She arranges the pans under sink which the County Attorney had shoved out of place.*)

MRS. PETERS: Of course it's no more than their duty.
150 MRS. HALE: Duty's all right, but I guess that deputy sheriff that came out to make the fire might have got a little of this on. (*Gives the

roller towel a pull.) Wish I'd thought of that sooner. Seems mean to talk about her for not having things slicked up when she had to come away in such a hurry.

MRS. PETERS *(Who has gone to a small table in the left rear corner of the room, and lifted one end of a towel that covers a pan.)*: She had bread set.

(Stands still.)

MRS. HALE *(Eyes fixed on a loaf of bread beside the breadbox, which is on a low shelf at the other side of the room. Moves slowly toward it.)*: She was going to put this in there. *(Picks up loaf, then abruptly drops it. In a manner of returning to familiar things.)* It's a shame about her fruit. I wonder if it's all gone. *(Gets up on the chair and looks.)* I think there's some here that's all right, Mrs. Peters. Yes—here; *(Holding it toward the window)* this is cherries, too. *(Looking again.)* I declare I believe that's the only one. *(Gets down, bottle in her hand. Goes to the sink and wipes it off on the outside.)* She'll feel awful bad after all her hard work in the hot weather. I remember the afternoon I put up my cherries last summer.

(She puts the bottle on the big kitchen table, center of the room. With a sigh, is about to sit down in the rocking-chair. Before she is seated realizes what chair it is; with a slow look at it, steps back. The chair which she has touched rocks back and forth.)

MRS. PETERS: Well, I must get those things from the front room closet. *(She goes to the door at the right, but after looking into the other room, steps back.)* You coming with me, Mrs. Hale? You could help me carry them.

(They go in the other room; reappear, Mrs. Peters carrying a dress and skirt, Mrs. Hale following with a pair of shoes.)

MRS. PETERS: My, it's cold in there.

(She puts the clothes on the big table, and hurries to the stove.)

MRS. HALE *(Examining her skirt.)*: Wright was close. I think maybe that's why she kept so much to herself. She didn't even belong to the Ladies Aid. I suppose she felt she couldn't do her part, and then you don't enjoy things when you feel shabby. She used to wear pretty clothes and be lively, when she was Minnie Foster, one of the town girls singing in the choir. But that—oh, that was thirty years ago. This all you was to take in?

MRS. PETERS: She said she wanted an apron. Funny thing to want, for there isn't much to get you dirty in jail, goodness knows. But I suppose just to make her feel more natural. She said they was in the top drawer in this cupboard. Yes, here. And then her little shawl that always hung behind the door. *(Opens stair door and looks.)* Yes, here it is.

160

170

180

(Quickly shuts door leading upstairs.)

MRS. HALE *(Abruptly moving toward her.)*: Mrs. Peters?

MRS. PETERS: Yes, Mrs. Hale?

MRS. HALE: Do you think she did it?

MRS. PETERS *(In a frightened voice.)*: Oh, I don't know.

MRS. HALE: Well, I don't think she did. Asking for an apron and her little shawl. Worrying about her fruit.

MRS. PETERS *(Starts to speak, glances up, where footsteps are heard in the room above. In a low voice.)*: Mr. Peters says it looks bad for her. Mr. Henderson is awful sarcastic in a speech and he'll make fun of her sayin' she didn't wake up.

MRS. HALE: Well, I guess John Wright didn't wake when they was slipping that rope under his neck.

MRS. PETERS: No, it's strange. It must have been done awful crafty and still. They say it was such a—funny way to kill a man, rigging it all up like that.

MRS. HALE: That's just what Mr. Hale said. There was a gun in the house. He says that's what he can't understand.

MRS. PETERS: Mr. Henderson said coming out that what was needed for the case was a motive; something to show anger, or—sudden feeling.

MRS. HALE *(Who is standing by the table.)*: Well, I don't see any signs of anger around here. *(She puts her hand on the dish towel which lies on the table, stands looking down at table, one half of which is clean, the other half messy.)* It's wiped to here. *(Makes a move as if to finish work, then turns and looks at loaf of bread outside the breadbox. Drops towel. In that voice of coming back to familiar things.)* Wonder how they are finding things upstairs. I hope she had it a little more red-up up there. You know, it seems kind of *sneaking*. Locking her up in town and then coming out here and trying to get her own house to turn against her!

MRS. PETERS: But Mrs. Hale, the law is the law.

MRS. HALE: I s'pose 'tis. *(Unbuttoning her coat.)* Better loosen up your things, Mrs. Peters. You won't feel them when you go out.

(Mrs. Peters takes off her fur tippet, goes to hang it on hook at back of room, stands looking at the under part of the small corner table.)

MRS. PETERS: She was piecing a quilt.

(She brings the large sewing basket and they look at the bright pieces.)

MRS. HALE: It's log cabin pattern. Pretty, isn't it? I wonder if she was goin' to quilt it or just knot it?

(Footsteps have been heard coming down the stairs. The Sheriff enters followed by Hale and the County Attorney.)

SHERIFF: They wonder if she was going to quilt it or just knot it!

(The men laugh; the women look abashed.)

COUNTY ATTORNEY *(Rubbing his hands over the stove.)*: Frank's fire didn't do much up there, did it? Well, let's go out to the barn and get that cleared up.

(The men go outside.)

MRS. HALE *(Resentfully.)*: I don't know as there's anything so strange, our takin' up our time with little things while we're waiting for them to get the evidence. *(She sits down at the big table smoothing out a block with decision.)* I don't see as it's anything to laugh about. 220

MRS. PETERS *(Apologetically.)*: Of course they've got awful important things on their minds.

(Pulls up a chair and joins Mrs. Hale at the table.)

MRS. HALE *(Examining another block.)*: Mrs. Peters, look at this one. Here, this is the one she was working on, and look at the sewing! All the rest of it has been so nice and even. And look at this! It's all over the place! Why, it looks as if she didn't know what she was about! 230

(After she has said this they look at each, then start to glance back at the door. After an instant Mrs. Hale has pulled at a knot and ripped the sewing.)

MRS. PETERS: Oh, what are you doing, Mrs. Hale?

MRS. HALE *(Mildly.)*: Just pulling out a stitch or two that's not sewed very good. *(Threading a needle.)* Bad sewing always made me fidgety.

MRS. PETERS *(Nervously.)*: I don't think we ought to touch things.

MRS. HALE: I'll just finish up this end. *(Suddenly stopping and leaning forward.)* Mrs. Peters?

MRS. PETERS: Yes, Mrs. Hale?

MRS. HALE: What do you suppose she was so nervous about?

MRS. PETERS: Oh—I don't know. I don't know as she was nervous. I sometimes sew awful queer when I'm just tired. *(Mrs. Hale starts to say something, looks at Mrs. Peters, then goes on sewing.)* Well, I must get these things wrapped up. They may be through sooner than we think. *(Putting apron and other things together.)* I wonder where I can find a piece of paper, and string. 240

MRS. HALE: In that cupboard, maybe.

MRS. PETERS *(Looking in cupboard.)*: Why, here's a birdcage. *(Holds it up.)* Did she have a bird, Mrs. Hale?

MRS. HALE: Why, I don't know whether she did or not—I've not been here for so long. There was a man around last year selling canaries cheap, but I don't know as she took one; maybe she did. She used to sing real pretty herself. 250

MRS. PETERS (*Glancing around.*): Seems funny to think of a bird here. But she must have had one, or why would she have a cage? I wonder what happened to it.

MRS. HALE: I s'pose maybe the cat got it.

MRS. PETERS: No, she didn't have a cat. She's got that feeling some people have about cats—being afraid of them. My cat got in her room and she was real upset and asked me to take it out.

260   MRS. HALE: My sister Bessie was like that. Queer, ain't it?

MRS. PETERS (*Examining the cage.*): Why, look at this door. It's broke. One hinge is pulled apart.

MRS. HALE (*Looking too.*): Looks as if someone must have been rough with it.

MRS. PETERS: Why, yes.

(*She brings the cage forward and puts it on the table.*)

MRS. HALE: I wish if they're going to find any evidence they'd be about it. I don't like this place.

MRS. PETERS: But I'm awful glad you came with me, Mrs. Hale. It would be lonesome for me sitting here alone.

270   MRS. HALE: It would, wouldn't it? (*Dropping her sewing.*) But I tell you what I do wish, Mrs. Peters. I wish I had come over sometimes when *she* was here. I—(*Looking round the room.*)—wish I had.

MRS PETERS: But of course you were awful busy, Mrs. Hale—your house and your children.

MRS. HALE: I could've come. I stayed away because it weren't cheerful—and that's why I ought to have come. I—I've never liked this place. Maybe because it's down in a hollow and you don't see the road. I dunno what it is but it's a lonesome place and always was. I wish I had come over to see Minnie Foster sometimes. I can see

280   now—

(*Shakes her head.*)

MRS. PETERS: Well, you mustn't reproach yourself, Mrs. Hale. Somehow we just don't see how it is with other folks until—something comes up.

MRS. HALE: Not having children makes less work—but it makes a quiet house, and Wright out to work all day, and no company when he did come in. Did you know John Wright, Mrs. Peters?

MRS. PETERS: Not to know him; I've seen him in town. They say he was a good man.

MRS. HALE: Yes—good; he didn't drink, and kept his word as well as
290   most, I guess, and paid his debts. But he was a hard man, Mrs. Peters. Just to pass the time of day with him—(*Shivers.*) Like a raw wind that gets to the bone. (*Pauses, her eye falling on the cage.*) I should think she would'a wanted a bird. But what do you suppose went with it?

MRS. PETERS: I don't know, unless it got sick and died.

(She reaches over and swings the broken door, swings it again. Both women watch it.)

MRS. HALE: You weren't raised round here, were you? *(Mrs. Peters shakes her head.)* You didn't know—her?

MRS. PETERS: Not till they brought her yesterday.

MRS. HALE: She—come to think of it, she was kind of a like a bird herself—real sweet and pretty, but kind of timid and—fluttery. How—she—did—change. *(Silence, then as if struck by a happy thought and relieved to get back to everyday things.)* Tell you what, Mrs. Peters, why don't you take the quilt in with you? It might take up her mind.   300

MRS. PETERS: Why, I think that's a real nice idea, Mrs. Hale. There couldn't possibly be an objection to it, could there? Now, just what would I take? I wonder if her patches are in here—and her things.

(They look in the sewing basket.)

MRS. HALE: Here's some red. I expect this has got sewing things in it. *(Brings out a fancy box.)* What a pretty box. Looks like something somebody would give you. Maybe her scissors are in here. *(Opens box. Suddenly puts her hand to her nose.)* Why—*(Mrs. Peters bends nearer, then turns her face away.)* There's something wrapped up in this piece of silk.   310

MRS. PETERS: Why, this isn't her scissors.

MRS. HALE *(Lifting the silk.)*: Oh, Mrs. Peters—it's—

(Mrs. Peters bends closer.)

MRS. PETERS: It's the bird.

MRS. HALE *(Jumping up.)*: But, Mrs. Peters—look at it! Its neck! Look at its neck! It's all—other side *to.*

MRS. PETERS: Somebody—wrung—its—neck.

(Their eyes meet. A look of growing comprehension, of horror. Steps are heard outside. Mrs. Hale slips box under quilt pieces, and sinks into her chair. Enter Sheriff and County Attorney. Mrs. Peters rises.)

COUNTY ATTORNEY *(As one turning from serious things to little pleasantries.)*: Well, ladies, have you decided whether she was going to quilt it or knot it?   320

MRS. PETERS: We think she was going to—knot it.

COUNTY ATTORNEY: Well, that's interesting, I'm sure. *(Seeing the birdcage.)* Has the bird flown?

MRS. HALE *(Putting more quilt pieces over the box.)*: We think the—cat got it.

COUNTY ATTORNEY *(Preoccupied.)*: Is there a cat?

(Mrs. Hale glances in a quick covert way at Mrs. Peters.)

MRS. PETERS: Well, not now. They're superstitious, you know. They leave.

COUNTY ATTORNEY *(To Sheriff Peters, continuing an interrupted con-*
330   *versation.)*: No sign at all of anyone having come from the outside.
Their own rope. Now let's go up again and go over it piece by
piece. *(They start upstairs.)* It would have to have been someone
who knew just the—

*(Mrs. Peters sits down. The two women sit there not looking at one
another, but as if peering into something and at the same time holding back. When they talk now it is in the manner of feeling their
way over strange ground, as if afraid of what they are saying, but as
if they can not help saying it.)*

MRS. HALE: She liked the bird. She was going to bury it in that pretty
box.

MRS. PETERS *(In a whisper.)*: When I was a girl—my kitten—there was
a boy took a hatchet, and before my eyes—and before I could get
there—*(Covers her face an instant)* If they hadn't held me back I
would have—*(Catches herself, looks upstairs where steps are heard,*
340   *falters weakly)*—hurt him.

MRS. HALE *(With a slow look around her.)*: I wonder how it would
seem never to have had any children around. *(pause)* No, Wright
wouldn't like the bird—a thing that sang. She used to sing. He
killed that, too.

MRS. PETERS *(Moving uneasily.)*: We don't know who killed the bird.

MRS. HALE: I knew John Wright.

MRS. PETERS: It was an awful thing was done in this house that night,
Mrs. Hale. Killing a man while he slept, slipping a rope around his
neck that choked the life out of him.

350   MRS. HALE: His neck. Choked the life out of him.

(Her hand goes out and rests on the birdcage.)

MRS. PETERS *(With rising voice.)*: We don't know who killed him. We
don't know.

MRS. HALE *(Her own feeling not interrupted.)*: If there'd been years
and years of nothing, then a bird to sing to you, it would be awful—still, after the bird was still.

MRS. PETERS *(Something within her speaking.)*: I know what stillness
is. When we homesteaded in Dakota, and my first baby died—after
he was two years old, and me with no other then—

MRS. HALE *(Moving.)*: How soon do you suppose they'll be through,
360   looking for the evidence?

MRS. PETERS: I know what stillness is. *(Pulling herself back.)* The law
has got to punish crime, Mrs. Hale.

MRS. HALE *(Not as if answering that.)*: I wish you'd seen Minnie Foster when she wore a white dress with blue ribbons and stood up
there in the choir and sang. *(A look around the room.)* Oh, I *wish*
I'd come over here once in a while! That was a crime! That was a
crime! Who's going to punish that?

MRS. PETERS *(Looking upstairs.):* We mustn't—take on.

MRS. HALE: I might have known she needed help! I know how things can be—for women. I tell you, it's queer, Mrs. Peters. We live close together and we live far apart. We all go through the same things— it's all just a different kind of the same thing. *(Brushes her eyes; noticing the bottle of fruit, reaches out for it.)* If I was you I wouldn't tell her her fruit was gone. Tell her it *ain't.* Tell her it's all right. Take this in to prove it to her. She—she may never know whether it was broke or not.

MRS. PETERS *(Takes the bottle, looks about for something to wrap it in; takes petticoat from the clothes brought from the other room, very nervously begins winding this around the bottle. In a false voice.):* My, it's a good thing the men couldn't hear us. Wouldn't they just laugh! Getting all stirred up over a little thing like a—dead canary. As if that could have anything to do with—with—wouldn't they *laugh!*

(The men are heard coming down stairs.)

MRS. HALE *(Under her breath.):* Maybe they would—maybe they wouldn't.

COUNTY ATTORNEY: No, Peters, it's all perfectly clear except a reason for doing it. Something to show—something to make a story about—a thing that would connect up with this strange way of doing it—

(The women's eyes meet for an instant. Enter Hale from outer door.)

HALE: Well, I've got the team around. Pretty cold out there.

COUNTY ATTORNEY: I'm going to stay here a while myself. *(To the Sheriff.)* You can send Frank out for me, can't you? I want to go over everything. I'm not satisfied that we can't do better.

SHERIFF: Do you want to see what Mrs. Peters is going to take in?

(The County Attorney goes to the table, picks up the apron, laughs.)

COUNTY ATTORNEY: Oh, I guess they're not very dangerous things the ladies have picked out. *(Moves a few things about, disturbing the quilt pieces which cover the box. Steps back.)* No, Mrs. Peters doesn't need supervising. For that matter, a sheriff's wife is married to the law. Ever think of it that way, Mrs. Peters?

MRS. PETERS: Not—just that way.

SHERIFF *(Chuckling.):* Married to the law. *(Moves toward the other room.)* I just want you to come in here a minute, George. We ought to take a look at these windows.

COUNTY ATTORNEY *(Scoffingly.):* Oh, windows!

SHERIFF: We'll be right out, Mr. Hale.

(Hale goes outside. The Sheriff follows the County Attorney into the other room. Then Mrs. Hale rises, hands tight together, looking

intensely at Mrs. Peters, whose eyes make a slow turn, finally meet-
ing Mrs. Hale's. A moment Mrs. Hale holds her, then her own eyes
point the way to where the box is concealed. Suddenly Mrs. Peters
throws back quilt pieces and tries to put the box in the bag she is
wearing. It is too big. She opens box, starts to take bird out, cannot
touch it, goes to pieces, stands there helpless. Sound of a knob turn-
ing in the other room. Mrs. Hale snatches the box and puts it in the
pocket of her big coat. Enter County Attorney and Sheriff.)

COUNTY ATTORNEY *(Facetiously.)*: Well, Henry, at least we found out
that she was not going to quilt it. She was going to—what is it you
call it, ladies?

MRS. HALE *(Her hand against her pocket.)*: We call it—knot it, Mr.
Henderson.

Curtain.

❏ Questions for Discussion

1. When Lewis Hale tells how he found John Wright's body,
   Hale's story is loose and rambling. How does County Attorney
   Henderson react to Hale's story? What does Henderson's reac-
   tion reveal about him? How much does Henderson learn from
   Hale's story? What can you learn from Hale's story that Hen-
   derson fails to learn?

2. What is **ironic** about the sheriff's saying, "Nothing here but
   kitchen things"? What is **ironic** about the play's title?

3. In what ways are the men in the story condescending to the
   women?

4. Putting together all the signs in the play, what conclusions can
   you draw about who killed Mr. Wright and about the killer's
   motive?

5. Glaspell changed the title of the play, *Trifles*, when she wrote
   the short story, "A Jury of Her Peers." Which title is more appropriate? Why?

❏ Suggestions for Exploration and Writing

1. In an essay, contrast the men's manner and approach to the
   investigation with that of the women. Why are the women able
   to solve the murder when the men are not?

2. For what reasons do Mrs. Peters and Mrs. Hale decide to with-
   hold evidence from the men?

3. Starting with the bird in the cage, explain how the various objects in the kitchen are **symbolic** of Minnie's life after her marriage.

4. From the clues given, write a **character analysis** of the dead man, John Wright.

5. Do you think people of the same sex communicate better with each other than with those of the opposite sex? Write an essay in which you explain your position.

C A S E B O O K
on Henrik Ibsen

HENRIK IBSEN (1828–1906)

*Norwegian playwright Henrik Ibsen is often called the father of modern drama. His early romantic plays were written in verse. In his plays, Ibsen established the tradition of realism in drama, of plays that attempt to imitate life faithfully. His most famous realistic plays, A Doll's House (1879), Ghosts (1881), and Hedda Gabler (1890), are also described as theater of ideas or **problem plays,** those that deal with social issues or depict social problems.*

A Doll's House caused immediate controversy when it was first produced, for it was performed before audiences accustomed to viewing a wife as virtually the property of her husband. When A Doll's House was followed by Ghosts, a play about inherited venereal disease, Ibsen was forced to leave Norway. Later when praised by leaders of the Women's Rights League for defending women's rights, Ibsen pointed out that he was describing all humanity in his plays. One reason for the continued popularity of A Doll's House is that it raises questions about the rights of women and about the multiple roles played by women—roles which sometimes pull women in different directions.

A Doll's House
Trans. Michael Meyer

List of Characters

TORVALD HELMER:	*a lawyer*
NORA:	*his wife*
DR. RANK	
MRS. LINDE	
NILS KROGSTAD:	*also a lawyer*
THE HELMERS' THREE SMALL CHILDREN	
ANNE-MARIE:	*their nurse*
HELEN:	*the maid*
A PORTER	

Scene

The action takes place in the Helmers' apartment.

ACT 1

A comfortably and tastefully, but not expensively furnished room. Backstage right a door leads out to the hall; backstage left, another door to Helmer's study. Between these two doors stands a piano. In the middle of the left-hand wall is a door, with a window downstage of it. Near the window, a round table with armchairs and a small sofa. In the right-hand wall, slightly upstage, is a door; downstage of this, against the same wall, a stove lined with porcelain tiles, with a couple of armchairs and a rocking-chair in front of it. Between the stove and the side door is a small table. Engravings on the wall. A what-not with china and other bric-a-brac; a small bookcase with leather-bound books. A carpet on the floor; a fire in the stove. A winter day.

A bell rings in the hall outside. After a moment we hear the front door being opened. Nora enters the room, humming contentedly to herself. She is wearing outdoor clothes and carrying a lot of parcels, which she puts down on the table right. She leaves the door to the hall open; through it, we can see a Porter carrying a Christmas tree and a basket. He gives these to the Maid, who had opened the door for them.

NORA: Hide that Christmas tree away, Helen. The children mustn't see it before I've decorated it this evening. (*To the Porter, taking out her purse.*) How much—?
PORTER: A shilling.
NORA: Here's half a crown. No, keep it.

The Porter touches his cap and goes. Nora closes the door. She continues to laugh happily to herself as she removes her coat, etc. She takes from her pocket a bag containing macaroons and eats a couple. Then she tiptoes across and listens at her husband's door.

NORA: Yes, he's here. (*Starts humming again as she goes over to the table, right.*)
HELMER (*from his room*): Is that my skylark twittering out there?
NORA (*opening some of the parcels*): It is!
HELMER: Is that my squirrel rustling?
NORA: Yes!   10
HELMER: When did my squirrel come home?
NORA: Just now. (*Pops the bag of macaroons in her pocket and wipes her mouth.*) Come out here, Torvald, and see what I've bought.
HELMER: You mustn't disturb me! (*Short pause; then he opens the door and looks in, his pen in his hand.*) Bought, did you say? All that? Has my little squanderbird been overspending again?
NORA: Oh, Torvald, surely we can let ourselves go a little this year! It's the first Christmas we don't have to scrape.
HELMER: Well, you know, we can't afford to be extravagant.
NORA: Oh yes, Torvald, we can be a little extravagant now. Can't we?   20
Just a tiny bit? You've got a big salary now, and you're going to make lots and lots of money.
HELMER: Next year, yes. But my new salary doesn't start till April.

NORA: Pooh; we can borrow till then.

HELMER: Nora! (*Goes over to her and takes her playfully by the ear.*)
What a little spendthrift you are! Suppose I were to borrow fifty
pounds today, and you spent it all over Christmas, and then on
New Year's Eve a tile fell off a roof on to my head—

NORA (*puts her hand over his mouth*): Oh, Torvald! Don't say such
30   dreadful things!

HELMER: Yes, but suppose something like that did happen? What
then?

NORA: If anything as frightful as that happened, it wouldn't make
much difference whether I was in debt or not.

HELMER: But what about the people I'd borrowed from?

NORA: Them? Who cares about them? They're strangers.

HELMER: Oh, Nora, Nora, how like a woman! No, but seriously,
Nora, you know how I feel about this. No debts! Never borrow! A
home that is founded on debts can never be a place of freedom and
40   beauty. We two have stuck it out bravely up to now; and we shall
continue to do so for the short time we still have to.

NORA (*goes over towards the stove*): Very well, Torvald. As you say.

HELMER (*follows her*): Now, now! My little songbird mustn't droop
her wings. What's this? Is little squirrel sulking? (*Takes out his
purse.*) Nora; guess what I've got here!

NORA (*turns quickly*): Money!

HELMER Look. (*Hands her some banknotes.*) I know how these small
expenses crop up at Christmas.

NORA (*counts them*): One—two—three—four. Oh, thank you, Tor-
50   vald, thank you! I should be able to manage with this.

HELMER: You'll have to.

NORA: Yes, yes of course I will. But come over here, I want to show
you everything I've bought. And so cheaply! Look, here are new
clothes for Ivar—and a sword. And a horse and a trumpet for Bob.
And a doll and a cradle for Emmy—they're nothing much, but she'll
pull them apart in a few days. And some bits of material and handkerchiefs for the maids. Old Anne-Marie ought to have had something better, really.

HELMER: And what's in that parcel?

60   NORA (*cries*): No, Torvald, you mustn't see that before this evening!

HELMER: Very well. But now, tell me, you little spendthrift, what do
you want for Christmas?

NORA: Me? Oh, pooh, I don't want anything.

HELMER: Oh, yes, you do. Now tell me, what, within reason, would
you most like?

NORA: No, I really don't know. Oh, yes—Torvald—!

HELMER: Well?

NORA (*plays with his coat-buttons; not looking at him*): If you really
want to give me something, you could—you could—

HELMER: Come on, out with it.   70

NORA (*quickly*): You could give me money, Torvald. Only as much as
you feel you can afford; then later I'll buy something with it.

HELMER: But, Nora—

NORA: Oh yes, Torvald dear, please! Please! Then I'll wrap up the
notes in pretty gold paper and hang them on the Christmas tree.
Wouldn't that be fun!

HELMER: What's the name of that little bird that can never keep any
money?

NORA: Yes, yes, squanderbird; I know. But let's do as I say, Torvald;
then I'll have time to think about what I need most. Isn't that the   80
best way? Mm?

HELMER (*smiles*): To be sure it would be, if you could keep what I
give you and really buy yourself something with it. But you'll spend
it on all sorts of useless things for the house, and then I'll have to
put my hand in my pocket again.

NORA: Oh, but Torvald—

HELMER: You can't deny it, Nora dear. (*Puts his arm round her
waist.*) The squanderbird's a pretty little creature, but she gets
through an awful lot of money. It's incredible what an expensive pet
she is for a man to keep.   90

NORA: For shame! How can you say such a thing? I save every penny I
can.

HELMER (*laughs*): That's quite true. Every penny you can. But you
can't.

NORA (*hums and smiles, quietly gleeful*): Hm. If you only knew how
many expenses we larks and squirrels have, Torvald.

HELMER: You're a funny little creature. Just like your father used to
be. Always on the look-out for some way to get money, but as soon
as you have any it just runs through your fingers, and you never
know where it's gone. Well, I suppose I must take you as you are.   100
It's in your blood. Yes, yes, yes, these things are hereditary, Nora.

NORA: Oh, I wish I'd inherited more of Papa's qualities.

HELMER: And I wouldn't wish my darling little songbird to be any different from what she is. By the way, that reminds me. You look awfully—how shall put it?—awfully guilty today.

NORA: Do I?

HELMER: Yes, you do. Look me in the eyes.

NORA (*looks at him*): Well?

HELMER (*wags his finger*): Has my little sweet-tooth been indulging
herself in town today, by any chance?   110

NORA: No, how can you think such a thing?

HELMER: Not a tiny little digression into a pastry shop?

NORA: No, Torvald, I promise—

HELMER: Not just a wee jam tart?

NORA: Certainly not.

HELMER: Not a little nibble at a macaroon?

NORA: No, Torvald—I promise you, honestly—

HELMER: There, there. I was only joking.

NORA (*goes over to the table, right*): You know I could never act
against your wishes.

HELMER: Of course not. And you've given me your word—(*Goes over
to her.*) Well, my beloved Nora, you keep your little Christmas secrets to yourself. They'll be revealed this evening, I've no doubt,
once the Christmas tree has been lit.

NORA: Have you remembered to invite Dr. Rank?

HELMER: No. But there's no need; he knows he'll be dining with us.
Anyway, I'll ask him when he comes this morning. I've ordered
some good wine. Oh, Nora, you can't imagine how I'm looking forward to this evening.

NORA: So am I. And, Torvald, how the children will love it!

HELMER: Yes, it's a wonderful thing to know that one's position is
assured and that one has an ample income. Don't you agree? It's
good to know that, isn't it?

NORA: Yes, it's almost like a miracle.

HELMER: Do you remember last Christmas? For three whole weeks
you shut yourself away every evening to make flowers for the
Christmas tree, and all those other things you were going to surprise
us with. Ugh, it was the most boring time I've ever had in my life.

NORA: I didn't find it boring.

HELMER (*smiles*): But it all came to nothing in the end, didn't it?

NORA: Oh, are you going to bring that up again? How could I help
the cat getting in and tearing everything to bits?

HELMER: No, my poor little Nora, of course you couldn't. You simply
wanted to make us happy, and that's all that matters. But it's good
that those hard times are past.

NORA: Yes, it's wonderful.

HELMER: I don't have to sit by myself and be bored. And you don't
have to tire you're pretty eyes and your delicate little hands—

NORA (*claps her hands*): No, Torvald, that's true, isn't it—I don't have
to any longer? Oh, it's really all just like a miracle. (*Takes his arm.*)
Now, I'm going to tell you what I thought we might do, Torvald.
As soon as Christmas is over—(*A bell rings in the hall.*) Oh, there's
the doorbell. (*Tidies up one or two things in the room.*) Someone's
coming. What a bore.

HELMER: I'm not at home to any visitors. Remember!

MAID (*in the doorway*): A lady's called, madam. A stranger.

NORA: Well, ask her to come in.

MAID: And the doctor's here too, sir.

HELMER: Has he gone to my room?

MAID: Yes, sir.

Helmer goes into his room. The Maid shows in Mrs. Linde, who is dressed in traveling clothes, and closes the door.

MRS. LINDE (*shyly and a little hesitantly*): Good evening, Nora.

NORA (*uncertainly*): Good evening—

MRS. LINDE: I don't suppose you recognize me.

NORA: No, I'm afraid I—Yes, wait a minute—surely—(*Exclaims.*) Why, Christine! Is it really you?

MRS. LINDE: Yes, it's me.

NORA: Christine! And I didn't recognize you! But how could I—? (*More quietly.*) How you've changed, Christine!

MRS. LINDE: Yes, I know. It's been nine years—nearly ten—

NORA: Is it so long? Yes, it must be. Oh, these last eight years have   170
been such a happy time for me! So you've come to town? All that way in winter! How brave of you!

MRS. LINDE: I arrived by the steamer this morning.

NORA: Yes, of course—to enjoy yourself over Christmas. Oh, how splendid! We'll have to celebrate! But take off your coat. You're not cold, are you? (*Helps her off with it.*) There! Now let's sit down here by the stove and be comfortable. No, you take the armchair. I'll sit here in the rocking chair. (*Clasps Mrs. Linde's hands.*) Yes, now you look like your old self. It was just at first that—you've got a little paler, though, Christine. And perhaps a bit thinner.   180

MRS. LINDE: And older, Nora. Much, much older.

NORA: Yes, perhaps a little older. Just a tiny bit. Not much. (*Checks herself suddenly and says earnestly.*) Oh, but how thoughtless of me to sit here and chatter away like this! Dear, sweet Christine, can you forgive me?

MRS. LINDE: What do you mean, Nora?

NORA (*quietly*): Poor Christine, you've become a widow.

MRS. LINDE: Yes. Three years ago.

NORA: I know, I know—I read it in the papers. Oh, Christine, I meant to write to you so often, honestly. But I always put it off, and some-   190
thing else always cropped up.

MRS. LINDE: I understand, Nora dear.

NORA: No, Christine, it was beastly of me. Oh, my poor darling, what you've gone through! And he didn't leave you anything?

MRS. LINDE: No.

NORA: No children, either?

MRS. LINDE: No.

NORA: Nothing at all, then?

MRS. LINDE: Not even a feeling of loss or sorrow.

NORA (*looks incredulously at her*): But, Christine, how is that possi-   200
ble?

MRS. LINDE (*smiles sadly and strokes Nora's hair*): Oh, these things happen, Nora.

NORA: All alone. How dreadful that must be for you. I've three lovely children. I'm afraid you can't see them now, because they're out with nanny. But you must tell me everything—

MRS. LINDE: No, no, no. I want to hear about you.

NORA: No, you start. I'm not going to be selfish today, I'm just going to think about you. Oh, but there's one thing I *must* tell you. Have you heard of the wonderful luck we've just had?

MRS. LINDE: No. What?

NORA: Would you believe it—my husband's just been made manager of the bank!

MRS. LINDE: Your husband? Oh, how lucky—!

NORA: Yes, isn't it? Being a lawyer is so uncertain, you know, especially if one isn't prepared to touch any case that isn't—well—quite nice. And of course Torvald's been very firm about that—and I'm absolutely with him. Oh, you can imagine how happy we are! He's joining the bank in the New Year, and he'll be getting a big salary, and lots of percentages too. From now on we'll be able to live quite differently—we'll be able to do whatever we want. Oh, Christine, it's such a relief! I feel so happy! Well, I mean, it's lovely to have heaps of money and not to have to worry about anything. Don't you think?

MRS. LINDE: It must be lovely to have enough to cover one's needs, anyway.

NORA: Not just our needs! We're going to have heaps and heaps of money!

MRS. LINDE (*smiles*): Nora, Nora, haven't you grown up yet? When we were at school you were a terrible little spendthrift.

NORA (*laughs quietly*): Yes, Torvald still says that. (*Wags her finger.*) But "Nora, Nora" isn't as silly as you think. Oh, we've been in no position for me to waste money. We've both had to work.

MRS. LINDE: You too?

NORA: Yes, little things—fancy work, crocheting, embroidery and so forth. (*Casually.*) And other things too. I suppose you know Torvald left the Ministry when we got married? There were no prospects of promotion in his department, and of course he needed more money. But the first year he overworked himself quite dreadfully. He had to take on all sorts of extra jobs, and worked day and night. But it was too much for him, and he became frightfully ill. The doctors said he'd have to go to a warmer climate.

MRS. LINDE: Yes, you spent a whole year in Italy, didn't you?

NORA: Yes. It wasn't easy for me to get away, you know. I'd just had Ivar. But of course we had to do it. Oh, it was a marvelous trip! And it saved Torvald's life. But it cost an awful lot of money, Christine.

MRS. LINDE: I can imagine.

NORA: Two hundred and fifty pounds. That's a lot of money, you
  know.   250
MRS. LINDE: How lucky you had it.
NORA: Well, actually, we got it from my father.
MRS. LINDE: Oh, I see. Didn't he die just about that time?
NORA: Yes, Christine, just about then. Wasn't it dreadful, I couldn't go
  and look after him. I was expecting little Ivar any day. And then I
  had my poor Torvald to care for—we really didn't think he'd live.
  Dear, kind Papa! I never saw him again, Christine. Oh, it's the sad-
  dest thing that's happened to me since I got married.
MRS. LINDE: I know you were very fond of him. But you went to
  Italy—?   260
NORA: Yes. Well, we had the money, you see, and the doctors said we
  mustn't delay. So we went the month after Papa died.
MRS. LINDE: And your husband came back completely cured?
NORA: Fit as a fiddle!
MRS. LINDE: But—the doctor?
NORA: How do you mean?
MRS. LINDE: I thought the maid said that the gentleman who arrived
  with me was the doctor.
NORA: Oh yes, that's Doctor Rank, but he doesn't come because any-
  one's ill. He's our best friend, and he looks us up at least once every   270
  day. No, Torvald hasn't had a moment's illness since we went away.
  And the children are fit and healthy and so am I (*Jumps up and
  claps her hands.*) Oh God, oh God, Christine, isn't it a wonderful
  thing to be alive and happy! Oh, but how beastly of me! I'm only
  talking about myself. (*Sits on a footstool and rests her arms on Mrs.
  Linde's knee.*) Oh, please don't be angry with me! Tell me, is it
  really true you didn't love your husband? Why did you marry him,
  then?
MRS. LINDE: Well, my mother was still alive; and she was helpless and
  bedridden. And I had my two little brothers to take care of. I didn't   280
  feel I could say no.
NORA: Yes, well, perhaps you're right. He was rich then, was he?
MRS. LINDE: Quite comfortably off, I believe. But his business was unsound, you see, Nora. When he died it went bankrupt, and there
  was nothing left.
NORA: What did you do?
MRS. LINDE: Well, I had to try to make ends meet somehow, so I
  started a little shop, and a little school, and anything else I could
  turn my hand to. These last three years have been just one endless
  slog for me, without a moment's rest. But now it's over, Nora. My   290
  poor dear mother doesn't need me any more; she's passed away.
  And the boys don't need me either; they've got jobs now and can
  look after themselves.

NORA: How relieved you must feel—

MRS. LINDE: No, Nora. Just unspeakably empty. No one to live for any more. (*Gets up restlessly.*) That's why I couldn't bear to stay out there any longer, cut off from the world. I thought it'd be easier to find some work here that will exercise and occupy my mind. If only I could get a regular job—office work of some kind—

300   NORA: Oh, but, Christine, that's dreadfully exhausting; and you look practically finished already. It'd be much better for you if you could go away somewhere.

MRS. LINDE (*goes over to the window*): I have no Papa to pay for my holidays, Nora.

NORA (*gets up*): Oh, please don't be angry with me.

MRS. LINDE: My dear Nora, it's I who should ask you not to be angry. That's the worst thing about this kind of situation—it makes one so bitter. One has no one to work for; and yet one has to be continually sponging for jobs. One has to live; and so one becomes com-

310   pletely egocentric. When you told me about this luck you've just had with Torvald's new job—can you imagine?—I was happy not so much on your account, as on my own.

NORA: How do you mean? Oh, I understand. You mean Torvald might be able to do something for you?

MRS. LINDE: Yes, I was thinking that.

NORA: He will too, Christine. Just you leave it to me. I'll lead up to it so delicately, so delicately; I'll get him in the right mood. Oh, Christine, I do so want to help you.

MRS. LINDE: It's sweet of you to bother so much about me, Nora. Es-

320   pecially since you know so little of the worries and hardships of life.

NORA: I? You say *I* know little of—?

MRS. LINDE (*smiles*): Well, good heavens—those bits of fancy work of yours—well, really—! You're a child, Nora.

NORA (*tosses her head and walks across the room*): You shouldn't say that so patronizingly.

MRS. LINDE: Oh?

NORA: You're like the rest. You all think I'm incapable of getting down to anything serious—

MRS. LINDE: My dear—

330   NORA: You think I've never had any worries like the rest of you.

MRS. LINDE: Nora dear, you've just told me about all your difficulties—

NORA: Pooh—that! (*Quietly.*) I haven't told you about the big thing.

MRS. LINDE: What big thing? What do you mean?

NORA: You patronize me, Christine; but you shouldn't. You're proud that you've worked so long and so hard for your mother.

MRS. LINDE: I don't patronize anyone, Nora. But you're right—I am both proud and happy that I was able to make my mother's last months on earth comparatively easy.

NORA: And you're also proud of what you've done for your brothers.

MRS. LINDE: I think I have a right to be.   340
NORA: I think so too. But let me tell you something, Christine. I too
  have done something to be proud and happy about.
MRS. LINDE: I don't doubt it. But—how do you mean?
NORA: Speak quietly! Suppose Torvald should hear! He mustn't, at
  any price—no one must know, Christine—no one but you.
MRS. LINDE: But what is this?
NORA: Come over here. (*Pulls her down on to the sofa beside her.*)
  Yes, Christine—I too have done something to be happy and proud
  about. It was I who saved Torvald's life.
MRS. LINDE: Saved his—? How did you save it?   350
NORA: I told you about our trip to Italy. Torvald couldn't have lived if
  he hadn't managed to get down there—
MRS. LINDE: Yes, well—your father provided the money—
NORA (*smiles*): So Torvald and everyone else thinks. But—
MRS. LINDE: Yes?
NORA: Papa didn't give us a penny. It was I who found the money.
MRS. LINDE: You? All of it?
NORA: Two hundred and fifty pounds. What do you say to that?
MRS. LINDE: But Nora, how could you? Did you win a lottery or
  something?   360
NORA (*scornfully*): Lottery? (*Sniffs.*) What would there be to be proud
  of in that?
MRS. LINDE: But where did you get it from, then?
NORA (*hums and smiles secretively*): Hm; tra-la-la-la!
MRS. LINDE: You couldn't have borrowed it.
NORA: Oh? Why not?
MRS. LINDE: Well, a wife can't borrow money without her husband's
  consent.
NORA (*tosses her head*): Ah, but when a wife has a little business
  sense, and knows how to be clever—   370
MRS. LINDE: But Nora, I simply don't understand—
NORA: You don't have to. No one has said I borrowed the money. I
  could have got it in some other way. (*Throws herself back on the
  sofa.*) I could have got it from an admirer. When a girl's as pretty as
  I am—
MRS. LINDE: Nora, you're crazy!
NORA: You're dying of curiosity now, aren't you, Christine?
MRS. LINDE: Nora dear, you haven't done anything foolish?
NORA (*sits up again*): Is it foolish to save one's husband's life?
MRS. LINDE: I think it's foolish if without his knowledge you—   380
NORA: But the whole point was that he mustn't know! Great heavens,
  don't you see? He hadn't to know how dangerously ill he was. I
  was the one they told that his life was in danger and that only going
  to a warm climate could save him. Do you suppose I didn't try to
  think of other ways of getting him down there? I told him how

wonderful it would be for me to go abroad like other young wives; I cried and prayed; I asked him to remember my condition, and said he ought to be nice and tender to me; and then I suggested he might quite easily borrow the money. But then he got almost angry with me, Christine. He said I was frivolous, and that it was his duty as a husband not to pander to my moods and caprices—I think that's what he called them. Well, well, I thought, you've got to be saved somehow. And then I thought of a way—

MRS. LINDE: But didn't your husband find out from your father that the money hadn't come from him?

NORA: No, never. Papa died just then. I'd thought of letting him into the plot and asking him not to tell. But since he was so ill—! And as things turned out, it didn't become necessary.

MRS. LINDE: And you've never told your husband about this?

NORA: For heaven's sake, no! What an idea! He's frightfully strict about such matters. And besides—he's so proud of being a *man*— it'd be so painful and humiliating for him to know that he owed anything to me. It'd completely wreck our relationship. This life we have built together would no longer exist.

MRS. LINDE: Will you never tell him?

NORA (*thoughtfully, half-smiling*): Yes—some time, perhaps. Years from now, when I'm no longer pretty. You mustn't laugh! I mean of course, when Torvald no longer loves me as he does now; when it no longer amuses him to see me dance and dress up and play the fool for him. Then it might be useful to have something up my sleeve. (*Breaks off.*) Stupid, stupid, stupid! That time will never come. Well, what do you think of my big secret, Christine? I'm not completely useless, am I? Mind you, all this has caused me a frightful lot of worry. It hasn't been easy for me to meet my obligations punctually. In case you don't know, in the world of business there are things called quarterly installments and interest, and they're a terrible problem to cope with. So I've had to scrape a little here and save a little there as best I can. I haven't been able to save much on the housekeeping money, because Torvald likes to live well; and I couldn't let the children go short of clothes—I couldn't take anything out of what he gives me for them. The poor little angels!

MRS. LINDE: So you've had to stint yourself, my poor Nora?

NORA: Of course. Well, after all, it was my problem. Whenever Torvald gave me money to buy myself new clothes, I never used more than half of it; and I always bought what was cheapest and plainest. Thank heaven anything suits me, so that Torvald's never noticed. But it made me a bit sad sometimes, because it's lovely to wear pretty clothes. Don't you think?

MRS. LINDE: Indeed it is.

NORA: And then I've found one or two other sources of income. Last winter I managed to get a lot of copying to do. So I shut myself

away and wrote every evening, late into the night. Oh, I often got
so tired, so tired. But it was great fun, though, sitting there working
and earning money. It was almost like being a man.

MRS. LINDE: But how much have you managed to pay off like this?

NORA: Well, I can't say exactly. It's awfully difficult to keep an exact
check on these kind of transactions. I only know I've paid everything I've managed to scrape together. Sometimes I really didn't
know where to turn. (*Smiles.*) Then I'd sit here and imagine some
rich old gentleman had fallen in love with me—   440

MRS. LINDE: What! What gentleman?

NORA: Silly! And that now he'd died and when they opened his will it
said in big letters: "Everything I possess is to be paid forthwith to
my beloved Mrs. Nora Helmer in cash."

MRS. LINDE: But, Nora dear, who was this gentleman?

NORA: Great heavens, don't you understand? There wasn't any old
gentleman; he was just something I used to dream up as I sat here
evening after evening wondering how on earth I could raise some
money. But what does it matter? The old bore can stay imaginary as
far as I'm concerned, because now I don't have to worry any longer!   450
(*Jumps up.*) Oh, Christine, isn't it wonderful? I don't have to worry
any more! No more troubles! I can play all day with the children, I
can fill the house with pretty things, just the way Torvald likes.
And, Christine, it'll soon be spring, and the air'll be fresh and the
skies blue,—and then perhaps we'll be able to take a little trip somewhere. I shall be able to see the sea again. Oh, yes, yes, it's a wonderful thing to be alive and happy!

The bell rings in the hall.

MRS. LINDE (*gets up*): You've a visitor. Perhaps I'd better go.

NORA: No, stay. It won't be for me. It's someone for Torvald—

MAID (*in the door*): Excuse me, madam, a gentleman's called who says   460
he wants to speak to the master. But I didn't know—seeing as the
doctor's with him—

NORA: Who is this gentleman?

KROGSTAD (*in the doorway*): It's me, Mrs. Helmer.

Mrs. Linde starts, composes herself, and turns away to the window.

NORA (*takes a step toward him and whispers tensely*): You? What is
it? What do you want to talk to my husband about?

KROGSTAD: Business—you might call it. I hold a minor post in the
bank, and I hear your husband is to become our new chief—

NORA: Oh—then it isn't—?

KROGSTAD: Pure business, Mrs. Helmer. Nothing more.   470

NORA: Well, you'll find him in his study.

*Nods indifferently as she closes the hall door behind him. Then she
walks across the room and sees to the stove.*

MRS. LINDE: Nora, who was that man?

NORA: A lawyer called Krogstad.

MRS. LINDE: It was him, then.

NORA: Do you know that man?

MRS. LINDE: I used to know him—some years ago. He was a solicitor's clerk in our town, for a while.

NORA: Yes, of course, so he was.

MRS. LINDE: How he's changed!

480 NORA: He was very unhappily married, I believe.

MRS. LINDE: Is he a widower now?

NORA: Yes, with a lot of children. Ah, now it's alight.

She closes the door of the stove and moves the rocking-chair a little to one side.

MRS. LINDE: He does—various things now, I hear?

NORA: Does he? It's quite possible—I really don't know. But don't let's talk about business. It's so boring.

Dr. Rank enters from Helmer's study.

RANK (*still in the doorway*): No, no, my dear chap, don't see me out. I'll go and have a word with your wife. (*Closes the door and notices Mrs. Linde.*) Oh, I beg your pardon. I seem to be *de trop* here too.

NORA: Not in the least. (*Introduces them.*) Dr. Rank. Mrs. Linde.

490 RANK: Ah! A name I have often heard in this house. I believe I passed you on the stairs as I came up.

MRS. LINDE: Yes. Stairs tire me; I have to take them slowly.

RANK: Oh, have you hurt yourself?

MRS. LINDE: No, I'm just a little run down.

RANK: Ah, is that all? Then I take it you've come to town to cure yourself by a round of parties?

MRS. LINDE: I have come here to find work.

RANK: Is that an approved remedy for being run down?

MRS. LINDE: One has to live, Doctor.

500 RANK: Yes, people do seem to regard it as a necessity.

NORA: Oh, really, Dr. Rank. I bet you want to stay alive.

RANK: You bet I do. However miserable I sometimes feel, I still want to go on being tortured for as long as possible. It's the same with all my patients; and with people who are morally sick, too. There's a moral cripple in with Helmer at this very moment—

MRS. LINDE (*softly*): Oh!

NORA: Whom do you mean?

RANK: Oh, a lawyer fellow called Krogstad—you wouldn't know him. He's crippled all right; morally twisted. But even he started off by

510 announcing, as though it were a matter of enormous importance, that he had to live.

NORA: Oh? What did he want to talk to Torvald about?

RANK: I haven't the faintest idea. All I heard was something about the bank.

NORA: I didn't know that Krog—that this man Krogstad had any connection with the bank.

RANK: Yes, he's got some kind of job down there. (*To Mrs. Linde.*) I wonder if in your part of the world you too have a species of human being that spends its time fussing around trying to smell out moral corruption? And when they find a case they give him some 520 nice, comfortable position so that they can keep a good watch on him. The healthy ones just have to lump it.

MRS. LINDE: But surely it's the sick who need care most?

RANK (*shrugs his shoulders*): Well, there we have it. It's that attitude that's turning human society into a hospital.

Nora, lost in her own thoughts, laughs half to herself and claps her hands.

RANK: Why are you laughing? Do you really know what society is?

NORA: What do I care about society? I think it's a bore. I was laughing at something else—something frightfully funny. Tell me, Dr. Rank— will everyone who works at the bank come under Torvald now?

RANK: Do you find that particularly funny? 530

NORA (*smiles and hums*): Never you mind! Never you mind! (*Walks around the room.*) Yes, I find it very amusing to think that we—I mean, Torvald—has obtained so much influence over so many people. (*Takes the paper bag from her pocket.*) Dr. Rank, would you like a small macaroon?

RANK: Macaroons! I say! I thought they were forbidden here.

NORA: Yes, well, these are some Christine gave me.

MRS. LINDE: What? I—?

NORA: All right, all right, don't get frightened. You weren't to know Torvald had forbidden them. He's afraid they'll ruin my teeth. But, 540 dash it—for once—! Don't you agree, Dr. Rank? Here! (*Pops a macaroon into his mouth.*) You too, Christine. And I'll have one too. Just a little one. Two at the most. (*Begins to walk around again.*) Yes, now I feel really, really happy. Now there's just one thing in the world I'd really love to do.

RANK: Oh? And what is that?

NORA: Just something I'd love to say to Torvald.

RANK: Well, why don't you say it?

NORA: No, I daren't. It's too dreadful.

MRS. LINDE: Dreadful? 550

RANK: Well, then, you'd better not. But you can say it to us. What is it you'd so love to say to Torvald?

NORA: I've the most extraordinary longing to say: "Bloody hell!"

RANK: Are you mad?

MRS. LINDE: My dear Nora—!

RANK: Say it. Here he is.

NORA (*hiding the bag of macaroons*): Ssh! Ssh!

> *Helmer, with his overcoat on his arm and his hat in his hand, enters from his study.*

NORA (*goes to meet him*): Well, Torvald dear, did you get rid of him?

HELMER: Yes, he's just gone.

560 NORA: May I introduce you—? This is Christine. She's just arrived in town.

HELMER: Christine—? Forgive me, but I don't think—

NORA: Mrs. Linde, Torvald dear. Christine Linde.

HELMER: Ah. A childhood friend of my wife's, I presume.

MRS. LINDE: Yes, we knew each other in earlier days.

NORA: And imagine, now she's traveled all this way to talk to you.

HELMER: Oh?

MRS. LINDE: Well, I didn't really—

NORA: You see, Christine's frightfully good at office work, and she's
570 mad to come under some really clever man who can teach her even more than she knows already—

HELMER: Very sensible, madam.

NORA: So when she heard you'd become head of the bank—it was in her local paper—she came here as quickly as she could and—Torvald, you will, won't you? Do a little something to help Christine? For my sake?

HELMER: Well, that shouldn't be impossible. You are a widow, I take it, Mrs. Linde?

MRS. LINDE: Yes.

580 HELMER: And you have experience of office work?

MRS. LINDE: Yes, quite a bit.

HELMER: Well then, it's quite likely I may be able to find some job for you—

NORA (*claps her hands*): You see, you see!

HELMER: You've come at a lucky moment, Mrs. Linde.

MRS. LINDE: Oh, how can I ever thank you—?

HELMER: There's absolutely no need. (*Puts on his overcoat.*) But now I'm afraid I must ask you to excuse me—

RANK: Wait. I'll come with you.

> *He gets his fur coat from the hall and warms it at the stove.*

590 NORA: Don't be long, Torvald dear.

HELMER: I'll only be an hour.

NORA: Are you going too, Christine?

MRS. LINDE (*puts on her outdoor clothes*): Yes, I must start to look round for a room.

HELMER: Then perhaps we can walk part of the way together.

NORA (*helps her*): It's such a nuisance we're so cramped here—I'm afraid we can't offer to—

MRS. LINDE: Oh, I wouldn't dream of it. Goodbye, Nora dear, and thanks for everything.

NORA: *Au revoir.* You'll be coming back this evening, of course. And you too, Dr. Rank. What? If you're well enough? Of course you'll be well enough. Wrap up warmly, though. 600

They go out, talking, into the hall. Children's voices are heard from the stairs.

NORA: Here they are! Here they are!

She runs out and opens the door. Anne-Marie, the nurse, enters with the children.

NORA: Come in, come in! (*Stoops down and kisses them.*) Oh, my sweet darlings—! Look at them, Christine! Aren't they beautiful?

RANK: Don't stand here chattering in this draught!

HELMER: Come, Mrs. Linde. This is for mothers only.

Dr. Rank, Helmer, and Mrs. Linde go down the stairs. The nurse brings the children into the room. Nora follows, and closes the door to the hall.

NORA: How well you look! What red cheeks you've got! Like apples and roses! (*The children answer her inaudibly as she talks to them.*) Have you had fun? That's splendid. You gave Emmy and Bob a ride 610 on the sledge? What, both together? I say! What a clever boy you are, Ivar! Oh, let me hold her for a moment, Anne-Marie! My sweet little baby doll! (*Takes the smallest child from the nurse and dances with her.*) Yes, yes, Mummy will dance with Bob too. What? Have you been throwing snowballs? Oh, I wish I'd been there! No, don't— I'll undress them myself, Anne-Marie. No, please let me; it's such fun. Go inside and warm yourself; you look frozen. There's some hot coffee on the stove. (*The nurse goes into the room on the left. Nora takes off the children's outdoor clothes and throws them anywhere while they all chatter simultaneously.*) What? A big dog ran after you? But he didn't bite you? No, dogs don't bite lovely little baby dolls. 620 Leave those parcels alone, Ivar. What's in them? Ah, wouldn't you like to know! No, no; it's nothing nice. Come on, let's play a game. What shall we play? Hide and seek. Yes, let's play hide and seek. Bob shall hide first. You want me to? All right, let me hide first.

Nora and the children play around the room, and in the adjacent room to the left, laughing and shouting. At length Nora hides under the table. The children rush in, look, but cannot find her. Then they hear her half-stifled laughter, run to the table, lift up the cloth, and see her. Great excitement. She crawls out as though to frighten them. Further excitement. Meanwhile, there has been a knock on the door leading from the hall, but no one has noticed it. Now the door is half-opened and Krogstad enters. He waits for a moment; the game continues.

KROGSTAD: Excuse me, Mrs. Helmer—

NORA (*turns with a stifled cry and half jumps up*): Oh! What do you want?

KROGSTAD: I beg your pardon; the front door was ajar. Someone must have forgotten to close it.

630   NORA (*gets up*): My husband is not at home, Mr. Krogstad.

KROGSTAD: I know.

NORA: Well, what do want here, then?

KROGSTAD: A word with you.

NORA: With—? (*To the children, quietly.*) Go inside to Anne-Marie. What? No the strange gentleman won't do anything to hurt Mummy. When he's gone we'll start playing again.

She takes the children into the room on the left and closes the door behind them.

NORA (*uneasy, tense*): You want to speak to me?

KROGSTAD: Yes.

NORA: Today? But it's not the first of the month yet.

640   KROGSTAD: No, it is Christmas Eve. Whether or not you have a merry Christmas depends on you.

NORA: What do you want? I can't give you anything today—

KROGSTAD: We won't talk about that for the present. There's something else. You have a moment to spare?

NORA: Oh, yes. Yes, I suppose so; though—

KROGSTAD: Good. I was sitting in the café down below and I saw your husband cross the street—

NORA: Yes.

KROGSTAD: With a lady.

650   NORA: Well?

KROGSTAD: Might I be so bold as to ask: was not that lady a Mrs. Linde?

NORA: Yes.

KROGSTAD: Recently arrived in town?

NORA: Yes, today.

KROGSTAD: She is a good friend of yours, is she not?

NORA: Yes, she is. But I don't see—

KROGSTAD: I used to know her too once.

NORA: I know.

660   KROGSTAD: Oh? You've discovered that. Yes, I thought you would. Well then, may I ask you a straight question: is Mrs. Linde to be employed at the bank?

NORA: How dare you presume to cross-examine me, Mr. Krogstad? You, one of my husband's employees? But since you ask, you shall have an answer. Yes, Mrs. Linde is to be employed by the bank. And I arranged it, Mr. Krogstad. Now you know.

KROGSTAD: I guessed right, then.

NORA (*walks up and down the room*): Oh, one has a little influence, you know. Just because one's a woman it doesn't necessarily mean that—When one is in a humble position, Mr. Krogstad, one should think twice before offending someone who—hm— 670

KROGSTAD: —who has influence?

NORA: Precisely.

KROGSTAD (*changes his tone*): Mrs. Helmer, will you have the kindness to use your influence on my behalf?

NORA: What? What do you mean?

KROGSTAD: Will you be so good as to see that I keep my humble position at the bank?

NORA: What do you mean? Who is thinking of removing you from your position? 680

KROGSTAD: Oh, you don't need to play innocent with me. I realize it can't be very pleasant for your friend to risk bumping into me; and now I also realize whom I have to thank for being hounded out like this.

NORA: But I assure you—

KROGSTAD: Look, let's not beat about the bush. There's still time, and I'd advise you to use your influence to stop it.

NORA: But, Mr. Krogstad, I have no influence!

KROGSTAD: Oh? I though you just said—

NORA: But I didn't mean it like that! I? How on earth could you imagine that I would have any influence over my husband? 690

KROGSTAD: Oh, I've known your husband since we were students together. I imagine he has his weaknesses like other married men.

NORA: If you speak impertinently of my husband, I shall show you the door.

KROGSTAD: You're a bold woman, Mrs. Helmer.

NORA: I'm not afraid of you any longer. Once the New Year is in, I'll soon be rid of you.

KROGSTAD (*more controlled*): Now listen to me, Mrs. Helmer. If I'm forced to, I shall fight for my little job at the bank as I would fight for my life. 700

NORA: So it sounds.

KROGSTAD: It isn't just the money; that's the last thing I care about. There's something else—well, you might as well know. It's like this, you see. You know of course, as everyone else does, that some years ago I committed an indiscretion.

NORA: I think I did hear something—

KROGSTAD: It never came into court; but from that day, every opening was barred to me. So I turned my hand to the kind of business you know about. I had to do something; and I don't think I was one of the worst. But now I want to give up all that. My sons are growing 710 up; for their sake, I must try to regain what respectability I can. This job in the bank was the first step on the ladder. And now your husband wants to kick me off that ladder back into the dirt.

NORA: But my dear Mr. Krogstad, it simply isn't in my power to help you.

KROGSTAD: You say that because you don't want to help me. But I have the means to make you.

NORA: You don't mean you'd tell my husband that I owe you money?

720   KROGSTAD: And if I did?

NORA: That'd be a filthy trick! (*Almost in tears.*) This secret that is my pride and my joy—that he should hear about it in such a filthy, beastly way—hear about it from you! It'd involve me in the most dreadful unpleasantness—

KROGSTAD: Only—unpleasantness?

NORA (*vehemently*): Allright, do it! You'll be the one who'll suffer. It'll show my husband the kind of man you are, and then you'll never keep your job.

KROGSTAD: I asked you whether it was merely domestic unpleasant-
730   ness you were afraid of.

NORA: If my husband hears about it, he will of course immediately pay you whatever is owing. And then we shall have nothing more to do with you.

KROGSTAD (*takes a step closer*): Listen, Mrs. Helmer. Either you've a bad memory or else you know very little about financial transactions. I had better enlighten you.

NORA: What do you mean?

KROGSTAD: When your husband was ill, you came to me to borrow two hundred and fifty pounds.

740   NORA: I didn't know anyone else.

KROGSTAD: I promised to find that sum for you—

NORA: And you did find it.

KROGSTAD: I promised to find that sum for you on certain conditions. You were so worried about your husband's illness and so keen to get the money to take him abroad that I don't think you bothered much about the details. So it won't be out of place if I refresh your memory. Well—I promised to get you the money in exchange for an I.O.U., which I drew up.

NORA: Yes, and which I signed.

750   KROGSTAD: Exactly. But then I added a few lines naming your father as security for the debt. This paragraph was to be signed by your father.

NORA: Was to be? He did sign it.

KROGSTAD: I left the date blank for your father to fill in when he signed this paper. You remember, Mrs. Helmer?

NORA: Yes, I think so—

KROGSTAD: Then I gave you back this I.O.U. for you to post to your father. Is that not correct?

NORA: Yes.

KROGSTAD: And of course you posted it at once; for within five or six days you brought it along to me with your father's signature on it. Whereupon I handed you the money. 760

NORA: Yes, well. Haven't I repaid the installments as agreed?

KROGSTAD: Mm—yes, more or less. But to return to what we were speaking about—that was a difficult time for you just then, wasn't it, Mrs. Helmer?

NORA: Yes, it was.

KROGSTAD: And your father was very ill, if I am not mistaken.

NORA: He was dying.

KROGSTAD: He did in fact die shortly afterwards? 770

NORA: Yes.

KROGSTAD: Tell me, Mrs. Helmer, do you by any chance remember the date of your father's death? The day of the month, I mean.

NORA: Papa died on the twenty-ninth of September.

KROGSTAD: Quite correct; I took the trouble to confirm it. And that leaves me with a curious little problem—(*Takes out a paper.*)—which I simply cannot solve.

NORA: Problem? I don't see—

KROGSTAD: The problem, Mrs. Helmer, is that your father signed this paper three days after his death. 780

NORA: What? I don't understand—

KROGSTAD: Your father died on the twenty-ninth of September. But look at this. Here your father has dated his signature the second of October. Isn't that a curious little problem, Mrs. Helmer? (*Nora is silent.*) Can you suggest any explanation? (*She remains silent.*) And there's another curious thing. The words "second of October" and the year are written in a hand which is not your father's, but which I seem to know. Well, there's a simple explanation to that. Your father could have forgotten to write in the date when he signed, and someone else could have added it before the news came of his death. 790 There's nothing criminal about that. It's the signature itself I'm wondering about. It *is* genuine, I suppose, Mrs. Helmer? It was your father who wrote his name here?

NORA (*after a short silence, throws back her head and looks defiantly at him*): No, it was not. It was I who wrote Papa's name there.

KROGSTAD: Look, Mrs. Helmer, do you realize this is a dangerous admission?

NORA: Why? You'll get your money.

KROGSTAD: May I ask you a question? Why didn't you send this paper to your father?

NORA: I couldn't. Papa was very ill. If I'd asked him to sign this, I'd 800 have had to tell him what the money was for. But I couldn't have told him in his condition that my husband's life was in danger. I couldn't have done that!

KROGSTAD: Then you would have been wiser to have given up your idea of a holiday.

NORA: But I couldn't! It was to save my husband's life. I couldn't put it off.

KROGSTAD: But didn't it occur to you that you were being dishonest towards me?

810   NORA: I couldn't bother about that. I didn't care about you. I hated you because of all the beastly difficulties you'd put in my way when you knew how dangerously ill my husband was.

KROGSTAD: Mrs. Helmer, you evidently don't appreciate exactly what you have done. But I can assure you that it is no bigger nor worse a crime than the one I once committed, and thereby ruined my whole social position.

NORA: You? Do you expect me to believe that you would have taken a risk like that to save your wife's life?

KROGSTAD: The law does not concern itself with motives.

820   NORA: Then the law must be very stupid.

KROGSTAD: Stupid or not, if I show this paper to the police, you will be judged according to it.

NORA: I don't believe that. Hasn't a daughter the right to shield her father from worry and anxiety when he's old and dying? Hasn't a wife the right to save her husband's life? I don't know much about the law, but there must be something somewhere that says that such things are allowed. You ought to know about that, you're meant to be a lawyer, aren't you? You can't be a very good lawyer, Mr. Krogstad.

830   KROGSTAD: Possibly not. But business, the kind of business we two have been transacting—I think you'll admit I understand something about that? Good. Do as you please. But I tell you this. If I get thrown into the gutter for a second time, I shall take you with me.

He bows and goes out through the hall.

NORA (*stands for a moment in thought, then tosses her head*): What nonsense! He's trying to frighten me! I'm not that stupid. (*Busies herself gathering together the children's clothes; then she suddenly stops.*) But—? No, it's impossible. I did it for love, didn't I?

CHILDREN (*in the doorway, left*): Mummy, the strange gentleman's gone out into the street.

NORA: Yes, yes, I know. But don't talk to anyone about the strange
840   gentleman. You hear? Not even to Daddy.

CHILDREN: No, Mummy. Will you play with us again now?

NORA: No, no. Not now.

CHILDREN: Oh but, Mummy, you promised!

NORA: I know, but I can't just now. Go back to the nursery. I've a lot to do. Go away, my darlings, go away. (*She pushes them gently into the other room, and closes the door behind them. She sits on the sofa, takes up her embroidery, stitches for a few moments, but soon stops.*) No! (*Throws the embroidery aside, gets up, goes to the door leading to the hall, and calls.*) Helen! Bring in the Christmas tree! (*She goes to the table on the left and opens the drawer in it; then pauses again.*) No, but it's utterly impossible!

MAID (*enters with tree*): Where shall I put it, madam?

NORA: There, in the middle of the room. 850

MAID: Will you be wanting anything else?

NORA: No, thank you, I have everything I need.

The maid puts down the tree and goes out.

NORA (*busy decorating the tree*): Now—candles here—and flowers here. That loathsome man! Nonsense, nonsense, there's nothing to be frightened about. The Christmas tree must be beautiful. I'll do everything that you like, Torvald. I'll sing for you, dance for you—

Helmer, with a bundle of papers under his arm, enters.

NORA: Oh—are you back already?

HELMER: Yes. Has anyone been here?

NORA: Here? No.

HELMER: That's strange. I saw Krogstad come out of the front door. 860

NORA: Did you? Oh yes, that's quite right—Krogstad was here for a few minutes.

HELMER: Nora, I can tell from your face, he's been here and asked you to put in a good word for him.

NORA: Yes.

HELMER: And you were to pretend you were doing it of your own accord? You weren't going to tell me he'd been here? He asked you to do that too, didn't he?

NORA: Yes, Torvald. But—

HELMER: Nora, Nora! And you were ready to enter into such a con- 870 spiracy? Talking to a man like that, and making him promises—and then, on top of it all, to tell me an untruth!

NORA: An untruth?

HELMER: Didn't you say no one had been here? (*Wags his finger.*) My little songbird must never do that again. A songbird must have a clean beak to sing with; otherwise she'll start twittering out of tune. (*Puts his arm round her waist.*) Isn't that the way we want things? Yes, of course it is. (*Lets go of her.*) So let's hear no more about that. (*Sits down in front of the stove.*) Ah, how cozy and peaceful it is here. (*Glances for a few moments at his papers.*) 880

NORA (*busy with the tree; after a short silence*): Torvald.

HELMER: Yes.

NORA: I'm terribly looking forward to that fancy dress ball at the Stenborgs on Boxing Day.

HELMER: And I'm terribly curious to see what you're going to surprise me with.

NORA: Oh, it's so maddening.

HELMER: What is?

NORA: I can't think of anything to wear. It all seems so stupid and 890   meaningless.

HELMER: So my little Nora's come to that conclusion, has she?

NORA (*behind his chair, resting her arms on its back*): Are you very busy, Torvald?

HELMER: Oh—

NORA: What are those papers?

HELMER: Just something to do with the bank.

NORA: Already?

HELMER: I persuaded the trustees to give me authority to make certain immediate changes in the staff and organization. I want to have ev- 900   erything straight by the New Year.

NORA: Then that's why this poor man Krogstad—

HELMER: Hm.

NORA (*still leaning over his chair, slowly strokes the back of his head*): If you hadn't been so busy, I was going to ask you an enormous favour, Torvald.

HELMER: Well, tell me. What was it to be?

NORA: You know I trust your taste more than anyone's. I'm so anxious to look really beautiful at the fancy dress ball. Torvald, couldn't you help me to decide what I shall go as, and what kind of costume I ought to wear?

910   HELMER: Aha! So little Miss Independent's in trouble and needs a man to rescue her, does she?

NORA: Yes, Torvald. I can't get anywhere without your help.

HELMER: Well, well, I'll give the matter thought. We'll find something.

NORA: Oh, how kind of you! (*Goes back to the tree. Pause.*) How pretty these red flowers look! But, tell me, is it so dreadful, this thing that Krogstad's done?

HELMER: He forged someone else's name. Have you any idea what that means?

NORA: Mightn't he have been forced to do it by some emergency?

920   HELMER: He probably just didn't think—that's what usually happens. I'm not so heartless as to condemn a man for an isolated action.

NORA: No, Torvald, of course not!

HELMER: Men often succeed in reestablishing themselves if they admit their crime and take their punishment.

NORA: Punishment?

HELMER: But Krogstad didn't do that. He chose to try and trick his way out of it; and that's what has morally destroyed him.

NORA: You think that would—?

HELMER: Just think how a man with that load on his conscience must always be lying and cheating and dissembling; how he must wear a mask even in the presence of those who are dearest to him, even his own wife and children! Yes, the children. That's the worst danger, Nora. 930

NORA: Why?

HELMER: Because an atmosphere of lies contaminates and poisons every corner of the home. Every breath that the children draw in such a house contains the germs of evil.

NORA (*comes closer behind him*): Do you really believe that?

HELMER: Oh, my dear, I've come across it so often in my work at the bar. Nearly all young criminals are the children of mothers who are constitutional liars. 940

NORA: Why do you say mothers?

HELMER: It's usually the mother; though of course the father can have the same influence. Every lawyer knows that only too well. And yet this fellow Krogstad has been sitting at home all these years poisoning his children with his lies and pretenses. That's why I say that, morally speaking, he is dead. (*Stretches out his hands toward her.*) So my pretty little Nora must promise me not to plead his case. Your hand on it. Come, come, what's this? Give me your hand. There. That's settled, now. I assure you it'd be quite impossible for me to work in the same building as him. I literally feel physically ill in the presence of a man like that. 950

NORA (*draws her hand from his and goes over to the other side of the Christmas tree*): How hot it is in here! And I've so much to do.

HELMER (*gets up and gathers his papers*): Yes, and I must try to get some of this read before dinner. I'll think about your costume too. And I may even have something up my sleeve to hang in gold paper on the Christmas tree. (*Lays his hand on her head.*) My precious little songbird!

He goes into his study and closes the door.

NORA (*softly, after a pause*): It's nonsense. It must be. It's impossible. It must be impossible! 960

NURSE (*in the doorway, left*): The children are asking if they can come in to Mummy.

NORA: No, no, no; don't let them in! You stay with them, Anne-Marie.

NURSE: Very good, madam. (*Closes the door.*)

NORA (*pale with fear*): Corrupt my little children—! Poison my home! (*Short pause. She throws back her head.*) It isn't true! It *couldn't* be true!

ACT 2

The same room. In the corner by the piano the Christmas tree stands, stripped and disheveled, its candles burned to their sockets. Nora's outdoor clothes lie on the sofa. She is alone in the room, walking restlessly to and fro. At length she stops by the sofa and picks up her coat.

NORA (*drops the coat again*): There's someone coming! (*Goes to the door and listens.*) No, it's no one. Of course—no one'll come today, it's Christmas Day. Nor tomorrow. But perhaps—! (*Opens the door and looks out.*) No. Nothing in the letter-box. Quite empty. (*Walks across the room.*) Silly, silly. Of course he won't do anything. It couldn't happen. It isn't possible. Why, I've three small children.

970

The Nurse, carrying a large cardboard box, enters from the room on the left.

NURSE: I found those fancy dress clothes at last, madam.
NORA: Thank you. Put them on the table.
NURSE (*does so*): They're all rumpled up.
NORA: Oh, I wish I could tear them into a million pieces!
NURSE Why, madam! They'll be all right. Just a little patience.
NORA: Yes, of course. I'll go and get Mrs. Linde to help me.
NURSE: What, out again? In this dreadful weather? You'll catch a chill, madam.

980

NORA: Well, that wouldn't be the worst. How are the children?
NURSE: Playing with their Christmas presents, poor little dears. But—
NORA: Are they still asking to see me?
NURSE: They're so used to having their Mummy with them.
NORA: Yes, but, Anne-Marie, from now on I shan't be able to spend so much time with them.
NURSE: Well, children get used to anything in time.
NORA: Do you think so? Do you think they'd forget their mother if she went away from them—for ever?

990

NURSE: Mercy's sake, madam! For ever!
NORA: Tell me, Anne-Marie—I've so often wondered. How could you bear to give your child away—to strangers?
NURSE: But I had to when I came to nurse my little Miss Nora.
NORA: Do you mean you wanted to?
NURSE: When I had the chance of such a good job? A poor girl what's got into trouble can't afford to pick and choose. That good-for-nothing didn't lift a finger.
NORA: But your daughter must have completely forgotten you.

1000

NURSE: Oh no, indeed she hasn't. She's written to me twice, once when she got confirmed and then again when she got married.
NORA (*hugs her*): Dear old Anne-Marie, you were a good mother to me.
NURSE: Poor little Miss Nora, you never had any mother but me.
NORA: And if my little ones had no one else, I know you would—no, silly, silly, silly! (*Opens the cardboard box.*) Go back to them, Anne-Marie. Now I must—Tomorrow you'll see how pretty I shall look.
NURSE: Why, there'll be no one at the ball as beautiful as my Miss Nora.

1010

She goes into the room, left.

NORA (*begins to unpack the clothes from the box, but soon throws them down again*): Oh, if only I dared to go out! If I could be sure no one would come, and nothing would happen while I was away! Stupid, stupid! No one will come. I just mustn't think about it. Brush this muff. Pretty gloves, pretty gloves! Don't think about it, don't think about it! One, two, three, four, five, six—(*Cries.*) Ah—they're coming—!

She begins to run toward the door, but stops uncertainly. Mrs. Linde enters from the hall where she has been taking off her outdoor clothes.

NORA: Oh, it's you, Christine. There's no one else out there, is there? Oh, I'm so glad you've come.

MRS. LINDE: I hear you were at my room asking for me.

NORA: Yes, I just happened to be passing. I want to ask you to help me with something. Let's sit down here on the sofa. Look at this. There's going to be a fancy dress ball tomorrow night upstairs at Consul Stenborg's, and Torvald wants me to go as a Neapolitan fisher-girl and dance the tarantella. I learned it on Capri. 1020

MRS. LINDE: I say, are you going to give a performance?

NORA: Yes, Torvald says I should. Look, here's the dress. Torvald had it made for me in Italy; but now it's all so torn, I don't know—

MRS. LINDE: Oh, we'll soon put that right; the stitching's just come away. Needle and thread? Ah, here we are.

NORA: You're being awfully sweet.

MRS. LINDE (*sews*): So you're going to dress up tomorrow, Nora? I must pop over for a moment to see how you look. Oh, but I've completely forgotten to thank you for that nice evening yesterday. 1030

NORA (*gets up and walks across the room*): Oh, I didn't think it was as nice as usual. You ought to have come to town a little earlier, Christine. . . . Yes, Torvald understands how to make a home look attractive.

MRS. LINDE: I'm sure you do, too. You're not your father's daughter for nothing. But, tell me. Is Dr. Rank always in such low spirits as he was yesterday?

NORA: No, last night it was very noticeable. But he's got a terrible disease; he's got spinal tuberculosis, poor man. His father was a frightful creature who kept mistresses and so on. As a result Dr. Rank has been sickly ever since he was a child—you understand— 1040

MRS. LINDE (*puts down her sewing*): But, my dear Nora, how on earth did you get to know about such things?

NORA (*walks about the room*): Oh, don't be silly, Christine—when one has three children, one comes into contact with women who—well, who know about medical matters, and they tell one a thing or two.

MRS. LINDE (*sews again; a short silence*): Does Dr. Rank visit you every day? 1050

NORA: Yes, every day. He's Torvald's oldest friend, and a good friend to me too. Dr. Rank's almost one of the family.

MRS. LINDE: But, tell me—is he quite sincere? I mean doesn't he rather say the sort of thing he thinks people want to hear?

NORA. No, quite the contrary. What gave you that idea?

MRS. LINDE: When you introduced me to him yesterday, he said he'd often heard my name mentioned here. But later I noticed your husband had no idea who I was. So how could Dr. Rank—?

NORA: Yes, that's quite right, Christine. You see, Torvald's so hopelessly in love with me that he wants to have me all to himself—those were his very words. When we were first married, he got quite jealous if I as much as mentioned any of my old friends back home. So naturally, I stopped talking about them. But I often chat with Dr. Rank about that kind of thing. He enjoys it, you see.

MRS. LINDE: Now listen, Nora. In many ways you're still a child; I'm a bit older than you and have a little more experience of the world. There's something I want to say to you. You ought to give up this business with Dr. Rank.

NORA: What business?

MRS. LINDE: Well, everything. Last night you were speaking about this rich admirer of yours who was going to give you money—

NORA: Yes, and who doesn't exist—unfortunately. But what's that got to do with—?

MRS. LINDE: Is Dr. Rank rich?

NORA: Yes.

MRS. LINDE: And he has no dependents?

NORA: No, no one. But—

MRS. LINDE: And he comes here to see you every day?

NORA: Yes, I've told you.

MRS. LINDE. But how dare a man of his education be so forward?

NORA: What on earth are you talking about?

MRS. LINDE: Oh, stop pretending, Nora. Do you think I haven't guessed who it was who lent you that two hundred pounds?

NORA: Are you out of your mind? How could you imagine such a thing? A friend, someone who comes here every day! Why, that'd be an impossible situation!

MRS. LINDE: Then it really wasn't him?

NORA: No, of course not. I've never for a moment dreamed of—anyway, he hadn't any money to lend then. He didn't come into that till later.

MRS. LINDE: Well, I think that was a lucky thing for you, Nora dear.

NORA: No, I could never have dreamed of asking Dr. Rank—Though I'm sure that if I ever did ask him—

MRS. LINDE: But of course you won't.

NORA: Of course not. I can't imagine that it should ever become necessary. But I'm perfectly sure that if I did speak to Dr. Rank—

MRS. LINDE: Behind your husband's back?

NORA: I've got to get out of this other business; and *that's* been going on behind his back. I've *got* to get out of it.

MRS. LINDE: Yes, well, that's what I told you yesterday. But— 1100

NORA (*walking up and down*): It's much easier for a man to arrange these things than a woman—

MRS. LINDE: One's own husband, yes.

NORA: Oh, bosh. (*Stops walking.*) When you've completely repaid a debt, you get your I.O.U. back, don't you?

MRS. LINDE: Yes, of course.

NORA: And you can tear it into a thousand pieces and burn the filthy, beastly thing!

MRS. LINDE (*looks hard at her, puts down her sewing, and gets up slowly*): Nora, you're hiding something from me.

NORA: Can you see that? 1110

MRS. LINDE: Something has happened since yesterday morning. Nora, what is it?

NORA (*goes toward her*): Christine! (*Listens.*) Ssh! There's Torvald. Would you mind going into the nursery for a few minutes? Torvald can't bear to see sewing around. Anne-Marie'll help you.

MRS. LINDE (*gathers some of her things together*): Very well. But I shan't leave this house until we've talked this matter out.

She goes into the nursery, left. As she does so, Helmer enters from the hall.

NORA (*runs to meet him*): Oh, Torvald dear, I've been so longing for you to come back!

HELMER: Was that the dressmaker? 1120

NORA: No, it was Christine. She's helping me mend my costume. I'm going to look rather splendid in that.

HELMER: Yes, that was quite a bright idea of mine, wasn't it?

NORA: Wonderful! But wasn't it nice of me to give in to you?

HELMER (*takes her chin in his hand*): Nice—to give in to your husband? All right, little silly, I know you didn't mean it like that. But I won't disturb you. I expect you'll be wanting to try it on.

NORA: Are you going to work now?

HELMER: Yes. (*Shows her a bundle of papers.*) Look at these. I've been down to the bank—(*Turns to go into his study.*) 1130

NORA: Torvald.

HELMER (*stops*): Yes.

NORA: If little squirrel asked you really prettily to grant her a wish—

HELMER: Well?

NORA: Would you grant it to her?

HELMER: First I should naturally have to know what it was.

NORA: Squirrel would do lots of pretty tricks for you if you granted her wish.

HELMER: Out with it, then.

1140 NORA: Your little skylark would sing in every room—

HELMER: My little skylark does that already.

NORA: I'd turn myself into a little fairy and dance for you in the moonlight, Torvald.

HELMER: Nora, it isn't that business you were talking about this morning?

NORA (*comes closer*): Yes, Torvald—oh, please! I beg of you!

HELMER: Have you really the nerve to bring that up again?

NORA: Yes, Torvald, yes, you must do as I ask! You must let Krogstad keep his place at the bank!

1150 HELMER: My dear Nora, his is the job I'm giving to Mrs. Linde.

NORA: Yes, that's terribly sweet of you. But you can get rid of one of the other clerks instead of Krogstad.

HELMER: Really, you're being incredibly obstinate. Just because you thoughtlessly promised to put in a word for him, you expect me to—

NORA: No, it isn't that, Helmer. It's for your own sake. The man writes for the most beastly newspapers—you said so yourself. He could do you tremendous harm. I'm so dreadfully frightened of him—

1160 HELMER: Oh, I understand. Memories of the past. That's what's frightening you.

NORA: What do you mean?

HELMER: You're thinking of your father, aren't you?

NORA: Yes, yes. Of course. Just think what those dreadful men wrote in the papers about Papa! The most frightful slanders. I really believe it would have lost him his job if the Ministry hadn't sent you down to investigate, and you hadn't been so kind and helpful to him.

1170 HELMER: But my dear little Nora, there's a considerable difference between your father and me. Your father was not a man of unassailable reputation. But I am; and I hope to remain so all my life.

NORA: But no one knows what spiteful people may not dig up. We could be so peaceful and happy now, Torvald—we could be free from every worry—you and I and the children. Oh, please, Torvald, please—!

HELMER: The very fact of your pleading his cause makes it impossible for me to keep him. Everyone at the bank already knows that I intend to dismiss Krogstad. If the rumor got about that the new manager had allowed his wife to persuade him to change his mind—

1180 NORA: Well, what then?

HELMER: Oh, nothing, nothing. As long as my little Miss Obstinate gets her way—Do you expect me to make a laughing-stock of myself before my entire staff—give people the idea that I am open to outside influence? Believe me, I'd soon feel the consequences! Besides—there's something else that makes it impossible for Krogstad to remain in the bank while I am its manager.

NORA: What is that?

HELMER: I might conceivably have allowed myself to ignore his moral obloquies—

NORA: Yes, Torvald, surely? 1190

HELMER: And I hear he's quite efficient at his job. But we—well, we were schoolfriends. It was one of those friendships that one enters into over-hastily and so often comes to regret late in life. I might as well confess the truth. We—well, we're on Christian name terms. And the tactless idiot makes no attempt to conceal it when other people are present. On the contrary, he thinks it gives him the right to be familiar with me. He shows off the whole time, with "Torvald this," and "Torvald that." I can tell you, I find it damned annoying. If he stayed, he'd make my position intolerable.

NORA: Torvald, you can't mean this seriously. 1200

HELMER: Oh? And why not?

NORA: But it's so petty.

HELMER: What did you say? Petty? You think *I* am petty?

NORA: No, Torvald dear, of course you're not. That's just why—

HELMER: Don't quibble! You call my motives petty. Then I must be petty too. Petty! I see. Well, I've had enough of this. (*Goes to the door and calls into the hall.*) Helen!

NORA: What are you going to do?

HELMER (*searching among his papers*): I'm going to settle this matter once and for all. (*The Maid enters.*) Take this letter downstairs at 1210 once. Find a messenger and see that he delivers it. Immediately! The address is on the envelope. Here's the money.

MAID: Very good, sir. (*Goes out with the letter.*)

HELMER (*putting his papers in order*): There now, little Miss Obstinate.

NORA (*tensely*): Torvald—what was in that letter?

HELMER: Krogstad's dismissal.

NORA: Call her back, Torvald! There's still time. Oh, Torvald, call her back! Do it for my sake—for your own sake—for the children! Do you hear me, Torvald? Please do it! You don't realize what this may 1220 do to us all!

HELMER: Too late.

NORA: Yes. Too late.

HELMER: My dear Nora, I forgive you this anxiety. Though it is a bit of an insult to me. Oh, but it is! Isn't it an insult to imply that I should be frightened by the vindictiveness of a depraved hack journalist? But I forgive you, because it so charmingly testifies to the love you bear me. (*Takes her in his arms.*) Which is as it should be,

my own dearest Nora. Let what will happen, happen. When the real
1230   crisis comes, you will not find me lacking in strength or courage. I
am man enough to bear the burden for us both.

NORA (*fearfully*): What do you mean?

HELMER: The whole burden, I say—

NORA (*calmly*): I shall never let you do that.

HELMER: Very well. We shall share it, Nora—as man and wife. And
that is as it should be. (*Caresses her.*) Are you happy now? There,
there, there; don't look at me with those frightened little eyes.
You're simply imagining things. You go ahead now and do your
tarantella, and get some practice on that tambourine. I'll sit in my
1240   study and close the door. Then I won't hear anything, and you can
make all the noise you want. (*Turns in the doorway.*) When Dr.
Rank comes, tell him where to find me. (*He nods to her, goes into
his room with his papers, and closes the door.*)

NORA (*desperate with anxiety, stands as though transfixed, and whispers*): He said he'd do it. He will do it. He will do it, and nothing'll
stop him. No, never that. I'd rather anything. There must be some
escape—Some way out—! (*The bell rings in the hall.*) Dr. Rank—!
Anything but that! Anything, I don't care—!

*She passes her hand across her face, composes herself, walks across,
and opens the door to the hall. Dr. Rank is standing there, hanging
up his fur coat. During the following scene, it begins to grow dark.*

NORA: Good evening, Dr. Rank. I recognized your ring. But you
mustn't go to Torvald yet. I think he's busy.

RANK: And—you?

1250   NORA (*as he enters the room and she closes the door behind him*): Oh,
you know very well I've always time to talk to you.

RANK: Thank you. I shall avail myself of that privilege as long as I can.

NORA: What do you mean by that? As long as you *can?*

RANK: Yes. Does that frighten you?

NORA: Well, it's rather a curious expression. Is something going to
happen?

RANK: Something I've been expecting to happen for a long time. But I
didn't think it would happen quite so soon.

NORA (*seizes his arm*): What is it? Dr. Rank, you must tell me!

1260   RANK (*sits down by the stove*): I'm on the way out. And there's nothing to be done about it.

NORA (*sighs with relief*): Oh, it's you—?

RANK: Who else? No, it's no good lying to oneself. I am the most
wretched of all my patients, Mrs. Helmer. These last few days I've
been going through the books of this poor body of mine, and I find
I am bankrupt. Within a month I may be rotting up there in the
churchyard.

NORA: Ugh, what a nasty way to talk!

RANK: The facts aren't exactly nice. But the worst is that there's so
much else that's nasty to come first. I've only one more test to 1270
make. When that's done I'll have a pretty accurate idea of when the
final disintegration is likely to begin. I want to ask you a favour.
Helmer's a sensitive chap, and I know how he hates anything ugly. I
don't want him to visit me when I'm in hospital—

NORA: Oh but, Dr. Rank—

RANK: I don't want him there. On any pretext. I shan't have him allowed in. As soon as I know the worst, I'll send you my visiting
card with a black cross on it, and then you'll know that the final
filthy process has begun.

NORA: Really, you're being quite impossible this evening. And I did 1280
hope you'd be in a good mood.

RANK: With death on my hands? And all this to atone for someone
else's sin? Is there justice in that? And in every single family, in one
way or another, the same merciless law of retribution is at work—

NORA (*holds her hands to her ears*): Nonsense! Cheer up! Laugh!

RANK: Yes, you're right. Laughter's all the damned thing's fit for. My
poor innocent spine must pay for the fun my father had as a gay
young lieutenant.

NORA (*at the table, left*): You mean he was too fond of asparagus and
foie gras? 1290

RANK: Yes, and truffles too.

NORA: Yes, of course, truffles, yes. And oysters too, I suppose?

RANK: Yes, oysters, oysters. Of course.

NORA: And all that port and champagne to wash them down. It's too
sad that all those lovely things should affect one's spine.

RANK: Especially a poor spine that never got any pleasure out of them.

NORA: Oh yes, that's the saddest thing of all.

RANK (*looks searchingly at her*): Hm—

NORA (*after a moment*): Why did you smile?

RANK: No, it was you who laughed. 1300

NORA: No, it was you who smiled, Dr. Rank!

RANK (*gets up*): You're a worse little rogue than I thought.

NORA: Oh, I'm full of stupid tricks today.

RANK: So it seems.

NORA (*puts both her hands on his shoulders*): Dear, dear. Dr. Rank,
you mustn't die and leave Torvald and me.

RANK: Oh, you'll soon get over it. Once one is gone, one is soon forgotten.

NORA (*looks at him anxiously*): Do you believe that?

RANK: One finds replacements, and then— 1310

NORA: Who will find a replacement?

RANK: You and Helmer both will, when I am gone. You seem to have
made a start already, haven't you? What was this Mrs. Linde doing
here yesterday evening?

NORA: Aha! But surely you can't be jealous of poor Christine?

RANK: Indeed I am. She will be my successor in this house. When I have moved on, this lady will—

NORA: Ssh—don't speak so loud! She's in there!

RANK: Today again? You see!

1320   NORA: She's only come to mend my dress. Good heavens, how unreasonable you are! (*Sits on the sofa.*) Be nice now, Dr. Rank. Tomorrow you'll see how beautifully I shall dance; and you must imagine that I'm doing it just for you. And for Torvald of course; obviously. (*Takes some things out of the box.*) Dr. Rank, sit down here and I'll show you something.

RANK (*sits*): What's this?

NORA: Look here! Look!

RANK: Silk stockings!

NORA: Flesh-colored. Aren't they beautiful? It's very dark in here now,
1330   of course, but tomorrow—No, no, no; only the soles. Oh well, I suppose you can look a bit higher if you want to.

RANK: Hm—

NORA: Why are you looking so critical? Don't you think they'll fit me?

RANK: I can't really give you a qualified opinion on that.

NORA (*looks at him for a moment*): Shame on you! (*Flicks him on the ear with the stockings.*) Take that. (*Puts them back in the box.*)

RANK: What other wonders are to be revealed to me?

NORA: I shan't show you anything else. You're being naughty.

She hums a little and looks among the things in the box.

1340   RANK (*after a short silence*): When I sit here like this being so intimate with you, I can't think—I cannot imagine what would have become of me if I had never entered this house.

NORA (*smiles*): Yes, I think you enjoy being with us, don't you?

RANK (*more quietly, looking into the middle distance*): And now to have to leave it all—

NORA: Nonsense. You're not leaving us.

RANK (*as before*): And not to be able to leave even the most wretched token of gratitude behind; hardly even a passing sense of loss; only an empty place, to be filled by the next comer.

NORA: Suppose I were to ask you to—? No—
1350   RANK: To do what?

NORA: To give me proof of your friendship—

RANK: Yes, yes?

NORA: No, I mean—to do me a very great service—

RANK: Would you really for once grant me that happiness?

NORA: But you've no idea what it is.

RANK: Very well, tell me, then.

NORA: No, but, Dr. Rank, I can't. It's far too much—I want your help and advice, and I want you to do something for me.

RANK: The more the better. I've no idea what it can be. But tell me. You do trust me, don't you? 1360

NORA: Oh, yes, more than anyone. You're my best and truest friend. Otherwise I couldn't tell you. Well then, Dr. Rank—there's something you must help me to prevent. You know how much Torvald loves me—he'd never hesitate for an instant to lay down his life for me—

RANK (*leans over toward her*): Nora—do you think he is the only one—?

NORA (*with a slight start*): What do you mean?

RANK: Who would gladly lay down his life for you?

NORA (*sadly*): Oh, I see. 1370

RANK: I swore to myself I would let you know that before I go. I shall never have a better opportunity. . . . Well, Nora, now you know that. And now you also know that you can trust me as you can trust nobody else.

NORA (*rises; calmly and quietly*): Let me pass, please.

RANK (*makes room for her but remains seated*): Nora—

NORA (*in the doorway to the hall*): Helen, bring the lamp. (*Goes over to the stove.*) Oh, dear Dr. Rank, this was really horrid of you.

RANK (*gets up*): That I have loved you as deeply as anyone else has? Was that horrid of me? 1380

NORA: No—but that you should go and tell me. That was quite unnecessary—

RANK: What do you mean? Did you know, then—?

The Maid enters with the lamp, puts it on the table, and goes out.

RANK: Nora—Mrs. Helmer—I am asking you, did you know this?

NORA: Oh, what do I know, what did I know, what didn't I know—I really can't say. How could you be so stupid, Dr. Rank? Everything was so nice.

RANK: Well, at any rate now you know that I am ready to serve you, body and soul. So—please continue.

NORA (*looks at him*): After this? 1390

RANK: Please tell me what it is.

NORA: I can't possibly tell you now.

RANK: Yes, yes! You mustn't punish me like this. Let me be allowed to do what I can for you.

NORA: You can't do anything for me now. Anyway, I don't need any help. It was only my imagination—you'll see. Yes, really. Honestly. (*Sits in the rocking chair, looks at him, and smiles.*) Well, upon my word you *are* a fine gentleman, Dr. Rank. Aren't you ashamed of yourself, now that the lamps been lit?

RANK: Frankly, no. But perhaps I ought to say—*adieu?* 1400

NORA: Of course not. You will naturally continue to visit us as before. You know quite well how Torvald depends on your company.

RANK: Yes, but you?

NORA: Oh, I always think it's enormous fun having you here.

RANK: That was what misled me. You're a riddle to me, you know. I'd often felt you'd just as soon be with me as with Helmer.

NORA: Well, you see, there are some people whom one loves, and others whom it's almost more fun to be with.

RANK: Oh yes, there's some truth in that.

1410   NORA: When I was at home, of course I loved Papa best. But I always used to think it was terribly amusing to go down and talk to the servants; because they never told me what I ought to do; and they were such fun to listen to.

RANK: I see. So I've taken their place?

NORA (*jumps up and runs over to him*): Oh, dear, sweet Dr. Rank, I didn't mean that at all. But I'm sure you understand—I feel the same about Torvald as I did abut Papa.

MAID (*enters from the hall*): Excuse me, madam. (*Whispers to her and hands her a visiting card.*)

NORA (*glances at the card*): Oh! (*Puts it quickly in her pocket.*)

1420   RANK: Anything wrong?

NORA: No, no, nothing at all. It's just something that—it's my new dress.

RANK: What? But your costume is lying over there.

NORA: Oh—that, yes—but there's another—I ordered it specially—Torvald mustn't know—

RANK: Ah, so that's your big secret?

NORA: Yes, yes. Go in and talk to him—he's in his study—keep him talking for a bit—

RANK: Don't worry. He won't get away from me. (*Goes into Helmer's study.*)

1430   NORA (*to the Maid*): Is he waiting in the kitchen?

MAID: Yes, madam, he came up the back way—

NORA: But didn't you tell him I had a visitor?

MAID: Yes, but he wouldn't go.

NORA: Wouldn't go?

MAID: No, madam, not until he'd spoken with you.

NORA: Very well, show him in; but quietly. Helen, you mustn't tell anyone about this. It's a surprise for my husband.

MAID: Very good, madam. I understand. (*Goes.*)

NORA: It's happening. It's happening after all. No, no, no, it can't hap-
1440   pen, it mustn't happen.

She walks across and bolts the door of Helmer's study. The Maid opens the door in the hall to admit Krogstad, and closes it behind him. He is wearing an overcoat, heavy boots, and a fur cap.

NORA (*goes towards him*): Speak quietly. My husband's at home.

KROGSTAD: Let him hear.

NORA: What do you want from me?

KROGSTAD: Information.

NORA: Hurry up, then. What is it?

KROGSTAD: I suppose you know I've been given the sack.

NORA: I couldn't stop it, Mr. Krogstad. I did my best for you, but it didn't help.

KROGSTAD: Does your husband love you so little? He knows what I can do to you, and yet he dares to— 1450

NORA: Surely you don't imagine I told him?

KROGSTAD: No. I didn't really think you had. It wouldn't have been like my old friend Torvald Helmer to show that much courage—

NORA: Mr. Krogstad, I'll trouble you to speak respectfully of my husband.

KROGSTAD: Don't worry, I'll show him all the respect he deserves. But since you're so anxious to keep this matter hushed up, I presume you're better informed than you were yesterday of the gravity of what you've done?

NORA: I've learned more than you could ever teach me. 1460

KROGSTAD: Yes, a bad lawyer like me—

NORA: What do you want from me?

KROGSTAD: I just wanted to see how things were with you, Mrs. Helmer. I've been thinking about you all day. Even duns and hack journalists have hearts, you know.

NORA: Show some heart, then. Think of my little children.

KROGSTAD: Have you and your husband thought of mine? Well, let's forget that. I just wanted to tell you, you don't need to take this business too seriously. I'm not going to take any action, for the present. 1470

NORA: Oh, no—you won't, will you? I knew it.

KROGSTAD: It can all be settled quite amicably. There's no need for it to become public. We'll keep it among the three of us.

NORA: My husband must never know about this.

KROGSTAD: How can you stop him? Can you pay the balance of what you owe me?

NORA: Not immediately.

KROGSTAD: Have you any means of raising the money during the next few days?

NORA: None that I would care to use. 1480

KROGSTAD: Well, it wouldn't have helped anyway. However much money you offered me now I wouldn't give you back that paper.

NORA: What are you going to do with it?

KROGSTAD: Just keep it. No one else need ever hear about it. So in case you were thinking of doing anything desperate—

NORA: I am.

KROGSTAD: Such as running away—

NORA: I am.

KROGSTAD: Or anything more desperate—

NORA: How did you know?

KROGSTAD: —just give up the idea.

NORA: How did you know?

KROGSTAD: Most of us think of that at first. I did. But I hadn't the courage—

NORA (*dully*): Neither have I.

KROGSTAD (*relieved*): It's true, isn't it? You haven't the courage either?

NORA: No. I haven't. I haven't.

KROGSTAD: It'd be a stupid thing to do anyway. Once the first little domestic explosion is over. . . . I've got a letter in my pocket here addressed to your husband—

NORA: Telling him everything?

KROGSTAD: As delicately as possible.

NORA (*quickly*): He must never see that letter. Tear it up. I'll find the money somehow—

KROGSTAD: I'm sorry, Mrs. Helmer, I thought I'd explained—

NORA: Oh, I don't mean the money I owe you. Let me know how much you want from my husband, and I'll find it for you.

KROGSTAD: I'm not asking your husband for money.

NORA: What do you want, then?

KROGSTAD: I'll tell you. I want to get on my feet again, Mrs. Helmer. I want to get to the top. And your husband's going to help me. For eighteen months now my record's been clean. I've been in hard straits all that time; I was content to fight my way back inch by inch. Now I've been chucked back into the mud, and I'm not going to be satisfied with just getting back my job. I'm going to get to the top, I tell you. I'm going to get back into the bank, and it's going to be higher up. Your husband's going to create a new job for me—

NORA: He'll never do that!

KROGSTAD: Oh, yes he will. I know him. He won't dare to risk a scandal. And once I'm in there with him, you'll see! Within a year I'll be his right-hand man. It'll be Nils Krogstad who'll be running that bank, not Torvald Helmer!

NORA: That will never happen.

KROGSTAD: Are you thinking of—?

NORA: Now I *have* the courage.

KROGSTAD: Oh, you can't frighten me. A pampered little pretty like you—

NORA: You'll see! You'll see!

KROGSTAD: Under the ice? Down in the cold, black water? And then, in the spring, to float up again, ugly, unrecognizable, hairless—?

NORA: You can't frighten me.

KROGSTAD: And you can't frighten me. People don't do such things, Mrs. Helmer. And anyway, what'd be the use? I've got him in my pocket.

NORA: But afterwards? When I'm no longer—?

KROGSTAD: Have you forgotten that then your reputation will be in my hands? (*She looks at him speechlessly.*) Well, I've warned you. Don't do anything silly. When Helmer's read my letter, he'll get in touch with me. And remember, it's your husband who's forced me to act like this. And for that I'll never forgive him. Goodbye, Mrs. Helmer. (*He goes out through the hall.*)

NORA (*runs to the hall door, opens it a few inches, and listens*): He's going. He's not going to give him the letter. Oh, no, no, it couldn't possibly happen. (*Opens the door a little wider.*) What's he doing? Standing outside the front door. He's not going downstairs. Is he changing his mind? Yes, he—!

A letter falls into the letter-box. Krogstad's footsteps die away down the stairs.

NORA (*with a stifled cry, runs across the room towards the table by the sofa. A pause*): In the letter-box. (*Steals timidly over towards the hall door.*) There it is! Oh, Torvald, Torvald! Now we're lost!

MRS. LINDE (*enters from the nursery with Nora's costume*): Well, I've done the best I can. Shall we see how it looks—?

NORA (*whispers hoarsely*): Christine, come here.

MRS. LINDE (*throws the dress on the sofa*): What's wrong with you? You look as though you'd seen a ghost!

NORA: Come here. Do you see that letter? There—look—through the glass of the letter-box.

MRS. LINDE: Yes, yes, I see it.

NORA: That letter's from Krogstad—

MRS. LINDE: Nora! It was Krogstad who lent you the money!

NORA: Yes. And now Torvald's going to discover everything.

MRS. LINDE: Oh, believe me, Nora, it'll be best for you both.

NORA: You don't know what's happened. I've committed a forgery—

MRS. LINDE: But, for heaven's sake—!

NORA: Christine, all I want is for you to be my witness.

MRS. LINDE: What do you mean? Witness what?

NORA: If I should go out of my mind—and it might easily happen—

MRS. LINDE: Nora!

NORA: Or if anything else should happen to me—so that I wasn't here any longer—

MRS. LINDE: Nora, Nora, you don't know what you're saying!

NORA: If anyone should try to take the blame, and say it was all his fault—you understand—?

MRS. LINDE: Yes, yes—but how can you think—?

NORA: Then you must testify that it isn't true, Christine. I'm not mad—I know exactly what I'm saying—and I'm telling you, no one else knows anything about this. I did it entirely on my own. Remember that.

MRS. LINDE: All right. But I simply don't understand—

NORA: Oh, how could you understand? A—miracle—is about to happen.

MRS. LINDE: Miracle?

1580   NORA: Yes. A miracle. But it's so frightening, Christine. It *mustn't* happen, not for anything in the world.

MRS. LINDE: I'll go over and talk to Krogstad.

NORA: Don't go near him. He'll only do something to hurt you.

MRS. LINDE: Once upon a time he'd have done anything for my sake.

NORA: He?

MRS. LINDE: Where does he live?

NORA: Oh, how should I know—? Oh, yes, wait a moment—(*Feels in her pocket.*) Here's his card. But the letter, the letter—!

HELMER (*in his study, knocks on the door*): Nora!

1590   NORA (*cries in alarm*): What is it?

HELMER: Now, now, don't get alarmed. We're not coming in; you've closed the door. Are you trying on your costume?

NORA: Yes, yes—I'm trying on my costume. I'm going to look so pretty for you, Torvald.

MRS. LINDE (*who has been reading the card*): Why, he lives just around the corner.

NORA: Yes; but it's no use. There's nothing to be done now. The letter's lying there in the box.

MRS. LINDE: And your husband has the key?

1600   NORA: Yes, he always keeps it.

MRS. LINDE: Krogstad must ask him to send the letter back unread. He must find some excuse—

NORA: But Torvald always opens the box at just about this time—

MRS. LINDE: You must stop him. Go in and keep him talking. I'll be back as quickly as I can.

She hurries out through the hall.

NORA (*goes over to Helmer's door, opens it and peeps in*): Torvald!

HELMER (*offstage*): Well, may a man enter his own drawing room again? Come on, Rank, now we'll see what—(*In the doorway.*) But what's this?

1610   NORA: What, Torvald dear?

HELMER: Rank's been preparing me for some great transformation scene.

RANK (*in the doorway*): So I understood. But I seem to have been mistaken.

NORA: Yes, no one's to be allowed to see me before tomorrow night.

HELMER: But, my dear Nora, you look quite worn out. Have you been practicing too hard?

NORA: No, I haven't practiced at all yet.

HELMER: Well, you must.

NORA: Yes, Torvald, I must, I know. But I can't get anywhere without

1620   your help. I've completely forgotten everything.

HELMER: Oh, we'll soon put that to rights.

NORA: Yes, help me, Torvald. Promise me you will? Oh, I'm so nervous. All those people—! You must forget everything except me this evening. You mustn't think of business—I won't even let you touch a pen. Promise me, Torvald?

HELMER: I promise. This evening I shall think of nothing but you—my poor, helpless little darling. Oh, there's just one thing I must see to—(*Goes toward the hall door.*)

NORA: What do you want out there?

HELMER: I'm only going to see if any letters have come.   1630

NORA: No, Torvald, no!

HELMER: Why, what's the matter?

NORA: Torvald, I beg you. There's nothing there.

HELMER: Well, I'll just make sure.

> *He moves towards the door. Nora runs to the piano and plays the first bar of the tarantella.*

HELMER (*at the door, turns*): Aha!

NORA: I can't dance tomorrow if I don't practice with you now.

HELMER (*goes over to her*): Are you really so frightened, Nora dear?

NORA: Yes, terribly frightened. Let me start practicing now, at once—we've still time before dinner. Oh, do sit down and play for me, Torvald dear. Correct me, lead me, the way you always do.   1640

HELMER: Very well, my dear, if you wish it.

> *He sits down at the piano. Nora seizes the tambourine and a long multi-colored shawl from the cardboard box, wraps the latter hastily around her, then takes a quick leap into the center of the room.*

NORA: Play for me! I want to dance!

> *Helmer plays and Nora dances. Dr. Rank stands behind Helmer at the piano and watches her.*

HELMER: Slower, slower!

NORA: I can't!

HELMER: Not so violently, Nora.

NORA: I must!

HELMER (*stops playing*): No, no, this won't do at all.

NORA (*laughs and swings her tambourine*): Isn't that what I told you?

RANK: Let me play for her.

HELMER (*gets up*): Yes, would you? Then it'll be easier for me to show   1650
her.

> *Rank sits down at the piano and plays. Nora dances more and more wildly. Helmer has stationed himself by the stove and tries repeatedly to correct her but she seems not to hear him. Her hair works loose and falls over her shoulders; she ignores it and continues to dance. Mrs. Linde enters.*

MRS. LINDE (*stands in the doorway as though tongue-tied*): Ah—!

NORA (*as she dances*): Oh, Christine, we're having such fun!

HELMER: But, Nora darling, you're dancing as if your life depended on it.

NORA: It does.

HELMER: Rank, stop it! This is sheer lunacy. Stop it, I say!

Rank ceases playing. Nora suddenly stops dancing.

HELMER (*goes over to her*): I'd never have believed it. You've forgotten everything I taught you.

1660 NORA (*throws away the tambourine*): You see!

HELMER: I'll have to show you every step.

NORA: You see how much I need you! You must show me every step of the way. Right to the end of the dance. Promise me you will, Torvald?

HELMER: Never fear. I will.

NORA: You mustn't think about anything but me—today or tomorrow. Don't open any letters—don't even open the letter-box—

HELMER: Aha, you're still worried about that fellow—

NORA: Oh, yes, yes, him too.

HELMER: Nora, I can tell from the way you're behaving, there's a let-1670 ter from him already lying there.

NORA: I don't know. I think so. But you mustn't read it now. I don't want anything ugly to come between us till it's all over.

RANK (*quietly, to Helmer*): Better give her her way.

HELMER (*puts his arm round her*): My child shall have her way. But tomorrow night, when your dance is over—

NORA: Then you will be free.

MAID (*appears in the doorway, right*): Dinner is served, madam.

NORA: Put out some champagne, Helen.

MAID: Very good, madam. (*Goes.*)

1680 HELMER: I say! What's this, a banquet?

NORA: We'll drink champagne until dawn! (*Calls.*) And, Helen! Put out some macaroons! Lots of macaroons—for once!

HELMER (*takes her hands in his*): Now, now, now. Don't get so excited. Where's my little songbird, the one I know?

NORA: All right. Go and sit down—and you too, Dr. Rank. I'll be with you in a minute. Christine, you must help me put my hair up.

RANK (*quietly, as they go*): There's nothing wrong, is there? I mean, she isn't—er—expecting—?

HELMER: Good heavens no, my dear chap. She just gets scared like a 1690 child sometimes—I told you before—

They go out right.

NORA: Well?

MRS. LINDE: He's left town.

NORA: I saw it from your face.

MRS. LINDE: He'll be back tomorrow evening. I left a note for him.

NORA: You needn't have bothered. You can't stop anything now. Anyway, it's wonderful really, in a way—sitting here and waiting for the miracle to happen.

MRS. LINDE: Waiting for what?

NORA: Oh, you wouldn't understand. Go in and join them. I'll be with you in a moment.   1700

Mrs. Linde goes into the dining-room.

NORA (*stands for a moment as though collecting herself. Then she looks at her watch*): Five o'clock. Seven hours till midnight. Then another twenty-four hours till midnight tomorrow. And then the tarantella will be finished. Twenty-four and seven? Thirty-one hours to live.

HELMER (*appears in the doorway, right*): What's happened to my little songbird?

NORA (*runs to him with her arms wide*): Your songbird is here!

ACT 3

The same room. The table which was formerly by the sofa has been moved into the center of the room; the chairs surround it as before. The door to the hall stands open. Dance music can be heard from the floor above. Mrs. Linde is seated at the table, absent-mindedly glancing through a book. She is trying to read, but seems unable to keep her mind on it. More than once she turns and listens anxiously towards the front door.

MRS. LINDE (*looks at her watch*): Not here yet. There's not much time left. Please God he hasn't—! (*Listens again.*) Ah, here he is. (*Goes out into the hall and cautiously opens the front door. Footsteps can be heard softly ascending the stairs. She whispers.*) Come in. There's   1710 no one here.

KROGSTAD (*in the doorway*): I found a note from you at my lodgings. What does this mean?

MRS. LINDE: I must speak with you.

KROGSTAD: Oh? And must our conversation take place in this house?

MRS. LINDE: We couldn't meet at my place; my room has no separate entrance. Come in. We're quite alone. The maid's asleep, and the Helmers are at the dance upstairs.

KROGSTAD (*comes into the room*): Well, well! So the Helmers are dancing this evening? Are they indeed?   1720

MRS. LINDE: Yes. Why not?

KROGSTAD: True enough. Why not?

MRS. LINDE: Well, Krogstad. You and I must have a talk together.

KROGSTAD: Have we two anything further to discuss?

MRS. LINDE: We have a great deal to discuss.

KROGSTAD: I wasn't aware of it.

MRS. LINDE: That's because you've never really understood me.

KROGSTAD: Was there anything to understand? It's the old story, isn't it—a woman chucking a man because something better turns up?

1730   MRS. LINDE: Do you really think I'm so utterly heartless? You think it was easy for me to give you up?

KROGSTAD: Wasn't it?

MRS. LINDE: Oh, Nils, did you really believe that?

KROGSTAD: Then why did you write to me the way you did?

MRS. LINDE: I had to. Since I had to break with you, I thought it my duty to destroy all the feelings you had for me.

KROGSTAD (*clenches his fists*): So that was it. And you did this for money!

1740   MRS. LINDE: You mustn't forget I had a helpless mother to take care of, and two little brothers. We couldn't wait for you, Nils. It would have been so long before you'd had enough to support us.

KROGSTAD: Maybe. But you had no right to cast me off for someone else.

MRS. LINDE: Perhaps not. I've often asked myself that.

KROGSTAD (*more quietly*): When I lost you, it was just as though all solid ground had been swept from under my feet. Look at me. Now I am a shipwrecked man clinging to a spar.

MRS. LINDE: Help may be near at hand.

KROGSTAD: It was near. But then you came, and stood between it and

1750   me.

MRS. LINDE: I didn't know, Nils. No one told me till today that this job I'd found was yours.

KROGSTAD: I believe you, since you say so. But now you know, won't you give it up?

MRS. LINDE: No—because it wouldn't help you even if I did.

KROGSTAD: Wouldn't it? I'd do it all the same.

MRS. LINDE: I've learned to look at things practically. Life and poverty have taught me that.

KROGSTAD: And life has taught me to distrust fine words.

1760   MRS. LINDE: Then it's taught you a useful lesson. But surely you still believe in actions?

KROGSTAD: What do you mean?

MRS. LINDE: You said you were like a shipwrecked man clinging to a spar.

KROGSTAD: I have good reason to say it.

MRS. LINDE: I'm in the same position as you. No one to care about, no one to care for.

KROGSTAD: You made your own choice.

MRS. LINDE: I had no choice—then.

1770   KROGSTAD: Well?

MRS. LINDE: Nils, suppose we two shipwrecked souls could join hands?

KROGSTAD: What are you saying?

MRS. LINDE: Castaways have a better chance of survival together than on their own.

KROGSTAD: Christine!

MRS. LINDE: Why do you suppose I came to this town?

KROGSTAD: You mean—you came because of me?

MRS. LINDE: I must work if I'm to find life worth living. I've always worked, for as long as I can remember; it's been the greatest joy of my life—my only joy. But now I'm alone in the world, and I feel so 1780 dreadfully lost and empty. There's no joy in working just for oneself. Oh, Nils, give me something—someone—to work for.

KROGSTAD: I don't believe all that. You're just being hysterical and romantic. You want to find an excuse for self-sacrifice.

MRS. LINDE: Have you ever known me to be hysterical?

KROGSTAD: You mean you really—? Is it possible? Tell me—you know all about my past?

MRS. LINDE: Yes.

KROGSTAD: And you know what people think of me here?

MRS. LINDE: You said just now that with me you might have become a 1790 different person.

KROGSTAD: I know I could have.

MRS. LINDE: Couldn't it still happen?

KROGSTAD: Christine—do you really mean this? Yes—you do—I see it in your face. Have you really the courage—?

MRS. LINDE: I need someone to be a mother to; and your children need a mother. And you and I need each other. I believe in you, Nils. I am afraid of nothing—with you.

KROGSTAD (*clasps her hands*): Thank you, Christine—thank you! Now I shall make the world believe in me as you do! Oh—but I'd 1800 forgotten—

MRS. LINDE (*listens*): Ssh! The tarantella! Go quickly, go!

KROGSTAD: Why? What is it?

MRS. LINDE: You hear that dance? As soon as it's finished, they'll be coming down.

KROGSTAD: All right, I'll go. It's no good, Christine. I'd forgotten—you don't know what I've just done to the Helmers.

MRS. LINDE: Yes, Nils. I know.

KROGSTAD: And yet you'd still have the courage to—?

MRS. LINDE: I know what despair can drive a man like you to. 1810

KROGSTAD: Oh, if only I could undo this!

MRS. LINDE: You can. Your letter is still lying in the box.

KROGSTAD: Are you sure?

MRS. LINDE: Quite sure. But—

KROGSTAD (*looks searchingly at her*): Is that why you're doing this? You want to save your friend at any price? Tell me the truth. Is that the reason?

MRS. LINDE: Nils, a woman who has sold herself once for the sake of others doesn't make the same mistake again.

1820 KROGSTAD: I shall demand my letter back.

MRS. LINDE: No, no.

KROGSTAD: Of course I shall. I shall stay here till Helmer comes down. I'll tell him he must give me back my letter—I'll say it was only to do with my dismissal, and that I don't want him to read it—

MRS. LINDE: No, Nils, you mustn't ask for that letter back.

KROGSTAD: But—tell me—wasn't that the real reason you asked me to come here?

MRS. LINDE: Yes—at first, when I was frightened. But a day has passed since then, and in that time I've seen incredible things happen in this

1830 house. Helmer must know the truth. This unhappy secret of Nora's must be revealed. They must come to a full understanding; there must be an end of all these shiftings and evasions.

KROGSTAD: Very well. If you're prepared to risk it. But one thing I can do—and at once—

MRS. LINDE (*listens*): Hurry! Go, go! The dance is over. We aren't safe here another moment.

KROGSTAD: I'll wait for you downstairs.

MRS. LINDE: Yes, do. You can see me home.

KROGSTAD: I've never been so happy in my life before!

He goes out through the front door. The door leading from the room into the hall remains open.

1840 MRS. LINDE (*tidies the room a little and gets her hat and coat*): What a change! Oh, what a change! Someone to work for—to live for! A home to bring joy into! I won't let this chance of happiness slip through my fingers. Oh, why don't they come? (*Listens.*) Ah, here they are. I must get my coat on.

She takes her hat and coat. Helmer's and Nora's voices become audible outside. A key is turned in the lock and Helmer leads Nora almost forcibly into the hall. She is dressed in an Italian costume with a large black shawl. He is in evening dress, with a black cloak.

NORA (*still in the doorway, resisting him*): No, no, no—not in here! I want to go back upstairs. I don't want to leave so early.

HELMER: But my dearest Nora—

NORA: Oh, please, Torvald, please! Just another hour!

HELMER: Not another minute, Nora, my sweet. You know what we

1850 agreed. Come along, now. Into the drawing-room. You'll catch cold if you stay out here.

He leads her, despite her efforts to resist him, gently into the room.

MRS. LINDE: Good evening.

NORA: Christine!

HELMER: Oh, hullo, Mrs. Linde. You still here?

MRS. LINDE: Please forgive me. I did so want to see Nora in her costume.

NORA: Have you been sitting here waiting for me?

MRS. LINDE: Yes. I got here too late, I'm afraid. You'd already gone up. And I felt I really couldn't go back home without seeing you.

HELMER (*takes off Nora's shawl*): Well, take a good look at her. She's   1860
worth looking at, don't you think? Isn't she beautiful, Mrs. Linde?

MRS. LINDE: Oh, yes, indeed —

HELMER: Isn't she unbelievably beautiful? Everyone at the party said so. But dreadfully stubborn she is, bless her pretty little heart. What's to be done about that? Would you believe it, I practically had to use force to get her away!

NORA: Oh, Torvald, you're going to regret not letting me stay — just half an hour longer.

HELMER: Hear that, Mrs. Linde? She dances her tarantella — makes a roaring success — and very well deserved — though possibly a trifle   1870
too realistic — more so than was aesthetically necessary, strictly speaking. But never mind that. Main thing is — she had a success — roaring success. Was I going to let her stay on after that and spoil the impression? No, thank you. I took my beautiful little Capri signorina — my capricious little Capricienne, what? — under my arm — a swift round of the ballroom, a curtsey to the company, and, as they say in novels, the beautiful apparition disappeared! An exit should always be dramatic, Mrs. Linde. But unfortunately that's just what I can't get Nora to realize. I say, it's hot in here. (*Throws his cloak on a chair and opens the door to his study.*) What's this? It's   1880
dark in here. Ah, yes, of course — excuse me. (*Goes in and lights a couple of candles.*)

NORA (*whispers swiftly, breathlessly*): Well?

MRS. LINDE (*quietly*): I've spoken to him.

NORA: Yes?

MRS. LINDE: Nora — you must tell your husband everything.

NORA (*dully*): I knew it.

MRS. LINDE: You've nothing to fear from Krogstad. But you must tell him.

NORA: I shan't tell him anything.

MRS. LINDE: Then the letter will.   1890

NORA: Thank you, Christine. Now I know what I must do. Ssh!

HELMER (*returns*): Well, Mrs. Linde, finished admiring her?

MRS. LINDE: Yes. Now I must say goodnight.

HELMER: Oh, already? Does this knitting belong to you?

MRS. LINDE (*takes it*): Thank you, yes. I nearly forgot it.

HELMER: You knit, then?

MRS. LINDE: Why, yes.

HELMER: Know what? You ought to take up embroidery.

MRS. LINDE: Oh? Why?

1900   HELMER: It's much prettier. Watch me, now. You hold the embroidery
in your left hand, like this, and then you take the needle in your
right hand and go in and out in a slow, steady movement—like this.
I am right, aren't I?

MRS. LINDE: Yes, I'm sure—

HELMER: But knitting, now—that's an ugly business—can't help it.
Look—arms all huddled up—great clumsy needles going up and
down—make you look like a damned Chinaman. I say, that really
was a magnificent champagne they served us.

MRS. LINDE: Well, good night, Nora. And stop being stubborn. Re-
1910   member!

HELMER: Quite right, Mrs. Linde!

MRS. LINDE: Good night, Mr. Helmer.

HELMER (*accompanies her to the door*): Good night, good night! I
hope you'll manage to get home all right? I'd gladly—but you
haven't far to go, have you? Good night, good night. (*She goes. He
closes the door behind her and returns.*) Well, we've got rid of her
at last. Dreadful bore that woman is!

NORA: Aren't you very tired, Torvald?

HELMER: No, not in the least.

1920   NORA: Aren't you sleepy?

HELMER: Not a bit. On the contrary, I feel extraordinarily exhilarated.
But what about you? Yes, you look very sleepy and tired.

NORA: Yes, I am very tired. Soon I shall sleep.

HELMER: You see, you see! How right I was not to let you stay longer!

NORA: Oh, you're always right, whatever you do.

HELMER (*kisses her on the forehead*): Now my little songbird's talking
just like real big human being. I say, did you notice how cheerful
Rank was this evening?

NORA: Oh? Was he? I didn't have a chance to speak with him.

1930   HELMER: I hardly did. But I haven't seen him in such a jolly mood for
ages. (*Looks at her for a moment, then comes closer.*) I say, it's nice
to get back to one's home again, and be all alone with you. Upon
my word, you're a distractingly beautiful young woman.

NORA: Don't look at me like that, Torvald!

HELMER: What, not look at my most treasured possession? At all this
wonderful beauty that's mine, mine alone, all mine.

NORA (*goes round to the other side of the table*): You mustn't talk to
me like that tonight.

HELMER (*follows her*): You've still the tarantella in your blood, I see.
1940   And that makes you even more desirable. Listen! Now the other
guests are beginning to go. (*More quietly.*) Nora—soon the whole
house will be absolutely quiet.

NORA: Yes, I hope so.

HELMER: Yes, my beloved Nora, of course you do! Do you know—
when I'm out with you among other people like we were tonight, do

you know why I say so little to you, why I keep so aloof from you, and just throw you an occasional glance? Do you know why I do that? It's because I pretend to myself that you're my secret mistress, my clandestine little sweetheart, and that nobody knows there's anything at all between us.

NORA: Oh, yes, yes, yes—I know you never think of anything but me.

HELMER: And then when we're about to go, and I wrap the shawl round your lovely young shoulders, over this wonderful curve of your neck—then I pretend to myself that you are my young bride, that we've just come from the wedding, that I'm taking you to my house for the first time—that, for the first time, I am alone with you—quite alone with you, as you stand there young and trembling and beautiful. All evening I've had no eyes for anyone but you. When I saw you dance the tarantella, like a huntress, a temptress, my blood grew hot, I couldn't stand it any longer! That was why I seized you and dragged you down here with me—

NORA: Leave me, Torvald! Get away from me! I don't want all this.

HELMER: What? Now, Nora, you're joking with me. Don't want, don't want—? Aren't I your husband—?

There is a knock on the front door.

NORA (*starts*): What was that?

HELMER (*goes toward the hall*): Who is it?

RANK (*outside*): It's me. May I come in for a moment?

HELMER (*quietly, annoyed*): Oh, what does he want now? (*Calls.*) Wait a moment. (*Walks over and opens the door.*) Well! Nice of you not to go by without looking in.

RANK: I thought I heard your voice, so I felt I had to say goodbye. (*His eyes travel swiftly around the room.*) Ah, yes—these dear rooms, how well I know them. What a happy, peaceful home you two have.

HELMER: You seemed to be having a pretty happy time yourself upstairs.

RANK: Indeed I did. Why not? Why shouldn't one make the most of this world? As much as one can, and for as long as one can. The wine was excellent—

HELMER: Especially the champagne.

RANK: You noticed that too? It's almost incredible how much I managed to get down.

NORA: Torvald drank a lot of champagne too, this evening.

RANK: Oh?

NORA: Yes. It always makes him merry afterwards.

RANK: Well, why shouldn't a man have a merry evening after a well-spent day?

HELMER: Well-spent? Oh, I don't know that I can claim that.

RANK (*slaps him across the back*): I can, though, my dear fellow!

1990 NORA: Yes, of course, Dr. Rank—you've been carrying out a scientific experiment today, haven't you?

RANK: Exactly.

HELMER: Scientific experiment! Those are big words for my little Nora to use!

NORA: And may I congratulate you on the finding?

RANK: You may indeed.

NORA: It was good, then?

RANK: The best possible finding—both for the doctor and the patient. Certainty.

2000 NORA (*quickly*): Certainty?

RANK: Absolute certainty. So aren't I entitled to have a merry evening after that?

NORA: Yes, Dr. Rank. You were quite right to.

HELMER: I agree. Provided you don't have to regret it tomorrow.

RANK: Well, you never get anything in this life without paying for it.

NORA: Dr. Rank—you like masquerades, don't you?

RANK: Yes, if the disguises are sufficiently amusing.

NORA: Tell me. What shall we two wear at the next masquerade?

HELMER: You little gadabout! Are you thinking about the next one
2010 already?

RANK: We two? Yes, I'll tell you. You must go as the Spirit of Happiness—

HELMER: You try to think of a costume that'll convey that.

RANK: Your wife need only appear as her normal, everyday self—

HELMER: Quite right! Well said! But what are you going to be? Have you decided that?

RANK: Yes, my dear friend. I have decided that.

HELMER: Well?

RANK: At the next masquerade, I shall be invisible.

2020 HELMER: Well, that's a funny idea.

RANK: There's a big, black hat—haven't you heard of the invisible hat? Once it's over your head, no one can see you any more.

HELMER (*represses a smile*): Ah yes, of course.

RANK: But I'm forgetting what I came for. Helmer, give me a cigar. One of your black Havanas.

HELMER: With the greatest pleasure. (*Offers him the box.*)

RANK (*takes one and cuts off the tip*): Thank you.

NORA (*strikes a match*): Let me give you a light.

RANK: Thank you. (*She holds out the match for him. He lights his ci-*
2030 *gar.*) And now—goodbye.

HELMER: Goodbye, my dear chap, goodbye.

NORA: Sleep well, Dr. Rank.

RANK: Thank you for that kind wish.

NORA: Wish me the same.

RANK: You? Very well—since you ask. Sleep well. And thank you for the light. (*He nods to them both and goes.*)

HELMER (*quietly*): He's been drinking too much.

NORA (*abstractedly*): Perhaps.

Helmer takes his bunch of keys from his pocket and goes out into the hall.

NORA: Torvald, what do you want out there?

HELMER: I must empty the letter-box. It's absolutely full. There'll be no room for the newspapers in the morning. 2040

NORA: Are you going to work tonight?

HELMER: You know very well I'm not. Hullo, what's this? Someone's been at the lock.

NORA: At the lock—?

HELMER: Yes, I'm sure of it. Who on earth—? Surely not one of the maids? Here's a broken hairpin. Nora, it's yours—

NORA (*quickly*): Then it must have been the children.

HELMER: Well, you'll have to break them of that habit. Hm, hm. Ah, that's done it. (*Takes out the contents of the box and calls into the kitchen.*) Helen! Put out the light on the staircase. (*Comes back into the drawing-room with the letters in his hand and closes the door to the hall.*) Look at this! You see how they've piled up? (*Glances through them.*) What on earth's this? 2050

NORA (*at the window*): The letter! Oh, no, Torvald no!

HELMER: Two visiting cards—from Rank.

NORA: From Dr. Rank?

HELMER (*looks at them*): Peter Rank, M.D. They were on top. He must have dropped them in as he left.

NORA: Has he written anything on them?

HELMER: There's a black cross above his name. Look. Rather grue- some, isn't it? It looks just as though he was announcing his death. 2060

NORA: He is.

HELMER: What? Do you know something? Has he told you anything?

NORA: Yes. When these cards come, it means he's said goodbye to us. He wants to shut himself up in his house and die.

HELMER: Ah, poor fellow. I knew I wouldn't be seeing him for much longer. But so soon—! And now he's going to slink away and hide like a wounded beast.

NORA: When the time comes, it's best to go silently. Don't you think so, Torvald? 2070

HELMER (*walks up and down*): He was so much a part of our life. I can't realize that he's gone. His suffering and loneliness seemed to provide a dark background to the happy sunlight of our marriage. Well, perhaps it's best this way. For him, anyway. (*Stops walking.*) And perhaps for us too, Nora. Now we have only each other.

(*Embraces her.*) Oh, my beloved wife—I feel as though I could never hold you close enough. Do you know, Nora, often I wish some terrible danger might threaten you, so that I could offer my life and my blood, everything, for your sake.

2080   NORA (*tears herself loose and says in a clear, firm voice*): Read your letters now, Torvald.

HELMER: No, no. Not tonight. Tonight I want to be with you, my darling wife—

NORA: When your friend is about to die—?

HELMER: You're right. This news has upset us both. An ugliness has come between us; thoughts of death and dissolution. We must try to forget them. Until then—you go to your room; I shall go to mine.

NORA (*throws her arms round his neck*): Good night, Torvald! Good night!

2090   HELMER (*kisses her on the forehead*): Good night, my darling little songbird. Sleep well, Nora. I'll go and read my letters.

He goes into the study with the letters in his hand, and closes the door.

NORA (*wild-eyed, fumbles around, seizes Helmer's cloak, throws it round herself and whispers quickly, hoarsely*): Never see him again. Never. Never. Never. (*Throws the shawl over her head.*) Never see the children again. Them too. Never. Never. Oh—the icy black water! Oh—that bottomless—that—! Oh, if only it were all over! Now he's got it—he's reading it. Oh, no, no! Not yet! Goodbye, Torvald! Goodbye, my darlings!

She turns to run into the hall. As she does so, Helmer throws open his door and stands there with an open letter in his hand.

HELMER: Nora!

NORA (*shrieks*): Ah—!

2100   HELMER: What is this? Do you know what is in this letter?

NORA: Yes, I know. Let me go! Let me go!

HELMER (*holds her back*): Go? Where?

NORA (*tries to tear herself loose*): You mustn't try to save me, Torvald!

HELMER (*staggers back*): Is it true? Is it true, what he writes? Oh, my God! No, no—it's impossible, it can't be true!

NORA: It *is* true. I've loved you more than anything else in the world.

HELMER: Oh, don't try to make silly excuses.

NORA (*takes a step toward him*): Torvald—

HELMER: Wretched woman! What have you done?

2110   NORA: Let me go! You're not going to suffer for my sake. I won't let you!

HELMER: Stop being theatrical. (*Locks the front door.*) You're going to stay here and explain yourself. Do you understand what you've done? Answer me! Do you understand?

NORA (*looks unflinchingly at him and, her expression growing colder, says*): Yes. Now I am beginning to understand.

HELMER (*walking around the room*): Oh, what a dreadful awakening! For eight whole years—she who was my joy and my pride—a hypocrite, a liar—worse, worse—a criminal! Oh, the hideousness of it! Shame on you, shame!

Nora is silent and stares unblinkingly at him.

HELMER (*stops in front of her*): I ought to have guessed that something 2120 of this sort would happen. I should have foreseen it. All your father's recklessness and instability—be quiet!—I repeat, all your father's recklessness and instability he had handed on to you. No religion, no morals, no sense of duty! Oh, how I have been punished for closing my eyes to his faults! I did it for your sake. And now you reward me like this.

NORA: Yes. Like this.

HELMER: Now you have destroyed all my happiness. You have ruined my whole future. Oh, it's too dreadful to contemplate! I am in the power of a man who is completely without scruples. He can do 2130 what he likes with me, demand what he pleases, order me to do anything—I dare not disobey him. I am condemned to humiliation and ruin simply for the weakness of a woman.

NORA: When I am gone from this world, you will be free.

HELMER: Oh, don't be melodramatic. Your father was always ready with that kind of remark. How would it help me if you were "gone from this world," as you put it? It wouldn't assist me in the slightest. He can still make all the facts public; and if he does, I may quite easily be suspected of having been an accomplice in your crime. People may think that I was behind it—that it was I who 2140 encouraged you! And for all this I have to thank you, you whom I have carried on my hands through all the years of our marriage! Now do you realize what you've done to me?

NORA (*coldly calm*): Yes.

HELMER: It's so unbelievable I can hardly credit it. But we must try to find some way out. Take off that shawl. Take it off, I say! I must try to buy him off somehow. This thing must be hushed up at any price. As regards our relationship—we must appear to be living together just as before. Only *appear*, of course. You will therefore continue to reside here. That is understood. But the children shall be 2150 taken out of your hands. I dare no longer entrust them to you. Oh, to have to say this to the woman I once loved so dearly—and whom I still—! Well, all that must be finished. Henceforth there can be no question of happiness; we must merely strive to save what shreds and tatters—(*The front bell rings. Helmer starts.*) What can that be? At this hour? Surely not—? He wouldn't—? Hide yourself, Nora. Say you're ill.

Nora does not move. Helmer goes to the door of the room and opens it. The maid is standing half-dressed in the hall.

MAID: A letter for madam.

HELMER: Give it to me. (*Seizes the letter and shuts the door.*) Yes, it's from him. You're not having it. I'll read this myself.

NORA: Read it.

HELMER (*by the lamp*): I hardly dare to. This may mean the end for us both. No, I must know. (*Tears open the letter hastily; reads a few lines; looks at a piece of paper which is enclosed with it; utters a cry of joy.*) Nora! (*She looks at him questioningly.*) Nora! No—I must read it once more. Yes, yes, it's true! I am saved! Nora, I am saved!

NORA: What about me?

HELMER: You too, of course. We're both saved, you and I. Look! He's returning your I.O.U. He writes that he is sorry for what has happened—a happy accident has changed his life—oh, what does it matter what he writes? We are saved, Nora! No one can harm you now. Oh, Nora, Nora—no, first let me destroy this filthy thing. Let me see—! (*Glances at the I.O.U.*) No, I don't want to look at it. I shall merely regard the whole business as a dream. (*He tears the I.O.U. and both letters into pieces, throws them into the stove, and watches them burn.*) There. Now they're destroyed. He wrote that ever since Christmas Eve you've been—oh, these must have been three dreadful days for you, Nora.

NORA: Yes. It's been a hard fight.

HELMER: It must have been terrible—seeing no way out except—no, we'll forget the whole sordid business. We'll just be happy and go on telling ourselves over and over again: "It's over! It's over!" Listen to me, Nora. You don't seem to realize. It's over! Why are you looking so pale? Ah, my poor little Nora, I understand. You can't believe that I have forgiven you. But I have, Nora. I swear it to you. I have forgiven you everything. I know that what you did you did for your love of me.

NORA: That is true.

HELMER: You have loved me as a wife should love her husband. It was simply that in your inexperience you chose the wrong means. But do you think I love you any the less because you don't know how to act on your own initiative? No, no. Just lean on me. I shall counsel you. I shall guide you. I would not be a true man if your feminine helplessness did not make you doubly attractive in my eyes. You mustn't mind the hard words I said to you in those first dreadful moments when my whole world seemed to be tumbling about my ears. I have forgiven you, Nora. I swear it to you; I have forgiven you.

NORA: Thank you for your forgiveness.

She goes out through the door, right.

HELMER: No, don't go—(*Looks in.*) What are you doing there?

NORA (*offstage*): Taking off my fancy dress.

HELMER (*by the open door*): Yes, do that. Try to calm yourself and get your balance again, my frightened little songbird. Don't be afraid. I have broad wings to shield you. (*Begins to walk around near the door.*) How lovely and peaceful this little home of ours is, Nora. You are safe here; I shall watch over you like a hunted dove which I have snatched unharmed from the claws of the falcon. Your wildly beating little heart shall find peace with me. It will happen, Nora; it will take time, but it will happen, believe me. Tomorrow all this will seem quite different. Soon everything will be as it was before. I shall no longer need to remind you that I have forgiven you; your own heart will tell you that it is true. Do you really think I could ever bring myself to disown you, or even to reproach you? Ah, Nora, you don't understand what goes on in a husband's heart. There is something indescribably wonderful and satisfying for a husband in knowing that he has forgiven his wife—forgiven her unreservedly, from the bottom of his heart. It means that she has become his property in a double sense; he has, as it were, brought her into the world anew; she is now not only his wife but also his child. From now on that is what you shall be to me, my poor, helpless, bewildered little creature. Never be frightened of anything again, Nora. Just open your heart to me. I shall be both your will and your conscience. What's this? Not in bed? Have you changed?

NORA (*in her everyday dress*): Yes, Torvald. I've changed.

HELMER: But why now—so late—?

NORA: I shall not sleep tonight.

HELMER: But, my dear Nora—

NORA (*looks at her watch*): It isn't that late. Sit down here, Torvald. You and I have a lot to talk about.

She sits down on one side of the table.

HELMER: Nora, what does this mean? You look quite drawn—

NORA: Sit down. It's going to take a long time. I've a lot to say to you.

HELMER (*sits down on the other side of the table*): You alarm me, Nora. I don't understand you.

NORA: No, that's just it. You don't understand me. And I've never understood you—until this evening. No, don't interrupt me. Just listen to what I have to say. You and I have got to face facts, Torvald.

HELMER: What do you mean by that?

NORA (*after a short silence*): Doesn't anything strike you about the way we're sitting here?

HELMER: What?

NORA: We've been married for eight years. Does it occur to you that this is the first time that we two, you and I, man and wife, have ever had a serious talk together?

HELMER: Serious? What do you mean, serious?

NORA: In eight whole years—no, longer—ever since we first met—we have never exchanged a serious word on a serious subject.

HELMER: Did you expect me to drag you into all my worries—worries you couldn't possibly have helped me with?

NORA: I'm not talking about worries. I'm simply saying that we have never sat down seriously to try to get to the bottom of anything.

HELMER: But, my dear Nora, what on earth has that got to do with you?

NORA: That's just the point. You have never understood me. A great wrong has been done to me, Torvald. First by Papa, and then by you.

HELMER: What? But we two have loved you more than anyone in the world!

NORA (*shakes her head*): You have never loved me. You just thought it was fun to be in love with me.

HELMER: Nora, what kind of a way is this to talk?

NORA: It's the truth, Torvald. When I lived with Papa, he used to tell me what he thought about everything, so that I never had any opinions but his. And if I did have any of my own, I kept them quiet, because he wouldn't have liked them. He called me his little doll, and he played with me just the way I played with my dolls. Then I came here to live in your house.

HELMER: What kind of a way is that to describe our marriage?

NORA (*undisturbed*): I mean, then I passed from Papa's hands into yours. You arranged everything the way you wanted it, so that I simply took over your taste in everything—or pretended I did—I don't really know—I think it was a little of both—first one and then the other. Now I look back on it, it's as if I've been living here like a pauper, from hand to mouth. I performed tricks for you, and you gave me food and drink. But that was how you wanted it. You and Papa have done me a great wrong. It's your fault that I have done nothing with my life.

HELMER: Nora, how can you be so unreasonable and ungrateful? Haven't you been happy here?

NORA: No; never. I used to think I was; but I haven't ever been happy.

HELMER: Not—not happy?

NORA: No. I've just had fun. You've always been very kind to me. But our home has never been anything but a playroom. I've been your doll-wife, just as I used to be Papa's doll-child. And the children have been my dolls. I used to think it was fun when you came in and played with me, just as they think it's fun when I go in and play games with them. That's all our marriage has been, Torvald.

HELMER: There may be a little truth in what you say, though you exaggerate and romanticize. But from now on it'll be different. Playtime is over. Now the time has come for education.

NORA: Whose education? Mine or the children's?

HELMER: Both yours and the children's, my dearest Nora.

NORA: Oh, Torvald, you're not the man to educate me into being the right wife for you.   2290

HELMER: How can you say that?

NORA: And what about me? Am I fit to educate the children?

HELMER: Nora!

NORA: Didn't you say yourself a few minutes ago that you dare not leave them in my charge?

HELMER: In a moment of excitement. Surely you don't think I meant it seriously?

NORA: Yes. You were perfectly right. I'm not fitted to educate them. There's something else I must do first. I must educate myself. And   2300 you can't help me with that. It's something I must do by myself. That's why I'm leaving you.

HELMER (*jumps up*): What did you say?

NORA: I must stand on my own feet if I am to find out the truth about myself and about life. So I can't go on living here with you any longer.

HELMER: Nora, Nora!

NORA: I'm leaving you now, at once. Christine will put me up for to-night—

HELMER: You're out of your mind! You can't do this! I forbid you!   2310

NORA: It's no use your trying to forbid me any more. I shall take with me nothing but what is mine. I don't want anything from you, now or ever.

HELMER: What kind of madness is this?

NORA: Tomorrow I shall go home—I mean, to where I was born. It'll be easiest for me to find some kind of job there.

HELMER: But you're blind! You've no experience of the world—

NORA: I must try to get some, Torvald.

HELMER: But to leave your home, your husband, your children! Have you thought what people will say?   2320

NORA: I can't help that. I only know that I must do this.

HELMER: But this is monstrous! Can you neglect your most sacred duties?

NORA: What do you call my most sacred duties?

HELMER: Do I have to tell you? Your duties towards your husband, and your children.

NORA: I have another duty which is equally sacred.

HELMER: You have not. What on earth could that be?

NORA: My duty towards myself.

HELMER: First and foremost you are a wife and a mother.   2330

NORA: I don't believe that any longer. I believe that I am first and foremost a human being, like you—or anyway, that I must try to become one. I know most people think as you do, Torvald, and I know there's something of the sort to be found in books. But I'm no longer prepared to accept what people say and what's written in books. I must think things out for myself, and try to find my own answer.

HELMER: Do you need to ask where your duty lies in your own home? Haven't you an infallible guide in such matters—your religion?

NORA: Oh, Torvald, I don't really know what religion means.

HELMER: What are you saying?

NORA: I only know what Pastor Hansen told me when I went to confirmation. He explained that religion meant this and that. When I get away from all this and can think things out on my own, that's one of the questions I want to look into. I want to find out whether what Pastor Hansen said was right—or anyway, whether it is right for me.

HELMER: But it's unheard of for so young a woman to behave like this! If religion cannot guide you, let me at least appeal to your conscience. I presume you have some moral feelings left? Or—perhaps you haven't? Well, answer me.

NORA: Oh, Torvald, that isn't an easy question to answer. I simply don't know. I don't know where I am in these matters. I only know that these things mean something quite different to me from what they do to you. I've learned now that certain laws are different from what I'd imagined them to be; but I can't accept that such laws can be right. Has a woman really not the right to spare her dying father pain, or save her husband's life? I can't believe that.

HELMER: You're talking like a child. You don't understand how society works.

NORA: No, I don't. But now I intend to learn. I must try to satisfy myself which is right, society or I.

HELMER: Nora, you're ill; you're feverish. I almost believe you're out of your mind.

NORA: I've never felt so sane and sure in my life.

HELMER: You feel sure that it is right to leave your husband and your children?

NORA: Yes. I do.

HELMER: Then there is only one possible explanation.

NORA: What?

HELMER: That you don't love me any longer.

NORA: No, that's exactly it.

HELMER: Nora! How can you say this to me?

NORA: Oh, Torvald, it hurts me terribly to have to say it, because you've always been so kind to me. But I can't help it. I don't love you any longer.

HELMER (*controlling his emotions with difficulty*): And you feel quite sure about this too?

NORA: Yes, absolutely sure. That's why I can't go on living here any longer. 2380

HELMER: Can you also explain why I have lost your love?

NORA: Yes, I can. It happened this evening, when the miracle failed to happen. It was then that I realized you weren't the man I'd thought you to be.

HELMER: Explain more clearly. I don't understand you.

NORA: I've waited so patiently, for eight whole years—well, good heavens, I'm not such a fool as to suppose that miracles occur every day. Then this dreadful thing happened to me, and then I *knew:* "Now the miracle will take place!" When Krogstad's letter was lay- 2390 ing out there, it never occurred to me for a moment that you would let that man trample over you. I *knew* that you would say to him: "Publish the facts to the world." And when he had done this—

HELMER: Yes, what then? When I'd exposed my wife's name to shame and scandal—

NORA: Then I was certain that you would step forward and take all the blame on yourself, and say: "I am the one who is guilty!"

HELMER: Nora!

NORA: You're thinking I wouldn't have accepted such a sacrifice from you? No, of course I wouldn't! But what would my word have counted for against yours? That was the miracle I was hoping for, 2400 and dreading. And it was to prevent it happening that I wanted to end my life.

HELMER: Nora, I would gladly work for you night and day, and en- dure sorrow and hardship for your sake. But no man can be ex- pected to sacrifice his honor, even for the person he loves.

NORA: Millions of women have done it.

HELMER: Oh, you think and talk like a stupid child.

NORA: That may be. But you neither think nor talk like the man I could share my life with. Once you'd got over your fright—and you weren't frightened of what might threaten me, but only of what 2410 threatened you—once the danger was past, then as far as you were concerned it was exactly as though nothing had happened. I was your little songbird just as before—your doll whom henceforth you would take particular care to protect from the world because she was so weak and fragile. (*Gets up.*) Torvald, in that moment I real- ized that for eight years I had been living here with a complete stranger, and had borne him three children—! Oh, I can't bear to think of it! I could tear myself to pieces!

HELMER (*sadly*): I see it, I see it. A gulf has indeed opened between us. Oh, but Nora—couldn't it be bridged? 2420

NORA: As I am now, I am no wife for you.

HELMER: I have the strength to change.

NORA: Perhaps—if your doll is taken from you.

HELMER: But to be parted—to be parted from you! No, no, Nora, I can't conceive of it happening!

NORA (*goes into the room, right*): All the more necessary that it should happen.

She comes back with her outdoor things and a small traveling bag, which she puts down on a chair by the table.

HELMER: Nora, Nora, not now! Wait till tomorrow!

2430   NORA (*puts on her coat*): I can't spend the night in a strange man's house.

HELMER: But can't we live here as brother and sister, then—?

NORA (*fastens her hat*): You know quite well it wouldn't last. (*Puts on her shawl.*) Goodbye, Torvald. I don't want to see the children. I know they're in better hands than mine. As I am now, I can be nothing to them.

HELMER: But some time, Nora—some time—?

NORA: How can I tell? I've no idea what will happen to me.

HELMER: But you are my wife, both as you are and as you will be.

2440   NORA: Listen, Torvald. When a wife leaves her husband's house, as I'm doing now, I'm told that according to the law he is freed of any obligations towards her. In any case, I release you from any such obligations. You mustn't feel bound to me in any way, however small, just as I shall not feel bound to you. We must both be quite free. Here is your ring back. Give me mine.

HELMER: That too?

NORA: That too.

HELMER: Here it is.

NORA: Good. Well, now it's over. I'll leave the keys here. The servants know about everything to do with the house—much better than I

2450   do. Tomorrow, when I have left town, Christine will come to pack the things I brought here from home. I'll have them sent on after me.

HELMER: This is the end then! Nora, will you never think of me any more?

NORA: Yes, of course. I shall often think of you and the children and this house.

HELMER: May I write to you, Nora?

NORA: No. Never. You mustn't do that.

HELMER: But at least you must let me send you—

NORA: Nothing. Nothing.

2460   HELMER: But if you should need help?—

NORA: I tell you, no. I don't accept things from strangers.

HELMER: Nora—can I never be anything but a stranger to you?

NORA (*picks up her bag*): Oh, Torvald! Then the miracle of miracles would have to happen.

HELMER: The miracle of miracles?

NORA: You and I would both have to change so much that—oh, Torvald, I don't believe in miracles any longer.

HELMER: But I want to believe in them. Tell me. We should have to change so much that—?

NORA: That life together between us two could become a marriage. 2470 Goodbye.

She goes out through the hall.

HELMER (*sinks down on a chair by the door and buries his face in his hands*): Nora! Nora! (*Looks round and gets up.*) Empty! She's gone! (*A hope strikes him.*) The miracle of miracles—?

The street door is slammed shut downstairs.

❑ Questions for Discussion
Act I

1. Why does Nora want money for her Christmas gift?

2. When Torvald says, "I wouldn't wish my darling little songbird to be any different from what she is," what are the qualities which he admires in Nora?

3. From the opening scene of the play until the last scene, Nora lies to Torvald. Why?

4. In what ways is Christine Linde a **dramatic foil** for Nora?

5. Why has Torvald not made a lot of money as a lawyer? In what ways does the knowledge of his attitude toward clients **foreshadow** his reaction to Nora's revelation?

6. Nora says of Torvald, ". . . he's so proud of being a *man*—it'd be so painful and humiliating for him to know that he owed anything to me." What attitudes does Nora here reveal about male-female relationships?

7. Examine Torvald's statements about Krogstad near the end of act I. How do these opinions foreshadow Torvald's reaction to Nora's revelation in act III?

Act II

1. Explain the **irony** of Torvald's statement: "When the real crisis comes, you will not find me lacking in strength or courage. I am man enough to bear the burden for us both."

2. Why does Dr. Rank refuse to let Torvald visit him in the hospital?

3. Explain Nora's statement to Dr. Rank that ". . . there are some people whom one loves, and others whom it's almost more fun to be with."

Act III

1. Why does Christine tell Krogstad *not* to take his letter back?

2. Explain Nora's statement to Torvald: "You don't understand me. And I've never understood you—until this evening."

3. Why would Nora's statement that she has a duty toward herself be so astonishing to a nineteenth-century audience? What would be the probable reaction of an audience today?

4. In what ways is Nora's situation at the end of the play more difficult than it would be for a woman today?

5. List the pet names that Torvald calls Nora and explain the implications of each.

6. Explain the significance of the play's title.

On The Poet's Vision[1]
(1874)

1   ... My private relations I have never made the direct subject of any poetical work. In the earlier hard times these relations were of less importance to me than I have afterwards often been able to justify to myself. When the nest of the eider duck was robbed the first and second and third time, it was of illusions and of great hopes of life that it was robbed. When at festival gatherings I have been sensible of recollections like the bear in the hands of his tamer, it has been because I have been co-responsible in a time which buried a glorious thought amid song and feasting.

2   And what is it then that constitutes a poet? As for me, it was long time before I realized that to be a poet, that is chiefly to see, but mark well, to see in such a manner that the thing seen is perceived by his audience just as the poet saw it. But thus is seen and thus is appreciated that only which has been lived through. And as regards the thing which has been lived through, that is just the secret of the literature of modern times. All that I have written, these last ten years, I have, mentally, lived through. But no poet lives through anything isolated. What he lives through all of his countrymen live through together with him. For if that were not so, what would establish the bridge of understanding between the producing and the receiving mind?

3   And what is it, then, that I have lived through and written on? The range has been large. Partly, I have written on that which only by

[1] Henrik Ibsen, *Speeches and New Letters*, trans. Arne Kildal (Boston, 1910), 319–20. Rpt. in Barrett H. Clark, ed. *European Theories of the Drama*, rev. ed. (New York: Crown Pub., 1918), 319–20.

glimpses and at my best moments I have felt stirring vividly within me as something great and beautiful. I have written on that which, so to speak, has stood higher than my daily self, and I have written on this in order to fasten it over against and within myself.

But I have also written on the opposite, on that which to introspective ⁴ contemplation appears as the dregs and sediment of one's own nature. The work of writing has in this case been to me like a bath which I have felt to leave cleaner, healthier, and freer. Yes, gentlemen, nobody can poetically present that to which he has not to a certain degree and at least at times the model within himself. And who is the man among us who has not now and then felt and acknowledged within himself a contradiction between word and action, between will and task, between life and teaching on the whole? Or who is there among us who has not, at least in some cases, selfishly been sufficient unto himself, and half unconsciously, half in good faith, has extenuated this conduct both to others and to himself?

. . . A poet by nature belongs to the far-sighted. Never have I seen the ⁵ fatherland and the actual life of the fatherland so fully, so clearly, and at a closer range than just from afar and during my absence. . . .

To The Norwegian Women's Rights League[1]
(1898)

I am not a member of the Women's Rights League. Whatever I have written has been without any conscious thought of making propaganda. I have been more poet and less social philosopher than people generally seem inclined to believe. I thank you for the toast, but must disclaim the honor of having consciously worked for the women's rights movement. I am not even quite clear as to just what this women's rights movement really is. To me it has seemed a problem of humanity in general. And if you read my books carefully you will understand this. True enough, it is desirable to solve the problem of women's rights, along with all the others; but that has not been the whole purpose. My task has been the *description of humanity*. To be sure, whenever such a description is felt to be reasonably true, the reader will insert his own feelings and sentiments into the work of the poet. These are attributed to the poet; but incorrectly so. Every reader remolds it so beautifully and nicely, each according to his own personality. Not only those who write, but also those who read are poets; they are collaborators; they are often more poetical than the poet himself. . . .

---

[1] Henrik Ibsen, *Speeches and New Letters*, trans. Arne Kildal (Boston, 1910), 320. Rpt. in Barrett H. Clark, ed., *European Theories of the Drama*, rev. ed. (New York: Crown Pub., 1918), 320.

from *Catiline's Dream*[1]

by James Hurt

Considering the tumultuous reception of *A Doll's House* as a major feminist document, Ibsen's words at a banquet given in his honor twenty years later by the Norwegian League for Women's Rights are rather surprising: "I am not a member of the Women's Rights League. Whatever I have written has been without any conscious thought of making propaganda. I have been more the poet and less the social philosopher than people generally seem inclined to believe. I thank you for the toast, but must disclaim the honor of having consciously worked for the women's rights movement. I am not even quite clear as to just what this women's rights movement really is. To me it has seemed a problem of mankind in general."

In *A Doll's House,* as in the other realistic plays, the "problem submitted to debate" is less fundamental to the action than the "problem of mankind in general" which underlies it: the struggle of the individual for liberation from the forces in his own character that hold him captive. Ibsen once wrote to Brandes that the fact that Brand was a priest was not important, he could equally well have been a sculptor or a politician. *A Doll's House* demonstrates that he could also have been a woman, for Nora's struggle with herself is fundamentally very much like Brand's self-conflict.

Such an interpretation is implicit in the opening scene of the play. No gloss on Norwegian marriage laws or nineteenth-century family life can explain why an apparently high-spirited young woman like Nora would submit to Helmer's repellent combination of bullying and baby-talk. Yet she humiliates herself by sneaking forbidden macaroons, begging for money, and playing "larks and squirrels" for the benefit of her insufferable husband. We very soon suspect what is later confirmed in the play: that Nora's childish behavior as a doll in a doll's house is not merely a role forced on her from without, but one which she herself has adopted to present to the outside world, including Helmer, while she lives a secret, inner life of her own.

We learn something of the origins of Nora's personality in her last-act conversation with Helmer, when she recalls her childhood:

NORA: A great wrong has been done to me, Torvald. First by Papa, and then by you. . . . When I lived with Papa, he used to tell me what he thought about everything, so that I never had any opinions but his. And if I did have any of my own, I kept them quiet, because he wouldn't have liked them. He called me his little doll, and he played with me just the way I played with my dolls. Then I came here to live in your house—

---

[1] James Hurt, *Catiline's Dream: An Essay on Ibsen's Plays* (Urbana: University of Illinois Press, 1972), 103–9.

TORVALD: What kind of a way is that to describe our marriage?
NORA *(undisturbed)*: I mean, then I passed from Papa's hands into
  yours. You arranged everything the way you wanted it, so that I
  simply took over your taste in everything—or pretended I did—I
  don't really know—I think it was a little of both—first one and then
  the other. Now I look back on it, it's as if I've been living here like
  a pauper, from hand to mouth. I performed tricks for you, and you
  gave me food and drink. But that was how you wanted it. You and
  Papa have done me a great wrong. It's your fault that I have done
  nothing with my life.

Nora emphasizes in this speech the stifling of her intellectual development in her childhood home and in Helmer's home, but as she half-
realizes, the psychological damage has been much greater than this. The
undercurrent of unconscious sexuality in Nora's descriptions here and
elsewhere of her relationship with her father is reminiscent of the combination of playfulness and flirtatiousness in the relationship between
Peer Gynt and Aase. Like Peer, Nora has found refuge from "troublesome thoughts" in compulsive fantasizing and role-playing. A surrogate
for her dead mother in her father's household, she felt deeply inadequate;
in a parallel situation, Peer Gynt dreams of being an emperor, Nora has
tried to remain a child.

Nora's primary home with her father became a tomb world for her; the
metaphor she chooses for it, "a doll's house," sums up its psychic threat
of turning her into an inanimate object, a "doll" without an identity of
its own. The home she found with Helmer during the early days of their
marriage was simply a continuation of this tomb world; she passed from
being a doll-child into being a doll-wife.

The first crisis in this situation was the trip to Italy, a year after
their marriage, and the circumstances surrounding it. Torvald became ill from overwork and the doctor told Nora that he had to go
to a warmer climate; his condition had to be kept a secret from Torvald, however. Nora begged Torvald to take her to Italy, but he refused, saying that she was "frivolous" and that it was his duty not to
"pander to her moods and caprices." Her father was seriously ill at the
time and died shortly thereafter, so she was unable to turn to him for
help. Her solution was to borrow the money, forging her father's name
to the note as security for the debt. By the time of the play, she has been
slowly repaying the debt over the period of six years since their return from Italy, using money saved from household accounts and from
secret jobs.

The most significant part of this sequence of events is Nora's attitudes
and motivations, as she reveals them to Christine Linde in Act I. She has
kept the debt a secret from Torvald even after his recovery because she
sees the secret as something to keep in reserve to help preserve her
marriage:

MRS. LINDE: Will you never tell him?

NORA *(thoughtfully, half-smiling)*: Yes—some time, perhaps. Years
   from now, when I'm no longer pretty. You mustn't laugh! I mean of
   course, when Torvald no longer loves me as he does now; when it
   no longer amuses him to see me dance and dress up and play the
   fool for him. Then it might be useful to have something up my
   sleeve.
   (Breaks off.) Stupid, stupid, stupid! That time will never come.

Nora's decision at the time of her husband's illness thus assumes much
broader implications than the immediate, practical ones. She has committed herself to preserving her marriage by playing the childlike role that
Torvald seems to want and by holding in reserve the secret of the loan for
the time when she can no longer keep his affection by the role-playing.
The other side of this decision is the rejection of the possibility of telling
Torvald the truth and thus demanding that he accept her as a mature
human being with whom he can enter into a mature relationship.

Nora's decision to borrow the money secretly constitutes the kind of
fundamental life-choice involved in a mythic ascent to the heights.
Threatened by the external forces which are turning her into a "doll," she
withdraws into her inner world and arms herself with a project of the
will, a source of personal security though it involves the rejection of free
and mature love.

Nora's inner division is represented by the antithetical figures of the
two men in her life: Helmer and Dr. Rank, the masculine correlative
of the gentle woman and fascinating woman figures in the earlier plays.
Helmer thinks of himself in sharp contrast to Nora's father; several
times in the course of the play, he expresses contempt for his father-in-
law's irresponsibility with money. In his anger after reading Krogstad's
letter, he tells Nora, "I ought to have guessed that something of this sort
would happen. I should have foreseen it. All your father's recklessness and instability—be quiet!—I repeat, all your father's recklessness
and instability he has handed on to you. No religion, no morals, no sense
of duty!"

Nevertheless, it is obvious that Helmer is closely identified with Nora's
father; as Nora herself comes to realize, he has taken over her father's
role with almost no break. The paternal elements in his relationship with
Nora lend a sinister undercurrent to their sexual relationship. The "larks
and squirrels" game seems to arouse him sexually, as does his fantasy of
deflowering the innocent:

HELMER: . . . I pretend to myself that you are my young bride, that
   we've just come from the wedding, that I'm taking you to my house
   for the first time—that, for the first time, I am alone with you—
   quite alone with you, as you stand there young and trembling and
   beautiful.

Nora, however, does not acknowledge the identification of Torvald with her father until after the insight she gains into their relationship when Torvald reads Krogstad's letter. It is Dr. Rank whom she has associated with dangerous and thrilling sexuality. She plays the same childish role with Rank that she does with her husband, and she refuses to acknowledge even to herself the powerful undercurrent of sexuality in their relationship, until after his open declaration of love in Act II. Sensual and diseased from birth, he suggests the sensuality which Nora has rejected for herself in her decision upon the heights.

The play opens, in accordance with the retrospective technique which Ibsen adopted for all the realistic plays, at a point just before the final collapse of the project of the will. Nora has been pursuing her project of the will for six years, and although she tells Mrs. Linde, "These last eight years have been such a happy time for me," she betrays the strain of her life in a number of ways, including the slightly hysterical edge to her "playful" relationship with Torvald.

That her secondary home has become a tomb world is visually suggested by the setting and lighting. The Helmer doll's house is actually an apartment on the lower floor of an apartment building. The Stenborg apartment, where the fancy-dress ball is held, is on an upper floor. It is Christmas time and bitterly cold outside; the Helmer doors and windows are kept tightly shut and the continually burning fire in the stove keeps the room overheated, as Nora, and even Helmer, complain several times. The first two acts take place in the early evening, the third late at night, and the room is dimly lighted by lamps throughout. During Act II, as Nora's possible avenues of escape are cut off, one by one, leaving her only the prospect of suicide, as she thinks, the room "begins to grow dark." When Nora realizes that Dr. Rank is in love with her and that she cannot borrow money from him, she quietly calls, "Helen, bring the lamp." Through the rest of this act and the following act, the lamp stands on the table, a small pool of light in the otherwise shadowy room. Nora and Helmer alternately approach this focal point and withdraw from it, as they work out their relationship. Helmer tends to turn lights out—he shouts to the maid to "put out the light on the staircase" just before he launches into his denunciation of Nora after reading Krogstad's letter—but Nora forces him to sit down with her by the lamp for their final confrontation. The dark, claustrophobic "doll's house" thus comes to suggest Nora's frightening inner world, as Brand's similarly stifling parsonage comes to suggest his, and in *A Doll's House,* as in *Brand,* the dim flame of the lamp suggests the threatened self.

The final collapse of Nora's project of the will comes with Torvald's reaction to Krogstad's letter revealing her forgery. She has built up an elaborate private fantasy of what would happen when Torvald learned the truth; in their final conversation she reveals it to Torvald:

NORA: I've waited so patiently, for eight whole years—well, good
   heavens, I'm not such a fool as to suppose that miracles occur
   every day. Then this dreadful thing happened to me, and then I
   knew: "Now the miracle will take place!" When Krogstad's letter
   was lying out there, it never occurred to me for a moment that
   you would let that man trample over you. I *knew* that you would
   say to him: "Publish the facts to the world." And when he had done
   this—
HELMER: Yes, what then? When I'd exposed my wife's name to shame
   and scandal—
NORA: Then I was certain that you would step forward and take all
   the blame on yourself, and say: "I am the one who is guilty!"

Helmer's reaction, of course, is totally different; he flies into a fury and
wildly attacks Nora for "condemning him to humiliation and ruin simply
for the weakness of a woman."

Nora's transformation at this point is parallel to Brand's when he
decides to "march under my own flag, even if none will follow" and
begins his ascent to the peaks. And the end of the play contains
many muted reminiscences of Brand's ascent to the peaks. Nora at
first "is silent and stares unblinkingly at him." Then she quietly goes
out and changes into her everyday clothes from her party costume. "What's this? Not in bed?" cries Torvald when she reenters. "Have
you changed?" She answers, "Yes, Torvald. I've changed." The conversation that follows is full of suggestions of death and rebirth. Nora
renounces the whole previous course of her life—as Brand does before the Ice Church—strips herself of all ties to Torvald including
his ring, and declares her intention of beginning her life over as a mature human being. The death of the old Nora is suggested in the
mythic "child-death" of the threat to her three children whom she is
abandoning. And her spectacular final exit, with its famous slamming door, is out of the stifling tomb world of the doll's house into the
December snow that recalls Brand's mountain peaks. Dawn is breaking as Nora renounces "upon the peaks" not merely the social pressures that have kept her a captive in her marriage but the psychological division that has made her a willing collaborator in her own imprisonment.

   A Doll's House is representative of Ibsen's realistic plays not only in
its focus upon a "problem for debate" and in its tight, closed construction, but also in the interplay it sets up between its social and psychological levels. The plot is logical and credible and the characters are
provided with explicit, conscious motivations for all their actions, but
there is more to the play than the brilliance of its surface structure. It
gains depth and power from the myth of the self which underlie the overt
plot and which gives Nora, unpretentious as she is, the stature of a
mythic figure.

The Doll's House *Backlash:*
Criticism, Feminism, and Ibsen[1]

by Joan Templeton

It is simply not true that Ibsen was not interested in feminism. It is also not true that "there is no indication that Ibsen was thinking of writing a feminist play when he first began to work seriously on *A Doll House* in the summer of 1879" (Valency 150). In the spring of that year, while Ibsen was planning his play, a scandalous incident, easily available in the biographies, took place that proves not only Ibsen's interest in women's rights but his passionate support for the movement. Ibsen had made two proposals to the Scandinavian Club in Rome, where he was living: that the post of librarian be opened to women candidates and that women be allowed to vote in club meetings. In the debate on the proposal, he made a long, occasionally eloquent speech, part of which follows:

> Is there anyone in this gathering who dares assert that our ladies are inferior to us in culture, or intelligence, or knowledge, or artistic talent? I don't think that many men would dare suggest that. Then what is it men fear? I hear there is a tradition here that women are cunning intriguers, and that therefore we don't want them. Well, I have encountered a good deal of male intrigue in my time. . . .
>
> (M. Meyer 449)

Ibsen's first proposal was accepted, the second not, failing by one vote. He left the club in a cold rage. A few days later, he astonished his compatriots by appearing at a gala evening. People thought he was penitent. But he was planning a surprise: facing the ballroom and its dancing couples, he interrupted the music to make a terrible scene, haranguing the celebrants with a furious tirade. He had tried to bring them progress, he shouted, but their cowardly resistance had refused it. The women were especially contemptible, for it was for them he had tried to fight. A Danish countess fainted and had to be removed, but Ibsen continued, growing more and more violent. Gunnar Heiberg, who was present, later gave this account of the event:

> As his voice thundered it was as though he were clarifying his own thoughts, as his tongue chastised it was as though his spirit were scouring the darkness in search of his present spiritual goal—his poem [*A Doll House*]—as though he were personally bringing out his theories, incarnating his characters. And when he was done, he went out into the hall, took his overcoat and walked home.
>
> (M. Meyer 450)

---

[1] Joan Templeton, "The *Doll's House* Backlash: Criticism, Feminism, and Ibsen," *PMLA* 104 (1989): 28–40.

In 1884, five years after *A Doll House* had made Ibsen a recognized champion of the feminist cause, he joined with H. E. Berner, president of the Norwegian Women's Rights League, and with his fellow Norwegian writers Bjornson, Lie, and Kielland, in signing a petition to the Storting, the Norwegian parliament, urging the passage of a bill establishing separate property rights for married women. When he returned the petition to Bjornson, Ibsen wryly commented that the Storting should not be interested in men's opinions: "To consult men in such a matter is like asking wolves if they desire better protection for the sheep" (*Letters* 228). He also spoke of his fears that the current campaign for universal suffrage would come to nothing. The solution, which he despaired of seeing, would be the formation of a "strong, resolute progressive party" that would include in its goals "the statutory improvement of the position of woman" (229).

It is foolish to apply the formalist notion that art is never sullied by argument to Ibsen's middle-period plays, written at a time when he was an out-spoken and direct fighter in what he called the "mortal combat between two epochs" (*Letters* 123). Ibsen was fiercely his own man, refusing all his life to be claimed by organizations or campaigns of many sorts, including the Women's Rights League and the movement to remove the mark of Sweden from the Norwegian flag. And he had a deeply conservative streak where manners were concerned (except when he lost his temper), for he was acutely suspicious of show. Temperamentally, Ibsen was a loner. But he was also, as Georg Brandes declared, "a born polemist" (47). While it is true that Ibsen never reduced life to "ideas," it is equally true that he was passionately interested in the events and ideas of his day. He was as deeply anchored in his time as any writer has been before or since. Writing to his German translator a year after the publication of *A Doll House*, Ibsen offered one of the truest self-appraisals a writer has ever made:

> Everything that I have written is intimately connected with what I have lived through, even if I have not lived it myself. Every new work has served me as emancipation and catharsis; for none of us can escape the responsibility and the guilt of the society to which we belong.
>
> (Hundreårsutgave 402; my trans.)

Works Cited

Ibsen, Henrik. *Hundreårsutgave. Henrik Ibsens Samlede Verker.* Ed. Francis Bull, Halvdan Koht, and Didrik Arup Seip. Vol. 17. Oslo: Gyldendal, 1946. 21 vols. 1928–58.

——. *Letters and Speeches.* Ed. and trans. Evert Sprinchorn. New York: Hill, 1964.

Meyer, Michael. *Ibsen.* Garden City: Doubleday, 1971.

Hats Off to Ibsen
Teresa Cochran
English 102

Henrik Ibsen's A Doll's House, published in 1879, was a topic of "worldwide controversy" (Hurt 102). Critics debated whether Ibsen was a defender of women's rights. Ibsen, speaking before The Norwegian Women's Rights League, stated:

> I thank you . . . , but must disclaim the honor of having consciously worked for the women's rights movement. I am not even quite clear as to just what this women's rights movement really is. ("To The Norwegian" 320)

Although he never acknowledged defending the cause, evidence in A Doll's House suggests he does uphold the rights of women.

The play was published well before women's rights were recognized, when male chauvinism was the rule, not the exception. It was a time when women were considered possessions of their husbands, a situation which is especially true for Nora, the leading lady of Ibsen's play. Her husband, Torvald, refers to her as his "most treasured possession" (296),* a trinket "worth looking at" (296), to be displayed at his whim. In the interim, she is to perform her "sacred duties" (301), first to her husband and then to her children.

Torvald represents the epitome of the condescending attitude of men toward women prevalent during the nineteenth-century. He rarely calls Nora by her given name; instead he calls her "skylark," "squirrel," and "squanderbird" (273). It is only when he becomes angry with her that Torvald calls Nora by name, in a tone much like that of a parent scolding a child. He infuriatingly refers to Nora as his "expensive pet" (274). Torvald exercises control over Nora's apparel, her finances, and her diet. He goes so far as to interrogate Nora when he suspects she may have eaten a macaroon (274). Obviously, Torvald wants to be certain his trinket is worthy of display at all times. Oddly enough, Nora allows herself to be treated in this manner. Hurt states:

> No gloss on Norwegian marriage laws or nineteenth-century family life can explain why an apparently high-spirited young woman like Nora would submit to [Torvald's] repellent combination of bullying and baby-talk. (103)

Torvald is self-centered and egotistical. His only concern is himself, his name, and his reputation. The previous Christmas, Nora handmade ornaments and gifts because there was no money to purchase any. This year, "[the] hard times are past," and "I don't have to sit by myself and

---

* All page numbers refer to *A Doll's House* as it appears in *Types of Drama*. (See "Works Cited")

be bored," Torvald exclaims (274). His concern is not for his wife but for himself. As Nora says, "he's so proud of being a man" (278), and he believes he is a step above the average man. His lack of success as an attorney certainly comes as no surprise since he refuses to accept cases that have a hint of immorality (276). He is of the opinion that most criminals are offspring of "mothers who are constitutional liars" (284). He goes into great detail about how lies invade and destroy the home and the children who live there (284). Nora, who in the technical sense has committed a crime and covered it with a lie, is devastated when Torvald makes this declaration. She feels that her behavior, far from being immoral, is a wonderful gift for Torvald. She is convinced that when she has lost her looks and her youth, she will also lose Torvald's love. At that point, she plans to tell him of the sacrifice she made in order to save his life. She believes with all her heart that he will be proud of her. After Torvald delivers his speech about the corruption of lies, Nora becomes wrapped in guilt and fears she has greatly harmed her children (284). Like most mothers, she would die to protect her children.

Torvald insinuates throughout the play that he will be there to protect Nora; however, he fails miserably. In the opening act of the play, he tells her she "needs a man to rescue her" (283). In the second act, he tells her, "Let what will happen, happen. When the real crisis comes, you will not find me lacking in strength or courage. I am man enough to bear the burden for us both" (287). Worst of all, in the final act, Torvald ironically tells Nora, "Often I wish some terrible danger might threaten you, so that I could offer my life and my blood, everything for your sake" (298). Yet when Nora needs Torvald, not to lay down his life but to defend her reputation, he casts her aside, concerned only for his name and reputation. He immediately tells her that she will be disowned but will be able to continue to live in his home. His concern is not about her living arrangements but about avoiding a scandal. Worst of all, Torvald denies her the right to care for her own children (299), saying, ". . . the children shall be taken out of your hands. I dare no longer entrust them to you."

Miraculously, the crisis is averted. Torvald takes a typical male approach and now assumes that all is well and that their lives will be as they were before. He yells, "I am saved," concerned again only for himself (299). He announces he "[has] broad wings to shield [her]" (300). Apparently his wings had stopped beating temporarily, but now he thinks they are fluttering like those of an angel and all is well. Torvald does not even seem to care that he has all but destroyed his wife; instead he thinks all is right with the world now that he has forgiven Nora.

Nora is in fact reborn. She announces, "I've changed" (301) and finally takes a stand. Nora now realizes Torvald has never really loved her (301). She compares their relationship to that of a monkey and a vendor: the better her performance, the larger her reward (302). When Torvald tells Nora, "no man can be expected to sacrifice his honor, not even for the person he loves" (302), Nora reveals, "Millions of women have done it" (302).

From this point on, Ibsen truly champions the rights of women. As James Hurt states, Nora has "passed from being a doll-child into being a doll-wife" (105). She was not allowed her own opinions as a child (A Doll's House 299) nor when she became an adult and married. Torvald has belittled her for eight years; he has all but destroyed any resemblance to a human being she may have had. Worst of all, he has convinced her she is not a fit mother for her children. Nora now acknowledges that she has a duty, "a sacred duty" (301), to herself. She wants to learn and to think for herself, to depend on no one. She does in fact leave her children. However, her reasons are purely unselfish; she does so because she believes that leaving them is the best she can possibly do for them, that they will be better off without her.

Templeton writes, "It is simply not true, then, that Ibsen was not interested in feminism" (37). Ibsen (as cited by Templeton 37), asked, "Is there anyone who dares assert that our ladies are inferior to us in culture, or intelligence, or knowledge, or artistic talent?" And finally, Ibsen said of himself:

> Everything that I have written is intimately connected with what I have lived through, even if I have not lived it myself. Every new work has served me as emancipation and catharsis; for none of us can escape the responsibility and the guilt of the society to which we belong. (as cited and translated by Templeton 38)

Obviously, Henrik Ibsen was concerned with humanity in general. However, it is clear he was deeply troubled by the way women were treated. When Ibsen said he was not consciously working for the rights of women, he was probably stressing his concern for rights of humanity in general. For Torvald has been wronged as well. He is not intentionally abusing Nora but is acting as society dictates. He simply behaves like most men of his time. Nora may well represent one of the first women to take a stand, to say, "I don't have to take this treatment any longer."

Over one hundred years have passed since Ibsen published A Doll's House. Certainly, times have changed and much progress has been made; however, many of the attitudes of the nineteenth-century are reflected in modern male-female relationships. Law books still contain ancient laws regarding women's rights and there are still a few male chauvinists with whom to deal. We could certainly do with a few more "Noras," perhaps another Ibsen as well.

Works Cited

Hurt, James. Cataline's Dream: an Essay on Ibsen's Plays. Urbana: University of Illinois Press, 1972. 102–09.

Ibsen, Henrik. A Doll's House. Trans. Michael Meyer. Types of Drama.

Ed. Sylvan Barnett, Morton Berman, and William Burto. 6th ed. New York: HarperCollins, 1993. 273–303.

——. "To the Norwegian Women's Rights League." Speeches and New Letters. Trans. Arne Kildall. Boston, 1910. Rpt. in European Theories of Drama. Ed. Barrett H. Clark. Rev. ed. New York: Crown, 1918. 320.

Templeton, Joan, "The Doll's House Backlash." PMLA 104 (Jan. 1989): 28–40.

❏ Suggestions for Research, Exploration, and Writing

1. What does Nora think Torvald will do when he learns the truth? How does her expectation make the reality even worse?

2. In an essay, explain the ironic contrast between Torvald's statements to Nora about protecting her and his actual behavior toward her.

3. In a cause-and-effect essay, explain why Nora has been, as Torvald says, for eight years "a hypocrite, [and] a liar."

4. Write an essay explaining why Nora leaves her children, even though she loves them.

5. In what ways does Nora misjudge both of the males in her life? Explain.

6. Write an essay explaining how you, as a modern wife or husband, would deal with a situation such as that faced by Nora or Torvald, or explain how you would conduct your life in such a way as to avoid facing such a situation.

7. Write a documented essay attacking or defending the following statement: Ibsen is defending the rights of women in *A Doll's House.*

8. Using the information in the critical essays and in *A Doll's House,* explain the controversy caused by the original performance of the play.

9. Write a documented paper showing how the setting, props, stage directions, and/or costumes symbolize or suggest themes or character traits.

❏ Writing Suggestions for Men and Women

1. Choose a character in one of the works in this unit and explain how this character dominates his or her spouse.

2. Five of the poems in this section deal with courtship: *"Corinna's* going a Maying," "To His Coy Mistress," Millay's Sonnet 42, "One Perfect Rose," and "Living in Sin." Using several of

3. Compare and/or contrast the problems faced by women and their methods of dealing with the problems in *A Doll's House* and *Trifles*.

4. Several of the poets use humor in their depiction of the male-female relationship. After re-reading the poems and reviewing your own knowledge and/or experience about such relationships, write a humorous poem, story, or essay describing the complexities of such relationships.

H U M A N
V U L N E R A B I L I T Y

A TELEVISION NEWS REPORT THAT a construction worker was killed in an accident, crushed into dust by the sheer weight of earth falling on him, brings home how vulnerable all humans are—mere quivering, soft, easily crushed masses. How then do we live with the knowledge of our vulnerability and our mortality? Such a question has haunted writers since time immemorial, puzzling the ever-patient Job, the great tragedians of ancient Athens, and religious thinkers of diverse cultures and times. Something, Annie Dillard says, exulting in the sheer power of spirit, "pummels us."

No matter how we try to protect ourselves with security systems, storm warnings, airbags, quake-resistant structures, and the like, violence constantly threatens us. It may threaten from outside ourselves, like the brutal violence Mathabane describes in "The Road to Alexandria" and the ghastly devastation of war described in Jarrell's brief poem "The Death of the Ball Turret Gunner." Perhaps more frighteningly, violence may threaten us from within ourselves, as it does the narrator in Madison Smartt Bell's "Customs of the Country." She reveals and must ultimately face the violence within herself which has led her to abuse her son and to assault the wife-abuser next door. Othello in Shakespeare's tragedy, twisted and manipulated by the evil Iago, struggles with jealousy so violent that it leads him to kill his innocent wife, Desdemona. Like Othello, we may live in an illusion of security until the seductive face of evil draws us into its violent maw.

How we face our common and fearful vulnerability defines us as human beings. Like Colonel Sanchez in Marquez's "Death Constant Beyond Love," we may hide from our mortality by erecting a massive structure of illusions. Others of us, like Dickinson's narrator in "I heard a Fly buzz," may face death with matter-of-fact dignity; still others, like Dylan Thomas's speaker in "Do Not Go Gentle into That Good Night," may fight death with every ounce of will and energy they can muster. However it may confront them, great literature does not ignore the horrors of evil in the world but reflects the extraordinary variety of our responses to them.

ESSAYS

ANNIE DILLARD (1945–)

Annie Dillard, born in Pittsburgh, Pennsylvania, is an American poet and essayist. Her essays in Pilgrim at Tinker Creek *(1974), from which the following essay is taken, and* Teaching a Stone to Talk *(1982) reveal a profound interest in, even fascination with, the natural world, dwelling lovingly on its details. Aware not only of nature's violence but also of the transcendental mystery that infuses it, Dillard reveals a sense of awe at the power of the divine driving the physical world.*

Heaven and Earth in Jest

1   I used to have a cat, an old fighting tom, who would jump through the open window by my bed in the middle of the night and land on my chest. I'd half-awaken. He'd stick his skull under my nose and purr, stinking of urine and blood. Some nights he kneaded my bare chest with his front paws, powerfully, arching his back, as if sharpening his claws, or pummeling a mother for milk. And some mornings I'd wake in daylight to find my body covered with paw prints in blood; I looked as though I'd been painted with roses.

2   It was hot, so hot the mirror felt warm. I washed before the mirror in a daze, my twisted summer sleep still hung about me like sea kelp. What blood was this, and what roses? It could have been the rose of union, the blood of murder, or the rose of beauty bare and the blood of some unspeakable sacrifice or birth. The sign on my body could have been an emblem or a stain, the keys to the kingdom or the mark of Cain. I never knew. I never knew as I washed, and the blood streaked, faded and finally disappeared, whether I'd purified myself or ruined the blood sign of the passover. We wake, if we ever wake at all, to mystery, rumors of death, beauty, violence. . . . "Seem like we're just set down here," a woman said to me recently "and don't nobody know why."

3   These are morning matters, pictures you dream as the final wave heaves you up on the sand to the bright light and drying air. You remember pressure, and a curved sleep you rested against, soft, like a scallop in its shell. But the air hardens your skin; you stand; you leave the lighted shore to explore some dim headland, and soon you're lost in the leafy interior, intent, remembering nothing.

4   I still think of that old tomcat, mornings, when I wake. Things are tamer now; I sleep with the window shut. The cat and our rites are gone and my life is changed, but the memory remains of something powerful

playing over me. I wake expectant, hoping to see a new thing. If I'm lucky I might be jogged awake by a strange birdcall. I dress in a hurry, imagining the yard flapping with auks, or flamingos. This morning it was a wood duck, down at the creek. It flew away.

I live by a creek, Tinker Creek, in a valley in Virginia's Blue Ridge. An 5 anchorite's hermitage is called an anchor-hold; some anchor-holds were simple sheds clamped to the side of a church like a barnacle to a rock. I think of this house clamped to the side of Tinker Creek as an anchor-hold. It holds me at anchor to the rock bottom of the creek itself and it keeps me steadied in the current, as a sea anchor does, facing the stream of light pouring down. It's a good place to live; there's a lot to think about. The creeks—Tinker and Carvin's—are an active mystery, fresh every minute. Theirs is the mystery of the continuous creation and all that providence implies: the uncertainty of vision, the horror of the fixed, the dissolution of the present, the intricacy of beauty, the pressure of fecundity, the elusiveness of the free, and the flawed nature of perfection. The mountains—Tinker and Brushy, McAfee's Knob and Dead Man—are a passive mystery, the oldest of all. Theirs is the one simple mystery of creation from nothing, of matter itself, anything at all, the given. Mountains are giant, restful, absorbent. You can heave your spirit into a mountain and the mountain will keep it, folded, and not throw it back as some creeks will. The creeks are the world with all its stimulus and beauty; I live there. But the mountains are home.

The wood duck flew away. I caught only a glimpse of something like 6 a bright torpedo that blasted the leaves where it flew. Back at the house I ate a bowl of oatmeal; much later in the day came the long slant of light that means good walking.

If the day is fine, any walk will do; it all looks good. Water in 7 particular looks its best, reflecting blue sky in the flat, and chopping it into graveled shallows and white chute and foam in the riffles. On a dark day, or a hazy one, everything's washed-out and lack-luster but the water. It carries its own lights. I set out for the railroad tracks, for the hill the flocks fly over, for the woods where the white mare lives. But I go to the water.

Today is one of those excellent January partly cloudies in which light 8 chooses an unexpected part of the landscape to trick out in gilt, and then shadow sweeps it away. You know you're alive. You take huge steps, trying to feel the planet's roundness arc between your feet. Kazantzakis says that when he was young he had a canary and a globe. When he freed the canary, it would perch on the globe and sing. All his life, wandering the earth, he felt as though he had a canary on top of his mind, singing.

West of the house, Tinker Creek makes a sharp loop, so that the creek 9 is both in back of the house, south of me, and also on the other side of the road, north of me. I like to go north. There the afternoon sun hits the creek just right, deepening the reflected blue and lighting the sides of trees on the banks. Steers from the pasture across the creek come down to drink; I always flush a rabbit or two there; I sit on a fallen trunk in the shade and watch the squirrels in the sun. There are two separated wooden fences suspended from cables that cross the creek just upstream from my tree-trunk bench. They keep the steers from escaping up or down the creek when they come to drink. Squirrels, the neighborhood children, and I use the downstream fence as a swaying bridge across the creek. But the steers are there today.

10   I sit on the downed tree and watch the black steers slip on the creek bottom. They are all bred beef: beef heart, beef hide, beef hocks. They're a human product like rayon. They're like a field of shoes. They have cast-iron shanks and tongues like foam insoles. You can't see through to their brains as you can with other animals; they have beef fat behind their eyes, beef stew.

11   I cross the fence six feet above the water, walking my hands down the rusty cable and tightroping my feet along the narrow edge of the planks. When I hit the other bank and terra firma, some steers are bunched in a knot between me and the barbed-wire fence I want to cross. So I suddenly rush at them in an enthusiastic spring, flailing my arms and hollering, "Lightning! Copperhead! Swedish meatballs!" They flee, still in a knot, stumbling across the flat pasture. I stand with the wind on my face.

12   When I slide under a barbed-wire fence, cross a field, and run over a sycamore trunk felled across the water, I'm on a little island shaped like a tear in the middle of Tinker Creek. On one side of the creek is a steep forested bank; the water is swift and deep on that side of the island. On the other side is the level field I walked through next to the steers' pasture; the water between the field and the island is shallow and sluggish. In summer's low water, flags and bulrushes grow along a series of shallow pools cooled by the lazy current. Water striders patrol the surface film, crayfish hump along the silt bottom eating filth, frogs shout and glare, and shiners and small bream hide among roots from the sulky green heron's eye. I come to this island every month of the year. I walk around it, stopping and staring, or I straddle the sycamore log over the creek, curling my legs out of the water in winter, trying to read. Today I sit on dry grass at the end of the island by the slower side of the creek. I'm drawn to this spot. I come to it as to an oracle; I return to it as a man years later will seek out the battlefield where he lost a leg or an arm.

13   A couple of summers ago I was walking along the edge of the island to see what I could see in the water, and mainly to scare frogs. Frogs have an inelegant way of taking off from invisible positions on the bank just ahead of your feet, in dire panic, emitting a froggy "Yike!" and splashing into the water. Incredibly, this amused me, and incredibly, it amuses me still. As I walked along the grassy edge of the island, I got better and better at seeing frogs both in and out of the water. I learned to recognize, slowing down, the difference in texture of the light reflected from mud-

bank, water, grass, or frog. Frogs were flying all around me. At the end of the island I noticed a small green frog. He was exactly half in and half out of the water, looking like a schematic diagram of an amphibian, and he didn't jump.

He didn't jump; I crept closer. At last I knelt on the island's winter-killed grass, lost, dumbstruck, staring at the frog in the creek just four feet away. He was a very small frog with wide, dull eyes. And just as I looked at him, he slowly crumpled and began to sag. The spirit vanished from his eyes as if snuffed. His skin emptied and drooped; his very skull seemed to collapse and settle like a kicked tent. He was shrinking before my eyes like a deflating football. I watched the taut, glistening skin on his shoulder ruck, and rumple, and fall. Soon, part of his skin, formless as a pricked balloon, lay in floating folds like bright scum on top of the water: it was a monstrous and terrifying thing. I gaped bewildered, appalled. An oval shadow hung in the water behind the drained frog; then the shadow glided away. The frog skin bag started to sink.

I had read about the giant water bug, but never seen one. "Giant water bug" is really the name of the creature, which is an enormous, heavy-bodied brown beetle. It eats insects, tadpoles, fish, and frogs. Its grasping forelegs are mighty and hooked inward. It seizes a victim with these legs, hugs it tight, and paralyzes it with enzymes injected during a vicious bite. That one bite is the only bite it ever takes. Through the puncture shoot the poisons that dissolve the victim's muscle and bone and organs—all but the skin—and through it the giant water bug sucks out the victim's body, reduced to a juice. This event is quite common in warm fresh water. The frog I saw was being sucked by a giant water bug. I had been kneeling on the island grass; when the unrecognizable flap of frog skin settled on the creek bottom, swaying, I stood up and brushed the knees of my pants. I couldn't catch my breath.

Of course, many carnivorous animals devour their prey alive. The usual method seems to be to subdue the victim by downing or grasping it so it can't flee, then eating it whole or in a series of bloody bites. Frogs eat everything whole, stuffing prey into the mouths with their thumbs. People have seen frogs with their wide jaws so full of live dragonflies they couldn't close them. Ants don't even have to catch their prey: in the spring they swarm over newly hatched, featherless birds in the nest and eat them tiny bite by bite.

That it's rough out there and chancy is no surprise. Every live thing is a survivor on a kind of extended emergency bivouac. But at the same time we are also created. In the Koran, Allah asks, "The heaven and the earth and all in between, thinkest thou I made them *in jest?*" It's a good question. What do we think of the created universe, spanning an un-thinkable void with an unthinkable profusion of forms? Or what do we think of nothingness, those sickening reaches of time in either direction? If the giant water bug was not made in jest, was it then made in earnest? Pascal uses a nice term to describe the notion of the creator's, once

14

15

16

17

having called forth the universe, turning his back to it: "Deus Absconditus." Is that what we think happened? Was the sense of it there, and God absconded with it, ate it, like a wolf who disappears round the edge of the house with the Thanksgiving turkey? "God is subtle," Einstein said, "but not malicious." Again, Einstein said that "nature conceals her mystery by means of her essential grandeur, not by her cunning." It could be that God has not absconded but spread, as our vision and understanding of the universe have spread, to a fabric of spirit and sense so grand and subtle, so powerful in a new way, that we can only feel blindly of its hem. In making the thick darkness a swaddling band for the sea, God "set bars and doors" and said, "hitherto shalt thou come, but no further." But have we come even that far? Have we rowed out to the thick darkness, or are we all playing pinochle in the bottom of the boat?

18   Cruelty is a mystery, and the waste of pain. But if we describe a world to compass these things, a world that is a long, brute game, then we bump against another mystery: the inrush of power and light, the canary that sings on the skull. Unless all ages and races of men have been deluded by the same mass hypnotist (who?), there seems to be such a thing as beauty, a grace wholly gratuitous. About five years ago I saw a mockingbird make a straight vertical descent from the roof gutter of a four-story building. It was an act as careless and spontaneous as the curl of a stem or the kindling of a star.

19   The mockingbird took a single step into the air and dropped. His wings were still folded against his sides as though he were singing from a limb and not falling, accelerating thirty-two feet per second per second, through empty air. Just a breath before he would have been dashed to the ground, he unfurled his wings with exact, deliberate care, revealing the broad bars of white, spread his elegant, white-banded tail, and so floated onto the grass. I had just rounded a corner when his insouciant step caught my eye; there was no one else in sight. The fact of his free fall was like the old philosophical conundrum about the tree that falls in the forest. The answer must be, I think, that beauty and grace are performed whether or not we will or sense them. The least we can do is try to be there.

20   Another time I saw another wonder: sharks off the Atlantic coast of Florida. There is a way a wave rises above the ocean horizon, a triangular wedge against the sky. If you stand where the ocean breaks on a shallow beach, you see the raised water in a wave is translucent, shot with lights. One late afternoon at low tide a hundred big sharks passed the beach near the mouth of a tidal river in a feeding frenzy. As each green wave rose from the churning water, it illuminated within itself the six- or eight-foot-long bodies of twisting sharks. The sharks disappeared as each wave rolled toward me; then a new wave would swell above the horizon, containing in it, like scorpions in amber, sharks that roiled and heaved. The sight held awesome wonders: power and beauty, grace tangled in a rapture with violence.

21   We don't know what's going on here. If these tremendous events are random combinations of matter run amok, the yield of millions of

monkeys at millions of typewriters, then what is it in us, hammered out of those same typewriters, that they ignite? We don't know. Our life is a faint tracing on the surface of mystery, like the idle, curved tunnels of leaf miners on the face of a leaf. We must somehow take a wider view, look at the whole landscape, really see it, and describe what's going on here. Then we can at least wail the right question into the swaddling band of darkness, or, if it comes to that, choir the proper praise.

At the time of Lewis and Clark, setting the prairies on fire was a 22 well-known signal that meant, "Come down to the water." It was an extravagant gesture, but we can't do less. If the landscape reveals one certainty, it is that the extravagant gesture is the very stuff of creation. After the one extravagant gesture of creation in the first place, the universe has continued to deal exclusively in extravagances, flinging intricacies and colossi down aeons of emptiness, heaping profusions on profligacies with ever-fresh vigor. The whole show has been on fire from the word go. I come down to the water to cool my eyes. But everywhere I look I see fire; that which isn't flint is tinder, and the whole world sparks and flames.

I have come to the grassy island late in the day. The creek is up; icy 23 water sweeps under the sycamore log bridge. The frog skin, of course, is utterly gone. I have stared at that one spot on the creek bottom for so long, focusing past the rush of water, that when I stand, the opposite bank seems to stretch before my eyes and flow grassily upstream. When the bank settles down I cross the sycamore log and enter again the big plowed field next to the steers' pasture.

The wind is terrific out of the west; the sun comes and goes. I can see 24 the shadow on the field before me deepen uniformly and spread like a plague. Everything seems so dull I am amazed I can even distinguish objects. And suddenly the light runs across the land like a comber, and up the trees, and goes again in a wink: I think I've gone blind or died. When it comes again, the light, you hold your breath, and if it stays you forget about it until it goes again.

It's the most beautiful day of the year. At four o'clock the eastern sky 25 is a dead stratus black flecked with low white clouds. The sun in the west illuminates the ground, the mountains, and especially the bare branches of trees, so that everywhere silver trees cut into the black sky like a photographer's negative of a landscape. The air and the ground are dry; the mountains are going on and off like neon signs. Clouds slide east as if pulled from the horizon, like a tablecloth whipped off a table. The hemlocks by the barbed-wire fence are flinging themselves east as though their backs would break. Purple shadows are racing east; the wind makes me face east, and again I feel the dizzying, drawn sensation I felt when the creek bank reeled.

At four-thirty the sky in the east is clear; how could that big blackness 26 be blown? Fifteen minutes later another darkness is coming overhead from the northwest; and it's here. Everything is drained of its light as if sucked. Only at the horizon do inky black mountains give way to distant, lighted mountains—lighted not by direct illumination but rather paled by glowing sheets of mist hung before them. Now the blackness is in the east; everything is half in shadow, half in sun, every clod, tree, mountain, and hedge. I can't see Tinker Mountain through the line of hemlock, till it comes on like a streetlight, ping, *ex nihilo.* Its sandstone cliffs pink and swell. Suddenly the light goes; the cliffs recede as if pushed. The sun hits a clump of sycamores between me and the mountains; the sycamore arms light up, and *I can't see the cliffs.* They're gone. The pale network of sycamore arms, which a second ago was transparent as a screen, is suddenly opaque, glowing with light. Now the sycamore arms snuff out, the mountains come on, and there are the cliffs again.

27   I walk home. By five-thirty the show has pulled out. Nothing is left but an unreal blue and a few banked clouds low in the north. Some sort of carnival magician has been here, some fast-talking worker of wonder who has the act backwards. "Something in this hand," he says, "something in this hand, something up my sleeve, something behind my back . . ." and abracadabra, he snaps his fingers, and it's all gone. Only the bland, blank-faced magician remains, in his unruffled coat, barehanded, acknowledging a smattering of baffled applause. When you look again the whole show has pulled up stakes and moved on down the road. It never stops. New shows roll in from over the mountains and the magician reappears unannounced from a fold in the curtain you never dreamed was an opening. Scarves of clouds, rabbits in plain view, disappear into the black hat forever. Presto chango. The audience, if there is an audience at all, is dizzy from head-turning, dazed.

28   Like the bear who went over the mountain, I went out to see what I could see. And, I might as well warn you, like the bear, all that I could see was the other side of the mountain: more of the same. On a good day I might catch a glimpse of another wooded ridge rolling under the sun like water, another bivouac. I propose to keep here what Thoreau called "a meteorological journal of the mind," telling some tales and describing some of the sights of this rather tamed valley, and exploring, in fear and trembling, some of the unmapped dim reaches and unholy fastnesses to which those tales and sights so dizzyingly lead.

29   I am no scientist. I explore the neighborhood. An infant who has just learned to hold his head up has a frank and forthright way of gazing about him in bewilderment. He hasn't the faintest clue where he is, and he aims to learn. In a couple of years, what he will have learned instead is how to fake it: he'll have the cocksure air of a squatter who has come to feel he owns the place. Some unwonted, taught pride diverts us from our original intent, which is to explore the neighborhood, view the landscape, to discover at least *where* it is that we have been so startlingly set down, if we can't learn why.

30   So I think about the valley. It is my leisure as well as my work, a game. It is a fierce game I have joined because it is being played anyway, a game

of both skill and chance, played against an unseen adversary—the conditions of time—in which the payoffs, which may suddenly arrive in a blast of light at any moment, might as well come to me as anyone else. I stake the time I'm grateful to have, the energies I'm glad to direct. I risk getting stuck on the board, so to speak, unable to move in any direction, which happens enough, God knows; and I risk the searing, exhausting nightmares that plunder rest and force me face down all night long in some muddy ditch seething with hatching insects and crustaceans.

But if I can bear the nights, the days are a pleasure. I walk out; I see   31
something, some event that would otherwise have been utterly missed and lost; or something sees me, some enormous power brushes me with its clean wing, and I resound like a beaten bell.

I am an explorer, then, and I am also a stalker, or the instrument of the   32
hunt itself. Certain Indians used to carve long grooves along the wooden shafts of their arrows. They called the grooves "lightning marks," because they resembled the curved fissure lightning slices down the trunks of trees. The function of lightning marks is this: if the arrow fails to kill the game, blood from a deep wound will channel along the lightning mark, streak down the arrow shaft, and spatter to the ground, laying a trail dripped on broadleaves, on stone, that the barefoot and trembling archer can follow into whatever deep or rare wilderness it leads. I am the arrow shaft, carved along my length by unexpected lights and gashes from the very sky, and this book is the straying trail of blood.

Something pummels us, something barely sheathed. Power broods and   33
lights. We're played on like a pipe; our breath is not our own. James Houston describes two young Eskimo girls sitting cross-legged on the ground, mouth on mouth, blowing by turns each other's throat cords, making a low, unearthly music. When I cross again the bridge that is really the steers' fence, the wind has thinned to the delicate air of twilight; it crumples the water's skin. I watch the running sheets of light raised on the creek's surface. The sight has the appeal of the purely passive, like the racing of light under clouds on a field, the beautiful dream at the moment of being dreamed. The breeze is the merest puff, but you yourself sail headlong and breathless under the gale force of the spirit.

❏ Questions for Discussion

1. What does the blood, repeatedly left on her body by the cat, suggest about Dillard?

2. Dillard says that Nikos Kazantzakis "felt as though he had a canary on top of his mind, singing." What does he mean? How is this quotation appropriate to Dillard's essay?

3. Dillard asks whether the giant water bug was "made in jest" or "in earnest." What is your answer? Why?

4. "Cruelty is a mystery," Dillard says. What does she mean? What else does she see as a mystery?

5. What does Dillard mean when she defines beauty as "a grace wholly gratuitous"? What meanings of the word *grace* might she have in mind?

6. Explain Dillard's comparison of herself to an arrowhead. What is she saying about herself and her environment?

7. What does Dillard mean when she says, "Something pummels us, something barely sheathed"?

❑ **Suggestions for Exploration and Writing**

1. Dillard's essay is rich in **imagery**. Examine the relationships between images of violence, power, light, dark, and grace. What dominant impression of people's place in the universe do these images suggest?

2. Compare the questions Dillard asks in this essay with the question Frost's speaker asks in the poem "Design."

SOPHRONIA LIU (1953–)

Liu writes autobiographical essays and stories. Originally from Hong Kong but educated in the United States, Liu recalls with pleasure, as well as with pain, growing up in Hong Kong. "So Tsi-fai" is just one of her memories.

So Tsi-fai

1   Voices, images, scene from the past—twenty-three years ago, when I was in sixth grade:

2   "Let us bow our heads in silent prayer for the soul of So Tsi-fai. Let us pray for God's forgiveness for this boy's rash taking of his own life . . ." Sister Marie (Mung Gu-liang). My sixth-grade English teacher. Missionary nun from Paris. Principal of The Little Flower's School. Disciplinarian, perfectionist, authority figure: awesome and awful in my ten-year-old eyes.

3   "I don't need any supper. I have drunk enough insecticide." So Tsi-fai. My fourteen-year-old classmate. Daredevil; good-for-nothing lazy-bones (according to Mung Gu-liang). Bright black eyes, disheveled hair, defiant sneer, creased and greasy uniform, dirty hands, careless walk, shuffling feet. Standing in the corner for being late, for forgetting his homework, for talking in class, for using foul language. ("Shame on you! Go wash your mouth with soap!" Mung Gu-liang's sharp command. He did, and came back with a grin.) So Tsi-fai: Sticking his tongue out behind Mung Gu-liang's back, passing secret notes to his friends, kept behind after school, sent to the Principal's office for repeated offense. So Tsi-fai: incorrigible, hopeless, and without hope.

It was a Monday in late November when we heard of his death, returning to school after the weekend with our parents' signatures on our midterm reports. So Tsi-fai also showed his report to his father, we were told later. He flunked three out of the fourteen subjects: English Grammar, Arithmetic, and Chinese Dictation. He missed each one by one to three marks. That wasn't so bad. But he was a hopeless case. Overaged, stubborn, and uncooperative; a repeated offender of school rules, scourge of all teachers; who was going to give him a lenient passing grade? Besides, being a few months over the maximum age—fourteen—for sixth graders, he wasn't even allowed to sit for the Secondary School Entrance Exam.

All sixth graders in Hong Kong had to pass the SSE before they could obtain a seat in secondary school. In 1964 when I took the exam, there were more than twenty thousand candidates. About seven thousand of us passed: four thousand were sent to government and subsidized schools, and the other three thousand to private and grant-in-aid schools. I came in around no. 2000; I was lucky. Without the public exam, there would be no secondary school for So Tsi-fai. His future was sealed.

Looking at the report with three red marks on it, his father was furious. So Tsi-fai was the oldest son. There were three younger children. His father was a vegetable farmer with a few plots of land in Wong Juk-hang, by the sea. His mother worked in a local factory. So Tsi-fai helped in the fields, cooked for the family, and washed his own clothes. ("Filthy, dirty boy!" gasped Mung Gu-liang. "Grime behind the ears, black rims on the fingernails, dirty collar, crumpled shirt. Why doesn't your mother iron your shirt?") Both his parents were illiterate. So Tsi-fai was their biggest hope: He made it to the sixth grade.

Who woke him up for school every morning and had breakfast waiting for him? Nobody. ("Time for school! Get up! Eat your rice!" Ma nagged and screamed. The aroma of steamed rice and Chinese sausages spread all over the house. "Drink your tea! Eat your oranges! Wash your face! And remember to wash behind your ears!") And who helped So Tsi-fai do his homework? Nobody. Did he have older brothers like mine who knew all about the arithmetic of rowing a boat against the currents or with the currents, how to count the feet of chickens and rabbits in the same cage, the present perfect continuous tense of "to live" and the future perfect tense of "to succeed"? None. Nil. So Tsi-fai was a lost cause.

I came first in both terms that year, the star pupil. So Tsi-fai was one of the last in the class: He was lazy; he didn't care. Or did he?

When his father scolded him, So Tsi-fai left the house. When he showed up again, late for supper, he announced, "I don't need any supper. I have drunk enough insecticide." Just like another one of his practical jokes. The insecticide was stored in the field for his father's vegetables. He was rushed to the hospital; dead upon arrival.

10   "He gulped for a last breath and was gone," an uncle told us at the funeral. "But his eyes wouldn't shut. So I said in his ear, 'You go now and rest in peace.' And I smoothed my hand over his eyelids. His face was all purple."

11   His face was still purple when we saw him in his coffin. Eyes shut tight, nostrils dilated and white as if fire and anger might shoot out, any minute.

12   In class that Monday morning, Sister Marie led us in prayer. "Let us pray that God will forgive him for his sins." We said the Lord's Prayer and the Hail Mary. We bowed our heads. I sat in my chair, frozen and dazed, thinking of the deadly chill in the morgue, the smell of disinfectant, ether, and dead flesh.

13   "Bang!" went a gust of wind, forcing open a leaf of the double door leading to the back balcony. "Flap, flap, flap." The door swung in the wind. We could see the treetops by the hillside rustling to and fro against a pale blue sky. An imperceptible presence had drifted in with the wind. The same careless walk and shuffling feet, the same daredevil air—except that the eyes were lusterless, dripping blood; the tongue hanging out, gasping for air. As usual, he was late. But he had come back to claim his place.

14   "I died a tragic death," his voice said. "I have as much right as you to be here. This is my seat." We heard him; we knew he was back.

15   . . . So Tsi-fai: Standing in the corner for being late, for forgetting his homework, for talking in class, for using foul language. So Tsi-fai: Palm outstretched, chest sticking out, holding his breath: "Tat. Tat. Tat." Down came the teacher's wooden ruler, twenty times on each hand. Never batting an eyelash: then back to facing the wall in the corner by the door. So Tsi-fai: grimy shirt, disheveled hair, defiant sneer. So Tsi-fai. Incorrigible, hopeless, and without hope.

16   The girls in front gasped and shrank back in their chairs. Mung Gu-liang went to the door, held the doorknob in one hand, poked her head out, and peered into the empty balcony. Then, with a determined jerk, she pulled the door shut. Quickly crossing herself, she returned to the teacher's desk. Her black cross swung upon the front of her gray habit as she hurried across the room. "Don't be silly!" she scolded the frightened girls in the front row.

17   What really happened? After all these years, my mind is still haunted by this scene. What happened to So Tsi-fai? What happened to me? What happened to all of us that year in sixth grade, when we were green and young and ready to fling our arms out for the world? All of a sudden, death claimed one of us and he was gone.

18   Who arbitrates between life and death? Who decides which life is worth preserving and prospering, and which to nip in its bud? How did it happen that I, at ten, turned out to be the star pupil, the lucky one, while my friend, a peasant's son, was shoveled under the heap and lost forever? How could it happen that this world would close off a young boy's life

at fourteen just because he was poor, undisciplined, and lacked the training and support to pass his exams? What really happened?

Today, twenty-three years later, So Tsi-fai's ghost still haunts me. "I died a tragic death. I have as much right as you to be here. This is my seat." The voice I heard twenty-three years ago in my sixth-grade classroom follows me in my dreams. Is there anything I can do to lay it to rest? 19

❏ Questions for Discussion

1. Why does So Tsi-fai commit suicide by insecticide? Is this act symbolic?

2. How does the treatment by his school, his peers, and his family impact on his self-esteem?

3. Liu calls So Tsi-fai a "lost cause." What does she mean? Why can he not progress in school like the others? Was there anything anyone could have done to prevent his death?

4. The **narrator** says that she is haunted by her memory of So Tsi-fai and by her guilt at her failure to help him. What was her attitude toward So Tsi-fai before his death and why was her attitude changed?

5. What is **ironic** about Sister Marie's praying for forgiveness of So Tsi-fai's sins?

❏ Suggestions for Exploration and Writing

1. Supplementing your own experience with research, write an essay examining in detail a particular kind of institutionalized injustice. You might consider a kind of injustice you see recurring in school.

2. How were nonconforming students treated in your high school? Analyze the treatment of these students by peers, the faculty, and/or the administration.

3. Write an essay describing a case in which the forces of environment and/or heredity seem to control a person's destiny.

MARK MATHABANE (1960–   )

Mark Mathabane, a black South African, grew up in Alexandra, a crowded, poverty-stricken ghetto outside Johannesburg. His autobiography, Kaffir Boy *(1986), from which the following selection comes, recounts his upbringing under the crushing weight of apartheid and his escape to the United States by means of a tennis scholarship. The word* kaffir *in the title is a racial epithet, a term used by South African whites to degrade and disparage blacks.*

The Road to Alexandra

1   It was early morning of a bitterly cold winter day in 1965. I was lying on a bed of cardboard, under a kitchen table, peering through a large hole in the blanket at the spooky darkness around me. I was wide awake and terrified. All night long I had been having nightmares in which throngs of black people sprawled dead in pools of red blood, surrounded by all sorts of slimy, creeping creatures. These nightmares had plagued me since I turned five two weeks ago. I thought of waking my mother in the next room, but my father's words of warning not to wake her on account of bad dreams stopped me. All was quiet, save for the snores of my sister Florah—three years old—huddled alongside me, under the same blanket, and the squeaks of rats in the cupboard. From time to time the moon shone eerily through the window. Afraid to go back to sleep lest I have another nightmare, I stayed awake, peering at the quivering blackness through the hole. The darkness seemed alive.

2   My father woke up and began arguing sharply with my mother in the bedroom. It was five o'clock by the *kikilihoo* (cock's crow), time for him to go to work. He always went to work at this time—and he was angry at my mother for forgetting to prepare his *scufftin* (food for work). Soon he emerged, holding a flickering tallow candle in one hand, and a worn-out Stetson hat in the other. He silently went about preparing his *scufftin* from what was left of yesterday's *pap 'n vleis* (porridge and meat). He wrapped the *scufftin* in sheets of old newspapers, took the family's *waslap* (facecloth) from the window, dampened it with water from a mug and wiped his face. He drank what was left of the water in the mug. Minutes later he was out through the door, on his way to work, but not before I had said to him: "Don't forget our fish and chips, Papa."

3   "Fish and chips is tomorrow, son. Today is Thursday. Payday is tomorrow."

4   " 'Bye, 'bye, Papa."

5   "Go back to sleep."

6   As soon as he was out through the door my mother, clad only in her skimpy underwear, came into the kitchen, chamber pot in hand. The chamber pot dripped and had a bad smell, like the one which always pervaded the yard whenever our neighbours hung urine-soaked blankets and cardboard on fences to dry under the blazing African sun.

7   "Where are you going, Mama?"

8   "To the outhouse."

9   "Those bad dreams came back, Mama."

10   "I'll be back soon."

11   Before she left, she blew out the candle to save it from burning out and took with her a book of matches. I lingered between sleep and wakefulness, anticipating my mother's speedy return. Twenty minutes passed without any sign of her. I grew more afraid of the darkness; I shut my eyes, pulled the blanket over my head and minutes later I was in dream-

land. I had been asleep but a short while when my mother came bursting through the door, yelling, in a winded voice, "Get up, Johannes! Get up quickly!" And as she yelled she reached under the table and shook me vigorously.

"Hunh?" I mumbled sleepily, stirring but not waking up, thinking it a dream. [12]

"Get up! Get up!" she yelled again, yanking the torn blanket covering Florah and me, and almost instantly I awoke and heard a door shut with a resounding slam. From then on things became rather entangled for me. Unaware that I was still under the table I jerked upward, and my head banged against the top of the table. I winced but didn't cry; my father had warned me that men and boys never cry, ever. Still only half awake, I began crawling upon my hands and knees from under the table, but the darkness was all around me, and I couldn't see where I was going. [13]

As I was crawling blindly my face rammed into one of the concrete slabs propping one of the table's legs. I let out a scream and drew back momentarily, dazed and smarting. At this point half my mind still told me that I was in a dream, but the hot pain all over my face convinced me otherwise. I resumed groping for a way from under the table, to find out where my mother had suddenly gone, and why she had awakened me. Finally I was out. I leaned myself for a while against the side of the table and waited for the throbbing pain in my head to cease. [14]

Suddenly, as I stood leaning against the table, from outside came a series of dreadful noises. Sirens blared, voices screamed and shouted, wood cracked and windows shattered, children bawled, dogs barked and footsteps pounded. I was bewildered; I had never heard such a racket before. I was instantly seized by a feeling of terror. [15]

"Mama! Where are you?" I screamed, groping about with one hand, the other clutching the table. I did not know whether my mother had gone back out, or was still in the house. [16]

"Over here," a voice suddenly whispered from somewhere behind me. It was my mother's voice, but it sounded so faint I could barely hear it. I turned my head and strained to see where it was coming from and saw nothing but darkness. Where was my mother? Why was it so dark? Why the dreadful noises outside? My imagination ran wild. The pitch-black room seemed alive with the voodoo spirits of my mother's tales, ready to pounce upon me if I as much as took a step from where I was standing. [17]

"Mama! Where are you?" I screamed again, fear mounting inside me. [18]

"I'm over here," the disembodied voice of my mother said from somewhere in the dark. [19]

I swung around and saw a candle coming out of the bedroom. It stopped briefly by the door. It was my mother. In the dim candlelight, her body, crouched like that of an animal cowering in fear, cast an oblong, eerie shadow on the flaking whitewashed wall. She stole over to where I stood transfixed, handed me the flickering candle and told me to keep it down and away from the window. [20]

21   "What's the matter, Mama?"

22   "Not so loud," she cautioned, a finger on her lips. Still clad only in her underwear, she hurriedly draped a tattered black shawl, which had been lying on a tin chair nearby, over her shoulders, but the shawl didn't cover much. She reached under the kitchen table and grabbed the torn blanket and draped it in place of the shawl and took the shawl and spread it over the newspapers and cardboard covering Florah.

23   "What's the matter, Mama?"

24   "Peri-Urban is here."

25   "Peri-Urban!" I gasped and stiffened at the name of the dreaded Alexandra Police Squad. To me nothing, short of a white man, was more terrifying; not even a bogeyman. Memories of previous encounters with the police began haunting me. Will the two fat black policemen with *sjamboks** and truncheons burst open the door again? And will the one with the twirled mustache and big hands grit his teeth at me while threatening, "Speak up, boy! or I'll let you taste my *sjambok!*" and thereafter spit in my face and hit me on the head with a truncheon for refusing to tell where my mother and father were hiding? And will the tall, carroty-haired white man in fatigues stand by the doorjamb again, whistling a strange tune and staring fear into Florah and me?

26   "W-where a-are t-they?" I stammered.

27   "Outside. Don't be afraid now. They're still in the next neighbourhood. I was in the outhouse when the alarm came." "When the alarm came" meant people leaping over fences in a mad dash to escape the police.

28   I nodded sheepishly, the sleep now completely gone from my eyes. I was now standing—naked, cold and trembling—in the middle of the room. My mother took the candle from my hand and told me to dress. I reached under the kitchen table for my patched khaki shorts and dressed hurriedly. Meanwhile the pandemonium outside was intensifying with each minute; the raid, it seemed, was gathering momentum. Suddenly a gust of wind puffed through the sackcloth covering the hole in the window; the candle flickered but did not go out. I felt something warm soak my groin and trickle down my legs. I tried to stem the flow of urine by pressing my thighs together, but I was too late; a puddle had formed about my feet, and I scattered it with my toes. My mother handed me the candle and headed toward the table in the corner. As she went along she said, without turning to face me, "Take good care of your brother and sister while I'm gone, you hear?"

29   "Yes, Mama." I knew she had to leave, she had to flee from the police and leave us children alone as she had done so many times before. By now my mother had reached the table, and her big brown eyes darted about its top, searching for something.

30   "Where's my passbook?" she asked in a frantic voice, her tense body

---

* An animal-hide whip used to enforce apartheid.

bent low over the table. "Bring the candle over here. Keep it down! Away from the window!" As I hurried the candle, which had now burnt to a stub, over to her, a loud scream leaped out from the dark outside. Alarmed, I stumbled and fell headlong into my mother's arms. As she steadied me she continued asking, "Where's my passbook? Where is it?" I did not know; I could not answer; I could not think; my mind had suddenly gone blank. She grabbed me by the shoulder and shook me, yelling frantically, "Where is it! Where is it! Oh, God. Where is it, child? Where is the book? Hurry, or they'll find me!"

"What book?" I said blankly.   31

"The little book I showed you and your sister last night, remember,"   32
she stared at me anxiously, but my eyes merely widened in confusion. No matter how hard I tried it seemed I could not rid my mind of the sinister force that had suddenly blotted out all memory.

"Remember the little black book with my picture in it. Where is it?"   33
my mother said, again grabbing me and shaking me, begging me to remember. I could not snap out of my amnesia.

The noise outside had risen to a dreadful crescendo. Suddenly several   34
gunshots rang out in quick succession. Shouts of "Follow that Kaffir! He can't get far! He's wounded!" followed the shots. Somehow it all jolted me back to consciousness, and I remembered where my mother's little black book was; under the pallet of cardboard where I had tucked it the night before, hoping to sneak it out the next day and show it to my friends at play—who had already shown me their mothers'—to see whose mother's picture was the most beautiful.

"It's under the table, Mama!" I cried out.   35

My mother thanked her ancestors. Hurriedly, she circled the table,   36
reached under it, rolled Florah away from the damp cardboard, lifted them up, and underneath, on the earthen floor, she found her little black book. I heaved a great sigh of relief as I watched her tuck it into her bosom.

My sister's naked, frail body, now on the bare floor, shook from the icy   37
cold seeping through a hole under the door. She coughed, then moaned—a prolonged rasping sound; but she did not wake up. My mother quickly straightened out the cardboard and rolled Florah back to sleep and covered her with more newspapers and cardboard. More screams came from outside as more doors and windows were being busted by the police; the vicious barking of dogs escalated, as did the thudding of running feet. Shouts of "*Mbambe! Mbambe!* (Grab him! Catch him!)" followed the screams of police whistles.

My mother was headed for the bedroom door when a shaft of very   38
bright light flashed through the uncurtained window and fell upon her. Instantly she leaped behind the door and remained hidden behind it. Alarmed, I dropped the candle, spilling the molten wax on my feet; the room was plunged into utter darkness, for the bright light disappeared barely seconds after it had flashed. As I groped about for the candle, the

bright light again flashed through the window and flooded the kitchen. This time it stayed. It seemed daylight.

39   My mother crept from behind the bedroom door and started toward the kitchen door, on tiptoe. As she neared it, my year-old brother, George, who slept with my mother and father on the only bed in the house, started screaming, piercing the tenuous stillness of the house. His screams stopped my mother dead in her tracks; she spun around and said to me, in a whisper, "Go quiet your brother."

40   "Yes, Mama," I said, but I did not go. I could not go. I seemed rooted to the spot by a terrifying fear of the unknown.

41   "I'll be gone a short while," my mother, now by the door, whispered. She stealthily opened it a crack, her blanketed body still in a crouch, her head almost touching the floor. She hesitated a moment or two before peering through the opening. The storm of screams that came through the door made me think that the world was somehow coming to an end. Through the opening I saw policemen, with flashlights and what looked like raised cavemen's clubs, move searchingly about several shacks across the street.

42   "Don't forget to lock the door securely behind me," my mother said as she ran her eyes up and down the street. More gunshots rang out; more screams and more shouts came from somewhere deep in the neighbourhood.

43   "Don't go, Mama!" I cried. "Please don't go! Don't leave us, please!"

44   She did not answer, but continued opening the door a little wider and inching her blanketed body, still bent low, slowly forward until she was halfway in and halfway out. Meantime in the bedroom George continued bawling. I hated it when he cried like that, for it heightened, and made more real, my feelings of confusion, terror and helplessness.

45   "Let him suck thumb," my mother said, now almost out of the house. She was still bent low. She spat on the doorknob twice, a ritual that, she once told me, protected the innocent and kept all evil spirits away, including the police. I felt vaguely reassured seeing her perform the ritual.

46   "And don't forget now," she said, "don't ever be afraid. I'll be back soon." Those were her last words; and as I watched her disappear behind the shacks, swallowed up by the ominous darkness and ominous sounds, her figure like that of a black-cloaked ghost, she seemed less of the mother I knew and loved, and more of a desperate fugitive fleeing off to her secret lair somewhere in the inky blackness.

47   I immediately slammed the door shut, bolted it in three places, blew out the candle and then scampered to the bedroom, where my brother was still crying. But as I flung open the bedroom door a new and more dreadful fear gripped me and made me turn and run back to the front door. I suddenly remembered how the police had smashed open the door during a raid one morning even though it had been bolted. I must barricade the door this time, I told myself; that will stop them. I started dragging things from all over the kitchen and piling them up against the

door—a barrel half-filled with drinking water, a scuttle half-filled with coal and several tin chairs. Satisfied that the door was now impregnable I then scuttled back to the bedroom and there leaped onto the bed by the latticed window.

"Shut up, you fool!" I yelled at my brother, but he did not quiet. I then uttered the phrase, "There's a white man outside," which to small black children had the same effect as "There's a bogeyman outside," but still he would not stop. I then stuck my thumb into his wide-open mouth, as my mother had told me. But George had other plans for my thumb; he sunk his teeth into it. Howling with pain, I grabbed him by the feet and tossed him over and spanked him on the buttocks. 48

"Don't ever do that!" 49

He became hysterical and went into a seizure of screams. His body writhed and his mouth frothed. Again I grabbed his tiny feet and shook him violently, begged him to stop screaming, but still he would not quiet. I screamed at him some more; that made him worse. In desperation I wrenched his ears, pinched him black and blue, but still he continued hollering. In despair I gave up, for the time being, attempts to quiet him. My head spun and did not know what to do. 50

I glanced at the window; it was getting light outside. I saw two black policemen breaking down a door at the far end of the yard. A half-naked, near-hysterical, jet-black woman was being led out of an outhouse by a fat laughing black policeman who, from time to time, prodded her private parts with a truncheon. The storm of noises had now subsided somewhat, but I could still hear doors and windows being smashed, and dogs barking and children screaming. I jerked George and pinned him against the window, hoping that he would somehow understand why I needed him to shut up; but that did not help, for his eyes were shut, and he continued to scream and writhe. My eyes roved frantically about the semidark room and came to rest on a heavy black blanket hanging limply from the side of the bed. Aha! I quickly grabbed it and pulled it over George's head to muffle his screams. I pinned it tightly with both hands over his small head as he lay writhing. It worked! For though he continued screaming, I could hardly hear him. He struggled and struggled and I pinned the blanket tighter and tighter. It never crossed my mind that my brother might suffocate. As he no longer screamed, I waited, from time to time glancing nervously at the window. 51

Suddenly I heard the bedroom door open and shut. Startled, I let go of my hold on the blanket and turned my head toward the door only to see Florah, her eyes wild with fear, come rushing in, screaming, her hands over her head. She came over to the bedside and began tugging frantically at the blanket. 52

"Where's Mama! I want Mama! Where's Mama!" 53

"Shut up!" I raged. "Go back to sleep before I hit you!" 54

She did not leave. 55

"I'm scared," she whimpered. "I want Mama." 56

57　"Shut up, you fool!" I screamed at her again. "The white man is outside, and he's going to get you and eat you!" I should not have said that; my sister became hysterical. She flung herself at the bed and tried to claw her way up. Enraged, I slapped her hard across the mouth; she staggered but did not fall. She promptly returned to the bedside and resumed her tugging of the blanket more determinedly. My brother too was now screaming. My head felt hot with confusion and desperation; I did not know what to do; I wished my mother were present; I wished the police were blotted off the surface of the earth.

58　I could still hear footsteps pounding, children screaming and dogs barking, so I quickly hauled my sister onto the bed, seeing that she was resolved not to return to the kitchen. We coiled together on the narrow bed, the three of us, but because of all the awkward movements everyone was making, the bricks propping the legs of the bed shifted, and it wobbled as if about to collapse. I held my breath, and the bed did not fall. I carefully pulled the blanket tautly over the three of us. Under the blanket I saw nothing but darkness.

59　But the din outside after a temporary lull surged and made its way through the bolted door, through the barricade, through the kitchen, through the blanket, through the blackness and into my finger-plugged ear, as if the bed were perched in the midst of all the pandemonium. My mind blazed with questions. What was really going on outside? Were the barking dogs police dogs? Who was shooting whom? Were the *Msomi** gangs involved? I had often been told that police dogs ate black people when given the order by white people—were they eating people this time? Suppose my mother had been apprehended, would the police dogs eat her up too? What was happening to my friends?

60　I ached with curiosity and fear. Should I go to the kitchen window and see what was going on in the streets? My sister had wet the bed, and it felt damp and cold. Childish curiosity finally overcame the fear, and I hopped out of bed and tiptoed to the kitchen window. I had barely reached the bedroom door when I heard my sister whimper.

61　"Where are you going? I'm scared." I looked over my shoulder and saw Florah on the edge of the bed, her legs dangling over the side, poised to follow.

62　"Shut up and go back to sleep!"

63　"I'm coming with you." She dropped her tiny feet to the floor.

64　"Dare and I'll whip you!"

65　She whined and retracted her body frame under the blanket. I slowly opened the bedroom door, taking care to keep low and away from the shaft of light still streaming through the uncurtained window. I reached the window. What next? A piece of sackcloth covered the bottom half of the window where several panes were missing, the result of a rock hurled from the street one night long ago. My father hadn't replaced the window but used the flap as a watchpost whenever police raided the neighbourhood.

---

* Legendary black gangsters of the fifties and early sixties in the mode of the Mafia.

With mounting excitement I raised myself toward the window and reached for the flap. I carefully pushed it to one side as I had seen my father do and then poked my head through; all the time my eyes were on the prowl for danger. My head was halfway in and halfway out when my eyes fell upon two tall black policemen emerging from a shack across the street. They joined two others standing alongside a white man by the entrance gate to one of the yards. The white man had a holstered gun slung low about his waist, as in the movies, and was pacing briskly about, shouting orders and pointing in all different directions. Further on in the yard, another white man, also with a gun, was supervising a group of about ten black policeman as they rounded up half-naked black men and women from the shacks. Children's screams issued from some of the shacks.

The sight had me spellbound. Suddenly the white man by the entrance gate pointed in the direction of our house. Two black policemen jumped and started across the street toward me. They were quickly joined by a third. I gasped with fear. A new terror gripped me and froze me by the window, my head still sticking halfway out. My mind went blank; I shut my eyes; my heart thumped somewhere in my throat. I overheard the three black policemen, as they came across the street, say to each other.

"That's number thirty-seven."

"Yes. But I don't think we'll find any of the *Msomi* gang in there."

"*Umlungu* [the white man] thinks there may be a few hiding in there. If we don't find them, we can still make easy money. The yard is a haven for people without passbooks."

"But I think everybody has fled. Look at those busted doors."

"There's a few over there still shut."

"All right, then, let's go in."

Suddenly there was a tremendous thud, as of something heavy crashing against the floor, and I heard George's screams of pain pierce the air. I opened my eyes momentarily and saw the three black policemen, only a few steps from the door, stop and look at one another. I quickly retracted my head but remained crouched under the window, afraid of going anywhere lest I be seen. I heard the three policemen say to one another:

"You hear that?"

"Yes. It's an infant crying."

"I bet you they left that one alone too."

Suddenly my sister came screaming out of the bedroom, her hands over her head.

"Yowee! Yowee!" she bawled. "Johannes! Come an' see! Come an' see!"

I stared at her, unable to move, not wanting to move.

"It's G-george," she stammered with horror; "B-blood, d-dead, b-blood, d-dead!" her voice trailed into sobs. She rushed over to where I stood and began pulling my hand, imploring me to go see my brother who, she said dramatically, was bleeding to death. My mouth contorted into frantic, inaudible "Go aways" and "shut ups" but she did not leave.

I heard someone pounding at the door. In the confusion that followed angry voices said:

82   "There's no point in going in. I've had enough of hollering infants."

83   "Me too."

84   "I bet you there's no one in there but the bloody children."

85   "You just took the words right out of my mouth."

86   "Then let's go back to the vans. We still have more streets to comb. This neighbourhood is about dry anyway."

87   They left. It turned out that George had accidently fallen off the bed and smashed his head against a pile of bricks at the foot of the bed, sustaining a deep cut across the forehead. The gash swelled and bled badly, stopping only after I had swathed his forehead with pieces of rags. The three of us cowered together in silence another three hours until my mother returned from the ditch where she had been hiding.

❏ Questions for Discussion

1. What details reveal the poverty of this family?

2. Why must the mother leave the house? Why is she so frantic to find her passbook?

3. Why are the police raiding the yard? If the family has done nothing wrong, why should the family fear the police?

4. The essay is told from the **point of view** of a five-year-old boy who seems wise for his age. What are the advantages of this point of view?

❏ Suggestions for Exploration and Writing

1. People whose jobs or life-styles require the frequent use of violence sometimes develop a tolerance for violence. In an essay discuss the development of a tolerance for violence in a group of people or propose methods for preventing the development of this tolerance.

2. Classify the fears of South African blacks as shown in this essay.

3. Could anything like this incident happen in the United States? In an essay, discuss the possibility.

FICTION

KATHERINE ANNE PORTER (1890–1980)

American short story writer Katherine Anne Porter considered herself an artist; and in her stories and her one novel, Ship of Fools

(1962), she proves her claim. For her subjects, Porter probed deeply into the minds and hearts of her characters, revealing both their dreams and aspirations and their disappointments and disillusionment. Her mastery of style, even in her early stories, was at least partly a result of her almost endless polishing.

The Grave

The grandfather, dead for more than thirty years, had been twice disturbed in his long repose by the constancy and possessiveness of his widow. She removed his bones first to Louisiana and then to Texas as if she had set out to find her own burial place, knowing well she would never return to the places she had left. In Texas she set up a small cemetery in a corner of her first farm, and as the family connection grew, and oddments of relations came over from Kentucky to settle, it contained at last about twenty graves. After the grandmother's death, part of her land was to be sold for the benefit of certain of her children, and the cemetery happened to lie in the part set aside for sale. It was necessary to take up the bodies and bury them again in the family plot in the big new public cemetery, where the grandmother had been buried. At last her husband was to lie beside her for eternity, as she had planned.

The family cemetery had been a pleasant small neglected garden of tangled rose bushes and ragged cedar trees and cypress, the simple flat stones rising out of uncropped sweet-smelling wild grass. The graves were lying open and empty one burning day when Miranda and her brother Paul, who often went together to hunt rabbits and doves, propped their twenty-two Winchester rifles carefully against the rail fence, climbed over and explored among the graves. She was nine years old and he was twelve.

They peered into the pits all shaped alike with such purposeful accuracy, and looking at each other with pleased adventurous eyes, they said in solemn tones: "These were graves!" trying by words to shape a special, suitable emotion in their minds, but they felt nothing except an agreeable thrill of wonder: they were seeing a new sight, doing something they had not done before. In them both there was also a small disappointment at the entire commonplaceness of the actual spectacle. Even if it had once contained a coffin for years upon years, when the coffin was gone a grave was just a hole in the ground. Miranda leaped into the pit that had held her grandfather's bones. Scratching around aimlessly and pleasurably as any young animal, she scooped up a lump of earth and weighed it in her palm. It had a pleasantly sweet, corrupt smell, being mixed with the cedar needles and small leaves, and as the crumbs fell apart, she saw a silver dove no larger than a hazel nut, with spread wings and a neat fan-shaped tail. The breast had a deep round hollow in it. Turning it up to the fierce sunlight, she saw that the inside of the hollow was cut in little whorls. She scrambled out, over the pile of loose earth that had fallen back into one end of the grave, calling to Paul that she had found something, he must guess what . . . His head appeared smiling over the rim of another grave.

He waved a closed hand at her. "I've got something too!" They ran to compare treasures, making a game of it, so many guesses each, all wrong, and a final show-down with opened palms. Paul had found a thin wide gold ring carved with intricate flowers and leaves. Miranda was smitten at sight of the ring and wished to have it. Paul seemed more impressed by the dove. They made a trade, with some little bickering. After he had got the dove in his hand, Paul said, "Don't you know what this is? This is a screw head for a *coffin!* . . . I'll bet nobody else in the world has one like this!"

4   Miranda glanced at it without covetousness. She had the gold ring on her thumb; it fitted perfectly. "Maybe we ought to go now," she said, "maybe one of the niggers 'll see us and tell somebody." They knew the land had been sold, the cemetery was no longer theirs, and they felt like trespassers. They climbed back over the fence, slung their rifles loosely under their arms—they had been shooting at targets with various kinds of firearms since they were seven years old—and set out to look for the rabbits and doves or whatever small game might happen along. On these expeditions Miranda always followed at Paul's heels along the path, obeying instructions about handling her gun when going through fences; learning how to stand it up properly so it would not slip and fire unexpectedly; how to wait her time for a shot and not just bang away in the air without looking, spoiling shots for Paul, who really could hit things if given a chance. Now and then, in her excitement at seeing birds whizz up suddenly before her face, or a rabbit leap across her very toes, she lost her head, and almost without sighting she flung her rifle up and pulled the trigger. She hardly ever hit any sort of mark. She had no proper sense of hunting at all. Her brother would be often completely disgusted with her. "You don't care whether you get your bird or not," he said. "That's no way to hunt." Miranda could not understand his indignation. She had seen him smash his hat and yell with fury when he had missed his aim. "What I like about shooting," said Miranda, with exasperating inconsequence, "is pulling the trigger and hearing the noise."

5   "Then, by golly," said Paul, "whyn't you go back to the range and shoot at bulls-eyes?"

6   "I'd just as soon," said Miranda, "only like this, we walk round more."

7   "Well, you just stay behind and stop spoiling my shots," said Paul, who, when he made a kill, wanted to be certain he had made it. Miranda, who alone brought down a bird once in twenty rounds, always claimed as her own any game they got when they fired at the same moment. It was tiresome and unfair and her brother was sick of it.

8   "Now, the first dove we see, or the first rabbit, is mine," he told her. "and the next will be yours. Remember that and don't get smarty."

9   "What about snakes?" asked Miranda idly. "Can I have the first snake?"

10   Waving her thumb gently and watching her gold ring glitter, Miranda lost interest in shooting. She was wearing her summer roughing outfit:

dark blue overalls, a light blue shirt, a hired-man's straw hat, and thick brown sandals. Her brother had the same outfit except his was a sober hickory-nut color. Ordinarily Miranda preferred her overalls to any other dress, though it was making rather a scandal in the countryside, for the year was 1903, and in the back country the law of female decorum had teeth in it. Her father had been criticized for letting his girls dress like boys and go careering around astride barebacked horses. Big sister Maria, the really independent and fearless one, in spite of her rather affected ways, rode at a dead run with only a rope knotted around her horse's nose. It was said that the motherless family was running down, with the Grandmother no longer there to hold it together. It was known that she had discriminated against her son Harry in her will, and that he was in straits about money. Some of his old neighbors reflected with vicious satisfaction that now he would probably not be so stiffnecked, nor have any more high-stepping horses either. Miranda knew this, though she could not say how. She had met along the road old women of the kind who smoked corn-cob pipes, who had treated her grandmother with most sincere respect. They slanted their gummy old eyes side-ways at the granddaughter and said, "Ain't you ashamed of yoself, Missy? It's aginst the Scriptures to dress like that. Whut yo Pappy thinkin about?" Miranda, with her powerful social sense, which was like a fine set of antennae radiating from every pore of her skin, would feel ashamed because she knew well it was rude and ill-bred to shock anybody, even bad-tempered old crones, though she had faith in her father's judgment and was perfectly comfortable in the clothes. Her father had said, "They're just what you need, and they'll save your dresses for school . . ." This sounded quite simple and natural to her. She had been brought up in rigorous economy. Wastefulness was vulgar. It was also a sin. These were truths; she had heard them repeated many times and never once disputed.

Now the ring, shining with the serene purity of fine gold on her rather grubby thumb, turned her feelings against her overalls and sockless feet, toes sticking through the thick brown leather straps. She wanted to go back to the farmhouse, take a good cold bath, dust herself with plenty of Maria's violet talcum powder—provided Maria was not present to ob-ject, of course—put on the thinnest, most becoming dress she owned, with a big sash, and sit in a wicker chair under the trees . . . These things were not all she wanted, of course; she had vague stirrings of desire for luxury and a grand way of living which could not take precise form in her imagination but were founded on family legend of past wealth and leisure. These immediate comforts were what she could have, and she wanted them at once. She lagged rather far behind Paul, and once she thought of just turning back without a word and going home. She stopped, thinking that Paul would never do that to her, and so she would have to tell him. When a rabbit leaped, she let Paul have it without dispute. He killed it with one shot.

12   When she came up with him, he was already kneeling, examining the wound, the rabbit trailing from his hands. "Right through the head," he said complacently, as if he had aimed for it. He took out his sharp, competent bowie knife and started to skin the body. He did it very cleanly and quickly. Uncle Jimbilly knew how to prepare the skins so that Miranda always had fur coats for her dolls, for though she never cared much for her dolls she liked seeing them in fur coats. The children knelt facing each other over the dead animal. Miranda watched admiringly while her brother stripped the skin away as if he were taking off a glove. The flayed flesh emerged dark scarlet, sleek, firm; Miranda with thumb and finger felt the long fine muscles with the silvery flat strips binding them to the joints. Brother lifted the oddly bloated belly. "Look," he said, in a low amazed voice. "It was going to have young ones."

13   Very carefully he slit the thin flesh from the center ribs to the flanks, and a scarlet bag appeared. He slit again and pulled the bag open, and there lay a bundle of tiny rabbits, each wrapped in a thin scarlet veil. The brother pulled these off and there they were, dark gray, their sleek wet down lying in minute even ripples, like a baby's head just washed, their unbelievably small delicate ears folded close, their little blind faces almost featureless.

14   Miranda said, "Oh, I want to *see*," under her breath. She looked and looked—excited but not frightened, for she was accustomed to the sight of animals killed in hunting—filled with pity and astonishment and a kind of shocked delight in the wonderful little creatures for their own sakes, they were so pretty. She touched one of them ever so carefully, "Ah, there's blood running over them," she said and began to tremble without knowing why. Yet she wanted most deeply to see and to know. Having seen, she felt at once as if she had known all along. The very memory of her former ignorance faded, she had always known just this. No one had ever told her anything outright, she had been rather unobservant of the animal life around her because she was so accustomed to animals. They seemed simply disorderly and unaccountably rude in their habits, but altogether natural and not very interesting. Her brother had spoken as if he had known about everything all along. He may have seen all this before. He had never said a word to her, but she knew now a part at least of what he knew. She understood a little of the secret, formless intuitions in her own mind and body, which had been clearing up, taking form, so gradually and so steadily she had not realized that she was learning what she had to know. Paul said cautiously, as if he were talking about something forbidden. "They were just about ready to be born." His voice dropped on the last word. "I know," said Miranda, "like kittens. I know, like babies." She was quietly and terribly agitated, standing again with her rifle under her arm, looking down at the bloody heap. "I don't want the skin," she said, "I won't have it." Paul buried the young rabbits again in their mother's body, wrapped the skin around her, carried her to a clump of sage bushes, and hid her away. He came out

again at once and said to Miranda, with an eager friendliness, a confidential tone quite unusual in him, as if he were taking her into an important secret on equal terms: "Listen now. Now you listen to me, and don't ever forget. Don't you ever tell a living soul that you saw this. Don't tell a soul. Don't tell Dad because I'll get into trouble. He'll say I'm leading you into things you ought not to do. He's always saying that. So now don't you go and forget and blab out sometime the way you're always doing . . . Now, that's a secret. Don't you tell."

Miranda never told, she did not even wish to tell anybody. She thought 15 about the whole worrisome affair with confused unhappiness for a few days. Then it sank quietly in her mind and was heaped over by accumulated thousands of impressions, for nearly twenty years. One day she was picking her path among the puddles and crushed refuse of a market street in a strange city of a strange country, when without warning, plain and clear in its true colors as if she looked through a frame upon a scene that had not stirred nor changed since the moment it happened, the episode of that far-off day leaped from its burial place before her mind's eye. She was so reasonlessly horrified she halted suddenly staring, the scene before her eyes dimmed by the vision back of them. An Indian vendor had held up before her a tray of dyed sugar sweets, in the shapes of all kinds of small creatures: birds, baby chicks, baby rabbits, lambs, baby pigs. They were in gay colors and smelled of vanilla, maybe. . . . It was a very hot day and the smell in the market, with its piles of raw flesh and wilting flowers, was like the mingled sweetness and corruption she had smelled that other day in the empty cemetery at home: the day she had remembered always until now vaguely as the time she and her brother had found treasure in the opened graves. Instantly upon this thought the dreadful vision faded, and she saw clearly her brother, whose childhood face she had forgotten, standing again in the blazing sunshine, again twelve years old, a pleased sober smile in his eyes, turning the silver dove over and over in his hands.

❑ Questions for Discussion

1. What is significant about the graveyard **setting?**

2. What is unusual about Miranda's appearance and interests?

3. Why does Paul insist that Miranda not tell about the incident? Why is she not supposed to know about such experiences?

4. How does Miranda react to the sight of the dead rabbit with her dead fetuses? Why does Miranda remember the scene with horror? Why is the experience with the rabbit so important to Miranda? Could it be described as an **epiphany?**

5. The story of the discoveries in the grave is framed by the scene of moving the remains of Miranda's grandfather and the later

scene in the Indian market. What significance do these framing scenes have?

❏ **Suggestions for Exploration and Writing**

1. Write an essay describing your first encounter with death.

2. Memories linger, especially memories of extremes: a violent or a peaceful scene, death or birth, marriage or painful divorce. In "So Tsi-fai," Liu is plagued by memories of the title character: "After all these years, my mind is still haunted by this scene." Porter also says, ". . . the episode of that far-off day leaped from its burial place before her mind's eye." Write an essay in which you describe a particularly vivid memory which haunts you.

3. In "A Summer Tragedy," Bontemps explores death from the **point of view** of an old black couple. In "The Grave," Porter explores the same subject from the point of view of two white children. Contrast the points of view in the two stories.

4. After carefully re-reading the descriptions of the ring, the dove, and the rabbit, write an essay explaining and illustrating what each symbolizes.

WILLIAM FAULKNER (1897–1962)

Born near Oxford, Mississippi, Faulkner used his home state as the setting for many of his short stories and novels. He invented an imaginary county—Yoknapatawpha—and peopled it with a variety of characters worthy of Shakespeare, from the noble members of the Sartoris family and the intellectual Quenton Compson to the Snopes family, most of whom are sneaky and self-serving. His most famous novels include The Sound and the Fury *(1929),* Light in August *(1932),* Absalom, Absalom! *(1936), and the Snopes trilogy:* The Hamlet *(1940),* The Town *(1957), and* The Mansion *(1958). In 1950, Faulkner was awarded the Nobel Prize for Literature.*

A Rose for Emily

I

1   When Miss Emily Grierson died, our whole town went to her funeral: the men through a sort of respectful affection for a fallen monument, the women mostly out of curiosity to see the inside of her house, which no one save an old manservant—a combined gardener and cook—had seen in at least ten years.

2   It was a big, squarish frame house that had once been white, decorated with cupolas and spires and scrolled balconies in the heavily lightsome

style of the seventies, set on what had once been our most select street. But garages and cotton gins had encroached and obliterated even the august names of that neighborhood; only Miss Emily's house was left, lifting its stubborn and coquettish decay above the cotton wagons and the gasoline pumps—an eyesore among eyesores. And now Miss Emily had gone to join the representatives of those august names where they lay in the cedar-bemused cemetery among the ranked and anonymous graves of Union and Confederate soldiers who fell at the battle of Jefferson.

Alive, Miss Emily had been a tradition, a duty, and a care; a sort of hereditary obligation upon the town, dating from that day in 1894 when Colonel Sartoris, the mayor—he who fathered the edict that no Negro woman should appear on the streets without an apron—remitted her taxes, the dispensation dating from the death of her father on into perpetuity. Not that Miss Emily would have accepted charity. Colonel Sartoris invented an involved tale to the effect that Miss Emily's father had loaned money to the town, which the town, as a matter of business, preferred this way of repaying. Only a man of Colonel Sartoris' generation and thought could have invented it and only a woman could have believed it.

When the next generation, with its more modern ideas, became mayors and aldermen, this arrangement created some little dissatisfaction. On the first of the year they mailed her a tax notice. February came, and there was no reply. They wrote her a formal letter, asking her to call at the sheriff's office at her convenience. A week later the mayor wrote her himself, offering to call or to send his car for her, and received in reply a note on paper of an archaic shape, in a thin, flowing calligraphy in faded ink, to the effect that she no longer went out at all. The tax notice was also enclosed, without comment.

They called a special meeting of the Board of Aldermen. A deputation waited upon her, knocked at the door through which no visitor had passed since she ceased giving china painting lessons eight or ten years earlier. They were admitted by the old Negro into a dim hall from which a stairway mounted into still more shadow. It smelled of dust and disuse—a close, dank smell. The Negro led them into the parlor. It was furnished in heavy, leather-covered furniture. When the Negro opened the blinds of one window, they could see that the leather was cracked; and when they sat down, a faint dust rose sluggishly about their thighs, spinning with slow motes in the single sun-ray. On a tarnished gilt easel before the fireplace stood a crayon portrait of Miss Emily's father.

They rose when she entered—a small, fat woman in black, with a thin gold chain descending to her waist and vanishing into her belt, leaning on an ebony cane with a tarnished gold head. Her skeleton was small and spare; perhaps that was why what would have been merely plumpness in another was obesity in her. She looked bloated, like a body long submerged in motionless water, and of that pallid hue. Her eyes, lost in the fatty ridges of her face, looked like two small pieces of coal pressed into a lump of dough as they moved from one face to another while the visitors stated their errand.

7   She did not ask them to sit. She just stood in the door and listened quietly until the spokesman came to a stumbling halt. Then they could hear the invisible watch ticking at the end of the gold chain.

8   Her voice was dry and cold. "I have no taxes in Jefferson. Colonel Sartoris explained it to me. Perhaps one of you can gain access to the city records and satisfy yourselves."

9   "But we have. We are the city authorities, Miss Emily. Didn't you get a notice from the sheriff, signed by him?"

10   "I received a paper, yes," Miss Emily said. "Perhaps he considers himself the sheriff . . . I have no taxes in Jefferson."

11   "But there is nothing on the books to show that, you see. We must go by the —"

12   "See Colonel Sartoris. I have no taxes in Jefferson."

13   "But, Miss Emily —"

14   "See Colonel Sartoris." (Colonel Sartoris had been dead almost ten years.) "I have no taxes in Jefferson. Tobe!" The Negro appeared. "Show these gentlemen out."

II

15   So she vanquished them, horse and foot, just as she had vanquished their fathers thirty years before about the smell. That was two years after her father's death and a short time after her sweetheart—the one we believed would marry her—had deserted her. After her father's death she went out very little; after her sweetheart went away, people hardly saw her at all. A few of the ladies had the temerity to call, but were not received, and the only sign of life about the place was the Negro man—a young man then—going in and out with a market basket.

16   "Just as if a man—any man—could keep a kitchen properly," the ladies said; so they were not surprised when the smell developed. It was another link between the gross, teeming world and the high and mighty Griersons.

17   A neighbor, a woman, complained to the mayor, Judge Stevens, eighty years old.

18   "But what will you have me do about it, madam?" he said.

19   "Why, send her word to stop it," the woman said. "Isn't there a law?"

20   "I'm sure that won't be necessary," Judge Stevens said. "It's probably just a snake or a rat that nigger of hers killed in the yard. I'll speak to him about it."

21   The next day he received two more complaints, one from a man who came in diffident deprecation. "We really must do something about it, Judge. I'd be the last one in the world to bother Miss Emily, but we've got to do something." That night the Board of Aldermen met—three graybeards and one younger man, a member of the rising generation.

22   "It's simple enough," he said. "Send her word to have her place cleaned up. Give her a certain time to do it in, and if she don't . . ."

"Dammit, sir," Judge Stevens said, "will you accuse a lady to her face 23
of smelling bad?"

So the next night, after midnight, four men crossed Miss Emily's lawn 24
and slunk about the house like burglars, sniffing along the base of the
brickwork and at the cellar openings while one of them performed a
regular sowing motion with his hand out of a sack slung from his
shoulder. They broke open the cellar door and sprinkled lime there, and
in all the outbuildings. As they recrossed the lawn, a window that had
been dark was lighted and Miss Emily sat in it, the light behind her, and
her upright torso motionless as that of an idol. They crept quietly across
the lawn and into the shadow of the locusts that lined the street. After a
week or two the smell went away.

That was when people had begun to feel really sorry for her. People in 25
our town, remembering how old lady Wyatt, her great-aunt, had gone
completely crazy at last, believed that the Griersons held themselves a
little too high for what they really were. None of the young men were
quite good enough for Miss Emily and such. We had long thought of
them as a tableau, Miss Emily a slender figure in white in the background, her father a spraddled silhouette in the foreground, his back to
her and clutching a horsewhip, the two of them framed by the back-flung
front door. So when she got to be thirty and was still single, we were not
pleased exactly, but vindicated; even with insanity in the family she
wouldn't have turned down all of her chances if they had really materi-
alized.

When her father died, it got about that the house was all that was left 26
to her; and in a way, people were glad. At last they could pity Miss Emily.
Being left alone, and a pauper, she had become humanized. Now she too
would know the old thrill and the old despair of a penny more or less.

The day after his death all the ladies prepared to call at the house and 27
offer condolence and aid, as is our custom. Miss Emily met them at the
door, dressed as usual and with no trace of grief on her face. She told
them that her father was not dead. She did that for three days, with the
ministers calling on her, and the doctors, trying to persuade her to let
them dispose of the body. Just as they were about to resort to law and
force, she broke down, and they buried her father quickly.

We did not say she was crazy then. We believed she had to do that. We 28
remembered all the young men her father had driven away, and we knew
that with nothing left, she would have to cling to that which had robbed
her, as people will.

III

She was sick for a long time. When we saw her again, her hair was cut 29
short, making her look like a girl, with a vague resemblance to those
angels in colored church windows—sort of tragic and serene.

The town had just let the contracts for paving the sidewalks, and in 30
the summer after her father's death they began the work. The construction company came with niggers and mules and machinery, and a

foreman named Homer Barron, a Yankee—a big, dark, ready man, with a big voice and eyes lighter than his face. The little boys would follow in groups to hear him cuss the niggers, and the niggers singing in time to the rise and fall of picks. Pretty soon he knew everybody in town. Whenever you heard a lot of laughing anywhere about the square, Homer Barron would be in the center of the group. Presently we began to see him and Miss Emily on Sunday afternoons driving in the yellow-wheeled buggy and the matched team of bays from the livery stable.

31   At first we were glad that Miss Emily would have an interest, because the ladies all said, "Of course a Grierson would not think seriously of a Northerner, a day laborer." But there were still others, older people, who said that even grief could not cause a real lady to forget *noblesse oblige*—without calling it *noblesse oblige*. They just said, "Poor Emily. Her kinsfolk should come to her." She had some kin in Alabama; but years ago her father had fallen out with them over the estate of old lady Wyatt, the crazy woman, and there was no communication between the two families. They had not even been represented at the funeral.

32   And as soon as the old people said, "Poor Emily," the whispering began. "Do you suppose it's really so?" they said to one another. "Of course it is. What else could . . ." This behind their hands; rustling of craned silk and satin behind jalousies closed upon the sun of Sunday afternoon as the thin, swift clop-clop-clop of the matched team passed: "Poor Emily."

33   She carried her head high enough—even when we believed that she was fallen. It was as if she demanded more than ever the recognition of her dignity as the last Grierson; as if it had wanted that touch of earthiness to reaffirm her imperviousness. Like when she bought the rat poison, the arsenic. That was over a year after they had begun to say "Poor Emily," and while the two female cousins were visiting her.

34   "I want some poison," she said to the druggist. She was over thirty then, still a slight woman, though thinner than usual, with cold, haughty black eyes in a face the flesh of which was strained across the temples and about the eyesockets as you imagine a lighthouse-keeper's face ought to look. "I want some poison," she said.

35   "Yes, Miss Emily. What kind? For rats and such? I'd recom—"

36   "I want the best you have. I don't care what kind."

37   The druggist named several. "They'll kill anything up to an elephant. But what you want is—"

38   "Arsenic," Miss Emily said, "Is that a good one?"

39   "Is . . . arsenic? Yes, ma'am. But what you want—"

40   "I want arsenic."

41   The druggist looked down at her. She looked back at him, erect, her face like a strained flag. "Why, of course," the druggist said. "If that's what you want. But the law requires you to tell what you are going to use it for."

Miss Emily just stared at him, her head tilted back in order to look him
eye for eye, until he looked away and went and got the arsenic and
wrapped it up. The Negro delivery boy brought her the package; the
druggist didn't come back. When she opened the package at home there
was written on the box, under the skull and bones: "For rats."

IV

So the next day we all said, "She will kill herself"; and we said it would
be the best thing. When she had first begun to be seen with Homer
Barron, we had said, "She will marry him." Then we said, "She will
persuade him yet," because Homer himself had remarked—he liked men,
and it was known that he drank with the younger men in the Elks'
Club—that he was not a marrying man. Later we said, "Poor Emily"
behind the jalousies as they passed on Sunday afternoon in the glittering
buggy, Miss Emily with her head high and Homer Barron with his hat
cocked and a cigar in his teeth, reins and whip in a yellow glove.

Then some of the ladies began to say that it was a disgrace to the town
and a bad example to the young people. The men did not want to
interfere, but at last the ladies forced the Baptist minister—Miss Emily's
people were Episcopal—to call upon her. He would never divulge what
happened during that interview, but he refused to go back again. The
next Sunday they again drove about the streets, and the following day the
minister's wife wrote to Miss Emily's relations in Alabama.

So she had blood-kin under her roof again and we sat back to watch
the developments. At first nothing happened. Then we were sure that
they were to be married. We learned that Miss Emily had been to the
jeweler's and ordered a man's toilet set in silver, with the letters H. B. on
each piece. Two days later we learned that she had bought a complete
outfit of men's clothing, including a nightshirt, and we said, "They are
married." We were really glad. We were glad because the two female
cousins were even more Grierson than Miss Emily had ever been.

So we were not surprised when Homer Barron—the streets had been
finished some time since—was gone. We were a little disappointed that
there was not a public blowing-off, but we believed that he had gone on
to prepare for Miss Emily's coming, or to give her a chance to get rid of
the cousins. (By that time it was a cabal, and we were all Miss Emily's
allies to help circumvent the cousins.) Sure enough, after another week
they departed. And, as we had expected all along, within three days
Homer Barron was back in town. A neighbor saw the Negro man admit
him at the kitchen door at dusk one evening.

And that was the last we saw of Homer Barron. And of Miss Emily for
some time. The Negro man went in and out with the market basket, but
the front door remained closed. Now and then we would see her at a
window for a moment, as the men did that night when they sprinkled the
lime, but for almost six months she did not appear on the streets. Then
we knew that this was to be expected too; as if that quality of her father

which had thwarted her woman's life so many times had been too virulent and too furious to die.

48   When we next saw Miss Emily, she had grown fat and her hair was turning gray. During the next few years it grew grayer and grayer until it attained an even pepper-and-salt iron-gray, when it ceased turning. Up to the day of her death at seventy-four it was still that vigorous iron-gray, like the hair of an active man.

49   From that time on her front door remained closed, save for a period of six or seven years, when she was about forty, during which she gave lessons in china-painting. She fitted up a studio in one of the downstairs rooms, where the daughters and granddaughters of Colonel Sartoris' contemporaries were sent to her with the same regularity and in the same spirit that they were sent to church on Sundays with a twenty-five-cent piece for the collection plate. Meanwhile her taxes had been remitted.

50   Then the newer generation became the backbone and the spirit of the town, and the painting pupils grew up and fell away and did not send their children to her with boxes of color and tedious brushes and pictures cut from the ladies' magazines. The front door closed upon the last one and remained closed for good. When the town got free postal delivery, Miss Emily alone refused to let them fasten the metal numbers above her door and attach a mailbox to it. She would not listen to them.

51   Daily, monthly, yearly we watched the Negro grow grayer and more stooped, going in and out with the market basket. Each December we sent her a tax notice, which would be returned by the post office a week later, unclaimed. Now and then we would see her in one of the downstairs windows—she had evidently shut up the top floor of the house—like the carven torso of an idol in a niche, looking or not looking at us, we could never tell which. Thus she passed from generation to generation—dear, inescapable, impervious, tranquil, and perverse.

52   And so she died. Fell ill in the house filled with dust and shadows, with only a doddering Negro man to wait on her. We did not even know she was sick; we had long since given up trying to get any information from the Negro. He talked to no one, probably not even to her, for his voice had grown harsh and rusty, as if from disuse.

53   She died in one of the downstairs rooms, in a heavy walnut bed with a curtain, her gray head propped on a pillow yellow and moldy with age and lack of sunlight.

V

54   The Negro met the first of the ladies at the front door and let them in, with their hushed, sibilant voices and their quick curious glances, and then he disappeared. He walked right through the house and out the back and was not seen again.

55   The two female cousins came at once. They held the funeral on the second day, with the town coming to look at Miss Emily beneath a mass of bought flowers, with the crayon face of her father musing profoundly

above the bier and the ladies sibilant and macabre; and the very old men — some in their brushed confederate uniforms — on the porch and the lawn, talking of Miss Emily as if she had been a contemporary of theirs, believing that they had danced with her and courted her perhaps, confusing time with its mathematical progression, as the old do, to whom all the past is not a diminishing road but, instead, a huge meadow which no winter ever quite touches, divided from them now by the narrow bottleneck of the most recent decade of years.

Already we knew that there was one room in that region above stairs   56 which no one had seen in forty years, and which would have to be forced. They waited until Miss Emily was decently in the ground before they opened it.

The violence of breaking down the door seemed to fill this room with   57 pervading dust. A thin, acrid pall as of the tomb seemed to lie everywhere upon this room decked and furnished as for a bridal: upon the valance curtains of faded rose color, upon the rose-shaded lights, upon the dressing table, upon the delicate array of crystal and the man's toilet things backed with tarnished silver, silver so tarnished that the monogram was obscured. Among them lay a collar and tie, as if they had just been removed, which, lifted, left upon the surface a pale crescent in the dust. Upon a chair hung the suit, carefully folded; beneath it the two mute shoes and the discarded socks.

The man himself lay in the bed.   58

For a long while we just stood there, looking down at the profound   59 and fleshless grin. The body had apparently once lain in the attitude of an embrace, but now the long sleep that outlasts love, that conquers even the grimace of love, had cuckolded him. What was left of him, rotted beneath what was left of the nightshirt, had become inextricable from the bed in which he lay; and upon him and upon the pillow beside him lay that even coating of the patient and biding dust.

Then we noticed that in the second pillow was the indentation of a   60 head. One of us lifted something from it, and leaning forward, that faint and invisible dust dry and acrid in the nostrils, we saw a long strand of iron-gray hair.

❏ Questions for Discussion

1. From whose **point of view** is the story told? How would you describe the narrators' attitude toward Miss Emily?

2. What is the relationship between the town and Miss Emily? In what sense(s) is she a "tradition, a duty, and a care"? Why does Colonel Sartoris feel obliged to remit her taxes and to make up an excuse for doing so?

3. Why is Miss Emily able to vanquish the authorities of Jefferson, to make them back down on taxes and on the smell? Why don't they just bring the force of the law to bear on her?

4. What does the description of the parlor reveal about the house and about Miss Emily?

5. What does the last sentence of the story reveal? What hints of the ending make it believable, if shocking?

❏ **Suggestions for Exploration and Writing**

1. Write an essay about a person you know who has refused to adapt to changing times.

2. In terms of the time and the environment in which she lives, explain Miss Emily's treatment by, and response to, the two men in her life.

Arna Bontemps (1902–1973)

Bontemps was born in Alexandria, Louisiana, but moved to Los Angeles, California, as a child. Because his parents resented their African-American heritage, they sent him to white schools, and he lived in white neighborhoods. Bontemps learned about his culture from his great uncle Buddy. As a result of his upbringing, Bontemps spent the rest of his life trying to rectify omissions in the history books and trying to increase interest in African-American literature and culture.

A Summer Tragedy

1   Old Jeff Patton, the black share farmer, fumbled with his bow tie. His fingers trembled, and the high, stiff collar pinched his throat. A fellow loses his hand for such vanities after thirty or forty years of simple life. Once a year, or maybe twice if there's a wedding among his kin-folks, he may spruce up; but generally fancy clothes do nothing but adorn the wall of the big room and feed the moths. That had been Jeff Patton's experience. He had not worn his stiff-bosomed shirt more than a dozen times in all his married life. His swallowtailed coat lay on the bed beside him, freshly brushed and pressed, but it was as full of holes as the overalls in which he worked on week days. The moths had used it badly. Jeff twisted his mouth into a hideous toothless grimace as he contended with the obstinate bow. He stamped his good foot and decided to give up the struggle.

2   "Jennie," he called.

3   "What's that, Jeff?" His wife's shrunken voice came out of the adjoining room like an echo. It was hardly bigger than a whisper.

4   "I reckon you'll have to he'p me wid this heah bow tie, baby," he said meekly. "Dog if I can hitch it up."

5   Her answer was not strong enough to reach him, but presently the old

woman came to the door, feeling her way with a stick. She had a wasted, dead-leaf appearance. Her body, as scrawny and gnarled as a stringbean, seemed less than nothing in the ocean of frayed and faded petticoats that surrounded her. These hung an inch or two above the tops of her heavy, unlaced shoes and showed little grotesque piles where the stockings had fallen down from her negligible legs.

"You oughta could do a heap mo' wid a thing like that 'n me—beingst as you got yo' good sight." 6

"Looks like I *oughta* could," he admitted. "But ma fingers is gone democrat on me. I get all mixed up in the looking glass an' can't tell whicha way to twist the devilish thing." 7

Jennie sat on the side of the bed and old Jeff Patton got down on one knee while she tied the bow knot. It was a slow and painful ordeal for each of them in this position. Jeff's bones cracked, his knee ached, and it was only after a half dozen attempts that Jennie worked a semblance of a bow into the tie. 8

"I got to dress maself now," the old woman whispered. "These is ma old shoes an' stockings, and I ain't so much as unwrapped ma dress." 9

"Well, don't worry 'bout me no mo', baby," Jeff said. "That 'bout finishes me. All I gotta do now is slip on that old coat 'n ves' an' I'll be fixed to leave." 10

Jennie disappeared again through the dim passage into the shed room. Being blind was no handicap to her in that black hole. Jeff heard the cane placed against the wall beside the door and knew that his wife was on easy ground. He put on his coat, took a battered top hat from the bed post, and hobbled to the front door. He was ready to travel. As soon as Jennie could get on her Sunday shoes and her old black silk dress, they would start. 11

Outside the tiny log house the day was warm and mellow with sunshine. A host of wasps was humming with busy excitement in the trunk of a dead sycamore. Grey squirrels were searching through the grass for hickory nuts and blue jays were in the trees, hopping from branch to branch. Pine woods stretched away to the left like a black sea. Among them were scattered scores of log houses like Jeff's, houses of black share farmers. Cows and pigs wandered freely among the trees. There was no danger of loss. Each farmer knew his own stock and knew his neighbor's as well as he knew his neighbor's children. 12

Down the slope to the right were the cultivated acres on which the colored folks worked. They extended to the river, more than two miles away, and they were today green with the unmade cotton crop. A tiny thread of a road, which passed directly in front of Jeff's place, ran through these green fields like a pencil mark. 13

Jeff, standing outside the door with his absurd hat in his left hand, surveyed the wide scene tenderly. He had been forty-five years on these acres. He loved them with the unexplained affection that others have for the countries to which they belong. 14

15   The sun was hot on his head, his collar still pinched his throat, and the Sunday clothes were intolerably hot. Jeff transferred the hat to his right hand and began fanning with it. Suddenly the whisper that was Jennie's voice came out of the shed room.

16   "You can bring the car round front whilst you's waitin'," it said feebly. There was a tired pause; then it added, "I'll soon be fixed to go."

17   "A'right, baby," Jeff answered. "I'll get it in a minute."

18   But he didn't move. A thought struck him that made his mouth fall open. The mention of the car brought to his mind, with new intensity, the trip he and Jennie were about to take. Fear came into his eyes; excitement took his breath. Lord, Jesus!

19   "Jeff . . . Oh Jeff," the old woman's whisper called.

20   He awakened with a jolt. "Hunh, baby?"

21   "What you doin'?"

22   "Nuthin. Jes studyin'. I jes been turnin' things round 'n round in ma mind."

23   "You could be gettin' the car," she said.

24   "Oh yes, right away, baby."

25   He started round to the shed, limping heavily on his bad leg. There were three frizzly chickens in the yard. All his other chickens had been killed or stolen recently. But the frizzly chickens had been saved somehow. That was fortunate indeed, for these curious creatures had a way of devouring "poison" from the yard and in that way protecting against conjure and bad luck and spells. But even the frizzly chickens seemed now to be in a stupor. Jeff thought they had some ailment; he expected all three of them to die shortly.

26   The shed in which the old model-T Ford stood was only a grass roof held up by four corner poles. It had been built by tremulous hands at a time when the little rattle-trap car had been regarded as a peculiar treasure. And, miraculously, despite wind and downpour, it still stood.

27   Jeff adjusted the crank and put his weight on it. The engine came to life with a sputter and bang that rattled the old car from radiator to tail light. Jeff hopped into the seat and put his foot on the accelerator. The sputtering and banging increased. The rattling became more violent. That was good. It was good banging, good sputtering and rattling, and it meant that the aged car was still in running condition. She could be depended on for this trip.

28   Again Jeff's thought halted as if paralyzed. The suggestion of the trip fell into the machinery of his mind like a wrench. He felt dazed and weak. He swung the car out into the yard, made a half turn, and drove around to the front door. When he took his hands off the wheel, he noticed that he was trembling violently. He cut off the motor and climbed to the ground to wait for Jennie.

29   A few moments later she was at the window, her voice rattling against the pane like a broken shutter.

30   "I'm ready, Jeff."

He did not answer, but limped into the house and took her by the arm. 31
He led her slowly though the big room, down the step, and across the
yard.

"You reckon I'd oughta lock the do'?" he asked softly. 32

They stopped and Jennie weighed the question. Finally she shook her 33
head.

"Ne' mind the do'," she said. "I don't see no cause to lock up things." 34

"You right," Jeff agreed. "No cause to lock up." 35

Jeff opened the door and helped his wife into the car. A quick shudder 36
passed over him. Jesus! Again he trembled.

"How come you shaking so?" Jennie whispered. 37

"I don't know," he said. 38

"You mus' be scairt, Jeff." 39

"No, baby, I ain't scairt." 40

He slammed the door after her and went around to crank up again. 41
The motor started easily. Jeff wished that it had not been so responsive.
He would have liked a few more minutes in which to turn things around
in his head. As it was, with Jennie chiding him about being afraid, he had
to keep going. He swung the car into the little pencil-mark road and
started off toward the river, driving very slowly, very cautiously.

Chugging across the green countryside, the small, battered Ford 42
seemed tiny indeed. Jeff felt a familiar excitement, a thrill, as they came
down the first slope to the immense levels on which the cotton was
growing. He could not help reflecting that the crops were good. He knew
what that meant, too; he had made forty-five of them with his own
hands. It was true that he had worn out nearly a dozen mules, but that
was the fault of old man Stevenson, the owner of the land. Major
Stevenson had the odd notion that one mule was all a share farmer
needed to work a thirty-acre plot. It was an expensive notion, the way it
killed mules from overwork, but the old man held to it. Jeff thought it
killed a good many share farmers as well as mules, but he had no
sympathy for them. He had always been strong, and he had been taught
to have no patience with weakness in men. Women or children might be
tolerated if they were puny, but a weak man was a curse. Of course, his
own children—

Jeff's thought halted there. He and Jennie never mentioned their dead 43
children any more. And naturally he did not wish to dwell upon them in
his mind. Before he knew it, some remark would slip out of his mouth
and that would make Jennie feel blue. Perhaps she would cry. A woman
like Jennie could not easily throw off the grief that comes from losing five
grown children within two years. Even Jeff was still staggered by the
blow. His memory had not been much good recently. He frequently
talked to himself. And, although he had kept it a secret he knew that his
courage had left him. He was terrified by the least unfamiliar sound at
night. He was reluctant to venture far from home in the daytime. And
that habit of trembling when he felt fearful was now far beyond his

control. Sometimes he became afraid and trembled without knowing what had frightened him. The feeling would just come over him like a chill.

44   The car rattled slowly over the dusty road. Jennie sat erect and silent, with a little absurd hat pinned to her hair. Her useless eyes seemed very large and very white in their deep sockets. Suddenly Jeff heard her voice, and he inclined his head to catch the words.

45   "Is we passed Delia Moore's house yet?" she asked.

46   "Not yet," he said.

47   "You must be drivin' mighty slow, Jeff."

48   "We jes as well take our time, baby."

49   There was a pause. A little puff of steam was coming out of the radiator of the car. Heat wavered above the hood. Delia Moore's house was nearly half a mile away. After a moment Jennie spoke again.

50   "You ain't really scairt, is you, Jeff?"

51   "Nah, baby, I ain't scairt."

52   "You know how we agreed—we gotta keep on goin'."

53   Jewels of perspiration appeared on Jeff's forehead. His eyes rounded, blinked, became fixed on the road.

54   "I don't know," he said with a shiver. "I reckon it's the only thing to do."

55   "Hm."

56   A flock of guinea fowls, pecking in the road, were scattered by the passing car. Some of them took to their wings; others hid under bushes. A blue jay, swaying on a leafy twig, was annoying a roadside squirrel. Jeff held an even speed till he came near Delia's place. Then he slowed down noticeably.

57   Delia's house was really no house at all, but an abandoned store building converted into a dwelling. It sat near a crossroads, beneath a single black cedar tree. There Delia, a catlike old creature of Jennie's age, lived alone. She had been there more years than anybody could remember, and long ago had won the disfavor of such women as Jennie. For in her young days Delia had been gayer, yellower, and saucier than seemed proper in those parts. Her ways with menfolks had been dark and suspicious. And the fact that she had had as many husbands as children did not help her reputation.

58   "Yonder's old Delia," Jeff said as they passed.

59   "What she doin'?"

60   "Jes sittin' in the do'," he said.

61   "She see us?"

62   "Hm," Jeff said. "Musta did."

63   That relieved Jennie. It strengthened her to know that her old enemy had seen her pass in her best clothes. That would give the old she-devil something to chew her gums and fret about, Jennie thought. Wouldn't she have a fit if she didn't find out? Old evil Delia! This would be just the thing for her. It would pay her back for being so evil. It would also pay

her, Jennie thought, for the way she used to grin at Jeff—long ago when her teeth were good.

The road became smooth and red, and Jeff could tell by the smell of the 64
air that they were nearing the river. He could see the rise where the road turned and ran along parallel to the stream. The car chugged on monotonously. After a long silent spell, Jennie leaned against Jeff and spoke.

"How many bale o' cotton you think we got standin'?" she said. 65

Jeff wrinkled his forehead as he calculated. 66

" 'Bout twenty-five, I reckon." 67

"How many you make las' year?" 68

"Twenty-eight," he said. "How come you ask that?" 69

"I's jes thinkin'," Jennie said quietly. 70

"It don't make a speck o' diff'ence though," Jeff reflected. "If we get 71
much or if we get little, we still gonna be in debt to old man Stevenson when he gets through counting up agin us. It's took us a long time to learn that."

Jennie was not listening to these words. She had fallen into a trance- 72
like meditation. Her lips twitched. She chewed her gums and rubbed her old gnarled hands nervously. Suddenly, she leaned forward, buried her face in the nervous hands, and burst into tears. She cried aloud in a dry, cracked voice that suggested the rattle of fodder on dead stalks. She cried aloud like a child, for she had never learned to suppress a genuine sob. Her slight old frame shook heavily and seemed hardly able to sustain such violent grief.

"What's the matter, baby?" Jeff asked awkwardly. "Why you cryin' 73
like all that?"

"I's jes thinkin'," she said. 74

"So you the one what's scairt now, hunh?" 75

"I ain't scairt, Jeff. I's jes thinkin' 'bout leavin' eve'thing like this— 76
eve'thing we been used to. It's right sad-like."

Jeff did not answer, and presently Jennie buried her face and continued 77
crying.

The sun was almost overhead. It beat down furiously on the dusty 78
wagon path road, on the parched roadside grass, and the tiny battered car. Jeff's hands, gripping the wheel, became wet with perspiration; his forehead sparkled. Jeff's lips parted and his mouth shaped a hideous grimace. His face suggested the face of a man being burned. But the torture passed and his expression softened again.

"You mustn't cry, baby," he said to his wife. "We gotta be strong. We 79
can't break down."

Jennie waited a few seconds, then said, "You reckon we oughta do it, 80
Jeff? You reckon we oughta go 'head an' do it really?"

Jeff's voice choked; his eyes blurred. He was terrified to hear Jennie say 81
the thing that had been in his mind all morning. She had egged him on when he had wanted more than anything in the world to wait, to reconsider, to think things over a little longer. Now *she* was getting cold

feet. Actually, there was no need of thinking the question through again. It would only end in making the same painful decision once more. Jeff knew that. There was no need of fooling around longer.

82   "We jes as well to do like we planned," he said. "They ain't nuthin else for us now—it's the bes' thing."

83   Jeff thought of the handicaps, the near impossibility, of making another crop with his leg bothering him more and more each week. Then there was always the chance that he would have another stroke, like the one that had made him lame. Another one might kill him. The least it could do would be to leave him helpless. Jeff gasped . . . Lord, Jesus! He could not bear to think of being helpless, like a baby, on Jennie's hands. Frail, blind Jennie.

84   The little pounding motor of the car worked harder and harder. The puff of steam from the cracked radiator became large. Jeff realized that they were climbing a little rise. A moment later the road turned abruptly and he looked down upon the face of the river.

85   "Jeff."

86   "Hunh?"

87   "Is that the water I hear?"

88   "Hm. That's it."

89   "Well, which way you goin' now?"

90   "Down this-a way," he answered. "The road runs 'long-side o' the water a lil piece."

91   She waited a while calmly. Then she said, "Drive faster."

92   "A'right, baby," Jeff said.

93   The water roared in the bed of the river. It was fifty or sixty feet below the level of the road. Between the road and the water there was a long smooth slope, sharply inclined. The slope was dry; the clay had been hardened by prolonged summer heat. The water below, roaring in a narrow channel, was noisy and wild.

94   "Jeff."

95   "Hunh?"

96   "How far you goin'?"

97   "Jes a lil piece down the road."

98   "You ain't scairt is you, Jeff?"

99   "Nah, baby," he was trembling. "I ain't scairt."

100   "Remember how we planned it, Jeff. We gotta do it like we said. Brave-like."

101   "Hm."

102   Jeff's brain darkened. Things suddenly seemed unreal, like figures in a dream. Thoughts swam in his mind foolishly, hysterically, like little blind fish in a pool within a dense cave. They rushed, crossed one another, jostled, collided, retreated, and rushed again. Jeff soon became dizzy. He shuddered violently and turned to his wife.

103   "Jennie, I can't do it. I can't." His voice broke pitifully.

104   She did not appear to be listening. All the grief had gone from her face. She sat erect, her unseeing eyes wide open, strained and frightful. Her

glossy black skin had become dull. She seemed as thin and as sharp and bony as a starved bird. Now, having suffered and endured the sadness of tearing herself away from beloved things, she showed no anguish. She was absorbed with her own thoughts, and she didn't even hear Jeff's voice shouting in her ear.

Jeff said nothing more. For an instant there was light in his cavernous brain. That chamber was, for less than a second, peopled by characters he knew and loved. They were simple, healthy creatures, and they behaved in a manner that he could understand. They had quality. But since he had already taken leave of them long ago, the remembrance did not break his heart again. Young Jeff Patton was among them, the Jeff Patton of fifty years ago who went down to New Orleans with a crowd of country boys to the Mardi Gras doings. The gay young crowd—boys with candy-striped shirts and rouged brown girls in noisy silks—was like a picture in his head. Yet it did not make him sad. On that very trip Slim Burns had killed Joe Beasley—the crowd had been broken up. Since then Jeff Patton's work had been the Greenbrier Plantation. If there had been other Mardi Gras carnivals, he had not heard of them. Since then there had been no time; the years had fallen on him like waves. Now he was old, worn out. Another paralytic stroke like the one he had already suffered would put him on his back for keeps. In that condition, with a frail blind woman to look after him, he would be worse off than if he were dead. 105

Suddenly Jeff's hands became steady. He actually felt brave. He slowed down the motor of the car and carefully pulled off the road. Below, the water of the stream boomed, a soft thunder in the deep channel. Jeff ran the car onto the clay slope, pointed it directly toward the stream, and put his foot heavily on the accelerator. The little car leaped furiously down the steep incline toward the water. The movement was nearly as swift and direct as a fall. The two old black folks, sitting quietly side by side, showed no excitement. In another instant the car hit the water and dropped immediately out of sight. 106

A little later it lodged in the mud of a shallow place. One wheel of the crushed and upturned little Ford became visible above the rushing water. 107

❏ Questions for Discussion

1. What does "gone democrat" mean?

2. Why does Bontemps take so much time to describe the old couple, the **setting,** and the model-T Ford?

3. What **foreshadows** the ending?

4. Analyze the feelings of Jeff Patton. Why does Jeff shiver or feel dazed? Why does he say to himself, "Women or children might be tolerated if they were puny, but a weak man was a curse"?

5. Analyze the feelings of Jennie Patton. Why does she want to get even with Delia Moore? Why does she cry?

6. What causes Jeff and Jennie to despair? What is Mr. Stevenson's role in their decision?

❑ **Suggestions for Exploration and Writing**

1. Bontemps says that "fear came into [Jeff Patton's] eyes; excitement took his breath." Sometimes fear is accompanied by excitement. Examine some activity that you are thrilled by and discuss both the thrill and the fear involved.

2. Jeff Patton thinks to himself: "Now he was old, worn out." Discuss why and how elderly people in some cultures are treated as if they are "worn out."

Gabriel Garcia Marquez (1928–)

Gabriel Garcia Marquez is probably the best known of the many South American writers who produced distinguished fiction in the sixties, seventies, and eighties. Much of his material is drawn from his native Columbia. Marquez helped develop the contemporary fictional technique of "magical realism," wherein fantastic events are given such detailed and realistic treatment that readers become immersed in a new and symbolic world. Marquez's great novel, One Hundred Years of Solitude (1967), translated into twenty-five languages, has, in its richness, given rise to an amazing diversity of interpretations. In 1982 Marquez received the Nobel Prize for Literature. The following short story illustrates, in miniature, the characteristics of Marquez's work: political realism, detail in rendering the fantastic, and rich symbolism.

Death Constant Beyond Love

1   Senator Onésimo Sánchez had six months and eleven days to go before his death when he found the woman of his life. He met her in Rosal del Virrey, an illusory village which by night was the furtive wharf for smugglers' ships, and on the other hand, in broad daylight looked like the most useless inlet on the desert, facing a sea that was arid and without direction and so far from everything no one would have suspected that someone capable of changing the destiny of anyone lived there. Even its name was a kind of joke, because the only rose in that village was being worn by Senator Onésimo Sánchez himself on the same afternoon when he met Laura Farina.

2   It was an unavoidable stop in the electoral campaign he made every four years. The carnival wagons had arrived in the morning. Then came

the trucks with the rented Indians who were carried into the towns in order to enlarge the crowds at public ceremonies. A short time before eleven o'clock, along with the music and rockets and jeeps of the retinue, the ministerial automobile, the color of strawberry soda, arrived. Senator Onésimo Sánchez was placid and weatherless inside the air-conditioned car, but as soon as he opened the door he was shaken by a gust of fire and his shirt of pure silk was soaked in a kind of light-colored soup and he felt many years older and more alone than ever. In real life he had just turned forty-two, had been graduated from Göttingen with honors as a metallurgical engineer, and was an avid reader, although without much reward, of badly translated Latin classics. He was married to a radiant German woman who had given him five children and they were all happy in their home, he the happiest of all until they told him, three months before, that he would be dead forever by next Christmas.

While the preparations for the public rally were being completed, the senator managed to have an hour alone in the house they had set aside for him to rest in. Before he lay down he put in a glass of drinking water the rose he had kept alive all across the desert, lunched on the diet cereals that he took with him so as to avoid the repeated portions of fried goat that were waiting for him during the rest of the day, and he took several analgesic pills before the time prescribed so that he would have the remedy ahead of the pain. Then he put the electric fan close to the hammock and stretched out naked for fifteen minutes in the shadow of the rose, making a great effort at mental distraction so as not to think about death while he dozed. Except for the doctors, no one knew that he had been sentenced to a fixed term, for he had decided to endure his secret all alone, with no change in his life, not because of pride but out of shame.   3

He felt in full control of his will when he appeared in public again at three in the afternoon, rested and clean, wearing a pair of coarse linen slacks and a floral shirt, and with his soul sustained by the anti-pain pills. Nevertheless, the erosion of death was much more pernicious than he had supposed, for as he went up onto the platform he felt a strange disdain for those who were fighting for the good luck to shake his hand, and he didn't feel sorry as he had at other times for the groups of barefoot Indians who could scarcely bear the hot saltpeter coals of the sterile little square. He silenced the applause with a wave of his hand, almost with rage, and he began to speak without gestures, his eyes fixed on the sea, which was sighing with heat. His measured, deep voice had the quality of calm water, but the speech that had been memorized and ground out so many times had not occurred to him in the nature of telling the truth, but, rather, as the opposite of a fatalistic pronouncement by Marcus Aurelius in the fourth book of his *Meditations*.   4

"We are here for the purpose of defeating nature," he began, against all his convictions. "We will no longer be foundlings in our own country,   5 orphans of God in a realm of thirst and bad climate, exiles in our own land. We will be different people, ladies and gentleman, we will be a great and happy people."

6   There was a pattern to his circus. As he spoke his aides threw clusters of paper birds into the air and the artificial creatures took on life, flew about the platform of planks, and went out to sea. At the same time, other men took some prop trees with felt leaves out of the wagons and planted them in the saltpeter soil behind the crowd. They finished by setting up a cardboard façade with make-believe houses of red brick that had glass windows, and with it they covered the miserable real-life shacks.

7   The senator prolonged his speech with two quotations in Latin in order to give the farce more time. He promised rain-making machines, portable breeders for table animals, the oils of happiness which would make vegetables grow in the saltpeter and clumps of pansies in the window boxes. When he saw that his fictional world was all set up, he pointed to it. "That's the way it will be for us, ladies and gentlemen," he shouted. "Look! That's the way it will be for us."

8   The audience turned around. An ocean liner made of painted paper was passing behind the houses and it was taller than the tallest houses in the artificial city. Only the senator himself noticed that since it had been set up and taken down and carried from one place to another the superimposed cardboard town had been eaten away by the terrible climate and that it was almost as poor and dusty as Rosal del Virrey.

9   For the first time in twelve years, Nelson Farina didn't go to greet the senator. He listened to the speech from his hammock amidst the remains of his siesta, under the cool bower of a house of unplaned boards which he had built with the same pharmacist's hands with which he had drawn and quartered his first wife. He had escaped from Devil's Island and appeared in Rosal del Virrey on a ship loaded with innocent macaws, with a beautiful and blasphemous black woman he had found in Paramaribo and by whom he had a daughter. The woman died of natural causes a short while later and she didn't suffer the fate of the other, whose pieces had fertilized her own cauliflower patch, but was buried whole and with her Dutch name in the local cemetery. The daughter had inherited her color and her figure along with her father's yellow and astonished eyes, and he had good reason to imagine that he was rearing the most beautiful woman in the world.

10   Ever since he had met Senator Onésimo Sánchez during his first electoral campaign, Nelson Farina had begged for his help in getting a false identity card which would place him beyond the reach of the law. The senator, in a friendly but firm way, had refused. Nelson Farina never gave up, and for several years, every time he found the chance, he would repeat his request with a different recourse. But this time he stayed in his hammock, condemned to rot alive in that burning den of buccaneers. When he heard the final applause, he lifted his head, and looking over the boards of the fence, he saw the back side of the farce: the props for the

buildings, the framework of the trees, the hidden illusionists who were pushing the ocean liner along. He spat without rancor.

"*Merde,*" he said. "*C'est le Blacamán de la politique.*" [11]

After the speech, as was customary, the senator took a walk through [12] the streets of the town in the midst of the music and the rockets and was besieged by the townspeople, who told him their troubles. The senator listened to them goodnaturedly and he always found some way to console everybody without having to do them any difficult favors. A woman up on the roof of a house with her six youngest children managed to make herself heard over the uproar and the fireworks.

"I'm not asking for much, Senator," she said. "Just a donkey to haul [13] water from Hanged Man's Well."

The senator noticed the six thin children. "What became of your [14] husband?" he asked.

"He went to find his fortune on the island of Aruba," the woman [15] answered good-humoredly, "and what he found was a foreign woman, the kind that put diamonds on their teeth."

The answer brought on a roar of laughter. [16]

"All right," the senator decided, "you'll get your donkey." [17]

A short while later an aide of his brought a good pack donkey to the [18] woman's house and on the rump it had a campaign slogan written in indelible paint so that no one would ever forget that it was a gift from the senator.

Along the short stretch of street he made other, smaller gestures, and [19] he even gave a spoonful of medicine to a sick man who had had his bed brought to the door of his house so he could see him pass. At the last corner, through the boards of the fence, he saw Nelson Farina in his hammock, looking ashen and gloomy, but nonetheless the senator greeted him, with no show of affection.

"Hello, how are you?" [20]

Nelson Farina turned in his hammock and soaked him in the sad [21] amber of his look.

"*Moi, vous savez,*" he said. [22]

His daughter came out into the yard when she heard the greeting. She [23] was wearing a cheap, faded Guajiro Indian robe, her head was decorated with colored bows, and her face was painted as protection against the sun, but even in that state of disrepair it was possible to imagine that there had never been another so beautiful in the whole world. The senator was left breathless. "I'll be damned!" he breathed in surprise. "The Lord does the craziest things!"

That night Nelson Farina dressed his daughter up in her best clothes [24] and sent her to the senator. Two guards armed with rifles who were nodding from the heat in the borrowed house ordered her to wait on the only chair in the vestibule.

The senator was in the next room meeting with the important people [25] of Rosal del Virrey, whom he had gathered together in order to sing for them the truths he had left out of his speeches. They looked so much like all the ones he always met in all the towns in the desert that even the senator himself was sick and tired of that perpetual nightly session. His shirt was soaked with sweat and he was trying to dry it on his body with the hot breeze from an electric fan that was buzzing like a horse fly in the heavy heat of the room.

26   "We, of course, can't eat paper birds," he said. "You and I know that the day there are trees and flowers in this heap of goat dung, the day there are shad instead of worms in the water holes, that day neither you nor I will have anything to do here, do I make myself clear?"

27   No one answered. While he was speaking, the senator had torn a sheet off the calendar and fashioned a paper butterfly out of it with his hands. He tossed it with no particular aim into the air current coming from the fan and the butterfly flew about the room and then went out through the half-open door. The senator went on speaking with a control aided by the complicity of death.

28   "Therefore," he said, "I don't have to repeat to you what you already know too well: that my reelection is a better piece of business for you than it is for me, because I'm fed up with stagnant water and Indian sweat, while you people, on the other hand, make your living from it."

29   Laura Farina saw the paper butterfly come out. Only she saw it because the guards in the vestibule had fallen asleep on the steps, hugging their rifles. After a few turns, the large lithographed butterfly unfolded completely, flattened against the wall, and remained stuck there. Laura Farina tried to pull it off with her nails. One of the guards, who woke up with the applause from the next room, noticed her vain attempt.

30   "It won't come off," he said sleepily. "It's painted on the wall."

31   Laura Farina sat down again when the men began to come out of the meeting. The senator stood in the doorway of the room with his hand on the latch, and he only noticed Laura Farina when the vestibule was empty.

32   "What are you doing here?"

33   "*C'est de la part de mon père*," she said.

34   The senator understood. He scrutinized the sleeping guards, then he scrutinized Laura Farina, whose unusual beauty was even more demanding than his pain, and he resolved then that death had made his decision for him.

35   "Come in," he told her.

36   Laura Farina was struck dumb standing in the doorway to the room: thousands of bank notes were floating in the air, flapping like the butterfly. But the senator turned off the fan and the bills were left without air and alighted on the objects in the room.

37   "You see," he said, smiling, "even shit can fly."

38   Laura Farina sat down on a schoolboy's stool. Her skin was smooth and firm, with the same color and the same solar density as crude oil, her hair was the mane of a young mare, and her huge eyes were brighter than

the light. The senator followed the thread of her look and finally found the rose, which had been tarnished by the saltpeter.

"It's a rose," he said. 39

"Yes," she said with a trace of perplexity. "I learned what they were in Riohacha." 40

The senator sat down on an army cot, talking about roses as he unbuttoned his shirt. On the side where he imagined his heart to be inside his chest he had a corsair's tattoo of a heart pierced by an arrow. He threw the soaked shirt to the floor and asked Laura Farina to help him off with his boots. 41

She knelt down facing the cot. The senator continued to scrutinize her, thoughtfully, and while she was untying the laces he wondered which one of them would end up with the bad luck of that encounter. 42

"You're just a child," he said. 43

"Don't you believe it," she said. "I'll be nineteen in April." 44

The senator became interested. 45

"What day?" 46

"The eleventh," she said. 47

The senator felt better. "We're both Aries," he said. And smiling, he added: 48

"It's the sign of solitude." 49

Laura Farina wasn't paying attention because she didn't know what to do with the boots. The senator, for his part, didn't know what to do with Laura Farina, because he wasn't used to sudden love affairs and, besides, he knew that the one at hand had its origins in indignity. Just to have some time to think, he held Laura Farina tightly between his knees, embraced her about the waist, and lay down on his back on the cot. Then he realized that she was naked under her dress, for her body gave off the dark fragrance of an animal of the woods, but her heart was frightened and her skin disturbed by a glacial sweat. 50

"No one loves us," he sighed. 51

Laura Farina tried to say something, but there was only enough air for her to breathe. He laid her down beside him to help her, he put out the light and the room was in the shadow of the rose. She abandoned herself to the mercies of her fate. The senator caressed her slowly, seeking her with his hand, barely touching her, but where he expected to find her, he came across something iron that was in the way. 52

"What have you got there?" 53

"A padlock," she said. 54

"What in hell!" the senator said furiously and asked what he knew only too well. "Where's the key?" 55

Laura Farina gave a breath of relief. 56

"My papa has it," she answered. "He told me to tell you to send one of your people to get it and to send along with him a written promise that you'll straighten out his situation." 57

58   The senator grew tense. "Frog bastard," he murmured indignantly. Then he closed his eyes in order to relax and he met himself in the darkness. *Remember,* he remembered, *that whether it's you or someone else, it won't be long before you'll be dead and it won't be long before your name won't even be left.*

59   He waited for the shudder to pass.

60   "Tell me one thing," he asked then. "What have you heard about me?"

61   "Do you want the honest-to-God truth?"

62   "The honest-to-God truth."

63   "Well," Laura Farina ventured, "they say you're worse than the rest because you're different."

64   The senator didn't get upset. He remained silent for a long time with his eyes closed, and when he opened them again he seemed to have returned from his most hidden instincts.

65   "Oh, what the hell," he decided. "Tell your son of a bitch of a father that I'll straighten out his situation."

66   "If you want, I can go get the key myself," Laura Farina said.

67   The senator held her back.

68   "Forget about the key," he said, "and sleep awhile with me. It's good to be with someone when you're so alone."

69   Then she laid his head on her shoulder with her eyes fixed on the rose. The senator held her about the waist, sank his face into the woods-animal armpit, and gave in to terror. Six months and eleven days later he would die in that same position, debased and repudiated because of the public scandal with Laura Farina and weeping with rage at dying without her.

❏ Questions for Discussion

1. As a politician, what has been Sánchez's primary purpose in life? How does he wage his political campaigns? Given his educational background and his powerful position, would you say his life has been productive?

2. How has Sánchez built up a fantasy life and protected himself against the intrusion of reality? How has he maintained control over his world? What is happening to his illusory world as he visits Rosal del Virrey?

3. How has Sánchez's awareness of impending death changed his perception of the villagers and of his political life? How does this awareness condition his reaction to Laura?

4. What does the rose symbolize?

5. Why does Sánchez leave his family and come to Rosal del Virrey when he has only six months to live?

6. Explain the multiple **ironies** of the final sentence.

❏ **Suggestions for Exploration and Writing**

1. In an extended **contrast,** analyze the illusions on which the senator's life rests. Consider the following contrasts: between the reality of Rosal del Virrey and Sánchez's campaign promises and illusions, between the people and the senator, and between his treatment of the people and the ideal implied by familiarity with Marcus Aurelius.

2. Have the illusions he has used to control the people fooled the senator himself? Discuss.

3. If you knew you had only a short time until your death, would you trade your good name or position in society for something that was forbidden, as Senator Onésimo Sánchez does? Discuss.

JOYCE CAROL OATES (1938–)

Joyce Carol Oates, a highly skilled and extraordinarily productive American writer of poems, criticism, and fiction, is best known for her more than twenty darkly violent novels. From Them *(1969), which won a National Book Award, to* Black Water *(1992), a short novel which inevitably reminds readers of Mary Jo Kopechne, Senator Edward Kennedy, and Chappaquidick, Oates' novels represent an unusually large body of distinguished achievement. Born a Roman Catholic in Lockport, New York, Oates depicts a world devoid of saving grace. A realistic writer whose characters speak a colloquial dialogue full of allusions to popular culture, Oates explores the nightmarish violence that erupts out of the empty, lost characters she creates.*

Where Are You Going, Where Have You Been?

For Bob Dylan

Her name was Connie. She was fifteen and she had a quick nervous giggling habit of craning her neck to glance into mirrors, or checking other people's faces to make sure her own was all right. Her mother, who noticed everything and knew everything and who hadn't much reason any longer to look at her own face, always scolded Connie about it. "Stop gawking at yourself, who are you? You think you're so pretty?" she would say. Connie would raise her eyebrows at these familiar complaints and look right through her mother, into a shadowy vision of herself as she was right at that moment: she knew she was pretty and that was everything. Her mother had been pretty once too, if you could believe those old snapshots in the album, but now her looks were gone and that was why she was always after Connie.

1

2   "Why don't you keep your room clean like your sister? How've you got your hair fixed—what the hell stinks? Hair spray? You don't see your sister using that junk."

3   Her sister June was twenty-four and still lived at home. She was a secretary in the high school Connie attended, and if that wasn't bad enough—with her in the same building—she was so plain and chunky and steady that Connie had to hear her praised all the time by her mother and her mother's sisters. June did this, June did that, she saved money and helped clean the house and cooked and Connie couldn't do a thing, her mind was all filled with trashy daydreams. Their father was away at work most of the time and when he came home he wanted supper and he read the newspaper at supper and after supper he went to bed. He didn't bother talking much to them, but around his bent head Connie's mother kept picking at her until Connie wished her mother was dead and she herself was dead and it was all over. "She makes me want to throw up sometimes," she complained to her friends. She had a high, breathless, amused voice which made everything she said sound a little forced, whether it was sincere or not.

4   There was one good thing: June went places with girl friends of hers, girls who were just as plain and steady as she, and so when Connie wanted to do that her mother had no objections. The father of Connie's best girl friend drove the girls the three miles to town and left them off at a shopping plaza, so that they could walk through the stores or go to a movie, and when he came to pick them up again at eleven he never bothered to ask what they had done.

5   They must have been familiar sights, walking around that shopping plaza in their shorts and flat ballerina slippers that always scuffed the sidewalk, with charm bracelets jingling on their thin wrists; they would lean together to whisper and laugh secretly if someone passed by who amused or interested them. Connie had long dark blond hair that drew anyone's eye to it, and she wore part of it pulled up on her head and puffed out and the rest of it she let fall down her back. She wore a pull-over jersey blouse that looked one way when she was at home and another way when she was away from home. Everything about her had two sides to it, one for home and one for anywhere that was not home: her walk that could be childlike and bobbing, or languid enough to make anyone think she was hearing music in her head, her mouth which was pale and smirking most of the time, but bright and pink on these evenings out, her laugh which was cynical and drawling at home—"Ha, ha, very funny"—but high-pitched and nervous anywhere else, like the jingling of the charms on her bracelet.

6   Sometimes they did go shopping or to a movie, but sometimes they went across the highway, ducking fast across the busy road, to a drive-in restaurant where older kids hung out. The restaurant was shaped like a big bottle, though squatter than a real bottle, and on its cap was a revolving figure of a grinning boy who held a hamburger aloft. One night

in mid-summer they ran across, breathless with daring, and right away someone leaned out a car window and invited them over, but it was just a boy from high school they didn't like. It made them feel good to be able to ignore him. They went up through the maze of parked and cruising cars to the bright-lit, fly-infested restaurant, their faces pleased and expectant as if they were entering a sacred building that loomed out of the night to give them what haven and what blessing they yearned for. They sat at the counter and crossed their legs at the ankles, their thin shoulders rigid with excitement, and listened to the music that made everything so good: the music was always in the background like music at a church service, it was something to depend upon.

A boy named Eddie came in to talk with them. He sat backwards on his stool, turning himself jerkily around in semi-circles and then stopping and turning again, and after a while he asked Connie if she would like something to eat. She said she did and so she tapped her friend's arm on her way out—her friend pulled her face up into a brave droll look—and Connie said she would meet her at eleven, across the way. "I just hate to leave her like that," Connie said earnestly, but the boy said that she wouldn't be alone for long. So they went out to his car and on the way Connie couldn't help but let her eyes wander over the windshields and faces all around her, her face gleaming with a joy that had nothing to do with Eddie or even this place; it might have been the music. She drew her shoulders up and sucked in her breath with the pure pleasure of being alive, and just at that moment she happened to glance at a face just a few feet from hers. It was a boy with shaggy black hair, in a convertible jalopy painted gold. He stared at her and then his lips widened into a grin. Connie slit her eyes at him and turned away, but she couldn't help glancing back and there he was still watching her. He wagged a finger and laughed and said, "Gonna get you, baby," and Connie turned away again without Eddie noticing anything. 7

She spent three hours with him, at the restaurant where they ate hamburgers and drank Cokes in wax cups that were always sweating, and then down an alley a mile or so away, and when he left her off at five to eleven only the movie house was still open at the plaza. Her girl friend was there, talking with a boy. When Connie came up the two girls smiled at each other and Connie said, "How was the movie?" and the girl said, "*You* should know." They rode off with the girl's father, sleepy and pleased, and Connie couldn't help but look at the darkened shopping plaza with its big empty parking lot and its signs that were faded and ghostly now, and over at the drive-in restaurant where cars were still circling tirelessly. She couldn't hear the music at this distance. 8

Next morning June asked her how the movie was and Connie said, "So-so." 9

She and that girl and occasionally another girl went out several times a week that way, and the rest of the time Connie spent around the house—it was summer vacation—getting in her mother's way and think- 10 ing, dreaming, about the boys she met. But all the boys fell back and dissolved into a single face that was not even a face, but an idea, a feeling, mixed up with the urgent insistent pounding of the music and the humid night air of July. Connie's mother kept dragging her back to the daylight by finding things for her to do or saying, suddenly, "What's this about the Pettinger girl?"

11   And Connie would say nervously, "Oh, her. That dope." She always drew thick clear lines between herself and such girls, and her mother was simple and kindly enough to believe her. Her mother was so simple, Connie thought, that it was maybe cruel to fool her so much. Her mother went scuffling around the house in old bedroom slippers and complained over the telephone to one sister about the other, then the other called up and the two of them complained about the third one. If June's name was mentioned her mother's tone was approving, and if Connie's name was mentioned it was disapproving. This did not really mean she disliked Connie and actually Connie thought that her mother preferred her to June because she was prettier, but the two of them kept up a pretense of exasperation, a sense that they were tugging and struggling over something of little value to either of them. Sometimes, over coffee, they were almost friends, but something would come up—some vexation that was like a fly buzzing suddenly around their heads—and their faces went hard with contempt.

12   One Sunday Connie got up at eleven—none of them bothered with church—and washed her hair so that it could dry all day long, in the sun. Her parents and sister were going to a barbecue at an aunt's house and Connie said no, she wasn't interested, rolling her eyes to let her mother know just what she thought of it. "Stay home alone then," her mother said sharply. Connie sat out back in a lawn chair and watched them drive away, her father quiet and bald, hunched around so that he could back the car out, her mother with a look that was still angry and not at all softened through the windshield, and in the back seat poor old June all dressed up as if she didn't know what a barbecue was, with all the running yelling kids and the flies. Connie sat with her eyes closed in the sun, dreaming and dazed with the warmth about her as if this were a kind of love, the caresses of love, and her mind slipped over onto thoughts of the boy she had been with the night before and how nice he had been, how sweet it always was, not the way someone like June would suppose but sweet, gentle, the way it was in movies and promised in songs; and when she opened her eyes she hardly knew where she was, the back yard ran off into weeds and a fence-line of trees and behind it the sky was perfectly blue and still. The asbestos "ranch house" that was now three years old startled her—it looked small. She shook her head as if to get awake.

13   It was too hot. She went inside the house and turned on the radio to drown out the quiet. She sat on the edge of her bed, barefoot, and listened

for an hour and a half to a program called XYZ Sunday Jamboree, record after record of hard, fast, shrieking songs she sang along with, interspersed by exclamations from "Bobby King": "An' look here you girls at Napoleon's—Son and Charley want you to pay real close attention to this song coming up!"

And Connie paid close attention herself, bathed in a glow of slow-pulsed joy that seemed to rise mysteriously out of the music itself and lay languidly about the airless little room, breathed in and breathed out with each gentle rise and fall of her chest.   14

After a while she heard a car coming up the drive. She sat up at once, startled, because it couldn't be her father so soon. The gravel kept crunching all the way in from the road—the driveway was long—and Connie ran to the window. It was a car she didn't know. It was an open jalopy, painted a bright gold that caught the sunlight opaquely. Her heart began to pound and her fingers snatched at her hair, checking it, and she whispered "Christ. Christ," wondering how bad she looked. The car came to a stop at the side door and the horn sounded four short taps as if this were a signal Connie knew.   15

She went into the kitchen and approached the door slowly, then hung out the screen door, her bare toes curling down off the step. There were two boys in the car and now she recognized the driver: he had shaggy, shabby black hair that looked crazy as a wig and he was grinning at her.   16

"I ain't late, am I?" he said.   17

"Who the hell do you think you are?" Connie said.   18

"Toldja I'd be out, didn't I?"   19

"I don't even know who you are."   20

She spoke sullenly, careful to show no interest or pleasure, and he spoke in a fast bright monotone. Connie looked past him to the other boy, taking her time. He had fair brown hair, with a lock that fell onto his forehead. His sideburns gave him a fierce, embarrassed look, but so far he hadn't even bothered to glance at her. Both boys wore sunglasses. The driver's glasses were metallic and mirrored everything in miniature.   21

"You wanta come for a ride?" he said.   22

Connie smirked and let her hair fall loose over one shoulder.   23

"Don'tcha like my car? New paint job," he said. "Hey."   24

"What?"   25

"You're cute."   26

She pretended to fidget, chasing flies away from the door.   27

"Don'tcha believe me, or what?" he said.   28

"Look, I don't even know who you are," Connie said in disgust.   29

"Hey, Ellie's got a radio, see. Mine's broke down." He lifted his friend's arm and showed her the little transistor the boy was holding, and now Connie began to hear the music. It was the same program that was playing inside the house.   30

"Bobby King?" she said.   31

32   "I listen to him all the time. I think he's great."

33   "He's kind of great," Connie said reluctantly.

34   "Listen, that guy's *great*. He knows where the action is."

35   Connie blushed a little, because the glasses made it impossible for her to see just what this boy was looking at. She couldn't decide if she liked him or if he was just a jerk, and so she dawdled in the doorway and wouldn't come down or go back inside. She said "What's all that stuff painted on your car?"

36   "Can'tcha read it?" He opened the door very carefully, as if he was afraid it might fall off. He slid out just as carefully, planting his feet firmly on the ground, the tiny metallic world in his glasses slowing down like gelatine hardening and in the midst of it Connie's bright green blouse. "This here is my name, to begin with," he said. ARNOLD FRIEND was written in tarlike black letters on the side, with a drawing of a round grinning face that reminded Connie of a pumpkin, except it wore sunglasses. "I wanta introduce myself, I'm Arnold Friend and that's my real name and I'm gonna be your friend, honey, and inside the car's Ellie Oscar, he's kinda shy." Ellie brought his transistor radio up to his shoulder and balanced it there. "Now these numbers are a secret code, honey," Arnold Friend explained. He read off the numbers 33, 19, 17 and raised his eyebrows at her to see what she thought of that, but she didn't think much of it. The left rear fender had been smashed and around it was written, on the gleaming gold background: DONE BY CRAZY WOMAN DRIVER. Connie had to laugh at that. Arnold Friend was pleased at her laughter and looked up at her. "Around the other side's a lot more—you wanta come and see them?"

37   "No."

38   "Why not?"

39   "Why should I?"

40   "Don'tcha wanta see what's on the car? Don'tcha wanta go for a ride?"

41   "I don't know."

42   "Why not?"

43   "I got things to do."

44   "Like what?"

45   "Things."

46   He laughed as if she had said something funny. He slapped his thighs. He was standing in a strange way, leaning back against the car as if he were balancing himself. He wasn't tall, only an inch or so taller than she would be if she came down to him. Connie liked the way he was dressed, which was the way all of them dressed: tight faded jeans stuffed into black, scuffed boots, a belt that pulled his waist in and showed how lean he was, and a white pull-over shirt that was a little soiled and showed the hard small muscles of his arms and shoulders. He looked as if he probably did hard work, lifting and carrying things. Even his neck looked muscular. And his face was a familiar face, somehow: the jaw and chin and cheeks slightly darkened, because he hadn't shaved for a day or two,

and the nose long and hawk-like, sniffing as if she were a treat he was going to gobble up and it was all a joke.

"Connie, you ain't telling the truth. This is your day set aside for a ride with me and you know it," he said, still laughing. The way he straightened and recovered from his fit of laughing showed that it had been all fake. 47

"How do you know what my name is?" she said suspiciously. 48

"It's Connie." 49

"Maybe and maybe not." 50

"I know my Connie," he said, wagging his finger. Now she remembered him even better, back at the restaurant, and her cheeks warmed at the thought of how she sucked in her breath just at the moment she passed him — how she must have looked to him. And he had remembered her. "Ellie and I come out here especially for you," he said. "Ellie can sit in back. How about it?" 51

"Where?" 52

"Where what?" 53

"Where're we going?" 54

He looked at her. He took off the sunglasses and she saw how pale the skin around his eyes was, like holes that were not in shadow but instead in light. His eyes were chips of broken glass that catch the light in an amiable way. He smiled. It was as if the idea of going for a ride somewhere, to some place, was a new idea to him. 55

"Just for a ride, Connie sweetheart." 56

"I never said my name was Connie," she said. 57

"But I know what it is. I know your name and all about you, lots of things," Arnold Friend said. He had not moved yet but stood still leaning back against the side of his jalopy. "I took a special interest in you, such a pretty girl, and found out all about you like I know your parents and sister are gone somewheres and I know where and how long they're going to be gone, and I know who you were with last night, and your best girlfriend's name is Betty. Right?" 58

He spoke in a simple lilting voice, exactly as if he were reciting the words to a song. His smile assured her that everything was fine. In the car, Ellie turned up the volume on his radio and did not bother to look around at them. 59

"Ellie can sit in the back seat," Arnold Friend said. He indicated his friend with a casual jerk of his chin, as if Ellie did not count and she should not bother with him. 60

"How'd you find out all that stuff?" Connie said. 61

"Listen: Betty Schultz and Tony Fitch and Jimmy Pettinger and Nancy Pettinger," he said, in a chant. "Raymond Stanley and Bob Hutter—" 62

"Do you know all those kids?" 63

"I know everybody." 64

"Look, you're kidding. You're not from around here." 65

"Sure." 66

67   "But—how come we never saw you before?"

68   "Sure you saw me before," he said. He looked down at his boots, as if he were a little offended. "You just don't remember."

69   "I guess I'd remember you," Connie said.

70   "Yeah?" He looked up at this, beaming. He was pleased. He began to mark time with the music from Ellie's radio, tapping his fists lightly together. Connie looked away from his smile to the car, which was painted so bright it almost hurt her eyes to look at it. She looked at that name, ARNOLD FRIEND. And up at the front fender was an expression that was familiar—MAN THE FLYING SAUCERS. It was an expression kids had used the year before, but didn't use this year. She looked at it for a while as if the words meant something to her that she did not yet know.

71   "What're you thinking about? Huh?" Arnold Friend demanded. "Not worried about your hair blowing around in the car, are you?"

72   "No."

73   "Think I maybe can't drive good?"

74   "How do I know?"

75   "You're a hard girl to handle. How come?" he said. "Don't you know I'm your friend? Didn't you see me put my sign in the air when you walked by?"

76   "What sign?"

77   "My sign." And he drew an X in the air, leaning out toward her. They were maybe ten feet apart. After his hand fell back to his side the X was still in the air, almost visible. Connie let the screen door close and stood perfectly still inside it, listening to the music from her radio and the boy's blend together. She stared at Arnold Friend. He stood there so stiffly relaxed, pretending to be relaxed, with one hand idly on the door handle as if he were keeping himself up that way and had no intention of ever moving again. She recognized most things about him, the tight jeans that showed his thighs and buttocks and the greasy leather boots and the tight shirt, and even that slippery friendly smile of his, that sleepy dreamy smile that all the boys used to get across ideas they didn't want to put into words. She recognized all this and also the singsong way he talked, slightly mocking, kidding, but serious and a little melancholy, and she recognized the way he tapped one fist against the other in homage to the perpetual music behind him. But all these things did not come together.

78   She said suddenly, "Hey, how old are you?"

79   His smile faded. She could see then that he wasn't a kid, he was much older—thirty, maybe more. At this knowledge her heart began to pound faster.

80   "That's a crazy thing to ask. Can'tcha see I'm your own age?"

81   "Like hell you are."

82   "Or maybe a couple years older, I'm eighteen."

83   "Eighteen?" she said doubtfully.

84   He grinned to reassure her and lines appeared at the corners of his mouth. His teeth were big and white. He grinned so broadly his eyes

became slits and she saw how thick the lashes were, thick and black as if painted with a black tarlike material. Then he seemed to become embarrassed, abruptly, and looked over his shoulder at Ellie. *"Him,* he's crazy," he said. "Ain't he a riot, he's a nut, a real character." Ellie was still listening to the music. His sunglasses told nothing about what he was thinking. He wore a bright orange shirt unbuttoned halfway to show his chest, which was a pale, bluish chest and not muscular like Arnold Friend's. His shirt collar was turned up all around and the very tips of the collar pointed out past his chin as if they were protecting him. He was pressing the transistor radio up against his ear and sat there in a kind of daze, right in the sun.

"He's kinda strange," Connie said.   85

"Hey, she says you're kinda strange! Kinda strange!" Arnold Friend   86
cried. He pounded on the car to get Ellie's attention. Ellie turned for the first time and Connie saw with shock that he wasn't a kid either — he had a fair, hairless face, cheeks reddened slightly as if the veins grew too close to the surface of his skin, the face of a forty-year-old baby. Connie felt a wave of dizziness rise in her at this sight and she stared at him as if waiting for something to change the shock of the moment, make it all right again. Ellie's lips kept shaping words, mumbling along, with the words blasting in his ear.

"Maybe you two better go away," Connie said faintly.   87

"What? How come?" Arnold Friend cried. "We come out here to take   88
you for a ride. It's Sunday." He had the voice of the man on the radio now. It was the same voice, Connie thought. "Don'tcha know it's Sunday all day and honey, no matter who you were with last night today you're with Arnold Friend and don't you forget it! — Maybe you better step out here," he said, and this last was in a different voice. It was a little flatter, as if the heat was finally getting to him.

"No. I got things to do."   89

"Hey."   90

"You two better leave."   91

"We ain't leaving until you come with us."   92

"Like hell I am—"   93

"Connie, don't fool around with me. I mean, I mean, don't fool   94
around," he said, shaking his head. He laughed incredulously. He placed his sunglasses on top of his head, carefully, as if he were indeed wearing a wig, and brought the stems down behind his ears. Connie stared at him, another wave of dizziness and fear rising in her so that for a moment he wasn't even in focus but was just a blur, standing there against his gold car, and she had the idea that he had driven up the driveway all right but had come from nowhere before that and belonged nowhere and that everything about him and even about the music that was so familiar to her was only half real.

"If my father comes and sees you—"   95

"He ain't coming. He's at the barbecue."   96

"How do you know that?"   97

98   "Aunt Tillie's. Right now they're—uh—they're drinking. Sitting around," he said vaguely, squinting as if he were staring all the way to town and over to Aunt Tillie's backyard. Then the vision seemed to get clear and he nodded energetically. "Yeah. Sitting around. There's your sister in a blue dress, huh? And high heels, the poor sad bitch—nothing like you, sweetheart! And your mother's helping some fat woman with the corn, they're cleaning the corn—husking the corn—"

99   "What fat woman?" Connie cried.

100   "How do I know what fat woman. I don't know every goddam fat woman in the world!" Arnold Friend laughed.

101   "Oh, that's Mrs. Hornby . . . . Who invited her?" Connie said. She felt a little light-headed. Her breath was coming quickly.

102   "She's too fat. I don't like them fat. I like them the way you are, honey," he said, smiling sleepily at her. They stared at each other for awhile, through the screen door. He said softly, "Now what you're going to do is this: you're going to come out that door. You're going to sit up front with me and Ellie's going to sit in the back, the hell with Ellie, right? This isn't Ellie's date. You're my date. I'm your lover, honey."

103   "What? You're crazy—"

104   "Yes, I'm your lover. You don't know what that is but you will," he said. "I know that too. I know all about you. But look: it's real nice and you couldn't ask for nobody better than me, or more polite. I always keep my word. I'll tell you how it is, I'm always nice at first, the first time. I'll hold you so tight you won't think you have to try to get away or pretend anything because you'll know you can't. And I'll come inside you where it's all secret and you'll give in to me and you'll love me—"

105   "Shut up! You're crazy!" Connie said. She backed away from the door. She put her hands against her ears as if she'd heard something terrible, something not meant for her. "People don't talk like that, you're crazy," she muttered. Her heart was almost too big now for her chest and its pumping made sweat break out all over her. She looked out to see Arnold Friend pause and then take a step toward the porch lurching. He almost fell. But, like a clever drunken man, he managed to catch his balance. He wobbled in his high boots and grabbed hold of one of the porch posts.

106   "Honey?" he said. "You still listening?"

107   "Get the hell out of here!"

108   "Be nice, honey. Listen."

109   "I'm going to call the police—"

110   He wobbled again and out of the side of his mouth came a fast spat curse, an aside not meant for her to hear. But even this "Christ!" sounded forced. Then he began to smile again. She watched this smile come, awkward as if he were smiling from inside a mask. His whole face was a mask, she thought wildly, tanned down onto his throat but then running out as if he had plastered make-up on his face but had forgotten about his throat.

"Honey—? Listen, here's how it is. I always tell the truth and I promise you this: I ain't coming in that house after you."

"You better not! I'm going to call the police if you—if you don't—"

"Honey," he said, talking right through her voice, "honey, I'm not coming in there but you are coming out here. You know why?"

She was panting. The kitchen looked like a place she had never seen before, some room she had run inside but which wasn't good enough, wasn't going to help her. The kitchen window had never had a curtain, after three years, and there were dishes in the sink for her to do— probably—and if you ran your hand across the table you'd probably feel something sticky there.

"You listening, honey? Hey?"

"—going to call the police—"

"Soon as you touch the phone I don't need to keep my promise and can come inside. You won't want that."

She rushed forward and tried to lock the door. Her fingers were shaking. "But why lock it," Arnold Friend said gently, talking right into her face. "It's just a screen door. It's just nothing." One of his boots was at a strange angle, as if his foot wasn't in it. It pointed out to the left, bent at the ankle. "I mean, anybody can break through a screen door and glass and wood and iron or anything else if he needs to, anybody at all and specially Arnold Friend. If the place got lit up with a fire honey you'd come running out into my arms, right into my arms and safe at home—like you knew I was your lover and'd stopped fooling around. I don't mind a nice shy girl but I don't like no fooling around." Part of those words were spoken with a slight rhythmic lilt, and Connie somehow recognized them—the echo of a song from last year, about a girl rushing into her boy friend's arms and coming home again—

Connie stood barefoot on the linoleum floor, staring at him. "What do you want?" she whispered.

"I want you," he said.

"What?"

"Seen you that night and thought, that's the one, yes sir. I never needed to look any more."

"But my father's coming back. He's coming to get me. I had to wash my hair first—" She spoke in a dry, rapid voice, hardly raising it for him to hear.

"No, your daddy is not coming and yes, you had to wash your hair and you washed it for me. It's nice and shining and all for me, I thank you, sweetheart," he said, with a mock bow, but again he almost lost his balance. He had to bend and adjust his boots. Evidently his feet did not go all the way down; the boots must have been stuffed with something so that he would seem taller. Connie stared out at him and behind him Ellie in the car, who seemed to be looking off toward Connie's right, into nothing. This Ellie said, pulling the words out of the air one after another as if he were just discovering them, "You want me to pull out the phone?"

125 "Shut your mouth and keep it shut," Arnold Friend said, his face red from bending over or maybe from embarrassment because Connie had seen his boots. "This ain't none of your business."

126 "What—what are you doing? What do you want?" Connie said. "If I call the police they'll get you, they'll arrest you—"

127 "Promise was not to come in unless you touch that phone, and I'll keep that promise," he said. He resumed his erect position and tried to force his shoulders back. He sounded like a hero in a movie, declaring something important. He spoke too loudly and it was as if he were speaking to someone behind Connie. "I ain't made plans for coming in that house where I don't belong but just for you to come out to me, the way you should. Don't you know who I am?"

128 "You're crazy," she whispered. She backed away from the door but did not want to go into another part of the house, as if this would give him permission to come through the door. "What do you . . . You're crazy, you . . ."

129 "Huh? What're you saying, honey?"

130 Her eyes darted everywhere in the kitchen. She could not remember what it was, this room.

131 "This is how it is, honey: you come out and we'll drive away, have a nice ride. But if you don't come out we're gonna wait till your people come home and then they're all going to get it."

132 "You want that telephone pulled out?" Ellie said. He held the radio away from his ear and grimaced, as if without the radio the air was too much for him.

133 "I toldja shut up, Ellie," Arnold Friend said, "you're deaf, get a hearing aid, right? Fix yourself up. This little girl's no trouble and's gonna be nice to me, so Ellie keep to yourself, this ain't your date—right? Don't hem in on me. Don't hog. Don't crush. Don't bird dog. Don't trail me," he said in a rapid meaningless voice, as if he were running through all the expressions he'd learned but was no longer sure which one of them was in style, then rushing on to new ones, making them up with his eyes closed, "Don't crawl under my fence, don't squeeze in my chipmunk hole, don't sniff my glue, suck my popsicle, keep your own greasy fingers on yourself!" He shaded his eyes and peered in at Connie, who was backed against the kitchen table. "Don't mind him honey he's just a creep. He's a dope. Right? I'm the boy for you and like I said you come out here nice like a lady and give me your hand, and nobody else gets hurt, I mean, your nice old bald-headed daddy and your mummy and your sister in her high heels. Because listen: why bring them in this?"

134 "Leave me alone," Connie whispered.

135 "Hey, you know that old woman down the road, the one with the chickens and stuff—you know her?"

136 "She's dead!"

"Dead? What? You know her?" Arnold Friend said. 137

"She's dead—" 138

"Don't you like her?" 139

"She's dead—she's—she isn't here any more—" 140

"But don't you like her, I mean, you got something against her? Some 141
grudge or something?" Then his voice dipped as if he were conscious of
a rudeness. He touched the sunglasses perched on top of his head as if to
make sure they were still there. "Now you be a good girl."

"What are you going to do?" 142

"Just two things, or maybe three," Arnold Friend said. "But I promise 143
it won't last long and you'll like me that way you get to like people you're
close to. You will. It's all over for you here, so come on out. You don't
want your people in any trouble, do you?"

She turned and bumped against a chair or something, hurting her leg, 144
but she ran into the back room and picked up the telephone. Something
roared in her ear, a tiny roaring, and she was so sick with fear that she
could do nothing but listen to it—the telephone was clammy and very
heavy and her fingers groped down to the dial but were too weak to
touch it. She began to scream into the phone, into the roaring. She cried
out, she cried for her mother, she felt her breath start jerking back and
forth in her lungs as if it were something Arnold Friend were stabbing her
with again and again with no tenderness. A noisy sorrowful wailing rose
all about her and she was locked inside it the way she was locked inside
the house.

After a while she could hear again. She was sitting on the floor with her 145
wet back against the wall.

Arnold Friend was saying from the door, "That's a good girl. Put the 146
phone back."

She kicked the phone away from her. 147

"No, honey. Pick it up. Put it back right." 148

She picked it up and put it back. The dial tone stopped. 149

"That's a good girl. Now come outside." 150

She was hollow with what had been fear, but what was now just an 151
emptiness. All that screaming had blasted it out of her. She sat, one leg
cramped under her, and deep inside her brain was something like a
pinpoint of light that kept going and would not let her relax. She thought,
I'm not going to see my mother again. She thought, I'm not going to sleep
in my bed again. Her bright green blouse was all wet.

Arnold Friend said, in a gentle-loud voice that was like a stage voice, 152
"The place where you came from ain't there any more, and where you
had in mind to go is cancelled out. This place you are now—inside your
daddy's house—is nothing but a cardboard box I can knock down any
time. You know that and always did know it. You hear me?"

She thought, I have got to think. I have to know what to do. 153

"We'll go out to a nice field, out in the country here where it smells so 154
nice and it's sunny," Arnold Friend said. "I'll have my arms around you

so you won't need to try to get away and I'll show you what love is like, what it does. The hell with this house! It looks solid all right," he said. He ran a fingernail down the screen and the noise did not make Connie shiver, as it would have the day before. "Now put your hand on your heart, honey. Feel that? That feels solid too but we know better, be nice to me, be sweet like you can because what else is there for a girl like you but to be sweet and pretty and give in? — and get away before her people come back?"

155   She felt her pounding heart. Her hand seemed to enclose it. She thought for the first time in her life that it was nothing that was hers, that belonged to her, but just a pounding, living thing inside this body that wasn't really hers either.

156   "You don't want them to get hurt," Arnold Friend went on. "Now get up, honey. Get up all by yourself."

157   She stood up.

158   "Now turn this way. That's right. Come over here to me — Ellie, put that away, didn't I tell you? You dope. You miserable creepy dope," Arnold said. His words were not angry but only part of an incantation. The incantation was kindly. "Now come out through the kitchen to me honey and let's see a smile, try it, you're a brave sweet little girl and now they're eating corn and hotdogs cooked to bursting over an outdoor fire, and they don't know one thing about you and never did and honey you're better than them because not a one of them would have done this for you."

159   Connie felt the linoleum under her feet; it was cool. She brushed her hair back out of her eyes. Arnold Friend let go of the post tentatively and opened his arms for her, his elbows pointing in toward each other and his wrists limp, to show that this was an embarrassed embrace and a little mocking, he didn't want to make her self-conscious.

160   She put out her hand against the screen. She watched herself push the door slowly open as if she were safe back somewhere in the other doorway, watching this body and this head of long hair moving out into the sunlight where Arnold Friend waited.

161   "My sweet little blue-eyed girl," he said, in a half-sung sigh that had nothing to do with her brown eyes but was taken up just the same by the vast sunlit reaches of the land behind him and on all sides of him, so much land that Connie had never seen before and did not recognize except to know that she was going to it.

❏ Questions for Discussion

1. How does Connie feel about her mother's constant nagging? How does Connie react?

2. What is most important to Connie? Why?

3. Why does Arnold Friend fake laughter and pretend to be a teenager even though he must know Connie will see through

his charade? What about Arnold and Ellie attracts Connie? What about them frightens her?

4. How does Arnold know so much about Connie? How does Arnold convince Connie that she is powerless before him?

5. What will happen to Connie?

❏ **Suggestions for Exploration and Writing**

1. Ultimately, as Arnold insists, Connie makes the decision to walk out the door to Arnold. What leads her to do so?

2. Compare Arnold Friend to Iago in *Othello* as embodiments of evil.

MADISON SMARTT BELL (1957–)

A prolific young writer, Madison Smartt Bell by the age of thirty-four had published six novels and two collections of short stories. His fiction creates a dark world of often violent characters who frequently, like the narrator-protagonist of "Customs of the Country," live or die in the face of apparent hopelessness.

Customs of the Country

I don't remember much about that place anymore. It was nothing but somewhere I came to put in some pretty bad time, though that was not what I had planned on when I went there. I had it in mind to improve things, but I didn't think you could fairly claim that's what I did. So that's one reason I might just as soon forget about it. And I didn't stay there all that long, not more than about nine months or so, about the same time, come to think, that the child I was there to try to get back had lived inside my body.

It was a cluster-housing thing a little ways north out of town from Roanoke, on a two-lane road that crossed the railroad cut and went about a mile farther up through the woods. The buildings looked something like a motel, a little raw still, though they weren't new. My apartment was no more than a place that would barely look all right and yet cost me little enough so I had something left over to give the lawyer. There was fresh paint on the walls and the trim in the kitchen and bathroom was in fair shape. And it was real quiet mostly, except that the man next door used to beat up his wife a couple of times a week. The place was soundproof enough I couldn't usually hear talk but I could hear yelling plain as day and when he got going good he would slam her bang into our common wall. If she hit in just the right spot it would send my pots and pans flying off the pegboard where I'd hung them above the stove.

3   Not that it mattered to me that the pots fell down, except for the noise and the time it took to pick them up again. Living alone like I was, I didn't have the heart to do much cooking and if I did fix myself something I mostly used an old iron skillet that hung there on the same wall. All the others I only had out for show. The whole apartment was done about the same way, made into something I kept spotless and didn't much care to use. I wore my hands out scrubbing everything clean and then saw to it that it stayed that way. I sewed slipcovers for that threadbare batch of Goodwill furniture I'd put in the place, and I hung curtains and found some sunshiny posters to tack on the walls, and I never cared a damn about any of it. It was an act, and I wasn't putting it on for me or for Davey, but for all the other people I expected to come to see it and judge it. And however good I could get it looking, it never felt quite right.

4   I felt even less at home there than I did at my job, which was waitressing three snake-bends of the counter at the Truckstops of America out at the I-81 interchange. The supervisor was a man named Tim that used to know my husband Patrick from before we had the trouble. He was nice about letting me take my phone calls there and giving me time off to see the lawyer, and in most other ways he was a decent man to work for, except that now and then he would have a tantrum over something or other and try to scream the walls down. Still, it never went beyond yelling, and he always acted sorry once he got through. The other waitress on my shift was an older lady named Prissy, and I liked her all right in spite of the name.

5   We were both on a swing shift that rolled over every ten days, which was the main thing I didn't like about that job. The six-to-two I hated the worst because it would have me getting back to my apartment building around three in the morning, not the time it looked its best. It was the kind of place where at that time of night I could expect to find the deputies out there looking for somebody, or else some other kind of trouble. I never got to know the neighbors any too well, but a lot of them were pretty sorry—small-time criminals, dope dealers and thieves, none of them much good at whatever it was they did. There was one check forger that I knew of, and a man who would break into the other apartments looking for whiskey. One thing and another, along that line.

6   The man next door, the one that beat up his wife, didn't do crimes or work either that I ever heard. He just seemed to lay around the place, maybe drawing some kind of welfare. There wasn't a whole lot of him, he was just a stringy little man, hair and mustache a dishwater-brown, cheap green tatoos running up his arms. Maybe he was stronger than he looked, but I did wonder how come his wife would take it from him, since she was about a head taller and must have outweighed him an easy ten pounds. I might have thought she was whipping on him—stranger things have been known to go on—but she was the one that seemed like

she might break out crying if you looked at her crooked. She was a big fine-looking girl with a lovely shape, and long brown hair real smooth and straight and shiny. I guess she was too hammered down most of the time to pay much attention to how she dressed, but still she had pretty brown eyes, big and long-lashed and soft, sort of like a cow's eyes, except I never saw a cow that looked that miserable.

At first I thought maybe I might make a friend of her, she was about the only one around there I felt like I might want to. Our paths crossed pretty frequent, either around the apartment building or in the Kwik Sack back toward town, where I'd find her running the register some days. But she was shy of me, shy of anybody I suppose. She would flinch if you did so much as say hello. So after a while I quit trying. She'd get hers about twice a week, maybe other times I wasn't around to hear it happen. It's a wonder all the things you can learn to ignore, and after a month or so I was that accustomed I barely noticed when they would start in. I would just wait till I thought they were good and through, and then get up and hang those pans back on the wall where they were supposed to go. And all the while I would just be thinking about some other thing, like what might be going on with my Davey.

The place where he had been fostered out was not all that far away, just about ten or twelve miles up the road, out there in the farm country. The people were named Baker. I never got to first names with them, just called them Mr. and Mrs. They were older than me, both just into their forties, and they didn't have any children of their own. The place was only a small farm but Mr. Baker grew tobacco on the most of it and I'm told he made it a paying thing. Mrs. Baker kept a milk cow or two and she grew a garden and canned in the old-time way. Thrifty people. They were real sweet to Davey and he seemed to like being with them pretty well. He had been staying there almost the whole two years, which was lucky too, since most children usually got moved around a whole lot more than that.

And that was the trouble, like the lawyer explained to me, it was just too good. Davey was doing too well out there. He'd made out better in the first grade than anybody would have thought. So nobody really felt like he needed to be moved. The worst of it was the Bakers had got to like him well enough they were saying they wanted to adopt him if they could. Well, it would have been hard enough for me without that coming into it.

Even though he was so close, I didn't go out to see Davey near as much as I would have liked to. The lawyer kept telling me it wasn't a good idea to look like I was pressing too hard. Better take it easy till all the evaluations came in and we had our court date and all. Still, I would call and go on out there maybe a little more than once a month, most usually on the weekends, since that seemed to suit the Bakers better. They never acted like it was any trouble, and they were always pleasant to me, or polite might be a better word yet. The way it sometimes seemed they didn't trust me did bother me a little. I would have liked to take him out to the movies a time or two, but I could see plain enough the Bakers wouldn't have been easy about me having him off their place.

11   But I can't remember us having a bad time, any of those times I went. He was always happy to see me, though he'd be quiet when we were in the house, with Mrs. Baker hovering. So I would get us outside quick as ever I could and, once we were out, we would just play like both of us were children. There was an open pasture, a creek with a patch of woods, a hay barn where we would play hide-and-go-seek. I don't know what all else we did, silly things mostly. That was how I could get near him the easiest, he didn't get a whole lot of playing in, way out there. The Bakers weren't what you would call playful and there weren't any other children living near. So that was the thing I could give him that was all mine to give. When the weather was good we would stay outside together most all the day and he would just wear me out. But over the winter those visits seemed to get shorter and shorter, like the days.

12   Davey called me Momma still, but I suppose he had come to think your mother was something more like a big sister or just some kind of a friend. Mrs. Baker was the one doing for him all the time. I don't know just what he remembered from before, or if he remembered any of the bad part. He would always mind me but he never acted scared around me, and if anybody says he did they lie. But I never really did get to know what he had going on in the back of his mind about the past. At first I worried the Bakers might have been talking against me, but after I had seen a little more of them I knew they wouldn't have done anything like that, wouldn't have thought it right. So I expect whatever Davey knew about the other time he remembered on his own. He never mentioned Patrick hardly and I think he really had forgotten about him. Thinking back I guess he never saw that much of Patrick even when we were all living together. But Davey had Patrick's mark all over him, the same eyes and the same red hair.

13   Patrick had thick wavy hair the shade of an Irish setter's, and a big rolling mustache the same color. Maybe that was his best feature, but he was a good-looking man altogether, still is I suppose, though the prison haircut don't suit him. If he ever had much of a thought in his head I suspect he had knocked it clean out with dope, yet he was always fun to be around. I wasn't but seventeen when I married him and I didn't have any better sense myself. Right to the end I never thought anything much was the matter, all his vices looked so small to me. He was good-tempered almost all the time, and good with Davey when he did notice him. Never once did he raise his hand to either one of us. In little ways he was unreliable, late, not showing up at all, gone out of the house for days sometimes. Hindsight shows me he ran with other women, but I managed not to know anything about that at the time. He had not quite

finished high school and the best job he could hold was being an orderly down at the hospital, but he made a good deal of extra money stealing pills out of there and selling them on the street.

That was something else I didn't allow myself to think on much back then. Patrick never told me a lot about it anyhow, always acted real mysterious about whatever he was up to in that line. He would disappear on one of his trips and come back with a whole mess of money, and I would spend up my share and be glad I had it too. I never thought much about where it was coming from, the money or the pills either one. He used to keep all manner of pills around the house, Valium and ludes and a lot of different kinds of speed, and we both took what we felt like whenever we felt in the mood. But what Patrick made the most on was Dilaudid. I used to take it without ever knowing what it really was, but once everything fell in on us I found out it was a bad thing, bad as heroin they said, and not much different, and it was what they gave Patrick most of his time for.

I truly was surprised to find out that it was the strongest dope we had, because I never really even felt like it made you all that high. You would just take one and kick back on a long slow stroke and whatever trouble you might have, it would not be able to find you. It came on like nothing but it was the hardest habit to lose, and I was a long time shaking it. I might be thinking about it yet if I would let myself, and there were times, all through the winter I spent in that apartment, I'd catch myself remembering the feeling.

You couldn't call it a real bad winter, there wasn't much snow or anything, but I was cold just about all the time, except when I was at work. All I had in the apartment was some electric baseboard heaters, and they cost too much for me to leave them running very long at a stretch. I'd keep it just warm enough so I couldn't see my breath, and spent my time in a hot bathtub or under a big pile of blankets on the bed. Or else I would just be cold.

There was some kind of strange quietness about that place all during the cold weather. If the phone rang it would make me jump. Didn't seem like there was any TV or radio ever playing next door. The only sound coming out of there was Susan getting beat up once in a while. That was her name, a sweet name, I think. I found it out from hearing him say it, which he used to do almost every time before he started on her. "Su-*san*," he'd call out, loud enough I could hear him through the wall. He'd do it a time or two, he might have been calling her to him, and I suppose she went. After that would come a bad silence that reminded you of a snake being somewhere around. Then a few minutes' worth of hitting sounds and then the big slam as she hit the wall, and the clatter of my pots falling on the floor. He'd throw her at the wall maybe once or twice, usually when he was about to get rough. By the time the pots had quit spinning on the floor it would be real quiet over there again, and the next time I saw Susan she'd be walking in that ginger way people have when they're hiding a hurt, and if I said hello to her she'd give a little jump and look away.

18   After a while I quit paying it much mind, it didn't feel any different to me than hearing the news on the radio. All their carrying on was not any more to me than a bump in the rut I had worked myself into, going back and forth from the job, cleaning that apartment till it hurt, calling up the lawyer about once a week to find out what was happening, which never was much. He was forever trying to get our case before some particular doctor or social worker or judge who'd be more apt to help us than another, so he said. I would call him up from the TOA, all eager to hear what news he had, and every time it was another delay. In the beginning I used to talk it all over with Tim or Prissy after I hung up, but after a while I got out of the mood to discuss it. I kept ahead making those calls but every one of them just wore out my hope a little more, like a drip of water wearing down a stone. And little by little I got in the habit of thinking that nothing really was going to change.

19   Somehow or other that winter passed by, with me going from one phone call to the next, going out to wait on that TOA counter, coming home to shiver and hold hands with myself and lie awake all through the night, or the day, depending what shift I was on. It was springtime, well into warm weather, before anything really happened at all. That was when the lawyer called *me,* for a change, and told me he had some people lined up to see me at last.

20   Well, I was all ready for them to come visit, come see how I'd fixed up my house and all the rest of my business to get set for having Davey back with me again. But as it turned out, nobody seemed to feel like they were called on to make that trip. "I don't think that will be necessary" was what one of them said, I don't recall which. They both talked about the same, in voices that sounded like filling out forms.

21   So all I had to do was drive downtown a couple of times and see them in their offices. That child psychologist was the first and I doubt he kept me more than half an hour. I couldn't tell the point of most of the questions he asked. My second trip I saw the social worker, who turned out to be a black lady once I got down there, though I never could have told it over the phone. Her voice sounded like it was coming out of the TV. She looked me in the eye while she was asking her questions, but I couldn't tell a thing about what she thought. It wasn't till I was back in the apartment that I understood that she must have already had her mind made up.

22   That came to me in a sort of a flash, while I was standing in the kitchen washing out a cup. Soon as I walked back in the door I saw my coffee mug left over from breakfast, and I kicked myself for letting it sit out. I was giving it a hard scrub with a scouring pad when I realized it didn't matter anymore. I might just as well have dropped it on the floor and got

what kick I could out of watching it smash, because it wasn't going to make any difference to anybody now. But all the same I rinsed it and set it in the drainer, careful as if it was an eggshell. Then I stepped backward out of the kitchen and took a long look around that cold shabby place and thought it might be for the best that nobody was coming. How could I have expected it to fool anybody else when it wasn't even good enough to fool me? A lonesomeness came over me, I felt like I was floating all alone in the middle of cold air, and then I began to remember some things I would just as soon as have not.

No, I never did like to think about this part, but I have had to think 23 about it time and again, with never a break for a long, long time, because I needed to get to understand it at least well enough to believe it never would ever happen anymore. And I had come to believe that, in the end. If I hadn't, I never would have come back at all. I had found a way to trust myself again, though it took me a full two years to do it, and though of course it still didn't mean that anybody else would trust me.

What had happened was that Patrick went off on one of his mystery 24 trips and stayed gone a deal longer than usual. Two nights away, I was used to that, but on the third I did start to wonder. He normally would have called at least, if he was going to be gone that long of a stretch. But I didn't hear a peep until about halfway through the fourth day. And it wasn't Patrick himself that called, but one of those public-assistance lawyers from downtown.

Seemed like the night before Patrick had got himself stopped on the 25 interstate loop down there. The troopers said he was driving like a blind man, and he was so messed up on whiskey and ludes I suppose he must have been pretty near blind at that. Well, maybe he would have just lost his license or something like that, only that the backseat of the car was loaded up with all he had lately stole out of the hospital.

So it was bad. It was so bad my mind just could not contain it, and 26 every hour it seemed to be getting worse. I spent the next couple of days running back and forth between the jail and that lawyer, and I had to haul Davey along with me wherever I went. He was too little for school and I couldn't find anybody to take him right then, though all that running around made him awful cranky. Patrick was just grim, he would barely speak. He already knew pretty well for sure that he'd be going to prison. The lawyer had told him there wasn't no use in getting a bondsman, he might just as well stay on in there and start pulling his time. I don't know how much he really saved himself that way, though, since what they ended up giving him was twenty-five years.

That was when all my troubles found me, quick. Two days after 27 Patrick got arrested, I came down real sick with something. I thought at first it was a bad cold or the flu. My nose kept running and I felt so wore out I couldn't hardly get up off the bed and yet at the same time I felt real restless, like all my nerves had been scraped bare. Well, I didn't really connect it up to the fact that I'd popped the last pill in the house a couple of days before. What was really the matter was me coming off that Dilaudid, but I didn't have any notion of that at the time.

28   I was laying there in bed not able to get up and about ready to jump right out of my skin at the same time when Davey got the drawer underneath the stove open. Of course he was getting restless himself with all that had been going on, and me not able to pay him much mind. All our pots and pans were down in that drawer then, and he began to take them out one at a time and throw them on the floor. It made a hell of a racket, and the shape I was in, I felt like he must be doing it on purpose to devil me. I called out to him and asked him to quit. Nice at first: "You stop that, now, Davey. Momma don't feel good." But he kept right ahead. All he wanted was to have my attention, I know, but my mind wasn't working right just then. I knew I should get up and just go lead him away from there, but I couldn't seem to get myself to move. I had a picture of myself doing the right thing, but I just wasn't doing it. I was still lying there calling to him to quit and he was still banging those pots around and before long I was screaming at him outright, and starting to cry at the same time. But he never stopped a minute. I guess I had scared him some already and he was just locked into doing it, or maybe he wanted to drown me out. Every time he flung a pot it felt like I was getting shot at. And the next thing I knew I got myself in the kitchen someway and I was snatching him up off the floor.

29   To this day I don't remember doing it, though I have tried and tried. I thought if I could call it back then maybe I could root it out of myself and be shed of it for good and all. But all I ever knew was one minute I was grabbing a hold of him and the next he was laying on the far side of the room with his right leg folded up funny where it was broke, not even crying, just looking surprised. And I knew that it had to be me that threw him over there because as sure as hell is real there was nobody else around that could have done it.

30   I drove him to the hospital myself. I laid him straight on the front seat beside me and drove with one hand all the way so I could hold on to him with the other. He was real quiet and real brave the whole time, never cried the least bit, just kept a tight hold on my hand with his. Well, after a while, we got there and they ran him off somewhere to get his leg set and pretty soon the doctor came back out and asked me how it had happened.

31   It was the same hospital where Patrick had worked and I even knew that doctor a little bit. Not that being connected to Patrick would have done me a whole lot of good around there at that time. Still, I have often thought since then that things might have come out better for me and Davey both if I just could have lied to that man, but I was not up to telling a lie that anybody would be apt to believe. All I could do was start to scream and jabber like a crazy person, and it ended up I stayed in that hospital quite a few days myself. They took me for a junkie and I guess

I really was one too, though I hadn't known it till that very day. And I never saw Davey again for a whole two years, not till the first time they let me go out to the Bakers'.

Sometimes you don't get but one mistake, if the one you pick is bad enough. Do as much as step in the road one time without looking, and your life could be over with then and there. But during those two years I taught myself to believe that this mistake of mine could be wiped out, that if I struggled hard enough with myself and the world I could make it like it never had been. 32

Three weeks went by after I went to see that social worker, and I didn't have any idea what was happening, or if anything was. Didn't call anybody, I expect I was afraid to. Then one day the phone rang for me out there at the TOA. It was the lawyer and I could tell right off from the sound of his voice I wasn't going to care for his news. Well, he told me all the evaluations had come in now, sure enough and they weren't running in our favor. They weren't against *me,* he made sure to say that, it was more like they were *for* the Bakers. And his judgement was it wouldn't pay me anything if we went on to court. It looked like the Bakers would get Davey for good anyhow, and they were likely to be easier about visitation if there wasn't any big tussle. But if I drug them into court, then we would have to start going back over the whole case history— 33

That was the word he used, *case history,* and it was around about there that I hung up. I went walking stiff-legged back across to the counter and just let myself sort of drop on a stool. Prissy had been covering my station while I was on the phone and she came right over to me then. 34

"What is it?" she said. I guess she could tell it was something by the look on my face. 35

"I lost him," I said. 36

"Oh, hon, you know I'm so sorry," she said. She reached out for my hand but I snatched it back. I know she meant it well but I just was not in the mood to be touched. 37

"There's no forgiveness," I said. I felt bitter about it. It had been a hard road for me to come as near forgiving myself as I ever could. And Davey forgave me, I really knew that, I could tell it in the way he acted when we were together. And if us two could do it, I didn't feel like it ought to be anybody else's business but ours. Tim walked up then and Prissy whispered something to him, and then he took a step nearer to me. 38

"I'm sorry," he told me. 39

"Not like I am," I said. "You don't know the meaning of the word." 40

"Go ahead and take off the rest of your shift if you feel like it," he said. "I'll wait on these tables myself, need be." 41

"I don't know it would make any difference," I said. 42

"Better take it easy on yourself," he said. "No use in taking it so hard. You're just going to have to get used to it." 43

44   "Is that a fact?" I said. And I lit myself a cigarette and turned my face away. We had been pretty busy, it was lunchtime, and the people were getting restless seeing all of us standing around there not doing a whole lot about bringing them their food. Somebody called out something to Tim, I didn't hear just what it was, but it set off one of his temper fits.

45   "Go on and get out of here if that's how you feel," he said. He was getting red in the face and waving his arms around to include everybody there in what he was saying. "Go on and clear out of here, every last one of you, and we don't care if you never come back. There's not one of you couldn't stand to miss a meal anyhow. Take a look at yourselves, you're all fat as hogs . . ."

46   It seemed like he might be going to keep it up a good while, and he had already said I could leave, so I hung up my apron and got my purse and I left. It was the first time he ever blew up at the customers that way, it had always been me or Prissy or one of the cooks. I never did find out what came of it all because I never went back to that place again.

47   I drove home in such a poison mood I barely knew I was driving a car or that there were any others on the road. I was ripe to get killed or kill somebody, and I wouldn't have cared much either way. I kept thinking about what Tim had said about having to get used to it. It came to me that I was used to it already, I really hadn't been all that surprised. That's what I'd been doing all those months, just gradually getting used to losing my child forever.

48   When I got back to the apartment I just fell in a chair and sat there staring across at the kitchen wall. It was in my mind to pack my traps and leave that place, but I hadn't yet figured out where I could go. I sat there a good while, I guess. The door was ajar from me not paying attention, but it wasn't cold enough out to make any difference. If I turned my head that way I could see a slice of the parking lot. I saw Susan drive up and park and come limping toward the building with an armload of groceries. Because of the angle I couldn't see her go into their apartment but I heard the door open and shut and after that it was quiet as a tomb. I kept on sitting there thinking about how used to everything I had got. There must have been generous numbers of other people too, I thought, who had got themselves accustomed to all kinds of things. Some were used to taking the pain and the rest were used to serving it up. About half of the world was screaming in misery, and it wasn't anything but a habit.

49   When I started to hear the hitting sounds come toward me through the wall, a smile came on my face like it was cut there with a knife. I'd been expecting it, you see, and the mood I was in I felt satisfied to see what I had expected was going to happen. So I listened a little more carefully than I'd been inclined to do before. It was *hit hit hit* going along together with a groan and a hiss of the wind being knocked out of her. I had to strain pretty hard to hear that breathing part, and I could hear him grunt too, when he got in a good one. There was about three minutes of that with some little breaks, and then a longer pause. When she hit the wall

it was the hardest she had yet, I think. It brought down every last one of my pots at one time, including the big iron skillet that was the only one I ever used.

It was the first time they'd managed to knock that skillet down, and I was so impressed that I went over and stood looking down at it like I needed to make sure it was a real thing. I stared at the skillet so long it went out of focus and started looking more like a big black hole in the floor. That's when it dawned on me that this was one thing I didn't really have to keep on being used to. [50]

It took three or four knocks before he came to the door, but that didn't worry me at all. I had faith, I knew he was going to come. I meant to stay right there till he did. When he came, he opened the door wide and stood there with his arms folded and his face all stiff with his secrets. It was fairly dark behind him, they had all the curtains drawn. I had that skillet held out in front of me in both my hands, like maybe I had come over to borrow a little hot grease or something. It was so heavy it kept wanting to dip down toward the floor like a water witch's rod. When I saw he wasn't expecting anything, I twisted the skillet back over my shoulder like baseball players do their bat, and I hit him bang across the face as hard as I knew how. He went down and out at the same time and fetched up on his back clear in the middle of the room. [51]

Then I went in after him with the skillet cocked and ready in case he made to get up. But he didn't look like there was a whole lot of fight left in him right then. He was awake, at least partly awake, but his nose was just spouting blood and it seemed like I'd knocked out a few of his teeth. I wish I could tell you I was sorry or glad, but I didn't feel much of anything really, just that high lonesome whistle in the blood I used to get when I took all that Dilaudid. Susan was sitting on the floor against the wall, leaning down on her knees and sniveling. Her eyes were red but she didn't have any bruises where they showed. He never did hit her on the face, that was the kind he was. There was a big crack coming down the wall behind her and I remember thinking it probably wouldn't be too much longer before it worked through to my side. [52]

"I'm going to pack and drive over to Norfolk," I told her. I hadn't thought of it before but once it came out my mouth I knew it was what I would do. "You can ride along with me if you want to. With your looks you could make enough money serving drinks to the sailors to buy that Kwik Sack and blow it up." [53]

She didn't say anything, just raised her head up and stared at me kind of bug-eyed. And after a minute I turned around and went out. It didn't take me any time at all to get ready. All I had was a suitcase and a couple of boxes of other stuff. The sheets and blankets I just pulled off the bed and stuffed in the trunk all in one big wad. I didn't care a damn about that furniture, I would have lit it on fire on a dare. [54]

When I was done I stuck my head back into the other apartment. The door was still open like I had left it. What was she doing but kneeling [55] down over that son of a bitch and trying to clean off his face with a washrag. I noticed he was making a funny sound when he breathed, and his nose was still bleeding pretty quick, so I thought maybe I had broke it. Well, I can't say that worried me much.

56   "Come on now if you're coming, girl," I said. She looked up at me, not telling me one word, just giving me a stare out of those big cow eyes of hers like I was the one had been beating on her that whole winter through. And I saw then that they were both of them stuck in their groove and that she would not be the one to step out of it. So I pulled back out of the doorway and went on down the steps to my car.

57   I was speeding on the road to Norfolk, doing seventy, seventy-five. I'd have liked to gone faster if the car had been up to it. I can't say I felt sorry for busting that guy, though I didn't enjoy the thought of it either. I just didn't know what difference it had made, and chances were it had made none at all. Kind of a funny thing, when you thought about it that way. It was the second time in my life I'd hurt somebody bad, and the other time I hadn't meant to do it at all. This time I'd known what I was doing for sure, but I still didn't know what I'd done.

❏ Questions for Discussion

1. Why does the **narrator** clean up the apartment even though she says she does not care how it looks and does not feel at home there? How does she feel when the expected social worker and other experts do not come to her apartment?

2. What events led the **narrator** to abuse Davey?

3. How would this story be different if it were told from another **point of view?** Could it be as effective?

4. What does the **narrator** mean when she says, "That's what I was doing all these months, just gradually getting used to losing my child forever"? How has she attempted to get used to losing her child? How successful has she been?

5. What kind of future can the narrator anticipate?

❏ Suggestions for Exploration and Writing

1. Is the **narrator,** a child-abuser and drug addict, simply an evil person, or does she have some redeeming qualities? Do you feel sympathy for her? If you do, explain how the writer has caused you to do so. If you have no sympathy for the **narrator** explain why, citing specific passages from the story.

2. In spite of his abuse, Susan is very tender toward her husband and refuses to leave him. Using research on spouse abuse, explain the reasons for Susan's behavior.

3. What factors are most often the causes of child abuse? In an essay, propose methods for stopping child abuse or treatments for abused children.

POETRY

EMILY DICKINSON (1830–1886)

Few people in Amherst, Massachusetts, where Emily Dickinson spent most of her life in seclusion, would have dreamed that within the confines of her yard a revolution in American poetry was taking place. Because her poetry was far ahead of her time both in form and content, the few poems which she published were poorly received, and the great bulk of her work—over a thousand poems—was discovered only after her death. In little packets sewn together with thread, Dickinson had confined an extraordinary outpouring of creativity. Her brief poems, punctuated primarily with dashes, present both the wealth of startling images and an intensity of thought which have made her one of America's most loved and studied poets.

I heard a Fly buzz

I heard a Fly buzz—when I died—
The Stillness in the Room
Was like the Stillness in the Air—
Between the Heaves of Storm—

The eyes around—had wrung them dry— 5
And Breaths were gathering firm
For the last Onset—when the King
Be witnessed—in the Room—

I willed my Keepsakes—Signed away
What portion of me be 10
Assignable—and then it was
There interposed a Fly—

With Blue—uncertain stumbling Buzz—
Between the light—and me—
And then the Windows failed—and then 15
I could not see to see—

❏ Questions for Discussion

1. Contrast the attitudes toward death of the spectator in the first two stanzas and the speaker in the third and fourth stanzas. What is the speaker's attitude toward death?

2. Who is the King?

3. What does the fly suggest about the speaker's attitude toward death and about the nature of death itself? Why does the speaker focus on the fly?

❏ Suggestions for Exploration and Writing

1. The speaker in Dickinson's poem says that she "willed [her] keepsakes" and the part of herself that could be signed over. Discuss how one does or does not achieve immortality through the things left to people or institutions.

2. If a person is near death, everything may seem magnified, even the buzz of a fly. From the opposite point of view, that of the person watching another die, write an analysis of what is magnified.

3. Analyze this poem, showing how **imagery,** sound, **diction,** and **syntax** all contribute to the poem's **tone**—the speaker's attitude toward death. Also consider the placement of dashes.

Because I could not stop for Death

Because I could not stop for Death—
He kindly stopped for me—
The Carriage held but just Ourselves—
And Immortality.

5 We slowly drove—He knew no haste
And I had put away
My labor and my leisure too,
For His Civility—

We passed the School, where Children strove
10 At Recess—in the Ring—
We passed the Fields of Gazing Grain—
We passed the Setting Sun—

Or rather—He passed Us—
The Dews drew quivering and chill—
15 For only Gossamer, my Gown—
My Tippet—only Tulle—

We paused before a House that seemed
A Swelling of the Ground—
The Roof was scarcely visible—
20 The Cornice—in the Ground—

Since then—'tis Centuries—and yet
Feels shorter than the Day
I first surmised the Horses Heads
Were toward Eternity—

❏ Suggestions for Exploration and Writing

1. Death, of course, is eternal, or as Dickinson states, ". . . the Horses Heads / Were toward Eternity." Is death ever preferred? Is it ever a blessing? Discuss.

2. Dickinson personifies death and says that in her carriage ride with death, she passes many things symbolic—first of life and then of death. Write an essay in which you point out and interpret each of the **symbols.**

My life closed twice

My life closed twice before its close;
It yet remains to see
If Immortality unveil
A third event to me,

So huge, so hopeless to conceive   5
As these that twice befel.
Parting is all we know of heaven,
And all we need of hell.

❏ Questions for Discussion

1. What kind of event is Dickinson referring to in this poem?

2. Explain the last two lines.

❏ Suggestion for Exploration and Writing

1. Write an essay describing an event in your life that is comparable to the event Dickinson describes here and explaining your ability to cope with the event.

Edwin Arlington Robinson (1869–1935)

*Edwin Arlington Robinson's life provided him with a wealth of material for his poetic portraits of lonely and tragic misfits. After a series of financial and physical tragedies decimated his family, Robinson moved to Greenwich Village in New York City where for a time he was practically destitute. Although he received Pulitzer prizes for his later work, primarily book-length **blank verse** poems* *on the Arthurian legends, Robinson is best remembered for his Tilbury Town poems, portraits of imaginary misfits who inhabit a town based on his hometown of Gardiner, Maine.*

Richard Cory

Whenever Richard Cory went down town,
We people on the pavement looked at him:
He was a gentleman from sole to crown,
Clean favored, and imperially slim.

5   And he was always quietly arrayed,
And he was always human when he talked;
But still he fluttered pulses when he said,
"Good-morning," and he glittered when he walked.

And he was rich—yes, richer than a king—
10   And admirably schooled in every grace:
In fine, we thought that he was everything
To make us wish that we were in his place.

So on we worked, and waited for the light,
And went without the meat, and cursed the bread;
15   And Richard Cory, one calm summer night,
Went home and put a bullet through his head.

❏ Questions for Discussion

1. From what **point of view** is the poem written?

2. What do the people see when they look at Richard Cory?

❏ Suggestions for Exploration and Writing

1. Situations and appearances are sometimes deceiving. Using the poem as the basis for an essay, discuss why the public makes assumptions about the seemingly rich lives of public figures.

2. Write an essay on the **symbols, images,** and sound devices used in this poem—the overall symbolism of kingship; the **metonymy** and **metaphor;** the **alliteration, assonance, consonance, rhyme,** and **rhythm.** Explain how these devices help to emphasize the observers' misperception of Richard Cory.

PAUL LAURENCE DUNBAR (1872–1906)

Paul Dunbar was born in Dayton, Ohio, to former slaves; however, his father, Joshua, escaped to Canada and fought in the Union army. Dunbar later wrote for The Tattler, printed by his classmate, Orville

Wright. Wanting more than Dayton could offer, Dunbar toured Europe giving readings of his poetry. During his lifetime, he wrote poems, among them the collection Oak and Ivy *(1892); novels, such as* The Sport of Gods *(1902); and musicals, including* Dream Lovers: An Operatic Romance *(1898). Dunbar gained recognition for his diverse accomplishments and for the use of dialect in his poems. His themes include the overt oppression of African Americans in all aspects of life and the ramifications of brutality imposed on the human soul.*

We Wear the Mask

We wear the mask that grins and lies,
It hides our cheeks and shades our eyes, —
This debt we pay to human guile;
With torn and bleeding hearts we smile,
And mouth with myriad subtleties.   5

Why should the world be overwise,
In counting all our tears and sighs?
Nay, let them only see us, while
    We wear the mask.

We smile, but, O great Christ, our cries   10
To Thee from tortured souls arise.
We sing, but oh, the clay is vile
Beneath our feet, and long the mile;
But let the world dream otherwise,
    We wear the mask.   15

❏ Questions for Discussion

1. To whom does the "we" refer?

2. What does the speaker mean by "with torn and bleeding hearts we smile"? Why torn and bleeding? At another point the speaker refers to "tortured souls" and says, "the clay is vile." Is the **tone** bitter? If so, why?

3. Why does the speaker say African Americans wish to mask their true feelings? Why is there a certain amount of fear involved in exposing the true feelings behind the mask?

❏ Suggestions for Exploration and Writing

1. Does the poem have to refer to just one racial or ethnic group? Discuss cultural, racial, or ethnic groups that wear masks.

2. Explain why people have to hide behind masks. What is there in society that causes people to conceal their true selves?

JOHN C. RANSOM (1888–1974)

American poet John Crowe Ransom was a member of a group of faculty members at Vanderbilt University who called themselves the Fugitives and founded a journal of literary criticism with the same title. He later moved to Kenyon College and started the Kenyon Review. *As a poet, primarily in the early years of his career, Ransom wrote witty, ironic poems which reflect both the depth of his knowledge and his concern with the problems faced by human beings in a changing, sometimes frightening world.*

Bells for John Whiteside's Daughter

There was such speed in her little body,
And such lightness in her footfall,
It is no wonder her brown study
Astonishes us all.

5   Her wars were bruited in our high window.
We looked among orchard trees and beyond
Where she took arms against her shadow,
Or harried unto the pond

The lazy geese, like a snow cloud
10   Dripping their snow on the green grass.
Tricking and stopping, sleepy and proud,
Who cried in goose, Alas,

For the tireless heart within the little
Lady with rod that made them rise
15   From their noon apple-dreams and scuttle
Goose-fashion under the skies!

But now go the bells, and we are ready,
In one house we are sternly stopped
To say we are vexed at her brown study,
20   Lying so primly propped.

❏ **Questions for Discussion**

1. Is the death of a child more horrid than the death of an adult? Discuss.

2. Why does Ransom describe the daughter's death as a "brown study"?

3. Why does Ransom use understatement to explain the death and the distress of the mourners? What makes this particular death so distressing?

Janet Waking

Beautifully Janet slept
Till it was deeply morning. She woke then
And thought about her dainty-feathered hen,
To see how it had kept.

One kiss she gave her mother.   5
Only a small one gave she to her daddy
Who would have kissed each curl of his shining baby;
No kiss at all for her brother.

"Old Chucky, old Chucky!" she cried,
Running across the world upon the grass   10
To Chucky's house, and listening. But alas,
Her Chucky had died.

It was a transmogrifying bee
Came droning down on Chucky's old bald head
And sat and put the poison. It scarcely bled,   15
But how exceedingly

And purply did the knot
Swell with the venom and communicate
Its rigor! Now the poor comb stood up straight
But Chucky did not.   20

So there was Janet
Kneeling on the wet grass, crying her brown hen
(Translated far beyond the daughters of men)
To rise and walk upon it.

And weeping fast as she had breath   25
Janet implored us, "Wake her from her sleep!"
And would not be instructed in how deep
Was the forgetful kingdom of death.

❏ Questions for Discussion

1. Why is the death of a hen such a significant incident for the
   little girl? Ransom emphasizes this significance by saying that
   the hen was killed by a "transmogrifying bee" and was "translated far beyond the daughters of men." Explain these phrases.

2. Ransom says that Janet "would not be instructed in how deep /
   Was the forgetful kingdom of death." Is failure to accept the
   finality of death a typical human reaction? Explain.

CLAUDE McKAY (1890–1948)

Claude McKay's poetry reflects his childhood in Jamaica and his adult life in America. His work is associated with the Harlem Renaissance, but he was often in conflict with the writers of that movement because of his political views. During the course of his life, McKay wrote lyrical poems, dialect poems, and sonnets.

If We Must Die

If we must die, let it not be like hogs
Hunted and penned in an inglorious spot,
While round us bark the mad and hungry dogs,
Making their mock at our accursed lot.
5   If we must die, O let us nobly die,
So that our precious blood may not be shed
In vain; then even the monsters we defy
Shall be constrained to honor us though dead!
O kinsmen! we must meet the common foe!
10   Though far outnumbered let us show us brave,
And for their thousand blows deal one deathblow!
What though before us lies the open grave?
Like men we'll face the murderous, cowardly pack,
Pressed to the wall, dying, but fighting back!

❏ Questions for Discussion

1. Whom does McKay refer to as "we" in the poem? McKay uses the terms "kinsmen" and the "common foe." Is his poem only about African Americans?

2. McKay has negative words for those he wants to oppose: "mad and hungry dogs," "the monsters," and "murderous, cowardly pack." Do you think McKay is being too biased or slanted?

❏ Suggestions for Exploration and Discussion

1. Martin Luther King, Jr., preached nonviolence; however, Claude McKay, writing a generation earlier, preaches violence. Using the poem as the basis for discussion, comment on McKay's justification for not backing down from retaliation or violence.

2. Is there any cause for which you would be willing to die? Discuss.

WILFRED OWEN (1893–1918)

Wilfred Owen is recognized as one of the greatest English war poets. He joined the British Army in 1915, fought as an officer in the First

World War, and was killed in that war on November 4, 1918, just seven days before it ended. Most of Owen's poems, which powerfully evoke the terror and inhumanity of war, were not published until after his death.

Dulce et Decorum Est

Bent double, like old beggars under sacks,
Knock-kneed, coughing like hags, we cursed through sludge,
Till on the haunting flares we turned our backs
And towards our distant rest began to trudge.
Men marched asleep. Many had lost their boots   5
But limped on, blood-shod. All went lame; all blind;
Drunk with fatigue; deaf even to the hoots
Of tired, outstripped Five-Nines that dropped behind.

Gas! GAS! Quick, boys!—An ecstasy of fumbling,
Fitting the clumsy helmets just in time;   10
But someone still was yelling out and stumbling
And flound'ring like a man in fire or lime . . .
Dim, through the misty panes and thick green light,
As under a green sea, I saw him drowning.

In all my dreams, before my helpless sight,   15
He plunges at me, guttering, choking, drowning.

If in some smothering dreams you too could pace
Behind the wagon that we flung him in,
And watch the white eyes writhing in his face,
His hanging face, like a devil's sick of sin;   20
If you could hear, at every jolt, the blood
Come gargling from the froth-corrupted lungs,
Obscene as cancer, bitter as the cud
Of vile, incurable sores on innocent tongues,—
My friend, you would not tell with such high zest   25
To children ardent for some desperate glory,
The old Lie: *Dulce et decorum est
Pro patria mori.*

❏ Questions for Discussion

1. This poem's last line, from Horace, *Odes*, III, ii, 13, means "It is sweet and proper to die for one's country." How does the realistic portrayal of war in the first stanza contrast with the patriotic sentiments the speaker attacks in the last few lines of the poem?

2. Why does Owen use the Latin quotation at the end?

❏ **Suggestion for Exploration and Writing**

1. Write a thorough analysis of this poem, examining how its **tone** changes from stanza to stanza and how **imagery**, sound, **diction**, and **syntax** develop tone.

COUNTEE CULLEN (1903–1948)

A New Yorker by birth, Cullen was a Phi Beta Kappa graduate of New York University. He wrote his first collection of poems, Color *(1945), while he was in college. Cullen also wrote a novel,* One Way to Heaven *(1932), and a version of Euripides' play* Medea. *Although a member of the Harlem Renaissance, Cullen later turned to teaching in order to earn a living.*

Incident

(For Eric Walrond)

Once riding in old Baltimore,
  Heart-filled, head-filled with glee,
I saw a Baltimorean
  Keep looking straight at me.

5   Now I was eight and very small,
  And he was no whit bigger,
And so I smiled, but he poked out
  His tongue, and called me, "Nigger."

I saw the whole of Baltimore
10   From May until December;
Of all the things that happened there
  That's all that I remember.

❏ **Question for Discussion**

1. Why does the speaker remember only this incident from a seven-month stay in the city?

❏ **Suggestion for Exploration and Writing**

1. Discuss the impact that a word such as "nigger" or another derogatory term can have on the self-esteem of an individual or a group.

DYLAN THOMAS (1914–1953)

Dylan Thomas was a Welsh poet known for his extraordinary reading voice. His most famous poems, exuberant and rich in sound and imagery, are nevertheless constructed with painstaking care, as the deceptively simple villanelle "Do Not Go Gentle into That Good Night" illustrates.

Do Not Go Gentle into That Good Night

Do not go gentle into that good night,
Old age should burn and rave at close of day;
Rage, rage against the dying of the light.

Though wise men at their end know dark is right,
Because their words had forked no lightning they   5
Do not go gentle into that good night.

Good men, the last wave by, crying how bright
Their frail deeds might have danced in a green bay,
Rage, rage against the dying of the light.

Wild men who caught and sang the sun in flight,   10
And learn, too late, they grieved it on its way,
Do not go gentle into that good night.

Grave men, near death, who see with blinding sight
Blind eyes could blaze like meteors and be gay,
Rage, rage against the dying of the light.   15

And you, my father, there on the sad height,
Curse, bless, me now with your fierce tears, I pray.
Do not go gentle into that good night.
Rage, rage against the dying of the light.

❏ Questions for Discussion

1. What is the effect of Thomas' repeating the two lines "Do not go gentle into that good night" and "Rage, rage against the dying of the light"?

2. Each of the middle stanzas describes a different kind of man facing death. Besides resisting death, what do the men have in common?

3. How effective is the longer, more specific last stanza after the first five? Why are the first five stanzas necessary if the main subject is the father's death?

4. Why does the speaker ask his father to "curse, bless" him? What does the speaker mean?

5. This poem is a **villanelle,** a form that is extremely difficult and rare in English poetry because of its rigidly patterned rhyme scheme. How does the extremely rigid form contribute to the **tone** of Thomas's poem?

❏ Suggestion for Exploration and Writing

1. Thomas repeats, "Rage, rage against the dying of the light." He obviously feels that everyone should live life to the fullest and challenge old age and eventual death. Using three of his reasons, discuss whether you would agree or disagree with Thomas.

RANDALL JARRELL (1914–1965)

Randall Jarrell was an American poet and critic. While some of his poems like the following one present a bleak, almost tragic vision, others present an innocent, almost childlike vision. Early war poems such as "The Death of the Ball Turret Gunner" arose out of Jarrell's service as a pilot and air traffic controller in World War II.

The Death of the Ball Turret Gunner

From my mother's sleep I fell into the State,
And I hunched in its belly till my wet fur froze.
Six miles from earth, loosed from its dream of life,
I woke to black flak and the nightmare fighters.

5 When I died they washed me out of the turret with a hose.

❏ Questions for Discussion

1. Based on the **imagery** of the poem, how do you picture the gunner?

2. What does the first line mean? What does it suggest about the gunner and his relationship to the military?

3. Note the references to "sleep," "dream," and "nightmare" in the poem. What do they suggest about the speaker's consciousness?

4. In the last line, to whom does "they" refer? Why does Jarrell use an unclear pronoun? What is the emotional effect of this line?

SHARON OLDS (1942–   )

Sharon Olds, a San Francisco-born American poet, has won a National Book Critics Circle Award for her poetry. Her three books of poems are Satan Days *(1980),* The Dead and the Living *(1983), and* The Gold Cell *(1987), which includes the following poem.*

On the Subway

The boy and I face each other.
His feet are huge, in black sneakers
laced with white in a complex pattern like a
set of intentional scars. We are stuck on
opposite sides of the car, a couple of   5
molecules stuck in a rod of light
rapidly moving through darkness. He has the
casual cold look of a mugger,
alert under hooded lids. He is wearing
red, like the inside of the body   10
exposed. I am wearing dark fur, the
whole skin of an animal taken and
used. I look at his raw face,
he looks at my fur coat, and I don't
know if I am in his power—   15
he could take my coat so easily, my
briefcase, my life—
or if he is in my power, the way I am
living off his life, eating the steak
he does not eat, as if I am taking   20
the food from his mouth. And he is black
and I am white, and without meaning or
trying to I must profit from his darkness,
the way he absorbs the murderous beams of the
nation's heart, as black cotton   25
absorbs the heat of the sun and holds it. There is
no way to know how easy this
white skin makes my life, this
life he could take so easily and
break across his knee like a stick the way his   30
own back is being broken, the
rod of his soul that at birth was dark and
fluid and rich as the heart of a seedling
ready to thrust up into any available light.

❏ **Questions for Discussion**

1. Examine the **images** of color and light in the poem. How are
   they important in creating the **tone** of the poem?

2. List the **images** of hurt and pain the speaker uses to describe
   the life of the man she meets. How do these and other images
   create a striking contrast between the speaker's life and that of
   the stranger?

3. Explain the contradiction of the speaker's saying:

> . . . I don't
> know if I am in his power—
> . . . .
> Or if he is in my power . . . .

To be in another's control can be very frightening. Who is in control of the lives in this poem—the boy, the speaker, both, or neither?

❏ **Suggestions for Exploration and Writing**

1. Write an essay explaining how the rich **similes** and **metaphors** add to both the visual effect of the poem and the depth of meaning.

2. Using the poem as background, analyze the factors leading to the fear of the white woman for the black man.

3. Discuss the meaning of the last three lines of the poem. According to Olds, what has happened to the rod of the black man's soul?

DRAMA

WILLIAM SHAKESPEARE (1564–1616)

William Shakespeare is generally regarded as the greatest writer ever to have written in English. Though Shakespeare also produced an often-admired sequence of 154 sonnets and several narrative poems, his extraordinary reputation rests primarily on his plays. Notable for their sheer number and diversity, the thirty-seven plays include thirteen **comedies,** *ten* **tragedies,** *ten history plays, and four* **romances.**

Using language that is rich and highly allusive yet conversational and informal, the plays reveal not only a sure sense of dramatic structure and tension but also a love of human diversity. As a member of an acting company that performed both in the outdoor Globe playhouse and in the indoor Blackfriars, Shakespeare was intimately familiar with the theater of his time and with its conventions. Among the most highly regarded of his plays are the comedies As You Like It, All's Well That Ends Well, *and* Twelfth Night; *the history plays* Henry IV, Part I *and* Henry IV, Part II; *the tragedies*

Hamlet, Othello, King Lear, *and* Macbeth; *and* The Tempest, *a romance generally thought to have been Shakespeare's last play.* Othello *displays the richness of language, character, and dramatic tension for which Shakespeare is justly celebrated.*

About Tragedy

Shakespeare's *Othello* is a **tragedy.** In its most general literary usage, the term **tragedy** refers to a particular kind of play in which a good person through some character flaw destroys himself or herself.

The most famous definition of tragedy comes from the ancient Greek philosopher Aristotle (384–322 B.C.). In his *Poetics,* Aristotle defines tragedy as

> a representation (*mimesis*) of an action (*praxis*) that is serious, complete, and of a certain magnitude . . . presented, not narrated [i.e., a drama not a story] . . . with incidents arousing pity and fear in such a way as to accomplish a purgation (*katharsis*) of such emotions. (296)

The purpose of tragedy according to Aristotle, then, is to make the audience feel "pity and fear" in order somehow to purge or cleanse these emotions. The most important elements of tragedy are **plot** and **character.** The plot must present an action that is complete, with a clear beginning and an ending that gives a sense of finality, and must be unified, so that every part contributes to the whole. The best plots feature reversal (**peripeteia**), a not improbable but unexpected 180-degree change in situation, and recognition (**anagnorisis**), the tragic hero's sudden understanding of his or her fate and its implications. A **tragic hero,** Aristotle maintains, must be good but flawed, must be aristocratic, must be believable, and must behave consistently.

Shakespeare, writing for a different audience in a different kind of theater at a different time, produced tragedies that are rich in language and character development but less dramatically unified than Aristotle prescribes. For example, Shakespeare did not hesitate to insert into his tragedies scenes containing the broadest farce, an impropriety of which Aristotle would almost certainly have disapproved. It is a testimony to Shakespeare's dramatic genius that he could include in his tragedies such richly comic scenes without disrupting their dramatic tension. Of all Shakespeare's tragedies, *Othello* is the most Aristotelian in its unity. Shakespearean in its **puns** and plays on words and in the diversity and fullness of such characters as Othello, Iago, Emilia, and Desdemona, *Othello* moves inexorably to its tragic conclusion.

Work Cited

Aristotle. "The Art of Poetry." From *Aristotle.* Sel. & trans. Philip Wheelwright. New York: Odyssey, 1951.

Othello, the Moor of Venice

The Names of the Actors

OTHELLO:	*the Moor*
BRABANTIO:	*[a senator,] father to Desdemona*
CASSIO:	*an honorable lieutenant [to Othello]*
IAGO:	*[Othello's ancient,] a villain*
RODERIGO:	*a gulled gentleman*
DUKE OF VENICE	
SENATORS [OF VENICE]	
MONTANO:	*Governor of Cyprus*
GENTLEMEN *of Cyprus*	
LODOVICO *and* GRATIANO:	*[kinsmen to Brabantio,] two noble Venetians*
SAILORS	
CLOWN	
DESDEMONA:	*[daughter to Brabantio and] wife to Othello*
EMILIA:	*wife to Iago*
BIANCA:	*a courtesan [and mistress to Cassio]*
A MESSENGER	
A HERALD	
A MUSICIAN	

servants, attendants, officers, senators, musicians, gentlemen

Scene

Venice; a seaport in Cyprus

1.1

Enter Roderigo and Iago.

RODERIGO
Tush, never tell me! I take it much unkindly   1
That thou, Iago, who has had my purse
As if the strings were thine, shouldst know of this.   3
IAGO 'Sblood, but you'll not hear me.   4
If ever I did dream of such a matter,
Abhor me.

1.1. Location: Venice. A street.
1 never tell me (An expression of incredulity, like "tell me another one.")   **3 this** i.e., Desdemona's elopement   **4 'Sblood** by His (Christ's) blood

RODERIGO
Thou toldst me thou didst hold him in thy hate.
IAGO   Despise me
If I do not. Three great ones of the city,
In personal suit to make me his lieutenant,
Off-capped to him; and by the faith of man,   11
I know my price, I am worth no worse a place.
But he, as loving his own pride and purposes,
Evades them with a bombast circumstance   14
Horribly stuffed with epithets of war,   15
And, in conclusion,
Nonsuits my mediators. For, "Certes," says he,   17
"I have already chose my officer."
And what was he?
Forsooth, a great arithmetician,   20
One Michael Cassio, a Florentine,
A fellow almost damned in a fair wife,   22
That never set a squadron in the field
Nor the division of a battle knows   24
More than a spinster unless the bookish theoric,   25
Wherein the togaed consuls can propose   26
As masterly as he. Mere prattle without practice
Is all his soldiership. But he, sir, had th' election;
And I, of whom his eyes had seen the proof   29
At Rhodes, at Cyprus, and on other grounds
Christened and heathen, must be beleed and calmed   31
By debitor and creditor. This countercaster,   32
He, in good time, must his lieutenant be,   33
And I—God bless the mark!—his Moorship's ancient.   34
RODERIGO
By heaven, I rather would have been his hangman.   35

---

11 him i.e., Othello   **14 bombast circumstance** wordy evasion. (*Bombast* is cotton padding.)   **15 epithets of war** military expressions   **17 Nonsuits** rejects the petition of. **Certes** certainly   **20 arithmetician** i.e., a man whose military knowledge is merely theoretical, based on books of tactics   **22 A ... wife** (Cassio does not seem to be married, but his counterpart in Shakespeare's source does have a woman in his house. See also 4.1.131.)   **24 division of a battle** disposition of a military unit   **25 a spinster** i.e., a housewife, one whose regular occupation is spinning. **theoric** theory   **26 togaed** wearing the toga. **consuls** counselors, senators. **propose** discuss   **29 his** i.e., Othello's   **31 Christened** Christian. **beleed and calmed** left to leeward without wind, becalmed. (A sailing metaphor.)   **32 debitor and creditor** (A name for a system of bookkeeping, here used as a contemptuous nickname for Cassio.) **countercaster** i.e., bookkeeper, one who tallies with *counters*, or "metal disks." (Said contemptuously.)   **33 in good time** opportunely, i.e., forsooth   **34 God bless the mark** (Perhaps originally a formula to ward off evil; here an expression of impatience.) **ancient** standard-bearer, ensign   **35 his hangman** the executioner of him

IAGO

Why, there's no remedy. 'Tis the curse of service;
Preferment goes by letter and affection,　　　　　　　　　37
And not by old gradation, where each second　　　　　　38
Stood heir to th' first. Now, sir, be judge yourself
Whether I in any just term am affined　　　　　　　　　40
To love the Moor.

RODERIGO　I would not follow him then.

IAGO　O sir, content you.　　　　　　　　　　　　　　43
I follow him to serve my turn upon him.
We cannot all be masters, nor all masters
Cannot be truly followed. You shall mark　　　　　　　46
Many a duteous and knee-crooking knave
That, doting on his own obsequious bondage,
Wears out his time, much like his master's ass,
For naught but provender, and when he's old, cashiered.　50
Whip me such honest knaves. Others there are　　　　　51
Who, trimmed in forms and visages of duty,　　　　　　52
Keep yet their hearts attending on themselves,
And, throwing but shows of service on their lords,
Do well thrive by them, and when they have lined their coats,　55
Do themselves homage. These fellows have some soul,　56
And such a one do I profess myself. For, sir,
It is as sure as you are Roderigo,
Were I the Moor I would not be Iago.　　　　　　　　59
In following him, I follow but myself—
Heaven is my judge, not I for love and duty,
But seeming so for my peculiar end.　　　　　　　　　62
For when my outward action doth demonstrate
The native act and figure of my heart　　　　　　　　64
In compliment extern, 'tis not long after　　　　　　　65
But I will wear my heart upon my sleeve
For daws to peck at. I am not what I am.　　　　　　67

---

37 Preferment promotion. **letter and affection** personal influence and favoritism
38 old gradation step-by-step seniority, the traditional way　**40 term** respect. **affined**
bound　**43 content you** don't you worry about that　**46 truly** faithfully　**50 cashiered**
dismissed from service　**51 Whip me** whip, as far as I'm concerned　**52 trimmed . . .**
duty dressed up in the mere form and show of dutifulness　**55 lined their coats** i.e.,
stuffed their purses　**56 Do themselves homage** i.e., attend to self-interest solely
59 Were . . Iago i.e., if I were able to assume command, I certainly would not choose to
remain a subordinate, or, I would keep a suspicious eye on a flattering subordinate
62 peculiar particular, personal　**64 native** innate. **figure** shape, intent　**65 compliment**
extern outward show (conforming in this case to the inner workings and intention of the
heart)　**67 daws** small crowlike birds, proverbially stupid and avaricious. **I am not what**
I am i.e., I am not one who wears his heart on his sleeve

RODERIGO
What a full fortune does the thick-lips owe   68
If he can carry 't thus!
IAGO   Call up her father.   69
Rouse him, make after him, poison his delight,
Proclaim him in the streets; incense her kinsmen,
And, though he in a fertile climate dwell,   72
Plague him with flies. Though that his joy be joy,   73
Yet throw such chances of vexation on 't   74
As it may lose some color.   75
RODERIGO
Here is her father's house. I'll call aloud.
IAGO
Do, with like timorous accent and dire yell   77
As when, by night and negligence, the fire   78
Is spied in populous cities.
RODERIGO
What ho, Brabantio! Signor Brabantio, ho!
IAGO
Awake! What ho, Brabantio! Thieves, thieves, thieves!
Look to your house, your daughter, and your bags!
Thieves, thieves!   83

Brabantio [enters] above [at a window].

BRABANTIO
What is the reason of this terrible summons?
What is the matter there?   85
RODERIGO
Signor, is all your family within?
IAGO
Are your doors locked?
BRABANTIO   Why, wherefore ask you this?
IAGO
Zounds, sir, you're robbed. For shame, put on your gown!   88
Your heart is burst; you have lost half your soul.
Even now, now, very now, an old black ram
Is tupping your white ewe. Arise, arise!   91

---

68 full swelling. **thick-lips** (Elizabethans often applied the term "Moor" to Negroes.)
owe own **69 carry 't thus** carry this off **72–73 though . . . flies** though he seems prosperous and happy now, vex him with misery **73 Though . . . be joy** although he seems
fortunate and happy. (Repeats the idea of line 72.) **74 changes of vexation** vexing
changes **75 As it may** that may cause it to. **some color** some of its fresh gloss **77 timorous** frightening **78 and negligence** i.e., by negligence **83 s.d. at a window** (This
stage direction, from the Quarto, probably calls for an appearance on the gallery above
and rearstage.) **85 the matter** your business **88 Zounds** by His (Christ's) wounds
91 tupping covering, copulating with. (Said of sheep.)

Awake the snorting citizens with the bell,   92
Or else the devil will make a grandsire of you.   93
Arise, I say!
BRABANTIO   What, have you lost your wits?
RODERIGO
Most reverend signor, do you know my voice?
BRABANTIO   Not I. What are you?
RODERIGO   My name is Roderigo.
BRABANTIO   The worser welcome.
I have charged thee not to haunt about my doors.
In honest plainness thou hast heard me say
My daughter is not for thee; and now, in madness,
Being full of supper and distempering drafts,   102
Upon malicious bravery dost thou come   103
To start my quiet.   104
RODERIGO
Sir, sir, sir—
BRABANTIO   But thou must needs be sure
My spirits and my place have in their power   106
To make this bitter to thee.
RODERIGO   Patience, good sir.
BRABANTIO
What tell'st thou me of robbing? This is Venice;
My house is not a grange.
RODERIGO   Most grave Brabantio,   109
In simple and pure soul I come to you.   110
IAGO   Zounds, sir, you are one of those that will not
serve God if the devil bid you. Because we come to do
you service and you think we are ruffians, you'll have
your daughter covered with a Barbary horse; you'll   114
have your nephews neigh to you; you'll have coursers   115
for cousins and jennets for germans.   116
BRABANTIO   What profane wretch art thou?
IAGO   I am one, sir, that comes to tell you your daughter
and the Moor are now making the beast with two
backs.
BRABANTIO
Thou art a villain.

---

92 **snorting** snoring   93 **the devil** (The devil was conventionally pictured as black.)
102 **distempering** intoxicating   103 **Upon malicious bravery** with hostile intent to defy
me   104 **start** startle, disrupt   106 **My spirits and my place** my temperament and my
authority of office. **have in** have it in   109 **grange** isolated country house   110 **simple**
sincere   114 **Barbary** from northern Africa (and hence associated with Othello)
115 **nephews** i.e., grandsons. **coursers** powerful horses   116 **cousins** kinsmen. **jennets**
small Spanish horses. **germans** near relatives

IAGO   You are a senator.   121

BRABANTIO

This thou shalt answer. I know thee, Roderigo.   122

RODERIGO

Sir, I will answer anything. But I beseech you,

If 't be your pleasure and most wise consent—   124

As partly I find it is—that your fair daughter,

At this odd-even and dull watch o' the night,   126

Transported with no worse nor better guard   127

But with a knave of common hire, a gondolier,   128

To the gross clasps of a lascivious Moor—

If this be known to you and your allowance   130

We then have done you bold and saucy wrongs.   131

But if you know not this, my manners tell me

We have your wrong rebuke. Do not believe

That, from the sense of all civility,   134

I thus would play and trifle with your reverence.   135

Your daughter, if you have not given her leave,

I say again, hath made a gross revolt,

Tying her duty, beauty, wit, and fortunes   138

In an extravagant and wheeling stranger   139

Of here and everywhere. Straight satisfy yourself.   140

If she be in her chamber or your house,

Let loose on me the justice of the state

For thus deluding you.

BRABANTIO   Strike on the tinder, ho!   144

Give me a taper! Call up all my people!

This accident is not unlike my dream.   146

Belief of it oppresses me already.

Light, I say, light!   *Exit* [*above*].

IAGO   Farewell, for I must leave you.

It seems not meet nor wholesome to my place   149

To be producted—as, if I stay, I shall—   150

Against the Moor. For I do know the state,

However this may gall him with some check,   152

121 **a senator** (Said with mock politeness, as though the word itself were an insult.)
122 **answer** be held accountable for   124 **wise** well-informed   126 **odd-even** between
one day and the next, i.e., about midnight   127 **with** by   128 **But with a knave** than
by a low fellow, a servant   130 **allowance** permission   131 **saucy** insolent   134 **from**
contrary to. **civility** good manners, decency   135 **your reverence** the respect due to you
138 **wit** intelligence   139 **extravagant** expatriate, wandering far from home. **wheeling**
roving about, vagabond. **stranger** foreigner   140 **Straight** straightway   144 **tinder**
charred linen ignited by a spark from flint and steel, used to light torches or *tapers* (lines
145, 170)   146 **accident** occurrence, event   149 **meet** fitting. **place** position (as ensign)
150 **producted** produced (as a witness)   152 **gall** rub; oppress. **check** rebuke

Cannot with safety cast him, for he's embarked 153
With such loud reason to the Cyprus wars, 154
Which even now stands in act, that, for their souls, 155
Another of his fathom they have none 156
To lead their business; in which regard, 157
Though I do hate him as I do hell pains,
Yet for necessity of present life 159
I must show out a flag and sign of love,
Which is indeed but sign. That you shall surely find him,
Lead to the Sagittary the raisèd search, 162
And there will I be with him. So farewell.   *Exit* 163

Enter [below] Brabantio [in his nightgown] with servants and torches.

BRABANTIO
It is too true an evil. Gone she is;
And what's to come of my despisèd time 165
Is naught but bitterness. Now, Roderigo,
Where didst thou see her?—O unhappy girl!—
With the Moor, sayst thou?—Who would be a father!—
How didst thou know 'twas she?—O, she deceives me
Past thought!—What said she to you?—Get more tapers.
Raise all my kindred.—Are they married, think you?
RODERIGO   Truly, I think they are.
BRABANTIO
O heaven! How got she out? O treason of the blood!
Fathers, from hence trust not your daughters' minds
By what you see them act. Is there not charms 175
By which the property of youth and maidhood 176
May be abused? Have you not read, Roderigo, 177
Of some such thing?
RODERIGO   Yes, sir, I have indeed.
BRABANTIO
Call up my brother.—O, would you had had her!—
Some one way, some another.—Do you know
Where we may apprehend her and the Moor?
RODERIGO
I think I can discover him, if you please 182
To get good guard and go along with me.

153 **cast** dismiss. **embarked** engaged   154 **loud reason** unanimous shout of confirmation (in the Senate)   155 **stands in act** are going on. **for their souls** to save themselves   156 **fathom** i.e., ability, depth of experience   157 **in which regard** out of regard for which   159 **life** livelihood   162 **Sagittary** (An inn or house where Othello and Desdemona are staying, named for its sign of Sagittarius, or Centaur.) **raisèd search** search party roused out of sleep   163 **s.d. nightgown** dressing gown. (This costuming is specified in the Quarto text.)   165 **time** i.e., remainder of life   175 **charms** spells   176 **property** special quality, nature   177 **abused** deceived   182 **discover** reveal, uncover

BRABANTIO

Pray you, lead on. At every house I'll call;
I may command at most.—Get weapons, ho!   185
And raise some special officers of night.—
On, good Roderigo. I will deserve your pains.   *Exeunt.*   187

1.2

Enter Othello, Iago, attendants with torches.

IAGO

Though in the trade of war I have slain men,
Yet do I hold it very stuff o' the conscience   2
To do no contrived murder. I lack iniquity   3
Sometimes to do me service. Nine or ten times
I had thought t' have yerked him here under the ribs.   5

OTHELLO

'Tis better as it is.

IAGO   Nay, but he prated,
And spoke such scurvy and provoking terms
Against your honor
That, with the little godliness I have,
I did full hard forbear him. But, I pray you, sir,   10
Are you fast married? Be assured of this,
That the magnifico is much beloved,   12
And hath in his effect a voice potential   13
As double as the Duke's. He will divorce you,
Or put upon you what restraint or grievance
The law, with all his might to enforce it on,
Will give him cable.

OTHELLO   Let him do his spite.   17
My services which I have done the seigniory   18
Shall out-tongue his complaints. 'Tis yet to know—   19
Which, when I know that boasting is an honor,
I shall promulgate—I fetch my life and being
From men of royal siege, and my demerits   22
May speak unbonneted to as proud a fortune   23
As this that I have reached. For know, Iago,

---

185 **command** demand assistance   187 **deserve** show gratitude for
1.2 Location: Venice. Another street, before Othello's lodgings.
2 **very stuff** essence, basic material (continuing the metaphor of *trade* from line 1)
3 **contrived** premeditated   5 **yerked** stabbed. **him** i.e., Roderigo   10 **I . . . him** I restrained myself with great difficulty from assaulting him   12 **magnifico** Venetian
grandee, i.e., Brabantio   13 **in his effect** at his command. **potential** powerful   17 **cable**
i.e., scope   18 **seigniory** Venetian government   19 **yet to know** not yet widely known
22 **siege** i.e., rank. (Literally, seat used by a person of distinction.) **demerits** deserts
23 **unbonneted** without removing the hat, i.e., on equal terms (? Or "with hat off," "in
all due modesty.")

But that I love the gentle Desdemona,
I would not my unhousèd free condition   26
Put into circumscription and confine   27
For the sea's worth. But look, what lights come yond?   28

Enter Cassio [and certain officers] with torches.

IAGO
Those are the raisèd father and his friends.
You were best go in.
OTHELLO   Not I. I must be found.
My parts, my title, and my perfect soul   31
Shall manifest me rightly. Is it they?
IAGO   By Janus, I think no.   33
OTHELLO
The servants of the Duke? And my lieutenant?
The goodness of the night upon you, friends!
What is the news?
CASSIO   The Duke does greet you, General,
And he requires your haste-post-haste appearance
Even on the instant.
OTHELLO   What is the matter, think you?   38
CASSIO
Something from Cyprus, as I may divine.   39
It is a business of some heat. The galleys   40
Have sent a dozen sequent messengers   41
This very night at one another's heels,
And many of the consuls, raised and met,   43
Are at the Duke's already. You have been hotly called for;
When, being not at your lodging to be found,
The Senate hath sent about three several quests   46
To search you out.
OTHELLO   'Tis well I am found by you.
I will but spend a word here in the house
And go with you.   [*Exit.*]
CASSIO   Ancient, what makes he here?   49
IAGO
Faith, he tonight hath boarded a land carrack.   50
If it prove lawful prize, he's made forever.   51

---

26 **unhousèd** unconfined, undomesticated   27 **circumscription and confine** restriction
and confinement   28 **the sea's worth** all the riches at the bottom of the sea. **s.d. officers**
(The Quarto text calls for "Cassio with lights, officers with torches.")   31 **My ... soul**
my natural gifts, my position or reputation, and my unflawed conscience   33 **Janus** Roman two-faced god of beginnings   38 **matter** business   39 **divine** guess   40 **heat** urgency   41 **sequent** successive   43 **consuls** senators   46 **about** all over the city. **several**
separate   49 **makes** does   50 **boarded** gone aboard and seized as an act of piracy (with
sexual suggestion). **carrack** large merchant ship   51 **prize** booty

CASSIO
I do not understand.
IAGO   He's married.
CASSIO   To who?
[Enter Othello.]
IAGO
Marry, to—Come,—Captain, will you go?   53
OTHELLO Have with you.   54
CASSIO
Here comes another troop to seek for you.   55
Enter Brabantio, Roderigo, with officers and torches.

IAGO
It is Brabantio. General, be advised.   56
He comes to bad intent.
OTHELLO   Holla! Stand there!
RODERIGO
Signor, it is the Moor.
BRABANTIO   Down with him, thief!
                    [They draw on both sides.]
IAGO
You, Roderigo! Come, sir, I am for you.
OTHELLO
Keep up your bright swords, for the dew will rust them. 60
Good signor, you shall more command with years
Than with your weapons.
BRABANTIO
O thou foul thief, where hast thou stowed my daughter?
Damned as thou art, thou hast enchanted her!
For I'll refer me to all things of sense,   65
If she in chains of magic were not bound
Whether a maid so tender, fair, and happy,
So opposite to marriage that she shunned
The wealthy curlèd darlings of our nation,
Would ever have, t' incur a general mock,
Run from her guardage to the sooty bosom   71
Of such a thing as thou—to fear, not to delight.
Judge me the world if 'tis not gross in sense   73
That thou hast practiced on her with foul charms,
Abused her delicate youth with drugs or minerals   75

53 **Marry** (An oath, originally "by the Virgin Mary"; here used with wordplay on *married*.)   54 **Have with you** i.e., let's go   55 s.d. **officers and torches** (The Quarto text calls for "others with lights and weapons.")   56 **be advised** be on your guard   60 **Keep up** keep in the sheath   65 **refer me** submit my case. **things of sense** commonsense understandings, or, creatures possessing common sense   71 **her guardage** my guardianship of her   73 **gross in sense** obvious   75 **minerals** i.e., poisons

That weakens motion. I'll have 't disputed on;   76
'Tis probable and palpable to thinking.
I therefore apprehend and do attach thee   78
For an abuser of the world, a practicer
Of arts inhibited and out of warrant. —   80
Lay hold upon him! If he do resist,
Subdue him at his peril.
OTHELLO   Hold your hands,
 Both you of my inclining and the rest.   83
 Were it my cue to fight, I should have known it
 Without a prompter. — Whither will you that I go
 To answer this your charge?
BRABANTIO   To prison, till fit time
 Of law and course of direct session   88
 Call thee to answer.
OTHELLO   What if I do obey?
 How may the Duke be therewith satisfied,
 Whose messengers are here about my side
 Upon some present business of the state
 To bring me to him?
OFFICER   'Tis true, most worthy signor.
 The Duke's in council, and your noble self,
 I am sure, is sent for.
BRABANTIO   How? The Duke in council?
 In this time of the night? Bring him away.   96
 Mine's not an idle cause. The Duke himself,   97
 Or any of my brothers of the state,
 Cannot but feel this wrong as 'twere their own;
 For if such actions may have passage free,   100
 Bondslaves and pagans shall our statesmen be.   *Exeunt.*

1.3

*Enter Duke [and] Senators [and sit at a table, with lights], and Of-
ficers. [The Duke and Senators are reading dispatches.]*

DUKE

There is no composition in these news   1
That gives them credit.

---

76 **weakens motion** impair the vital faculties. **disputed on** argued in court by professional counsel, debated by experts   78 **attach** arrest   80 **arts inhibited** prohibited arts,
black magic.   83 **inclining** following, party   88 **course of direct session** regular or specially convened legal proceedings   96 **away** right along   97 **idle** trifling   100 **have passage free** are allowed to go unchecked
1.3 Location: Venice. A council chamber.
s.d. Enter . . . Officers (The Quarto text calls for the Duke and senators to "sit at a table
with lights and attendants.")   1 **composition** consistency

FIRST SENATOR   Indeed, they are disproportioned. 3
My letters say a hundred and seven galleys.
DUKE
And mine, a hundred forty.
SECOND SENATOR   And mine, two hundred.
But though they jump not on a just account— 6
As in these cases, where the aim reports 7
'Tis oft with difference—yet do they all confirm
A Turkish fleet, and bearing up to Cyprus.
DUKE
Nay, it is possible enough to judgment.
I do not so secure me in the error 11
But the main article I do approve 12
In fearful sense.
SAILOR *(within)*   What ho, what ho, what ho!
Enter Sailor.
OFFICER   A messenger from the galleys.
DUKE   Now, what's the business?
SAILOR
The Turkish preparation makes for Rhodes. 16
So was I bid report here to the state
By Signor Angelo.
DUKE
How say you by this change?
FIRST SENATOR   This cannot be 19
By no assay of reason. 'Tis a pageant 20
To keep us in false gaze. When we consider 21
Th' importancy of Cyprus to the Turk,
And let ourselves again but understand
That, as it more concerns the Turk than Rhodes,
So may he with more facile question bear it, 25
For that it stands not in such warlike brace, 26
But altogether lacks th' abilities 27
That Rhodes is dressed in—if we make thought of this, 28
We must not think the turk is so unskillful 29
To leave the latest which concerns him first, 30
Neglecting an attempt of ease and gain
To wake and wage a danger profitless. 32

3 **disproportioned** inconsistent   6 **jump** agree. **just** exact   7 **the aim** conjecture
11–12 I do not . . . approve I do not take such (false) comfort in the discrepancies that I
fail to perceive the main point, i.e., that the Turkish fleet is threatening   16 **preparation**
fleet prepared for battle   19 **by** about   20 **assay** test. **pageant** mere show   21 **in false
gaze** looking the wrong way   25 **So may . . . it** so also he (the Turk) can more easily
capture it (Cyprus)   26 **For that** since. **brace** state of defense   27 **abilities** means of self-
defense   28 **dressed in** equipped with   29 **unskillful** deficient in judgment   30 **latest**
last   32 **wake** stir up. **wage** risk

DUKE
Nay, in all confidence, he's not for Rhodes.
OFFICER   Here is more news.

Enter a Messenger.

MESSENGER
The Ottomites, reverend and gracious,
Steering with due course toward the isle of Rhodes,
Have there injointed them with an after fleet.   37
FIRST SENATOR
Ay, so I thought. How many, as you guess?
MESSENGER
Of thirty sail; and now they do restem   39
Their backward course, bearing with frank appearance   40
Their purposes toward Cyprus. Signor Montano,
Your trusty and most valiant servitor,   42
With his free duty recommends you thus,   43
And prays you to believe him.
DUKE   'Tis certain then for Cyprus.
Marcus Luccicos, is not he in town?
FIRST SENATOR   He's now in Florence.
DUKE
Write from us to him, post-post-haste. Dispatch.
FIRST SENATOR
Here comes Brabantio and the valiant Moor.

Enter Brabantio, Othello, Cassio, Iago, Roderigo, and officers.

DUKE
Valiant Othello, we must straight employ you   50
Against the general enemy Ottoman.   51
[*To Brabantio.*] I did not see you; welcome, gentle signor.   52
We lacked your counsel and your help tonight.
BRABANTIO
So did I yours. Good Your Grace, pardon me;
Neither my place nor aught I heard of business   55
Hath raised me from my bed, nor doth the general care
Take hold on me, for my particular grief   57
Is of so floodgate and o'erbearing nature   58
That it engluts and swallows other sorrows   59
And it is still itself.

---

37 **injointed them** joined themselves. **after** second, following   39–40 **restem . . . course**
retrace their original course   40 **frank appearance** undisguised intent   42 **servitor** officer under your command   43 **free duty** freely given and loyal service. **recommends**
commends himself and reports to   50 **straight** straightway   51 **general enemy** universal
enemy to all Christendom   52 **gentle** noble   55 **place** official position   57 **particular**
personal   58 **floodgate** i.e., overwhelming (as when floodgates are opened)   59 **engluts**
engulfs

DUKE   Why, what's the matter?   60
BRABANTIO
My daughter! O, my daughter!
DUKE AND SENATORS   Dead?
BRABANTIO   Ay, to me.
She is abused, stol'n from me, and corrupted   62
By spells and medicines bought of mountebanks;
For nature so preposterously to err,
Being not deficient, blind, or lame of sense,   65
Sans witchcraft could not.   66
DUKE
Whoe'er he be that in this foul proceeding
Hath thus beguiled your daughter of herself,
And you of her, the bloody book of law
You shall yourself read in the bitter letter
After your own sense—yea, though our proper son   71
Stood in your action.
BRABANTIO   Humbly I thank Your Grace.   72
Here is the man, this Moor, whom now it seems
Your special mandate for the state affairs
Hath hither brought.
ALL   We are very sorry for 't.
DUKE [*to Othello*]
What, in your own part, can you say to this?
BRABANTIO Nothing, but this is so.
OTHELLO
Most potent, grave, and reverend signors,
My very noble and approved good masters: 79
That I have ta'en away this old man's daughter,
It is most true; true, I have married her.
The very head and front of my offending   82
Hath this extent, no more. Rude am I in my speech,   83
And little blessed with the soft phrase of peace;
For since these arms of mine had seven years' pith,   85
Till now some nine moons wasted, they have used   86
Their dearest action in the tented field;   87
And little of this great world can I speak
More than pertains to feats of broils and battle,
And therefore little shall I grace my cause

60 **is still itself** remains undiminished   62 **abused** deceived   65 **deficient** defective. **lame of sense** deficient in sensory perception   66 **Sans** without   71 **After . . . sense** according to your own interpretation. **our proper** my own   72 **Stood . . . action** were under your accusation   79 **approved** proved, esteemed   82 **head and front** height and breadth, entire extent   83 **Rude** unpolished   85 **since . . . pith** i.e., since I was seven. **pith** strength, vigor   86 **Till . . . wasted** until some nine months ago (since when Othello has evidently not been on active duty, but in Venice)   87 **dearest** most valuable

In speaking for myself. Yet, by your gracious patience,
I will a round unvarnished tale deliver   92
Of my whole course of love—what drugs, what charms,
What conjuration, and what mighty magic,
For such proceeding I am charged withal,   95
I won his daughter.

BRABANTIO   A maiden never bold;
Of spirit so still and quiet that her motion   97
Blushed at herself; and she, in spite of nature,   98
Of years, of country, credit, everything,   99
To fall in love with what she feared to look on!
It is a judgment maimed and most imperfect
That will confess perfection so could err   102
Against all rules of nature, and must be driven
To find out practices of cunning hell   104
Why this should be. I therefore vouch again   105
That with some mixtures powerful o'er the blood,   106
Or with some dram conjured to this effect,   107
He wrought upon her.

DUKE   To vouch this is no proof,
Without more wider and more overt test   109
Than these thin habits and poor likelihoods   110
Of modern seeming do prefer against him.   111

FIRST SENATOR   But Othello, speak.
Did you by indirect and forcèd courses   113
Subdue and poison this young maid's affections?
Or came it by request and such fair question   115
As soul to soul affordeth?

OTHELLO   I do beseech you,
Send for the lady to the Sagittary
And let her speak of me before her father.
If you do find me foul in her report,
The trust, the office I do hold of you
Not only take away, but let your sentence
Even fall upon my life.

DUKE   Fetch Desdemona hither.

OTHELLO
Ancient, conduct them. You best know the place.

---

92 round plain   **95 withal** with   **97–98 her . . . herself** i.e., she blushed easily at herself. (*Motion* can suggest the impulse of the soul or of the emotions, or physical movement.)   **99 years** i.e., difference in age. **credit** virtuous reputation   **102 confess** concede (that)   **104 practices** plots   **105 vouch** assert   **106 blood** passions   **107 dram . . . effect** dose made by magical spells to have this effect   **109 more wider** fuller. **test** testimony   **110 habits** garments, i.e., appearances. **poor likelihoods** weak inferences   **111 modern seeming** commonplace assumption. **prefer** bring forth   **113 forcèd courses** means used against her will   **115 question** conversation

[Exeunt Iago and attendants.]
And, till she come, as truly as to heaven
I do confess the vices of my blood,   125
So justly to your grave ears I'll present   126
How I did thrive in this fair lady's love,
And she in mine.
DUKE   Say it, Othello.
OTHELLO
Her father loved me, oft invited me,
Still questioned me the story of my life   131
From year to year—the battles, sieges, fortunes
That I have passed.
I ran it through, even from my boyish days
To th' very moment that he bade me tell it,
Wherein I spoke of most disastrous chances,
Of moving accidents by flood and field,   137
Of hairbreadth scapes i' th' imminent deadly breach,   138
Of being taken by the insolent foe
And sold to slavery, of my redemption thence,
And portance in my travels' history,   141
Wherein of antres vast and deserts idle,   142
Rough quarries, rocks, and hills whose heads touch heaven,   143
It was my hint to speak—such was my process—   144
And of the Cannibals that each other eat,
The Anthropophagi, and men whose heads   146
Do grow beneath their shoulders. These things to hear
Would Desdemona seriously incline;
But still the house affairs would draw her thence,
Which ever as she could with haste dispatch
She'd come again, and with a greedy ear
Devour up my discourse. Which I, observing,
Took once a pliant hour, and found good means   153
To draw from her a prayer of earnest heart
That I would all my pilgrimage dilate,   155
Whereof by parcels she had something heard,   156
But not intentively. I did consent,   157
And often did beguile her of her tears,
When I did speak of some distressful stroke
That my youth suffered. My story being done,

125 **blood** passions, human nature   126 **justly** truthfully, accurately   131 **Still** continually   137 **moving accidents** stirring happenings   138 **imminent . . . breach** death-
threatening gaps made in a fortification   141 **portance** conduct   142 **antres** caverns.
idle barren, desolate   143 **Rough quarries** rugged rock formations   144 **hint** occasion,
opportunity   146 **Anthropophagi** man-eaters. (A term from Pliny's *Natural History*.)
153 **pliant** well-suiting   155 **dilate** relate in detail   156 **by parcels** piecemeal   157 **intentively** with full attention, continuously

She gave me for my pains a world of sighs.
She swore, in faith, 'twas strange, 'twas passing strange,   162
'Twas pitiful, 'twas wondrous pitiful.
She wished she had not heard it, yet she wished
That heaven had made her such a man. She thanked me,   165
And bade me, if I had a friend that loved her,
I should but teach him how to tell my story,
And that would woo her. Upon this hint I spake.   168
She loved me for the dangers I had passed,
And I loved her that she did pity them.
This only is the witchcraft I have used.
Here comes the lady. Let her witness it.

Enter Desdemona, Iago, [and] attendants.

DUKE
I think this tale would win my daughter too.
Good Brabantio,
Take up this mangled matter at the best.   175
Men do their broken weapons rather use
Than their bare hands.
BRABANTIO   I pray you, hear her speak.
If she confess that she was half the wooer,
Destruction on my head if my bad blame
Light on the man!—Come hither, gentle mistress.
Do you perceive in all this noble company
Where most you owe obedience?
DESDEMONA   My noble Father,
I do perceive here a divided duty.
To you I am bound for life and education;   184
My life and education both do learn me   185
How to respect you. You are the lord of duty;   186
I am hitherto your daughter. But here's my husband,
And so much duty as my mother showed
To you, preferring you before her father,
So much I challenge that I may profess   190
Due to the Moor my lord.
BRABANTIO   God be with you! I have done.
Please it Your Grace, on to the state affairs.
I had rather to adopt a child than get it.   194
Come hither, Moor.   [*He joins the hands of Othello
                                        and Desdemona.*]

---

162 passing exceedingly   **165 made her** created her to be   **168 hint** opportunity.
(Othello does not mean that she was dropping hints.)   **175 Take . . . best** make the best
of a bad bargain   **184 education** upbringing   **185 learn** teach   **186 of duty** to whom
duty is due   **190 challenge** claim   **194 get** beget

I here do give thee that with all my heart 196
Which, but thou hast already, with all my heart 197
I would keep from thee.—For your sake, jewel, 198
I am glad at soul I have no other child,
For thy escape would teach me tyranny, 200
To hang clogs on them.—I have done, my lord. 201

DUKE

Let me speak like yourself, and lay a sentence 202
Which, as a grece or step, may help these lovers 203
Into your favor.
When remedies are past, the griefs are ended 205
By seeing the worst, which late on hopes depended. 206
To mourn a mischief that is past and gone 207
Is the next way to draw new mischief on. 208
What cannot be preserved when fortune takes, 209
Patience her injury a mockery makes. 210
The robbed that smiles steals something from the thief;
He robs himself that spends a bootless grief. 212

BRABANTIO

So let the Turk of Cyprus us beguile,
We lose it not, so long as we can smile.
He bears the sentence well that nothing bears 215
But the free comfort which from thence he hears, 216
But he bears both the sentence and the sorrow 217
That, to pay grief, must of poor patience borrow. 218
These sentences, to sugar or to gall, 219
Being strong on both sides, are equivocal. 220
But words are words. I never yet did hear
That the bruisèd heart was piercèd through the ear. 222
I humbly beseech you, proceed to th' affairs of state.

DUKE The Turk with a most mighty preparation makes
for Cyprus. Othello, the fortitude of the place is best 225

---

196 with all my heart wherein my whole affection has been engaged   **197 with all my heart** willingly, gladly   **198 For your sake** on your account   **200 escape** elopement   **201 clogs** (Literally, blocks of wood fastened to the legs of criminals or convicts to inhibit escape.)   **202 like yourself** i.e., as you would, in your proper temper. **lay a sentence** apply a maxim   **203 grece** step   **205 remedies** hopes of remedy   **206 which . . . depended** which griefs were sustained until recently by hopeful anticipation   **207 mischief** misfortune, injury   **208 next** nearest   **209 What** whatever   **210 Patience . . . makes** patience laughs at the injury inflicted by fortune (and thus eases the pain)   **212 spends a bootless grief** indulges in unavailing grief   **215–218 He bears . . . borrow** a person well bears out your maxim who can enjoy its platitudinous comfort, free of all genuine sorrow, but anyone whose grief bankrupts his poor patience is left with your saying and his sorrow, too. (*Bears the sentence* also plays on the meaning, "receives judicial sentence.")   **219–220 These . . . equivocal** these fine maxims are equivocal, either sweet or bitter in their application   **222 piercèd . . . ear** i.e., surgically lanced and cured by mere words of advice   **225 fortitude** strength

known to you; and though we have there a substitute 226
of most allowed sufficiency, yet opinion, a sovereign 227
mistress of effects, throws a more safer voice on you. 228
You must therefore be content to slubber the gloss of 229
your new fortunes with this more stubborn and 230
boisterous expedition.

OTHELLO
  The tyrant custom, most grave senators,
  Hath made the flinty and steel couch of war
  My thrice-driven bed of down. I do agnize 234
  A natural and prompt alacrity
  I find in hardness, and do undertake 236
  These present wars against the Ottomites.
  Most humbly therefore bending to your state, 238
  I crave fit disposition for my wife,
  Due reference of place and exhibition, 240
  With such accommodation and besort 241
  As levels with her breeding. 242

DUKE
  Why, at her father's.

BRABANTIO   I will not have it so.

OTHELLO
  Nor I.

DESDEMONA   Nor I. I would not there reside,
  To put my father in impatient thoughts
  By being in his eye. Most gracious Duke,
  To my unfolding lend your prosperous ear, 247
  And let me find a charter in your voice, 248
  T' assist my simpleness.

DUKE What would you, Desdemona?

DESDEMONA
  That I did love the Moor to live with him,
  My downright violence and storm of fortunes 252

226 **substitute** deputy   227 **allowed** acknowledged   227–228 **opinion . . . on you** general opinion, an important determiner of affairs, chooses you as the best man
229 **slubber** soil, sully   230 **stubborn** harsh, rough   234 **thrice-driven** thrice sifted, winnowed. **agnize** know in myself, acknowledge   236 **hardness** hardship   238 **bending . . . state** bowing or kneeling to your authority   240 **reference . . . exhibition** provision of appropriate place to live and allowance of money   241 **accommodation** suitable provision. **besort** attendance   242 **levels** equals, suits. **breeding** social position, upbringing   247 **unfolding** explanation, proposal. **prosperous** propitious   248 **charter** privilege, authorization   252 **My . . . fortunes** my plain and total breach of social custom, taking my future by storm and disrupting my whole life

May trumpet to the world. My heart's subdued 253
Even to the very quality of my lord. 254
I saw Othello's visage in his mind,
And to his honors and his valiant parts 256
Did I my soul and fortunes consecrate.
So that, dear lords, if I be left behind
A moth of peace, and he go to the war, 259
The rites for why I love him are bereft me, 260
And I a heavy interim shall support
By his dear absence. Let me go with him. 262
OTHELLO   Let her have your voice. 263
Vouch with me, heaven, I therefor beg it not
To please the palate of my appetite,
Nor to comply with heat—the young affects 266
In me defunct—and proper satisfaction, 267
But to be free and bounteous to her mind. 268
And heaven defend your good souls that you think 269
I will your serious and great business scant
When she is with me. No, when light-winged toys
Of feathered Cupid seel with wanton dullness 272
My speculative and officed instruments, 273
That my disports corrupt and taint my business, 274
Let huswives make a skillet of my helm,
And all indign and base adversities 276
Make head against my estimation! 277
DUKE
Be it as you shall privately determine,
Either for her stay or going. Th' affair cries haste,
And speed must answer it.
A SENATOR   You must away tonight.
DESDEMONA
Tonight, my lord?
DUKE   This night.
OTHELLO   With all my heart.

253–254 **My heart's . . . lord** my heart is brought wholly into accord with Othello's virtues; I love him for his virtues   256 **parts** qualities   259 **moth** i.e., one who consumes
merely   260 **rites** rites of love (with a suggestion, too, of "rights," sharing)   262 **dear**
(1) heartfelt (2) costly   263 **voice** consent   266 **heat** sexual passion. **young affects** passions of youth, desires   267 **proper** personal   268 **free** generous   269 **defend** forbid.
think should think   272 **seel** i.e., making blind (as in falconry, by sewing up the eyes of
the hawk during training)   273 **speculative . . . instruments** eyes and other faculties used
in the performance of duty   274 **That** so that. **disports** sexual pastimes. **taint** impair
276 **indign** unworthy, shameful   277 **Make head** raise an army. **estimation** reputation

DUKE
　At nine i' the morning here we'll meet again.
　Othello, leave some officer behind,
　And he shall our commission bring to you,
　With such things else of quality and respect   285
　As doth import you.
OTHELLO　　　　　　So please Your Grace, my ancient;   286
　A man he is of honesty and trust.
　To his conveyance I assign my wife,
　With what else needful Your Good Grace shall think
　To be sent after me.
DUKE　　　　　　　Let it be so.
　Good night to everyone. [*To Brabantio.*] And, noble signor,
　If virtue no delighted beauty lack,   292
　Your son-in-law is far more fair than black.
FIRST SENATOR
　Adieu, brave Moor. Use Desdemona well.
BRABANTIO
　Look to her, Moor, if thou hast eyes to see.
　She has deceived her father, and may thee.
　　　　Exeunt [Duke, Brabantio, Cassio, Senators and officers].
OTHELLO
　My life upon her faith! Honest Iago,
　My Desdemona must I leave to thee.
　I prithee, let thy wife attend on her,
　And bring them after in the best advantage.   300
　Come, Desdemona. I have but an hour
　Of love, of worldly matters and direction,   302
　To spend with thee. We must obey the time.   303
　　　　　　　　　　　Exit [with Desdemona].
RODERIGO　Iago—
IAGO　What sayst thou, noble heart?
RODERIGO　What will I do, think'st thou?
IAGO　Why, go to bed and sleep.
RODERIGO　I will incontinently drown myself.   308
IAGO　If thou dost, I shall never love thee after. Why,
　thou silly gentleman?
RODERIGO　It is silliness to live when to live is torment;
　and then have we a prescription to die when death is   312
　our physician.

285 **of quality and respect** of importance and relevance　286 **import** concern　292 **delighted** capable of delighting　300 **in . . . advantage** at the most favorable opportunity　302 **direction** instructions　303 **the time** the urgency of the present crisis　308 **incontinently** immediately, without self-restraint　312 **prescription** (1) right based on long-established custom (2) doctor's prescription

IAGO   O villainous! I have looked upon the world for   314
   four times seven years, and, since I could distinguish
   betwixt a benefit and an injury, I never found man
   that knew how to love himself. Ere I would say I
   would drown myself for the love of a guinea hen, I   318
   would change my humanity with a baboon.

RODERIGO   What should I do? I confess it is my shame
   to be so fond, but it is not in my virtue to amend it.   321

IAGO   Virtue? A fig! 'Tis in ourselves that we are thus or   322
   thus. Our bodies are our gardens, to the which our
   wills are gardeners; so that if we will plant nettles or
   sow lettuce, set hyssop and weed up thyme, supply it   325
   with one gender of herbs or distract it with many,   326
   either to have it sterile with idleness or manured with   327
   industry—why, the power and corrigible authority of   328
   this lies in our wills. If the beam of our lives had not   329
   one scale of reason to poise another of sensuality, the   330
   blood and baseness of our natures would conduct us   331
   to most preposterous conclusions. But we have reason
   to cool our raging motions, our carnal stings, our   333
   unbitted lusts, whereof I take this that you call love to   334
   be a sect or scion.   335

RODERIGO   It cannot be.

IAGO   It is merely a lust of the blood and a permission
   of the will. Come, be a man. Drown thyself? Drown
   cats and blind puppies. I have professed me thy friend,
   and I confess me knit to thy deserving with cables of
   perdurable toughness. I could never better stead thee   341
   than now. Put money in thy purse. Follow thou the
   wars; defeat thy favor with an usurped beard. I say,   343
   put money in thy purse. It cannot be long that Desdemona should continue her love to the Moor—put
   money in thy purse—nor he his to her. It was a violent commencement in her, and thou shalt see an an-   347
   swerable sequestration—put but money in thy purse.   348
   These moors are changeable in their wills—fill thy   349
   purse with money. The food that to him now is as

---

314 villainous i.e., what perfect nonsense   **318 guinea hen** (A slang term for a prostitute.)   **321 fond** infatuated. **virtue** strength, nature   **322 fig** (To give a fig is to thrust the thumb between the first and second fingers in a vulgar and insulting gesture)
325 hyssop a herb of the mint family   **326 gender** kind. **distract it with** divide it among
327 idleness want of cultivation   **328 corrigible authority** power to correct   **329 beam** balance   **330 poise** counterbalance   **331 blood** natural passions   **333 motions** appetites
334 unbitted unbridled, uncontrolled   **335 sect or scion** cutting or offshoot   **341 perdurable** very durable. **stead** assist   **343 defeat thy favor** disguise your face. **usurped** (The suggestion is that Roderigo is not man enough to have a beard of his own.)
347–348 an answerable sequestration a corresponding separation or estrangement
349 wills carnal appetites

luscious as locusts shall be to him shortly as bitter as   351
coloquintida. She must change for youth; when she is   352
sated with his body, she will find the error of her
choice. She must have change, she must. Therefore
put money in thy purse. If thou wilt needs damn thyself, do it a more delicate way than drowning. Make   356
all the money thou canst. If sanctimony and a frail vow   357
betwixt an erring barbarian and a supersubtle Vene-   358
tian be not too hard for my wits and all the tribe of
hell, thou shalt enjoy her. Therefore make money. A
pox of drowning thyself! It is clean out of the way.   361
Seek thou rather to be hanged in compassing thy joy   362
than to be drowned and go without her.

RODERIGO   Wilt thou be fast to my hopes if I depend on   364
the issue?   365

IAGO   Thou art sure of me. Go, make money. I have
told thee often, and I retell thee again and again, I hate
the Moor. My cause is hearted; thine hath no less rea-   368
son. Let us be conjunctive in our revenge against him.   369
If thou canst cuckold him, thou dost thyself a pleasure,
me a sport. There are many events in the womb of
time which will get delivered. Traverse, go, provide thy   372
money. We will have more of this tomorrow. Adieu.

RODERIGO   Where shall we meet i' the morning?

IAGO   At my lodging.

RODERIGO   I'll be with thee betimes. [*He starts to leave.*]   376

IAGO   Go to, farewell. — Do you hear, Roderigo?

RODERIGO   What say you?

IAGO   No more of drowning, do you hear?

RODERIGO   I am changed.

IAGO   Go to, farewell. Put money enough in your
purse.

RODERIGO   I'll sell my land.   *Exit.*

IAGO

Thus do I ever make my fool my purse;
For I mine own gained knowledge should profane
If I would time expend with such a snipe   386
But for my sport and profit. I hate the Moor;
And it is thought abroad that twixt my sheets   388

---

351 **locusts** fruit of the carob tree (see Matthew 3:4), or perhaps honeysuckle   352 **colo-quintida** colocynth or bitter apple, a purgative   356 **Make** raise, collect   357 **sanctimony** sacred ceremony   358 **erring** wandering, vagabond, unsteady   361 **clean . . . way** entirely unsuitable as a course of action   362 **compassing** encompassing, embracing   364 **fast** true   365 **issue** (successful) outcome   368 **hearted** fixed in the heart, heartfelt   369 **conjunctive** united   372 **Traverse** (A military marching term.)   376 **betimes** early   386 **snipe** woodcock, i.e., fool   388 **it is thought abroad** it is rumored

He's done my office. I know not if 't be true; 389
But I, for mere suspicion in that kind,
Will do as if for surety. He holds me well; 391
The better shall my purpose work on him.
Cassio's a proper man. Let me see now: 393
To get his place and to plume up my will 394
In double knavery—How, how?—Let's see:
After some time, to abuse Othello's ear 396
That he is too familiar with his wife. 397
He hath a person and a smooth dispose 398
To be suspected, framed to make women false.
The Moor is of a free and open nature, 400
That thinks men honest that but seem to be so,
And will as tenderly be led by the nose 402
As asses are.
I have 't. It is engendered. Hell and night
Must bring this monstrous birth to the world's light.

[*Exit.*]

2.1

Enter Montano and two Gentlemen.

MONTANO
What from the cape can you discern at sea?
FIRST GENTLEMAN
Nothing at all. It is a high-wrought flood. 2
I cannot, twixt the heaven and the main, 3
Descry a sail.
MONTANO
Methinks the wind hath spoke aloud at land;
A fuller blast ne'er shook our battlements.
If it hath ruffianed so upon the sea, 7
What ribs of oak, when mountains melt on them, 8
Can hold the mortise? What shall we hear of this? 9
SECOND GENTLEMAN
A segregation of the Turkish fleet. 10
For do but stand upon the foaming shore,

---

389 my office i.e., my sexual function as husband **391 do . . . surety** act as if on certain knowledge. **holds me well** regards me favorably **393 proper** handsome
394 plume up put a feather in the cap of, i.e., glorify, gratify **396 abuse** deceive
397 he i.e., Cassio **398 dispose** disposition **400 free** frank, generous. **open** unsuspicious **402 tenderly** readily
2.1. Location: A seaport in Cyprus. An open place near the quay.
2 high-wrought flood very agitated sea **3 main** ocean (also at line 41) **7 ruffianed** raged **8 mountains** i.e., of water **9 hold the mortise** hold their joints together. (A mortise is the socket hollowed out in fitting timbers.) **10 segregation** dispersal

The chidden billow seems to pelt the clouds;   12
The wind-shaked surge, with high and monstrous mane,   13
Seems to cast water on the burning Bear   14
And quench the guards of th' ever-fixèd pole.
I never did like molestation view   16
On the enchafèd flood.   17
MONTANO   If that the Turkish fleet   18
Be not ensheltered and embayed, they are drowned;   19
It is impossible to bear it out.   20

Enter a [Third] Gentleman.

THIRD GENTLEMAN   News, lads! Our wars are done.
The desperate tempest hath so banged the Turks
That their designment halts. A noble ship of Venice   23
Hath seen a grievous wreck and sufferance   24
On most part of their fleet.
MONTANO   How? Is this true?
THIRD GENTLEMAN   This ship is here put in,
A Veronesa; Michael Cassio,   28
Lieutenant to the warlike Moor Othello,
Is come on shore; the Moor himself at sea,
And is in full commission here for Cyprus.
MONTANO
I am glad on 't. 'Tis a worthy governor.
THIRD GENTLEMAN
But this same Cassio, though he speak of comfort
Touching the Turkish loss, yet he looks sadly   34
And prays the Moor be safe, for they were parted
With foul and violent tempest.
MONTANO   Pray heaven he be,
For I have served him, and the man commands
Like a full soldier. Let's to the seaside, ho!   38
As well to see the vessel that's come in
As to throw out our eyes for brave Othello,
Even till we make the main and the' aerial blue   41
An indistinct regard.

---

12 chidden i.e., rebuked, repelled (by the shore), and thus shot into the air   13 monstrous mane (The surf is like the mane of a wild beast.)   14 the burning Bear i.e., the constellation Ursa Minor or the Little Bear, which includes the polestar (and hence regarded as the *guards of th' ever-fixèd pole* in the next line; sometimes the term *guards* is applied to the two "pointers" of the Big Bear or Dipper, which may be intended here.)
16 like molestation comparable disturbance   17 enchafèd angry   18 If that if   19 embayed sheltered by a bay   20 bear it out survive, weather the storm   23 designment design, enterprise. halts is lame   24 wreck shipwreck. sufferance damage, disaster
28 Veronesa i.e., fitted out in Verona for Venetian service, or possibly *Verennessa* (the Folio spelling), i.e., *verrinessa*, a cutter (from *verrinare*, "to cut through")   34 sadly gravely   38 full perfect   41 the main . . . blue the sea and the sky

THIRD GENTLEMAN   Come, let's do so,   42
  For every minute is expectancy   43
  Of more arrivance.   44

Enter Cassio.

CASSIO
  Thanks, you the valiant of this warlike isle,
  That so approve the Moor! O, let the heavens   46
  Give him defense against the elements,
  For I have lost him on a dangerous sea.
MONTANO   Is he well shipped?
CASSIO
  His bark is stoutly timbered, and his pilot
  Of very expert and approved allowance;   51
  Therefore my hopes, not surfeited to death,   52
  Stand in bold cure.
        [A cry] within: "A sail, a sail, a sail!"   53
CASSIO   What noise?
A GENTLEMAN
  The town is empty. On the brow o' the sea   55
  Stand ranks of people, and they cry "A sail!"
CASSIO
  My hopes do shape him for the governor.   57
              [A shot within.]
SECOND GENTLEMAN
  They do discharge their shot of courtesy;   58
  Our friends at least.
CASSIO   I pray you, sir, go forth,
  And give us truth who 'tis that is arrived.
SECOND GENTLEMAN   I shall.   *Exit.*
MONTANO
  But, good Lieutenant, is your general wived?
CASSIO
  Most fortunately. He hath achieved a maid
  That paragons description and wild fame,   64
  One that excels the quirks of blazoning pens,   65
  And in th' essential vesture of creation   66

42 **An indistinct regard** indistinguishable in our view 43 **is expectancy** gives expectation 44 **arrivance** arrival 46 **approve** admire, honor 51 **approved allowance** tested
reputation 52 **surfeited to death** i.e., overextended, worn thin through repeated application or delayed fulfillment 53 **in bold cure** in strong hopes of fulfillment 55 **brow o'
the sea** cliff-edge 57 **My . . . for** I hope it is 58 **discharge . . . courtesy** fire a salute in
token of respect and courtesy 64 **paragons** surpasses. **wild fame** extravagant report
65 **quirks** witty conceits. **blazoning** setting forth as though in heraldic language
66–67 **in . . . enginer** in her real, God-given, beauty, (she) defeats any attempt to praise
her. **enginer** engineer, i.e, poet, one who devises. s.d. **Second Gentleman** (So identified in
the Quarto text here and in lines 58, 61, 68, and 96; the Folio calls him a gentleman.)

Does tire the enginer.

Enter [Second] Gentleman.

How now? Who has put in?   67

SECOND GENTLEMAN
'Tis one Iago, ancient to the General.

CASSIO
He's had most favorable and happy speed.
Tempests themselves, high seas, and howling winds,
The guttered rocks and congregated sands—   71
Traitors ensteeped to clog the guiltless keel—   72
As having sense of beauty, do omit   73
Their mortal natures, letting go safely by   74
The divine Desdemona.

MONTANO   What is she?

CASSIO
She that I spake of, our great captain's captain,
Left in the conduct of the bold Iago,
Whose footing here anticipates our thoughts   78
A sennight's speed. Great Jove, Othello guard,   79
And swell his sail with thine own powerful breath,
That he may bless this bay with his tall ship,   81
Make love's quick pants in Desdemona's arms,
Give renewed fire to our extinct spirits,
And bring all Cyprus comfort!

Enter Desdemona, Iago, Roderigo, and Emilia.

O, behold,
The riches of the ship is come on shore!
You men of Cyprus, let her have your knees.
        [*The gentleman make curtsy to Desdemona.*]
Hail to thee, lady! And the grace of heaven
Before, behind thee, and on every hand
Enwheel thee round!

DESDEMONA   I thank you, valiant Cassio.
What tidings can you tell me of my lord?

CASSIO
He is not yet arrived, nor know I aught.
But that he's well and will be shortly here.

DESDEMONA
O, but I fear—How lost you company?

CASSIO
The great contention of the sea and skies

---

67 **put in** i.e., to harbor   71 **guttered** jagged, trenched   72 **ensteeped** lying under water
73 **As** as if. **omit** forbear to exercise   74 **mortal** deadly   78 **footing** landing   79 **sennight's** week's   81 **tall** splendid, gallant

Parted our fellowship.

                (Within) "A sail, a sail!" [*A shot.*]

                But hark. A sail!

SECOND GENTLEMAN

They give their greeting to the citadel.

This likewise is a friend.

CASSIO   See for the news

                [*Exit Second Gentleman.*]

Good Ancient, you are welcome. [*Kissing Emilia.*]

    Welcome, mistress.

Let it not gall your patience, good Iago,

That I extend my manners; 'tis my breeding   100

That gives me this bold show of courtesy.

IAGO

Sir, would she give you so much of her lips

As of her tongue she often bestows on me,

You would have enough.

DESDEMONA   Alas, she has no speech!   105

IAGO   In faith, too much.

I find it still, when I have list to sleep.   107

Marry, before your ladyship, I grant,

She puts her tongue a little in her heart

And chides with thinking.

EMILIA   You have little cause to say so.   110

IAGO

Come on, come on. You are pictures out of doors,   111

Bells in your parlors, wildcats in your kitchens,   112

Saints in your injuries, devils being offended,   113

Players in your huswifery, and huswives in your beds. 114

DESDEMONA   O, fie upon thee, slanderer!

IAGO

Nay, it is true, or else I am a Turk.   116

You rise to play, and go to bed to work.

EMILIA

You shall not write my praise.

IAGO   No, let me not.

DESDEMONA

What wouldst write of me, if thou shouldst praise me?

---

100 extend give scope to. **breeding** training in the niceties of etiquette   **105 she has no speech** i.e., she's not a chatterbox, as you allege   **107 still** always. **list** desire   **110 with thinking** i.e., in her thoughts only   **111 pictures out of doors** i.e., silent and well-behaved in public   **112 Bells** i.e., jangling, noisy, and brazen. **in your kitchens** i.e., in domestic affairs. (Ladies would not do the cooking.)   **113 Saints** martyrs   **114 Players** idlers, triflers, or deceivers. **huswifery** housekeeping. **huswives** hussies (i.e., women are "busy" in bed, or unduly thrifty in dispensing sexual favors)   **116 A Turk** an infidel, not to be believed

IAGO
>   O gentle lady, do not put me to 't,
>   For I am nothing if not critical.   121

DESDEMONA
>   Come on, essay.—There's one gone to the harbor?   122

IAGO   Ay, madam.

DESDEMONA
>   I am not merry, but I do beguile
>   The thing I am by seeming otherwise.   125
>   Come, how wouldst thou praise me?

IAGO
>   I am about it, but indeed my invention
>   Comes from my pate as birdlime does from frieze—   128
>   It plucks out brains and all. But my Muse labors,   129
>   And thus she is delivered:
>   If she be fair and wise, fairness and wit,
>   The one's for use, the other useth it.   132

DESDEMONA
>   Well praised! How if she be black and witty?   133

IAGO
>   If she be black, and thereto have a wit,
>   She'll find a white that shall her blackness fit.   135

DESDEMONA
>   Worse and worse.

EMILIA   How if fair and foolish?

IAGO
>   She never yet was foolish that was fair,
>   For even her folly helped her to an heir.   138

DESDEMONA These are old fond paradoxes to make fools   139
>   laugh i' th' alehouse. What miserable praise hast thou
>   for her that's foul and foolish?   141

IAGO
>   There's none so foul and foolish thereunto,   142
>   But does foul pranks which fair and wise ones do.   143

DESDEMONA O heavy ignorance! Thou praisest the worst
>   best. But what praise couldst' thou bestow on a deserving

---

121 **critical** censorious   122 **essay** try   125 **The thing I am** i.e., my anxious self
128 **birdlime** sticky substance used to catch small birds. **frieze** coarse woolen cloth
129 **labors** (1) exerts herself (2) prepares to deliver a child (with a following pun on *delivered* in line 130)   132 **The one's . . . it** i.e., her cleverness will make use of her beauty
133 **black** dark-complexioned, brunette   135 **a white** a fair person (with wordplay on
"wight," a person). **fit** (with sexual suggestion of mating)   138 **folly** (with added meaning of "lechery, wantonness"). **to an heir** i.e., to bear a child   139 **fond** foolish
141 **foul** ugly   142 **thereunto** in addition   143 **foul** sluttish

woman indeed, one that, in the authority of her merit,
did justly put on the vouch of very malice itself? 147

IAGO

She that was ever fair, and never proud,
Had tongue at will, and yet was never loud,
Never lacked gold and yet went never gay, 150
Fled from her wish, and yet said, "Now I may," 151
She that being angered, her revenge being nigh,
Bade her wrong stay and her displeasure fly, 153
She that in wisdom never was so frail
To change the cod's head for the salmon's tail, 155
She that could think and ne'er disclose her mind,
See suitors following and not look behind,
She was a wight, if ever such wight were—

DESDEMONA To do what?

IAGO

To suckle fools and chronicle small beer. 160

DESDEMONA O most lame and impotent conclusion! Do
not learn of him, Emilia, though he be thy husband.
How say you, Cassio? Is he not a most profane and 163
liberal counselor? 164

CASSIO He speaks home, madam. You may relish him 165
more in the soldier than in the scholar. 166

[*Cassio and Desdemona stand together, conversing
intimately.*]

IAGO [*aside*] He takes her by the palm. Ay, well said, 167
whisper. With as little a web as this will I ensnare as
great a fly as Cassio. Ay, smile upon her, do; I will
gyve thee in thine own courtship. You say true; 'tis so, 170
indeed. If such tricks as these strip you out of your
lieutenantry, it had been better you had not kissed
your three fingers so oft, which now again you are
most apt to play the sir in. Very good; well kissed! An 174
excellent courtesy! 'Tis so, indeed. Yet again your fingers
to your lips? Would they were clyster pipes for your 176
sake! [*Trumpet within.*] The Moor! I know his trumpet.

147 **put . . . vouch** compel the approval 150 **gay** extravagantly clothed 151 **Fled . . . may** avoided temptation where the choice was hers 153 **Bade . . . stay** i.e., resolved to put up with her injury patiently 155 **To . . . tail** i.e., to exchange a lackluster husband for a sexy lover (?) (*Cod's head* is slang for "penis," and *tail*, for "pudendum.")
160 **suckle fools** breastfeed babies. **chronicle small beer** i.e., keep petty household accounts, keep track of trivial matters 163 **profane** irreverent, ribald 164 **liberal** licentious, free-spoken 165 **home** right to the target. (A term from fencing.) **relish** appreciate 166 **in** in the character of 167 **well said** well done 170 **gyve** fetter, shackle. **courtship** courtesy, show of courtly manners. **You say true** i.e., that's right, go ahead 174 **the sir** i.e., the fine gentleman 176 **clyster pipes** tubes used for enemas and douches

CASSIO 'Tis truly so.
DESDEMONA Let's meet him and receive him.
CASSIO Lo, where he comes!

Enter Othello and attendants.

OTHELLO
O my fair warrior!
DESDEMONA   My dear Othello!
OTHELLO
It gives me wonder great as my content
To see you here before me. O my soul's joy,
If after every tempest come such calms,
May the winds blow till they have wakened death,
And let the laboring bark climb hills of seas
Olympus-high, and duck again as low
As hell's from heaven! If it were now to die,
'Twere now to be most happy, for I fear
My soul hath her content so absolute
That not another comfort like to this
Succeeds in unknown fate.
DESDEMONA   The heavens forbid   192
But that our loves and comforts should increase
Even as our days do grow!
OTHELLO   Amen to that, sweet powers!
I cannot speak enough of this content.
It stops me here; it is too much of joy.
And this, and this, the greatest discords be   198

                                        [*They kiss*]

That e'er our hearts shall make!
IAGO [*aside*]   O, you are well tuned now!
But I'll set down the pegs that make this music,   201
As honest as I am.   202
OTHELLO   Come, let us to the castle.
News, friends! Our wars are done, the Turks are drowned.
How does my old acquaintance of this isle? —
Honey, you shall be well desired in Cyprus;   206
I have found great love amongst them. O my sweet,
I prattle out of fashion, and I dote   208
In mine own comforts. — I prithee, good Iago,
Go to the bay and disembark my coffers.   210
Bring thou the master to the citadel;   211

192 **Succeeds . . . fate** i.e., can follow in the unknown future   198 **s.d. They kiss** (The direction is from the Quarto.)   201 **set down** loosen (and hence untune the instrument)   202 **As . . . I am** for all my supposed honesty   206 **desired** welcomed   208 **out of fashion** irrelevantly, incoherently (?)   210 **coffers** chests, baggage   211 **master** ship's captain

He is a good one, and his worthiness
Does challenge much respect.—Come, Desdemona.—   213
Once more, well met at Cyprus!
   Exeunt Othello and Desdemona [and all but Iago
             and Roderigo].
IAGO [*to an attendant*] Do thou meet me presently at
 the harbor. [*To Roderigo.*] Come hither. If thou be'st
 valiant—as, they say, base men being in love have   217
 then a nobility in their natures more than is native to
 them—list me. The Lieutenant tonight watches on   219
 the court of guard. First, I must tell thee this: 220
 Desdemona is directly in love with him.
RODERIGO With him? Why, 'tis not possible.
IAGO Lay thy finger thus, and let thy soul be instructed.   223
 Mark me with what violence she first loved the Moor,
 but for bragging and telling her fantastical lies. To love   225
 him still for prating? Let not thy discreet heart think it.
 Her eye must be fed; and what delight shall she have
 to look on the devil? When the blood is made dull with
 the act of sport, there should be, again to inflame it   229
 and to give satiety a fresh appetite, loveliness in favor,   230
 sympathy in years, manners, and beauties all which   231
 the Moor is defective in. Now, for want of these
 required conveniences, her delicate tenderness will   233
 find itself abused, begin to heave the gorge, disrelish   234
 and abhor the Moor. Very nature will instruct her in it   235
 and compel her to some second choice. Now, sir, this
 granted—as it is a most pregnant and unforced   237
 position—who stands so eminent in the degree of this   238
 fortune as Cassio does? A knave very voluble, no   239
 further conscionable than in putting on the mere form   240
 of civil and humane seeming for the better compass-   241
 ing of his salt and most hidden loose affection. Why,   242
 none, why, none. A slipper and subtle knave, a finder   243
 out of occasions, that has an eye can stamp and   244
 counterfeit advantages, though true advantage never   245

---

213 **challenge** lay claim to, deserve 217 **base men** even lowly born men 219 **list** listen
to 220 **court of guard** guardhouse. (Cassio is in charge of the watch.) 223 **thus** i.e.,
on your lips 225 **but** only 229 **the act of sport** sex 230 **favor** appearance 231 **sympathy** correspondence, similarity 233 **required conveniences** things conducive to sexual
compatibility 234 **abused** cheated, revolted. **heave the gorge** experience nausea
235 **Very nature** her very instincts 237 **pregnant** evident, cogent 238 **in . . . of** as next
in line for 239 **voluble** facile, glib 240 **conscionable** conscientious, conscience-bound
241 **humane** polite, courteous 242 **salt** licentious. **affection** passion 243 **slipper** slippery 244 **an eye can stamp** an eye that can coin, create 245 **advantages** favorable opportunities

present itself; a devilish knave. Besides, the knave is
handsome, young, and hath all those requisites in him
that folly and green minds look after. A pestilent   248
complete knave, and the woman hath found him   249
already.

RODERIGO   I cannot believe that in her. She's full of
most blessed condition.   252

IAGO   Blessed fig's end! The wine she drinks is made of   253
grapes. If she had been blessed, she would never have
loved the Moor. Blessed pudding! Didst thou not see   255
her paddle with the palm of his hand? Didst not mark
that?

RODERIGO   Yes, that I did; but that was but courtesy.

IAGO   Lechery, by this hand. An index an obscure pro-   259
logue to the history of lust and foul thoughts. They
met so near with their lips that their breaths embraced
together. Villainous thoughts, Roderigo! When these
mutualities so marshal the way, hard at hand comes   263
the master and main exercise, th' incorporate conclu-   264
sion. Pish! But, sir, be you ruled by me. I have brought
you from Venice. Watch you tonight; for the com-   266
mand, I'll lay 't upon you. Cassio knows you not. I'll   267
not be far from you. Do you find some occasion to
anger Cassio, either by speaking too loud, or tainting   269
his discipline, or from what other course you please,
which the time shall more favorably minister.   271

RODERIGO   Well.

IAGO   Sir, he's rash and very sudden in choler, and hap-   273
ly may strike at you. Provoke him that he may, for   274
even out of that will I cause these of Cyprus to mutiny,   275
whose qualification shall come into no true taste again   276
but by the displanting of Cassio. So shall you have a
shorter journey to your desires by the means I shall
then have to prefer them, and the impediment most   279
profitably removed, without the which there were no
expectation of our prosperity.

---

248 folly wantonness. **green** immature   **249 found him** sized him up, perceived his intent   **252 condition** disposition   **253 fig's end** (See 1.3.322 for the vulgar gesture of the
fig.)   **255 pudding** sausage   **259 index** table of contents. **obscure** (i.e., the *lust and foul
thoughts,* line 260, are secret, hidden from view)   **263 mutualities** exchanges, intima-
cies. **hard at hand** closely following   **264 incorporate** carnal   **266 Watch you** stand
watch   **266–267 for the command . . . you** I'll arrange for you to be appointed, given
orders   **269 tainting** disparaging   **271 minister** provide   **273 choler** wrath
273–274 haply perhaps   **275 mutiny** riot   **276 qualification** appeasement. **true taste**
i.e., acceptable state   **279 prefer** advance

RODERIGO   I will do this, if you can bring it to any
opportunity.
IAGO   I warrant thee. Meet me by and by at the citadel.   284
I must fetch his necessaries ashore. Farewell.
RODERIGO   Adieu.   *Exit.*
IAGO
That Cassio loves her, I do well believe 't;
That she loves him, 'tis apt and of great credit.   288
The Moor, howbeit that I endure him not,
Is of a constant, loving, noble nature,
And I dare think he'll prove to Desdemona
A most dear husband. Now, I do love her too,
Not out of absolute lust—though peradventure
I stand accountant for as great a sin—   294
But partly led to diet my revenge   295
For that I do suspect the lusty Moor
Hath leaped into my seat, the thought whereof
Doth, like a poisonous mineral, gnaw my innards;
And nothing can or shall content my soul
Till I am evened with him, wife for wife,
Or failing so, yet that I put the Moor
At least into a jealousy so strong
That judgment cannot cure. Which thing to do,
If this poor trash of Venice, whom I trace   304
For his quick hunting, stand the putting on,   305
I'll have our Michael Cassio on the hip,   306
Abuse him to the Moor in the rank garb—   307
For I fear Cassio with my nightcap too—   308
Make the Moor thank me, love me, and reward me
For making him egregiously an ass
And practicing upon his peace and quiet   311
Even to madness. 'Tis here, but yet confused.
Knavery's plain face is never seen till used.   *Exit.*

---

284 warrant assure. **by and by** immediately   **288 apt** probable. **credit** credibility
294 accountant accountable   **295 diet** feed   **304 trace** i.e., train, or follow (?), or perhaps *trash*, a hunting term, meaning to put weights on a hunting dog in order to slow
him down   **305 For** to make more eager. **stand . . . on** respond properly when I incite
him to quarrel   **306 on the hip** at my mercy, where I can throw him. (A wrestling
term.)   **307 Abuse** slander. **rank garb** coarse manner, gross fashion   **308 with my
nightcap** i.e., as a rival in my bed, as one who gives me cuckold's horns   **311 practicing
upon** plotting against

2.2

Enter Othello's Herald with a proclamation.

HERALD   It is Othello's pleasure, our noble and valiant
general, that, upon certain tidings now arrived, im-
porting the mere perdition of the Turkish fleet, every   3
man put himself into triumph: some to dance, some to   4
make bonfires, each man to what sport and revels his
addiction leads him. For, besides these beneficial   6
news, it is the celebration of his nuptial. So much was
his pleasure should be proclaimed. All offices are open,   8
and there is full liberty of feasting from this present
hour of five till the bell have told eleven. Heaven bless
the isle of Cyprus and our noble general Othello!

Exit.

2.3

Enter Othello, Desdemona, Cassio, and attendants.

OTHELLO
Good Michael, look you to the guard tonight.
Let's teach ourselves that honorable stop   2
Not to outsport discretion   3
CASSIO
Iago hath direction what to do,
But notwithstanding, with my personal eye
Will I look to 't.
OTHELLO   Iago is most honest.
Michael, good night. Tomorrow with your earliest   7
Let me have speech with you. [*To Desdemona.*]
    Come, my dear love,
The purchase made, the fruits are to ensue;   9
That profit's yet to come 'tween me and you.—   10
Good night.
Exit [Othello, with Desdemona and attendants].

Enter Iago.

CASSIO   Welcome, Iago. We must to the watch.
IAGO   Not this hour, Lieutenant; 'tis not yet ten o' the   13
clock. Our general cast us thus early for the love of his   14

2.2. Location: Cyprus. A street.
3 **mere perdition** complete destruction   4 **triumph** public celebration   6 **addiction** inclination   8 **offices** rooms where food and drink are kept
2.3. Location: Cyprus. The citadel.
2 **stop** restraint   3 **outsport** celebrate beyond the bounds of   7 **with your earliest** at
your earliest convenience   9–10 **The purchase . . . you** i.e., though married, we haven't
yet consummated our love   13 **Not this hour** not for an hour yet   14 **cast** dismissed

Desdemona; who let us not therefore blame. He hath 15
not yet made wanton the night with her, and she is
sport for Jove.

CASSIO She's a most exquisite lady.

IAGO And, I'll warrant her, full of game.

CASSIO Indeed, she's a most fresh and delicate creature.

IAGO What an eye she has! Me thinks it sounds a parley 21
to provocation.

CASSIO An inviting eye, and yet methinks right modest.

IAGO And when she speaks, is it not an alarum to love? 24

CASSIO She is indeed perfection.

IAGO Well, happiness to their sheets! Come, Lieutenant,
I have a stoup of wine, and here without are a brace of 27
Cyprus gallants that would fain have a measure to the 28
health of black Othello.

CASSIO Not tonight, good Iago. I have very poor and
unhappy brains for drinking. I could well wish courtesy would invent some other custom of entertainment.

IAGO O, they are our friends. But one cup! I'll drink for 34
you. 35

CASSIO I have drunk but one cup tonight and that was
craftily qualified too, and behold what innovation it 37
makes here. I am unfortunate in the infirmity and 38
dare not task my weakness with any more.

IAGO What, man? 'Tis a night of revels. The gallants
desire it.

CASSIO Where are they?

IAGO Here at the door. I pray you, call them in.

CASSIO I'll do 't, but it dislikes me.   *Exit.* 44

IAGO
If I can fasten but one cup upon him,
With that which he hath drunk tonight already,
He'll be as full of quarrel and offense 47
As my young mistress' dog. Now, my sick fool Roderigo,
Whom love hath turned almost the wrong side out,
To Desdemona hath tonight caroused 50
Potations pottle-deep; and he's to watch. 51

---

15 who i.e, Othello **21 sounds a parley** calls for a conference, issues an invitation
24 alarum signal calling men to arms (continuing the military metaphor of *parley,* line
21) **27 stoup** measure of liquor, two quarts. **without** outside. **brace** pair **28 fain have
a measure** gladly drink a toast **34–35 for you** in your place. (Iago will do the steady
drinking to keep the gallants company while Cassio has only one cup.) **37 qualified**
diluted. **innovation** disturbance, insurrection **38 here** i.e., in my head **44 it dislikes me**
i.e., I'm reluctant **47 offense** readiness to take offense **50 caroused** drunk off
52 pottle-deep to the bottom of the tankard. **watch** stand watch

Three lads of Cyprus—noble swelling spirits,   52
That hold their honors in a wary distance,   53
The very elements of this warlike isle—   54
Have I tonight flustered with flowing cups,
And they watch too. Now, 'mongst this flock of drunkards   56
Am I to put our Cassio in some action
That may offend the isle. But here they come.

Enter Cassio, Montano, and gentlemen; [servants
following with wine].

If consequence do but approve my dream,   59
My boat sails freely both with wind and stream.   60
CASSIO   'Fore God, they have given me a rouse already,   61
MONTANO   Good faith, a little one; not past a pint, as I
am a soldier.
IAGO   Some wine, ho!
  [*He sings.*] "And let me the cannikin clink, clink,   65
          And let me the cannikin clink.
      A soldier's a man,
      O, man's life's but a span;   68
    Why, then, let a soldier drink."
Some wine, boys!
CASSIO   'Fore God, an excellent song.
IAGO   I learned it in England, where indeed they are
most potent in potting. Your Dane, your German, and   73
your swag-bellied Hollander—drink, ho!—are noth-
ing to your English.
CASSIO   Is your Englishman so exquisite in his drinking?
IAGO   Why, he drinks you, with facility, your Dane   77
dead drunk; he sweats not to overthrow your Almain;   78
he gives your Hollander a vomit ere the next pottle can
be filled.
CASSIO   To the health of our general!
MONTANO   I am for it, Lieutenant, and I'll do yo justice.   82
IAGO   O sweet England! [*He sings.*]

"King Stephen was and-a worthy peer,
    His breeches cost him but a crown;

---

52 **swelling** proud   53 **hold . . . distance** i.e., are extremely sensitive of their honor
54 **very elements** typical sort   56 **watch** are members of the guard   59 **If . . . dream** if
subsequent events will only substantiate my scheme   60 **stream** current   61 **rouse** full
draft of liquor   65 **cannikin** small drinking vessel   68 **span** brief span of time. (Compare Psalm 39:5 as rendered in the Book of Common Prayer: "Thou hast made my days
as it were a span long.")   73 **potting** drinking   77 **drinks you** drinks. **your Dane** your
typical Dane   78 **sweats not** i.e., need not exert himself. **Almain** German   82 **I'll . . .
justice** i.e., I'll drink as much as you

He held them sixpence all too dear,
    With that he called the tailor lown. 87

He was a wight of high renown,
    And thou art but of low degree.
'Tis pride that pulls the country down; 90
    Then take thy auld cloak about thee." 91

Some wine, ho!

CASSIO   'Fore God, this is a more exquisite song than
the other.

IAGO   Will you hear 't again?

CASSIO   No, for I hold him to be unworthy of his place
that does those things. Well, God's above all; and
there be souls must be saved, and there be souls must
not be saved.

IAGO   It's true, good Lieutenant.

CASSIO   For mine own part—no offense to the General,
nor any man of quality—I hope to be saved. 102

IAGO   And so do I too, Lieutenant.

CASSIO   Ay, but, by your leave, not before me; the lieutenant is to be saved before the ancient. Let's have no
more of this; let's to our affairs.—God forgive us our
sins!—Gentleman, let's look to our business. Do not
think, gentleman, I am drunk. This is my ancient; this
is my right hand, and this is my left. I am not drunk
now. I can stand well enough, and speak well enough.

GENTLEMEN   Excellent well.

CASSIO   Why, very well then; you must not think then
that I am drunk.   *Exit.*

MONTANO
To th' platform, masters. Come, let's set the watch. 114

               [Exeunt Gentlemen.]

IAGO
You see this fellow that is gone before.
He's a soldier fit to stand by Caesar
And give direction; and do but see his vice.
'Tis to his virtue a just equinox, 118
The one as long as the' other. 'Tis pity of him.
I fear the trust Othello puts him in,
On some odd time of his infirmity,
Will shake this island.

MONTANO   But is he often thus?

---

87 **lown** lout, rascal   90 **pride** i.e., extravagance in dress   91 **auld** old   102 **quality**
rank   114 **set the watch** mount the guard   118 **just equinox** exact counterpart. (*Equinox* is an equal length of days and nights.)

IAGO
'Tis evermore the prologue to his sleep.
He'll watch the horologe a double set,   124
If drink rock not his cradle.
MONTANO   It were well
The General were put in mind of it.
Perhaps he sees it not, or his good nature
Prizes the virtue that appears in Cassio
And looks not on his evils. Is not this true?

Enter Roderigo.

IAGO [*aside to him*] How now, Roderigo?
I pray you, after the Lieutenant; go. [*Exit Roderigo.*]
MONTANO
And 'tis great pity that the noble Moor
Should hazard such a place as his own second   133
With one of an engraffed infirmity.   134
It were an honest action to say so
To the Moor.
IAGO   Not I, for this fair island.
I do love Cassio well and would do much
To cure him of this evil.   [*Cry within:* "Help! Help!"]
          But, hark! What noise?   138

Enter Cassio, pursuing Roderigo.

CASSIO   Zounds, you rogue! You rascal!
MONTANO   What's the matter, Lieutenant?
CASSIO   A knave teach me my duty? I'll beat the knave
into a twiggen bottle.   142
RODERIGO   Beat me?
CASSIO   Dost thou prate, rogue?   [*He strikes Roderigo.*]
MONTANO   Nay, good Lieutenant. [*Restraining him.*] I
pray you, sir, hold your hand.
CASSIO   Let me go, sir, or I'll knock you o'er the
mazard.   148
MONTANO   Come, come, you're drunk.
CASSIO   Drunk?   [*They fight.*]
IAGO [*aside to Roderigo*]
Away, I say. Go out and cry a mutiny.   151

                                      [*Exit Roderigo.*]
Nay, good Lieutenant—God's will, gentlemen—

---

124 watch . . . set stay awake twice around the clock or *horologe*   **133–134 hazard . . .
With** risk giving such an important position as his second in command to   **134 engraffed** engrafted, inveterate   **138 s.d. pursuing** (The Quarto text reads, "driving in.")
142 twiggen wicker-covered. (Cassio vows to assail Roderigo until his skin resembles
wickerwork or until he has driven Roderigo through the holes in a wickerwork.)
148 mazard i.e., head. (Literally, a drinking vessel.)   **151 mutiny** riot

Help, ho!—Lieutenant—sir—Montano—sir—
Help, masters!—Here's a goodly watch indeed! 154

[*A bell rings.*]

Who's that which rings the bell?—Diablo, ho! 155
The town will rise. God's will, Lieutenant, hold! 156
You'll be ashamed forever.

Enter Othello and attendants [with weapons].

OTHELLO
What is the matter here?
MONTANO   Zounds, I bleed still.
I am hurt to th' death. He dies! [*He thrusts at Cassio.*]
OTHELLO   Hold, for your lives!
IAGO
Hold, ho! Lieutenant—sir—Montano—gentlemen—
Have you forgot all sense of place and duty?
Hold! The General speaks to you. Hold, for shame!
OTHELLO
Why, how now, ho! From whence ariseth this?
Are we turned Turks, and to ourselves do that 164
Which heaven hath forbid the Ottomites? 165
For Christian shame, put by this barbarous brawl!
He that stirs next to carve for his own rage 167
Holds his soul light; he dies upon his motion. 168
Silence that dreadful bell. It frights the isle
From her propriety. What is the matter, masters? 170
Honest Iago, that looks dead with grieving,
Speak. Who began this? On thy love, I charge thee.
IAGO
I do not know. Friends all but now, even now,
In quarter and in terms like bride and groom 174
Devesting them for bed; and then, but now— 175
As if some planet had unwitted men—
Swords out, and tilting one at others' breasts
In opposition bloody. I cannot speak 178
Any beginning to this peevish odds; 179
And would in action glorious I had lost
Those legs that brought me to a part of it!

---

154 masters sirs. **s.d. A bell rings** (This direction is from the Quarto, as are *Exit Rod-erigo* at line 131, *They fight* at line 150, and *with weapons* at line 157.) **155 Diablo** the devil **156 rise** grow riotous **164–165 to ourselves . . . Ottomites** inflict on ourselves the harm that heaven has prevented the Turks from doing (by destroying their fleet) **167 carve for** i.e., indulge, satisfy with his sword **168 Holds . . . light** i.e., places little value on his life. **upon his motion** if he moves **170 propriety** proper state or condition **174 In quarter** in friendly conduct, within bounds. **in terms** on good terms **175 Devesting them** undressing themselves **178 speak** explain **179 peevish odds** childish quarrel

OTHELLO

How comes it, Michael, you are thus forgot?   182

CASSIO

I pray you, pardon me. I cannot speak.

OTHELLO

Worthy Montano, you were wont be civil;   184
The gravity and stillness of your youth   185
The world hath noted, and your name is great
In mouths of wisest censure. What's the matter   187
That you unlace your reputation thus   188
And spend your rich opinion for the name   189
Of a night-brawler? Give me answer to it.

MONTANO

Worthy Othello, I am hurt to danger.
Your officer, Iago, can inform you—
While I spare speech, which something now offends me—   193
Of all that I do know; nor know I aught
By me that's said or done amiss this night,
Unless self-charity be sometimes a vice,
And to defend ourselves it be a sin
When violence assails us.

OTHELLO   Now, by heaven,
My blood begins my safer guides to rule,   199
And passion, having my best judgment collied,   200
Essays to lead the way. Zounds, if I stir,   201
Or do but lift this arm, the best of you
Shall sink in my rebuke. Give me to know
How this foul rout began, who set it on;   204
And he that is approved in this offense,   205
Though he had twinned with me, both at a birth,
Shall lose me. What? In a town of war   207
Yet wild, the people's hearts brim full of fear,
To manage private and domestic quarrel?   209
In night, and on the court and guard of safety?   210
'Tis monstrous. Iago, who began 't?

MONTANO [*to Iago*]

If partially affined, or leagued in office,   212

---

182 **are thus forgot** have forgotten yourself thus   184 **wont be** accustomed to be
185 **stillness** sobriety   187 **censure** judgment   188 **unlace** undo, lay open (as one might
loose the strings of a purse containing reputation)   189 **opinion** reputation   193 **something** somewhat. **offends** pains   199 **blood** passion (of anger). **guides** i.e., reason
200 **collied** darkened   201 **Essays** undertakes   204 **rout** riot   205 **approved in** found
guilty of   207 **town of** town garrisoned for   209 **manage** undertake   210 **on . . . safety**
at the main guardhouse or headquarters and on watch   212 **partially affined** made partial by some personal relationship. **leagued in office** in league as fellow officers

Thou dost deliver more or less than truth,
Thou art no soldier.
IAGO   Touch me not so near.
   I had rather have this tongue cut from my mouth
   Than it should do offense to Michael Cassio;
   Yet, I persuade myself, to speak the truth
   Shall nothing wrong him. Thus it is, General.
   Montano and myself being in speech,
   There comes a fellow crying out for help,
   And Cassio following him with determined sword
   To execute upon him. Sir, this gentleman   222
                                 [*indicating Montano*]
   Steps in to Cassio and entreats his pause.   223
   Myself the crying fellow did pursue,
   Lest by his clamor—as it so fell out—
   The town might fall in fright. He, swift of foot,
   Outran my purpose, and I returned, the rather   227
   For that I heard the clink and fall of swords
   And Cassio high in oath, which till tonight
   I ne'er might say before. When I came back—
   For this was brief—I found them close together
   At blow and thrust, even as again they were
   When you yourself did part them.
   More of this matter cannot I report.
   But men are men; the best sometimes forget.   235
   Though Cassio did some little wrong to him,
   As men in rage strike those that wish them best,   237
   Yet surely Cassio, I believe, received
   From him that fled some strange indignity,
   Which patience could not pass.
OTHELLO   I know, Iago,   240
   Thy honesty and love doth mince this matter,
   Making it light to Cassio. Cassio, I love thee,
   But nevermore be officer of mine.

Enter Desdemona, attended.

   Look if my gentle love be not raised up.
   I'll make thee an example.
DESDEMONA
   What is the matter, dear?
OTHELLO   All's well now, sweeting;
   Come away to bed. [*To Montano.*] Sir, for your hurts,

---

222 execute give effect to (his anger)   **223 his pause** him to stop   **227 rather** sooner
235 forget forget themselves   **237 those . . . best** i.e., even those who are well disposed   **240 pass** pass over, overlook

Myself will be your surgeon.—Lead him off.   248

[*Montano is led off.*]

Iago, look with care about the town
And silence those whom this vile brawl distracted.
Come, Desdemona. 'Tis the soldiers' life
To have their balmy slumbers waked with strife.

Exit [*with all but Iago and Cassio*].

IAGO   What, are you hurt, Lieutenant?

CASSIO   Ay, past all surgery.

IAGO   Marry, God forbid!

CASSIO   Reputation, reputation, reputation! O, I have
lost my reputation! I have lost the immortal part of
myself, and what remains is bestial. My reputation,
Iago, my reputation!

IAGO   As I am an honest man, I thought you had
received some bodily wound; there is more sense in
that than in reputation. Reputation is an idle and most
false imposition, oft got without merit and lost with-   263
out deserving. You have lost no reputation at all,
unless you repute yourself such a loser. What, man,
there are more ways to recover the General again. You   266
are but now cast in his mood—a punishment more in   267
policy than in malice, even so as one would beat his   268
offenseless dog to affright an imperious lion. Sue to   269
him again and he's yours.

CASSIO   I will rather sue to be despised than to deceive
so good a commander with so slight, so drunken, and   272
so indiscreet an officer. Drunk? And speak parrot?   273
And squabble? Swagger? Swear? And discourse fus-
tian with one's own shadow? O thou invisible spirit
of wine, if thou hast no name to be known by, let us
call thee devil!

IAGO   What was he that you followed with your sword?
What had he done to you?

CASSIO   I know not.

IAGO   Is 't possible?

CASSIO   I remember a mass of things, but nothing
distinctly; a quarrel, but nothing wherefore. O God,   283
that men should put an enemy in their mouths to steal

---

248 **be your surgeon** i.e., make sure you receive medical attention   263 **false imposition**
thing artificially imposed and of no real value   266 **recover** regain favor with   267 **cast**
in his mood dismissed in a moment of anger   267–268 **in policy** done for expediency's
sake and as a public gesture   268–269 **would . . . lion** i.e., would make an example of
a minor offender in order to deter more important and dangerous offenders   269 **Sue**
petition   272 **slight** worthless   273 **speak parrot** talk nonsense, rant. (*Discourse fustian,*
lines 274–275, has much the same meaning.)   283 **wherefore** why

away their brains! That we should with joy, pleasance,
revel, and applause transform ourselves into beasts!   286

IAGO   Why, but you are now well enough. How came
you thus recovered?

CASSIO   It hath pleased the devil drunkenness to give
place to the devil wrath. One unperfectness shows me
another, to make me frankly despise myself.

IAGO   Come, you are too severe a moraler. As the time,   293
the place, and the condition of this country stand, I
could heartily wish this had not befallen; but since it is
as it is, mend it for your own good.

CASSIO   I will ask him for my place again; he shall tell
me I am a drunkard. Had I as many mouths as Hydra,   298
such an answer would stop them all. To be now a
sensible man, by and by a fool, and presently a beast!
O, strange! Every inordinate cup is unblessed, and the
ingredient is a devil.

IAGO   Come, come, good wine is a good familiar
creature, if it be well used. Exclaim no more against it.
And, good Lieutenant, I think you think I love you.

CASSIO   I have well approved it, sir. I drunk!   306

IAGO   You or any man living may be drunk at a time,   307
man. I'll tell you what you shall do. Our general's wife
is now the general—I may say so in this respect, for   309
that he hath devoted and given up himself to the   310
contemplation, mark, and denotement of her parts   311
and graces. Confess yourself freely to her; importune
her help to put you in your place again. She is of so
free, so kind, so apt, so blessed a disposition, she   314
holds it a vice in her goodness not to do more than she
is requested. This broken joint between you and her
husband entreat her to splinter; and, my fortunes   317
against any lay worth naming, this crack of your love   318
shall grow stronger than it was before.

CASSIO   You advise me well.

IAGO   I protest, in the sincerity of love and honest   321
kindness.

CASSIO   I think it freely; and betimes in the morning I   323

---

286 **applause** desire for applause   293 **moraler** moralizer   298 **Hydra** the Lernaean Hydra, a monster with many heads and the ability to grow two heads when one was cut
off, slain by Hercules as the second of his twelve labors   306 **approved** proved
307 **at a time** at one time or another   309–310 **in . . . that** in view of this fact, that
311 **mark, and denotement** (Both words mean "observation.") parts qualities   314 **free**
generous   317 **splinter** bind with splints   318 **lay** stake, wager   321 **protest** insist, declare   323 **freely** unreservedly

will beseech the virtuous Desdemona to undertake for
me. I am desperate of my fortunes if they check me
here.   325
IAGO   You are in the right. Good night, Lieutenant. I
must to the watch.
CASSIO   Good night, Honest Iago.   *Exit Cassio.*
IAGO
And what's he then that says I play the villain,
When this advice is free I give, and honest,   331
Probal to thinking, and indeed the course   332
To win the Moor again? For 'tis most easy
Th' inclining Desdemona to subdue   334
In any honest suit; she's framed as fruitful   335
As the free elements. And then for her   336
To win the Moor—were 't to renounce his baptism,
All seals and symbols of redeemèd sin—
His soul is so enfettered to her love
That she may make, unmake, do what she list,
Even as her appetite shall play the god   341
With his weak function. How am I then a villain,   342
To counsel Cassio to this parallel course   343
Directly to his good? Divinity of hell!   344
When devils will the blackest sins put on,   345
They do suggest at first with heavenly shows,   346
As I do now. For whiles this honest fool
Plies Desdemona to repair his fortune,
And she for him pleads strongly to the Moor,
I'll pour this pestilence into his ear,
That she repeals him for her body's lust;   351
And by how much she strives to do him good,
She shall undo her credit with the Moor.
So will I turn her virtue into pitch,   354
And out of her own goodness make the net
That shall enmesh them all.
Enter Roderigo.

                                    How now, Roderigo?
RODERIGO   I do follow here in the chase, not like a
hound that hunts, but one that fills up the cry. My   358

325 **check** repulse   331 **free** (1) free from guile (2) freely given   332 **Probal** probable,
reasonable   334 **inclining** favorably disposed. **subdue** persuade   335 **framed as fruitful**
created as generous   336 **free elements** i.e., earth, air, fire, and water, unrestrained and
spontaneous   341 **her appetite** her desire, or, perhaps, his desire for her   342 **function**
exercise of faculties (weakened by his fondness for her)   343 **parallel** corresponding to
these facts and to his best interests   344 **Divinity of hell** inverted theology of hell
(which seduces the soul to its damnation)   345 **put on** further, instigate   346 **suggest**
tempt   351 **repeals him** attempts to get him restored   354 **pitch** i.e., (1) foul blackness
(2) a snaring substance   358 **fills up the cry** merely takes part as one of the pack

money is almost spent; I have been tonight exceedingly well cudgeled; and I think the issue will be I shall
have so much experience for my pains, and so,   361
with no money at all and a little more wit, return again
to Venice.

IAGO
How poor are they that have not patience!
What wound did ever heal but by degrees?
Thou know'st we work by wit, and not by witchcraft,
And wit depends on dilatory time.
Does 't not go well? Cassio hath beaten thee,
And thou, by that small hurt, hast cashiered Cassio.   369
Though other things grow fair against the sun,   370
Yet fruits that blossom first will first be ripe.   371
Content thyself awhile. By the Mass, 'tis morning!
Pleasure and action make the hours seem short.
Retire thee; go where thou art billeted.
Away, I say! Thou shalt know more hereafter.
Nay, get thee gone.   *Exit Roderigo.*
            Two things are to be done.
My wife must move for Cassio to her mistress;   377
I'll set her on;
Myself the while to draw the Moor apart
And bring him jump when he may Cassio find   380
Soliciting his wife. Ay, that's the way.
Dull not device by coldness and delay.   *Exit.*   382

3.1

Enter Cassio [and] Musicians.

CASSIO
Masters, play here—I will content your pains—   1
Something that's brief, and bid "Good morrow, General."
                              [*They play.*]

[*Enter*] *Clown*

CLOWN Why, masters, have your instruments been in
  Naples, that they speak i' the nose thus?   4
A MUSICIAN How, sir, how?

---

361 **so much** just so much and no more   369 **cashiered** dismissed from service   370–
371 **Though . . . ripe** i.e., plans that are well prepared and set expeditiously in motion
will soonest ripen into success   377 **move** plead   380 **jump** precisely   382 **device** plot.
coldness lack of zeal
3.1. Location: **Before the chamber of Othello and Desdemona.**
1 **content your pains** reward your efforts   4 **speak i' the nose** (1) sound nasal (2) sound
like one whose nose has been attacked by syphilis. (Naples was popularly supposed to
have a high incidence of venereal disease.)

CLOWN Are these, I pray you, wind instruments?

A MUSICIAN Ay, marry, are they, sir.

CLOWN O, thereby hangs a tail.

A MUSICIAN Whereby hangs a tale, sir?

CLOWN Marry, sir, by many a wind instrument that I know. 10
    But, masters, here's money for you. [*He gives money.*]
    And the General so likes your music that he desires
    you, for love's sake, to make no more noise with it. 13

A MUSICIAN Well, sir, we will not.

CLOWN If you have any music that may not be heard, 16
    to 't again; but, as they say, to hear music the General
    does not greatly care.

A MUSICIAN We have none such, sir.

CLOWN Then put up your pipes in your bag, for I'll 20
    away. Go, vanish into air, away! *Exeunt Musicians.* 21

CASSIO Dost thou hear, mine honest friend?

CLOWN No, I hear not your honest friend; I hear you.

CASSIO Prithee, keep up thy quillets. There's a poor 24
    piece of gold for thee. [*He gives money.*] If the gentle-
    woman that attends the General's wife be stirring, tell
    her there's one Cassio entreats her a little favor of 27
    speech. Wilt thou do this? 28

CLOWN She is stirring, sir. If she will stir hither, I shall 29
    seem to notify unto her. 30

CASSIO
Do, good my friend. *Exit Clown.*

Enter Iago.

               In happy time, Iago. 31

IAGO You have not been abed, then?

CASSIO Why, no. The day had broke
Before we parted. I have made bold, Iago,
To send in to your wife. My suit to her
Is that she will to virtuous Desdemona
Procure me some access.

IAGO   I'll send her to you presently;
And I'll devise a means to draw the Moor
Out of the way, that your converse and business
May be more free.

---

10 **wind instrument** (With a joke on flatulence. The *tail*, line 8, that hangs nearby the *wind instrument* suggests the penis) 13 **for love's sake** (1) out of friendship and affection (2) for the sake of lovemaking in Othello's marriage 16 **may not** cannot 20–21 **I'll away** (Possibly a misprint, or a snatch of song?) 24 **keep up** do not bring out, do not use. **quillets** quibbles, puns 27–28 **a little … speech** the favor of a brief talk 29 **stir** bestir herself (with a play on *stirring,* "rousing herself from rest") 30 **seem** deem it good, think fit 31 **In happy time** i.e., well met

CASSIO

  I humbly thank you for 't.   *Exit [Iago].*

                    I never knew

  A Florentine more kind and honest.   43

  Enter Emilia.

EMILIA

  Good morrow, good Lieutenant. I am sorry

  For your displeasure; but all will sure be well.   45

  The General and his wife are talking of it,

  And she speaks for you stoutly. The Moor replies   47

  That he you hurt is of great fame in Cyprus   48

  And great affinity, and that in wholesome wisdom   49

  He might not but refuse you; but he protests he loves you   50

  And needs no other suitor but his likings

  To take the safest occasion by the front   52

  To bring you in again.

CASSIO   Yet I beseech you,

  If you think fit, or that it may be done,

  Give me advantage of some brief discourse

  With Desdemon alone.

EMILIA   Pray you, come in.

  I will bestow you where you shall have time

  To speak your bosom freely.   58

CASSIO I am much bound to you.   [*Exeunt.*]

<h3 style="text-align:center">3.2</h3>

Enter Othello, Iago, and Gentlemen.

OTHELLO [*giving letters*]

  These letters give, Iago, to the pilot,

  And by him do my duties to the Senate.   2

  That done, I will be walking on the works;   3

  Repair there to me.

IAGO   Well, my good lord, I'll do 't.   4

OTHELLO

  This fortification, gentlemen, shall we see 't?

GENTLEMEN   We'll wait upon your lordship.   *Exeunt.*   6

43 Florentine i.e., even a fellow Florentine. (Iago is a Venetian; Cassio is a Florentine.) **45 displeasure** fall from favor **47 stoutly** spiritedly **48 fame** reputation, importance **49 affinity** kindred, family connection **50 protests** insists **52 occasion . . . front** opportunity by the forelock **58 bosom** inmost thoughts
3.2. Location: The citadel.
2 do my duties convey my respects **3 works** breastworks, fortifications **4 Repair** return, come **6 wait upon** attend

3.3

Enter Desdemona, Cassio, and Emilia.

DESDEMONA
Be thou assured, good Cassio, I will do
All my abilities in thy behalf.

EMILIA
Good madam, do. I warrant it grieves my husband
As if the cause were his.

DESDEMONA
O, that's an honest fellow. Do not doubt, Cassio,
But I will have my lord and you again
As friendly as you were.

CASSIO   Bounteous madam,
Whatever shall become of Michael Cassio,
He's never anything but your true servant.

DESDEMONA
I know 't. I thank you. You do love my lord;
You have known him long, and be you well assured
He shall in strangeness stand no farther off   12
Than in a politic distance.

CASSIO   Ay, but lady,   13
That policy may either last so long,
Or feed upon such nice and waterish diet,   15
Or breed itself so out of circumstance,   16
That, I being absent and my place supplied,   17
My general will forget my love and service.

DESDEMONA
Do not doubt that. Before Emilia here   19
I give thee warrant of thy place. Assure thee,   20
If I do vow a friendship I'll perform it
To the last article. My lord shall never rest.
I'll watch him tame and talk him out of patience;   23
His bed shall seem a school, his board a shrift;   24
I'll intermingle everything he does
With Cassio's suit. Therefore be merry, Cassio,
For thy solicitor shall rather die   27
Than give thy cause away.   28

3.3. Location: The garden of the citadel.
12 **strangeness** aloofness   13 **politic** required by wise policy   15 **Or . . . diet** or sustain
itself at length upon such trivial and meager technicalities   16 **breed . . . circumstance**
continually renew itself so out of chance events, or yield so few chances for my being
pardoned   17 **supplied** filled by another person   19 **doubt** fear   20 **warrant** guarantee
23 **watch him tame** tame him by keeping him from sleeping. (A term from falconry.)
out of patience past his endurance   24 **board** dining table. **shrift** confessional   27 **solicitor** advocate   28 **away** up

Enter Othello and Iago [at a distance].

EMILIA   Madam, here comes my lord.

CASSIO   Madam, I'll take my leave.

DESDEMONA   Why, stay, and hear me speak.

CASSIO
Madam, not now. I am very ill at ease,
Unfit for mine own purposes.

DESDEMONA   Well, do your discretion.   *Exit Cassio.*   34

IAGO   Ha? I like not that.

OTHELLO   What dost thou say?

IAGO
Nothing, my lord; or if—I know not what.

OTHELLO
Was not that Cassio parted from my wife?

IAGO
Cassio, my lord? No, sure, I cannot think it,
That he would steal away so guiltylike,
Seeing you coming.

OTHELLO   I do believe 'twas he.

DESDEMONA   How now, my lord?
I have been talking with a suitor here.
A man that languishes in your displeasure.

OTHELLO   Who is 't you mean?

DESDEMONA
Why, your lieutenant, Cassio. Good my lord,
If I have any grace or power to move you,
His present reconciliation take;   49
For if he be not one that truly loves you,
That errs in ignorance and not in cunning,   51
I have no judgment in an honest face.
I prithee, call him back.

OTHELLO   Went he hence now?

DESDEMONA   Yes, faith, so humbled
That he hath left part of his grief with me
To suffer with him. Good love, call him back.

OTHELLO
Not now, sweet Desdemon. Some other time.

DESDEMONA   But shall 't be shortly?

OTHELLO   The sooner, sweet, for you.

DESDEMONA   Shall 't be tonight at supper?

OTHELLO   No, not tonight.

DESDEMONA   Tomorrow dinner, then?   63

---

34 do your discretion act according to your own discretion   **49 His . . . take** let him be reconciled to you right away   **51 in cunning** wittingly   **63 dinner** (the noontime meal.)

OTHELLO   I shall not dine at home.
I meet the captains at the citadel.
DESDEMONA
Why, then, tomorrow night, or Tuesday morn,
On Tuesday noon, or night, on Wednesday morn.
I prithee, name the time, but let it not
Exceed three days. In faith, he's penitent;
And yet his trespass, in our common reason—   70
Save that, they say, the wars must make example   71
Out of her best—is not almost a fault   72
T' incur a private check. When shall he come?   73
Tell me, Othello. I wonder in my soul
What you would ask me that I should deny,
Or stand so mammering on. What? Michael Cassio,   76
That came a-wooing with you, and so many a time,
When I have spoke of you dispraisingly,
Hath ta'en your part—to have so much to do
To bring him in! By 'r Lady, I could do much—   80
OTHELLO
Prithee, no more. Let him come when he will;
I will deny thee nothing.
DESDEMONA   Why, this is not a boon.
'Tis as I should entreat you wear your gloves,
Or feed on nourishing dishes, or keep you warm,
Or sue to you to do a peculiar profit   86
To your own person. Nay, when I have a suit
Wherein I mean to touch your love indeed,   88
It shall be full of poise and difficult weight,   89
And fearful to be granted.
OTHELLO   I will deny thee nothing.
Whereon, I do beseech thee, grant me this,   92
To leave me but a little to myself.
DESDEMONA
Shall I deny you? No. Farewell, my lord.
OTHELLO
Farewell, my Desdemona. I'll come to thee straight.   95
DESDEMONA
Emilia, come.—Be as your fancies teach you;   96
Whate'er you be, I am obedient.   *Exit [with Emilia].*

---

70 **common reason** everyday judgments   71–72 **Save . . . best** were it not that, as the
saying goes, military discipline requires making an example of the very best men. (*Her*
refers to *wars* as a singular concept)   72 **not almost** scarcely   73 **a private check** even a
private reprimand   76 **mammering on** wavering about   80 **bring him in** restore him to
favor   86 **peculiar** particular, personal   88 **touch** test   89 **poise** weight, heaviness; or
equipoise, delicate balance involving hard choice   92 **Whereon** in return for which
95 **straight** straightway   96 **fancies** inclinations

OTHELLO

    Excellent wretch! Perdition catch my soul   98

    But I do love thee! And when I love thee not,   99

    Chaos is come again.   100

IAGO My noble lord—

OTHELLO What doest thou say, Iago?

IAGO

    Did Michael Cassio, when you wooed my lady,

    Know of your love?

OTHELLO

    He did, from first to last. Why dost thou ask?

IAGO

    But for a satisfaction of my thought;

    No further harm.

OTHELLO   Why of thy thought, Iago?

IAGO

    I did not think he had been acquainted with her.

OTHELLO

    O, yes, and went between us very oft.

IAGO Indeed?

OTHELLO

    Indeed? Ay, indeed. Discern'st thou aught in that?

    Is he not honest?

IAGO Honest, my lord?

OTHELLO Honest. Ay, honest?

IAGO My lord, for aught I know.

OTHELLO What dost thou think?

IAGO Think, my lord?

OTHELLO

    "Think, my lord?" By heaven, thou echo'st me,

    As if there were some monster in thy thought

    Too hideous to be shown. Thou dost mean something.

    I heard thee say even now, thou lik'st not that,

    When Cassio left my wife. What didst not like?

    And when I told thee he was of my counsel   123

    In my whole course of wooing, thou criedst "Indeed?"

    And didst contract and purse thy brow together   125

    As if thou then hadst shut up in thy brain

    Some horrible conceit. If thou dost love me,   127

    Show me thy thought.

IAGO My lord, you know I love you.

---

98 wretch (A term of affectionate endearment.) **99–100 And . . . again** i.e., my love for you will last forever, until the end of time when chaos will return. (But with an unconscious, ironic suggestion that, if anything should induce Othello to cease loving Desdemona, the result would be chaos.) **123 of my counsel** in my confidence **125 purse** knit **127 conceit** fancy

OTHELLO   I think thou dost;
   And for I know thou'rt full of love and honesty,   131
   And weigh'st thy words before thou giv'st them breath,
   Therefore these stops of thine fright me the more;   133
   For such things in a false disloyal knave
   Are tricks of custom, but in a man that's just   135
   They're close dilations, working from the heart   136
   That passion cannot rule.
IAGO   For Michael Cassio,   137
   I dare be sworn I think that he is honest.
OTHELLO
   I think so too.
IAGO   Men should be what they seem;
   Or those that be not, would they might seem none!   140
OTHELLO
   Certain, men should be what they seem.
IAGO
   Why, then, I think Cassio's an honest man.
OTHELLO   Nay, yet there's more in this.
   I prithee, speak to me as to thy thinkings,
   As thou dost ruminate, and give thy worst of thoughts
   The worst of words.
IAGO   Good my lord, pardon me.
   Though I am bound to every act of duty,
   I am not bound to that all slaves are free to.   148
   Utter my thoughts? Why, say they are vile and false,
   As where's that palace where into foul things
   Sometimes intrude not? Who has that breast so pure
   But some uncleanly apprehensions
   Keep leets and law days, and in sessions sit   153
   With meditations lawful?   154
OTHELLO
   Thou dost conspire against thy friend, Iago,   155
   If thou but think'st him wronged and mak'st his ear
   A stranger to thy thoughts.
IAGO   I do beseech you,
   Though I perchance am vicious in my guess—   158
   As I confess it is my nature's plague

---

131 for because **133 stops** pauses **135 of custom** customary **136 close dilations** secret or involuntary expressions or delays **137 That passion cannot rule** i.e., that are too passionately strong to be restrained (referring to the workings), or, that cannot rule its own passions (referring to the heart). For as for **140 none** i.e., not to be men, or not seem to be honest **148 that** that which. **free to** free with respect to **153 Keep leets and law days** i.e., hold court, set up their authority in one's heart. (*Leets* are a kind of manor court; *law days* are the days courts sit in session, or those sessions.) **154 With** along with. **lawful** innocent **155 thy friend** i.e., Othello **158 vicious** wrong

To spy into abuses, and oft my jealousy   160
Shapes faults that are not—that your wisdom then,   161
From one that so imperfectly conceits,   162
Would take no notice, nor build yourself a trouble
Out of his scattering and unsure observance.   164
It were not for your quiet nor your good,
Nor for my manhood, honesty, and wisdom,
To let you know my thoughts.
OTHELLO   What dost thou mean?
IAGO
Good name in man and woman, dear my lord,
Is the immediate jewel of their souls.   169
Who steals my purse steals trash; 'tis something, nothing;
'Twas mine, 'tis his, and has been slave to thousands;
But he that filches from me my good name
Robs me of that which not enriches him
And makes me poor indeed.
OTHELLO   By heaven, I'll know thy thoughts.
IAGO
You cannot, if my heart were in your hand,   176
Nor shall not, whilst 'tis in my custody.
OTHELLO   Ha?
IAGO   O, beware, my lord, of jealousy.
It is the green-eyed monster which doth mock   179
The meat it feeds on. That cuckold lives in bliss   180
Who, certain of his fate, loves not his wronger;   181
But O, what damnèd minutes tells he o'er   182
Who dotes, yet doubts, suspects, yet fondly loves!
OTHELLO   O misery!
IAGO
Poor and content is rich, and rich enough,   185
But riches fineless is as poor as winter   186
To him that ever fears he shall be poor.
Good God, the souls of all my tribe defend
From jealousy!
OTHELLO   Why, why is this?
Think'st thou I'd make a life of jealousy,

---

160 **jealousy** suspicious nature   161 **then** on that account   162 **one** i.e., myself, Iago.
conceits judges, conjectures   164 **scattering** random   169 **immediate** essential, most
precious   176 **if** even if   179–180 **doth mock . . . on** mocks and torments the heart of
its victim, the man who suffers jealousy   181 **his wronger** i.e., his faithless wife. (The
unsuspecting cuckold is spared the misery of loving his wife only to discover she is
cheating on him.)   182 **tells** counts   185 **Poor . . . enough** to be content with what little
one has is the greatest wealth of all. (Proverbial.)   186 **fineless** boundless

To follow still the changes of the moon   192
With fresh suspicions? No! To be once in doubt   193
Is once to be resolved. Exchange me for a goat   194
When I shall turn the business of my soul
To such exsufflicate and blown surmises   196
Matching thy inference. 'Tis not to make me jealous   197
To say my wife is fair, feeds well, loves company,
Is free of speech, sings, plays, and dances well;
Where virtue is, these are more virtuous.
Nor from mine own weak merits will I draw
The smallest fear or doubt of her revolt,   202
For she had eyes, and chose me. No, Iago,
I'll see before I doubt; when I doubt, prove;
And on the proof, there is no more but this—
Away at once with love or jealousy.

IAGO
I am glad of this, for now I shall have reason
To show the love and duty that I bear you
With franker spirit. Therefore, as I am bound,
Receive it from me. I speak not yet of proof.
Look to your wife; observe her well with Cassio.
Wear your eyes thus, not jealous nor secure.   212
I would not have your free and noble nature,
Out of self-bounty, be abused. Look to 't.   214
I know our country disposition well;
In Venice they do let God see the pranks
They dare not show their husbands; their best conscience
Is not to leave 't undone, but keep 't unknown.

OTHELLO   Dost thou say so?

IAGO
She did deceive her father, marrying you;
And when she seemed to shake and fear your looks,
She loved them most.

OTHELLO   And so she did.

IAGO   Why, go to, then!   222
She that, so young, could give out such a seeming,   223
To seel her father's eyes up close as oak,   224
He thought 'twas witchcraft! But I am much to blame.

192–193 **To follow . . . suspicions** to be constantly imagining new causes for suspicion, changing incessantly like the moon   194 **once** once and for all. **resolved** free of doubt, having settled the matter   196 **exsufflicate and blown** inflated and blown up, rumored about, or, spat out and flyblown, hence, loathsome, disgusting   197 **inference** description or allegation   202 **doubt . . . revolt** fear of her unfaithfulness   212 **not** neither. **secure** free from uncertainty   214 **self-bounty** inherent or natural goodness and generosity. **abused** deceived   222 **go to** (An expression of impatience.)   223 **seeming** false appearance   224 **seel** blind. (A term from falconry.) **oak** (A close-grained wood.)

I humbly do beseech you of your pardon
For too much loving you.

OTHELLO   I am bound to thee forever.   228

IAGO
I see this hath a little dashed your spirits.

OTHELLO
Not a jot, not a jot.

IAGO   I' faith, I fear it has.
I hope you will consider what is spoke
Comes from my love. But I do see you're moved.
I am to pray you not to strain my speech
To grosser issues nor to larger reach   234
Than to suspicion.

OTHELLO   I will not.

IAGO   Should you do so, my lord,
My speech should fall into such vile success   238
Which my thoughts aimed not. Cassio's my worthy friend.
My lord, I see you're moved.

OTHELLO   No, not much moved.
I do not think but Desdemona's honest.   241

IAGO
Long live she so! And long live you to think so!

OTHELLO
And yet, how nature erring from itself—

IAGO
Ay, there's the point! As—to be bold with you—
Not to affect many proposèd matches   245
Of her own clime, complexion, and degree,   246
Whereto we see in all things nature tends—
Foh! One may smell in such a will most rank,   248
Foul disproportion, thoughts unnatural.   249
But pardon me. I do not in position   250
Distinctly speak of her, though I may fear
Her will, recoiling to her better judgment,   252
May fall to match you with her country forms   253
And happily repent.

OTHELLO   Farewell, farewell!   254
If more thou dost perceive, let me know more.
Set on thy wife to observe. Leave me, Iago.

---

228 bound indebted (but perhaps with ironic sense of "tied")   **234 issues** significance.
reach meaning, scope   **238 success** effect, result   **241 honest** chaste   **245 affect** prefer,
desire   **246 clime . . . degree** country, color, and social position   **248 will** sensuality,
appetite   **249 disproportion** abnormality   **250 position** argument, proposition   **252
recoiling** reverting. **better** i.e., more natural and reconsidered   **253 fall . . . forms** undertake to compare you with Venetian norms of handsomeness   **254 happily repent** haply
repent her marriage

IAGO [*going*]   My lord, I take my leave.

OTHELLO

Why did I marry? This honest creature doubtless
Sees and knows more, much more, than he unfolds.

IAGO [*returning*]

My Lord, I would I might entreat your honor
To scan this thing no farther. Leave it to time.   261
Although 'tis fit that Cassio have his place—
For, sure, he fills it up with great ability—
Yet, if you please to hold him off awhile,
You shall by that perceive him and his means.   265
Note if your lady strain his entertainment   266
With any strong or vehement importunity;
Much will be seen in that. In the meantime,
Let me be thought too busy in my fears—   269
As worthy cause I have to fear I am—
And hold her free, O do beseech your honor.   271

OTHELLO   Fear not my government.   272

IAGO   I once more take my leave.   *Exit.*

OTHELLO

This fellow's of exceeding honesty,
And knows all qualities, with a learnèd spirit,   275
Of human dealings. If I do prove her haggard,   276
Though that her jesses were my dear heartstrings,   277
I'd whistle her off and let her down the wind   278
To prey at fortune. Haply, for I am black   279
And have not those soft parts of conversation   280
That chamberers have, or for I am declined   281
Into the vale of years—yet that's not much—
She's gone. I am abused, and my relief   283
Must be to loathe her. O curse of marriage,
That we can call these delicate creatures ours
And not their appetites! I had rather be a toad
And live upon the vapor of a dungeon
Than keep a corner in the thing I love
For others' uses. Yet, 'tis the plague of great ones;

---

261 scan scrutinize   **265 his means** the method he uses (to regain his post)   **266 strain his entertainment** urge his reinstatement   **269 busy** interfering   **271 hold her free** regard her as innocent   **272 government** self-control, conduct   **275 qualities** natures, types   **276 haggard** wild (like a wild female hawk)   **277 jesses** straps fastened around the legs of a trained hawk   **278 I'd . . . wind** i.e., I'd let her go forever. (To release a hawk downwind was to invite it not to return.)   **279 prey at fortune** fend for herself in the wild. **Haply, for** perhaps because   **280 soft . . . conversation** pleasing graces of social behavior   **281 chamberers** gallants   **283 abused** deceived

Prerogatived are they less than the base. 290
'Tis destiny unshunnable, like death.
Even then this forkèd plague is fated to us 292
When we do quicken. Look where she comes. 293

Enter Desdemona and Emilia.

If she be false, O, then heaven mocks itself!
I'll not believe 't.
DESDEMONA   How now, my dear Othello?
Your dinner, and the generous islanders 296
By you invited, do attend your presence. 297
OTHELLO
I am to blame.
DESDEMONA   Why do you speak so faintly?
Are you not well?
OTHELLO
I have a pain upon my forehead here.
DESDEMONA
Faith, that's with watching. 'Twill away again. 301
                    [*She offers her handkerchief.*]
Let me but bind it hard, within this hour
It will be well.
OTHELLO   Your napkin is too little. 303
Let it alone. Come, I'll go in with you. 304
    [*He puts the handkerchief from him, and it drops.*]
DESDEMONA
I am very sorry that you are not well.
                    Exit [*with Othello*].
EMILIA [*picking up the handkerchief*]
I am glad I have found this napkin.
This was her first remembrance from the Moor.
My wayward husband hath a hundred times 308
Wooed me to steal it, but she so loves the token—
For he conjured her she should ever keep it—
That she reserves it evermore about her
To kiss and talk to. I'll have the work ta'en out, 312
And give 't Iago. What he will do with it

290 **Prerogatived** privileged (to have honest wives). **the base** ordinary citizens. (Socially prominent men are especially prone to the unavoidable destiny of being cuckolded and to the public shame that goes with it.)   292 **forkèd** (An allusion to the horns of the cuckold.)   293 **quicken** receive life. (*Quicken* may also mean to swarm with maggots as the body festers, as in 4.2.69, in which case lines 292–293 suggest that *even then,* in death, we are cuckolded by *forkèd* worms.)   296 **generous** noble   297 **attend** await   301 **watching** too little sleep   303 **napkin** handkerchief   304 **Let it alone** i.e., never mind   308 **wayward** capricious   312 **work ta'en out** design of the embroidery copied

Heaven knows, not I;
I nothing but to please his fantasy.   315

Enter Iago.

IAGO
How now? What do you here alone?
EMILIA
Do not you chide. I have a thing for you.
IAGO
You have a thing for me? It is a common thing—   318
EMILIA   Ha?
IAGO   To have a foolish wife.
EMILIA
O, is that all? What will you give me now
For that same handkerchief?
IAGO   What handkerchief?
EMILIA   What handkerchief?
Why, that the Moor first gave to Desdemona;
That which so often you did bid me steal.
IAGO   Hast stolen it from her?
EMILIA
No, faith. She let it drop by negligence,
And to th' advantage, I, being here, took 't up.   329
Look, here 'tis.
IAGO   A good wench! Give it me.
EMILIA
What will you do with 't, that you have been so earnest
To have me filch it?
IAGO [*snatching it*]   Why, what is that to you?
EMILIA
If it be not for some purpose of import,
Give 't me again. Poor lady, she'll run mad
When she shall lack it.
IAGO   Be not acknown on 't.   335
I have use for it. Go, leave me.   *Exit Emilia.*
I will in Cassio's lodging lose this napkin   337
And let him find it. Trifles light as air
Are to the jealous confirmations strong
As proofs of Holy Writ. This may do something.
The Moor already changes with my poison.

---

315 fantasy whim   **318 common thing** (With bawdy suggestion; *common* suggests
coarseness and availability to all comers, and *thing* is a slang term for the pudendum.)
329 to th' advantage taking the opportunity   **335 lack** miss. **Be ... on 't** do not confess knowledge of it   **337 lose** (The Folio spelling, *loose,* is a normal spelling for "lose,"
but may also contain the idea of "let go," "release.")

Dangerous conceits are in their natures poisons, 342
Which at the first are scarce found to distaste, 343
But with a little act upon the blood 344
Burn like the mines of sulfur.

Enter Othello.

                        I did say so.
Look where he comes! Not poppy nor mandragora 346
Nor all the drowsy syrups of the world
Shall ever medicine thee to that sweet sleep
Which thou owedst yesterday.
OTHELLO   Ha, ha, false to me? 349
IAGO
  Why, how now, General? No more of that.
OTHELLO
  Avaunt! Begone! Thou hast set me on the rack.
  I swear 'tis better to be much abused
  Than but to know 't a little.
IAGO   How now, my lord?
OTHELLO
  What sense had I of her stolen hours of lust?
  I saw 't not, thought it not, it harmed not me.
  I slept the next night well, fed well, was free and merry; 356
  I found not Cassio's kisses on her lips.
  He that is robbed, not wanting what is stolen, 358
  Let him not know 't and he's not robbed at all.
IAGO   I am sorry to hear this.
OTHELLO
  I had been happy if the general camp,
  Pioners and all, had tasted her sweet body, 362
  So I had nothing known. O, now, forever 363
  Farewell the tranquil mind! Farewell content!
  Farewell the plumèd troops and the big wars 365
  That makes ambition virtue! Oh, farewell!
  Farewell the neighing steed and the shrill trump,
  The spirit-stirring drum, th' ear-piercing fife,
  The royal banner, and all quality, 369
  Pride, pomp, and circumstance of glorious war! 370
  And O, you mortal engines, whose rude throats 371

---

342 conceits fancies, ideas **343 distaste** be distasteful **344 act** action, working
346 mandragora an opiate made of the mandrake root **349 thou owedst** you did own
356 free carefree **358 wanting** missing **362 Pioners** diggers of mines, the lowest grade
of soldiers **363 So** provided **365 big** stately **369 quality** character, essential nature
370 Pride rich display. **circumstance** pageantry **371 mortal engines** i.e., cannon. (*Mortal* means "deadly.")

Th' immortal Jove's dread clamors counterfeit,   372
Farewell! Othello's occupation's gone.
IAGO Is 't possible, my lord?
OTHELLO
Villain, be sure thou prove my love a whore!
Be sure of it. Give me the ocular proof,
Or, by the worth of mine eternal soul,
Thou hadst been better have been born a dog
Than answer my waked wrath!
IAGO   Is 't come to this?
OTHELLO
Make me to see 't, or at least so prove it
That the probation bear no hinge nor loop   381
To hang a doubt on, or woe upon thy life!
IAGO My noble lord—
OTHELLO
If thou dost slander her and torture me,
Never pray more; abandon all remorse;   385
On horror's head horrors accumulate;   386
Do deeds to make heaven weep, all earth amazed;   387
For nothing canst thou to damnation add
Greater than that.
IAGO   O grace! O heaven forgive me!
Are you a man? Have you a soul or sense?
God b' wi' you; take mine office. O wretched fool,   391
That lov'st to make thine honesty a vice!   392
O monstrous world! Take note, take note, O world,
To be direct and honest is not safe.
I thank you for this profit, and from hence   395
I'll love no friend, sith love breeds such offense.   396
OTHELLO Nay, stay. Thou shouldst be honest.   397
IAGO
I should be wise, for honesty's a fool
And loses that it works for.
OTHELLO   By the world,   399
I think my wife be honest and think she is not;
I think that thou art just and think thou are not.
I'll have some proof. My name, that was as fresh

---

372 **Jove's dread clamors** i.e., thunder   381 **probation** proof   385 **remorse** pity, penitent hope for salvation   386 **horrors accumulate** add still more horrors   387 **amazed**
confounded with horror   391 **O wretched fool** (Iago addresses himself as a fool for
having carried honesty too far.)   392 **vice** failing, something overdone   395 **profit** profitable instruction. **hence** henceforth   396 **sith** since. **offense** i.e., harm to the one who
offers help and friendship   397 **Thou shouldst be** It appears that you are. (But Iago replies in the sense of "ought to be.")   399 **that** what

As Dian's visage, is now begrimed and black 403
As mine own face. If there be cords, or knives,
Poison, or fire, or suffocating streams,
I'll not endure it. Would I were satisfied!

IAGO
I see, sir, you are eaten up with passion.
I do repent me that I put it to you.
You would be satisfied?

OTHELLO   Would? Nay, and I will.

IAGO
And may; but how? How satisfied, my lord?
Would you, the supervisor, grossly gape on? 411
Behold her topped?

OTHELLO   Death and damnation! O!

IAGO
It were a tedious difficulty, I think,
To bring them to that prospect. Damn them then, 414
If ever mortal eyes do see them bolster 415
More than their own. What then? How then? 416
What shall I say? Where's satisfaction?
It is impossible you should see this,
Were they as prime as goats, as hot as monkeys, 419
As salt as wolves in pride, and fools as gross 420
As ignorance made drunk. But yet I say,
If imputation and strong circumstances 422
Which lead directly to the door of truth
Will give you satisfaction, you might have 't.

OTHELLO
Give me a living reason she's disloyal.

IAGO   I do not like the office.
But sith I am entered in this cause so far, 427
Pricked to 't by foolish honesty and love, 428
I will go on. I lay with Cassio lately,
And being troubled with a raging tooth
I could not sleep. There are a kind of men
So loose of soul that in their sleeps will mutter
Their affairs. One of this kind is Cassio.
In sleep I heard him say, "Sweet Desdemona,
Let us be wary, let us hide our loves!"
And then, sir, would he grip and wring my hand,

403 **Dian** Diana, goddess of the moon and of chastity   411 **supervisor** onlooker
414 **Damn them then** i.e., they would have to be really incorrigible   415 **bolster** go to
bed together, share a bolster   416 **More** other. **own** own eyes   419 **prime** lustful
420 **salt** wanton, sensual. **pride** heat   422 **imputation . . . circumstances** strong circum-
stantial evidence   427 **sith** since   428 **Pricked** spurred

Cry "O sweet creature!", then kiss me hard,
As if he plucked up kisses by the roots
That grew upon my lips; then laid his leg
Over my thigh, and sighed, and kissed, and then
Cried, "Cursèd fate that gave thee to the Moor!"

OTHELLO
O monstrous! Monstrous!

IAGO   Nay, this was but his dream.

OTHELLO
But this denoted a foregone conclusion.   443
'Tis a shrewd doubt, though it be but a dream.   444

IAGO
And this may help to thicken other proofs
That do demonstrate thinly.

OTHELLO   I'll tear her all to pieces.

IAGO
Nay, but be wise. Yet we see nothing done;
She may be honest yet. Tell me but this:
Have you not sometimes seen a handkerchief
Spotted with strawberries in your wife's hand?   450

OTHELLO
I gave her such a one. 'Twas my first gift.

IAGO
I know not that; but such a handkerchief—
I am sure it was your wife's—did I today
See Cassio wipe his beard with.

OTHELLO   If it be that—

IAGO
If it be that, or any that was hers,
It speaks against her with the other proofs.

OTHELLO
O, that the slave had forty thousand lives!   457
One is too poor, too weak for my revenge.
Now do I see 'tis true. Look here, Iago,
All my fond love thus do I blow to heaven.   460
'Tis gone.
Arise, black vengeance, from the hollow hell!
Yield up, O love, thy crown and hearted throne   463
To tyrannous hate! Swell, bosom, with thy freight,   464
For 'tis of aspics' tongues!   465

---

443 **foregone conclusion** concluded experience or action   444 **shrewd doubt** suspicious
circumstance   450 **Spotted with strawberries** embroidered with a strawberry pattern
457 **the slave** i.e., Cassio   460 **fond** foolish (but also suggesting "affectionate")
463 **hearted** fixed in the heart   464 **freight** burden   465 **aspics'** venemous serpents'

IAGO   Yet be content.   466
OTHELLO   O, blood, blood, blood!
IAGO
  Patience, I say. Your mind perhaps may change.
OTHELLO
  Never, Iago. Like to the Pontic Sea,   469
  Whose icy current and compulsive course
  Ne'er feels retiring ebb, but keeps due on
  To the Propontic and the Hellespont,   472
  Even so my bloody thoughts with violent pace
  Shall ne'er look back, ne'er ebb to humble love,
  Till that a capable and wide revenge   475
  Swallow them up. Now, by yond marble heaven,   476
  [*Kneeling*] In the due reverence of a sacred vow
  I here engage my words.
IAGO   Do not rise yet.
  [*He kneels.*] Witness, you ever-burning lights above,   479
  You elements that clip us round about,   480
  Witness that here Iago doth give up
  The execution of his wit, hands, heart,   482
  To wronged Othello's service. Let him command,
  And to obey shall be in me remorse,   484
  What bloody business ever.   [*They rise.*]
OTHELLO   I greet thy love,   485
  Not with vain thanks, but with acceptance bounteous,
  And will upon the instant put thee to 't.   487
  Within these three days let me hear thee say
  That Cassio's not alive.
IAGO   My friend is dead;
  'Tis done at your request. But let her live.
OTHELLO
  Damn her, lewd minx! O, damn her, damn her!   491
  Come, go with me apart. I will withdraw
  To furnish me with some swift means of death
  For the fair devil. Now art thou my lieutenant.
IAGO   I am your own forever.   *Exeunt.*

---

466 content calm   **469 Pontic Sea** Black Sea   **472 Propontic** Sea of Marmora, between
the Black Sea and the Aegean. **Hellespont** Dardanelles, straits where the Sea of Marmora
joins with the Aegean   **475 capable** ample, comprehensive   **476 marble** i.e., gleaming
like marble and unrelenting   **479 s.d. He kneels** (In the Quarto text, Iago kneels here
after Othello has knelt at line 477.)   **480 clip** encompass   **482 execution** exercise, action. **wit** mind   **484 remorse** pity (for Othello's wrongs)   **485 ever** soever   **487 to 't** to
the proof   **491 minx** wanton

3.4

Enter Desdemona, Emilia, and Clown.

DESDEMONA   Do you know, sirrah, where Lieutenant   1
Cassio lies?   2

CLOWN   I dare not say he lies anywhere.

DESDEMONA   Why, man?

CLOWN   He's a soldier, and for me to say a soldier lies,
'tis stabbing.

DESDEMONA   Go to. Where lodges he?

CLOWN   To tell you where he lodges is to tell you where
I lie.

DESDEMONA   Can anything be made of this?

CLOWN   I know not where he lodges, and for me to devise a lodging and say he lies here, or he lies there,
were to lie in mine own throat.   13

DESDEMONA   Can you inquire him out, and be edified
by report?

CLOWN   I will catechize the world for him; that is, make
questions, and by them answer.

DESDEMONA   Seek him, bid him come hither. Tell him I
have moved my lord on his behalf and hope all will be   19
well.

CLOWN   To do this is within the compass of man's wit,
and therefore I will attempt the doing it.   *Exit Clown.*

DESDEMONA
Where should I lose that handkerchief, Emilia?

EMILIA   I know not, madam.

DESDEMONA
Believe me, I had rather have lost my purse
Full of crusadoes; and but my noble Moor   26
Is true of mind and made of no such baseness
As jealous creatures are, it were enough
To put him to ill thinking.

EMILIA   Is he not jealous?

DESDEMONA
Who, he? I think the sun where he was born
Drew all such humors from him.

EMILIA   Look where he comes.   31

Enter Othello.

3.4. Location: Before the citadel.
1 sirrah (A form of address to an inferior.)   **2 lies** lodges. (But the Clown makes the
obvious pun.)   **13 lie ... throat** (1) lie egregiously and deliberately (2) use the windpipe
to speak a lie   **19 moved** petitioned   **26 crusadoes** Portuguese gold coins   **31 humors**
(Refers to the four bodily fluids thought to determine temperament.)

DESDEMONA
I will not leave him now till Cassio
Be called to him. How is 't with you, my lord?
OTHELLO
Well, my good lady. [*Aside.*] O, hardness to dissemble! —
How do you, Desdemona?
DESDEMONA   Well, my good lord.
OTHELLO
Give me your hand. [*She gives her hand.*] This hand is moist, my
lady.
DESDEMONA
It yet hath felt no age nor known no sorrow.
OTHELLO
This argues fruitfulness and liberal heart.   38
Hot, hot, and moist. This hand of yours requires
A sequester from liberty, fasting and prayer,   40
Much castigation, exercise devout;   41
For here's a young and sweating devil here
That commonly rebels. 'Tis a good hand,
A frank one.
DESDEMONA   You may indeed say so,   44
For 'twas that hand that gave away my heart.
OTHELLO
A liberal hand. The hearts of old gave hands,   46
But our new heraldry is hands, not hearts.   47
DESDEMONA
I cannot speak of this. Come now, your promise.
OTHELLO   What promise, chuck?   49
DESDEMONA
I have sent to bid Cassio come speak with you.
OTHELLO
I have a salt and sorry rheum offends me;   51
Lend me thy handkerchief.
DESDEMONA   Here, my lord.   [*She offers a handkerchief*]
OTHELLO
That which I gave you.
DESDEMONA   I have it not about me.

---

38 **argues** gives evidence of. **fruitfulness** generosity, amorousness, and fecundity. **liberal** generous and sexually free   40 **sequester** separation, sequestration   41 **castigation** corrective discipline. **exercise devout** i.e., prayer, religious meditation, etc.   44 **frank** generous, open (with sexual suggestion)   46 **The hearts ... hands** i.e., in former times, people would give their hearts when they gave their hands to something   47 **But ... hearts** i.e., in our decadent times, the joining of hands is no longer a badge to signify the giving of hearts   49 **chuck** (A term of endearment.)   51 **salt ... rheum** distressful head cold or watering of the eyes

OTHELLO   Not?

DESDEMONA   No, faith, my lord.

OTHELLO

That's a fault. That handkerchief
Did an Egyptian to my mother give.
She was a charmer, and could almost read   59
The thoughts of people. She told her, while she kept it
'Twould make her amiable and subdue my father   61
Entirely to her love, but if she lost it
Or made a gift of it, my father's eye
Should hold her loathèd and his spirits should hunt
After new fancies. She, dying, gave it me,   65
And bid me, when my fate would have me wived,
To give it her. I did so; and take heed on 't;   67
Make it a darling like your precious eye.
To lose 't or give 't away were such perdition   69
As nothing else could match.

DESDEMONA   Is 't possible?

OTHELLO

'Tis true. There's magic in the web of it.   71
A sibyl, that had numbered in the world
The sun to course two hundred compasses,   73
In her prophetic fury sewed the work;   74
The worms were hallowed that did breed the silk,
And it was dyed in mummy which the skillful   76
Conserved of maiden's hearts.

DESDEMONA   I' faith! Is 't true?   77

OTHELLO

Most veritable. Therefore look to 't well.

DESDEMONA

Then would to God that I had never seen 't!

OTHELLO   Ha? Wherefore?

DESDEMONA

Why do you speak so startingly and rash?   81

OTHELLO

Is 't lost? Is 't gone? Speak, is 't out o' the way?   82

DESDEMONA   Heaven bless us!

OTHELLO   Say you?

---

59 charmer sorceress   **61 amiable** desirable   **65 fancies** loves   **67 her** i.e., to my wife
69 perdition loss   **71 web** fabric, weaving   **73 compasses** annual circlings. (The *sibyl,*
or prophetess, was two hundred years old.)   **74 prophetic fury** frenzy of prophetic inspiration. **work** embroidered pattern   **76 mummy** medicinal or magical preparation
drained from mummified bodies   **77 Conserved of** prepared or preserved out of
81 startingly and rash disjointedly and impetuously, excitedly   **82 out o' the way** lost,
misplaced

DESDEMONA
It is not lost; but what an if it were? 85
OTHELLO How?
DESDEMONA
I say it is not lost.
OTHELLO   Fetch 't, let me see 't.
DESDEMONA
Why, so I can, sir, but I will not now.
This is a trick to put me from my suit.
Pray you, let Cassio be received again.
OTHELLO
Fetch me the handkerchief! My mind misgives.
DESDEMONA Come, come,
You'll never meet a more sufficient man. 93
OTHELLO
The handkerchief!
DESDEMONA   I pray, talk me of Cassio. 94
OTHELLO
The handkerchief!
DESDEMONA   A man that all his time 95
Hath founded his good fortunes on your love,
Shared dangers with you—
OTHELLO The handkerchief!
DESDEMONA I' faith, you are to blame.
OTHELLO Zounds!   *Exit Othello.*
EMILIA Is not this man jealous?
DESDEMONA I ne'er saw this before.
Sure, there's some wonder in this handkerchief.
I am most unhappy in the loss of it.
EMILIA
'Tis not a year or two shows us a man. 105
They are all but stomachs, and we all but food; 106
They eat us hungerly, and when they are full 107
They belch us.
Enter Iago and Cassio.
            Look you, Cassio and my husband.
IAGO [*to Cassio*]
There is no other way; 'tis she must do 't.
And, lo, the happiness! Go and importune her. 110
DESDEMONA
How now, good Cassio? What's the news with you?

---

85 an if if   **93 sufficient** able, complete   **94 talk** talk to   **95 all his time** throughout his career   **105 'Tis . . . man** i.e., you can't really know a man even in a year or two of experience (?), or, real men come along seldom (?)   **106 but** nothing but   **107 hungerly** hungrily   **110 the happiness** in happy time, fortunately met

CASSIO
  Madam, my former suit. I do beseech you
  That by your virtuous means I may again   113
  Exist and be a member of his love
  Whom I, with all the office of my heart,   115
  Entirely honor. I would not be delayed.
  If my offense be of such mortal kind   117
  That nor my service past, nor present sorrows,   118
  Nor purposed merit in futurity
  Can ransom me into his love again,
  But to know so must be my benefit;   121
  So shall I clothe me in a forced content,
  And shut myself up in some other course,   123
  To fortune's alms.
DESDEMONA   Alas, thrice-gentle Cassio,   124
  My advocation is not now in tune.   125
  My lord is not my lord; nor should I know him,
  Were he in favor as in humor altered.   127
  So help me every spirit sanctified
  As I have spoken for you all my best
  And stood within the blank of his displeasure   130
  For my free speech! You must awhile be patient.
  What I can do I will, and more I will
  Than for myself I dare. Let that suffice you.
IAGO
  Is my lord angry?
EMILIA   He went hence but now.
  And certainly in strange unquietness.
IAGO
  Can he be angry? I have seen the cannon
  When it hath blown his ranks into the air,
  And like the devil from his very arm
  Puffed his own brother—and is he angry?
  Something of moment then. I will go meet him.   140
  There's matter in 't indeed, if he be angry.
DESDEMONA
  I prithee, do so.   *Exit* [*Iago*].
            Something, sure of state,   142

113 **virtuous** efficacious   115 **office** loyal service   117 **mortal** fatal   118 **nor . . . nor** neither . . . nor   121 **But . . . benefit** merely to know that my case is hopeless will have to content me (and will be better than uncertainty)   123 **shut . . . in** confine myself to   124 **To fortune's alms** throwing myself on the mercy of fortune   125 **advocation** advocacy   127 **favor** appearance. **humor** mood   130 **within the blank** within point-blank range. (The *blank* is the center of the target.)   140 **of moment** of immediate importance, momentous   142 **of state** concerning state affairs

Either from Venice, or some unhatched practice   143
Made demonstrable here in Cyprus to him,
Hath puddled his clear spirit; and in such cases   145
Men's natures wrangle with inferior things,
Though great ones are their object. 'Tis even so;
For let our finger ache, and it indues   148
Our other, healthful members even to a sense
Of pain. Nay, we must think men are not gods,
Nor of them look for such observancy   151
As fits the bridal. Beshrew me much, Emilia,   152
I was, unhandsome warrior as I am,   153
Arraigning his unkindness with my soul;   154
But now I find I had suborned the witness,   155
And he's indicted falsely.

EMILIA   Pray heaven it be
State matters, as you think, and no conception
Nor no jealous toy concerning you.   158

DESDEMONA
Alas the day! I never gave him cause.

EMILIA
But jealous souls will not be answered so;
They are not ever jealous for the cause,
But jealous for they're jealous. It is a monster   162
Begot upon itself, born on itself.   163

DESDEMONA
Heaven keep that monster from Othello's mind!

EMILIA Lady, amen.

DESDEMONA
I will go seek him. Cassio, walk hereabout.
If I do find him fit, I'll move your suit
And seek to effect it to my uttermost.

CASSIO
I humbly thank your ladyship.

Exit [Desdemona with Emilia].

Enter Bianca.

BIANCA
Save you, friend Cassio!

---

143 **unhatched practice** as yet unexecuted or undiscovered plot   145 **puddled** muddied
148 **indues** brings to the same condition   151 **observancy** attentiveness   152 **bridal**
wedding (when a bridegroom is newly attentive to his bride). **Beshrew me** (A mild oath.)
153 **unhandsome** insufficient, unskillful   154 **with** before the bar of   155 **suborned the**
witness induced the witness to give false testimony   158 **toy** fancy   162 **for** because   163 **Begot upon itself** generated solely from itself

CASSIO   What make you from home?   170
  How is 't with you, my most fair Bianca?
  I' faith, sweet love, I was coming to your house.
BIANCA
  And I was going to your lodging, Cassio.
  What, keep a week away? Seven days and nights?
  Eightscore-eight hours? And lovers' absent hours   175
  More tedious than the dial eightscore times?   176
  O weary reckoning!
CASSIO   Pardon me, Bianca.
  I have this while with leaden thoughts been pressed;
  But I shall, in a more continuate time,   179
  Strike off this score of absence. Sweet Bianca,   180
                [giving her Desdemona's handkerchief]
  Take me this work out.
BIANCA   O Cassio, whence came this?   181
  This is some token from a newer friend.   182
  To the felt absence now I feel a cause.
  Is 't come to this? Well, well.
CASSIO   Go to, woman!
  Throw your vile guesses in the devil's teeth,
  From whence you have them. You are jealous now
  That this is from some mistress, some remembrance.
  No, by my faith, Bianca.
BIANCA   Why, whose is it?
CASSIO
  I know not, neither. I found it in my chamber.
  I like the work well. Ere it be demanded—   190
  As like enough it will—I would have it copied.   191
  Take it and do 't, and leave me for this time.
BIANCA Leave you? Wherefore?
CASSIO
  I do attend here on the General,
  And think it no addition, nor my wish,   195
  To have him see me womaned.
BIANCA Why, I pray you?
CASSIO Not that I love you not.
BIANCA But that you do not love me.
  I pray you, bring me on the way a little,   200
  And say if I shall see you soon at night.

---

170 Save God save. **make** do   **175 Eightscore-eight** one hundred sixty-eight, the number of hours in a week   **176 the dial** a complete revolution of the clock   **179 continuate** uninterrupted   **180 Strike . . . score** settle this account   **181 Take . . . out** copy this embroidery for me   **182 friend** mistress   **190 demanded** inquired for   **191 like** likely   **195 addition** i.e., addition to my reputation   **200 bring** accompany

CASSIO
  'Tis but a little way that I can bring you,
  For I attend here; but I'll see you soon.
BIANCA
  'Tis very good. I must be circumstanced.   204

Exeunt omnes.

4.1

Enter Othello and Iago.

IAGO
  Will you think so?
OTHELLO   Think so, Iago?
IAGO   What,
  To kiss in private?
OTHELLO   An unauthorized kiss!
IAGO
  Or to be naked with her friend in bed
  An hour or more, not meaning any harm?
OTHELLO
  Naked in bed, Iago, and not mean harm?
  It is hypocrisy against the devil.
  They that mean virtuously and yet do so,
  The devil their virtue tempts, and they tempt heaven.
IAGO
  If they do nothing, 'tis a venial slip.   9
  But if I give my wife a handkerchief—
OTHELLO What then?
IAGO
  Why then, 'tis hers, my lord, and being hers,
  She may, I think, bestow 't on any man.
OTHELLO
  She is protectress of her honor too.
  May she give that?
IAGO
  Her honor is an essence that's not seen;
  They have it very oft that have it not.   17
  But, for the handkerchief—
OTHELLO
  By heaven, I would most gladly have forgot it.
  Thou saidst—O, it comes o'er my memory

---

204 **be circumstanced** be governed by circumstance, yield to your conditions
4.1. Location: Before the citadel.
9 **venial** pardonable   17 **They have it** i.e., they enjoy a reputation for it

As doth the raven o'er the infectious house,　　　　　　21
Boding to all—he had my handkerchief.
IAGO
　Ay, what of that?
OTHELLO　　　　　　That's not so good now.
IAGO　　　　　　　　　　　　　　　　　　What
　If I had said I had seen him do you wrong?
　Or heard him say—as knaves by such abroad,　　　　25
　Who having, by their own importunate suit,
　Or voluntary dotage of some mistress,　　　　　　　27
　Convincèd or supplied them, cannot choose　　　　　28
　But they must blab—
OTHELLO　　　　　　Hath he said anything?
IAGO
　He hath, my lord; but, be you well assured,
　No more than he'll unswear.
OTHELLO　　　　　　What hath he said?
IAGO
　Faith, that he did—I know not what he did.
OTHELLO　What? What?
IAGO
　Lie—
OTHELLO　With her?
IAGO　　　　　　With her, on her; what you will.
OTHELLO　Lie with her? Lie on her? We say "lie on her"
　when they belie her. Lie with her? Zounds, that's ful-　　36
　some.—Handkerchief—confessions—handkerchief!　　37
　—To confess and be hanged for his labor—first to be　　38
　hanged and then to confess.—I tremble at it. Nature　　39
　would not invest herself in such shadowing passion　　40
　without some instruction. It is not words that shakes　　41
　me thus. Pish! Noses, ears, and lips.—Is 't pos-
　sible?—Confess—handkerchief!—O devil!
　　　　　　　　　　　　　　　　　Falls in a trance.
IAGO　Work on,
　My medicine, work! Thus credulous fools are caught,
　And many worthy and chaste dames even thus,

---

21 raven . . . house (Allusion to the belief that the raven hovered over a house of sickness or infection, such as one visited by the plague.)　**25 abroad** around about　**27 voluntary dotage** willing infatuation　**28 Convincèd or supplied** seduced or sexually gratified　**36 belie** slander　**36–37 fulsome** foul　**38–39 first . . to confess** (Othello reverses the proverbial *confess and be hanged;* Cassio is to be given no time to confess before he dies.)　**39–41 Nature . . . instruction** i.e., without some foundation in fact, nature would not have dressed herself in such an overwhelming passion that comes over me now and fills my mind with images, or in such a lifelike fantasy as Cassio had in his dream of lying with Desdemona　**41 words** mere words

All guiltless, meet reproach.—What, ho! My lord!
My lord, I say! Othello!

Enter Cassio.

How now,Cassio?

CASSIO What's the matter?

IAGO

My lord is fall'n into an epilepsy.
This is his second fit. He had one yesterday.

CASSIO

Rub him about the temples.

IAGO   No, forbear.
The lethargy must have his quiet course.   53
If not, he foams at mouth, and by and by
Breaks out to savage madness. Look, he stirs.
Do you withdraw yourself a little while.
He will recover straight. When he is gone,
I would on great occasion speak with you.   58

                                        [*Exit Cassio.*]

How is it, General? Have you not hurt your head?

OTHELLO

Dost thou mock me?

IAGO   I mock you not, by heaven.   60
Would you would bear your fortune like a man!

OTHELLO

A hornèd man's a monster and a beast.

IAGO

There's many a beast then in a populous city,
And many a civil monster.   64

OTHELLO Did he confess it?

IAGO Good sir, be a man.
Think every bearded fellow that's but yoked   67
May draw with you. There's millions now alive   68
That nightly lie in those unproper beds   69
Which they dare swear peculiar. Your case is better.   70
O, 'tis the spite of hell, the fiend's arch-mock,
To lip a wanton in a secure couch   72
And to suppose her chaste! No, let me know,
And knowing what I am, I know what she shall be.   74

---

53 lethargy coma. **his** its   **58 on great occasion** on a matter of great importance
60 mock me (Othello takes Iago's question about hurting his head to be a mocking reference to the cuckold's horns)   **64 civil** i.e., dwelling in a city   **67 yoked** (1) married
(2) put into the yoke of infamy and cuckoldry   **68 draw with you** pull as you do, like
oxen who are yoked, i.e., share your fate as cuckold   **69 unproper** not exclusively their
own   **70 peculiar** private, their own. **better** i.e., because you know the truth   **72 lip**
kiss. **secure** free from suspicion   **74 what I am** i.e., a cuckold. **she shall be** will happen
to her

OTHELLO   O, thou art wise. 'Tis certain.
IAGO   Stand you awhile apart;
   Confine yourself but in a patient list.   77
   Whilst you were here o'erwhelmèd with your grief—
   A passion most unsuiting such a man—
   Cassio came hither. I shifted him away,   80
   And laid good 'scuse upon your ecstasy,   81
   Bade him anon return and here speak with me,
   The which he promised. Do but encave yourself   83
   And mark the fleers, the gibes, and notable scorns   84
   That dwell in every region of his face;
   For I will make him tell the tale anew,
   Where, how, how oft, how long ago, and when
   He hath and is again to cope your wife.   88
   I say, but mark his gesture. Marry, patience!
   Or I shall say you're all-in-all in spleen,   90
   And nothing of a man.
OTHELLO   Dost thou hear, Iago?
   I will be found most cunning in my patience;
   But dost thou hear?—most bloody.
IAGO   That's not amiss;
   But yet keep time in all. Will you withdraw?   94

                              [Othello stands apart.]
   Now will I question Cassio of Bianca,
   A huswife that by selling her desires   96
   Buys herself bread and clothes. It is a creature
   That dotes on Cassio—as 'tis the strumpet's plague
   To beguile many and be beguiled by one.
   He, when he hears of her, cannot restrain   100
   From the excess of laughter. Here he comes.

   Enter Cassio.

   As he shall smile, Othello shall go mad;
   And his unbookish jealousy must conster   103
   Poor Cassio's smiles, gestures, and light behaviors
   Quite in the wrong.—How do you now, Lieutenant?
CASSIO
   The worser that you give me the addition   106
   Whose want even kills me.   107

---

77 **in . . . list** within the bounds of patience 80 **shifted him away** used a dodge to get rid of him 81 **ecstasy** trance 83 **encave** conceal 84 **fleers** sneers. **notable** obvious 88 **cope** encounter with, have sex with 90 **all-in-all in spleen** utterly governed by passionate impulses 94 **keep time** keep yourself steady (as in music) 96 **huswife** hussy 100 **restrain** refrain 103 **unbookish** uninstructed. **conster** construe 106 **addition** title 107 **Whose want** the lack of which

IAGO
Ply Desdemona well and you are sure on 't.
[*Speaking lower.*] Now, if this suit lay in Bianca's power,
How quickly should you speed!
CASSIO [*laughing*]   Alas, poor caitiff!   111
OTHELLO [*aside*]   Look how he laughs already!
IAGO
I never knew a woman love man so.
CASSIO
Alas, poor rogue! I think, i' faith, she loves me.
OTHELLO
Now he denies it faintly, and laughs it out.
IAGO
Do you hear, Cassio?
OTHELLO   Now he importunes him
To tell it o'er. Go to! Well said, well said.   117
IAGO
She gives it out that you shall marry her.
Do you intend it?
CASSIO   Ha, ha, ha!
OTHELLO
Do you triumph, Roman? Do you triumph?   121
CASSIO   I marry her? What? A customer? Prithee, bear   122
some charity to my wit; do not think it so unwhole-   123
some. Ha, ha, ha!
OTHELLO   So, so, so, so! They laugh that win.   125
IAGO   Faith, the cry goes that you shall marry her.   126
CASSIO   Prithee, say true.
IAGO   I am a very villain else.   128
OTHELLO   Have you scored me? Well.   129
CASSIO   This is the monkey's own giving out. She is
persuaded I will marry her out of her own love and
flattery, not out of my promise.   132
OTHELLO   Iago beckons me. Now he begins the story.   133
CASSIO   She was here even now; she haunts me in every
place. I was the other day talking on the seabank with   135

---

111 **caitiff** wretch   117 **Go to** (An expression of remonstrance.)   **Well said** well done
121 **Roman** (The Romans were noted for their *triumphs* or triumphal processions.)
122 **customer** i.e., prostitute   122–123 **bear ... wit** be more charitable to my judgment
125 **They ... win** i.e., they that laugh last laugh best   126 **cry** rumor   128 **I ... else**
call me a complete rogue if I'm not telling the truth   129 **scored me** scored off me,
beaten me, made up my reckoning, branded me   132 **flattery** self-flattery, self-deception
133 **beckons** signals   135 **seabank** seashore

certain Venetians, and thither comes the bauble, and,   136
by this hand, she falls thus about my neck—   137

[He embraces Iago.]

OTHELLO   Crying, "O dear Cassio!" as it were; his gesture imports it.

CASSIO   So hangs and lolls and weeps upon me, so shakes
and pulls me. Ha, ha, ha!

OTHELLO   Now he tells how she plucked him to my
chamber. O, I see that nose of yours, but not that dog   143
I shall throw it to.   144

CASSIO   Well, I must leave her company.

IAGO   Before me, look where she comes.   146

Enter Bianca [with Othello's handkerchief].

CASSIO   'Tis such another fitchew! Marry, a perfumed   147
one. What do you mean by this haunting of me?

BIANCA   Let the devil and his dam haunt you! What did   148
you mean by that same handkerchief you gave me
even now? I was a fine fool to take it. I must take out
the work? A likely piece of work, that you should find   152
it in your chamber and know not who left it there!
This is some minx's token, and I must take out the
work? There; give it your hobbyhorse. *[She gives him*   155
the handkerchief.] Wheresoever you had it, I'll take out
no work on't.

CASSIO   How now, my sweet Bianca? How now? How
now?

OTHELLO   By heaven, that should be my handkerchief!   159

BIANCA   If you'll come to supper tonight, you may; if
you will not, come when you are next prepared for.   161

Exit.

IAGO   After her, after her.

CASSIO   Faith, I must. She'll rail in the streets else.

IAGO   Will you sup there?

CASSIO   Faith, I intend so.

IAGO   Well, I may chance to see you, for I would very
fain speak with you.

CASSIO   Prithee, come. Will you?

IAGO   Go to. Say no more.   *[Exit Cassio.]* 169

---

136 **bauble** plaything   137 **by this hand** I make my vow   143–144 **not . . . to** (Othello
imagines himself cutting off Cassio's nose and throwing it to a dog.)   146 **Before me**
i.e., on my soul   147 **'Tis . . . fitchew** what a polecat she is! Just like all the others.
fitchew (Polecats were often compared with prostitutes because of their rank smell and
presumed lechery.)   149 **dam** mother   152 **A likely . . . work** a fine story   155 **hobbyhorse** harlot   159 **should be** must be   161 **when . . . for** when I'm ready for you (i.e.,
never)   169 **Go to** (An expression of remonstrance.)

OTHELLO [*advancing*]   How shall I murder him, Iago?

IAGO   Did you perceive how he laughed at his vice?

OTHELLO   O, Iago!

IAGO   And did you see the handkerchief?

OTHELLO   Was that mine?

IAGO   Yours, by this hand. And to see how he prizes
the foolish woman your wife! She gave it him, and he
hath given it his whore.

OTHELLO   I would have him nine years a-killing. A fine
woman! A fair woman! A sweet woman!

IAGO   Nay, you must forget that.

OTHELLO   Ay, let her rot and perish, and be damned
tonight, for she shall not live. No, my heart is turned
to stone; I strike it, and it hurts my hand. O, the world
hath not a sweeter creature! She might lie by an emperor's side and command him tasks.

IAGO   Nay, that's not your way.   186

OTHELLO   Hang her! I do but say what she is. So delicate
with her needle! An admirable musician! O, she will
sing the savageness out of a bear. Of so high and plen-
teous wit and invention!   190

IAGO   She's the worse for all this.

OTHELLO   O, a thousand, a thousand times! And then,
of so gentle a condition!   193
                                                                    194
IAGO   Ay, too gentle.

OTHELLO   Nay, that's certain. But yet the pity of it, Iago!
O, Iago, the pity of it, Iago!

IAGO   If you are so fond over her iniquity, give her patent   197
to offend, for if it touch not you it comes near nobody.

OTHELLO   I will chop her into messes. Cuckold me?   199

IAGO   O, 'tis foul in her.

OTHELLO   With mine officer?

IAGO   That's fouler.

OTHELLO   Get me some poison, Iago, this night. I'll not
expostulate with her, lest her body and beauty unpro-   204
vide my mind again. This night, Iago.   205

IAGO   Do it not with poison. Strangle her in her bed,
even the bed she hath contaminated.

OTHELLO   Good, good! The justice of it pleases. Very good.

IAGO   And for Cassio, let me be his undertaker. You   209
shall hear more by midnight.

---

186 your way i.e. the way you should think of her   **190 invention** imagination   **193
gentle a condition** wellborn and well-bred   **194 gentle** generous, yielding (to other men)
197 fond foolish. **patent** license   **199 messes** portions of meat, i.e., bits   **204–205 un-
provide** weaken, render unfit   **209 be his undertaker** undertake to dispatch him

OTHELLO

Excellent good. [*A trumpet within.*] What trumpet is that same?

IAGO   I warrant, something from Venice.

Enter Lodovico, Desdemona, and attendants.

'Tis Lodovico. This comes from the Duke.

See, your wife's with him.

LODOVICO

God save you, worthy General!

OTHELLO   With all my heart, sir.   215

LODOVICO [*giving him a letter*]

The duke and the senators of Venice greet you.

OTHELLO

I kiss the instrument of their pleasures.

                              [*He opens the letter, and reads.*]

DESDEMONA

And what's the news, good cousin Lodovico?

IAGO

I am very glad to see you, signor.

Welcome to Cyprus.

LODOVICO

I thank you. How does Lieutenant Cassio?

IAGO   Lives sir.

DESDEMONA

Cousin, there's fall'n between him and my lord

An unkind breach; but you shall make all well.   224

OTHELLO   Are you sure of that?

DESDEMONA   My lord?

OTHELLO [*reads*]   "This fail you not to do, as you will—"

LODOVICO

He did not call; he's busy in the paper.

Is there division twixt my lord and Cassio?

DESDEMONA

A most unhappy one. I would do much

T' atone them, for the love I bear to Cassio.   231

OTHELLO   Fire and brimstone!

DESDEMONA   My lord?

OTHELLO   Are you wise?

DESDEMONA

What, is he angry?

LODOVICO   Maybe the letter moved him;

For, as I think, they do command him home,

Deputing Cassio in his government.   237

---

215 With all my heart i.e., I thank you most heartily   **224 unkind** unnatural, contrary
to their natures; hurtful   **231 atone** reconcile   **237 government** office

DESDEMONA By my troth, I am glad on 't.   238
OTHELLO Indeed?
DESDEMONA My lord?
OTHELLO I am glad to see you mad.   241
DESDEMONA Why, sweet Othello—
OTHELLO [*striking her*] Devil!
DESDEMONA I have not deserved this.
LODOVICO
  My lord, this would not be believed in Venice,
  Though I should swear I saw 't. 'Tis very much.   246
  Make her amends; she weeps.
OTHELLO   O devil, devil!
  If that the earth could teem with woman's tears,   248
  Each drop she falls would prove a crocodile.   249
  Out of my sight!
DESDEMONA   I will not stay to offend you.   [*Going.*]
LODOVICO Truly, an obedient lady.
  I do beseech your lordship, call her back.
OTHELLO Mistress!
DESDEMONA [*returning*] My lord?
OTHELLO What would you with her, sir?   255
LODOVICO Who, I, my lord?
OTHELLO
  Ay, you did wish that I would make her turn.
  Sir, she can turn, and turn, and yet go on
  And turn again; and she can weep, sir, weep;
  And she's obedient, as you say, obedient,   260
  Very obedient.—Proceed you in your tears.—
  Concerning this, sir—O well-painted passion!—   262
  I am commanded home.—Get you away;
  I'll send for you anon.—Sir, I obey the mandate
  And will return to Venice.—Hence, avaunt!
                                      [*Exit Desdemona.*]
  Cassio shall have my place. And, sir, tonight
  I do entreat that we may sup together.
  You are welcome, sir, to Cyprus.—Goats and monkeys!
                                      Exit.   268
LODOVICO
  Is this the noble Moor whom our full Senate

238 on 't of it 241 I am . . . mad i.e., I am glad to see that you are insane enough to rejoice in Cassio's promotion (? Othello bitterly plays on Desdemona's *I am glad.*) 246 very much too much, outrageous 248 teem breed, be impregnated 249 falls lets fall. crocodile (Crocodiles were supposed to weep hypocritical tears for their victims.) 255 What . . . sir (Othello implies that Desdemona is pliant and will do a *turn*, lines 257–259, for any man.) 260 obedient (With much the same sexual connotation as *turn* in lines 257–59.) 262 passion i.e., grief 268 Goats and monkeys (See 3.3.419.)

Call all in all sufficient? Is this the nature
Whom passion could not shake? Whose solid virtue
The shot of accident nor dart of chance
Could neither graze nor pierce?

IAGO   He is much changed.

LODOVICO
Are his wits safe? Is he not light of brain?

IAGO
He's that he is. I may not breathe my censure   275
What he might be. If what he might he is not,   276
I would to heaven he were!

LODOVICO   What, strike his wife?   277

IAGO
Faith, that was not so well; yet would I knew
That stroke would prove the worst!

LODOVICO   Is it his use?   279
Or did the letters work upon his blood   280
And new-create his fault?

IAGO   Alas, alas!
It is not honesty in me to speak
What I have seen and known. You shall observe him,
And his own courses will denote him so   284
That I may save my speech. Do but go after,
And mark how he continues.

LODOVICO
I am sorry that I am deceived in him.   *Exeunt.*

4.2

Enter Othello and Emilia.

OTHELLO   You have seen nothing then?

EMILIA
Nor ever heard, nor ever did suspect.

OTHELLO
Yes, you have seen Cassio and she together.

EMILIA
But then I saw no harm, and then I heard
Each syllable that breath made up between them.

OTHELLO   What, did they never whisper?

EMILIA   Never, my lord.

OTHELLO   Nor send you out o' the way?

275–277 **I may . . . were** i.e., I dare not venture an opinion as to whether he's of unsound mind, as you suggest, but, if he isn't, then it might be better to wish he were in fact insane, since only that could excuse his wild behavior   279 **use** custom   280 **blood** passions   284 **courses will denote** actions will reveal
4.2. Location: The citadel.

EMILIA   Never.

OTHELLO

To fetch her fan, her gloves, her mask, nor nothing?

EMILIA   Never, my lord.

OTHELLO   That's strange.

EMILIA

I durst, my lord, to wager she is honest,

Lay down my soul at stake. If you think other,   14

Remove your thought; it doth abuse your bosom.   15

If any wretch have put this in your head,

Let heaven requite it with the serpent's curse!   17

For if she be not honest, chaste, and true,

There's no man happy; the purest of their wives

Is foul as slander.

OTHELLO   Bid her come hither. Go.

Exit Emilia.

She says enough; yet she's a simple bawd   21

That cannot say as much. This is a subtle whore,   22

A closet lock and key of villainous secrets.   23

And yet she'll kneel and pray; I have seen her do't.

Enter Desdemona and Emilia.

DESDEMONA   My lord, what is your will?

OTHELLO   Pray you, chuck, come hither.

DESDEMONA

What is your pleasure?

OTHELLO   Let me see your eyes.

Look in my face.

DESDEMONA   What horrible fancy's this?

OTHELLO [*to Emilia*]   Some of your function, mistress   29

Leave procreants alone and shut the door;   30

Cough or cry "hem" if anybody come.

Your mystery, your mystery! Nay, dispatch.   32

Exit Emilia.

DESDEMONA [*kneeling*]

Upon my knees, what doth your speech import?

I understand a fury in your words,

But not the words.

---

14 **at stake** as the wager   15 **abuse your bosom** deceive you   17 **the serpent's curse** the curse pronounced by God on the serpent for deceiving Eve, just as some man has done to Othello and Desdemona. (See Genesis 3:14.)   21–22 **she's . . . much** i.e., any procuress or go-between who couldn't make up as plausible a story as Emilia's would have to be pretty stupid   22 **This** i.e., Desdemona   23 **closet lock and key** i.e, concealer   29 **Some . . . function** i.e., practice your chosen profession, that of bawd (by guarding the door)   30 **procreants** mating couples   32 **mystery** trade, occupation

OTHELLO
Why, what art thou?
DESDEMONA   Your wife, my lord, your true
And loyal wife.
OTHELLO   Come, swear it, damn thyself,
Lest, being like one of heaven, the devils themselves   38
Should fear to seize thee. Therefore be double damned:
Swear thou art honest.
DESDEMONA   Heaven doth truly know it.
OTHELLO
Heaven truly knows that thou art false as hell.
DESDEMONA
To whom, my lord? With whom? How am I false?
OTHELLO [*weeping*]
Ah, Desdemon! Away, away, away!
DESDEMONA
Alas the heavy day! Why do you weep?
Am I the motive of these tears, my lord?   45
If haply you my father do suspect
An instrument of this your calling back,
Lay not your blame on me. If you have lost him,
I have lost him too.
OTHELLO   Had it pleased heaven
To try me with affliction, had they rained   50
All kinds of sores and shames on my bare head,
Steeped me in poverty to the very lips,
Given to captivity me and my utmost hopes,
I should have found in some place of my soul
A drop of patience. But, alas, to make me
A fixèd figure for the time of scorn   56
To point his slow and moving finger at!   57
Yet could I bear that too, well, very well.
But there where I have garnered up my heart,   59
Where either I must live or bear no life,
The fountain from the which my current runs   61
Or else dries up to be discarded thence!
Or keep it as a cistern for foul toads   63
To knot and gender in! Turn thy complexion there,   64

---

38 **being . . . heaven** looking like an angel   45 **motive** cause   50 **they** i.e., heavenly
powers   56 **time of scorn** i.e., scornful world   57 **his** its. **slow and moving finger** i.e.,
hour hand of the clock, moving so slowly it seems hardly to move at all. (Othello envis-
ages himself as being eternally pointed at by the scornful world as the numbers on a
clock are pointed at by the hour hand.)   59 **garnered** stored   61 **fountain** spring   63
cistern cesspool   64 **knot** couple. **gender** engender. **Turn . . . there** change your color,
grow pale, at such a sight

Patience, thou young and rose-lipped cherubin— 65
Ay, there look grim as hell! 66

DESDEMONA
I hope my noble lord esteems me honest. 67

OTHELLO
O, ay, as summer flies are in the shambles, 68
That quicken even with blowing. O thou weed, 69
Who art so lovely fair and smell'st so sweet
That the sense aches at thee, would thou hadst ne'er been born!

DESDEMONA
Alas, what ignorant sin have I committed? 72

OTHELLO
Was this fair paper, this most goodly book,
Made to write "whore" upon? What committed?
Committed? O thou public commoner! 75
I should make very forges of my cheeks,
That would to cinders burn up modesty,
Did I but speak thy deeds. What committed?
Heaven stops the nose at it and the moon winks; 79
The bawdy wind, that kisses all it meets, 80
Is hushed within the hollow mine of earth 81
And will not hear 't. What committed?
Impudent strumpet!

DESDEMONA   By heaven, you do me wrong.

OTHELLO
Are not you a strumpet?

DESDEMONA   No, as I am a Christian.
If to preserve this vessel for my lord 86
From any other foul unlawful touch
Be not to be a strumpet, I am none.

OTHELLO   What, not a whore?

DESDEMONA   No, as I shall be saved.

OTHELLO   Is 't possible?

DESDEMONA
O, heaven forgive us!

OTHELLO   I cry you mercy, then. 92
I took you for that cunning whore of Venice
That married with Othello. [*Calling out.*] You, mistress,

65–66 **Patience . . . hell** (Even Patience, that rose-lipped cherub, will look grim and pale at this spectacle.)   67 **honest** chaste   68 **shambles** slaughterhouse   69 **quicken** come to life. **with blowing** i.e., with the puffing up of something rotten in which maggots are breeding   72 **ignorant sin** sin in ignorance   75 **commoner** prostitute   79 **winks** closes her eyes. (The moon symbolizes chastity.)   80 **bawdy** kissing one and all   81 **mine** cave (where the winds were thought to dwell)   86 **vessel** body   92 **cry you mercy** beg your pardon

That have the office opposite to Saint Peter
And keep the gate of hell!
Enter Emilia.

                        You, you, ay, you!
We have done our course. There's money for your pains.
                        [*He gives money.*]   97
I pray you, turn the key and keep our counsel. *Exit.*
EMILIA
Alas, what does this gentleman conceive?   99
How do you, madam? How do you, my good lady?
DESDEMONA   Faith, half asleep.   101
EMILIA
Good madam, what's the matter with my lord?
DESDEMONA   With who?
EMILIA   Why, with my lord, madam.
DESDEMONA
Who is thy lord?
EMILIA   He that is yours, sweet lady.
DESDEMONA
I have none. Do not talk to me, Emilia.
I cannot weep, nor answers have I none
But what should go by water. Prithee, tonight   108
Lay on my bed my wedding sheets, remember;
And call thy husband hither.
EMILIA   Here's a change indeed!   *Exit.*
DESDEMONA
'Tis meet I should be used so, very meet.   112
How have I been behaved, that he might stick   113
The small'st opinion on my least misuse?   114
Enter Iago and Emilia.

IAGO
What is your pleasure, madam? How is 't with you?
DESDEMONA
I cannot tell. Those that do teach young babes
Do it with gentle means and easy tasks.
He might have chid me so, for, in good faith,
I am a child to chiding.
IAGO   What is the matter, lady?
EMILIA
Alas, Iago, my lord hath so bewhored her,

97 **course** business (with an indecent suggestion of "trick," turn at sex)   99 **conceive** suppose, think   101 **half asleep** i.e., dazed   108 **go by water** be expressed by tears   112 **meet** fitting   113 **stick** attach   114 **opinion** censure. **least misuse** slightest misconduct

Thrown such despite and heavy terms upon her,
That true hearts cannot bear it.
DESDEMONA   Am I that name, Iago?
IAGO   What name, fair lady?
DESDEMONA
Such as she said my lord did say I was.
EMILIA
He called her whore. A begger in his drink
Could not have laid such terms upon his callet.   128
IAGO   Why did he so?
DESDEMONA [weeping]
I do not know. I am sure I am none such.
IAGO   Do not weep, do not weep. Alas the day!
EMILIA
Hath she forsook so many noble matches,
Her father and her country and her friends,
To be called whore? Would it not make one weep?
DESDEMONA
It is my wretched fortune.
IAGO   Beshrew him for 't!   135
How comes this trick upon him?
DESDEMONA   Nay, heaven doth know.   136
EMILIA
I will be hanged if some eternal villain,   137
Some busy and insinuating rogue,   138
Some cogging, cozening slave, to get some office,   139
Have not devised this slander. I will be hanged else.
IAGO
Fie, there is no such man. It is impossible.
DESDEMONA
If any such there be, heaven pardon him!
EMILIA
A halter pardon him! And hell gnaw his bones!   143
Why should he call her whore? Who keeps her company?
What place? What time? What form? What likelihood?   145
The Moor's abused by some most villainous knave,
Some base notorious knave, some scurvy fellow.
O heaven, that such companions thou'dst unfold,   148
And put in every honest hand a whip
To lash the rascals naked through the world
Even from the east to th' west!
IAGO   Speak within door.   151

128 **callet** whore   135 **Beshrew** curse   136 **trick** strange behavior, delusion   137 **eternal** inveterate   138 **insinuating** ingratiating, fawning, wheedling   139 **cogging** cheating. **cozening** defrauding   143 **halter** hangman's noose   145 **form** appearance, circumstance   148 **that** would that. **companions** fellows. **unfold** expose   151 **within door** i.e., not so loud

EMILIA

O, fie upon them! Some such squire he was   152
That turned your wit the seamy side without   153
And made you to suspect me with the Moor.

IAGO

You are a fool. Go to.

DESDEMONA   Alas, Iago,   155
What shall I do to win my lord again?
Good friend, go to him; for, by this light of heaven,
I know not how I lost him. Here I kneel. [*She kneels.*]
If e'er my will did trespass 'gainst his love,
Either in discourse of thought or actual deed,   160
Or that mine eyes, mine ears, or any sense   161
Delighted them in any other form;   162
Or that I do not yet, and ever did,   163
And ever will—though he do shake me off
To beggarly divorcement love him dearly,
Comfort forswear me! Unkindness may do much,   166
And his unkindness may defeat my life,   167
But never taint my love. I cannot say "whore."
It does abhor me now I speak the word;   169
To do the act that might the addition earn   170
Not the world's mass of vanity could make me.   171

                                        [*She rises.*]

IAGO

I pray you, be content. 'Tis but his humor.   172
The business of the state does him offense,
And he does chide with you.

DESDEMONA   If 'twere no other—

IAGO   It is but so, I warrant.   [*Trumpets within.*]
Hark, how these instruments summon you to supper!
The messengers of Venice stays the meat.   178
Go in, and weep not. All things shall be well.
                    Exeunt Desdemona and Emilia.

Enter Roderigo

How now, Roderigo?

RODERIGO   I do not find that thou deal'st justly with me.

IAGO   What in the contrary?

---

152 **squire** fellow   153 **seamy side without** wrong side out   155 **Go to** i.e., that's
enough   160 **discourse of thought** process of thinking   161 **that** if. (Also in line 163.)
162 **Delighted them** took delight   163 **yet** still   166 **Comfort forswear** may heavenly
comfort forsake   167 **defeat** destroy   169 **abhor** (1) fill me with abhorrence (2) make
me whorelike   170 **addition** title   171 **vanity** showy splendor   172 **humor** mood
178 **stays the meat** are waiting to dine

RODERIGO   Every day thou daff'st me with some de- 183
vice, Iago, and rather, as it seems to me now, keep'st 184
from me all conveniency than suppliest me with the 185
least advantage of hope. I will indeed no longer 186
endure it, nor am I yet persuaded to put up in peace 187
what already I have foolishly suffered.

IAGO   Will you hear me, Roderigo?

RODERIGO   Faith, I have heard too much, for your words
and performances are no kin together.

IAGO   You charge me most unjustly.

RODERIGO   With naught but truth. I have wasted myself
out of my means. The jewels you have had from me to
deliver Desdemona would half have corrupted a vo- 195
tarist. You have told me she hath received them and 196
returned me expectations and comforts of sudden re- 197
spect and acquaintance, but I find none. 198

IAGO   Well, go to, very well.

RODERIGO   "Very well"! "Go to"! I cannot go to, man, 200
nor 'tis not very well. By this hand, I think it is scurvy,
and begin to find myself fopped in it. 202

IAGO   Very well.

RODERIGO   I tell you 'tis not very well. I will make myself 204
known to Desdemona. If she will return me my jewels,
I will give over my suit and repent my unlawful solic-
itation; if not, assure yourself I will seek satisfaction 207
of you.

IAGO   You have said now? 209

RODERIGO   Ay, and said nothing but what I protest
intendment of doing. 211

IAGO   Why, now I see there's mettle in thee, and even
from this instant do build on thee a better opinion
than ever before. Give me thy hand, Roderigo. Thou
hast taken against me a most just exception; but yet I
protest I have dealt most directly in thy affair.

RODERIGO   It hath not appeared.

IAGO   I grant indeed it hath not appeared, and your
suspicion is not without wit and judgment. But,

183 thou daff'st me you put me off   183–184 device excuse, trick   185 conveniency advantage, opportunity   186 advantage increase   187 put up submit to, tolerate
195 deliver deliver to   195–196 votarist nun   197–198 sudden respect immediate consideration   200 I cannot go to (Roderigo changes Iago's go to, an expression urging patience, to I cannot go to, "I have no opportunity for success in wooing.")
202 fopped fooled, duped   204 not very well (Roderigo changes Iago's very well, "all right then," to not very well, "not at all good.")   207 satisfaction repayment. (The term normally means settling of accounts in a duel)   209 You . . . now have you finished?
211 intendment intention

Roderigo, if thou hast that in thee indeed which I have
greater reason to believe now than ever—I mean
purpose, courage, and valor—this night show it. If
thou the next night following enjoy not Desdemona,
take me from this world with treachery and devise
engines for my life.   225

RODERIGO Well, what is it? Is it within reason and
compass?

IAGO Sir, there is especial commission come from Venice to
depute Cassio in Othello's place.

RODERIGO Is that true? Why, then Othello and Desdemona return again to Venice.

IAGO O, no; he goes into Mauritania and takes away
with him the fair Desdemona, unless his abode be
lingered here by some accident; wherein none can be
so determinate as the removing of Cassio.   235

RODERIGO How do you mean, removing of him?

IAGO Why, by making him uncapable of Othello's
place—knocking out his brains.

RODERIGO And that you would have me to do?

IAGO Ay, if you dare do yourself a profit and a right.
He sups tonight with a harlotry, and thither will I go to   241
him. He knows not yet of his honorable fortune. If
you will watch his going thence, which I will fashion
to fall out between twelve and one, you may take him   244
at your pleasure. I will be near to second your attempt,
and he shall fall between us. Come, stand not amazed
at it, but go along with me. I will show you such a
necessity in his death that you shall think yourself
bound to put it on him. It is now high suppertime,   249
and the night grows to waste. About it.   250

RODERIGO I will hear further reason for this.

IAGO And you shall be satisfied.   *Exeunt.*

4.3

Enter Othello, Lodovico, Desdemona, Emilia, and attendants.

LODOVICO
I do beseech you, sir, trouble yourself no further.

OTHELLO
O, pardon me; 'twill do me good to walk.

LODOVICO
Madam, good night. I humbly thank your ladyship.

---

225 **engines for** plots against   235 **determinate** conclusive   241 **harlotry** slut   244 **fall
out** occur   249 **high** fully   250 **grows to waste** wastes away
4.3. Location: The citadel.

DESDEMONA

Your honor is most welcome.

OTHELLO   Will you walk, sir?

O, Desdemona!

DESDEMONA   My lord?

OTHELLO   Get you to bed on th' instant. I will be returned forthwith. Dismiss your attendant there. Look
't be done.

DESDEMONA   I will my lord.

Exit [*Othello, with Lodovico and attendants*].

EMILIA   How goes it now? He looks gentler than he did.

DESDEMONA

He says he will return incontinent,   12

And hath commanded me to go to bed,

And bid me to dismiss you.

EMILIA   Dismiss me?

DESDEMONA

It was his bidding. Therefore, good Emilia,

Give me my nightly wearing, and adieu.

We must not now displease him.

EMILIA   I would you had never seen him!

DESDEMONA

So would not I. My love doth so approve him

That even his stubbornness, his checks, his frowns—   21

Prithee, unpin me—have grace and favor in them.

[*Emilia prepares Desdemona for bed.*]

EMILIA   I have laid those sheets you bade me on the
bed.

DESDEMONA

All's one. Good faith, how foolish are our minds!   25

If I do die before thee, prithee shroud me

In one of these same sheets.

EMILIA   Come, come, you talk.   27

DESDEMONA

My mother had a maid called Barbary.

She was in love, and he she loved proved mad   29

And did forsake her. She had a song of "Willow."

An old thing 'twas, but it expressed her fortune,

And she died singing it. That song tonight

Will not go from my mind; I have much to do   33

But to go hang my head all at one side   34

And sing it like poor Barbary. Prithee, dispatch.

12 incontinent immediately   **21 stubbornness** roughness. **checks** rebukes   **25 All's one**
all right. It doesn't really matter   **27 talk** i.e., prattle   **29 mad** wild, i.e., faithless   **33–
34 I . . . hang** I can scarcely keep myself from hanging

EMILIA   Shall I go fetch your nightgown?   36
DESDEMONA   No, unpin me here.
   This Lodovico is a proper man.   38
EMILIA   A very handsome man.
DESDEMONA   He speaks well.
EMILIA   I know a lady in Venice would have walked
   barefoot to Palestine for a touch of his nether lip.
DESDEMONA [*singing*]
   "The poor soul sat sighing by a sycamore tree,
   Sing all a green willow;   44
   Her hand on her bosom, her head on her knee,
   Sing willow, willow, willow.
   The fresh streams ran by her and murmured her moans;
   Sing willow, willow, willow;
   Her salt tears fell from her, and softened the stones —"
   Lay by these.
   [*Singing*.] "Sing willow, willow, willow —"
   Prithee, hie thee. He'll come anon.   52
   [*Singing*.] "Sing all a green willow must be my garland.
   Let nobody blame him; his scorn I approve —"
   Nay, that's not next. — Hark! Who is 't that knocks?
EMILIA   It's the wind.
DESDEMONA [*singing*]
   "I called my love false love; but what said he then?
   Sing willow, willow, willow;
   If I court more women, you'll couch with more men."
   So, get thee gone. Good night. Mine eyes do itch;
   Doth that bode weeping?
EMILIA   'Tis neither here not there.
DESDEMONA
   I have heard it said so. O, these men, these men!
   Dost thou in conscience think — tell me, Emilia —
   That there be women do abuse their husbands   64
   In such gross kind?
EMILIA   There be some such, no question.
DESDEMONA
   Wouldst thou do such a deed for all the world?
EMILIA
   Why, would not you?
DESDEMONA   No, by this heavenly light!
EMILIA
   Nor I neither by this heavenly light;
   I might do 't as well i' the dark.

---

36 nightgown dressing gown   **38 proper** handsome   **44 willow** (A conventional emblem of disappointed love.)   **52 hie thee** hurry. **anon** right away   **64 abuse** deceive

DESDEMONA
Wouldst thou do such a deed for all the world?

EMILIA
The world's a huge thing. It is a great price
For a small vice.

DESDEMONA
Good troth, I think thou wouldst not.

EMILIA   By my troth, I think I should, and undo 't when
I had done. Marry, I would not do such a thing for a
joint ring, nor for measures of lawn, nor for gowns,   76
petticoats, nor caps, nor any petty exhibition. But for   77
all the whole world! Uds pity, who would not make   78
her husband a cuckold to make him a monarch? I
should venture purgatory for 't.

DESDEMONA
Beshrew me if I would do such a wrong
For the whole world.

EMILIA   Why, the wrong is but a wrong i' the world, and
having the world for your labor, 'tis a wrong in your
own world, and you might quickly make it right.

DESDEMONA
I do not think there is any such woman.

EMILIA   Yes, a dozen, and as many
To th' vantage as would store the world they played for.   88
But I do think it is their husbands' faults
If wives do fall. Say that they slack their duties   90
And pour our treasures into foreign laps,   91
Or else break out in peevish jealousies,
Throwing restraint upon us? Or say they strike us,   93
Or scant our former having in despite?   94
Why, we have galls, had though we have some grace,   95
Yet have we some revenge. Let husbands know
Their wives have sense like them. They see, and smell,   97
And have their palates both for sweet and sour,
As husbands have. What is it that they do
When they change us for others? Is it sport?   100
I think it is. And doth affection breed it?   101
I think it doth. Is 't frailty that thus errs?
It is so, too. And have not we affections,

---

76 **joint ring** a ring made in separate halves. **lawn** fine linen   77 **exhibition** gift
78 **Uds** God's   88 **To th' vantage** in addition, to boot. **store** populate. **played** (1) gam-
bled (2) sport sexually   90 **duties** marital duties   91 **pour . . . laps** i.e., are unfaithful,
give what is rightfully ours (semen) to other women   93 **Throwing . . . us** i.e, jealously
restricting our freedom to see other men   94 **scant . . . despite** reduce our allowance to
spite us   95 **have galls** i.e, are capable of resenting injury and insult   97 **sense** physical
sense   100 **sport** sexual pastime   101 **affection** passion

Desires for sport, and frailty, as men have?
Then let them sue us well; else let them know,
The ills we do, their ills instruct us so.

DESDEMONA
Good night, good night. God me such uses send   107
Not to pick bad from bad, but by bad mend!   108

                                                    Exeunt.

5.1

Enter Iago and Roderigo.

IAGO
Here stand behind this bulk. Straight will he come.   1
Wear thy good rapier bare, and put it home.   2
Quick, quick! Fear nothing. I'll be at thy elbow.
It makes us or it mars us. Think on that,
And fix most firm thy resolution.

RODERIGO
Be near at hand. I may miscarry in 't.

IAGO
Here, at thy hand. Be bold, and take thy stand.
          [*Iago stands aside. Roderigo conceals himself.*]

RODERIGO
I have no great devotion to the deed;
And yet he hath given me satisfying reasons.
'Tis but a man gone. Forth, my sword! He dies.

                                          [*He draws.*]

IAGO
I have rubbed this young quat almost to the sense,   11
And he grows angry. Now, whether he kill Cassio
Or Cassio him, or each do kill the other,
Every way makes my gain. Live Roderigo,   14
He calls me to a restitution large
Of gold and jewels that I bobbed from him   16
As gifts to Desdemona.
It must not be. If Cassio do remain,
He hath a daily beauty in his life
That makes me ugly; and besides, the Moor
May unfold me to him; there stand I in much peril.   21
No, he must die. Be 't so. I hear him coming.

107 uses habit, practice   108 Not .. . mend i.e, not to learn bad conduct from others'
badness (as Emilia has suggested women learn from men), but to mend my ways by perceiving what badness is, making spiritual benefit out of evil and adversity
5.1. Location: A street in Cyprus.
1 bulk framework projecting from the front of a shop   2 bare unsheathed   11 quat
pimple, pustule. to the sense to the quick   14 Live Roderigo if Roderigo lives
16 bobbed swindled   21 unfold expose

Enter Cassio.

RODERIGO [*coming forth*]
  I know his gait, 'tis he.—Villain, thou diest!
                                    [*He attacks Cassio.*]

CASSIO
  That thrust had been mine enemy indeed,
  But that my coat is better than thou know'st.   25
  I will make proof of thine.
                        [*He draws, and wounds Roderigo.*]
RODERIGO   O, I am slain!   [*He falls.*]   26
        [*Iago, from behind, wounds Cassio in the leg, and exit.*]
CASSIO
  I am maimed forever. Help, ho! Murder! Murder!

Enter Othello.

OTHELLO
  The voice of Cassio! Iago keeps his word.
RODERIGO O, villain that I am!
OTHELLO It is even so.
CASSIO O, help, ho! Light! A surgeon!
OTHELLO
  'Tis he. O brave Iago, honest and just,
  That hast such noble sense of thy friend's wrong!
  Thou teachest me. Minion, your dear lies dead,   34
  And your unblest fate hies. Strumpet, I come.   35
  Forth of my heart those charms, thine eyes, are blotted;   36
  Thy bed, lust-stained, shall with lust's blood be spotted.
                                          Exit Othello.

Enter Lodovico and Gratiano.

CASSIO
  What ho! No watch? No passage? Murder! Murder!   38
GRATIANO
  'Tis some mischance. The voice is very direful.
CASSIO O, help!
LODOVICO Hark!
RODERIGO O wretched villain!
LODOVICO
  Two or three groan. 'Tis heavy night;   43
  These may be counterfeits. Let's think 't unsafe
  To come in to the cry without more help.   45
                        [*They remain near the entrance.*]

---

25 coat (Possibly a garment of mail under the outer clothing, or simply a tougher coat
than Roderigo expected.)   **26 proof** a test   **34 Minion** hussy (i.e., Desdemona)   **35 hies**
hastens on   **36 Forth of** from out   **38 passage** people passing by   **43 heavy** thick, dark
45 come in to approach

RODERIGO

Nobody come? Then shall I bleed to death.

Enter Iago [in his shirtsleeves, with a light].

LODOVICO Hark!

GRATIANO

Here's one comes in his shirt, with light and weapons.

IAGO

Who's there? Whose noise is this that cries on murder?   49

LODOVICO

We do not know.

IAGO   Did not you hear a cry?

CASSIO

Here, here! for heaven's sake, help me!

IAGO   What's the matter?

[*He moves toward Cassio.*]

GRATIANO [*to Lodovico*]

This is Othello's ancient, as I take it.

LODOVICO [*to Gratiano*]

The same indeed, a very valiant fellow.

IAGO [*to Cassio*]

What are you here that cry so grievously?   54

CASSIO

Iago? O, I am spoiled, undone by villains!   55

Give me some help.

IAGO

O me, Lieutenant! What villains have done this?

CASSIO

I think that one of them is hereabout,

And cannot make away.

IAGO   O treacherous villains!   59

[*To Lodovico and Gratiano.*] What are you there? Come

in, and give me some help.   [*They advance.*]

RODERIGO O, help me there!

CASSIO

That's one of them.

IAGO   O murderous slave! O villain!

[*He stabs Roderigo.*]

RODERIGO

O damned Iago! O inhuman dog!

IAGO

Kill men i' the dark?—Where be these bloody thieves?—

How silent is this town!—Ho! Murder, murder!—

[*To Lodovico and Gratiano.*] What may you be? Are you of good

or evil?

---

49 cries on cries out   **54 What** who (also at lines 60 and 66)   **55 spoiled** ruined, done
for   **59 make** get

LODOVICO   As you shall prove us, praise us.   67
IAGO   Signor Lodovico?
LODOVICO   He, sir.
IAGO
I cry you mercy. Here's Cassio hurt by villains.   70
GRATIANO   Cassio?
IAGO   How is 't, brother?
CASSIO   My leg is cut in two.
IAGO   Marry, heaven forbid!
Light, gentlemen! I'll bind it with my shirt.
[*He hands them the light, and tends to Cassio's wound.*]

Enter Bianca.

BIANCA
What is the matter, ho? Who is 't that cried?
IAGO   Who is 't that cried?
BIANCA   O my dear Cassio!
My sweet Cassio! O Cassio, Cassio, Cassio!
IAGO
O notable strumpet! Cassio, may you suspect
Who they should be that have thus mangled you?
CASSIO   No.
GRATIANO
I am sorry to find you thus. I have been to seek you.
IAGO
Lend me a garter. [*He applies a tourniquet.*] So.—O, for a chair,   83
To bear him easily hence!
BIANCA
Alas, he faints! O Cassio, Cassio, Cassio!
IAGO
Gentlemen all, I do suspect this trash
To be a party in this injury.—
Patience awhile, good Cassio.—Come, come;
Lend me a light. [*He shines the light on Roderigo.*]
   Know we this face or no?
Alas, my friend and my dear countryman
Roderigo! No.—Yes, sure.—O heaven! Roderigo!
GRATIANO   What, of Venice?
IAGO   Even he, sir. Did you know him?
GRATIANO   Know him? Ay.
IAGO
Signor Gratiano? I cry your gentle pardon.   95
These bloody accidents must excuse my manners   96
That so neglected you.

---

67 praise appraise   **70 I cry you mercy** I beg your pardon   **83 chair** litter   **95 gentle**
noble   **96 accidents** sudden events

GRATIANO   I am glad to see you.

IAGO

How do you, Cassio? O, a chair, a chair!

GRATIANO   Roderigo!

IAGO

He, he, 'tis he. [*A litter is brought in.*] O, that's well said; the
    chair.   100
Some good man bear him carefully from hence;
I'll fetch the General's surgeon. [*To Bianca.*] For you, mistress,
Save you your labor.—He that lies slain here, Cassio,   103
Was my dear friend. What malice was between you?   104

CASSIO

None in the world, nor do I know the man.

IAGO [*to Bianca*]

What, look you pale?—O, bear him out o' th' air.   106

                [*Cassio and Roderigo are borne off.*]
Stay you, good gentlemen.—Look you pale, mistress?—   107
Do you perceive the gastness of her eye?—   108
Nay, if you stare, we shall hear more anon.—   109
Behold her well; I pray you, look upon her.
Do you see, gentlemen? Nay, guiltiness
Will speak, though tongues were out of use.

[*Enter Emilia.*]

EMILIA

'Las, what's the matter? What's the matter, husband?

IAGO

Cassio hath here been set on in the dark
By Roderigo and fellows that are scaped.
He's almost slain, and Roderigo dead.

EMILIA

Alas, good gentleman! Alas, good Cassio!

IAGO

This is the fruits of whoring. Prithee, Emilia,
Go know of Cassio where he supped tonight.   119
[*To Bianca.*] What, do you shake at that?

BIANCA

He supped at my house, but I therefore shake not.

IAGO

O, did he so? I charge you go with me.

EMILIA   O, fie upon thee, strumpet!

---

100 well said well done   **103 Save ... labor** i.e., never you mind tending Cassio
104 malice enmity   **106 bear ... air** (Fresh air was thought to be dangerous for a
wound.)   **107 Stay you** (Lodovico and Gratiano are evidently about to leave.)   **108
gastness** terror   **109 stare** (Iago pretends to interpret Bianca's wild looks as an involuntary confession of guilt.)   **119 know** learn

BIANCA

I am no strumpet, but of life as honest   124
  As you that thus abuse me.

EMILIA As I? Faugh! Fie upon thee!

IAGO

Kind gentlemen, let's go see poor Cassio dressed. —   127
Come, mistress, you must tell 's another tale.
Emilia, run you to the citadel
And tell my lord and lady what hath happed. —
Will you go on afore? [*Aside.*] This is the night
That either makes me or fordoes me quite.   *Exeunt.*   132

5.2

Enter Othello [with a light], and Desdemona in her bed.

OTHELLO

It is the cause, it is the cause, my soul.   1
Let me not name it to you, you chaste stars!
It is the cause. Yet I'll not shed her blood,
Nor scar that whiter skin of hers than snow,
And smooth as monumental alabaster.   5
Yet she must die, else she'll betray more men.
Put out the light, and then put out the light.   7
If I quench thee, thou flaming minister,   8
I can again thy former light restore,
Should I repent me; but once put out thy light,   10
Thou cunning'st pattern of excelling nature,   11
I know not where is that Promethean heat   12
That can thy light relume. When I have plucked thy rose, 13
I cannot give it vital growth again;
It needs must wither. I'll smell thee on the tree.

                        [*He kisses her.*]

O balmy breath, that dost almost persuade
Justice to break her sword! One more, one more.
Be thus when thou art dead, and I will kill thee,
And love thee after. One more, and that's the last.

124 **honest** chaste 127 **Cassio dressed** Cassio's wounds dressed 132 **fordoes** undoes, ruins
5.2. Location: A bedchamber in the citadel.
s.d. in her bed (Either the curtains are drawn back to reveal the bed in a recessed area backstage, or the bed is "thrust out" onstage as the scene begins.) 1 **cause** i.e., cause of justice, the offense itself, which Othello must correct as an agent of justice 5 **monumental** i.e., used in making tombs and funeral monuments 7 **the light . . . light** the torch or lamp . . . Desdemona's life 8 **flaming minister** torch or lamp that serves me 10 **repent me** change my mind 11 **Thou . . . pattern** you skillfully wrought perfect example 12 **Promethean heat** divine fire. (Alluding to the theft of fire from heaven by Prometheus.) 13 **relume** rekindle

[He kisses her.]

So sweet was ne'er so fatal. I must weep,
But they are cruel tears. This sorrow's heavenly;   21
It strikes where it doth love. She wakes.   22

DESDEMONA   Who's there? Othello?

OTHELLO   Ay, Desdemona.

DESDEMONA   Will you come to bed, my lord?

OTHELLO   Have you prayed tonight, Desdemon?

DESDEMONA   Ay, my lord.

OTHELLO

If you bethink yourself of any crime   28
Unreconciled as yet to heaven and grace,
Solicit for it straight.   30

DESDEMONA

Alack, my lord, what may you mean by that?

OTHELLO

Well, do it, and be brief. I will walk by.
I would not kill thy unpreparèd spirit.
No, heaven forfend! I would not kill thy soul.   34

DESDEMONA

Talk you of killing?

OTHELLO   Ay, I do.

DESDEMONA   Then heaven
Have mercy on me!

OTHELLO   Amen, with all my heart!

DESDEMONA

If you say so, I hope you will not kill me.

OTHELLO Humh!

DESDEMONA

And yet I fear you; for you're fatal then
When your eyes roll so. Why I should fear I know not,
Since guiltiness I know not; but yet I feel I fear.

OTHELLO

Think on thy sins.

DESDEMONA   They are loves I bear to you.   42

OTHELLO   Ay, and for that thou diest.

DESDEMONA

That death's unnatural that kills for loving.
Alas, why gnaw you so your nether lip?
Some bloody passion shakes your very frame.

---

21 **cruel** unrelenting   22 **It . . . love** (Compare Hebrews 12:6: "For whom the Lord loveth he chasteneth.")   28 **crime** sin   30 **Solicit** petition, pray. **straight** immediately   34 **forfend** forbid   42 **They are . . . you** i.e., if I sinned, it was in loving you more than my father or more than God

These are portents; but yet I hope, I hope,
They do not point on me.   48
OTHELLO   Peace, and be still!
DESDEMONA   I will so. What's the matter?
OTHELLO
That handkerchief which I so loved and gave thee
Thou gav'st to Cassio.
DESDEMONA   No, by my life and soul!
Send for the man and ask him.
OTHELLO
Sweet soul, take heed, take heed of perjury.
Thou art on thy deathbed.
DESDEMONA
Ay, but not yet to die.
OTHELLO   Yes, presently.   56
Therefore confess thee freely of thy sin;
For to deny each article with oath
Cannot remove nor choke the strong conception   59
That I do groan withal. Thou art to die.   60
DESDEMONA
Then Lord have mercy on me!
OTHELLO   I say, amen.
DESDEMONA
And have you mercy too! I never did
Offend you in my life; never loved Cassio   63
But with such general warranty of heaven   64
As I might love. I never gave him token.
OTHELLO
By heaven, I saw my handkerchief in 's hand.
O perjured woman! Thou dost stone my heart,   67
And makes me call what I intend to do
A murder, which I thought a sacrifice.
I saw the handkerchief.
DESDEMONA   He found it, then.
I never gave it him. Send for him hither;
Let him confess a truth.
OTHELLO   He hath confessed.
DESDEMONA   What, my lord?
OTHELLO
That he hath used thee.
DESDEMONA   How? Unlawfully?

---

48 point on point at, predict what is to happen to   **56 presently** immediately   **59 conception** (1) belief in your guilt (2) plan in my mind   **60 groan withal** (1) groan at in sorrow (2) as in giving birth   **63 Offend** wrong   **64 warranty** sanction   **67 stone** turn to stone, harden

OTHELLO   Ay.

DESDEMONA
  He will not say so.

OTHELLO   No, his mouth is stopped;
  Honest Iago hath ta'en order for 't.   76

DESDEMONA
  O, my fear interprets. What, is he dead?

OTHELLO
  Had all his hairs been lives, my great revenge
  Had stomach for them all.

DESDEMONA
  Alas, he is betrayed and I undone!   [*She weeps.*]

OTHELLO
  Out, strumpet! Weep'st thou for him to my face?

DESDEMONA
  O, banish me, my lord, but kill me not!

OTHELLO   Down, strumpet!

DESDEMONA
  Kill me tomorrow; let me live tonight!

OTHELLO   Nay, if you strive—

DESDEMONA
  But half an hour!

OTHELLO   Being done, there is no pause.   86

DESDEMONA
  But while I say one prayer!

OTHELLO   It is too late.

                                      Smothers her.

EMILIA (*at the door*)
  My lord, my lord! What, ho! My lord, my lord!

OTHELLO
  What noise is this? Not dead? Not yet quite dead?
  I that am cruel am yet merciful;
  I would not have thee linger in thy pain.

                                [*He dispatches her.*]
  So, so.

EMILIA (*within*)   What, ho! My lord, my lord!

OTHELLO   Who's there?

EMILIA [*within*]
  O, good my lord, I would speak a word with you!

OTHELLO
  Yes, 'tis Emilia.—By and by.—She's dead.
  'Tis like she comes to speak of Cassio's death.—   95

---

76 **ta'en order** taken measures   86 **Being done** i.e., since justice has begun its relentless
course   95 **like** likely that

The noise was here. Ha! No more moving?   96
Still as the grave. Shall she come in? Were 't good? —
I think she stirs again. No. What's best to do?
If she come in, she'll sure speak to my wife.
My wife! My wife! What wife? I have no wife.
O, insupportable! O heavy hour!
Methinks it should be now a huge eclipse
Of sun and moon, and that th' affrighted globe
Should yawn at alteration.
EMILIA [*within*]   I do beseech you   104
That I may speak with you, O, good my lord!
OTHELLO
I had forgot thee. O, come in, Emilia. —
Soft, by and by. Let me the curtains draw. —   107
[*He closes the bed-curtains and opens the door.*]
Where art thou?
Enter Emilia.
           What's the matter with thee now?
EMILIA
O, my good lord, yonder's foul murders done!
OTHELLO   What, now?
EMILIA   But now, my lord.
OTHELLO
It is the very error of the moon;   112
She comes more nearer earth than she was wont,
And makes men mad.
EMILIA
Cassio, my lord, hath killed a young Venetian
Called Roderigo.
OTHELLO   Roderigo killed?
And Cassio killed?
EMILIA   No, Cassio is not killed.
OTHELLO
Not Cassio killed? Then murder's out of tune,
And sweet revenge grows harsh.
DESDEMONA   O, falsely, falsely murdered!
EMILIA   O Lord, what cry is that?
OTHELLO   That? What?

---

96 here (The Folio's *high* is possible, suggesting that the commotion of the attack on Cassio was loud.)   **104 yawn** gape in amazement, i.e., move in an earthquake. (According to Pliny, earthquakes often happen during eclipses.) **at alteration** at these cataclysmic events in nature, well suited to express the horror of Desdemona's death   **107 Soft** wait a minute   **112 error** aberration, irregularity

EMILIA
Out and alas, that was my lady's voice.   123

> [*She opens the bed-curtains.*]

Help, help, ho, help! O lady, speak again!
Sweet Desdemona! O sweet mistress, speak!

DESDEMONA A guiltless death I die.

EMILIA O, who hath done this deed?

DESDEMONA Nobody; I myself. Farewell.
Commend me to my kind lord. O, farewell! [*She dies.*]

OTHELLO
Why, how should she be murdered?

EMILIA   Alas, who knows?

OTHELLO
You heard her say herself it was not I.

EMILIA
She said so. I must needs report the truth.

OTHELLO
She's like a liar gone to burning hell!
'Twas I that killed her.

EMILIA   O, the more angel she,
And you the blacker devil!

OTHELLO
She turned to folly, and she was a whore.   136

EMILIA
Thou dost belie her, and thou art a devil.   137

OTHELLO She was false as water.

EMILIA Thou art rash as fire to say
That she was false. O, she was heavenly true!

OTHELLO
Cassio did top her. Ask thy husband else.   141
O, I were damned beneath all depth in hell
But that I did proceed upon just grounds
To this extremity. Thy husband knew it all.

EMILIA My husband?

OTHELLO Thy husband.

EMILIA That she was false to wedlock?

OTHELLO
Ay, with Cassio. Nay, had she been true,
If heaven would make me such another world
Of one entire and perfect chrysolite,   150
I'd not have sold her for it.

EMILIA My husband?

---

123 Out (A cry of dismay, intensifying *alas.*)   136 folly i.e., wantonness, fleshly sin
137 belie slander   141 else i.e., if you don't believe me   150 chrysolite precious topaz

OTHELLO
Ay, 'twas he that told me on her first.
An honest man he is, and hates the slime
That sticks on filthy deeds.
EMILIA My husband?
OTHELLO
What needs this iterance, woman? I say thy husband.   157
EMILIA
O mistress, villainy hath made mocks with love!   158
My husband say she was false?
OTHELLO   He, woman;
I say thy husband. Dost understand the word?
My friend, thy husband, honest, honest Iago.
EMILIA
If he say so, may his pernicious soul
Rot half a grain a day! He lies to th' heart.
She was too fond of her most filthy bargain.
OTHELLO Ha?   [*He draws.*]
EMILIA Do thy worst!
This deed of thine is no more worthy heaven
Than thou wast worthy her.
OTHELLO   Peace, you were best.   168
EMILIA
Thou hast not half that power to do me harm
As I have to be hurt. O gull! O dolt!   170
As ignorant as dirt! Thou hast done a deed—
I care not for thy sword; I'll make thee known,
Though I lost twenty lives.—Help! Help, ho, help!
The Moor hath killed my mistress! Murder, murder!

Enter Montano, Gratiano, and Iago.

MONTANO
What is the matter? How now, General?
EMILIA
O, are you come, Iago? You have done well,
That men must lay their murders on your neck.
GRATIANO What is the matter?
EMILIA [*to Iago*]
Disprove this villain, if thou be'st a man.
He says thou toldst him that his wife was false.
I know thou didst not; thou'rt not such a villain.
Speak, for my heart is full.

157 **iterance** iteration, repetition 158 **made mocks with** derided, made sport of
168 **you were best** it would be best for you 170 **to be hurt** i.e, to endure hurt. **gull**
dupe

IAGO

I told him what I thought, and told no more
Than what he found himself was apt and true.   184

EMILIA

But did you ever tell him she was false?

IAGO   I did.

EMILIA

You told a lie, an odious, damnèd lie!
Upon my soul, a lie, a wicked lie.
She false with Cassio? Did you say with Cassio?

IAGO

With Cassio, mistress. Go to, charm your tongue.   190

EMILIA

I will not charm my tongue; I am bound to speak.
My mistress here lies murdered in her bed—

ALL   O heavens forfend!

EMILIA

And your reports have set the murder on.

OTHELLO

Nay, stare not, masters. It is true indeed.

GRATIANO   'Tis a strange truth.

MONTANO

O monstrous act!

EMILIA   Villainy, villainy, villainy!
I think upon 't—I think I smell 't! O villainy!
I thought so then—I'll kill myself for grief—   199
O villainy, villainy!

IAGO

What, are you mad? I charge you, get you home.

EMILIA

Good gentlemen, let me have leave to speak.
'Tis proper I obey him, but not now.
Perchance, Iago, I will ne'er go home.

OTHELLO

O! O! O!   [*Othello falls on the bed.*]

EMILIA   Nay, lay thee down and roar,   205
For thou hast killed the sweetest innocent
That e'er did lift up eye.

OTHELLO [*rising*]   O, she was foul!   207
I scarce did know you, uncle. There lies your niece,

---

184 apt plausible   **190 charm** keep silent (as though by a magic spell)   **199 then** (Perhaps at 3.3.331–332 and 4.2.137–154.)   **205 s.d. Othello . . . bed** (This direction is from the Quarto, as also *He kisses her* at line 19 and *She dies* at line 129.)   **207 lift up eye** i.e., lift her eyes to heaven

Whose breath indeed these hands have newly stopped.
I know this act shows horrible and grim.   210

GRATIANO
Poor Desdemon! I am glad thy father's dead.
Thy match was mortal to him, and pure grief
Shore his old thread in twain. Did he live now,   213
This sight would make him do a desperate turn,   214
Yea, curse his better angel from his side,
And fall to reprobance.   216

OTHELLO
'Tis pitiful. But yet Iago knows
That she with Cassio hath the act of shame
A thousand times committed. Cassio confessed it;
And she did gratify his amorous works   220
With that recognizance and pledge of love   221
Which I first gave her. I saw it in his hand;
It was a handkerchief, an antique token
My father gave my mother.

EMILIA   O God! O heavenly God!

IAGO
Zounds, hold your peace.

EMILIA   'Twill out, 'twill out! I peace?
No, I will speak as liberal as the north.   227
Let heaven and men and devils, let them all,
All, all, cry shame against me, yet I'll speak.

IAGO
Be wise, and get you home.

EMILIA   I will not.
                            [*Iago threatens Emilia.*]

GRATIANO   Fie,
Your sword upon a woman?

EMILIA
O thou dull Moor! That handkerchief thou speak'st of
I found by fortune and did give my husband;
For often, with a solemn earnestness,
More than indeed belonged to such a trifle,   235
He begged of me to steal 't.

IAGO   Villainous whore!

EMILIA
She give it Cassio? No, alas! I found it,
And I did give 't my husband.

---

210 shows looks   **213 Shore ... thread** sheared the thread of his old age (as Atropos, one of the three Fates, was thought to do)   **214 turn** deed   **216 reprobance** damnation, i.e., suicide   **220 gratify** reward   **221 recognizance** token   **227 liberal as the north** freely as the north wind (blows)   **235 belonged** was appropriate

IAGO   Filth, thou liest!

EMILIA

By heaven, I do not, I do not, gentlemen.
O murderous coxcomb! What should such a fool   240
Do with so good a wife?

OTHELLO   Are there no stones in heaven   242
But what serves for the thunder?—Precious villain!   243
    [*He runs at Iago; Montano disarms Othello. Iago,*
from behind, stabs Emilia.]

GRATIANO

The woman falls! Sure he hath killed his wife.

EMILIA

Ay, ay. O, lay me by my mistress' side.

                                        [*Exit Iago.*]

GRATIANO   He's gone, but his wife's killed.

MONTANO

'Tis a notorious villain. Take you this weapon,
Which I have here recovered from the Moor.
Come, guard the door without. Let him not pass,
But kill him rather. I'll after that same villain,
For 'tis a damnèd slave.
        Exit [*with all but Othello and Emilia, who has been*
laid by Desdemona's side].

OTHELLO   I am not valiant neither,
But every puny whipster gets my sword.   253
But why should honor outlive honesty?   254
Let it go all.

EMILIA   What did thy song bode, lady?
Hark, canst thou hear me? I will play the swan,
And die in music. [*She sings.*] "Willow, willow, willow."
Moor, she was chaste. She loved thee, cruel Moor.
So come my soul to bliss as I speak true.
So speaking as I think, alas, I die.   [*She dies.*]

OTHELLO

I have another weapon in this chamber;
It was a sword of Spain, the ice-brook's temper—   262
O, here it is. [*He finds a sword.*] Uncle, I must come forth.

---

240 **coxcomb** fool. (Addressed to Othello.)   242 **stones** bolts, such as those used for
thunderbolts   243 **Precious** i.e., arrant, utter.   **s.d. He . . . Emilia** (The Quarto text reads,
"The Moor runs at Iago. Iago kills his wife." The Quarto also specifies the exit of Iago
at line 245 and the death of Emilia at line 260.)   253 **whipster** contemptible fellow (one
who is always ready to whip out his sword)   254 **honor** i.e., the bravery for which one
enjoys a soldier's reputation.   **honesty** true integrity   262 **the icebrook's temper** tempered in ice-cold water

GRATIANO [*within*]

If thou attempt it, it will cost thee dear.

Thou hast no weapon, and perforce must suffer.

OTHELLO

Look in upon me then and speak with me,

Or, naked as I am, I will assault thee. 267

[*Enter Gratiano.*]

GRATIANO

What is the matter?

OTHELLO   Behold, I have a weapon;

A better never did itself sustain

Upon a soldier's thigh. I have seen the day

That, with this little arm and this good sword,

I have made my way through more impediments

Than twenty times your stop. But O, vain boast! 273

Who can control his fate? 'Tis not so now.

Be not afraid, though you do see me weaponed;

Here is my journey's end, here is my butt 276

And very seamark of my utmost sail. 277

                              [*Gratiano steps back.*]

Do you go back dismayed? 'Tis a lost fear; 278

Man but a rush against Othello's breast 279

And he retires. Where should Othello go?

                              [*He turns to Desdemona.*]

Now, how dost thou look now? O ill-starred wench!

Pale as thy smock! When we shall meet at compt, 282

This look of thine will hurl my soul from heaven,

And fiends will snatch at it. Cold, cold, my girl?

Even like thy chastity. O cursèd, cursèd slave! 285

Whip me, ye devils,

From the possession of this heavenly sight!

Blow me about in winds! Roast me in sulfur!

Wash me in steep-down gulfs of liquid fire!

O Desdemon! Dead, Desdemon! Dead! O! O! 290

Enter Lodovico, Cassio [carried in a litter], Montano, and Iago
[prisoner], with officers.

LODOVICO

Where is this rash and most unfortunate man?

OTHELLO

That's he that was Othello. Here I am.

---

267 **naked** unarmed   273 **stop** power (to stop)   276 **butt** goal, limit. (An archery term.)
277 **seamark** beacon (marking his destination or limit)   278 **lost** wasted, unneeded
279 **Man . . . rush** wield no more than a reed   282 **compt** account, judgment day
285 **slave** i.e., Othello himself   290 **s.d. in a litter** (The Quarto specifies that Cassio is
"in a chair.")

LODOVICO
  Where is that viper? Bring the villain forth.
                              [*Iago is led forward.*]
OTHELLO
  I look down towards his feet; but that's a fable.   294
  If that thou be'st a devil, I cannot kill thee.
                              [*He wounds Iago.*]
LODOVICO
  Wrench his sword from him.   [*Othello is disarmed.*]
IAGO   I bleed, sir, but not killed.
OTHELLO
  I am not sorry neither. I'd have thee live,
  For in my sense 'tis happiness to die.   298
LODOVICO
  O thou Othello that was once so good,
  Fall'n in the practice of a cursèd slave,   300
  What shall be said to thee?
OTHELLO   Why, anything.
  An honorable murderer, if you will,
  For naught I did in hate, but all in honor.
LODOVICO
  This wretch hath part confessed his villainy.
  Did you and he consent in Cassio's death?   305
OTHELLO   Ay.
CASSIO
  Dear General, I never gave you cause.
OTHELLO
  I do believe it, and I ask your pardon.
  Will you, I pray, demand that demi-devil
  Why he hath thus ensnared my soul and body?
IAGO
  Demand me nothing. What you know, you know.
  From this time forth I never will speak word.
LODOVICO   What, not to pray?
GRATIANO   Torments will ope your lips.   314
OTHELLO   Well, thou dost best.
LODOVICO
  Sir, you shall understand what hath befall'n,
  Which, as I think, you know not. Here is a letter
  Found in the pocket of the slain Roderigo;
  And here another. [*He produces letters.*] The one of them imports

---

294 towards his feet i.e., to see if they are cloven, as the devil's are fabled to be   **298 in my sense** to one who feels as I do   **300 in the practice** through the plotting, into the snare. **slave** villain   **305 consent** agree   **314 Torments** torture

The death of Cassio, to be undertook
By Roderigo.

OTHELLO
O villain!

CASSIO   Most heathenish and most gross!   322

LODOVICO [*showing another paper*]
Now here's another discontented paper   323
Found in his pocket too. And this, it seems,
Roderigo meant t' have sent this damnèd villain;
But that belike Iago in the interim   326
Came in and satisfied him.   327

OTHELLO   O thou pernicious caitiff!—
How came you, Cassio, by that handkerchief
That was my wife's?

CASSIO   I found it in my chamber;
And he himself confessed but even now
That there he dropped it for a special purpose
Which wrought to his desire.

OTHELLO   O fool, fool, fool!   333

CASSIO
There is besides in Roderigo's letter
How he upbraids Iago, that he made him
Brave me upon the watch, whereon it came   336
That I was cast; and even but now he spake,   337
After long seeming dead, Iago hurt him,
Iago set him on.

LODOVICO [*to Othello*]
You must forsake this room and go with us.
Your power and your command is taken off,   341
And Cassio rules in Cyprus. For this slave,
If there be any cunning cruelty
That can torment him much and hold him long,   344
It shall be his. You shall close prisoner rest   345
Till that the nature of your fault be known
To the Venetian state.—Come, bring away.

OTHELLO
Soft you; a word or two before you go.   348
I have done the state some service, and they know 't.
No more of that. I pray you, in your letters,

---

322 **gross** monstrous   323 **discontented** full of discontent   326 **belike** most likely
327 **Came . . . him** interposed and gave him satisfactory explanation   333 **wrought . . .
desire** worked out as he wished, fitted in with his plan   336 **Brave** defy.   **whereon it
came** whereof it came about   337 **cast** dismissed   341 **taken off** taken away   344 **hold
him long** keep him alive a long time (during his torture)   345 **rest** remain   348 **Soft
you** one moment

When you shall these unlucky deeds relate,   351
Speak of me as I am; nothing extenuate,
Nor set down aught in malice. Then must you speak
Of one that loved not wisely but too well;
Of one not easily jealous but, being wrought,   355
Perplexed in the extreme; of one whose hand,   356
Like the base Indian, threw a pearl away   357
Richer than all his tribe; of one whose subdued eyes,   358
Albeit unusèd to the melting mood,
Drops tears as fast as the Arabian trees
Their medicinable gum. Set you down this;   361
And say besides that in Aleppo once,
Where a malignant and a turbaned Turk
Beat a Venetian and traduced the state,
I took by th' throat the circumcisèd dog
And smote him, thus.   [*He stabs himself.*]   366
LODOVICO   O bloody period!   367
GRATIANO   All that is spoke is marred.
OTHELLO
I kissed thee ere I killed thee. No way but this,
Killing myself, to die upon a kiss.
                          [*He kisses Desdemona and*] *dies.*
CASSIO
This did I fear, but thought he had no weapon;
For he was great of heart.
LODOVICO [*to Iago.*]   O Spartan dog,   372
More fell than anguish, hunger, or the sea!   373
Look on the tragic loading of this bed.
This is thy work. The object poisons sight;
Let it be hid. Gratiano, keep the house,   376
                    [*The bed curtains are drawn*]
And seize upon the fortunes of the Moor,   377
For they succeed on you. [*To Cassio.*] To you, Lord Governor,   378
Remains the censure of this hellish villain,   379
The time, the place, the torture. O, enforce it!
Myself will straight aboard, and to the state
This heavy act with heavy heart relate.   *Exeunt.*

351 **unlucky** unfortunate   355 **wrought** worked upon, worked into a frenzy   356 **Perplexed** distraught   357 **Indian** (This reading from the Quarto pictures an ignorant savage who cannot recognize the value of a precious jewel. The Folio reading, *Iudean* or *Judean*, i.e., infidel or disbeliever, may refer to Herod, who slew Miriamne in a fit of jealousy, or to Judas Iscariot, the betrayer of Christ.)   358 **subdued** i.e., overcome by grief   361 **gum** i.e., myrrh   366 **s.d. He stabs himself** (This direction is in the Quarto text.)   367 **period** termination, conclusion   372 **Spartan dog** (Spartan dogs were noted for their savagery and silence.)   373 **fell** cruel   376 **Let it be hid** i.e., draw the bed curtains. (No stage direction specifies that the dead are to be carried offstage at the end of the play.) **keep** remain in   377 **seize upon** take legal possession of   378 **succeed on** pass as though by inheritance to   379 **censure** sentencing

❏ Questions for Discussion
Act I

1. What are Iago's motives for disliking Othello? What does he mean by " 'Tis in ourselves that we are thus or thus" (1.3.322)? Why does Iago tell Roderigo he hates Othello, then advise Othello of danger in the next scene?

2. When Brabantio and Roderigo draw swords to attack Othello, the latter says, "Keep up your bright swords, for the dew will rust them" (1.2.60). What does this line reveal about Othello's character?

3. What are the qualities in Othello which cause Desdemona to fall in love with him?

Act II

1. Why must Othello punish Cassio so severely? Is Cassio to blame? Is Othello punishing Cassio unjustly?

2. Why is Iago so adept when talking to Roderigo but so inept in producing flattering verses to please Desdemona? How do Iago's apparent ineptness in flattery and bluntness of speech serve his purpose?

3. What seems to be Iago's attitude toward women and sexuality? How does the **imagery** he uses reveal this attitude?

4. Why does Shakespeare have the ordinarily deceptive Iago reveal his true character in such **soliloquies** as:

> . . . Divinity of hell!
> When devils will the blackest sins put on,
> They do suggest at first with heavenly shows,
> As I do now. (2.3.344–47)

Act III

1. How does Iago lead Othello to begin doubting and suspecting Cassio?

2. Iago says in 3.3.341, "The Moor already changes with my poison." When Othello begins to doubt Desdemona, how else does his character change? Does his language change? If so, how does that reveal a character change? See 3.3.274–93 and 3.3.361–73.

3. What is significant about the handkerchief?

4. Explain the **foreshadowing** of Othello's speech,

> . . . Perdition catch my soul
> But I do love thee! And when I love thee not,
> Chaos is come again. (3.3.98–100)

5. Explain the truth and the **irony** of Iago's speech,

> Who steals my purse steals trash; 'tis something, nothing;
> 'Twas mine, 'tis his, and has been slave to thousands;
> But he that filches from me my good name
> Robs me of that which not enriches him
> And makes me poor indeed. (3.3.170–74)

Act IV

1. How does Iago manipulate Cassio into incriminating himself and Desdemona?

2. Do Othello's speech and actions in this act make sense? What has happened to him? How does Lodovico's speech in 4.1.269–73 reflect the extent of Othello's fall?

3. Does Desdemona show the slightest sign of disobedience or unfaithfulness to Othello? How innocent is she? How does she respond to bad treatment from him? Support your response with references to the text. See, in particular, 4.3.62–65 and 4.3.81–82.

4. In what ways is Emilia a **dramatic foil** for Desdemona?

Act V

1. Why does Othello say, "Put out the light, and then put out the light" (5.2.7)?

2. How does Othello feel about killing Desdemona as he prepares to do so? See his soliloquy at 5.2.1–22.

3. How does Othello's speech at 5.2.268–90 reflect the extent of his fall?

4. What is Othello's motivation to kill Desdemona? Would he have been justified in doing so even if he had incontrovertible evidence of her infidelity? What flaw in his character leads him to fall for Iago's trap?

5. Why, after having explained his motives in **soliloquies** and conversations earlier in the play, does Iago now (5.2.312) say, "From this time forth I never will speak word"?

6. In what sense is Othello's death a triumph? Has he managed to retain any of his former dignity?

❏ **Suggestions for Exploration and Writing**

1. Examine Iago's **motivation.** Is there any adequate motive that can explain the intensity of his malevolence? Is his evil ultimately explainable? Is it diabolic?

2. Analyze the means by which Iago poisons Othello's mind.

3. Examine in detail the change Othello undergoes. How does jealousy change not only his attitude toward Desdemona and Cassio, but his language, his sleep, and his attitudes toward his work as a soldier—indeed his entire personality?

4. Discuss in detail how **imagery** defines one or more of the major characters—Iago, Desdemona, Othello, or Cassio. For example, you might choose to show how Iago's use of animal imagery reveals his character.

5. In *Poetics,* Aristotle describes the **tragic hero** as a good man who holds a high position and falls because of a flaw within himself. Write an essay explaining how Othello does or does not fit this definition.

CASEBOOK

on Robert Frost

ROBERT FROST (1874–1963)

Robert Frost's life, like many of his poems, was filled with ironies. Known as a New England poet, Frost was born in San Francisco and named after Robert E. Lee. When his poetry was not recognized in the United States, he moved to England and there published his first books of poetry, A Boy's Will *(1913) and* North of Boston *(1914). When he returned to the United States, his fame as a poet was already established. Early criticism identified Frost with the kindly New England speaker of many of his poems, and even now his most famous poems are those about nature which often emphasize rising above life's problems.*

Frost had more than his share of family tragedies, however, and was always aware of the darker side of life. Even his famous definition of poetry as a "momentary stay against confusion" in "The Figure a Poem Makes" emphasizes the complexities of life and the necessity of finding ways to manage life's ambiguities. For Frost, precise form in poetry is one of those ways: As a master craftsman, he uses traditional poetic form so skillfully that he seems to recreate the natural speech patterns of the New England characters in his **dialogues** *and* **monologues,** *and he adds to the meaning of his poems by using such tight forms as the* **sonnet** *and* **terza rima.** *Poems reflecting Frost's more optimistic views may be found in the Quest unit.*

Design

I found a dimpled spider, fat and white,
On a white heal-all, holding up a moth
Like a white piece of rigid satin cloth—
Assorted characters of death and blight
5　Mixed ready to begin the morning right,
Like the ingredients of a witches' broth—
A snow-drop spider, a flower like a froth,
And dead wings carried like a paper kite.

What had that flower to do with being white,
10　The wayside blue and innocent heal-all?
What brought the kindred spider to that height,
Then steered the white moth thither in the night?
What but design of darkness to appall?—
If design govern in a thing so small.

❑ **Question for Discussion**

1. The traditional Italian **sonnet** asks a question in the **octave** and answers it in the **sestet**. In "Design," Frost changes the traditional form by asking questions in the sestet. What do these questions imply? How does Frost's reversal of the traditional form emphasize the meaning of the poem?

Desert Places

Snow falling and night falling fast, oh, fast
In a field I looked into going past,
And the ground almost covered smooth in snow,
But a few weeds and stubble showing last.

The woods around it have it—it is theirs.   5
All animals are smothered in their lairs.
I am too absent-spirited to count;
The loneliness includes me unawares.

And lonely as it is, that loneliness
Will be more lonely ere it will be less—   10
A blanker whiteness of benighted snow
With no expression, nothing to express.

They cannot scare me with their empty spaces
Between stars—on stars where no human race is.
I have it in me so much nearer home   15
To scare myself with my own desert places.

❑ **Questions for Discussion**

1. To what does "it" in line 5 refer?

2. Explain the last four lines of the poem. How do they relate to the description of the snow-covered landscape? What kind of desert places might exist within a person?

Acquainted with the Night

I have been one acquainted with the night.
I have walked out in rain—and back in rain.
I have outwalked the furthest city light.

I have looked down the saddest city lane.
I have passed by the watchman on his beat.   5
And dropped my eyes, unwilling to explain.

I have stood still and stopped the sound of feet
When far away an interrupted cry
Came over houses from another street,

10
But not to call me back or say good-by;
And further still at an unearthly height
One luminary clock against the sky

Proclaimed the time was neither wrong nor right.
I have been one acquainted with the night.

❏ **Questions for Discussion**

1. This poem is written in **terza rima**, the interlocking rhyme scheme in iambic pentameter created by Dante for the *Divine Comedy*. Explain how the use of this form and other poetic devices such as **anaphora, alliteration,** and **caesura** help to unify the poem and emphasize its meaning.

2. Explain lines 12–13.

3. What does Frost mean by "I have been one acquainted with the night"?

Neither Out Far Nor In Deep

The people along the sand
All turn and look one way.
They turn their back on the land.
They look at the sea all day.

5
As long as it takes to pass
A ship keeps raising its hull;
The wetter ground like glass
Reflects a standing gull.

10
The land may vary more;
But wherever the truth may be—
The water comes ashore,
And the people look at the sea.

They cannot look out far.
They cannot look in deep.
15
But when was that ever a bar
To any watch they keep?

❏ **Questions for Discussion**

1. What do the land and the sea symbolize in this poem?

2. What is Frost saying about human nature in the last four lines?

Once By the Pacific

The shattered water made a misty din.
Great waves looked over others coming in,

And thought of doing something to the shore
That water never did to land before.
The clouds were low and hairy in the skies,   5
Like locks blown forward in the gleam of eyes.
You could not tell, and yet it looked as if
The shore was lucky in being backed by cliff,
The cliff in being backed by continent;
It looked as if a night of dark intent   10
Was coming, and not only a night, an age.
Someone had better be prepared for rage.
There would be more than ocean-water broken
Before God's last *Put out the Light* was spoken.

❑ Questions for Discussion

1. How does the **personification** of the ocean make the poem
   threatening?

2. What is the threat implied in the last five lines of the poem?

Home Burial

He saw her from the bottom of the stairs
Before she saw him. She was starting down,
Looking back over her shoulder at some fear.
She took a doubtful step and then undid it
To raise herself and look again. He spoke   5
Advancing toward her: "What is it you see
From up there always?—for I want to know."
She turned and sank upon her skirts at that,
And her face changed from terrified to dull.
He said to gain time: "What is it you see?"   10
Mounting until she cowered under him.
"I will find out now—you must tell me, dear."
She, in her place, refused him any help,
With the least stiffening of her neck and silence.
She let him look, sure that he wouldn't see,   15
Blind creature; and awhile he didn't see.
But at last he murmured, "Oh," and again, "Oh."

"What is it—what?" she said.

                    "Just that I see."

"You don't," she challenged. "Tell me what it is."   20

"The wonder is I didn't see at once.
I never noticed it from here before.
I must be wonted to it—that's the reason.
The little graveyard where my people are!

25 So small the window frames the whole of it.
    Not so much larger than a bedroom, is it?
    There are three stones of slate and one of marble,
    Broad-shouldered little slabs there in the sunlight
30 On the sidehill. We haven't to mind *those*.
    But I understand: it is not the stones,
    But the child's mound——"

                    "Don't, don't, don't,

        don't," she cried.

    She withdrew, shrinking from beneath his arm
35 That rested on the banister, and slid downstairs;
    And turned on him with such a daunting look,
    He said twice over before he knew himself:
    "Can't a man speak of his own child he's lost?"

    "Not you!—Oh, where's my hat? Oh, I don't need it!
40 I must get out of here. I must get air.—
    I don't know rightly whether any man can."

    "Amy! Don't go to someone else this time.
    Listen to me. I won't come down the stairs."
    He sat and fixed his chin between his fists.
45 "There's something I should like to ask you, dear."

    "You don't know how to ask it."

                        "Help me, then."

    Her fingers moved the latch for all reply.

    "My words are nearly always an offense.
50 I don't know how to speak of anything
    So as to please you. But I might be taught,
    I should suppose. I can't say I see how.
    A man must partly give up being a man
    With womenfolk. We could have some arrangement
55 By which I'd bind myself to keep hands off
    Anything special you're a-mind to name.
    Though I don't like such things 'twixt those that love.
    Two that don't love can't live together without them.
    But two that do can't live together with them."
60 She moved the latch a little. "Don't—don't go.
    Don't carry it to someone else this time.
    Tell me about it if it's something human.
    Let me into your grief. I'm not so much
    Unlike other folks as your standing there
65 Apart would make me out. Give me my chance.
    I do think, though, you overdo it a little.
    What was it brought you up to think it the thing

To take your mother-loss of a first child
So inconsolably—in the face of love.
You'd think his memory might be satisfied——"   70

"There you go sneering now!"

                       "I'm not, I'm not!

You make me angry. I'll come down to you.
God, what a woman! And it's come to this,
A man can't speak of his own child that's dead."   75

"You can't because you don't know how to speak.
If you had any feelings, you that dug
With your own hand—how could you?—his little grave;
I saw you from that very window there,
Making the gravel leap and leap in air,   80
Leap up, like that, like that, and land so lightly
And roll back down the mound beside the hole.
I thought, Who is that man? I didn't know you.
And I crept down the stairs and up the stairs
To look again, and still your spade kept lifting.   85
Then you came in. I heard your rumbling voice
Out in the kitchen and I don't know why,
But I went near to see with my own eyes.
You could sit there with the stains on your shoes
Of the fresh earth from your own baby's grave   90
And talk about your everyday concerns.
You had stood the spade up against the wall
Outside there in the entry, for I saw it."

"I shall laugh the worst laugh I ever laughed.
I'm cursed. God, if I don't believe I'm cursed."   95

"I can repeat the very words you were saying:
'Three foggy mornings and one rainy day
Will rot the best birch fence a man can build.'
Think of it, talk like that at such a time!
What had how long it takes a birch to rot   100
To do with what was in the darkened parlor?
You *couldn't* care! The nearest friends can go
With anyone to death, comes so far short
They might as well not try to go at all.
No, from the time when one is sick to death,   105
One is alone, and he dies more alone.
Friends make pretense of following to the grave,
But before one is in it, their minds are turned
And making the best of their way back to life
And living people, and things they understand.   110

But the world's evil. I won't have grief so
If I can change it. Oh, I won't, I won't!"

"There, you have said it all and you feel better.
You won't go now. You're crying. Close the door.
115 The heart's gone out of it: why keep it up?
Amy! There's someone coming down the road!"

"*You*—oh, you think the talk is all. I must go—
Somewhere out of this house. How can I make you——"

"If—you—do!" She was opening the door wider.
120 "Where do you mean to go? First tell me that.
I'll follow and bring you back by force. I *will*!—"

❏ Questions for Discussion

1. Explain the double meaning of the poem's title.

2. The husband says, "A man must partly give up being a man /
   With womenfolk." Explain these lines and agree or disagree
   with the husband's claim.

3. Explain Amy's statement in lines 100–07.

A Servant to Servants

I didn't make you know how glad I was
To have you come and camp here on our land.
I promised myself to get down some day
And see the way you lived, but I don't know!
5 With a houseful of hungry men to feed
I guess you'd find. . . . It seems to me
I can't express my feelings, any more
Than I can raise my voice or want to lift
My hand (oh, I can lift it when I have to).
10 Did ever you feel so? I hope you never.
It's got so I don't even know for sure
Whether I *am* glad, sorry, or anything.
There's nothing but a voice-like left inside
That seems to tell me how I ought to feel,
15 And would feel if I wasn't all gone wrong.
You take the lake. I look and look at it.
I see it's a fair, pretty sheet of water.
I stand and make myself repeat out loud
The advantages it has, so long and narrow,
20 Like a deep piece of some old running river
Cut short off at both ends. It lies five miles
Straightaway through the mountain notch

From the sink window where I wash the plates,
And all our storms come up toward the house,
Drawing the slow waves whiter and whiter and whiter.   25
It took my mind off doughnuts and soda biscuit
To step outdoors and take the water dazzle
A sunny morning, or take the rising wind
About my face and body and through my wrapper,
When a storm threatened from the Dragon's Den,   30
And a cold chill shivered across the lake.
I see it's a fair, pretty sheet of water,
Our Willoughby! How did you hear of it?
I expect, though, everyone's heard of it.
In a book about ferns? Listen to that!   35
You let things more like feathers regulate
Your going and coming. And you like it here?
I can see how you might. But I don't know!
It would be different if more people came,
For then there would be business. As it is,   40
The cottages Len built, sometimes we rent them,
Sometimes we don't. We've a good piece of shore
That ought to be worth something, and may yet.
But I don't count on it as much as Len.
He looks on the bright side of everything,   45
Including me. He thinks I'll be all right
With doctoring. But it's not medicine—
Lowe is the only doctor's dared to say so—
It's rest I want—there, I have said it out—
From cooking meals for hungry hired men   50
And washing dishes after them—from doing
Things over and over that just won't stay done.
By good rights I ought not to have so much
Put on me, but there seems no other way.
Len says one steady pull more ought to do it.   55
He says the best way out is always through.
And I agree to that, or in so far
As that I can see no way out but through—
Leastways for me—and then they'll be convinced.
It's not that Len don't want the best for me.   60
It was his plan our moving over in
Beside the lake from where that day I showed you
We used to live—ten miles from anywhere.
We didn't change without some sacrifice,
But Len went at it to make up the loss.   65
His work's a man's, of course, from sun to sun,
But he works when he works as hard as I do—
Though there's small profit in comparisons.

(Women and men will make them all the same.)
70   But work ain't all. Len undertakes too much.
He's into everything in town. This year
It's highways, and he's got too many men
Around him to look after that make waste.
They take advantage of him shamefully,
75   And proud, too, of themselves for doing so.
We have four here to board, great good-for-nothings,
Sprawling about the kitchen with their talk
While I fry their bacon. Much they care!
No more put out in what they do or say
80   Than if I wasn't in the room at all.
Coming and going all the time, they are:
I don't learn what their names are, let alone
Their characters, or whether they are safe
To have inside the house with doors unlocked.
85   I'm not afraid of them, though, if they're not
Afraid of me. There's two can play at that.
I have my fancies: it runs in the family.
My father's brother wasn't right. They kept him
Locked up for years back there at the old farm.
90   I've been away once—yes, I've been away.
The State Asylum. I was prejudiced;
I wouldn't have sent anyone of mine there;
You know the old idea—the only asylum
Was the poorhouse, and those who could afford,
95   Rather than send their folks to such a place,
Kept them at home; and it does seem more human.
But it's not so: the place is the asylum.
There they have every means proper to do with,
And you aren't darkening other people's lives—
100   Worse than no good to them, and they no good
To you in your condition; you can't know
Affection or the want of it in that state.
I've heard too much of the old-fashioned way.
My father's brother, he went mad quite young.
105   Some thought he had been bitten by a dog,
Because his violence took on the form
Of carrying his pillow in his teeth;
But it's more likely he was crossed in love,
Or so the story goes. It was some girl.
110   Anyway all he talked about was love.
They soon saw he would do someone a mischief
If he wa'n't kept strict watch of, and it ended
In father's building him a sort of cage,
Or room within a room, of hickory poles,

Like stanchions in the barn, from floor to ceiling— 115
A narrow passage all the way around.
Anything they put in for furniture
He'd tear to pieces, even a bed to lie on.
So they made the place comfortable with straw,
Like a beast's stall, to ease their consciences. 120
Of course they had to feed him without dishes.
They tried to keep him clothed, but he paraded
With his clothes on his arm—all of his clothes.
Cruel—it sounds. I s'pose they did the best
They knew. And just when he was at the height, 125
Father and mother married, and mother came,
A bride, to help take care of such a creature,
And accommodate her young life to his.
That was what marrying father meant to her.
She had to lie and hear love things made dreadful 130
By his shouts in the night. He'd shout and shout
Until the strength was shouted out of him,
And his voice died down slowly from exhaustion.
He'd pull his bars apart like bow and bowstring,
And let them go and make them twang, until 135
His hands had worn them smooth as any oxbow.
And then he'd crow as if he thought that child's play—
The only fun he had. I've heard them say, though,
They found a way to put a stop to it.
He was before my time—I never saw him; 140
But the pen stayed exactly as it was,
There in the upper chamber in the ell,
A sort of catchall full of attic clutter.
I often think of the smooth hickory bars.
It got so I would say—you know, half fooling— 145
"It's time I took my turn upstairs in jail"—
Just as you will till it becomes a habit.
No wonder I was glad to get away.
Mind you, I waited till Len said the word.
I didn't want the blame if things went wrong. 150
I was glad though, no end, when we moved out,
And I looked to be happy, and I was,
As I said, for a while—but I don't know!
Somehow the change wore out like a prescription.
And there's more to it than just window views 155
And living by a lake. I'm past such help—
Unless Len took the notion, which he won't,
And I won't ask him—it's not sure enough.
I s'pose I've got to go the road I'm going:
Other folks have to, and why shouldn't I? 160

I almost think if I could do like you,
Drop everything and lie out on the ground—
But it might be, come night, I shouldn't like it,
Or a long rain. I should soon get enough,
165   And be glad of a good roof overhead.
I've lain awake thinking of you, I'll warrant,
More than you have yourself, some of these nights.
The wonder was the tents weren't snatched away
From over you as you lay in your beds.
170   I haven't courage for a risk like that.
Bless you, of course you're keeping me from work,
But the thing of it is, I need to *be* kept.
There's work enough to do—there's always that;
But behind's behind. The worst that you can do
175   Is set me back a little more behind.
I shan't catch up in this world, anyway.
I'd *rather* you'd not go unless you must.

❏ Question for Discussion

1. Why would the speaker prefer the insane asylum to staying at home?

Robert Frost and the Darkness of Nature[1]

by Roberts W. French

Rightly or wrongly, Robert Frost has achieved a reputation as a poet of nature; and it is true that one tends to think of him posed against the landscapes of rural New England. He may in his poems be looking at birches, or stopping by woods on a snowy evening, or picking apples, or listening to the thrush or the oven bird; wherever he is, he seems to be participating in the life of nature, deriving sustenance from it, and finding in it a deeply satisfying source of pleasure.

Certainly Frost's poetry is filled with the imagery of nature; but to think of him as a "nature poet," or as a celebrant of nature, is to distort his poetry by overlooking its darker complexities. While Frost has written poems that express a certain joy in nature—"Mowing," for example, or "Putting in the Seed," or "Two Look at Two"—he is far from being a lover of nature; reading through his works, one finds that a major tone involves feelings of profound uneasiness, even of fear, toward nature. Frost may present himself in a natural landscape, but he is far from comfortable there. . . .

Frost shares something of Thoreau's concern for the distance between man and nature. "Birches," for example—one of his best known and

[1] From *Critical Essays on Robert Frost*, ed. Philip L. Gerber (Boston: G. K. Hall & Co., 1982), 155–62.

most misunderstood poems—is not a poem about birches, primarily, but about the desirability of escaping from this world, if only temporarily; "I'd like to get away from earth awhile," he writes, "And then come back to it and begin over." Birch trees provide the poet with a useful metaphor, since a properly chosen birch tree will lower a person back to earth if he climbs it high enough; but the poem shows no great feeling for such trees, or for any trees. The dominant mood, rather, is one of confused exhaustion; the poet is "weary of consideration," "And life is too much like a pathless wood. . . ." In a similar mood, the young Wordsworth went to nature for consolation and spiritual renewal, but Frost never does that; nature offers no such blessings for him. His way out, if there is one, is not to go *into* nature, but to go beyond nature. In "Birches," as in some other poems, nature has at best a morally neutral value; if it does not oppress, neither does it comfort. . . .

In "An Old Man's Winter Night" nature is a malevolent voyeur; in "Storm Fear" nature is portrayed as an active diabolical opponent:

> When the wind works against us in the dark,
> And pelts with snow
> The lower chamber window on the east,
> And whispers with a sort of stifled bark,
> The beast,
> 'Come out! Come out!'—
> It costs no inward struggle not to go,
> Ah, no! . . . .

Nature is bestial, savage, intent on luring man to his destruction; and even worse, nature is portrayed as scheming and deceptive, whispering its cruel invitation to disaster. Faced with such active malevolence, the poet feels a deep sense of human inadequacy. What chance is there against such an opponent? One can only try to survive from day to day, but the uncertainty of the struggle leaves the poet troubled: "And my heart owns a doubt / Whether 'tis in us to arise with day / And save ourselves unaided."

Among the darkest of Frost's works, surely, is the five-poem sequence, "The Hill Wife," in which Frost takes an apparently idyllic situation—a young couple on a remote farm—and turns it into a nightmare of loneliness and fear. Like *Heart of Darkness* and *Lord of the Flies*, "The Hill Wife" is an anti-pastoral of the first order. The wife has all the resources of nature at hand, but she can find no solace or satisfaction in them. "One ought not," she complains to her husband,

> to have to care
> So much as you and I
> Care when the birds come round the house
> To seem to say good-by;

> Or care so much when they come back
>   With whatever it is they sing. . . .

They *have* to care, she laments; there is no alternative, because there is nothing else. Being secluded in nature, they must turn to nature for their satisfactions; and for the wife, it is clear, this is not enough. She knows that they feel "too sad" when the birds leave and "too glad" when they return, and she resents being made so dependent on them, especially when she realizes that the birds are totally indifferent toward her (they only *seem* to say good-by, because that is what she would have them do; but she recognizes the illusion for what it is). Nature she has, in abundance; but nature will not serve her human needs. What she wants, nature cannot give; as a human, she is distinctly uncomfortable in a natural world.

Nature is not only unsatisfactory, however, as a source of spiritual sustenance; what is worse, nature seems actively hostile, a constant threat, and the wife has learned to fear it:

> She had no saying dark enough
>   For the dark pine that kept
> Forever trying the window-latch
>   Of the room where they slept.

As in "An Old Man's Winter Night" and "Storm Fear," nature—here represented by the "dark pine"—is just beyond the barriers (a house, a window) that protect humans from nature's force; but the barriers are weak and unreliable, and nature tries ceaselessly to penetrate them. The time may come when the barriers will prove inadequate; and then? Not surprisingly, the Hill Wife has nightmares about the dark pine outside her window:

> It never had been inside the room,
>   And only one of the two
> Was afraid in an oft-repeated dream
>   Of what the tree might do.

Such desperate fears push the wife to the limits of control and finally past the limits: on a moment's impulse she runs away, disappearing into the woods, and that is the last we hear of her. She has been tried by nature, and she has been found insufficiently strong; she is one of the failures. Again and again Frost's poetry insists that in this life we must be tough, resourceful, and resilient if we are to endure; lacking these qualities, the Hill Wife goes down to defeat. . . .

With springtime's momentary beauty gone, the rest of the year appears as a time of deficiency: "a diminished thing," as "The Oven Bird" tells us. In this poem, the bird of the title is left to contemplate the ruin that is summer, a time when other birds have ceased to sing, when most flowers have disappeared, when pear and cherry blossoms have fallen to earth, when "the highway dust is over all." There is not much left that is attractive, and the oven bird knows it ("the question that he frames in all but words / Is what to make of a diminished thing"). Unlike the Hill Wife, however, he can take whatever life gives him; he is a realist who sees exactly what is happening and can make the proper adjustments. He knows that the summer is a time of loss, and he refuses to sing, for singing would be inappropriate. With his metallic chatter, however, he will at least make a noise. The sound is not beautiful, but it's something; probably it's better than no sound at all. It's not what we would like, but it's as much as we have any right to expect. The oven bird knows how to adapt to circumstances; he is a survivor. He knows a lesser world when he sees one, and he shows us what to do.

"The Oven Bird" leaves us with a world in disarray; nature is drab and desolate, and it has no message for us, either of grief or consolation. In this regard it stands opposed to those nature writings (like Wordsworth's "Prelude" or Faulkner's "The Bear") that center upon moments of illumination, when nature deigns to speak to man, to make some gesture in his direction. At such times the veil is removed and nature stands revealed; one is permitted an insight into essential truth. If Frost's poetry insists on anything, however, it insists on the impenetrable barrier between man and nature: we live in a world that we cannot know, for it will not reveal itself; and yet we yearn for some sort of communion. The speaker in "The Most Of It," for example, fervently asks for a revelation:

> Some morning from the boulder-broken beach
> He would cry out on life, that what it wants
> Is not its own love back in copy speech,
> But counter love, original response.

He searches for reassurance that he does not live in a world that ignores him and is totally indifferent toward his welfare; he is looking for a *sign:*

> And nothing ever came of what he cried
> Unless it was the embodiment that crashed
> In the cliff's talus on the other side,
> And then in the far distant water splashed,
> But after a time allowed for it to swim,
> Instead of proving human when it neared
> And someone else additional to him,
> As a great buck it powerfully appeared,
> Pushing the crumpled water up ahead,
> And landed pouring like a waterfall,
> And stumbled through the rocks with horny tread,
> And forced the underbrush—and that was all.

And that was all. Does he get an answer? Is this the sign he wanted? We cannot say, for the poem is deliberately uncertain on this point (Characteristically, a Frost poem deals with questions, not with solutions). If this *is* an answer, however, it is not the answer that was sought. The speaker was asking for "counter love"; but this "embodiment" of a great buck, if it is a sign of anything, is a sign of *power*. It knows nothing of love. . . .

. . . In "Neither Out Far Nor In Deep" Frost depicts the futility of the human search for certainty: people line the beach, their backs turned to the land, and stare all day at the sea—

> They cannot look out far.
> They cannot look in deep.
> But when was that ever a bar
> To any watch they keep?

The watch is maintained continuously, as though the people were waiting for an imminent sign; but there is no sign, only the overwhelming indifference of an unresponsive nature.

Faced with rejection, Frost does not yearn for any deep relationship with nature; he is no Shelley, crying out for union with powers beyond him. Like the oven bird, he adjusts to the situation and carries on a separate existence; he sees the way things are, and he knows what must be. When, in "The Need of Being Versed in Country Things," he describes the human tragedy of a house destroyed by fire, he does not lament; for tragedy depends on how you see a thing, and Frost realizes that the human perspective is not the only one possible. For the phoebes that flocked around the ruined house, "there was nothing really sad." They went about their ways as usual; human sorrows were none of their business, and in any case, life is like that: one must go on, one must survive. Perhaps the barest (and most effective) statement of this theme in Frost's poetry is in " 'Out, Out—,' " a poem describing the death of a child when a buzz-saw accidentally cuts through his wrist. Dead, he is useless: "No more to build on there." The survivors carry on: "And they, since they / Were not the one dead, turned to their affairs." That is what happens; that is the way it must be. . . .

"My Kind of Fooling":
The Deceptiveness of Robert Frost[1]

by James L. Potter

If the public image of Robert Frost as a man and as a poet is deceptive, the fault is partly his and partly ours. He helped to foster his image as a kindly and humorous rural sage in his public appearances and his poetry, and many people have been unable or unwilling to see anything else. Thoughtful readers of Frost are inevitably distressed by the limitations and falsifications of the Frost myth in its simple form; it persists mainly

[1] From *Robert Frost Handbook* (University Park: Pennsylvania State University Press, 1980), 47–68.

because many readers find comfort in it, because it answers a need to preserve various myths, some merely popular, some central to our culture.[2] Fortunately it has been revised by increasing knowledge about Frost and his work. Anyone who reads much of his poetry intently, or who has read the studies of his poetry of such critics and scholars as Lawrance Thompson, Reginald L. Cook, John F. Lynen, Reuben A. Brower, and Frank Lentricchia, knows how much more complex Frost is than the simple myth indicates.

Thompson's biography of Frost has made clear that the myth was partly created and significantly developed and propagated by the poet himself.[3] We have learned of many episodes in Frost's life when he deliberately worked up his public image directly or indirectly. Certainly that image corresponded to much that he actually was—but not to all that he was. He was often kind, thoughtful, and helpful, and even more, often wise; frequently he seemed most content with the simplicities of the rural life—as his persistent "botanizing" suggests—in contrast to the difficulties of urban existence. Thus the Frost myth is valid to a significant degree. But at the same time, Frost was often riddled with doubts about his position, his role in relation to his family and friends, and even his poetic powers. Evidently, he was often angry and bitter, sometimes despairing, and perhaps even suicidal at moments. One is reluctant to consider Frost a "tortured soul," but the mixture in him of attitudes, motives, and often unacknowledged characteristics leaves no doubt that a more complex image is needed than that of the Frost myth. As one comes to know the poet and his work well, one becomes uncertain of his basic character, and of the stance manifested in the poetry. Thompson has shown in biographical terms that Frost often concealed much of himself, good and bad, from many people, even from himself. Certainly, we have learned, he wore a mask in public much of the time, concealing his personal problems and complexities from his reading and listening audiences. Most accurately, we can say that Frost tried simultaneously to reach out to others and to hide from them. In his writings, too, he tried to put himself forward and remain in the background at the same time, and as a result produced poetry that is often quite deceptive—sometimes half-intentionally—for many readers.

Our concern is with Frost's poetry; the main question is, "Are we reading his poetry correctly?" To begin with, if we accede to the Frost myth, we oversimplify our reading. The myth implies, for one thing, that Frost's work is explicit, that everything in it is immediately available on the surface. Further, it suggests that his work is not so much "poetry" as "verse" (to make the snobbish distinction), hence less worth critical attention. It may be taken as simple stuff, casually tossed off—or at least

---

[2] See Dendinger, "Robert Frost, The Popular and the Central Poetic Images," pp. 792–804.

[3] *Early Years* and *Years of Triumph*.

not as painstakingly wrought as the poetry of Eliot or Yeats—and therefore not worth as much aesthetic attention. . . .

This Frost myth is also modified by the "darkness" in his poetry that Lionel Trilling emphasized when he called Frost a "terrifying" poet.[4] His vision is not only of pleasant farmland, gentle deer, and friendly people, but also of a darker universe:

> *Once by the Pacific*
> The shattered water made a misty din.
> Great waves looked over others coming in,
> And thought of doing something to the shore
> That water never did to land before.
>
> . . . .
>
> It looked as if a night of dark intent
> Was coming, and not only a night, an age.
> Someone had better be prepared for rage.
> There would be more than ocean-water broken
> Before God's last *Put out the Light* was spoken.

. . . "Once by the Pacific" . . . is a prophecy of doomsday. Frost always considered himself something of a prophet, and on at least one occasion referred to this poem as a vision of the horrors of World Wars I and II.[5] Whether the poem is prophetic or not, the natural world he decries here is far from benevolent. On the contrary, the emphasis is on the darkness and violence which man regards fearfully but powerlessly.

More important, the vision is of nature personified. The clouds and waves become savage embodiments of a universal enmity. Metaphysically, the poem suggests not merely an indifferent universe, but a brutally malevolent one, which is—since the poem indicates no justification for the "dark intent"—incomprehensible to us human victims and what is perhaps worst, the last two lines indicate that God himself is using this savage embodiment as His instrument, or is at least sanctioning its violence, as a preparation for the end of the world: God's command here is a counterpart of "Let there be light" in Genesis, but in contrast, there is no reason man can understand for the violent destruction of the world. This vision almost goes beyond the Old Testament God of Wrath or the Puritan's harsh deity, especially considering the dark humor of God's saying "Put out the light" as if to children, to signal the end of the world. Certainly, Frost is "terrifying" in much of his best poetry. . . .

When we acknowledge that Frost's work is more elusive than it appears, we begin to recognize how complex and indeed ambiguous it is. We find it difficult to identify his poetic stance with certainty. No doubt other contemporary poets are more profound; certainly many are more obviously complex. But Frost, because he hides behind a simple front, has

---

[4] Trilling, "A Speech on Robert Frost: A Cultural Episode," p. 451.
[5] *Years of Triumph*, pp. 304, 626, 725–726.

proven more difficult of access in practical terms. His superficial simplicity is being deeply penetrated, however, and the implicit tension that lies beneath the surface of much of his work is making itself felt more acutely. His work embodies opposing or inconsistent attitudes and impulses of many kinds, and out of this opposition comes the uncertainty that modern readers have become so sensitive to. . . .

From the circumstances of its composition we know that "Design" was originally aimed at the Reverend William Hayes Ward, who maintained a very rigid and narrow conception of divinity and of God's relationship with man and the world.[6] The version of the poem we have is poetically superior to the original, but thematically it is almost the same. The only significant difference in meaning appears in the last line, which first read, "Design, design! Do I use the word aright?," thereby leaving the theme just a little more uncertain than in the revision. The original reason for the hedging here, then, was to conceal the mockery aimed at the distinguished clergyman.

There are other equivocations involved in the history of the poem, however, revolving around the fact that most readers now interpret "Design" rather differently from the way Frost intended it. Usually [readers] see the poem as one of two things, either a suggestion that darkness or evil does design the universe, or that there is no design at all, merely chance. If design does govern in these particular small things, then it would seem to be evil. Or there may be no design at all—it may be simply long-worked-out odds that set up the white spider-flower-moth combination. "Natural selection," a refinement of chance, evidently may determine the colors of insects, with due allowance for "sports" like the white heal-all.

In a way, however, we are "deceived" in these two interpretations—they are not what the poem evidently meant to Frost. What he wanted to suggest to the Reverend Ward was: "If you insist that God's design governs every minute detail in the universe, you may find that some details suggest a dark and malevolent God." This argument is based on Frost's confidence in the goodness of God's design, which is nevertheless a general one, subject to partial and momentary anomalies. He was not seriously suggesting that God was evil, nor that He did not exist. By revising the last line Frost tried to make clearer his basic point, but the sonnet still was ambiguous—and, surprisingly, Frost allowed it to remain so. Our common interpretations are perfectly legitimate, of course, when we take the poem by itself; the "deception" lies in Frost's tacitly permitting those interpretations by refraining from further revision and explanations to clarify his original point (which he sometimes provided for "The Road Not Taken"). Frost may have sympathized with our interpretations; as Thompson suggests, he sometimes felt the power of

[6] *Early Years*, pp. 381–388, 582.

darkness strongly enough to do so.[7] In any case he refused to be more explicit about the theme of "Design," either because he felt it was clear enough as it stood, or because he was reticent about his intimate thoughts and emotions. Perhaps both motives were involved. . . .

One typical way Frost conceals himself is by his wit and humor. His work is pervaded by his sense of humor—he is continually joking, punning, indulging in what seems like sheer whimsy. Very few of his poems lack some touch of fooling, or at least of wittiness, sardonic though it may be at times. . . .

There are two basic reasons for this fooling. It is often a weapon, first of all, as in "A Hundred Collars" and "Departmental," where we are made to laugh at a stuffy professor on the one hand and at mankind in general, represented by the ants, on the other. Secondly, and more generally, Frost uses humor as a mask, to prevent others from seeing where he is most vulnerable. When he uses humor or wit as a weapon in irony, it also serves as a shield; "Irony is simply a kind of guardedness," he said. But he added, "So is a twinkle. It keeps the reader from criticism."[8] In other words, both aggressive wit and good-humored fooling enable him to hide from the reader. During his life he generally felt threatened; this would explain his wanting to hide in his poetry the real intensity of his feelings. More important, in many of his poems we can feel that intensity if we penetrate the surface humor. The perceptive reader can see beneath the tonal mask to the fundamental seriousness. . . .

Some poems of Frost's middle years manifest his sense of fun, such as "Departmental," "A Considerable Speck," and "The Literate Farmer and the Planet Venus." The rhythm of "Departmental," for one thing, is "good fun" and helps to set a similar tone for the poem; and then there are the phrases like "feelers calmly atwiddle," not to mention the general imagery of the earnest little ants, all going about their business.

In Frost's later volumes, from the forties on, the fooling seems to increase, but at the same time it is mixed more thoroughly with ironic notes. Typical is "It Bids Pretty Fair":

> The play seems out for an almost infinite run.
> Don't mind a little thing like the actors fighting.
> The only thing I worry about is the sun.
> We'll be all right if nothing goes wrong with the lighting.

This version of "all the world's a stage" is presented tongue-in-cheek, but it also has a satiric point at the expense of mankind in general and social critics in particular. . . .

---

[7] *Years of Triumph*, p. 388.

[8] Letter of 10 March 1924, *The Letters of Robert Frost to Louis Untermeyer*, pp. 165–166.

Often, Frost's wit takes the form of puns. Sometimes these are so inconsequential and awkward, like "pitching throne," that they seem whimsical. But usually Frost's puns are functional, helping to develop the themes of his poems fairly directly. In "Mending Wall," for instance, lines 31–33 raise the question of giving "offense" in building the wall. The pun on "a fence" directly concerns the validity of stone walls — the word play may be outrageous but it keeps the focus on a main issue in the poem. The same is true in a better-known case, that of "morning right" in "Design." There, "right" suggests "rite," and "morning" may suggest "mourning," both appropriately. Indeed, the conception of a ritual effectively intensifies the problematic question of universal design: If the white spider-flower-moth collocation embodies a ritual (as it must if only to the extent of being a breakfast scene), then what a design there may be for us all!

Puns are only one manifestation of Frost's wit, however, for his poetry abounds in clever phrasing and unexpected figures of speech. The epigrams represent the most obvious exercise of verbal cleverness, and it is tempting to chuckle at the phrasing without seriously considering Frost's meaning. The lines about his "fooling" quoted earlier are a case in point; the following are equally good:

(Forgive, O Lord)

Forgive, O Lord, my little jokes on Thee
And I'll forgive Thy great big one on me.

The neatly turned parallel phrasing reinforces and partly exemplifies the point of the explicit statement: This epigram itself is one of Frost's "little jokes" on God, and because he has made it, he can better endure God's "big joke," the difficulty and uncertainty of satisfying Him. The interrelated concepts that the two lines embody could serve as keys to Frost's moral and poetic philosophies, as we shall see later. . . .

. . . Frost's wit is not simply epigrammatic, however, for it is evident in the basic medium of his poetry, his imagery and figures of speech, and his diction, even in passages where he is at his most serious. He gives the woman speaker in "A Servant to Servants," who knows she is slowly going insane, a wry sense of humor:

Bless, you, of course you're keeping me from work,
But the thing of it is, I need to *be* kept.
There's work enough to do — there's always that;
But behind's behind. The worst that you can do
Is set me back a little more behind.
I shan't catch up in this world, anyway.

This speaker is like many others in Frost's dramatic pieces — they have a flair for a half-humorous, neat, and rather original turn of phrase, like Frost himself. And like Frost, they try to dissipate their worries by joking about them. They are exemplars of mythic rural New Englanders, whom Frost has adopted as his type. His public and literary image is founded partly on this type, and as personae in his poetry, they are partly him, despite their individual differences.

A similar rural New England wit comes more directly from Frost in the monosyllabic opening of "Directive": "Back out of all this now too much for us. . . ." Equally wittily, in a different way he later writes, "if you'll let a guide direct you / Who only has at heart your getting lost" (to the complexities of the modern world, of course). This kind of mild wit very often appears simply as understatement appropriate to the myth of the laconic Yankee, and is one of the most effective ways Frost's wit operates in serious contexts to shield him from the eyes of the reader. The severely understated ending of " 'Out, Out—,' " for instance, has seemed to some altogether too callous:

> They listened at his heart.
> Little—less—nothing!—and that ended it.
> No more to build on there. And they, since they
> Were not the one dead, turned to their affairs.

But one point of this conclusion is that it tries to mitigate the tragedy, as the woman in "A Servant" accepts hers, by accepting its inevitability and underplaying it. We get an even flatter understatement in "Acquainted with the Night," where the anti-emotional line "I have been one acquainted with the night" is the keynote and frame of the poem. . . .

Self-consciousness was an important element in the deceptiveness of "Design" and "The Road Not Taken" and in Frost's use of wit and humor. He held himself back knowingly, enjoying the fact that his more private or deeper thoughts and feelings were hidden from the reader. But this process must have become just as much a habit of mind as a deliberate technique. If it was a response to a real need he felt, it must have become second nature—and indeed it persisted and increased throughout his life.

Even more clearly, the element of irony is basic in Frost. Here, he does not try deliberately to deceive or maintain a pretense. Rather, most of the irony in his poetry reflects his cast of mind. There are some poems in which he establishes the classic ironic position of saying the opposite of what he really means, but for the most part, he is in the position of Northrop Frye's *eiron,* the persona who "makes himself invulnerable . . . , appearing to be less than [he] is."[9] Frost's use of understatement achieves a wit that often partakes of this kind of irony. But there are further examples which indicate that it is more than merely a manner of speaking. It is, one comes to realize, a central position for Frost, enabling him on the one hand to show the inadequacy of man's

---

[9] *Anatomy of Criticism,* p. 40.

expectations of life and the universe, and on the other to maintain one kind of defense against the incomprehensible powers and conditions surrounding him.[10] . . .

We find the same situation to some extent in a number of other poems like "The Vantage Point," "After Apple-Picking," and "All Revelation." Here he provides more specific hints about the implications of the poems, but that is all. We are still left with the job of exploring them. In "After Apple-Picking," for instance, Frost does say:

> For I have had too much
> Of apple-picking: I am overtired
> Of the great harvest I myself desired.

and he concludes,

> One can see what will trouble
> This sleep of mine, whatever sleep it is.
> Were he not gone,
> The woodchuck could say whether it's like his
> Long sleep, as I describe its coming on,
> Or just some human sleep.

On top of the description of apple-picking and its aftermath, these hints make it obvious that the poet is talking about considerably more than simply picking apples. We understand that he is concerned profoundly with the nature of man's life and his work and perhaps of his death, and even with further metaphysical considerations. But it is up to us to explore these. Frost is too reticent, even too diffident, to impose them on us explicitly. . . .

This objectivity and balance is even more obvious in the dramatic poems. Monologues like "A Servant to Servants" and "The Pauper Witch of Grafton" are almost completely objective character studies; Frost keeps himself out of them. There are, too, dialogues like "Home Burial" and "West-Running Brook," and a few dramatic poems with three or more speakers, like "Snow," all of which are considerably more objective than the *Masques*. In "Home Burial," typically, each speaker is partly at fault and partly justified in his attitude toward the other. The husband is rather callous, though not hard-hearted, and considerably more sensible; the wife is warmer and more sensitive, but almost neurotically unrealistic as well as imperceptive of her husband's real grief. In "Snow," similarly, we find ourselves sympathizing with each of the three *dramatis personae*, even Meserve for responding to the challenge of the storm.

"A Servant to Servants" is one of Frost's most strikingly successful dramatic monologues; the speaker, a farmer's wife, tells a silent inter-locutor about her situation, which she can perceive all too well, and

---

[10] See Greiner, "The Use of Irony in Robert Frost."

manifests half-consciously in the course of the narration the desperate effects of her entrapment, especially as it reflects the entrapment of the whole society of isolated farmers which she represents. She is imprisoned particularly by the work:

> It's rest I want—there, I have said it out—
> From cooking meals for hungry hired men
> And washing dishes after them—from doing
> Things over and over that just won't stay done.
> By good rights I ought not to have so much
> Put on me, but there seems no other way.

She is trapped also by the insanity in her family:

> I have my fancies: it runs in the family.
> My father's brother wasn't right. They kept him
> Locked up for years back there at the old farm.
> I've been away once—yes, I've been away.
> The State Asylum. . . .

She feels she cannot avoid these traps, but she does want to prevent her family's falling into the one that the "old-fashioned way" of keeping the insane at home represents.

> I've heard too much of the old-fashioned way.
> My father's brother, he went mad quite young.
> . . . .
> They soon saw he would do someone a mischief
> If he wa'n't kept strict watch of, and it ended
> In father's building him a sort of cage,
> Or room within a room, of hickory poles,
> Like stanchions in the barn, from floor to ceiling—
> . . . .
> Cruel—it sounds. I s'pose they did the best
> They knew. And just when he was at the height,
> Father and mother married, and mother came,
> A bride, to help take care of such a creature,
> And accommodate her young life to his.

She recognizes some of the effects on herself of her imprisonment, but only some of them—she knows that she can feel little, emotionally, but she is not conscious of her neurotic vagueness and uncertainty:

> I promised myself to get down some day
> And see the way you lived, but I don't know!
> With a houseful of hungry men to feed
> I guess you'd find . . . It seems to me
> I can't express my feelings, any more
> Than I can raise my voice or want to lift

My hand (oh, I can lift it when I have to).
Did you ever feel so? I hope you never.
It's got so I don't even know for sure
Whether I *am* glad, sorry, or anything.

Without a single word from her interlocutor, she is allowed to ramble
through her thoughts and stories and emerge as one of Frost's most
thoroughly individualized and realistic characters, as well as one of the
most uncomplaining yet pathetic victims of circumstance. Frost makes no
direct appeal for our sympathy; he stays in the authorial background and
lets the woman speak for herself. This objectivity of Frost's, coupled with
the woman's stoicism, keeps the poem from being sentimental.

What makes it truly difficult for readers of Frost is that he stays in the
background and puts himself forward simultaneously. He is a writer with
marked character—we can recognize his style and tone easily, and we
are familiar with his typical subjects. And in his lyrics, he seems to be
speaking in his own person. Yet he is elusive. Sometimes he seems to
confront us directly and explicitly, as in "Two Tramps in Mud Time" or
"Birches," where the conclusion is practically a spelled-out moral. But
usually he withholds or conceals himself to some extent. He may seem
on the surface to be saying one thing, while implying another; he may
seem to be half-joking, while really being serious; he may even half-
deliberately allow us to be misled for a time in interpreting certain poems.

What we see on the surface is certainly Frost, and we are sometimes
deceived, like the man in "The most of It," into thinking that that is all.
The more closely we examine Frost and his work, however, the more
clearly we see that much lies beneath the surface, that his work is
complex and ambiguous. The inconsistency between the surface impression of his poetry and the subtext is in itself a mark of that complexity.

Works Cited Compiled from Potter's Bibliography

Dendinger, Lloyd N. "Robert Frost: The Popular and the Central Poetic
  Images." *American Quarterly* 21 (1969): 792–804.
Frost, Robert. *The Letters of Robert Frost to Louis Untermeyer.* Ed.
  Louis Untermeyer. New York, 1963.
Frye, Northrop. *Anatomy of Criticism.* Princeton, 1957.
Greiner, Donald J. "The Use of Irony in Robert Frost." *South Atlantic
  Bulletin* 38 (1973): 21–37.
Thompson, Lawrance. *Robert Frost: The Early Years, 1874–1915.* New
  York, 1966.
———. *Robert Frost: The Years of Triumph, 1915–1938.* New York,
  1970.
———, and R. H. Winnick. *The Later Years, 1838–1963.* New York,
  1976.
Trilling, Lionel. "A Speech on Robert Frost: A Cultural Episode." *Par-
  tisan Review* 26 (1959): 445–52.

The Indispensable Robert Frost[1]

by Donald J. Greiner

On 6 April 1935, just before the publication of his last book, Edwin Arlington Robinson died. Soon after, Macmillan and Company, Robinson's publisher, asked Robert Frost to write a preface to the forthcoming *King Jasper*. Following several fits and starts, including a draft that was more about himself than Robinson, Frost completed one of his best essays which is known today as the "Introduction" to *King Jasper*. And in that essay, he wrote one of his clearest descriptions of the poet's goal: "The utmost of ambition is to lodge a few poems where they will be hard to get rid of. . . ."[2] Most readers will agree that Robert Frost lodged more than his share.

What is not easy to agree on, however is *which* of Frost's poems are lodged forever in American literature. Very few lists of the twelve best poems by Robert Frost would be identical. This is as it should be, for personal preferences always affect judgments of art. Just as difficult—and personal—is the task of examining Frost's canon to determine not only what is best but what is essential. The charge might be put this way: Which dozen parts of Frost's entire corpus, including poems, prose, letters, and remarks, are indispensable to the reader who would be conversant with the poet's achievement? In many cases, of course, the best and the essential are one and the same—but not always. This essay is one man's effort to answer the question. . . .

"Home Burial" was first published in *North of Boston* (1914). It is the best of the renowned dialogue poems not only because it movingly details a failing marriage but also because of its dazzling combination of sentence sounds and blank verse. Lawrance Thompson reports that Frost recalled writing the poem in 1912 or 1913 and that his inspiration was the marital estrangement between Nathaniel and Leona Harvey following the death of their first-born child in 1895.[3] Mrs. Harvey was Frost's wife's older sister. But as numerous scholars and Thompson himself point out, the composition of "Home Burial" cannot be totally separated

[1] From *Critical Essays on Robert Frost*, ed. Philip L. Gerber (Boston: G. K. Hall & Co., 1982), 220–40.

[2] Robert Frost, "Introduction" to Edwin Arlington Robinson, *King Jasper,* in *Selected Prose of Robert Frost,* eds. Hyde Cox and Edward Connery Lathem (New York: Holt, Rinehart and Winston, 1966), p. 63. The original is Edwin Arlington Robinson, *King Jasper* (New York: Macmillan, 1935).

[3] Thompson, II, pp. 597–598. [Greiner's original footnote 3 includes the following information: Lawrance Thompson, *Robert Frost: The Early Years, 1874–1915* (New York: Holt, Rinehart and Winston, 1966), p. 417. The other two volumes of the Frost biography are Thompson, *Robert Frost: The Years of Triumph, 1915–1938* (New York: Holt, Rinehart and Winston, 1970); and Thompson and R. H. Winnick, *Robert Frost: The Later Years, 1938–1963* (New York: Holt, Rinehart and Winston, 1976). Further references to these three volumes will be noted by volume and page number. All quotations of Frost's poetry are taken from *The Poetry of Robert Frost*, ed. Edward Connery Lathem (New York: Holt, Rinehart and Winston, 1969).]

from the death of Frost and Elinor's own first-born child, Elliott, in 1900 at age four. Mrs. Frost could not ease her grief following Elliott's death, and Frost later reported that she knew then that the world was evil. Amy in "Home Burial" makes the same observation. Further evidence that the poem may be partly autobiographical is Thompson's recollection of Frost's once telling him that he could never read "Home Burial" in public because it was "too sad." These biographical particulars are relevant when one remembers the American public's misconception of Frost's forty-three year marriage to Elinor as idyllic and serene.

But even if one dismisses biographical significance, one had to admire the technical virtuosity of "Home Burial." Frost himself did. In a letter (27 July 1914) to John Cournos, he explains both his pleasure with the poem and his innovative technique:

> I also think well of those four "don'ts" in Home Burial. They would be good in prose and they gain something from the way they are placed in the verse. Then there is the threatening
>
> "If—you—do!" (Last of Home Burial)
>
> It is that particular kind of imagination that I cultivate rather than the kind that merely sees things, the hearing imagination rather than the seeing imagination though I should not want to be without the latter.
>
> I am not bothered by the question whether anyone will be able to hear or say those three words ("If—you—do!") as I mean them to be said or heard. I should say that they were sufficiently self expressive.[4]

Frost was correct. These words are "sufficiently self expressive," and they illustrate his theory of sentence sounds as well as his letter to John Bartlett of 22 February 1914 explains it. His decision to combine the irregular rhythms of colloquial diction and normal speech patterns with the regularity of iambic pentameter revolutionized blank verse. The revolution was so total, in fact, that not only did such perspicacious critics as Ford Madox Heuffer feel bewildered but also such less perceptive readers as Jessie B. Rittenhouse, then the secretary of the Poetry Society of America, wondered if Frost would not be better off leaving the complexities of poetry for the relative safety of the short story.[5]

The four "don'ts" are a case in point. Frost positions them on the page so that the regularity of the iambic pentameter rhythm gives way to the irregularity of the husband's declaration and the wife's despairing response:

[4] *Selected Letters of Robert Frost,* p. 130. Greiner's original footnote 2 includes the following information: *Selected Letters of Robert Frost,* ed. Lawrance Thompson (New York: Holt, Rinehart and Winston, 1064).

[5] Jessie B. Rittenhouse, "*North of Boston:* Robert Frost's Poems of New England Farm Life," *New York Times Book Review,* 16 May 1915, p. 189.

"But the child's mound—"

                                              "Don't, don't don't,
don't," she cried.

The stresses fall on "child," "mound," and the first three "don'ts" to make the pentameter line. Frost then leaves incomplete the line of " 'don't', she cried" to illustrate the shattered communication between husband and wife that is the theme of "Home Burial."

A home is truly buried in this poem. Marital love is so engulfed by the disaster of the baby's death that the husband and wife exchange the effort to discuss their differences for a tense outbreak of accusations. The development of this theme is as important as the innovative technique in making "Home Burial" indispensable. For sexual love—itself a form of communication—also breaks down. Although the sexual allusions are never explicit, they reverberate throughout the poem from the very beginning: Amy cowers under the husband's "mounting," and their bedroom is equated with a graveyard:

> The little graveyard where my people are!
> So small the window frames the whole of it.
> Not so much larger than a bedroom, is it?

In recent years more and more readers have admitted that the difficulties of communication via sex as well as talk were always major considerations in Frost's work. This theme reaches its climax in the disturbing "The Subverted Flower," published in 1942, but it plays a key role in poems as early as "Love and A Question" and "A Prayer in Spring" in *A Boy's Will* (1913). Despite Frost's comments to the contrary, it seems certain that at least part of his personal experiences went into the writing of "Home Burial." Death and the threat of insanity were inextricably mixed with sex and love in his long marriage to Elinor, and his poetic rendering of this baffling mixture is one of the highlights of his career. "Home Burial" is a masterpiece, as modern in theme as it is in technique.

"After Apple-Picking" was first published in *North of Boston* (1914), and it is my nomination for Frost's greatest poem. In the letter to John Cournos (27 July 1914), Frost explains that "After Apple-Picking" is the only poem in his second book that "will intone."[6] Although he does not elaborate, he means that the rest of the poems sound like human speech whereas "After Apple-Picking" is a lyrical meditation on the tension between a job well done and the uncertainties accompanying the end of something significant. Note that the first word in the title is "After." Frost's refusal to specify what has ended, other than apple-picking, is one of the glories of the poem.

---

[6] *Selected Letters of Robert Frost*, pp. 129–130.

The other glories are the examples of technical brilliance. The rhymes alone are worth the reading. Every one of the forty-two lines is rhymed, but Frost eschews the tradition of rhyme scheme altogether. The result is a beautiful, even haunting, rendering of the natural progression of a person's meditation as he uneasily ponders the ambiguities which suddenly well up before him now that his job is done. Similarly, the brilliant use of irregular iambic pentameter, first experimented with in "Storm Fear," to suggest the uncertain balance between the poet figure's need to maintain form in the face of confusion and the threat to his effort cast in the form of truncated lines illustrates the union of technique and theme when Frost is at his best. Although the poem begins with its longest line, the iambic heptameter "My long two-pointed ladder's sticking through a tree,"[7] and includes a line as short as "For all," the meter invariably returns to the predominant rhythm of iambic pentameter as the meditator struggles to keep his balance in uncertainty as he has kept it on the ladder of his life.

Nuances of aspiration, satisfaction, completion, rest, and death echo throughout "After Apple-Picking" beginning with the title. Like the speaker, the reader never knows how far to pursue the mythical associations between apple and man's expulsion from Eden. If such associations are to be dismissed, then the speaker has safely and satisfactorily completed his task—whatever it literally is—of harvesting the "ten thousand thousand fruit." The phrase "after apple-picking" thus suggests rest. But the genius of the poem is that the speaker is never sure. If the associations between apples and Eden are not to be dismissed, then the poet figure has finished his life's work only to be confronted with an overwhelming uncertainty about what awaits him now. "After Apple-Picking" thus suggests death.

The imagery of hazy speculation is precise. The phrase "toward heaven" indicates the speaker's ultimate aspiration, and the line "Essence of winter sleep is on the night" reverberates with suggestions of termination and the question of rebirth. The point is that the poet figure needs answers to questions he will not pose, and he can only see as through a glass darkly:

> I cannot rub the strangeness from my sight
> I got from looking through a pane of glass
> I skimmed this morning from the drinking trough. . . .

The woodchuck, so unthinkingly confident of rebirth from its winter hibernation, cannot help him. "After Apple-Picking" is a poem of encroaching fear because it is a poem of uncertainty. Although the religious connotations are never obtrusive, this great poem is another of Frost's

---

[7] Accents fall on both "two" and "point. . . ."

explorations of what he considered to be man's greatest terror: that our best may not be good enough in Heaven's sight. . . .

"Design," first published in *American Poetry, 1922, A Miscellany* (1922) before being collected in *A Further Range* (1936), was begun in late 1911 or early 1912. On 15 January 1912, Frost sent a sonnet entitled "In White" to Susan Hayes Ward, one of the editors of the *Independent*, the journal that had first published a Frost poem in 1894. Part of the need to write "In White" came from an argument between Frost and Miss Ward's brother, William Hayes Ward, about the religious qualities of Henri Bergson's *Creative Evolution*. Frost defended Bergson against Ward's charge of atheism, and he wrote the first drafts of the poem that would become "Design" partly to answer Ward and partly in response to his reading of Bergson and of William James's *Pragmatism*.[8]

Questions about the benevolence of an all-powerful deity may have been in the background when Frost began "Design," but readers familiar with the scope of American literature will note its affinity with Poe's *The Narrative of Gordon Pym* and Melville's chapter in *Moby-Dick* titled "The Whiteness of the Whale." In each case the association between the color white and ambiguity leads to uncertainty or terror. Frost's poem builds from the confidence of "I found" through a series of questions to the crucial word "If."

Yet "Design" is indispensable as much for its form as for its theme. It is one of the most unusual and perfect sonnets by one of the finest sonneteers among major American poets. "Design" is an Italian sonnet with significant variations determined by theme. In the traditional Italian sonnet, the fourteen lines are divided into an octave and a sestet so that the sestet answers a question or solves a problem posed in the octave. The rhyme scheme may vary, but normally no more than five rhymes are permitted. Such a poem suggests the confidence of order; the sonnet fulfills the reader's expectations of developing form because both poem and problem are wrapped up at the end.

Not so in "Design." Writing a poem of uncertainty and fear, Frost reverses the traditional division of the Italian sonnet and describes a scene in the octave which he then questions in the sestet. The sestet is composed of three questions and a final line beginning with "If"—hardly the stuff of confidence. Equally important are the rhymes, for Frost limits the rhyme scheme to three rhymes as if he were keeping the tightest possible hold on a baffling scene that could engulf him.

The matter-of-fact beginning—"I found a dimpled spider, fat and white"—dissolves to a vision of evil in the guise of innocence. No allusion to a fat, white, dimpled baby can answer the question of why the blue flower is freakishly white, simultaneously attracting the white moth to it for protection and camouflaging the white spider that will devour

---

[8] The sonnet "In White" may be read in Thompson, I, p. 582.

the moth. "Design" is a nature poem in which the entire natural scene reeks of unnaturalness. Visions of Melville's albino whale hover behind it, but whereas Melville's whale is associated with both destruction and grandeur, Frost's tableau suggests only the void.

Frost's poet figure tries everything he can to stay his confusion: hints of innocence in such words as "dimpled," "snow-drop," and "flower"; puns on "right" and "appall"; allusions to *Macbeth*. But all of his efforts crumble before the relentless message of possible manipulation in such words as "mixes," "brought," "steered," and "govern." Although he hopes to temper his fear with the word "If" in the final line—"If design govern in a thing so small"—his situation is precarious no matter how he answers the query. If design does govern in such small matters, then what greater terror awaits man, who surely counts for more than a spider and a moth? If design does not govern, then what is man to do in the face of such mindless destruction?

This brilliant sonnet uses an unexpected relationship between octave and sestet and an unusual rhyme scheme to illustrate an unnatural experience. Perverted natural form affects poetic form, and deviation on two levels results. And yet the affirmation of technique counters the pessimism of theme. In the "Letter to *The Amherst Student*" (25 March 1935), Frost writes, "When in doubt there is always form for us to go on with. . . . To me any little form I assert upon it is velvet, as the saying is, and to be considered for how much more it is than nothing."[9] This is the case in "Design." The poet figure may fall to uncertainty, but not the poet. Writing a poem was Frost's way of asserting himself against the void. Faced with a baffling scene and the terrifying prospect of questions forever raised and always unanswered, Frost stays his confusion, if only momentarily, by casting it in the shape of one of the most ordered forms in all poetry, the sonnet. . . .

"Directive" (*Steeple Bush*, 1947) was first published in the *Virginia Quarterly Review* for Winter 1946. The poem was probably written between 1944 and 1946; for like two important poems composed during these years, *A Masque of Reason* (1945) and *A Masque of Mercy* (1947), it illustrates Frost's concern at that time with religious matters. Additional evidence that the poem may have been written in the middle 1940s is Theodore Morrison's essay "The Agitated Heart" in which he recalls a conversation between Frost and Hyde Cox during which Cox explained that Christ spoke in parables not because they were easy to understand but because they prevented the wrong listeners from grasping the message.[10] According to Cox, Frost was delighted with this comment. It is indeed probable, then, that the following lines in "Directive" have their genesis in Frost's conversation with Cox:

[9] *Selected Letters of Robert Frost*, pp. 418–419.
[10] Theodore Morrison, "The Agitated Heart," *Atlantic Monthly* (July 1967), 72–79.

A broken drinking goblet like the Grail
Under a spell so the wrong ones can't find it,
So can't get saved, as Saint Mark says they mustn't.[11]

Although Frost is reported to have joked once that "Directive" is his "Eliot poem" because it mentions the Holy Grail, the religious trappings are not throw-aways. Allusions to the Crucifixion ("tatters hung on barb and thorn") and to God as the final source ("Too lofty and original to rage") are offered seriously to those readers who would experience the poem as a religious statement. Frost himself pointed to the word "source" as the center of "Directive": "the key lines, if you want to know, are 'Cold as a spring as yet so near its source, / Too lofty and original to rage.' . . . But the key word in the whole poem is source — whatever source it is."[12]

Despite the importance of the religious tone, the poem is indispensable because it nudges the reader to consider sources beyond religion. Frost hints as much when he comments on "whatever source it is," thus suggesting an extra-religious dimension. Similarly, Morrison quotes Frost as saying, "You can't be saved unless you understand poetry — or you can't be saved unless you have some poetry in you." Yet even if the reader is unaware of Frost's comments about the poem, he should not overlook the crucial hint within it.

"Directive" ends with the word "confusion": "Here are your waters and your watering place. / Drink and be whole again beyond confusion." A significant word in the Frost canon, "confusion" is probably best known as part of the memorable phrase in his essay "The Figure a Poem Makes" when he talks about "a momentary stay against confusion." Although the literal meaning of the phrase is that the completed poem stays the confusion which the poet experiences when he first begins to write, the context of the entire essay suggests that any consciously created form, but especially poetry, is a momentary stay against the permanence of confusion. Form stays chaos, but only for a while. Poems must be written again and again.

If this suggestion has merit, then the last great poem of Frost's career is as much about poetry as it is about religion. The source that helps mankind to be "whole again beyond confusion" will be different things to different people, but for Frost himself the source is poetry — it always was. The technique of "Directive" testifies to his artistic prowess in old age; he was seventy three when *Steeple Bush* was published. One can only marvel at the stately blank verse, the sudden opening line of mono-syllables, the metaphors of quest and home and child. But "Directive" is a major poem by any standard because it insists on the close relationship

---

[11] The biblical allusion is to Mark 4:11–12.
[12] Thompson and Winnick, III, p. 406.

between artistic creation and religious faith. Those familiar with the Frost biography know how his commitment to poetry clashed with his commitment to family. Frost was a survivor. He would not be beaten down by anyone's death but his own. When pressure threatened and chaos called, he always had poetry to go on with. Art was his source. To create it was to affirm wholeness.

Affirmation of creativity is the heart of Frost's canon. Even in his darkest verse, those lyrics and dialogue poems that unsettle the reader with glimpses of universal terror and portrayals of domestic fear, the affirmation of technique balances the pessimistic theme. He lodged so many poems in American literature that his best work will be forever necessary to the cultural health of the nation. The phrase "the indispensable Robert Frost" thus cuts two ways: it describes the stature of a major author, and it invites a discussion of those parts of his canon that the reader who would understand his work should know. Frost himself might not have agreed with the choices examined here, but eager to hold the spotlight he would have been pleased that the examination was taking place.

The Effects of Death on a Marriage
Beth Fowler
English 101

Robert Frost was a man well-acquainted with family tragedy. Many scholars believe that some of his poems parallel his own life. For example, Frost and his wife experienced the death of their four-year-old son, and his wife had much difficulty adjusting to this death. Frost's poem "Home Burial" deals with a couple whose marriage has become strained after the loss of their firstborn. The failed marriage is due not only to the loss of the child but also to the lack of communication between the couple and the different ways they have of dealing with their grief.

The death of a family member causes the greatest sense of loss a person can experience. The death of a child, especially the firstborn, can be exceptionally painful. During the time following the death, emotions are very intense. If these emotions are not dealt with properly, they can almost destroy family ties. Husbands and wives may react with hostility and blame toward each other. The husband and wife in a strong marriage may be able to work through these emotions and even become closer as a result, but a weak marriage may well fall apart under the stress.

The marriage portrayed in "Home Burial" is weakened by a lack of communication. The wife, Amy, feels that her husband "couldn't care" about their child's death. However, the husband's apparent apathy stems from his way of dealing with grief. Believing that her husband is cold and callous, Amy refuses to share her feelings with him and instead takes her problems "to someone else". The husband realizes that unless they can communicate more effectively, their marriage will not survive. However, without Amy's help, there is little he can do to build a more open and understanding marriage.

The husband in "Home Burial" has a realistic and practical sense of grief. To help with his sorrow, he digs the child's "little grave". He tries to go on with his daily routine to ease his pain. He prefers to talk about "everyday concerns" rather than about the child's death. It is common for men in American society to have difficulty in openly expressing their feelings. He has trouble relating to his wife because his concept of grief is so radically different from hers. As he states in the poem, "My words are nearly always an offense."

Amy's misconception that her husband does not care that their child is dead seriously threatens their marriage. She feels that mourning in her husband's fashion is hard-hearted and uncaring. She even states, "I won't have grief so." Amy believes that she should continue grieving for her child until she reaches the grave herself. She claims that others only "make pretense of following to the grave." Because he tries to get on with this life, Amy believes that her husband feels no sorrow with regard to their dead child.

The death of the child in "Home Burial" precipitates the death of the relationship between the husband and wife. In this poem, Frost skillfully conveys the impact that losing a child can have on a marriage. The dialogue he uses demonstrates the devastating effect that the lack of communication can have in this circumstance. He describes the different ways of grieving by the husband and the wife in a powerful manner. One could assume that the realism of the poem may have been influenced by the reality of Frost's life.

Work Cited

Frost, Robert. "Home Burial." The Poetry of Robert Frost. Ed. Edward C. Lathem. 1st ed. New York: Holt, Rinehart & Winston, 1967. 51–55.

❏ Suggestions for Exploration and Writing

1. Write an essay explaining the causes for the failed marriage in "Home Burial."

2. Using the poem and the critical essays, explain how the speaker in "A Servant to Servants" is trapped by both heredity and environment. What is her attitude about the situation?

3. The husband in "Home Burial" says:

> We could have some arrangement
> By which I'd bind myself to keep hands off
> Anything special you're a-mind to name.

Though I don't like such things 'twixt those that love.
Two that don't love can't live together without them.
But two that do can't live together with them.

In an essay, attack or defend the husband's position.

4. Using the poems "Once by the Pacific," "Desert Places," and "Design" and the critical essays, write a documented essay on Frost's view of the "dark side" of nature.

5. Robert Frost presents a realistic—not a dark—view of life in his poems. Using at least two of the poems and information from the critical essays in this section, attack or defend this statement.

❏ **Suggestions for Writing**

1. One consistent **theme** in many of the works in this unit is that death is the ultimate equalizer since everyone has to die. Choose one or more of the works and show how death is an equalizer.

2. People are constantly susceptible to fears, prejudice, discrimination, and abuse of one sort or another. Describe an incident in which you were a victim of, or a witness to, one of these examples of human vulnerability.

3. Write an essay on racial, cultural, or gender vulnerability, examining one of the selections that deals with a race, culture, or gender other than your own.

4. Use two of the short stories to show how people try to deal with their own vulnerability by clinging to others.

5. Select at least two poems which deal with the reaction of the living to the death of a loved one. Write an essay discussing the survivors' emotions.

6. Human beings often react violently when they realize their own vulnerability. Using one or more of the selections in this unit to illustrate and support your points, classify and describe these violent reactions.

FREEDOM AND
RESPONSIBILITY

AMERICANS ARE ACCUSTOMED TO CELEBRATING their freedom without much thought. Seldom do they stop to realize what that freedom means or what it requires of them. The most seminal of American documents, the Declaration of Independence, espouses a doctrine that even today seems astoundingly revolutionary—the idea that governments "derive all power from the consent of the governed" and that when governments fail to serve their purpose in protecting citizens' rights, those citizens have the right—even the responsibility—to overthrow such governments. When Henry David Thoreau refused to pay a poll tax and when Martin Luther King led peaceful protests against the segregation and brutal treatment of African Americans, they were simply acting on ideas—those of freedom and equality—contained in Jefferson's great founding document.

Freedom entails responsibilities and choices that can be a burden. In his lighthearted essay "A Chinese Reporter on Cape Cod," Guan Keguang deplores the bewildering variety of choices he faces simply in eating lunch. Sometimes the desire for freedom may compete with personal responsibilities to family and community as in Soyinka's play *The Lion and the Jewel*.

Often Americans fail to realize the extent to which those great values—freedom and equality—may be mutually exclusive. As Kurt Vonnegut's "Harrison Bergeron" demonstrates, an exact and universal equality may not only reduce freedom but produce a world that is culturally sterile. Nowhere is the terrible cost of freedom more graphically exemplified than in "The Ones Who Walk Away from Omelas," where the freedom and the comfort of a whole society depend on the brutal suffering of a single poor wretch.

Finally, several of the poems and Thoreau's essay demonstrate that freedom can be as much a mental state as a physical state. Just as Thoreau can declare himself free even while in prison, so the speakers in the poems by Wordsworth, Jarrell, Sexton, and Rich are, at least, in part, imprisoned by or freed by their own perceptions.

Essays

Thomas Jefferson (1743–1826)

Thomas Jefferson, the third president of the United States and author of the Declaration of Independence, was truly a Renaissance man—a statesman, a scientist, an architect, and an author. The son of a successful planter and a member of the famous Randolph family of Virginia, Jefferson spent most of his life in Virginia. As an architect, he designed both his home, Monticello, and the buildings of the University of Virginia. Jefferson is considered by many historians to be the foremost symbol of the American desire for individual freedom.

The Declaration of Independence

1   When in the course of human events, it becomes necessary for one people to dissolve the political bands which have connected them with another, and to assume among the powers of the earth, the separate and equal station to which the Laws of Nature and of Nature's God entitle them, a decent respect to the opinions of mankind requires that they should declare the causes which impel them to the separation.

2   We hold these truths to be self-evident, that all men are created equal, that they are endowed by their Creator with certain inalienable rights, that among these are life, liberty, and the pursuit of happiness. That to secure these rights, governments are instituted among men, deriving their just powers from the consent of the governed. That whenever any form of government becomes destructive of these ends, it is the right of the people to alter or to abolish it, and to institute new government, laying its foundation on such principles and organizing its powers in such form, as to them shall seem most likely to effect their safety and happiness. Prudence, indeed, will dictate that governments long established should not be changed for light and transient causes; and accordingly all experience hath shown, that mankind are more disposed to suffer, while evils are sufferable, than to right themselves by abolishing the forms to which they are accustomed. But when a long train of abuses and usurpations, pursuing invariably the same object, evinces a design to reduce them under absolute despotism, it is their right, it is their duty, to throw off such government, and to provide new guards for their future security. Such has been the patient sufferance of these Colonies; and such is now the necessity which constrains them to alter their former systems of government. The history of the present King of Great Britain is a history of repeated injuries and usurpations, all having in direct object the establishment of an absolute tyranny over these States. To prove this, let facts be submitted to a candid world.

He has refused his assent to laws, the most wholesome and necessary for the public good. 3

He has forbidden his Governors to pass laws of immediate and pressing importance, unless suspended in their operation till his assent should be obtained; and when so suspended, he has utterly neglected to attend to them. 4

He has refused to pass other laws for the accommodation of large districts of people, unless those people would relinquish the right of representation in the legislature, a right inestimable to them and formidable to tyrants only. 5

He has called together legislative bodies at places unusual, uncomfortable, and distant from the depository of their public records, for the sole purpose of fatiguing them into compliance with his measures. 6

He has dissolved representative houses repeatedly, for opposing with manly firmness his invasions on the rights of the people. 7

He has refused for a long time, after such dissolutions, to cause others to be elected; whereby the legislative powers, incapable of annihilation, have returned to the people at large for their exercise; the State remaining in the meantime exposed to all the dangers of invasion from without and convulsions within. 8

He has endeavoured to prevent the population of these states; for that purpose obstructing the laws for naturalization of foreigners; refusing to pass others to encourage their migration hither, and raising the conditions of new appropriations of lands. 9

He has obstructed the administration of justice, by refusing his assent to laws for establishing judiciary powers. 10

He has made judges dependent on his will alone, for the tenure of their office, and the amount and payment of their salaries. 11

He has erected a multitude of new offices, and sent hither swarms of officers to harass our people, and eat out their substance. 12

He has kept among us, in times of peace, standing armies without the consent of our legislatures. 13

He has affected to render the military independent of and superior to the civil power. 14

He has combined with others to subject us to a jurisdiction foreign of our constitution, and unacknowledged by our laws; giving his assent to their acts of pretended legislation: 15

For quartering large bodies of armed troops among us: 16

For protecting them, by a mock trial, from punishment for any murders which they should commit on the inhabitants of these States: 17

For cutting off our trade with all parts of the world: 18

For imposing taxes on us without our consent: 19

For depriving us in many cases of the benefits of trial by jury: 20

For transporting us beyond seas to be tried for pretended offenses: 21

For abolishing the free system of English laws in a neighbouring Province, establishing therein an arbitrary government, and enlarging its 22 boundaries so as to render it at once an example and fit instrument for introducing the same absolute rule into these Colonies:

23   For taking away our Charters, abolishing our most valuable laws, and altering fundamentally the forms of our governments:

24   For suspending our own legislatures, and declaring themselves invested with power to legislate for us in all cases whatsoever.

25   He has abdicated government here, by declaring us out of his protection and waging war against us.

26   He has plundered our seas, ravaged our coasts, burnt our towns, and destroyed the lives of our people.

27   He is at this time transporting large armies of foreign mercenaries to complete the works of death, desolation, and tyranny, already begun with circumstances of cruelty and perfidy scarcely paralleled in the most barbarous ages, and totally unworthy the head of a civilized nation.

28   He has constrained our fellow citizens taken captive on the high seas to bear arms against their country, to become the executioners of their friends and brethren, or to fall themselves by their hands.

29   He has excited domestic insurrections amongst us, and has endeavored to bring on the inhabitants of our frontiers, the merciless Indian savages, whose known rule of warfare, is an undistinguished destruction of all ages, sexes, and conditions.

30   In every stage of these oppressions we have petitioned for redress in the most humble terms: our repeated petitions have been answered only by repeated injury. A prince whose character is thus marked by every act which may define a tyrant is unfit to be the ruler of a free people.

31   Nor have we been wanting in attention to our British brethren. We have warned them from time to time of attempts by their legislature to extend an unwarrantable jurisdiction over us. We have reminded them of the circumstances of our emigration and settlement here. We have appealed to their native justice and magnanimity, and we have conjured them by the ties of our common kindred to disavow these usurpations, which would inevitably interrupt our connections and correspondence. They too have been deaf to the voice of justice and of consanguinity. We must, therefore, acquiesce in the necessity, which denounces our separation, and hold them, as we hold the rest of mankind, enemies in war, in peace friends.

32   We, therefore, the Representatives of the United States of America, in General Congress assembled, appealing to the Supreme Judge of the world for the rectitude of our intentions, do, in the name, and by authority of the good people of these Colonies, solemnly publish and declare, That these United Colonies are, and of right ought to be, Free and Independent States; that they are absolved from all allegiance to the British Crown, and that all political connection between them and the state of Great Britain, is and ought to be totally dissolved; and that as Free and Independent States, they have full power to levy war, conclude peace, contract alliances, establish commerce, and to do all other acts and

things which Independent States may of right do. And for the support of this declaration, with a firm reliance on the protection of Divine Providence, we mutually pledge to each other our lives, our fortunes, and our sacred honor.

❏ **Questions for Discussion**

1. Since the outcome of the rebellion will be determined by war in any case, why do Jefferson and his fellow patriots feel compelled to explain their reasons for rebellion?

2. What are the premises of Jefferson's argument?

3. What, according to Jefferson, is the purpose of government?

4. What are the abuses of power with which the Declaration charges King George III of England?

❏ **Suggestion for Exploration and Writing**

1. To what degree have governments and government agencies in the United States today—local, state, and federal—failed in their purpose and ignored the source of their power? To what degree have they succeeded? Cite specific examples.

HENRY DAVID THOREAU (1817–1862)

Henry David Thoreau exemplified American individualism, asserting the authority of free people against the dehumanizing effects of industrialization and coercive government. His most famous book, Walden *(1854), recounts two years he spent living in solitude in a cabin he built in the woods on Walden Pond. "Civil Disobedience," written after Thoreau spent a night in jail because he would not pay a poll tax that supported the Mexican War and slavery, influenced both Mahatma Gandhi and Martin Luther King, Jr.*

Civil Disobedience

I heartily accept the motto,—"That government is best which governs 1 least;" and I should like to see it acted up to more rapidly and systematically. Carried out, it finally amounts to this, which also I believe,— "That government is best which governs not at all;" and when men are prepared for it, that will be the kind of government which they will have. Government is at best but an expedient; but most governments are usually, and all governments are sometimes, inexpedient. The objections which have been brought against a standing army, and they are many and weighty, and deserve to prevail, may also at last be brought against a standing government. The standing army is only an arm of the standing government. The government itself, which is only the mode which the people have chosen to execute their will, is equally liable to be abused and perverted before the people can act through it. Witness the present Mexican war, the work of comparatively a few individuals using the standing government as their tool; for, in the outset, the people would not have consented to this measure.

2   This American government,—what is it but a tradition, though a recent one, endeavoring to transmit itself unimpaired to posterity, but each instant losing some of its integrity? It has not the vitality and force of a single living man; for a single man can bend it to his will. It is a sort of wooden gun to the people themselves; and, if ever they should use it in earnest as a real one against each other, it will surely split. But it is not the less necessary for this; for the people must have some complicated machinery or other, and hear its din, to satisfy that idea of government which they have. Governments show thus how successfully men can be imposed on, even impose on themselves, for their own advantage. It is excellent, we must allow; yet this government never of itself furthered any enterprise, but by the alacrity with which it got out of its way. *It* does not keep the country free. *It* does not settle the West. *It* does not educate. The character inherent in the American people has done all that has been accomplished; and it would have done somewhat more, if the government had not sometimes got in its way. For government is an expedient by which men would fain succeed in letting one another alone; and, as has been said, when it is more expedient, the governed are most let alone by it. Trade and commerce, if they were not made of India rubber, would never manage to bounce over the obstacles which legislators are continually putting in their way; and, if one were to judge these men wholly by the effects of their actions, and not partly by their intentions, they would deserve to be classed and punished with those mischievous persons who put obstructions on the railroads.

3   But, to speak practically and as a citizen, unlike those who call themselves no-government men, I ask for, not at once no government, but *at once* a better government. Let every man make known what kind of government would command his respect, and that will be one step toward obtaining it.

4   After all, the practical reason why, when the power is once in the hands of the people, a majority are permitted, and for a long period continue, to rule, is not because they are most likely to be in the right, nor because this seems fairest to the minority, but because they are physically the strongest. But a government in which the majority rule in all cases cannot be based on justice, even as far as men understand it. Can there not be a government in which majorities do not virtually decide right and wrong, but conscience?—in which majorities decide only those questions to which the rule of expediency is applicable? Must the citizen ever for a moment, or in the least degree, resign his conscience to the legislator? Why has every man a conscience then? I think that we should be men first, and subjects afterward. It is not desirable to cultivate a respect for

the law, so much as for the right. The only obligation which I have a right to assume, is to do at any time what I think right. It is truly enough said, that a corporation has no conscience; but a corporation of conscientious men is a corporation with a conscience. Law never made men a whit more just; and, by means of their respect for it, even the well-disposed are daily made the agents of injustice. A common and natural result of an undue respect for law is, that you may see a file of soldiers, colonel, captain, corporal, privates, powder-monkeys and all, marching in admirable order over hill and dale to the wars, against their wills, aye, against their common sense and consciences, which makes it very steep marching indeed, and produces a palpitation of the heart. They have no doubt that it is a damnable business in which they are concerned; they are all peaceably inclined. Now, what are they? Men at all? or small moveable forts and magazines, at the service of some unscrupulous man in power? Visit the Navy Yard, and behold a marine, such a man as an American government can make, or such as it can make a man with its black arts, a mere shadow and reminiscence of humanity, a man laid out alive and standing, and already, as one may say, buried under arms with funeral accompaniments, though it may be

"Not a drum was heard, nor a funeral note,
 As his corse to the ramparts we hurried;
Not a soldier discharged his farewell shot
 O'er the grave where our hero we buried."

The mass of men serve the State thus, not as men mainly, but as machines, with their bodies. They are the standing army, and the militia, jailers, constables, *posse comitatus,* &c. In most cases there is no free exercise whatever of the judgment or of the moral sense; but they put themselves on a level with wood and earth and stones; and wooden men can perhaps be manufactured that will serve the purpose as well. Such command no more respect than men of straw, or a lump of dirt. They have the same sort of worth only as horses and dogs. Yet such as these even are commonly esteemed good citizens. Others, as most legislators, politicians, lawyers, ministers, and office-holders, serve the State chiefly with their heads; and, as they rarely make any moral distinctions, they are as likely to serve the devil, without intending it, as God. A very few, as heroes, patriots, martyrs, reformers in the great sense, and *men,* serve the State with their consciences also, and so necessarily resist it for the most part; and they are commonly treated by it as enemies. A wise man will only be useful as a man, and will not submit to be "clay," and "stop a hole to keep the wind away," but leave that office to his dust at least: —

"I am too high-born to be propertied,
 To be a secondary at control,
 Or useful serving-man and instrument
 To any sovereign state throughout the world."

6   He who gives himself entirely to his fellow-men appears to them useless and selfish; but he who gives himself partially to them is pronounced a benefactor and philanthropist.

7   How does it become a man to behave toward this American government to-day? I answer that he cannot without disgrace be associated with it. I cannot for an instant recognize that political organization as *my* government which is the *slave's* government also.

8   All men recognize the right of revolution; that is, the right to refuse allegiance to and to resist the government, when its tyranny or its inefficiency are great and unendurable. But almost all say that such is not the case now. But such was the case, they think, in the Revolution of '75. If one were to tell me that this was a bad government because it taxed certain foreign commodities brought to its ports, it is most probable that I should not make an ado about it, for I can do without them: all machines have their friction; and possibly this does enough good to counterbalance the evil. At any rate, it is a great evil to make a stir about it. But when the friction comes to have its machine, and oppression and robbery are organized, I say, let us not have such a machine any longer. In other words, when a sixth of the population of a nation which has undertaken to be the refuge of liberty are slaves, and a whole country is unjustly overrun and conquered by a foreign army, and subjected to military law, I think that it is not too soon for honest men to rebel and revolutionize. What makes this duty the more urgent is the fact, that the country so overrun is not our own, but ours is the invading army.

9   Paley, a common authority with many on moral questions, in his chapter on the "Duty of Submission to Civil Government," resolves all civil obligation into expedience; and he proceeds to say, "that so long as the interest of the whole society requires it, that is, so long as the established government cannot be resisted or changed without public inconveniency, it is the will of God that the established government be obeyed, and no longer."—"This principle being admitted, the justice of every particular case of resistance is reduced to a computation of the quantity of the danger and grievance on the one side, and of the probability and expense of redressing it on the other." Of this, he says, every man shall judge for himself. But Paley appears never to have contemplated those cases to which the rule of expediency does not apply, in which a people, as well as an individual, must do justice, cost what it may. If I have unjustly wrested a plank from a drowning man, I must restore it to him though I drown myself. This, according to Paley, would be inconvenient. But he that would save his life, in such a case, shall lose it. This people must cease to hold slaves, and to make war on Mexico, though it cost them their existence as a people.

10   In their practice, nations agree with Paley; but does any one think that Massachusetts does exactly what is right at the present crisis?

> "A drab of state, a cloth-o'-silver slut,
>   To have her train borne up, and her soul trail in the dirt."

Practically speaking, the opponents to a reform in Massachusetts are not a hundred thousand politicians at the South, but a hundred thousand merchants and farmers here, who are more interested in commerce and agriculture than they are in humanity, and are not prepared to do justice to the slave and to Mexico, *cost what it may.* I quarrel not with far-off foes, but with those who, near at home, co-operate with, and do the bidding of those far away, and without whom the latter would be harmless. We are accustomed to say, that the mass of men are unprepared; but improvement is slow, because the few are not materially wiser or better than the many. It is not so important that many should be as good as you, as that there be some absolute goodness somewhere; for that will leaven the whole lump. There are thousands who are *in opinion* opposed to slavery and to the war, who yet in effect do nothing to put an end to them; who, esteeming themselves children of Washington and Franklin, sit down with their hands in their pockets, and say that they know not what to do, and do nothing; who even postpone the question of freedom to the question of free-trade, and quietly read the prices-current along with the latest advices from Mexico, after dinner, and, it may be, fall asleep over them both. What is the price-current of an honest man and patriot to-day? They hesitate, and they regret, and sometimes they petition; but they do nothing in earnest and with effect. They will wait, well disposed, for others to remedy the evil, that they may no longer have it to regret. At most, they give only a cheap vote, and a feeble countenance and God-speed, to the right, as it goes by them. There are nine hundred and ninety-nine patrons of virtue to one virtuous man; but it is easier to deal with the real possessor of a thing than with the temporary guardian of it.

All voting is a sort of gaming, like chequers or backgammon, with a slight moral tinge to it, a playing with right and wrong, with moral questions; and betting naturally accompanies it. The character of the voters is not staked. I cast my vote, perchance, as I think right; but I am not vitally concerned that the right should prevail. I am willing to leave it to the majority. Its obligation, therefore, never exceeds that of expedience. Even voting *for the right* is *doing* nothing for it. It is only expressing to men feebly your desire that it should prevail. A wise man will not leave the right to the mercy of chance, nor wish it to prevail through the power of the majority. There is but little virtue in the action of masses of men. When the majority shall at length vote for the abolition of slavery, it will be because they are indifferent to slavery, or because there is but little slavery left to be abolished by their vote. *They* will then be the only slaves. Only *his* vote can hasten the abolition of slavery who asserts his own freedom by his vote. 11

I hear of a convention to be held at Baltimore, or elsewhere, for the selection of a candidate for the Presidency, made up chiefly of editors, and men who are politicians by profession; but I think, what is it to any independent, intelligent, and respectable man what decision they may come to, shall we not have the advantage of his wisdom and honesty, 12 nevertheless? Can we not count upon some independent votes? Are there not many individuals in the country who do not attend conventions? But no: I find that the respectable man, so called, has immediately drifted from his position, and despairs of his country, when his country has more reason to despair of him. He forthwith adopts one of the candidates thus selected as the only *available* one, thus proving that he is himself *available* for any purposes of the demagogue. His vote is of no more worth than that of an unprincipled foreigner or hireling native, who may have been bought. Oh for a man who is a *man*, and, as my neighbor says, has a bone in his back which you cannot pass your hand through! Our statistics are at fault: the population has been returned too large. How many *men* are there to a square thousand miles in this country? Hardly one. Does not America offer any inducement for men to settle here? The American has dwindled into an Odd Fellow,—one who may be known by the development of his organ of gregariousness, and a manifest lack of intellect and cheerful self-reliance; whose first and chief concern, on coming into the world, is to see that the alms-houses are in good repair; and, before yet he has lawfully donned the virile garb, to collect a fund for the support of the widows and orphans that may be; who, in short, ventures to live only by the aid of the mutual insurance company, which has promised to bury him decently.

13   It is not a man's duty, as a matter of course, to devote himself to the eradication of any, even the most enormous wrong; he may still properly have other concerns to engage him; but it is his duty, at least, to wash his hands of it, and, if he gives it no thought longer, not to give it practically his support. If I devote myself to other pursuits and contemplations, I must first see, at least, that I do not pursue them sitting upon another man's shoulders. I must get off him first, that he may pursue his contemplations too. See what gross inconsistency is tolerated. I have heard some of my townsmen say, "I should like to have them order me out to help put down an insurrection of the slaves, or to march to Mexico,—see if I would go;" and yet these very men have each, directly by their allegiance, and so indirectly, at least, by their money, furnished a substitute. The soldier is applauded who refuses to serve in an unjust war by those who do not refuse to sustain the unjust government which makes the war; is applauded by those whose own act and authority he disregards and sets at nought; as if the State were penitent to that degree that it hired one to scourge it while it sinned, but not to that degree that it left off sinning for a moment. Thus, under the name of order and civil government, we are all made at last to pay homage to and support our own meanness. After the first blush of sin, comes its indifference; and from immoral it becomes, as it were, *un*moral, and not quite unnecessary to that life which we have made.

14   The broadest and most prevalent error requires the most disinterested virtue to sustain it. The slight reproach to which the virtue of patriotism is commonly liable, the noble are most likely to incur. Those who, while

they disapprove of the character and measures of a government, yield to it their allegiance and support, are undoubtedly its most conscientious supporters, and so frequently the most serious obstacles to reform. Some are petitioning the State to dissolve the Union, to disregard the requisitions of the President. Why do they not dissolve it themselves,—the union between themselves and the State,—and refuse to pay their quota into its treasury? Do not they stand in the same relation to the State, that the State does to the Union? And have not the same reasons prevented the State from resisting the Union, which have prevented them from resisting the State?

How can a man be satisfied to entertain an opinion merely, and enjoy   15
it? Is there any enjoyment in it, if his opinion is that he is aggrieved? If you are cheated out of a single dollar by your neighbor, you do not rest satisfied with knowing that you are cheated, or with saying that you are cheated, or even with petitioning him to pay you your due; but you take effectual steps at once to obtain the full amount, and see that you are never cheated again. Action from principle,—the perception and the performance of right,—changes things and relations; it is essentially revolutionary, and does not consist wholly with any thing which was. It not only divides states and churches, it divides families; aye, it divides the *individual,* separating the diabolical in him from the divine.

Unjust laws exist: shall we be content to obey them, or shall we   16
endeavor to amend them, and obey them until we have succeeded, or shall we transgress them at once? Men generally, under such a government as this, think that they ought to wait until they have persuaded the majority to alter them. They think that, if they should resist, the remedy would be worse than the evil. But it is the fault of the government itself that the remedy *is* worse than the evil. *It* makes it worse. Why is it not more apt to anticipate and provide for reform? Why does it not cherish its wise minority? Why does it cry and resist before it is hurt? Why does it not encourage its citizens to be on the alert to point out its faults, and *do* better than it would have them? Why does it always crucify Christ, and excommunicate Copernicus and Luther, and pronounce Washington and Franklin rebels?

One would think, that a deliberate and practical denial of its authority   17
was the only offence never contemplated by government; else, why has it not assigned its definite, its suitable and proportionate penalty? If a man who has no property refuses but once to earn nine shillings for the State, he is put in prison for a period unlimited by any law that I know, and determined only by the discretion of those who placed him there; but if he should steal ninety times nine shillings from the State, he is soon permitted to go at large again.

If the injustice is part of the necessary friction of the machine of   18
government, let it go, let it go: perchance it will wear smooth,—certainly the machine will wear out. If the injustice has a spring, or a pulley, or a rope, or a crank, exclusively for itself, then perhaps you may consider

whether the remedy will not be worse than the evil; but if it is of such a nature that it requires you to be the agent of injustice to another, then, I say, break the law. Let your life be a counter friction to stop the machine. What I have to do is to see, at any rate, that I do not lend myself to the wrong which I condemn.

19   As for adopting the ways which the State has provided for remedying the evil, I know not of such ways. They take too much time, and a man's life will be gone. I have other affairs to attend to. I came into this world, not chiefly to make this a good place to live in, but to live in it, be it good or bad. A man has not every thing to do, but something; and because he cannot do *every thing,* it is not necessary that he should do *something* wrong. It is not my business to be petitioning the governor or the legislator any more than it is theirs to petition me; and, if they should not hear my petition, what should I do then? But in this case the State has provided no way: its very Constitution is the evil. This may seem to be harsh and stubborn and unconciliatory; but it is to treat with the utmost kindness and consideration the only spirit that can appreciate or deserves it. So is all change for the better, like birth and death which convulse the body.

20   I do not hesitate to say, that those who call themselves abolitionists should at once effectually withdraw their support, both in person and property, from the government of Massachusetts, and not wait till they constitute a majority of one, before they suffer the right to prevail through them. I think that it is enough if they have God on their side, without waiting for that other one. Moreover, any man more right than his neighbors, constitutes a majority of one already.

21   I meet this American government, or its representative the State government, directly, and face to face, once a year, no more, in the person of its tax-gatherer; this is the only mode in which a man situated as I am necessarily meets it; and it then says distinctly, Recognize me; and the simplest, the most effectual, and, in the present posture of affairs, the indispensablest mode of treating with it on this head, of expressing your little satisfaction with and love for it, is to deny it then. My civil neighbor, the tax-gatherer, is the very man I have to deal with,—for it is, after all, with men and not with parchment that I quarrel,—and he has voluntarily chosen to be an agent of the government. How shall he ever know well what he is and does as an officer of the government, or as a man, until he is obliged to consider whether he shall treat me, his neighbor, for whom he has respect, as a neighbor and well-disposed man, or as a maniac and disturber of the peace, and see if he can get over this obstruction to his neighborliness without a ruder and more impetuous thought or speech corresponding with his action? I know this well, that if one thousand, if one hundred, if ten men whom I could name,—if ten *honest* men only,— aye, if *one* HONEST man, in this State of Massachusetts, *ceasing to hold slaves,* were actually to withdraw from this co-partnership, and be locked up in the county jail therefor, it would be the abolition of slavery in

America. For it matters not how small the beginning may seem to be: what is once well done is done for ever. But we love better to talk about it: that we say is our mission. Reform keeps many scores of newspapers in its service, but not one man. If my esteemed neighbor, the State's ambassador, who will devote his days to the settlement of the question of human rights in the Council Chamber, instead of being threatened with the prisons of Carolina, were to sit down the prisoner of Massachusetts, that State which is so anxious to foist the sin of slavery upon her sister, — though at present she can discover only the act of inhospitality to be the ground of a quarrel with her, — the Legislature would not wholly waive the subject the following winter.

Under a government which imprisons any unjustly, the true place for a just man is also a prison. The proper place to-day, the only place which Massachusetts has provided for her freer and less desponding spirits, is in her prisons, to be put out and locked out of the State by her own act, as they have already put themselves out by their principles. It is there that the fugitive slave, and the Mexican prisoner on parole, and the Indian come to plead the wrongs of his race, should find them; on that separate, but more free and honorable ground, where the State places those who are not *with* her but *against* her, — the only house in a slave-state in which a free man can abide with honor. If any think that their influence would be lost there, and their voices no longer afflict the ear of the State, that they would not be as an enemy within its walls, they do not know by how much truth is stronger than error, nor how much more eloquently and effectively he can combat injustice who has experienced a little in his own person. Cast your whole vote, not a strip of paper merely, but your whole influence. A minority is powerless while it conforms to the majority; it is not even a minority then; but it is irresistible when it clogs by its whole weight. If the alternative is to keep all just men in prison, or give up war and slavery, the State will not hesitate which to choose. If a thousand men were not to pay their tax-bills this year, that would not be a violent and bloody measure, as it would be to pay them, and enable the State to commit violence and shed innocent blood. This is, in fact, the definition of a peaceable revolution, if any such is possible. If the tax-gatherer, or any other public officer, asks me, as one has done, "But what shall I do?" my answer is, "If you really wish to do any thing, resign your office." When the subject has refused allegiance, and the officer has resigned his office, then the revolution is accomplished. But even suppose blood should flow. Is there not a sort of blood shed when the conscience is wounded? Through this wound a man's real manhood and immortality flow out, and he bleeds to an everlasting death. I see this blood flowing now.

22

I have contemplated the imprisonment of the offender, rather than the seizure of his goods, — though both will serve the same purpose, — because they who assert the purest right, and consequently are most dangerous to a corrupt State, commonly have not spent much time in

23

accumulating property. To such the State renders comparatively small service, and a slight tax is wont to appear exorbitant, particularly if they are obliged to earn it by special labor with their hands. If there were one who lived wholly without the use of money, the State itself would hesitate to demand it of him. But the rich man—not to make any invidious comparison—is always sold to the institution which makes him rich. Absolutely speaking, the more money, the less virtue; for money comes between a man and his objects, and obtains them for him; and it was certainly no great virtue to obtain it. It puts to rest many questions which he would otherwise be taxed to answer; while the only new question which it puts is the hard but superfluous one, how to spend it. Thus his moral ground is taken from under his feet. The opportunities of living are diminished in proportion as what are called the "means" are increased. The best thing a man can do for his culture when he is rich is to endeavour to carry out those schemes which he entertained when he was poor. Christ answered the Herodians according to their condition. "Show me the tribute-money," said he;—and one took a penny out of his pocket;—If you use money which has the image of Caesar on it, and which he has made current and valuable, that is, *if you are men of the State,* and gladly enjoy the advantages of Caesar's government, then pay him back some of his own when he demands it; "Render therefore to Caesar that which is Caesar's, and to God those things which are God's,"—leaving them no wiser than before as to which was which; for they did not wish to know.

24   When I converse with the freest of my neighbors, I perceive that, whatever they may say about the magnitude and seriousness of the question, and their regard for the public tranquillity, the long and the short of the matter is, that they cannot spare the protection of the existing government, and they dread the consequences of disobedience to it to their property and families. For my own part, I should not like to think that I ever rely on the protection of the State. But, if I deny the authority of the State when it presents its tax-bill, it will soon take and waste all my property, and so harass me and my children without end. This is hard. This makes it impossible for a man to live honestly and at the same time comfortably in outward respects. It will not be worth the while to accumulate property; that would be sure to go again. You must hire or squat somewhere, and raise but a small crop, and eat that soon. You must live within yourself, and depend upon yourself, always tucked up and ready for a start, and not have many affairs. A man may grow rich in Turkey even, if he will be in all respects a good subject of the Turkish government. Confucius said,—"If a State is governed by the principles of reason, poverty and misery are subjects of shame; if a State is not governed by the principles of reason, riches and honors are the subjects of shame." No: until I want the protection of Massachusetts to be extended to me in some distant southern port, where my liberty is

endangered, or until I am bent solely on building up an estate at home by peaceful enterprise, I can afford to refuse allegiance to Massachusetts, and her right to my property and life. It costs me less in every sense to incur the penalty of disobedience to the State, than it would to obey. I should feel as if I were worth less in that case.

Some years ago, the State met me in behalf of the church, and commanded me to pay a certain sum toward the support of a clergyman whose preaching my father attended, but never I myself. "Pay it," it said, "or be locked up in the jail." I declined to pay. But, unfortunately, another man saw fit to pay it. I did not see why the schoolmaster should be taxed to support the priest, and not the priest the schoolmaster; for I was not the State's schoolmaster, but I supported myself by voluntary subscription. I did not see why the lyceum should not present its tax-bill, and have the State to back its demand, as well as the church. However, at the request of the selectmen, I condescended to make some such statement as this in writing: — "Know all men by these presents, that I, Henry Thoreau, do not wish to be regarded as a member of any incorporated society which I have not joined." This I gave to the town-clerk; and he has it. The State, having thus learned that I did not wish to be regarded as a member of that church, has never made a like demand on me since; though it said that it must adhere to its original presumption that time. If I had known how to name them, I should then have signed off in detail from all the societies which I never signed on to; but I did not know where to find a complete list.

I have paid no poll-tax for six years. I was put into a jail once on this account, for one night; and, as I stood considering the walls of solid stone, two or three feet thick, the door of wood and iron, a foot thick, and the iron grating which strained the light, I could not help being struck with the foolishness of that institution which treated me as if I were mere flesh and blood and bones, to be locked up. I wondered that it should have concluded at length that this was the best use it could put me to, and had never thought to avail itself of my services in some way. I saw that, if there was a wall of stone between me and my townsmen, there was a still more difficult one to climb or break through, before they could get to be as free as I was. I did not for a moment feel confined, and the walls seemed a great waste of stone and mortar. I felt as if I alone of all my townsmen had paid my tax. They plainly did not know how to treat me, but behaved like persons who are underbred. In every threat and in every compliment there was a blunder; for they thought that my chief desire was to stand the other side of that stone wall. I could not but smile to see how industriously they locked the door on my meditations, which followed them out again without let or hinderance, and *they* were really all that was dangerous. As they could not reach me, they had resolved to punish my body; just as boys, if they cannot come at some person against whom they have a spite, will abuse his dog. I saw that the

State was half-witted, that it was timid as a lone woman with her silver spoons, and that it did not know its friends from its foes, and I lost all my remaining respect for it, and pitied it.

27   Thus the State never intentionally confronts a man's sense, intellectual or moral, but only his body, his senses. It is not armed with superior wit or honesty, but with superior physical strength. I was not born to be forced. I will breathe after my own fashion. Let us see who is the strongest. What force has a multitude? They only can force me who obey a higher law than I. They force me to become like themselves. I do not hear of *men* being *forced* to live this way or that by masses of men. What sort of life were that to live? When I meet a government which says to me, "Your money or your life," why should I be in haste to give it my money? It may be in a great strait, and not know what to do: I cannot help that. It must help itself; do as I do. It is not worth the while to snivel about it. I am not responsible for the successful working of the machinery of society. I am not the son of the engineer. I perceive that, when an acorn and a chestnut fall side by side, the one does not remain inert to make way for the other, but both obey their own laws, and spring and grow and flourish as best they can, till one, perchance, overshadows and destroys the other. If a plant cannot live according to its nature, it dies; and so a man.

28   The night in prison was novel and interesting enough. The prisoners in their shirt-sleeves were enjoying a chat and the evening air in the door-way, when I entered. But the jailer said, "Come, boys, it is time to lock up;" and so they dispersed, and I heard the sound of their steps returning into the hollow apartments. My room-mate was introduced to me by the jailer, as "a first-rate fellow and a clever man." When the door was locked, he showed me where to hang my hat, and how he managed matters there. The rooms were whitewashed once a month; and this one, at least, was the whitest, most simply furnished, and probably the neatest apartment in the town. He naturally wanted to know where I came from, and what brought me there; and, when I had told him, I asked him in my turn how he came there, presuming him to be an honest man, of course; and, as the world goes, I believe he was. "Why," said he, "they accuse me of burning a barn; but I never did it." As near as I could discover, he had probably gone to bed in a barn when drunk, and smoked his pipe there; and so a barn was burnt. He had the reputation of being a clever man, had been there some three months waiting for his trial to come on, and would have to wait as much longer; but he was quite domesticated and contented, since he got his board for nothing, and thought that he was well treated.

29   He occupied one window, and I the other; and I saw, that if one stayed there long, his principal business would be to look out the window. I had soon read all the tracts that were left there, and

examined where former prisoners had broken out, and where a grate had been sawed off, and heard the history of the various occupants of that room; for I found that even here there was a history and a gossip which never circulated beyond the walls of the jail. Probably this is the only house in the town where verses are composed, which are afterward printed in a circular form, but not published. I was shown quite a long list of verses which were composed by some young men who had been detected in an attempt to escape, who avenged themselves by singing them.

I pumped my fellow-prisoner as dry as I could, for fear I should never see him again; but at length he showed me which was my bed, and left me to blow out the lamp.   30

It was like travelling into a far country, such as I had never expected to behold, to lie there for one night. It seemed to me that I never had heard the town-clock strike before, nor the evening sounds of the village; for we slept with the windows open, which were inside the grating. It was to see my native village in the light of the middle ages, and our Concord was turned into a Rhine stream, and visions of knights and castles passed before me. They were the voices of old burghers that I heard in the streets. I was an involuntary spectator and auditor of whatever was done and said in the kitchen of the adjacent village-inn,—a wholly new and rare experience to me. It was a closer view of my native town. I was fairly inside of it. I never had seen its institutions before. This is one of its peculiar institutions; for it is a shire town. I began to comprehend what its inhabitants were about.   31

In the morning, our breakfasts were put through the hole in the door, in small oblong-square tin pans, made to fit, and holding a pint of chocolate, with brown bread, and an iron spoon. When they called for the vessels again, I was green enough to return what bread I had left; but my comrade seized it, and said that I should lay that up for lunch or dinner. Soon after, he was let out to work at haying in a neighboring field, whither he went every day, and would not be back till noon; so he bade me good-day, saying that he doubted if he should see me again.   32

When I came out of prison,—for some one interfered, and paid the tax,—I did not perceive that great changes had taken place on the common, such as he observed who went in a youth, and emerged a tottering and gray-headed man; and yet a change had to my eyes come over the scene,—the town, and State, and country,—greater than any that mere time could effect. I saw yet more distinctly the State in which I lived. I saw to what extent the people among whom I lived could be trusted as good neighbors and friends; that their friendship was for summer weather only; that they did not greatly purpose to do right; that they were a distinct race from me by their prejudices and superstitions, as the Chinamen   33 and Malays are; that, in their sacrifices to humanity, they ran no risks, not even to their property; that, after all, they were not so noble but they treated the thief as he had treated them, and hoped, by a certain outward observance and a few prayers, and by walking in a particular straight though useless path from time to time, to save their souls. This may be to judge my neighbors harshly; for I believe that most of them are not aware that they have such an institution as the jail in their village.

34   It was formerly the custom in our village, when a poor debtor came out of jail, for his acquaintances to salute him, looking through their fingers, which were crossed to represent the grating of a jail window, "How do ye do?" My neighbors did not thus salute me, but first looked at me, and then at one another, as if I had returned from a long journey. I was put into jail as I was going to the shoemaker's to get a shoe which was mended. When I was let out the next morning, I proceeded to finish my errand, and, having put on my mended shoe, joined a huckleberry party, who were impatient to put themselves under my conduct; and in half an hour,—for the horse was soon tackled,—was in the midst of a huckleberry field, on one of the highest hills, two miles off; and then the State was nowhere to be seen.

35   This is the whole history of "My Prisons."

36   I have never declined paying the highway tax, because I am as desirous of being a good neighbor as I am of being a bad subject; and, as for supporting schools, I am doing my part to educate my fellow-countrymen now. It is for no particular item in the tax-bill that I refuse to pay it. I simply wish to refuse allegiance to the State, to withdraw and stand aloof from it effectually. I do not care to trace the course of my dollar, if I could, till it buys a man, or a musket to shoot one with,—the dollar is innocent,—but I am concerned to trace the effects of my allegiance. In fact, I quietly declare war with the State, after my fashion, though I will still make what use and get what advantage of her I can, as is usual in such cases.

37   If others pay the tax which is demanded of me, from a sympathy with the State, they do but what they have already done in their own case, or rather they abet injustice to a greater extent than the State requires. If they pay the tax from a mistaken interest in the individual taxed, to save his property or prevent his going to jail, it is because they have not considered wisely how far they let their private feelings interfere with the public good.

38   This, then, is my position at present. But one cannot be too much on his guard in such a case, lest his action be biassed by obstinacy, or an undue regard for the opinions of men. Let him see that he does only what belongs to himself and to the hour.

I think sometimes, Why, this people mean well; they are only ignorant;   39
they would do better if they knew how: why give your neighbors this
pain to treat you as they are not inclined to? But I think, again, this is no
reason why I should do as they do, or permit others to suffer much
greater pain of a different kind. Again, I sometimes say to myself, When
many millions of men, without heat, without ill-will, without personal
feeling of any kind, demand of you a few shillings only, without the
possibility, such is their constitution, of retracting or altering their
present demand, and without the possibility, on your side, of appeal to
any other millions, why expose yourself to this overwhelming brute
force? You do not resist cold and hunger, the winds and the waves, thus
obstinately; you quietly submit to a thousand similar necessities. You do
not put your head into the fire. But just in proportion as I regard this as
not wholly a brute force, but partly a human force, and consider that I
have relations to those millions as to so many millions of men, and not
of mere brute or inanimate things, I see that appeal is possible, first and
instantaneously, from them to the Maker of them, and secondly, from
them to themselves. But, if I put my head deliberately into the fire, there
is no appeal to fire or to the Maker of fire, and I have only myself to
blame. If I could convince myself that I have any right to be satisfied with
men as they are, and to treat them accordingly, and not according, in
some respects, to my requisitions and expectations of what they and I
ought to be, then, like a good Mussulman and fatalist, I should endeavor
to be satisfied with things as they are, and say it is the will of God. And,
above all, there is this difference between resisting this and a purely brute
or natural force, that I can resist this with some effect; but I cannot
expect, like Orpheus, to change the nature of the rocks and trees and
beasts.

I do not wish to quarrel with any man or nation. I do not wish to split   40
hairs, to make fine distinctions, or set myself up as better than my
neighbors. I seek rather, I may say, even an excuse for conforming to the
laws of the land. I am but too ready to conform to them. Indeed I have
reason to suspect myself on this head; and each year, as the tax-gatherer
comes round, I find myself disposed to review the acts and position of the
general and state governments, and the spirit of the people, to discover a
pretext for conformity. I believe that the State will soon be able to take
all my work of this sort out my hands, and then I shall be no better a
patriot than my fellow-countrymen. Seen from a lower point of view, the
Constitution, with all its faults, is very good; the law and the courts are
very respectable; even this State and this American government are, in
many respects, very admirable and rare things, to be thankful for, such as
a great many have described them; but seen from a point of view a little
higher, they are what I have described them; seen from a higher still, and
the highest, who shall say what they are, or that they are worth looking
at or thinking of at all?

41   However, the government does not concern me much, and I shall bestow the fewest possible thoughts on it. It is not many moments that I live under a government, even in this world. If a man is thought-free, fancy-free, imagination-free, that which *is not* never for a long time appearing *to be* to him, unwise rulers or reformers cannot fatally interrupt him.

42   I know that most men think differently from myself; but those whose lives are by profession devoted to the study of these or kindred subjects, content me as little as any. Statesmen and legislators, standing so completely within the institution, never distinctly and nakedly behold it. They speak of moving society, but have no resting-place without it. They may be men of a certain experience and discrimination, and have no doubt invented ingenious and even useful systems, for which we sincerely thank them; but all their wit and usefulness lie within certain not very wide limits. They are wont to forget that the world is not governed by policy and expediency. Webster never goes behind government, and so cannot speak with authority about it. His words are wisdom to those legislators who contemplate no essential reform in the existing government; but for thinkers, and those who legislate for all time, he never once glances at the subject. I know of those whose serene and wise speculations on this theme would soon reveal the limits of his mind's range and hospitality. Yet, compared with the cheap professions of most reformers, and the still cheaper wisdom and eloquence of politicians in general, his are almost the only sensible and valuable words, and we thank Heaven for him. Comparatively, he is always strong, original, and, above all, practical. Still his quality is not wisdom, but prudence. The lawyer's truth is not Truth, but consistency, or a consistent expediency. Truth is always in harmony with herself, and is not concerned chiefly to reveal the justice that may consist with wrong-doing. He well deserves to be called as he has been called, the Defender of the Constitution. There are really no blows to be given by him but defensive ones. He is not a leader, but a follower. His leaders are the men of '87. "I have never made an effort," he says, "and never propose to make an effort; I have never countenanced an effort, and never mean to countenance an effort, or disturb the arrangement as originally made, by which the various States came into the Union." Still thinking of the sanction which the Constitution gives to slavery, he says, "Because it was a part of the original compact,—let it stand." Notwithstanding his special acuteness and ability, he is unable to take a fact out of its merely political relations, and behold it as it lies absolutely to be disposed of by the intellect,—what, for instance, it behooves a man to do here in America to-day with regard to slavery, but ventures, or is driven, to make some such desperate answer as the following, while professing to speak absolutely, and as a private man,— from which what new and singular code of social duties might be inferred?—"The manner," says he, "in which the government of those

States where slavery exists are to regulate it, is for their own consideration, under their responsibility to their constituents, to the general laws of propriety, humanity, and justice, and to God. Associations formed elsewhere, springing from a feeling of humanity, or any other cause, have nothing whatever to do with it. They have never received any encouragement from me, and they never will."

They who know of no purer sources of truth, who have traced up its 43 stream no higher, stand, and wisely stand, by the Bible and the Constitution, and drink at it there with reverence and humility; but they who behold where it comes trickling into this lake or that pool, gird up their loins once more, and continue their pilgrimage toward its fountainhead.

No man with a genius for legislation has appeared in America. They 44 are rare in the history of the world. There are orators, politicians, and eloquent men, by the thousand; but the speaker has not yet opened his mouth to speak, who is capable of settling the much-vexed questions of the day. We love eloquence for its own sake, and not for any truth which it may utter, or any heroism it may inspire. Our legislators have not yet learned the comparative value of free-trade and of freedom, of union, and of rectitude, to a nation. They have no genius or talent for comparatively humble questions of taxation and finance, commerce and manufactures and agriculture. If we were left solely to the wordy wit of legislators in Congress for our guidance, uncorrected by the seasonable experience and the effectual complaints of the people, America would not long retain her rank among the nations. For eighteen hundred years, though perchance I have no right to say it, the New Testament has been written; yet where is the legislator who has wisdom and practical talent enough to avail himself of the light which it sheds on the science of legislation?

The authority of government, even such as I am willing to submit 45 to,—for I will cheerfully obey those who know and can do better than I, and in many things even those who neither know nor can do so well,—is still an impure one: to be strictly just, it must have the sanction and consent of the governed. It can have no pure right over my person and property but what I concede to it. The progress from an absolute to a limited monarchy, from a limited monarchy to a democracy, is a progress toward a true respect for the individual. Is a democracy, such as we know it, the last improvement possible in government? Is it not possible to take a step further towards recognizing and organizing the rights of man? There will never be a really free and enlightened State, until the State comes to recognize the individual as a higher and independent power, from which all its own power and authority are derived, and treats him accordingly. I please myself with imagining a State at last which can afford to be just to all men, and to treat the individual with respect as a neighbor; which even would not think it inconsistent with its own repose, if a few were to live aloof from it, not meddling with it, nor embraced by it, who fulfilled all the duties of neighbors and fellowmen. A State which bore this kind of fruit, and suffered it to drop off as fast as it ripened, would prepare the way for a still more perfect and glorious State, which also I have imagined, but not yet anywhere seen.

❏ Questions for Discussion

1. How does Thoreau feel about government? How does he feel about law? Explain your answers.

2. Why does Thoreau advocate revolution? What, according to Thoreau, are the limits of governmental authority? What has the government done to which Thoreau objects?

3. Why does Thoreau insist that it was useless to put him in jail? How does he regard being in jail? How does his stay there alter his view of his friends and neighbors?

4. Thoreau says, "There will never be a really free and enlightened State until the State comes to recognize the individual as a higher and independent power, from which all its own power and authority are derived, and treats him accordingly." Where did Thoreau get such a revolutionary idea?

❏ Suggestions for Exploration and Writing

1. Do you agree with Thoreau's statement that "there are nine-hundred and ninety-nine patrons of virtue to one virtuous man"? Write an essay in support of your response.

2. Attack or defend this statement: "Under a government that imprisons any unjustly, the true place for a just man is also a prison."

MARTIN LUTHER KING, JR. (1929–1968)

Martin Luther King, Jr., an ordained minister at the age of eighteen, was born in Atlanta, Georgia. He received degrees from Morehouse College, Crozer Theological Seminary, and Boston University. A leader of the civil rights movement, King organized the Montgomery, Alabama, bus boycott after Rosa Parks refused to give up her seat. He was also the founder and president of the Southern Christian Leadership Conference (SCLC), which espoused King's philosophy of nonviolence. This letter from jail was written in response to the local clergy who had questioned King's approach and methodology.

Letter from Birmingham City Jail

My dear Fellow Clergymen,

While confined here in Birmingham city jail, I came across your recent statement calling our present activities "unwise and untimely." Seldom, if ever, do I pause to answer criticism of my work and ideas. If I sought to answer all of the criticisms that cross my desk, my secretaries would be engaged in little else in the course of the day, and I would have no time for constructive work. But since I feel that you are men of genuine good will and your criticisms are sincerely set forth, I would like to answer your statement in what I hope will be patient and reasonable terms.

I think I should give the reason for my being in Birmingham, since you have been influenced by the argument of "outsiders coming in." I have the honor of serving as president of the Southern Christian Leadership Conference, an organization operating in every southern state, with headquarters in Atlanta, Georgia. We have some eighty-five affiliate organizations all across the South—one being the Alabama Christian Movement for Human Rights. Whenever necessary and possible we share staff, educational and financial resources with our affiliates. Several months ago our local affiliate here in Birmingham invited us to be on call to engage in a nonviolent direct-action program if such were deemed necessary. We readily consented and when the hour came we lived up to our promises. So I am here, along with several members of my staff, because we were invited here. I am here because I have basic organizational ties here.

Beyond this, I am in Birmingham because injustice is here. Just as the eighth century prophets left their little villages and carried their "thus saith the Lord" far beyond the boundaries of their hometowns; and just as the Apostle Paul left his little village of Tarsus and carried the gospel of Jesus Christ to practically every hamlet and city of the Graeco-Roman world, I too am compelled to carry the gospel of freedom beyond my particular hometown. Like Paul, I must constantly respond to the Macedonian call for aid.

Moreover, I am cognizant of the interrelatedness of all communities and states. I cannot sit idly by in Atlanta and not be concerned about what happens in Birmingham. Injustice anywhere is a threat to justice everywhere. We are caught in an inescapable network of mutuality, tied in a single garment of destiny. Whatever affects one directly affects all indirectly. Never again can we afford to live with the narrow, provincial "outside agitator" idea. Anyone who lives in the United States can never be considered an outsider anywhere in this country.

You deplore the demonstrations that are presently taking place in Birmingham. But I am sorry that your statement did not express a similar concern for the conditions that brought the demonstrations into being. I am sure that each of you would want to go beyond the superficial social analyst who looks merely at effects, and does not grapple with underlying causes. I would not hesitate to say that it is unfortunate that so-called demonstrations are taking place in Birmingham at this time, but I would say in more emphatic terms that it is even more unfortunate that the white power structure of this city left the Negro community with no other alternative.

7   In any nonviolent campaign there are four basic steps: (1) collection of the facts to determine whether injustices are alive, (2) negotiation, (3) self-purification, and (4) direct action. We have gone through all of these steps in Birmingham. There can be no gainsaying of the fact that racial injustice engulfs this community.

8   Birmingham is probably the most thoroughly segregated city in the United States. Its ugly record of police brutality is known in every section of this country. Its injust treatment of Negroes in the courts is a notorious reality. There have been more unsolved bombings of Negro homes and churches in Birmingham than any city in this nation. These are the hard, brutal and unbelievable facts. On the basis of these conditions Negro leaders sought to negotiate with the city fathers. But the political leaders consistently refused to engage in good faith negotiation.

9   Then came the opportunity last September to talk with some of the leaders of the economic community. In these negotiating sessions certain promises were made by the merchants—such as the promise to remove the humiliating racial signs from the stores. On the basis of these promises Rev. Shuttlesworth and the leaders of the Alabama Christian Movement for Human Rights agreed to call a moratorium on any type of demonstrations. As the weeks and months unfolded we realized that we were the victims of a broken promise. The signs remained. Like so many experiences of the past we were confronted with blasted hopes, and the dark shadow of a deep disappointment settled upon us. So we had no alternative except that of preparing for direct action, whereby we would present our very bodies as a means of laying our case before the conscience of the local and national community. We were not unmindful of the difficulties involved. So we decided to go through a process of self-purification. We started having workshops on nonviolence and repeatedly asked ourselves the questions, "Are you able to accept blows without retaliating?" "Are you able to endure the ordeals of jail?" We decided to set our direct-action program around the Easter season, realizing that with the exception of Christmas, this was the largest shopping period of the year. Knowing that a strong economic withdrawal program would be the by-product of direct action, we felt that this was the best time to bring pressure on the merchants for the needed changes. Then it occurred to us that the March election was ahead and so we speedily decided to postpone action until after election day. When we discovered that Mr. Connor was in the run-off, we decided again to postpone action so that the demonstrations could not be used to cloud

the issues. At this time we agreed to begin our nonviolent witness the day after the run-off.

This reveals that we did not move irresponsibly into direct action. We too wanted to see Mr. Connor defeated; so we went through postponement after postponement to aid in this community need. After this we felt that direct action could be delayed no longer. 10

You may well ask, "Why direct action? Why sit-ins, marches, etc.? Isn't negotiation a better path?" You are exactly right in your call for negotiation. Indeed, this is the purpose of direct action. Nonviolent direct action seeks to create such a crisis and establish such creative tension that a community that has constantly refused to negotiate is forced to confront the issue. It seeks so to dramatize the issue that it can no longer be ignored. I just referred to the creation of tension as a part of the work of the nonviolent resister. This may sound rather shocking. But I must confess that I am not afraid of the word tension. I have earnestly worked and preached against violent tension, but there is a type of constructive nonviolent tension that is necessary for growth. Just as Socrates felt that it was necessary to create a tension in the mind so that individuals could rise from the bondage of myths and half-truths to the unfettered realm of creative analysis and objective appraisal, we must see the need of having nonviolent gadflies to create the kind of tension in society that will help men to rise from the dark depths of prejudice and racism to the majestic heights of understanding and brotherhood. So the purpose of the direct action is to create a situation so crisis-packed that it will inevitably open the door to negotiation. We, therefore, concur with you in your call for negotiation. Too long has our beloved Southland been bogged down in the tragic attempt to live in monologue rather than dialogue. 11

One of the basic points in your statement is that our acts are untimely. Some have asked, "Why didn't you give the new administration time to act?" The only answer that I can give to this inquiry is that the new administration must be prodded about as much as the outgoing one before it acts. We will be sadly mistaken if we feel that the election of Mr. Boutwell will bring the millennium to Birmingham. While Mr. Boutwell is much more articulate and gentle than Mr. Connor, they are both segregationists, dedicated to the task of maintaining the status quo. The hope I see in Mr. Boutwell is that he will be reasonable enough to see the futility of massive resistance to desegregation. But he will not see this without pressure from the devotees of civil rights. My friends, I must say to you that we have not made a single gain in civil rights without determined legal and nonviolent pressure. History is the long and tragic story of the fact that privileged groups seldom give up their privileges voluntarily. Individuals may see the moral light and voluntarily give up their unjust posture; but as Reinhold Niebuhr has reminded us, groups are more immoral than individuals. 12

13   We know through painful experience that freedom is never voluntarily given by the oppressor; it must be demanded by the oppressed. Frankly, I have never yet engaged in a direct action movement that was "well-timed," according to the timetable of those who have not suffered unduly from the disease of segregation. For years now I have heard the words "Wait!" It rings in the ear of every Negro with a piercing familiarity. This "Wait" has almost always meant "Never." It has been a tranquilizing thalidomide, relieving the emotional stress for a moment, only to give birth to an ill-formed infant of frustration. We must come to see with the distinguished jurist of yesterday that "justice too long delayed is justice denied." We have waited for more than 340 years for our constitutional and God-given rights. The nations of Asia and Africa are moving with jetlike speed toward the goal of political independence, and we still creep at horse and buggy pace toward the gaining of a cup of coffee at a lunch counter. I guess it is easy for those who have never felt the stinging darts of segregation to say, "Wait." But when you have seen vicious mobs lynch your mothers and fathers at will and drown your sisters and brothers at whim; when you have seen hate-filled policemen curse, kick, brutalize and even kill your black brothers and sisters with impunity; when you see the vast majority of your twenty million Negro brothers smothering in an airtight cage of poverty in the midst of an affluent society; when you suddenly find your tongue twisted and your speech stammering as you seek to explain to your six-year-old daughter why she can't go to the public amusement park that has just been advertised on television, and see tears welling up in her little eyes when she is told that Funtown is closed to colored children, and see the depressing clouds of inferiority begin to form in her little mental sky, and see her begin to distort her little personality by unconsciously developing a bitterness toward white people; when you have to concoct an answer for a five-year-old son asking in agonizing pathos: "Daddy, why do white people treat colored people so mean?"; when you take a cross-country drive and find it necessary to sleep night after night in the uncomfortable corners of your automobile because no motel will accept you; when you are humiliated day in and day out by nagging signs reading "white" and "colored"; when your first name becomes "nigger" and your middle name becomes "boy" (however old you are) and your last name becomes "John," and when your wife and mother are never given the respected title "Mrs."; when you are harried by day and haunted by night by the fact that you are a Negro, living constantly at tiptoe stance never quite knowing what to expect next, and plagued with inner fears and outer resentments; when you are forever fighting a degenerating sense of "nobodiness"; then you will understand why we find it difficult to wait. There comes a time when the cup of endurance runs over, and men are no longer willing to be plunged into an abyss of injustice where they experience the blackness of corroding despair. I hope, sirs, you can understand our legitimate and unavoidable impatience.

You express a great deal of anxiety over our willingness to break laws. 14
This is certainly a legitimate concern. Since we so diligently urge people
to obey the Supreme Court's decision of 1954 outlawing segregation in
the public schools, it is rather strange and paradoxical to find us consciously breaking laws. One may well ask, "How can you advocate
breaking some laws and obeying others?" The answer is found in the fact
that there are two types of laws: there are *just* and there are *unjust* laws.
I would agree with Saint Augustine that "An unjust law is no law at all."

Now what is the difference between the two? How does one determine 15
when a law is just or unjust? A just law is a man-made code that squares
with the moral law or the law of God. An unjust law is a code that is out
of harmony with the moral law. To put it in the terms of Saint Thomas
Aquinas, an unjust law is a human law that is not rooted in eternal and
natural law. Any law that uplifts human personality is just. Any law that
degrades human personality is unjust. All segregation statutes are unjust
because segregation distorts the soul and damages the personality. It
gives the segregator a false sense of superiority, and the segregated a false
sense of inferiority. To use the words of Martin Buber, the great Jewish
philosopher, segregation substitutes an "I-it" relationship for the "I-
thou" relationship, and ends up relegating persons to the status of things.
So segregation is not only politically, economically and sociologically
unsound, but it is morally wrong and sinful. Paul Tillich has said that sin
is separation. Isn't segregation an existential expression of man's tragic
separation, an expression of his awful estrangement, his terrible sinful-
ness? So I can urge men to disobey segregation ordinances because they
are morally wrong.

Let us turn to a more concrete example of just and unjust laws. An 16
unjust law is a code that a majority inflicts on a minority that is not
binding on itself. This is difference made legal. On the other hand a just
law is a code that a majority compels a minority to follow that it is
willing to follow itself. This is sameness made legal.

Let me give another explanation. An unjust law is a code inflicted upon 17
a minority which that minority had no part in enacting or creating
because they did not have the unhampered right to vote. Who can say
that the legislature of Alabama which set up the segregation laws was
democratically elected? Throughout the state of Alabama all types of
conniving methods are used to prevent Negroes from becoming registered voters and there are some counties without a single Negro registered to vote despite the fact that the Negro constitutes a majority of the
population. Can any law set up in such a state be considered democratically structured?

These are just a few examples of unjust and just laws. There are some 18
instances when a law is just on its face and unjust in its application. For
instance, I was arrested Friday on a charge of parading without a permit.
Now there is nothing wrong with an ordinance which requires a permit
for a parade, but when the ordinance is used to preserve segregation and

to deny citizens the First Amendment privilege of peaceful assembly and peaceful protest, then it becomes unjust.

19   I hope you can see the distinction I am trying to point out. In no sense do I advocate evading or defying the law as the rabid segregationist would do. This would lead to anarchy. One who breaks an unjust law must do it *openly, lovingly* (not hatefully as the white mothers did in New Orleans when they were seen on television screaming, "nigger, nigger, nigger"), and with a willingness to accept the penalty. I submit that an individual who breaks a law that conscience tells him is unjust, and willingly accepts the penalty by staying in jail to arouse the conscience of the community over its injustice, is in reality expressing the very highest respect for law.

20   Of course, there is nothing new about this kind of civil disobedience. It was seen sublimely in the refusal of Shadrach, Meshach and Abednego to obey the laws of Nebuchadnezzar because a higher moral law was involved. It was practiced superbly by the early Christians who were willing to face hungry lions and the excruciating pain of chopping blocks, before submitting to certain unjust laws of the Roman Empire. To a degree academic freedom is a reality today because Socrates practiced civil disobedience.

21   We can never forget that everything Hitler did in Germany was "legal" and everything the Hungarian freedom fighters did in Hungary was "illegal." It was "illegal" to aid and comfort a Jew in Hitler's Germany. But I am sure that if I had lived in Germany during that time I would have aided and comforted my Jewish brothers even though it was illegal. If I lived in a Communist country today where certain principles dear to the Christian faith are suppressed, I believe I would openly advocate disobeying these anti-religious laws. I must make two honest confessions to you, my Christian and Jewish brothers. First, I must confess that over the last few years I have been gravely disappointed with the white moderate. I have almost reached the regrettable conclusion that the Negro's great stumbling block in the stride toward freedom is not the White Citizen's Counciler or the Ku Klux Klanner, but the white moderate who is more devoted to "order" than to justice; who prefers a negative peace which is the absence of tension to a positive peace which is the presence of justice; who constantly says, "I agree with you in the goal you seek, but I can't agree with your methods of direct action"; who paternalistically feels that he can set the timetable for another man's freedom; who lives by the myth of time and who constantly advised the Negro to wait until a "more convenient season." Shallow understanding from people of good will is more frustrating than absolute misunderstanding from people of ill will. Lukewarm acceptance is much more bewildering than outright rejection.

22   I had hoped that the white moderate would understand that law and order exist for the purpose of establishing justice, and that when they fail to do this they become dangerously structured dams that block the flow

of social progress. I had hoped that the white moderate would understand that the present tension of the South is merely a necessary phase of the transition from an obnoxious negative peace, where the Negro passively accepted his unjust plight, to a substance-filled positive peace, where all men will respect the dignity and worth of human personality. Actually, we who engage in nonviolent direct action are not the creators of tension. We merely bring to the surface the hidden tension that is already alive. We bring it out in the open where it can be seen and dealt with. Like a boil that can never be cured as long as it is covered up but must be opened with all its pus-flowing ugliness to the natural medicines of air and light, injustice must likewise be exposed, with all of the tension its exposing creates, to the light of human conscience and the air of national opinion before it can be cured.

In your statement you asserted that our actions, even though peaceful, must be condemned because they precipitate violence. But can this assertion be logically made? Isn't this like condemning the robbed man because his possession of money precipitated the evil act of robbery? Isn't this like condemning Socrates because his unswerving commitment to truth and his philosophical delvings precipitated the misguided popular mind to make him drink the hemlock? Isn't this like condemning Jesus because His unique God-consciousness and never-ceasing devotion to his will precipitated the evil act of crucifixion? We must come to see, as federal courts have consistently affirmed, that it is immoral to urge an individual to withdraw his efforts to gain his basic constitutional rights because the quest precipitates violence. Society must protect the robbed and punish the robber. 23

I had also hoped that the white moderate would reject the myth of time. I received a letter this morning from a white brother in Texas which said: "All Christians know that the colored people will receive equal rights eventually, but it is possible that you are in too great of a religious hurry. It has taken Christianity almost two thousand years to accomplish what it has. The teachings of Christ take time to come to earth." All that is said here grows out of a tragic misconception of time. It is the strangely irrational notion that there is something in the very flow of time that will inevitably cure all ills. Actually time is neutral. It can be used either destructively or constructively. I am coming to feel that the people of ill will have used time much more effectively than the people of good will. We will have to repent in this generation not merely for the vitriolic words and actions of the bad people, but for the appalling silence of the good people. We must come to see that human progress never rolls in on wheels of inevitability. It comes through the tireless efforts and persistent work of men willing to be co-workers with God, and without this hard work time itself becomes an ally of the forces of social stagnation. We must use time creatively, and forever realize that the time is always ripe to do right. Now is the time to make real the promise of democracy, and 24 transform our pending national elegy into a creative psalm of brother-hood. Now is the time to lift our national policy from the quicksand of racial injustice to the solid rock of human dignity.

25   You spoke of our activity in Birmingham as extreme. At first I was rather disappointed that fellow clergymen would see my nonviolent efforts as those of the extremist. I started thinking about the fact that I stand in the middle of two opposing forces in the Negro community. One is a force of complacency made up of Negroes who, as a result of long years of oppression, have been so completely drained of self-respect and a sense of "somebodiness" that they have adjusted to segregation, and, of a few Negroes in the middle class who, because of a degree of academic and economic security, and because at points they profit by segregation, have unconsciously become insensitive to the problems of the masses. The other force is one of bitterness and hatred, and comes perilously close to advocating violence. It is expressed in the various black nation-alist groups that are springing up over the nation, the largest and best known being Elijah Muhammad's Muslim movement. This movement is nourished by the contemporary frustration over the continued existence of racial discrimination. It is made up of people who have lost faith in America, who have absolutely repudiated Christianity, and who have concluded that the white man is an incurable "devil." I have tried to stand between these two forces, saying that we need not follow the "do-nothingism" of the complacent or the hatred and despair of the black nationalist. There is the more excellent way of love and nonviolent protest. I'm grateful to God that, through the Negro church, the dimen-sion of nonviolence entered our struggle. If this philosophy had not emerged, I am convinced that by now many streets of the South would be flowing with floods of blood. And I am further convinced that if our white brothers dismiss us as "rabble-rousers" and "outside agitators" those of us who are working through the channels of nonviolent direct action and refuse to support our nonviolent efforts, millions of Negroes, out of frustration and despair, will seek solace and security in black nationalist ideologies, a development that will lead inevitably to a fright-ening racial nightmare.

26   Oppressed people cannot remain oppressed forever. The urge for freedom will eventually come. This is what happened to the American Negro. Something within has reminded him of his birthright of freedom; something without has reminded him that he can gain it. Consciously and unconsciously, he has been swept in by what the Germans call the *Zeitgeist,* and with his black brothers of Africa, and his brown and yellow brothers of Asia, South America and the Caribbean, he is moving with a sense of cosmic urgency toward the promised land of racial justice. Recognizing this vital urge that has engulfed the Negro community, one should readily understand public demonstrations. The Negro has many pent-up resentments and latent frustrations. He has to get them out. So let him march sometime; let him have his prayer pilgrimages to the city

hall; understand why he must have sit-ins and freedom rides. If his repressed emotions do not come out in these nonviolent ways, they will come out in ominous expressions of violence. This is not a threat; it is a fact of history. So I have not said to my people "get rid of your discontent." But I have tried to say that this normal and healthy discontent can be channelized through the creative outlet of nonviolent direct action. Now this approach is being dismissed as extremist. I must admit that I was initially disappointed in being so categorized.

But as I continued to think about the matter I gradually gained a bit of satisfaction from being considered an extremist. Was not Jesus an extremist in love—"Love your enemies, bless them that curse you, pray for them that despitefully use you." Was not Amos an extremist for justice—"Let justice roll down like waters and righteousness like a mighty steam." Was not Paul an extremist for the gospel of Jesus Christ—"I bear in my body the marks of the Lord Jesus." Was not Martin Luther an extremist—"Here I stand; I can do none other so help me God." Was not John Bunyan an extremist—"I will stay in jail to the end of my days before I make a butchery of my conscience." Was not Abraham Lincoln an extremist—"This nation cannot survive half slave and half free." Was not Thomas Jefferson an extremist—"We hold these truths to be self-evident, that all men are created equal." So the question is not whether we will be extremist but what kind of extremist will we be. Will we be extremists for hate or will we be extremists for love? Will we be extremists for the preservation of injustice—or will we be extremists for the cause of justice? In that dramatic scene on Calvary's hill, three men were crucified. We must not forget that all three were crucified for the same crime—the crime of extremism. Two were extremists for immorality, and thusly fell below their environment. The other, Jesus Christ, was an extremist for love, truth and goodness, and thereby rose above his environment. So, after all, maybe the South, the nation and the world are in dire need of creative extremists.   27

I had hoped that the white moderate would see this. Maybe I was too optimistic. Maybe I expected too much. I guess I should have realized that few members of a race that has oppressed another race can understand or appreciate the deep groans and passionate yearnings of those that have been oppressed and still fewer have the vision to see that injustice must be rooted out by strong, persistent and determined action. I am thankful, however, that some of our white brothers have grasped the meaning of this social revolution and committed themselves to it. They are still all too small in quantity, but they are big in quality. Some like Ralph McGill, Lillian Smith, Harry Golden and James Dabbs have written about our struggle in eloquent, prophetic and understanding terms. Others have marched with us down nameless streets of the South. They have languished in filthy roach-infested jails, suffering the abuse and brutality of angry policemen who see them as "dirty nigger-lovers." They, unlike so many of their moderate brothers and sisters, have   28 recognized the urgency of the moment and sensed the need for powerful "action" antidotes to combat the disease of segregation.

29   Let me rush on to mention my other disappointment. I have been so greatly disappointed with the white church and its leadership. Of course, there are some notable exceptions. I am not unmindful of the fact that each of you has taken some significant stands on this issue. I commend you, Rev. Stallings, for your Christian stance on this past Sunday, in welcoming Negroes to your worship service on a non-segregated basis. I commend the Catholic leaders of this state for integrating Springhill College several years ago.

30   But despite these notable exceptions I must honestly reiterate that I have been disappointed with the church. I do not say that as one of the negative critics who can always find something wrong with the church. I say it as a minister of the gospel, who loves the church; who was nurtured in its bosom; who has been sustained by its spiritual blessing and who will remain true to it as long as the cord of life shall lengthen.

31   I had the strange feeling when I was suddenly catapulted into the leadership of the bus protest in Montgomery several years ago that we would have the support of the white church. I felt that the white ministers, priests and rabbis of the South would be some of our strongest allies. Instead, some have been outright opponents, refusing to understand the freedom movement and misrepresenting its leaders; all too many others have been more cautious than courageous and have remained silent behind the anesthetizing security of the stained-glass windows.

32   In spite of my shattered dreams of the past, I came to Birmingham with the hope that the white religious leadership of this community would see the justice of our cause, and with deep moral concern, serve as the channel through which our just grievances would get to the power structure. I had hoped that each of you would understand. But again I have been disappointed. I have heard numerous religious leaders of the South call upon their worshippers to comply with a desegregation decision because it is the *law,* but I have longed to hear white ministers say, "Follow this decree because integration is morally *right* and the Negro is your brother." In the midst of blatant injustices inflicted upon the Negro, I have watched white churches stand on the sideline and merely mouth pious irrelevancies and sanctimonious trivialities. In the midst of a mighty struggle to rid our nation of racial and economic injustice, I have heard so many ministers say, "Those are social issues with which the gospel has no concern," and I have watched so many churches commit themselves to a completely otherworldly religion which made a strange distinction between body and soul, the sacred and the secular.

33   So here we are moving toward the exit of the twentieth century with a religious community largely adjusted to the status quo, standing as a taillight behind other community agencies rather than a headlight leading men to higher levels of justice.

I have traveled the length and breadth of Alabama, Mississippi and all the other southern states. On sweltering summer days and crisp autumn mornings I have looked at her beautiful churches with their lofty spires pointing heavenward. I have beheld the impressive outlay of her massive religious education buildings. Over and over again I have found myself asking: "What kind of people worship here? Who is their God? Where were their voices when the lips of Governor Barnett dripped with words of interposition and nullification? Where were they when Governor Wallace gave the clarion call for defiance and hatred? Where were their voices of support when tired, bruised and weary Negro men and women decided to rise from the dark dungeons of complacency to the bright hills of creative protest?" 34

Yes, these questions are still in my mind. In deep disappointment, I have wept over the laxity of the church. But be assured that my tears have been tears of love. There can be no deep disappointment where there is not deep love. Yes, I love the church; I love her sacred walls. How could I do otherwise? I am in the rather unique position of being the son, the grandson and the great-grandson of preachers. Yes, I see the church as the body of Christ. But, oh! How we have blemished and scarred that body through social neglect and fear of being nonconformists. 35

There was a time when the church was very powerful. It was during that period when the early Christians rejoiced when they were deemed worthy to suffer for what they believed. In those days the church was not merely a thermometer that recorded the ideas and principles of popular opinion; it was a thermostat that transformed the mores of society. Wherever the early Christians entered a town the power structure got disturbed and immediately sought to convict them for being "disturbers of the peace" and "outside agitators." But they went on with the conviction that they were "a colony of heaven," and had to obey God rather than man. They were small in number but big in commitment. They were too God-intoxicated to be "astronomically intimidated." They brought an end to such ancient evils as infanticide and gladiatorial contest. 36

Things are different now. The contemporary church is often a weak, ineffectual voice with an uncertain sound. It is so often the arch-supporter of the status quo. Far from being disturbed by the presence of the church, the power structure of the average community is consoled by the church's silent and often vocal sanction of things as they are. 37

But the judgment of God is upon the church as never before. If the church of today does not recapture the sacrificial spirit of the early church, it will lose its authentic ring, forfeit the loyalty of millions, and be dismissed as an irrelevant social club with no meaning for the twentieth century. I am meeting young people every day whose disappointment with the church has risen to outright disgust. 38

Maybe again, I have been too optimistic. Is organized religion too inextricably bound to the status quo to save our nation and the world? 39

Maybe I must turn my faith to the inner spiritual church, the church within the church, as the true *ecclesia* and the hope of the world. But again I am thankful to God that some noble souls from the ranks of organized religion have broken loose from the paralyzing chains of conformity and joined us as active partners in the struggle for freedom. They have left their secure congregations and walked the streets of Albany, Georgia, with us. They have gone through the highways of the South on tortuous rides for freedom. Yes, they have gone to jail with us. Some have been kicked out of their churches, and lost support of their bishops and fellow ministers. But they have gone with the faith that right defeated is stronger then evil triumphant. These men have been the leaven in the lump of the race. Their witness has been the spiritual salt that has preserved the true meaning of the gospel in these troubled times. They have carved a tunnel of hope through the dark mountain of disappointment.

40   I hope the church as a whole will meet the challenge of this decisive hour. But even if the church does not come to the aid of justice, I have no despair about the future. I have no fear about the outcome of our struggle in Birmingham, even if our motives are presently misunderstood. We will reach the goal of freedom in Birmingham and all over the nation, because the goal of America is freedom. Abused and scorned though we may be, our destiny is tied up with the destiny of America. Before the Pilgrims landed at Plymouth we were here. Before the pen of Jefferson etched across the pages of history the majestic words of the Declaration of Independence, we were here. For more than two centuries our foreparents labored in this country without wages; they made cotton king; and they built the homes of their masters in the midst of brutal injustice and shameful humiliation—and yet out of a bottomless vitality they continued to thrive and develop. If the inexpressible cruelties of slavery could not stop us, the opposition we now face will surely fail. We will win our freedom because the sacred heritage of our nation and the eternal will of God are embodied in our echoing demands.

41   I must close now. But before closing I am impelled to mention one other point in your statement that troubled me profoundly. You warmly commended the Birmingham police force for keeping "order" and "preventing violence." I don't believe you would have so warmly commended the police force if you had seen its angry violent dogs literally biting six unarmed, nonviolent Negroes. I don't believe you would so quickly commend the policemen if you would observe their ugly and inhuman treatment of Negroes here in the city jail; if you would watch them push and curse old Negro women and young Negro girls; if you would see them slap and kick old Negro men and young boys; if you will observe them, as they did on two occasions, refuse to give us food because we wanted to sing our grace together. I'm sorry that I can't join you in your praise for the police department.

It is true that they have been rather disciplined in their public handling   42
of the demonstrators. In this sense they have been rather publicly "nonviolent." But for what purpose? To preserve the evil system of segregation. Over the last few years I have consistently preached that nonviolence demands that the means we use must be as pure as the ends we seek.
So I have tried to make it clear that it is wrong to use immoral means to
attain moral ends. But now I must affirm that it is just as wrong, or even
more so, to use moral means to preserve immoral ends. Maybe Mr.
Connor and his policemen have been rather publicly nonviolent, as Chief
Pritchett was in Albany, Georgia, but they have used the moral means of
nonviolence to maintain the immoral end of flagrant racial injustice. T. S.
Eliot has said that there is no greater treason than to do the right deed for
the wrong reason.

I wish you had commended the Negro sit-inners and demonstrators of   43
Birmingham for their sublime courage, their willingness to suffer and
their amazing discipline in the midst of the most inhuman provocation.
One day the South will recognize its real heroes. They will be the James
Merediths, courageously and with a majestic sense of purpose facing
jeering and hostile mobs and the agonizing loneliness that characterizes
the life of the pioneer. They will be old, oppressed, battered Negro
women, symbolized in the seventy-two-year-old woman of Montgomery,
Alabama, who rose up with a sense of dignity and with her people
decided not to ride the segregated buses, and responded to one who
inquired about her tiredness with ungrammatical profundity: "My feet is
tired, but my soul is rested." They will be the young high school and
college students, young ministers of the gospel and a host of their elders
courageously and nonviolently sitting-in at lunch counters and willingly
going to jail for conscience's sake. One day the South will know that
when these disinherited children of God sat down at lunch counters they
were in reality standing up for the best in the American dream and the
most sacred values in our Judeo-Christian heritage, and thusly, carrying
our whole nation back to those great wells of democracy which were dug
deep by the Founding Fathers in the formulation of the Constitution and
the Declaration of Independence.

Never before have I written a letter this long (or should I say a book?).   44
I'm afraid that it is much too long to take your precious time. I can assure
you that it would have been much shorter if I had been writing from a
comfortable desk, but what else is there to do when you are alone for
days in the dull monotony of a narrow jail cell other than write long
letters, think strange thoughts, and pray long prayers?

If I have said anything in this letter that is an overstatement of the truth   45
and is indicative of an unreasonable impatience, I beg you to forgive me.
If I have said anything in this letter that is an understatement of the truth
and is indicative of my having a patience that makes me patient with
anything less than brotherhood, I beg God to forgive me.

46   I hope this letter finds you strong in the faith. I also hope that circumstances will soon make it possible for me to meet each of you, not as an integrationist or a civil rights leader, but as a fellow clergyman and a Christian brother. Let us all hope that the dark clouds of racial prejudice will soon pass away and the deep fog of misunderstanding will be lifted from our fear-drenched communities and in some not too distant tomorrow the radiant stars of love and brotherhood will shine over our great nation with all of their scintillating beauty.

47   Yours for the cause of Peace and Brotherhood,

48   Martin Luther King, Jr.

❏ Questions for Discussion

1. What are the conditions which King and others in Birmingham are protesting? How does King respond to the charge that he is an "outside agitator"?

2. What are the four basic steps in a nonviolent action campaign? How were they carried out in Birmingham?

3. How does King use the word *untimely?* How does he prove invalid the charge that the demonstrations are untimely? Explain how "wait" becomes "never."

4. Under what circumstances does King consider breaking the law justified? What precedents does he cite for doing so? Discuss the dichotomy between *just* and *unjust* law and the difference between *"difference* made legal" and *"sameness* made legal."

5. Explain King's claim that "Injustice anywhere is a threat to justice everywhere."

6. Explain the "tension in the mind" which King discusses. How can it "help men to rise from the dark depths of prejudice and racism to the majestic heights of understanding and brotherhood"?

❏ Suggestions for Exploration and Writing

1. Select one of the following quotations from King's letter and agree or disagree with it:

> History is the long and tragic story of the fact that privileged groups seldom give up their privileges voluntarily.

> Shallow understanding from people of good will is more frustrating than absolute misunderstanding from people of ill will. Lukewarm acceptance is much more bewildering than outright rejection.

2. King was influenced by both the Bible and the Declaration of Independence. In an essay, show how King's letter reflects the ideas and styles of these documents.

3. Analyze the style of this letter, showing how the rhythmic cadences of a sermon, the rhetorical questions, and the metaphors help to make the letter persuasive.

4. Write an essay explaining how poverty can be "an airtight cage."

5. King says that if people's frustrations and contained anger are not released, people will resort to violence. Discuss this concept.

6. Argue for or against this statement: Churches and their leaders have a moral responsibility to speak out against hatred and injustice and to speak for love and justice.

7. Agree or disagree with this statement: If the cause is right or just, I would participate in a boycott, march, or other nonviolent action.

MAYA ANGELOU (1929–)

Marguerita Johnson, who later changed her name to Maya Angelou, was born in St. Louis but spent her childhood in Stamps, Arkansas, and in California. Angelou has written five autobiographical books, the first, I Know Why the Caged Bird Sings *(1970), being the most popular. In addition, she excels in many areas: writing essays, novels, and short fiction; acting and directing; and participating in civil-rights activities. Maya Angelou is a colorful and popular speaker. At Bill Clinton's Presidential Inauguration in January 1993, Angelou read her poem "On the Pulse of Morning."*

from *I Know Why the Caged Bird Sings*

Recently a white woman from Texas, who would quickly describe   1
herself as a liberal, asked me about my hometown. When I told her that in Stamps my grandmother had owned the only Negro general merchandise store since the turn of the century, she exclaimed, "Why, you were a debutante." Ridiculous and even ludicrous. But Negro girls in small southern towns, whether poverty-stricken or just munching along on a few of life's necessities, were given as extensive and irrelevant preparations for adulthood as rich white girls shown in magazines. Admittedly the training was not the same. While white girls learned to waltz and sit gracefully with a tea cup balanced on their knees, we were lagging

behind, learning the mid-Victorian values with very little money to indulge them. (Come and see Edna Lomax spending the money she made picking cotton on five balls of ecru tatting thread. Her fingers are bound to snag the work and she'll have to repeat the stitches time and time again. But she knows that when she buys the thread.)

2   We were required to embroider and I had trunkfuls of colorful dish-towels, pillowcases, runners and handkerchiefs to my credit. I mastered the art of crocheting and tatting, and there was a lifetime's supply of dainty doilies that would never be used in sacheted dresser drawers. It went without saying that all girls could iron and wash, but the finer touches around the home, like setting a table with real silver, baking roasts and cooking vegetables without meat, had to be learned elsewhere. Usually at the source of those habits. During my tenth year, a white woman's kitchen became my finishing school.

3   Mrs. Viola Cullinan was a plump woman who lived in a three-bedroom house somewhere behind the post office. She was singularly unattractive until she smiled, and then the lines around her eyes and mouth which made her look perpetually dirty disappeared, and her face looked like the mask of an impish elf. She usually rested her smile until late afternoon when her women friends dropped in and Miss Glory, the cook, served them cold drinks on the closed-in porch.

4   The exactness of her house was inhuman. This glass went here and only here. That cup had its place and it was an act of impudent rebellion to place it anywhere else. At twelve o'clock the table was set. At 12:15 Mrs. Cullinan sat down to dinner (whether her husband had arrived or not). At 12:16 Miss Glory brought out the food.

5   It took me a week to learn the difference between a salad plate, a bread plate and a dessert plate.

6   Mrs. Cullinan kept up the tradition of her wealthy parents. She was from Virginia. Miss Glory, who was a descendant of slaves that had worked for the Cullinans, told me her history. She had married beneath her (according to Miss Glory). Her husband's family hadn't had their money very long and what they had "didn't 'mount to much."

7   As ugly as she was, I thought privately, she was lucky to get a husband above or beneath her station. But Miss Glory wouldn't let me say a thing against her mistress. She was very patient with me, however, over the housework. She explained the dishware, silverware and servants' bells. The large round bowl in which soup was served wasn't a soup bowl, it was a tureen. There were goblets, sherbet glasses, ice-cream glasses, wine glasses, green glass coffee cups with matching saucers and water glasses. I had a glass to drink from, and it sat with Miss Glory's on a separate shelf from the others. Soup spoons, gravy boat, butter knives, salad forks and carving platter were additions to my vocabulary and in fact almost represented a new language. I was fascinated with the novelty, with the fluttering Mrs. Cullinan and her Alice-in-Wonderland house.

Her husband remains, in my memory, undefined. I lumped him with all the other white men that I had ever seen and tried not to see. 8

On our way home one evening, Miss Glory told me that Mrs. Cullinan couldn't have children. She said that she was too delicate-boned. It was hard to imagine bones at all under those layers of fat. Miss Glory went on to say that the doctor had taken out all her lady organs. I reasoned that a pig's organs included the lungs, heart and liver, so if Mrs. Cullinan was walking around without those essentials, it explained why she drank alcohol out of unmarked bottles. She was keeping herself embalmed. 9

When I spoke to Bailey about it, he agreed that I was right, but he also informed me that Mr. Cullinan had two daughters by a colored lady and that I knew them very well. He added that the girls were the spitting image of their father. I was unable to remember what he looked like, although I had just left him a few hours before, but I thought of the Coleman girls. They were very lightskinned and certainly didn't look very much like their mother (no one ever mentioned Mr. Coleman). 10

My pity for Mrs. Cullinan preceded me the next morning like the Cheshire cat's smile. Those girls, who could have been her daughters, were beautiful. They didn't have to straighten their hair. Even when they were caught in the rain, their braids still hung down straight like tame snakes. Their mouths were pouty little cupid's bows. Mrs. Cullinan didn't know what she missed. Or maybe she did. Poor Mrs. Cullinan. 11

For weeks after, I arrived early, left late and tried very hard to make up for her barrenness. If she had had her own children, she wouldn't have had to ask me to run a thousand errands from her back door to the back door of her friends. Poor old Mrs. Cullinan. 12

Then one evening Miss Glory told me to serve the ladies on the porch. After I set the tray down and turned toward the kitchen, one of the women asked, "What's your name, girl?" It was the speckled-faced one. Mrs. Cullinan said, "She doesn't talk much. Her name's Margaret." 13

"Is she dumb?" 14

"No. As I understand it, she can talk when she wants to but she's usually quiet as a little mouse. Aren't you, Margaret?" 15

I smiled at her. Poor thing. No organs and couldn't even pronounce my name correctly. 16

"She's a sweet little thing, though." 17

"Well, that may be, but the name's too long. I'd never bother myself. I'd call her Mary if I was you." 18

I fumed into the kitchen. That horrible woman would never have the chance to call me Mary because if I was starving I'd never work for her. I decided I wouldn't pee on her if her heart was on fire. Giggles drifted in off the porch and into Miss Glory's pots. I wondered what they could be laughing about. 19

White folks were so strange. Could they be talking about me? Everybody knew that they stuck together better than the Negroes did. It was 20 possible that Mrs. Cullinan had friends in St. Louis who heard about a girl from Stamps being in court and wrote to tell her. Maybe she knew about Mr. Freeman.

21 My lunch was in my mouth a second time and I went outside and relieved myself on the bed of four-o'clocks. Miss Glory thought I might be coming down with something and told me to go on home, and that Momma would give me some herb tea, and she'd explain to her mistress.

22 I realized how foolish I was being before I reached the pond. Of course Mrs. Cullinan didn't know. Otherwise she wouldn't have given me the two nice dresses that Momma cut down, and she certainly wouldn't have called me a "sweet little thing." My stomach felt fine, and I didn't mention anything to Momma.

23 That evening I decided to write a poem on being white, fat, old and without children. It was going to be a tragic ballad. I would have to watch her carefully to capture the essence of her loneliness and pain.

24 The very next day, she called me by the wrong name. Miss Glory and I were washing up the lunch dishes when Mrs. Cullinan came to the doorway. "Mary?"

25 Miss Glory asked, "Who?"

26 Mrs. Cullinan, sagging a little, knew and I knew. "I want Mary to go down to Mrs. Randall's and take her some soup. She's not been feeling well for a few days."

27 Miss Glory's face was a wonder to see. "You mean Margaret, ma'am. Her name's Margaret."

28 "That's too long. She's Mary from now on. Heat that soup from last night and put it in the china tureen and, Mary, I want you to carry it carefully."

29 Every person I knew had a hellish horror of being "called out of his name." It was a dangerous practice to call a Negro anything that could be loosely construed as insulting because of the centuries of their having been called niggers, jigs, dinges, blackbirds, crows, boots and spooks.

30 Miss Glory had a fleeting second of feeling sorry for me. Then as she handed me the hot tureen she said, "Don't mind, don't pay that no mind. Sticks and stones may break your bones, but words . . . You know, I been working for her for twenty years."

31 She held the back door open for me. "Twenty years. I wasn't much older than you. My name used to be Hallelujah. That's what Ma named me, but my mistress give me 'Glory,' and it stuck. I likes it better too."

32 I was in the little path that ran behind the houses when Miss Glory shouted, "It's shorter too."

33 For a few seconds it was a tossup over whether I would laugh (imagine being named Hallelujah) or cry (imagine letting some white women rename you for her convenience). My anger saved me from either outburst. I had to quit the job, but the problem was going to be how to do it. Momma wouldn't allow me to quit for just any reason.

"She's a peach. That woman is a real peach." Mrs. Randall's maid was talking as she took the soup from me, and I wondered what her name used to be and what she answered to now.

For a week I looked into Mrs. Cullinan's face as she called me Mary. She ignored my coming late and leaving early. Miss Glory was a little annoyed because I had begun to leave egg yolk on the dishes and wasn't putting much heart in polishing the silver. I hoped that she would complain to our boss, but she didn't.

Then Bailey solved my dilemma. He had me describe the contents of the cupboard and the particular plates she liked best. Her favorite piece was a casserole shaped like a fish and the green glass coffee cups. I kept his instructions in mind, so on the next day when Miss Glory was hanging out clothes and I had again been told to serve the old biddies on the porch, I dropped the empty serving tray. When I heard Mrs. Cullinan scream, "Mary!" I picked up the casserole and two of the green glass cups in readiness. As she rounded the kitchen door I let them fall on the tiled floor.

I could never absolutely describe to Bailey what happened next, because each time I got to the part where she fell on the floor and screwed up her ugly face to cry, we burst out laughing. She actually wobbled around on the floor and picked up shards of the cups and cried, "Oh Momma. Oh, dear Gawd. It's Momma's china from Virginia. Oh, Momma, I sorry."

Miss Glory came running in from the yard and the women from the porch crowded around. Miss Glory was almost as broken up as her mistress. "You mean to say she broke our Virginia dishes? What we gone do?"

Mrs. Cullinan cried louder, "That clumsy nigger. Clumsy little black nigger."

Old speckled-face leaned down and asked, "Who did it, Viola? Was it Mary? Who did it?"

Everything was happening so fast I can't remember whether her action preceded her words, but I know that Mrs. Cullinan said, "Her name's Margaret, goddamn it, her name's Margaret." And she threw a wedge of the broken plate at me. It could have been the hysteria which put her aim off, but the flying crockery caught Miss Glory right over her ear and she started screaming.

I left the front door wide open so all the neighbors could hear.

Mrs. Cullinan was right about one thing. My name wasn't Mary.

34

35

36

37

38

39

40

41

42

43

❏ Questions for Discussion

1. Why does Angelou say that the idea of "Negro" girls being debutantes is "ridiculous and even ludicrous"? Why does Angelou refer to her "preparations for adulthood" as "extensive and irrelevant"?

2. What is Angelou's **tone** when she talks about her "finishing school" being in a white woman's kitchen?

3. How are the names of the kitchen utensils a new language? What is being communicated?

4. Why does Mrs. Cullinan feel so hostile toward Mr. Cullinan?

5. What is the significance of the white woman's referring to Margaret (Marguerita) as Mary? Why is being " 'called out of [her] name' " insulting? Why does Miss "Glory" accept that name?

6. What is your reaction when Margaret breaks Mrs. Cullinan's favorite plate, laughs at her, and leaves the front door open so all the neighbors can hear Mrs. Cullinan cry?

7. What is the connection between a debutante and the finished Maya at the end of the essay?

❏ Suggestions for Exploration and Writing

1. Write a character analysis of Mrs. Cullinan. What does Mrs. Cullinan reveal about herself by nonverbal signs—her smile, her exactness about time, and her insistence on proper place-ment of dishes and silver? By what nonverbal signs does Mrs. Cullinan expose her racism and her feeling that Glory and Margaret are her inferiors?

2. Contrast Miss Glory and Margaret.

3. In "The Incident" by Countee Cullen and in Angelou's essay the authors imply that language has the power to liberate or restrict a person. Discuss this implication.

4. Write an essay discussing Margaret's sense of humor. To what extent does her sense of humor contribute to her control of her destiny?

GUAN KEGUANG (1938–   )

Guan Keguang, a 1960 graduate of Shanghai International Studies University, has traveled extensively in the United States, writing for many newspapers. As a result of his travels, he has become ac-quainted with many sections of the country and has written exten-sively about New England for the Cape Cod Times *(1986–1987).*

A Chinese Reporter on Cape Cod

Next to the newsroom in the *Cape Cod Times* main office building there is a "lunchroom." My colleagues and I sometimes go there to buy something to eat or drink from the vending machines. 1

The experience has been quite a novelty for me. I put in some coins, push a button, and out comes what I want. 2

The machines offer a variety of food and drinks. Many of them are new to me and the labels don't tell me much about what's inside. The operation is simple and automatic. But so many decisions! 3

Such a process epitomizes what I have experienced while struggling hard to adapt my traditional ways of thinking and doing things to an American environment, which demands constantly considering alternatives and making decisions. 4

This has been no easy job for me. 5

For almost half a century I have lived in a culture where choices and decisions are made by authorities and circumstances rather than by individuals and personal preferences. 6

It's OK for young children to have things arranged for them by their parents, because they are inexperienced in life and not wise enough to make important decisions. But when they reach their late teens they don't like to be treated that way — even in China. They yearn for independence and freedom, as the recent demonstrations have shown. They are frustrated when things don't go their way and they find themselves helpless and unable to do anything about their fate. 7

When the time comes to enter the work force, however, reality sets in. They are assigned a job, and that's it. Moreover, the job assignment determines where you must live. 8

If you have completed twelve years' schooling, but you fail in the college entrance examination and are not admitted, the government will assign you a job — perhaps as a factory worker, a store clerk, or a bus driver. Very likely that will be your lifelong job, because you can't freely pick and choose or change your job. Once you are in a job you will have to stick to it, unless the authorities want to transfer you to another job. You could negotiate with the authorities, but the government always has the final say. 9

Students do have an opportunity to state their preference among university and courses of study — and if you pass your exams with flying colors, with scores much higher than others, you will be admitted into a department of a university of your own choice. But once you get into a university you stay in your major for four or five years without a break. You do not change your major. You take the courses given to you, pass all the exams, behave well and toe the party line, earn your bachelor's degree and graduate. 10

Then, you just wait until a job is assigned to you. During the waiting period, students with "connections" seek to influence the decision. A few 11 succeed. In any event, until the decision is made, you will not know where you will go and what your lifelong career will be.

12   Your job assignment notice is more than a certificate with which you report for duty. It is also a certificate for your residence registration and your daily necessity rations. If you don't like the job assigned to you and refuse to take it, you are jobless. Because you don't have an official permission to live in any place other than where the job is, you won't get your ration coupons.

13   Your choice, therefore, is very simple: to eat or not to eat.

14   Every graduate is guaranteed a job. Each job affords the same starting salary. Engineer, schoolteacher, office clerk, truck driver, scientist—the difference in salary is negligible. That is the socialist way.

15   No matter if you like it or not, you stay with your job.

16   No matter if you are liked or not, you stay with your job.

17   If you are not very ambitious, life can be very easy for you. Its pace won't be so maddeningly fast as it is here in America. You don't have to worry about choosing alternatives or making decisions. You don't have to worry about getting laid off.

18   Since you don't have much to choose from and everything is planned and arranged for you, you will be better off if you take things easy. As an old Chinese saying goes: "Those who are content are forever happy."

19   People like that—who have been content to let their decisions be made for them—would find it hard to get used to the American lifestyle, to keep their eyes open to opportunities, to be searching constantly for a better job, a better place to live. Such a way of life would be too risky, too precarious, too challenging.

20   Our old tradition taught us to be humble, modest, unassuming, moderate, and passive. Even when a Chinese host treats a guest to a dinner consisting of twelve courses and costing half of his monthly salary, he still apologizes repeatedly to the guest between the courses for the "inadequate" meal he has prepared for his honorable guest. Meanwhile, the guest politely and humbly refuses to accept the food his host keeps piling up on his dish, because he feels he shouldn't assume that he deserves so much good food and he should leave more good stuff for the host family, even though he is very hungry at the moment and he likes the food immensely.

21   The other day while I was going through the classified ads in the magazine *Editor & Publisher,* I came across ads placed by publications in search of "aggressive, talented, hungry" reporters.

22   What could I do if I wanted such a position?

23   If I were hungry, I would try every face-saving means not to admit it.

24   If I were talented, I would (or should) be modest enough not to advertise it.

25   Even if I were desperately in need of the position, I still wouldn't know how to be aggressive.

26   I wonder if I should take a crash course, teaching me how to be aggressive, talented, and hungry.

❏ Questions for Discussion

1. Why does Keguang begin with the situation in the lunchroom? How does it develop his point? How does the vending machine represent America and the American way of life to Keguang?

2. How is this statement about China true: "Your choice, therefore, is very simple: to eat or not to eat"? Explain some of the choices you make that a Chinese student would not be able to make. Why is adjusting to American freedom and opportunity difficult for Keguang?

3. Discuss Keguang's reaction to the newspaper advertisements for " 'aggressive, talented, hungry' reporters."

❏ Suggestions for Exploration and Writing

1. Compare the attempt to equalize everyone in Kurt Vonnegut's short story "Harrison Bergeron" with the reality of conditions in China as Keguang describes them.

2. Keguang says that unambitious people can thrive in China because they do not have to make decisions and they have jobs for life. Why would some Americans have difficulty thriving in China?

3. Several times, Keguang discusses the collective personality of the Chinese people. For example, he says that the Chinese are taught to be "humble, modest, unassuming, moderate, and passive." He seems to imply that the Americans are the opposite. What words would you use to describe the American character? Discuss.

4. In a short comic **narrative,** imagine a group of friends who are apologetic, humble, and polite eating in a Chinese-American restaurant.

FICTION

RICHARD WRIGHT (1908–1960)

Richard Wright, born in Natchez, Mississippi, settled after high school in New York where he became a journalist. He began to write seriously about the plight of African-American men when he wrote Uncle Tom's Children *(1938), a collection of five stories;* Native Son *(1940), a story of racial conflict in urban America; and* Black Boy

(1945), an autobiography. In 1946 Wright moved to Paris where he lived the rest of his life. He wrote realistically but often experimented with various literary techniques, including the mix of dialect and standard English.

The Man Who Was Almost A Man

1   Dave struck out across the fields, looking homeward through paling light. Whut's the use talkin wid em niggers in the field? Anyhow, his mother was putting supper on the table. Them niggers can't understan nothing. One of these days he was going to get a gun and practice shooting, then they couldn't talk to him as though he were a little boy. He slowed, looking at the ground. Shucks, Ah ain scareda them even ef they are biggern me! Aw, Ah know whut Ahma do. Ahm going by ol Joe's sto n git that Sears Roebuck catlog n look at them guns. Mebbe Ma will lemme buy one when she gits mah pay from ol man Hawkins. Ahma beg her t gimme some money. Ahm ol ernough to hava gun. Ahm seventeen. Almost a man. He strode, feeling his long loose-jointed limbs. Shucks, a man oughta hava little gun aftah he done worked hard all day.

2   He came in sight of Joe's store. A yellow lantern glowed on the front porch. He mounted steps and went through the screen door, hearing it bang behind him. There was a strong smell of coal oil and mackerel fish. He felt very confident until he saw fat Joe walk in through the rear door, then his courage began to ooze.

3   "Howdy Dave! Whutcha want?"

4   "How yuh, Mistah Joe? Aw, Ah don wanna buy nothing. Ah jus wanted t see ef yuhd lemme look at tha catlog erwhile."

5   "Sure! You wanna see it here?"

6   "Nawsuh. Ah wans t take it home wid me. Ah'll bring it back termorrow when Ah come in from the fiels."

7   "You plannin on buying something?"

8   "Yessuh."

9   "Your ma lettin you have your own money now?"

10   "Shucks. Mistah Joe, Ahm gittin t be a man like anybody else!"

11   Joe laughed and wiped his greasy white face with a red bandanna.

12   "Whut you plannin on buyin?"

13   Dave looked at the floor, scratched his head, scratched his thigh, and smiled. Then he looked up shyly.

14   "Ah'll tell yuh, Mistah Joe, ef yuh promise yuh won't tell."

15   "I promise."

16   "Waal, Ahma buy a gun."

17   "A gun? Whut you want with a gun?"

18   "Ah wanna keep it."

19   "You ain't nothing but a boy. You don't need a gun."

20   "Aw, lemme have the catlog, Mistah Joe. Ah'll bring it back."

21   Joe walked through the rear door. Dave was elated. He looked around at barrels of sugar and flour. He heard Joe coming back. He craned his

neck to see if he were bringing the book. Yeah, he's got it. Gawddog, he's got it!

"Here, but be sure you bring it back. It's the only one I got." 22

"Sho, Mistah Joe." 23

"Say, if you wanna buy a gun, why don't you buy one from me? I gotta gun to sell." 24

"Will it shoot?" 25

"Sure it'll shoot." 26

"Whut kind is it?" 27

"Oh, it's kinda old . . . a left-hand Wheeler. A pistol. A big one." 28

"Is it got bullets in it?" 29

"It's loaded." 30

"Kin Ah see it?" 31

"Where's your money?" 32

"Whut yuh wan fer it?" 33

"I'll let you have it for two dollars." 34

"Just two dollahs? Shucks, Ah could buy tha when Ah git mah pay." 35

"I'll have it here when you want it." 36

"Awright, suh. Ah be in fer it." 37

He went through the door, hearing it slam again behind him. Ahma git 38
some money from Ma n buy me a gun! Only two dollahs! He tucked the
thick catalogue under his arm and hurried.

"Where yuh been, boy?" His mother held a steaming dish of black- 39
eyed peas.

"Aw, Ma, Ah jus stopped down the road t talk wid the boys." 40

"Yuh know bettah t keep suppah waitin." 41

He sat down, resting the catalogue on the edge of the table. 42

"Yuh git up from there and git to the well n wash yosef! Ah ain feedin 43
no hogs in mah house!"

She grabbed his shoulder and pushed him. He stumbled out of the 44
room, then came back to get the catalogue.

"Whut this?" 45

"Aw, Ma, it's jusa catlog." 46

"Who yuh git it from?" 47

"From Joe, down at the sto." 48

"Waal, thas good. We kin use it in the outhouse." 49

"Naw, Ma." He grabbed for it. "Gimme ma catlog, Ma." 50

She held onto it and glared at him. 51

"Quit hollerin at me! Whut's wrong wid yuh? Yuh crazy?" 52

"But Ma, please. It ain mine! It's Joe's! He tol me t bring it back t im 53
termorrow."

She gave up the book. He stumbled down the back steps, hugging the 54
thick book under his arm. When he had splashed water on his face and
hands, he groped back to the kitchen and fumbled in a corner for the
towel. He bumped into a chair; it clattered to the floor. The catalogue
sprawled at his feet. When he had dried his eyes he snatched up the book
and held it again under his arm. His mother stood watching him.

55   "Now, ef yuh gonna act a fool over that ol book, Ah'll take it n burn it up."

56   "Naw, Ma, please."

57   "Waal, set down n be still!"

58   He sat down and drew the oil lamp close. He thumbed page after page, unaware of the food his mother set on the table. His father came in. Then his small brother.

59   "Whutcha got there, Dave?" his father asked.

60   "Jusa catlog," he answered, not looking up.

61   "Yeah, here they is!" His eyes glowed at blue-and-black revolvers. He glanced up, feeling sudden guilt. His father was watching him. He eased the book under the table and rested it on his knees. After the blessing was asked, he ate. He scooped up peas and swallowed fat meat without chewing. Buttermilk helped to wash it down. He did not want to mention money before his father. He would do much better by cornering his mother when she was alone. He looked at his father uneasily out of the edge of his eye.

62   "Boy, how com yuh don quit foolin wid tha book n eat yo suppah?"

63   "Yessuh."

64   "How you n ol man Hawkins gitten erlong?"

65   "Suh?"

66   "Can't yuh hear? Why don yuh lissen? Ah ast yu how wuz yuh n ol man Hawkins gittin erlong?"

67   "Oh, swell, Pa. Ah plows mo lan than anybody over there."

68   "Waal, yuh oughta keep yo mind on whut yuh doin."

69   "Yessuh."

70   He poured his plate full of molasses and sopped it up slowly with a chunk of cornbread. When his father and brother had left the kitchen, he still sat and looked again at the guns in the catalogue, longing to muster courage enough to present his case to his mother. Lawd, ef Ah only had tha pretty one! He could almost feel the slickness of the weapon with his fingers. If he had a gun like that he would polish it and keep it shining so it would never rust. N Ah'd keep it loaded, by Gawd!

71   "Ma?" His voice was hesitant.

72   "Hunh?"

73   "Ol man Hawkins give yuh mah money yit?"

74   "Yeah, but ain no usa yuh thinking bout throwin nona it erway. Ahm keepin tha money sos yuh kin have cloes t go to school this winter."

75   He rose and went to her side with the open catalogue in his palms. She was washing dishes, her head bent low over a pan. Shyly he raised the book. When he spoke, his voice was husky, faint.

76   "Ma, Gawd knows Ah wans one of these."

77   "One of whut?" she asked, not raising her eyes.

78   "One of these," he said again, not daring even to point. She glanced up at the page, then at him with wide eyes.

79   "Nigger, is yuh gone plumb crazy?"

80   "Aw, Ma—"

"Git outta here! Don yuh talk t me bout no gun! Yuh a fool!"   81

"Ma, Ah kin buy one fer two dollahs."   82

"Not ef Ah knows it, yuh ain!"   83

"But yuh promised me one—"   84

"Ah don care whut Ah promised! Yuh ain nothing but a boy yit!"   85

"Ma, ef yuh lemme buy one Ah'll *never* ast yuh fer nothing no mo."   86

"Ah tol yuh t git outta here! Yuh ain gonna toucha penny of tha money   87
for no gun! Thas how come Ah has Mistah Hawkins t pay yo wages t me,
cause Ah knows yuh ain got no sense."

"But, Ma, we needa gun. Pa ain got no gun. We needa gun in the   88
house. Yuh kin never tell whut might happen."

"Now don yuh try to maka fool outta me, boy! Ef we did hava gun,   89
yuh wouldn't have it!"

He laid the catalogue down and slipped his arm around her waist.   90

"Aw, Ma, Ah done worked hard alla summer n ain ast yuh fer nothin,   91
is Ah, now?"

"Thas whut yuh spose to do!"   92

"But Ma, Ah wans a gun. Yuh kin lemme have two dollahs outta   93
mah money. Please, Ma. I kin give it to Pa . . . Please, Ma! Ah loves yuh,
Ma."

When she spoke her voice came soft and low.   94

"Whut yu wan wida gun, Dave? Yuh don need no gun. Yuh'll git in   95
trouble. N ef yo pa jus thought Ah let yuh have money t buy a gun he'd
hava fit."

"Ah'll hide it, Ma. It ain but two dollahs."   96

"Lawd, chil, whut's wrong wid yuh?"   97

"Ain nothin wrong, Ma. Ahm almos a man now. Ah wans a gun."   98

"Who gonna sell yuh a gun?"   99

"Ol Joe at the sto."   100

"N it don cos but two dollahs?"   101

"Thas all, Ma. Jus two dollahs. Please, Ma."   102

She was stacking the plates away; her hands moved slowly, reflectively.   103
Dave kept an anxious silence. Finally, she turned to him.

"Ah'll let yuh git the gun ef yuh promise me one thing."   104

"Whut's tha, Ma?"   105

"Yuh bring it straight back t me, yuh hear? It be fer Pa."   106

"Yessum! Lemme go now, Ma."   107

She stooped, turned slightly to one side, raised the hem of her dress,   108
rolled down the top of her stocking, and came up with a slender wad of
bills.

"Here," she said. "Lawd knows yuh don need no gun. But yer pa does.   109
Yuh bring it right back to me, yuh hear? Ahma put it up. Now ef yuh
don, Ahma have yuh pa lick yuh so hard yuh won fergit it."

"Yessum."   110

He took the money, ran down the steps, and across the yard.   111

"Dave! Yuuuuuh Daaaaave!"   112

He heard, but he was not going to stop now. "Naw, Lawd!"   113

114   The first movement he made the following morning was to reach under his pillow for the gun. In the gray light of dawn he held it loosely, feeling a sense of power. Could kill a man with a gun like this. Kill anybody, black or white. And if he were holding his gun in his hand, nobody could run over him; they would have to respect him. It was a big gun, with a long barrel and a heavy handle. He raised and lowered it in his hand, marveling at its weight.

115   He had not come straight home with it as his mother had asked; instead he had stayed out in the fields, holding the weapon in his hand, aiming it now and then at some imaginary foe. But he had not fired it; he had been afraid that his father might hear. Also he was not sure he knew how to fire it.

116   To avoid surrendering the pistol he had not come into the house until he knew that they were all asleep. When his mother had tiptoed to his bedside later that night and demanded the gun, he had first played possum; then he had told her that the gun was hidden outdoors, that he would bring it to her in the morning. Now he lay turning it slowly in his hands. He broke it, took out the cartridges, felt them, and then put them back.

117   He slid out of bed, got a long strip of old flannel from a trunk, wrapped the gun in it, and tied it to his naked thigh while it was still loaded. He did not go in to breakfast. Even though it was not yet daylight, he started for Jim Hawkins' plantation. Just as the sun was rising he reached the barns where the mules and plows were kept.

118   "Hey! That you, Dave?"

119   He turned. Jim Hawkins stood eyeing him suspiciously.

120   "What're yuh doing here so early?"

121   "Ah didn't know Ah wuz gittin up so early, Mistah Hawkins. Ah wuz fixin t hitch up ol Jenny n take her t the fiels."

122   "Good. Since you're so early, how about plowing that stretch down by the woods?"

123   "Suits me, Mistah Hawkins."

124   "O.K. Go to it!"

125   He hitched Jenny to a plow and started across the fields. Hot dog! This was just what he wanted. If he could get down by the woods, he could shoot his gun and nobody would hear. He walked behind the plow, hearing the traces creaking, feeling the gun tied tight to his thigh.

126   When he reached the woods, he plowed two whole rows before he decided to take out the gun. Finally, he stopped, looked in all directions, then untied the gun and held it in his hand. He turned to the mule and smiled.

127   "Know whut this is, Jenny? Naw, yuh wouldn know! Yuhs jusa old mule! Anyhow, this is a gun, n it kin shoot, by Gawd!"

128   He held the gun at arm's length. Whut t hell, Ahma shoot this thing! He looked at Jenny again.

129   "Lissen here, Jenny! When Ah pull this ol trigger, Ah don wan yuh t run n acka fool now!"

Jenny stood with head down, her short ears pricked straight. Dave   130
walked off about twenty feet, held the gun far out from him at arm's
length, and turned his head. Hell, he told himself, Ah ain afraid. The gun
felt loose in his fingers; he waved it wildly for a moment. Then he shut
his eyes and tightened his forefinger. Bloom! A report half deafened him
and he thought his right hand was torn from his arm. He heard Jenny
whinnying and galloping over the field, and he found himself on his
knees, squeezing his fingers hard between his legs. His hand was numb;
he jammed it into his mouth, trying to warm it, trying to stop the pain.
The gun lay at his feet. He did not quite know what had happened. He
stood up and stared at the gun as though it were a living thing. He gritted
his teeth and kicked the gun. Yuh almos broke mah arm! He turned to
look for Jenny; she was far over the fields, tossing her head and kicking
wildly.

"Hol on there, ol mule!"   131

When he caught up with her she stood trembling, walling her big white   132
eyes at him. The plow was far away; the traces had broken. Then Dave
stopped short, looking, not believing. Jenny was bleeding. Her left side
was red and wet with blood. He went closer. Lawd, have mercy! Wondah
did Ah shoot this mule? He grabbed for Jenny's mane. She flinched,
snorted, whirled, tossing her head.

"Hol on now! Hol on."   133

Then he saw the hole in Jenny's side, right between the ribs. It was   134
round, wet, red. A crimson stream streaked down the front leg, flowing
fast. Good Gawd! Ah wuzn't shootin at tha mule. He felt panic. He knew
he had to stop that blood, or Jenny would bleed to death. He had never
seen so much blood in all his life. He chased the mule for half a mile,
trying to catch her. He caught her mane and led her back to where the
plow and gun lay. Then he stooped and grabbed handfuls of damp black
earth and tried to plug the bullet hole. Jenny shuddered, whinnied, and
broke from him.

"Hol on! Hol on now!"   135

He tried to plug it again, but blood came anyhow. His fingers were hot   136
and sticky. He rubbed dirt into his palms, trying to dry them. Then again
he attempted to plug the bullet hole, but Jenny shied away, kicking her
heels high. He stood helpless. He had to do something. He ran at Jenny;
she dodged him. He watched a red stream of blood flow down Jenny's leg
and form a bright pool at her feet.

"Jenny . . . Jenny," he called weakly.   137

His lips trembled. She's bleeding t death! He looked in the direction of   138
home, wanting to go back, wanting to get help. But he saw the pistol laying
in the damp black clay. He had a queer feeling that if he only did something, this would not be; Jenny would not be there bleeding to death.

When he went to her this time, she did not move. She stood with   139
sleepy, dreamy eyes; and when he touched her she gave a low-pitched
whinny and knelt to the ground, her front knees slopping in blood.

140   "Jenny . . . Jenny . . ." he whispered.

141   For a long time she held her neck erect; then her head sank, slowly. Her ribs swelled with a mighty heave and she went over.

142   Dave's stomach felt empty, very empty. He picked up the gun and held it gingerly between his thumb and forefinger. He buried it at the foot of a tree. He took a stick and tried to cover the pool of blood with dirt—but what was the use? There was Jenny lying with her mouth open and her eyes walled and glassy. He could not tell Jim Hawkins he had shot his mule. But he had to tell something. Yeah, Ah'll tell em Jenny started gittin wil n fell on the joint of the plow. . . . But that would hardly happen to a mule. He walked across the field slowly, head down.

143   It was sunset. Two of Jim Hawkins' men were over near the edge of the woods digging a hole in which to bury Jenny. Dave was surrounded by a knot of people, all of whom were looking down at the dead mule.

144   "I don't see how in the world it happened," said Jim Hawkins for the tenth time.

145   The crowd parted and Dave's mother, father, and small brother pushed into the center.

146   "Where Dave?" his mother called.

147   "There he is," said Jim Hawkins.

148   His mother grabbed him.

149   "Whut happened, Dave? Whut yuh done?"

150   "Nothin."

151   "C mon, boy, talk," his father said.

152   Dave took a deep breath and told the story he knew nobody believed.

153   "Waal," he drawled. "Ah brung ol Jenny down here sos Ah could do mah plowing. Ah plowed bout two rows, just like yuh see." He stopped and pointed at the long rows of upturned earth. "Then somethin musta been wrong wid ol Jenny. She wouldn ack right a-tall. She started snortin n kickin her heels. Ah tried t hol her, but she pulled erway, rearin n goin in. Then when the point of the plow was stickin up in the air, she swung erroun n twisted herself back on it . . . She stuck herself n started t bleed. N fo Ah could do anything, she wuz dead."

154   "Did you ever hear of anything like that in all your life?" asked Jim Hawkins.

155   There were white and black standing in the crowd. They murmured. Dave's mother came close to him and looked hard into his face. "Tell the truth, Dave," she said.

156   "Looks like a bullet hole to me," said one man.

157   "Dave, whut yuh do wid the gun?" his mother asked.

158   The crowd surged in, looking at him. He jammed his hands into his pockets, shook his head slowly from left to right, and backed away. His eyes were wide and painful.

159   "Did he hava gun?" asked Jim Hawkins.

"By Gawd, Ah tol yuh tha wuz a gun wound," said a man, slapping his thigh. 160

His father caught his shoulders and shook him till his teeth rattled. 161

"Tell whut happened, yuh rascal! Tell whut . . ." 162

Dave looked at Jenny's stiff legs and began to cry. 163

"Whut yuh do wid tha gun?" his mother asked. 164

"Whut wuz he doin wida gun?" his father asked. 165

"Come on and tell the truth," said Hawkins. "Ain't nobody going to hurt you . . ." 166

His mother crowded close to him. 167

"Did yuh shoot that mule, Dave?" 168

Dave cried, seeing blurred white and black faces. 169

"Ahh ddinn gggo tt sshooot hher . . . Ah ssswear ffo Gawd Ahh ddin. . . . Ah wuz a-tryin t sssee ef the old gggun would sshoot—" 170

"Where yuh git the gun from?" his father asked. 171

"Ah got it from Joe, at the sto." 172

"Where yuh git the money?" 173

"Ma give it t me." 174

"He kept worryin me, Bob. Ah had t. Ah tol im t bring the gun right back t me . . . It was fer yuh, the gun." 175

"But how yuh happen to shoot that mule?" asked Jim Hawkins. 176

"Ah wuzn shootin at the mule, Mistah Hawkins. The gun jumped when Ah pulled the trigger . . . N fo Ah knowed anythin Jenny was there a-bleedin." 177

Somebody in the crowd laughed. Jim Hawkins walked close to Dave and looked into his face. 178

"Well, looks like you have bought you a mule, Dave." 179

"Ah swear fo Gawd, Ah didn go t kill the mule, Mistah Hawkins!" 180

"But you killed her!" 181

All the crowd was laughing now. They stood on tiptoe and poked heads over one another's shoulders. 182

"Well, boy, looks like yuh done bought a dead mule! Hahaha!" 183

"Ain tha ershame." 184

"Hohohohoho." 185

Dave stood, head down, twisting his feet in the dirt. 186

"Well, you needn't worry about it, Bob," said Jim Hawkins to Dave's father. "Just let the boy keep on working and pay me two dollars a month." 186

"Whut yuh wan fer yo mule, Mistah Hawkins?" 188

Jim Hawkins screwed up his eyes. 189

"Fifty dollars." 190

"Whut yuh do wid tha gun?" Dave's father demanded. 191

Dave said nothing. 192

"Yuh wan me t take a tree n beat yuh till yuh talk!" 193

"Nawsuh!" 194

"Whut yuh do wid it?" 195

196   "Ah throwed it erway."

197   "Where?"

198   "Ah . . . Ah throwed it in the creek."

199   "Waal, c mon home. N firs thing in the mawnin git to tha creek n fin tha gun."

200   "Yessuh."

201   "Whut yuh pay fer it?"

202   "Two dollahs."

203   "Take tha gun n git yo money back n carry it to Mistah Hawkins, yuh hear? N don fergit Ahma lam you black bottom good fer this! Now march yosef on home, suh!"

204   Dave turned and walked slowly. He heard people laughing. Dave glared, his eyes welling with tears. Hot anger bubbled in him. Then he swallowed and stumbled on.

205   That night Dave did not sleep. He was glad that he had gotten out of killing the mule so easily, but he was hurt. Something hot seemed to turn over inside him each time he remembered how they had laughed. He tossed on his bed, feeling his hard pillow. N Pa says he's gonna beat me . . . He remembered other beatings, and his back quivered. Naw, naw, Ah sho don wan im t beat me tha way no mo. Dam em all! Nobody ever gave him anything. All he did was work. They treat me like a mule, n then they beat me. He gritted his teeth. N Ma had t tell on me.

206   Well, if he had to, he would take old man Hawkins that two dollars. But that meant selling the gun. And he wanted to keep that gun. Fifty dollars for a dead mule.

207   He turned over, thinking how he had fired the gun. He had an itch to fire it again. Ef other men kin shoota gun, by Gawd, Ah kin! He was still, listening. Mebbe they all sleepin now. The house was still. He heard the soft breathing of his brother. Yes, now! He would go down and get that gun and see if he could fire it! He eased out of bed and slipped into overalls.

208   The moon was bright. He ran almost all the way to the edge of the woods. He stumbled over the ground, looking for the spot where he had buried the gun. Yeah, here it is. Like a hungry dog scratching for a bone, he pawed it up. He puffed his black cheeks and blew dirt from the trigger and barrel. He broke it and found four cartridges unshot. He looked around; the fields were filled with silence and moonlight. He clutched the gun stiff and hard in his fingers. But, as soon as he wanted to pull the trigger, he shut his eyes and turned his head. Naw, Ah can't shoot wid mah eyes closed n mah head turned. With effort he held his eyes open; then he squeezed. *Blooooom!* He was stiff, not breathing. The gun was still in his hands. Dammit, he'd done it! He fired again. *Blooooom!* He smiled. *Blooooom! Blooooom! Click, click.* There! It was empty. If anybody could shoot a gun, he could. He put the gun into his hip pocket and started across the fields.

209   When he reached the top of a ridge he stood straight and proud in the moonlight, looking at Jim Hawkins' big white house, feeling the gun

sagging in his pocket. Lawd, ef Ah had just one mo bullet Ah'd taka shot at tha house. Ah'd like t scare ol man Hawkins jusa little . . . Jusa enough t let im know Dave Saunders is a man.

To his left the road curved, running to the tracks of the Illinois Central. He jerked his head, listening. From far off came a faint *hoooof-hoooof; hoooof-hoooof; hoooof-hoooof.* . . . He stood rigid. Two dollahs a mont. Les see now . . . Tha means it'll take bout two years. Shucks! Ah'll be dam!

He started down the road, toward the tracks. Yeah, here she comes! He stood beside the track and held himself stiffly. Here she comes, erroun the ben . . . C mon, yuh slow poke! C mon! He had his hand on his gun; something quivered in his stomach. Then the train thundered past, the gray and brown box cars rumbling and clinking. He gripped the gun tightly; then he jerked his hand out of his pocket. Ah betcha Bill wouldn't do it! Ah betcha . . . The cars slid past, steel grinding upon steel. Ahm ridin yuh ternight, so hep me Gawd! He was hot all over. He hesitated just a moment; then he grabbed, pulled atop of a car, and lay flat. He felt his pocket; the gun was still there. Ahead the long rails were glinting in the moonlight, stretching away, away to somewhere, somewhere where he could be a man . . .

☐ Questions for Discussion

1. The African Americans in the story call each other "nigger" at various times. Why?

2. Why does Dave want a gun? What does the gun symbolize to him? Is his mother right to give in to Dave's desire to have a gun?

3. Why does Dave lie about the gun? Why does the laughter bother him?

4. Why does Dave sneak out of his house to fire the gun and use up all the bullets?

5. What would having to work two years for Hawkins to pay for the dead mule do to Dave? Why does Dave hop the train to leave home?

☐ Suggestions for Exploration and Writing

1. Discuss the various **ironies** of the story, including the irony of the title.

2. Do guns still play a role in the manhood of some people? Discuss.

3. What responsibilities should accompany the freedom to own guns? Use the story as a basis for an essay.

KURT VONNEGUT, JR. (1922–   )

Kurt Vonnegut, Jr., a self-acknowledged pessimist, is one of America's foremost science fiction writers. In his short stories and novels he satirizes the dilemmas which humans have created: unimaginably destructive wars, out-of-control technology, pollution, and racism. His most famous novels are Cat's Cradle *(1963), which ends with the freezing of the world, and* Slaughterhouse-Five *(1969). In addition to fiction, Vonnegut writes plays and television adaptations of his stories.*

Harrison Bergeron

1   The year was 2081, and everybody was finally equal. They weren't only equal before God and the law. They were equal every which way. Nobody was smarter than anybody else. Nobody was better looking than anybody else. Nobody was stronger or quicker than anybody else. All this equality was due to the 211th, 212th, and 213th Amendments to the Constitution, and to the unceasing vigilance of agents of the United States Handicapper General.

2   Some things about living still weren't quite right, though. April, for instance, still drove people crazy by not being springtime. And it was in that clammy month that the H-G men took George and Hazel Bergeron's fourteen-year-old son, Harrison, away.

3   It was tragic, all right, but George and Hazel couldn't think about it very hard. Hazel had a perfectly average intelligence, which meant she couldn't think about anything except in short bursts. And George, while his intelligence was way above normal, had a little mental handicap radio in his ear. He was required by law to wear it at all times. It was tuned to a government transmitter. Every twenty seconds or so, the transmitter would send out some sharp noise to keep people like George from taking unfair advantage of their brains.

4   George and Hazel were watching television. There were tears on Hazel's cheeks, but she'd forgotten for the moment what they were about.

5   On the television screen were ballerinas.

6   A buzzer sounded in George's head. His thoughts fled in panic, like bandits from a burglar alarm.

7   "That was a really pretty dance, that dance they just did," said Hazel.

8   "Huh?" said George.

9   "That dance—it was nice," said Hazel.

10   "Yup," said George. He tried to think a little about the ballerinas. They weren't really very good—no better than anybody else would have been, anyway. They were burdened with sashweights and bags of bird-shot, and their faces were masked, so that no one, seeing a free and graceful gesture or a pretty face, would feel like something the cat drug in. George was toying with the vague notion that maybe dancers shouldn't be handicapped. But he didn't get very far with it before another noise in his ear radio scattered his thoughts.

George winced. So did two out of the eight ballerinas. 11

Hazel saw him wince. Having no mental handicap herself, she had to 12
ask George what the latest sound had been.

"Sounded like somebody hitting a milk bottle with a ball peen ham- 13
mer," said George.

"I'd think it would be real interesting, hearing all the different 14
sounds," said Hazel, a little envious. "All the things they think up."

"Um," said George. 15

"Only, if I was Handicapper General, you know what I would do?" 16
said Hazel. Hazel, as a matter of fact, bore a strong resemblance to the
Handicapper General, a woman named Diana Moon Glampers. "If I was
Diana Moon Glampers," said Hazel, "I'd have chimes on Sunday—just
chimes. Kind of in honor of religion."

"I could think, if it was just chimes," said George. 17

"Well—maybe make 'em real loud," said Hazel. "I think I'd make a 18
good Handicapper General."

"Good as anybody else," said George. 19

"Who knows better'n I do what normal is?" said Hazel. 20

"Right," said George. He began to think glimmeringly about his 21
abnormal son who was now in jail, about Harrison, but a twenty-one-
gun salute in his head stopped that.

"Boy!" said Hazel, "that was a doozy, wasn't it?" 22

It was such a doozy that George was white and trembling, and tears 23
stood on the rims of his red eyes. Two of the eight ballerinas had
collapsed to the studio floor, were holding their temples.

"All of a sudden you look so tired," said Hazel. "Why don't you 24
stretch out on the sofa, so's you can rest your handicap bag on the
pillows, honeybunch." She was referring to the forty-seven pounds of
birdshot in a canvas bag, which was padlocked around George's neck.
"Go on and rest the bag for a little while," she said. "I don't care if you're
not equal to me for a while."

George weighed the bag with his hands. "I don't mind it," he said. "I 25
don't notice it any more. It's just a part of me."

"You been so tired lately—kind of wore out," said Hazel. "If there was 26
just some way we could make a little hole in the bottom of the bag, and
just take out a few of them lead balls. Just a few."

"Two years in prison and two thousand dollars fine for every ball I 27
took out," said George. "I don't call that a bargain."

"If you could just take a few out when you came home from work," 28
said Hazel. "I mean—you don't compete with anybody around here. You
just set around."

"If I tried to get away with it," said George, "then other people'd get 29
away with it—and pretty soon we'd be right back to the dark ages again,
with everybody competing against everybody else. You wouldn't like
that, would you?"

"I'd hate it," said Hazel. 30

31   "There you are," said George. "The minute people start cheating on laws, what do you think happens to society?"

32   If Hazel hadn't been able to come up with an answer to this question, George couldn't have supplied one. A siren was going off in his head.

33   "Reckon it'd fall all apart," said Hazel.

34   "What would?" said George blankly.

35   "Society," said Hazel uncertainly. "Wasn't that what you just said?"

36   "Who knows?" said George.

37   The television program was suddenly interrupted for a news bulletin. It wasn't clear at first as to what the bulletin was about, since the announcer, like all announcers, had a serious speech impediment. For about half a minute, and in a state of high excitement, the announcer tried to say, "Ladies and gentlemen—"

38   He finally gave up, handed the bulletin to a ballerina to read.

39   "That's all right—" Hazel said of the announcer, "he tried. That's the big thing. He tried to do the best he could with what God gave him. He should get a nice raise for trying so hard."

40   "Ladies and gentlemen—" said the ballerina, reading the bulletin. She must have been extraordinarily beautiful, because the mask she wore was hideous. And it was easy to see that she was the strongest and most graceful of all the dancers, for her handicap bags were as big as those worn by two-hundred-pound men.

41   And she had to apologize at once for her voice, which was a very unfair voice for a woman to use. Her voice was a warm, luminous, timeless melody. "Excuse me—" she said, and she began again, making her voice absolutely uncompetitive.

42   "Harrison Bergeron, age fourteen," she said in a grackle squawk, "has just escaped from jail, where he was held on suspicion of plotting to overthrow the government. He is a genius and an athlete, is under-handicapped, and should be regarded as extremely dangerous."

43   A police photograph of Harrison Bergeron was flashed on the screen— upside down, then sideways, upside down again, then right side up. The picture showed the full length of Harrison against a background calibrated in feet and inches. He was exactly seven feet tall.

44   The rest of Harrison's appearance was Halloween and hardware. Nobody had ever borne heavier handicaps. He had outgrown hindrances faster than the H-G men could think them up. Instead of a little ear radio for a mental handicap, he wore a tremendous pair of earphones, and spectacles with thick wavy lenses. The spectacles were intended to make him not only half blind, but to give him whanging headaches besides.

45   Scrap metal was hung all over him. Ordinarily, there was a certain symmetry, a military neatness to the handicaps issued to strong people, but Harrison looked like a walking junkyard. In the race of life, Harrison carried three hundred pounds.

46   And to offset his good looks, the H-G men required that he wear at all

times a red rubber ball for a nose, keep his eyebrows shaved off, and cover his even white teeth with black caps at snaggle-tooth random.

"If you see this boy," said the ballerina, "do not—I repeat, do not—try to reason with him." 47

There was the shriek of a door being torn from its hinges. 48

Screams and barking cries of consternation came from the television set. The photograph of Harrison Bergeron on the screen jumped again and again, as though dancing to the tune of an earthquake. 49

George Bergeron correctly identified the earthquake, and well he might have—for many was the time his own home had danced to the same crashing tune. "My God—" said George, "that must be Harrison." 50

The realization was blasted from his mind instantly by the sound of an automobile collision in his head. 51

When George could open his eyes again, the photograph of Harrison was gone. A living, breathing Harrison filled the screen. 52

Clanking, clownish, and huge, Harrison stood in the center of the studio. The knob of the uprooted studio door was still in his hand. Ballerinas, technicians, musicians, and announcers cowered on their knees before him, expecting to die. 53

"I am the Emperor!" cried Harrison. "Do you hear? I am the Emperor! Everybody must do what I say at once!" He stamped his foot and the studio shook. 54

"Even as I stand here—" he bellowed, "crippled, hobbled, sickened—I am a greater ruler than any man who ever lived! Now watch me become what I *can* become!" 55

Harrison tore the straps of his handicap harness like wet tissue paper, tore straps guaranteed to support five thousand pounds. 56

Harrison's scrap-iron handicaps crashed to the floor. 57

Harrison thrust his thumbs under the bar of the padlock that secured his head harness. The bar snapped like celery. Harrison smashed his headphones and spectacles against the wall. 58

He flung away his rubber-ball nose, revealed a man that would have awed Thor, the god of thunder. 59

"I shall now select my Empress!" he said, looking down on the cowering people. "Let the first woman who dares rise to her feet claim her mate and her throne!" 60

A moment passed, and then a ballerina arose, swaying like a willow. 61

Harrison plucked the mental handicap from her ear, snapped off her physical handicaps with marvellous delicacy. Last of all, he removed her mask. 62

She was blindingly beautiful. 63

"Now—" said Harrison, taking her hand, "shall we show the people the meaning of the word dance? Music!" he commanded. 64

The musicians scrambled back into their chairs, and Harrison stripped them of their handicaps, too. "Play your best," he told them, "and I'll make you barons and dukes and earls." 65

66   The music began. It was normal at first—cheap, silly, false. But Harrison snatched two musicians from their chairs, waved them like batons as he sang the music as he wanted it played. He slammed them back into their chairs.

67   The music began again and was much improved.

68   Harrison and his Empress merely listened to the music for a while—listened gravely, as though synchronizing their heartbeats with it.

69   They shifted their weights to their toes.

70   Harrison placed his big hands on the girl's tiny waist, letting her sense the weightlessness that would soon be hers.

71   And then, in an explosion of joy and grace, into the air they sprang!

72   Not only were the laws of the land abandoned, but the law of gravity and the laws of motion as well.

73   They reeled, whirled, swiveled, flounced, capered, gamboled, and spun.

74   They leaped like deer on the moon.

75   The studio ceiling was thirty feet high, but each leap brought the dancers nearer to it.

76   It became their obvious intention to kiss the ceiling.

77   They kissed it.

78   And then, neutralizing gravity with love and pure will, they remained suspended in air inches below the ceiling, and they kissed each other for a long, long time.

79   It was then that Diana Moon Glampers, the Handicapper General, came into the studio with a double-barreled ten-gauge shotgun. She fired twice, and the Emperor and the Empress were dead before they hit the floor.

80   Diana Moon Glampers loaded the gun again. She aimed it at the musicians and told them they had ten seconds to get their handicaps back on.

81   It was then that the Bergerons' television tube burned out.

82   Hazel turned to comment about the blackout to George. But George had gone out into the kitchen for a can of beer.

83   George came back in with the beer, paused while a handicap signal shook him up. And then he sat down again. "You been crying?" he said to Hazel.

84   "Yup," she said.

85   "What about?" he said.

86   "I forget," she said. "Something real sad on television."

87   "What was it?" he said.

88   "It's all kind of mixed up in my mind," said Hazel.

89   "Forget sad things," said George.

90   "I always do," said Hazel.

91   "That's my girl," said George. He winced. There was the sound of a rivetting gun in his head.

92   "Gee—I could tell that one was a doozy," said Hazel.

93   "You can say that again," said George.

94   "Gee—" said Hazel, "I could tell that one was a doozy."

❑ Questions for Discussion

1. What are the effects of enforced equality in this story? Why are people handicapped? What is lost in this society because of enforced equality?

2. What is the effect of telling the story from George and Hazel Bergeron's **point of view?** How would the story be different if told from Harrison's point of view?

3. What effect would 213 amendments have on the U.S. constitution?

4. What is the significance of Hazel's repeating herself at the end of the story?

❑ Suggestions for Exploration and Writing

1. The society of "Harrison Bergeron" extends to its logical conclusion: Jefferson's premise that "all men are created equal." In what ways does the society described in this story violate other principles enunciated in the Declaration of Independence?

2. Discuss current trends in education or society which parallel the kind of equality established in this story.

3. George Bergeron says, " 'The minute people start cheating on laws, what do you think happens to society?' " Hazel responds, " 'Reckon it'd fall all apart.' " Argue for or against Hazel's assessment.

4. "Harrison Bergeron" makes a statement about the clash between equality and competition. In an essay, discuss the conflict between equality and competition in a free society.

URSULA K. LEGUIN (1929–)

Ursula K. LeGuin is one of the most prolific writers of this century and one of the hardest to classify. She has written poetry, short stories, novels, and children's books. At times the genres seem to overlap, for her fiction is beautifully lyric, often symbolic, and philosophically titillating. Though she is usually classified as a writer of science fiction or fantasy, LeGuin's works are also realistic. Her fiction is sometimes based on recorded mythology, but often the myths are LeGuin originals. Her most famous and most admired novels are those included in The Earthsea Trilogy *(1968, 1971, 1972).*

The Ones Who Walk Away From Omelas

1   With a clamor of bells that set the swallows soaring, the Festival of Summer came to the city Omelas, bright-towered by the sea. The rigging of the boats in harbor sparkled with flags. In the streets between houses with red roofs and painted walls, between old moss-grown gardens and under avenues of trees, past great parks and public buildings, processions moved. Some were decorous: old people in long stiff robes of mauve and grey, grave master workmen, quiet, merry women carrying their babies and chatting as they walked. In other streets the music beat faster, a shimmering of gong and tambourine, and the people went dancing, the procession was a dance. Children dodged in and out, their high calls rising like the swallows' crossing flights over the music and the singing. All the processions wound towards the northside of the city, where on the great water-meadow called the Green Fields boys and girls, naked in the bright air, with mud-stained feet and ankles and long, lithe arms, exercised their restive horses before the race. The horses wore no gear at all but a halter without bit. Their manes were braided with streamers of silver, gold, and green. They flared their nostrils and pranced and boasted to one another; they were vastly excited, the horse being the only animal who has adopted our ceremonies as his own. Far off to the north and west the mountains stood up half encircling Omelas on her bay. The air of morning was so clear that the snow still crowning the Eighteen Peaks burned with white-gold fire across the miles of sunlit air, under the dark blue of the sky. There was just enough wind to make the banners that marked the racecourse snap and flutter now and then. In the silence of the broad green meadows one could hear the music winding through the city streets, farther and nearer and ever approaching, a cheerful faint sweetness of the air that from time to time trembled and gathered together and broke into the great joyous clanging of the bells.

2   Joyous! How is one to tell about joy? How describe the citizens of Omelas?

3   They were not simple folk, you see, though they were happy. But we do not say the words of cheer much any more. All smiles have become archaic. Given a description such as this one tends to make certain assumptions. Given a description such as this one tends to look next for the King, mounted on a splendid stallion and surrounded by his noble knights, or perhaps in a golden litter borne by great-muscled slaves. But there was no king. They did not use swords, or keep slaves. They were not barbarians. I do not know the rules and laws of their society, but I suspect that they were singularly few. As they did without monarchy and slavery, so they also got on without the stock exchange, the advertisement, the secret police, and the bomb. Yet I repeat that these were not simple folk, not dulcet shepherds, noble savages, bland utopians. They were not less complex than us. The trouble is that we have a bad habit,

encouraged by pedants and sophisticates, of considering happiness as something rather stupid. Only pain is intellectual, only evil interesting. This is the treason of the artist: a refusal to admit the banality of evil and the terrible boredom of pain. If you can't lick 'em, join 'em. If it hurts, repeat it. But to praise despair is to condemn delight, to embrace violence is to lose hold of everything else. We have almost lost hold; we can no longer describe a happy man, nor make any celebration of joy. How can I tell you about the people of Omelas? They were not naïve and happy children—though their children were, in fact, happy. They were mature, intelligent, passionate adults whose lives were not wretched. O miracle! but I wish I could describe it better. I wish I could convince you. Omelas sounds in my words like a city in a fairy tale, long ago and far away, once upon a time. Perhaps it would be best if you imagined it as your own fancy bids, assuming it will rise to the occasion, for certainly I cannot suit you all. For instance, how about technology? I think that there would be no cars or helicopters in and above the streets; this follows from the fact that the people of Omelas are happy people. Happiness is based on a just discrimination of what is necessary, what is neither necessary nor destructive, and what is destructive. In the middle category, however—that of the unnecessary but undestructive, that of comfort, luxury, exuberance, etc.—they could perfectly well have central heating, subway trains, washing machines, and all kinds of marvelous devices not yet invented here, floating light-sources, fuelless power, a cure for the common cold. Or they could have none of that: it doesn't matter. As you like it. I incline to think that people from towns up and down the coast have been coming in to Omelas during the last days before the Festival on very fast little trains and double-decked trams, and that the train station of Omelas is actually the handsomest building in town, though plainer than the magnificent Farmer's Market. But even granted trains, I fear that Omelas so far strikes some of you as goody-goody. Smiles, bells, parades, horses, bleh. If so, please add an orgy. If an orgy would help, don't hesitate. Let us not, however, have temples from which issue beautiful nude priests and priestesses already half in ecstasy and ready to copulate with any man or woman, lover or stranger, who desires union with the deep godhead of the blood, although that was my first idea. But really it would be better not to have any temples in Omelas—at least, not manned temples. Religion yes, clergy no. Surely the beautiful nudes can just wander about, offering themselves like divine soufflés to the hunger of the needy and the rapture of the flesh. Let them join the processions. Let tambourines be struck above the copulations, and the glory of desire be proclaimed upon the gongs, and (a not unimportant point) let the offspring of these delightful rituals be beloved and looked after by all. One thing I know there is none of in Omelas is guilt. But what else should there be? I thought at first there were no drugs, but that is puritanical. For those who like it, the faint insistent sweetness of *drooz* may perfume the ways of the city, *drooz* which first brings a great lightness and brilliance to the mind and limbs, and then after some hours a dreamy languor, and wonderful visions at least of the very arcana and inmost secrets of the Universe, as well as exciting the pleasure of sex beyond all belief; and it is not habit-forming. For more modest tastes I think there ought to be beer. What else, what else belongs in the joyous city? The sense of victory, surely, the celebration of courage. But as we did without clergy, let us do without soldiers. The joy built upon successful slaughter is not the right kind of joy; it will not do; it is fearful and it is trivial. A boundless and generous contentment, a magnanimous triumph felt not against some outer enemy but in communion with the finest and fairest in the souls of all men everywhere and the splendor of the world's summer: this is what swells the hearts of the people of Omelas, and the victory they celebrate is that of life. I really don't think many of them need to take *drooz*.

4   Most of the processions have reached the Green Fields by now. A marvelous smell of cooking goes forth from the red and blue tents of the provisioners. The faces of small children are amiably sticky; in the benign grey beard of a man a couple of crumbs of rich pastry are entangled. The youths and girls have mounted their horses and are beginning to group around the starting line of the course. An old woman, small, fat, and laughing, is passing out flowers from a basket, and tall young men wear her flowers in their shining hair. A child of nine or ten sits at the edge of the crowd, alone, playing on a wooden flute. People pause to listen, and they smile, but they do not speak to him, for he never ceases playing and never sees them, his dark eyes wholly rapt in the sweet, thin magic of the tune.

5   He finishes, and slowly lowers his hands holding the wooden flute.

6   As if that little private silence were the signal, all at once a trumpet sounds from the pavilion near the starting line: imperious, melancholy, piercing. The horses rear on their slender legs, and some of them neigh in answer. Sober-faced, the young riders stroke the horses' necks and soothe them, whispering, "Quiet, quiet, there my beauty, my hope. . . ." They begin to form in rank along the starting line. The crowds along the racecourse are like a field of grass and flowers in the wind. The Festival of Summer has begun.

7   Do you believe? Do you accept the festival, the city, the joy? No? Then let me describe one more thing.

8   In a basement under one of the beautiful public buildings of Omelas, or perhaps in the cellar of one of its spacious private homes, there is a room. It has one locked door, and no window. A little light seeps in dustily between cracks in the boards, secondhand from a cobwebbed window somewhere across the cellar. In one corner of the little room a couple of mops, with stiff, clotted, foul-smelling heads, stand near a rusty bucket. The floor is dirt, a little damp to the touch, as cellar dirt usually

is. The room is about three paces long and two wide: a mere broom closet or disused tool room. In the room a child is sitting. It could be a boy or a girl. It looks about six, but actually is nearly ten. It is feeble-minded. Perhaps it was born defective, or perhaps it has become imbecile through fear, malnutrition, and neglect. It picks its nose and occasionally fumbles vaguely with its toes or genitals, as it sits hunched in the corner farthest from the bucket and the two mops. It is afraid of the mops. It finds them horrible. It shuts its eyes, but it knows the mops are still standing there; and the door is locked; and nobody will come. The door is always locked; and nobody ever comes, except that sometimes—the child has no understanding of time or interval—sometimes the door rattles terribly and opens, and a person, or several people, are there. One of them may come in and kick the child to make it stand up. The others never come close, but peer in at it with frightened, disgusted eyes. The food bowl and the water jug are hastily filled, the door is locked, the eyes disappear. The people at the door never say anything, but the child, who has not always lived in the tool room, and can remember sunlight and its mother's voice, sometimes speaks. "I will be good," it says. "Please let me out. I will be good!" They never answer. The child used to scream for help at night, and cry a good deal, but now it only makes a kind of whining, "eh-haa, eh-haa," and it speaks less and less often. It is so thin there are no calves to its legs; its belly protrudes; it lives on a half-bowl of corn meal and grease a day. It is naked. Its buttocks and thighs are a mass of festered sores, as it sits in its own excrement continually.

They all know it is there, all the people of Omelas. Some of them have come to see it, others are content merely to know it is there. They all know that it has to be there. Some of them understand why, and some do not, but they all understand that their happiness, the beauty of their city, the tenderness of their friendships, the health of their children, the wisdom of their scholars, the skill of their makers, even the abundance of their harvest and the kindly weathers of their skies, depend wholly on this child's abominable misery.

This is usually explained to children when they are between eight and twelve, whenever they seem capable of understanding; and most of those who come to see the child are young people, though often enough an adult comes, or comes back, to see the child. No matter how well the matter has been explained to them, these young spectators are always shocked and sickened at the sight. They feel disgust, which they had thought themselves superior to. They feel anger, outrage, impotence, despite all the explanations. They would like to do something for the child. But there is nothing they can do. If the child were brought up into the sunlight out of that vile place, if it were cleaned and fed and comforted, that would be a good thing, indeed; but if it were done, in that day and hour all the prosperity and beauty and delight of Omelas would wither and be destroyed. Those are the terms. To exchange all the goodness and grace of every life in Omelas for that single, small improvement: to throw away the happiness of thousands for the chance of the happiness of one: that would be to let guilt within the walls indeed.

11   The terms are strict and absolute; there may not even be a kind word spoken to the child.

12   Often the young people go home in tears, or in a tearless rage, when they have seen the child and faced this terrible paradox. They may brood over it for weeks or years. But as time goes on they begin to realize that even if the child could be released, it would not get much good of its freedom: a little vague pleasure of warmth and food, no doubt, but little more. It is too degraded and imbecile to know any real joy. It has been afraid too long ever to be free of fear. Its habits are too uncouth for it to respond to humane treatment. Indeed, after so long it would probably be wretched without walls about it to protect it, and darkness for its eyes, and its own excrement to sit in. Their tears at the bitter injustice dry when they begin to perceive the terrible justice of reality, and to accept it. Yet it is their tears and anger, the trying of their generosity and the acceptance of their helplessness, which are perhaps the true source of the splendor of their lives. Theirs is no vapid, irresponsible happiness. They know that they, like the child, are not free. They know compassion. It is the existence of the child, and their knowledge of its existence, that makes possible the nobility of their architecture, the poignancy of their music, the profundity of their science. It is because of the child that they are so gentle with children. They know that if the wretched one were not there snivelling in the dark, the other one, the flute-player, could make no joyful music as the young riders line up in their beauty for the race in the sunlight of the first morning of summer.

13   Now do you believe in them? Are they not more credible? But there is one more thing to tell, and this is quite incredible.

14   At times one of the adolescent girls or boys who go to see the child does not go home to weep or rage, does not, in fact, go home at all. Sometimes also a man or woman much older falls silent for a day or two, and then leaves home. These people go out into the street, and walk down the street alone. They keep walking, and walk straight out of the city of Omelas, through the beautiful gates. They keep walking across the farmlands of Omelas. Each one goes alone, youth or girl, man or woman. Night falls; the traveler must pass down village streets, between the houses with yellow-lit windows, and on out into the darkness of the fields. Each alone, they go west or north, towards the mountains. They go on. They leave Omelas, they walk ahead into the darkness, and they do not come back. The place they go towards is a place even less imaginable to most of us than the city of happiness. I cannot describe it at all. It is possible that it does not exist. But they seem to know where they are going, the ones who walk away from Omelas.

❏ Questions for Discussion

1. What descriptive details might lead you to infer that Omelas is a utopia? How does LeGuin involve you in making her description of Omelas believable? What is the significance of telling you what the people are *not?*

2. LeGuin's narrator accuses writers and artists of having a bias against happiness and joy, of seeing happiness as simpleminded. What writers that you have read in this anthology seem to have such a bias?

3. Why does the happiness of Omelas depend on the misery of a feebleminded child locked in a closet? Why is the child referred to as "it"?

4. Why are the young offended, and why do they eventually walk away from Omelas? Why does the story emphasize the people who stay and the title emphasize the ones who walk away?

5. Omelas will have religion but no clergy. What is the logic behind this proposal? Similarly, Omelas has no soldiers. Why?

❏ Suggestions for Exploration and Writing

1. Would you walk away from Omelas? Give detailed reasons for your position. If you left Omelas, where would you go?

2. Should the prosperity of the majority be considered over the "rights" of the minority? Apply this story to the United States today.

TONI CADE BAMBARA (1939–)

Toni Cade adopted the name Bambara from a name she found in a sketchbook in her great grandmother's trunk. This renaming of herself, with an emphasis on personal history, demonstrates her fascination with the myths, music, and history of African Americans. After receiving a bachelor of arts degree in theater art and English from Queens College and studying at Commedia del'Arte in Milan, Italy, Bambara taught at several colleges throughout the Northeast. She settled in Atlanta and taught at Spelman College. Many of her works skillfully portray adolescents coming to grips with their environment and show the politics and cultural activities of the urban community.

Blues Ain't No Mockin Bird

1   The puddle had frozen over, and me and Cathy went stompin in it. The twins from next door, Tyrone and Terry, were swingin so high out of sight we forgot we were waitin our turn on the tire. Cathy jumped up and came down hard on her heels and started tap-dancin. And the frozen patch splinterin every which way underneath kinda spooky. "Looks like a plastic spider web," she said. "A sort of weird spider, I guess, with many mental problems." But really it looked like the crystal paperweight Granny kept in the parlor. She was on the back porch, Granny was, making the cakes drunk. The old ladle dripping rum into the Christmas tins, like it used to drip maple syrup into the pails when we lived in the Judson's woods, like it poured cider into the vats when we were on the Cooper place, like it used to scoop buttermilk and soft cheese when we lived at the dairy.

2   "Go tell that man we ain't a bunch of trees."

3   "Ma'am?"

4   "I said to tell that man to get away from here with that camera." Me and Cathy look over toward the meadow where the men with the station wagon'd been roamin around all mornin. The tall man with a huge camera lassoed to his shoulder was buzzin our way.

5   "They're makin movie pictures," yelled Tyrone, stiffenin his legs and twistin so the tire'd come down slow so they could see.

6   "They're makin movie pictures," sang out Terry.

7   "That boy don't never have anything original to say," says Cathy grown-up.

8   By the time the man with the camera had cut across our neighbor's yard, the twins were out of the trees swingin low and Granny was onto the steps, the screen door bammin soft and scratchy against her palms. "We thought we'd get a shot or two of the house and everything and then—"

9   "Good mornin," Granny cut him off. And smiled that smile.

10   "Good mornin," he said, head all down the way Bingo does when you yell at him about the bones on the kitchen floor. "Nice place you got here, aunty. We thought we'd take a—"

11   "Did you?" said Granny with her eyebrows. Cathy pulled up her socks and giggled.

12   "Nice things here," said the man, buzzin his camera over the yard. The pecan barrels, the sled, me and Cathy, the flowers, the printed stones along the driveway, the trees, the twins, the toolshed.

13   "I don't know about the thing, the it, and the stuff," said Granny, still talkin with her eyebrows. "Just people here is what I tend to consider."

14   Camera man stopped buzzin. Cathy giggled into her collar.

15   "Mornin, ladies," a new man said. He had come up behind us when we weren't lookin. "And gents," discoverin the twins givin him a nasty look.

"We're filmin for the county," he said with a smile. "Mind if we shoot a bit around here?"

"I do indeed," said Granny with no smile. Smilin man was smiling up a storm. So was Cathy. But he didn't seem to have another word to say, so he and the camera man backed on out the yard, but you could hear the camera buzzin still. "Suppose you just shut that machine off," said Granny real low through her teeth, and took a step down off the porch and then another.

"Now, aunty," Camera said, pointin the thing straight at her.

"Your mama and I are not related."

Smilin man got his notebook out and a chewed-up pencil. "Listen," he said movin back into our yard, "we'd like to have a statement from you . . . for the film. We're filmin for the county, see. Part of the food stamp campaign. You know about the food stamps?"

Granny said nuthin.

"Maybe there's somethin you want to say for the film. I see you grow your own vegetables," he smiled real nice. "If more folks did that, see, there'd be no need—"

Granny wasn't sayin nothin. So they backed on out, buzzin at our clothes line and the twins' bicycles, then back on down to the meadow. The twins were danglin in the tire, lookin at Granny. Me and Cathy were waitin, too, cause Granny always got somethin to say. She teaches steady with no let-up. "I was on this bridge one time," she started off. "Was a crowd cause this man was goin to jump, you understand. And a minister was there and the police and some other folks. His woman was there, too."

"What was they doin?" asked Tyrone.

"Trying to talk him out of it was what they was doin. The minister talkin about how it was a mortal sin, suicide. His woman takin bites out of her own hand and not even knowin it, so nervous and cryin and talkin fast."

"So what happened?" asked Tyrone.

"So here comes . . . this person . . . with a camera, takin pictures of the man and the minister and the woman. Takin pictures of the man in his misery about to jump, cause life so bad and people been messin with him so bad. This person takin up the whole roll of film practically. But savin a few, of course."

"Of course," said Cathy, hatin the person. Me standin there wonderin how Cathy knew it was "of course" when I didn't and it was *my* grandmother.

After a while Tyrone say, "Did he jump?"

"Yeh, did he jump?" say Terry all eager.

And Granny just stared at the twins till their faces swallow up the eager and they don't even care any more about the man jumpin. Then she goes back onto the porch and lets the screen door go for itself. I'm lookin to Cathy to finish the story cause she knows Granny's whole story before me even. Like she knew how come we move so much and Cathy ain't but a third cousin we picked up on the way last Thanksgivin visitin. But she knew it was on account of people drivin Granny crazy till she'd get up in the night and start packin. Mumblin and packin and wakin everybody up saying, "Let's get on away from here before I kill me somebody." Like people wouldn't pay her for things like they said they would. Or Mr. Judson bringin us boxes of old clothes and raggedy magazines. Or Mrs. Cooper comin in our kitchen and touchin everything and sayin how clean it all was. Granny goin crazy, and Granddaddy Cain pullin her off the people, sayin, "Now, now, Cora." But next day loadin up the truck, with rocks all in his jaw, madder than Granny in the first place.

31   "I read a story once," said Cathy soundin like Granny teacher. "About this lady Goldilocks who barged into a house that wasn't even hers. And not invited, you understand. Messed over the people's groceries and broke up the people's furniture. Had the nerve to sleep in the folks' bed."

32   "Then what happened?" asked Tyrone. "What they do, the folks, when they come in to all this mess?"

33   "Did they make her pay for it?" asked Terry, makin a first. "I'd've made her pay me."

34   I didn't even ask. I could see Cathy actress was very likely to just walk away and leave us in mystery about this story which I heard was about some bears.

35   "Did they throw her out?" asked Tyrone, like his father sounds when he's bein extra nasty-plus to the washin-machine man.

36   "Woulda," said Terry. "I woulda gone upside her head with my fist and—"

37   "You woulda done whatcha always do—go cry to Mama, you big baby," said Tyrone. So naturally Terry starts hittin on Tyrone, and next thing you know they tumblin out the tire and rollin on the ground. But Granny didn't say a thing or send the twins home or step out on the steps to tell us bout how we can't afford to be fightin amongst ourselves. She didn't say nuthin. So I get into the tire to take my turn. And I could see her leanin up against the pantry table, starin at the cakes she was puttin up for the Christmas sale, mumblin real low and grumpy and holdin her forehead like it wanted to fall off and mess up the rum cakes.

38   Behind me I hear before I can see Granddaddy Cain comin through the woods in his field boots. Then I twist around to see the shiny black oilskin cuttin through what little left there was of yellows, reds, and oranges. His great white head not quite round cause of this bloody thing high on his shoulder, like he was wearin a cap on sideways. He takes the shortcut through the pecan grove, and the sound of twigs snapping overhead and underfoot travels clear and cold all the way up to us. And here comes Smilin and Camera up behind him like they was goin to do somethin. Folks like to go for him sometimes. Cathy say it's because he's so tall and quiet and like a king. And people just can't stand it. But Smilin and Camera don't hit him in the head or nuthin. They just buzz on him

as he stalks by with the chicken hawk slung over his shoulder, squawkin, drippin red down the back of the oilskin. He passes the porch and stops a second for Granny to see he's caught the hawk at last, but she's just starin and mumblin, and not at the hawk. So he nails the bird to the toolshed door, the hammerin rackin through the eardrums. And the bird flappin himself to death and droolin down the door to paint the gravel in the driveway red, then brown, then black. And the two men movin up on tiptoe like they was invisible or we were blind, one.

"Get them persons out of my flower bed, Mister Cain," say Granny   39
moanin real low like a funeral.

"How come your grandmother calls her husband 'Mister Cain' all the   40
time?" Tyrone whispers all loud and noisy and from the city and don't
know no better. Like his mama, Miss Myrtle, tell us never mind the
formality as if we had no better breeding than to call her Myrtle, plain.
And then this awful thing—a giant hawk—come wailin up over the
meadow, flyin low and tilted and screamin, zigzaggin through the pecan
grove, breakin branches and hollerin, snappin past the clothesline, flyin
every which way, flyin into things reckless with crazy.

"He's come to claim his mate," say Cathy fast, and ducks down. We   41
all fall quick and flat into the gravel driveway, stones scrapin my face. I
squinch my eyes open again at the hawk on the door, trying to fly up out
of her death like it was just a sack flown into by mistake. Her body holdin
her there on that nail, though. The mate beatin the air overhead and
clutchin for hair, for heads, for landin space.

The camera man duckin and bendin and runnin and fallin, jigglin the   42
camera and scared. And Smilin jumpin up and down swipin at the huge
bird, tryin to bring the hawk down with just his raggedy ole cap.
Granddaddy Cain straight up and silent, watchin the circles of the hawk,
then aimin the hammer off his wrist. The giant bird fallin, silent and
slow. Then here comes Camera and Smilin all big and bad now that the
awful screechin thing is on its back and broken, here they come, and
Granddaddy Cain looks up at them like it was the first time noticin, but
not payin them too much mind cause he's listenin, we all listen, to that
low groanin music coming from the porch. And we figure any minute,
somethin in my back tells me any minute now, Granny gonna bust
through that screen with somethin in her hand and murder on her mind.
So Granddaddy say above the buzzin, but quiet, "Good day, gentlemen."
Just like that. Like he'd invited them in to play cards and they'd stayed
too long and all the sandwiches were gone and Reverend Webb was
droppin by and it was time to go.

They didn't know what to do. But like Cathy say, folks can't stand   43
Granddaddy tall and silent and like a king. They can't neither. The smile
the men smilin is pullin the mouth back and showin the teeth. Lookin like
the wolf man, both of them. Then Granddaddy holds his hand out—this
huge hand I used to sit in when I was a baby and he'd carry me through
the house to my mother like I was a gift on a tray. Like he used to on the

trains. They called the other men just waiters. But they spoke of Grand-daddy separate and said, The Waiter. And said he had engines in his feet and motors in his hands and couldn't no train throw him off and couldn't nobody turn him round. They were big enough for motors, his hands were. He held that one hand out all still and it gettin to be not at all a hand but a person in itself.

44   "He wants you to hand him the camera," Smilin whispers to Camera, tiltin his head to talk secret like they was in the jungle or somethin and come upon a native that don't speak the language. The men start untyin the straps, and they put the camera into that great hand speckled with the hawk's blood all black and crackly now. And the hand don't even drop with the weight, just the fingers move, curl up around the machine. But Granddaddy lookin straight at the men. They lookin at each other and everywhere but at Granddaddy's face.

45   "We filmin for the county, see," say Smilin. "We puttin together a movie for the food stamp program . . . filmin all around these parts. Uhh, filmin for the county."

46   "Can I have my camera back?" say the tall man with no machine on his shoulder, but still keepin it high like the camera was still there or needed to be. "Please, sir."

47   Then Granddaddy's other hand flies up like a sudden and gentle bird, slaps down fast on top of the camera and lifts off half like it was a calabash cut for sharing.

48   "Hey," Camera jumps forward. He gathers up the parts into his chest and everything unrollin and fallin all over. "Whatcha tryin to do? You'll ruin the film." He looks down into his chest of metal reels and things like he's protectin a kitten from the cold.

49   "You standin in the misses' flower bed," say Granddaddy. "This is our own place."

50   The two men look at him, then at each other, then back at the mess in the camera man's chest, and they just back off. One sayin over and over all the way down to the meadow, "Watch it, Bruno. Keep ya fingers off the film." Then Granddaddy picks up the hammer and jams it into the oilskin pocket, scrapes his boots, and goes into the house. And you can hear the squish of his boots headin through the house. And you can see the funny shadow he throws from the parlor window onto the ground by the string-bean patch. The hammer draggin the pocket of the oilskin out so Granddaddy looked even wider. Granny was hummin now—high, not low and grumbly. And she was doin the cakes again, you could smell the molasses from the rum.

51   "There's this story I'm goin to write one day," say Cathy dreamer. "About the proper use of the hammer."

52   "Can I be in it?" Tyrone say with his hand up like it was a matter of first come, first served.

53   "Perhaps," say Cathy, climbin onto the tire to pump us up. "If you there and ready."

❏ Questions for Discussion

1. Why are the men taking pictures of the house and of the people? Why does Cathy secretly laugh when the men attempt to talk to Granny? What does she know that they don't?

2. Why is Granny offended by the familiar term "aunty"? What else had offended her in the past?

3. What is Granny's point in the story that she tells about a man who was going to jump off a bridge? What is the significance of Cathy's story of Goldilocks?

4. Why do the men give the camera to Granddaddy Cain? Explain why Cathy says that he is "so tall and quiet and like a king." Why do the men leave?

5. What is the significance of the hawks in the story?

6. Who is the **narrator** in this story? What do you estimate the narrator's age to be? How does this age affect his or her reliability as a narrator?

❏ Suggestions for Exploration and Writing

1. Examine the title of the story. What is meant by "blues" and by "mockin bird"? Who has the blues, and how do the blues relate to a mocking bird? Using the story for support, write an essay about the meaning of the title.

2. A photograph has the remarkable ability to tell the truth, and people are free to tell their own brand of the truth in America; but words and photographs can also misrepresent reality. Using this story and Giovanni's poem, "Nikki-Rosa," discuss how writers and photographers can distort the truth about people.

3. Analyze Granddaddy's reasons for smashing the men's camera. Is he simply brutal? What right is he trying to protect?

4. Giving examples from the story, discuss the dignity and nobility of Granny and Granddaddy.

LESLIE MARMON SILKO (1948–)

A native American born on the Laguna (NM) Pueblo Indian Reservation, Leslie Silko explores the conflict between native American values and rituals and the dominant culture. Her fiction reveals native Americans forced by the dominant white culture to accept sanitized modern "improvements" which conflict with their traditions. Her novel Ceremony *(1977) was the first ever published in the United States by a Native American woman.*

Lullaby

1   The sun had gone down but the snow in the wind gave off its own light. It came in thick tufts like new wool—washed before the weaver spins it. Ayah reached out for it like her own babies had, and she smiled when she remembered how she had laughed at them. She was an old woman now, and her life had become memories. She sat down with her back against the wide cottonwood tree, feeling the rough bark on her back bones; she faced east and listened to the wind and snow sing a high-pitched Yeibechei song. Out of the wind she felt warmer, and she could watch the wide fluffy snow fill in her tracks, steadily, until the direction she had come from was gone. By the light of the snow she could see the dark outline of the big arroyo a few feet away. She was sitting on the edge of Cebolleta Creek, where in the springtime the thin cows would graze on grass already chewed flat to the ground. In the wide deep creek bed where only a trickle of water flowed in the summer, the skinny cows would wander, looking for new grass along winding paths splashed with manure.

2   Ayah pulled the old Army blanket over her head like a shawl. Jimmie's blanket—the one he had sent to her. That was a long time ago and the green wool was faded, and it was unraveling on the edges. She did not want to think about Jimmie. So she thought about the weaving and the way her mother had done it. On the tall wooden loom set into the sand under a tamarack tree for shade. She could see it clearly. She had been only a little girl when her grandma gave her the wooden combs to pull the twigs and burrs from the raw, freshly washed wool. And while she combed the wool, her grandma sat beside her, spinning a silvery strand of yarn around the smooth cedar spindle. Her mother worked at the loom with yarns dyed bright yellow and red and gold. She watched them dye the yarn in boiling black pots full of beeweed petals, juniper berries, and sage. The blankets her mother made were soft and woven so tight that rain rolled off them like birds' feathers. Ayah remembered sleeping warm on cold windy nights, wrapped in her mother's blankets on the hogan's sandy floor.

3   The snow drifted now, with the northwest wind hurling it in gusts. It drifted up around her black overshoes—old ones with little metal buckles. She smiled at the snow which was trying to cover her little by little. She could remember when they had no black rubber overshoes; only the high buckskin leggings that they wrapped over their elk-hide moccasins. If the snow was dry or frozen, a person could walk all day and not get wet; and in the evenings the beams of the ceiling would hang with lengths of pale buckskin leggings, drying out slowly.

4   She felt peaceful remembering. She didn't feel cold any more. Jimmie's blanket seemed warmer than it had ever been. And she could remember the morning he was born. She could remember whispering to her mother

who was sleeping on the other side of the hogan, to tell her it was time now. She did not want to wake the others. The second time she called to her, her mother stood up and pulled on her shoes; she knew. They walked to the old stone hogan together, Ayah walking a step behind her mother. She waited alone, learning the rhythms of the pains while her mother went to call the old woman to help them. The morning was already warm even before dawn and Ayah smelled the bee flowers blooming and the young willow growing at the springs. She could remember that so clearly, but his birth merged into the births of the other children and to her it became all the same birth. They named him for the summer morning and in English they called him Jimmie.

It wasn't like Jimmie died. He just never came back, and one day a 5 dark blue sedan with white writing on its doors pulled up in front of the boxcar shack where the rancher let the Indians live. A man in a khaki uniform trimmed in gold gave them a yellow piece of paper and told them that Jimmie was dead. He said the Army would try to get the body back and then it would be shipped to them; but it wasn't likely because the helicopter had burned after it crashed. All of this was told to Chato because he could understand English. She stood inside the doorway holding the baby while Chato listened. Chato spoke English like a white man and he spoke Spanish too. He was taller than the white man and he stood straighter too. Chato didn't explain why; he just told the military man they could keep the body if they found it. The white man looked bewildered; he nodded his head and he left. Then Chato looked at her and shook his head. "Goddamn," he said in English, and then he told her "Jimmie isn't coming home anymore," and when he spoke, he used the words to speak of the dead. She didn't cry then, but she hurt inside with anger. And she mourned him as the years passed, when a horse fell with Chato and broke his leg, and the white rancher told them he wouldn't pay Chato until he could work again. She mourned Jimmie because he would have worked for his father then; he would have saddled the big bay horse and ridden the fence lines each day, with wire cutters and heavy gloves, fixing the breaks in the barbed wire and putting the stray cattle back inside again.

She mourned him after the white doctors came to take Danny and Ella 6 away. She was at the shack alone that day when they came. It was back in the days before they hired Navajo women to go with them as interpreters. She recognized one of the doctors. She had seen him at the children's clinic at Cañoncito about a month ago. They were wearing khaki uniforms and they waved papers at her and a black ball point pen, trying to make her understand their English words. She was frightened by the way they looked at the children, like the lizard watches the fly. Danny was swinging on the tire swing in the elm tree behind the rancher's house, and Ella was toddling around the front door, dragging the broomstick horse Chato made for her. Ayah could see they wanted her to sign the papers, and Chato had taught her to sign her name. It was something she was proud of. She only wanted them to go, and to take their eyes away from her children.

7   She took the pen from the man without looking at his face and she signed the papers in three different places he pointed to. She stared at the ground by their feet and waited for them to leave. But they stood there and began to point and gesture at the children. Danny stopped swinging. Ayah could see his fear. She moved suddenly and grabbed Ella into her arms; the child squirmed, trying to get back to her toys. Ayah ran with the baby toward Danny; she screamed for him to run and then she grabbed him around his chest and carried him too. She ran south into the foothills of juniper trees and black lava rock. Behind her she heard the doctors running, but they had been taken by surprise, and as the hills became steeper and the cholla cactus were thicker, they stopped. When she reached the top of the hill, she stopped too to listen in case they were circling around her. But in a few minutes she heard a car engine start and they drove away. The children had been too surprised to cry while she ran with them. Danny was shaking and Ella's little fingers were gripping Ayah's blouse.

8   She stayed up in the hills for the rest of the day, sitting on a black lava boulder in the sunshine where she could see for miles all around her. The sky was light blue and cloudless, and it was warm for late April. The sun warmth relaxed her and took the fear and anger away. She lay back on the rock and watched the sky. It seemed to her that she could walk into the sky, stepping through clouds endlessly. Danny played with little pebbles and stones, pretending they were birds, eggs and then little rabbits. Ella sat at her feet and dropped fistfuls of dirt into the breeze, watching the dust and particles of sand intently. Ayah watched a hawk soar high above them, dark wings gliding; hunting or only watching, she did not know. The hawk was patient and he circled all afternoon before he disappeared around the high volcanic peak the Mexicans call Guadalupe.

9   Late in the afternoon, Ayah looked down at the gray boxcar shack with the paint all peeled from the wood; the stove pipe on the roof was rusted and crooked. The fire she had built that morning in the oil drum stove had burned out. Ella was asleep in her lap now and Danny sat close to her, complaining that he was hungry; he asked when they would go to the house. "We will stay up here until your father comes," she told him, "because those white men were chasing us." The boy remembered then and he nodded at her silently.

10   If Jimmie had been there he could have read those papers and explained to her what they said. Ayah would have known, then, never to sign them. The doctors came back the next day and they brought a BIA policeman with them. They told Chato they had her signature and that was all they needed. Except for the kids. She listened to Chato sullenly; she hated him when he told her it was the old woman who died in the

winter, spitting blood; it was her old grandma who had given the children this disease. "They don't spit blood," she said coldly, "The whites lie." She held Ella and Danny close to her, ready to run to the hills again. "I want a medicine man first," she said to Chato, not looking at him. He shook his head. "It's too late now. The policeman is with them. You signed the paper." His voice was gentle.

It was worse than if they had died: to lose the children and to know that somewhere, in a place called Colorado, in a place full of sick and dying strangers, her children were without her. There had been babies that died soon after they were born, and one that died before he could walk. She had carried them herself, up to the boulders and great pieces of the cliff that long ago crashed down from Long Mesa; she laid them in the crevices of sandstone and buried them in fine brown sand with round quartz pebbles that washed down from the hills in the rain. She had endured it because they had been with her. But she could not bear this pain. She did not sleep for a long time after they took her children. She stayed up on the hill where they had fled the first time, and she slept rolled up in the blanket Jimmie had sent her. She carried the pain in her belly and it was fed by everything she saw: the blue sky of their last day together and the dust and pebbles they played with; the swing in the elm tree and broomstick horse chocked life from her. The pain filled her stomach and there was no room for food or for her lungs to fill with air. The air and the food would have been theirs.

She hated Chato, not because he let the policeman and doctors put the screaming children in the government care, but because he had taught her to sign her name. Because it was like the old ones always told her about learning their language or any of their ways: it endangered you. She slept alone on the hill until the middle of November when the first snows came. Then she made a bed for herself where the children had slept. She did not lay down beside Chato again until many years later, when he was sick and shivering and only her body could keep him warm. The illness came after the white rancher told Chato he was too old to work for him any more, and Chato and his old woman should be out of the shack by the next afternoon because the rancher had hired new people to work there. That had satisfied her. To see how the white man repaid Chato's years of loyalty and work. All of Chato's fine-sounding English talk didn't change things.

II

It snowed steadily and the luminous light from the snow gradually diminished into the darkness. Somewhere in Cebolleta a dog barked and other village dogs joined with it. Ayah looked in the direction she had come, from the bar where Chato was buying the wine. Sometimes he told her to go on ahead and wait; and then he never came. And when she finally went back looking for him, she would find him passed out at the bottom of the wooden steps to Azzie's Bar. All the wine would be gone and most of the money too, from the pale blue check that came to them once a month in a government envelope. It was then that she would look at his face and his hands, scarred by ropes and the barbed wire of all those years, and she would think 'this man is a stranger'; for 40 years she had smiled at him and cooked his food, but he remained a stranger. She stood up again, with the snow almost to her knees, and she walked back to find Chato.

14   It was hard to walk in the deep snow and she felt the air burn in her lungs. She stopped a short distance from the bar to rest and readjust the blanket. But this time he wasn't waiting for her on the bottom step with his old Stetson hat pulled down and his shoulders hunched up in his long wool overcoat.

15   She was careful not to slip on the wooden steps. When she pushed the door open, warm air and cigarette smoke hit her face. She looked around slowly and deliberately, in every corner, in every dark place that the old man might find to sleep. The bar-owner didn't like Indians in there, especially Navajos, but he let Chato come in because he could talk Spanish like he was one of them. The men at the bar stared at her, and the bartender saw that she left the door open wide. Snow flakes were flying inside like moths and melting into a puddle on the oiled wood floor. He motioned at her to close the door, but she did not see him. She held herself straight and walked across the room slowly, searching the room with every step. The snow in her hair melted and she could feel it on her forehead. At the far corner of the room, she saw red flames at the mica window of the old stove door; she looked behind the stove just to make sure. The bar got quiet except for the Spanish polka music playing on the jukebox. She stood by the stove and shook the snow from her blanket and held it near the stove to dry. The wet wool smell reminded her of new-born goats in early March, brought inside to warm near the fire. She felt calm.

16   In past years they would have told her to get out. But her hair was white now and her face was wrinkled. They looked at her like she was a spider crawling slowly across the room. They were afraid; she could feel the fear. She looked at their faces steadily. They reminded her of the first time the white people brought her children back to her that winter. Danny had been shy and hid behind the thin white woman who brought them. And the baby had not known her until Ayah took her into her arms, and then Ella had nuzzled close to her as she had when she was nursing. The blonde woman was nervous and kept looking at a dainty gold watch on her wrist. She sat on the bench near the small window and watched the dark snow clouds gather around the mountains; she was worrying about the unpaved road. She was frightened by what she saw inside too: the strips of venison drying on a rope across the ceiling and the children jabbering excitedly in a language she did not know. So they stayed for only a few hours. Ayah watched the government car disappear down the road and she knew they were already being weaned from these

lava hills and from this sky. The last time they came was in early June, and Ella stared at her the way the men in the bar were now staring. Ayah did not try to pick her up; she smiled at her instead and spoke cheerfully to Danny. When he tried to answer her, he could not seem to remember and he spoke English words with the Navajo. But he gave her a scrap of paper that he had found somewhere and carried in his pocket; it was folded in half, and he shyly looked up at her and said it was a bird. She asked Chato if they were home for good this time. He spoke to the white woman and she shook her head. "How much longer," he asked, and she said she didn't know; but Chato saw how she stared at the box car shack. Ayah turned away then. She did not say good-bye.

III

She felt satisfied that the men in the bar feared her. Maybe it was her 17 face and the way she held her mouth with teeth clenched tight, like there was nothing anyone could do to her now. She walked north down the road, searching for the old man. She did this because she had the blanket, and there would be no place for him except with her and the blanket in the old adobe barn near the arroyo. They always slept there when they came to Cebolleta. If the money and the wine were gone, she would be relieved because then they could go home again; back to the old hogan with a dirt roof and rock walls where she herself had been born. And the next day the old man could go back to the few sheep they still had, to follow along behind them, guiding them into dry sandy arroyos where sparse grass grew. She knew he did not like walking behind old ewes when for so many years he rode big quarter horses and worked with cattle. But she wasn't sorry for him; he should have known all along what would happen.

There had not been enough rain for their garden in five years; and that 18 was when Chato finally hitched a ride into the town and brought back brown boxes of rice and sugar and big tin cans of welfare peaches. After that, at the first of the month they went to Cebolleta to ask the postmaster for the check; and then Chato would go to the bar and cash it. They did this as they planted the garden every May, not because anything would survive the summer dust, but because it was time to do this. And the journey passed the days that smelled silent and dry like the caves above the canyon with yellow painted buffaloes on their walls.

IV

He was walking along the pavement when she found him. He did not 19 stop or turn around when he heard her behind him. She walked beside him and she noticed how slowly he moved now. He smelled strong of woodsmoke and urine. Lately he had been forgetting. Sometimes he called her by his sister's name and she had been gone for a long time. Once she had found him wandering on the road to the white man's ranch, and she asked him why he was going that way; he laughed at her and said "you know they can't run that ranch without me," and he walked on determined, limping on the leg that had been crushed many years before. Now he looked at her curiously, as if for the first time, but he kept shuffling along, moving slowly along the side of the highway. His gray hair had grown long and spread out on the shoulders of the long overcoat. He wore the old felt hat pulled down over his ears. His boots were worn out at the toes and he had stuffed pieces of an old red shirt in the holes. The rags made his feet look like little animals up to their ears in snow. She laughed at his feet; the snow muffled the sound of her laugh. He stopped and looked at her again. The wind had quit blowing and the snow was falling straight down; the southeast sky was beginning to clear and Ayah could see a star.

20   "Let's rest awhile," she said to him. They walked away from the road and up the slope to the giant boulders that had tumbled down from the red sandrock mesa throughout the centuries of rainstorms and earth tremors. In a place where the boulders shut out the wind, they sat down with their backs against the rock. She offered half of the blanket to him and they sat wrapped together.

21   The storm passed swiftly. The clouds moved east. They were massive and full, crowding together across the sky. She watched them with the feeling of horses—steely blue-gray horses startled across the sky. The powerful haunches pushed into the distances and the tail hairs streamed white mist behind them. The sky cleared. Ayah saw that there was nothing between her and the stars. The light was crystalline. There was no shimmer, no distortion through earth haze. She breathed the clarity of the night sky; she smelled the purity of the half moon and the stars. He was lying on his side with his knees pulled up near his belly for warmth. His eyes were closed now, and in the light from the stars and the moon, he looked young again.

22   She could see it descend out of the night sky: an icy stillness from the edge of the thin moon. She recognized the freezing. It came gradually, sinking snow flake by snow flake until the crust was heavy and deep. It had the strength of the stars in Orion, and its journey was endless. Ayah knew that with the wine he would sleep. He would not feel it. She tucked the blanket around him, remembering how it was when Ella had been with her; and she felt the rush so big inside her heart for the babies. And she sang the only song she knew to sing for babies. She could not remember if she had ever sung it to her children, but she knew that her grandmother had sung it and her mother had sung it:

> The earth is your mother,
>   she holds you.
> The sky is your father,
>   he protects you.
>
> sleep,
> sleep,

Rainbow is your sister,
>   she loves you.
The winds are your brothers,
>   they sing to you.

sleep,
sleep,
We are together always
We are together always
There never was a time
when this
was not so.

❏ Questions for Discussion

1. List examples from the story which show how little the "white men" understand the native American culture. Do the native Americans understand the white culture? What are the primary barriers to understanding?

2. Although Ayah's life apparently has been a series of tragic events, "her life [has] become memories," and many of her memories are full of vivid sensory detail. Find at least five **similes** or **metaphors** which reflect a poet's soul within Ayah and which bring her culture alive for readers.

3. Why does Ayah like being feared by the men in the bar? Do you think men really fear her? If so, why?

4. William Faulkner in his Nobel Prize acceptance speech says that the human race will endure. In what way is this statement true of Ayah? Why do Ayah and Chato continue to plant their garden every May even though they know it will die? Of what might this futile planting be **symbolic?**

5. How does the first paragraph of the story **foreshadow** the ending? Why is the lullaby a fitting end to the story? Whom does it comfort?

❏ Suggestions for Exploration and Writing

1. Examine the forces in contemporary culture that destroy families.

2. Discuss the relationship between Ayah and Chato in terms of Ayah's words, "This man is a stranger."

3. Underlying the story is the hostility between the Navajos, the Spanish men in the bar, and the white men. Discuss the causes and meaning of this anger and hostility.

4. The function of government rules and bureaucracy presumably is to protect and insure freedom, yet in Ayah's case they restrict freedom. In an essay, discuss ways in which government bureaucracy has applied rules too strictly, thereby restricting your freedom or the freedom of people you know.

POETRY

WILLIAM BLAKE (1757–1827)

William Blake was an English mystical poet and engraver. He sought to release Christianity from the constraints of early industrial materialism, Enlightenment rationalism, and puritanical sexual repression. He developed his own philosophical and mythological system expressed in such long, complex, and extremely difficult prophetic works as The Book of Thel *(1789) and* Jerusalem *(1804–1820). Much more accessible are the lyrics in* Songs of Innocence *(1789) and its companion volume* Songs of Experience *(1794), poems which express Blake's sympathy with the oppressed and his rage at the human institutions that perpetuate oppression.*

London

I wander through each chartered street,
Near where the chartered Thames does flow,
And mark in every face I meet
Marks of weakness, marks of woe.

5 In every cry of every man,
In every infant's cry of fear,
In every voice, in very ban,
The mind-forged manacles I hear.

How the chimney-sweeper's cry
10 Every black'ning church appalls
And the hapless soldier's sigh
Runs in blood down palace walls.

But most through midnight streets I hear
How the youthful harlot's curse
15 Blasts the new born infant's tear
And blights with plagues the marriage hearse.

❏ Questions for Discussion

1. What does Blake mean by calling the London streets and the Thames River "chartered"?

2. Look up the word *appalls*. What different meanings of the word seem appropriate here?

3. What "plagues" is Blake referring to in the final line? What is the "youthful harlot's curse"?

4. How, according to Blake's poem, is the revolt of the oppressed expressed?

❏ **Suggestions for Exploration and Writing**

1. Discuss what Blake means by "The mind-forg'd manacles I hear."

2. Observe the faces of the people in a city near you. What "marks of weakness, marks of woe" as well as marks of strength and marks of happiness do you find in these faces? Discuss.

WILLIAM WORDSWORTH (1770–1850)

William Wordsworth was a leading poet of the Romantic movement in England. His collaboration with Samuel Taylor Coleridge on the book of poems Lyrical Ballads *in 1798 is often cited as the beginning of the Romantic movement in England. Wordsworth rebelled against the order and restraint of the Enlightenment, supported the French Revolution, and sought in nature and in the lives of ordinary people an answer to the complexity and materialism of industrial England. In his poetry, he tried to use the plain language of ordinary people. As the supreme English nature poet, Wordsworth changed forever the view of nature in his culture and in ours.*

The World Is Too Much with Us

The world is too much with us; late and soon,
Getting and spending, we lay waste our powers;
Little we see in Nature that is ours;
We have given our hearts away, a sordid boon!
This Sea that bares her bosom to the moon;   5
The winds that will be howling at all hours,
And are up-gathered now like sleeping flowers;
For this, for everything, we are out of tune;
It moves us not. Great God! I'd rather be
A Pagan suckled in a creed outworn;   10
So might I, standing on this pleasant lea,
Have glimpses that would make me less forlorn;
Have sight of Proteus rising from the sea;
Or hear old Triton blow his wreathed horn.

❏ Questions for Discussion

1. According to Wordsworth, what has the world made us "out of tune" for? In what sense have we "given our hearts away"?

2. What does Wordsworth mean by "a Pagan suckled in a creed outworn"? Why would he prefer being a pagan?

3. Proteus was an ancient Greek god of the sea who could change his shape whenever and however he wished. Triton, another ancient Greek sea god, had the upper body of a man and the lower body of a fish. In what ways might the sight of Proteus and the sound of Triton's horn be consoling to the poem's speaker?

4. Compare the **theme** and subject of this poem to those of Hopkins' "God's Grandeur" in the Quest unit.

❏ Suggestion for Exploration and Writing

1. Wordsworth speaks of a former time when nature still awed humanity and life was simple. He says, however, "we have given our hearts away, a sordid boon!" Discuss some of the ways that people have given their hearts away.

RANDALL JARRELL (1914–1965)

The Woman at the Washington Zoo

The saris go by me from the embassies.

Cloth from the moon. Cloth from another planet.
They look back at the leopard like the leopard.
And I. . . .

5   this print of mine, that has kept its color
Alive through so many cleanings; this dull null
Navy I wear to work, and wear from work, and so
To my bed, so to my grave, with no
Complaints, no comment: neither from my chief,
10 The Deputy Chief Assistant, nor his chief—
Only I complain. . . . this serviceable
Body that no sunlight dyes, no hand suffuses
But, dome-shadowed, withering among columns,
Wavy beneath fountains—small, far-off, shining
15 In the eyes of animals, these beings trapped
As I am trapped but not, themselves, the trap,

Aging, but without knowledge of their age,
Kept safe here, knowing not of death, for death—
Oh, bars of my own body, open, open!

The world goes by my cage and never sees me.   20
And there come not to me, as come to these,
The wild beasts, sparrows pecking the llamas' grain,
Pigeons settling on the bears' bread, buzzards
Tearing the meat the flies have clouded. . . .
                        Vulture,   25
When you come for the white rat that the foxes left,
Take off the red helmet of your head, the black
Wings that have shadowed me, and step to me as man:
The wild brother at whose feet the white wolves fawn,
To whose hand of power the great lioness   30
Stalks, purring. . . .
               You know what I was,
You see what I am: change me, change me!

❑ Questions for Discussion

1. How does the speaker contrast with the other women she
   sees? What does she mean by "They look back at the leopard
   like the leopard"?

2. How does such repetition as "so to my bed, so to my grave"
   reveal the speaker's feeling of entrapment?

3. How does the speaker compare herself to the animals she
   sees?

4. Briefly **paraphrase** the speaker's concluding **apostrophe** to the
   vulture. Why would she choose to address this short speech to
   such a bird?

❑ Suggestions for Exploration and Writing

1. How does the speaker feel about her condition? How do
   sound, **diction, syntax,** and **imagery** develop her feeling?

2. What does Jarrell mean by "Oh, bars of my own body, open,
   open"? Using this poem and Blake's "London," write an essay
   about the cages and/or bars that people build for themselves.

3. At one point the woman thinks, ". . . Change me, change
   me!" To what extent is she not free to change? Discuss.

4. Would you have noticed the woman at the zoo? Why are some
   people almost invisible while others are not?

ANNE SEXTON (1928–1974)

*Anne Sexton believed that as a child she had been unwanted and
rejected. Before she was twenty years old, she married Alfred Muller
Sexton III. In 1954, shortly after the birth of her first daughter,
Sexton suffered her first mental breakdown. The birth of her second
daughter in 1955 was followed by a second breakdown. The psychiatrist who treated her at this time convinced her that she was both
intelligent and talented, and he encouraged her to write poetry.
Sexton found a form of salvation in writing poems about her tendency toward suicide, her mental breakdowns, and the problems she
faced as a woman. In 1974, after a lifetime of feeling that death was
calling her, Sexton committed suicide. The following poem was included in her first collection,* To Bedlam and Part Way Back *(1960).*

Ringing The Bells

And this is the way they ring
the bells in Bedlam
and this is the bell-lady
who comes each Tuesday morning
5   to give us a music lesson
and because the attendants make you go
and because we mind by instinct,
like bees caught in the wrong hive,
we are the circle of the crazy ladies
10 who sit in the lounge of the mental house
and smile at the smiling woman
who passes us each a bell,
who points at my hand
that holds my bell, E flat,
15 and this is the gray dress next to me
who grumbles as if it were special
to be old, to be old,
and this is the small hunched squirrel girl
on the other side of me
20 who picks at the hairs over her lip, not.
who picks at the hairs over her lip all day,
and this is how the bells really sound,
as untroubled and clean
as a workable kitchen,
25 and this is always my bell responding
to my hand that responds to the lady
who points at me, E flat;
although we are no better for it,
they tell you to go. And you do.

❑ **Questions for Discussion**

1. What is the music lesson supposed to do for the "crazy la-dies"? What does it actually do for them?

2. How does the speaker feel about the music lesson? How do the structure and **diction** of the poem reveal feeling? What does Sexton's use of **anaphora** add to the poem?

3. What does the animal imagery reveal about the women in the poem?

ADRIENNE RICH (1929–   )

Aunt Jennifer's Tigers

Aunt Jennifer's tigers prance across a screen,
Bright topaz denizens of a world of green.
They do not fear the men beneath the tree;
They pace in sleek chivalric certainty.

Aunt Jennifer's fingers fluttering through her wool   5
Find even the ivory needle hard to pull.
The massive weight of Uncle's wedding band
Sits heavily upon Aunt Jennifer's hand.

When Aunt is dead, her terrified hands will lie
Still ringed with ordeals she was mastered by.   10
The tigers in the panel that she made
Will go on prancing, proud and unafraid.

❑ **Questions for Discussion**

1. What does the narrator imply by saying that Aunt Jennifer's wedding band is "massive" and "sits heavily on Aunt Jennifer's hand"?

2. Why does Aunt Jennifer create such powerful tigers?

3. Why do you suppose Rich chose the restrictive form of **cou-plets** for this poem? How are the couplets and the regularity of **meter** appropriate to the subject?

❑ **Suggestions for Exploration and Writing**

1. The woman in the poem is the opposite of the tigers on the screen. Contrast the lack of freedom Aunt Jennifer experiences with that of the tigers she creates.

2. This poem was written in the 1950s. Discuss whether women have more freedom today than they did when Rich wrote this poem.

ALICIA OSTRIKER (1937–   )

Watching the Feeder

Snow has been falling, and the purple finches
Attack the feeder, diving like air aces.
A half a dozen squirrels
Do their Olympic leaps through the weak sunlight
5   Spilling sunflower seeds and seedhusks
Together over the drifts. The doves are pacing
And nodding, with the utmost
Placidity, like bourgeois wives and husbands.
Apparently they are going shopping—
10   I can almost see the stoutness of their billfolds,
Their station wagons, their wine cellars.
Snow falls through standing trees, my patch of the world's
    hair.

I have Vivaldi on the stereo,
Another cup of coffee. It is peaceful but hard
15   Growing older, no
Birds in my nest.

Now I can ask: What about my life?
What do I desire, now
That it has come to this? Snow coming down
20   Harder and harder this morning, the back yard
Becomes mysterious, the feeder
Is finally deserted.
I remember that I was hoping to be grateful
For existence itself.

❏ Questions for Discussion

1. Identify and explain the two **similes** which Ostriker uses to personify the birds.

2. Of what do the birds, and later the deserted feeder, remind the speaker? Now that she has the freedom and the time to ask herself "What about my life? / What do I desire," why is she sad?

3. Explain the last two lines of the poem.

❏ Suggestions for Exploration and Writing

1. How can women prepare themselves for the time when their nests are empty?

2. What responsibilities, if any, do children have to their parents after the children are grown?

PAT MORA (1942–)

Pat Mora is a Southwestern poet from El Paso, Texas. Of Mexican-American parentage, she has written two books of poems, Chants *(1984) and* Borders *(1986), from which the following poem comes. Her poems explore her heritage.*

Immigrants

wrap their babies in the American flag,
feed them mashed hot dogs and apple pie,
name them Bill and Daisy,
buy them blonde dolls that blink blue
eyes or a football and tiny cleats   5
before the baby can even walk,
speak to them in thick English,
    hallo, babee, hallo,
whisper in Spanish or Polish
when the babies sleep, whisper   10
in a dark parent bed, that dark
parent fear, "Will they like
our boy, our girl, our fine american
boy, our fine american girl?"

❏ Questions for Discussion

1. What American qualities do the immigrants seek for their children? Why?

2. Why do immigrants "whisper in Spanish or Polish while the babies sleep"?

3. What is the source of the immigrants' anxiety?

4. The United States is often described as a "melting pot." What does this poem imply may be melted away?

❏ Suggestions for Exploration and Writing

1. Explain the advantages and disadvantages of conforming to the society into which you have immigrated.

2. Mora speaks of the ultimate fear of the immigrant parents: the children will not fit in despite all attempts to Americanize them. Discuss your attitude or the attitudes of your community toward people who are different.

3. Discuss the responsibilities of immigrants to their new country. Or discuss the responsibilities of citizens to newcomers.

JOY HARJO (1951–   )

Joy Harjo, a Creek Indian born in Tulsa, Oklahoma, has won wide acclaim for her poetry. Most of her poems deal with her Creek heritage or the struggles of her people to avoid assimilation. Harjo's style usually mirrors the rhythm of the Creek language.

The Woman Hanging from the Thirteenth Floor Window

She is the woman hanging from the 13th floor
window. Her hands are pressed white against the
concrete moulding of the tenement building. She
hangs from the 13th floor window in east Chicago,
with a swirl of birds over her head. They could   5
be a halo, or a storm of glass waiting to crush her.

She thinks she will be set free.

The woman hanging from the 13th floor window
on the east side of Chicago is not alone.

She is a woman of children, of the baby, Carlos,   10
and of Margaret, and of Jimmy who is the oldest.
She is her mother's daughter and her father's son.
She is several pieces between the two husbands
she has had. She is all the women of the apartment
building who stand watching her, watching themselves.   15

When she was young she ate wild rice on scraped down
plates in warm wood rooms. It was in the farther
north and she was the baby then. They rocked her.

She sees Lake Michigan lapping at the shores of
herself. It is a dizzy hole of water and the rich   20
live in tall glass houses at the edge of it. In some
places Lake Michigan speaks softly, here, it just sputters
and butts itself against the asphalt. She sees
other buildings just like hers. She sees other

women hanging from many-floored windows 25
counting their lives in the palms of their hands
and in the palms of their children's hands.

She is the woman hanging from the 13th floor window
on the Indian side of town. Her belly is soft from
her children's births, her worn levis swing down below 30
her waist, and then her feet, and then her heart.
She is dangling.

The woman hanging from the 13th floor hears voices.
They come to her in the night when the lights have gone
dim. Sometimes they are little cats mewing and scratching 35
at the door, sometimes they are her grandmother's voice,
and sometimes they are gigantic men of light whispering
to her to get up, to get up, to get up. That's when she wants
to have another child to hold onto in the night, to be able
to fall back into dreams. 40

And the woman hanging from the 13th floor window
hears other voices. Some of them scream out from below
for her to jump, they would push her over. Others cry softly
from the sidewalks, pull their children up like flowers and
    gather
them into their arms. They would help her, like themselves. 45

But she is the woman hanging from the 13th floor window,
and she knows she is hanging by her own fingers, her
own skin, her own thread of indecision.

She thinks of Carlos, of Margaret, of Jimmy.
She thinks of her father, and of her mother. 50
She thinks of all the women she has been, of all
the men. She thinks of the color of her skin, and
of Chicago streets, and of waterfalls and pines.
She thinks of moonlight nights, and of cool spring storms.
Her mind chatters like neon and northside bars. 55
She thinks of the 4 a.m. lonelinesses that have folded
her up like death, discordant, without logical and
beautiful conclusion. Her teeth break off at the edges.
She would speak.

The woman hangs from the 13th floor window crying for 60
the lost beauty of her own life. She sees the
sun falling west over the grey plane of Chicago.
She thinks she remembers listening to her own life
break loose, as she falls from the 13th floor
window on the east side of Chicago, or as she 65
climbs back up to claim herself again.

❏ Questions for Discussion

1. Explain the significance of "13th floor window," "a tenement building in East Chicago," and "on the Indian side of town"?

2. Why does the hanging woman represent all the watching women? What do the references to the children mean in the overall context of the poem?

3. Why does the woman think she "will be set free"? Explain whether or not she will be set free.

4. Why does Harjo end the poem with two choices? What do you think she is trying to say about freedom and responsibility?

❏ Suggestions for Exploration and Writing

1. Using the poem to support your opinion, write an essay explaining what the woman's decision is and why she makes that decision.

2. From the poem, select one passage that makes a political statement. Write an essay that discusses the significance of this passage, or write an essay that discusses whether you agree or disagree with the passage.

DWIGHT OKITA (1958–)

Dwight Okita, a native of Chicago, is a poet of Japanese-American descent. His mother spent World War II in a relocation center, one of ten such centers in the Western states. In response to the Japanese attack on Pearl Harbor, the United States government, without due process, forced over 100,000 Japanese Americans into these centers.

In Response to Executive Order 9066: All Americans of Japanese Descent Must Report to Relocation Centers

Dear Sirs:
Of course I'll come. I've packed my galoshes
and three packets of tomato seeds. Janet calls them
"love apples." My father says where we're going
they won't grow.

I am a fourteen-year-old girl with bad spelling
and a messy room. If it helps any, I will tell you

I have always felt funny using chopsticks
and my favorite food is hot dogs.
My best friend is a white girl named Denise—   10
we look at boys together. She sat in front of me
all through grade school because of our names:
O'Connor, Ozawa. I know the back of Denise's head very well.
I tell her she's going bald. She tells me I copy on tests.
We're best friends.   15

I saw Denise today in Geography class.
She was sitting on the other side of the room.
"You're trying to start a war," she said, "giving secrets away
to the Enemy, Why can't you keep your big mouth shut?"
I didn't know what to say.   20
I gave her a packet of tomato seeds
and asked her to plant them for me, told her
when the first tomato ripened
she'd miss me.

❏ Questions for Discussion

1. What seems to be the speaker's attitude toward the executive
   order to report to a relocation center? Why does she say that
   she likes hot dogs and feels uncomfortable using chopsticks?

2. Contrast the relationship between the speaker and Denise in
   stanza two with their relationship in stanza three. What has
   happened to their friendship? Why does Denise sit on the
   other side of the room?

3. How does the speaker's attitude here compare to that of the
   speaker in "Immigrants"?

4. Why does the speaker give her friend Denise tomato plants?

❏ Suggestions for Exploration and Writing

1. Discuss some of the travesties of relocation centers as shown
   by the letter of the fourteen-year-old Japanese girl and by the
   behavior of her friend Denise.

2. How appropriate is it to refer to people born in the United
   States as Japanese Americans, African Americans, Native Americans, and so forth? In what ways is the United States a melting
   pot of different cultures homogenized and blended? In what
   ways is it a stew of different cultures maintaining their distinc-
   tiveness? Discuss.

DRAMA

WOLE SOYINKA (1934–   )

Wole Soyinka, a Nigerian poet, novelist, playwright, translator, and essayist, was educated at Leeds College in England. Both Yoruban tribal culture and European culture can be found in his works. At various times in his career he has taught school and worked at the Royal Court Theatre where The Swamp Dwellers *was produced in 1955. Both* The Swamp Dwellers *and* The Lion and the Jewel *(1963) were produced in Ibadan, then the capital of Western Nigeria. Soyinka has been imprisoned many times for his satirical political writings or for his supposed political alliances. His many themes include power struggles between corrupt forces, the clash of African values with European ideas, and death and rebirth.* The Lion and the Jewel *is a farcical play with a good example of the trickster hero who appears in much of African folklore.*

The Lion and the Jewel

Characters

SIDI:	the Village Belle
LAKUNLE:	School teacher
BAROKA:	the 'Bale' of Ilujinle
SADIKU:	His head wife

THE FAVOURITE
VILLAGE GIRLS
A WRESTLER
A SURVEYOR
SCHOOLBOYS
ATTENDANTS ON THE 'BALE'
MUSICIANS, DANCERS, MUMMERS,
PRISONERS, TRADERS, THE VILLAGE

MORNING

A clearing on the edge of the market, dominated by an immense 'odan' tree. It is the village centre. The wall of the bush school flanks the stage on the right, and a rude window opens on to the stage from the wall. There is a chant of the 'Arithmetic Times' issuing from this window. It begins a short while before the action begins. Sidi enters from left, carrying a small pail of water on her head. She is a slim girl with plaited hair. A true village belle. She balances the pail on her head with accustomed ease. Around her is wrapped the familiar broad cloth which is folded just above her breasts, leaving her shoulders bare.

*Almost as soon as she appears on the stage, the schoolmaster's
face also appears at the window. (The chanting continues—'Three
times two are six', 'Three times three are nine', etc.) The teacher
Lakunle, disappears. He is replaced by two of his pupils, aged
roughly eleven, who make a buzzing noise at Sidi, repeatedly
clapping their hands across the mouth. Lakunle now re-appears
below the window and makes for Sidi, stopping only to give the
boys admonitory whacks on the head before they can duck. They
vanish with a howl and he shuts the window on them. The
chanting dies away. The schoolmaster is nearly twenty-three. He
is dressed in an old-style English suit, threadbare but not ragged,
clean but not ironed, obviously a size or two too small. His tie is
done in a very small knot, disappearing beneath a shiny black
waistcoat. He wears twenty-three-inch-bottom trousers, and
blanco-white tennis shoes.*

LAKUNLE: Let me take it.
SIDI: No.
LAKUNLE: Let me. [*Seizes the pail. Some water spills on him.*]
SIDI: [*delighted.*]
    There. Wet for your pains.
    Have you no shame?
LAKUNLE: That is what the stewpot said to the fire.
    Have you no shame—at your age
    Licking my bottom? But she was tickled
    Just the same.
SIDI: The school teacher is full of stories   10
    This morning. And now, if the lesson
    Is over, may I have the pail?
LAKUNLE: No. I have told you not to carry loads
    On your head. But you are as stubborn
    As an illiterate goat. It is bad for the spine.
    And it shortens your neck, so that very soon
    You will have no neck at all. Do you wish to look
    Squashed like my pupils' drawings?
SIDI: Why should that worry me? Haven't you sworn
    That my looks do not affect your love?   20
    Yesterday, dragging your knees in the dust
    You said, Sidi, if you were crooked or fat,
    And your skin was scaly like a . . .
LAKUNLE: Stop!
SIDI: I only repeat what you said.
LAKUNLE: Yes, and I will stand by every word I spoke.
    But must you throw away your neck on that account?
    Sidi, it is so unwomanly. Only spiders
    Carry loads the way you do.

SIDI: [*huffily, exposing the neck to advantage.*]
30   Well, it is my neck, not your spider.
      LAKUNLE: [*looks, and gets suddenly agitated.*]
      And look at that! Look, look at that!
      [*Makes a general sweep in the direction of her breasts.*]
      Who was it talked of shame just now?
      How often must I tell you, Sidi, that
      A grown-up girl must cover up her . . .
      Her . . . shoulders? I can see quite . . . quite
      A good portion of—that! And so I imagine
      Can every man in the village. Idlers
      All of them, good-for-nothing shameless men
      Casting their lustful eyes where
40   They have no business . . .
      SIDI: Are you at that again? Why, I've done the fold
      So high and so tight, I can hardly breathe.
      And all because you keep at me so much.
      I have to leave my arms so I can use them . . .
      Or don't you know that?
      LAKUNLE: You could wear something.
      Most modest women do. But you, no.
      You must run about naked in the streets.
      Does it not worry you . . . the bad names,
50   The lewd jokes, the tongue-licking noises
      Which girls, uncovered like you,
      Draw after them?
      SIDI: This is too much. Is it you, Lakunle,
      Telling me that I make myself common talk?
      When the whole world knows of the madman
      Of Ilujinle, who calls himself a teacher!
      Is it Sidi who makes the men choke
      In their cups, or you, with your big loud words
      And no meaning? You and your ragged books
60   Dragging your feet to every threshold
      And rushing them out again as curses
      Greet you instead of welcome. Is it Sidi
      They call a fool—even the children—
      Or you with your fine airs and little sense!
      LAKUNLE: [*first indignant, then recovers composure.*]
      For that, what is a jewel to pigs?
      If now I am misunderstood by you
      And your race of savages, I rise above taunts
      And remain unruffled.
      SIDI: [*furious, shakes both fists at him.*]
      O . . . oh, you make me want to pulp your brain.
      LAKUNLE: [*retreats a little, but puts her aside with a very lofty gesture.*]

A natural feeling, arising out of envy; 70
For, as a woman, you have a smaller brain
Than mine.
SIDI: [*madder still.*]
Again! I'd like to know
Just what gives you these thoughts
Of manly conceit.
LAKUNLE: [*very very, patronizing.*]
No, no. I have fallen for that trick before.
You can no longer draw me into arguments
Which go above your head.
SIDI: [*can't find the right words, chokes back.*]
Give me the pail now. And if you ever dare 80
To stop me in the streets again . . .
LAKUNLE: Now, now, Sidi . . .
SIDI: Give it or I'll . . .
LAKUNLE: [*holds on to her.*]
Please, don't be angry with me.
I didn't mean you in particular.
And anyway, it isn't what I say.
The scientists have proved it. It's in my books.
Women have a smaller brain than men
That's why they are called the weaker sex.
SIDI: [*throws him off.*]
The weaker sex, is it?
Is it a weaker breed who pounds the yam 90
Or bends all day to plant the millet
With a child strapped to her back?
LAKUNLE: That is all part of what I say.
But don't you worry. In a year or two
You will have machines which will do
Your pounding, which will grind your pepper
Without it getting in your eyes.
SIDI: O-oh. You really mean to turn
The whole world upside down.
LAKUNLE: The world? Oh, that. Well, maybe later. 100
Charity, they say, begins at home.
For now, it is this village I shall turn
Inside out. Beginning with that crafty rogue,
Your past master of self-indulgence—Baroka.
SIDI: Are you still on about the Bale?
What has he done to you?
LAKUNLE: He'll find out. Soon enough, I'll let him know.
SIDI: These thoughts of future wonders—do you buy them
Or merely go mad and dream of them?
LAKUNLE: A prophet has honour except 110

In his own home. Wise men have been called mad
Before me and after, many more shall be
So abused. But to answer you, the measure
Is not entirely of my own coinage.
What I boast is known in Lagos, that city
Of magic, in Badagry where Saro women bathe
In gold, even in smaller towns less than
Twelve miles from here . . .

SIDI: Well go there. Go to these places where
120   Women would understand you
If you told them of your plans with which
You oppress me daily. Do you not know
What name they give you here?
Have you lost shame completely that jeers
Pass you over.

LAKUNLE: No. I have told you no. Shame belongs
Only to the ignorant.

SIDI: Well, I am going.
Shall I take the pail or not?

130   LAKUNLE: Not till you swear to marry me.
[*Takes her hand, instantly soulful.*]
Sidi, a man must prepare to fight alone.
But it helps if he has a woman
To stand by him, a woman who . . .
Can understand . . . like you.

SIDI: I do?

LAKUNLE: Sidi, my love will open your mind
Like the chaste leaf in the morning, when
The sun first touches it.

SIDI: If you start that I will run away.
140   I had enough of that nonsense yesterday.

LAKUNLE: Nonsense? Nonsense? Do you hear?
Does anybody listen? Can the stones
Bear to listen to this? Do you call it
Nonsense that I poured the waters of my soul
To wash your feet?

SIDI: You did what!

LAKUNLE: Wasted! Wasted! Sidi, my heart
Bursts into flowers with my love.
But you, you and the dead of this village
150   Trample it with feet of ignorance.

SIDI: [*shakes her head in bafflement.*]
If the snail finds splinters in his shell
He changes house. Why do you stay?

LAKUNLE: Faith. Because I have faith.
Oh Sidi, vow to me your own undying love

And I will scorn the jibes of these bush minds
Who know no better. Swear, Sidi,
Swear you will be my wife and I will
Stand against earth, heaven, and the nine
Hells . . .
SIDI: Now there you go again.   160
One little thing
And you must chirrup like a cockatoo.
You talk and talk and deafen me
With words which always sound the same
And make no meaning.
I've told you, and I say it again
I shall marry you today, next week
Or any day you name.
But my bride-price must first be paid.
Aha, now you turn away.   170
But I tell you, Lakunle, I must have
The full bride-price. Will you make me
A laughing-stock? Well, do as you please.
But Sidi will not make herself
A cheap bowl for the village spit.
LAKUNLE: On my head let fall their scorn.
SIDI: They will say I was no virgin
That I was forced to sell my shame
And marry you without a price.
LAKUNLE: A savage custom, barbaric, out-dated,   180
Rejected, denounced, accursed,
Excommunicated, archaic, degrading,
Humiliating, unspeakable, redundant.
Retrogressive, remarkable, unpalatable.
SIDI: Is the bag empty? Why did you stop?
LAKUNLE: I own only the Shorter Companion
Dictionary, but I have ordered
The Longer One—you wait!
SIDI: Just pay the price.
LAKUNLE: [*with a sudden shout.*]
An ignoble custom, infamous, ignominious   190
Shaming our heritage before the world.
Sidi, I do not seek a wife
To fetch and carry,
To cook and scrub,
To bring forth children by the gross . . .
SIDI: Heaven forgive you! Do you now scorn
Child-bearing in a wife?
LAKUNLE: Of course I do not. I only mean . . .
Oh Sidi, I want to wed

200   Because I love,
       I seek a life-companion, . . .
       [*pulpit-declamatory.*]
       'And the man shall take the woman
       And the two shall be together
       As one flesh.'
       Sidi, I seek a friend in need.
       An equal partner in my race of life.
SIDI: [*attentive no more. Deeply engrossed in counting the beads on
       her neck.*]
       Then pay the price.
LAKUNLE: Ignorant girl, can you not understand?
       To pay the price would be
210   To buy a heifer off the market stall.
       You'd be my chattel, my mere property.
       No, Sidi! [*very tenderly.*]
       When we are wed, you shall not walk or sit
       Tethered, as it were, to my dirtied heels.
       Together we shall sit at table
       —Not on the floor—and eat,
       Not with fingers, but with knives
       And forks, and breakable plates
       Like civilized beings.
220   I will not have you wait on me
       Till I have dined my fill.
       No wife of mine, no lawful wedded wife
       Shall eat the leavings off my plate—
       That is for the children.
       I want to walk beside you in the street,
       Side by side and arm in arm
       Just like the Lagos couples I have seen
       High-heeled shoes for the lady, red paint
       On her lips. And her hair is stretched
230   Like a magazine photo. I will teach you
       The waltz and we'll both learn the foxtrot
       And we'll spend the week-end in night-clubs at Ibadan.
       Oh I must show you the grandeur of towns
       We'll live there if you like or merely pay visits.
       So choose. Be a modern wife, look me in the eye
       And give me a little kiss—like this.
       [*Kisses her.*]
SIDI: [*backs away.*]
       No, don't! I tell you I dislike
       This strange unhealthy mouthing you perform.
       Every time, your action deceives me

Making me think that you merely wish   240
  To whisper something in my ear.
  Then comes this licking of my lips with yours.
  It's so unclean. And then,
  The sound you make—'Pyout!'
  Are you being rude to me?
LAKUNLE: [*wearily*] It's never any use.
  Bush-girl you are, bush-girl you'll always be;
  Uncivilized and primitive—bush-girl!
  I kissed you as all educated men—
  And Christians—kiss their wives.   250
  It is the way of civilized romance.
SIDI: [*lightly.*] A way you mean, to avoid
  Payment of lawful bride-price
  A cheating way, mean and miserly.
LAKUNLE: [*violently.*] It is not.
  [*Sidi bursts out laughing. Lakunle changes his tone to a soulful one,
  both eyes dreamily shut.*]
  Romance is the sweetening of the soul
  With fragrance offered by the stricken heart.
SIDI: [*looks at him in wonder for a while.*]
  Away with you. The village says you're mad,
  And I begin to understand.
  I wonder that they let you run the school.   260
  You and your talk. You'll ruin your pupils too
  And then they'll utter madness just like you.
  [*Noise off-stage.*]
  There are people coming
  Give me the bucket or they'll jeer.
  [*Enter a crowd of youths and drummers, the girls being in various
  stages of excitement.*]
FIRST GIRL: Sidi, he has returned. He came back just as he said he
  would.
SIDI: Who has?
FIRST GIRL: The stranger. The man from the outside world. The clown
  who fell in the river for you.
  [*They all burst out laughing.*]
SIDI: The one who rode on the devil's own horse?   270
SECOND GIRL: Yes, the same. The stranger with the one-eyed box.
  [*She demonstrates the action of a camera amidst admiring titters.*]
THIRD GIRL: And he brought his new horse right into the village
  square this time. This one has only two feet. You should have seen
  him. B-r-r-r-r.
  [*Runs around the platform driving an imaginary motor-bike.*]
SIDI: And has he brought . . . ?

FIRST GIRL: The images? He brought them all. There was hardly any
part of the village which does not show in the book.
[*Clicks the imaginary shutter.*]

SIDI: The book? Did you see the book?
Had he the precious book

280
That would bestow upon me
Beauty beyond the dreams of a goddess?
For so he said.
The book which would announce
This beauty to the world —
Have you seen it?

THIRD GIRL: Yes, yes, he did. But the Bale is still feasting his eyes on
the images. Oh, Sidi, he was right. You *are* beautiful. On the cover
of the book is an image of you from here [*touches the top of her
head*] to here [*her stomach*]. And in the middle leaves, from the be-

290
ginning of one leaf right across to the end of another, is one of you
from head to toe. Do you remember it? It was the one for which he
made you stretch your arms toward the sun. [*Rapturously.*] Oh,
Sidi, you looked as if, at that moment, the sun himself had been
your lover. [*They all gasp with pretended shock at this blasphemy
and one slaps her playfully on the buttocks.*]

FIRST GIRL: The Bale is jealous, but he pretends to be proud of you.
And when this man tells him how famous you are in the capital, he
pretends to be pleased, saying how much honour and fame you have
brought to the village.

SIDI: [*with amazement.*] Is not Baroka's image in the book at all?

300
SECOND GIRL: [*contemptuous.*] Oh yes, it is. But it would have been
much better for the Bale if the stranger had omitted him altogether.
His image is in a little corner somewhere in the book, and even that
corner he shares with one of the village latrines.

SIDI: Is that the truth? Swear! Ask Ogun to
Strike you dead.

GIRL: Ogun strike me dead if I lie.

SIDI: If that is true, then I am more esteemed
Than Bale Baroka,
The Lion of Ilujinle.

310
This means that I am greater than
The Fox of the Undergrowth,
The living god among men . . .

LAKUNLE: [*peevishly.*] And devil among women.

SIDI: Be silent, you.
You are merely filled with spite.

LAKUNLE: I know him what he is. This is
Divine justice that a mere woman
Should outstrip him in the end.

SIDI: Be quiet;

Or I swear I'll never speak to you again. 320
[*Affects sudden coyness.*]
In fact, I am not so sure I'll want to wed you now.
LAKUNLE: Sidi!
SIDI: Well, why should I?
Known as I am to the whole wide world,
I would demean my worth to wed
A mere village school teacher.
LAKUNLE: [*in agony.*] Sidi!
SIDI: And one who is too mean
To pay the bride-price like a man.
LAKUNLE: Oh, Sidi, don't! 330
SIDI: [*plunging into an enjoyment of Lakunle's misery.*]
Well, don't you know?
Sidi is more important even than the Bale.
More famous than that panther of the trees.
He is beneath me now—
Your fearless rake, the scourge of womanhood!
But now,
He shares the corner of the leaf
With the lowest of the low—
With the dug-out village latrine!
While I—How many leaves did my own image take? 340
FIRST GIRL: Two in the middle and . . .
SIDI: No, no. Let the school teacher count!
How many were there, teacher-man?
LAKUNLE: Three leaves.
SIDI: [*threateningly.*] One leaf for every heart that I shall break.
Beware!
[*Leaps suddenly into the air.*]
Hurray! I'm beautiful!
Hurray for the wandering stranger!
CROWD: Hurray for the Lagos man!
SIDI: [*wildly excited.*] I know. Let us dance the dance of the lost Trav- 350
eller.
SHOUTS: Yes, let's.
SIDI: Who will dance the devil-horse?
You, you, you and you.
[*The four girls fall out.*]
A python. Who will dance the snake?
Ha ha! Your eyes are shifty and your ways are sly.
[*The selected youth is pushed out amidst jeers.*]
The stranger. We've got to have the being
from the mad outer world . . . You there,
No, you have never felt the surge
Of burning liquor in your milky veins. 360

Who can we pick that knows the walk of drunks?
You? . . . No, the thought itself
Would knock you out as sure as wine . . . Ah!
[*Turns round slowly to where Lakunle is standing with a kindly,
fatherly smile for the children at play.*]
Come on book-worm, you'll play his part.

LAKUNLE: No, no. I've never been drunk in all my life.

SIDI: We know. But your father drank so much,
He must have drunk your share, and that
Of his great grandsons.

LAKUNLE: [*tries to escape.*] I won't take part.

370 SIDI: You must.

LAKUNLE: I cannot stay. It's nearly time to take
Primary four in Geography.

SIDI: [*goes over to the window and throws it open.*]
Did you think your pupils would remain in school
Now that the stranger has returned?
The village is on holiday, you fool.

LAKUNLE: [*as they drag him towards the platform.*]
No, no. I won't. This foolery bores me.
It is a game of idiots. I have work of more importance.

SIDI: [*bending down over Lakunle who has been seated forcibly on
the platform.*]
You are dressed like him
You look like him
380 You speak his tongue
You think like him
You're just as clumsy
In your Lagos ways—
You'll do for him!

[*This chant is taken up by all and they begin to dance round
Lakunle, speaking the words in a fast rhythm. The drummers join in
after the first time, keeping up a steady beat as the others whirl
round their victim. They go faster and faster and chant faster and
faster with each round. By the sixth or seventh, Lakunle has obviously had enough.*]

LAKUNLE: [*raising his voice above the din.*] All right! I'll do it.
Come now, let's get it over with.

[*A terrific shout and a clap of drums. Lakunle enters into the spirit
of the dance with enthusiasm. He takes over from Sidi, stations his
cast all over the stage as the jungle, leaves the right top-stage clear
for the four girls who are to dance the motor-car. A mime follows
of the visitor's entry into Ilujinle, and his short stay among the villagers. The four girls crouch on the floor, as four wheels of a car.*]

Lakunle directs their spacing, then takes his place in the middle, and sits on air. He alone does not dance. He does realistic miming. Soft throbbing drums, gradually swelling in volume, and the four 'wheels' begin to rotate the upper halves of their bodies in perpendicular circles. Lakunle clowning the driving motions, obviously enjoying this fully. The drums gain tempo, faster, faster, faster. A sudden crash of drums and the girls quiver and dance the stall. Another effort at rhythm fails, and the 'stalling wheels' give a corresponding shudder, finally, and let their faces fall on to their laps. Lakunle tampers with a number of controls, climbs out of the car and looks underneath it. His lips indicate that he is swearing violently. Examines the wheels, pressing them to test the pressure, betrays the devil in him by seizing his chance to pinch the girls' bottoms. One yells and bites him on the ankle. He climbs hurriedly back into the car, makes a final attempt to re-start it, gives it up and decides to abandon it. Picks up his camera and his helmet, pockets a flask of whisky from which he takes a swig, before beginning the trek. The drums resume beating, a different, darker tone and rhythm, varying with the journey. Full use of 'gangan' and 'iya ilu'. The 'trees' perform a subdued and unobtrusive dance on the same spot. Details as a snake slithering out of the branches and posing over Lakunle's head when he leans against a tree for a rest. He flees, restoring his nerves shortly after by a swig. A monkey drops suddenly in his path and gibbers at him before scampering off. A roar comes from somewhere, etc. His nerves go rapidly and he recuperates himself by copious draughts. He is soon tipsy, battles violently with the undergrowth and curses silently as he swats the flies off his tortured body.

Suddenly, from somewhere in the bush comes the sound of a girl singing. The Traveller shakes his head but the sound persists. Convinced he is suffering from sun-stroke, he drinks again. His last drop, so he tosses the bottle in the direction of the sound, only to be rewarded by a splash, a scream and a torrent of abuse, and finally, silence again. He tip-toes, clears away the obstructing growth, blinks hard and rubs his eyes. Whatever he has seen still remains. He whistles softly, unhitches his camera and begins to jockey himself into a good position for a take. Backwards and forwards, and his eyes are so closely glued to the lens that he puts forward a careless foot and disappears completely. There is a loud splash and the invisible singer alters her next tone to a sustained scream. Quickened rhythm and shortly afterwards, amidst sounds of splashes, Sidi appears on the stage, with a piece of cloth only partially covering her. Lakunle follows a little later, more slowly, trying to wring out the water from his clothes. He has lost all his appendages except the camera. Sidi has run right across the stage, and returns a short while later, accompanied by the Villagers. The same cast has disappeared and re-forms behind Sidi as the Villagers. They are in an ugly mood, and in spite of his protests, haul him off to the town centre, in front of the 'Odan' tree.

Everything comes to a sudden stop as Baroka the Bale, wiry, goateed, tougher than his sixty-two years, himself emerges at this point from behind the tree. All go down prostrate or kneeling with the greetings of 'Kabiyesi' 'Baba' etc. All except Lakunle who begins to sneak off.]

BAROKA: Akowe. Teacher wa. Misita Lakunle.

[*As the others take up the cry 'Misita Lakunle' he is forced to stop. He returns and bows deeply from the waist.*]

LAKUNLE: A good morning to you sir.

BAROKA: Guru morin guru morin, ngh-hn! That is
All we get from 'alakowe'. You call at his house
Hoping he sends for beer, but all you get is
Guru morin. Will guru morin wet my throat?
Well, well our man of knowledge, I hope you have no
Query for an old man today.

LAKUNLE: No complaints.

BAROKA: And we are not feuding in something
I have forgotten.

LAKUNLE: Feuding sir? I see no cause at all.

BAROKA: Well, the play was much alive until I came.
And now everything stops, and you were leaving
Us. After all, I knew the story and I came in
Right on cue. It makes me feel as if I was
Chief Baseje.

LAKUNLE: One hardly thinks the Bale would have the time
For such childish nonsense.

BAROKA: A-ah Mister Lakunle. Without these things you call
Nonsense, a Bale's life would be pretty dull.
Well, now that you say I am welcome, shall we
Resume your play?
[*Turns suddenly to his attendants*]
Seize him!

LAKUNLE: [*momentarily baffled.*] What for? What have I done?

BAROKA: You tried to steal our village maidenhead
Have your forgotten? If he has, serve him a slap
To wake his brain.

[*An uplifted arm being proferred, Lakunle quickly recollects and nods his head vigorously. So the play is back in performance. The Villagers gather round threatening, clamouring for his blood. Lakunle tries bluff, indignation, appeasement in turn. At a sudden signal from the Bale, they throw him down prostrate on his face. Only then does the Chief begin to show him sympathy, appear to*

*understand the Stranger's plight, and pacify the villagers on his be-
half. He orders dry clothes for him, seats him on his right and orders a feast in his honour. The Stranger springs up every second to
take photographs of the party, but most of the time his attention is
fixed on Sidi dancing with abandon. Eventually he whispers to the
Chief, who nods in consent, and Sidi is sent for. The Stranger arranges Sidi in all sorts of magazine postures and takes innumerable
photographs of her. Drinks are pressed upon him; he refuses at first,
eventually tries the local brew with skepticism, appears to relish it,
and drinks profusely. Before long, however, he leaves the party to
be sick. They clap him on the back as he goes out, and two drummers who insist on dancing round him nearly cause the calamity to
happen on the spot. However, he rushes out with his hand held to
the mouth. Lakunle's exit seems to signify the end of the mime. He
returns almost at once and the others discard their roles.]*

SIDI: [*delightedly.*] What did I say? You played him to the bone,
A court jester would have been the life for you,
Instead of school.
[*Points contemptuously to the school.*]
BAROKA: And where would the village be, robbed of
Such wisdom as Mister Lakunle dispenses
Daily? Who would tell us where we go wrong?
Eh, Mister Lakunle?   420
SIDI: [*hardly listening, still in the full grip of her excitement.*]
Who comes with me to find the man?
But Lakunle, you'll have to come and find sense
In his clipping tongue. You see book-man
We cannot really do
Without your head.
[*Lakunle begins to protest, but they crowd him and try to bear him
down. Suddenly he breaks free and takes to his heels with all the
women in full pursuit. Baroka is left sitting by himself—his wrestler,
who accompanied him on his entry, stands a respectful distance
away—staring at the flock of women in flight. From the folds of his
agbada he brings out his copy of the magazine and admires the heroine of the publication. Nods slowly to himself.*]
BAROKA: Yes, yes . . . it is five full months since last
I took a wife . . . five full months . . .

NOON

*A road by the market. Enter Sidi, happily engrossed in the pictures
of herself in the magazine. Lakunle follows one or two paces behind
carrying a bundle of firewood which Sidi has set out to obtain. They
are met in the centre by Sadiku, who has entered from the opposite
side. Sadiku is an old woman, with a shawl over her head.*

SADIKU: Fortune is with me. I was going to your house to see you.

430 SIDI: [*startled out of her occupation.*] What! Oh, it is you, Sadiku.

SADIKU: The Lion sent me. He wishes you well.

SIDI: Thank him for me.

[*Then excitedly.*]

Have you seen these?

Have you seen these images of me

Wrought by the man from the capital city?

Have you felt the gloss? [*Caresses the page.*]

Smoother by far than the parrot's breast.

SADIKU: I have. I have. I saw them as soon as the city man came ...

Sidi, I bring a message from my lord. [*Jerks her head at Lakunle.*]

440 Shall we draw aside a little?

SIDI: Him? Pay no more heed to that

Than you would a eunuch.

SADIKU: Then, in as few words as it takes to tell, Baroka wants you

for a wife.

LAKUNLE: [*bounds forward, dropping the wood.*]

What! The greedy dog!

Insatiate camel of a foolish, doting race;

Is he at his tricks again?

SIDI: Be quiet, 'Kunle. You get so tiresome.

The message is for me, not you.

LAKUNLE: [*down on his knees at once. Covers Sidi's hands with kisses.*]

450 My Ruth, my Rachel, Esther, Bathsheba

Thou sum of fabled perfections

From Genesis to the Revelations

Listen not to the voice of this infidel ...

SIDI: [*snatches her hand away.*]

Now that's your other game;

Giving me funny names you pick up

In your wretched books.

My name is Sidi. And now, let me be.

My name is Sidi, and I am beautiful.

The stranger took my beauty

460 And placed it in my hands.

Here, here it is. I need no funny names

To tell me of my fame.

Loveliness beyond the jewels of a throne—

That is what he said.

SADIKU: [*gleefully.*] Well, will you be Baroka's own jewel?

Will you be his sweetest princess, soothing him on weary nights?

What answer shall I give my lord?

SIDI: [*wags her finger playfully at the woman.*]

Ha ha. Sadiku of the honey tongue.

Sadiku, head of the Lion's wives.

You'll make no prey of Sidi with your wooing tongue   470
Not this Sidi whose fame has spread to Lagos
And beyond the seas.

[*Lakunle beams with satisfaction and rises.*]

SADIKU: Sidi, have you considered what a life of bliss awaits you?
Baroka swears to take no other wife after you. Do you know what
it is to be the Bale's last wife? I'll tell you. When he dies—and that
should not be long; even the Lion has to die sometime—well, when
he does, it means that you will have the honour of being the senior
wife of the new Bale. And just think, until Baroka dies, you shall be
his favourite. No living in the outhouses for you, my girl. Your
place will always be in the palace; first as the latest bride, and after-   480
wards, as the head of the new harem . . . It is a rich life, Sidi. I
know. I have been in that position for forty-one years.

SIDI: You waste your breath.
Why did Baroka not request my hand
Before the stranger
Brought his book of images?
Why did the Lion not bestow his gift
Before my face was lauded to the world?
Can you not see? Because he sees my worth
Increased and multiplied above his own;   490
Because he can already hear
The ballad-makers and their songs
In praise of Sidi, the incomparable,
While the Lion is forgotten.
He seeks to have me as his property
Where I must fade beneath his jealous hold.
Ah, Sadiku,
The school-man here has taught me certain things
And my images have taught me all the rest.
Baroka merely seeks to raise his manhood   500
Above my beauty
He seeks new fame
As the one man who has possessed
The jewel of Ilujinle!

SADIKU: [*shocked, bewildered, incapable of making any sense of Sidi's
words.*] But Sidi, are you well? Such nonsense never passed your lips
before. Did you not sound strange, even in your own hearing?
[*Rushes suddenly at Lakunle.*] Is this your doing, you popinjay?
Have you driven the poor girl mad at last? Such rubbish . . . I will
beat your head for this!

LAKUNLE: [*retreating in panic.*] Keep away from me, old hag.   510

SIDI: Sadiku, let him be.
Tell your lord that I can read his mind,
That I will none of him.

Look—judge for yourself.
[*Opens the magazine and points out the pictures.*]
He's old. I never knew till now,
He was that old . . .
[*During the rest of her speech, Sidi runs her hand over the surface
of the relevant part of the photographs, tracing the contours with
her fingers.*]
    . . . To think I took
No notice of my velvet skin.
How smooth it is!
520   And no man ever thought
To praise the fullness of my breasts . . .
LAKUNLE: [*laden with guilt and full of apology.*]
Well, Sidi, I did think . . .
But somehow it was not the proper thing.
SIDI: [*ignores the interruption.*]
See I hold them to the warm caress
[*unconsciously pushes out her chest.*]
Of a desire-filled sun.
[*Smiles mischievously.*]
There's a deceitful message in my eyes
Beckoning insatiate men to certain doom.
And teeth that flash the sign of happiness,
Strong and evenly, beaming full of life.
530   Be just, Sadiku,
Compare my image and your lord's—
An age of difference!
See how the water glistens on my face
Like the dew-moistened leaves on a Harmattan morning
But he—his face is like a leather piece
Torn rudely from the saddle of his horse,
[*Sadiku gasps.*]
Sprinkled with the musty ashes
From a pipe that is long over-smoked.
And this goat-like tuft
540   Which I once thought was manly;
It is like scattered twists of grass—
Not even green—
But charred and lifeless, as after a forest fire!
Sadiku, I am young and brimming; he is spent.
I am the twinkle of a jewel
But he is the hind-quarters of a lion!
SADIKU: [*recovering at last from helpless amazement.*] May Sango re-
store your wits. For most surely some angry god has taken posses-
sion of you. [*Turns around and walks away. Stops again as she re-
550   members something else.*] Your ranting put this clean out of my

head. My lord says that if you would not be his wife, would you at
least come to supper at his house tonight. There is a small feast in
your honour. He wishes to tell you how happy he is that the great
capital city has done so much honour to a daughter of Ilujinle. You
have brought great fame to your people.

SIDI: Ho ho! Do you think that I was only born
Yesterday?
The tales of Baroka's little suppers,
I know all.
Tell your lord that Sidi does not sup with   560
Married men.

SADIKU: They are lies, lies. You must not believe everything you hear.
Sidi, would I deceive you? I swear to you .. .

SIDI: Can you deny that
Every woman who has supped with him one night,
Becomes his wife or concubine the next.

LAKUNLE: Is it for nothing he is called the Fox?

SADIKU: [advancing on him.] You keep out of this, or so Sango be my
witness . . .

LAKUNLE: [retreats just a little, but continues to talk.]
His wiliness is known even in the larger towns.   570
Did you never hear
Of how he foiled the Public Works attempt
To build the railway through Ilujinle.

SADIKU: Nobody knows the truth of that. It is all hearsay.

SIDI: I love hearsays. Lakunle, tell me all.

LAKUNLE: Did you not know it? Well sit down and listen.
My father told me, before he died. And few men
Know of this trick—oh he's a die-hard rogue
Sworn against our progress . . . yes . . . it was . . . somewhere here
The track should have been laid just along   580
The outskirts. Well, the workers came, in fact
It was prisoners who were brought to do
The harder part . . . to break the jungle's back . . .
[Enter the prisoners, guarded by two warders. A white surveyor examines his map (khaki helmet, spats, etc.) The foreman runs up
with his camp stool, table etc., erects the umbrella over him and
unpacks the usual box of bush comforts—soda siphon, whisky bottle and geometric sandwiches. His map consulted, he directs the
sweat team where to work. They begin felling, matchet swinging,
log dragging, all to the rhythm of the work gang's metal percussion
(rod on gong or rude triangle, etc.) The two performers are also the
song leaders and the others fill the chorus. 'N'ijo itoro;', 'Amuda
el'ebe l'aiya' 'Gbe je on'ipa' etc.]

LAKUNLE: They marked the route with stakes, ate
Through the jungle and began the tracks. Trade,

Progress, adventure, success, civilization,
Fame, international conspicuousity . . . it was
All within the grasp of Ilujinle . . .
[*The wrestler enters, stands horrified at the sight and flees. Returns
later with the Bale himself who soon assesses the situation. They
disappear. The work continues, the surveyor occupies himself with
the fly-whisk and whisky. Shortly after, a bull-roarer is heard. The
prisoners falter a little, pick up again. The bull-roarer continues on
its way, nearer and farther, moving in circles, so that it appears to
come from all round them. The foreman is the first to break and
then the rest is chaos. Sole survivor of the rout is the surveyor who
is too surprised to move. Baroka enters a few minutes later accompanied by some attendants and preceded by a young girl bearing a
calabash bowl. The surveyor, angry and threatening, is prevailed
upon to open his gift. From it he reveals a wad of pound notes and
kola nuts. Mutual understanding is established. The surveyor frowns
heavily, rubs his chin and consults his map. Re-examines the contents of the bowl, shakes his head. Baroka adds more money, and a
coop of hens. A goat follows, and more money. This time 'truth'
dawns on him at last, he has made a mistake. The track really
should go the other way. What an unfortunate error, discovered just
in time! No, no, no possibility of a mistake this time, the track
should be much further away. In fact (scooping up the soil) the
earth is most unsuitable, couldn't possibly support the weight of a
railway engine. A gourd of palm wine is brought to seal the agreement and a kola nut is broken. Baroka's men help the surveyor
pack and they leave with their arms round each other followed by
the surveyor's booty.*]

LAKUNLE: [*as the last of the procession disappears, shakes his fist at
them, stamping on the ground.*]
Voluptuous beast! He loves this life too well
590   To bear to part from it. And motor roads
And railways would do just that, forcing
Civilization at his door. He foresaw it
And he barred the gates, securing fast
His dogs and horses, his wives and all his
Concubines . . . ah, yes . . . all those concubines
Baroka has such a selective eye, none suits him
But the best . . .
[*His eyes truly light up. Sidi and Sadiku snigger, tip-toe off stage.*]
. . . Yes, one must grant him that.
Ah, I sometimes wish I led his kind of life.
600   Such luscious bosoms make his nightly pillow.
I am sure he keeps a time-table just as
I do at school. Only way to ensure fair play.
He must be healthy to keep going as he does.

I don't know what the women see in him. His eyes
Are small and always red with wine. He must
Possess some secret . . . No! I do not envy him!
Just the one woman for me. Alone I stand
For progress, with Sidi my chosen soul-mate, the one
Woman of my life . . . Sidi! Sidi where are you?
[*Rushes out after them, returns to fetch the discarded firewood and
runs out again.*]

*

[*Baroka in bed, naked except for baggy trousers, calf-length. It is a
rich bedroom covered in animal skins and rugs. Weapons round the
wall. Also a strange machine, a most peculiar contraption with a
long lever. Kneeling beside the bed is Baroka's current Favourite,
engaged in plucking the hairs from his armpit. She does this by first
massaging the spot around the selected hair very gently with her
forefinger. Then, with hardly a break, she pulls out the hair between
her finger and the thumb with a sudden sharp movement. Baroka
twitches slightly with each pull. Then an aspirated 'A-ah', and a
look of complete beatitude spreads all over his face.*]

FAVOURITE: Do I improve my lord?   610
BAROKA: You are still somewhat over-gentle with the pull
   As if you feared to hurt the panther of the trees.
   Be sharp and sweet
   Like the swift sting of a vicious wasp
   For there the pleasure lies—the cooling aftermath.
FAVOURITE: I'll learn my lord.
BAROKA: You have not time, my dear.
   Tonight I hope to take another wife.
   And the honour of this task, you know,
   Belongs by right to my latest choice.   620
   But—A-ah—Now that was sharp.
   It had in it the scorpion's sudden sting
   Without its poison.
   It was an angry pull; you tried to hurt
   For I had made you wrathful with my boast.
   But now your anger flows in my blood-stream.
   How sweet it is! A-ah! That was sweeter still.
   I think perhaps that I shall let you stay,
   The sole out-puller of my sweat-bathed hairs.
   Ach!   630
[*Sits up suddenly and rubs the sore point angrily.*]
      Now that had far more pain than pleasure
Vengeful creature, you did not caress
The area of extraction long enough!
[*Enter Sadiku. She goes down on her knees at once and bows her
head into her lap.*]

Aha! Here comes Sadiku.
Do you bring some balm,
To soothe the smart of my misused armpit?
Away, you enemy!
[*Exit the Favourite.*]
SADIKU: My lord . . .
BAROKA: You have my leave to speak.
640   What did she say?
SADIKU: She will not, my lord. I did my best, but she will have none
of you.
BAROKA: It follows the pattern—a firm refusal
At the start. Why will she not?
SADIKU: That is the strange part of it. She say's you're much too old.
If you ask me, I think that she is really off her head. All this excite-
ment of the books has been too much for her.
BAROKA: [*springs to his feet.*]
She says . . . That I am old
That I am much too old? Did a slight
650   Unripened girl say this of me?
SADIKU: My lord, I heard the incredible words with my ears, and I
thought the world was mad.
BAROKA: But is it possible, Sadiku? Is this right?
Did I not, at the festival of Rain,
Defeat the men in the log-tossing match?
Do I not still with the most fearless ones,
Hunt the leopard and the boa at night
And save the farmers' goats from further harm?
And does she say I'm old?
660   Did I not, to announce the Harmattan,
Climb to the top of the silk-cotton tree,
Break the first pod, and scatter tasselled seeds
To the four winds—and this but yesterday?
Do any of my wives report
A failing in my manliness?
The strongest of them all
Still wearies long before the Lion does!
And so would she, had I the briefest chance
To teach this unfledged birdling
670   That lacks the wisdom to embrace
The rich mustiness of age . . . if I could once . . .
Come hither, soothe me, Sadiku
For I am wroth at heart.
[*Lies back on the bed, staring up as before. Sadiku takes her place
at the foot of the bed and begins to tickle the soles of his feet.
Baroka turns to the left suddenly, reaches down the side, and comes*

*up with a copy of the magazine. Opens it and begins to study the
pictures. He heaves a long sigh.*]
That is good, Sadiku, very good.
[*He begins to compare some pictures in the book, obviously his own
and Sidi's. Flings the book away suddenly and stares at the ceiling
for a second or two. Then, unsmiling.*]
Perhaps it is as well, Sadiku.

SADIKU: My lord, what did you say?

BAROKA: Yes, faithful one, I say it is as well.
The scorn, the laughter and the jeers
Would have been bitter.
Had she consented and my purpose failed,   680
I would have sunk with shame.

SADIKU: My lord, I do not understand.

BAROKA: The time has come when I can fool myself
No more. I am no man, Sadiku. My manhood
Ended near a week ago.

SADIKU: The gods forbid.

BAROKA: I wanted Sidi because I still hoped—
A foolish thought I know, but still—I hoped
That, with a virgin young and hot within,
My failing strength would rise and save my pride.   690
[*Sadiku begins to moan.*]
A waste of hope. I knew it even then.
But it's a human failing never to accept
The worst; and so I pandered to my vanity.
When manhood must, it ends.
The well of living, tapped beyond its depth,
Dries up, and mocks the wastrel in the end.
I am withered and unsapped, the joy
Of ballad-mongers, the aged butt
Of youth's ribaldry.

SADIKU: [*tearfully.*] The Gods must have mercy yet.   700

BAROKA: [*as if suddenly aware of her presence, starts up.*]
I have told this to no one but you,
Who are my eldest, my most faithful wife.
But if you dare parade my shame before the world . . .
[*Sadiku shakes her head in protest and begins to stroke the soles of
his feet with renewed tenderness. Baroka sighs and falls back
slowly.*]
How irritable I have grown of late
Such doubts to harbour of your loyalty . . .
But this disaster is too much for one
Checked thus as I upon the prime of youth.
That rains that blessed me from my birth

Number a meagre sixty-two;
710   While my grandfather, that man of teak,
Fathered two sons, late on sixty-five.
But Okiki, my father beat them all
Producing female twins at sixty-seven.
Why then must I, descendant of these lions
Forswear my wives at a youthful sixty-two
My veins of life run dry, my manhood gone!
[*His voice goes drowsy; Sadiku sighs and moans and caresses his
feet. His face lights up suddenly with rapture.*]
Sango bear witness! These weary feet
Have felt the loving hands of much design
In women.
720   My soles have felt the scratch of harsh,
Gravelled hands.
They have borne the heaviness of clumsy,
Gorilla paws.
And I have known the tease of tiny,
Dainty hands,
Toy-like hands that tantalized
My eager senses,
Promised of thrills to come
Remaining
730   Unfulfilled because the fingers
Were too frail
The touch too light and faint to pierce
The incredible thickness of my soles.
But thou Sadiku, thy plain unadorned hands
Encase a sweet sensuality which age
Will not destroy. A-ah,
Oyayi! Beyond a doubt Sadiku,
Thou art the queen of them all.
[*Falls asleep.*]

NIGHT

*The village centre. Sidi stands by the Schoolroom window, admiring
her photos as before. Enter Sadiku with a longish bundle. She is
very furtive. Unveils the object which turns out to be a carved figure
of the Bale, naked and in full detail. She takes a good look at it,
bursts suddenly into derisive laughter, sets the figure standing in
front of the tree. Sidi stares in utter amazement.*

SADIKU: So we did for you too did we? We did for you in the end. Oh
740   high and mighty lion, have we really scotched you? A—ya-ya-ya . . .
we women undid you in the end. I was there when it happened to
your father, the great Okiki. I did for him, I, the youngest and

freshest of the wives. I killed him with my strength. I called him and
he came at me, but no, for him, this was not like other times. I,
Sadiku, was I not flame itself and he the flax on old women's spin-
dles? I ate him up! Race of mighty lions, we always consume you, at
our pleasure we spin you, at our whim we make you dance; like the
foolish top you think the world revolves around you . . . fools!
fools! . . . it is you who run giddy while we stand still and watch,
and draw your frail thread from you, slowly, till nothing is left but   750
a runty old stick. I scotched Okiki, Sadiku's unopened treasure-
house demanded sacrifice, and Okiki came with his rusted key. Like
a snake he came at me, like a rag he went back, a limp rag, smeared
in shame. . . . [*Her ghoulish laugh re-possesses her.*] Ah, take warning my masters, we'll scotch you in the end . . [*With a yell she leaps
up, begins to dance round the tree, chanting.*]
Take warning, my masters
We'll scotch you in the end.
[*Sidi shuts the window gently, comes out, Sadiku, as she comes
round again, gasps and is checked in mid-song.*]

SADIKU: Oh it is you my daughter. You should have chosen a better
time to scare me to death. The hour of victory is no time for any
woman to die.   760

SIDI: Why? What battle have you won?

SADIKU: Not me alone girl. You too. Every woman. Oh my daughter,
that I have lived to see this day . . . To see him fizzle with the drab-
best puff of a mis-primed 'sakabula'.
[*Resumes her dance.*]
Take warning, my masters
We'll scotch you in the end.

SIDI: Wait Sadiku. I cannot understand.

SADIKU: You will my girl. You will.
Take warning my masters . . .

SIDI: Sadiku, are you well?   770

SADIKU: Ask no questions my girl. Just join my victory dance. Oh
Sango my lord, who of us possessed your lightning and ran like fire
through that lion's tail . . .

SIDI: [*holds her firmly as she is about to go off again.*]
Stop your loose ranting. You will not
Move from here until you make some sense.

SADIKU: Oh you are troublesome. Do you promise to tell no one?

SIDI: I swear it. Now tell me quickly.
[*As Sadiku whispers, her eyes widen.*]
O-ho-o-o-o-!
But Sadiku, if he knew the truth, why
Did he ask me to . . .   780
[*Again Sadiku whispers.*]
Ha ha! Some hope indeed. Oh Sadiku

I suddenly am glad to be a woman.
[*Leaps in the air.*]
We won! We won! Hurray for womankind!
[*Falls in behind Sadiku.*]
Take warning, my masters
We'll scotch you in the end. [*Lakunle enters unobserved.*]
LAKUNLE: The full moon is not yet, but
The women cannot wait.
They must go mad without it.
[*The dancing stops. Sadiku frowns.*]
SADIKU: The scarecrow is here. Begone fop! This is the world of women. At this moment our star sits in the centre of the sky. We are supreme. What is more, we are about to perform a ritual. If you remain, we will chop you up, we will make you the sacrifice.
LAKUNLE: What is the hag gibbering?
SADIKU: [*advances menacingly.*] You less than man, you less than the littlest woman, I say begone!
LAKUNLE: [*nettled.*] I will have you know that I am a man
As you will find out if you dare
To lay a hand on me.
SADIKU: [*throws back her head in laughter.*] You a man? Is Baroka not more of a man than you? And if he is no longer a man, then what are you? [*Lakunle, understanding the meaning, stands rooted, shocked.*] Come on, dear girl, let him look on if he will. After all, only *men* are barred from watching this ceremony.
Take warning, my masters
We'll . . .
SIDI: Stop. Sadiku stop. Oh such an idea
Is running in my head. Let me to the palace for
This supper he promised me. Sadiku, what a way
To mock the devil. I shall ask forgiveness
For my hasty words . . . No need to change
My answer and consent to be his bride—he might
Suspect you've told me. But I shall ask a month
To think on it.
SADIKU: [*somewhat doubtful.*] Baroka is no child you know, he will know I have betrayed him.
SIDI: No, he will not. Oh Sadiku let me go.
I long to see him thwarted, to watch his longing
His twitching hands which this time cannot
Rush to loosen his trouser cords.
SADIKU: You will have to match the Fox's cunning. Use your bashful looks and be truly repentant. Goad him my child, torment him until he weeps for shame.
SIDI: Leave it to me. He will never suspect you
of deceit.

790

800

810

820

SADIKU: [*with another of her energetic leaps.*] Yo-rooo o! Yo-rororo o!
   Shall I come with you?
SIDI: Will that be wise? You forget
   We have not seen each other.
SADIKU: Away then. Away woman. I shall bide here.
   Haste back and tell Sadiku how the no-man is.
   Away, my lovely child.   830
LAKUNLE: [*he has listened with increasing horror.*]
   No, Sidi, don't. If you care
   One little bit for what I feel,
   Do not go to torment the man.
   Suppose he knows that you have come to jeer—
   And he will know, if he is not a fool—
   He is a savage thing, degenerate
   He would beat a helpless woman if he could . . .
SIDI: [*running off gleefully.*] Ta-raa school teacher. Wait here for me.
LAKUNLE: [*stamps his foot helplessly.*]
   Foolish girl! . . . And this is all your work.
   Could you not keep a secret?   840
   Must every word leak out of you
   As surely as the final drops
   Of mother's milk
   Oozed from your flattened breast
   Generations ago?
SADIKU: Watch your wagging tongue, unformed creature!
LAKUNLE: If any harm befalls her . . .
SADIKU: Woman though she is, she can take better care of herself than
   you can of her. Fancy a thing like you actually wanting a girl like
   that, all to your little self. [*Walks round him and looks him up and*   850
   down.] Ah! Oba Ala is an accommodating god. What a poor figure
   you cut!
LAKUNLE: I wouldn't demean myself to bandy words
   With a woman of the bush.
SADIKU: At this moment, your betrothed is supping
   with the Lion.
LAKUNLE: [*pleased at the use of the word 'Betrothed'.*]
   Well, we are not really betrothed as yet,
   I mean, she is not promised yet.
   But it will come in time, I'm sure.
SADIKU: [*bursts into her cackling laughter,*] The bride-price, is that   860
   paid?
LAKUNLE: Mind your own business.
SADIKU: Why don't you do what other men have done. Take a farm
   for a season. One harvest will be enough to pay the price, even for a
   girl like Sidi. Or will the smell of the wet soil be too much for your
   delicate nostrils?

LAKUNLE: I said mind your own business.

SADIKU: A—a—ah. It is true what they say then. You are going to
convert the whole village so that no one will ever pay the bride-
price again. Ah, you're a clever man. I must admit that it is a good
way for getting out of it, but don't you think you'd use more time
and energy that way than you would if . . .

LAKUNLE: [*with conviction.*] Within a year or two, I swear,
This town shall see a transformation
Bride-price will be a thing forgotten
And wives shall take their place by men.
A motor road will pass this spot.
And bring the city ways to us.
We'll buy saucepans for all the women
Clay pots are crude and unhygienic
No man shall take more wives than one
That's why they're impotent too soon.
The ruler shall ride cars, not horses
Or a bicycle at the very least.
We'll burn the forest, cut the trees
Then plant a modern park for lovers
We'll print newspapers every day
With pictures of seductive girls.
The world will judge our progress by
The girls that win beauty contests.
While Lagos builds new factories daily
We only play 'ayo' and gossip.
Where is our school of Ballroom dancing?
Who here can throw a cocktail party?
We must be modern with the rest
Or live forgotten by the world
We must reject the palm wine habit.
And take to tea, with milk and sugar.
[*Turns on Sadiku who has been staring at him in terror. She re-
treats, and he continues to talk down at her as they go round, then
down and off-stage, Lakunle's hectoring voice trailing away in the
distance.*]
This is my plan, you withered face
And I shall start by teaching you.
From now you shall attend my school
And take your place with twelve-year olds.
For though you're nearly seventy,
Your mind is simple and unformed.
Have you no shame that at your age,
You neither read nor write nor think?
You spend your days as senior wife,
Collecting brides for Baroka.

And now because you've sucked him dry,
You send my Sidi to his shame. . . . 910
[*The scene changes to Baroka's bedroom. On the left in a one-knee-on-floor posture, two men are engaged in a kind of wrestling, their arms clasped round each other's waist, testing the right moment to leave. One is Baroka, the other a short squat figure of apparent muscular power. The contest is still in the balanced stage. In some distant part of the house, Sidi's voice is heard lifted in the familiar general greeting, addressed to no one in particular.*]
SIDI: A good day to the head and people
Of this house.
[*Baroka lifts his head, frowns as if he is trying to place the voice.*]
A good day to the head and people
Of this house.
[*Baroka now decides to ignore it and to concentrate on the contest. Sidi's voice draws progressively nearer. She enters nearly backwards, as she is still busy admiring the room through which she has just passed. Gasps on turning round to see the two men.*]
BAROKA: [*without looking up.*] Is Sadiku not at home then?
SIDI: [*absent-mindedly.*] Hm?
BAROKA: I asked, is Sadiku not at home?
SIDI: [*recollecting herself, she curtsys quickly.*] I saw no one, Baroka.
BAROKA: No one? Do you mean there was no one
To bar unwanted strangers from my privacy? 920
SIDI: [*retreating.*] The house . . . seemed . . . empty.
BAROKA: Ah, I forget. This is the price I pay
Once every week, for being progressive.
Prompted by the school teacher, my servants
Were prevailed upon to form something they call
The Palace Workers' Union. And in keeping
With the habits—I am told—of modern towns,
This is their day off.
SIDI: [*seeing that Baroka seems to be in a better mood, she becomes somewhat bolder. Moves forward—saucily.*]
Is this also a day off
For Baroka's wives? 930
BAROKA: [*looks up sharply, relaxes and speaks with a casual voice.*]
No, the madness has not gripped them—yet.
Did you not meet with one of them?
SIDI: No, Baroka. There was no one about.
BAROKA: Not even Ailatu, my favourite?
Was she not at her usual place,
Beside my door?
SIDI: [*absently. She is deeply engrossed in watching the contest.*]
Her stool is there. And I saw
The slippers she was embroidering.

BAROKA: Hm. Hm. I think I know
940   Where she'll be found. In a dark corner
    Sulking like a slighted cockroach.
    By the way, look and tell me
    If she left her shawl behind.
    [*So as not to miss any part of the tussle, she moves backwards,
    darts a quick look round the door and back again.*]
SIDI: There is a black shawl on the stool.
BAROKA: [*a regretful sigh.*]
    Then she'll be back tonight. I had hoped
    My words were harsh enough
    To free me from her spite for a week or more.
SIDI: Did Ailatu offend her husband?
BAROKA: Offend? My armpit still weeps blood
950   For the gross abuse I suffered from one
    I called my favourite.
SIDI: [*in a disappointed voice.*]
    Oh. Is that all?
BAROKA: Is that not enough? Why child?
    What more could the woman do?
SIDI: Nothing. Nothing, Baroka. I thought perhaps—
    Well—young wives are known to be—
    Forward—sometimes—to their husbands.
BAROKA: In an ill-kept household perhaps. But not
    Under Baroka's roof. And yet,
960   Such are the sudden spites of women
    That even I cannot foresee them all.
    And child—if I lose this little match
    Remember that my armpit
    Burns and itches turn by turn.
    [*Sidi continues watching for some time, then clasps her hand over
    her mouth as she remembers what she should have done to begin
    with. Doubtful how to proceed, she hesitates for some moments,
    then comes to a decision and kneels.*]
SIDI: I have come, Bale, as a repentant child.
BAROKA: What?
SIDI: [*very hesitantly, eyes to the floor, but she darts a quick look up
    when she thinks the Bale isn't looking.*]
    The answer which I sent to the Bale
    Was given in a thoughtless moment . . .
BAROKA: Answer, child? To what?
970 SIDI: A message brought by . . .
BAROKA: [*groans and strains in a muscular effort.*]
    Will you say that again? It is true that for supper
    I did require your company. But up till now
    Sadiku has brought no reply.

SIDI: [*amazed.*] But the other matter! Did not the Bale
Send . . . did Baroka not send . . . ?
BAROKA: [*with sinister encouragement.*]
What did Baroka not, my child?
SIDI: [*cowed, but angry, rises.*]
It is nothing, Bale. I only hope
That I am here at the Bale's invitation.
BAROKA: [*as if trying to understand, he frowns as he looks at her.*]
A-ah, at last I understand. You think
I took offence because you entered   980
Unannounced?
SIDI: I remember that the Bale called me
An unwanted stranger.
BAROKA: That could be expected. Is a man's bedroom
To be made naked to any flea
That chances to wander through?
[*Sidi turns away, very hurt.*]
Come, come, my child. You are too quick
To feel aggrieved. Of course you are
More than welcome. But I expected Ailatu
To tell me you were here.   990
[*Sidi curtsys briefly with her back to Baroka. After a while, she
turns round. The mischief returns to her face. Baroka's attitude of
denial has been a set-back but she is now ready to pursue her
mission.*]
SIDI: I hope the Bale will not think me
Forward. But, like everyone, I had thought
The Favourite was a gentle woman.
BAROKA: And so had I.
SIDI: [*slyly.*] One would hardly think that *she*
Would give offence without a cause
Was the Favourite . . . in some way . . .
Dissatisfied . . . with her lord and husband?
[*With a mock curtsy, quickly executed as Baroka begins to look
up.*]
BAROKA: [*slowly turns towards her.*]
                             Now that
Is a question which I never thought to hear   1000
Except from a school teacher. Do you think
The Lion has such leisure that he asks
The whys and wherefores of a woman's
Squint?
[*Sidi steps back and curtsys. As before, and throughout this scene,
she is easily cowed by Baroka's change of mood, all the more easily
as she is, in any case, frightened by her own boldness.*]
SIDI: I meant no disrespect . . .

BAROKA: [*gently.*] I know. [*Breaks off.*] Christians on my
Father's shrines, child!
Do you think I took offence? A—aw
Come in and seat yourself. Since you broke in
1010   Unawares, and appear resolved to stay,
Try, if you can, not to make me feel
A humourless old ram. I allow no one
To watch my daily exercise, but as we say,
The woman gets lost in the woods one day
And every wood deity dies the next.
[*Sidi curtsys, watches and moves forward warily, as if expecting the
two men to spring apart too suddenly.*]
SIDI: I think he will win.
BAROKA: Is that a wish, my daughter?
SIDI: No, but—[*Hesitates, but boldness wins.*]
                         If the tortoise cannot tumble
1020   It does not mean that he can stand.
[*Baroka looks at her, seemingly puzzled. Sidi turns away,
humming.*]
BAROKA: When the child is full of riddles, the mother
Has one water-pot the less.
[*Sidi tiptoes to Baroka's back and pulls asses' ears at him.*]
SIDI: I think he will win.
BAROKA: He knows he must. Would it profit me
To pit my strength against a weakling?
Only yesterday, this son of—I suspect—
A python for a mother, and fathered beyond doubt
By a blubber-bottomed baboon,
[*The complimented man grins.*]
Only yesterday, he nearly
1030   Ploughed my tongue with my front teeth
In a friendly wrestling bout.
WRESTLER: [*encouraged, makes an effort.*] Ugh. Ugh.
SIDI: [*bent almost over them. Genuinely worried.*]
Oh! Does it hurt?
BAROKA: Not yet . . . but, as I was saying
I change my wrestlers when I have learnt
To throw them. I also change my wives
When I have learnt to tire them.
SIDI: And is this another . . . changing time
For the Bale?
1040   BAROKA: Who knows? Until the finger nails
Have scraped the dust, no one can tell
Which insect released his bowels.
[*Sidi grimaces in disgust and walks away. Returns as she thinks up a
new idea.*]

SIDI: A woman spoke to me this afternoon.

BAROKA: Indeed. And does Sidi find this unusual—
    That a woman speak with her in the afternoon?

SIDI: [*stamping.*] No. She had the message of a go-between.

BAROKA: Did she? Then I rejoice with you.
    [*Sidi stands biting her lips. Baroka looks at her, this time with delib-
    erate appreciation.*]
    And now I think of it, why not?
    There must be many men who
    Build their loft to fit your height.   1050

SIDI: [*unmoving, pointedly.*] Her message came from one
    With many lofts.

BAROKA: Ah! Such is the greed of men.

SIDI: If Baroka were my father
    [*aside*]—which many would take him to be—
    [*Makes a rude sign.*]
    Would he pay my dowry to this man
    And give his blessings?

BAROKA: Well, I must know his character.
    For instance, is the man rich?

SIDI: Rumour has it so.   1060

BAROKA: Is he repulsive?

SIDI: He is old. [*Baroka winces.*]

BAROKA: Is he mean and miserly?

SIDI: To strangers—no. There are tales
    Of his open-handedness, which are never
    Quite without a motive. But his wives report
    —To take one little story—
    How he grew the taste for ground corn
    And pepper—because he would not pay
    The price of snuff!   1070
    [*With a sudden burst of angry energy, Baroka lifts his opponent and
    throws him over his shoulder.*]

BAROKA: A lie! The price of snuff
    Had nothing to do with it.

SIDI: [*too excited to listen.*] You won!

BAROKA: By the years on my beard, I swear
    They slander me!

SIDI: [*excitedly.*] You won. You won!
    [*She breaks into a kind of shoulder dance and sings.*]
    Yokolu Yokolu. Ko ha tan bi
    Iyawo gb'oko san'le
    Oko yo'ke . . .
    [*She repeats this throughout Baroka's protests. Baroka is pacing an-
    grily up and down. The defeated man, nursing a hip, goes to the
    corner and lifts out a low 'ako' bench. He sits on the floor, and*]

soon, Baroka joins him; using only their arms now, they place their elbows on the bench and grip hands. Baroka takes his off again, replaces it, takes it off again and so on during the rest of his outburst.]

1080   BAROKA: This means nothing to me of course. Nothing!
But I know the ways of women, and I know
Their ruinous tongues.
Suppose that, as a child—only suppose—
Suppose then, that as a child, I—
And remember, I only use myself
To illustrate the plight of many men . . .
So, once again, suppose that as a child
I grew to love 'tanfiri'—with a good dose of pepper
And growing old, I found that—
1090   Sooner than die away, my passion only
Bred itself upon each mouthful of
Ground corn and pepper I consumed.
Now, think child, would it be seemly
At my age, and the father of children,
To be discovered, in public
Thrusting fistfuls of corn and pepper
In my mouth? Is it not wise to indulge
In the little masquerade of a dignified
Snuff-box!—But remember, I only make
1100   A pleading for this prey of women's
Malice. I feel his own injustice,
Being myself, a daily fellow-sufferer!
[*Baroka seems to realize for the first time that Sidi has paid no attention to his explanation. She is, in fact, still humming and shaking her shoulders. He stares questioningly at her. Sidi stops, somewhat confused and embarrassed, points sheepishly to the wrestler.*]
SIDI: I think this time he will win.
[*Baroka's grumbling subsides slowly. He is now attentive to the present bout.*]
BAROKA: Now let us once again take up
The questioning. [*Almost timidly.*] Is this man
Good and kindly.
SIDI: They say he uses well
His dogs and horses.
BAROKA: [*desperately.*]
Well is he fierce then? Reckless!
1110   Does the bush cow run to hole
When he hears his beaters' Hei-ei-wo-rah!
SIDI: There are heads and skins of leopards
Hung around his council room.
But the market is also
Full of them.

BAROKA: Is he not wise? Is he not sagely?
　Do the young and old not seek
　His counsel?
SIDI: The Fox is said to be wise
　So cunning that he stalks and dines on　　　　　　　　1120
　New-hatched chickens.
BAROKA: [*more and more desperate.*]
　Does he not beget strength on wombs?
　Are his children not tall and stout-limbed?
SIDI: Once upon a time.
BAROKA: Once upon a time?
　What do you mean, girl?
SIDI: Just once upon a time.
　Perhaps his children have of late
　Been plagued with shyness and refuse
　To come into the world. Or else　　　　　　　　　　1130
　He is so tired with the day's affairs
　That at night, he turns his buttocks
　To his wives. But there have been
　No new reeds cut by his servants,
　No new cots woven.
　And his household gods are starved
　For want of child-naming festivities
　Since the last two rains went by.
BAROKA: Perhaps he is a frugal man.
　Mindful of years to come,　　　　　　　　　　　　1140
　Planning for a final burst of life, he
　Husbands his strength.
SIDI: [*giggling. She is actually stopped, half-way, by giggling at the
　cleverness of her remark.*]
　To husband his wives surely ought to be
　A man's first duties — at all times.
BAROKA: My beard tells me you've been a pupil,
　A most diligent pupil of Sadiku.
　Among all shameless women,
　The sharpest tongues grow from that one
　Peeling bark — Sadiku, my faithful lizard!
　[*Growing steadily warmer during this speech, he again slaps down
　his opponent's arm as he shouts 'Sadiku'.*]
SIDI: [*backing away, aware that she has perhaps gone too far and be-
　trayed knowledge of the 'secret'.*]
　I have learnt nothing of anyone.　　　　　　　　　1150
BAROKA: No more. No more.
　Already I have lost a wrestler
　On your account. This town-bred daring
　Of little girls, awakes in me

A seven-horned devil of strength.
Let one woman speak a careless word
And I can pin a wriggling—Bah!
[*Lets go the man's arm. He has risen during the last speech but held
on to the man's arm, who is forced to rise with him.*]
The tappers should have called by now.
See if we have a fresh gourd by the door.
[*The wrestler goes out. Baroka goes to sit on the bed, Sidi eyeing
him, doubtfully.*]

1160   What an ill-tempered man I daily grow
Towards. Soon my voice will be
The sand between two grinding stones.
But I have my scattered kindliness
Though few occasions serve to herald it.
And Sidi, my daughter, you do not know
The thoughts which prompted me
To ask the pleasure that I be your host
This evening, I would not tell Sadiku,
Meaning to give delight
1170   With the surprise of it. Now, tell me, child
Can you guess a little at this thing?
SIDI: Sadiku told me nothing.
BAROKA: You are hasty with denial. For how indeed
Could Sadiku, since I told her
Nothing of my mind, But, my daughter,
Did she not, perhaps . . . invent some tale?
For I know Sadiku loves to be
All-knowing.
SIDI: She said no more, except the Bale
1180   Begged my presence.
BAROKA: [*rises quickly to the bait.*]
Begged? Bale Baroka begged?
[*Wrestler enters with gourd and calabash-cups. Baroka relapses.*]
Ah! I see you love to bait your elders.
One way the world remains the same,
The child still thinks she is wiser than
The cotton head of age.
Do you think Baroka deaf or blind
To little signs? But let that pass.
Only, lest you fall victim to the schemes
Of busy women, I will tell you this—
1190   I know Sadiku plays the match-maker
Without the prompting. If I look
On any maid, or call her name
Even in the course of harmless, neighbourly
Well-wishing—How fares your daughter?

—Is your sister now recovered from her
Whooping cough?—How fast your ward
Approaches womanhood! Have the village lads
Begun to gather at your door?—
Or any word at all which shows I am
The thoughtful guardian of the village health,   1200
If it concerns a woman, Sadiku straightway
Flings herself into the role of go-between
And before I even don a cap, I find
Yet another stranger in my bed!
SIDI: It seems a Bale's life
Is full of great unhappiness.
BAROKA: I do not complain. No, my child
I accept the sweet and sour with
A ruler's grace. I lose my patience
Only when I meet with   1210
The new immodesty with women.
Now, my Sidi, you have not caught
This new and strange disease, I hope.
SIDI: [*curtsying.*] The threading of my smock—
Does Baroka not know the marking
Of the village loom?
BAROKA: But will Sidi, the pride of mothers,
Will she always wear it?
SIDI: Will Sidi, the proud daughter of Baroka,
Will she step out naked?   1220
[*A pause. Baroka surveys Sidi in an almost fatherly manner and she
bashfully drops her eyes.*]
BAROKA: To think that once I thought,
Sidi is the eye's delight, but
She is vain, and her head
Is feather-light, and always giddy
With a trivial thought. And now
I find her deep and wise beyond her years.
[*Reaches under his pillow, brings out the now familiar magazine,
and also an addressed envelope. Retains the former and gives her
the envelope.*]
Do you know what this means?
The trim red piece of paper
In the corner?
SIDI: I know it. A stamp. Lakunle receives   1230
Letters from Lagos marked with it.
BAROKA: [*obviously disappointed.*]
Hm. Lakunle. But more about him
Later. Do you know what it means—
This little frippery?

SIDI: [*very proudly.*]
> Yes. I know that too. Is it not a tax on
> The habit of talking with paper?

BAROKA: Oh. Oh. I see you dip your hand
> Into the pockets of the school teacher
> And retrieve it bulging with knowledge.
> [*Goes to the strange machine, and pulls the lever up and down.*]

1250
> Now this, not even the school teacher can tell
> What magic this performs. Come nearer,
> It will not bite.

SIDI: I have never seen the like.

BAROKA: The work dear child, of the palace blacksmiths
> Built in full secrecy. All is not well with it—
> But I will find the cause and then Ilujinle
> Will boast its own tax on paper, made with
> Stamps like this. For long I dreamt it
> And here it stands, child of my thoughts.

1260
SIDI: [*wonder-struck.*] You mean . . . this will work some day?

BAROKA: Ogun has said the word. And now my girl
> What think you of that image on the stamp
> This spiderwork of iron, wood and mortar?

SIDI: Is it not a bridge?

BAROKA: It is a bridge. The longest—so they say
> In the whole country. When not a bridge,
> You'll find a print of groundnuts
> Stacked like pyramids,
> Or palm trees, or cocoa-trees, and farmers

1270
> Hacking pods, and workmen
> Felling trees and tying skinned logs
> Into rafts. A thousand thousand letters
> By road, by rail, by air,
> From one end of the world to another,
> And not one human head among them;
> Not one head of beauty on the stamp?

SIDI: But I once saw Lakunle's letter
> With a head of bronze.

BAROKA: A figurehead, my child, a lifeless work

1280
> Of craft, with holes for eyes, and coldness
> For the warmth of life and love
> In youthful cheeks like yours,
> My daughter . . .
> [*Pauses to watch the effect on Sidi.*]
> . . . Can you see it, Sidi?
> Tens of thousands of these dainty prints
> And each one with this legend of Sidi.
> [*Flourishes the magazine, open in the middle.*]

The village goddess, reaching out
Towards the sun, her lover.
Can you see it, my daughter!
[*Sidi drowns herself totally in the contemplation, takes the magazine
but does not even look at it. Sits on the bed.*]
BAROKA: [*very gently.*]
    I hope you will not think it too great   1290
A burden, to carry the country's mail
All on your comeliness.
[*Walks away, an almost business-like tone.*]
                                  Our beginnings will
Of course be modest. We shall begin
By cutting stamps for our own village alone.
As the schoolmaster himself would say—
Charity begins at home.
[*Pause. Faces Sidi from nearly the distance of the room.*]
                          For a long time now,
The town-dwellers have made up tales
Of the backwardness of Ilujinle   1300
Until it hurts Baroka, who holds
The welfare of his people deep at heart.
Now, if we do this thing, it will prove more
Than any single town has done!
[*The wrestler, who has been listening open-mouthed, drops his cup
in admiration. Baroka, annoyed, realizing only now in fact that he
is still in the room, waves him impatiently out.*]
I do not hate progress, only its nature
Which makes all roofs and faces look the same.
And the wish of one old man is
That here and there,
[*Goes progressively towards Sidi, until he bends over her, then sits
beside her on the bed.*]
Among the bridges and the murderous roads,
Below the humming birds which   1310
Smoke the face of Sango, dispenser of
The snake-tongue lightning; between this moment
And the reckless broom that will be wielded
In these years to come, we must leave
Virgin plots of lives, rich decay
And the tang of vapour rising from
Forgotten heaps of compost, lying
Undisturbed . . . But the skin of progress
Masks, unknown, the spotted wolf of sameness . . .
Does sameness not revolt your being,   1320
My daughter?
[*Sidi is capable only of a bewildered nod, slowly.*]

BAROKA: [*sighs, hands folded piously on his lap.*]
  I find my soul is sensitive, like yours,
  Indeed, although there is one—no more think I—
  One generation between yours and mine,
  Our thoughts fly crisply through the air
  And meet, purified, as one.
  And our first union
  Is the making of this stamp.
  The one redeeming grace on any paper-tax
1330 Shall be your face. And mine,
  The soul behind it all, worshipful
  Of Nature for her gift of youth
  And beauty to our earth. Does this
  Please you, my daughter?
SIDI: I can no longer see the meaning, Baroka.
  Now that you speak
  Almost like the school teacher, except
  Your words fly on a different path,
  I find . . .
1340 BAROKA: It is a bad thing, then, to sound
  Like your school teacher?
SIDI: No Bale, but words are like beetles
  Boring at my ears, and my head
  Becomes a jumping bean. Perhaps after all,
  As the school teacher tells me often,
  [*Very miserably.*]
  I have a simple mind.
BAROKA: [*pats her kindly on the head.*]
  No, Sidi, not simple, only straight and truthful
  Like a fresh-water reed. But I do find
  Your school teacher and I are much alike.
1350 The proof of wisdom is the wish to learn
  Even from children. And the haste of youth
  Must learn its temper from the gloss
  Of ancient leather, from a strength
  Knit close along the grain. The school teacher
  And I, must learn one from the other.
  Is this not right?
  [*A tearful nod.*]
BAROKA: The old must flow into the new, Sidi,
  Not blind itself or stand foolishly
  Apart. A girl like you must inherit
1360 Miracles which age alone reveals.
  Is this not so?
SIDI: Everything you say, Bale,
  Seems wise to me.

BAROKA: Yesterday's wine alone is strong and blooded, child,
And though the Christians' holy book denies
The truth of this, old wine thrives best
Within a new bottle. The coarseness
Is mellowed down, and the rugged wine
Acquires a full and rounded body . . .
Is this not so—my child?   1370
[*Quite overcome, Sidi nods.*]
BAROKA: Those who know little of Baroka think
His life one pleasure-living course.
But the monkey sweats, my child,
The monkey sweats,
It is only the hair upon his back
Which still deceives the world . . .
[*Sidi's head falls slowly on the Bale's shoulder. The Bale remains in
his final body-weighed-down-by-burdens-of-State attitude.*

*Even before the scene is completely shut off a crowd of dancers
burst in at the front and dance off at the opposite side without
slackening pace. In their brief appearance it should be apparent that
they comprise a group of female dancers pursuing a masked male.
Drumming and shouts continue quite audibly and shortly afterwards. They enter and re-cross the stage in the same manner.*

*The shouts fade away and they next appear at the market clear-
ing. It is now full evening. Lakunle and Sadiku are still waiting for
Sidi's return. The traders are beginning to assemble one by one,
ready for the evening market. Hawkers pass through with oil-lamps
beside their ware. Food sellers enter with cooking-pots and food-
stuffs, set up their 'adogan' or stone hearth and build a fire.*

*All this while, Lakunle is pacing wretchedly, Sadiku looks on
placidly.*]
LAKUNLE: [*he is pacing furiously.*]
He's killed her.
I warned you. You know him,
And I warned you.
[*Goes up all the approaches to look.*]
She's been gone half the day. It will soon   1380
Be daylight. And still no news.
Women have disappeared before.
No trace. Vanished. Now we know how.
[*Checks, turns round.*]
And why!
Mock an old man, will you? So?
You can laugh? Ha ha! You wait.
I'll come and see you
Whipped like a dog. Baroka's head wife
Driven out of the house for plotting

1390 With a girl.
[*Each approaching footstep brings Lakunle to attention, but it is only a hawker or a passer-by. The wrestler passes. Sadiku greets him familiarly. Then, after he has passed, some significance of this breaks on Sadiku and she begins to look a little puzzled.*]
LAKUNLE: I know he has dungeons. Secret holes
Where a helpless girl will lie
And rot for ever. But not for nothing
Was I born a man. I'll find my way
To rescue her. She little deserves it, but
I shall risk my life for her.
[*The mummers can now be heard again, distantly. Sadiku and Lakunle become attentive as the noise approaches, Lakunle increasingly uneasy. A little, but not too much notice is paid by the market people.*]
What is that?
SADIKU: If my guess is right, it will be mummers.
[*Adds slyly.*]
Somebody must have told them the news.
1400 LAKUNLE: What news?
[*Sadiku chuckles darkly and comprehension breaks on the School teacher.*]
Baroka! You dared . . . ?
Woman, is there no mercy in your veins?
He gave you children, and he stood
Faithfully by you and them.
He risked his life that you may boast
A warrior-hunter for your lord . . . But you—
You sell him to the rhyming rabble
Gloating in your disloyalty . . .
SADIKU: [*calmly dips her hand in his pocket.*]
Have you any money?
LAKUNLE: [*snatching out her hand.*]
1410 Why? What? . . . Keep away, witch! Have you
Turned pickpocket in your dotage?
SADIKU: Don't be a miser. Will you let them go without giving you a special performance?
LAKUNLE: If you think I care for their obscenity . . .
SADIKU: [*wheedling.*] Come on, school teacher. They'll expect it of you . . . The man of learning . . . the young sprig of foreign wisdom . . . You must not demean yourself in their eyes . . . you must give them money to perform for your lordship . . .

[*Re-enter the mummers, dancing straight through (more centrally this time) as before. Male dancer enters first, pursued by a number of young women and other choral idlers. The man dances in tortured movements. He and about half of his pursuers have already danced off-stage on the opposite side when Sadiku dips her hand briskly in Lakunle's pocket, this time with greater success. Before Lakunle can stop her, she has darted to the drummers and pressed a coin apiece on their foreheads, waving them to possession of the floor. Tilting their heads backwards, they drum her praises. Sadiku denies the credit, points to Lakunle as the generous benefactor. They transfer their attention to him where he stands biting his lips at the trick. The other dancers have now been brought back and the drummers resume the beat of the interrupted dance. The treasurer removes the coins from their foreheads and places them in a pouch. Now begins the dance of virility which is of course none other than the Baroka story. Very athletic movements. Even in his prime, 'Baroka' is made a comic figure, held in a kind of tolerant respect by his women. At his decline and final downfall, they are most un- sparing in their taunts and tantalizing motions. Sadiku has never stopped bouncing on her toes through the dance, now she is done the honour of being invited to join at the kill. A dumb show of bashful refusals, then she joins them, reveals surprising agility for her age, to the wild enthusiasm of the rest who surround and spur her on.*

With 'Baroka' finally scotched, the crowd dances away to their incoming movement, leaving Sadiku to dance on oblivious of their departure. The drumming becomes more distant and she unwraps her eyelids. Sighs, looks around her and walks contentedly towards Lakunle. As usual he has enjoyed the spectacle in spite of himself, showing especial relish where 'Baroka' gets the worst of it from his women. Sadiku looks at him for a moment while he tries to replace his obvious enjoyment with disdain. She shouts 'Boo' at him, and breaks into a dance movement, shakes a sudden leg at Lakunle.]

SADIKU: Sadiku of the duiker's feet . . . that's what the men used to call me. I could twist and untwist my waist with the smoothness of a water snake . . .   1420

LAKUNLE: No doubt. And you are still just as slippery.
I hope Baroka kills you for this.
When he finds out what your wagging tongue
Has done to him, I hope he beats you
Till you choke on your own breath . . .
[*Sidi bursts in, she has been running all the way. She throws herself on the ground against the tree and sobs violently, beating herself on the ground.*]

SADIKU: [*on her knees beside her.*] Why, child. What is the matter?
SIDI: [*pushes her off.*]
Get away from me. Do not touch me.
LAKUNLE: [*with a triumphant smile, he pulls Sadiku away and takes her place.*]
Oh, Sidi, let me kiss your tears . . .

SIDI: [*pushes him so hard that he sits down abruptly.*]
1430   Don't touch me.

LAKUNLE: [*dusting himself.*]
     He must have beaten her.
     Did I not warn you both?
     Baroka is a creature of the wilds,
     Untutored, mannerless, devoid of grace.
     [*Sidi only cries all the more, beats on the ground with clenched fists
     and stubs her toes in the ground.*]
     Chief though he is,
     I shall kill him for this . . .
     No. Better still, I shall demand
     Redress from the central courts.
     I shall make him spend
1440   The remainder of his wretched life
     In prison—with hard labour.
     I'll teach him
     To beat defenceless women . . .

SIDI: [*lifting her head.*]
     Fool! You little fools! It was a lie.
     The frog. The cunning frog!
     He lied to you, Sadiku.

SADIKU: Sango forbid!

SIDI: He told me . . . afterwards, crowing.
     It was a trick.
1450   He knew Sadiku would not keep it to herself,
     That I, or maybe other maids would hear of it
     And go to mock his plight.
     And how he laughed!
     How his frog-face croaked and croaked
     And called me little fool!
     Oh how I hate him! How I loathe
     And long to kill the man!

LAKUNLE: [*retreating.*] But Sidi, did he . . . ? I mean . . .
     Did you escape?
     [*Louder sobs from Sidi.*]
1460   Speak, Sidi, this is agony.
     Tell me the worst; I'll take it like a man.
     Is it the fright which effects you so,
     Or did he . . . ? Sidi, I cannot bear the thought.
     The words refuse to form.
     Do not unman me, Sidi. Speak
     Before I burst in tears.

SADIKU: [*raises Sidi's chin in her hand.*]
     Sidi, are you a maid or not?
     [*Sidi shakes her head violently and bursts afresh in tears.*]

LAKUNLE: The Lord forbid!
SADIKU: Too late for prayers. Cheer up. It happens to the best of us.
LAKUNLE: Oh heavens, strike me dead! 1470
    Earth, open up and swallow Lakunle.
    For he no longer has the wish to live.
    Let the lightning fall and shrivel me
    To dust and ashes . . .
    [*Recoils.*]
    No, that wish is cowardly. This trial is my own.
    Let Sango and his lightning keep out of this. It
    Is my cross, and let it not be spoken that
    In the hour of need, Lakunle stood
    Upon the scales and was proved wanting.
    My love is selfless—the love of spirit 1480
    Not of flesh.
    [*Stands over Sidi.*]
    Dear Sidi, we shall forget the past.
    This great misfortune touches not
    The treasury of my love.
    But you will agree, it is only fair
    That we forget the bride-price totally
    Since you no longer can be called a maid.
    Here is my hand; if on these terms,
    You'll be my cherished wife.
    We'll take an oath, between us three 1490
    That this shall stay
    A secret to our dying days . . .
    [*Takes a look at Sadiku and adds quickly.*]
    Oh no, a secret even after we're dead and gone.
    And if Baroka dares to boast of it,
    I'll swear he is a liar—and swear by Sango too!
    [*Sidi raises herself slowly, staring at Lakunle with unbelieving eyes.*
    She is unsmiling, her face a puzzle.]
SIDI: You would? You would marry me?
LAKUNLE: [*puffs out his chest.*] Yes.
    [*Without a change of expression, Sidi dashes suddenly off the stage.*]
SADIKU: What on earth has got into her?
LAKUNLE: I wish I knew
    She took off suddenly 1500
    Like a hunted buck.
    [*Looks off-stage.*]
    I think—yes, she is,
    She is going home.
    Sadiku, will you go?
    Find out if you can
    What she plans to do.

[*Sadiku nods and goes. Lakunle walks up and down.*]
And now I know I am the biggest fool
That ever walked this earth.
There are women to be found
In every town or village in these parts,
And every one a virgin.
But I obey my books.
[*Distant music. Light drums, flutes, box-guitars, 'sekere'.*]
'Man takes the fallen woman by the hand'
And ever after they live happily.
Moreover, I will admit,
It solves the problem of her bride-price too.
A man must live or fall by his true
Principles. That, I had sworn,
Never to pay.
[*Enter Sadiku.*]

SADIKU: She is packing her things. She is gathering her clothes and
trinkets together, and oiling herself as a bride does before her
wedding.

LAKUNLE: Heaven help us! I am not impatient.
Surely she can wait a day or two at least.
There is the asking to be done,
And then I have to hire a praise-singer,
And such a number of ceremonies
Must firstly be performed.

SADIKU: Just what I said but she only laughed at me and called me a
. . . a . . . what was it now . . . a bra . . . braba . . . brabararian. It
serves you right. It all comes of your teaching. I said what about the
asking and the other ceremonies. And she looked at me and said,
leave all that nonsense to savages and brabararians.

LAKUNLE: But I must prepare myself.
I cannot be
A single man one day and a married one the next.
It must come gradually.
I will not wed in haste.
A man must have time to prepare,
To learn to like the thought.
I must think of my pupils too:
Would they be pleased if I were married
Not asking their consent . . . ?
[*The singing group is now audible even to him.*]
What is that? The musicians?
Could they have learnt so soon?

SADIKU: The news of a festivity travels fast. You ought to know that.

LAKUNLE: The goddess of malicious gossip
Herself must have a hand in my undoing.

1510

1520

1530

1540

The very spirits of the partial air
Have all conspired to blow me, willy-nilly   1550
Down the slippery slope of grim matrimony.
What evil have I done . . . ? Ah, here they come!
[*Enter crowd and musicians.*]
Go back. You are not needed yet. Nor ever.
Hence parasites, you've made a big mistake.
There is no one getting wedded; get you home.
[*Sidi now enters. In one hand she holds a bundle, done up in a
richly embroidered cloth: in the other the magazine. She is radiant,
jewelled, lightly clothed, and wears light leather-thong sandals. They
all go suddenly silent except for the long-drawn O-Ohs of admira-
tion. She goes up to Lakunle and hands him the book.*]
SIDI: A present from Sidi.
    I tried to tear it up
    But my fingers were too frail.
    [*To the crowd.*]
    Let us go.
    [*To Lakunle.*]
    You may come too if you wish,   1560
    You are invited.
LAKUNLE: [*lost in the miracle of transformation.*]
    Well I should hope so indeed
    Since I am to marry you.
SIDI: [*turns round in surprise.*]
    Marry who . . . ? You thought . . .
    Did you really think that you, and I . . .
    Why, did you think that after him,
    I could endure the touch of another man?
    I who have felt the strength,
    The perpetual youthful zest
    Of the panther of the trees?   1570
    And would I choose a watered-down,
    A beardless version of unripened man?
LAKUNLE: [*bars her way.*]
    I shall not let you.
    I shall protect you from yourself.
SIDI: [*gives him a shove that sits him down again, hard against the
    tree base.*]
    Out of my way, book-nourished shrimp.
    Do you see what strength he has given me?
    That was not bad. For a man of sixty,
    It was the secret of God's own draught
    A deed for drums and ballads.
    But you, at sixty, you'll be ten years dead!   1580
    In fact, you'll not survive your honeymoon . . .

Come to my wedding if you will. If not . . .
[*She shrugs her shoulders. Kneels down at Sadiku's feet.*]
Mother of brides, your blessing . . .

SADIKU: [*lays her hand on Sidi's head.*] I invoke the fertile gods. They will stay with you. May the time come soon when you shall be as round-bellied as a full moon in a low sky.

SIDI: [*hands her the bundle.*]
Now bless my worldly goods.
[*Turns to the musicians.*]
Come, sing to me of seeds
Of children, sired of the lion stock.
[*The Musicians resume their tune. Sidi sings and dances.*]

1590
Mo te'ni. Mo te'ni.
Mo te'ni. Mo te'ni.
Sun mo mi, we mo mi
Sun mo mi, fa mo mi
Yarabi lo m'eyi t'o le d'omo . . .

[*Festive air, fully pervasive. Oil lamps from the market multiply as traders desert their stalls to join them. A young girl flaunts her dancing buttocks at Lakunle and he rises to the bait. Sadiku gets in his way as he gives chase. Tries to make him dance with her. Lakunle last seen, having freed himself of Sadiku, clearing a space in the crowd for the young girl.*

The crowd repeat the song after Sidi.]

Tolani Tolani
T'emi ni T'emi ni
Sun mo mi, we mo mi
Sun mo mi, fa mo mi
Yarabi lo m'eyi t'o le d'omo.

❏ Questions for Discussion
Morning

1. What causes the conflict between Sidi and Lakunle? How thorough or deep is Lakunle's understanding and imitation of Western culture?

2. How does Western culture conflict with the village culture? How does the photograph in the magazine change Sidi?

3. Why is the custom of the bride-price so important to Sidi? Why is it just the opposite for Lakunle?

Afternoon

1. What is the position of Baroka, the Bale? What are his titles?

2. What would happen to Sidi if she married the Bale? Why does she not want to marry him?

Night

1. How does the Bale compare in wisdom and understanding with the other characters? What kind of a ruler is he and what kind of relationship does he have with his people?

2. Why is the word *jewel* emphasized? In what ways is Sidi like a jewel?

3. How or why does Sadiku think that she is stronger than the Lion? What does she mean by "Ah, take warning, my masters, we'll scotch you in the end"?

4. What tricks does Baroka use to seduce Sidi? What does he mean by "old wine thrives best / within a new bottle"? Is he simply deceptive, or is there truth in what he says?

5. One might say the essential conflict in this play pits a beautiful young girl's desire for freedom against the community and tribal tradition. In the world of this play which is more important? Why?

6. In a traditional tragic plot the action moves from disorder to order at great cost. On the other hand, in a traditional comic plot the action moves from disorder to order without great cost. What are the sources of disorder and order in Soyinka's play? What is the cost of restoring order?

7. The play is divided into "Morning," "Afternoon," and "Night" rather than conventional acts and scenes. Why do you think Soyinka chose these divisions?

❏ **Suggestions for Exploration and Writing**

1. Examine the dramatic function of the three elaborately described dance scenes in the play. How do the dances enhance the play's **comedy?** How do they develop its **theme, plot,** and **characters?**

2. Analyze in detail the **conflict** developed in this play between tribal or family tradition and individual dignity and freedom.

3. Trace the growth of Sidi through the course of the play.

4. Lakunle does not convert the village to modernism: modern roads, revocation of the bride-price, monogamy, and so forth.

Write an essay discussing aspects of your culture or ethnic group that you do not want absorbed into the overall American culture.

5. Using the play as background, compare and/or contrast modern American marriage customs and the Yoruban customs depicted in Soyinka's play.

❏ **Suggestions for Writing**

1. Using one selection from this unit, discuss how the author shows the delicate balance between freedom and responsibility.

2. Choose one short story from this section and relate what that work says about the responsibilities a person has to others in society.

3. When is an individual obligated to disobey government regulations or laws? Using at least one work from this section, write an essay answering this question.

4. From your own experience or knowledge, explain how one's own freedom may be limited by the obligation to allow others to be free.

5. Write an essay describing the responsibilities to others that members of a civilized and organized society are expected to fulfill. Or write an essay describing the results, in the United States or in another country, of a failure to fulfill such responsibilities.

ART AND
LANGUAGE

WE ARE ALL ARTISTS, AND ART IS FOR ALL OF US. Too often our society treats art as ancient Egyptian priests treated the gods they worshipped: as the exclusive preserve of an initiated elite to be revered and protected from the uninitiated masses. We distort paintings by putting them behind glass in museums, and we dutifully applaud a Beethoven symphony at just the right moment, looking with frozen faces and condemnatory nods at those uninitiated who applaud at inappropriate times. Such treasures as great paintings and symphonies, we seem to say, need to be preserved and are not, as Dee-Wangero says of her sister's quilts in Alice Walker's story, for "everyday use."

As surely as in the painting by Renoir, the Beethoven played to a dutifully hushed audience, and the Shakespeare play delivered in resonant British accent, art is found in the street guitarist, the break dancer whose energy and grace leave spectators breathless, and the joke artfully told with perfect timing between (or even during) classes. Shakespeare's original audiences probably had more in common with the audience at a modern professional wrestling match or a hockey game than with the audience at a modern production of one of his plays. As Chinua Achebe shows in his essay "Africa and Her Writers," in most traditional cultures, art has been produced by and for people, not for an initiated elite. In the elaborate Igbo art festival called Mbari, Achebe finds art that embodies the heritage and values of and that is produced for, and even in a sense by, a whole people. Similarly, the quilts, gardens, and blues songs in Alice Walker's essay and stories represent a whole way of life—the expression of a people's experience, heritage, and values. And even a highly regarded and difficult mainstream poet like William Butler Yeats (see "Sailing to Byzantium" in the Quest unit), longed for a shared mythology that could integrate his art with the practical and religious life of his people.

Art, then, is an expression of the life of a community. It draws sustenance from that life and in turn enriches and directs it. For the men in Walter Van Tilburg Clark's "The Portable Phonograph," art alone gives them a direction and reason for living in a bleak world. The line between life and art is obscured in Woody Allen's hilarious short story "The Kugelmass Episode" as Kugelmass enters the fictional world of Gustave Flaubert's Madame Bovary to have an affair with the title character. Finally, art may even threaten to consume the reader as it does at the end of Allen's story and in Ishmael Reed's "beware : do not read this poem."

One might broadly define art as an expression of the human mind as it plays with various materials, called media. Such play is serious business. Though work may be thought of as serious and play as trivial, play is often taken much more seriously than work and is given much more attention. Our performance on the golf course or our favorite team's play on the football field often excites us more than anything we do at work. Art is a particularly serious and concentrated form of play. Paradoxically, it is also intensely pleasurable. In "Persimmons," for example, Li-Young Lee has great fun exploring the full implications of the word *persimmons* at the expense of his pedantic teacher. In the tales of hunters analyzed by Barry Lopez in "Landscape and Narrative," serious attention to the right word, the right detail, is both pleasurable and essential. The resulting artful tale gives a tremendous sense of order and satisfaction. From the magnificent quilts and the immaculate gardens of black women, to the artfully told tales of hunters, to the hilarious misadventures of Kugelmass transported into a classic novel, the works in this unit are variations on the common theme of the paradoxical nature of artistic play, at once intensely serious and intensely joyful.

ESSAYS

CHINUA ACHEBE (1930–   )

Chinua Achebe, a Nigerian novelist and man of letters who writes in English, is among the most highly respected and influential contemporary African authors. Achebe's early novels, Things Fall Apart *(1959),* No Longer at Ease *(1962), and* Arrow of Gold *(1964), explore the conflict between traditional tribal customs and the European values introduced by colonists. His later novels,* A Man of the People *(1964) and* Anthills of the Savannah *(1988), expose the corruption and conflicts in postcolonial Nigerian politics.* Morning Yet on Creation Day *(1975), from which the following essay comes, is a collection of essays on the search for a genuinely Nigerian voice in letters.*

Africa and Her Writers

1   Some time ago, in a very testy mood, I began a lecture with these words: *Art for art's sake is just another piece of deodorized dog shit.*

Today, and particularly in these sublime and hallowed precincts,[1] I should be quite prepared to modify my language if not my opinion. In other words I will still insist that art is, and was always, in the service of man. Our ancestors created their myths and legends and told their stories for a human purpose (including, no doubt, the excitation of wonder and pure delight); they made their sculptures in wood and terra cotta, stone and bronze to serve the needs of their times. Their artists lived and moved and had their being in society and created their works for the good of that society.

I have just used the word *good,* which no decent man uses in polite society these days, and must hasten to explain. By *good* I do not mean moral uplift, although—why not?—that would be part of it; I mean *good* in the sense in which God at the end of each day's work of putting the world together saw that what He had made was good. Then, and only then, did He count it a day's job. *Good* in that sense does not mean pretty.

In the beginning art was good and useful; it always had its airy and magical qualities, of course; but even the magic was often intended to minister to a basic human need, to serve a down-to-earth necessity, as when the cavemen drew pictures on the rock of animals they hoped to kill in their next hunt!

But somewhere in the history of European civilization the idea that art should be accountable to no one, and needed to justify itself to nobody except itself, began to emerge. In the end it became a minor god and its devotees became priests urging all who are desirous to approach its altar to banish entirely from their hearts and minds such doubts and questions as *What use is this to me?* as the ultimate irreverence and profanation. Words like *use, purpose, value* are beneath the divine concerns of this Art, and so are we, the vulgarians craving the message and the morality. This Art exists independently of us, of all mankind. Man and his world may indeed pass away but not a jot from the laws of this Art.

Do I exaggerate? Perhaps a little, but not too much, I think. True, Edgar Allan Poe's famous lecture, "The Poetic Principle," may not now be the gospel it was to earlier generations, but the romantic idea of "the poem written solely for the poem's sake" still exerts a curious fascination on all kinds of people. I remember my surprise a few years ago at a conference of African writers when some obscure Rhodesian poet announced solemnly that a good poem writes itself. I very rarely wish writers ill, but that day I would have been happy if Shango had silenced that one with a nicely aimed thunderbolt and given his ghost the eternal joy of watching new poems surface onto his earthly notebook (or whatever he scribbled his verses on).

---

[1] Eliot House, Harvard University.

6   Strangely enough (or perhaps not so strangely—perhaps we should
rather say, appropriately) there is from the same European mainspring
another stream flowing down the slopes on the other side of the hill,
watering a different soil and sustaining a different way of life. There, on
these other slopes, a poet is not a poet until the Writers' Union tells him
so. Between these two peoples, an acrimonious argument rages. Each side
hurls invective over the hill into the other camp. *Monstrous philistines!*
Corrupt, decadent! So loud and bitter does the recrimination become that
it is often difficult to believe that these two peoples actually live on two
slopes of the same hill.

7   Once upon a time (according to my own adaptation of a favorite
Yoruba story), two farmers were working their farms on either side of a
road. As they worked they made friendly conversation across the road.
Then Eshu, god of fate and lover of confusion, decided to upset the state
of peace between them. A god with a sharp and nimble imagination, he
took his decision as quickly as lightning. He rubbed one side of his body
with white chalk and the other side with charcoal and walked *up* the road
with considerable flourish between the farmers. As soon as he passed
beyond earshot the two men jumped from their work at the same time.
And one said: "Did you notice that extraordinary white man who has
just gone up the road?" In the same breath the other asked: "Did you see
that incredible black man I have just seen?" In no time at all the friendly
questions turned into a violent argument and quarrel, and finally into a
fight. As they fought they screamed: *He was white! He was black!* After
they had belabored themselves to their heart's content they went back to
their farms and resumed their work in gloomy and hostile silence. But no
sooner had they settled down than Eshu returned and passed with even
greater flourish between them *down* the road. Immediately the two men
sprang up again. And one said: "I am sorry, my good friend. You were
right; the fellow is white." And in the same breath the other farmer was
saying: "I do apologize for my blindness. The man is indeed black, just
as you said." And in no time again the two were quarreling and then
fighting. As they fought this time, they shouted: *I was wrong! No, I was*
wrong!

8   The recrimination between capitalist and communist aesthetics in our
time is, of course, comparable to the first act of the farmers' drama—the
fight for the exclusive claim on righteousness and truth. Perhaps Eshu
will return one day and pass again between them down the road and
inaugurate the second act—the fight for self-abasement, for a monopoly
on guilt.

9   As African writers emerge onto the world stage, they come under
pressure to declare their stand. Now, I am not one for opposing an idea
or a proposition simply on the grounds that it is "un-African"—a common enough ploy of obscurantist self-interest; thus a modern leader
anxious to continue unchallenged his business of transforming public
wealth into a dynastic fortune will often tell you that socialism (which,

quite rightly scares the daylights out of him) is un-African. We are not talking about *his* concern for Africanness. But there seems to me to be a genuine need for African writers to pause momentarily and consider whether anything in traditional African aesthetics will fit their contemporary condition.

Let me give one example from Nigeria. Among the Owerri Igbo there was a colorful ceremony called *mbari,* a profound affirmation of the people's belief in the indivisibility of art and society. Mbari was performed at the behest of the Earth goddess, Ala, the most powerful deity in the Igbo pantheon, for she was not only the owner of the soil but also controller of morality and creativity, artistic and biological. Every so many years Ala would instruct the community through her priest to prepare a festival of images in her honor. That night the priest would travel through the town, knocking on many doors to announce to the various households whom of their members Ala had chosen for the great work. These chosen men and women then moved into seclusion in a forest clearing, and under the instruction and guidance of master artists and craftsmen, began to build a house of images. The work might take a year or even two, but as long as it lasted the workers were deemed to be hallowed and were protected from undue contact from, and distraction by, the larger community. 10

The finished temple was architecturally simple—two side walls and a back wall under a high thatched roof. Steps ran the full width of the temple, ascending backward and upward almost to the roof. But in spite of the simplicity of its structure, mbari was often a miracle of artistic achievement—a breathtaking concourse of images in bright, primary colors. Since the enterprise was in honor of Ala, most of the work was done in her own materials—simple molded earth. But the execution turned this simple material into finished images of startling power and diversity. The goddess had a central seat, usually with a child on her knee—a telling juxtaposition of formidable (even, implacable) power and gentleness. Then there were other divinities; there were men, women, beasts, and birds, real or imaginary. Indeed, the total life of the community was reflected—scenes of religious duty, of day-to-day tasks and diversions, and even of village scandal. The work completed, the village declared a feast and a holiday to honor the goddess of creativity and her children, the makers of images. 11

This brief and inadequate description can give no idea of the impact of mbari. Even the early Christian missionaries who were shocked by the frankness of some of the portrayals couldn't quite take their eyes off! But all I want to do is to point out one or two of the aesthetic ideas underlying mbari. First, the making of art is not the exclusive concern of a particular caste or secret society. Those young men and women whom the goddess chose for the re-enactment of creation were not "artists." They were ordinary members of society. Next time around, the choice would fall on other people. Of course, mere nomination would not turn 12 every man into an artist—not even divine appointment could guarantee it. The discipline, instruction, and guidance of a master artist would be necessary. But not even a conjunction of those two conditions would insure infallibly the emergence of a new, exciting sculptor or painter. But mbari was not looking for that. It was looking for, and saying, something else: *There is no rigid barrier between makers of culture and its consumers. Art belongs to all and is a "function" of society.* When Senghor insists with such obvious conviction that every man is a poet, he is responding, I think, to this holistic concern of our traditional societies.

13   All this will, I dare say, sound like abominable heresy in the ears of mystique lovers. For their sake and their comfort, let me hasten to add that the idea of mbari does not deny the place or importance of the master with unusual talent and professional experience. Indeed it highlights such gift and competence by bringing them into play on the seminal potentialities of the community. Again, mbari does not deny the need for the creative artist to go apart from time to time so as to commune with himself, to look inwardly into his own soul. For when the festival is over, the villagers return to their normal lives again, and the master artists to their work and contemplation. But they can never after this experience, this creative communal enterprise, become strangers again to one another. And by logical and physical extension the greater community, which comes to the unveiling of the art and then receives its makers again into its normal life, becomes a beneficiary—indeed an active partaker—of this experience.

14   If one believes, as many seem to do in some so-called advanced cultures, that the hallmark of a true artist is the ability to ignore society (and paradoxically demand at the same time its attention and homage), then one must find the ruling concerns of mbari somewhat undramatic. Certainly no artist reared within the mbari culture could aspire to humiliate his community by hanging his canvas upside down in an exhibition and, withdrawing to a corner, watching viewers extol its many fine and hidden points with much nodding of the head and outpouring of sophisticated jargon. Could a more appalling relationship be imagined? And the artist who so blatantly dramatizes it has more to answer for than all those pathetic courtiers lost in admiration of the emperor's new clothes, desperately hiding in breathless garrulity the blankness of their vision. *They* are only victims of an irresponsible monarch's capriciousness. And quite rightly, it is not they but the emperor himself who suffers the ultimate humiliation.

15   There is, of course, a deep political implication to all this. The Igbo society from which the example of mbari was taken is notorious for its unbridled republicanism. A society that upholds and extols an opposing political system is likely to take a different cultural viewpoint. For example, the European aesthetic, which many African writers are accepting so uncritically, developed in a rigid oligarchical culture in which kings and their nobilities in the past cultivated a taste different from the

common appetite. And since they monopolized the resources of the realm, they were able to buy over the artists in the society through diverse bribes, inducements, and patronage to minister to this taste. Thus over many generations a real differentiation occurred between aristocratic culture and the common culture. The latter, having no resources to develop itself, went into stagnation. Of course, there is such a thing as poetic justice, and in the fullness of time the high culture, living so long in rarefied reaches of the upper atmosphere, became sick. Somehow it sensed that unless it made contact again with the ground it would surely die. So it descended to the earthy, stagnant pool of the common culture and began to fish out between delicate beaks such healing tidbits as four-letter words.

Where does the African writer come in, in all this? Quite frankly he is   16
confused. Sometimes—in a spasmodic seizure of confidence—he feels called upon to save Europe and the West by giving them Africa's peculiar gifts of healing, irrigating (in the words of Senghor) the Cartesian rationalism of Europe with black sensitivity through the gift of emotion. In his poem *Prayer to Masks* we are those very children called to sacrifice their lives like the poor man his last garment,

> So that hereafter we may cry "hear" at the rebirth of the
>   world being the leaven that the white flour needs.
> For who else would teach rhythm to the world that has
> died   of machines and cannons?
> For who else should ejaculate the cry of joy that arouses
> the   dead and the wise in a new dawn?
> Say who else could return the memory of life to men with a
>   torn hope?

And in his famous poem *New York* he tells that amazing metropolis   17
what it must do to be saved.

> New York! I say to you: New York let black blood flow
> into   your blood
> That it may rub the rust from your steel joints, like an oil
> of   life
> That it may give to your bridges the bend of buttocks and
> the   suppleness of creepers.

The trouble is that personally I am not so sure of things to be able to   18
claim for Africa such a messianic mission in the world. In the first place we would be hard put to it "in our present condition of health" (to use a common Nigerian cliché) to save anybody. In the second place the world may not wish to be saved, even if Africa had the power to.

In talking about the world here we really mean Europe and the West.   19
But we have all got into the bad habit of regarding that slice of the globe as the whole thing. That an African writer can so easily slip into this error is a tribute to its hold upon the contemporary imagination. For those of

Europe and the West, such a habit if not entirely excusable is at least understandable. It can even be amusing in a harmless way, as when, for example, a game between Cincinnati and Minnesota is called the World Series. But it ceases to be funny when it consigns other continents and peoples into a kind of limbo; and it begins to border on the grotesque when these continents and peoples come to accept this view of the world and of themselves.

20 Senghor's solicitude for the health and happiness of Europe may indeed have a ring of quixotic adventure about it, but at least it seems to be rooted in a positive awareness of self. Not so some of the more recent—and quite bizarre—fashions in African literature; for example, the near-pathological eagerness to contract the sicknesses of Europe in the horribly mistaken belief that our claim to sophistication is improved thereby. I am talking, of course, about the *human-condition* syndrome. Presumably European art and literature have every good reason for going into a phase of despair. But ours does not. The worst we can afford at present is disappointment. Perhaps when we too have overreached our-selves in technical achievement without spiritual growth, we shall be entitled to despair. Or, who knows? We may even learn from the history of others and avoid that particular fate. But whether we shall learn or not, there seems to me no sense whatever in rushing out now, so prematurely, to an assignation with a cruel destiny that will not be stirring from her place for a long time yet.

21 There is a brilliant Ghanaian novelist, Ayi Kwei Armah, who seems to me to be in grave danger of squandering his enormous talent and energy in pursuit of the *human condition*. In an impressive first novel, *The Beautyful Ones Are Not Yet Born,* he gives us a striking parable of corruption in Ghana society and of one man who refuses to be contaminated by this filth.

22 It is a well-written book. Armah's command of language and imagery is of a very high order indeed. But it is a sick book. Sick, not with the sickness of Ghana, but with the sickness of the *human condition.* The hero, pale and passive and nameless—a creation in the best manner of existentialist writing—wanders through the story in an anguished half-sleep, neck-deep in despair and human excrement of which we see rather a lot in the book. Did I say he *refused* to be corrupted? He did not do anything as positive as refusing. He reminded me very strongly of that man and woman in a Jean-Paul Sartre novel who sit in anguished gloom in a restaurant and then in a sudden access of nihilistic energy seize table knives and stab their hands right through to the wood—to prove some very obscure point to each other. Except that Armah's hero would be quite incapable of suffering any seizure.

23 Ultimately the novel failed to convince me. And this was because Armah insists that this story is happening in Ghana and not in some modern, existentialist no man's land. He throws in quite a few realistic ingredients like Kwame Nkrumah to prove it. And that is a mistake. Just

as the hero is nameless, so should everything else be; and Armah might have gotten away with a modern, "universal" story. Why did he not opt simply for that easy choice? I don't know. But I am going to be super-stitious and say that Africa probably seized hold of his subconscious and insinuated there this deadly obligation—deadly, that is, to universalistic pretentions—to use his considerable talents in the service of a particular people and a particular place. Could it be that under this pressure Armah attempts to tell what Europe would call a modern story and Africa a moral fable, at the same time; to relate the fashions of European litera-ture to the men and women of Ghana? He tried very hard. But his Ghana is unrecognizable. This aura of cosmic sorrow and despair is as foreign and unusable as those monstrous machines Nkrumah was said to have imported from Eastern European countries. Said, that is, by critics like Armah.

True, Ghana was sick. And what country is not? But everybody has his 24 own brand of ailment. Ayi Kwei Armah imposes so much foreign met-aphor on the sickness of Ghana that it ceases to be true. And finally, the suggestion (albeit existentially tentative) of the hero's personal justifica-tion without faith nor works is grossly inadequate in a society where even a lunatic walking stark naked through the highways of Accra has an extended family somewhere suffering vicarious shame.

Armah is clearly an alienated writer, a modern writer complete with all 25 the symptoms. Unfortunately Ghana is not a modern existentialist coun-try. It is just a Western African state struggling to become a nation. So there is enormous distance between Armah and Ghana. There is some-thing scornful, cold and remote about Armah's obsession with the filth of Ghana:

> Left-hand fingers in their careless journey from a hasty anus sliding all the way up the banister as their owners made the return trip from the lavatory downstairs to the office above. Right-hand fin-gers still dripping with the after-piss and the stale sweat from fat crotches. The callused palms of messengers after they had blown their clogged noses reaching for a convenient place to leave the well-rubbed moisture. Afternoon hands not entirely licked clean of palm soup and remnants of *kenkey*. . . .

You have to go to certain European writers on Africa to find something 26 of the same attitude and icy distance:

> Fada is the ordinary native town of the Western Sudan. It has no beauty, convenience or health. It is a dwelling place at one stage from the rabbit warren and the badger burrow; and not so cleanly kept as the latter. It is . . . built on its own rubbish heaps, without charm even of antiquity. Its squalor and its stinks are all new. . . . All its mud walls are eaten as if by small-pox. . . . Its people would not know the change if time jumped back fifty thousand years.

> They live like mice or rats in a palace floor; all the magnificence and variety of the arts, the learning and the battles of civilization go on over their heads and they do not even imagine them.

27   That is from Joyce Cary's famous novel, *Mister Johnson,* "the best novel ever written about Africa" according to *Time* magazine. Joyce Cary was an alien writing about Africa; Ayi Kwei Armah is the alienated native. It seems that to achieve the modern alienated stance an African writer will end up writing like some white District Officer.

28   There are African writers who are prepared to say they are not African writers but just writers. It is a sentiment guaranteed to win applause in Western circles. But it is a statement of defeat. A man is never more defeated than when he is running away from himself. When Pablo Neruda received the Nobel Prize for Literature in 1971, he said:

> I belong to all the people of Latin America, a little of whose soul I have tried to interpret.

29   I wonder what an African writer would have said. Perhaps "I belong to the universe, all of whose soul I have successfully interpreted."

30   I know the source of our problem, of course. *Anxiety.* Africa has had such a fate in the world that the very adjective *African* can still call up hideous fears of rejection. Better then to cut all links with this homeland, this liability, and become in one giant leap the universal man. Indeed, I understand the anxiety. But running away from myself seems to me a very inadequate way of dealing with an anxiety. And if writers should opt for such escapism, who is to meet the challenge?

31   Sometimes this problem appears in almost comical forms. A young Nigerian poet living and teaching in New York sent me in Nigeria a poem for the literary magazine I edit. It was a good poem but in one of his lines he used a plural Italian word as if it were a singular. And there was no reason I could see for invoking poetic license. So I made the slightest alteration imaginable in the verb to correct this needless error. The bright, young poet, instead of thanking me, wrote an angry and devastating letter in which he accused me of being a grammarian. I didn't mind that, really; it was a new kind of accusation. But in his final crushing statement he contrasted the linguistic conservatism of those who live in the outposts of the empire with the imaginative freedom of the dwellers of the metropolis.

32   At first I thought of replying but in the end decided it was a waste of my time. If I had replied, I would have agreed with him about our respective locations, but would have gone on to remind him that the outposts had always borne the historic role of defending the empire from the constant threat of the barbarian hordes; and so needed always to be awake and alert, unlike the easygoing, soft-living metropolis.

33   But jokes apart, this incident is really a neat parable of the predicament of the African writer in search of universality. He has been misled into

thinking that the metropolis belongs to him. Well, not yet. For him there is still the inescapable grammar of values to straighten out, the confused vocabulary of fledgling polities. Ease and carelessness in our circumstance will only cause a total breakdown of communications.

But you might say: What does it really matter? A man could have the 34 wrongest ideas and yet write good poems and good novels, while another with impeccable notions writes terrible books. This may be true. Certainly those who will write bad books will probably write bad books whatever ideas they may hold. It is the good, or the potentially good, writer who should interest us. And for him I will sooner risk good ideas than bad. I don't believe he will come to much harm by asking himself a few pointed questions.

The late Christopher Okigbo was perhaps a good example of an artist 35 who sometimes had, and expressed, confusing ideas while producing immaculate poetry. He was, in the view of many, Africa's finest poet of our time. For while other poets wrote good poems, Okigbo conjured up for us an amazing, haunting poetic firmament of a wild and violent beauty. Well, Christopher Okigbo once said that he wrote his poems only for other poets: thus putting himself not just beyond the African pale but in a position that would have shocked the great English Romantic poet who defined himself as a man writing for men. On another occasion Okigbo said: "There is no African literature. There is good writing and bad writing—that's all." But quite quickly we are led to suspect that this was all bluff. For when Okigbo was asked why he turned to poetry, he said:

> The turning point came in 1958 when I found myself wanting to know myself better, and I had to turn and look at myself from inside. . . . And when I talk of looking inward to myself, I mean turning inward to examine myselves. This, of course, takes account of ancestors. . . . Because I do not exist apart from my ancestors.

And then, as though to spell it out clearly that ancestors does not mean 36 some general psychological or genetic principle, Okigbo tells us specifically that he is the reincarnation of his maternal grandfather, a priest in the shrine of the Earth goddess. In fact, poetry becomes for him an anguished journey back from alienation to resumption of ritual and priestly functions. His voice becomes the voice of the sunbird of Igbo mythology, mysterious and ominous.

But it was not a simple choice or an easy return journey for Okigbo to 37 make, for he never underrated his indebtedness to the rest of the world. He brought into his poetry all the heirlooms of his multiple heritage; he ranged with ease through Rome and Greece and Babylon, through the rites of Judaism and Catholicism, through European and Bengali literatures, through modern music and painting. But at least one perceptive Nigerian critic has argued that Okigbo's true voice only came to him in his last sequence of poems, *Path of Thunder,* when he had finally and

decisively opted for an African inspiration. This opinion may be con-
tested, though I think it has substantial merit. The trouble is that Okigbo
is such a bewitching poet, able to cast such a powerful spell that,
whatever he cares to say or sing, we stand breathless at the sheer beauty
and grace of his sound and imagery. Yet there is that undeniable fire in
his last poems which was something new. It was as though the goddess
he sought in his poetic journey through so many alien landscapes, and
ultimately found at home, had given him this new thunder. Unfortunately, when he was killed in 1967 he left us only that little, tantalizing
hint of the new self he had found. But perhaps he will be reincarnated in
other poets and sing for us again like his sunbird whose imperishable
song survived the ravages of the eagles.

❏ **Questions for Discussion**

1. Achebe says, "Our ancestors created their myths and legends
   and told their stories for a human purpose. . . ." What does
   Achebe consider to be the "human purpose" of art? What do
   you consider to be the "human purpose" of art?

2. Why does Achebe say that "no decent man uses [the word
   good] in polite society"? Judging from the rest of the essay,
   what is the **tone** of his statement?

3. What kinds of **images** does Mbari include and what do they
   symbolize? What purposes for art does Mbari suggest? What
   point does Achebe make through the example of Mbari?

4. Achebe calls Mbari a "reenactment of creation"? What does he
   mean?

5. Is Achebe being fair when he argues that "the European aesthetic . . . developed in a rigid oligarchical culture"?

❏ **Suggestions for Exploration and Writing**

1. Write an essay about a local equivalent of Mbari in your home
   town, a kind of art which is unique to your community, which
   expresses your community's values, and in which a substantial
   part of your community participates. Think of art in broad
   terms: a style of play, a local game, a festival, or a community
   picnic or parade.

2. Analyze the degree to which other works in this anthology exemplify or contradict Achebe's theories about art.

3. In an essay, discuss a person, like one Achebe mentions, who
   used art to humiliate you as if you were vulgar and unworthy
   of art.

ANNE TYLER (1941–)

Fiction writer Anne Tyler lives in Baltimore with her husband, Iranian psychiatrist and writer Taghi Moderessi, and their children. The warm, tolerant, and amused tone of "Still Just Writing" is characteristic of much of Tyler's fiction, which focuses on family life. Among her novels are Dinner at the Homesick Restaurant *(1982) and* The Accidental Tourist *(1985), which won the National Book Critics Circle Award. This essay shows her characteristic modesty, wit, and gentleness, along with her distinctive voice, as she juggles the often competing roles of wife, mother, and writer.*

Still Just Writing

While I was painting the downstairs hall I thought of a novel to write. 1 Really I just thought of a character; he more or less wandered into my mind, wearing a beard and a broad-brimmed leather hat. I figured that if I sat down and organized this character on paper, a novel would grow up around him. But it was March and the children's spring vacation began the next day, so I waited.

After spring vacation the children went back to school, but the dog got 2 worms. It was a little complicated at the vet's and I lost a day. By then it was Thursday; Friday is the only day I can buy the groceries, pick up new cedar chips for the gerbils, scrub the bathrooms. I waited till Monday. Still, that left me four good weeks in April to block out the novel.

By May I was ready to start actually writing, but I had to do it in 3 patches. There was the follow-up treatment at the vet, and then a half-day spent trailing the dog with a specimen tin so the lab could be sure the treatment had really worked. There were visits from the washing machine repairman and the Davey tree man, not to mention briefer interruptions by the meter reader, five Jehovah's Witnesses, and two Mormons. People telephoned wanting to sell me permanent light bulbs and waterproof basements. An Iranian cousin of my husband's had a baby; the cousin's uncle died; then the cousin's mother decided to go home to Iran and needed to know where to buy a black American coat before she left. There *are* no black American coats; don't Americans wear mourning? I told her no, but I checked around at all the department stores anyway because she didn't speak English. Then I wrote chapters one and two. I had planned to work till 3:30 every day, but it was a month of early quittings: once for the children's dental appointment, once for the cat's rabies shot, once for our older daughter's orthopedist, and twice for her gymnastics meets. Sitting on the bleachers in the school gymnasium, I told myself I could always use this in a novel someplace, but I couldn't really picture writing a novel about 20 little girls in leotards trying to walk the length of a wooden beam without falling off. By the time I'd written chapter three, it was Memorial Day and the children were home again.

Characters on Hold

4   I knew I shouldn't expect anything from June. School was finished then and camp hadn't yet begun. I put the novel away. I closed down my mind and planted some herbs and played cribbage with the children. Then on the 25th, we drove one child to a sleepaway camp in Virginia and entered the other in a day camp, and I was ready to start work again. First I had to take my car in for repairs and the mechanics lost it, but I didn't get diverted. I sat in the garage on a folding chair while they hunted my car all one afternoon, and I hummed a calming tune and tried to remember what I'd planned to do next in my novel. Or even what the novel was about, for that matter. My character wandered in again in his beard and his broad-brimmed hat. He looked a little pale and knuckly, like someone scrabbling at a cliff edge so as not to fall away entirely.

5   I had high hopes for July, but it began with a four-day weekend, and on Monday night we had a long-distance call from our daughter's camp in Virginia. She was seriously ill in a Charlottesville hospital. We left our youngest with friends and drove three hours in a torrent of rain. We found our daughter frightened and crying, and another child (the only other child I knew in all of Virginia) equally frightened and crying down in the emergency room with possible appendicitis, so I spent that night alternating between a chair in the pediatric wing and a chair in the emergency room. By morning, it had begun to seem that our daughter's illness was typhoid fever. We loaded her into the car and took her back to Baltimore, where her doctor put her on drugs and prescribed a long bed-rest. She lay in bed six days, looking wretched and calling for fluids and cold cloths. On the seventh day she got up her same old healthy self, and the illness was declared to be not typhoid fever after all but a simple virus, and we shipped her back to Virginia on the evening train. The next day I was free to start writing again but sat, instead, on the couch in my study, staring blankly at the wall.

Part-time Creativity

6   I could draw some conclusions here about the effect that being a woman/wife/mother has upon my writing, except that I am married to a writer who is also a man/husband/father. He published his first novel while he was a medical student in Iran; then he came to America to finish his training. His writing fell by the wayside, for a long while. You can't be on call in the emergency room for 20 hours and write a novel during the other four. Now he's a child psychiatrist, fulltime, and he writes his novels in the odd moments here and there—when he's not preparing a lecture, when he's not on the phone with a patient, when he's not attending classes at the psychoanalytic institute. He writes in Persian, still, in those black-and-white speckled composition books. Sometimes one of the children will interrupt him in English and he will answer in Persian, and they'll say, "What?" and he'll look up blankly, and it seems

a sheet has to fall from in front of his eyes before he remembers where he is and switches to English. Often, I wonder what he would be doing now if he didn't have a family to support. He cares deeply about his writing and he's very good at it, but every morning at 5:30 he gets up and puts on a suit and tie and drives in the dark to the hospital. Both of us, in different ways, seem to be hewing our creative time in small, hard chips from our living time.

Drained and Drawn

Occasionally, I take a day off. I go to a friend's house for lunch, or   7 weed the garden, or rearrange the linen closet. I notice that at the end of one of these days, when my husband asks me what I've been doing, I tend to exaggerate any hardships I may have encountered. ("A pickup nearly sideswiped me on Greenspring Avenue. I stood in line an hour just trying to buy the children some flip-flops.") It seems sinful to have lounged around so. Also, it seems sinful that I have more choice than my husband as to whether or not to undertake any given piece of work. I can refuse to do an article if it doesn't appeal to me, refuse to change a short story, refuse to hurry a book any faster than it wants to go—all luxuries. My husband, on the other hand, is forced to rise and go off to that hospital every blessed weekday of his life. *His* luxury is that no one expects him to drop all else for two weeks when a child has chicken pox. The only person who has no luxuries at all, it seems to me, is the woman writer who is the sole support of her children. I often think about how she must manage. I think that if I were in that position, I'd have to find a job involving manual labor. I have spent so long erecting partitions around the part of me that writes—learning how to close the door on it when ordinary life intervenes, how to close the door on ordinary life when it's time to start writing again—that I'm not sure I could fit the two parts of me back together now.

Before we had children I worked in a library. It was a boring job, but   8 I tend to like doing boring things. I would sit on a stool alphabetizing Russian catalogue cards and listening to the other librarians talking around me. It made me think of my adolescence, which was spent listening to the tobacco stringers while I handled tobacco. At night I'd go home from the library and write. I never wrote what the librarians said, exactly, but having those voices in my ears all day helped me summon up my own characters' voices. Then our first baby came along—an insomniac. I quit work and stayed home all day with her and walked her all night. Even if I had found the time to write, I wouldn't have had the insides. I felt drained; too much care and feeling were being drawn out of me. And the only voices I heard now were by appointment—people who came to dinner, or invited us to dinner, and who therefore felt they had to make deliberate conversation. That's one thing writers never have, and I still miss it: the easy-going, on-again-off-again, gossipy murmurs of people working alongside each other all day.

Free and Useful

9   I enjoyed tending infants (though I've much preferred the later ages), but it was hard to be solely, continually in their company and not to be able to write. And I couldn't think of any alternative. I know it must be possible to have a child raised beautifully by a housekeeper, but every such child I've run into has seemed dulled and doesn't use words well. So I figured I'd better stick it out. As it happened, it wasn't that long—five years, from the time our first daughter was born till our second started nursery school and left me with my mornings free. But while I was going through it I thought it would be a lot longer. I couldn't imagine any end to it. I felt that everything I wanted to write was somehow coagulating in my veins and making me fidgety and slow. Then after a while I didn't have anything to write anyhow, but I still had the fidgets. I felt useless, no matter how many diapers I washed or strollers I pushed. The only way I could explain my life to myself was to imagine that I was living in a very small commune. I had spent my childhood in a commune, or what would nowadays be called a commune, and I was used to the idea of division of labor. What we had here, I told myself, was a perfectly sensible arrangement: One member was the liaison with the outside world, bringing in money; another was the caretaker, reading the Little Bear books to the children and repairing the electrical switches. This second member might have less physical freedom, but she had much more freedom to arrange her own work schedule. I must have sat down a dozen times a week and very carefully, consciously thought it all through. Often, I was merely trying to convince myself that I really did pull my own weight.

Strung Up

10   This Iranian cousin who just had the baby: She sits home now and cries a lot. She was working on her master's degree and is used to being out in the world more. "Never mind," I tell her, "you'll soon be out again. This stage doesn't last long."

11   "How long?" she asks.

12   "Oh . . . three years, if you just have the one."

13   "Three years!"

14   I can see she's appalled. Her baby is beautiful, very dark and Persian; and what's more, he sleeps—something I've rarely seen a baby do. What I'm trying to say to her (but of course, she'll agree without really hearing me) is that he's worth it. It seems to me that since I've had children, I've grown richer and deeper. They may have slowed down my writing for a while, but when I did write, I had more of a self to speak from. After all, who else in the world do you *have* to love, no matter what? Who else can you absolutely not give up on? My life seems more intricate. Also more dangerous.

15   After the children started school, I put up the partitions in my mind. I would rush around in the morning braiding their hair, packing their

lunches; then the second they were gone I would grow quiet and climb the stairs to my study. Sometimes a child would come home early and I would feel a little tug between the two parts of me; I'd be absent-minded and short-tempered. Then gradually I learned to make the transition more easily. It feels like a sort of string that I tell myself to loosen. When the children come home, I drop the string and close the study door and that's the end of it. It doesn't always work perfectly, of course. There are times when it doesn't work at all: If a child is sick, for instance, I can't possibly drop the children's end of the string, and I've learned not to try. It's easier just to stop writing for a while. Or if they're home but otherwise occupied, I no longer attempt to sneak off to my study to finish that one last page; I know that instantly, as if by magic, assorted little people will be pounding on my door requiring Band-Aids, tetanus shots, and a complete summation of the facts of life.

Last spring, I bought a midget tape recorder to make notes on. I'd   16
noticed that my best ideas come while I was running the vacuum cleaner, but I was always losing them. I thought this little recorder would help. I carried it around in my shirt pocket. But I was ignoring the partitions, is what it was; I was letting one half of my life intrude upon the other. A child would be talking about her day at school and suddenly I'd whip out the tape recorder and tell it, "Get Morgan out of that cocktail party; he's not the type to drink." "Huh?" the child would say. Both halves began to seem ludicrous, unsynchronized. I took the recorder back to Radio Shack.

Faith and Adaptation

A few years ago, my parents went to the Gaza Strip to work for the   17
American Friends Service Committee. It was a lifelong dream of my father's to do something with the AFSC as soon as all his children were grown, and he'd been actively preparing for it for years. But almost as soon as they got there, my mother fell ill with a mysterious fever that neither the Arab nor the Israeli hospitals could diagnose. My parents had to come home for her treatment, and since they'd sublet their house in North Carolina, they had to live with us. For four months, they stayed here—but only on a week-to-week basis, not knowing when they were going back, or whether they were going back at all, or how serious my mother's illness was. It was hard for her, of course, but it should have been especially hard in another way for my father, who had simply to hang in suspended animation for four months while my mother was whisked in and out of hospitals. However, I believe he was as pleased with life as he always is. He whistled Mozart and puttered around insulating our windows. He went on long walks collecting firewood. He strolled over to the meetinghouse and gave a talk on the plight of the Arab refugees. "Now that we seem to have a little time," he told my mother, "why not visit the boys?" and during one of her outpatient periods he took her on a gigantic cross-country trip to see all my brothers

and any other relatives they happened upon. Then my mother decided she ought to go to a faith healer. (She wouldn't usually do such a thing, but she was desperate.) "Oh. Okay," my father said, and he took her to a faith healer, whistling all the way. And when the faith healer didn't work, my mother said, "I think this is psychosomatic. Let's go back to Gaza." My father said, "Okay," and reserved two seats on the next plane over. The children and I went to see them the following summer: My mother's fever was utterly gone, and my father drove us down the Strip, weaving a little Renault among the tents and camels, cheerfully whistling Mozart.

18   I hold this entire, rambling set of events in my head at all times, and remind myself of it almost daily. It seems to me that the way my father lives (infinitely adapting, and looking around him with a smile to say, "Oh! so *this* is where I am!") is also the way to slip gracefully through a choppy life of writing novels, plastering the dining room ceiling, and presiding at slumber parties. I have learned, bit by bit, to accept a school snow-closing as an unexpected holiday, an excuse to play 17 rounds of Parcheesi instead of typing up a short story. When there's a midweek visitation of uncles from Iran (hordes of great, bald, yellow men calling for their glasses of tea, sleeping on guest beds, couches, two armchairs pushed together, and discarded crib mattresses), I have decided that I might as well listen to what they have to say, and work on my novel tomorrow instead. I smile at the uncles out of a kind of clear, swept space inside me. What this takes, of course, is a sense of limitless time, but I'm getting that. My life is beginning to seem unusually long. And there's a danger to it: I could wind up as passive as a piece of wood on a wave. But I try to walk a middle line.

Wait for Heaven

19   I was standing in the schoolyard waiting for a child when another mother came up to me. "Have you found work yet?" she asked. "Or are you still just writing?"

20   Now, how am I supposed to answer that?

21   I could take offense, come to think of it. Maybe the reason I didn't is that I halfway share her attitude. They're *paying* me for this? For just writing down untruthful stories? I'd better look around for more permanent employment. For I do consider writing to be a finite job. I expect that any day now, I will have said all I have to say; I'll have used up all my characters, and then I'll be free to get on with my real life. When I make a note of new ideas on index cards, I imagine I'm clearing out my head, and that soon it will be empty and spacious. I file the cards in a little blue box, and I can picture myself using the final card one day—ah! through at last!—and throwing the blue box away. I'm like a dentist who continually fights tooth decay, working toward the time when he's conquered it altogether and done himself out of a job. But my head keeps

loading up again; the little blue box stays crowded and messy. Even when I feel I have no ideas at all, and can't possibly start the next chapter, I have a sense of something still bottled in me, trying to get out.

People have always seemed funny and strange to me, and touching in unexpected ways. I can't shake off a sort of mist or irony that hangs over whatever I see. Probably that's what I'm trying to put across when I write; I may believe that I'm the one person who holds this view of things. And I'm always hurt when a reader says that I choose only bizarre or eccentric people to write about. It's not a matter of choice; it just seems to me that even the most ordinary person, in real life, will turn out to have something unusual at his center. I like to think that I might meet up with one of my past characters at the very next street corner. The odd thing is, sometimes I have. And if I were remotely religious, I'd believe that a little gathering of my characters would be waiting for me in heaven when I died. *"Then* what happened?" I'd ask them. "How have things worked out, since the last time I saw you?" 22

Eudora's Legacy

I think I was born with the impression that what happened in books was much more reasonable, and interesting, and *real,* in some ways, than what happened in life. I hated childhood, and spent it sitting behind a book waiting for adulthood to arrive. When I ran out of books I made up my own. At night, when I couldn't sleep, I made up stories in the dark. Most of my plots involved girls going west in covered wagons. I was truly furious that I'd been born too late to go west in a covered wagon. 23

I know a poet who says that in order to be a writer, you have to have had rheumatic fever in your childhood. I've never had rheumatic fever, but I believe that any kind of setting-apart situation will do as well. In my case, it was emerging from that commune—really an experimental Quaker community in the wilderness—and trying to fit into the outside world. I was eleven. I had never used a telephone and could strike a match on the soles of my bare feet. All the children in my new school looked very peculiar to me, and I certainly must have looked peculiar to them. I am still surprised, to this day, to find myself where I am. My life is so streamlined and full of modern conveniences. How did I get here? I have given up hope, by now, of ever losing my sense of distance; in fact, I seem to have come to cherish it. Neither I nor any of my brothers can stand being out among a crowd of people for any length of time at all. 24

I spent my adolescence planning to be an artist, not a writer. After all, books had to be about major events, and none had ever happened to me. All I knew were tobacco workers, stringing the leaves I handed them and talking up a storm. Then I found a book of Eudora Welty's short stories in the high school library. She was writing about Edna Earle, who was so slow-witted she could sit all day just pondering how the tail of the *C* got through the loop of the *L* on the Coca-Cola sign. Why, I knew Edna 25

Earle. You mean you could *write* about such people? I have always meant to send Eudora Welty a thank-you note, but I imagine she would find it a little strange.

The Write of Passage

26   I wanted to go to Swarthmore College, but my parents suggested Duke instead, where I had a full scholarship, because my three brothers were coming along right behind me and it was more important for boys to get a good education than for girls. That was the first and last time that my being female was ever a serious issue. I still don't think it was just, but I can't say it ruined my life. After all, Duke had Reynolds Price, who turned out to be the only person I ever knew who could actually teach writing. It all worked out, in the end.

27   I believe that for many writers, the hardest time is that dead spot after college (where they're wonder-children, made much of) and before their first published work. Luckily, I didn't notice that part; I was so vague about what I wanted to do that I could hardly chafe at not yet doing it. I went to graduate school in Russian studies; I scrubbed decks on a boat in Maine; I got a job ordering books from the Soviet Union. Writing was something that crept in around the edges. For a while I lived in New York, where I became addicted to riding any kind of train or subway, and while I rode I often felt I was nothing but an enormous eye, taking things in and turning them over and sorting them out. But who would I tell them to, once I'd sorted them? I have never had more than three or four close friends, at any period of my life; and anyway, I don't talk well. I am the kind of person who wakes up at four in the morning and suddenly thinks of what she should have said yesterday at lunch. For me, writing something down was the only road out.

Rewarding Routines and Rituals

28   You would think, since I waited so long and so hopefully for adulthood, that it would prove to be a disappointment. Actually, I figure it was worth the wait. I like everything about it but the paperwork—the income tax and protesting the Sears bill and renewing the Triple-A membership. I always did count on having a husband and children, and here they are. I'm surprised to find myself a writer but have fitted it in fairly well, I think. The only real trouble that writing has ever brought me is an occasional sense of being invaded by the outside world. Why do people imagine that writers, having chosen the most private of professions, should be any good at performing in public, or should have the slightest desire to tell their secrets to interviewers from ladies' magazines? I feel I am only holding myself together by being extremely firm and decisive about what I will do and what I will not do. I will write my books and raise the children. Anything else just fritters me away. I know this makes me seem narrow, but in fact, I *am* narrow. I like routine and rituals and

I hate leaving home; I have a sense of digging my heels in. I refuse to drive on freeways. I dread our annual vacation. Yet I'm continually prepared for travel: It is physically impossible for me to buy any necessity without buying a travel-sized version as well. I have a little toilet kit, with soap and a nightgown, forever packed and ready to go. How do you explain that?

As the outside world grows less dependable, I keep buttressing my 29 inside world, where people go on meaning well and surprising other people with little touches of grace. There are days when I sink into my novel like a pool and emerge feeling blank and bemused and used up. Then I drift over to the schoolyard, and there's this mother wondering if I'm doing anything halfway useful yet. Am I working? Have I found a job? No, I tell her.

I'm still just writing. 30

❏ Questions for Discussion

1. What reasons does Tyler cite for putting her writing "on hold"?

2. How does Tyler feel about her husband's role in the family?

3. Why is Tyler's story about her father relevant?

4. What influence did Eudora Welty have on Tyler as a writer?

5. How does this essay change your idea of what a novelist's life is like?

❏ Suggestion for Exploration and Writing

1. Basing your analysis on Tyler's **tone** as created by her **diction, imagery,** sentence structure, and explicit statements about herself, write a **character analysis** of Tyler as a person.

GARRISON KEILLOR (1942–   )

Garrison Keillor, a storyteller, humorist, and radio personality from rural Minnesota, is best known for A Prairie Home Companion, *his popular radio show broadcast for many years on National Public Radio. The fictional town of Lake Wobegon, Minnesota, originally created on the radio show, is also the setting for Keillor's book* Lake Wobegon Days *(1985). In both the radio show and the book, Keillor, with gentle humor, celebrates the people and customs of rural Minnesota, investing the local and particular with a universal resonance and revealing the wonder of the commonplace. The following essay comes from Keillor's* Happy to be Here *(1982), a collection of short stories and essays.*

Attitude

1   Long ago I passed the point in life when major-league ballplayers begin to be younger than yourself. Now all of them are, except for a few aging trigenarians and a couple of quadros who don't get around on the fastball as well as they used to and who sit out the second games of double-headers. However, despite my age (thirty-nine), I am still active and have a lot of interests. One of them is slow-pitch softball, a game that lets me go through the motions of baseball without getting beaned or having to run too hard. I play on a pretty casual team, one that drinks beer on the bench and substitutes freely. If a player's wife or girlfriend wants to play, we give her a glove and send her out to right field, no questions asked, and if she lets a pop fly drop six feet in front of her, nobody agonizes over it.

2   Except me. This year. For the first time in my life, just as I am entering the dark twilight of my slow-pitch career, I find myself taking the game seriously. It isn't the bonehead play that bothers me especially—the pop fly that drops untouched, the slow roller juggled and the ball then heaved ten feet over the first baseman's head and into the next diamond, the routine singles that go through outfielders' legs for doubles and triples with gloves flung after them. No, it isn't our stone-glove fielding or pussyfoot base-running or limp-wristed hitting that gives me fits, though these have put us on the short end of some mighty ridiculous scores this summer. It's our attitude.

3   Bottom of the ninth, down 18–3, two outs, a man on first and a woman on third, and our third baseman strikes out. *Strikes out!* In slow-pitch, not even your grandmother strikes out, but this guy does, and after his third strike—a wild swing at a ball that bounces on the plate—he topples over in the dirt and lies flat on his back, laughing. *Laughing!*

4   Same game, earlier. They have the bases loaded. A weak grounder is hit toward our second baseperson. The runners are running. She picks up the ball, and she looks at them. She looks at first, at second, at home. We yell. "Throw it! throw it!," and she throws it, underhand, at the pitcher, who has turned and run to back up the catcher. The ball rolls across the third-base line and under the bench. Three runs score. The batter, a fatso, chugs into second. The other team hoots and hollers, and what does she do? She shrugs and smiles ("Oh, silly me"); after all, it's only a game. Like the aforementioned strikeout artist, she treats her error as a joke. They have forgiven themselves instantly, which is unforgivable. It is *we* who should forgive them, who can say, "It's all right, it's only a game." They are supposed to throw up their hands and kick the dirt and hang their heads, as if this boner, even if it is their sixteenth of the afternoon—*this* is the one that really and truly breaks their hearts.

5   That attitude sweetens the game for everyone. The sinner feels sweet remorse. The fatso feels some sense of accomplishment; this is no bunch of rumdums he forced into an error but a team with some class. We, the

sinner's teammates, feel momentary anger at her—dumb! dumb play!—but then, seeing her grief, we sympathize with her in our hearts (any one of us might have made that mistake or one worse), and we yell encouragement, including the shortstop, who, moments before, dropped an easy throw for a force at second. "That's all right! Come on! We got 'em!" we yell. "Shake it off! These turkeys can't hit!" This makes us all feel good, even through the turkeys now lead us by ten runs. We're getting clobbered, but we have a wining attitude.

Let me say this about attitude: Each player is responsible for his or her 6 own attitude, and to a considerable degree you can *create* a good attitude by doing certain little things on the field. There are certain little things that ballplayers do in the Bigs, and we ought to be doing them in the Slows.

1. When going up to bat, don't step right into the batter's box as if 7 it were an elevator. The box is your turf, your stage. Take possession of it slowly and deliberately, starting with a lot of back-bending, knee-stretching, and torso-revolving in the on-deck circle. Then, approaching the box, stop outside it and tap the dirt off your spikes with your bat. You don't have spikes, you have sneakers, of course, but the significance of the tapping is the same. Then, upon entering the box, spit on the ground. It's a way of saying, "This here is mine. This is where I get my hits."

2. Spit frequently. Spit at all crucial moments. Spit correctly. Spit 8 should be *blown,* not ptuied weakly with the lips, which often results in dribble. Spitting should convey forcefulness of purpose, concentration, pride. Spit down, not in the direction of others. Spit in the glove and on the fingers, especially after making a real knucklehead play; it's a way of saying, "I dropped the ball because my glove was dry."

3. At the bat and in the field, pick up dirt. Rub dirt in the fingers 9 (especially after spitting on them). Toss dirt, as if testing the wind for velocity and direction. Smooth the dirt. Be involved with dirt. If no dirt is available (e.g., in the outfield), pluck tufts of grass. Fielders should be grooming their areas constantly between plays, flicking away tiny sticks and bits of gravel.

4. Take your time. Tie your laces. Confer with your teammates about 10 possible situations that may arise and conceivable options in dealing with them. Extend the game. Three errors on three consecutive plays can be humiliating if the plays occur within the space of a couple of minutes, but if each error is separated from the next by extensive conferences on the mound, lace-tying, glove adjustments, and arguing close calls (if any), the effect on morale is minimized.

5. Talk. Not just an occasional "Let's get a hit now" but continuous 11 rhythmic chatter, a flow of syllables; "Hey babe hey babe c'mon babe good stick now hey babe long tater take him downtown babe . . . hey good eye good eye."

12   Infield chatter is harder to maintain. Since the slow-pitch pitch is required to be a soft underhand lob, infielders hesitate to say, "Smoke him babe hey low heat hey throw it on the black babe chuck it in there back him up babe no hit no hit." Say it anyway.

13   6. One final rule, perhaps the most important of all: When your team is up and has made the third out, the batter and the players who were left on base do not come back to the bench for their gloves. *They remain on the field, and their teammates bring their gloves out to them.* This requires some organization and discipline, but it pays off big in morale. It says, "Although we're getting our pants knocked off, still we must conserve our energy."

14   Imagine that you have bobbled two fly balls in this rout and now you have just tried to stretch a single into a double and have been easily thrown out sliding into second base, where the base runner ahead of you had stopped. It was the third out and a dumb play, and your opponents smirk at you as they run off the field. You are the goat, a lonely and tragic figure sitting in the dirt. You curse yourself, jerking your head sharply forward. You stand up and kick the base. How miserable! How degrading! Your utter shame, though brief, bears silent testimony to the worthiness of your teammates, whom you have let down, and they appreciate it. They call out to you now as they take the field, and as the second baseman runs to his position he says, "Let's get 'em now," and tosses you your glove. Lowering your head, you trot slowly out to right. There you do some deep knee bends. You pick grass. You find a pebble and fling it into foul territory. As the first batter comes to the plate, you check the sun. You get set in your stance, poised to fly. Feet spread, hands on hips, you bend slightly at the waist and spit the expert spit of a veteran ballplayer—a player who has known the agony of defeat but who always bounces back, a player who has lost a stride on the base paths but can still make the big play.

15   This is *ball*, ladies and gentlemen. This is what it's all about.

❏ Questions for Discussion

1. Keillor appears to be less concerned about the quality of his team's hitting and fielding than about such apparently minor details as spitting correctly and knocking dirt from one's cleats? Why? What is his point in focusing on such details?

2. What are these middle-aged men trying to accomplish by playing softball? What do they try to communicate through their elaborate gestures and rituals?

3. Why does the speaker consider it unpardonable for players who make major mistakes instantly to forgive themselves?

4. Clearly the speaker is not serious in his criticism of his team-mates' attitudes. What is the serious point he is trying to make?

❏ **Suggestion for Exploration and Writing**

1. Discuss in detail a particular role you play in which apparently minor details take on exaggerated importance.

BARRY LOPEZ (1945–)

Barry Lopez reveals in his nonfiction books a passionate reverence for nature. In Arctic Dreams, *which won the National Book Award for nonfiction in 1986, he celebrates the richness of vast, seemingly barren Arctic landscapes. In* Crossing Open Ground *(1988), a collection of essays including "Landscape and Narrative," Lopez explores humanity's interaction and integration with the landscape.*

Landscape and Narrative

One summer evening in a remote village in the Brooks Range of Alaska, I sat among a group of men listening to hunting stories about the trapping and pursuit of animals. I was particularly interested in several incidents involving wolverine, in part because a friend of mine was studying wolverine in Canada, among the Cree, but, too, because I find this animal such an intense creature. To hear about its life is to learn more about fierceness.

Wolverines are not intentionally secretive, hiding their lives from view, but they are seldom observed. The range of their known behavior is less than that of, say, bears or wolves. Still, that evening no gratuitous details were set out. This was somewhat odd, for wolverine easily excite the imagination; they can loom suddenly on the landscape with authority, with an aura larger than their compact physical dimensions, drawing one's immediate and complete attention. Wolverine also have a deserved reputation for resoluteness in the worst winters, for ferocious strength. But neither did these attributes induce the men to embellish.

I listened carefully to these stories, taking pleasure in the sharply observed detail surrounding the dramatic thread of events. The story I remember most vividly was about a man hunting a wolverine from a snow machine in the spring. He followed the animal's tracks for several miles over rolling tundra in a certain valley. Soon he caught sight ahead of a dark spot on the crest of a hill—the wolverine pausing to look back. The hunter was catching up, but each time he came over a rise the wolverine was looking back from the next rise, just out of range. The hunter topped one more rise and met the wolverine bounding toward him. Before he could pull his rifle from its scabbard the wolverine flew across the engine cowl and the windshield, hitting him square in the chest. The hunter scrambled his arms wildly, trying to get the wolverine out of his lap, and fell over as he did so. The wolverine jumped clear as the snow machine rolled over, and fixed the man with a stare. He had not bitten, not even scratched the man. Then the wolverine walked away. The man thought of reaching for the gun, but no, he did not.

4   The other stories were like this, not so much making a point as evoking something about contact with wild animals that would never be completely understood.

5   When the stories were over, four or five of us walked out of the home of our host. The surrounding land, in the persistent light of a far northern summer, was still visible for miles—the striated, pitched massifs of the Brooks Range; the shy, willow-lined banks of the John River flowing south from Anaktuvuk Pass; and the flat tundra plain, opening with great affirmation to the north. The landscape seemed alive because of the stories. It was precisely these ocherous tones, this kind of willow, exactly this austerity that had informed the wolverine narratives. I felt exhilaration, and a deeper confirmation of the stories. The mundane tasks which awaited me I anticipated now with pleasure. The stories had renewed in me a sense of the purpose of my life.

6   This feeling, an inexplicable renewal of enthusiasm after storytelling, is familiar to many people. It does not seem to matter greatly what the subject is, as long as the context is intimate and the story is told for its own sake, not forced to serve merely as the vehicle for an idea. The tone of the story need not be solemn. The darker aspects of life need not be ignored. But I think intimacy is indispensable—a feeling that derives from the listener's trust and a storyteller's certain knowledge of his subject and regard for his audience. This intimacy deepens if the storyteller tempers his authority with humility, or when terms of idiomatic expression, or at least the physical setting for the story, are shared.

7   I think of two landscapes—one outside the self, the other within. The external landscape is the one we see—not only the line and color of the land and its shading at different times of the day, but also its plants and animals in season, its weather, its geology, the record of its climate and evolution. If you walk up, say, a dry arroyo in the Sonoran Desert you will feel a mounding and rolling of sand and silt beneath your foot that is distinctive. You will anticipate the crumbling of the sedimentary earth in the arroyo bank as your hand reaches out, and in that tangible evidence you will sense a history of water in the region. Perhaps a black-throated sparrow lands in a paloverde bush—the resiliency of the twig under the bird, that precise shade of yellowish-green against the milk-blue sky, the fluttering whir of the arriving sparrow, are what I mean by "the landscape." Draw on the smell of creosote bush, or clack stones together in the dry air. Feel how light is the desiccated dropping of

the kangaroo rat. Study an animal track obscured by the wind. These are all elements of the land, and what makes the landscape comprehensible are the relationships between them. One learns a landscape finally not by knowing the name or identity of everything in it, but by perceiving the relationships in it—like that between the sparrow and the twig. The difference between the relationships and the elements is the same as that between written history and a catalog of events.

The second landscape I think of is an interior one, a kind of projection within a person of a part of the exterior landscape. Relationships in the exterior landscape include those that are named and discernible, such as the nitrogen cycle, or a vertical sequence of Ordovician limestone, and others that are uncodified or ineffable, such as winter light falling on a particular kind of granite, or the effect of humidity on the frequency of a blackpoll warbler's burst of song. That these relationships have purpose and order, however inscrutable they may seem to us, is a tenet of evolution. Similarly, the speculations, intuitions, and formal ideas we refer to as "mind" are a set of relationships in the interior landscape with purpose and order; some of these are obvious, many impenetrably subtle. The shape and character of these relationships in a person's thinking, I believe, are deeply influenced by where on this earth one goes, what one touches, the patterns one observes in nature—the intricate history of one's life in the land, even a life in the city, where wind, the chirp of birds, the line of a falling leaf, are known. These thoughts are arranged, further, according to the thread of one's moral, intellectual, and spiritual development. The interior landscape responds to the character and subtlety of an exterior landscape; the shape of the individual mind is affected by land as it is by genes.

In stories like those I heard at Anaktuvuk Pass about wolverine, the relationship between separate elements in the land is set forth clearly. It is put in a simple framework of sequential incidents and apposite detail. If the exterior landscape is limned well, the listener often feels that he has heard something pleasing and authentic—trustworthy. We derive this sense of confidence I think not so much from verifiable truth as from an understanding that lying has played no role in the narrative. The storyteller is obligated to engage the reader with a precise vocabulary, to set forth a coherent and dramatic rendering of incidents—and to be ingenuous.

When one hears a story one takes pleasure in it for different reasons— the euphony of its phrases, an aspect of the plot, or because one identifies with one of the characters. With certain stories certain individuals may experience a deeper, more profound sense of well-being. This latter phenomenon, in my understanding, rests at the heart of storytelling as an elevated experience among aboriginal peoples. It results from bringing two landscapes together. The exterior landscape is organized according to principles or laws or tendencies beyond human control. It is understood to contain an integrity that is beyond human analysis and unimpeachable. Insofar as the storyteller depicts various subtle and obvious relationships in the exterior landscape accurately in his story, and insofar as he orders them along traditional lines of meaning to create the narrative, the narrative will "ring true." The listener who "takes the story to heart" will feel a pervasive sense of congruence within himself and also with the world.

11   Among the Navajo and, as far as I know, many other native peoples, the land is thought to exhibit a sacred order. That order is the basis of ritual. The rituals themselves reveal the power in that order. Art, architecture, vocabulary, and costume, as well as ritual, are derived from the perceived natural order of the universe—from observations and meditations on the exterior landscape. An indigenous philosophy—metaphysics, ethics, epistemology, aesthetics, and logic—may also be derived from a people's continuous attentiveness to both the obvious (scientific) and ineffable (artistic) orders of the local landscape. Each individual, further, undertakes to order his interior landscape according to the exterior landscape. To succeed in this means to achieve a balanced state of mental health.

12   I think of the Navajo for a specific reason. Among the various sung ceremonies of this people—Enemyway, Coyoteway, Red Antway, Uglyway—is one called Beautyway. In the Navajo view, the elements of one's interior life—one's psychological makeup and moral bearing—are subject to a persistent principle of disarray. Beautyway is, in part, a spiritual invocation of the order of the exterior universe, that irreducible, holy complexity that manifests itself as all things changing through time (a Navajo definition of beauty, hózhǫ́ǫ́). The purpose of this invocation is to recreate in the individual who is the subject of the Beautyway ceremony that same order, to make the individual again a reflection of the myriad enduring relationships of the landscape.

13   I believe story functions in a similar way. A story draws on relationships in the exterior landscape and projects them onto the interior landscape. The purpose of storytelling is to achieve harmony between the two landscapes, to use all the elements of story—syntax, mood, figures of speech—in a harmonious way to reproduce the harmony of the land in the individual's interior. Inherent in story is the power to reorder a state of psychological confusion through contact with the pervasive truth of those relationships we call "the land."

14   These thoughts, of course, are susceptible to interpretation. I am convinced, however, that these observations can be applied to the kind of prose we call nonfiction as well as to traditional narrative forms such as the novel and the short story, and to some poems. Distinctions between fiction and nonfiction are sometimes obscured by arguments over what constitutes "the truth." In the aboriginal literature I am familiar with, the first distinction made among narratives is to separate the authentic from the inauthentic. Myth, which we tend to regard as fictitious or "merely

metaphorical," is as authentic, as real, as the story of a wolverine in a man's lap. (A distinction is made, of course, about the elevated nature of myth—and frequently the circumstances of myth-telling are more rigorously prescribed than those for the telling of legends or vernacular stories—but all of these narratives are rooted in the local landscape. To violate *that* connection is to call the narrative itself into question.)

The power of narrative to nurture and heal, to repair a spirit in disarray, rests on two things: the skillful invocation of unimpeachable sources and a listener's knowledge that no hypocrisy or subterfuge is involved. This last simple fact is to me one of the most imposing aspects of the Holocene history of man. 15

We are more accustomed now to thinking of "the truth" as something that can be explicitly stated, rather than as something that can be evoked in a metaphorical way outside science and Occidental culture. Neither can truth be reduced to aphorism or formulas. It is something alive and unpronounceable. Story creates an atmosphere in which it becomes discernible as a pattern. For a storyteller to insist on relationships that do not exist is to lie. Lying is the opposite of story. (I do not mean to confuse ignorance with deception, or to imply that a storyteller can perceive all that is inherent in the land. Every storyteller falls short of a perfect limning of the landscape—perception and language both fail. But to make up something that is not there, something which can never be corroborated in the land, to knowingly set forth a false relationship, is to be lying, no longer telling a story.) 16

Because of the intricate, complex nature of the land, it is not always possible for a storyteller to grasp what is contained in a story. The intent of the storyteller, then, must be to evoke, honestly, some single aspect of all that the land contains. The storyteller knows that because different individuals grasp the story at different levels, the focus of his regard for truth must be at the primary one—with who was there, what happened, when, where, and why things occurred. The story will then possess similar truth at other levels—the integrity inherent at the primary level of meaning will be conveyed everywhere else. As long as the storyteller carefully describes the order before him, and uses his storytelling skill to heighten and emphasize certain relationships, it is even possible for the story to be more successful than the storyteller himself is able to imagine. 17

I would like to make a final point about the wolverine stories I heard at Anaktuvuk Pass. I wrote down the details afterward, concentrating especially on aspects of the biology and ecology of the animals. I sent the information on to my friend living with the Cree. When, many months later, I saw him, I asked whether the Cree had enjoyed these insights of the Nunamiut into the nature of the wolverine. What had they said? 18

"You know," he told me, "how they are. They said, 'That could happen.'" 19

20   In these uncomplicated words the Cree declared their own knowledge of the wolverine. They acknowledged that although they themselves had never seen the things that Nunamiut spoke of, they accepted
them as accurate observations, because they did not consider story a
context for misrepresentation. They also preserved their own dignity by
not overstating their confidence in the Nunamiut, a distant and unknown
people.

21   Whenever I think of this courtesy on the part of the Cree I think of the
dignity that is ours when we cease to demand the truth and realize that
the best we can have of those substantial truths that guide our lives is
metaphorical—a story. And the most of it we are likely to discern comes
only when we accord one another the respect the Cree showed the
Nunamiut. Beyond this—that the interior landscape is a metaphorical
representation of the exterior landscape, that the truth reveals itself most
fully not in dogma but in the paradox, irony, and contradictions that
distinguish compelling narratives—beyond this there are only failures of
imagination: reductionism in science; fundamentalism in religion; fas-
cism in politics.

22   Our national literatures should be important to us insofar as they
sustain us with illumination, and heal us. They can always do that so long
as they are written with respect for both the source and the reader, and
with an understanding of why the human heart and the land have been
brought together so regularly in human history.

❏ Questions for Discussion

1. What point is Lopez making in citing the story of the hunter
   and the wolverine? How might the story have "renewed [in
   Lopez] a sense of the purpose of [his] life"?

2. Lopez says, "One learns a landscape finally not by knowing the
   name or identity of everything in it, but by perceiving the relationships in it—like that between the sparrow and the twig."
   Lopez is referring to natural landscapes. To what degree can
   the same be said of artificial landscapes—cities, villages, or
   communities? Cite examples to illustrate your response.

3. What does Lopez mean by "internal landscapes"? Can we read
   other people's "internal landscapes" as we can "external landscapes"? If so, how?

4. What is the relationship between "internal landscape" and "external landscape"?

5. What special power does Lopez attribute to stories? Have you
   ever heard or read stories that gave you a "profound sense of
   well-being"?

❏ Suggestions for Exploration and Writing

1. Write an essay about a story that gave you a sense of order and comfort.

2. Lopez says about Navajo ritualistic dances, "Art, architecture, vocabulary, and costume, as well as ritual, are derived from the perceived natural order of the universe." How do the Igbo festival of Mbari described in Achebe's "Africa and Her Writers" and the dances incorporated into Soyinka's *The Lion and the Jewel* exemplify Lopez's point? Explain.

3. Write an essay on how a story or movie, through its portrayal of external landscape, touched your internal landscape.

FICTION

WALTER VAN TILBURG CLARK (1909–1972)

Walter Van Tilburg Clark, American novelist, short-story writer, and teacher, first achieved fame with the publication of his novel The Ox-Bow Incident *in 1940. This novel illustrates most of Clark's major themes: his love of landscape and concern with preserving humans' relationship to the land; his strong concern with morality; and his realization of the ambiguities which complicate life when people's aspirations for success and their desire to conform conflict with their love of the land and their own morality. In this story, taken from* The Watchful Gods and Other Stories *(1950), Clark presents a view of the importance of art to the survival of humanity.*

The Portable Phonograph

The red sunset with narrow, black cloud strips like threads across it, 1 lay on the curved horizon of the prairie. The air was still and cold, and in it settled the mute darkness and greater cold of night. High in the air there was wind, for through the veil of the dusk the clouds could be seen gliding rapidly south and changing shapes. A queer sensation of torment, of two-sided, unpredictable nature, arose from the stillness of the earth air beneath the violence of the upper air. Out of the sunset, through the dead, matted grass and isolated weed stalks of the prairie, crept the narrow and deeply rutted remains of a road. In the road, in places, there were crusts of shallow, brittle ice. There were little islands of an old oiled pavement in the road too, but most of it was mud, now frozen rigid. The frozen mud still bore the toothed impress of great tanks, and a wanderer on the neighboring undulations might have stumbled, in this light, into large, partially filled-in and weed-grown cavities, their banks channeled and beginning to spread into badlands. These pits were such as might have been made by falling meteors, but they were not. They were the scars of gigantic bombs, their rawness already made a little natural by rain, seed, and time. Along the road, there were rakish remnants of fence. There was also, just visible, one portion of tangled and multiple barbed wire still erect, behind which was a shelving ditch with small caves, now very quiet and empty, at intervals in its back wall. Otherwise there was no structure or remnant of a structure visible over the dome of the darkling earth, but only, in sheltered hollows, the darker shadows of young trees trying again.

2   Under the withering arch of the high wind a V of wild geese fled south. The rush of their pinions sounded briefly, and the faint, plaintive notes of their expeditionary talk. Then they left a still greater vacancy. There was the smell and expectation of snow as there is likely to be when the wild geese fly south. From the remote distance, towards the red sky, came faintly the protracted howl and quick yap-yap of a prairie wolf.

3   North of the road, perhaps a hundred yards, lay the parallel and deeply intrenched course of a small creek, lined with leafless alders and willows. The creek was already silent under ice. Into the bank above it was dug a sort of cell, with a single opening, like the mouth of a mine tunnel. Within the cell there was a little red of fire, which showed dully through the opening, like a reflection or a deception of the imagination. The light came from the chary burning of four blocks of poorly aged peat, which gave off a petty warmth and much acrid smoke. But the precious remnants of wood, old fence posts and timbers from the long-deserted dugouts, had to be saved for the real cold, for the time when a man's breath blew white, the moisture in his nostrils stiffened at once when he stepped out, and the expansive blizzards paraded for days over the vast open, swirling and settling and thickening, till the dawn of the cleared day when the sky was thin blue-green and the terrible cold, in which a man could not live for three hours unwarmed, lay over the uniformly drifted swell of the plain.

4   Around the smoldering peat, four men were seated cross-legged. Behind them, traversed by their shadows, was the earth bench, with two old and dirty army blankets, where the owner of the cell slept. In a niche in the opposite wall were a few tin utensils which caught the glint of the coals. The host was rewrapping in a piece of daubed burlap four fine, leather-bound books. He worked slowly and very carefully, and at last tied the bundle securely with a piece of grass-woven cord. The other three looked intently upon the process, as if a great significance lay in it. As the host tied the cord, he spoke. He was an old man, his long, matted beard and hair gray to nearly white. The shadows made his brows and cheekbones appear gnarled, his eyes and cheeks deeply sunken. His big hands, rough with frost and swollen by rheumatism, were awkward but gentle at their task. He was like a prehistoric priest performing a fateful

ceremonial rite. Also his voice had in it a suitable quality of deep, reverent despair, yet perhaps at the moment, a sharpness of selfish satisfaction.

"When I perceived what was happening," he said, "I told myself, 'It is 5
the end. I cannot take much; I will take these.' "

"Perhaps I was impractical," he continued. "But for myself, I do not 6
regret, and what do we know of those who will come after us? We are the
doddering remnant of a race of mechanical fools. I have saved what I
love; the soul of what was good in us is here; perhaps the new ones will
make a strong enough beginning not to fall behind when they become
clever."

He rose with slow pain and placed the wrapped volumes in the niche 7
with his utensils. The others watched him with the same ritualistic gaze.

"Shakespeare, the Bible, *Moby Dick*,[1] the *Divine Comedy*," one of 8
them said softly. "You might have done worse, much worse."

"You will have a little soul left until you die," said another harshly. 9
"That is more than is true of us. My brain becomes thick, like my hands."
He held the big, battered hands, with their black nails, in the glow to be
seen.

"I want paper to write on," he said. "And there is none." 10

The fourth man said nothing. He sat in the shadow farthest from the 11
fire, and sometimes his body jerked in its rags from the cold. Although he
was still young, he was sick and coughed often. Writing implied a greater
future than he now felt able to consider.

The old man seated himself laboriously, and reached out, groaning at 12
the movement, to put another block of peat on the fire. With bowed
heads and averted eyes, his three guests acknowledged his magnanimity.

"We thank you, Doctor Jenkins, for the reading," said the man who 13
had named the books.

They seemed then to be waiting for something. Doctor Jenkins under- 14
stood, but was loath to comply. In an ordinary moment he would have
said nothing. But the words of *The Tempest*,[2] which he had been reading,
and the religious attention of the three made this an unusual occasion.

"You wish to hear the phonograph," he said grudgingly. 15

The two middle-aged men stared into the fire, unable to formulate and 16
expose the enormity of their desire.

The young man, however, said anxiously, between suppressed coughs, 17
"Oh, please," like an excited child.

The old man rose again in his difficult way, and went to the back of the 18
cell. He returned and placed tenderly upon the packed floor, where the
firelight might fall upon it, an old portable phonograph in a black case.

---

[1] *Moby Dick*, a nineteenth century American novel by Herman Melville, is a richly
symbolic story of Ahab, captain of the whaling ship *Pequod*, who is obsessed with a desire
to kill the white whale Moby Dick, and Ishmael, a voyager and observer who survives to
tell what he has learned.

[2] *The Tempest*, Shakespeare's last play, was considered his farewell to the theater.

He smoothed the top with his hand, and then opened it. The lovely green-felt-covered disk became visible.

19   "I have been using thorns as needles," he said. "But tonight, because we have a musician among us"—he bent his head to the young man, almost invisible in the shadow—"I will use a steel needle. There are only three left."

20   The two middle-aged men stared at him in speechless adoration. The one with the big hands, who wanted to write, moved his lips, but the whisper was not audible.

21   "Oh, don't!" cried the young man, as if he were hurt. "The thorns will do beautifully."

22   "No," the old man said. "I have become accustomed to the thorns, but they are not really good. For you, my young friend, we will have good music tonight."

23   "After all," he added generously, and beginning to wind the phonograph, which creaked, "they can't last forever."

24   "No, nor we," the man who needed to write said harshly. "The needle, by all means."

25   "Oh, thanks," said the young man. "Thanks," he said again in a low, excited voice, and then stifled his coughing with a bowed head.

26   "The records, though," said the old man when he had finished winding, "are a different matter. Already they are very worn. I do not play them more than once a week. One, once a week, this what I allow myself."

27   "More than a week I cannot stand it; not to hear them," he apologized.

28   "No, how could you?" cried the young man. "And with them here like this."

29   "A man can stand anything," said the man who wanted to write, in his harsh, antagonistic voice.

30   "Please, the music," said the young man.

31   "Only the one," said the old man. "In the long run, we will remember more that way."

32   He had a dozen records with luxuriant gold and red seals. Even in that light the others could see that the threads of the records were becoming worn. Slowly he read out the titles and the tremendous, dead names of the composers and the artists and the orchestras. The three worked upon the names in their minds, carefully. It was difficult to select from such a wealth what they would at once most like to remember. Finally, the man who wanted to write named Gershwin's "New York."

33   "Oh, no," cried the sick young man, and then could say nothing more because he had to cough. The others understood him, and the harsh man withdrew his selection and waited for the musician to choose.

34   The musician begged Doctor Jenkins to read the titles again, very slowly, so that he could remember the sounds. While they were read, he lay back against the wall, his eyes closed, his thin, horny hand pulling at

his light beard, and listened to the voices and the orchestras and the single instruments in his mind.

When the reading was done he spoke despairingly. "I have forgotten,"   35
he complained; "I cannot hear them clearly."

"There are things missing," he explained.   36

"I know," said Doctor Jenkins. "I thought that I knew all of Shelley[3]   37
by heart. I should have brought Shelley."

"That's more soul than we can use," said the harsh man. "*Moby Dick*   38
is better."

"By God, we can understand that," he emphasized.   39

The Doctor nodded.   40

"Still," said the man who had admired the books, "we need the   41
absolute if we are to keep a grasp on anything."

"Anything but these sticks and peat clods and rabbit snares," he said   42
bitterly.

"Shelley desired an ultimate absolute," said the harsh man. "It's too   43
much," he said. "It's no good; no earthly good."

The musician selected a Debussy nocturne. The others considered and   44
approved. They rose to their knees to watch the Doctor prepare for the playing, so that they appeared to be actually in an attitude of worship. The peat glow showed the thinness of their bearded faces and the deep lines in them, and revealed the condition of their garments. The other two continued to kneel as the old man carefully lowered the needle onto the spinning disk, but the musician suddenly drew back against the wall again, with his knees up, and buried his face in his hands.

At the first notes of the piano the listeners were startled. They stared at   45
each other. Even the musician lifted his head in amazement, but then quickly bowed it again, strangely, as if he were suffering from a pain he might not be able to endure. They were all listening deeply, without movement. The wet, blue-green notes tinkled forth from the old machine, and were individual, delectable presences in the cell. The individual, delectable presences swept into a sudden tide of unbearably beautiful dissonance, and then continued fully the swelling and ebbing of that tide, the dissonant inpourings, and the resolutions, and the diminishments, and the little, quiet wavelets of interlude lapping between. Every sound was piercing and singularly sweet. In all the men except the musician, there occurred rapid sequences of tragically heightened recollection. He heard nothing but what was there. At the final, whispering disappearance, but moving quietly so that the others would not hear him and look at him, he let his head fall back in agony, as if it were drawn there by the hair, and clenched the fingers of one hand over his teeth. He sat that way

[3] Percy Bysshe Shelley was a nineteenth century Romantic poet who wrote about nature, sorrow, and the role of the poet.

while the others were silent, and until they began to breathe again normally. His drawn-up legs were trembling violently.

46   Quickly Doctor Jenkins lifted the needle off, to save it and not to spoil the recollection with scraping. When he had stopped the whirling of the sacred disk, he courteously left the phonograph open and by the fire, in sight.

47   The others, however, understood. The musician rose last, but then abruptly, and went quickly out at the door without saying anything. The others stopped at the door and gave their thanks in low voices. The Doctor nodded magnificently.

48   "Come again," he invited, "in a week. We will have the 'New York.'"

49   When the two had gone together, out towards the rimed road, he stood in the entrance, peering and listening. At first, there was only the resonant boom of the wind overhead, and then far over the dome of the dead, dark plain, the wolf cry lamenting. In the rifts of clouds the Doctor saw four stars flying. It impressed the Doctor that one of them had just been obscured by the beginning of a flying cloud at the very moment he heard what he had been listening for, a sound of suppressed coughing. It was not nearby, however. He believed that down against the pale alders he could see the moving shadow.

50   With nervous hands he lowered the piece of canvas which served as his door, and pegged it at the bottom. Then quickly and quietly, looking at the piece of canvas frequently, he slipped the records into the case, snapped the lid shut, and carried the phonograph to his couch. There, pausing often to stare at the canvas and listen, he dug earth from the wall and disclosed a piece of board. Behind this was a deep hole in the wall, into which he put the phonograph. After a moment's consideration, he went over and reached down his bundle of books and inserted it also. Then, guardedly, he once more sealed up the hole with the board and the earth. He also changed his blankets, and the grass-stuffed sack which served as a pillow, so that he could lie facing the entrance. After carefully placing two more blocks of peat upon the fire, he stood for a long time watching the stretched canvas, but it seemed to billow naturally with the first gusts of a lowering wind. At last he prayed, and got in under his blankets, and closed his smoke-smarting eyes. On the inside of the bed, next the wall, he could feel with his hand the comfortable piece of lead pipe.

❏ Questions for Discussion

1. Only one of the characters is given a name. How does the author characterize each of the other characters?

2. Explain Dr. Jenkins' choices of literature and music in light of his statement that "I have saved what I love; the soul of what was good in us is here. . . ." Why do the survivors prefer to have Melville's *Moby Dick* rather than the poetry of Shelley?

3. How does the elaborately described natural setting enhance this story?

4. What do literature and music mean to these men? Why?

5. Explain the significance of Dr. Jenkins' elaborate precautions at the end of the story.

❏ **Suggestions for Exploration and Writing**

1. If you were faced with a similar situation, what would you choose to save? Why?

2. Write a researched paper in which you point out the parallels between "The Portable Phonograph" and Shakespeare's *Tempest,* especially those between Dr. Jenkins and Prospero.

MARGUERITE YOURCENAR (1913–1987)

Marguerite Yourcenar, a French writer who was born Marguerite de Crayencour in Brussels, lived most of her life in the United States. Many of her works were written in her native French and later translated into English. In 1980 she became the first female member of the French Academy. Yourcenar is noted for her historical novels, Memoirs of Hadrian *(1951) and* The Abyss *(1968). Her specialty, however, was in retelling the ancient myths and legends.* Fires *(1974) is an attempt to modernize the legends of ancient Greece in prose poems;* Oriental Tales *(1938), which contains "How Wang-Fo Was Saved," derives from Taoist and Hindu stories, Japanese literature, Balkan legends, and even an item in a newspaper.*

How Wang-Fo Was Saved

The old painter Wang-Fo and his disciple Ling were wandering along the roads of the Kingdom of Han. 1

They made slow progress because Wang-Fo would stop at night to watch the stars and during the day to observe the dragonflies. They carried hardly any luggage, because Wang-Fo loved the image of things and not the things themselves, and no object in the world seemed to him worth buying, except brushes, pots of lacquer and China ink, and rolls of silk and rice paper. They were poor, because Wang-Fo would exchange his paintings for a ration of boiled millet, and paid no attention to pieces of silver. Ling, his disciple, bent beneath the weight of a sack full of sketches, bowed his back with respect as if he were carrying the heavens' vault, because for Ling the sack was full of snow-covered mountains, torrents in spring, and the face of the summer moon. 2

Ling had not been born to trot down the roads, following an old man who seized the dawn and captured the dusk. His father had been a 3 banker who dealt in gold, his mother the only child of a jade merchant who had left her all his worldly possessions, cursing her for not being a son. Ling had grown up in a house where wealth made him shy: he was afraid of insects, of thunder and the face of the dead. When Ling was fifteen, his father chose a bride for him, a very beautiful one because the thought of the happiness he was giving his son consoled him for having reached the age in which the night is meant for sleep. Ling's wife was as frail as a reed, childish as milk, sweet as saliva, salty as tears. After the wedding, Ling's parents became discreet to the point of dying, and their son was left alone in a house painted vermilion, in the company of his young wife who never stopped smiling and a plum tree that blossomed every spring with pale-pink flowers. Ling loved this woman of a crystal-clear heart as one loves a mirror that will never tarnish, or a talisman that will protect one forever. He visited the teahouses to follow the dictates of fashion, and only moderately favored acrobats and dancers.

4   One night, in the tavern, Wang-Fo shared Ling's table. The old man had been drinking in order to better paint a drunkard, and he cocked his head to one side as if trying to measure the distance between his hand and his bowl. The rice wine undid the tongue of the taciturn craftsman, and that night Wang spoke as if silence were a wall and words the colors with which to cover it. Thanks to him, Ling got to know the beauty of the drunkards' faces blurred by the vapors of hot drink, the brown splendor of the roasts unevenly brushed by tongues of fire, and the exquisite blush of wine stains strewn on the tablecloths like withered petals. A gust of wind broke the window: the downpour entered the room. Wang-Fo leaned out to make Ling admire the livid zebra stripes of lightning, and Ling, spellbound, stopped being afraid of storms.

5   Ling paid the old painter's bill, and as Wang-Fo was both without money and without lodging, he humbly offered him a resting place. They walked away together; Ling held a lamp whose light projected unexpected fires in the puddles. That evening, Ling discovered with surprise that the walls of his house were not red, as he had always thought, but the color of an almost rotten orange. In the courtyard, Wang-Fo noticed the delicate shape of a bush to which no one had paid any attention until then, and compared it to a young woman letting down her hair to dry. In the passageway, he followed with delight the hesitant trail of an ant along the cracks in the wall, and Ling's horror of these creatures vanished into thin air. Realizing that Wang-Fo had just presented him with the gift of a new soul and a new vision of the world, Ling respectfully offered the old man the room in which his father and mother had died.

6   For many years now, Wang-Fo had dreamed of painting the portrait of a princess of olden days playing the lute under a willow. No woman was sufficiently unreal to be his model, but Ling would do because he was not a woman. Then Wang-Fo spoke of painting a young prince shooting an arrow at the foot of a large cedar tree. No young man of the present was sufficiently unreal to serve as his model, but Ling got his own wife to pose

under the plum tree in the garden. Later on, Wang-Fo painted her in a fairy costume against the clouds of twilight, and the young woman wept because it was an omen of death. As Ling came to prefer the portraits painted by Wang-Fo to the young woman herself, her face began to fade, like a flower exposed to warm winds and summer rains. One morning they found her hanging from the branches of the pink plum tree: the ends of the scarf that was strangling her floated in the wind, entangled with her hair. She looked even more delicate than usual, and as pure as the beauties celebrated by the poets of days gone by. Wang-Fo painted her one last time, because he loved the green hue that suffuses the face of the dead. His disciple Ling mixed the colors and the task needed such concentration that he forgot to shed tears.

One after the other, Ling sold his slaves, his jades, and the fish in his   7
pond to buy his master pots of purple ink that came from the West. When the house was emptied, they left it, and Ling closed the door of his past behind him. Wang-Fo felt weary of a city where the faces could no longer teach him secrets of ugliness or beauty, and the master and his disciple walked away together down the roads of the Kingdom of Han.

Their reputation preceded them into the villages, to the gateway of   8
fortresses, and into the atrium of temples where restless pilgrims halt at dusk. It was murmured that Wang-Fo had the power to bring his paintings to life by adding a last touch of color to their eyes. Farmers would come and beg him to paint a watchdog, and the lords would ask him for portraits of their best warriors. The priests honored Wang-Fo as a sage; the people feared him as a sorcerer. Wang enjoyed these differences of opinion which gave him the chance to study expressions of gratitude, fear, and veneration.

Ling begged for food, watched over his master's rest, and took advan-   9
tage of the old man's raptures to massage his feet. With the first rays of the sun, when the old man was still asleep, Ling went in pursuit of timid landscapes hidden behind bunches of reeds. In the evening, when the master, disheartened, threw down his brushes, he would carefully pick them up. When Wang became sad and spoke of his old age, Ling would smile and show him the solid trunk of an old oak; when Wang felt happy and made jokes, Ling would humbly pretend to listen.

One day, at sunset, they reached the outskirts of the Imperial City   10
and Ling sought out and found an inn in which Wang-Fo could spend the night. The old man wrapped himself up in rags, and Ling lay down next to him to keep him warm because spring had only just begun and the floor of beaten earth was still frozen. At dawn, heavy steps echoed in the corridors of the inn; they heard the frightened whispers of the innkeeper and orders shouted in a foreign, barbaric tongue. Ling trembled, remembering that the night before, he had stolen a rice cake for his master's supper. Certain that they would come to take him to prison, he asked himself who would help Wang-Fo ford the next river on the following day.

11   The soldiers entered carrying lanterns. The flames gleaming through the motley paper cast red and blue lights on their leather helmets. The string of a bow quivered over their shoulders, and the fiercest among them suddenly let out a roar for no reason at all. A heavy hand fell on Wang-Fo's neck, and the painter could not help noticing that the soldiers' sleeves did not match the color of their coats.

12   Helped by his disciple, Wang-Fo followed the soldiers, stumbling along uneven roads. The passing crowds made fun of these two criminals who were certainly going to be beheaded. The soldiers answered Wang's questions with savage scowls. His bound hands hurt him, and Ling in despair looked smiling at his master, which for him was a gentler way of crying.

13   They reached the threshold of the Imperial Palace, whose purple walls rose in broad daylight like a sweep of sunset. The soldiers led Wang-Fo through countless square and circular rooms whose shapes symbolized the seasons, the cardinal points, the male and the female, longevity, and the prerogatives of power. The doors swung on their hinges with a musical note, and were placed in such a manner that one followed the entire scale when crossing the palace from east to west. Everything combined to give an impression of superhuman power and subtlety, and one could feel that here the simplest orders were as final and as terrible as the wisdom of the ancients. At last, the air became thin and the silence so deep that not even a man under torture would have dared to scream. A eunuch lifted a tapestry; the soldiers began to tremble like women, and the small troop entered the chamber in which the Son of Heaven sat on a high throne.

14   It was a room without walls, held up by thick columns of blue stone. A garden spread out on the far side of the marble shafts, and each and every flower blooming in the greenery belonged to a rare species brought here from across the oceans. But none of them had any perfume, so that the Celestial Dragon's meditations would not be troubled by fine smells. Out of respect for the silence in which his thoughts evolved, no bird had been allowed within the enclosure, and even the bees had been driven away. An enormous wall separated the garden from the rest of the world, so that the wind that sweeps over dead dogs and corpses on the battlefield would not dare brush the Emperor's sleeve.

15   The Celestial Master sat on a throne of jade, and his hands were wrinkled like those of an old man, though he had scarcely reached the age of twenty. His robe was blue to symbolize winter, and green to remind one of spring. His face was beautiful but blank, like a looking glass placed too high, reflecting nothing except the stars and the immutable heavens. To his right stood his Minister of Perfect Pleasures, and to his left his Counselor of Just Torments. Because his courtiers, lined along the base of the columns, always lent a keen ear to the slightest sound from his lips, he had adopted the habit of speaking in a low voice.

"Celestial Dragon," said Wang-Fo, bowing low, "I am old, I am poor, [16] I am weak. You are like summer; I am like winter. You have Ten Thousand Lives; I have but one, and it is near its close. What have I done to you? My hands have been tied, these hands that never harmed you."

"You ask what you have done to me, old Wang-Fo?" said the Em- [17] peror.

His voice was so melodious that it made one want to cry. He raised his [18] right hand, to which the reflections from the jade pavement gave a pale sea-green hue like that of an underwater plant, and Wang-Fo marveled at the length of those thin fingers, and hunted among his memories to discover whether he had not at some time painted a mediocre portrait of either the Emperor or one of his ancestors that would not merit a sentence of death. But it seemed unlikely because Wang-Fo had not been an assiduous visitor at the Imperial Court. He preferred the farmers' huts or, in the cities, the courtesans' quarters and the taverns along the harbor where the dockers liked to quarrel.

"You ask me what it is you have done, old Wang-Fo?" repeated the [19] Emperor, inclining his slender neck toward the old man waiting attentively. "I will tell you. But, as another man's poison cannot enter our veins except through our nine openings, in order to show you your offenses I must take you with me down the corridors of my memory and tell you the story of my life. My father had assembled a collection of your work and hidden it in the most secret chamber in the palace, because he judged that the people in your paintings should be concealed from the world since they cannot lower their eyes in the presence of profane viewers. It was in those same rooms that I was brought up, old Wang-Fo, surrounded by solitude. To prevent my innocence from being sullied by other human souls, the restless crowd of my future subjects had been driven away from me, and no one was allowed to pass my threshold, for fear that his or her shadow would stretch out and touch me. The few aged servants that were placed in my service showed themselves as little as possible; the hours turned in circles; the colors of your paintings bloomed in the first hours of the morning and grew pale at dusk. At night, when I was unable to sleep, I gazed at them, and for nearly ten years I gazed at them every night. During the day, sitting on a carpet whose design I knew by heart, I dreamed of the joys the future had in store for me. I imagined the world, with the Kingdom of Han at the center, to be like the flat palm of my hand crossed by the fatal lines of the Five Rivers. Around it lay the sea in which monsters are born, and farther away the mountains that hold up the heavens. And to help me visualize these things I used your paintings. You made me believe that the sea looked like the vast sheet of water spread across your scrolls, so blue that if a stone were to fall into it, it would become a sapphire; that women opened and closed like flowers, like the creatures that come forward, pushed by the wind, along the paths of your painted gardens; and that the young, slim-waisted warriors who mount guard in the fortresses along the frontier were themselves like arrows that could pierce my heart. At sixteen I saw the doors that separated me from the world open once again; I climbed onto the balcony of my palace to look at the clouds, but they were far less beautiful than those in your sunsets. I ordered my litter; bounced along roads on which I had not foreseen either mud or stones, I traveled across the provinces of the Empire without ever finding your gardens full of women like fireflies, or a woman whose body was in itself a garden. The pebbles on the beach spoiled my taste for oceans; the blood of the tortured is less red than the pomegranates in your paintings; the village vermin prevented me from seeing the beauty of the rice fields; the flesh of mortal women disgusted me like the dead meat hanging from the butcher's hook, and the coarse laughter of my soldiers made me sick. You lied, Wang-Fo, you old impostor. The world is nothing but a mass of muddled colors thrown into the void by an insane painter, and smudged by out tears. The Kingdom of Han is not the most beautiful of kingdoms, and I am not the Emperor. The only empire which is worth reigning over is that which you alone can enter, old Wang, by the road of One Thousand Curves and Ten Thousand Colors. You alone reign peacefully over mountains covered in snow that cannot melt, and over fields of daffodils that cannot die. And that is why, Wang-Fo, I have conceived a punishment for you, for you whose enchantment has filled me with disgust at everything I own, and with desire for everything I shall never possess. And in order to lock you up in the only cell from which there is no escape, I have decided to have your eyes burned out, because your eyes, Wang-Fo, are the two magic gates that open onto your kingdom. And as your hands are the two roads of ten forking paths that lead to the heart of your kingdom, I have decided to have your hands cut off. Have you understood, old Wang-Fo?"

20   Hearing the sentence, Ling, the disciple, tore from his belt an old knife and leaped toward the Emperor. Two guards immediately seized him. The Son of Heaven smiled and added, with a sigh: "And I also hate you, old Wang-Fo, because you have known how to make yourself beloved. Kill that dog."

21   Ling jumped to one side so that his blood would not stain his master's robe. One of the soldiers lifted his sword and Ling's head fell from his neck like a cut flower. The servants carried away the remains, and Wang-Fo, in despair, admired the beautiful scarlet stain that his disciple's blood made on the green stone floor.

22   The Emperor made a sign and the two eunuchs wiped Wang's eyes.

23   "Listen, old Wang-Fo," said the Emperor, "and dry your tears, because this is not the time to weep. Your eyes must be clear so that the little light that is left to them is not clouded by your weeping. Because it is not only the grudge I bear you that makes me desire your death; it is not only the cruelty in my heart that makes me want to see you suffer. I have other plans, old Wang-Fo. I possess among your work a remarkable

painting in which the mountains, the river estuary, and the sea reflect each other, on a very small scale certainly, but with a clarity that surpasses the real landscapes themselves, like objects reflected on the walls of a metal sphere. But that painting is unfinished, Wang-Fo; your masterpiece is but a sketch. No doubt, when you began your work, sitting in a solitary valley, you noticed a passing bird, or a child running after the bird. And the bird's beak or the child's cheeks made you forget the blue eyelids of the sea. You never finished the frills of the water's cloak, or the seaweed hair of the rocks. Wang-Fo, I want you to use the few hours of light that are left to you to finish this painting, which will thus contain the final secrets amassed during your long life. I know that your hands, about to fall, will not tremble on the silken cloth, and infinity will enter your work through those unhappy cuts. I know that your eyes, about to be put out, will discover bearings far beyond all human senses. This is my plan, old Wang-Fo, and I can force you to fulfill it. If you refuse, before blinding you, I will have all your paintings burned, and you will be like a father whose children are slaughtered and all hopes of posterity extinguished. However, believe, if you wish, that this last order stems from nothing but my kindness, because I know that the silken scroll is the only mistress you ever deigned to touch. And to offer you brushes, paints, and inks to occupy your last hours is like offering the favors of a harlot to a man condemned to death."

Upon a sign from the Emperor's little finger, two eunuchs respectfully brought forward the unfinished scroll on which Wang-Fo had outlined the image of the sea and the sky. Wang-Fo dried his tears and smiled, because that small sketch reminded him of his youth. Everything in it spoke of a fresh new spirit which Wang-Fo could no longer claim as his, and yet something was missing from it, because when Wang had painted it he had not yet looked long enough at the mountains or at the rocks bathing their naked flanks in the sea, and he had not yet penetrated deep enough into the sadness of the evening twilight. Wang-Fo selected one of the brushes which a slave held ready for him and began spreading wide strokes of blue on the unfinished sea. A eunuch crouched by his feet, mixing the colors; he carried out his task with little skill, and more than ever Wang-Fo lamented the loss of his disciple Ling.   24

Wang began by adding a touch of pink to the tip of the wing of a cloud perched on a mountain. Then he painted onto the surface of the sea a few small lines that deepened the perfect feeling of calm. The jade floor became increasingly damp, but Wang-Fo, absorbed as he was in his painting, did not seem to notice that he was working with his feet in water.   25

The fragile rowboat grew under the strokes of the painter's brush and now occupied the entire foreground of the silken scroll. The rhythmic sound of the oars rose suddenly in the distance, quick and eager like the beating of wings. The sound came nearer, gently filling the whole room, then ceased, and a few trembling drops appeared on the boatman's oars.   26

The red iron intended for Wang's eyes lay extinguished on the executioner's coals. The courtiers, motionless as etiquette required, stood in
water up to their shoulders, trying to lift themselves onto the tips of their
toes. The water finally reached the level of the imperial heart. The silence
was so deep one could have heard a tear drop.

27   It was Ling. He wore his everyday robe, and his right sleeve still had a
hole that he had not had time to mend that morning before the soldiers'
arrival. But around his neck was tied a strange red scarf.

28   Wang-Fo said to him softly, while he continued painting, "I thought
you were dead."

29   "You being alive," said Ling respectfully, "how could I have died?"

30   And he helped his master into the boat. The jade ceiling reflected itself
in the water, so that Ling seemed to be inside a cave. The pigtails of
submerged courtiers rippled up toward the surface like snakes, and the
pale head of the Emperor floated like a lotus.

31   "Look at them," said Wang-Fo sadly. "These wretches will die, if they
are not dead already. I never thought there was enough water in the sea
to drown an Emperor. What are we to do?"

32   "Master, have no fear," murmured the disciple. "They will soon be dry
again and will not even remember that their sleeves were ever wet. Only
the Emperor will keep in his heart a little of the bitterness of the sea.
These people are not the kind to lose themselves inside a painting."

33   And he added: "The sea is calm, the wind high, the seabirds fly to their
nests. Let us leave, Master, and sail to the land beyond the waves."

34   "Let us leave," said the old painter.

35   Wang-Fo took hold of the helm, and Ling bent over the oars. The
sound of rowing filled the room again, strong and steady like the beating of a heart. The level of the water dropped unnoticed around the
large vertical rocks that became columns once more. Soon only a few
puddles glistened in the hollows of the jade floor. The courtiers' robes
were dry, but a few wisps of foam still clung to the hem of the Emperor's
cloak.

36   The painting finished by Wang-Fo was leaning against a tapestry. A
rowboat occupied the entire foreground. It drifted away little by little,
leaving behind it a thin wake that smoothed out into the quiet sea. One
could no longer make out the faces of the two men sitting in the boat, but
one could still see Ling's red scarf and Wang-Fo's beard waving in the
breeze.

37   The beating of the oars grew fainter, then ceased, blotted out the
distance. The Emperor, leaning forward, a hand above his eyes, watched
Wang's boat sail away till it was nothing but an imperceptible dot in the
paleness of the twilight. A golden mist rose and spread over the water.
Finally the boat veered around a rock that stood at the gateway to the
ocean; the shadow of a cliff fell across it; its wake disappeared from the
deserted surface, and the painter Wang-Fo and his disciple Ling vanished
forever on the jade-blue sea that Wang-Fo had just created.

❏ **Questions for Discussion**

1. Why does the Emperor want Wang-Fo dead? What has Wang-Fo discovered about the relationship between art and reality?

2. When Wang-Fo admires the beautiful stain on the stone floor—a stain created from the blood of his loyal disciple Ling—how does this simple observation of beauty reveal Wang-Fo's complete devotion to his art? How has art transcended reality for him?

3. Wang-Fo paints a picture, supposedly his last act of freedom before death. Wang-Fo, however, sails off across the "jade-blue sea" with Ling, thereby saving himself and resurrecting Ling. What is suggested by this last scene?

❏ **Suggestions for Exploration and Writing**

1. Write an essay attacking or defending an artist's right to depict life, people, colors, and mood as he or she sees them rather than as others may perceive them.

2. As Wang-Fo and Ling sail off, Ling reflects upon the Emperor and his men: "These people are not the kind to lose themselves inside a painting." Write an essay analyzing the type of persons who could "lose" themselves inside a painting or any other work of art.

WOODY ALLEN (1935–)

Born Allen Stewart Konigsberg, Woody Allen exhibited an early interest in writing and at the age of seventeen joined NBC as a staff writer. There he wrote for The Garry Moore Show *and Sid Caesar's* Your Show of Shows. *His first screenplay,* What's New Pussycat? *(1964), decided his future as a director. Since then he has written, directed, and starred in over fifteen films as an Academy Award-winning filmmaker and one of the few directors with total control over production. Many of Allen's films and stories are parodies, science fiction, and spoofs of nineteenth-century Russian novels; and they often use wordplay, allusions, and juxtapositions of unusual elements. "The Kugelmass Episode," first published in the* New Yorker, *won an O. Henry Award as one of the best stories of 1978.*

The Kugelmass Episode

Kugelmass, a professor of humanities at City College, was unhappily   1
married for the second time. Daphne Kugelmass was an oaf. He also had
two dull sons by his first wife, Flo, and was up to his neck in alimony and
child support.

2   "Did I know it would turn out so badly?" Kugelmass whined to his analyst one day. "Daphne had promise. Who suspected she'd let herself go and swell up like a beach ball? Plus she had a few bucks, which is not in itself a healthy reason to marry a person, but it doesn't hurt, with the kind of operating nut I have. You see my point?"

3   Kugelmass was bald and as hairy as a bear, but he had soul.

4   "I need to meet a new woman," he went on. "I need to have an affair. I may not look the part, but I'm a man who needs romance. I need softness, I need flirtation. I'm not getting younger, so before it's too late I want to make love in Venice, trade quips at '21,' and exchange coy glances over red wine and candlelight. You see what I'm saying?"

5   Dr. Mandel shifted in his chair and said, "An affair will solve nothing. You're so unrealistic. Your problems run much deeper."

6   "And also this affair must be discreet," Kugelmass continued. "I can't afford a second divorce. Daphne would really sock it to me."

7   "Mr. Kugelmass—"

8   "But it can't be anyone at City College, because Daphne also works there. Not that anyone on the faculty at C.C.N.Y. is any great shakes, but some of those co-eds . . ."

9   "Mr. Kugelmass—"

10   "Help me. I had a dream last night. I was skipping through a meadow holding a picnic basket and the basket was marked 'Options.' And then I saw there was a hole in the basket."

11   "Mr. Kugelmass, the worst thing you could do is act out. You must simply express your feelings here, and together we'll analyze them. You have been in treatment long enough to know there is no overnight cure. After all, I'm an analyst, not a magician."

12   "Then perhaps what I need is a magician," Kugelmass said, rising from his chair. And with that he terminated his therapy.

13   A couple of weeks later, while Kugelmass and Daphne were moping around in their apartment one night like two pieces of old furniture, the phone rang.

14   "I'll get it," Kugelmass said. "Hello."

15   "Kugelmass?" a voice said. "Kugelmass, this is Persky."

16   "Who?"

17   "Persky. Or should I say The Great Persky?"

18   "Pardon me?"

19   "I hear you're looking all over town for a magician to bring a little exotica into your life? Yes or no?"

20   "Sh-h-h," Kugelmass whispered. "Don't hang up. Where are you calling from, Persky?"

21   Early the following afternoon, Kugelmass climbed three flights of stairs in a broken-down apartment house in the Bushwick section of Brooklyn. Peering through the darkness of the hall, he found the door he was looking for and pressed the bell. I'm going to regret this, he thought to himself.

Seconds later, he was greeted by a short, thin, waxy-looking man.   22
"*You're* Persky the Great?" Kugelmass said.   23
"The Great Persky. You want a tea?"   24
"No, I want romance. I want music. I want love and beauty."   25
"But not tea, eh? Amazing. O.K., sit down."   26
Persky went to the back room, and Kugelmass heard the sounds of   27
boxes and furniture being moved around. Persky reappeared, pushing
before him a large object on squeaky roller-skate wheels. He removed
some old silk handkerchiefs that were lying on its top and blew away a
bit of dust. It was a cheap-looking Chinese cabinet, badly lacquered.
"Persky," Kugelmass said, "what's your scam?"   28
"Pay attention," Persky said. "This is some beautiful effect. I devel-   29
oped it for a Knights of Pythias date last year, but the booking fell
through. Get into the cabinet."
"Why, so you can stick it full of swords of something?"   30
"You see any swords?"   31
Kugelmass made a face and, grunting, climbed into the cabinet. He   32
couldn't help noticing a couple of ugly rhinestones glued onto the raw
plywood just in front of his face. "If this is a joke," he said.
"Some joke. Now, here's the point. If I throw any novel into this   33
cabinet with you, shut the doors, and tap it three times, you will find
yourself projected into that book."
Kugelmass made a grimace of disbelief.   34
"It's the emess," Persky said "My hand to God. Not just a novel,   35
either. A short story, a play, a poem. You can meet any of the women
created by the world's best writers. Whoever you dreamed of. You could
carry on all you like with a real winner. Then when you've had enough
you give a yell, and I'll see you're back here in a split second."
"Persky, are you some kind of outpatient?"   36
"I'm telling you it's on the level," Persky said.   37
Kugelmass remained skeptical. "What are you telling me—that this   38
cheesy homemade box can take me on a ride like you're describing?"
"For a double sawbuck."   39
Kugelmass reached for his wallet. "I'll believe this when I see it," he   40
said.
Persky tucked the bills in his pants pocket and turned toward his   41
bookcase. "So who do you want to meet? Sister Carrie?[1] Hester Prynne?[2]
Ophelia?[3] Maybe someone by Saul Bellow?[4] Hey, what about Temple
Drake?[5] Although for a man your age she'd be a workout."
"French. I want to have an affair with a French lover."   42

[1] Sister Carrie, a character in Theodore Dreiser's novel of the same name, becomes a prostitute.
[2] Hester Prynne, a character in Hawthorne's *Scarlet Letter,* wears an "A" for adultery.
[3] Ophelia in Shakespeare's *Hamlet* is the young woman whom Hamlet loves.
[4] Saul Bellow is a contemporary American novelist.
[5] In William Faulkner's novel *Sanctuary,* Popeye rapes Temple Drake with a corncob.

43   "Nana?"[6]

44   "I don't want to have to pay for it."

45   "What about Natasha in *War and Peace?*"

46   "I said French. I know! What about Emma Bovary?[7] That sounds to me perfect."

47   "You got it Kugelmass. Give me a holler when you've had enough." Persky tossed in a paperback copy of Flaubert's novel.

48   "You sure this is safe?" Kugelmass asked as Persky began shutting the cabinet doors.

49   "Safe. Is anything safe in this crazy world?" Persky rapped three times on the cabinet and then flung open the doors.

50   Kugelmass was gone. At the same moment, he appeared in the bedroom of Charles and Emma Bovary's house at Yonville. Before him was a beautiful woman, standing alone with her back turned to him as she folded some linen. I can't believe this, thought Kugelmass, staring at the doctor's ravishing wife. This is uncanny. I'm here. It's her.

51   Emma turned in surprise. "Goodness, you startled me," she said. "Who are you?" She spoke in the same fine English translation as the paperback.

52   It's simply devastating, he thought. Then, realizing that it was he whom she had addressed, he said, "Excuse me. I'm Sidney Kugelmass. I'm from City College. A professor of humanities. C.C.N.Y.? Uptown. I—oh, boy!"

53   Emma Bovary smiled flirtatiously and said, "Would you like a drink? A glass of wine, perhaps?"

54   She is beautiful, Kugelmass thought. What a contrast with the troglodyte who shared his bed! He felt a sudden impulse to take this vision into his arms and tell her she was the kind of woman he had dreamed of all his life.

55   "Yes, some wine," he said hoarsely. "White. No, red. No, white. Make it white."

56   "Charles is out for the day," Emma said, her voice full of playful implication.

57   After the wine, they went for a stroll in the lovely French countryside. "I've always dreamed that some mysterious stranger would appear and rescue me from the monotony of this crass rural existence," Emma said, clasping his hand. They passed a small church. "I love what you have on," she murmured. "I've never seen anything like it around here. It's so . . . so modern."

58   "It's called a leisure suit," he said romantically. "It was marked down." Suddenly he kissed her. For the next hour they reclined under a tree and whispered together and told each other deeply meaningful things with their eyes. Then Kugelmass sat up. He had just remembered he had

---

[6] Nana is the sensuous heroine of Zola's *Nana.*
[7] Emma Bovary is the faithless wife in Flaubert's *Madame Bovary.*

to meet Daphne at Bloomingdale's. "I must go," he told her. "But don't worry, I'll be back."

"I hope so," Emma said.

He embraced her passionately, and the two walked back to the house. He held Emma's face cupped in his palms, kissed her again, and yelled, "O.K., Persky! I got to be at Bloomingdale's by three-thirty."

There was an audible pop, and Kugelmass was back in Brooklyn.

"So? Did I lie?" Persky asked triumphantly.

"Look, Persky, I'm right now late to meet the ball and chain at Lexington Avenue, but when can I go again? Tomorrow?"

"My pleasure. Just bring a twenty. And don't mention this to anybody."

"Yeah. I'm going to call Rupert Murdoch."[8]

Kugelmass hailed a cab and sped off to the city. His heart danced on point. I am in love, he thought, I am the possessor of a wonderful secret. What he didn't realize was that at this very moment students in various classrooms across the country were saying to their teachers, "Who is this character on page 100? A bald Jew is kissing Madame Bovary?" A teacher in Sioux Falls, South Dakota, sighed and thought, Jesus, these kids, with their pot and acid. What goes through their minds!

Daphne Kugelmass was in the bathroom-accessories department at Bloomingdale's when Kugelmass arrived breathlessly. "Where've you been?" she snapped. "It's four-thirty."

"I got held up in traffic," Kugelmass said.

Kugelmass visited Persky the next day, and in a few minutes was again passing magically to Yonville. Emma couldn't hide her excitement at seeing him. The two spent hours together, laughing and talking about their different backgrounds. Before Kugelmass left, they made love. "My God, I'm doing it with Madame Bovary!" Kugelmass whispered to himself. "Me, who failed freshman English."

As the months passed, Kugelmass saw Persky many times and developed a close and passionate relationship with Emma Bovary. "Make sure and always get me into the book before page 120," Kugelmass said to the magician one day. "I always have to meet her before she hooks up with this Rodolphe character."

"Why?" Persky asked. "You can't beat his time?"

"Beat his time. He's landed gentry. Those guys have nothing better to do than flirt and ride horses. To me, he's one of those faces you see in the pages of *Women's Wear Daily*. With the Helmut Berger hairdo. But to her he's hot stuff."

"And her husband suspects nothing?"

"He's out of his depth. He's a lacklustre little paramedic who's thrown

---

[8] Rupert Murdoch is a wealthy Australian publisher and owner of several sensational tabloids.

in his lot with a jitterbug. He's ready to go to sleep by ten, and she's putting on her dancing shoes. Oh, well . . . See you later."

75   And once again Kugelmass entered the cabinet and passed instantly to the Bovary estate at Yonville. "How you doing, cupcake?" he said to Emma.

76   "Oh, Kugelmass," Emma sighed. "What I have to put up with. Last night at dinner, Mr. Personality dropped off to sleep in the middle of the dessert course. I'm pouring my heart out about Maxim's and the ballet, and out of the blue I hear snoring."

77   "It's O.K., darling. I'm here now," Kugelmass said, embracing her. I've earned this, he thought, smelling Emma's French perfume and burying his nose in her hair. I've suffered enough. I've paid enough analysts. I've searched till I'm weary. She's young and nubile, and I'm here a few pages after Leon and just before Rodolphe. By showing up during the correct chapters, I've got the situation knocked.

78   Emma, to be sure, was just as happy as Kugelmass. She had been starved for excitement, and his tales of Broadway night life, of fast cars and Hollywood and TV stars, enthralled the young French beauty.

79   "Tell me again about O. J. Simpson," she implored that evening, as she and Kugelmass strolled past Abbé Bournisien's church.

80   "What can I say? The man is great. He sets all kinds of rushing records. Such moves. They can't touch him."

81   "And the Academy Awards?" Emma said wistfully. "I'd give anything to win one."

82   "First you've got to be nominated."

83   "I know. You explained it. But I'm convinced I can act. Of course, I'd want to take a class or two. With Strasberg maybe. Then if I had the right agent—"

84   "We'll see, we'll see. I'll speak to Persky."

85   That night, safely returned to Persky's flat, Kugelmass brought up the idea of having Emma visit him in the big city.

86   "Let me think about it," Persky said. "Maybe I could work it. Stranger things have happened." Of course, neither of them could think of one.

87   "Where the hell do you go all the time?" Daphne Kugelmass barked at her husband as he returned home late that evening. "You got a chippie stashed somewhere?"

88   "Yeah, sure, I'm just the type," Kugelmass said wearily. "I was with Leonard Popkin. We were discussing Socialist agriculture in Poland. You know Popkin. He's a freak on the subject."

89   "Well, you've been very odd lately," Daphne said. "Distant. Just don't forget about my father's birthday. On Saturday?"

90   "Oh, sure, sure," Kugelmass said, heading for the bathroom.

91   "My whole family will be there. We can see the twins. And Cousin Hamish. You should be more polite to Cousin Hamish—he likes you."

92   "Right, the twins," Kugelmass said, closing the bathroom door and shutting out the sound of his wife's voice. He leaned against it and took

a deep breath. In a few hours, he told himself, he would be back in Yonville again, back with his beloved. And this time, if all went well, he would bring Emma back with him.

At three-fifteen the following afternoon, Persky worked his wizardry again. Kugelmass appeared before Emma, smiling and eager. The two spent a few hours at Yonville with Binet and then remounted the Bovary carriage. Following Persky's instructions, they held each other tightly, closed their eyes, and counted to ten. When they opened them, the carriage was just drawing up at the side door of the Plaza Hotel, where Kugelmass had optimistically reserved a suite earlier in the day. 93

"I love it! It's everything I dreamed it would be," Emma said as she swirled joyously around the bedroom, surveying the city from their window. "There's F.A.O. Schwarz. And there's Central Park, and the Sherry is which one? Oh, there—I see. It's too divine." 94

On the bed there were boxes from Halston and Saint Laurent. Emma unwrapped a package and held up a pair of black velvet pants against her perfect body. 95

"The slacks suit is by Ralph Lauren," Kugelmass said. "You'll look like a million bucks in it. Come on, sugar, give us a kiss." 96

"I've never been so happy!" Emma squealed as she stood before the mirror. "Let's go out on the town. I want to see *Chorus Line* and the Guggenheim and this Jack Nicholson character you always talk about. Are any of his flicks showing?" 97

"I cannot get my mind around this," a Stanford professor said. "First a strange character named Kugelmass, and now she's gone from the book. Well, I guess the mark of a classic is that you can reread it a thousand times and always find something new." 98

The lovers passed a blissful weekend. Kugelmass had told Daphne he would be away at a symposium in Boston and would return Monday. Savoring each moment, he and Emma went to the movies, had dinner in Chinatown, passed two hours at a discothèque, and went to bed with a TV movie. They slept till noon on Sunday, visited SoHo, and ogled celebrities at Elaine's. They had caviar and champagne in their suite on Sunday night and talked until dawn. That morning, in the cab taking them to Persky's apartment, Kugelmass thought, It was hectic, but worth it. I can't bring her here too often, but now and then it will be a charming contrast with Yonville. 99

At Persky's, Emma climbed into the cabinet, arranged her new boxes of clothes neatly around her, and kissed Kugelmass fondly. "My place next time," she said with a wink. Persky rapped three times on the cabinet. Nothing happened. 100

"Hmmm," Persky said, scratching his head. He rapped again, but still no magic. "Something must be wrong," he mumbled. 101

"Persky, you're joking!" Kugelmass cried. "How can it not work?" 102

"Relax, relax. Are you still in the box, Emma?" 103

"Yes." 104

105   Persky rapped again—harder this time.

106   "I'm still here, Persky."

107   "I know, darling. Sit tight."

108   "Persky, we *have* to get her back," Kugelmass whispered. "I'm a married man, and I have a class in three hours. I'm not prepared for anything more than a cautious affair at this point."

109   "I can't understand it," Persky muttered. "It's such a reliable little trick."

110   But he could do nothing. "It's going to take a little while," he said to Kugelmass. "I'm going to have to strip it down. I'll call you later."

111   Kugelmass bundled Emma into a cab and took her back to the Plaza. He barely made to his class on time. He was on the phone all day, to Persky and to his mistress. The magician told him it might be several days before he got to the bottom of the trouble.

112   "How was the symposium?" Daphne asked him that night.

113   "Fine, fine," he said, lighting the filter end of a cigarette.

114   "What's wrong? You're as tense as a cat."

115   "Me? Ha, that's a laugh. I'm as calm as a summer night. I'm just going to take a walk." He eased out the door, hailed a cab, and flew to the Plaza.

116   "This is no good," Emma said. "Charles will miss me."

117   "Bear with me, sugar," Kugelmass said. He was pale and sweaty. He kissed her again, raced to the elevators, yelled at Persky over a pay phone in the Plaza lobby, and just made it home before midnight.

118   "According to Popkin, barley prices in Kraków have not been this stable since 1971," he said to Daphne, and smiled wanly as he climbed into bed.

119   The whole week went by like that.

120   On Friday night, Kugelmass told Daphne there was another symposium he had to catch, this one in Syracuse. He hurried back to the Plaza, but the second weekend there was nothing like the first. "Get me back into the novel or marry me," Emma told Kugelmass. "Meanwhile, I want to get a job or go to class, because watching TV all day is the pits."

121   "Fine. We can use the money," Kugelmass said. "You consume twice your weight in room service."

122   "I met an Off Broadway producer in Central Park yesterday, and he said I might be right for a project he's doing," Emma said.

123   "Who is this clown?" Kugelmass asked.

124   "He's not a clown. He's sensitive and kind and cute. His name's Jeff Something-or-Other, and he's up for a Tony."

125   Later that afternoon, Kugelmass showed up at Persky's drunk.

126   "Relax," Persky told him. "You'll get a coronary."

127   "Relax. The man says relax. I've got a fictional character stashed in a hotel room, and I think my wife is having me tailed by a private shamus."

"O.K., O.K. We know there's a problem." Persky crawled under the cabinet and started banging on something with a large wrench. 128

"I'm like a wild animal." Kugelmass went on. "I'm sneaking around town, and Emma and I have had it up to here with each other. Not to mention a hotel tab that reads like the defense budget." 129

"So what should I do? This is the world of magic," Persky said. "It's all nuance." 130

"Nuance, my foot. I'm pouring Dom Pérignon and black eggs into this little mouse, plus her wardrobe, plus she's enrolled at the Neighborhood Playhouse and suddenly needs professional photos. Also, Persky, Professor Fivish Kopkind, who teaches Comp Lit and who has always been jealous of me, has identified me as the sporadically appearing character in the Flaubert book. He's threatened to go to Daphne. I see ruin and alimony; jail. For adultery with Madame Bovary, my wife will reduce me to beggary." 131

"What do you want me to say? I'm working on it night and day. As far as your personal anxiety goes, that I can't help you with. I'm a magician, not an analyst." 132

By Sunday afternoon, Emma had locked herself in the bathroom and refused to respond to Kugelmass's entreaties. Kugelmass stared out the window at the Wollman Rink and contemplated suicide. Too bad this is a low floor, he thought, or I'd do it right now. Maybe if I ran away to Europe and started life over. . . . Maybe I could sell the *International Herald Tribune*, like those young girls used to. 133

The phone rang. Kugelmass lifted it to his ear mechanically. 134

"Bring her over," Persky said. "I think I got the bugs out of it." 135

Kugelmass's heart leaped. "You're serious?" he said. "You got it licked?" 136

"It was something in the transmission. Go figure." 137

"Persky, you're a genius. We'll be there in a minute. Less than a minute." 138

Again the lovers hurried to the magician's apartment, and again Emma Bovary climbed into the cabinet with her boxes. This time there was no kiss. Persky shut the doors, took a deep breath, and tapped the box three times. There was the reassuring popping noise, and when Persky peered inside, the box was empty. Madame Bovary was back in her novel. Kugelmass heaved a great sigh of relief and pumped the magician's hand. 139

"It's over," he said. "I learned my lesson. I'll never cheat again, I swear it." He pumped Persky's hand again and made a mental note to send him a necktie. 140

Three weeks later, at the end of a beautiful spring afternoon, Persky answered his doorbell. It was Kugelmass, with a sheepish expression on his face. 141

"O.K., Kugelmass," the magician said. "Where to this time?" 142

143   "It's just this once," Kugelmass said. "The weather is so lovely, and I'm not getting any younger. Listen, you've read *Portnoy's Complaint?*[9] Remember The Monkey?"[10]

144   "The price is now twenty-five dollars, because the cost of living is up, but I'll start you off with one freebie, due to all the trouble I caused you."

145   "You're good people," Kugelmass said, combing his few remaining hairs as he climbed into the cabinet again. "This'll work all right?"

146   "I hope. But I haven't tried it much since all that unpleasantness."

147   "Sex and romance," Kugelmass said from inside the box. "What we go through for a pretty face."

148   Persky tossed in a copy of *Portnoy's Complaint* and rapped three times on the box. This time, instead of a popping noise there was a dull explosion, followed by a series of crackling noises and a shower of sparks. Persky leaped back, was seized by a heart attack, and dropped dead. The cabinet burst into flames, and eventually the entire house burned down.

149   Kugelmass, unaware of this catastrophe, had his own problems. He had not been thrust into *Portnoy's Complaint,* or into any other novel, for that matter. He had been projected into an old textbook, *Remedial Spanish,* and was running for his life over a barren, rocky terrain as the word *tener* ("to have")—a large and hairy irregular verb—raced after him on its spindly legs.

❏ Questions for Discussion

1. Why does Kugelmass want to have a love affair?

2. Kugelmass is given the option of meeting and loving any woman in any work of literature. If you were given the option of so choosing a man or woman, whom would you choose? Why?

3. Why does Persky mention as options such characters as Hester Prynne, Ophelia, Temple Drake, or Nana? How do these allusions add depth to the humor of the story?

4. What relationship between life and art does this story suggest? In what ways does it give new meaning to the term "escapist literature"?

❏ Suggestions for Exploration and Writing

1. If you have read *Madame Bovary,* choose a scene before the entry of Rodolphe and rewrite it, adding Kugelmass. If you

[9] *Portnoy's Complaint* is a novel by Philip Roth which, when it was first published, was a favorite of undergraduates because of its sexual explicitness.

[10] The Monkey is a sexually athletic young woman in *Portnoy's Complaint.*

have not read *Madame Bovary,* write an imagined scene set in either France or New York City from the point of view of Emma Bovary as she is seen in Allen's story.

2. At the end of Allen's story, Kugelmass becomes a character with "few remaining hairs" being chased by "a large and hairy irregular verb" in a remedial Spanish book. Compare his situation to becoming a character in a Stephen King novel or a similar work.

3. In a comic narrative, imagine yourself or a friend transported to a story or play in this anthology.

4. Cast yourself as a character in a recent movie and explain your reasons for selecting that character.

RAYMOND CARVER (1938–1988)

Cathedral

This blind man, an old friend of my wife's, he was on his way to spend the night. His wife had died. So he was visiting the dead wife's relatives in Connecticut. He called my wife from his in-laws'. Arrangements were made. He would come by train, a five-hour trip, and my wife would meet him at the station. She hadn't seen him since she worked for him one summer in Seattle ten years ago. But she and the blind man had kept in touch. They made tapes and mailed them back and forth. I wasn't enthusiastic about his visit. He was no one I knew. And his being blind bothered me. My idea of blindness came from the movies. In the movies, the blind moved slowly and never laughed. Sometimes they were led by seeing-eye dogs. A blind man in my house was not something I looked forward to.

That summer in Seattle she had needed a job. She didn't have any money. The man she was going to marry at the end of the summer was in officers' training school. He didn't have any money, either. But she was in love with the guy, and he was in love with her, etc. She'd seen something in the paper: HELP WANTED—*Reading to Blind Man,* and a telephone number. She phoned and went over, was hired on the spot. She'd worked with this blind man all summer. She read stuff to him, case studies, reports, that sort of thing. She helped him organize his little office in the county social-service department. They'd become good friends, my wife and the blind man. How do I know these things? She told me. And she told me something else. On her last day in the office, the blind man asked if he could touch her face. She agreed to this. She told me he touched his fingers to every part of her face, her nose—even her neck! She never forgot it. She even tried to write a poem about it. She was always trying to write a poem. She wrote a poem or two every year, usually after something really important had happened to her.

3   When we first started going out together, she showed me the poem. In the poem, she recalled his fingers and the way they had moved around over her face. In the poem, she talked about what she had felt at the time, about what went through her mind when the blind man touched her nose and lips. I can remember I didn't think much of the poem. Of course, I didn't tell her that. Maybe I just don't understand poetry. I admit it's not the first thing I reach for when I pick up something to read.

4   Anyway, this man who'd first enjoyed her favors, the officer-to-be, he'd been her childhood sweetheart. So okay. I'm saying that at the end of the summer she let the blind man run his hands over her face, said good-bye to him, married her childhood etc., who was now a commissioned officer, and she moved away from Seattle. But they'd kept in touch, she and the blind man. She made the first contact after a year or so. She called him up one night from an Air Force base in Alabama. She wanted to talk. They talked. He asked her to send a tape and tell him about her life. She did this. She sent the tape. On the tape, she told the blind man about her husband and about their life together in the military. She told the blind man she loved her husband but she didn't like it where they lived and she didn't like it that he was part of the military-industrial thing. She told the blind man she'd written a poem and he was in it. She told him that she was writing a poem about what it was like to be an Air Force officer's wife. The poem wasn't finished yet. She was still writing it. The blind man made a tape. He sent her the tape. She made a tape. This went on for years. My wife's officer was posted to one base and then another. She sent tapes from Moody AFB, McGuire, McConnell, and finally Travis, near Sacramento, where one night she got to feeling lonely and cut off from people she kept losing in that moving-around life. She got to feeling she couldn't go it another step. She went in and swallowed all the pills and capsules in the medicine chest and washed them down with a bottle of gin. Then she got into a hot bath and passed out.

5   But instead of dying, she got sick. She threw up. Her officer—why should he have a name? He was the childhood sweetheart, and what more does he want?—came home from somewhere, found her, and called the ambulance. In time, she put it all on a tape and sent the tape to the blind man. Over the years, she put all kinds of stuff on tapes and sent the tapes off lickety-split. Next to writing a poem every year, I think it was her chief means of recreation. On one tape, she told the blind man she'd decided to live away from her officer for a time. On another tape, she told him about their divorce. She and I began going out, and of course she told her blind man about it. She told him everything, or so it seemed to me. Once she asked me if I'd like to hear the latest tape from the blind man. This was a year ago. I was on the tape, she said. So I said okay, I'd listen to it. I got us drinks and we settled down in the living room. We made

ready to listen. First she inserted the tape into the player and adjusted a couple of dials. Then she pushed a lever. The tape squeaked and someone began to talk in this loud voice. She lowered the volume. After a few minutes of harmless chitchat, I heard my own name in the mouth of this stranger, this blind man I didn't even know! And then this: "From all you've said about him, I can only conclude—" But we were interrupted, a knock at the door, something, and we didn't ever get back to the tape. Maybe it was just as well. I'd heard all I wanted to.

Now this same blind man was coming to sleep in my house.   6

"Maybe I could take him bowling," I said to my wife. She was at the   7 draining board doing scalloped potatoes. She put down the knife she was using and turned around.

"If you love me," she said, "you can do this for me. If you don't love   8 me, okay. But if you had a friend, any friend, and the friend came to visit, I'd make him feel comfortable." She wiped her hands with the dish towel.

"I don't have any blind friends," I said.   9

"You don't have *any* friends," she said. "Period. Besides," she said,   10 "goddamn it, his wife's just died! Don't you understand that? The man's lost his wife!"

I didn't answer. She'd told me a little about the blind man's wife. Her   11 name was Beulah. Beulah! That's a name for a colored woman.

"Was his wife a Negro?" I asked.   12

"Are you crazy?" my wife said. "Have you just flipped or something?"   13 She picked up a potato. I saw it hit the floor, then roll under the stove. "What's wrong with you?" she said. "Are you drunk?"

"I'm just asking," I said.   14

Right then my wife filled me in with more detail than I cared to know.   15 I made a drink and sat at the kitchen table to listen. Pieces of the story began to fall into place.

Beulah had gone to work for the blind man the summer after my wife   16 had stopped working for him. Pretty soon Beulah and the blind man had themselves a church wedding. It was a little wedding—who'd want to go to such a wedding in the first place?—just the two of them, plus the minister and the minister's wife. But it was a church wedding just the same. It was what Beulah had wanted, he'd said. But even then Beulah must have been carrying the cancer in her glands. After they had been inseparable for eight years—my wife's word, *inseparable*—Beulah's health went into a rapid decline. She died in a Seattle hospital room, the blind man sitting beside the bed and holding on to her hand. They'd married, lived and worked together, slept together—had sex, sure—and then the blind man had to bury her. All this without his having ever seen what the goddamned woman looked like. It was beyond my understanding. Hearing this, I felt sorry for the blind man for a little bit. And then I found myself thinking what a pitiful life this woman must have led. Imagine a woman who could never see herself as she was seen in the eyes of her loved one. A woman who could go on day after day and never receive the smallest compliment from her beloved. A woman whose husband could never read the expression on her face, be it misery or something better. Someone who could wear makeup or not—what difference to him? She could, if she wanted, wear green eye-shadow around one eye, a straight pin in her nostril, yellow slacks, and purple shoes, no matter. And then to slip off into death, the blind man's hand on her hand, his blind eyes streaming tears—I'm imagining now—her last thought maybe this: that he never even knew what she looked like, and she on an express to the grave. Robert was left with a small insurance policy and a half of a twenty-peso Mexican coin. The other half of the coin went into the box with her. Pathetic.

17   So when the time rolled around, my wife went to the depot to pick him up. With nothing to do but wait—sure, I blamed him for that—I was having a drink and watching the TV when I heard the car pull into the drive. I got up from the sofa with my drink and went to the window to have a look.

18   I saw my wife laughing as she parked the car. I saw her get out of the car and shut the door. She was still wearing a smile. Just amazing. She went around to the other side of the car to where the blind man was already starting to get out. This blind man, feature this, he was wearing a full beard! A beard on a blind man! Too much, I say. The blind man reached into the backseat and dragged out a suitcase. My wife took his arm, shut the car door, and, talking all the way, moved him down the drive and then up the steps to the front porch. I turned off the TV. I finished my drink, rinsed the glass, dried my hands. Then I went to the door.

19   My wife said, "I want you to meet Robert. Robert, this is my husband. I've told you all about him." She was beaming. She had this blind man by his coat sleeve.

20   The blind man let go of his suitcase and up came his hand.

21   I took it. He squeezed hard, held my hand, and then he let it go.

22   "I feel like we've already met," he boomed.

23   "Likewise," I said. I didn't know what else to say. Then I said, "Welcome, I've heard a lot about you." We began to move then, a little group, from the porch into the living room, my wife guiding him by the arm. The blind man was carrying his suitcase in his other hand. My wife said things like, "To your left here, Robert. That's right. Now watch it, there's a chair. That's it. Sit down right here. This is the sofa. We just bought this sofa two weeks ago."

24   I started to say something about the old sofa. I'd liked that old sofa. But I didn't say anything. Then I wanted to say something else, small-talk, about the scenic ride along the Hudson. How coming *to* New York, you should sit on the right-hand side of the train, and coming *from* New York, the left-hand.

25   "Did you have a good train ride?" I said. "Which side of the train did you sit on, by the way?"

"What a question, which side!" my wife said. "What's it matter which side?" she said. 26

"I just asked," I said. 27

"Right side," the blind man said. "I hadn't been on a train in nearly forty years. Not since I was a kid. With my folks. That's been a long time. I'd nearly forgotten the sensation. I have winter in my beard now," he said. "So I've been told, anyway. Do I look distinguished, my dear?" the blind man said to my wife. 28

"You look distinguished, Robert," she said. "Robert," she said. "Robert, it's just so good to see you." 29

My wife finally took her eyes off the blind man and looked at me. I had the feeling she didn't like what she saw. I shrugged. 30

I've never met, or personally known, anyone who was blind. This blind man was late forties, a heavy-set, balding man with stooped shoulders, as if he carried a great weight there. He wore brown slacks, brown shoes, a light-brown shirt, a tie, a sports coat. Spiffy. He also had this full beard. But he didn't use a cane and he didn't wear dark glasses. I'd always thought dark glasses were a must for the blind. Fact was, I wished he had a pair. At first glance, his eyes looked like anyone else's eyes. But if you looked close, there was something different about them. Too much white in the iris, for one thing, and the pupils seemed to move around in the sockets without his knowing it or being able to stop it. Creepy. As I stared at his face, I saw the left pupil turn in toward his nose while the other made an effort to keep in one place. But it was only an effort, for that eye was on the roam without his knowing it or wanting it to be. 31

I said, "Let me get you a drink. What's your pleasure? We have a little of everything. It's one of our pastimes." 32

"Bub, I'm a Scotch man myself," he said fast enough in this big voice. 33

"Right," I said. Bub! "Sure you are. I knew it." 34

He let his fingers touch his suitcase, which was sitting alongside the sofa. He was taking his bearings. I didn't blame him for that. 35

"I'll move that up to your room," my wife said. 36

"No, that's fine," the blind man said loudly. "It can go up when I go up." 37

"A little water with the Scotch?" I said. 38

"Very little," he said. 39

"I knew it," I said. 40

He said, "Just a tad. The Irish actor, Barry Fitzgerald? I'm like that fellow. When I drink water, Fitzgerald said, I drink water. When I drink whiskey, I drink whiskey." My wife laughed. The blind man brought his hand up under his beard. He lifted his beard slowly and let it drop. 41

I did the drinks, three big glasses of Scotch with a splash of water in each. Then we made ourselves comfortable and talked about Robert's travels. First the long flight from the West Coast to Connecticut, we covered that. Then from Connecticut up here by train. We had another drink concerning that leg of the trip. 42

43   I remembered having read somewhere that the blind didn't smoke because, as speculation had it, they couldn't see the smoke they exhaled. I thought I knew that much and that much only about blind people. But this blind man smoked his cigarette down to the nubbin and then lit another one. This blind man filled his ashtray and my wife emptied it.

44   When we sat down at the table for dinner, we had another drink. My wife heaped Robert's plate with cube steak, scalloped potatoes, green beans. I buttered him up two slices of bread. I said, "Here's bread and butter for you." I swallowed some of my drink. "Now let us pray," I said, and the blind man lowered his head. My wife looked at me, her mouth agape. "Pray the phone won't ring and the food doesn't get cold," I said.

45   We dug in. We ate everything there was to eat on the table. We ate like there was no tomorrow. We didn't talk. We ate. We scarfed. We grazed that table. We were into serious eating. The blind man had right away located his foods, he knew just where everything was on his plate. I watched with admiration as he used his knife and fork on the meat. He'd cut two pieces of meat, fork the meat into his mouth, and then go all out for the scalloped potatoes, the beans next, and then he'd tear off a hunk of buttered bread and eat that. He'd follow this up with a drink of milk. It didn't seem to bother him to use his fingers once in a while, either.

46   We finished everything, including half a strawberry pie. For a few moments, we sat as if stunned. Sweat beaded on our faces. Finally, we got up from the table and left the dirty plates. We didn't look back. We took ourselves into the living room and sank into our places again. Robert and my wife sat on the sofa. I took the big chair. We had us two or three more drinks while they talked about the major things that had come to pass for them in the past ten years. For the most part, I just listened. Now and then I joined in. I didn't want him to think I'd left the room, and I didn't want her to think I was feeling left out. They talked of things that had happened to them—to them!—these past ten years. I waited in vain to hear my name on my wife's sweet lips: "And then my dear husband came into my life"—something like that. But I heard nothing of the sort. More talk of Robert. Robert had done a little of everything, it seemed, a regular blind jack-of-all-trades. But most recently he and his wife had had an Amway distributorship, from which, I gathered, they'd earned their living, such as it was. The blind man was also a ham radio operator. He talked in his loud voice about conversations he'd had with fellow operators in Guam, in the Philippines, in Alaska, and even in Tahiti. He said he'd have a lot of friends there if he ever wanted to go visit those places. From time to time, he'd turn his blind face toward me, put his hand under his beard, ask me something. How long had I been in my present position? (Three years.) Did I like my work? (I didn't.) Was I going to stay with it? (What were the options?) Finally, when I thought he was beginning to run down, I got up and turned on the TV.

47   My wife looked at me with irritation. She was heading toward a boil. Then she looked at the blind man and said, "Robert, do you have a TV?"

The blind man said, "My dear, I have two TVs. I have a color set and a black-and-white thing, an old relic. It's funny, but if I turn the TV on, and I'm always turning it on, I turn on the color set. It's funny, don't you think?" 48

I didn't know what to say to that. I had absolutely nothing to say to that. No opinion. So I watched the news program and tried to listen to what the announcer was saying. 49

"This is a color TV," the blind man said. "Don't ask me how, but I can tell." 50

"We traded up a while go," I said. 51

The blind man had another taste of his drink. He lifted his beard, sniffed it, and let it fall. He leaned forward on the sofa. He positioned his ashtray on the coffee table, then put the lighter to his cigarette. He leaned back on the sofa and crossed his legs at the ankles. 52

My wife covered her mouth, and then she yawned. She stretched. She said, "I think I'll go upstairs and put on my robe. I think I'll change into something else. Robert, you make yourself comfortable," she said. 53

"I'm comfortable," the blind man said. 54

"I want you to feel comfortable in this house," she said. 55

"I am comfortable," the blind man said. 56

After she'd left the room, he and I listened to the weather report and then to the sports roundup. By that time, she'd been gone so long I didn't know if she was going to come back. I thought she might have gone to bed. I wished she'd come back downstairs. I didn't want to be left alone with a blind man. I asked him if he wanted another drink, and he said sure. Then I asked if he wanted to smoke some dope with me. I said I'd just rolled a number. I hadn't, but I planned to do so in about two shakes. 57

"I'll try some with you," he said. 58

"Damn right," I said. "That's the stuff." 59

I got our drinks and sat down on the sofa with him. Then I rolled us two fat numbers. I lit one and passed it. I brought it to his fingers. He took it and inhaled. 60

"Hold it as long as you can," I said. I could tell he didn't know the first thing. 61

My wife came back downstairs wearing her pink robe and her pink slippers. 62

"What do I smell?" she said. 63

"We thought we'd have us some cannabis," I said. 64

My wife gave me a savage look. Then she looked at the blind man and said, "Robert, I didn't know you smoked." 65

He said, "I do now, my dear. There's a first time for everything. But I don't feel anything yet." 66

"This stuff is pretty mellow," I said. "This stuff is mild. It's dope you can reason with," I said. "It doesn't mess you up." 67

"Not much it doesn't, bub," he said, and laughed. 68

69   My wife sat on the sofa between the blind man and me. I passed her the number. She took it and toked and then passed it back to me. "Which way is this going?" she said. Then she said, "I shouldn't be smoking this. I can hardly keep my eyes open as it is. That dinner did me in. I shouldn't have eaten so much."

70   "It was the strawberry pie," the blind man said. "That's what did it," he said, and he laughed his big laugh. Then he shook his head.

71   "There's more strawberry pie," I said.

72   "Do you want some more, Robert?" my wife said.

73   "Maybe in a little while," he said.

74   We gave our attention to the TV. My wife yawned again. She said, "Your bed is made up when you feel like going to bed, Robert. I know you must have had a long day. When you're ready to go to bed, say so." She pulled his arm. "Robert?"

75   He came to and said, "I've had a real nice time. This beats tapes, doesn't it?"

76   I said, "Coming at you," and I put the number between his fingers. He inhaled, held the smoke, and then let it go. It was like he'd been doing it since he was nine years old.

77   "Thanks, bub," he said. "but I think this is all for me. I think I'm beginning to feel it," he said. He held the burning roach out for my wife.

78   "Same here," she said. "Ditto. Me, too." She took the roach and passed it to me. "I may just sit here for a while between you two guys with my eyes closed. But don't let me bother you, okay? Either one of you. If it bothers you, say so. Otherwise, I may just sit here with my eyes closed until you're ready to go to bed," she said. "Your bed's made up, Robert, when you're ready. It's right next to our room at the top of the stairs. We'll show you up when you're ready. You wake me up now, you guys, if I fall asleep." She said that and then she closed her eyes and went to sleep.

79   The news program ended. I got up and changed the channel. I sat back down on the sofa. I wished my wife hadn't pooped out. Her head lay across the back of the sofa, her mouth open. She'd turned so that her robe slipped away from her legs, exposing a juicy thigh. I reached to draw her robe back over her, and it was then that I glanced at the blind man. What the hell! I flipped the robe open again.

80   "You say when you want some strawberry pie," I said.

81   "I will," he said.

82   I said, "Are you tired? Do you want me to take you up to your bed? Are you ready to hit the hay?"

83   "Not yet," he said. "No, I'll stay up with you, bub. If that's all right. I'll stay up until you're ready to turn in. We haven't had a chance to talk. Know what I mean? I feel like me and her monopolized the evening." He lifted his beard and he let it fall. He picked up his cigarettes and his lighter.

84   "That's all right," I said. Then I said, "I'm glad for the company."

And I guess I was. Every night I smoked dope and stayed up as long as   85
I could before I fell asleep. My wife and I hardly ever went to bed at the
same time. When I did go to sleep, I had these dreams. Sometimes I'd
wake up from one of them, my heart going crazy.

Something about the church and the Middle Ages was on the TV. Not   86
your run-of-the-mill TV fare. I wanted to watch something else. I turned
to the other channels. But there was nothing on them, either. So I turned
back to the first channel and apologized.

"Bub, it's all right," the blind man said. "It's fine with me. Whatever   87
you want to watch is okay. I'm always learning something. Learning
never ends. It won't hurt me to learn something tonight. I got ears," he
said.

We didn't say anything for a time. He was leaning forward with his   88
head turned at me, his right ear aimed in the direction of the set. Very
disconcerting. Now and then his eyelids drooped and then they snapped
open again. Now and then he put his fingers into his beard and tugged,
like he was thinking about something he was hearing on the television.

On the screen, a group of men wearing cowls was being set upon and   89
tormented by men dressed in skeleton costumes and men dressed as
devils. The men dressed as devils wore devil masks, horns, and long tails.
This pageant was part of a procession. The Englishman who was narrating the thing said it took place in Spain once a year. I tried to explain
to the blind man what was happening.

"Skeletons," he said. "I know about skeletons," he said, and he   90
nodded.

The TV showed this one cathedral. Then there was a long, slow look   91
at another one. Finally, the picture switched to the famous one in Paris,
with its flying buttresses and its spires reaching up to the clouds. The
camera pulled away to show the whole of the cathedral rising above the
skyline.

There were times when the Englishman who was telling the thing   92
would shut up, would simply let the camera move around the cathedrals.
Or else the camera would tour the countryside, men in fields walking
behind oxen. I waited as long as I could. Then I felt I had to say
something. I said, "They're showing the outside of this cathedral now.
Gargoyles. Little statues carved to look like monsters. Now I guess
they're in Italy. Yeah, they're in Italy. There's paintings on the walls of
this one church."

"Are those fresco paintings, bub?" he asked, and he sipped from his   93
drink.

I reached for my glass. But it was empty. I tried to remember what I   94
could remember. "You're asking me are those frescoes?" I said. "That's
a good question. I don't know."

The camera moved to a cathedral outside Lisbon. The differences in   95
the Portuguese cathedral compared with the French and Italian were not

that great. But they were there. Mostly the interior stuff. Then something occurred to me, and I said, "Something has occurred to me. Do you have any idea what a cathedral is? What they look like, that is? Do you follow me? If somebody says cathedral to you, do you have any notion what they're talking about? Do you know the difference between that and a Baptist church, say?"

96   He let the smoke dribble from his mouth. "I know they took hundreds of workers fifty or a hundred years to build," he said. "I just heard the man say that, of course. I know generations of the same families worked on a cathedral. I heard him say that too. The men who began their life's work on them, they never lived to see the completion of their work. In that wise, bub, they're no different from the rest of us, right?" He laughed. Then his eyelids drooped again. His head nodded. He seemed to be snoozing. Maybe he was imagining himself in Portugal. The TV was showing another cathedral now. This one was in Germany. The Englishman's voice droned on. "Cathedrals," the blind man said. He sat up and rolled his head back and forth. "If you want the truth, bub, that's about all I know. What I just said. What I heard him say. But maybe you could describe one to me? I wish you'd do it. I'd like that. If you want to know, I really don't have a good idea."

97   I stared hard at the shot of the cathedral on the TV. How could I even begin to describe it? But say my life depended on it. Say my life was being threatened by an insane guy who said I had to do it or else.

98   I stared some more at the cathedral before the picture flipped off into the countryside. There was no use. I turned to the blind man and said, "To begin with, they're very tall." I was looking around the room for clues. "They reach way up. Up and up. Toward the sky. They're so big, some of them, they have to have these supports. To help hold them up, so to speak. These supports are called buttresses. They remind me of viaducts, for some reasons. But maybe you don't know viaducts, either? Sometimes the cathedrals have devils and such carved in the front. Sometimes lords and ladies. Don't ask me why this is," I said.

99   He was nodding. The whole upper part of his body seemed to be moving back and forth.

100   "I'm not doing so good, am I?" I said.

101   He stopped nodding and leaned forward on the edge of the sofa. As he listened to me, he was running his fingers through his beard. I wasn't getting through to him, I could see that. But he waited for me to go on just the same. He nodded, like he was trying to encourage me. I tried to think what else to say. "They're really big," I said. "They're massive. They're built of stone. Marble, too, sometimes. In those olden days, when they built cathedrals, men wanted to be close to God. In those olden days, God was an important part of everyone's life. You could tell this from their cathedral-building. I'm sorry," I said, "but it looks like that's the best I can do for you. I'm just no good at it."

102   "That's all right, bub," the blind man said. "Hey, listen. I hope you

don't mind my asking you. Can I ask you something? Let me ask you a simple question, yes or no. I'm just curious and there's no offense. You're my host. But let me ask if you are in any way religious? You don't mind my asking?"

I shook my head. He couldn't see that, though. A wink is the same as a nod to a blind man. "I guess I don't believe in it. In anything. Sometimes it's hard. You know what I'm saying?" 103

"Sure, I do," he said. 104

"Right," I said. 105

The Englishman was still holding forth. My wife sighed in her sleep. She drew a long breath and went on with her sleeping. 106

"You'll have to forgive me," I said. "But I can't tell you what a cathedral looks like. It just isn't in me to do it. I can't do any more than I've done." 107

The blind man sat very still, his head down, as he listened to me. 108

I said, "The truth is, cathedrals don't mean anything special to me. Nothing. Cathedrals. They're something to look at on late-night TV. That's all they are." 109

It was then that the blind man cleared his throat. He brought something up. He took a handkerchief from his back pocket. Then he said, "I get it, bub. It's okay. It happens. Don't worry about it," he said. "Hey, listen to me. Will you do me a favor? I got an idea. Why don't you find us some heavy paper? And a pen. We'll do something. We'll draw one together. Get us a pen and some heavy paper. Go on, bub, get the stuff," he said. 110

So I went upstairs. My legs felt like they didn't have any strength in them. They felt like they did after I'd done some running. In my wife's room, I looked around. I found some ballpoints in a little basket on her table. And then I tried to think where to look for the kind of paper he was talking about. 111

Downstairs, in the kitchen, I found a shopping bag with onion skins in the bottom of the bag. I emptied the bag and shook it. I brought it into the living room and sat down with it near his legs. I moved some things, smoothed the wrinkles from the bag, spread it out on the coffee tale. 112

The blind man got down from the sofa and sat next to me on the carpet. 113

He ran his fingers over the paper. He went up and down the sides of the paper. The edges, even the edges. He fingered the corners. 114

"All right," he said. "All right, let's do her." 115

He found my hand, the hand with the pen. He closed his hand over my hand. "Go ahead, bub, draw," he said. "Draw. You'll see. I'll follow along with you. It'll be okay. Just begin now like I'm telling you. You'll see. Draw," the blind man said. 116

So I began. First I drew a box that looked like a house. It could have been the house I lived in. Then I put a roof on it. At either end of the roof, I drew spires. Crazy. 117

118   "Swell," he said. "Terrific. You're doing fine," he said. "Never thought anything like this could happen in your lifetime, did you, bub? Well, it's a strange life, we all know that. Go on now. Keep it up."

119   I put in windows with arches. I drew flying buttresses. I hung great doors. I couldn't stop. The TV station went off the air. I put down the pen and closed and opened my fingers. The blind man felt around over the paper. He moved the tips of his fingers over the paper, all over what I had drawn, and he nodded.

120   "Doing fine," the blind man said.

121   I took up the pen again, and he found my hand. I kept at it. I'm no artist. But I kept drawing just the same.

122   My wife opened up her eyes and gazed at us. She sat up on the sofa, her robe hanging open. She said, "What are you doing? Tell me, I want to know."

123   I didn't answer her.

124   The blind man said, "We're drawing a cathedral. Me and him are working on it. Press hard," he said to me. "That's right. That's good," he said. "Sure. You got it, bub, I can tell. You didn't think you could. But you can, can't you? You're cooking with gas now. You know what I'm saying? We're going to really have us something here in a minute. How's the old arm?" he said. "Put some people in there now. What's a cathedral without people?"

125   My wife said, "What's going on? Robert, what are you doing? What's going on?"

126   "It's all right," he said to her. "Close your eyes now," the blind man said to me.

127   I did it. I closed them just like he said.

128   "Are they closed?" he said. "Don't fudge."

129   "They're closed," I said.

130   "Keep them that way," he said. He said, "Don't stop now. Draw."

131   So we kept on with it. His fingers rode my fingers as my hand went over the paper. It was like nothing else in my life up to now.

132   Then he said, "I think that's it. I think you got it," he said. "Take a look. What do you think?"

133   But I had my eyes closed. I thought I'd keep them that way for a little longer. I thought it was something I ought to do.

134   "Well?" he said. "Are you looking?"

135   My eyes were still closed. I was in my house. I knew that. But I didn't feel like I was inside anything.

136   "It's really something," I said.

❏ Questions for Discussion

1. How does the **narrator** feel about the blind man's visit? Why? What is the narrator's attitude toward blind people and toward other people in general?

2. What kind of relationship does the narrator have with his wife? What kind of relationship does the blind man have with the narrator's wife?

3. Why is the narrator's wife upset at such actions as his turning on the television? What attitude do his behavior and conversation betray?

4. What is the difference between the narrator's **dialogue** with the blind man about cathedrals and their earlier conversation? What allows the narrator and the blind man finally to communicate with each other and to begin bonding?

5. Imagine what the narrator and the blind man look like drawing together on the floor. How is this event a major change in the narrator's life? Why is it "like nothing else in [his] life up to [then]"?

❏ **Suggestions for Exploration and Writing**

1. Through a detailed contrast between the narrator before and after he begins to talk about and draw the cathedral, analyze the ways in which he changes.

2. Contrast the narrator and the blind man. Which man is healthier and more complete?

3. This story is about communication through traditional language and nonverbal signs. Discuss how the narrator's ability to communicate improves as the story unfolds.

POETRY

JOHN KEATS (1795–1821)

John Keats was, along with William Wordsworth, Samuel Taylor Coleridge, Lord Byron, and Percy Bysshe Shelley, one of the leading poets of the Romantic period in England. Nearly all of his greatest poems were written in one year, 1818–1819, and published in Lamia, Isabella, and Other Poems *(1820). Keats' poetry celebrates beauty in rich, lush images; and his magnificent collected letters, a work of art in their own right, have gained increasing attention in the twentieth century. Keats was stricken with tuberculosis and died at the age of twenty-five.*

Ode to a Nightingale

I

My heart aches, and a drowsy numbness pains
   My sense, as though of hemlock I had drunk,
Or emptied some dull opiate to the drains
   One minute past, and Lethe-wards had sunk:
'Tis not through envy of thy happy lot,
   But being too happy in thine happiness,—
     That thou, light-winged Dryad of the trees,
      In some melodious plot
   Of beechen green, and shadows numberless,
   Singest of summer in full-throated ease.

II

O, for a draught of vintage! that hath been
   Cool'd a long age in the deep-delved earth,
Tasting of Flora and the country green,
   Dance, and Provençal song, and sunburnt mirth!
O for a beaker full of the warm South,
   Full of the true, the blushful Hippocrene,
     With beaded bubbles winking at the brim,
      And purple-stained mouth;
   That I might drink, and leave the world unseen,
   And with thee fade away into the forest dim:

III

Fade far away, dissolve, and quite forget
   What thou among the leaves hast never known,
The weariness, the fever, and the fret
   Here, where men sit and hear each other groan;
Where palsy shakes a few, sad, last gray hairs,
   Where youth grows pale, and spectre-thin, and dies;
     Where but to think is to be full of sorrow
      And leaden-eyed despairs,
   Where Beauty cannot keep her lustrous eyes,
   Or new Love pine at them beyond to-morrow.

IV

Away! away! for I will fly to thee,
   Not charioted by Bacchus and his pards,
But on the viewless wings of Poesy,
   Though the dull brain perplexes and retards:
Already with thee! tender is the night,
   And haply the Queen-Moon is on her throne,
     Cluster'd around by all her starry Fays;
      But here there is no light,
Save what from heaven is with the breezes blown
   Through verdurous glooms and winding mossy ways.

V

I cannot see what flowers are at my feet,
  Nor what soft incense hangs upon the boughs,
But, in embalmed darkness, guess each sweet
  Wherewith the seasonable month endows
The grass, the thicket, and the fruit-tree wild;   45
  White hawthorn, and the pastoral eglantine:
    Fast fading violets cover'd up in leaves;
      And mid-May's eldest child,
  The coming musk-rose, full of dewy wine,
    The murmurous haunt of flies on summer eves.   50

VI

Darkling I listen; and, for many a time
  I have been half in love with easeful Death,
Call'd him soft names in many a mused rhyme,
  To take into the air my quiet breath;
Now more than ever seems it rich to die,   55
  To cease upon the midnight with no pain,
    While thou art pouring forth thy soul abroad
      In such an ecstasy!
  Still wouldst thou sing, and I have ears in vain—
    To thy high requiem become a sod.   60

VII

Thou wast not born for death, immortal Bird!
  No hungry generations tread thee down;
The voice I hear this passing night was heard
  In ancient days by emperor and clown:
Perhaps the self-same song that found a path   65
  Through the sad heart of Ruth, when, sick for home,
    She stood in tears amid the alien corn;
      The same that oft-times hath
  Charm'd magic casements, opening on the foam
    Of perilous seas, in faery lands forlorn.   70

VIII

Forlorn! the very word is like a bell
  To toll me back from thee to my sole self!
Adieu! the fancy cannot cheat so well
  As she is fam'd to do, deceiving elf.
Adieu! adieu! thy plaintive anthem fades   75
  Past the near meadows, over the still stream,
    Up the hill-side; and now 'tis buried deep
      In the next valley-glades:
  Was it a vision, or a waking dream?
    Fled is that music:—Do I wake or sleep?   80

❏ **Questions for Discussion**

1. To what does the speaker compare his state of mind? How has the nightingale produced that state of mind?

2. What **images** characterize the rich imagined world symbolized by the nightingale?

3. What does Keats mean by "Thou wast not born for death, immortal Bird"? How can a bird be immortal?

4. Why does Keats end the poem with two questions rather than with answers?

❏ **Suggestions for Exploration and Writing**

1. Examine the elaborately developed **symbolism** of the nightingale. How does the speaker feel about the bird and what it represents to him?

2. In an essay, discuss the contrast the speaker makes between his own world and that of the nightingale.

Ode On A Grecian Urn

I

Thou still unravish'd bride of quietness,
    Thou foster-child of silence and slow time,
Sylvan historian, who canst thus express
    A flowery tale more sweetly than our rhyme:
5   What leaf-fring'd legend haunts about thy shape
        Of deities or mortals, or of both,
           In Tempe or the dales of Arcady?
        What men or gods are these? What maidens loth?
What mad pursuit? What struggle to escape?
10   What pipes and timbrels? What wild ecstasy?

II

Heard melodies are sweet, but those unheard
    Are sweeter; therefore, ye soft pipes, play on;
Not to the sensual ear, but, more endear'd,
    Pipe to the spirit ditties of no tone:
15   Fair youth, beneath the trees, thou canst not leave
        Thy song, nor ever can those trees be bare;
           Bold Lover, never, never canst thou kiss,
Though winning near the goal—yet, do not grieve;
        She cannot fade, though thou hast not thy bliss,
20   For ever wilt thou love, and she be fair!

III

Ah, happy, happy boughs! that cannot shed
   Your leaves, nor ever bid the Spring adieu;
And, happy melodist, unwearied,
   For ever piping songs for ever new;
More happy love! more happy, happy love!   25
   For ever warm and still to be enjoy'd,
      For ever panting, and for ever young;
All breathing human passion far above,
   That leaves a heart high-sorrowful and cloy'd,
      A burning forehead, and a parching tongue.   30

IV

Who are these coming to the sacrifice?
   To what green altar, O mysterious priest,
Lead'st thou that heifer lowing at the skies,
   And all her silken flanks with garlands drest?
What little town by river or sea shore,   35
   Or mountain-built with peaceful citadel,
      Is emptied of this folk, this pious morn?
And, little town, thy streets for evermore
   Will silent be; and not a soul to tell
      Why thou art desolate, can e'er return.   40

V

O Attic shape! Fair attitude! with brede
   Of marble men and maidens overwrought,
With forest branches and the trodden weed;
   Thou, silent form, dost tease us out of thought
As doth eternity: Cold Pastoral!   45
   When old age shall this generation waste,
      Thou shalt remain, in midst of other woe
Than ours, a friend to man, to whom thou say'st,
   'Beauty is truth, truth beauty,'—that is all
      Ye know on earth, and all ye need to know.   50

❏ Questions for Discussion

1. Keats begins by addressing an urn or vase. What does he mean
   when he calls the urn a "still unravish'd bride of quietness," a
   "foster-child of silence and slow time," and a "Sylvan historian"?

2. How can "unheard" melodies be "sweeter" than "heard" ones?

3. At the beginning of the second stanza, Keats addresses the
   "pipes," and midway through the second stanza, he addresses
   lovers. In the third stanza, Keats addresses "happy boughs" and
   in the fourth a priest. Where did he find the pipes, the lovers,
   the boughs, and the priest? What do they all have in common?

4. How can the speaker say to the lovers, "For ever wilt thou love, and she be fair"?

❑ **Suggestion for Exploration and Writing**

1. Supporting your answer with references to your own experience, argue for or against the statement: " 'Beauty is truth, truth beauty.' "

LEWIS CARROLL (1832–1898)

Charles Lutwidge Dodgson, mathematician, photographer, and author, took the pen name Lewis Carroll for his delightful fantasies Alice in Wonderland *and* Through the Looking Glass *(1872). His pleasure in using language for light* **satire** *and wordplay is obvious in both his longer works and his poems. "Jabberwocky," a poem in a "looking-glass book," which must be read in a mirror, is in the first chapter of* Through the Looking Glass.

Jabberwocky

'Twas brillig, and the slithy toves
    Did gyre and gimble in the wabe:
All mimsy were the borogoves,
    And the mome raths outgrabe.

5 "Beware the Jabberwock, my son!
    The jaws that bite, the claws that catch!
Beware the Jubjub bird, and shun
    The frumious Bandersnatch!"

He took his vorpal sword in hand;
10   Long time the manxome foe he sought—
So rested he by the Tumtum tree
    And stood awhile in thought.

And, as in uffish thought he stood,
    The Jabberwock, with eyes of flame,
15 Came whiffling through the tulgey wood,
    And burbled as it came!

One, two! One, two! And through and through
    The vorpal blade went snicker-snack!
He left it dead, and with its head
20   He went galumphing back.

"And hast thou slain the Jabberwock?
    Come to my arms, my beamish boy!
O frabjous day! Callooh, Callay!"
    He chortled in his joy.

'Twas brillig, and the slithy toves   25
　　Did gyre and gimble in the wabe:
All mimsy were the borogoves,
　　And the mome raths outgrabe.

❏ Suggestions for Exploration and Writing

1. Lewis Carroll plays with words in this poem, mixing existing words with invented ones. Look up the words that you do not know. Then make up definitions for the ones you do not find, being sure that your definitions fit in the context of the poem.

2. Using the same techniques that Carroll does, write an essay or a poem in which you combine existing words with your original words. Your essay might, for example, recommend the adoption of your words into the English language.

3. If you are fluent in more than one language, write an essay explaining the advantages to individuals and to their community of knowing more than one language.

A. E. HOUSMAN (1859–1936)

A. E. Housman was a brilliant classical scholar, professor of Latin, and writer of deceptively simple poems. His very formal, spare poems are often heartrending in their carefully controlled understatement. In directness and laconic stoicism, "Terence, This Is Stupid Stuff" typifies Housman's poetic style.

Terence, This Is Stupid Stuff

'Terence, this is stupid stuff:
You eat your victuals fast enough;
There can't be much amiss, 'tis clear,
To see the rate you drink your beer.
But oh, good Lord, the verse you make,   5
It gives a chap the belly-ache.
The cow, the old cow, she is dead;
It sleeps well, the horned head:
We poor lads, 'tis our turn now
To hear such tunes as killed the cow.   10
Pretty friendship 'tis to rhyme
Your friends to death before their time
Moping melancholy mad:
Come, pipe a tune to dance to, lad.'

Why, if 'tis dancing you would be,   15
There's brisker pipes than poetry.

Say, for what were hop-yards meant,
Or why was Burton built on Trent?
Oh many a peer of England brews
20   Livelier liquor than the Muse,
And malt does more than Milton can
To justify God's ways to man.
Ale, man, ale's the stuff to drink
For fellows whom it hurts to think:
25   Look into the pewter pot
To see the world as the world's not.
And faith, 'tis pleasant till 'tis past:
The mischief is that 'twill not last.
Oh I have been to Ludlow fair
30   And left my necktie God knows where,
And carried halfway home, or near,
Pints and quarts of Ludlow beer:
Then the world seemed none so bad,
And I myself a sterling lad;
35   And down in lovely muck I've lain,
Happy till I woke again.
Then I saw the morning sky:
Heigho, the tale was all a lie;
The world, it was the old world yet,
40   I was I, my things were wet,
And nothing now remained to do
But begin the game anew.

Therefore, since the world has still
Much good, but much less good than ill,
45   And while the sun and moon endure
Luck's a chance, but trouble's sure,
I'd face it as a wise man would,
And train for ill and not for good.
'Tis true, the stuff I bring for sale
50   Is not so brisk a brew as ale:
Out of a stem that scored the hand
I wrung it in a weary land.
But take it: if the smack is sour,
The better for the embittered hour;
55   It should do good to heart and head
When your soul is in my soul's stead;
And I will friend you, if I may,
In the dark and cloudy day.

There was a king reigned in the East:
60   There, when kings will sit to feast,
They get their fill before they think
With poisoned meat and poisoned drink.

He gathered all that springs to birth
From the many-venomed earth;
First a little, thence to more,   65
He sampled all her killing store;
And easy, smiling, seasoned sound,
Sate the king when healths went round.
They put arsenic in his meat
And stared aghast to watch him eat;   70
They poured strychnine in his cup
And shook to see him drink it up:
They shook, they stared as white's their shirt:
Them it was their poison hurt.
—I tell the tale that I heard told.   75
Mithridates, he died old.

❏ **Questions for Discussion**

1. Why does the first speaker complain about Terence's poetry?
   What kind of poetry does this speaker request? What place
   does such poetry have?

2. Terence alludes to John Milton's **epic** poem *Paradise Lost*,
   which has as its stated purpose "To justify the ways of God to
   man." What does Terence mean by "malt does more than
   Milton can / To justify God's ways to man"?

3. What does Terence claim is the purpose of his poetry? How
   does the story of Mithridates illustrate his point?

❏ **Suggestion for Exploration and Writing**

1. Based on your own experience, how valid do you consider
   Terence's claim for poetry?

MARIANNE MOORE (1887–1972)

*Marianne Moore, who spent most of her life in Brooklyn, was
influential in twentieth-century American poetry both as a poet
and as a critic. She published in* Poetry *magazine and edited the*
Dial, *both of which were instrumental in shaping modern American
poetry.*

Poetry

I, too, dislike it: there are things that are important beyond
all this fiddle.
   Reading it, however, with a perfect contempt for it, one
   discovers in it after all, a place for the genuine.

5 Hands that can grasp, eyes
       that can dilate, hair that can rise
           if it must, these things are important not because a
   high-sounding interpretation can be put upon them but
       because they are useful. When they become so derivative
10   as to become unintelligible, the same thing may be said
   for all of us, that we
       do not admire what
   we cannot understand: the bat
       holding on upside down or in quest of something to
15 eat, elephants pushing, a wild horse taking a roll, a tireless
   wolf under a tree, the immovable critic twitching his skin
   like a horse that feels
       a flea, the base-
   ball fan, the statistician—
20   nor is it valid
           to discriminate against "business documents and
   school-books"; all these phenomena are important. One
   must make a distinction
       however: when dragged into prominence by half poets,
25 the result is not poetry,
       nor till the poets among us can be
       "literalists of
       the imagination"—above
           insolence and triviality and can present
30 for inspection, "imaginary gardens with real toads in
   them," shall we have it. In the meantime, if you demand
   on the one hand,
       the raw material of poetry in
           all its rawness and
35   that which is on the other hand
               genuine, you are interested in poetry.

❑ Questions for Discussion

1. Though Moore begins by saying "I, too, dislike it," she then
   says that poetry is "useful" when it is "genuine." Explain.

2. Explain Moore's description of poets as " 'literalists of the
   imagination' " and of poetry as " 'imaginary gardens with real
   toads in them.' "

❑ Suggestions for Exploration and Writing

1. In an essay, give your opinion of what a poem is.

2. Write a poem which you believe would fulfill the criteria
   Moore outlines for poetry.

ARCHIBALD MACLEISH (1892–1982)

Archibald MacLeish was an American scholar, teacher, poet, essay-
ist, critic, and playwright. He served for five years (1939–1944) as
Librarian of Congress. Primarily known for his short poems, Mac-
Leish also received a Pulitzer Prize for J.B., a verse dramatization of
the biblical story of Job. Though MacLeish was not one of the first
Imagists, *his "Ars Poetica" is often mentioned as one of the best*
examples of Imagist writing.

Ars Poetica

A poem should be palpable and mute
As a globed fruit,

Dumb
As old medallions to the thumb,

Silent as the sleeve-worn stone   5
Of casement ledges where the moss has grown—

A poem should be wordless
As the flight of birds.

*

A poem should be motionless in time
As the moon climbs,   10

Leaving, as the moon releases
Twig by twig the night-entangled trees,

Leaving, as the moon behind the winter leaves,
Memory by memory the mind—

A poem should be motionless in time   15
As the moon climbs.

*

A poem should be equal to:
Not true.

For all the history of grief
An empty doorway and a maple leaf.   20

For love
The leaning grasses and two lights above the sea—

A poem should not mean
But be.

❏ Questions for Discussion

1. Explain each of the three statements that MacLeish makes
   about poetry.

1. What pictures do the **similes** and **metaphors** provide? In what ways do these devices communicate, even more clearly than expository writing can, a definition of poetry?

❏ **Suggestion for Exploration and Writing**

1. Both Moore and MacLeish use poetic form to give their definitions of poetry. In a **comparison contrast** essay, examine these definitions of poetry. If possible, explain the poets' selection of the poetic form for their definitions.

LANGSTON HUGHES (1902–1967)

Langston Hughes, born in Joplin, Missouri, was a novelist and poet who wrote dialect poems in imitation of Paul Laurence Dunbar. A graduate of Lincoln University in 1929, Hughes was a noteworthy member of the Harlem Renaissance. He also founded theaters, produced plays, and traveled to such locales as Haiti, the Soviet Union, and Spain, where he covered the Spanish Civil War. Hughes' many works include the Semple tales and the novels Not Without Laughter *(1930),* Ask Your Mama *(1961), and* Tambourines to Glory *(1959).*

Theme for English B

The instructor said,

> *Go home and write*
> *a page tonight.*
> *And let that page come out of you—*
> *Then, it will be true.*

5

I wonder if it's that simple?

I am twenty-two, colored, born in Winston-Salem.
I went to school there, then Durham, then here
to this college on the hill above Harlem.
10 I am the only colored student in my class.
The steps from the hill lead down into Harlem,
through a park, then I cross St. Nicholas,
Eighth Avenue, Seventh, and I come to the Y,
the Harlem Branch Y, where I take the elevator
15 up to my room, sit down, and write this page:

It's not easy to know what is true for you or me
at twenty-two, my age. But I guess I'm what
I feel and see and hear. Harlem, I hear you:
hear you, hear me—we two—you, me, talk on this page.
20 (I hear New York, too.) Me—who?

Well, I like to eat, sleep, drink, and be in love.
I like to work, read, learn, and understand life.
I like a pipe for a Christmas present,
or records—Bessie, bop, or Bach.
I guess being colored doesn't make me *not* like   25
the same things other folks like who are other races.

So will my page be colored that I write?
Being me, it will not be white.
But it will be
a part of you, instructor.   30
You are white—
yet a part of me, as I am a part of you.
That's American.
Sometimes perhaps you don't want to be a part of me.
Nor do I often want to be a part of you.   35
But we are, that's true!
As I learn from you,
I guess you learn from me—
although you're older—and white—
and somewhat more free.   40

This is my page for English B.

❏ Questions for Discussion

1. What does the college teacher mean when he or she says,
   " 'And let the page come out of you' "? What conflict does the
   speaker see in that assignment?

2. What does the speaker mean by "Me—who"?

3. In what ways are the white teacher and the African-American
   student both a part of each other even though they often do
   not want to be?

❏ Suggestion for Exploration and Writing

1. Hughes wonders whether his theme and his writing will be
   "colored" or reflect himself. How might the way he constructs
   his sentences, the way he uses words, and his word choices
   make him vulnerable? Discuss.

W. H. AUDEN (1907–1973)

*W. H. Auden, a major twentieth-century poet who was born in
England, became a citizen of the United States in 1946. A precocious
writer, he published* Poems *in 1930 and* Orators *in 1932. Also in the*

1930s, Auden experimented with different forms of drama, includ-
ing verse plays and plays which used music. A winner of many
literary prizes, he was praised for his expertise in lyrical poetry and
for his technical proficiency. Auden, who influenced many of the
poets of his age, is noted as a poet, critic, essayist, and playwright.

Musée des Beaux Arts

About suffering they were never wrong,
The Old Masters: how well they understood
Its human position; how it takes place
While someone else is eating or opening a window or just
    walking dully along;
How, when the aged are reverently, passionately waiting
For the miraculous birth, there always must be
Children who did not specially want it to happen, skating
On a pond at the edge of the wood:
They never forgot
That even the dreadful martyrdom must run its course
Anyhow in a corner, some untidy spot
Where the dogs go on with their doggy life and the
    torturer's horse
Scratches its innocent behind on a tree.
In Brueghel's *Icarus,* for instance: how everything turns
    away
Quite leisurely from the disaster; the ploughman may
Have heard the splash, the forsaken cry,
But for him it was not an important failure; the sun shone
As it had to on the white legs disappearing into the green
Water; and the expensive delicate ship that must have seen
Something amazing, a boy falling out of the sky,
Had somewhere to get to and sailed calmly on.

❏ Questions for Discussion

1. What is "the miraculous birth"?

2. What can the "Old Masters" reveal about suffering?

3. Find a reproduction of Brueghel's *The Fall of Icarus.* The background of this painting depicts the fall of Icarus after he has
disregarded the advice of his father, Daedalus, and has flown
too close to the sun, melting the wax that held his wings together. Explain how the painting supports Auden's claim about
the "Old Masters."

❏ **Suggestion for Exploration and Writing**

1. Write an essay describing a work of art which you admire, explaining what special meaning it has for you.

LAWRENCE FERLINGHETTI (1919–)

*Lawrence Ferlinghetti is an American poet, novelist, and playwright who was an important member of the **Beat** movement. He opened the first paperback bookstore in the United States, a shop which became a center for jazz performances and poetry readings. Many of his poems use irony and sarcasm to protest the status quo. Ferlinghetti believes that poetry can improve society.*

Constantly Risking Absurdity

Constantly risking absurdity
             and death
     whenever he performs
         above the heads
            of his audience   5
 the poet like an acrobat
       climbs on rime
         to a high wire of his own making
and balancing on eyebeams
           above a sea of faces   10
      paces his way
        to the other side of day
    performing entrechats
        and slight-of-foot tricks
  and other high theatrics   15
        and all without mistaking
     any thing
       for what it may not be
   For he's the super realist
         who must perforce perceive   20
   taut truth
       before the taking of each stance or step
 in his supposed advance
       toward that still higher perch
where Beauty stands and waits   25
       with gravity
        to start her death-defying leap

And he
　　　a little charleychaplin man
　　　　　　　　　　　　　who may or may not catch
　　　　her fair eternal form
　　　　　　　　　　　spreadeagled in the empty air
　　　of existence

❏ Questions for Discussion

1. In one long sentence Ferlinghetti compares the poet to the high-wire acrobat. In what ways are they alike? Why do they both take risks?

2. What effect does the reading aloud of "must perforce perceive / taut truth" have on the speed of the poem? How is this speed relevant to that of a tightrope walker?

3. Why is a poet a "super realist"? How does this statement compare with Moore's description of poets as " 'literalists of the imagination' "?

4. Explain the use of "charleychaplin." Describe the image conveyed by this **allusion.**

5. What effect does the arrangement of the lines have on the meaning of the poem?

❏ Suggestions for Exploration and Writing

1. In an **expository** essay, describe the skills and talents which you think make a person a poet.

2. Write an essay agreeing or disagreeing with this statement: The profession of poet is costly for the person who chooses it.

JOHN HOLLANDER (1929–　)

John Hollander has written many books of poems and criticism, including Types of Shape *(1969) and* The Night Mirror *(1970), from which "Adam's Task" comes. His poems show technical mastery and often, like "Adam's Task," a playful wit and fascination with language.*

Adam's Task

"And Adam gave names to all cattle, and to the fowl of the air, and to every beast of the field . . ."—Gen. 2:20

The "30" in margin near top: 30

Thou, paw-paw-paw; thou, glurd; thou, spotted
  Glurd; thou, whitestap, lurching through
The high-grown brush; thou, pliant-footed,
  Implex; thou, awagabu.

Every burrower, each flier   5
  Came for the name he had to give:
Gay, first work, ever to be prior,
  Not yet sunk to primitive.

Thou, verdle; thou, McFleery's pomma;
  Thou; thou; thou—three types of grawl;   10
Thou, flisket; thou, kabasch; thou, comma-
  Eared mashawk; thou, all; thou, all.

Were, in fire of becoming,
  Laboring to be burned away,
Then work, half-measuring, half-humming,   15
  Would be as serious as play.

Thou, pambler; thou, rivarn; thou, greater
  Wherret, and thou, lesser one;
Thou, sproal; thou, zant; thou, lily-eater.
  Naming's over. Day is done.   20

❏ **Questions for Discussion**

1. What situation does the poem ask the reader to imagine?

2. The poem has two distinct speakers, two voices. Who is speaking in the first, third, and fifth stanzas? How does the perspective of the speaker in the second and fourth stanzas differ from that of the speaker in the other stanzas?

3. What is appropriate about the nonsense words?

4. Briefly **paraphrase** stanzas two and four. Be particularly careful in paraphrasing the **paradoxes** in the fourth stanza. How do stanzas two and four relate to the rest of the poem?

5. How does the speaker in the first, third, and fifth stanza feel about his or her work? How do the speaker's attitudes toward language and work differ from those of many people today?

❏ **Suggestions for Exploration and Writing**

1. In what ways is the creation of language an artistic act? In what ways is it like a child's play? Discuss.

2. Analyze the poem, showing how sound and **diction** differentiate the voice and **tone** of each speaker.

AUDRE LORDE (1934–1992)

Born to Granadian parents, Audre Lorde attended school and lived most of her life in New York. Inarticulate as a small child, she spoke in rhythm or in poetry form to express herself. Lorde wrote about subjects that lead to confrontation. As a feminist poet, she portrays strong African-American women who challenge the status quo.

The Art of Response

The first answer was incorrect
the second was
sorry   the third trimmed its toenails
on the Vatican steps
5   the fourth went mad
the fifth
nursed a grudge until it bore twins
that drank poisoned grape juice in Jonestown
the sixth   wrote a book about it
10   the seventh
argued a case before the Supreme Court
against taxation on Girl Scout Cookies
the eighth held a news conference
while four Black babies
15   and one other   picketed New York City
for a hospital bed to die in
the ninth and tenth swore
Revenge on the Opposition
and the eleventh dug their graves
20   next to Eternal Truth
the twelfth
processed funds from a Third World country
that provides doctors for Central Harlem
the thirteenth
25   refused
the fourteenth sold cocaine and shamrocks
near a toilet in the Big Apple circus
the fifteenth
changed the question.

❑ Questions for Discussion

1. How does Lorde build the "art" of answering a question? What is the significance of the fifteenth's response?

2. Why isn't the question to which all are responding ever given?

3. Select one response and discuss its humor or its deeper implications.

❑ **Suggestions for Exploration and Writing**

1. Write an essay explaining what you think the question is and why. Or explain what the question is and what the fifteenth person's change is.

2. Explain how responding to essay questions on an exam can be an art form.

ISHMAEL REED (1938–)

*Ishmael Reed is a controversial American poet and novelist. A savage **satirist**, Reed attacks what he believes to be a dying Western cultural tradition as incompatible with African and Asian traditions. His poems sometimes take the form of rituals designed to separate readers and African-American poets from the influence of the dominant culture.*

beware   :   do not read this poem

tonite ,   thriller was
abt an ol woman   , so vain she
surrounded herself w/
     many mirrors

it got so bad that finally she   5
locked herself indoors & her
whole life became the
     mirrors

one day the villagers broke
into her house ,   but she was too   10
swift for them .   she disappeared
     into a mirror

each tenant who bought the house
after that ,   lost a loved one to
     the ol woman in the mirror   :   15
     first a little girl
     then a young woman
     then the young woman/s husband

the hunger of this poem is legendary
it has taken in many victims   20

back off from this poem
it has drawn in yr feet
back off from this poem
it has drawn in yr legs

25   back off from this poem
it is a greedy mirror
you are into this poem   .   from
      the waist down
nobody can hear you can they   ?
30   this poem has had you up to here
      belch
this poem aint got no manners
you cant call out frm this poem
relax now & go w/ this poem
35   move & roll on to this poem
do not resist this poem
this poem has yr eyes
this poem has his head
this poem has his arms
40   this poem has his fingers
this poem has his fingertips

this poem is the reader & the
reader this poem

statistic   :   the us bureau of missing persons reports
45   that in 1968 over 100,000 people disappeared
      leaving no solid clues
              nor trace   only
    a space   in the lives of their friends

❏ Questions for Discussion

1. Reed attacks the common conception of poetry as pretty, nice, and innocuous. What claims does this poem make for the power of art?

2. What does this poem imply about the subjects of art?

3. In what sense(s) might a work of art or a culture consume one?

4. What is the point of the statistic at the end of the poem?

RAY YOUNG BEAR (1950–   )

A native American of Mesquakie ancestry, Ray Young Bear lives in Tama, Iowa, a Mesquakie community. Though he writes poetry in English, Young Bear speaks the traditional language of his people.

Frequently anthologized, Young Bear has written one book of poems, Winter of the Salamander *(1980).*

Wadasa Nakamoon, Vietnam Memorial

Last night when the yellow moon
of November broke through the last line
of turbulent Midwestern clouds,
a lone frog, the same one
who probably announced   5
the premature spring floods,
attempted to sing.
Veterans' Day, and it was
sore-throat weather.
In reality the invisible musician   10
reminded me of my own doubt.
The knowledge that my grandfathers
were singers as well as composers—
one of whom felt the simple utterance
of a vowel made for the start   15
of a melody—did not produce
the necessary memory or feeling
to make a Wadasa Nakamoon,
Veterans' Song.
All I could think of   20
was the absence of my name
on a distant black rock.
Without this monument
I felt I would not be here.
For a moment, I questioned   25
why I had to immerse myself
in country, controversy and guilt,
but I wanted to honor them.
Surely, the song they presently
listened to along with my grandfathers   30
was the ethereal kind which did not stop.

❏ Questions for Discussion

1. Of what does the frog, "the invisible musician," remind the speaker? What does it mean to the speaker?

2. Why does the speaker refer to "my grandfathers"? What have they to do with the frog, the Vietnam Memorial in Washington, and Veterans' Day?

3. What feelings are aroused in the speaker by the "absence of my name / on a distant black rock"?

4. How does the last sentence relate to the speaker's guilt for being unable to produce a song? Ultimately, what is the song?

LI-YOUNG LEE (1957–)

Of Chinese descent, Li-Young Lee is a native of Indonesia. He has written two highly regarded books of poems, Rose *(1986), which includes "Persimmons," and* City in Which I Love You *(1990). Among the strongest influences on his poetry have been his father, a minister in the Presbyterian Church, and the King James Version of the Bible.*

Persimmons

In sixth grade Mrs. Walker
slapped the back of my head
and made me stand in the corner
for not knowing the difference
5 between *persimmon* and *precision.*
How to choose

persimmons. This is precision.
Ripe ones are soft and brown-spotted.
Sniff the bottoms. The sweet one
10 will be fragrant. How to eat:
put the knife away, lay down newspaper.
Peel the skin tenderly, not to tear the meat.
Chew the skin, suck it,
and swallow. Now, eat
15 the meat of the fruit,
so sweet,
all of it, to the heart.

Donna undresses, her stomach is white.
In the yard, dewy and shivering
20 with crickets, we lie naked,
face-up, face-down.
I teach her Chinese.
Crickets: *chiu chiu.* Dew: I've forgotten.
Naked: I've forgotten.
25 *Ni, wo:*   you and me.
I part her legs,
remember to tell her
she is beautiful as the moon.

Other words
30 that got me into trouble were

fight and *fright, wren* and *yarn.*
Fight was what I did when I was frightened,
fright was what I felt when I was fighting.
Wrens are small, plain birds,
yarn is what one knits with.   35
Wrens are soft as yarn.
My mother made birds out of yarn.
I loved to watch her tie the stuff;
a bird, a rabbit, a wee man.

Mrs. Walker brought a persimmon to class   40
and cut it up
so everyone could taste
a *Chinese apple.* Knowing
it wasn't ripe or sweet, I didn't eat
but watched the other faces.   45

My mother said every persimmon has a sun
inside, something golden, glowing,
warm as my face.

Once, in the cellar, I found two wrapped in newspaper,
forgotten and not yet ripe.   50
I took them and set both on my bedroom windowsill,
where each morning a cardinal
sang, *The sun, the sun.*

Finally understanding
he was going blind,   55
my father sat up all one night
waiting for a song, a ghost.
I gave him the persimmons,
swelled, heavy as sadness,
and sweet as love.   60

This year, in the muddy lighting
of my parents' cellar, I rummage, looking
for something I lost.
My father sits on the tired, wooden stairs,
black cane between his knees,   65
hand over hand, gripping the handle.

He's so happy that I've come home.
I ask how his eyes are, a stupid question.
All gone, he answers.

Under some blankets, I find a box.   70
inside the box I find three scrolls.
I sit beside him and untie
three paintings by my father:

Hibiscus leaf and a white flower.
75   Two cats preening.
Two persimmons, so full they want to drop from the cloth.

He raises both hands to touch the cloth,
asks, *Which is this?*

This is persimmons, Father.

80   *Oh, the feel of the wolftail on the silk,*
the strength, the tense
precision in the wrist.
I painted them hundreds of times
eyes closed. These I painted blind.
85   *Some things never leave a person:*
scent of the hair of one you love,
the texture of persimmons,
in your palm, the ripe weight.

❏ Questions for Discussion

1. What does the word *persimmon* mean to the speaker? What associations does it bring to mind? How is it related to the word *precision*?

2. How does the erotic episode with Donna relate in the narrator's mind to persimmons?

3. How sensitive is the speaker to the subtle meanings of and relationships between words? How sensitive is the teacher to them?

4. What languages besides English and Chinese are represented in this poem?

5. What have the father's painting and his blindness to do with the rest of the poem?

❏ Suggestions for Exploration and Writing

1. This poem implicitly asks what is meant by the word *meaning*. When a word is used, it may refer to an object, action, or idea, or it may refer to a whole series of associations it symbolizes. In an analysis of Lee's poem, contrast the speaker's sense of the symbolic richness of language with the teacher's insistence that words correctly signify one's meaning.

2. In an essay discuss in detail the rich private and personal associations brought to mind by a particular concrete noun.

DRAMA

TINA HOWE (1937–)

Tina Howe was born in New York City and currently lives there. Among her plays are Museum, *which opened in Los Angeles in 1976;* The Art of Dining, *which was coproduced by the New York Shakespeare Festival and the Kennedy Center in 1979;* Painting Churches, *which was first produced in New York City in 1983, won several major awards, and was televised in 1986; and* Coastal Disturbances, *which was produced in New York City and nominated for a Tony award in 1986. Howe is an avowed admirer of the Marx Brothers, and this influence is obvious in the hilarious slapstick of her comedies.*

Painting Churches

Characters

FANNY SEDGWICK CHURCH:	a Bostonian from a fine old family, in her sixties
GARDNER CHURCH:	her husband, an eminent New England poet from a finer family, in his seventies
MARGARET CHURCH (MAGS):	their daughter, a painter, in her early thirties

Time

Several years ago.

Place

Boston, Massachusetts.

ACT ONE

SCENE I

The living room of the Churches' townhouse on Beacon Hill one week before everything will be moved to Cape Cod. Empty packing cartons line the room and all the furniture has been tagged with brightly colored markers. At first glance it looks like any discreet Boston interior, but on closer scrutiny one notices a certain flamboyance. Oddities from secondhand stores are mixed in with the fine old furniture, and exotic handmade curios vie with tasteful family objets d'art. What makes the room remarkable, though, is the play of light that pours through three soaring arched windows. At one hour it's hard edged and brilliant; the next, it's dappled and yielding. It transforms whatever it touches, giving the room a distinct feeling of unreality. It's several years ago, a bright spring morning.

Fanny is sitting on the sofa, wrapping a valuable old silver coffee
service. She's wearing a worn bathrobe and fashionable hat. As
she works, she makes a list of everything on a yellow legal pad.
Gardner can be heard typing in his study down the hall.

FANNY *(Picks up a coffee pot):* God, this is good-looking! I'd forgotten
how handsome Mama's old silver was! It's probably worth a fortune. It certainly weighs enough! *(Calling)* GARRRRRRRRRRRR-
RRRRRDNERRRRRRRRRRRR? . . . Well, it should bring us a
pretty penny, that's for sure. *(Wraps it, places it in a carton, and*
then picks up the tray that goes with it. She holds it up like a mirror
and adjusts her hat. Louder in another register) OH, GARRRRRR-
RRRRRRRRRRDNERRRRR?

   (Gardner continues typing. She then reaches for a small box and
   opens it with reverence) Grandma's Paul Revere teaspoons! . . . *(She*
   takes out several and fondles them) I don't care how desperate
10   things get, these will never go! One has to maintain some standards!
   (She writes on her list) Grandma's Paul Revere teaspoons, Cotuit!
   . . . WASN'T IT THE AMERICAN WING OF THE METROPOLI-
   TAN MUSEUM OF ART THAT WANTED GRANDMA'S PAUL
   REVERE TEASPOONS SO BADLY? . . . *(She looks at her reflection*
   in the tray again) This is a very good-looking hat, if I do say so. I
   was awfully smart to grab it up. *(Silence)*
      DON'T YOU REMEMBER A DISTINGUISHED-LOOKING
   MAN COMING TO THE HOUSE AND OFFERING US FIFTY
   THOUSAND DOLLARS FOR GRANDMA'S PAUL REVERE TEA-
20   SPOONS? . . . HE HAD ON THESE MARVELOUS SHOES! THEY
   WERE SO POINTED AT THE ENDS WE COULDN'T IMAGINE
   HOW HE EVER GOT THEM ON AND THEY WERE SHINED
   TO WITHIN AN INCH OF THEIR LIVES AND I REMEMBER
   HIM SAYING HE CAME FROM THE . . . AMERICAN WING OF
   THE METROPOLITAN MUSEUM OF ART! . . . HELLO? . . .
   GARDNER? . . . ARE YOU THERE! *(The typing stops)* YOO-
   HOOOOOOO . . . *(Like a foghorn)* GARRRRRRRRRRRDNER-
   RRRRR?

GARDNER *(Offstage; from his study):* YES, DEAR . . . IS THAT YOU?
30   FANNY: OF COURSE IT'S ME! WHO ELSE COULD IT POSSIBLY
   BE? . . . DARLING, PLEASE COME HERE FOR A MINUTE. *(The*
   typing resumes) FOR GOD'S SAKE, WILL YOU STOP THAT
   DREADFUL TYPING BEFORE YOU SEND ME STRAIGHT TO
   THE NUT HOUSE? . . . *(In a new register)* GARRRRRRRRRRR-
   RRDNERRRRRR?

He stops.

GARDNER *(Offstage):* WHAT'S   FANNY: I SAID . . . Lord, I hate
THAT? MAGS IS BACK   this yelling. . . . PLEASE . . .
FROM THE NUT HOUSE?   COME . . . HERE!

Brief silence.

GARDNER *(Offstage)*: I'LL BE
WITH YOU IN A MOMENT,
I DIDN'T HEAR HER RING.
(Starts singing) "Nothing could
be finer than to be in Carolina."

FANNY: It's a wonder I'm not in a
straitjacket already. Actually, it   40
might be rather nice for a
change . . . peaceful. DARLING
. . . I WANT TO SHOW YOU
MY NEW HAT!

*Silence. Gardner enters, still singing. He's wearing mismatched
tweeds and is holding a stack of papers which keep drifting to the
floor.*

GARDNER: Oh, don't you look nice! Very attractive, very attractive!

FANNY: But I'm still in my bathrobe.

GARDNER *(Looking around the room, leaking more papers)*: Well,
where's Mags?

FANNY: Darling, you're dropping your papers all over the floor.

GARDNER *(Spies the silver tray)*: I remember this! Aunt Alice gave it to   50
us, didn't she? *(He picks it up)* Good Lord, it's heavy. What's it
made of? Lead?!

FANNY: No, Aunt Alice did *not* give it to us. It was Mama's.

GARDNER: Oh, yes . . . *(He starts to exit with it)*

FANNY: Could I have it back, please?

GARDNER *(Hands it to her, dropping more papers)*: Oh, sure thing. . . .
Where's Mags? I thought you said she was here.

FANNY: I didn't say Mags was here, I asked *you* to come here.

GARDNER *(Papers spilling)*: Damned papers keep falling . . .

FANNY: I wanted to show you my new hat. I bought it in honor of   60
Mags' visit. Isn't it marvelous?

GARDNER *(Picking up the papers as more drop)*: Yes, yes, very nice . . .

FANNY: Gardner, you're not even looking at it!

GARDNER: Very becoming . . .

FANNY: You don't think it's too bright, do you? I don't want to look
like a traffic light. Guess how much it cost?

GARDNER *(A whole sheaf of papers slides to the floor; he dives for
them)*: OH, SHIT!

FANNY *(Gets to them first)*: It's all right, I've got them, I've got them.
(She hands them to him)

GARDNER: You'd think they had wings on them . . .

FANNY: Here you go . . .

GARDNER: . . . damned things   70
won't hold still!

FANNY: Gar . . . ?

GARDNER *(Engrossed in one of the pages)*: Mmmmm?

FANNY: HELLO?

GARDNER *(Startled)*: What's that?

FANNY *(In a whisper)*: My hat. Guess how much it cost.

GARDNER: Oh, yes. Let's see . . . ten dollars?

FANNY: Ten dollars . . . IS THAT ALL?

GARDNER: Twenty?

80 FANNY: GARDNER, THIS HAPPENS TO BE A DESIGNER HAT! DESIGNER HATS START AT FIFTY DOLLARS . . . SEVENTY-FIVE!

GARDNER *(Jumps)*: Was that the door bell?

FANNY: No, it wasn't the door bell. Though it's high time Mags were here. She was probably in a train wreck!

GARDNER *(Looking through his papers)*: I'm beginning to get fond of Wallace Stevens again.

FANNY: This damned move is going to kill me! Send me straight to my grave!

GARDNER *(Reading from a page)*:

90 "The mules that angels ride come slowly down
The blazing passes, from beyond the sun.
Descensions of their tinkling bells arrive.
These muleteers are dainty of their way . . ."[1]
(Pause) Don't you love that! "These muleteers are *dainty* of their way"!?

FANNY: Gar, the hat. How much? *(Gardner sighs)* Darling . . . ?

GARDNER: Oh, yes. Let's see . . . fifty dollars? Seventy-five?

FANNY: It's French.

GARDNER: Three hundred!

100 FANNY *(Triumphant)*: No, eighty-five cents.

GARDNER: Eighty-five cents! . . . I thought you said . . .

FANNY: That's right . . . eighty . . . five . . . *cents*!

GARDNER: Well, you sure had me fooled!

FANNY: I found it at the thrift shop.

GARDNER: I thought it cost at least fifty dollars or seventy-five. You know, designer hats are very expensive!

FANNY: It was on the markdown table. *(She takes it off and shows him the label)* See that? Lily Daché! When I saw that label, I nearly keeled over right into the fur coats!

110 GARDNER *(Handling it)*: Well, what do you know, that's the same label that's in my bathrobe.

FANNY: Darling, Lily Daché designed hats, not men's bathrobes!

GARDNER: Yup . . . Lily Daché . . . same name . . .

FANNY: If you look again, I'm sure you'll see . . .

GARDNER: . . . same script, same color, same size. I'll show you. *(He exits)*

FANNY: Poor lamb can't keep anything straight anymore. *(Looks at herself in the tray again)* God, this is a good-looking hat!

---

[1] From Wallace Stevens, "Le Monocle de Mon Oncle." Stevens was a twentieth-century American poet.

GARDNER *(Returns with a nondescript plaid bathrobe. He points to the label)*: See that? . . . What does it say?

FANNY *(Refusing to look at it)*: Lily Daché was a *hat* designer! She designed ladies' *hats*!   120

GARDNER: What . . . does . . . it . . . say?

FANNY: Gardner, you're being ridiculous.

GARDNER *(Forcing it on her)*: Read . . . the label!

FANNY: Lily Daché did *not* design this bathrobe, I don't care what the label says!

GARDNER: READ! *(Fanny reads it)* ALL RIGHT, NOW WHAT DOES IT SAY?

FANNY *(Chagrined)*: Lily Daché.

GARDNER: I told you!

FANNY: Wait a minute, let me look at that again. *(She does; then   130
throws the robe at him in disgust)* Gar, Lily Daché never designed a bathrobe in her life! Someone obviously ripped the label off one of her hats and then sewed it into the robe.

GARDNER *(Puts it on over his jacket)*: It's damned good-looking. I've always loved this robe. I think you gave it to me. . . . Well, I've got to get back to work. *(He abruptly exits)*

FANNY: Where did you get that robe anyway? . . . I didn't give it to you, did I . . . ?

Silence. Gardner resumes typing.

FANNY *(Holding the tray up again and admiring herself)*: You know, I think I *did* give it to him. I remember how excited I was when I   140
found it at the thrift shop . . . fifty cents and never worn! *I* couldn't have sewn that label in to impress him, could I? . . . I can't be that far gone! . . . The poor lamb wouldn't even notice it, let alone understand its cachet. . . . Uuuuuuh, this damned tray is even heavier than the coffee pot. They must have been amazons in the old days! *(Writes on her pad)* "Empire tray, Parke-Bernet Galleries," and good riddance! *(She wraps it and drops it into the carton with the coffee pot)* Where *is* that wretched Mags? It would be just like her to get into a train wreck! She was supposed to be here hours ago. Well, if she doesn't show up soon, I'm going to drop dead of exhaus-   150
tion. God, wouldn't that be wonderful? . . . Then they could just cart me off into storage with all the old chandeliers and china . . .

The doorbell rings.

| FANNY: IT'S MAGS, IT'S MAGS! *(A pause. Dashing out of the room, colliding into Gardner)* GOOD GOD, LOOK AT ME! I'M STILL IN MY BATH-ROBE! | GARDNER *(Offstage)*: COMING, COMING . . . I'VE GOT IT . . . COMING! *(Dashing into the room, colliding into Fanny)* I'VE GOT IT . . . HOLD ON . . . COMING . . . COM-ING . . . |

160   FANNY *(Offstage)*: MAGS IS HERE! IT'S MAGS. . . . SHE'S FI-
NALLY HERE!

*Gardner exits to open the front door. Mags comes staggering in car-
rying a suitcase and an enormous duffel bag. She wears wonderfully
distinctive clothes and has very much her own look. She's extremely
out of breath and too wrought up to drop her heavy bags.*

MAGS: I'm sorry. . . . I'm sorry I'm so late. . . . Everything went wrong!
A passenger had a heart attack outside of New London and we had
to stop. . . . It was terrifying! All these medics and policemen came
swarming onto the train and the conductor kept running up and
down the aisles telling everyone not to leave their seats under any
circumstances. . . . Then the New London fire department came
screeching down to the tracks, sirens blaring, lights whirling, and all
these men in black rubber suits started pouring through the

170   doors. . . . *That* took two hours . . .

FANNY *(Offstage)*: DARLING . . . DARLING . . . WHERE ARE YOU?

MAGS: *Then,* I couldn't get a cab at the station. There just weren't
any! I must have circled the block fifteen times. Finally I just
stepped out into the traffic with my thumb out, but no one would
pick me up . . . so I walked . . .

FANNY *(Offstage)*: Damned zipper's stuck . . .

GARDNER: You walked all the way from the South Station?

MAGS: Well actually, I ran . . .

GARDNER: You had poor Mum scared to death.

180   MAGS *(Finally puts the bags down with a deep sigh)*: I'm sorry. . . . I'm
really sorry. It was a nightmare.

*Fanny reenters the room, her dress over her head. The zipper's
stuck; she staggers around blindly.*

FANNY: Damned zipper! Gar, will you please help me with this?

MAG: I sprinted all the way up Beacon Hill.

GARDNER *(Opening his arms wide)*: Well come here and let's get a
look at you. *(He hugs her)* Mags!

MAGS *(Squeezing him tight)*: Oh, Daddy . . . Daddy!

GARDNER: My Mags!

MAGS: I never thought I'd get here! . . . Oh, you look wonderful!

GARDNER: Well, you don't look so bad yourself!

190   MAGS: I love your hair. It's gotten so . . . white!

FANNY *(Still lost in her dress, struggling with the zipper)*: This is *so*
typical . . . just as Mags arrives, my zipper has to break! *(She grunts
and struggles)*

MAGS *(Waves at her)*: Hi, Mum . . .

FANNY: Just a minute, dear, my zipper's . . .

GARDNER *(Picks up Mags' bags)*: Well, sit down and take a load off
your feet . . .

MAGS: I was so afraid I'd never make it . . .

GARDNER *(Staggering under the weight of the bags)*: What have you got in here? Lead weights?

MAGS: I can't believe you're finally letting me do you.   200

Fanny flings her arms around Mags, practically knocking her over.

FANNY: OH, DARLING . . . MY PRECIOUS MAGS, YOU'RE HERE AT LAST.   GARDNER *(Lurching around in circles)*: Now let's see . . . where should I put these . . . ?

FANNY: I was sure your train had derailed and you were lying dead in some ditch!

MAGS *(Pulls away from Fanny to come to Gardner's rescue)*: Daddy, please, let me . . . these are much too heavy.

FANNY *(Finally noticing Mags)*: GOOD LORD, WHAT HAVE YOU DONE TO YOUR HAIR?!

MAGS *(Struggling to take the bags from Gardner)*: Come on, give them   210
to me . . . please? *(She sets them down by the sofa)*

FANNY *(As her dress starts to slide off one shoulder)*: Oh, not again!
. . . Gar, would you give me a hand and see what's wrong with this zipper. One minute it's stuck, the next it's falling to pieces.

Gardner goes to her and starts fussing with it.

MAGS *(Pacing)*: I don't know, it's been crazy all week. Monday, I forgot to keep an appointment I'd made with a new model. . . . Tuesday, I overslept and stood up my advanced painting students. . . . Wednesday, the day of my meeting with Max Zoll, I forgot to put on my underpants . . .

FANNY: GODDAMMIT, GAR, CAN'T YOU DO ANYTHING   220
ABOUT THIS ZIPPER?!

MAGS: I mean, there I was, racing down Broome Street in this gauzy Tibetan skirt when I tripped and fell right at his feet . . . SPLATTT! My skirt goes flying over my head and there I am . . . everything staring him in the face . . .

FANNY: COME ON, GAR, USE A LITTLE MUSCLE!

MAGS *(Laughing)*: Oh, well, all that matters is that I finally got here. . . . I mean . . . there you are . . .

GARDNER *(Struggling with the zipper)*: I can't see it, it's too small!

FANNY *(Whirls away from Gardner, pulling her dress off altogether)*:
OH, FORGET IT! JUST FORGET IT! The trolley's probably miss-   230
ing half its teeth, just like someone else I know. *(To Mags)* I grind my teeth in my sleep now, I've worn them all down to stubs. Look at that! *(She flings open her mouth and points)* Nothing left but the gums!

GARDNER: I never hear you grind your teeth . . .

FANNY: That's because I'm snoring so loud. How could you hear anything through all that racket? It even wakes me up. It's no wonder poor Daddy has to sleep downstairs.

MAGS *(Looking around)*: Jeez, look at the place! So, you're finally do-
240   ing it . . . selling the house and moving to Cotuit year round. I don't
believe it. I just don't believe it!

GARDNER: Well, how about a drink to celebrate Mags' arrival?

MAGS: You've been here so long. Why move now?

FANNY: Gardner, what are you wearing that bathrobe for?

MAGS: You can't move. I won't let you!

FANNY *(Softly to Gardner)*: Really, darling, you ought to pay more
attention to your appearance.

MAGS: You love this house. *I* love this house . . . the room . . . the
light.

250   GARDNER: So, Mags, how about a little . . . *(he drinks from an imaginary glass)* to wet your whistle?

FANNY: We can't start drinking now, it isn't even noon yet!

MAGS: I'm starving. I've got to get something to eat before I collapse!
(She exits towards the kitchen)

FANNY: What *have* you done to your hair, dear? The color's so queer
and all your nice curl is gone.

GARDNER: It looks to me as if she dyed it.

FANNY: Yes, that's it. You're absolutely right! It's a completely different color. She dyed it bright red!

Mags can be heard thumping and thudding through the icebox.

FANNY: NOW, MAGS, I DON'T WANT YOU FILLING UP ON
260   SNACKS. . . . I'VE MADE A PERFECTLY BEAUTIFUL LEG OF
LAMB FOR LUNCH! . . . HELLO? . . . DO YOU HEAR ME? . . .
(To Gardner) No one in our family has *ever* had red hair, it's so
common looking.

GARDNER: I like it. It brings out her eyes.

FANNY: WHY ON EARTH DID YOU DYE YOUR HAIR *RED,* OF
ALL COLORS?!

MAGS *(Returns, eating Saltines out of the box)*: I didn't dye my hair, I
just added some highlight.

FANNY: I suppose that's what your arty friends in New York do . . .
270   dye their hair all the colors of the rainbow!

GARDNER: Well, it's damned attractive if you ask me . . . damned attractive!

*Mags unzips her duffel bag and rummages around in it while eating
the Saltines.*

FANNY: Darling, I told you not to bring a lot of stuff with you. We're
trying to get rid of things.

MAGS *(Pulls out a folding easel and starts setting it up)*: AAAAAHHH-
HHH, here it is. Isn't it a beauty? I bought it just for you!

FANNY: Please don't get crumbs all over the floor. Crystal was just
here yesterday. It was her last time before we move.

MAGS *(At her easel)*: God, I can hardly wait! I can't believe you're finally letting me do you.   280

FANNY: *Do* us? . . . What *are* you talking about?

GARDNER *(Reaching for the Saltines)*: Hey, Mags, could I have a couple of those?

MAGS *(Tosses him the box)*: Sure! *(To Fanny)* Your portrait.

GARDNER: Thanks. *(He starts munching on a handful)*

FANNY: You're planning to paint our portrait now? While we're trying to move . . . ?

GARDNER *(Sputtering Saltines)*: Mmmmm, I'd forgotten just how delicious Saltines are!

MAGS: It's a perfect opportunity. There'll be no distractions; you'll be   290
completely at my mercy. Also, you promised.

FANNY: I did?

MAGS: Yes, you did.

FANNY: Well, I must have been off my rocker.

MAGS: No, you said, "You can paint us, you can dip us in concrete, you can do anything you want with us just so long as you help us get out of here!"

GARDNER *(Offering the box of Saltines to Fanny)*: You really ought to try some of these, Fan, they're absolutely delicious!

FANNY *(Taking a few)*: Why, thank you.   300

MAGS: I figure we'll pack in the morning and you'll pose in the afternoons. It'll be a nice diversion.

FANNY: These *are* good!

GARDNER: Here, dig in . . . take some more.

MAGS: I have some wonderful news . . . amazing news! I wanted to wait till I got here to tell you.

Gardner and Fanny eat their Saltines, passing the box back and forth as Mags speaks.

MAGS: You'll die! Just fall over into the packing cartons and die! Are you ready? . . . BRACE YOURSELVES. . . . OKAY, HERE
GOES. . . . I'm being given a one-woman show at one of the most
important galleries in New York this fall. Me, Margaret Church,   310
exhibited at Castelli's, 420 West Broadway. . . . Can you believe it?!
. . . MY PORTRAITS HANGING IN THE SAME ROOMS THAT
HAVE SHOWN RAUSCHENBERG, JOHNS, WARHOL, KELLY,
LICHTENSTEIN, STELLA, SERRA,[2] ALL THE HEAVIES. . . . It's
incredible, beyond belief . . . I mean, at my age. . . . Do you know
how good you have to be to get in there? It's a miracle . . . an honest-to-God, star-spangled miracle!

Pause.

---

[2] Contemporary American painters.

FANNY *(Mouth full)*: Oh, darling, that's wonderful. We're so happy for you!

GARDNER *(Mouth full)*: No one deserves it more, no one deserves it more!

MAGS: Through some fluke, some of Castelli's people showed up at our last faculty show at Pratt and were knocked out . . .

FANNY *(Reaching for the box of Saltines)*: More, more . . .

MAGS: They said they hadn't seen anyone handle light like me since the French Impressionists.[3] They said I was this weird blend ofPierre Bonnard, Mary Cassatt and David Hockney . . .[4]

GARDNER *(Swallowing his mouthful)*: I told you they were good.

MAGS: Also, no one's doing portraits these days. They're considered passé. I'm so out of it, I'm in.

GARDNER: Well, you're loaded with talent and always have been.

FANNY: She gets it all from Mama, you know. Her miniature of Henry James is still one of the main attractions at the Atheneum. Of course no woman of breeding could be a professional artist in her day. It simply wasn't done. But talk about talent . . . that woman had talent to burn!

MAGS: I want to do one of you for the show.

FANNY: Oh, do Daddy, he's the famous one.

MAGS: No, I want to do you both. I've always wanted to do you and now I've finally got a good excuse.

FANNY: It's high time somebody painted Daddy again! I'm sick to death of that dreadful portrait of him in the National Gallery they keep reproducing. He looks like an undertaker!

GARDNER: Well, I think you should just do Mum. She's never looked handsomer.

FANNY: Oh, come on, I'm a perfect fright and you know it.

MAGS: I want to do you both. Side by side. In this room. Something really classy. You look so great. Mum with her crazy hats and everything and you with that face. If I could just get you to hold still long enough and actually pose.

GARDNER *(Walking around, distracted)*: Where are those papers I just had? Goddammit, Fanny . . .

MAGS: I have the feeling it's either now or never.

GARDNER: I can't hold on to anything around here. *(He exits to his study)*

MAGS: I've always wanted to do you. It would be such a challenge.

FANNY *(Pulling Mags onto the sofa next to her)*: I'm so glad you're finally here, Mags. I'm very worried about Daddy.

MAGS: Mummy, please. I just got here.

---

[3] A school of late nineteenth-century painters including Renoir and Monet.

[4] Pierre Bonnard was a French Impressionist painter. Mary Cassatt was an American Impressionist painter. David Hockney is a contemporary English realistic and pop art painter.

FANNY: He's getting quite gaga.

MAGS: Mummy . . . !

FANNY: You haven't seen him in almost a year. Two weeks ago he   360
walked through the front door of the Codman's house, kissed Emily
on the cheek and settled down in the maid's room, thinking he was
home!

MAGS: Oh, come on, you're exaggerating.

FANNY: He's as mad as a hatter and getting worse every day! It's this
damned new book of his. He works on it around the clock. I've
read some of it, and it doesn't make one word of sense, it's all at
sixes and sevens . . .

GARDNER (*Pokes his head back in the room, spies some of his papers
on a table and grabs them*): Ahhh, here they are. (*He exits*)

FANNY (*Voice lowered*): Ever since this dry spell with his poetry, he's   370
been frantic, absolutely . . . frantic!

MAGS: I hate it when you do this.

FANNY: I'm just trying to get you to face the facts around here.

MAGS: There's nothing wrong with him! He's just as sane as the next
man. Even saner, if you ask me.

FANNY: You know what he's doing now? You couldn't guess in a million years! . . . He's writing criticism! Daddy! (*She laughs*) Can you
believe it? The man doesn't have one analytic bone in his body. His
mind is a complete jumble and always has been!

There's a loud crash from Gardner's study.

GARDNER (*Offstage*): SHIT!   380

MAGS: He's abstracted. . . . That's the way he is.

FANNY: He doesn't spend any time with me anymore. He just holes up
in that filthy study with Toots. God, I hate that bird! Though actually they're quite cunning together. Daddy's teaching him Gray's
Elegy.[5] You ought to see them in there, Toots perched on top of
Daddy's head, spouting out verse after verse . . . Daddy, tap-tap-
tapping away on his typewriter. They're quite a pair.

GARDNER (*Pokes his head back in*): Have you seen that Stevens' poem
I was reading before?

FANNY (*Long-suffering*): NO, I HAVEN'T SEEN THAT STEVENS'   390
POEM YOU WERE READING BEFORE! . . . Things are getting
very tight around here, in case you haven't noticed. Daddy's last
Pulitzer didn't even cover our real estate tax, and now that he's too
doddery to give readings anymore, that income is gone . . . (*Suddenly handing Mags the sugar bowl she'd been wrapping*) Mags, *do*
take this sugar bowl. You can use it to serve tea to your students at
that wretched art school of yours . . .

---

[5] "Elegy Written in a Country Churchyard," most famous poem of Thomas Gray, a
mid-eighteenth century English poet.

MAGS: It's called Pratt! The Pratt Institute.

FANNY: Pratt, Splatt, whatever . . .

400   MAGS: And I don't serve tea to my students, I teach them how to paint.

FANNY: Well, I'm sure none of them has ever seen a sugar bowl as handsome as this before.

GARDNER *(Reappearing again)*: You're sure you haven't seen it?

FANNY *(Loud and angry)*: YES, I'M SURE I HAVEN'T SEEN IT! I JUST TOLD YOU I HAVEN'T SEEN IT!

GARDNER *(Retreating)*: Right you are, right you are. *(He exits)*

FANNY: God!

Silence.

MAGS: What do you have to yell at him like that for?

410   FANNY: Because the poor thing's as deaf as an adder!

Mags sighs deeply; silence. Fanny, suddenly exuberant, leads her over to a lamp.

FANNY: Come, I want to show you something.

MAGS *(Looking at it)*: What is it?

FANNY: Something I made. *(Mags is about to turn it on)* WAIT, DON'T TURN IT ON YET! It's got to be dark to get the full effect. *(She rushes to the windows and pulls down the shades)*

MAGS: What *are* you doing?

FANNY: Hold your horses a minute. You'll see . . . *(As the room gets darker and darker)* Poor me, you wouldn't believe the lengths I go to to amuse myself these days . . .

MAGS *(Touching the lampshade)*: What is this? It looks like a scene of
420   some sort.

FANNY: It's an invention I made . . . a kind of magic lantern.

MAGS: Gee . . . it's amazing . . .

FANNY: What I did was buy an old engraving of the Grand Canal . . .

MAGS: You *made* this?

FANNY: . . . and then color it in with crayons. Next, I got out my sewing scissors and cut out all the street lamps and windows . . . anything that light would shine through. Then I pasted it over a plain lampshade, put the shade on this old horror of a lamp, turned on the switch and . . . *(She turns it on)* VOILÀ . . . VENICE
430   TWINKLING AT DUSK! It's quite effective, don't you think . . . ?

MAGS *(Walking around it)*: Jeeez . . .

FANNY: And see, I poked out all the little lights on the gondolas with a straight pin.

MAGS: Where on earth did you get the idea?

FANNY: Well, you know, idle minds . . . *(She spins the shade, making the lights whirl)*

MAGS: It's really amazing. I mean, you could sell this in a store!

GARDNER *(Enters)*: HERE IT IS. IT WAS RIGHT ON TOP OF MY DESK THE WHOLE TIME. *(He crashes into a table)* OOOOOWWWWW! 440

FANNY: LOOK OUT, LOOK OUT!

MAGS *(Rushes over to Gardner)*: Oh, Daddy, are you all right?

FANNY: WATCH WHERE YOU'RE GOING, WATCH WHERE YOU'RE GOING!

GARDNER *(Hopping up and down on one leg)*: GODDAMMIT! . . . I HIT MY SHIN.

FANNY: I was just showing Mags my lamp . . .

GARDNER *(Limping over to it)*: Oh, yes, isn't that something? Mum is awfully clever with that kind of thing. . . . It was all her idea. Buying the engraving, coloring it in, cutting out all those little dots. 450

FANNY: Not "dots" . . . lights and windows, lights and windows!

GARDNER: Right, right . . . lights and windows.

FANNY: Well, we'd better get some light back in here before someone breaks their neck. *(She zaps the shades back up)*

GARDNER *(Puts his arm around Mags)*: Gee, it's good to have you back.

MAGS: It's good to be back.

GARDNER: And I like that new red hair of yours. It's very becoming.

MAGS: But I told you, I hardly touched it . . .

GARDNER: Well, something's different. You've got a glow. So . . . how 460 do you want us to pose for this grand portrait of yours . . . ? *(He poses self-consciously)*

MAGS: Oh, Daddy, setting up a portrait takes a lot of time and thought. You've got to figure out the background, the lighting, what to wear, the sort of mood you want to—

FANNY: OOOOH, LET'S DRESS UP, LET'S DRESS UP! *(She grabs a packing blanket, drapes it around herself and links arms with Gardner, striking an elegant pose)* This *is* going to be fun. She was absolutely right! Come on, Gar, look distinguished!

MAGS: Mummy, please, it's not a game!

FANNY *(More and more excited)*: You still have your tuxedo, don't you? And I'll wear my marvelous long black dress that makes me 470 look like that fascinating woman in the Sargent paining! *(She strikes the famous profile pose)*

MAGS: MUMMY?!

FANNY: I'm sorry, we'll behave, just tell us what to do.

Fanny and Gardner settle down next to each other.

GARDNER: That's right, you're the boss.

FANNY: Yes, you're the boss.

MAGS: But I'm not ready yet; I haven't set anything up.

FANNY: Relax, darling, we just want to get the hang of it . . .

Fanny and Gardner stare straight ahead, trying to look like suitable subjects, but they can't hold still. They keep making faces, lifting an eyebrow, wriggling a nose, twitching a lip. Nothing big and grotesque, just flickering changes; a half-smile here, a self-important frown there. They steal glances at each other every so often.

GARDNER: How am I doing, Fan?

FANNY: Brilliantly, absolutely brilliantly!

480   MAGS: But you're making faces.

FANNY: *I'm* not making faces. (*Turning to Gardner and making a face*) Are *you* making faces, Gar?

GARDNER (*Instantly making one*): Certainly not! I'm the picture of restraint!

Without meaning to, Fanny and Gardner get sillier and sillier. They start giggling, then laughing.

490   MAGS (*Can't help but join in*): You two are impossible . . . completely impossible! I was crazy to think I could ever pull this off! (*Laughing away*) Look at you . . . just . . . look at you!

Blackout.

SCENE 2

Two days later, around five in the afternoon. Half of the Church household has been dragged into the living room for packing. Overflowing cartons are everywhere. They're filled with pots and pans, dishes and glasses, and the entire contents of two linen closets. Mags has placed a stepladder under one of the windows. A pile of tablecloths and curtains is flung beneath it. Two side chairs are in readiness for the eventual pose.

Mags has just pulled a large crimson tablecloth out of a carton. She unfurls it with one shimmering toss.

MAGS: PERFECT . . . PERFECT!

FANNY (*Seated on the sofa, clutches an old pair of galoshes to her chest*): Look at these old horrors; half the rubber is rotted away and
500   the fasteners are falling to pieces. . . . GARDNER? . . . OH, GARRRRRRRRRDNERRRRR?

MAGS (*Rippling out the tablecloth with shorter snapping motions*): Have you ever seen such a color?

FANNY: I'VE FOUND YOUR OLD SLEDDING GALOSHES IN WITH THE POTS AND PANS. DO YOU STILL WANT THEM?

MAGS: It's like something out of a Rubens![6]

---

[6] Seventeenth-century Flemish painter of richly colored, brilliantly lighted canvases.

Mags slings the tablecloth over a chair and then sits on a footstool to finish the Sara Lee banana cake she started. As she eats, she looks at the tablecloth, making happy grunting sounds. Fanny lovingly puts the galoshes on over her shoes and wiggles her feet.

FANNY: God, these bring back memories! There were real snowstorms in the old days. Not these pathetic little two-inch droppings we have now. After a particularly heavy one, Daddy and I used to go sledding on the Common. This was way before you were born. . . . God, it was a hundred years ago! . . . Daddy would stop writing early, put on these galoshes and come looking for me, jingling the fasteners like castanets. It was a kind of mating call, almost . . . *(She jingles them)* The Common was always deserted after a storm; we had the whole place to ourselves. It was so romantic. . . . We'd haul the sled up Beacon Street, stop under the State House, and aim it straight down to the Park Street Church, which was much further away in those days. . . . Then Daddy would lie down on the sled, I'd lower myself on top of him, we'd rock back and forth a few times to gain momentum and then . . . WHOOOOOOOOOSSSSSSSHH-HHH . . . down we'd plunge like a pair of eagles locked in a spasm of lovemaking. God, it was wonderful! . . . The city whizzing past us at ninety miles an hour . . . the cold . . . the darkness . . . Daddy's hair in my mouth . . . GAR . . . REMEMBER HOW WE USED TO GO SLEDDING IN THE OLD DAYS? . . . Sometimes he'd lie on top of me. That was fun. I liked that even more. *(In her foghorn voice)* GARRRRRRRRRDNERRRRR?

MAGS: Didn't he say he was going out this afternoon?

FANNY: Why, so he did! I completely forgot. *(She takes off the galoshes)* I'm getting just as bad as him. *(She drops them into a different carton—wistful)* Gar's galoshes, Cotuit.

A pause. Mags picks up the tablecloth again, holds it high over her head.

MAGS: Isn't this fabulous? . . . *(She then wraps Fanny in it)* It's the perfect backdrop. Look what it does to your skin.

FANNY: Mags, what *are* you doing?

MAGS: It makes you glow like a pomegranate . . . *(She whips it off her)* Now all I need is a hammer and nails . . . *(She finds them)* YES! *(She climbs up the stepladder and starts hammering a corner of the cloth into the molding of one of the windows)* This is going to look so great! . . . I've never seen such color!

FANNY: Darling, what is going on . . . ?

MAGS: Rembrandt, eat your heart out! You seventeenth-century Dutch has-been, you. *(She hammers more furiously)*

FANNY: MARGARET, THIS IS NOT A CONSTRUCTION SITE. . . . PLEASE . . . STOP IT. . . . YOO-HOOOOO . . . DO YOU HEAR ME?

Gardner suddenly appears, dressed in a raincoat.

GARDNER: YES, DEAR, HERE I AM. I JUST STEPPED OUT FOR A WALK DOWN CHESTNUT STREET. BEAUTIFUL AFTERNOON, ABSOLUTELY BEAUTIFUL! ... WHY, THAT LOOKS VERY NICE, MAGS, very nice indeed ...

FANNY *(To Mags)*: YOU'RE GOING TO RUIN THE WALLS TO SAY NOTHING OF MAMA'S BEST TABLECLOTH. ... MAGS, DO YOU HEAR ME? ... YOO-HOO! ... DARLING, I MUST INSIST you stop that dreadful ...

550

MAGS *(Steps down; stands back and looks at the tablecloth)*: That's it. That's *IT!*

FANNY *(To Gardner, worried)*: Where have *you* been?

Mags kisses her fingers at the backdrop and settles back into her banana cake.

GARDNER *(To Fanny)*: You'll never guess who I ran into on Chestnut Street ... Pate Baldwin!

Gardner takes his coat off and drops it on the floor. He sits in one of the posing chairs.

MAGS *(Mouth full of cake)*: Oh, Daddy, I'm nowhere near ready for you yet.

560

FANNY *(Picks up Gardner's coat and hands it to him)*: Darling, coats do *not* go on the floor.

GARDNER *(Rises, but forgets where he's supposed to go)*: He was in terrible shape. I hardly recognized him. Well, it's the Parkinson's disease ...

FANNY: You mean, Hodgkin's disease ...

GARDNER: Hodgkin's disease ... ?

MAGS *(Leaves her cake and returns to the tablecloth)*: Now to figure out exactly how to use this gorgeous light ...

570

FANNY: Yes, Pate has Hodgkin's disease, not Parkinson's disease. Sammy Bishop has Parkinson's disease. In the closet ... your coat goes ... in the closet!

GARDNER: You're absolutely right! Pate has Hodgkin's disease. *(He stands motionless, the coat over his arm)*

FANNY: And Goat Davis has Addison's disease.

GARDNER: I always get them confused.

FANNY *(Pointing towards the closet)*: That way ...

Gardner exits to the closet; Fanny calls after him.

FANNY: Grace Phelps has it too, I think. Or, it might be Hodgkin's, like Pate. I can't remember.

GARDNER *(Returns with a hanger)*: Doesn't The Goat have Parkinson's disease?

FANNY: No, that's Sammy Bishop.   580

GARDNER: God, I haven't seen The Goat in ages! *(The coat still over his arm, he hands Fanny the hanger)*

FANNY: He hasn't been well.

GARDNER: Didn't Heppy . . . *die?!*

FANNY: What are you giving me this for? . . . Oh, Heppy's been dead for years. She died on the same day as Luster Bright, don't you remember?

GARDNER: I always liked her.

FANNY *(Gives Gardner back the hanger)*: Here, I don't want this.

GARDNER: She was awfully attractive.

FANNY: Who?   590

GARDNER: Heppy!

FANNY: Oh, yes, Heppy had real charm.

MAGS *(Keeps adjusting the tablecloth)*: Better . . . better . . .

GARDNER: Which is something The Goat is short on, if you ask me. He has Hodgkin's disease, doesn't he? *(Puts his raincoat back on and sits down)*

FANNY: Darling, what *are* you doing? I thought you wanted to hang up your coat!

GARDNER *(After a pause)*: OH, YES, THAT'S RIGHT!

Gardner goes back to the closet; a pause.

FANNY: Where were we?

GARDNER *(Returns with yet another hanger)*: Let's see . . .   600

FANNY *(Takes both hangers from him)*: FOR GOD'S SAKE, GAR, PAY ATTENTION!

GARDNER: It was something about The Goat . . .

FANNY *(Takes the coat from Gardner)*: HERE, LET ME DO IT! . . . *(Under her breath to Mags)* See what I mean about him? You don't know the half of it!

Fanny hangs the raincoat up in the closet.

FANNY: Not the half.

MAGS *(Still tinkering with the backdrop)*: Almost . . . almost . . .

GARDNER *(Sitting back down in one of the posing chairs)*: Oh, Fan, did I tell you, I ran into Pate Baldwin just now. I'm afraid he's not   610
long for this world.

FANNY *(Returning)*: Well, it's that Hodgkin's disease . . . *(She sits on the posing chair next to him)*

GARDNER: God, I'd hate to see him go. He's one of the great editors of our times. I couldn't have done it without him. He gave me everything, everything!

MAGS *(Makes a final adjustment)*: Yes, that's it! *(She stands back and gazes at them)* You look wonderful!

FANNY: Isn't it getting to be . . . *(She taps at an imaginary watch on her wrist and drains an imaginary glass)* cocktail time?!

620   GARDNER *(Looks at his watch)*: On the button, on the button! *(He rises)*

FANNY: I'll have the usual, please. Do join us, Mags! Daddy bought some Dubonnet especially for you!

MAGS: Hey. I was just getting some ideas.

GARDNER *(To Mags, as he exits for the bar)*: How about a little . . . *Dubonnet* to wet your whistle?

FANNY: Oh, Mags, it's like the old times having you back with us like this!

GARDNER *(Offstage)*: THE USUAL FOR YOU, FAN?

FANNY: I wish we saw more of you. . . . PLEASE! . . . Isn't he darling?
630   Have you ever known anyone more darling than Daddy?

GARDNER *(Offstage; hums Jolson's "You Made Me Love You")*: MAGS, HOW ABOUT YOU? . . . A LITTLE . . . DUBONNET?

FANNY: Oh, *do* join us!   MAGS *(To Gardner)*: No, nothing, thanks.

FANNY: Well, what do you think of your aged parents picking up and moving to Cotuit year round? Pretty crazy, eh what? . . . Nothing but the gulls, oysters and us!

GARDNER *(Returns with Fanny's drink)*: Here you go . . .

FANNY: Why thank you, Gar. *(To Mags)* You sure you won't join us?

GARDNER *(Lifts his glass towards Fanny and Mags)*: Cheers!

Gardner and Fanny take that first lifesaving gulp.

640   FANNY: Aaaaahhhhh!   GARDNER: Hits the spot, hits the spot!

MAGS: Well, I certainly can't do you like that!

FANNY: Why not? I think we look very . . . *comme il faut!*[7]

Fanny slouches into a rummy pose; Gardner joins her.

FANNY: WAIT . . . I'VE GOT IT! I'VE GOT IT! *(She whispers excitedly to Gardner)*

MAGS: Come on, let's not start this again!

GARDNER: What's that? . . . Oh, yes . . . yes, yes . . . I know the one you mean. Yes, right, right . . . of course.

A pause.

FANNY: How's . . . *this?!*

Fanny grabs a large serving fork and she and Gardner fly into an imitation of Grant Wood's American Gothic.[8]

---

[7] French meaning *as appropriate* or *appropriate.*

[8] Famous painting of a farmer and his wife standing in front of a barn and looking very serious and self-righteous.

MAGS: And I wonder why it's taken me all these years to get you to pose for me. You just don't take me seriously! Poor old Mags and her ridiculous portraits . . .

FANNY: Oh, darling, your portraits aren't *ridiculous!* They may not be all that one *hopes* for, but they're certainly not—

MAGS: Remember how you behaved at my first group show in Soho? . . . Oh, come on, you remember. It was a real circus! Think back. . . . It was about six years ago. . . . Daddy had just been awarded some presidential medal of achievement and you insisted he wear it around his neck on a bright red ribbon, and you wore this . . . *huge* feathered hat to match! I'll never forget it! It was the size of a giant pizza with twenty-inch red turkey feathers shooting straight up into the air. . . . Oh, come on, you remember, don't you?

FANNY *(Leaping to her feet)*: HOLD EVERYTHING! THIS IS IT! THIS IS REALLY IT! Forgive me for interrupting, Mags darling, it'll just take a minute. *(She whispers excitedly to Gardner)*

MAGS: I had about eight portraits in the show, mostly of friends of mine, except for this old one I'd done of Mrs. Crowninshield.

GARDNER: All right, all right . . . let's give it a whirl.

A pause; then they mime Michelangelo's Pieta[9] *with Gardner lying across Fanny's lap as the dead Christ.*

MAGS *(Depressed)*: The *Pietà.* Terrific!

FANNY *(Jabbing Gardner in the ribs)*: Hey, we're getting good at this.

GARDNER: Of course it would help if we didn't have all these modern clothes on.

MAGS: AS I WAS SAYING . . .

FANNY: Sorry, Mags . . . sorry . . .

Huffing and creaking with the physical exertion of it all, Fanny and Gardner return to their seats.

MAGS: As soon as you stepped foot in the gallery you spotted it and cried out, "MY GOD, WHAT'S MILLICENT CROWNINSHIELD DOING HERE?" Everyone looked up, what with Daddy's clanking medal and your amazing hat which I was sure would take off and start flying around the room. A crowd gathered. . . . Through some utter fluke, you latched on to *the* most important critic in the city, I mean . . . Mr. Modern Art himself, and you hauled him over to the painting, trumpeting out for all to hear, "THAT'S MILLICENT CROWNINSHIELD! I GREW UP WITH HER. SHE LIVES RIGHT DOWN THE STREET FROM US IN BOSTON. BUT IT'S A VERY POOR LIKENESS, IF YOU ASK ME! HER NOSE ISN'T NEARLY THAT LARGE AND SHE DOESN'T HAVE SOMETHING QUEER GROWING OUT OF HER CHIN! THE CROWNINSHIELDS ARE

---

[9] Famous sculpture of the Virgin Mary holding the body of Christ.

REALLY QUITE GOOD-LOOKING, STUFFY, BUT GOOD-
LOOKING NONETHELESS!"

690 GARDNER *(Suddenly jumps up, ablaze)*: WAIT, WAIT . . . IF IT'S
MICHELANGELO YOU WANT . . . I'm sorry, Mags. . . . One
more . . . just one more . . . please?

MAGS: Sure, why not? Be my guest.

GARDNER: *Fanny, prepare yourself!*

More whispering.

FANNY: But I think *you* should be God.

GARDNER: Me? . . . Really?

FANNY: Yes, it's much more appropriate.

GARDNER: Well, if you say so . . .

*Fanny and Gardner ease down to the floor with some difficulty and
lie on their sides, Fanny as Adam, Gardner as God, their fingers
inching closer and closer in the attitude of Michelangelo's* The Creation. *Finally they touch. Mags cheers, whistles, applauds.*

MAGS: THREE CHEERS . . . VERY GOOD . . . NICELY DONE,
NICELY DONE!

*Fanny and Gardner hold the pose a moment more, flushed with plea-
sure; then rise, dust themselves off and grope back to their chairs.*

MAGS: So, there we were . . .

700 FANNY: Yes, *do* go on!

MAGS: . . . huddled around Millicent Crowninshield, when you
whipped into your pocketbook and suddenly announced, "HOLD
EVERYTHING! I'VE GOT A PHOTOGRAPH OF HER RIGHT
HERE, THEN YOU CAN SEE WHAT SHE REALLY LOOKS
LIKE!" . . . You then proceeded to crouch down to the floor and
dump everything out of your bag, and I mean . . . *everything!* . . .
leaking packets of sequins and gummed stars, seashells, odd pieces
of fur, crochet hooks, a monarch butterfly embedded in plastic, dental floss, antique glass buttons, small jingling bells, lace . . . I

710 thought I'd die! Just sink to the floor and quietly die! . . . You
couldn't find it, you see. I mean, you spent the rest of the afternoon
on your hands and knees crawling through this ocean of junk, muttering, "It's *got* to be here somewhere; I know I had it with me!"
. . . Then Daddy pulled me into the thick of it all and said, "By the
way, have you met our daughter Mags yet? She's the one who did
all these pictures . . . paintings . . . . portraits . . . whatever you call
them." *(She drops to her hands and knees and begins crawling out
of the room)* By this time, Mum had somehow crawled out of the
gallery and was lost on another floor. She began calling for me . . .

720 "YOO-HOO, MAGS . . . WHERE ARE YOU? . . . OH, MAGS,
DARLING . . . HELLO? . . . ARE YOU THERE?" *(She reenters and
faces them)* This was at my *first* show.

Blackout.

SCENE 3

Twenty-four hours later. The impact of the impending move has struck with hurricane force. Fanny has lugged all their clothing into the room and dumped it in various cartons. There are coats, jackets, shoes, skirts, suits, hats, sweaters, dresses, the works. She and Gardner are seated on the sofa, going through it all. Fanny, wearing a different hat and dress, holds up a ratty overcoat.

FANNY: What about this gruesome old thing?

Gardner is wearing several sweaters and vests, a Hawaiian holiday shirt, and a variety of scarves and ties around his neck. He holds up a pair of shoes.

GARDNER: God . . . remember these shoes? Pound gave them to me when he came back from Italy. I remember it vividly.

FANNY: *Do* let me give it to the thrift shop! *(She stuffs the coat into the appropriate carton)*

GARDNER: He bought them for me in Rome. Said he couldn't resist; bought himself a pair too since we both wore the same size. God, I miss him! *(Pause)* HEY, WHAT ARE YOU DOING WITH MY OVERCOAT?!   730

FANNY: Darling, it's threadbare!

GARDNER: But that's my overcoat! *(He grabs it out of the carton)* I've been wearing it every day for the past thirty-five years!

FANNY: That's just my point: it's had it.

GARDNER *(Puts it on over everything else)*: There's nothing wrong with this coat!

FANNY: I trust you remember that the cottage is an eighth the size of this place and you simply won't have room for half this stuff! *(She holds up a sports jacket)* This dreary old jacket, for instance. You've had it since Hector was a pup!   740

GARDNER *(Grabs the jacket and puts it on over his coat)*: Oh, no, you don't . . .

FANNY: And this God-awful hat . . .

GARDNER: Let me see that.

Gardner stands next to Fanny and they fall into a lovely tableau. Mags suddenly pops out from behind a wardrobe carton with a flash camera and takes a picture of them.

MAGS: PERFECT!

FANNY *(Hands flying to her face)*: GOOD GOD, WHAT WAS THAT . . . ?	GARDNER *(Hands flying to his heart)*: JESUS CHRIST, I'VE BEEN SHOT!

MAGS *(Walks to the center of the room, advancing the film)*: That was terrific. See if you can do it again.

FANNY: What *are* you doing . . . ?   750

GARDNER *(Feeling his chest)*: Is there blood?

FANNY: I see lace everywhere . . .

MAGS: It's all right, I was just taking a picture of you. I often use a Polaroid at this stage.

FANNY *(Rubbing her eyes)*: Really, Mags, you might have given us some warning!

MAGS: But that's the whole point: to catch you unawares!

GARDNER *(Rubbing his eyes)*: It's the damndest thing. . . . I see lace everywhere.

760   FANNY: Yes, so do I . . .

GARDNER: It's rather nice, actually. It looks as if you're wearing a veil.

FANNY: I *am* wearing a veil!

The camera spits out the photograph.

MAGS: OH GOODY, HERE COMES THE PICTURE!

FANNY *(Grabs the partially developed print out of her hands)*: Let me see, let me see . . .

GARDNER: Yes, let's have a look.

Gardner and Fanny have another quiet moment together looking at the photograph. Mags tiptoes away from them and takes another picture.

MAGS: YES!

FANNY: NOT AGAIN! PLEASE,   GARDNER: WHAT WAS THAT?
DARLING!   . . . WHAT HAPPENED?

Fanny and Gardner stagger towards each other.

770   MAGS: I'm sorry, I just couldn't resist. You looked so—

FANNY: WHAT ARE YOU TRYING TO DO . . . *BLIND* US?!

GARDNER: Really, Mags, enough is enough . . .

Gardner and Fanny keep stumbling about kiddingly.

FANNY: Are you still there, Gar?

GARDNER: Right as rain, right as rain!

MAGS: I'm sorry; I didn't mean to scare you. It's just a photograph can show you things you weren't aware of. Here, have a look. *(She gives them to Fanny)* Well, I'm going out to the kitchen to get something to eat. Anybody want anything? *(She exits)*

780   FANNY *(Looking at the photos, half-amused, half-horrified)*: Oh, Gardner, have you ever . . . ?

GARDNER *(Looks at the photos and laughs)*: Good grief . . .

MAGS *(Offstage; from the kitchen)*: IS IT ALL RIGHT IF I TAKE THE REST OF THIS TAPIOCA FROM LAST NIGHT?

FANNY: IT'S ALL RIGHT WITH ME. How about you, Gar?

GARDNER: Sure, go right ahead. I've never been that crazy about tapioca.

FANNY: What are you talking about, tapioca is one of your favorites.

MAGS *(Enters, slurping from a large bowl)*: Mmmmmmmm . . .

FANNY: Really, Mags, I've never seen anyone eat as much as you.

MAGS *(Takes the photos back)*: It's strange. I only do this when I come home.

FANNY: What's the matter, don't I feed you enough?

GARDNER: Gee, it's hot in here! *(Starts taking off his coat)*

FANNY: God knows, you didn't eat anything as a child! I've never seen such a fussy eater. Gar, what are you doing?

GARDNER *(Shedding clothes to the floor)*: Taking off some of these clothes. It's hotter than Tophet in here!

MAGS *(Looking at her photo)*: Yes, I like you looking at each other like that . . .

FANNY *(To Gardner)*: Please watch where you're dropping things; I'm trying to keep some order around here.

GARDNER *(Picks up what he dropped, dropping even more in the process)*: Right, right . . .

MAGS: Now all I've got to do is figure out what you should wear.

FANNY: Well, I'm going to wear my long black dress, and you'd be a fool not to do Daddy in his tuxedo. He looks so distinguished in it, just like a banker!

MAGS: I haven't really decided yet.

FANNY: Just because you walk around looking like something the cat dragged in, doesn't mean Daddy and I want to, do we Gar?

Gardner is making a worse and worse tangle of his clothes.

FANNY: HELLO . . . ?

GARDNER *(Looks up at Fanny)*: Oh, yes, awfully attractive, awfully attractive!

FANNY *(To Mags)*: If you don't mind me saying so, I've never seen you looking so forlorn. You'll never catch a husband looking that way. Those peculiar clothes, that God-awful hair . . . really, Mags, it's very distressing!

MAGS: I don't think my hair's so bad, not that it's terrific or anything . . .

FANNY: Well, I don't see other girls walking around like you. I mean, girls from your background. What would Lyman Wigglesworth think if he saw you in the street?

MAGS: Lyman Wigglesworth?! . . . Uuuuuuughhhhhhh! *(She shudders)*

FANNY: All right then, that brilliant Cabot boy . . . what *is* his name?

GARDNER: Sammy.

FANNY: No, not Sammy . . .

GARDNER: Stephen . . . Stanley . . . Stuart . . . Sheldon . . . Sherlock . . . Sherlock! It's *Sherlock!*

MAGS: Spence!

FANNY: SPENCE, THAT'S IT!   GARDNER: THAT'S IT . . .
HIS NAME IS SPENCE!   SPENCE! SPENCE CABOT!

FANNY: Spence Cabot was first in his class at Harvard.

MAGS: Mum, he has no facial hair.

FANNY: He has his own law firm on Arlington Street.

MAGS: Spence Cabot has six fingers on his right hand!

FANNY: So, he isn't the best-looking thing in the world. Looks isn't everything. He can't help it if he has extra fingers. Have a little sympathy!

MAGS: But the extra one has this weird nail on it that looks like a talon. . . . It's long and black and . . . (*She shudders*)

FANNY: No one's perfect, darling. He has lovely handwriting and an absolutely saintly mother. Also, he's as rich as Croesus! He's a lot more promising than some of those creatures you've dragged home. What was the name of that dreadful Frenchman who smelled like sweaty socks? . . . Jean Duke of Scripto?

MAGS (*Laughing*): Jean-Luc Zichot!

FANNY: And that peculiar little Oriental fellow with all the teeth! Really, Mags, he could have been put on display at the circus!

MAGS: Oh, yes, Tsu Chin. He was strange, but very sexy . . .

FANNY (*Shudders*): He had such tiny . . . feet! Really, Mags, you've got to bear down. You're not getting any younger. Before you know it, all the nice young men will be taken and then where will you be? . . . All by yourself in that grim little apartment of yours with those peculiar clothes and that bright red hair . . .

MAGS: MY HAIR IS NOT BRIGHT RED!

FANNY: I only want what's best for you, you know that. You seem to go out of your way to look wanting. I don't understand it. . . . Gar, what *are* you putting your coat on for? . . . You look like some derelict out on the street. We don't wear coats in the house. (*She helps him out of it*) That's the way. . . . I'll just put this in the carton along with everything else . . . (*She drops it into the carton, then pauses*) Isn't it about time for . . . *cocktails!*

GARDNER: What's that?

Fanny taps her wrist and mimes drinking.

GARDNER (*Looks at his watch*): Right you are, right you are! (*Exits to the bar*) THE USUAL . . . ?

FANNY: *Please!*

GARDNER (*Offstage*): HOW ABOUT SOMETHING FOR YOU MAGS?

MAGS: SURE, WHY NOT? . . . LET 'ER RIP!

GARDNER (*Offstage*): WHAT'S THAT . . . ?

FANNY: SHE SAID YES. SHE   MAGS: I'LL HAVE SOME
    SAID YES!   DUBONNET!

GARDNER (*Poking his head back in*): How about a little Dubonnet?

FANNY: That's just what she said. . . . She'd like some Dubonnet!

GARDNER (*Goes back to the bar and hums another Jolson tune*): GEE, IT'S GREAT HAVING YOU BACK LIKE THIS, MAGS . . . IT'S JUST GREAT! (*More singing*)

FANNY *(Leaning closer to Mags)*: You have such *potential,* darling! It breaks my heart to see how you've let yourself go. If Lyman Wigglesworth . . .

MAGS: Amazing as it may seem, I don't *care* about Lyman Wigglesworth!

FANNY: From what I've heard, he's quite a lady killer!

MAGS: But with whom? . . . Don't think I haven't heard about his fling   880 with . . . Hopie Stonewall!

FANNY *(Begins to laugh)*: Oh, God, let's not get started on Hopie Stonewall again . . . ten feet tall with spots on her neck . . . *(To Gardner)* OH, DARLING, DO HURRY BACK! WE'RE TALKING ABOUT PATHETIC HOPIE STONEWALL!

MAGS: It's not so much her incredible height and spotted skin; it's those tiny pointed teeth and the size eleven shoes!

FANNY: I love it when you're like this!

Mags starts clomping around the room making tiny pointed-teeth nibbling sounds.

FANNY: GARDNER . . . YOU'RE MISSING EVERYTHING! *(Still laughing)* Why is it Boston girls are always so . . . tall?   890

MAGS: Hopie Stonewall isn't a Boston girl; she's a giraffe. *(She prances around the room with an imaginary dwarf-sized Lyman)* She's perfect for Lyman Wigglesworth!

GARDNER *(Returns with Fanny's drink, which he hands her)*: Now, where were we . . . ?

FANNY *(Trying not to laugh)*: HOPIE STONEWALL . . . !

GARDNER: Oh, yes, she's the very tall one, isn't she?

Fanny and Mags burst into gales.

MAGS: The only hope for us . . . "Boston girls" is to get as far away from our kind as possible.

FANNY: She always asks after you, darling. She's very fond of you, you   900 know.

MAGS: Please, I don't want to hear!

FANNY: Your old friends are *always* asking after you.

MAGS: It's not so much how creepy they all are, as how much they remind me of myself!

FANNY: But you're not "creepy," darling . . . just . . . shabby!

MAGS: I mean, give me a few more inches and some brown splotches here and there, and Hopie and I could be sisters!

FANNY *(In a whisper to Gardner)*: Don't you love it when Mags is like this? I could listen to her forever!   910

MAGS: I mean . . . look at me!

FANNY *(Gasping)*: Don't stop, don't stop!

MAGS: Awkward . . . plain . . . I don't know how to dress, I don't know how to talk. When people find out Daddy's my father, they're always amazed. . . . "Gardner Church is YOUR father?! Aw, come on, you're kidding?!"

FANNY *(In a whisper)*: Isn't she divine . . . ?

MAGS: Sometimes I don't even tell them. I pretend I grew up in the
Midwest somewhere . . . farming people . . . we work with our
920   hands.

GARDNER *(To Mags)*: Well, how about a little refill . . . ?

MAGS: No, no more thanks.

   Pause.

FANNY: What did you have to go and interrupt her for? She was just
getting up a head of steam . . .

MAGS *(Walking over to her easel)*: The great thing about being a portrait painter, you see, is it's the *other* guy that's exposed; you're
safely hidden behind the canvas and easel. *(Standing behind it)* You
can be as plain as a pitchfork, as inarticulate as mud, but it doesn't
matter because you're completely concealed: Your body, your face,
930   your intentions. Just as you make your most intimate move, throw
open your soul . . . they stretch and yawn, remembering the dog has
to be let out at five. . . . To be so invisible while so enthralled . . . it
takes your breath away!

GARDNER: Well put, Mags. Awfully well put!

MAGS: That's why I've always wanted to paint you, to see if I'm up to
it. It's quite a risk. Remember what I went through as a child with
my great masterpiece . . . ?

FANNY: You painted a masterpiece when you were a child . . . ?

MAGS: Well, it was a masterpiece to me.

940   FANNY: I had no idea you were precocious as a child. Gardner, do you
remember Mags painting a masterpiece as a child?

MAGS: I didn't paint it. It was something I made!

FANNY: Well, this is all news to me! Gar, *do* get me another drink! I
haven't had this much fun in years! *(She hands him her glass and
reaches for Mags's)* Come on darling, join me . . .

MAGS: No, no more, thanks. I don't really like the taste.

FANNY: Oh, come on, kick up your heels for once!

MAGS: No, nothing . . . really.

FANNY: Please? Pretty please? . . . To keep me company?!

950   MAGS *(Hands Gardner her glass)*: Oh, all right, what the hell . . .

FANNY: That's a good girl!   GARDNER *(Exiting)*: Coming right
up, coming right up!

FANNY *(Yelling after Gardner)*: DON'T GIVE ME TOO MUCH
NOW. THE LAST ONE WAS AWFULLY STRONG . . . AND
HURRY BACK SO YOU DON'T MISS ANYTHING! . . . Daddy's
so cunning, I don't know what I'd do without him. If anything
should happen to him, I'd just . . .

MAGS: Mummy, nothing's going to happen to him . . . !

FANNY: Well, wait till you're our age, it's no garden party. Now . . .
960   where were we . . . ?

MAGS: My first masterpiece . . .

FANNY: Oh, yes, but *do* wait till Daddy gets back so he can hear it too. . . . YOO-HOO . . . GARRRRRRDNERRRRRR? . . . ARE YOU COMING? *(Silence)* Go and check on him, will you?

Gardner enters with both drinks. He's very shaken.

GARDNER: I couldn't find the ice.

FANNY: Well, *finally!*

GARDNER: It just up and disappeared . . . *(Hands Fanny her drink)* There you go. *(Fanny kisses her fingers and takes a hefty swig)* Mags. *(He hands Mags her drink)*

MAGS: Thanks, Daddy.   970

GARDNER: Sorry about the ice.

MAGS: No problem, no problem.

Gardner sits down; silence

FANNY *(To Mags)*: Well, drink up, drink up! *(Mags downs it in one gulp)* GOOD GIRL! . . . Now, what's all this about a masterpiece . . . ?

MAGS: I did it during that winter you sent me away from the dinner table. I was about nine years old.

FANNY: We sent you from the dinner table?

MAGS: I was banished for six months.

FANNY: You *were?* . . . How extraordinary!   980

MAGS: Yes, it *was* rather extraordinary!

FANNY: But why?

MAGS: Because I played with my food.

FANNY: You did?

MAGS: I used to squirt it out between my front teeth.

FANNY: Oh, I remember that! God, it used to drive me crazy, absolutely . . . crazy! *(Pause)* "MARGARET, STOP THAT OOZING RIGHT THIS MINUTE, YOU ARE *NOT* A TUBE OF TOOTH-PASTE!"

GARDNER: Oh, yes . . .

FANNY: It was perfectly disgusting!   990

GARDNER: I remember. She used to lean over her plate and squirt it out in long runny ribbons . . .

FANNY: That's enough, dear.

GARDNER: They were quite colorful, actually; decorative almost. She made the most intricate designs. They looked rather like small, moist Oriental rugs . . .

FANNY *(To Mags)*: But why, darling? What on earth possessed you to do it?

MAGS: I couldn't swallow anything. My throat just closed up. I don't know, I must have been afraid of choking or something.   1000

GARDNER: I remember one in particular. We'd had chicken fricassee and spinach. . . . She made the most extraordinary—

FANNY *(To Gardner)*: WILL YOU PLEASE SHUT UP?! *(Pause)* Mags, what *are* you talking about? You never choked in your entire life! This is the most distressing conversation I've ever had. Don't you think it's distressing, Gar?

GARDNER: Well, that's not quite the word I'd use.

FANNY: What word *would* you use, then?

GARDNER: I don't know right off the bat, I'd have to think about it.

1010   FANNY: THEN, THINK ABOUT IT!

Silence.

MAGS: I guess I was afraid of making a mess. I don't know; you were awfully strict about table manners. I was always afraid of losing control. What if I started to choke and began spitting up over every- thing . . . ?

FANNY: All right, dear, that's enough.

MAGS: No, I was really terrified about making a mess; you always got so mad whenever I spilled. If I just got rid of everything in neat little curlicues beforehand, you see . . .

FANNY: I SAID: THAT'S ENOUGH!

Silence

1020   MAGS: *I* thought it was quite ingenious, but you didn't see it that way. You finally sent me from the table with, "When you're ready to eat like a human being, you can come back and join us!" . . . So, it was off to my room with a tray. But I couldn't seem to eat there either. I mean, it was so strange settling down to dinner in my *bedroom.* . . . So I just flushed everything down the toilet and sat on my bed lis- tening to you: clinkity-clink, clatter clatter, slurp, slurp . . . but that got pretty boring after a while, so I looked around for something to do. It was wintertime, because I noticed I'd left some crayons on top of my radiator and they'd melted down into these beautiful shim-

1030   mering globs, like spilled jello, trembling and pulsing . . .

GARDNER (*Overlapping; eyes closed*):
"This luscious and impeccable fruit of life
Falls, it appears, of its own weight to earth . . ."

MAGS: Naturally, I wanted to try it myself, so I grabbed a red one and pressed it down against the hissing lid. It oozed and bubbled like raspberry jam!

GARDNER:
"When you were Eve, its acrid juice was sweet,
Untasted, in its heavenly, orchard air . . ."

MAGS: I mean, that radiator was really hot! It took incredible will power not to let go, but I held on, whispering, "Mags, if you let go

1040   of this crayon, you'll be run over by a truck on Newberry Street, so help you God!" . . . So I pressed down harder, my fingers steaming and blistering . . .

FANNY: I had no idea about any of this, did you, Gar?

MAGS: Once I'd melted one, I was hooked! I finished off my entire

supply in one night, mixing color over color until my head swam!
. . . The heat, the smell, the brilliance that sank and rose . . . I'd
never felt such exhilaration! . . . Every week I spent my allowance
on crayons. I must have cleared out every box of Crayolas in the
city!

GARDNER *(Gazing at Mags)*: You know, I don't think I've ever seen   1050
you looking prettier! You're awfully attractive when you get going!

FANNY: Why, what a lovely thing to say.

MAGS: AFTER THREE MONTHS THAT RADIATOR WAS . . .
SPECTACULAR! I MEAN IT, IT LOOKED LIKE SOME COLOS-
SAL FRUITCAKE, FIVE FEET TALL . . . !

FANNY: It sounds perfectly hideous.

MAGS: It was a knockout; shimmering with pinks and blues, lavenders
and maroons, turquoise and golds, oranges and creams. . . . For every color, I imagined a taste . . . YELLOW: lemon curls dipped in
sugar . . . RED: glazed cherries laced with rum . . . GREEN: tiny   1060
peppermint leaves veined with chocolate . . . PURPLE: —

FANNY: That's quite enough!

MAGS: And then the frosting . . . ahhhh, the frosting! A satiny mix of
white and silver . . . I kept it hidden under blankets during the day.
. . . My huge . . . *(She starts laughing)* looming . . . teetering sweet—

FANNY: I ASKED YOU TO STOP! GARDNER, WILL YOU PLEASE
GET HER TO STOP!

GARDNER: See here, Mags, Mum asked you to—

MAGS: I was so . . . *hungry* . . . losing weight every week. I looked like
a scarecrow what with the bags under my eyes and bits of crayon   1070
wrapper leaking out of my clothes. It's a wonder you didn't notice.
But finally you came to my rescue . . . if you could call what happened a rescue. It was more like a rout!

FANNY: Darling . . . *please!*   GARDNER: Now, look, young
                                             lady—

MAGS: The winter was almost over. . . . It was very late at night. . . . I
must have been having a nightmare because suddenly you and
Daddy were at my bed, shaking me. . . . I quickly glanced towards
the radiator to see if it was covered. . . . *It wasn't!* It glittered and
towered in the moonlight like some . . . gigantic Viennese pastry!   1080
You followed my gaze and saw it. Mummy screamed . . . "WHAT
HAVE YOU GOT IN HERE? . . . MAGS, WHAT HAVE YOU
BEEN DOING?" . . . She crept forward and touched it, and then
jumped back. "IT'S FOOD!" she cried . . . "IT'S ALL THE FOOD
SHE'S BEEN SPITTING OUT! OH, GARDNER, IT'S A MOUN-
TAIN OF ROTTING GARBAGE!"

FANNY *(Softly)*: Yes . . . it's coming back . . . it's coming back . . .

MAGS: Daddy exited as usual; left the premises. He fainted, just keeled
over onto the floor . . .

1090 GARDNER: Gosh, I don't remember any of this . . .

MAGS: My heart stopped! I mean, I knew it was all over. My lovely creation didn't have a chance. Sure enough . . . out came the blowtorch. Well, it couldn't have *really* been a blowtorch, I mean, where would you have ever gotten a blowtorch? . . . I just have this very strong memory of you standing over my bed, your hair streaming around your face, aiming this . . . flamethrower at my confection . . . my cake . . . my tart . . . my strudel . . . "IT'S GOT TO BE DESTROYED IMMEDIATELY! THE THING'S ALIVE WITH VERMIN! . . . JUST LOOK AT IT! . . . IT'S PRACTICALLY CRAWL-

1100 ING ACROSS THE ROOM!" . . . Of course in a sense you were right. It *was* a monument of my castoff dinners, only I hadn't built it with food. . . . I found my own materials. I was languishing with hunger, but oh, dear Mother . . . I FOUND MY OWN MATERIALS . . . !

FANNY: Darling . . . *please?!*

MAGS: I tried to stop you, but you wouldn't listen. . . . OUT SHOT THE FLAME! . . . I remember these waves of wax rolling across the room and Daddy coming to, wondering what on earth was going on. . . . Well, what did you know about my abilities? . . . You see, I

1110 had . . . I mean, I *have* abilities . . . (*Struggling to say it*) I have abilities. I have . . . strong abilities. I have . . . very strong abilities. They are very strong . . . very, very strong . . .

Mags rises and runs out of the room overcome as Fanny and Gardner watch, speechless. The curtain falls.

ACT TWO
SCENE I

Three days later. Miracles have been accomplished. Almost all of the Churches' furniture has been moved out, and the cartons of dishes and clothing are gone. All that remains are odds and ends. Mags's tableau looms, impregnable. Fanny and Gardner are dressed in their formal evening clothes, frozen in their pose. They hold absolutely still. Mags stands at her easel, her hands covering her eyes.

FANNY: All right, you can look now.

MAGS (*Removes her hands*): Yes! . . . I told you you could trust me on the pose.

FANNY: Well, thank God you let us dress up. It makes all the difference. Now we really look like something.

MAGS (*Starts to sketch them*): I'll say . . .

A silence as she sketches.

GARDNER (*Recites Yeats's "The Song of Wandering Aengus" in a wonderfully resonant voice as they pose*):
"I went out to the hazel wood,

1120 Because a fire was in my head,

And cut and peeled a hazel wand,
And hooked a berry to a thread,
And when white moths were on the wing,
And moth-like stars were flickering out,
I dropped the berry in a stream
And caught a little silver trout.

When I had laid it on the floor
I went to blow the fire a-flame,
But something rustled on the floor,
And someone called me by my name: 1130
It had become a glimmering girl
With apple blossoms in her hair
Who called me by my name and ran
And faded through the brightening air.

Though I am old with wandering
Through hollow lands and hilly lands,
I will find out where she has gone,
And kiss her lips and take her hands;
And walk among long dappled grass,
And pluck till time and times are done,   1140
The silver apples of the moon,
The golden apples of the sun."

FANNY: That's lovely, dear. Just lovely. Is it one of yours?

GARDNER: No, no, it's Yeats. I'm using it in my book.

FANNY: Well, you recited it beautifully, but then you've always recited
beautifully. That's how you wooed me, in case you've forgotten . . .
You must have memorized every love poem in the English language!
There was no stopping you when you got going . . . your Shakespeare, Byron, and Shelley . . . you were shameless . . . *shameless!*

GARDNER *(Eyes closed)*:
"I will find out where she has gone,   1150
And kiss her lips and take her hands . . ."

FANNY: And then there was your own poetry to do battle with; your
sonnets and quatrains. When you got going with them, there was
nothing left of me! You could have had your pick of any girl in Boston! Why you chose me, I'll never understand. I had no looks to
speak of and nothing much in the brains department. . . . Well, what
did you know about women and the world? . . . What did any of us
know . . . ?

Silence

FANNY: GOD, MAGS, HOW LONG ARE WE SUPPOSED TO SIT
LIKE THIS? . . . IT'S AGONY!   1160

MAGS *(Working away)*: You're doing fine . . . just fine . . .

FANNY *(Breaking her pose)*: It's so . . . boring!

MAGS: Come on, don't move. You can have a break soon.

FANNY: I had no idea it would be so boring!

GARDNER: Gee, I'm enjoying it.

FANNY: You would . . . !

A pause.

GARDNER *(Begins reciting more Yeats, almost singing it)*:
"He stood among a crowd at Drumahair;
His heart hung all upon a silken dress,
And he had known at last some tenderness,
Before earth made of him her sleepy care;
But when a man poured fish into a pile,
It seemed they raised their little silver heads . . ."[10]

FANNY: Gar . . . PLEASE! *(She lurches out of her seat)* God, I can't take this anymore!

MAGS *(Keeps sketching Gardner)*: I know it's tedious at first, but it gets easier . . .

FANNY: It's like a Chinese water torture! *(Crosses to Mags and looks at Gardner posing)* Oh, darling, you look marvelous, absolutely marvelous! Why don't you just do Daddy!?

MAGS: Because you look marvelous too. I want to do you both!

FANNY: Please! . . . I have one foot in the grave and you know it! Also, we're way behind in our packing. There's still one room left which everyone seems to have forgotten about!

GARDNER: Which one is that?

FANNY: You know perfectly well which one it is!

GARDNER: I do . . . ?

FANNY: Yes, you do!

GARDNER: Well, it's news to me.

FANNY: I'll give you a hint. It's in . . . *that* direction. *(She points)*

GARDNER: The dining room?

FANNY: No.

GARDNER: The bedroom?

FANNY: No.

GARDNER: Mags' room?

FANNY: No.

GARDNER: The kitchen?

FANNY: *Gar?!*

GARDNER: The guest room?

FANNY: Your God-awful study!

GARDNER: Oh, shit!

FANNY: That's right, "Oh, shit!" It's books and papers up to the ceiling! If you ask me, we should just forget it's there and quietly tiptoe away . . .

---

[10] From Yeats' poem "The Man Who Dreamed of Fairyland."

GARDNER: My study . . . !

FANNY: Let the new owners dispose of everything . . .

GARDNER *(Gets out of his posing chair)*: Now, just one minute . . .

FANNY: You never look at half the stuff in there!

GARDNER: I don't want you touching those books! They're mine!

FANNY: Darling, we're moving to a cottage the size of a handkerchief! Where, pray tell, is there room for all your books?   1210

GARDNER: I don't know. We'll just have to make room!

MAGS *(Sketching away)*: RATS!

FANNY: I don't know what we're doing fooling around with Mags like this when there's still so much to do . . .

GARDNER *(Sits back down, overwhelmed)*: My study . . . !

FANNY: You can stay with her if you'd like, but one of us has got to tackle those books! *(She exits to his study)*

GARDNER: I'm not up to this.

MAGS: Oh, good, you're staying!

GARDNER: There's a lifetime of work in there . . .   1220

MAGS: Don't worry, I'll help. Mum and I will be able to pack everything up in no time.

GARDNER: God . . .

MAGS: It won't be so bad . . .

GARDNER: I'm just not up to it.

MAGS: We'll all pitch in . . .

Gardner sighs, speechless. A silence as Fanny comes staggering in with an armload of books, which she drops to the floor with a crash.

GARDNER: WHAT WAS THAT?!   MAGS: GOOD GRIEF!

FANNY *(Sheepish)*: Sorry, sorry . . . *(She exits for more)*

GARDNER: I don't know if I can take this . . .

MAGS: Moving is awful . . . I know . . .   1230

GARDNER *(Settling back into his pose)*: Ever since Mum began tearing the house apart, I've been having these dreams. . . . I'm a child again back at 16 Louisberg Square . . . and this stream of moving men is carrying furniture into our house . . . van after van of tables and chairs, sofas and love seats, desks and bureaus . . . rugs, bathtubs, mirrors, chiming clocks, pianos, iceboxes, china cabinets . . . but what's amazing is that all of it is familiar . . .

Fanny comes in with another load, which she drops on the floor. She exits for more.

GARDNER: No matter how many items appear, I've seen every one of them before. Since my mother is standing in the midst of it directing traffic, I ask her where it's all coming from, but she doesn't hear me   1240
because of the racket . . . so finally I just scream out . . . "WHERE IS ALL THIS FURNITURE COMING FROM?" . . . Just as a

moving man is carrying Toots into the room, she looks at me and says, "Why, from the land of Skye!" . . . The next thing I know, *people* are being carried in along with it . . .

Fanny enters with her next load; drops it and exits.

GARDNER: People I've never seen before are sitting around our dining-room table. A group of foreigners is going through my books, chattering in a language I've never heard before. A man is playing a Chopin polonaise on Aunt Alice's piano. Several children are taking baths in our tubs from Cotuit . . .

MAGS: It sounds marvelous.

GARDNER: Well, it isn't marvelous at all because all of these perfect strangers have taken over our things . . .

Fanny enters, hurls down another load and exits.

MAGS: How odd . . .

GARDNER: Well, it *is* odd, but then something even odder happens . . .

MAGS *(Sketching away):* Tell me, tell me!

GARDNER: Well, our beds are carried in. They're all made up with sheets and everything, but instead of all these strange people in them, *we're* in them . . . !

MAGS: What's so odd about that?

GARDNER: Well, you and Mum are brought in, both sleeping like angels . . . Mum snoring away to beat the band . . .

MAGS: Yes . . .

Fanny enters with another load lets it fall.

GARDNER: But there's no one in mine. It's completely empty, never even been slept in! It's as if I were dead or had never even existed . . .

Fanny exits.

GARDNER: "HEY . . . WAIT UP!" I yell to the moving men . . . "THAT'S MY BED YOU'VE GOT THERE!" But they don't stop; they don't even acknowledge me. . . . "HEY, COME BACK HERE . . . I WANT TO GET INTO MY BED!" I cry again and I start running after them . . . down the hall, through the dining room, past the library. . . . Finally I catch up to them and hurl myself right into the center of the pillow. Just as I'm about to land, the bed suddenly vanishes and I go crashing down to the floor like some insect that's been hit by a fly swatter!

Fanny staggers in with her final load; she drops it with a crash and then collapses in her posing chair.

FANNY: THAT'S IT FOR ME! I'M DEAD!

Silence.

FANNY: Come on, Mags, how about you doing a little work around here.

MAGS: That's all I've been doing! This is the first free moment you've given me!

FANNY: You should see all the books in there . . . and papers! There are enough loose papers to sink a ship!

GARDNER: Why is it we're moving, again . . . ?

FANNY: Because life is getting too complicated here.

GARDNER (*Remembering*): Oh, yes . . .

FANNY: And we can't afford it anymore.

GARDNER: That's right, that's right . . .

FANNY: We don't have the . . . *income* we used to!

GARDNER: Oh, yes . . . *income!*

FANNY (*Assuming her post again*): Of course, we have our savings and various trust funds, but I wouldn't dream of touching those!

GARDNER: No, no, you must never dip into capital!

FANNY: I told Daddy I'd be perfectly happy to buy a gun and put a bullet through our heads so we could avoid all this, but he wouldn't hear of it!

MAGS (*Sketching away*): No, I shouldn't think so.

Pause.

FANNY: I've always admired people who kill themselves when they get to our stage of life. Well, no one can touch my Uncle Edmond in that department . . .

MAGS: I know, I know . . .

FANNY: The day before his seventieth birthday he climbed to the top of the Old North Church and hurled himself face down into Salem Street! They had to scrape him up with a spatula! God, he was a remarkable man . . . state senator, president of Harvard . . .

GARDNER (*Rises and wanders over to his books*): Well, I guess I'm going to have to do something about all of these . . .

FANNY: Come on, Mags, help Daddy! Why don't you start bringing in his papers . . .

Gardner sits on the floor; he picks up a book and soon is engrossed in it. Mags keeps sketching, oblivious. Silence.

FANNY (*To Mags*): Darling? . . . HELLO? . . . God, you two are impossible! Just look at you . . . heads in the clouds! No one would ever know we've got to be out of here in two days. If it weren't for me, nothing would get done around here . . . (*She starts stacking Gardner's books into piles*) There! That's all the maroon ones!

GARDNER (*Looks up*): What do you mean, *maroon* ones?!

FANNY: All your books that are maroon are in *this* pile . . . and your books that are green in *that* pile! . . . I'm trying to bring some order into your life for once. This will make unpacking so much easier.

GARDNER: But, my dear Fanny, it's not the color of the book that distinguishes it, but what's *inside* it!

FANNY: This will be a great help, you'll see. Now what about this awful
1320   striped thing? *(She picks up a slim, aged volume)* Can't it go . . . ?

GARDNER: No!

FANNY: But it's as queer as Dick's hatband! There are no others like it.

GARDNER: Open it and read. Go on . . . open it!

FANNY: We'll get nowhere at this rate.

GARDNER: I said . . . READ!

FANNY: Really, Gar, I—

GARDNER: Read the dedication!

FANNY *(Opens and reads)*: "To Gardner Church, you led the way.
    With gratitude and affection, Robert Frost." *(She closes it and
    hands it to him)*

1330 GARDNER: It was published the same year as my *Salem Gardens.*

FANNY *(Picking up a very worn book)*: Well, what about this dreadful
    thing? It's filthy. *(She blows off a cloud of dust)*

GARDNER: Please . . . *please?!*

FANNY *(Looking through it)*: It's all in French.

GARDNER *(Snatching it away from her)*: André Malraux[11] gave me
    that . . . !

FANNY: I'm just trying to help

GARDNER: It's a first edition of Baudelaire's *Fleurs du mal.*[12]

FANNY *(Giving it back)*: Well, pardon me for living!

1340 GARDNER: Why do you have to drag everything in here in the first
    place . . . ?

FANNY: Because there's no room in your study. You ought to see the
    mess in there! . . . WAKE UP, MAGS, ARE YOU GOING TO
    PITCH IN OR NOT?!

GARDNER: I'm not up to this.

FANNY: Well, you'd better be unless you want to be left behind!

MAGS *(Stops her sketching)*: All right, all right . . . I just hope you'll
    give me some more time later this evening.

FANNY *(To Mags)*: Since you're young and in the best shape, why
1350   don't you bring in the books and I'll cope with the papers. *(She
    exits to the study)*

GARDNER: Now just a minute . . .

FANNY *(Offstage)*: WE NEED A STEAM SHOVEL FOR THIS!

MAGS: Okay, what do you want me to do?

GARDNER: Look, I don't want you messing around with my—

*Fanny enters with an armful of papers, which she drops into an
empty carton.*

GARDNER: HEY, WHAT'S GOING ON HERE?!

---

[11] Twentieth-century French novelist and man of letters.

[12] *Flowers of Evil,* a book of poems by nineteenth-century French poet Charles Baudelaire.

FANNY: I'm packing up your papers. COME ON, MAGS, LET'S GET CRACKING! *(She exits for more papers)*

GARDNER *(Plucks several papers out of the carton)*: What is this . . . ?

MAGS *(Exits into his study)*: GOOD LORD, WHAT HAVE YOU DONE IN HERE?!   1360

GARDNER *(Reading)*: This is my manuscript.

Fanny enters with another batch, which she tosses on top of the others.

GARDNER: What *are* you doing?!

FANNY: Packing, darling . . . PACKING! *(She exits for more)*

GARDNER: SEE HERE, YOU CAN'T MANHANDLE MY THINGS THIS WAY!

Mags enters, staggering under a load of books, which she sets down on the floor.

GARDNER: *I* PACK MY MANUSCRIPT! I KNOW WHERE EVERY-THING IS!

FANNY *(Offstage)*: IF IT WERE UP TO YOU, WE'D NEVER GET OUT OF HERE! WE'RE UNDER A TIME LIMIT, GARDNER. KITTY'S PICKING US UP IN TWO DAYS . . . TWO . . . DAYS!   1370
(She enters with a larger batch of papers and heads for the carton)

GARDNER *(Grabbing Fanny's wrist)*: NOW, HOLD IT! . . . JUST . . . HOLD IT RIGHT THERE!

FANNY: OOOOOWWWWWWWW!

GARDNER: *I* PACK MY THINGS!

FANNY: LET GO, YOU'RE HURTING ME!

GARDNER: THAT'S MY MANUSCRIPT! GIVE IT TO ME!

FANNY *(Lifting the papers high over her head)*: I'M IN CHARGE OF THIS MOVE, GARDNER! WE'VE GOT TO GET CRACKING!

GARDNER: I said . . . GIVE IT TO ME!

MAGS: Come on, Mum, let him have it.   1380

Fanny and Gardner struggle.

GARDNER *(Finally wrenches the pages from Fanny)*: LET . . . ME . . . HAVE IT! . . . THAT'S MORE LIKE IT!

FANNY *(Soft and weepy)*: You see what he's like? . . . I try and help with his packing and what does he do . . . ?

GARDNER *(Rescues the rest of his papers from the carton)*: YOU DON'T JUST THROW EVERYTHING INTO A BOX LIKE A PILE OF GARBAGE! THIS IS A BOOK, FANNY. SOMETHING I'VE BEEN WORKING ON FOR TWO YEARS! *(Trying to assem-ble his papers, but only making things worse, dropping them all over the place)* You show a little respect for my things . . . You don't just throw them around every which way. . . . It's tricky trying   1390
to make sense of poetry; it's much easier to write the stuff . . . that is, if you've still got it in you . . .

MAGS: Here, let me help . . . *(Taking some of the papers)*

GARDNER: Criticism is tough sledding. You can't just dash off a few images here, a few rhymes there . . .

MAGS: Do you have these pages numbered in any way?

FANNY *(Returning to her posing chair)*: HA!

GARDNER: This is just the introduction.

MAGS: I don't see any numbers on these.

1400 GARDNER *(Exiting to his study)*: The important stuff is in my study . . .

FANNY *(To Mags)*: You don't know the half of it . . . *not the half* . . . !

GARDNER *(Offstage; thumping around)*: HAVE YOU SEEN THOSE YEATS POEMS I JUST HAD . . . ?

MAGS *(Reading over several pages)*: What is this? . . . It doesn't make sense. It's just fragments . . . pieces of poems.

FANNY: That's it, honey! That's his book. His great critical study! Now that he can't write his own poetry, he's trying to explain other people's. The only problem is, he can't get beyond typing them out. The poor lamb doesn't have the stamina to get beyond the opening

1410 stanzas, let alone trying to make sense of them.

GARDNER *(Thundering back with more papers, which keep falling)*: GODDAMMIT, FANNY, WHAT DID YOU DO IN THERE? I CAN'T FIND ANYTHING!

FANNY: I just took the papers that were on your desk.

GARDNER: Well, the entire beginning is gone. *(He exits)*

FANNY: I'M TRYING TO HELP YOU, DARLING!

GARDNER *(Returns with another armload)*: SEE THAT? . . . NO SIGN OF CHAPTER ONE OR TWO . . . *(He flings it all down to the floor)*

FANNY: Gardner . . . PLEASE?!

GARDNER *(Kicking through the mess)*: I TURN MY BACK FOR ONE

1420 MINUTE AND WHAT HAPPENS? . . . MY ENTIRE STUDY IS TORN APART! *(He exits)*

MAGS: Oh, Daddy . . . don't . . . please . . . Daddy . . . *please?!*

GARDNER *(Returns with a new batch of papers, which he tosses up into the air)*: THROWN OUT! . . . THE BEST PART IS THROWN OUT! . . . LOST . . . *(He starts to exit again)*

MAGS *(Reads one of the fragments to steady herself)*:
"I have known the inexorable sadness of pencils,
Neat in their boxes, dolor of pad and paper-weight,
All the misery of manila folders and mucilage . . ."[13]
They're beautiful . . . just beautiful.

GARDNER *(Stops)*: Hey, what's that you've got there?

1430 FANNY: It's your manuscript, darling. You see, it's right where you left it.

GARDNER *(To Mags)*: Read that again.

[13] From "Dolor," a poem by twentieth-century American poet Theodore Roethke.

MAGS:
"I have known the inexorable sadness of pencils,
Neat in their boxes, dolor of pad and paper-weight,
All the misery of manila folders and mucilage . . ."
GARDNER: Well, well, what do you know . . .
FANNY *(Hands him several random papers)*: You see . . . no one lost
anything. Everything's here, still intact.
GARDNER *(Reads)*:
"I knew a woman, lovely in her bones,
When small birds sighed, she would sigh back at them;
Ah, when she moved, she moved more ways than one:
The shapes a bright container can contain! . . ."[14]
FANNY *(Hands him another)*: And . . .
GARDNER *(Reads)*: Ahh . . . Frost . . .
"Some say the world will end in fire,
Some say in ice.
From what I've tasted of desire
I hold with those who favor fire."[15]
FANNY *(Under her breath to Mags)*: He can't give up the words. It's
the best he can do. *(Handing him another)* Here you go, here's
more.
GARDNER:
"Farm boys wild to couple
With anything   with soft-wooded trees
With mounds of earth   mounds
Of pinestraw   will keep themselves off
Animals by legends of their own . . ."[16]
MAGS *(Eyes shut)*: Oh, Daddy, I can't bear it . . . I . . .
FANNY: Of course no one will ever publish this.
GARDNER: Oh, here's a marvelous one. Listen to this!
"There came a Wind like a Bugle—
It quivered through the Grass
And a Green Chill upon the Heat
So ominous did pass
We barred the Windows and the Doors
As from an Emerald Ghost—
The Doom's electric Moccasin . . ."[17]
SHIT, WHERE DID THE REST OF IT GO . . . ?
FANNY: Well, don't ask *me*.
GARDNER: It just stopped in mid-air!
FANNY: Then go look for the original.

[14] From Roethke's "I Knew a Woman."
[15] From Robert Frost's poem "Fire and Ice."
[16] From "The Sheep Child," a poem by contemporary American poet James Dickey.
[17] From nineteenth-century American poet Emily Dickinson's poem number 1593.

GARDNER: Good idea, good idea! *(He exits to his study)*

FANNY *(To Mags)*: He's incontinent now, too. He wets his pants, in case you haven't noticed. *(She starts laughing)* You're not laughing. Don't you think it's funny? Daddy needs diapers. . . . I don't know about you, but I could use a drink! GAR . . . WILL YOU GET ME A SPLASH WHILE YOU'RE OUT THERE . . . ?

MAGS: STOP IT!

FANNY: It means we can't go out anymore. I mean, what would people say . . . ?

1480   MAGS: Stop it. Just stop it.

FANNY: My poet laureate can't hold it in! *(She laughs harder)*

MAGS: That's enough . . . STOP IT . . . Mummy . . . I beg of you . . . *please stop it!*

Gardner enters with a book and indeed a large stain has blossomed on his trousers. He plucks it away from his leg.

GARDNER: Here we go . . . I found it . . .

FANNY *(Pointing at it)*: See that? See? . . . he just did it again! *(Goes off into a shower of laughter)*

MAGS *(Looks, turns away)*: SHUT . . . UP! . . . *(Building up to a howl)* WILL YOU PLEASE JUST . . . SHUT . . . UP!

FANNY *(To Gardner)*: Hey, what about that drink?

GARDNER: Oh, yes . . . sorry, sorry . . . *(He heads towards the bar)*

1490   FANNY: Never mind, I'll get it, I'll get it.

Fanny exits, convulsed. Silence.

GARDNER: Well, where were we?

MAGS *(Near tears)*: Your poem.

GARDNER: Oh, yes . . . the Dickinson. *(He shuts his eyes, reciting from memory, holding the book against his chest)*
"There came a Wind like a Bugle—
It quivered through the Grass
And a Green Chill upon the Heat
So ominous did pass
We barred the Windows and the Doors

1500   As from an Emerald Ghost—"
(Opens the book and starts riffling through it) Let's see now, where's the rest? . . . *(He finally finds it)* Ahhh, here we go . . . !

FANNY *(Reenters, drink in hand)*: I'm back! *(Takes one look at Gardner and bursts out laughing again)*

MAGS: I don't believe you! How you can laugh at him?!

They all speak simultaneously as Mags gets angrier and angrier.

FANNY: I'm sorry, I wish I could stop, but there's really nothing else to do. Look at him . . . just . . . look at him . . . !

MAGS: It's so cruel. . . . You're so . . . incredibly cruel to him. . . . I mean, YOUR DISDAIN REALLY TAKES MY BREATH AWAY!

YOU'RE IN A CLASS BY YOURSELF WHEN IT COMES TO
HUMILIATION!
GARDNER *(Reading)*:
"The Doom's electric Moccasin   1510
That very instant passed—
On a strange Mob of panting Trees
And Fences fled away
And Rivers where the Houses ran
Those looked that lived—that Day—
The Bell within the steeple wild
The flying tidings told—
How much can come
And much can go,
And yet abide the World!"[18]   1520
*(He shuts the book with a bang, pauses and looks around the room,
confused)* Now, where was I . . . ?
FANNY: Safe and sound in the middle of the living room with Mags
and me.
GARDNER: But I was looking for something, wasn't I . . . ?
FANNY: Your manuscript.
GARDNER: THAT'S RIGHT! MY MANUSCRIPT! My manuscript!
FANNY: And here it is all over the floor. See, you're standing on it.
GARDNER *(Picks up a few pages and looks at them)*: Why, so I am . . .
FANNY: Now all we have to do is get it up off the floor and packed
neatly into these cartons!   1530
GARDNER: Yes, yes, that's right. Into the cartons.
FANNY *(Kicks a carton over to him)*: Here, you use this one and I'll
start over here . . . *(She starts dropping papers into a carton nearby)*
BOMBS AWAY! . . . Hey . . . this is fun!
GARDNER *(Picks up his own pile, lifts it high over his head and flings it
down into the carton)*: BOMBS AWAY. . . . This *is* fun!
FANNY: I told you! The whole thing is to figure out a system!
GARDNER: I don't know what I'd do without you, Fan. I thought I'd
lost everything.
FANNY *(Makes dive-bomber noises and machine-gun explosions as she
wheels more and more papers into the carton)*: TAKE THAT AND
THAT AND THAT!   1540
GARDNER *(Joins in the fun, outdoing her with dips, dives and blastings
of his own)*: BLAM BLAM BLAM BLAM! . . . ZZZZZZZZ-
RAAAAAA FOOM! . . . BLATTY-DE-BLATTY-DE-BLATTY-DE-
KABOOOOOOOOM! . . . WHAAAAAAA . . . DA-DAT-DAT-
DAT-DAT-DAT . . . WHEEEEEEEE AAAAAAAAAAAA . . .
FOOOOOO . . .

[18] From Dickinson's poem number 1593.

They get louder and louder as papers fly every which way.

FANNY *(Mimes getting hit with a bomb)*: AEEEEEEIIIIIIIIIIII! YOU
GOT ME RIGHT IN THE GIZZARD! *(She collapses on the floor
and starts going through death throes, having an absolute ball)*

GARDNER: TAKE THAT AND THAT AND THAT AND THAT . . .
(A series of explosions follow)

MAGS *(Furious)*: This is how you help him? . . . THIS IS HOW YOU
1550   PACK HIS THINGS?

FANNY: I keep him company. I get involved . . . which is a hell of a lot
more than you do!

MAGS *(Wild with rage)*: BUT YOU'RE MAKING A MOCKERY OF
HIM. . . . YOU TREAT HIM LIKE A CHILD OR SOME DIM-
WITTED SERVING BOY. HE'S JUST AN AMUSEMENT TO YOU!

FANNY *(Fatigue has finally overtaken her. She's calm, almost serene)*:
And to you who see him once a year, if that . . . what is he to *you*?
. . . I mean, what do you give him from yourself that costs you
something? . . . Hmmmmmm? . . . *(Imitating Mags)* "Oh, hi Daddy,
it's great to see you again. How have you been? . . . Gee, I love your
1560   hair. It's gotten so . . . *white*!" . . . What color do you expect it to
get when he's this age? . . . I mean, if you care so much how he
looks, why don't you come and see him once in a while? . . . But
oh, no . . . you have your paintings to do and your shows to put on.
You just come and see us when the whim strikes. *(Imitating Mags)*
"Hey, you know what would be really great? . . . To do a portrait
of you! I've always wanted to paint you, you're such great subjects!" *Paint* us?! . . . What about opening your eyes and really *seeing* us? . . . Noticing what's going on around here for a change! It's
all over for Daddy and me. This is it! "Finita la commedia!" . . . All
1570   I'm trying to do is exit with a little flourish; have some fun. . . .
What's so terrible about that? . . . It can get pretty grim around
here, in case you haven't noticed . . . Daddy, tap-tap-tapping out his
nonsense all day; me traipsing around to the thrift shops to amuse
myself. . . . He never keeps me company anymore; never takes me
out anywhere. . . . I'd put a bullet through my head in a minute, but
then who'd look after him? . . . What do you think we're moving to
the cottage for? So I can watch him like a hawk and make sure he
doesn't get lost. Do you think that's anything to look forward to?
. . . Being Daddy's nursemaid out in the middle of nowhere? I'd
1580   much rather stay here in Boston with the few friends I have left, but
you can't always do what you want in this world! "L'homme propose, Dieu dispose!" . . . If you want to paint us so badly, you
ought to paint us as we really are. There's your picture!

Fanny points to Gardner, who's quietly playing with a paper glide.

FANNY: Daddy spread out on the floor with all his toys and me hovering over him to make sure he doesn't hurt himself! *(She goes over to him)* YOO-HOO . . . GAR? . . . HELLO?

GARDNER *(Looks up at her)*: Oh, hi there, Fan. What's up?

FANNY: How's the packing coming . . . ?

GARDNER: Packing . . . ?

FANNY: Yes, you were packing your manuscript, remember? *(She lifts up a page and lets it fall into a carton)*   1590

GARDNER: Oh, yes . . .

FANNY: Here's your picture, Mags. Face over this way . . . turn your easel over here . . . *(She lets a few more papers fall)* Up, up . . . and away . . .

Blackout.

SCENE 2

The last day. All the books and boxes are gone. The room is completely empty except for Mags's backdrop. Late afternoon light dapples the walls; it changes from pale peach to deeper violet. The finished portrait sits on the easel, covered with a cloth. Mags is taking down the backdrop.

FANNY *(Offstage; to Gardner)*: DON'T FORGET TOOTS!

GARDNER *(Offstage; from another part of the house)*: WHAT'S THAT?

FANNY *(Offstage)*: I SAID: DON'T FORGET TOOTS! HIS CAGE IS SITTING IN THE MIDDLE OF YOUR STUDY!

Silence.

FANNY *(Offstage)*: HELLO? . . .   GARDNER *(Offstage)*: I'LL BE
ARE YOU THERE?   RIGHT WITH YOU; I'M JUST   1600
                                                       GETTING TOOTS!

GARDNER *(Offstage)*: WHAT'S THAT? I CAN'T HEAR YOU?

FANNY *(Offstage)*: I'M GOING THROUGH THE ROOMS ONE MORE TIME TO MAKE SURE WE DIDN'T FORGET ANYTHING. . . . KITTY'S PICKING US UP IN FIFTEEN MINUTES, SO PLEASE BE READY. . . . SHE'S DROPPING MAGS OFF AT THE STATION AND THEN IT'S OUT TO ROUTE 3 AND THE CAPE HIGHWAY . . .

GARDNER *(Enters, carrying Toots in his cage)*: Well, this is it. The big moment has finally come, eh what, Toots? *(He sees Mags)* Oh, hi   1610
there, Mags, I didn't see you . . .

MAGS: Oh, hi, Daddy, I'm just taking this down . . . *(She does and walks over to Toots)* Oh, Toots, I'll miss you. *(She makes little chattering noises into his cage)*

GARDNER: Come on, recite a little Gray's *Elegy* for Mags before we go.

MAGS: Yes, Mum said he was really good at it now.

GARDNER: Well, the whole thing is to keep at it every day. *(Slowly to Toots)*

"The curfew tolls the knell of parting day,
The lowing herd wind slowly o'er the lea . . ."
Come on, show Mags your stuff! *(Slower)*

1620

"The curfew tolls the knell of parting day,
The lowing herd wind slowly o'er the lea . . ."

Silence; Gardner makes little chattering sounds.

GARDNER: Come on, Toots, old boy . . .
MAGS: How does it go?
GARDNER *(To Mags)*:
    "The curfew tolls the knell of parting day,
    The lowing herd wind slowly o'er the lea . . ."
MAGS *(Slowly to Toots)*:
    The curfew tolls for you and me,
    As quietly the herd winds down . . .
GARDNER: No, no, it's "The curfew tolls the knell of parting *day* . . ."!
MAGS *(Repeating after him)*: "The curfew tolls the knell of parting

1630

    day . . ."
GARDNER: "The lowing herd wind slowly o'er the lea . . ."
MAGS *(With a deep breath)*:
    The curfew tolls at parting day,
    The herd low slowly down the lea . . . no, *knell!*
    They come winding down the *knell!*
GARDNER: Listen, Mags . . . *listen!*

A pause.

TOOTS *(Loud and clear with Gardner's inflection)*:
    "The curfew tolls the knell of parting day,
    The lowing herd wind slowly o'er the lea,
    The ploughman homeward plods his weary way,
    And leaves the world to darkness and to me."

1640

MAGS: HE SAID IT. . . . HE SAID IT! . . . AND IN YOUR VOICE!
    . . . OH, DADDY, THAT'S AMAZING!
GARDNER: Well, Toots is very smart, which is more than I can say for
    a lot of people I know . . .
MAGS *(To Toots)*: Polly want a cracker? Polly want a cracker?
GARDNER: You can teach a parakeet to say anything; all you need is
    patience . . .
MAGS: But *poetry* . . . that's so hard . . .

*Fanny enters carrying a suitcase and Gardner's typewriter in its
case. She's dressed in her traveling suit, wearing a hat to match.*

FANNY: WELL, THERE YOU ARE! I THOUGHT YOU'D DIED!
MAGS *(To Fanny)*: HE SAID IT! I FINALLY HEARD TOOTS RE-

1650

    CITE GRAY'S *ELEGY*. (*She makes silly clucking sounds into the
    cage.*)

FANNY: Isn't it uncanny how much he sounds like Daddy? Sometimes when I'm alone here with him, I've actually thought he *was* Daddy and started talking to him. Oh, yes, Toots and I have had quite a few meaty conversations together!

Fanny wolf-whistles into the cage; then draws back. Gardner covers the cage with a traveling cloth. Silence.

FANNY *(Looking around the room)*: God, the place looks so bare.

MAGS: I still can't believe it . . . Cotuit, year round. I wonder if there'll be any phosphorus when you get there?

FANNY: What on earth are you talking about? *(She carries the discarded backdrop out into the hall)*

MAGS: Remember that summer when the ocean was full of phosphorus?   1660

GARDNER *(Taking Toots out into the hall)*: Oh, yes . . .

MAGS: It was a great mystery where it came from or why it settled in Cotuit. But one evening when Daddy and I were taking a swim, suddenly it was there!

GARDNER *(Returns)*: I remember.

MAGS: I don't know where Mum was . . .

FANNY *(Reentering)*: Probably doing the dishes!

MAGS *(To Gardner)*: As you dove into the water, this shower of silvery green sparks erupted all around you. It was incredible! I thought you were turning into a saint or something; but then you told me to   1670 jump in too and the same thing happened to me . . .

GARDNER: Oh, yes, I remember that . . . the water smelled all queer.

MAGS: What *is* phosphorus, anyway?

GARDNER: Chemicals, chemicals . . .

FANNY: No, it isn't. Phosphorus is a green liquid inside insects. Fireflies have it. When you see sparks in the water it means insects are swimming around . . .

GARDNER: Where on earth did you get that idea . . . ?

FANNY: If you're bitten by one of them, it's fatal!

MAGS: And the next morning it was still there . . .   1680

GARDNER: It was the damndest stuff to get off! We'd have to stay in the shower a good ten minutes. It comes from the chemical waste, you see . . .

MAGS: Our bodies looked like mercury as we swam around . . .

GARDNER: It stained all the towels a strange yellow green.

MAGS: I was in heaven, and so were you for that matter. You'd finished your day's poetry and would turn somersaults like some happy dolphin . . .

FANNY: Damned dishes . . . why didn't I see any of this?!

MAGS: I remember one night in particular. . . . We sensed the phosphorus was about to desert us; blow off to another town. We were   1690 chasing each other under water. At one point I lost you, the brilliance was so intense . . . but finally your foot appeared . . . then your leg. I grabbed it! . . . I remember wishing the moment would hold forever; that we could just be fixed there, laughing and iridescent. . . . Then I began to get panicky because I knew it would pass; it was passing already. You were slipping from my grasp. The summer was almost over. I'd be going back to art school; you'd be going back to Boston. . . . Even as I was reaching for you, you were gone. We'd never be like that again.

1700

Silence. Fanny spies Mags's portrait covered on the easel.

FANNY: What's that over there? Don't tell me we forgot something!

MAGS: It's your portrait. I finished it.

FANNY: You finished it! How on earth did you manage that?

MAGS: I stayed up all night.

FANNY: You did? . . . *I* didn't hear you, did you hear her, Gar . . . ?

GARDNER: Not a peep, not a peep!

MAGS: Well, I wanted to get it done before you left. You know, see what you thought. It's not bad, considering . . . I mean, I did it almost completely from memory. The light was terrible and I was trying to be quiet so I wouldn't wake you. It was hardly an ideal situation . . . I mean, you weren't the most cooperative models . . . *(She suddenly panics and snatches the painting off the easel. She hugs it to her chest and starts dancing around the room with it)* Oh, God, you're going to hate it! You're going to hate it! How did I ever get into this! . . . Listen, you don't really want to see it . . . it's nothing . . . just a few dabs here and there. . . . It was awfully late when I finished it. The light was really impossible and my eyes were hurting like crazy. . . . Look, why don't we just go out to the sidewalk and wait for Kitty so she doesn't have to honk—

1710

GARDNER *(Snatches the painting out from under her grasp)*: WOULD YOU JUST SHUT UP A MINUTE AND LET US SEE IT?

1720

MAGS *(Laughing and crying)*: But it's nothing, Daddy . . . *really!* . . . I've done better with my eyes closed! It was so late I could hardly see anything and then I spilled a whole bottle of thinner into my palette . . .

GARDNER *(Sets the portrait down on the easel and stands back to look at it)*: THERE!

MAGS *(Dancing around them in a panic)*: Listen, it's just a quick sketch. . . . It's still wet. . . . I didn't have enough time. . . . It takes at least forty hours to do a decent portrait . . .

Suddenly it's very quiet as Fanny and Gardner stand back to look at the painting. More and more beside herself, Mags keeps leaping around the room wrapping her arms around herself, making little whimpering sounds.

MAGS: Please don't . . . no . . . don't . . . oh, please! . . . Come on, don't look. . . . Oh, God, don't . . . please . . .

1730

An eternity passes as Fanny and Gardner gaze at their portrait.

GARDNER: Well . . .

FANNY: Well . . .

More silence.

FANNY: I think it's perfectly dreadful!

GARDNER: Awfully clever, awfully clever!

FANNY: What on earth did you do to my face . . . ?

GARDNER: I particularly like Mum!

FANNY: Since when do I have purple skin?!

MAGS: I told you it was nothing, just a silly—

GARDNER: She looks like a million dollars!

FANNY: AND WILL YOU LOOK AT MY HAIR . . . IT'S BRIGHT ORANGE!

1740

GARDNER (*Views the painting from another angle*): It's really very good!

FANNY (*Pointing*): That doesn't look anything like me!

GARDNER: First-rate!

FANNY: Since when do I have purple skin and bright orange hair?!

MAGS (*Trying to snatch the painting off the easel*): Listen, you don't have to worry about my feelings . . . really . . . I—

GARDNER (*Blocking her way*): NOT SO FAST . . .

FANNY: And look at how I'm sitting! I've never sat like that in my life!

1750

GARDNER (*Moving closer to the painting*): Yes, yes, it's awfully clever . . .

FANNY: I HAVE NO FEET!

GARDNER: The whole thing is quite remarkable!

FANNY: And what happened to my legs, pray tell? . . . They just vanish below the knees! . . . At least my dress is presentable. I've always loved that dress.

GARDNER: It sparkles somehow . . .

FANNY (*To Gardner*): Don't you think it's becoming?

GARDNER: Yes, very becoming, awfully becoming . . .

1760

FANNY (*Examining it at closer range*): Yes, she got the dress very well, how it shows off what's left of my figure. . . . My smile is nice too.

GARDNER: Good and wide . . .

FANNY: I love how the corners of my mouth turn up . . .

GARDNER: It's very clever . . .

FANNY: They're almost quivering . . .

GARDNER: Good lighting effects!

FANNY: Actually, I look quite . . . *young,* don't you think?

GARDNER (*To Mags*): You're awfully good with those highlights.

1770 FANNY (*Looking at it from different angles*): And *you* look darling . . . !

GARDNER: Well, I don't know about that . . .

FANNY: No, you look absolutely darling. Good enough to eat!

MAGS (*In a whisper*): They like it. . . . They like it!

A silence as Fanny and Gardner keep gazing at their portrait.

FANNY: You know what it is? The wispy brush strokes make us look like a couple in a French Impressionist painting.

GARDNER: Yes, I see what you mean . . .

FANNY: A Manet or Renoir . . .

GARDNER: It's very evocative.

FANNY: There's something about the light . . .

They back up to survey the picture from a distance.

1780 FANNY: You know those Renoir café scenes . . . ?

GARDNER: She doesn't lay on the paint with a trowel; it's just touches here and there . . .

MAGS: They *like* it . . . !

FANNY: You know the one with the couple dancing?[19] . . . Not that we're dancing. There's just something similar in the mood . . . a kind of gaiety, almost. . . . The man has his back to you and he's swinging the woman around . . . OH, GAR, YOU'VE SEEN IT A MILLION TIMES! IT'S HANGING IN THE MUSEUM OF FINE ARTS! . . . They're dancing like this . . .

Fanny goes up to Gardner and puts an arm on his shoulders.

1790 MAGS: They like it. . . . They like it!

FANNY: She's got on this wonderful flowered dress with ruffles at the neck and he's holding her like this. . . . that's right . . . and she's got the most rhapsodic expression on her face . . .

Getting into the spirit of it, Gardner takes Fanny in his arms and slowly begins to dance around the room.

GARDNER: Oh, yes . . . I know the one you mean. . . . They're in a sort of haze . . . and isn't there a little band playing off to one side . . . ?

FANNY: Yes, that's it!

Kitty's horn honks outside. Mags is the only one who hears it.

MAGS: There's Kitty! (*She's torn and keeps looking towards the door, but finally gives in to their stolen moment*)

FANNY: And there's a man in a dark suit playing the violin and some-one's conducting, I think. . . . And aren't Japanese lanterns strung

1800 up . . . ?

Fanny and Gardner pick up speed, dipping and whirling around the room. Strains of a faraway Chopin waltz are heard.

---

[19] Possibly an allusion to Renoir's painting *Dance at Bougival*.

GARDNER: Oh, yes! There are all these little lights twinkling in the trees . . .

FANNY: And doesn't the woman have a hat on? . . . A big red hat . . . ?

GARDNER: . . . and lights all over the dancers, too. Everything shimmers with this marvelous glow. Yes, yes . . . I can see it perfectly! The whole thing is absolutely extraordinary!

The lights become dreamy and dappled as Fanny and Gardner dance around the room. Mags watches them, moved to tears as slowly the curtain falls.

❏ Questions for Discussion
Act I

1. Howe is known for her rich and elaborate settings. What does the setting of *Painting Churches*—a townhouse in a very old, very wealthy section of downtown Boston—tell you about the Churches? In what sense is this interior a work of art in its own right?

2. What does Fanny think of portraits? On what basis does she judge them? How else might one judge them?

3. How does Fanny react to Mags' and Gardner's enthusiasm over their art? Why does she choose to misunderstand it? Why did she behave so abysmally at Mags' first art show?

4. What about Gardner and Fanny would make them fascinating subjects for a portrait?

5. Though she is certainly a zany character, Fanny will not tolerate some kinds of behavior and talk. What will she not tolerate? Why?

6. Mags says, "The great thing about being a portrait painter, you see, is it's the other guy that's exposed, you're safely hidden behind the canvas and easel." Why would Mags be attracted to such anonymity? What can a portrait reveal about its painter?

Act II

1. Why does Gardner memorize poems and recite them at inappropriate times?

2. Why is Fanny so insistently anti-intellectual and anti-artistic?

3. Fanny maintains that she is the only practical member of the family: "If it weren't for me, nothing would ever get done around here." How practical is she? Why does she insist on taking charge of the move?

4. Gardner says, "Criticism is tough sledding. You can't just dash off a few images here, a few rhymes there. . . . " Why does he make writing poetry sound so easy?

5. Why does Fanny laugh at Gardner's incontinence and ineptitude?

6. Why does Mags fear that her parents will hate her portrait of them? Why is she so apologetic? In what way is she no longer "safely hidden behind canvas and easel"?

❏ **Suggestions for Exploration and Writing**

1. Mags says about painting portraits, "Just as you make your most intimate move, throw open your soul . . . they stretch and yawn, remembering the dog has to be let out at five . . . . To be so invisible while so enthralled . . . it takes your breath away!" What, then, in portraiture attracts Mags? How does this passage not only explain her preference for portraiture but also describe her relationship with her family?

2. In what sense is Fanny's taking a blowtorch to Mags's child-hood masterpiece symbolic of their relationship? What does Mags mean when she asks Fanny, "What do you know about my abilities?!"

3. In describing her "masterpiece," Mags associates particular colors with particular tastes. Write an essay in which you define certain tastes or moods in terms of particular colors and explain the reasons for your color choices.

4. Fanny says to Mags, "Paint us?! . . . What about opening your eyes and really seeing us? . . . Noticing what's going on around here for a change! It's all over for Daddy and me. This is it! 'Finita la commedia!' . . . All I'm trying to do is exit with a little flourish; have some fun." Using this passage as a starting point, write an analysis of Gardner and Fanny as a couple.

5. Fanny says, "If you want to paint us so badly, you ought to paint us as we really are. There's your picture!" Explain how you could possibly capture on canvas the extraordinary energy, confusion, and hilarity of the Churches' household.

6. Find a good reproduction of Renoir's *Dance at Bougival*, the painting to which Fanny compares Mags' portrait. Compare and/or contrast the Churches to the couple in the painting.

CASEBOOK
on Alice Walker

ALICE WALKER (1944–)

Alice Walker, writer of novels, short stories, and essays, is perhaps best known for her popular novel The Color Purple *(1982), which was made into a movie. Many of her earlier works, including* The Color Purple *and the stories included here, draw on her rural Southern upbringing; however, Walker's latest novel,* Possessing the Secret of Joy *(1992), is set in Africa. The selections in this casebook celebrate the complex, rich art of rural Southern African-American women.*

Everyday Use
for your grandmama

I will wait for her in the yard that Maggie and I made so clean and 1
wavy yesterday afternoon. A yard like this is more comfortable than most people know. It is not just a yard. It is like an extended living room. When the hard clay is swept clean as a floor and the fine sand around the edges lined with tiny, irregular grooves, anyone can come and sit and look up into the elm tree and wait for the breezes that never come inside the house.

Maggie will be nervous until after her sister goes: she will stand 2
hopelessly in corners, homely and ashamed of the burn scars down her arms and legs, eying her sister with a mixture of envy and awe. She thinks her sister has held life always in the palm of one hand, that "no" is a word the world never learned to say to her.

You've no doubt seen those TV shows where the child who has "made 3
it" is confronted, as a surprise, by her own mother and father, tottering in weakly from backstage. (A pleasant surprise, of course: What would they do if parent and child came on the show only to curse out and insult each other?) On TV mother and child embrace and smile into each other's faces. Sometimes the mother and father weep, the child wraps them in her arms and leans across the table to tell how she would not have made it without their help. I have seen these programs.

Sometimes I dream a dream in which Dee and I are suddenly brought 4
together on a TV program of this sort. Out of a dark and soft-seated limousine I am ushered into a bright room filled with many people. There I meet a smiling, gray, sporty man like Johnny Carson who shakes my hand and tells me what a fine girl I have. Then we are on the stage and

Dee is embracing me with tears in her eyes. She pins on my dress a large orchid, even though she has told me once that she thinks orchids are tacky flowers.

5   In real life I am a large, big-boned woman with rough, man-working hands. In the winter I wear flannel nightgowns to bed and overalls during the day. I can kill and clean a hog as mercilessly as a man. My fat keeps me hot in zero weather. I can work outside all day, breaking ice to get water for washing; I can eat pork liver cooked over the open fire minutes after it comes steaming from the hog. One winter I knocked a bull calf straight in the brain between the eyes with a sledge hammer and had the meat hung up to chill before nightfall. But of course all this does not show on television. I am the way my daughter would want me to be: a hundred pounds lighter, my skin like an uncooked barley pancake. My hair glistens in the hot bright lights. Johnny Carson has much to do to keep up with my quick and witty tongue.

6   But that is a mistake. I know even before I wake up. Who ever knew a Johnson with a quick tongue? Who can even imagine me looking a strange white man in the eye? It seems to me I have talked to them always with one foot raised in flight, with my head turned in whichever way is farthest from them. Dee, though. She would always look anyone in the eye. Hesitation was no part of her nature.

7   "How do I look, Mama?" Maggie says, showing just enough of her thin body enveloped in pink skirt and red blouse for me to know she's there, almost hidden by the door.

8   "Come out into the yard," I say.

9   Have you ever seen a lame animal, perhaps a dog run over by some careless person rich enough to own a car, sidle up to someone who is ignorant enough to be kind to him? That is the way my Maggie walks. She has been like this, chin on chest, eyes on ground, feet in shuffle, ever since the fire that burned the other house to the ground.

10   Dee is lighter than Maggie, with nicer hair and a fuller figure. She's a woman now, though sometimes I forget. How long ago was it that the other house burned? Ten, twelve years? Sometimes I can still hear the flame and feel Maggie's arms sticking to me, her hair smoking and her dress falling off her in little black papery flakes. Her eyes seemed stretched open, blazed open by the flames reflected in them. And Dee. I see her standing off under the sweet gum tree she used to dig gum out of; a look of concentration on her face as she watched the last dingy gray board of the house fall in toward the red-hot brick chimney. Why don't you do a dance around the ashes? I'd wanted to ask her. She had hated the house that much.

11   I used to think she hated Maggie, too. But that was before we raised the money, the church and me, to send her to Augusta to school. She used to read to us without pity; forcing words, lies, other folks' habits, whole lives upon us two, sitting trapped and ignorant underneath her voice. She washed us in a river of make-believe, burned us with a lot of knowledge

we didn't necessarily need to know. Pressed us to her with the serious way she read, to shove us away at just the moment, like dimwits, we seemed about to understand.

Dee wanted nice things. A yellow organdy dress to wear to her graduation from high school; black pumps to match a green suit she'd made from an old suit somebody gave me. She was determined to stare down any disaster in her efforts. Her eyelids would not flicker for minutes at a time. Often I fought off the temptation to shake her. At sixteen she had a style of her own: and knew what style was.

I never had an education myself. After second grade the school was closed down. Don't ask me why: in 1927 colored asked fewer questions than they do now. Sometimes Maggie reads to me. She stumbles along good-naturedly but can't see well. She knows she is not bright. Like good looks and money, quickness passed her by. She will marry John Thomas (who has mossy teeth in an earnest face) and then I'll be free to sit here and I guess just sing church songs to myself. Although I never was a good singer. Never could carry a tune. I was always better at a man's job. I used to love to milk till I was hooked in the side in '49. Cows are soothing and slow and don't bother you, unless you try to milk them the wrong way.

I have deliberately turned my back on the house. It is three rooms, just like the one that burned, except the roof is tin; they don't make shingle roofs any more. There are no real windows, just some holes cut in the sides, like the portholes in a ship, but not round and not square, with rawhide holding the shutters up on the outside. This house is in a pasture too, like the other one. No doubt when Dee sees it she will want to tear it down. She wrote me once that no matter where we "choose" to live, she will manage to come see us. But she will never bring her friends. Maggie and I thought about this and Maggie asked me, "Mama, when did Dee ever *have* any friends?"

She had a few. Furtive boys in pink shirts hanging about on washday after school. Nervous girls who never laughed. Impressed with her they worshiped the well-turned phrase, the cute shape, the scalding humor that erupted like bubbles in lye. She read to them.

When she was courting Jimmy T she didn't have much time to pay to us, but turned all her faultfinding power on him. He *flew* to marry a cheap city girl from a family of ignorant flashy people. She hardly had time to recompose herself.

When she comes I will meet—but there they are!

Maggie attempts to make a dash for the house, in her shuffling way, but I stay her with my hand. "Come back here," I say. And she stops and tries to dig a well in the sand with her toe.

It is hard to see them clearly through the strong sun. But even the first glimpse of leg out of the car tells me it is Dee. Her feet were always neat-looking, as if God himself had shaped them with a certain style.

From the other side of the car comes a short, stocky man. Hair is all over his head a foot long and hanging from his chin like a kinky mule tail. I hear Maggie suck in her breath. "Uhnnnh," is what it sounds like. Like when you see the wriggling end of a snake just in front of your foot on the road. "Uhnnnh."

20   Dee next. A dress down to the ground, in this hot weather. A dress so loud it hurts my eyes. There are yellows and oranges enough to throw back the light of the sun. I feel my whole face warming from the heat waves it throws out. Earrings gold, too, and hanging down to her shoulders. Bracelets dangling and making noises when she moves her arm up to shake the folds of the dress out of her armpits. The dress is loose and flows, and as she walks closer, I like it. I hear Maggie go "Uhnnnh" again. It is her sister's hair. It stands straight up like the wool on a sheep. It is black as night and around the edges are two long pigtails that rope about like small lizards disappearing behind her ears.

21   "Wa-su-zo-Tean-o!" she says, coming on in that gliding way the dress makes her move. The short stocky fellow with the hair to his navel is all grinning and he follows up with "Asalamalakim, my mother and sister!" He moves to hug Maggie but she falls back, right up against the back of my chair. I feel her trembling there and when I look up I see the perspiration falling off her chin.

22   "Don't get up," says Dee. Since I am stout it takes something of a push. You can see me trying to move a second or two before I make it. She turns, showing white heels through her sandals, and goes back to the car. Out she peeks next with a Polaroid. She stoops down quickly and lines up picture after picture of me sitting there in front of the house with Maggie cowering behind me. She never takes a shot without making sure the house is included. When a cow comes nibbling around the edge of the yard she snaps it and me and Maggie *and* the house. Then she puts the Polaroid in the back seat of the car, and comes up and kisses me on the forehead.

23   Meanwhile Asalamalakim is going through motions with Maggie's hand. Maggie's hand is as limp as a fish, and probably as cold, despite the sweat, and she keeps trying to pull it back. It looks like Asalamalakim wants to shake hands but wants to do it fancy. Or maybe he don't know how people shake hands. Anyhow, he soon gives up on Maggie.

24   "Well," I say. "Dee."

25   "No, Mama," she says. "Not 'Dee,' Wangero Leewanika Kemanjo!"

26   "What happened to 'Dee'?" I wanted to know.

27   "She's dead," Wangero said. "I couldn't bear it any longer, being named after the people who oppress me."

28   "You know as well as me you was named after your aunt Dicie," I said. Dicie is my sister. She named Dee. We called her "Big Dee" after Dee was born.

29   "But who was *she* named after?" asked Wangero.

30   "I guess after Grandma Dee," I said.

"And who was she named after?" asked Wangero.   31

"Her mother," I said, and saw Wangero was getting tired. "That's   32
about as far back as I can trace it," I said. Though, in fact, I probably
could have carried it back beyond the Civil War through the branches.

"Well," said Asalamalakim, "there you are."   33

"Uhnnnh," I heard Maggie say.   34

"There I was not," I said, "before 'Dicie' cropped up in our family, so   35
why should I try to trace it that far back?"

He just stood there grinning, looking down on me like somebody   36
inspecting a Model A car. Every once in a while he and Wangero sent eye
signals over my head.

"How do you pronounce this name?" I asked.   37

"You don't have to call me by it if you don't want to," said Wangero.   38

"Why shouldn't I?" I asked. "If that's what you want us to call you,   39
we'll call you."

"I know it might sound awkward at first," said Wangero.   40

"I'll get used to it," I said. "Ream it out again."   41

Well, soon we got the name out of the way. Asalamalakim had a name   42
twice as long and three times as hard. After I tripped over it two or three
times he told me to just call him Hakim-a-barber. I wanted to ask him
was he a barber, but I didn't really think he was, so I didn't ask.

"You must belong to those beef-cattle peoples down the road," I said.   43
They said "Asalamalakim" when they met you, too, but they didn't
shake hands. Always too busy: feeding the cattle, fixing the fences,
putting up salt-lick shelters, throwing down hay. When the white folks
poisoned some of the herd the men stayed up all night with rifles in their
hands. I walked a mile and a half just to see the sight.

Hakim-a-barber said, "I accept some of their doctrines, but farming   44
and raising cattle is not my style." (They didn't tell me, and I didn't ask,
whether Wangero (Dee) had really gone and married him.)

We sat down to eat and right away he said he didn't eat collards and   45
pork was unclean. Wangero, though, went on through the chitlins and
corn bread, the greens and everything else. She talked a blue streak over
the sweet potatoes. Everything delighted her. Even the fact that we still
used the benches her daddy made for the table when we couldn't afford
to buy chairs.

"Oh, Mama!" she cried. Then turned to Hakim-a-barber. "I never   46
knew how lovely these benches are. You can feel the rump prints," she
said, running her hands underneath her and along the bench. Then she
gave a sigh and her hand closed over Grandma Dee's butter dish. "That's
it!" she said. "I knew there was something I wanted to ask you if I could
have." She jumped up from the table and went over in the corner where
the churn stood, the milk in it clabber by now. She looked at the churn
and looked at it.

"This churn top is what I need," she said. "Didn't Uncle Buddy whittle   47
it out of a tree you all used to have?"

48   "Yes," I said.

49   "Uh huh," she said happily. "And I want the dasher, too."

50   "Uncle Buddy whittle that, too?" asked the barber.

51   Dee (Wangero) looked up at me.

52   "Aunt Dee's first husband whittled the dash," said Maggie so low you almost couldn't hear her. "His name was Henry, but they called him Stash."

53   "Maggie's brain is like an elephant's," Wangero said, laughing. "I can use the churn top as a centerpiece for the alcove table," she said, sliding a plate over the churn, "and I'll think of something artistic to do with the dasher."

54   When she finished wrapping the dasher the handle stuck out. I took it for a moment in my hands. You didn't even have to look close to see where hands pushing the dasher up and down to make butter had left a kind of sink in the wood. In fact, there were a lot of small sinks; you could see where thumbs and fingers had sunk into the wood. It was a beautiful light yellow wood, from a tree that grew in the yard where Big Dee and Stash had lived.

55   After dinner Dee (Wangero) went to the trunk at the foot of my bed and started rifling through it. Maggie hung back in the kitchen over the dishpan. Out came Wangero with two quilts. They had been pieced by Grandma Dee and then Big Dee and me had hung them on the quilt frames on the front porch and quilted them. One was in the Lone Star pattern. The other was Walk Around the Mountain. In both of them were scraps of dresses Grandma Dee had worn fifty and more years ago. Bits and pieces of Grandpa Jarrell's Paisley shirts. And one teeny faded blue piece, about the size of a penny matchbox, that was from Great Grandpa Ezra's uniform that he wore in the Civil War.

56   "Mama," Wangero said sweet as a bird. "Can I have these old quilts?"

57   I heard something fall in the kitchen, and a minute later the kitchen door slammed.

58   "Why don't you take one or two of the others?" I asked. "These old things was just done by me and Big Dee from some tops your grandma pieced before she died."

59   "No," said Wangero. "I don't want those. They are stitched around the borders by machine."

60   "That'll make them last better," I said.

61   "That's not the point," said Wangero. "These are all pieces of dresses Grandma used to wear. She did all this stitching by hand. Imagine!" She held the quilts securely in her arms, stroking them.

62   "Some of the pieces, like those lavender ones, come from old clothes her mother handed down to her," I said, moving up to touch the quilts. Dee (Wangero) moved back just enough so that I couldn't reach the quilts. They already belonged to her.

63   "Imagine!" she breathed again, clutching them closely to her bosom.

64   "The truth is," I said, "I promised to give them quilts to Maggie, for when she marries John Thomas."

She gasped like a bee had stung her.   65

"Maggie can't appreciate these quilts!" she said. "She'd probably be   66
backward enough to put them to everyday use."

"I reckon she would," I said. "God knows I been saving 'em for long   67
enough with nobody using 'em. I hope she will!" I didn't want to bring
up how I had offered Dee (Wangero) a quilt when she went away to
college. Then she had told me they were old-fashioned, out of style.

"But they're *priceless!*" she was saying now, furiously; for she has a   68
temper. "Maggie would put them on the bed and in five years they'd be
in rags. Less than that!"

"She can always make some more," I said. "Maggie knows how to   69
quilt."

Dee (Wangero) looked at me with hatred. "You just will not under-   70
stand. The point is these quilts, *these* quilts!"

"Well," I said, stumped. "What would *you* do with them?"   71

"Hang them," she said. As if that was the only thing you *could* do with   72
quilts.

Maggie by now was standing in the door. I could almost hear the   73
sound her feet made as they scraped over each other.

"She can have them, Mama," she said, like somebody used to never   74
winning anything, or having anything reserved for her. "I can 'member
Grandma Dee without the quilts."

I looked at her hard. She had filled her bottom lip with checkerberry   75
snuff and it gave her face a kind of dopey, hangdog look. It was Grandma
Dee and Big Dee who taught her how to quilt herself. She stood there
with her scarred hands hidden in the folds of her skirt. She looked at her
sister with something like fear but she wasn't mad at her. This was
Maggie's portion. This was the way she knew God to work.

When I looked at her like that something hit me in the top of my head   76
and ran down to the soles of my feet. Just like when I'm in church and
the spirit of God touches me and I get happy and shout. I did something
I never had done before: hugged Maggie to me, then dragged her on into
the room, snatched the quilts out of Miss Wangero's hands and dumped
them into Maggie's lap. Maggie just sat there on my bed with her mouth
open.

"Take one or two of the others," I said to Dee.   77

But she turned without a word and went out to Hakim-a-barber.   78

"You just don't understand," she said, as Maggie and I came out to the   79
car.

"What don't I understand?" I wanted to know.   80

"Your heritage," she said. And then she turned to Maggie, kissed her,   81
and said, "You ought to try to make something of yourself, too, Maggie.
It's really a new day for us. But from the way you and Mama still live
you'd never know it."

She put on some sunglasses that hid everything above the tip of her   82
nose and her chin.

Maggie smiled; maybe at the sunglasses. But a real smile, not scared.   83

After we watched the car dust settle I asked Maggie to bring me a dip of snuff. And then the two of us sat there just enjoying, until it was time to go in the house and go to bed.

❏ Questions for Discussion

1. What does the narrating mother's opening description of the yard tell you about her and Maggie?

2. What does the mother's recurring dream and her response to it reveal about her relationship to Maggie?

3. The narrator says of Dee, "She used to read to us without pity: forcing words, lies, other folks' habits, whole lives upon us two, sitting trapped and ignorant underneath her voice." Why does the narrator feel trapped by, rather than appreciative of, Dee's reading? Is the narrator merely ignorant and insensitive? Why does she regard what she hears as lies?

4. Why do Dee and her male friend use a strange language, and why has Dee changed her name?

5. Note that after the arrival of Dee, the narrator's style changes, becoming less formal and more colloquial. Why might Walker have chosen to change the style here?

6. What is the distinction between the mother's use of the churn and Dee's proposed use of it?

7. What is the significance of Maggie's saying, "I can 'member Grandma Dee without the quilts"?

Nineteen Fifty-five
1955

1   The car is a brandnew red Thunderbird convertible, and it's passed the house more than once. It slows down real slow now, and stops at the curb. An older gentleman dressed like a Baptist deacon gets out on the side near the house, and a young fellow who looks about sixteen gets out on the driver's side. They are white, and I wonder what in the world they are doing in this neighborhood.

2   Well, I say to J. T., put your shirt on, anyway, and let me clean these glasses offa the table.

3   We had been watching the ballgame on TV. I wasn't actually watching, I was sort of daydreaming, with my foots up in J. T.'s lap.

4   I seen 'em coming on up the walk, brisk, like they coming to sell something, and then they rung the bell, and J. T. declined to put on a shirt but instead disappeared into the bedroom where the other television is. I turned down the one in the living room; I figured I'd be rid of these two double quick and J. T. could come back out again.

Are you Gracie Mae Still? asked the old guy, when I opened the door   5
and put my hand on the lock inside the screen.

And I don't need to buy a thing, said I.   6

What makes you think we're sellin'? he asks, in that hearty Southern   7
way that makes my eyeballs ache.

Well, one way or another and they're inside the house and the first   8
thing the young fellow does is raise the TV a couple of decibels. He's
about five feet nine, sort of womanish looking, with real dark white skin
and a red pouting mouth. His hair is black and curly and he looks like a
Loosianna creole.

About one of your songs, says the deacon. He is maybe sixty, with   9
white hair and beard, white silk shirt, black linen suit, black tie, and
black shoes. His cold gray eyes look like they're sweating.

One of my songs?   10

Traynor here just *loves* your songs. Don't you, Traynor? He nudges   11
Traynor with his elbow. Traynor blinks, says something I can't catch in
a pitch I don't register.

The boy learned to sing and dance livin' round you people out in the   12
country. Practically cut his teeth on you.

Traynor looks up at me and bites his thumbnail.   13

I laugh.   14

Well, one way or another they leave with my agreement that they can   15
record one of my songs. The deacon writes me a check for five hundred
dollars, the boy grunts his awareness of the transaction, and I am
laughing all over myself by the time I rejoin J. T.

Just as I am snuggling down beside him though I hear the front door   16
bell going off again.

Forgit his hat? asks J. T.   17

I hope not, I say.   18

The deacon stands there leaning on the door frame and once again I'm   19
thinking of those sweaty-looking eyeballs of his. I wonder if sweat makes
your eyeballs pink because his are sure pink. Pink and gray and it strikes
me that nobody I'd care to know is behind them.

I forgot one little thing, he says pleasantly. I forgot to tell you Traynor   20
and I would like to buy up all of those records you made of the song. I
tell you we sure do love it.

Well, love it or not, I'm not so stupid as to let them do that without   21
making 'em pay. So I says, Well, that's gonna cost you. Because, really,
that song never did sell all that good, so I was glad they was going to buy
it up. But on the other hand, them two listening to my song by themselves, and nobody else getting to hear me sing it, give me a pause.

Well, one way or another the deacon showed me where I would come   22
out ahead on any deal he had proposed so far. Didn't I give you five
hundred dollars? he asked. What white man—and don't even mention
colored—would give you more? We buy up all your records of that
particular song: first, you git royalties. Let me ask you, how much you

sell that song for in the first place? Fifty dollars? A hundred, I say. And no royalties from it yet, right? Right. Well, when we buy up all of them records you gonna git royalties. And that's gonna make all them race record shops sit up and take notice of Gracie Mae Still. And they gonna push all them other records of yourn they got. And you no doubt will become one of the big name colored recording artists. And then we can offer you another five hundred dollars for letting us do all this for you. And by God you'll be sittin' pretty! You can go out and buy you the kind of outfit a star should have. Plenty sequins and yards of red satin.

23   I had done unlocked the screen when I saw I could get some more money out of him. Now I held it wide open while he squeezed through the opening between me and the door. He whipped out another piece of paper and I signed it.

24   He sort of trotted out to the car and slid in beside Traynor, whose head was back against the seat. They swung around in a u-turn in front of the house and then they was gone.

25   J. T. was putting his shirt on when I got back to the bedroom. Yankees beat the Orioles 10–6, he said. I believe I'll drive out to Paschal's pond and go fishing. Wanta go?

26   While I was putting on my pants J. T. was holding the two checks.

27   I'm real proud of a woman that can make cash money without leavin' home, he said. And I said *Umph*. Because we met on the road with me singing in first one little low-life jook after another, making ten dollars a night for myself if I was lucky, and sometimes bringin' home nothing but my life. And J. T. just loved them times. The way I was fast and flashy and always on the go from one town to another. He loved the way my singin' made the dirt farmers cry like babies and the womens shout Honey, hush! But that's mens. They loves any style to which you can get 'em accustomed.

1956

28   My little grandbaby called me one night on the phone: Little Mama, Little Mama, there's a white man on the television singing one of your songs! Turn on channel 5.

29   Lord, if it wasn't Traynor. Still looking half asleep from the neck up, but kind of awake in a nasty way from the waist down. He wasn't doing too bad with my song either, but it wasn't just the song that people in the audience was screeching and screaming over, it was that nasty little jerk he was doing from the waist down.

30   Well, Lord have mercy, I said, listening to him. If I'da closed my eyes, it could have been me. He had followed every turning of my voice, side streets, avenues, red lights, train crossings and all. It give me a chill.

31   Everywhere I went I heard Traynor singing my song, and all the little white girls just eating it up. I never had so many ponytails switched across my line of vision in my life. They was so *proud*. He was a *genius*.

Well, all that year I was trying to lose weight anyway and that and high   32
blood pressure and sugar kept me pretty well occupied. Traynor had
made a smash from a song of mine, I still had seven hundred dollars of
the original one thousand dollars in the bank, and I felt if I could just
bring my weight down, life would be sweet.

1957

I lost ten pounds in 1956. That's what I give myself for Christmas. And   33
J. T. and me and the children and their friends and grandkids of all
description had just finished dinner—over which I had put on nine and
a half of my lost ten—when who should appear at the front door but
Traynor. Little Mama, Little Mama! It's that white man who sings
_____. The children didn't call it my song anymore. Nobody
did. It was funny how that happened. Traynor and the deacon had
bought up all my records, true, but on his record he had put "written by
Gracie Mae Still." But that was just another name on the label, like
"produced by Apex Records."

On the TV he was inclined to dress like the deacon told him. But now   34
he looked presentable.

Merry Christmas, said he.   35

And same to you, Son.   36

I don't know why I called him Son. Well, one way or another they're   37
all our sons. The only requirement is that they be younger than us. But
then again, Traynor seemed to be aging by the minute.

You looks tired, I said. Come on in and have a glass of Christmas   38
cheer.

J. T. ain't never in his life been able to act decent to a white man he   39
wasn't working for, but he poured Traynor a glass of bourbon and water,
then he took all the children and grandkids and friends and whatnot out
to the den. After while I heard Traynor's voice singing the song, coming
from the stereo console. It was just the kind of Christmas present my kids
would consider cute.

I looked at Traynor, complicit. But he looked like it was the last thing   40
in the world he wanted to hear. His head was pitched forward over his
lap, his hands holding his glass and his elbows on his knees.

I done sung that song seem like a million times this year, he said. I sung   41
it on the Grand Ole Opry, I sung it on the Ed Sullivan show. I sung it on
Mike Douglas, I sung it at the Cotton Bowl, the Orange Bowl. I sung it
at Festivals. I sung it at Fairs. I sung it overseas in Rome, Italy, and once
in a submarine *underseas*. I've sung it and sung it, and I'm making forty
thousand dollars a day offa it, and you know what, I don't have the
faintest notion what that song means.

Whatchumean, what do it mean? It mean what it says. All I could   42
think was: These suckers is making forty thousand a *day* offa my song
and now they gonna come back and try to swindle me out of the original
thousand.

43   It's just a song, I said. Cagey. When you fool around with a lot of no count mens you sing a bunch of 'em. I shrugged.

44   Oh, he said. Well. He started brightening up. I just come by to tell you I think you are a great singer.

45   He didn't blush, saying that. Just said it straight out.

46   And I brought you a little Christmas present too. Now you take this little box and you hold it until I drive off. Then you take it outside under that first streetlight back up the street aways in front of that greenhouse. Then you open the box and see . . . Well, just *see*.

47   What had come over this boy, I wondered, holding the box. I looked out the window in time to see another white man come up and get in the car with him and then two more cars full of white mens start out behind him. They was all in long black cars that looked like a funeral procession.

48   Little Mama, Little Mama, what it is? One of my grandkids come running up and started pulling at the box. It was wrapped in gay Christmas paper — the thick, rich kind that's hard to picture folks making just to throw away.

49   J. T. and the rest of the crowd followed me out of the house, up the street to the streetlight and in front of the greenhouse. Nothing was there but somebody's gold-grilled white Cadillac. Brandnew and most distracting. We got to looking at it so till I almost forgot the little box in my hand. While the others were busy making 'miration I carefully took off the paper and ribbon and folded them up and put them in my pants pocket. What should I see but a pair of genuine solid gold caddy keys.

50   Dangling the keys in front of everybody's nose, I unlocked the caddy, motioned for J. T. to git in on the other side, and us didn't come back home for two days.

1960

51   Well, the boy was sure nuff famous by now. He was still a mite shy of twenty but already they was calling him the Emperor of Rock and Roll.

52   Then what should happen but the draft.

53   Well, says J. T. There goes all the Emperor of Rock and Roll business.

54   But even in the army the womens was on him like white on rice. We watched it on the News.

55   *Dear Gracie Mae* [he wrote from Germany],

56   *How you? Fine I hope as this leaves me doing real well. Before I come in the army I was gaining a lot of weight and gitting jittery from making all them dumb movies. But now I exercise and eat right and get plenty of rest. I'm more awake than I been in ten years.*

57   *I wonder if you are writing any more songs?*

58   *Sincerely,*
59   *Traynor*

I wrote him back: 60

Dear Son,   61

   We is all fine in the Lord's good grace and hope this finds you the   62
same. J. T. and me be out all times of the day and night in that car you
give me—which you know you didn't have to do. Oh, and I do appreciate
the mink and the new self-cleaning oven. But if you send anymore stuff to
eat from Germany I'm going to have to open up a store in the neighbor-
hood just to get rid of it. Really, we have more than enough of everything.
The Lord is good to us and we don't know Want.
   Glad to here you is well and gitting your right rest. There ain't nothing 63
like exercising to help that along. J. T. and me work some part of every
day that we don't go fishing in the garden.
   Well, so long Soldier.   64

                                                       Sincerely,   65
                                                       Gracie Mae   66
He wrote: 67

Dear Gracie Mae,   68

   I hope you and J. T. like that automatic power tiller I had one of the   69
stores back home send you. I went through a mountain of catalogs look-
ing for it—I wanted something that even a woman could use.
   I've been thinking about writing some songs of my own but every time   70
I finish one it don't seem to be about nothing I've actually lived myself.
My agent keeps sending me other people's songs but they just sound
mooney. I can hardly git through 'em without gagging.
   Everybody still loves that song of yours. They ask me all the time what   71
do I think it means, really. I mean, they want to know just what I want
to know. Where out of your life did it come from?

                                                       Sincerely,   72
                                                       Traynor   73

1968

   I didn't see the boy for seven years. No. Eight. Because just about   74
everybody was dead when I saw him again. Malcolm X, King, the
president and his brother, and even J. T. J. T. died of a head cold. It just
settled in his head like a block of ice, he said, and nothing we did moved
it until one day he just leaned out the bed and died.
   His good friend Horace helped me put him away, and then about a   75
year later Horace and me started going together. We was sitting out on
the front porch swing one summer night, dusk-dark, and I saw this great
procession of lights winding to a stop.
   Holy Toledo! said Horace. (He's got a real sexy voice like Ray   76
Charles.) Look *at* it. He meant the long line of flashy cars and the white
men in white summer suits jumping out on the drivers' sides and standing
at attention. With wings they could pass for angels, with hoods they
could be the Klan.

77   Traynor comes waddling up the walk.

78   And suddenly I know what it is he could pass for. An Arab like the ones you see in storybooks. Plump and soft and with never a care about weight. Because with so much money, who cares? Traynor is almost dressed like someone from a storybook too. He has on, I swear, about ten necklaces. Two sets of bracelets on his arms, at least one ring on every finger, and some kind of shining buckles on his shoes, so that when he walks you get a quite a few twinkling lights.

79   Gracie Mae, he says, coming up to give me a hug. J. T.

80   I explain that J. T. passed. That this is Horace.

81   Horace, he says, puzzled but polite, sort of rocking back on his heels, Horace.

82   That's it for Horace. He goes in the house and don't come back.

83   Looks like you and me is gained a few, I say.

84   He laughs. The first time I ever heard him laugh. It don't sound much like a laugh and I can't swear that it's better than no laugh a'tall.

85   He's gitting fat for sure, but he's still slim compared to me. I'll never see three hundred pounds again and I've just about said (excuse me) fuck it. I got to thinking about it one day an' I thought: aside from the fact that they say it's unhealthy, my fat ain't never been no trouble. Mens always have loved me. My kids ain't never complained. Plus they's fat. And fat like I is I looks distinguished. You see me coming and know somebody's *there*.

86   Gracie Mae, he says, I've come with a personal invitation to you to my house tomorrow for dinner. He laughed. What did it sound like? I couldn't place it. See them men out there? he asked me. I'm sick and tired of eating with them. They don't never have nothing to talk about. That's why I eat so much. But if you come to dinner tomorrow we can talk about the old days. You can tell me about that farm I bought you.

87   I sold it, I said.

88   You did?

89   Yeah, I said, I did. Just cause I said I liked to exercise by working in a garden didn't mean I wanted five hundred acres! Anyhow, I'm a city girl now. Raised in the country it's true. Dirt poor—the whole bit—but that's all behind me now.

90   Oh well, he said, I didn't mean to offend you.

91   We sat a few minutes listening to the crickets.

92   Then he said: You wrote that song while you was still on the farm, didn't you, or was it right after you left?

93   You had somebody spying on me? I asked.

94   You and Bessie Smith got into a fight over it once, he said.

95   You *is* been spying on me!

96   But I don't know what the fight was about, he said. Just like I don't know what happened to your second husband. Your first one died in the Texas electric chair. Did you know that? Your third one beat you up,

stole your touring costumes and your car and retired with a chorine to Tuskegee. He laughed. He's still there.

I had been mad, but suddenly I calmed down. Traynor was talking very dreamily. It was dark but seems like I could tell his eyes weren't right. It was like some*thing* was sitting there talking to me but not necessarily with a person behind it.   97

You gave up on marrying and seem happier for it. He laughed again. I married but it never went like it was supposed to. I never could squeeze any of my own life either into it or out of it. It was like singing somebody else's record. I copied the way it was sposed to be *exactly* but I never had a clue what marriage meant.   98

I bought her a diamond ring big as your fist. I bought her clothes. I built her a mansion. But right away she didn't want the boys to stay there. Said they smoked up the bottom floor. Hell, there were *five* floors.   99

No need to grieve, I said. No need to. Plenty more where she come from.   100

He perked up. That's part of what that song means, ain't it? No need to grieve. Whatever it is, there's plenty more down the line.   101

I never really believed that way back when I wrote that song, I said. It was all bluffing then. The trick is to live long enough to put your young bluffs to use. Now if I was to sing that song today I'd tear it up. 'Cause I done lived long enough to know it's *true*. Them words could hold me up.   102

I ain't lived that long, he said.   103

Look like you on your way, I said. I don't know why, but the boy seemed to need some encouraging. And I don't know, seem like one way or another you talk to rich white folks and you end up reassuring *them*. But what the hell, by now I feel something for the boy. I wouldn't be in his bed all alone in the middle of the night for nothing. Couldn't be nothing worse than being famous the world over for something you don't even understand. That's what I tried to tell Bessie. She wanted that same song. Overheard me practicing it one day, said, with her hands on her hips: Gracie Mae, I'ma sing your song tonight. I *likes* it.   104

Your lips be too swole to sing, I said. She was mean and she was strong, but I trounced her.   105

Ain't you famous enough with your own stuff? I said. Leave mine alone. Later on, she thanked me. By then she was Miss Bessie Smith to the World, and I was still Miss Gracie Mae Nobody from Notasulga.   106

The next day all these limousines arrived to pick me up. Five cars and twelve bodyguards. Horace picked that morning to start painting the kitchen.   107

Don't paint the kitchen, fool, I said. The only reason that dumb boy of ours is going to show me his mansion is because he intends to present us with a new house.   108

What you gonna do with it? he asked me, standing there in his shirtsleeves stirring the paint.   109

110   Sell it. Give it to the children. Live in it on weekends. It don't matter what I do. He sure don't care.

111   Horace just stood there shaking his head. Mama you sure looks *good*, he says. Wake me up when you git back.

112   *Fool*, I say, and pat my wig in front of the mirror.

113   The boy's house is something else. First you come to this mountain, and then you commence to drive and drive up this road that's lined with magnolias. Do magnolias grow on mountains? I was wondering. And you come to lakes and you come to ponds and you come to deer and you come up on some sheep. And I figure these two is sposed to represent England and Wales. Or something out of Europe. And you just keep on coming to stuff. And it's all pretty. Only the man driving my car don't look at nothing but the road. Fool. And then *finally*, after all this time, you begin to go up the driveway. And there's more magnolias—only they're not in such good shape. It's sort of cool up this high and I don't think they're gonna make it. And then I see this building that looks like if it had a name it would be The Tara Hotel. Columns and steps and outdoor chandeliers and rocking chairs. Rocking chairs? Well, and there's the boy on the steps dressed in a dark green satin jacket like you see folks wearing on TV late at night, and he looks sort of like a fat Dracula with all that house rising behind him, and standing beside him there's this little white vision of loveliness that he introduces as his wife.

114   He's nervous when he introduces us and he says to her: This is Gracie Mae Still, I want you to know me. I mean . . . and she gives him a look that would fry meat.

115   Won't you come in, Gracie Mae, she says, and that's the last I see of her.

116   He fishes around for something to say or do and decides to escort me to the kitchen. We go through the entry and the parlor and the breakfast room and the dining room and the servants' passage and finally get there. The first thing I notice is that, altogether, there are five stoves. He looks about to introduce me to one.

117   Wait a minute, I say. Kitchens don't do nothing for me. Let's go sit on the front porch.

118   Well, we hike back and we sit in the rocking chairs rocking until dinner.

119   Gracie Mae, he says down the table, taking a piece of fried chicken from the woman standing over him, I got a little surprise for you.

120   It's a house, ain't it? I ask, spearing a chitlin.

121   You're getting *spoiled*, he says. And the way he says *spoiled* sounds funny. He slurs it. It sounds like his tongue is too thick for his mouth. Just that quick he's finished the chicken and is now eating chitlins *and* a pork chop. *Me* spoiled, I'm thinking.

122   I already got a house. Horace is right this minute painting the kitchen. I bought that house. My kids feel comfortable in that house.

But this one I bought you is just like mine. Only a little smaller. 123

I still don't need no house. And anyway who would clean it? 124

He looks surprised. 125

Really, I think, some peoples advance *so* slowly. 126

I hadn't thought of that. But what the hell, I'll get you somebody to 127
live in.

I don't want other folks living 'round me. Makes me nervous. 128

You *don't*? It *do*? 129

What I want to wake up and see folks I don't even know for? 130

He just sits there downtable staring at me. Some of that feeling is in the 131
song, ain't it? Not the words, the *feeling*. What I want to wake up and see
folks I don't even know for? But I see twenty folks a day I don't even
know, including my wife.

This food wouldn't be bad to wake up to though, I said. The boy had 132
found the genius of corn bread.

He looked at me real hard. He laughed. Short. They want what you got 133
but they don't want you. They want what I got only it ain't mine. That's
what makes 'em so hungry for me when I sing. They getting the flavor of
something but they ain't getting the thing itself. They like a pack of
hound dogs trying to gobble up a scent.

You talking 'bout your fans? 134

Right. Right. He says. 135

Don't worry 'bout your fans, I say. They don't know their asses from 136
a hole in the ground. I doubt there's a honest one in the bunch.

That's the point. Dammit, that's the point! He hits the table with his 137
fist. It's so solid it don't even quiver. You need a honest audience! You
can't have folks that's just gonna lie right back to you.

Yeah, I say, it was small compared to yours, but I had one. It would 138
have been worth my life to try to sing 'em somebody else's stuff that I
didn't know nothing about.

He must have pressed a buzzer under the table. One of his flunkies 139
zombies up.

Git Johnny Carson, he says. 140

On the phone? asks the zombie. 141

On the phone, says Traynor, what you think I mean, git him offa the 142
front porch? Move your ass.

So two weeks later we's on the Johnny Carson show. 143

Traynor is all corseted down nice and looks a little bit fat but mostly 144
good. And all the women that grew up on him and my song squeal and
squeal. Traynor says: The lady who wrote my first hit record is here with
us tonight, and she's agreed to sing it for all of us, just like she sung it
forty-five years ago. Ladies and Gentlemen, the great Gracie Mae Still!

Well, I had tried to lose a couple of pounds my own self, but failing 145
that I had me a very big dress made. So I sort of rolls over next to

Traynor, who is dwarfted by me, so that when he puts his arm around back of me to try to hug me it looks funny to the audience and they laugh.

146   I can see this pisses him off. But I smile out there at 'em. Imagine squealing for twenty years and not knowing why you're squealing? No more sense of endings and beginnings than hogs.

147   It don't matter, Son, I say. Don't fret none over me.

148   I commence to sing. And I sound—wonderful. Being able to sing good ain't all about having a good singing voice a'tall. A good singing voice helps. But when you come up in the Hard Shell Baptist church like I did you understand early that the fellow that sings is the singer. Them that waits for programs and arrangements and letters from home is just good voices occupying body space.

149   So there I am singing my own song, my own way. And I give it all I got and enjoy every minute of it. When I finish Traynor is standing up clapping and clapping and beaming at first me and then the audience like I'm his mama for true. The audience claps politely for about two seconds.

150   Traynor looks disgusted.

151   He comes over and tries to hug me again. The audience laughs.

152   Johnny Carson looks at us like we both weird.

153   Traynor is mad as hell. He's supposed to sing something called a love ballad. But instead he takes the mike, turns to me and says: Now see if my imitation still holds up. He goes into the same song, *our song*, I think, looking out at his flaky audience. And he sings it just the way he always did. My voice, my tone, my inflection, everything. But he forgets a couple of lines. Even before he's finished the matronly squeals begin.

154   He sits down next to me looking whipped.

155   It don't matter, Son, I say, patting his hand. You don't even know those people. Try to make the people you know happy.

156   Is that in the song? he asks.

157   Maybe. I say.

1977

158   For a few years I hear from him, then nothing. But trying to lose weight takes all the attention I got to spare. I finally faced up to the fact that my fat is the hurt I don't admit, not even to myself, and that I been trying to bury it from the day I was born. But also when you git real old, to tell the truth, it ain't as pleasant. It gits lumpy and slack. Yuck. So one day I said to Horace, I'ma git this shit offa me.

159   And he fell in with the program like he always try to do and Lord such a procession of salads and cottage cheese and fruit juice!

160   One night I dreamed Traynor had split up with his fifteenth wife. He said: *You meet 'em for no reason. You date 'em for no reason. You marry 'em for no reason. I do it all but I swear it's just like somebody else doing it. I feel like I can't remember Life.*

161   The boy's in trouble, I said to Horace.

162   You've always said that, he said.

I have? 163

Yeah. You always said he looked asleep. You can't sleep through life 164
if you wants to live it.

You not such a fool after all, I said, pushing myself up with my cane 165
and hobbling over to where he was. Let me sit down on your lap, I said,
while this salad I ate takes effect.

In the morning we heard Traynor was dead. Some said fat, some said 166
heart, some said alcohol, some said drugs. One of the children called
from Detroit. Them dumb fans of his is on a crying rampage, she said.
You just ought to turn on the t.v.

But I didn't want to see 'em. They was crying and crying and didn't 167
even know what they was crying for. One day this is going to be a pitiful
country, I thought.

❏ Questions for Discussion

1. What has Gracie Mae Still's singing experience been like? How does it compare to Traynor's experience?

2. Why does Traynor fail to understand the meaning of Gracie Mae's song? Why does he give her gifts, write to her, and keep renewing his contact with her?

3. What do Traynor's letters reveal about him—his songs, his life, and his attraction to Gracie Mae?

4. What does Gracie Mae mean by "that fellow that sings is the singer"?

5. Why does Gracie Mae advise Traynor, "Try to make the people you know happy"? What has following this advice done for her?

6. Explain the significance of Gracie Mae's final remark: "One day this is going to be a pitiful country."

In Search of Our Mothers' Gardens

I described her own nature and temperament. Told how they
needed a larger life for their expression. . . . I pointed out that in
lieu of proper channels, her emotions had overflowed into paths
that dissipated them. I talked, beautifully I thought, about an art
that would be born, an art that would open the way for women the
likes of her. I asked her to hope, and build up an inner life against
the coming of that day. . . . I sang, with a strange quiver in my
voice, a promise song.

—*Jean Toomer, "Avey,"*
CANE

1   The poet speaking to a prostitute who falls asleep while he's talking—

2   When the poet Jean Toomer walked through the South in the early twenties, he discovered a curious thing: black women whose spirituality was so intense, so deep, so *unconscious,* that they were themselves unaware of the richness they held. They stumbled blindly through their lives; creatures so abused and mutilated in body, so dimmed and confused by pain, that they considered themselves unworthy even of hope. In the selfless abstractions their bodies became to the men who used them, they became more than "sexual objects," more even than mere women: they became "Saints." Instead of being perceived as whole persons, their bodies became shrines: what was thought to be their minds became temples suitable for worship. These crazy Saints stared out at the world, wildly, like lunatics—or quietly, like suicides; and the "God" that was in their gaze was as mute as a great stone.

3   Who were these Saints? These crazy, loony, pitiful women?

4   Some of them, without a doubt, were our mothers and grandmothers.

5   In the still heat of the post-Reconstruction South, this is how they seemed to Jean Toomer: exquisite butterflies trapped in an evil honey, toiling away their lives in an era, a century, that did not acknowledge them, except as "the *mule* of the world." They dreamed dreams that no one knew—not even themselves, in any coherent fashion—and saw visions no one could understand. They wandered or sat about the countryside crooning lullabies to ghosts, and drawing the mother of Christ in charcoal on courthouse walls.

6   They forced their minds to desert their bodies and their striving spirits sought to rise, like frail whirlwinds from the hard red clay. And when those frail whirlwinds fell, in scattered particles, upon the ground, no one mourned. Instead, men lit candles to celebrate the emptiness that remained, as people do who enter a beautiful but vacant space to resurrect a God.

7   Our mothers and grandmothers, some of them: moving to music not yet written. And they waited.

8   They waited for a day when the unknown thing that was in them would be made known; but guessed, somehow in their darkness, that on the day of their revelation they would be long dead. Therefore to Toomer they walked, and even ran, in slow motion. For they were going nowhere immediate, and the future was not yet within their grasp. And men took our mothers and grandmothers, "but got no pleasure from it." So complex was their passion and their calm.

9   To Toomer, they lay vacant and fallow as autumn fields, with harvest time never in sight: and he saw them enter loveless marriages, without joy; and become prostitutes, without resistance; and become mothers of children, without fulfillment.

10   For these grandmothers and mothers of ours were not Saints, but Artists; driven to a numb and bleeding madness by the springs of creativity in them for which there was no release. They were Creators,

who lived lives of spiritual waste, because they were so rich in spiritual-ity—which is the basis of Art—that the strain of enduring their unused and unwanted talent drove them insane. Throwing away this spirituality was their pathetic attempt to lighten the soul to a weight their work-worn, sexually abused bodies could bear.

What did it mean for a black woman to be an artist in our grandmoth-ers' time? In our great-grandmothers' day? It is a question with an answer cruel enough to stop the blood. 11

Did you have a genius of a great-great-grandmother who died under some ignorant and depraved white overseer's lash? Or was she required to bake biscuits for a lazy backwater tramp, when she cried out in her soul to paint watercolors of sunsets, or the rain falling on the green and peaceful pasturelands? Or was her body broken and forced to bear children (who were more often than not sold away from her)—eight, ten, fifteen, twenty children—when her one joy was the thought of modeling heroic figures of rebellion, in stone or clay? 12

How was the creativity of the black woman kept alive, year after year and century after century, when for most of the years black people have been in America, it was a punishable crime for a black person to read or write? And the freedom to paint, to sculpt, to expand the mind with action did not exist. Consider, if you can bear to imagine it, what might have been the result if singing, too, had been forbidden by law. Listen to the voices of Bessie Smith, Billie Holiday, Nina Simone, Roberta Flack, and Aretha Franklin, among others, and imagine those voices muzzled for life. Then you may begin to comprehend the lives of our "crazy," "Sainted" mothers and grandmothers. The agony of the lives of women who might have been Poets, Novelists, Essayists, and Short-Story Writers (over a period of centuries) who died with their great gifts stifled within them. 13

And, if this were the end of the story, we would have cause to cry out in my paraphrase of Okot p'Bitek's great poem: 14

> O, my clanswomen
> Let us all cry together!
> Come,
> Let us mourn the death of our mother,
> The death of a Queen
> The ash that was produced
> By a great fire!
> O, this homestead is utterly dead
> Close the gates
> With *lacari* thorns,
> For our mother
> The creator of the Stool is lost!
> And all the young women
> Have perished in the wilderness!

But this is not the end of the story, for all the young women—our mothers and grandmothers, *ourselves*—have not perished in the 15 wilderness. And if we ask ourselves why, and search for and find the answer, we will know beyond all efforts to erase it from our minds, just exactly who, and of what, we black American women are.

16   One example, perhaps the most pathetic, most misunderstood one, can provide a backdrop for our mothers' work: Phillis Wheatley, a slave in the 1700s.

17   Virginia Woolf, in her book *A Room of One's Own,* wrote that in order for a woman to write fiction she must have two things, certainly: a room of her own (with key and lock) and enough money to support herself.

18   What then are we to make of Phillis Wheatley, a slave, who owned not even herself? This sickly, frail black girl who required a servant of her own at times—her health was so precarious—and who, had she been white, would have been easily considered the intellectual superior of all the women and most of the men in the society of her day.

19   Virginia Woolf wrote further, speaking of course not of our Phillis, that "any woman born with a great gift in the sixteenth century [insert "eighteenth century," insert "black woman," insert "born or made a slave"] would certainly have gone crazed, shot herself, or ended her days in some lonely cottage outside the village, half witch, half wizard [insert "Saint,"], feared and mocked at. For it needs little skill and psychology to be sure that a highly gifted girl who had tried to use her gift for poetry would have been so thwarted and hindered by contrary instincts [add "chains, guns, the lash, the ownership of one's body by someone else, submission to an alien religion"], that she must have lost her health and sanity to a certainty."

20   The key words, as they relate to Phillis, are "contrary instincts." For when we read the poetry of Phillis Wheatley—as when we read the novels of Nella Larsen or the oddly false-sounding autobiography of that freest of all black women writers, Zora Hurston—evidence of "contrary instincts" is everywhere. Her loyalties were completely divided, as was, without question, her mind.

21   But how could this be otherwise? Captured at seven, a slave of wealthy, doting whites who instilled in her the "savagery" of the Africa they "rescued" her from . . . one wonders if she was even able to remember her homeland as she had known it, or as it really was.

22   Yet, because she did try to use her gift for poetry in a world that made her a slave, she was "so thwarted and hindered by . . . contrary instincts, that she . . . lost her health. . . ." In the last years of her brief life, burdened not only with the need to express her gift but also with a penniless, friendless "freedom" and several small children for whom she was forced to do strenuous work to feed, she lost her health, certainly. Suffering from malnutrition and neglect and who knows what mental agonies, Phillis Wheatley died.

23   So torn by "contrary instincts" was black, kidnapped, enslaved Phillis that her description of "the Goddess"—as she poetically called the

Liberty she did not have—is ironically, cruelly humorous. And, in fact, has held Phillis up to ridicule for more than a century. It is usually read prior to hanging Phillis's memory as that of a fool. She wrote:

> The Goddess comes, she moves divinely fair,
> Olive and laurel binds her *golden* hair.
> Wherever shines this native of the skies,
> Unnumber'd charms and recent graces rise. [My italics]

It is obvious that Phillis, the slave, combed the "Goddess's" hair every 24
morning; prior, perhaps, to bringing in the milk, or fixing her mistress's lunch. She took her imagery from the one thing she saw elevated above all others.

With the benefit of hindsight we ask, "How could she?" 25

But at last, Phillis, we understand. No more snickering when your stiff, 26
struggling, ambivalent lines are forced on us. We know now that you were not an idiot or a traitor; only a sickly little black girl, snatched from your home and country and made a slave; a woman who still struggled to sing the song that was your gift, although in a land of barbarians who praised you for your bewildered tongue. It is not so much what you sang, as that you kept alive, in so many of our ancestors, *the notion of song.*

Black women are called, in the folklore that so aptly identifies one's 27
status in society, "the *mule* of the world," because we have been handed the burdens that everyone else—*everyone* else—refused to carry. We have also been called "Matriarchs," "Superwomen," and "Mean and Evil Bitches." Not to mention "Castraters" and "Sapphire's Mama." When we have pleaded for understanding, our character has been distorted; when we have asked for simple caring, we have been handed empty inspirational appellations, then stuck in the farthest corner. When we have asked for love, we have been given children. In short, even our plainer gifts, our labors of fidelity and love, have been knocked down our throats. To be an artist and a black woman, even today, lowers our status in many respects, rather than raises it: and yet, artists we will be.

Therefore we must fearlessly pull out of ourselves and look at and 28
identify with our lives the living creativity some of our great-grandmothers were not allowed to know. I stress *some* of them because it is well known that the majority of our great-grandmothers knew, even without "knowing" it, the reality of their spirituality, even if they didn't recognize it beyond what happened in the singing at church—and they never had any intention of giving it up.

How they did it—those millions of black women who were not Phillis 29
Wheatley, or Lucy Terry or Frances Harper or Zora Hurston or Nella Larsen or Bessie Smith; or Elizabeth Catlett, or Katherine Dunham, either—brings me to the title of this essay, "In Search of Our Mothers' Gardens," which is a personal account that is yet shared, in its theme and

its meaning, by all of us. I found, while thinking about the far-reaching world of the creative black woman, that often the truest answer to a question that really matters can be found very close.

30   In the late 1920s my mother ran away from home to marry my father. Marriage, if not running away, was expected of seventeen-year-old girls. By the time she was twenty, she had two children and was pregnant with a third. Five children later, I was born. And this is how I came to know my mother: she seemed a large, soft, loving-eyed woman who was rarely impatient in our home. Her quick, violent temper was on view only a few times a year, when she battled with the white landlord who had the misfortune to suggest to her that her children did not need to go to school.

31   She made all the clothes we wore, even my brothers' overalls. She made all the towels and sheets we used. She spent the summers canning vegetables and fruits. She spent the winter evenings making quilts enough to cover all our beds.

32   During the "working" day, she labored beside—not behind—my father in the fields. Her day began before sunup, and did not end until late at night. There was never a moment for her to sit down, undisturbed, to unravel her own private thoughts; never a time free from interruption—by work or the noisy inquiries of her many children. And yet, it is to my mother—and all our mothers who were not famous—that I went in search of the secret of what has fed that muzzled and often mutilated, but vibrant, creative spirit that the black woman has inherited, and that pops out in wild and unlikely places to this day.

33   But when, you will ask, did my overworked mother have time to know or care about feeding the creative spirit?

34   The answer is so simple that many of us have spent years discovering it. We have constantly looked high, when we should have looked high—and low.

35   For example: in the Smithsonian Institution in Washington, D.C., there hangs a quilt unlike any other in the world. In fanciful, inspired, and yet simple and identifiable figures, it portrays the story of the Crucifixion. It is considered rare, beyond price. Though it follows no known pattern of quilt-making, and though it is made of bits and pieces of worthless rags, it is obviously the work of a person of powerful imagination and deep spiritual feeling. Below this quilt I saw a note that says it was made by "an anonymous Black woman in Alabama, a hundred years ago."

36   If we could locate this "anonymous" black woman from Alabama, she would turn out to be one of our grandmothers—an artist who left her mark in the only materials she could afford, and in the only medium her position in society allowed her to use.

37   As Virginia Woolf wrote further, in *A Room of One's Own:*

Yet genius of a sort must have existed among women as it must have existed among the working class. [Change this to "slaves" and "the wives and daughters of sharecroppers."] Now and again an Emily Brontë or a Robert Burns [change this to "a Zora Hurston or a Richard Wright"] blazes out and proves its presence. But certainly it never got itself on to paper. When, however, one reads of a witch being ducked, of a woman possessed by devils [or "Sainthood"], of a wise woman selling herbs [our root workers], or even a very remarkable man who had a mother, then I think we are on the track of a lost novelist, a suppressed poet, of some mute and inglorious Jane Austen. . . . Indeed, I would venture to guess that Anon, who wrote so may poems without signing them, was often a woman. . . .

And so our mothers and grandmothers have, more often than not 38 anonymously, handed on the creative spark, the seed of the flower they themselves never hoped to see; or like a sealed letter they could not plainly read.

And so it is, certainly, with my own mother. Unlike "Ma" Rainey's 39 songs, which retained their creator's name even while blasting forth from Bessie Smith's mouth, no song or poem will bear my mother's name. Yet so many of the stories that I write, that we all write, are my mother's stories. Only recently did I fully realize this: that through years of listening to my mother's stories of her life, I have absorbed not only the stories themselves, but something of the manner in which she spoke, something of the urgency that involves the knowledge that her stories—like her life—must be recorded. It is probably for this reason that so much of what I have written is about characters whose counterparts in real life are so much older than I am.

But the telling of these stories, which came from my mother's lips as 40 naturally as breathing, was not the only way my mother showed herself as an artist. For stories, too, were subject to being distracted, to dying without conclusion. Dinners must be started, and cotton must be gathered before the big rains. The artist that was and is my mother showed itself to me only after many years. This is what I finally noticed:

Like Mem, a character in *The Third Life of Grange Copeland,* my 41 mother adorned with flowers whatever shabby house we were forced to live in. And not just your typical straggly country stand of zinnias, either. She planted ambitious gardens—and still does—with over fifty different varieties of plants that bloom profusely from early March until late November. Before she left home for the fields, she watered her flowers, chopped up the grass, and laid out new beds. When she returned from the fields she might divide clumps of bulbs, dig a cold pit, uproot and replant roses, or prune branches from her taller bushes or trees—until night came and it was too dark to see.

Whatever she planted grew as if by magic, and her fame as a grower of 42 flowers spread over three counties. Because of her creativity with her flowers, even my memories of poverty are seen through a screen of blooms—sunflowers, petunias, roses, dahlias, forsythia, spirea, delphiniums, verbena . . . and on and on.

43   And I remember people coming to my mother's yard to be given cuttings from her flowers; I hear again the praise showered on her because whatever rocky soil she landed on, she turned into a garden. A garden so brilliant with colors, so original in its design, so magnificent with life and creativity, that to this day people drive by our house in Georgia—perfect strangers and imperfect strangers—and ask to stand or walk among my mother's art.

44   I notice that it is only when my mother is working in her flowers that she is radiant, almost to the point of being invisible—except as Creator: hand and eye. She is involved in work her soul must have. Ordering the universe in the image of her personal conception of Beauty.

45   Her face, as she prepares the art that is her gift, is a legacy of respect she leaves to me, for all that illuminates and cherishes life. She has handed down respect for the possibilities—and the will to grasp them.

46   For her, so hindered and intruded upon in so many ways, being an artist has still been a daily part of her life. This ability to hold on, even in very simple ways, is work black women have done for a very long time.

47   This poem is not enough, but it is something, for the woman who literally covered the holes in our walls with sunflowers:

          They were women then
          My mama's generation
          Husky of voice—Stout of
          Step
          With fists as well as
          Hands
          How they battered down
          Doors
          And ironed
          Starched white
          Shirts
          How they led
          Armies
          Headragged Generals
          Across mined
          Fields
          Booby-trapped
          Kitchens
          To discover books
          Desks
          A place for us

How they knew what we
Must know
Without knowing a page
Of it
Themselves.

Guided by my heritage of a love of beauty and a respect for strength   48
—in search of my mother's garden, I found my own.

And perhaps in Africa over two hundred years ago, there was just such   49
a mother; perhaps she painted vivid and daring decorations in oranges
and yellows and greens on the walls of her hut; perhaps she sang—in a
voice like Roberta Flack's—*sweetly* over the compounds of her village;
perhaps she wove the most stunning mats or told the most ingenious
stories of all the village storytellers. Perhaps she was herself a poet—
though only her daughter's name is signed to the poems that we know.

Perhaps Phillis Wheatley's mother was also an artist.   50

Perhaps in more than Phillis Wheatley's biological life is her mother's   51
signature made clear.

❏ Questions for Discussion

1. What does Walker mean by "spirituality . . . is the basis of art"?

2. What unspeakable sufferings did Southern black women endure? Why is the Southern black woman sometimes referred to as "the mule of the world"?

3. What unusual means of creative expression did black women find when their artistry was thwarted?

4. What did creating gardens do for Walker's mother?

Women's Blues:
Toni Cade Bambara and Alice Walker[1]

by Keith E. Byerman

"1955" develops another aspect of the relationship of art and culture. Here we have the parallel developments of a legendary blues singer and a successful white singer who tries to understand the meaning of her music. The moral of the story is rather obvious: the white man, patterned after Elvis Presley, gains great success by singing her songs, but he fails to find either meaning or happiness in life. She, on the other hand, has much less but lives a fully human life and is around at the end to comment on his death and the superficiality of society.

[1] From Keith E. Byerman, *Fingering the Jagged Grain: Tradition and Form in Recent Black Fiction* (Athens: University of Georgia Press, 1985), 159–61.

What makes the story more than a simplistic allegory is the quest for the meaning of the song. From beginning to end, Traynor is obsessed with finding out what Gracie Mae Still's song means. Even though he sings it well enough to launch a meteoric career, he believes that it contains a secret only she can reveal. The form of the story is a series of repetitions of this quest. The dating of the various sections shows how Traynor changes externally but never with regard to the song. In each, he pays his respects to Gracie Mae, offers her some grand gift, and then renews his questioning. The first meeting after his initial celebrity establishes the pattern.

> I done sung that song seem like a million times this year, he said. I sung it on the Grand Ole Opry, I sung it on the Ed Sullivan show, I sung it on Mike Douglas, I sung it at the Cotton Bowl. . . . I don't have the faintest notion of what that song means. Watchumean, what do it mean? It mean what it says. All I could think was: These suckers is making forty thousand a *day* offa my song and now they gonna come back and try to swindle me out of the original thousand. It's just a song, I said. Cagey. When you fool around with a lot of no count mens you sing a bunch of 'em. I shrugged. (*Good Woman*, 8)

He then gives her a new white Cadillac as a Christmas gift.

What Traynor never understands, because he cannot, is that the song grows out of the concrete history of this particular black woman and her community. It thus expresses a reality that cannot be purchased or investigated by himself or even articulated by Gracie Mae herself except by singing. The central problem is history:

> Now if I was to sing that song today I'd tear it up. 'Cause I done lived long enough to know it's *true*. Them words could hold me up.
> I ain't lived that long, he said. (*Good Woman*, 14)

Because he has not lived the life, he cannot truly sing the song. And this absence robs him of the enjoyment of his success. The relationship between the two is dialectical: the success came initially because he could effectively bring to the popular culture an inherently dishonest version of the song because he performed it with its history erased. But that very success, with its forms empty of content, became his history and thus made it even more difficult to comprehend the meaning.

Thus, the story becomes a comment on the relative natures and values of popular and folk art forms. The popular ones empty out the content that is the history: even Gracie Mae's children and grandchildren talk of the song as though it were Traynor's. In this manner the forms become meaningless but infinitely communicable. Thus, Gracie Mae's name appears on millions of copies of the record, but the meaning of her act is lost. On the other hand, the folk art maintains an organic connection between form and content, but for this reason, the art cannot be mass produced. It functions within history, and its meaning is subject to that history. Gracie Mae cannot tell Traynor what the song absolutely means because that meaning changes with each experience of her life, including her dealings with him. His death suggests the death-wish inherent in the drive for control and empty forms, while her continued life and energy constitute an appreciation of the vitality of the "dying" folk arts. . . .

Work Cited

Walker, Alice. *You Can't Keep a Good Woman Down*. New York: Harcourt, Brace, Jovanovich, 1981.

Alice Walker: the Black Woman as Wayward[1]

by Barbara Christian

Walker is drawn to the integral and economical process of quilt making as a model for her own craft, for through it, one can create out of seemingly disparate, everyday materials patterns of clarity, imagination, and beauty. Two of her works especially emphasize the idea of this process: her classic essay "In Search of Our Mothers' Gardens" and her short story "Everyday Use." Each piece complements the other and articulates the precise meaning of the quilt as idea and process for this writer.

In "In Search of Our Mothers' Gardens," Walker directly asks the question that every writer must: From whence do I, as a writer, come? What is my tradition? In pursuing the question she focuses most intensely on her female heritage, in itself a point of departure from the route most writers have taken. Walker traces the images of black women in the literature as well as those few who were able to be writers. However, as significant as the tracing of that literary history is, Walker's major insight in the essay is her illumination of the creative legacy of "ordinary" black women of the South, a focus that complements but finally transcends literary history. In her insistence on honesty, on examining the roots of *her own* creativity, she invokes not so much the literature of black women, which was probably unknown to her as a budding child writer, but the creativity of her mother, her grandmother, the women around her.

What did some slave women or black women of this century do with the creativity that might have, in a less restrictive society, expressed itself in paint, words, clay? Walker reflects on a truth so obvious it is seldom acknowledged: They used the few media left them by a society that

[1] From Barbara Christian, *Black Feminist Criticism: Perspectives on Black Women Writers* (New York: Pergamon Press, 1985), 85–87.

labeled them lowly, menial. Some, like Walker's mother, expressed it in the growing of magnificent gardens; some in cooking; others in quilts of imagination and passion like the one Walker saw at the Smithsonian Institution. Walker's description of that quilt's impact on her brings together essential elements of her more recent work: the theme of the black woman's creativity, her transformation, despite opposition, of the bits and pieces allowed her by society into a work of functional beauty.

But Walker does not merely acknowledge quilts (or the art black women created out of "low" media) as high art, a tendency now fostered by many women who have discovered the works of their maternal ancestors. She is also impressed by their *functional* beauty and by the process that produced them. Her short story "Everyday Use" is in some ways a conclusion in fiction to her essay. Just as she juxtaposed the history of black women writers with the creative legacy of ordinary black women, so she complemented her own essay, a search for the roots of her own creativity, with a story that embodies the idea itself.

In "Everyday Use," Walker again scrutinized a popular premise of the times. The story, which is dedicated to "your grandmama," is about the use and misuse of the concept of heritage. The mother of two daughters, one selfish and stylish, the other scarred and caring, passes on to us its true definition. Dee, the sister who has always despised the backward ways of her southern rural family, comes back to visit her old home. She has returned to her black roots because now they are fashionable. So she glibly delights in the artifacts of her heritage: the rough benches her father made, the handmade butter churn that she intends to use for a decorative centerpiece, the quilts made by her grandma Dee after whom she was named—the *things* that have been passed on. Ironically, in keeping with the times, Dee has changed her name to Wangero, denying the existence of her namesake, even as she covets the quilts she made.

On the other hand, her sister Maggie is not aware of the word *heritage*. But she loves her grandma and cherishes her memory in the quilts she made. Maggie has accepted the *spirit* that was passed on to her. The contrast between the two sisters is aptly summarized in Dee's focal line in the story: " 'Maggie can't appreciate these quilts!' she said. 'She'd probably be backward enough to put them to everyday use.' " Which her mother counters with: "She can always make some more. Maggie knows how to quilt."

The mother affirms the functional nature of their heritage and insists that it must continually be renewed rather than fixed in the past. The mother's succinct phrasing of the meaning of *heritage* is underscored by Dee's lack of knowledge about the bits and pieces that make up these quilts, the process of quilting that Maggie knows. For Maggie appreciates the people who made them, while Dee can only possess the "priceless" products. Dee's final words, ironically, exemplify her misuse of the concept of heritage, of what is passed on:

"What don't I understand?" I wanted to know.

"Your heritage," she said. And then she turned to Maggie, kissed her and said, "You ought to try to make something of yourself, too, Maggie. It's a new day for us. But from the way you and mama still live you'd never know it."

In critically analyzing the uses of the concept of heritage, Walker arrived at important distinctions. As an abstraction rather than a living idea, its misuse can subordinate people to artifact, can elevate culture above the community. And because she used, as the artifact, quilts that were made by southern black women, she focused attention on those supposedly backward folk who never heard the word heritage but fashioned a functional tradition out of little matter and much spirit.

In "Everyday Use," the mother, seemingly in a fit of contrariness, snatches the beautiful quilts out of the hands of the "black" Wangero and gives them to the "backward" Maggie. This story is one of eleven in Walker's first collection of short stories, *In Love and Trouble*. Though written over a period of some five years, the volume is unified by two of Walker's most persistent characteristics: her use of a southern black woman character as the protagonist, and that character's insistence on challenging convention, on being herself, sometimes in spite of herself. . . .

Patches: Quilts and Community in Alice Walker's "Everyday Use"[1]

by Houston A. Baker, Jr. and Charlotte Pierce-Baker

During the Depression and really hard time, people often paid their debts with quilts, and sometimes their tithe to the church too.

—*The Quilters*

A patch is a fragment. It is a vestige of wholeness that stands as a sign of loss and a challenge to creative design. As a remainder or remnant, the patch may symbolize rupture and impoverishment; it may be defined by the faded glory of the already gone. But as a fragment, it is also rife with explosive potential of the yet-to-be-discovered. Like woman, it is a liminal element between wholes.

Weaving, shaping, sculpting, or quilting in order to create a kaleidoscopic and momentary array is tantamount to providing an improvisational response to chaos. Such activity represents a nonce response to ceaseless scattering; it constitutes survival strategy and motion in the face of dispersal. A patchwork quilt, laboriously and affectionately crafted from bits of worn overalls, shredded uniforms, tattered petticoats, and

[1] From *The Southern Review* 21 (July 1985): 706–720.

outgrown dresses stands as a signal instance of a patterned wholeness in the African diaspora.

Traditional African cultures were scattered by the European slave trade throughout the commercial time and space of the New World. The transmutation of quilting, a European, feminine tradition, into a black women's folk art, represents an innovative fusion of African cloth manufacture, piecing, and appliqué with awesome New World experiences—and expediencies. The product that resulted was, in many ways, a double patch. The hands that pieced the master's rigidly patterned quilts by day were often the hands that crafted a more functional design in slave cabins by night. The quilts of Afro-America offer a *sui generis* context (a weaving together) of experiences and a storied, vernacular representation of lives conducted in the margins, ever beyond an easy and acceptable wholeness. In many ways, the quilts of Afro-America resemble the work of all those dismembered gods who transmute fragments and remainders into the light and breath of a new creation. And the sorority of quilt-makers, fragment weavers, holy patchers, possesses a sacred wisdom that it hands down from generation to generation of those who refuse the center for the ludic and unconfined spaces of the margins.

Those positioned outside the sorority and enamored of wholeness often fail to comprehend the dignity inherent in the quiltmakers' employment of remnants and conversion of fragments into items of everyday use. Just as the mysteries of, say, the blues remain hidden from those in happy circumstances, so the semantic intricacies of quiltmaking remain incomprehensible to the individualistic sensibility invested in myths of a postindustrial society. All of the dark, southern energy that manifests itself in the conversion of a sagging cabin—a shack really—into a "happy home" by stringing a broom wire between two nails in the wall and making the joint jump, or that shows itself in the "crazy quilt" patched from crumbs and remainders, seems but a vestige of outmoded and best-forgotten customs.

To relinquish such energy, however, is to lose an enduring resourcefulness that has ensured a distinctive aesthetic tradition and a unique code of everyday, improvisational use in America. The tradition-bearers of the type of Afro-American energy we have in mind have always included ample numbers of southern, black women who have transmuted fragments of New World displacement into a quilted eloquence scarcely appreciated by traditional spokespersons for wholeness. To wit: even the perspicacious and vigilant lion of abolitionism Frederick Douglass responded as follows to Monroe A. Majors' request for inclusions in his book *Noted Negro Women:*

> We have many estimable women of our variety but not many famous ones. It is not well to claim too much for ourselves before the public. Such extravagance invites contempt rather than

approval. I have thus far seen no book of importance written by a negro woman and I know of no one among us who can appropriately be called famous.

Southern black women have not only produced quilts of stunning beauty, they have also crafted books of monumental significance, works that have made them appropriately famous. In fact, it has been precisely the appropriation of energy drawn from sagging cabins and stitched remainders that has constituted the world of the quiltmakers' sorority. The energy has flowed through such women as Harriet Brent Jacobs, Zora Neale Hurston, and Margaret Walker, enabling them to continue an ancestral line elegantly shared by Alice Walker.

In a brilliant essay entitled "Alice Walker: The Black Woman Artist as Wayward," Professor Barbara Christian writes: "Walker is drawn to the integral and economical process of quilt making as a model for her own craft. For through it, one can create out of seemingly disparate everyday materials patterns of clarity, imagination, and beauty." Professor Christian goes on to discuss Walker's frequently cited "In Search of Our Mothers' Gardens" and her short story "Everyday Use." She convincingly argues that Walker employs quilts as signs of functional beauty and spiritual heritage that provide exemplars of challenging convention and radical individuality, or "artistic waywardness."

The patchwork quilt as a trope for understanding black women's creativity in the United States, however, presents an array of interpretive possibilities that is not exhausted by Professor Christian's adept criticism of Walker. For example, if one takes a different tack and suggests that the quilt as metaphor presents not a stubborn contrariness, a wayward individuality, but a communal bonding that confounds traditional definitions of art and of the artist, then one plays on possibilities in the quilting trope rather different from those explored by Christian. What we want to suggest in our own adaptation of the trope is that it opens a fascinating interpretive window on vernacular dimensions of lived, creative experience in the United States. Quilts, in their patched and many-colored glory offer not a counter to tradition, but, in fact, an instance of the only legitimate tradition of "the people" that exists. They are representations of the stories of the vernacular natives who make up the ninety-nine percent of the American population unendowed with money and control. The class distinction suggested by "vernacular" should not overshadow the gender specificity of quilts as products of a universal woman's creativity—what Pattie Chase in *The Contemporary Quilt* calls "an ancient affinity between women and cloth." They are the testimony of "mute and inglorious" generations of women gone before. The quilt as interpretive sign opens up a world of *difference,* a nonscripted territory whose creativity with fragments is less a matter of "artistic" choice than of economic and functional necessity. "So much in the habit of sewing something," says Walker's protagonist in the remarkable novel *The Color Purple,* "[that] I stitch up a bunch of scraps, try to see what I can make."

The Johnson women, who populate the generations represented in Walker's short story "Everyday Use," are inhabitants of southern cabins who have always worked with "scraps" and seen what they could make of them. The result of their labor has been a succession of mothers and daughters surviving the ignominies of Jim Crow life and passing on ancestral blessings to descendants. The guardians of the Johnson homestead when the story commences are the mother—"a large, big-boned woman with rough, man-working hands"—and her daughter Maggie, who has remained with her "chin on chest, eyes on ground, feet in shuffle, ever since the fire that burned the other house to the ground" ten or twelve years ago. The mood at the story's beginning is one of ritualistic "waiting": "I will wait for her in the yard that Maggie and I made so clean and wavy yesterday afternoon." The subject awaited is the other daughter, Dee. Not only has the yard (as ritual ground) been prepared for the arrival of a goddess, but the sensibilities and costumes of Maggie and her mother have been appropriately attuned for the occasion. The mother daydreams of television shows where parents and children are suddenly—and pleasantly—reunited, banal shows where chatty hosts oversee tearful reunions. In her fantasy, she weighs a hundred pounds less, is several shades brighter in complexion, and possesses a devastatingly quick tongue. She returns abruptly to real life meditation, reflecting on her own heroic, agrarian accomplishments in slaughtering hogs and cattle and preparing their meat for winter nourishment. She is a robust provider who has gone to the people of her church and raised money to send her light-complexioned, lithe-figured, and ever-dissatisfied daughter Dee to college. Today, as she waits in the purified yard, she notes the stark differences between Maggie and Dee and recalls how the "last dingy gray board of the house [fell] in toward the red-hot brick chimney" when her former domicile burned. Maggie was scarred horribly by the fire, but Dee, who had hated the house with an intense fury, stood "off under the sweet gum tree . . . a look of concentration on her face." A scarred and dull Maggie, who has been kept at home and confined to everyday offices, has but one reaction to the fiery and vivacious arrival of her sister: "I hear Maggie suck in her breath. 'Uhnnnh,' is what it sounds like. Like when you see the wriggling end of a snake just in front of your foot on the road. 'Uhnnnh'."

Indeed the question raised by Dee's energetic arrival is whether there are words adequate to her flair, her brightness, her intense colorfulness of style which veritably blocks the sun. She wears "a dress so loud it hurts my eyes. There are yellows and oranges enough to throw back the light of the sun. I feel my whole face warming from the heat waves it throws out." Dee is both serpent and fire introduced with bursting esprit into the calm pasture that contains the Johnson's tin-roofed, three-room, windowless shack and grazing cows. She has joined the radical, black nationalists of the 1960s and 1970s, changing her name from Dee to Wangero and cultivating a suddenly fashionable, or stylish, interest in what she passionately describes as her "heritage." If there is one quality that Dee (Wangero) possesses in abundance, it is "style": "At sixteen she had a style of her own: and knew what style was."

But in her stylishness, Dee is not an example of the indigenous rapping and styling out of Afro-America. Rather, she is manipulated by the style-makers, the fashion designers whose semiotics the French writer Roland Barthes has so aptly characterized. "Style" for Dee is the latest vogue—the most recent fantasy perpetuated by American media. When she left for college, her mother had tried to give her a quilt whose making began with her grandmother Dee, but the bright daughter felt such patched coverings were "old-fashioned and out of style." She has returned at the commencement of "Everyday Use," however, as one who now purports to know the value of the work of black women as holy patchers.

The dramatic conflict of the story surrounds the definition of holiness. The ritual purification and expectant atmosphere akin to that of Beckett's famous drama ("I will wait for her in the yard that Maggie and I made so clean and wavy yesterday afternoon.") prepare us for the narrator's epiphanic experience at the story's conclusion.

Near the end of "Everyday Use," the mother (who is the tale's narrator) realizes that Dee (a.k.a., Wangero) is a *fantasy* child, a perpetrator and victim of: "words, lies, other folks's habits." The energetic daughter is as frivolously careless of other peoples' lives as the fiery conflagration that she had watched ten years previously. Assured by the makers of American fashion that "black" is currently "beautiful," she has conformed her own "style" to that notion. Hers is a trendy "blackness" cultivated as "art" and costume. She wears "a dress down to the ground . . . bracelets dangling and making noises when she moves her arm up to shake the folds of the dress out of her armpits." And she says of quilts she has removed from a trunk at the foot of her mother's bed: "Maggie can't appreciate these quilts! She'd probably be backward enough to put them to everyday use." "Art" is, thus, juxtaposed with "everyday use" in Walker's short story, and the fire goddess Dee, who has achieved literacy only to burn "us with a lot of knowledge we didn't necessarily need to know," is revealed as a perpetuator of institutional theories of aesthetics. (Such theories hold that "art" is, in fact, defined by social institutions such as museums, book reviews, and art dealers.) Of the two quilts that she has extracted from the trunk, she exclaims: "But they're 'priceless.' " And so the quilts are by "fashionable" standards of artistic value, standards that motivate the answer that Dee provides to her mother's question: " 'Well,' I said, stumped. 'What would *you* do with them?' " Dee's answer: "Hang them." The stylish daughter's entire life has been one of "framed" experience; she has always sought a fashionably "aesthetic" distance from southern expediencies. (And how unlike quilt frames that signal social activity and a coming to completeness are her *frames*.) Her concentrated detachment from the fire, which so nearly symbolizes her role vis-à-vis the Afro-American community (her black friends "worshipped . . . the scalding humor that erupted like bubbles in lye") is characteristic of her attitude. Her goals include the appropriation of exactly what *she* needs to remain fashionable in the eyes of a world of pretended wholeness, a world of banal television shows, framed and institutionalized art, and polaroid cameras—devices that instantly process and record experience as "framed" photograph. Ultimately, the framed polaroid photograph represents the limits of Dee's vision.

Strikingly, the quilts whose *tops* have been stitched by her grandmother from fragments of outgrown family garments and quilted after the grandmother's death by Aunt Dee and her sister (the mother who narrates the story) are perceived in Dee's polaroid sensibility as merely "priceless" works of an institutionally, or stylishly, defined "arty world." In a reversal of perception tantamount to the acquisition of sacred knowledge by initiates in a rite of passage, the mother/narrator realizes that she has always worshipped at the altars of a "false" goddess. As her alter ego, Dee has always expressed that longing for the "other" that characterizes inhabitants of oppressed, "minority" cultures. Situated in an indisputably black and big-boned skin, the mother has secretly admired the "good hair," full figure, and well-turned (i.e., "whitely trim") ankle of Dee (Wangero). Sacrifices and sanctity have seemed in order. But in her epiphanic moment of recognition, she perceives the fire-scarred Maggie—the stay-at-home victim of southern scarifications—in a revised light. When Dee grows belligerent about possessing the quilts, Maggie emerges from the kitchen and says with a contemptuous gesture of dismissal: "She can have them, Mama. . . . I can 'member Grandma Dee without quilts." The mother's response to what she wrongly interprets as Maggie's hang-dog resignation before Dee is a radical awakening to godhead:

> When I looked at her . . . something hit me in the top of my head and ran down to the soles of my feet. Just like when I'm in church and the spirit of God touches me and I get happy and shout. I did something I never had done before: hugged Maggie to me, then dragged her on into the room, snatched the quilts out of Miss Wangero's hands and dumped them into Maggie's lap.

Maggie is the arisen goddess of Walker's story; she is the sacred figure who bears the scarifications of experience and knows how to convert patches into robustly patterned and beautifully quilted wholes. As an earth-rooted and quotidian goddess, she stands in dramatic contrast to the stylishly fiery and other-oriented Wangero. The mother says in response to Dee's earlier cited accusation that Maggie would reduce quilts to rags by putting them to everyday use: " 'She can always make some more,' I said. 'Maggie knows how to quilt.' " And, indeed, Maggie, the emergent goddess of New World improvisation and long ancestral memory, does know how to quilt. Her mind and imagination are capable of preserving the wisdom of grandmothers and aunts without material prompts: "I can 'member . . . without the quilts," she says. The secret to employing beautiful quilts as items of everyday use is the secret of crafty dues.

In order to comprehend the transient nature of all wholes, one must first become accustomed to living and working with fragments. Maggie has learned the craft of fragment weaving from her women ancestors: "It was Grandma Dee and Big Dee who taught her how to quilt herself." The conjunction of "quilt" and "self" in Walker's syntax may be simply a serendipitous accident of style. Nonetheless, the conjunction works magnificently to capture the force of black woman's quilting in "Everyday Use." Finally, it is the "self," or a version of humanness that one calls the Afro-American self, that must, in fact, be crafted from fragments on the basis of wisdom gained from preceding generations.

What is at stake in the world of Walker's short story, then, is not the prerogatives of Afro-American women as "wayward artists." Individualism and a flouting of convention in order to achieve "artistic" success constitute acts of treachery in "Everyday Use." For Dee, if she is anything, *is* a fashionable denizen of America's art/fantasy world. She is removed from the "everyday uses" of a black community that she scorns, misunderstands, burns. Certainly, she is "unconventionally" black. As such, however, she is an object of holy contempt from the archetypal weaver of black wholeness from tattered fragments. Maggie's "Uhnnnh" and her mother's designation "Miss Wangero" are gestures of utter contempt. Dee's sellout to fashion and fantasy in a television-manipulated world of "artistic" frames is a representation of the *complicity of the clerks.* Not "art," then, but use or function is the signal in Walker's fiction of sacred creation.

Quilts designed for everyday use, pieced wholes defying symmetry and pattern, are signs of the scarred generations of women who have always been alien to a world of literate words and stylish fantasies. The crafted fabric of Walker's story is the very weave of blues and jazz traditions in the Afro-American community, daringly improvisational modes that confront breaks in the continuity of melody (or theme) by riffing. The asymmetrical quilts of southern black women are like the off-centered stomping of the jazz solo or the innovative musical showmanship of the blues interlude. They speak a world in which the deceptively shuffling Maggie is capable of a quick change into goddess, an unlikely holy figure whose dues are paid in full. Dee's anger at her mother is occasioned principally by the mother's insistence that paid dues make Maggie a more likely bearer of sacredness, tradition, and true value than the "brighter" sister. "You just don't understand," she says to her mother. Her assessment is surely correct where institutional theories and systems of "art" are concerned. The mother's cognition contains no categories for framed art. The mother works according to an entirely different scale of use and value, finally assigning proper weight to the virtues of Maggie and to the ancestral importance of the pieced quilts that she has kept out of use for so many years. Smarting, perhaps, from Dee's designation of the quilts as "old-fashioned," the mother has buried the covers away in a trunk. At the end of Walker's story, however, she has become aware of her own mistaken value judgments, and she pays homage that is due to Maggie. The unlikely daughter is a *griot* of the vernacular who remembers actors and events in a distinctively black "historical" drama.

Before Dee departs, she "put on some sunglasses that hid everything above the tip of her nose and her chin." Maggie smiles at the crude symbolism implicit in this act, for she has always known that her sister saw "through a glass darkly." But it is the mother's conferral of an ancestral blessing (signaled by her deposit of the quilts in Maggie's lap) that constitutes the occasion for the daughter's first "real smile." Maggie knows that it is only communal recognition by elders of the tribe that confers ancestral privileges on succeeding generations. The mother's holy recognition of the scarred daughter's sacred status as quilter is the best gift of a hard-pressed womankind to the fragmented goddess of the present.

At the conclusion of "Everyday Use," which is surely a fitting precursor to *The Color Purple,* with its sewing protagonist and its scenes of sisterly quilting, Maggie and her mother relax in the ritual yard after the dust of Dee's departing car has settled. They dip snuff in the manner of African confreres sharing cola nuts. The moment is past when a putatively "new" generation has confronted scenes of black, everyday life. A change has taken place, but it is a change best described by Amiri Baraka's designation for Afro-American music's various styles and discontinuities. The change in Walker's story is the "changing same." What has been reaffirmed at the story's conclusion is the value of the quiltmaker's motion and strategy in the precincts of a continuously undemocratic South.

But the larger appeal of "Everyday Use" is its privileging of a distinctively woman's craft as *the* signal mode of confronting chaos through a skillful blending of patches. In *The Color Purple,* Celie's skill as a fabric worker completely transmutes the order of Afro-American existence. Not only do her talents with a needle enable her to wear the pants in the family, they also allow her to become the maker of pants par excellence. Hence, she becomes a kind of unifying goddess of patch and stitch, and instructress of mankind who bestows the gift of consolidating fragments. Her abusive husband Albert says: "When I was growing up . . . I use to try to sew along with mama cause that's what she was always doing. But everybody laughed at me. But you know, I liked it." "Well," says Celie, "nobody gon laugh at you now. . . . Here, help me stitch in these pockets."

A formerly "patched" separateness of woman is transformed through fabric craft into a new unity. Quilting, sewing, stitching are bonding activities that begin with the godlike authority and daring of women, but that are given (as a gift toward community) to men. The old disparities are transmuted into a vision best captured by the scene that Shug suggests to Celie: "But, Celie, try to imagine a city full of these shining, blueblack people wearing brilliant blue robes with designs like fancy quilt patterns." The heavenly city of quilted design is a form of unity wrested by the sheer force of the woman quiltmaker's will from chaos. As a community, it stands as both a sign of the potential effects of black women's creativity in America, and as an emblem of the effectiveness of women's skillful confrontation of patches. Walker's achievement as a southern, black, woman novelist is her own successful application of the holy patching that was a staple of her grandmother's and great-grandmother's hours of everyday ritual. "Everyday Use" is, not surprisingly, dedicated to "your grandmama": to those who began the line of converting patches into works of southern genius.

The Value of Art
Clare Schmitt
English 102

The definition of art is held in the eye of the beholder. As a result, people view art in many different ways. Most people consider the monetary value without acknowledging any other aspect of the art's value. However, to fully appreciate the real value of art, its history and possibly heritage must also be taken into consideration. Alice Walker clearly illustrates society's displaced valuation of art in her two stories "Everyday Use" and "Nineteen Fifty-five." In "Everyday Use," she depicts Dee to be a very shallow person who places importance on materialism instead of her heritage. On the other hand, Dee's mother pays homage to her heritage by passing on the tradition of quilting. In the story "Nineteen Fifty-five," Walker again portrays another character, Traynor, to be materialistic and selfish. In contrast, Gracie Mae Still sings blues songs that come directly out of her experience.

In the story, "Everyday Use," Dee intrudes upon her mother. Dee bases her lifestyle on the media's definition of fashion. To be accepted by society, Dee believes that she must be in style. Houston and Charlotte Pierce-Baker believe that "her goals include the appropriation of exactly what she needs to remain fashionable in the eyes of a world of pretended wholeness . . ." (717)[*]. This expectation causes her to conform to society's standards so that she appears to be very superficial and materialistic. It is her way, perhaps, to rebel against the impoverished life she has lived, in which she was unable to attain things that society

---

[*] See "Works Cited" for page references.

viewed as valuable. Having always been uncomfortable with her family's poverty-stricken lifestyle, Dee is never able to accept it. This leads her to detach herself from her heritage. By distancing herself from her family roots, Dee is unable to acknowledge the value of her heritage. Baker and Pierce-Baker feel that to reject such a heritage "is to lose an enduring resourcefulness that has ensured a distinctive aesthetic tradition and a unique code of everyday, improvisational use in America" (713).

However, when the media declare being " 'black' " to be in style, Dee returns home to acquire "fashionable art" (Baker and Pierce-Baker 1439). Baker and Pierce-Baker say,

> Assured by the makers of American fashion that "black" is currently "beautiful," [Dee] has conformed her own "style" to that notion. Hers is a trendy "blackness" cultivated as "art" and costume. (716)

Barbara Christian speculates that Dee "misuses the concept of heritage" (86). When she goes home, she informs her mother that she has changed her name because "I couldn't bear it any longer, being named after the people who oppress me" (53). The fear of not being in fashion has led her to change her name and possibly symbolizes her desire to eliminate the links to her past. Although she discards the person whom she was named after, she wants to possess the quilts created by her ancestors (Christian 86). She is unaware of the ancestral value of the quilts. For example, some of the fragments which make up the quilt were from dresses that her grandmother wore over fifty years ago, and one piece was from her Great Grandfather's Civil War uniform (55). This ancestral aspect of the quilt is not important to Dee: What is important to her is the materialistic value. Houston Baker and Charlotte Pierce-Baker say,

> Those positioned outside the sorority and enamored of wholeness often fail to comprehend the dignity inherent in the quiltmaker's employment of remnants and conversion of fragments into items of everyday use. ... the semantic intricacies of quiltmaking remain incomprehensible to the individualistic sensibility invested in myths of a post industrial society. (713)

Society's assessment of art is the only thing that Dee considers to be important. Dee believes in the "institutional theories of aesthetics" (716). In the story she says of the quilts, "But they're priceless!" (57) a statement which implies the value society places on these works of art. She could not imagine someone putting these quilts to everyday use; she would appreciate their value by "hang[ing] them" (58).

In contrast, Dee's mother has never incorporated society's influence into her lifestyle. She is not a materialistic person, and she enjoys the simple pleasures of life. She does not assess the value or importance of a person according to the current style or fashion. She appreciates people for who they are. Obviously, money and style are of little importance to her. Her family's ancestry and traditions have instilled the values in which she believes. For her, the most important aspect of life itself is her heritage. She values the quilts as pieces of art because of the quilts' history, not because of the monetary value or the fashionable style. Grandma Dee had "pieced the quilts and then Big Dee and [Dee's mother] had hung them on the quilt frames . . . and quilted them" (56). The scraps of fifty year old dresses and a small piece of Great Grandpa Ezra's Civil War uniform create the history and beauty of the quilts. According to Barbara Christian, the tradition of quilting establishes the real value because these women were able to design "patterns of clarity, imagination, and beauty" with miniscule scraps of material (qtd in Baker & Pierce-Baker 714). She appreciates not only the value and the beauty of the quilts but also the person who designed the quilts.

Although the quilts are beautiful pieces of art, Dee's mother does not believe that they should be preserved for mere decoration. She feels that to fully understand the tradition of quilting, quilts should continue to be created as time passes and their creation should never cease. Part of the idea behind the tradition of quilting is the idea that the person creating the quilt will be able to pass the tradition of quilting on to the next generation (Christian 87). Dee's mother is able to remember her mother creating a quilt and to save the memories without actually keeping the material. This is clearly illustrated when Dee says, " 'Maggie would put them on the bed and in five years they'd be in rags. Less than that!' " Her mother responds, " 'She can always make some more. Maggie knows how to quilt' " (57, 58). Houston Baker and Charlotte Pierce-Baker say,

> Her [Maggie's] mind and imagination are capable of preserving the wisdom of grandmothers and mother without material prompts. . . . The secret to employing beautiful quilts as items of everyday use is the secret of crafty dues. (718)

A similar conflict between art as a product of experience and tradition and art as a consumer product occurs in "Nineteen Fifty-five." In the story "Nineteen Fifty-five," Traynor first intrudes upon Gracie Mae Still when he goes to her house wanting to "record one of [her] songs" (520). Gracie's song become Traynor's song, and he turns into an overnight success with it. Money is an important and dominating factor in Traynor's life. Traynor lives a fast paced, stylish lifestyle. He experiences the finer things in life, including fancy cars, jewelry, and houses. Even though he acquires expensive luxuries, his life remains empty. He tries to substitute money for love, but the emptiness inside of him still remains. These materialistic items are unable to create happiness for him. Throughout his life, Traynor copies everybody else; he has no real history of his own. This becomes apparent when he says, "it was like singing somebody else's record. I copied the way it was sposed to be exactly but I never had a clue what marriage meant" (525). As a result,

Traynor is unable to appreciate the real value of songs or people. Initially, the song's monetary value appears to be important to Traynor. However, his search for the real meaning behind the song becomes more important to him as time passes. Although he has become successful, he is unable to "reap the rewards." He realizes that his lack of knowledge about the song hinders him from appreciating the song's artistic value. Keith Byerman says that Traynor is unable to understand the song because he sang an "inherently dishonest version of the song and performed it with its history erased" (160–161). Traynor appears before Gracie's door several times to inquire about the meaning of her song. However, even if she did explain the meaning, he would not be able to fully understand the song because it's about Gracie's life and her experiences. According to Keith Byerman, Gracie's life history as a black woman allows the song to be created. However, when Traynor sings the song, the real meaning is lost because he is a white man singing a black woman's song (Byerman 160). Since Traynor hasn't lived a black woman's life, he is unable to sing it with his heart and soul. This inability, in itself, does not allow the full artistic value to be recognized.

Gracie Mae Still, on the other hand, has lived a long and hard life. Throughout her life, she has constantly struggled to survive. The struggle enables her to appreciate the things that most people take for granted. This struggle allows her to be thankful for the simple things in life. As a result, expensive "toys" are not needed to bring fulfillment to her life. One simple pleasure of hers is singing. Her songs are a form of art because they reveal her black history and her personal experiences (Byerman 160). Although the song is important to her, she is able to sell her possession of it to Traynor without losing the memory or its significance in her life. She is the only person who can fully appreciate its artistic value because its "content is not erased" (Byerman 161).

In "Everyday Use" and "Nineteen Fifty-five," Alice Walker reveals not only the real meaning of art, but also the value that society should place on it. The true value of art goes beyond money. These stories emphasize the importance of the heritage and history behind a piece of art, compelling readers to think about their attitudes toward art and possibly reconsider their assessment of art to include and appreciate its history.

Works Cited

Baker, Houston A., Jr., and Charlotte Pierce-Baker. "Patches: Quilts and Community in Alice Walker's 'Everyday Use.'" The Southern Review 21 (July 1985): 706–20.

Byerman, Keith. Fingering the Jagged Grain: Tradition and Form in Recent Black Fiction. Athens: University of Georgia Press, 1985.

Christian, Barbara. "Alice Walker: the Black Woman as Wayward." New York: Pergamon Press, 1985.

Walker, Alice. "Everyday Use." In Love and Trouble. New York: Harcourt Brace Jovanovich, Inc., 1973. 47–59.

———. "Nineteen Fifty-five." <u>You Can't Keep a Good Woman Down</u>. New York: Harcourt Brace Jovanovich, Inc., 1981. Rpt. in <u>The Conscious Reader</u>. 4th ed. Ed. Caroline Shrodes, Harry Finestone, and Michael Shugrue. New York: Macmillan Publishing Company, 1988. 519–29.

❏ Suggestions for Exploration, Research, and Writing

1. In the two Walker stories, Dee and Traynor are intruders on their hosts, Dee's mother and Gracie Mae Still. In a researched essay, contrast the distinctively different life-styles of the intruders with those of their hosts, and explain how these life-styles affect their attitudes toward art.

2. Walker is adept at using gestures to reveal her characters. In a researched essay on "Everyday Use" and "Nineteen Fifty-five" analyze Walker's use of such gestures to create her characters.

3. In a researched essay, contrast the conception of " 'heritage' " exemplified by Dee and Traynor with that exemplified by Maggie and Gracie Mae Still. Explain whether a heritage is best preserved by protecting it or by living it.

4. In an essay, show how Alice Walker's concept of art compares with that of Achebe in "Africa and Her Writers," with that of Lopez in "Landscape and Narrative," and/or with that of the villagers in Soyinka's play *The Lion and the Jewel*.

5. Toni Cade Bambara's "Blues Ain't No Mockin Bird" and the stories by Walker portray strong, rural Southern black women. Each is an extraordinarily complex person. Moreover, though these women share some qualities, they also differ markedly. In a researched essay, contrast two of these women in order to demonstrate the uniqueness and complexity of each.

❏ Suggestions for Writing

1. The title of this section suggests that art and language are closely related. Using one or more works from this unit, show how language creates art. What languages other than verbal ones create works of art?

2. Is art only about what the artist perceives? Compare and/or contrast the idea of art exemplified in Tina Howe's play *Painting Churches* with that exemplified in Yourcenar's "How Wang-Fo Was Saved."

3. Select three poems and use quotations from them to write an essay giving a definition of poetry.

4. Using any three works in this unit, explain the relationship of creator (writer, artist, reader, etc.,) to creation.

5. In what ways does a work of art belong to everyone? Explain using examples from any section of this book.

6. Use any of the poems in this unit to illustrate the possibilities and/or problems of communicating accurately with language.

QUEST

AWARENESS THAT HUMANITY cannot "live by bread alone" (Matthew 4:4) predates Christ by thousands of years. The theme of the quest, which ultimately reveals humanity in a search for meaning, for a truth beyond the purely physical, is older than written literature. It finds expression in ancient religions and myths, in the Babylonian epic of *Gilgamesh,* and in the great oral epics of Homer, particularly *The Odyssey.* The human need for a defining direction, order, and meaning expresses itself in all art, in all mythology, and in all religions. In a sense, then, the quest, the search for an ultimate truth, might be seen as one defining characteristic of humanity.

The quest for truth begins not in certainty but in doubt—in questioning. By questioning the wisdom of his teachers, Golding, in "Thinking as a Hobby," arrives at a higher conception of truth; and Ozzie, in "The Conversion of the Jews," is so tormented by his elders' refusal to take seriously his very serious questions that he ends up casting doubt on all they have believed in. Plato's quest for truth—his philosophy—begins, proceeds, and ends with question after question. The wisdom of Jesus' Sermon on the Mount arises out of his questioning of received wisdom—his refusal to accept the status quo. Blake asks without answering the question whether the God who made the Lamb could make the Tyger.

Anguished questioning torments even writers and characters of profound faith. Faith seems not to end the quest but to begin it anew. Hopkins' "God's Grandeur," though written in praise of God and though ending in a strongly affirmative sestet, nevertheless reveals in its second quatrain grave doubts about humans' capacity to know God; and Donne's Holy Sonnets reveal a soul almost tortured by doubts about the adequacy of its quest for God. The narrator of Gish Jen's "The Water-Faucet Vision" grows through questioning from a naive faith to a more mature one; but the growth is agonizing, commencing with the father's throwing the mother out a window. Flannery O'Connor, a devout Catholic, sees modern men and women as so immersed in the world as to be wholly unaware of their own inadequacy. For O'Connor, only the inexplicable and often violent grace of God can give a person some sense of order and meaning. O'Connor's quest cannot even begin without grace.

The quest for truth may sometimes be quite costly. Oedipus' persistence in seeking the truth results in his wife's death and in his own blinding and banishment. In William Faulkner's "Barn Burning,"

Sarty's quest for truth ultimately leads him to betray his father. Because he regards his quest as too costly, Prufrock, the narrator of T.S. Eliot's "The Love Song of J. Alfred Prufrock," is unable even to ask his most superficial question. We see in him the predicament of much of contemporary humanity, unable to believe in God or in any ultimate truth, thoroughly disoriented, searching in spite of themselves for truth and direction in a world which apparently offers neither.

In spite of the difficulty of the quest, the search for a truth that transcends the merely physical world continues. Plato's philosopher finds his way out of the cave. Writers as different as the Old Testament psalmist, William Butler Yeats, and Robert Frost offer us a vision of what we might attain, of a transcendent existence beyond the ravages of pain and age, of a peace where people can, if only during a momentary refuge from the quest, "drink and be whole again beyond confusion."

The quest continues. As the persistent questioning of Socrates, the endless searching of Tennyson's Ulysses, and the eloquent frozen action of Keats' Grecian urn make clear, often the joy, meaning, and order we seek are in the quest itself. Even one of the most devout of Christian mystics, the monk Brother Lawrence, saw his vocation not as resting in God, but as constantly *practicing* God's presence. Like Tennyson's Ulysses, we feel compelled to search: "to strive, to seek, to find, and not to yield."

ESSAYS

PLATO (C. 429–347 B.C.)

The philosopher and teacher Plato was a high-born Athenian who studied under Socrates and taught Aristotle. Plato founded a school in the grove sacred to the hero Academus and called it the Academy. The Republic, Plato's plan for a utopia, incudes the most famous of all allegories, the **allegory** *of the cave, which delineates his philosophical view of reality. Plato customarily wrote in* **dialogues**, *often using Socrates as a character. Because of its emphasis on the transcendent, Plato's philosophy influenced many later religions, including Christianity and Islam.*

Allegory of the Cave[1]

1   And now, I said, let me show in a figure how far our nature is enlightened or unenlightened: —Behold! human beings living in an underground den, which has a mouth open towards the light and reaching all along the den; here they have been from their childhood, and have their legs and necks chained so that they cannot move, and can only see before

---

[1] From Plato's *The Republic*, translated by Benjamin Jowett.

them, being prevented by the chains from turning round their heads. Above and behind them a fire is blazing at a distance, and between the fire and the prisoners there is a raised way; and you will see, if you look, a low wall built along the way, like the screen which marionette players have in front of them, over which they show the puppets.

I see. 2

And do you see, I said, men passing along the wall carrying all sorts of 3 vessels, and statues and figures of animals made of wood and stone and various materials, which appear over the wall? Some of them are talking, others silent.

You have shown me a strange image, and they are strange prisoners. 4

Like ourselves, I replied; and they see only their own shadows, or the 5 shadows of one another, which the fire throws on the opposite wall of the cave?

True, he said; how could they see anything but the shadows if they 6 were never allowed to move their heads?

And of the objects which are being carried in like manner they would 7 only see the shadows?

Yes, he said. 8

And if they were able to converse with one another, would they not 9 suppose that they were naming what was actually before them?

Very true. 10

And suppose further that the prison had an echo which came from the 11 other side, would they not be sure to fancy when one of the passers-by spoke that the voice which they heard came from the passing shadow?

No question, he replied. 12

To them, I said, the truth would be literally nothing but the shadows 13 of the images.

That is certain. 14

And now look again, and see what will naturally follow if the prisoners 15 are released and disabused of their error. At first, when any of them is liberated and compelled suddenly to stand up and turn his neck round and walk and look towards the light, he will suffer sharp pains; the glare will distress him, and he will be unable to see the realities of which in his former state he had seen the shadows; and then conceive some one saying to him, that what he saw before was an illusion, but that now, when he is approaching nearer to being and his eye is turned towards more real existence, he has a clearer vision,—what will be his reply? And you may further imagine that his instructor is pointing to the objects as they pass and requiring him to name them,—will he not be perplexed? Will he not fancy that the shadows which he formerly saw are truer than the objects which are now shown to him?

Far truer. 16

And if he is compelled to look straight at the light, will he not have a 17 pain in his eyes which will make him turn away to take refuge in the objects of vision which he can see, and which he will conceive to be in reality clearer than the things which are now being shown to him?

18   True, he said.

19   And suppose once more, that he is reluctantly dragged up a steep and rugged ascent, and held fast until he is forced into the presence of the sun himself, is he not likely to be pained and irritated? When he approaches the light his eyes will be dazzled, and he will not be able to see anything at all of what are now called realities.

20   Not all in a moment, he said.

21   He will require to grow accustomed to the sight of the upper world. And first he will see the shadows best, next the reflections of men and other objects in the water, and then the objects themselves; then he will gaze upon the light of the moon and the stars and the spangled heaven; and he will see the sky and the stars by night better than the sun or the light of the sun by day?

22   Certainly.

23   Last of all he will be able to see the sun, and not mere reflections of him in the water, but he will see him in his own proper place, and not in another; and he will contemplate him as he is.

24   Certainly.

25   He will then proceed to argue that this is he who gives the season and the years, and is the guardian of all that is in the visible world, and in a certain way the cause of all things which he and his fellows have been accustomed to behold?

26   Clearly, he said, he would first see the sun and then reason about him.

27   And when he remembered his old habitation, and the wisdom of the den and his fellow-prisoners, do you not suppose that he would felicitate himself on the change, and pity them?

28   Certainly, he would.

29   And if they were in the habit of conferring honours among themselves on those who were quickest to observe the passing shadows and to remark which of them went before, and which followed after, and which were together; and who were therefore best able to draw conclusions as to the future, do you think that he would care for such honours and glories, or envy the possessors of them? Would he not say with Homer,

> "Better to be the poor servant of a poor master,"

and to endure anything, rather than think as they do and live after their manner?

30   Yes, he said, I think that he would rather suffer anything than entertain these false notions and live in this miserable manner.

31   Imagine once more, I said, such an one coming suddenly out of the sun to be replaced in his old situation; would he not be certain to have his eyes full of darkness?

32   To be sure, he said.

33   And if there were a contest, and he had to compete in measuring the shadows with the prisoners who had never moved out of the den, while his sight was still weak, and before his eyes had become steady (and the time which would be needed to acquire this new habit of sight might be

very considerable), would he not be ridiculous? Men would say of him that up he went and down he came without his eyes; and that it was better not even to think of ascending; and if any one tried to loose another and lead him up to the light, let them only catch the offender, and they would put him to death.

No question, he said.

34

This entire allegory, I said, you may now append, dear Glaucon, to the previous argument; the prison-house is the world of sight, the light of the fire is the sun, and you will not misapprehend me if you interpret the journey upwards to be the ascent of the soul into the intellectual world according to my poor belief, which, at your desire, I have expressed— whether rightly or wrongly God knows. But, whether true or false, my opinion is that in the world of knowledge the idea of good appears last of all, and is seen only with an effort; and, when seen, is also inferred to be the universal author of all things beautiful and right, parent of light and of the lord of light in this visible world, and the immediate source of reason and truth in the intellectual; and that this is the power upon which he who would act rationally either in public or private life must have his eye fixed.

35

I agree, he said, as far as I am able to understand you.

36

Moreover, I said, you must not wonder that those who attain to this beatific vision are unwilling to descend to human affairs; for their souls are ever hastening into the upper world where they desire to dwell; which desire of theirs is very natural, if our allegory may be trusted.

37

Yes, very natural.

38

And is there anything surprising in one who passes from divine con-templations to the evil state of man, misbehaving himself in a ridiculous manner; if, while his eyes are blinking and before he has become accus-tomed to the surrounding darkness, he is compelled to fight in courts of law, or in other places, about the images or the shadows of images of justice, and is endeavouring to meet the conceptions of those who have never yet seen absolute justice?

39

Anything but surprising, he replied.

40

Any one who has common sense will remember that the bewilderments of the eyes are of two kinds, and arise from two causes, either from coming out of the light or from going into the light, which is true of the mind's eye, quite as much as of the bodily eye; and he who remembers this when he sees any one whose vision is perplexed and weak, will not be too ready to laugh; he will first ask whether that soul of man has come out of the brighter life, and is unable to see because unaccustomed to the dark, or having turned from darkness to the day is dazzled by excess of light. And he will count the one happy in his condition and state of being, and he will pity the other; or, if he have a mind to laugh at the soul which comes from below into the light, there will be more reason in this than in the laugh which greets him who returns from above out of the light into the den.

41

That, he said, is a very just distinction.

42

43   But then, if I am right, certain professors of education must be wrong when they say that they can put a knowledge into the soul which was not there before, like sight into blind eyes.

44   They undoubtedly say this, he replied.

45   Whereas, our argument shows that the power and capacity of learning exists in the soul already; and that just as the eye was unable to turn from darkness to light without the whole body, so too the instrument of knowledge can only by the movement of the whole soul be turned from the world of becoming into that of being, and learn by degrees to endure the sight of being, and of the brightest and best of being, or in other words, of the good.

46   Very true.

47   And must there not be some art which will effect conversion in the easiest and quickest manner; not implanting the faculty of sight, for that exists already, but has been turned in the wrong direction, and is looking away from the truth?

48   Yes, he said, such an art may be presumed.

49   And whereas the other so-called virtues of the soul seem to be akin to bodily qualities, for even when they are not originally innate they can be implanted later by habit and exercise, the virtue of wisdom more than anything else contains a divine element which always remains, and by this conversion is rendered useful and profitable; or, on the other hand, hurtful and useless. Did you never observe the narrow intelligence flashing from the keen eye of a clever rogue—how eager he is, how clearly his paltry soul sees the way to his end; he is the reverse of blind, but his keen eye-sight is forced into the service of evil, and he is mischievous in proportion to his cleverness?

50   Very true, he said.

51   But what if there had been a circumcision of such natures in the days of their youth; and they had been severed from those sensual pleasures, such as eating and drinking, which, like leaden weights, were attached to them at their birth, and which drag them down and turn the vision of their souls upon the things that were below—if, I say, they had been released from these impediments and turned in the opposite direction, the very same faculty in them would have seen the truth as keenly as they see what their eyes are turned to now.

52   Very likely.

53   Yes, I said; and there is another thing which is likely, or rather a necessary inference from what has preceded, that neither the uneducated and uninformed of the truth, nor yet those who never make an end of their education, will be able ministers of State; not the former, because they have no single aim of duty which is the rule of all their actions, private as well as public; nor the latter, because they will not act at all except upon compulsion, fancying that they are already dwelling apart in the Islands of the Blest.

54   Very true, he replied.

Then, I said, the business of us who are the founders of the State will be to compel the best minds to attain that knowledge which we have already shown to be the greatest of all—they must continue to ascend until they arrive at the good; but when they have ascended and seen enough we must not allow them to do as they do now. 55

What do you mean? 56

I mean that they remain in the upper world: but this must not be allowed; they must be made to descend again among the prisoners in the den, and partake of their labours and honours, whether they are worth having or not. 57

But is not this unjust? he said; ought we to give them a worse life, when they might have a better? 58

You have again forgotten, my friend, I said, the intention of the legislator, who did not aim at making any one class in the State happy above the rest; the happiness was to be in the whole State, and he held the citizens together by persuasion and necessity, making them benefactors of the State, and therefore benefactors of one another; to this end he created them, not to please themselves, but to be his instruments in binding up the State. 59

True, he said, I had forgotten. 60

Observe, Glaucon, that there will be no injustice in compelling our philosophers to have a care and providence of others; we shall explain to them that in other States, men of their class are not obliged to share in the toils of politics: and this is reasonable, for they grow up at their own sweet will, and the government would rather not have them. Being self-taught, they cannot be expected to show any gratitude for a culture which they have never received. But we have brought you into the world to be rulers of the hive, kings of yourselves and of the other citizens, and have educated you far better and more perfectly than they have been educated, and you are better able to share in the double duty. Wherefore each of you, when his turn comes, must go down to the general underground abode, and get the habit of seeing in the dark. When you have acquired the habit, you will see ten thousand times better than the inhabitants of the den, and you will know what the several images are, and what they represent, because you have seen the beautiful and just and good in their truth. And thus our State which is also yours will be a reality, and not a dream only, and will be administered in a spirit unlike that of other States, in which men fight with one another about shadows only and are distracted in the struggle for power, which in their eyes is a great good. Whereas the truth is that the State in which the rulers are most reluctant to govern is always the best and most quietly governed, and the State in which they are most eager, the worst. 61

Quite true, he replied. 62

And will our pupils, when they hear this, refuse to take their turn at the toils of State, when they are allowed to spend the greater part of their time with one another in the heavenly light? 63

Impossible, he answered; for they are just men, and the commands which we impose upon them are just; there can be no doubt that every one will take office as a stern necessity, and not after the fashion of our present rulers of State.

64 Impossible, he answered; for they are just men, and the commands which we impose upon them are just; there can be no doubt that every one will take office as a stern necessity, and not after the fashion of our present rulers of State.

65 Yes, my friend, I said; and there lies the point. You must contrive for your future rulers another and a better life than that of a ruler, and then you may have a well ordered State; for only in the State which offers this, will they rule who are truly rich, not in silver and gold, but in virtue and wisdom, which are the true blessings of life. Whereas if they go to the administration of public affairs, poor and hungering after their own private advantage, thinking that hence they are to snatch the chief good, order there can never be; for they will be fighting about office, and the civil and domestic broils which thus arise will be the ruin of the rulers themselves and of the whole State.

66 Most true, he replied.

67 And the only life which looks down upon the life of political ambition is that of true philosophy. Do you know of any other?

68 Indeed, I do not, he said.

69 And those who govern ought not to be lovers of the task? For, if they are, there will be rival lovers, and they will fight.

70 No question.

71 Who then are those whom we shall compel to be guardians? Surely they will be the men who are wisest about affairs of State, and by whom the State is best administered, and who at the same time have other honours and another and a better life than that of politics?

72 They are the men, and I will choose them, he replied.

73 And now shall we consider in what way such guardians will be produced, and how they are to be brought from darkness to light,—as some are said to have ascended from the world below to the gods?

74 By all means, he replied.

❏ Questions for Discussion

1. Why does Socrates, the first-person **narrator** of this dialogue, ask questions rather than make statements?

2. An **allegory** is a story in which concrete elements signify specific things or ideas other than themselves. Explain the significance of the following elements in Plato's allegory: the cave, the sun, the men in the cave, the one man who escapes, his first reaction to the sun's light, and his subsequent actions and their results.

3. Why, according to Socrates, do those who attain knowledge of "the idea of the good" have difficulty concentrating on ordinary human affairs? Can you cite examples of highly educated people who lack common sense? How does Plato's allegory explain this lack?

4. According to Socrates, how valid is the justice of most societies?

5. What difficulty in finding ideal rulers does Socrates see?

6. What does the allegory of the cave suggest about most human intelligence?

❏ **Suggestions for Exploration and Writing**

1. Apply Socrates' allegory to contemporary politics. First assess the quality of the United States' political leaders; then explain, based on the cave allegory, the reasons for their quality or lack thereof.

2. Argue for or against the following statement: "The State in which the rulers are most reluctant to govern is always the best and most quietly governed, and the State in which they are most eager, the worst."

MATTHEW

Little is known about Matthew, the author of the first gospel; in fact, he is not mentioned elsewhere in the New Testament. He has traditionally been called "Matthew the tax collector" and been identified with Levi the Apostle. The fifth chapter of Matthew, the first chapter of the Sermon on the Mount, is probably the clearest exposition of Jesus' moral teachings in the four gospels.

The Sermon on the Mount

Chapter 5

And seeing the multitudes, he went up into a mountain: and when he was set, his disciples came unto him:

2 And he opened his mouth, and taught them, saying,

3 Blessed *are* the poor in spirit: for theirs is the kingdom of heaven.

4 Blessed *are* they that mourn: for they shall be comforted.

5 Blessed *are* the meek: for they shall inherit the earth.

6 Blessed *are* they which do hunger and thirst after righteousness: for they shall be filled.

7 Blessed *are* the merciful: for they shall obtain mercy.

8 Blessed *are* the pure in heart: for they shall see God.

9 Blessed *are* the peacemakers: for they shall be called the children of God.

10 Blessed *are* they which are persecuted for righteousness' sake: for theirs is the kingdom of heaven.

11 Blessed are ye, when *men* shall revile you, and persecute *you*, and shall say all manner of evil against you falsely, for my sake.

12 Rejoice, and be exceeding glad: for great *is* your reward in heaven: for so persecuted they the prophets which were before you.

13 Ye are the salt of the earth: but if the salt have lost his savour, wherewith shall it be salted? it is thenceforth good for nothing, but to be cast out, and to be trodden under foot of men.

14 Ye are the light of the world. A city that is set on an hill cannot be hid.

15 Neither do men light a candle, and put it under a bushel, but on a candlestick; and it giveth light unto all that are in the house.

16 Let your light so shine before men, that they may see your good works, and glorify your Father which is in heaven.

17 Think not that I am come to destroy the law, or the prophets: I am not come to destroy, but to fulfil.

18 For verily I say unto you, Till heaven and earth pass, one jot or one tittle shall in no wise pass from the law, till all be fulfilled.

19 Whosoever therefore shall break one of these least commandments, and shall teach men so, he shall be called the least in the kingdom of heaven: but whosoever shall do and teach *them,* the same shall be called great in the kingdom of heaven.

20 For I say unto you, That except your righteousness shall exceed *the righteousness* of the scribes and Pharisees, ye shall in no case enter into the kingdom of heaven.

21 Ye have heard that it was said by them of old time, Thou shalt not kill; and whosoever shall kill shall be in danger of the judgment:

22 But I say unto you, That whosoever is angry with his brother without a cause shall be in danger of the judgment: and whosoever shall say to his brother, Raca, shall be in danger of the council: but whosoever shall say, *Thou fool,* shall be in danger of hell fire.

23 Therefore if thou bring thy gift to the altar, and there rememberest that thy brother hath ought against thee;

24 Leave there thy gift before the altar, and go thy way; first be reconciled to thy brother, and then come and offer thy gift.

25 Agree with thine adversary quickly, whiles thou art in the way with him; lest at any time the adversary deliver thee to the judge, and the judge deliver thee to the officer, and thou be cast into prison.

26 Verily I say unto thee, Thou shalt by no means come out thence, till thou hast paid the uttermost farthing.

27 Ye have heard that it was said by them of old time, Thou shalt not commit adultery:

28 But I say unto you, That whosoever looketh on a woman to lust after her hath committed adultery with her already in his heart.

29 And if thy right eye offend thee, pluck it out, and cast *it* from thee: for it is profitable for thee that one of thy members should perish, and not *that* thy whole body should be cast into hell.

30 And if thy right hand offend thee, cut it off, and cast *it* from thee; for it is profitable for thee that one of thy members should perish, and not *that* thy whole body should be cast into hell.

31 It hath been said, Whosoever shall put away his wife, let him give her a writing of divorcement:

32 But I say unto you, That whosoever shall put away his wife, saving for the cause of fornication, causeth her to commit adultery: and whosoever shall marry her that is divorced committeth adultery.

33 Again, ye have heard that it hath been said by them of old time, Thou shalt not forswear thyself, but shalt perform unto the Lord thine oaths:

34 But I say unto you, Swear not at all; neither by heaven; for it is God's throne;

35 Nor by the earth; for it is his footstool: neither by Jerusalem; for it is the city of the great King.

36 Neither shalt thou swear by thy head, because thou canst not make one hair white or black.

37 But let your communication be, Yea, yea; Nay, nay: for whatsoever is more than these cometh of evil.

38 Ye have heard that it hath been said, An eye for an eye, and a tooth for a tooth:

39 But I say unto you, That ye resist not evil: but whosoever shall smite thee on thy right cheek, turn to him the other also.

40 And if any man will sue thee at the law, and take away thy coat, let him have *thy* cloak also.

41 And whosoever shall compel thee to go a mile, go with him twain.

42 Give to him that asketh thee, and from him that would borrow of thee turn not thou away.

43 Ye have heard that it hath been said, Thou shalt love thy neighbour, and hate thine enemy.

44 But I say unto you, Love your enemies, bless them that curse you, do good to them that hate you, and pray for them which despitefully use you, and persecute you;

45 That ye may be the children of your Father which is in heaven: for he maketh his sun to rise on the evil and on the good, and sendeth rain on the just and on the unjust.

46 For if ye love them which love you, what reward have ye? do not even the publicans the same?

47 And if ye salute your brethren only, what do ye more *than others?* do not even the publicans so?

48 Be ye therefore perfect, even as your Father which is in heaven is perfect.

❏ Questions for Discussion

1. Many of the Beatitudes, the nine statements beginning with "Blessed," are **paradoxes.** Explain what is paradoxical about them.

2. What commandments does Jesus recall? How does he expand or extend them?

3. Is the gospel of Jesus, as taught here to his disciples, easier or harder to fulfill than the old Jewish law? How easy is it to love as Jesus asks his disciples to love? Is it practical to do so? Why or why not? Can you cite examples of people today who follow Jesus' example?

4. What do the **metaphors** of salt and light reveal about the work the disciples will be asked to do?

❏ **Suggestion for Exploration and Discussion**

1. Write a narrative in which you place in a contemporary social situation a person who behaves as Jesus prescribes. How do you imagine people would react to him or her?

WILLIAM GOLDING (1911–1993)

British novelist and essayist William Golding is best known for his first novel, Lord of the Flies *(1954). His works, usually **allegorical**, are enriched with **image** clusters and **symbols** and often have unique **points of view**. The Inheritors (1955), for example, is seen primarily through the eyes of Neanderthals. Golding received the Nobel Prize for Literature in 1983 and was knighted by Queen Elizabeth in 1988.*

Thinking As a Hobby

1   While I was still a boy, I came to the conclusion that there were three grades of thinking; and since I was later to claim thinking as my hobby, I came to an even stranger conclusion—namely, that I myself could not think at all.

2   I must have been an unsatisfactory child for grownups to deal with. I remember how incomprehensible they appeared to me at first, but not, of course, how I appeared to them. It was the headmaster of my grammar school who first brought the subject of thinking before me—though neither in the way, nor with the result he intended. He had some statuettes in his study. They stood on a high cupboard behind his desk. One was a lady wearing nothing but a bath towel. She seemed frozen in an eternal panic lest the bath towel slip down any farther; and since she had no arms, she was in an unfortunate position to pull the towel up again. Next to her, crouched the statuette of a leopard, ready to spring down at the top drawer of a filing cabinet labeled A-AH. My innocence interpreted this as the victim's last despairing cry. Beyond the leopard was a naked, muscular gentleman, who sat, looking down, with his chin on his fist and his elbow on his knee. He seemed utterly miserable.

3   Some time later, I learned about these statuettes. The headmaster had placed them where they would face delinquent children, because they

symbolized to him the whole of life. The naked lady was the Venus of
Milo. She was Love. She was not worried about the towel. She was just
busy being beautiful. The leopard was nature, and he was being natural.
The naked, muscular gentleman was not miserable. He was Rodin's
Thinker, an image of pure thought. It is easy to buy small plaster models
of what you think life is like.

I had better explain that I was a frequent visitor to the headmaster's   4
study because of the latest thing I had done or left undone. As we now
say, I was not integrated. I was, if anything, disintegrated; and I was
puzzled. Grownups never made sense. Whenever I found myself in a
penal position before the headmaster's desk, with the statuettes glimmering whitely above him, I would sink my head, clasp my hands behind my
back and writhe one shoe over the other.

The headmaster would look opaquely at me through flashing specta-   5
cles.

"What are we going to do with you?"   6

Well, what *were* they going to do with me? I would writhe my shoe   7
some more and stare down at the worn rug.

"Look up, boy! Can't you look up?"   8

Then I would look up at the cupboard, where the naked lady was   9
frozen in her panic and the muscular gentleman contemplated the hind-
quarters of the leopard in endless gloom. I had nothing to say to the
headmaster. His spectacles caught the light so that you could see nothing
human behind them. There was no possibility of communication.

"Don't you ever think at all?"   10

No, I didn't think, wasn't thinking, couldn't think—I was simply   11
waiting in anguish for the interview to stop.

"Then you'd better learn—hadn't you?"   12

On one occasion the headmaster leaped to his feet, reached up and   13
plunked Rodin's masterpiece on the desk before me.

"That's what a man looks like when he's really thinking."   14

I surveyed the gentleman without interest or comprehension.   15

"Go back to your class."   16

Clearly there was something missing in me. Nature had endowed the   17
rest of the human race with a sixth sense and left me out. This must be
so, I mused, on my way back to the class, since whether I had broken a
window, or failed to remember Boyle's Law, or been late for school, my
teachers produced me one, adult answer: "Why can't you think?"

As I saw the case, I had broken the window because I had tried to hit   18
Jack Arney with a cricket ball and missed him; I could not remember
Boyle's Law because I had never bothered to learn it; and I was late for
school because I preferred looking over the bridge into the river. In fact,
I was wicked. Were my teachers, perhaps, so good that they could not
understand the depths of my depravity? Were they clear, untormented
people who could direct their every action by this mysterious business of
thinking? The whole thing was incomprehensible. In my earlier years, I

found even the statuette of the Thinker confusing. I did not believe any of my teachers were naked, ever. Like someone born deaf, but bitterly determined to find out about sound, I watched my teachers to find out about thought.

19   There was Mr. Houghton. He was always telling me to think. With a modest satisfaction, he would tell me that he had thought a bit himself. Then why did he spend so much time drinking? Or was there more sense in drinking than there appeared to be? But if not, and if drinking were in fact ruinous to health — and Mr. Houghton was ruined, there was no doubt about that — why was he always talking about the clean life and the virtues of fresh air? He would spread his arms wide with the action of a man who habitually spent his time striding along mountain ridges.

20   "Open air does me good, boys — I know it!"

21   Sometimes, exalted by his own oratory, he would leap from his desk and hustle us outside into a hideous wind.

22   "Now, boys! Deep breaths! Feel it right down inside you — huge draughts of God's good air!"

23   He would stand before us, rejoicing in his perfect health, an open-air man. He would put his hands on his waist and take a tremendous breath. You could hear the wind, trapped in the cavern of his chest and struggling with all the unnatural impediments. His body would reel with shock and his ruined face go white at the unaccustomed visitation. He would stagger back to his desk and collapse there, useless for the rest of the morning.

24   Mr. Houghton was given to high-minded monologues about the good life, sexless and full of duty. Yet in the middle of one of these monologues, if a girl passed the window, tapping along on her neat little feet, he would interrupt his discourse, his neck would turn of itself and he would watch her out of sight. In this instance, he seemed to me ruled not by thought but by an invisible and irresistible spring in his nape.

25   His neck was an object of great interest to me. Normally it bulged a bit over his collar. But Mr. Houghton had fought in the First World War alongside both Americans and French, and had come — by who knows what illogic? — to a settled detestation of both countries. If either country happened to be prominent in current affairs, no argument could make Mr. Houghton think well of it. He would bang the desk, his neck would bulge still further and go red. "You can say what you like," he would cry, "but I've thought about this — and I know what I think!"

26   Mr. Houghton thought with his neck.

27   There was Miss Parsons. She assured us that her dearest wish was our welfare, but I knew even then, with the mysterious clairvoyance of childhood, that what she wanted most was the husband she never got. There was Mr. Hands — and so on.

28   I have dealt at length with my teachers because this was my introduction to the nature of what is commonly called thought. Through them I

discovered that thought is often full of unconscious prejudice, ignorance and hypocrisy. It will lecture on disinterested purity while its neck is being remorselessly twisted toward a skirt. Technically, it is about as proficient as most businessmen's golf, as honest as most politician's intentions, or—to come near my own preoccupation—as coherent as most books that get written. It is what I came to call grade-three thinking, though more properly, it is feeling, rather than thought.

True, often there is a kind of innocence in prejudices, but in those days   29
I viewed grade-three thinking with an intolerant contempt and an incautious mockery. I delighted to confront a pious lady who hated the Germans with the proposition that we should love our enemies. She taught me a great truth in dealing with grade-three thinkers; because of her, I no longer dismiss lightly a mental process which for nine-tenths of the population is the nearest they will ever get to thought. They have immense solidarity. We had better respect them, for we are outnumbered and surrounded. A crowd of grade-three thinkers, all shouting the same thing, all warming their hands at the fire of their own prejudices, will not thank you for pointing out the contradictions in their beliefs. Man is a gregarious animal, and enjoys agreement as cows will graze all the same way on the side of a hill.

Grade-two thinking is the detection of contradictions. I reached grade   30
two when I trapped the poor, pious lady. Grade-two thinkers do not stampede easily, though often they fall into the other fault and lag behind. Grade-two thinking is a withdrawal, with eyes and ears open. It became my hobby and brought satisfaction and loneliness in either hand. For grade-two thinking destroys without having the power to create. It set me watching the crowds cheering His Majesty the King and asking myself what all the fuss was about, without giving me anything positive to put in the place of that heady patriotism. But there were compensations. To hear people justify their habit of hunting foxes and tearing them to pieces by claiming that the foxes liked it. To hear our Prime Minister talk about the great benefit we conferred on India by jailing people like Pandit Nehru and Gandhi. To hear American politicians talk about peace in one sentence and refuse to join the League of Nations in the next. Yes, there were moments of delight.

But I was growing toward adolescence and had to admit that Mr.   31
Houghton was not the only one with an irresistible spring in his neck. I, too, felt the compulsive hand of nature and began to find that pointing out contradiction could be costly as well as fun. There was Ruth, for example, a serious and attractive girl. I was an atheist at the time. Grade-two thinking is a menace to religion and knocks down sects like skittles. I put myself in a position to be converted by her with an hypocrisy worthy of grade three. She was a Methodist—or at least, her parents were, and Ruth had to follow suit. But, alas, instead of relying on the Holy Spirit to convert me, Ruth was foolish enough to open her

pretty mouth in argument. She claimed that the Bible (King James Version) was literally inspired. I countered by saying that the Catholics believed in the literal inspiration of Saint Jerome's *Vulgate,* and the two books were different. Argument flagged.

32   At last she remarked there were an awful lot of Methodists, and they couldn't be wrong, could they—not all those millions? That was too easy, said I restively (for the nearer you were to Ruth, the nicer she was to be near to) since there were more Roman Catholics than Methodists anyway; and they couldn't be wrong, could they—not all those hundreds of millions? An awful flicker of doubt appeared in her eyes. I slid my arm round her waist and murmured breathlessly that if we were counting heads, the Buddhists were the boys for my money. But Ruth had *really* wanted to do me good, because I was so nice. She fled. The combination of my arm and those countless Buddhists was too much for her.

33   That night her father visited my father and left, red-cheeked and indignant. I was given the third degree to find out what had happened. It was lucky we were both of us only fourteen. I lost Ruth and gained an undeserved reputation as a potential libertine.

34   So grade-two thinking could be dangerous. It was in this knowledge, at the age of fifteen, that I remember making a comment from the heights of grade two, on the limitations of grade three. One evening I found myself alone in the school hall, preparing it for a party. The door of the headmaster's study was open. I went in. The headmaster had ceased to thump Rodin's Thinker down on the desk as an example to the young. Perhaps he had not found any more candidates, but the statuettes were still there, glimmering and gathering dust on top of the cupboard. I stood on a chair and rearranged them. I stood Venus in her bath towel on the filing cabinet, so that now the top drawer caught its breath in a gasp of sexy excitement. "A-ah!" The portentous Thinker I placed on the edge of the cupboard so that he looked down at the bath towel and waited for it to slip.

35   Grade-two thinking, though it filled life with fun and excitement, did not make for content. To find out the deficiencies of our elders bolsters the young ego but does not make for personal security. I found that grade two was not only the power to point out contradictions. It took the swimmer some distance from the shore and left him there, out of his depth. I decided that Pontius Pilate was a typical grade-two thinker. "What is truth?" he said, a very common grade-two thought, but one that is used always as the end of an argument instead of the beginning. There is a still higher grade of thought which says, "What is truth?" and sets out to find it.

36   But these grade-one thinkers were few and far between. They did not visit my grammar school in the flesh though they were there in books. I aspired to them, partly because I was ambitious and partly because I now saw my hobby as an unsatisfactory thing if it went no further. If you set

out to climb a mountain, however high you climb, you have failed if you cannot reach the top.

I *did* meet an undeniably grade-one thinker in my first year at Oxford. I was looking over a small bridge in Magdalen Deer Park, and a tiny mustached and hatted figure came and stood by my side. He was a German who had just fled from the Nazis to Oxford as a temporary refuge. His name was Einstein. 37

But Professor Einstein knew no English at that time and I knew only two words of German. I beamed at him, trying wordlessly to convey by my bearing all the affection and respect that the English felt for him. It is possible—and I have to make the admission—that I felt here were two grade-one thinkers standing side by side; yet I doubt if my face conveyed more than a formless awe. I would have given my Greek and Latin and French and a good slice of my English for enough German to communicate. But we were divided; he was as inscrutable as my headmaster. For perhaps five minutes we stood together on the bridge, undeniable grade-one thinker and breathless aspirant. With true greatness, Professor Einstein realized that any contact was better than none. He pointed to a trout wavering in midstream. 38

He spoke *"Fisch."* 39

My brain reeled. Here I was, mingling with the great, and yet helpless as the veriest grade-three thinker. Desperately I sought for some sign by which I might convey that I, too, revered pure reason. I nodded vehemently. In a brilliant flash I used up half of my German vocabulary. *"Fisch. Ja. Ja."* 40

For perhaps another five minutes we stood side by side. Then Professor Einstein, his whole figure still conveying good will and amiability, drifted away out of sight. 41

I, too, would be a grade-one thinker. I was irreverent at the best of times. Political and religious systems, social customs, loyalties and traditions, they all came tumbling down like so many rotten apples off a tree. This was a fine hobby and a sensible substitute for cricket, since you could play it all the year round. I came up in the end with what must always remain the justification for grade-one thinking, its sign, seal and charter. I devised a coherent system for living. It was a moral system, which was wholly logical. Of course, as I readily admitted, conversion of the world to my way of thinking might be difficult, since my system did away with a number of trifles, such as big business, centralized government, armies, marriage. . . . 42

It was Ruth all over again. I had some very good friends who stood by me, and still do. But my acquaintances vanished, taking the girls with them. Young women seemed oddly contented with the world as it was. They valued the meaningless ceremony with a ring. Young men, while willing to concede the chaining sordidness of marriage, were hesitant about abandoning the organizations which they hoped would give them 43 a career. A young man on the first rung of the Royal Navy, while perfectly agreeable to doing away with big business and marriage, got as red-necked as Mr. Houghton when I proposed a world without any battleships in it.

44   Had the game gone too far? Was it a game any longer? In those prewar days, I stood to lose a great deal, for the sake of a hobby.

45   Now you are expecting me to describe how I saw the folly of my ways and came back to the warm nest, where prejudices are so soften called loyalties, where pointless actions are hallowed into custom by repetition, where we are content to say we think when all we do is feel.

46   But you would be wrong. I dropped my hobby and turned professional.

47   If I were to go back to the headmaster's study and find the dusty statuettes still there, I would arrange them differently. I would dust Venus and put her aside, for I have come to love her and know her for the fair things she is. But I would put the Thinker, sunk in his desperate thought, where there were shadows before him — and at his back, I would put the leopard, crouched and ready to spring.

❏ Questions for Discussion

1. Golding uses the three statuettes both symbolically and structurally. Explain what they mean to him as a young boy, as an adolescent, and as an adult.

2. Define the three grades of thinkers according to Golding.

3. Golding implies that most people are grade-three thinkers, dominated by prejudices and unwilling to examine their assumptions. Do you agree? Why or why not?

4. Explain the appropriateness of describing grade-three thinkers as cows that "graze all the same way on the side of a hill." Why are grade-three thinkers dangerous? What is dangerous about grade-two thinking?

5. How does Golding's assessment of most human intelligence compare to that of Socrates in the allegory of the cave?

❏ Suggestions for Exploration and Writing

1. In an essay, explain your own classification of thinkers.

2. Discuss how education and experience can change a person's level of thinking.

3. Write an essay using Golding's classification but developing it by using your own acquaintances and experience as examples.

FICTION

WILLIAM FAULKNER (1897–1962)

Barn Burning

The store in which the Justice of the Peace's court was sitting smelled   1
of cheese. The boy, crouched on his nail keg at the back of the crowded
room, knew he smelled cheese, and more: from where he sat he could see
the ranked shelves close-packed with the solid, squat, dynamic shapes of
tin cans whose labels his stomach read, not from the lettering which
meant nothing to his mind but from the scarlet devils and the silver curve
of fish—this, the cheese which he knew he smelled and the hermetic meat
which his intestines believed he smelled coming in intermittent gusts
momentary and brief between the other constant one, the smell and sense
just a little of fear because mostly of despair and grief, the old fierce pull
of blood. He could not see the table where the Justice sat and before
which his father and his father's enemy (*our enemy* he thought in that
despair: *ourn! mine and hisn both! He's my father!*) stood, but he could
hear them, the two of them that is, because his father had said no word
yet:

"But what proof have you, Mr. Harris?"   2

"I told you. The hog got into my corn. I caught it up and sent it back   3
to him. He had no fence that would hold it. I told him so, warned him.
The next time I put the hog in my pen. When he came to get it I gave him
enough wire to patch up his pen. The next time I put the hog up and kept
it. I rode down to his house and saw the wire I gave him still rolled on to
the spool in his yard. I told him he could have the hog when he paid me
a dollar pound fee. That evening a nigger came with the dollar and got
the hog. He was a strange nigger. He said, 'He say to tell you wood and
hay kin burn.' I said, 'What?' 'That whut he say to tell you,' the nigger
said. 'Wood and hay kin burn.' That night my barn burned. I got the
stock out but I lost the barn."

"Where's the nigger? Have you got him?"   4

"He was a strange nigger, I tell you. I don't know what became of   5
him."

"But that's not proof. Don't you see that's not proof?"   6

"Get that boy up here. He knows." For a moment the boy thought too   7
that the man meant his older brother until Harris said, "Not him. The
little one. The boy," and, crouching, small for his age, small and wiry like
his father, in patched and faded jeans even too small for him, with
straight, uncombed, brown hair and eyes gray and wild as storm scud, he
saw the men between himself and the table part and become a lane of
grim faces, at the end of which he saw the Justice, a shabby, collarless,

graying man in spectacles, beckoning him. He felt no floor under his bare feet; he seemed to walk beneath the palpable weight of the grim turning faces. His father, still in his black Sunday coat donned not for the trial but for the moving, did not even look at him. *He aims for me to lie,* he thought, again with that frantic grief and despair. *And I will have to do hit.*

8   "What's your name, boy?" the Justice said.

9   "Colonel Sartoris Snopes," the boy whispered.

10   "Hey?" the Justice said. "Talk louder. Colonel Sartoris? I reckon anybody named for Colonel Sartoris in this country can't help but tell the truth, can they?" The boy said nothing. *Enemy! Enemy!* he thought; for a moment he could not even see, could not see that the Justice's face was kindly nor discern that his voice was troubled when he spoke to the man named Harris: "Do you want me to question this boy?" But he could hear, and during those subsequent long seconds while there was absolutely no sound in the crowded little room save that of quiet and intent breathing it was as if he had swung outward at the end of a grape vine, over a ravine, and at the top of the swing had been caught in a prolonged instant of mesmerized gravity, weightless in time.

11   "No!" Harris said violently, explosively. "Damnation! Send him out of here!" Now time, the fluid world rushed beneath him again, the voices coming to him again through the smell of cheese and sealed meat, the fear and despair and the old grief of blood:

12   "This case is closed. I can't find against you, Snopes, but I can give you advice. Leave this country and don't come back to it."

13   His father spoke for the first time, his voice cold and harsh, level, without emphasis: "I aim to. I don't figure to stay in a country among people who . . ." he said something unprintable and vile, addressed to no one.

14   "That'll do," the Justice said. "Take your wagon and get out of this country before dark. Case dismissed."

15   His father turned, and he followed the stiff black coat, the wiry figure walking a little stiffly from where a Confederate provost's man's musket ball had taken him in the heel on a stolen horse thirty years ago, followed the two backs now, since his older brother had appeared from somewhere in the crowd, no taller than the father but thicker, chewing tobacco steadily, between the two lines of grim-faced men and out of the store and across the worn gallery and down the sagging steps and among the dogs and half-grown boys in the mild May dust, where as he passed a voice hissed:

16   "Barn burner!"

17   Again he could not see, whirling; there was a face in a red haze, moonlike, bigger than the full moon, the owner of it half again his size, he leaping in the red haze toward the face, feeling no blow, feeling no shock when his head struck the earth, scrabbling up and leaping again,

feeling no blow this time either and tasting no blood, scrabbling up to see the other boy in full flight and himself already leaping into pursuit as his father's hand jerked him back, the harsh, cold voice speaking above him: "Go get in the wagon."

It stood in a grove of locusts and mulberries across the road. His two 18 hulking sisters in their Sunday dresses and his mother and her sister in calico and sunbonnets were already in it, sitting on and among the sorry residue of the dozen and more movings which even the boy could remember—the battered stove, the broken beds and chairs, the clock inlaid with mother-of-pearl, which would not run, stopped at some fourteen minutes past two o'clock of a dead and forgotten day and time, which had been his mother's dowry. She was crying, though when she saw him she drew her sleeve across her face and began to descend from the wagon. "Get back," the father said.

"He's hurt. I got to get some water and wash his . . ." 19

"Get back in the wagon," his father said. He got in too, over the 20 tail-gate. His father mounted to the seat where the older brother already sat and struck the gaunt mules two savage blows with the peeled willow, but without heat. It was not even sadistic; it was exactly that same quality which in later years would cause his descendants to over-run the engine before putting a motor car into motion, striking and reining back in the same movement. The wagon went on, the store with its quiet crowd of grimly watching men dropped behind; a curve in the road hid it. *Forever* he thought. *Maybe he's done satisfied now, now that he has . . .* stopping himself, not to say it aloud even to himself. His mother's hand touched his shoulder.

"Does hit hurt?" she said. 21

"Naw," he said. "Hit don't hurt. Lemme be." 22

"Can't you wipe some of the blood off before hit dries?" 23

"I'll wash tonight," he said. "Lemme be, I tell you." 24

The wagon went on. He did not know where they were going. None of 25 them ever did or ever asked, because it was always somewhere, always a house of sorts waiting for them a day or two days or even three days away. Likely his father had already arranged to make a crop on another farm before he . . . Again he had to stop himself. He (the father) always did. There was something about his wolflike independence and even courage when the advantage was at least neutral which impressed strangers, as if they got from his latent ravening ferocity not so much a sense of dependability as a feeling that his ferocious conviction in the rightness of his own actions would be of advantage to all whose interest lay with his.

That night they camped, in a grove of oaks and beeches where a spring 26 ran. The nights were still cool and they had a fire against it, of a rail lifted from a nearby fence and cut into lengths—a small fire, neat, niggard almost, a shrewd fire; such fires were his father's habit and custom always, even in freezing weather. Older, the boy might have remarked this and wondered why not a big one; why should not a man who had not only seen the waste and extravagance of war, but who had in his blood an inherent voracious prodigality with material not his own, have burned everything in sight? Then he might have gone a step farther and thought that that was the reason: that niggard blaze was the living fruit of nights passed during those four years in the woods hiding from all men, blue and gray, with his strings of horses (captured horses, he called them). And older still, he might have divined the true reason: that the element of fire spoke to some deep mainspring of his father's being, as the element of steel or of powder spoke to other men, as the one weapon for the preservation of integrity, else breath were not worth the breathing, and hence to be regarded with respect and used with discretion.

27   But he did not think this now and he had seen those same niggard blazes all his life. He merely ate his supper beside it and was already half asleep over his iron plate when his father called him, and once more he followed the stiff back, the stiff and ruthless limp, up the slope and on to the starlit road where, turning, he could see his father against the stars but without face or depth—a shape black, flat, and bloodless as though cut from tin in the iron folds of the frock-coat which had not been made for him, the voice harsh like tin and without heat like tin:

28   "You were fixing to tell them. You would have told him."

29   He didn't answer. His father struck him with the flat of his hand on the side of the head, hard but without heat, exactly as he had struck the two mules at the store, exactly as he would strike either of them with any stick in order to kill a horse fly, his voice without heat or anger: "You're getting to be a man. You got to learn. You got to learn to stick to your own blood or you ain't going to have any blood to stick to you. Do you think either of them, any man there this morning, would? Don't you know all they wanted was a chance to get at me because they knew I had them beat? Eh?" Later, twenty years later, he was to tell himself, "If I had said they wanted only truth, justice, he would have hit me again." But now he said nothing. He was not crying. He just stood there. "Answer me," his father said.

30   "Yes," he whispered. His father turned.

31   "Get on to bed. We'll be there tomorrow."

32   Tomorrow they were there. In the early afternoon the wagon stopped before a paintless two-room house identical almost with the dozen others it had stopped before even in the boy's ten years, and again, as on the other dozen occasions, his mother and aunt got down and began to unload the wagon, although his two sisters and his father and brother had not moved.

33   "Likely hit ain't fitten for hawgs," one of the sisters said.

34   "Nevertheless, fit it will and you'll hog it and like it," his father said. "Get out of them chairs and help your Ma unload."

35   The two sisters got down, big, bovine, in a flutter of cheap ribbons; one of them drew from the jumbled wagon bed a battered lantern, the other

a worn broom. His father handed the reins to the older son and began to climb stiffly over the wheel. "When they get unloaded, take the team to the barn and feed them." Then he said, and at first the boy thought he was still speaking to his brother: "Come with me."

"Me?" he said.   36

"Yes," his father said. "You."   37

"Abner," his mother said. His father paused and looked back—the   38
harsh level stare beneath the shaggy, graying irascible brows.

"I reckon I'll have a word with the man that aims to begin tomorrow   39
owning me body and soul for the next eight months."

They went back up the road. A week ago—or before last night, that   40
is—he would have asked where they were going, but not now. His father
had struck him before last night but never before had he paused afterward to explain why; it was as if the blow and the following calm,
outrageous voice still rang, repercussed, divulging nothing to him save
the terrible handicap of being young, the light weight of his few years,
just heavy enough to prevent his soaring free of the world as it seemed to
be ordered but not heavy enough to keep him footed solid in it, to resist
it and try to change the course of its events.

Presently he could see the grove of oaks and cedars and the other   41
flowering trees and shrubs where the house would be, though not the
house yet. They walked beside a fence massed with honeysuckle and
Cherokee roses and came to a gate swinging open between two brick
pillars, and now, beyond a sweep of drive he saw the house for the first
time and at that instant he forgot his father and the terror and despair
both, and even when he remembered his father again (who had not
stopped) the terror and despair did not return. Because, for all the twelve
movings, they had sojourned until now in a poor country, a land of small
farms and fields and houses, and he had never seen a house like this
before. *Hit's big as a courthouse* he thought quietly, with a surge of peace
and joy whose reason he could not have thought into words, being too
young for that: *They are safe from him. People whose lives are a part of
this peace and dignity are beyond his touch, he no more to them than a
buzzing wasp: capable of stinging for a little moment but that's all; the
spell of this peace and dignity rendering even the barns and stable and
cribs which belong to it impervious to the puny flames he might contrive
. . .* this, the peace and joy, ebbing for an instant as he looked again at the
stiff black back, the stiff and implacable limp of the figure which was not
dwarfed by the house, for the reason that it had never looked big
anywhere and which now, against the serene columned backdrop, had
more than ever that impervious quality of something cut ruthlessly from
tin, depthless, as though, sidewise to the sun, it would cast no shadow.
Watching him, the boy remarked the absolutely undeviating course
which his father held and saw the stiff foot come squarely down in a pile
of fresh droppings where a horse had stood in the drive and which his
father could have avoided by a simple change of stride. But it ebbed only

a moment, though he could not have thought this into words either, walking on in the spell of the house, which he could even want but without envy, without sorrow, certainly never with that ravening and jealous rage which unknown to him walked in the ironlike black coat before him: *Maybe he will feel it too. Maybe it will even change him now from what maybe he couldn't help but be.*

42   They crossed the portico. Now he could hear his father's stiff foot as it came down on the boards with clocklike finality, a sound out of all proportion to the displacement of the body it bore and which was not dwarfed either by the white door before it, as though it had attained to a sort of vicious and ravening minimum not to be dwarfed by anything—the flat, wide, black hat, the formal coat of broadcloth which had once been black but which had now that friction-glazed greenish cast of the bodies of old house flies, the lifted sleeve which was too large, the lifted hand like a curled claw. The door opened so promptly that the boy knew the Negro must have been watching them all the time, an old man with neat grizzled hair, in a linen jacket, who stood barring the door with his body, saying, "Wipe yo foots, white man, fo you come in here. Major ain't home nohow."

43   "Get out of my way, nigger," his father said, without heat too, flinging the door back and the Negro also and entering, his hat still on his head. And now the boy saw the prints of the stiff foot on the doorjamb and saw them appear on the pale rug behind the machinelike deliberation of the foot which seemed to bear (or transmit) twice the weight which the body compassed. The Negro was shouting "Miss Lula! Miss Lula!" somewhere behind them, then the boy, deluged as though by a warm wave by a suave turn of the carpeted stair and a pendant glitter of chandeliers and a mute gleam of gold frames, heard the swift feet and saw her too, a lady—perphaps he had never seen her like before either—in a gray, smooth gown with lace at the throat and an apron tied at the waist and the sleeves turned back, wiping cake or biscuit dough from her hands with a towel as she came up the hall, looking not at his father at all but at the tracks on the blond rug with an expression of incredulous amazement.

44   "I tried," the Negro cried. "I tole him to . . ."

45   "Will you please go away?" she said in a shaking voice. "Major de Spain is not at home. Will you please go away?"

46   His father had not spoken again. He did not speak again. He did not even look at her. He just stood stiff in the center of the rug, in his hat, the shaggy iron-gray brows twitching slightly above the pebble-colored eyes as he appeared to examine the house with brief deliberation. Then with the same deliberation he turned; the boy watched him pivot on the good leg and saw the stiff foot drag around the arc of the turning, leaving a final long and fading smear. His father never looked at it, he never once looked down at the rug. The Negro held the door. It closed behind them, upon the hysteric and indistinguishable woman-wail. His father stopped at the top of the steps and scraped his boot clean on the edge of it. At the

gate he stopped again. He stood for a moment, planted stiffly on the stiff foot, looking back at the house. "Pretty and white, ain't it?" he said. "That's sweat. Nigger sweat. Maybe it ain't white enough yet to suit him. Maybe he wants to mix some white sweat with it."

Two hours later the boy was chopping wood behind the house within which his mother and aunt and the two sisters (the mother and aunt, not the two girls, he knew that; even at this distance and muffled by walls the flat loud voices of the two girls emanated an incorrigible idle inertia) were setting up the stove to prepare a meal, when he heard the hooves and saw the linen-clad man on a fine sorrel mare, whom he recognized even before he saw the rolled rug in front of the Negro youth following on a fat bay carriage horse—a suffused, angry face vanishing, still at full gallop, beyond the corner of the house where his father and brother were sitting in the two tilted chairs; and a moment later, almost before he could have put the axe down, he heard the hooves again and watched the sorrel mare go back out of the yard, already galloping again. Then his father began to shout one of the sisters' names, who presently emerged backward from the kitchen door dragging the rolled rug along the ground by one end while the other sister walked behind it. 47

"If you ain't going to tote, go on and set up the wash pot," the first said. 48

"You, Sarty!" the second shouted. "Set up the wash pot!" His father appeared at the door, framed against that shabbiness, as he had been against that other bland perfection, impervious to either, the mother's anxious face at his shoulder. 49

"Go on," the father said. "Pick it up." The two sisters stooped, broad, lethargic; stooping, they presented an incredible expanse of pale cloth and a flutter of tawdry ribbons. 50

"If I thought enough of a rug to have to git hit all the way from France I wouldn't keep hit where folks coming in would have to tromp on hit," the first said. They raised the rug. 51

"Abner," the mother said. "Let me do it." 52

"You go back and git dinner," his father said. "I'll tend to this." 53

From the woodpile through the rest of the afternoon the boy watched them, the rug spread flat in the dust beside the bubbling wash pot, the two sisters stooping over it with that profound and lethargic reluctance, while the father stood over them in turn, implacable and grim, driving them though never raising his voice again. He could smell the harsh homemade lye they were using; he saw his mother come to the door once and look toward them with an expression not anxious now but very like despair; he saw his father turn, and he fell to with the axe and saw from the corner of his eye his father raise from the ground a flattish fragment of field stone and examine it and return to the pot, and this time his mother actually spoke: "Abner. Abner. Please don't. Please, Abner." 54

Then he was done too. It was dusk; the whippoorwills had already begun. He could smell coffee from the room where they would presently 55 eat the cold food remaining from the mid-afternoon meal, though when he entered the house he realized they were having coffee again probably because there was a fire on the hearth, before which the rug now lay spread over the backs of the two chairs. The tracks of his father's foot were gone. Where they had been were now long, water-cloudy scoriations resembling the sporadic course of a lilliputian mowing machine.

56   It still hung there while they ate the cold food and then went to bed, scattered without order or claim up and down the two rooms, his mother in one bed, where his father would later lie, the older brother in the other, himself, the aunt, and the two sisters on pallets on the floor. But his father was not in bed yet. The last thing the boy remembered was the depthless, harsh silhouette of the hat and coat bending over the rug and it seemed to him that he had not even closed his eyes when the silhouette was standing over him, the fire almost dead behind it, the stiff foot prodding him awake. "Catch up the mule," his father said.

57   When he returned with the mule his father was standing in the black door, the rolled rug over his shoulder. "Ain't you going to ride?" he said.

58   "No. Give me your foot."

59   He bent his knee into his father's hand, the wiry, surprising power flowed smoothly, rising, he rising with it, on to the mule's bare back (they had owned a saddle once; the boy could remember it though not when or where) and with the same effortlessness his father swung the rug up in front of him. Now in the starlight they retraced the afternoon's path, up the dusty road rife with honeysuckle, through the gate and up the black tunnel of the drive to the lightless house, where he sat on the mule and felt the rough warp of the rug drag across his thighs and vanish.

60   "Don't you want me to help?" he whispered. His father did not answer and now he heard again that stiff foot striking the hollow portico with that wooden and clocklike deliberation, that outrageous overstatement of the weight it carried. The rug, hunched, not flung (the boy could tell that even in the darkness) from his father's shoulder struck the angle of wall and floor with a sound unbelievably loud, thunderous, then the foot again, unhurried and enormous; a light came on in the house and the boy sat, tense, breathing steadily and quietly and just a little fast, though the foot itself did not increase its beat at all, descending the steps now; now the boy could see him.

61   "Don't you want to ride now?" he whispered. "We kin both ride now," the light within the house altering now, flaring up and sinking. *He's coming down the stairs now,* he thought. He had already ridden the mule up beside the horse block; presently his father was up behind him and he doubled the reins over and slashed the mule across the neck, but before the animal could begin to trot the hard, thin arm came around him, the hard, knotted hand jerking the mule back to a walk.

62   In the first red rays of the sun they were in the lot, putting plow gear on the mules. This time the sorrel mare was in the lot before he heard it

at all, the rider collarless and even bareheaded, trembling, speaking in a shaking voice as the woman in the house had done, his father merely looking up once before stooping again to the hame he was buckling, so that the man on the mare spoke to his stooping back:

"You must realize you have ruined that rug. Wasn't there anybody here, any of your women . . ." he ceased, shaking, the boy watching him, the older brother leaning now in the stable door, chewing, blinking slowly and steadily at nothing apparently. "It cost a hundred dollars. But you never had a hundred dollars. You never will. So I'm going to charge you twenty bushels of corn against your crop. I'll add it in your contract and when you come to the commissary you can sign it. That won't keep Mrs. de Spain quiet but maybe it will teach you to wipe your feet off before you enter her house again." 63

Then he was gone. The boy looked at his father, who still had not spoken or even looked up again, who was now adjusting the logger-head in the hame. 64

"Pap," he said. His father looked at him—the inscrutable face, the shaggy brows beneath where the gray eyes glinted coldly. Suddenly the boy went toward him, fast, stopping as suddenly. "You done the best you could!" he cried. "If he wanted hit done different why didn't he wait and tell you how? He won't git no twenty bushels! He won't git none! We'll gather hit and hide hit! I kin watch . . ." 65

"Did you put the cutter back in that straight stock like I told you?" 66

"No, sir," he said. 67

"Then go do it." 68

That was Wednesday. During the rest of that week he worked steadily, at what was within his scope and some which was beyond it, with an industry that did not need to be driven nor even commanded twice; he had this from his mother, with the difference that some at least of what he did he liked to do, such as splitting wood with the half-size axe which his mother and aunt had earned, or saved money somehow, to present him with at Christmas. In company with the two older women (and on one afternoon, even one of the sisters), he built pens for the shoat and the cow which were a part of his father's contract with the landlord, and one afternoon, his father being absent, gone somewhere on one of the mules, he went to the field. 69

They were running a middle buster now, his brother holding the plow straight while he handled the reins, and walking beside the straining mule, the rich black soil shearing cool and damp against his bare ankles, he thought *Maybe this is the end of it. Maybe even that twenty bushels that seems hard to have to pay for just a rug will be a cheap price for him to stop forever and always from being what he used to be;* thinking, dreaming now, so that his brother had to speak sharply to him to mind the mule: *Maybe he even won't collect the twenty bushels. Maybe it will all add up and balance and vanish—corn, rug, fire; the terror and grief;* 70

the being pulled two ways like between two teams of horses — gone, done with for ever and ever.

71   Then it was Saturday; he looked up from beneath the mule he was harnessing and saw his father in the black coat and hat. "Not that," his father said. "The wagon gear." And then, two hours later, sitting in the wagon bed behind his father and brother on the seat, the wagon accomplished a final curve, and he saw the weathered paintless store with its tattered tobacco- and patent-medicine posters and the tethered wagons and saddle animals below the gallery. He mounted the gnawed steps behind his father and brother, and there again was the lane of quiet, watching faces for the three of them to walk through. He saw the man in spectacles sitting at the plank table and he did not need to be told this was a Justice of the Peace; he sent one glare of fierce, exultant, partisan defiance at the man in collar and cravat now, whom he had seen but twice before in his life, and that on a galloping horse, who now wore on his face an expression not of rage but of amazed unbelief which the boy could not have known was at the incredible circumstance of being sued by one of his own tenants, and came and stood against his father and cried at the Justice: "He ain't done it! He ain't burnt . . ."

72   "Go back to the wagon," his father said.

73   "Burnt?" the Justice said. "Do I understand this rug was burned too?"

74   "Does anybody here claim it was?" his father said. "Go back to the wagon." But he did not, he merely retreated to the rear of the room, crowded as that other had been, but not to sit down this time, instead, to stand pressing among the motionless bodies, listening to the voices:

75   "And you claim twenty bushels of corn is too high for the damage you did to the rug?"

76   "He brought the rug to me and said he wanted the tracks washed out of it. I washed the tracks out and took the rug back to him."

77   "But you didn't carry the rug back to him in the same condition it was in before you made the tracks on it."

78   His father did not answer, and now for perhaps half a minute there was no sound at all save that of breathing, the faint, steady suspiration of complete and intent listening.

79   "You decline to answer that, Mr. Snopes?" Again his father did not answer. "I'm going to find against you, Mr. Snopes. I'm going to find that you were responsible for the injury to Major de Spain's rug and hold you liable for it. But twenty bushels of corn seems a little high for a man in your circumstances to have to pay. Major de Spain claims it cost a hundred dollars. October corn will be worth about fifty cents. I figure that if Major de Spain can stand a ninety-five dollar loss on something he paid cash for, you can stand a five-dollar loss you haven't earned yet. I hold you in damages to Major de Spain to the amount of ten bushels of corn over and above your contract with him, to be paid to him out of your crop at gathering time. Court adjourned."

It had taken no time hardly, the morning was but half begun. He   80
thought they would return home and perhaps back to the field, since they
were late, far behind all other farmers. But instead his father passed on
behind the wagon, merely indicating with his hand for the older brother
to follow with it, and crossed the road toward the blacksmith shop
opposite, pressing on after his father, overtaking him, speaking, whispering up at the harsh, calm face beneath the weathered hat: "He won't
git no ten bushels either. He won't git one. We'll . . ." until his father
glanced for an instant down at him, the face absolutely calm, the grizzled
eyebrows tangled above the cold eyes, the voice almost pleasant, almost
gentle:

"You think so? Well, we'll wait till October anyway."   81

The matter of the wagon—the setting of a spoke or two and the   82
tightening of the tires—did not take long either, the business of the tires
accomplished by driving the wagon into the spring branch behind the
shop and letting it stand there, the mules nuzzling into the water from
time to time, and the boy on the seat with the idle reins, looking up the
slope and through the sooty tunnel of the shed where the slow hammer
rang and where his father sat on an upended cypress bolt, easily, either
talking or listening, still sitting there when the boy brought the dripping
wagon up out of the branch and halted it before the door.

"Take them on to the shade and hitch," his father said. He did so and   83
returned. His father and the smith and a third man squatting on his heels
inside the door were talking, about crops and animals; the boy, squatting
too in the ammoniac dust and hoof-parings and scales of rust, heard his
father tell a long and unhurried story out of the time before the birth of
the older brother even when he had been a professional horsetrader. And
then his father came up beside him where he stood before a tattered last
year's circus poster on the other side of the store, gazing rapt and quiet
at the scarlet horses, the incredible poisings and convulsions of tulle and
tights and the painted leers of comedians, and said, "It's time to eat."

But not at home. Squatting beside his brother against the front wall, he   84
watched his father emerge from the store and produce from a paper sack
a segment of cheese and divide it carefully and deliberately into three
with his pocket knife and produce crackers from the same sack. They all
three squatted on the gallery and ate, slowly, without talking; then in the
store again, they drank from a tin dipper tepid water smelling of the
cedar bucket and of living beech trees. And still they did not go home. It
was a horse lot this time, a tall rail fence upon and along which men
stood and sat and out of which one by one horses were led, to be walked
and trotted and then cantered back and forth along the road while the
slow swapping and buying went on and the sun began to slant westward,
they—the three of them—watching and listening, the older brother with
his muddy eyes and his steady, inevitable tobacco, the father commenting
now and then on certain of the animals, to no one in particular.

85 It was after sundown when they reached home. They ate supper by lamplight, then, sitting on the doorstep, the boy watched the night fully accomplish, listening to the whippoorwills and the frogs, when he heard his mother's voice: "Abner! No! No! Oh, God. Oh, God. Abner!" and he rose, whirled, and saw the altered light through the door where a candle stub now burned in a bottle neck on the table and his father, still in the hat and coat, at once formal and burlesque as though dressed carefully for some shabby and ceremonial violence, emptying the reservoir of the lamp back into the five-gallon kerosene can from which it had been filled, while the mother tugged at his arm until he shifted the lamp to the other hand and flung her back, not savagely or viciously, just hard, into the wall, her hands flung out against the wall for balance, her mouth open and in her face the same quality of hopeless despair as had been in her voice. Then his father saw him standing in the door.

86 "Go to the barn and get that can of oil we were oiling the wagon with," he said. The boy did not move. Then he could speak.

87 "What . . ." he cried. "What are you . . ."

88 "Go get that oil," his father said. "Go."

89 Then he was moving, running, outside the house, toward the stable: this the old habit, the old blood which he had not been permitted to choose for himself, which had been bequeathed him willy nilly and which had run for so long (and who knew where, battening on what of outrage and savagery and lust) before it came to him. *I could keep on,* he thought. *I could run on and on and never look back, never need to see his face again. Only I can't. I can't,* the rusted can in his hand now, the liquid sploshing in it as he ran back to the house and into it, into the sound of his mother's weeping in the next room, and handed the can to his father.

90 "Ain't you going to even send a nigger?" he cried. "At least you sent a nigger before!"

91 This time his father didn't strike him. The hand came even faster than the blow had, the same hand which had set the can on the table with almost excruciating care flashing from the can toward him too quick for him to follow it, gripping him by the back of his shirt and on to tiptoe before he had seen it quit the can, the face stooping at him in breathless and frozen ferocity, the cold, dead voice speaking over his to the older brother who leaned against the table, chewing with that steady, curious, sidewise motion of cows:

92 "Empty the can into the big one and go on. I'll catch up with you."

93 "Better tie him up to the bedpost," the brother said.

94 "Do like I told you," the father said. Then the boy was moving, his bunched shirt and the hard, bony hand between his shoulder-blades, his toes just touching the floor, across the room and into the other one, past the sisters sitting with spread heavy thighs in the two chairs over the cold hearth, and to where his mother and aunt sat side by side on the bed, the aunt's arm about his mother's shoulders.

95 "Hold him," the father said. The aunt made a startled movement. "Not

you," the father said. "Lennie. Take hold of him. I want to see you do it."
His mother took him by the wrist. "You'll hold him better than that. If
he gets loose don't you know what he is going to do? He will go up
yonder." He jerked his head toward the road. "Maybe I'd better tie him."

"I'll hold him," his mother whispered.   96

"See you do then." Then his father was gone, the stiff foot heavy and   97
measured upon the boards, ceasing at last.

Then he began to struggle. His mother caught him in both arms, he   98
jerking and wrenching at them. He would be stronger in the end, he knew
that. But he had no time to wait for it. "Lemme go!" he cried. "I don't
want to have to hit you!"

"Let him go!" the aunt said. "If he don't go, before God, I am going   99
up there myself!"

"Don't you see I can't?" his mother cried. "Sarty! Sarty! No! No! Help   100
me, Lizzie!"

Then he was free. His aunt grasped at him but it was too late. He   101
whirled, running, his mother stumbled forward on to her knees behind
him, crying to the nearer sister: "Catch him, Net! Catch him!" But that
was too late too, the sister (the sisters were twins, born at the same time,
yet either of them now gave the impression of being, encompassing as
much living meat and volume and weight as any other two of the family)
not yet having begun to rise from the chair, her head, face, alone merely
turned, presenting to him in the flying instant an astonishing expanse of
young female features untroubled by any surprise even, wearing only an
expression of bovine interest. Then he was out of the room, out of the
house, in the mild dust of the starlit road and the heavy rifeness of
honeysuckle, the pale ribbon unspooling with terrific slowness under his
running feet, reaching the gate at last and turning in, running, his heart
and lungs drumming, on up the drive toward the lighted house, the
lighted door. He did not knock, he burst in, sobbing for breath, incapable
for the moment of speech; he saw the astonished face of the Negro in the
linen jacket without knowing when the Negro had appeared.

"De Spain!" he cried, panted. "Where's . . ." then he saw the white   102
man too emerging from a white door down the hall. "Barn!" he cried.
"Barn!"

"What?" the white man said. "Barn?"   103

"Yes!" the boy cried. "Barn!"   104

"Catch him!" the white man shouted.   105

But it was too late this time too. The Negro grasped his shirt, but the 106
entire sleeve, rotten with washing, carried away, and he was out that
door too and in the drive again, and had actually never ceased to run even
while he was screaming into the white man's face.

Behind him the white man was shouting. "My horse! Fetch my horse!"   107
and he thought for an instant of cutting across the park and climbing the
fence into the road, but he did not know the park nor how the vine-
massed fence might be and he dared not risk it. So he ran on down the

drive, blood and breath roaring; presently he was in the road again though he could not see it. He could not hear either: the galloping mare was almost upon him before he heard her, and even then he held his course, as if the very urgency of his wild grief and need must in a moment more find him wings, waiting until the ultimate instant to hurl himself aside and into the seed-choked roadside ditch as the horse thundered past and on, for an instant in furious silhouette against the stars, the tranquil early summer night sky which, even before the shape of the horse and rider vanished, stained abruptly and violently upward: a long, swirling roar incredible and soundless, blotting the stars, and springing up and into the road again, running again, knowing it was too late yet still running even after he heard the shot and an instant later, two shots, pausing now without knowing he had ceased to run, crying, "Pap! Pap!", running again before he knew he had begun to run, stumbling, tripping over something and scrabbling up again without ceasing to run, looking backward over his shoulder at the glare as he got up, running on among the invisible trees, panting, sobbing, "Father! Father!"

108   At midnight he was sitting on the crest of a hill. He did not know it was midnight and he did not know how far he had come. But there was no glare behind him now and he sat now, his back toward what he had called home for four days anyhow, his face toward the dark woods which he would enter when breath was strong again, small, shaking steadily in the chill darkness, hugging himself into the remainder of his thin, rotten shirt, the grief and despair now no longer terror and fear but just grief and despair. *Father. My father,* he thought. "He was brave!" he cried suddenly, aloud but not loud, no more than a whisper. "He was! He was in the war! He was in Colonel Sartoris' cav'ry!" not knowing that his father had gone to that war a private in the fine old European sense, wearing no uniform, admitting the authority of and giving fidelity to no man or army or flag, going to war as Malbrouck himself did: for booty—it meant nothing and less than nothing to him if it were enemy booty or his own.

109   The slow constellations wheeled on. It would be dawn and then sun-up after a while and he would be hungry. But that would be tomorrow and now he was only cold, and walking would cure that. His breathing was easier now and he decided to get up and go on, and then he found that he had been asleep because he knew it was almost dawn, the night almost over. He could tell that from the whippoorwills. They were everywhere now among the dark trees below him, constant and inflectioned and ceaseless, so that, as the instant for giving over to the day birds drew nearer and nearer, there was no interval at all between them. He got up. He was a little stiff, but walking would cure that too as it would the cold, and soon there would be the sun. He went on down the hill, toward the dark woods within which the liquid silver voices of the birds called unceasing—the rapid and urgent beating of the urgent and quiring heart of the late spring night. He did not look back.

❏ **Questions for Discussion**

1. What do the Snopes own? Where and how do they live? How do poverty and illiteracy affect the family's behavior?

2. What is the contractual relationship between Abner Snopes and Major de Spain? How are the size and magnificence of Major de Spain's home important to the story? Why does Abner Snopes soil Major de Spain's rug, then destroy it when asked to wash it?

3. Why does Sarty think of some people outside his family as "enemies"? Why is he loyal to a man who has burned barns and defied the law? How does Sarty demonstrate loyalty to his father?

4. This story is told from the **point of view** of a young boy, yet in the paragraph that begins "That night they camped . . . ," Faulkner theorizes about what the boy might conclude if he were older. What does this variation allow Faulkner to add to the story? Where else in the story does he use this technique?

5. "Barn Burning" could be described as an **initiation story,** one in which a character achieves significant growth toward maturity and recognizes that growth. What is the nature of Sarty's initiation?

6. What does fire symbolize to Abner Snopes? What is the **symbolism** of the time of day at the end of the story?

❏ **Suggestions for Exploration and Writing**

1. Faulkner describes Sarty as "being pulled two ways like between two teams of horses." Write an essay discussing the forces that cause Sarty's conflict and his search for a resolution to this conflict.

2. Does Sarty betray his father at the end of the story? Is his behavior justified? Why or why not?

3. Discuss the dynamics of the Snopes' family. Does the mother/wife have any control over what happens to the family?

Arthur C. Clarke (1917–)

Arthur C. Clarke, a British physicist and mathematician, writes both fiction and nonfiction. His works, selling in the millions, have been translated into dozens of languages. A 1945 paper published in Wireless World *helped to set the stage for modern telecommunications. Clarke is, however, probably best known for the screenplay* for Stanley Kubrick's 2001: A Space Odyssey, *based on Clarke's* short story "Sentinel of Eternity." "The Star," published in 1955, won a Hugo award for excellence in science fiction.

The Star

1   It is three thousand light years to the Vatican. Once, I believed that space could have no power over faith, just as I believed that the heavens declared the glory of God's handiwork. Now I have seen that handiwork, and my faith is sorely troubled. I stare at the crucifix that hangs on the cabin wall above the Mark VI Computer, and for the first time in my life I wonder if it is no more than an empty symbol.

2   I have told no one yet, but the truth cannot be concealed. The facts are there for all to read, recorded on the countless miles of magnetic tape and the thousands of photographs we are carrying back to Earth. Other scientists can interpret them as easily as I can, and I am not one who would condone that tampering with the truth which often gave my order a bad name in the olden days.

3   The crew are already sufficiently depressed: I wonder how they will take this ultimate irony. Few of them have any religious faith, yet they will not relish using this final weapon in their campaign against me—that private, good-natured, but fundamentally serious, war which lasted all the way from Earth. It amused them to have a Jesuit as chief astrophysicist: Dr. Chandler, for instance, could never get over it (why are medical men such notorious atheists?). Sometimes he would meet me on the observation deck, where the lights are always low so that the stars shine with undiminished glory. He would come up to me in the gloom and stand staring out of the great oval port, while the heavens crawled slowly around us as the ship turned end over end with the residual spin we had never bothered to correct.

4   "Well, Father," he would say at last, "it goes on forever and forever, and perhaps *Something* made it. But how you can believe that Something has a special interest in us and our miserable little world—that just beats me." Then the argument would start, while the stars and nebulae would swing around us in silent, endless arcs beyond the flawlessly clear plastic of the observation port.

5   It was, I think, the apparent incongruity of my position that caused most amusement to the crew. In vain I would point to my three papers in the *Astrophysical Journal* my five in the *Monthly Notices of the Royal Astronomical Society.* I would remind them that my order has long been famous for its scientific works. We may be few now, but ever since the eighteenth century we have made contributions to astronomy and geophysics out of all proportion to our numbers. Will my report on the Phoenix Nebula end our thousand years of history? It will end, I fear, much more than that.

6   I do not know who gave the nebula its name, which seems to me a very bad one. If it contains a prophecy, it is one that cannot be verified for several billion years. Even the word nebula is misleading: this is a far

smaller object than those stupendous clouds of mist—the stuff of unborn stars—that are scattered throughout the length of the Milky Way. On the cosmic scale, indeed, the Phoenix Nebula is a tiny thing—a tenuous shell of gas surrounding a single star.

Or what is left of a star . . .   7

The Rubens engraving of Loyola seems to mock me as it hangs there   8
above the spectrophotometer tracings. What would *you*, Father, have made of this knowledge that has come into my keeping, so far from the little world that was all the universe you knew? Would your faith have risen to the challenge, as mine has failed to do?

You gaze into the distance, Father, but I have traveled a distance   9
beyond any that you could have imagined when you founded our order a thousand years ago. No other survey ship has been so far from Earth: we are at the very frontiers of the explored universe. We set out to reach the Phoenix Nebula, we succeeded, and we are homeward bound with our burden of knowledge. I wish I could lift that burden from my shoulders, but I call to you in vain across the centuries and the light-years that lie between us.

On the book you are holding the words are plain to read. AD MAJOREM   10
DEI GLORIAM, the message runs, but it is a message I can no longer believe. Would you still believe it, if you could see what we have found?

We knew, of course, what the Phoenix Nebula was. Every year, in our   11
galaxy alone, more than a hundred stars explode, blazing for a few hours or days with thousands of times their normal brilliance before they sink back into death and obscurity. Such are the ordinary novae—the commonplace disasters of the universe. I have recorded the spectrograms and light curves of dozens since I started working at the Lunar Observatory.

But three or four times in every thousand years occurs something   12
beside which even a nova pales into total insignificance.

When a star becomes a *supernova*, it may for a little while outshine all 13
the massed suns of the galaxy. The Chinese astronomers watched this happen in A.D. 1054, not knowing what it was they saw. Five centuries later, in 1572, a supernova blazed in Cassiopeia so brilliantly that it was visible in the daylight sky. There have been three more in the thousand years that have passed since then.

Our mission was to visit the remnants of such a catastrophe, to   14
reconstruct the events that led up to it, and, if possible, to learn its cause. We came slowly in through the concentric shells of gas that had been blasted out six thousand years before, yet were expanding still. They were immensely hot, radiating even now with a fierce violet light, but were far too tenuous to do us any damage. When the star had exploded, its outer layers had been driven upward with such speed that they had escaped completely from its gravitational field. Now they formed a hollow shell large enough to engulf a thousand solar systems, and at its center burned the tiny, fantastic object which the star had now become —a White Dwarf, smaller than the Earth, yet weighing a million times as much.

15   The glowing gas shells were all around us, banishing the normal night of interstellar space. We were flying into the center of a cosmic bomb that had detonated millennia ago and whose incandescent fragments were still hurling apart. The immense scale of the explosion, and the fact that the debris already covered a volume of space many billions of miles across, robbed the scene of any visible movement. It would take decades before the unaided eye could detect any motion in these tortured wisps and eddies of gas, yet the sense of turbulent expansion was overwhelming.

16   We had checked our primary drive hours before, and were drifting slowly toward the fierce little star ahead. Once it had been a sun like our own, but it had squandered in a few hours the energy that should have kept it shining for a million years. Now it was a shrunken miser, hoarding its resources as if trying to make amends for its prodigal youth.

17   No one seriously expected to find planets. If there had been any before the explosion, they would have been boiled into puffs of vapor, and their substance lost in the greater wreckage of the star itself. But we made the automatic search, as we always do when approaching an unknown sun, and presently we found a single small world circling the star at an immense distance. It must have been the Pluto of this vanished solar system, orbiting on the frontiers of the night. Too far from the central sun ever to have known life, its remoteness had saved it from the fate of all its lost companions.

18   The passing fires had seared its rocks and burned away the mantle of frozen gas that must have covered it in the days before the disaster. We landed, and we found the Vault.

19   Its builders had made sure that we should. The monolithic marker that stood above the entrance was now a fused stump, but even the first long-range photographs told us that here was the work of intelligence. A little later we detected the continent-wide pattern of radio-activity that had been buried in the rock. Even if the pylon above the Vault had been destroyed, this would have remained, an immovable and all but eternal beacon calling to the stars. Our ship fell toward this gigantic bull's-eye like an arrow into its target.

20   The pylon must have been a mile high when it was built, but now it looked like a candle that had melted down into a puddle of wax. It took us a week to drill through the fused rock, since we did not have the proper tools for a task like this. We were astronomers, not archaeologists, but we could improvise. Our original purpose was forgotten: this lonely monument, reared with such labor at the greatest possible distance from the doomed sun, could have only one meaning. A civilization that knew it was about to die had made its last bid for immortality.

21   It will take us generations to examine all the treasures that were placed in the Vault. They had plenty of time to prepare, for their sun must have given its first warnings many years before the final detonation. Everything that they wished to preserve, all the fruit of their genius, they brought here to this distant world in the days before the end, hoping that

some other race would find it and that they would not be utterly forgotten. Would we have done as well, or would we have been too lost in our own misery to give thought to a future we could never see or share?

If only they had had a little more time! They could travel freely enough 22 between the planets of their own sun, but they had not yet learned to cross the interstellar gulfs, and the nearest solar system was a hundred light-years away. Yet even had they possessed the secret of the Transfinite Drive, no more than a few millions could have been saved. Perhaps it was better thus.

Even if they had not been so disturbingly human as their sculpture 23 shows, we could not have helped admiring them and grieving for their fate. They left thousands of visual records and the machines for projecting them, together with elaborate pictorial instructions from which it will not be difficult to learn their written language. We have examined many of these records, and brought to life for the first time in six thousand years the warmth and beauty of a civilization that in many ways must have been superior to our own. Perhaps they only showed us the best, and one can hardly blame them. But their words were very lovely, and their cities were built with a grace that matches anything of man's. We have watched them at work and play, and listened to their musical speech sounding across the centuries. One scene is still before my eyes—a group of children on a beach of strange blue sand, playing in the waves as children play on Earth. Curious whiplike trees line the shore, and some very large animal is wading in the shadows yet attracting no attention at all.

And sinking into the sea, still warm and friendly and life-giving, is the 24 sun that will soon turn traitor and obliterate all this innocent happiness.

Perhaps if we had not been so far from home and so vulnerable to 25 loneliness, we should not have been so deeply moved. Many of us had seen the ruins of ancient civilizations on other worlds, but they had never affected us so profoundly. This tragedy was unique. It is one thing for a race to fail and die, as nations and cultures have done on Earth. But to be destroyed so completely in the full flower of its achievement, leaving no survivors—how could that be reconciled with the mercy of God?

My colleagues have asked me that, and I have given what answers I 26 can. Perhaps you could have done better, Father Loyola, but I have found nothing in the *Exercitia Spiritualia* that helps me here. They were not an evil people: I do not know what gods they worshiped, if indeed they worshiped any. But I have looked back at them across the centuries, and have watched while the loveliness they used their last strength to preserve was brought forth again into the light of their shrunken sun. They could have taught us much: why were they destroyed?

I know the answers that my colleagues will give when they get back to 27 Earth. They will say that the universe has no purpose and no plan, that since a hundred suns explode every year in our galaxy, at this very moment some race is dying in the depths of space. Whether that race has done good or evil during its lifetime will make no difference in the end: there is no divine justice, for there is no God.

28   Yet, of course, what we have seen proves nothing of the sort. Anyone who argues thus is being swayed by emotion, not logic. God has no need to justify His actions to man. He who built the universe can destroy it when He chooses. It is arrogance—it is perilously near blasphemy—for us to say what He may or may not do.

29   This I could have accepted, hard though it is to look upon whole worlds and peoples thrown into the furnace. But there comes a point when even the deepest faith must falter, and now, as I look at the calculations lying before me, I know I have reached that point at last.

30   We could not tell, before we reached the nebula, how long ago the explosion took place. Now, from the astronomical evidence and the record in the rocks of that one surviving planet, I have been able to date it very exactly. I know in what year the light of this colossal conflagration reached our Earth. I know how brilliantly the supernova whose corpse now dwindles behind our speeding ship once shone in terrestrial skies. I know how it must have blazed low in the east before sunrise, like a beacon in that oriental dawn.

31   There can be no reasonable doubt: the ancient mystery is solved at last. Yet, oh God, there were so many stars you could have used. What was the need to give these people to the fire, that the symbol of their passing might shine above Bethlehem?

❑ Questions for Discussion

1. What is the **point of view** in "The Star"? Why is it crucial to the **irony** of the ending?

2. Is this Jesuit priest an exacting scientist? Why does he face a spiritual crisis? Explain the Jesuit's statement at the beginning of the story: "Once, I believed that space could have no power over faith, just as I believed that the heavens declared the glory of God's handiwork. Now I have seen that handiwork, and my faith is sorely troubled."

3. What is the priest's answer to skeptics who argue that "the universe has no purpose and no plan" and that "there is no God"? Is the priest comfortable with his answer?

PHILIP ROTH (1933–)

Born in Newark, New Jersey, Philip Roth is a contemporary American novelist, short story writer, and man of letters. Goodbye, Columbus (1955), his first book, is a collection of short stories including "The Conversion of the Jews." Roth frequently takes as his subject the urban Jews among whom he grew up. His novels, often comic, include the hilarious Portnoy's Complaint (1969), *about a*

Jewish man afflicted with an insatiable sexual desire for gentile women; Letting Go *(1962);* The Great American Novel *(1973); and the Zuckerman trilogy:* Zuckerman Bound *(1985),* The Counterlife *(1988), and* Deception *(1990).*

The Conversion of the Jews

"You're a real one for opening your mouth in the first place," Itzie said. "What do you open your mouth all the time for?"   1

"I didn't bring it up, Itz, I didn't," Ozzie said.   2

"What do you care about Jesus Christ for anyway?"   3

"I didn't bring up Jesus Christ. He did. I didn't even know what he was talking about. Jesus is historical, he kept saying. Jesus is historical." Ozzie mimicked the monumental voice of Rabbi Binder.   4

"Jesus was a person that lived like you and me," Ozzie continued. "that's what Binder said—"   5

"Yeah? . . . so what! What do I give two cents whether he lived or not. And what do you gotta open your mouth!" Itzie Lieberman favored closed-mouthedness, especially when it came to Ozzie Freedman's questions. Mrs. Freedman had to see Rabbi Binder twice before about Ozzie's questions and this Wednesday at four-thirty would be the third time. Itzie preferred to keep *his* mother in the kitchen; he settled for behind-the-back subtleties such as gestures, faces, snarls and other less delicate barnyard noises.   6

"He was a real person, Jesus, but he wasn't like God, and we don't believe he is God." Slowly, Ozzie was explaining Rabbi Binder's position to Itzie, who had been absent from Hebrew School the previous afternoon.   7

"The Catholics," Itzie said helpfully, "they believe in Jesus Christ, that he's God." Itzie Lieberman used "the Catholics" in its broadest sense—to include the Protestants.   8

Ozzie received Itzie's remark with a tiny head bob, as though it were a footnote, and went on. "His mother was Mary, and his father probably was Joseph," Ozzie said. "But the New Testament says his real father was God."   9

"His *real* father?"   10

"Yeah," Ozzie said, "that's the big thing, his father's supposed to be God."   11

"Bull."   12

"That's what Rabbi Binder says, that it's impossible—"   13

"Sure it's impossible. That stuff's all bull. To have a baby you gotta get laid," Itzie theologized. "Mary hadda get laid."   14

"That's what Binder says: 'the only way a woman can have a baby is to have intercourse with a man.'"   15

"He said *that,* Ozz?" For a moment it appeared that Itzie had put the theological question aside. "He said that, intercourse?" A little curled smile shaped itself in the lower half of Itzie's face like a pink mustache. "What you guys do, Ozz, you laugh or something?"   16

17 "I raised my hand."

18 "Yeah? Whatja say?"

19 "That's when I asked the question."

20 Itzie's face lit up. "Whatja ask about—intercourse?"

21 "No, I asked the question about God, how if He could create the heaven and earth in six days, and make all the animals and the fish and the light in six days—the light especially, that's what always gets me, that He could make the light. Making fish and animals, that's pretty good—"

22 "That's damn good." Itzie's appreciation was honest but unimaginative: it was as though God had just pitched a one-hitter.

23 "But making light . . . I mean when you think about it, it's really something," Ozzie said. "Anyway, I asked Binder if He could make all that in six days, and He could *pick* the six days he wanted right out of nowhere, why couldn't He let a woman have a baby without having intercourse."

24 "You said intercourse, Ozz, to Binder?"

25 "Yeah."

26 "Right in class?"

27 "Yeah."

28 Itzie smacked the side of his head.

29 "I mean, no kidding around," Ozzie said, "that'd really be nothing. After all that other stuff, that'd practically be nothing."

30 Itzie considered a moment. "What'd Binder say?"

31 "He started all over again explaining how Jesus was historical and how he lived like you and me but he wasn't God. So I said I under*stood* that. What I wanted to know was different."

32 What Ozzie wanted to know was always different. The first time he had wanted to know how Rabbi Binder could call the Jews "The Chosen People" if the Declaration of Independence claimed all men to be created equal. Rabbi Binder tried to distinguish for him between political equality and spiritual legitimacy, but what Ozzie wanted to know, he insisted vehemently, was different. That was the first time his mother had to come.

33 Then there was the plane crash. Fifty-eight people had been killed in a plane crash at La Guardia. In studying a casualty list in the newspaper his mother had discovered among the list of those dead eight Jewish names (his grandmother had nine but she counted Miller as a Jewish name); because of the eight she said the plane crash was "a tragedy." During free-discussion time on Wednesday Ozzie had brought to Rabbi Binder's attention this matter of "some of his relations" always picking out the Jewish names. Rabbi Binder had begun to explain cultural unity and some other things when Ozzie stood up at his seat and said that what he wanted to know was different. Rabbi Binder insisted that he sit down and it was then that Ozzie shouted that he wished all fifty-eight were Jews. That was the second time his mother came.

34 "And he kept explaining about Jesus being historical, and so I kept asking him. No kidding, Itz, he was trying to make me look stupid."

"So what he finally do?" 35

"Finally he starts screaming that I was deliberately simple-minded and 36
a wise guy, and that my mother had to come, and this was the last time.
And that I'd never get bar-mitzvahed if he could help it. Then, Itz, then
he starts talking in that voice like a statue, real slow and deep, and he says
that I better think over what I said about the Lord. He told me to go to
his office and think it over." Ozzie leaned his body towards Itzie.

"Itz, I thought it over for a solid hour, and now I'm convinced God 37
could do it."

Ozzie had planned to confess his latest transgression to his mother as 38
soon as she came home from work. But it was a Friday night in November and already dark, and when Mrs. Freedman came through the door
she tossed off her coat, kissed Ozzie quickly on the face, and went to the
kitchen table to light the three yellow candles, two for the Sabbath and
one for Ozzie's father.

When his mother lit the candles she would move her two arms slowly 39
towards her, dragging them through the air, as though persuading people
whose minds were half made up. And her eyes would get glassy with
tears. Even when his father was alive Ozzie remembered that her eyes had
gotten glassy, so it didn't have anything to do with his dying. It had
something to do with lighting the candles.

As she touched the flaming match to the unlit wick of a Sabbath candle, 40
the phone rang, and Ozzie, standing only a foot from it, plucked it off the
receiver and held it muffled to his chest. When his mother lit candles Ozzie
felt there should be no noise; even breathing, if you could manage it,
should be softened. Ozzie pressed the phone to his breast and watched his
mother dragging whatever she was dragging, and he felt his own eyes get
glassy. His mother was a round, tired, gray-haired penguin of a woman
whose gray skin had begun to feel the tug of gravity and the weight of her
own history. Even when she was dressed up she didn't look like a chosen
person. But when she lit candles she looked like something better; like a
woman who knew momentarily that God could do anything.

After a few mysterious minutes she was finished. Ozzie hung up the 41
phone and walked to the kitchen table where she was beginning to lay the
two places for the four-course Sabbath meal. He told her that she would
have to see Rabbi Binder next Wednesday at four-thirty, and then he told
her why. For the first time in their life together she hit Ozzie across the
face with her hand.

All through the chopped liver and chicken soup part of the dinner 42
Ozzie cried; he didn't have any appetite for the rest.

On Wednesday, in the largest of the three basement classrooms of the 43
synagogue, Rabbi Marvin Binder, a tall, handsome, broad-shouldered
man of thirty with thick strong-fibered black hair, removed his watch
from his pocket and saw that it was four o'clock. At the rear of the room
Yakov Blotnik, the seventy-one-year-old custodian, slowly polished the

large window, mumbling to himself, unaware that it was four o'clock or six o'clock, Monday or Wednesday. To most of the students Yakov Blotnik's mumbling, along with his brown curly beard, scythe nose, and two heel-trailing black cats, made of him an object of wonder, a foreigner, a relic, towards whom they were alternately fearful and disrespectful. To Ozzie the mumbling had always seemed a monotonous, curious prayer; what made it curious was that old Blotnik had been mumbling so steadily for so many years, Ozzie suspected he had memorized the prayers and forgotten all about God.

44   "It is now free-discussion time," Rabbi Binder said. "Feel free to talk about any Jewish matter at all—religion, family, politics, sports—"

45   There was silence. It was a gusty, clouded November afternoon and it did not seem as though there ever was or could be a thing called baseball. So nobody this week said a word about that hero from the past, Hank Greenberg—which limited free discussion considerably.

46   And the soul-battering Ozzie Freedman had just received from Rabbi Binder had imposed its limitation. When it was Ozzie's turn to read aloud from the Hebrew book the rabbi had asked him petulantly why he didn't read more rapidly. He was showing no progress. Ozzie said he could read faster but that if he did he was sure not to understand what he was reading. Nevertheless, at the rabbi's repeated suggestion Ozzie tried, and showed a great talent, but in the midst of a long passage he stopped short and said he didn't understand a word he was reading, and started in again at a drag-footed pace. Then came the soul-battering.

47   Consequently when free-discussion time rolled around none of the students felt too free. The rabbi's invitation was answered only by the mumbling of feeble old Blotnik.

48   "Isn't there anything at all you would like to discuss?" Rabbi Binder asked again, looking at his watch. "No questions or comments?"

49   There was a small grumble from the third row. The rabbi requested that Ozzie rise and give the rest of the class the advantage of his thought.

50   Ozzie rose. "I forget it now," he said, and sat down in his place.

51   Rabbi Binder advanced a seat towards Ozzie and poised himself on the edge of the desk. It was Itzie's desk and the rabbi's frame only a dagger's-length away from his face snapped him to sitting attention.

52   "Stand up again, Oscar," Rabbi Binder said calmly, "and try to assemble your thoughts."

53   Ozzie stood up. All his classmates turned in their seats and watched as he gave an unconvincing scratch to his forehead.

54   "I can't assemble any," he announced and plunked himself down.

55   "Stand up!" Rabbi Binder advanced from Itzie's desk to the one directly in front of Ozzie; when the rabbinical back was turned Itzie gave it five-fingers off the tip of his nose, causing a small titter in the room. Rabbi Binder was too absorbed in squelching Ozzie's nonsense once and for all to bother with titters. "Stand up, Oscar. What's your question about?"

Ozzie pulled a word out of the air. It was the handiest word. "Reli- 56
gion."

"Oh, now you remember." 57

"Yes." 58

"What is it?" 59

Trapped, Ozzie blurted the first thing that came to him. "Why can't He 60
make anything He wants to make!"

As Rabbi Binder prepared an answer, a final answer, Itzie, ten feet 61
behind him, raised one finger on his left hand, gestured it meaningfully
towards the rabbi's back, and brought the house down.

Binder twisted quickly to see what had happened and in the midst of 62
the commotion Ozzie shouted into the rabbi's back what he couldn't
have shouted to his face. It was a loud, toneless sound that had the timbre
of something stored inside for about six days.

"You don't know! You don't know anything about God!" 63

The rabbi spun back towards Ozzie. "What?" 64

"You don't know—you don't—" 65

"Apologize, Oscar, apologize!" It was a threat. 66

"You don't—" 67

Rabbi Binder's hand flicked out at Ozzie's cheek. Perhaps had only 68
been meant to clamp the boy's mouth shut, but Ozzie ducked and the
palm caught him squarely on the nose.

The blood came in a short, red spurt on to Ozzie's shirt front. 69

The next moment was all confusion. Ozzie screamed, "You bastard, 70
you bastard!" and broke for the classroom door. Rabbi Binder lurched a
step backwards, as though his own blood had started flowing violently in
the opposite direction, then gave a clumsy lurch forward and bolted out
the door after Ozzie. The class followed after the rabbi's huge blue-suited
back, and before old Blotnik could turn from his window, the room was
empty and everyone was headed full speed up the three flights leading to
the roof.

If one should compare the light of day to the life of man: sunrise to 71
birth; sunset—the dropping down over the edge—to death; then as Ozzie
Freedman wiggled through the trapdoor of the synagogue roof, his feet
kicking backwards bronco-style at Rabbi Binder's outstretched arms—
at that moment the day was fifty years old. As a rule, fifty or fifty-five
reflects accurately the age of late afternoons in November, for it is that
month, during those hours, that one's awareness of light seems no longer
a matter of seeing, but of hearing: light begins clicking away. In fact, as
Ozzie locked shut the trapdoor in the rabbi's face, the sharp click of the
bolt into the lock might momentarily have been mistaken for the sound
of the heavier gray that had just throbbed through the sky.

With all his weight Ozzie kneeled on the locked door; any instant he 72
was certain that Rabbi Binder's shoulder would fling it open, splintering
the wood into shrapnel and catapulting his body into the sky. But the

door did not move and below him he heard only the rumble of feet, first loud then dim, like thunder rolling away.

73   A question shot through his brain. "Can this be *me*?" For a thirteen-year-old who had just labeled his religious leader a bastard, twice, it was not an improper question. Louder and louder the question came to him— "Is it me? It is me?"—until he discovered himself no longer kneeling, but racing crazily towards the edge of the roof, his eyes crying, his throat screaming, and his arms flying everywhichway as though not his own.

74   "Is it me? Is it me Me Me Me Me! It has to be me—but is it!"

75   It is the question a thief must ask himself the night he jimmies open his first window, and it is said to be the question with which bridegrooms quiz themselves before the altar.

76   In the few wild seconds it took Ozzie's body to propel him to the edge of the roof, his self-examination began to grow fuzzy. Gazing down at the street, he became confused as to the problem beneath the question: was it, is-it-me-who-called-Binder-a-bastard? or, is-it-me-prancing-around-on-the-roof? However, the scene below settled all, for there is an instant in any action when whether it is you or somebody else is academic. The thief crams the money in his pockets and scoots out the window. The bridegroom signs the hotel register for two. And the boy on the roof finds a streetful of people gaping at him, necks stretched backwards, faces up, as though he were the ceiling of the Hayden Planetarium. Suddenly you know it's you.

77   "Oscar! Oscar Freedman!" A voice rose from the center of the crowd, a voice that, could it have been seen, would have looked like the writing on scroll. "Oscar Freedman, get down from there. Immediately!" Rabbi Binder was pointing one arm stiffly up at him; and at the end of that arm, one finger aimed menacingly. It was the attitude of a dictator, but one —the eyes confessed all—whose personal valet had spit neatly in his face.

78   Ozzie didn't answer. Only for a blink's length did he look towards Rabbi Binder. Instead his eyes began to fit together the world beneath him, to sort out people from places, friends from enemies, participants from spectators. In little jagged starlike clusters his friends stood around Rabbi Binder, who was still pointing. The topmost point on a star compounded not of angels but of five adolescent boys was Itzie. What a world it was, with those stars below, Rabbi Binder below . . . Ozzie, who a moment earlier hadn't been able to control his own body, started to feel the meaning of the word control: he felt Peace and he felt Power.

79   "Oscar Freedman, I'll give you three to come down."

80   Few dictators give their subjects three to do anything; but, as always, Rabbi Binder only looked dictatorial.

81   "Are you ready, Oscar?"

82   Ozzie nodded his head yes, although he had no intention in the world —the lower one of the celestial one he'd just entered—of coming down even if Rabbi Binder should give him a million.

83   "All right then," said Rabbi Binder. He ran a hand through his black

Samson hair as though it were the gesture prescribed for uttering the first
digit. Then, with his other hand cutting a circle out of the small piece of
sky around him, he spoke. "One!"

There was no thunder. On the contrary, at that moment, as though
"one" was the cue for which he had been waiting, the world's least
thunderous person appeared on the synagogue steps. He did not so much
come out the synagogue door as lean out, onto the darkening air. He
clutched at the doorknob with one hand and looked up at the roof.

"Oy!"

Yakov Blotnik's old mind hobbled slowly, as if on crutches, and
though he couldn't decide precisely what the boy was doing on the roof,
he knew it wasn't good—that is, it wasn't-good-for-the-Jews. For Yakov
Blotnik life had fractionated itself simply: things were either good-for-
the-Jews or no-good-for-the-Jews.

He smacked his free hand to his in-sucked cheek, gently. "Oy, Gut!"
And then quickly as he was able, he jacked down his head and surveyed
the street. There was Rabbi Binder (like a man at an auction with only
three dollars in his pocket, he had just delivered a shakey "Two!"), there
were the students, and that was all. So far it-wasn't-so-bad-for-the-Jews.
But the boy had to come down immediately, before anybody saw. The
problem: how to get the boy off the roof?

Anybody who has ever had a cat on the roof knows how to get him
down. You call the fire department. Or first you call the operator and you
ask her for the fire department. And the next thing there is great jamming
of brakes and clanging of bells and shouting of instructions. And then the
cat is off the roof. You do the same thing to get a boy off the roof.

That is, you do the same thing if you are Yakov Blotnik and you once
had a cat on the roof.

When the engines, all four of them, arrived, Rabbi Binder had four
times given Ozzie the count of three. The big hook-and-ladder swung
around the corner and one of the firemen leaped from it, plunging
headlong towards the yellow fire hydrant in front of the synagogue. With
a huge wrench he began to unscrew the top nozzle. Rabbi Binder raced
over to him and pulled at his shoulder.

"There's no fire . . ."

The fireman mumbled back over his shoulder and, heatedly, continued
working at the nozzle.

"But there's no fire, there's no fire . . ." Binder shouted. When the
fireman mumbled again, the rabbi grasped his face with both his hands
and pointed it up at the roof.

To Ozzie it looked as though Rabbi Binder was trying to tug the
fireman's head out of his body, like a cork from a bottle. He had to
giggle at the picture they made: it was a family portrait—rabbi in black
skullcap, fireman in red fire hat, and the little yellow hydrant squatting
beside like a kid brother, bareheaded. From the edge of the roof Ozzie

waved at the portrait, a one-handed, flapping, mocking wave; in doing it his right foot slipped from under him. Rabbi Binder covered his eyes with his hands.

95   Firemen work fast. Before Ozzie had even regained his balance, a big, round, yellowed net was being held on the synagogue lawn. The firemen who held it looked up at Ozzie with stern, feelingless faces.

96   One of the firemen turned his head towards Rabbi Binder. "What, is the kid nuts or something?"

97   Rabbi Binder unpeeled his hands from his eyes, slowly, painfully, as if they were tape. Then he checked: nothing on the sidewalk, no dents in the net.

98   "Is he gonna jump, or what?" the fireman shouted.

99   In a voice not at all like a statue, Rabbi Binder finally answered. "Yes, Yes, I think so . . . He's been threatening to . . ."

100   Threatening to? Why, the reason he was on the roof, Ozzie remembered, was to get away; he hadn't even thought about jumping. He had just run to get away, and the truth was that he hadn't really headed for the roof as much as he'd been chased there.

101   "What's his name, the kid?"

102   "Freedman," Rabbi Binder answered. "Oscar Freedman."

103   The fireman looked up at Ozzie. "What is it with you, Oscar? You gonna jump, or what?"

104   Oscar did not answer. Frankly, the question had just arisen.

105   "Look, Oscar, if you're gonna jump, jump—and if you're not gonna jump, don't jump. But don't waste our time, willya?"

106   Ozzie looked at the fireman and then at Rabbi Binder. He wanted to see Rabbi Binder cover his eyes one more time.

107   "I'm going to jump."

108   And then he scampered around the edge of the roof to the corner, where there was no net below, and he flapped his arms at his sides, swishing the air and smacking his palms to his trousers on the downbeat. He began screaming like some kind of engine, "Wheeeee . . . wheeeeee," and leaning way out over the edge with the upper half of his body. The firemen whipped around to cover the ground with the net. Rabbi Binder mumbled a few words to Somebody and covered his eyes. Everything happened quickly, jerkily, as in a silent movie. The crowd, which had arrived with the fire engines, gave out a long, Fourth-of-July fireworks oooh-aahhh. In the excitement no one had paid the crowd much heed, except, of course, Yakov Blotnik, who swung from the doorknob counting heads. "Fier und tsvansik . . . finf und tsvantsik . . . Oy, Gut!" It wasn't like this with the cat.

109   Rabbi Binder peeked through his fingers, checked the sidewalk and net. Empty. But there was Ozzie racing to the other corner. The firemen raced with him but were unable to keep up. Whenever Ozzie wanted to he might jump and splatter himself upon the sidewalk, and by the time the firemen scooted to the spot all they could do with their net would be to cover the mess.

"Wheeeee . . . wheeeee . . ." 110

"Hey, Oscar," the winded fireman yelled, "What the hell is this, a 111
game or something?"

"Wheeeee . . . wheeeee . . ." 112

"Hey, Oscar—" 113

"But he was off now to the other corner, flapping his wings fiercely. 114
Rabbi Binder couldn't take it any longer—the fire engines from nowhere,
the screaming suicidal boy, the net. He fell to his knees, exhausted, and
with his hands curled together in front of his chest like a little dome, he
pleaded, "Oscar, stop it, Oscar. Don't jump, Oscar. Please come down
. . . Please don't jump."

And further back in the crowd a single voice, a single young voice, 115
shouted a lone word to the boy on the roof.

"Jump!" 116

It was Itzie. Ozzie momentarily stopped flapping. 117

"Go ahead, Ozz—jump!" Itzie broke off his point of the star and 118
courageously, with the inspiration not of a wise-guy but of a disciple,
stood alone. "Jump, Ozz, jump!"

Still on his knees, his hands still curled, Rabbi Binder twisted his body 119
back. He looked at Itzie, then, agonizingly, back to Ozzie.

"OSCAR, DON'T JUMP! PLEASE, DON'T JUMP . . . please please . . ." 120

"Jump!" This time it wasn't Itzie but another point of the star. By the 121
time Mrs. Freedman arrived to keep her four-thirty appointment with
Rabbi Binder, the whole little upside down heaven was shouting and
pleading for Ozzie to jump, and Rabbi Binder no longer was pleading
with him not to jump, but was crying into the dome of his hands.

Understandably Mrs. Freeman couldn't figure out what her son was 122
doing on the roof. So she asked. "Ozzie, my Ozzie, what are you doing?
My Ozzie, what is it?"

Ozzie stopped wheeeeeing and slowed his arms down to a cruising flap, 123
the kind birds use in soft winds, but he did not answer. He stood against
the low, clouded, darkening sky—light clicked down swiftly now, as on
a small gear—flapping softly and gazing down at the small bundle of
woman who was his mother.

"What are you doing, Ozzie?" She turned towards the kneeling Rabbi 124
Binder and rushed so close that only a paper-thickness of dusk lay
between her stomach and his shoulders.

"What is my baby doing?" 125

Rabbi Binder gaped up at her but he too was mute. All that moved was 126
the dome of his hands; it shook back and forth like a weak pulse.

"Rabbi, get him down! He'll kill himself. Get him down, my only 127
baby . . ."

"I can't," Rabbi Binder said, "I can't . . ." and he turned his handsome 128
head towards the crowd of boys behind him. "It's them. Listen to them."

And for the first time Mrs. Freedman saw the crowd of boys, and she 129
heard what they were yelling.

130   "He's doing it for them. He won't listen to me. It's them." Rabbi
Binder spoke like one in a trance.

131   "For them?"

132   "Yes."

133   "Why for them?"

134   "They want him to . . ."

135   Mrs. Freeman raised her two arms upward as though she were conducting the sky. "For them he's doing it!" And then in a gesture older
than pyramids, older than prophets and floods, her arms came slapping
down to her sides. "A martyr I have. Look!" She tilted her head to the
roof. Ozzie was still flapping softly. "My martyr."

136   "Oscar, come down, *please*," Rabbi Binder groaned.

137   In a startlingly even voice Mrs. Freedman called to the boy on the roof.
"Ozzie, come down, Ozzie. Don't be a martyr, my baby."

138   As though it were a litany, Rabbi Binder repeated her words. "Don't
be a martyr, my baby. Don't be a martyr."

139   "Gawhead, Ozz—*be* a Martin!" It was Itzie. "Be a Martin, be a Martin," and all the voices joined in singing for Martindom, whatever *it* was.
"Be a Martin, be a Martin . . ."

140   Somehow when you're on a roof the darker it gets the less you can
hear. All Ozzie knew was that two groups wanted two new things: his
friends were spirited and musical about what they wanted; his mother
and the rabbi were even-toned, chanting, about what they didn't want.
The rabbi's voice was without tears now and so was his mother's.

141   The big net stared up at Ozzie like a sightless eye. The big, clouded sky
pushed down. From beneath it looked like a gray corrugated board.
Suddenly, looking up into that unsympathetic sky, Ozzie realized all the
strangeness of what these people, his friends, were asking: they wanted
him to jump, to kill himself; they were singing about it now—it made
them happy. And there was an even greater strangeness: Rabbi Binder
was on his knees, trembling. If there was a question to be asked now it
was not "Is it me?" but rather "Is it us? . . . Is it us?"

142   Being on the roof, it turned out, was a serious thing. If he jumped
would the singing become dancing? Would it? What would jumping
stop? Yearningly, Ozzie wished he could rip open the sky, plunge his
hands through, and pull out the sun; and on the sun, like a coin, would
be stamped JUMP or DON'T JUMP.

143   Ozzie's knees rocked and sagged a little under him as though they were
setting him for a dive. His arms tightened, stiffened, froze, from shoulders to fingernails. He felt as if each part of his body were going to vote
as to whether he should kill himself or not—and each part as though it
were independent of *him*.

144   The light took an unexpected click down and the new darkness, like a
gag, hushed the friends singing for this and the mother and rabbi chanting for that.

Ozzie stopped counting votes, and in a curiously high voice, like one who wasn't prepared for speech, he spoke. 145

"Mamma?" 146

"Yes, Oscar." 147

"Mamma, get down on your knees, like Rabbi Binder." 148

"Oscar—" 149

"Get down on your knees," he said, "or I'll jump." 150

Ozzie heard a whimper, then a quick rustling, and when he looked down where his mother had stood he saw the top of a head and beneath that a circle of dress. She was kneeling beside Rabbi Binder. 151

He spoke again. "Everybody kneel." There was the sound of everybody kneeling. 152

Ozzie looked around. With one hand he pointed towards the synagogue entrance. "Make *him* kneel." 153

There was a noise, not of kneeling, but of body-and-cloth stretching. Ozzie could hear Rabbi Binder saying in a gruff whisper, ". . . or he'll *kill* himself," and when next he looked there was Yakov Blotnik off the doorknob and for the first time in his life upon his knees in the Gentile posture of prayer. 154

As for the firemen—it is not as difficult as one might imagine to hold a net taut while you are kneeling. 155

Ozzie looked around again; and then he called to Rabbi Binder. 156

"Rabbi?" 157

"Yes, Oscar." 158

"Rabbi Binder, do you believe in God." 159

"Yes." 160

"Do you believe God can do Anything?" Ozzie leaned his head out into the darkness. "Anything?" 161

"Oscar, I think—" 162

"Tell me you believe God can do Anything." 163

There was a second's hesitation. Then: "God can do Anything." 164

"Tell me you believe God can make a child without intercourse." 165

"He can." 166

"Tell me!" 167

"God," Rabbi Binder admitted, "can make a child without intercourse." 168

"Mamma, you tell me." 169

"God can make a child without intercourse," his mother said. 170

"Make *him* tell me." There was no doubt who *him* was. 171

In a few moments Ozzie heard an old comical voice say something to the increasing darkness about God. 172

Next, Ozzie made everybody say it. And then he made them all say they believed in Jesus Christ—first one at a time, then all together. 173

When the catechizing was through it was the beginning of evening. From the street it sounded as if the boy on the roof might have sighed. 174

"Ozzie?" A woman's voice dared to speak. "You'll come down now?" 175

176   There was no answer, but the woman waited, and when a voice finally did speak it was thin and crying, and exhausted as that of an old man who has just finished pulling the bells.

177   "Mamma, don't you see—you shouldn't hit me. He shouldn't hit me. You shouldn't hit me about God, Mamma. You should never hit anybody about God—"

178   "Ozzie, please come down now."

179   "Promise me, promise me you'll never hit anybody about God."

180   He had asked only his mother, but for some reason everyone kneeling in the street promised he would never hit anybody about God.

181   Once again there was silence.

182   "I can come down now, Mamma," the boy on the roof finally said. He turned his head both ways as though checking the traffic lights. "Now I can come down . . ."

183   And he did, right into the center of the yellow net that glowed in the evening's edge like an overgrown halo.

❏ Questions for Discussion

1. How do Itzie's interests contrast to Ozzie's? If you applied Golding's three levels of thinking to Itzie and Ozzie, which class would each fit in? Which class would the Rabbi fit in?

2. Why do adults have difficulty with Ozzie's questions? Is Ozzie, as Rabbi Binder maintains, "deliberately simple-minded"? Are Ozzie's questions intended to be irreverent? Are they valid questions?

3. How effectively does Ozzie's mother handle his questions? How effectively does Rabbi Binder handle them?

4. Why does Ozzie run to the roof? Does he have any serious intention of jumping? Why do Itzie and Ozzie's other friends shout for him to jump?

5. Why does Ozzie make the Rabbi, his mother, and all his friends kneel and declare their belief in Jesus Christ? Given their religious beliefs, what does such a declaration mean?

6. Discuss the **irony** of the title.

❏ Suggestions for Exploration and Writing

1. Ozzie's asking his Rabbi, his mother, and his friends to declare their belief in Jesus is an extreme action. In effect, he is requiring them to repudiate their faith. Analyze the causes of Ozzie's extreme action.

2. Attack or defend this statement: Efforts to stifle a child's quest for truth result in rebellion.

3. Ozzie calls Rabbi Binder a "bastard" twice. Do you agree with this assessment? Write a character analysis of Rabbi Binder.

Toni Cade Bambara (1939–)

Raymond's Run

I don't have much work to do around the house like some girls. My 1
mother does that. And I don't have to earn my pocket money by hustling;
George runs errands for the big boys and sells Christmas cards. And
anything else that's got to get done, my father does. All I have to do in
life is mind my brother Raymond, which is enough.

Sometimes I slip and say my little brother Raymond. But as any fool 2
can see he's much bigger and he's older too. But a lot of people call him
my little brother cause he needs looking after cause he's not quite right.
And a lot of smart mouths got lots to say about that too, especially when
George was minding him. But now, if anybody has anything to say to
Raymond, anything to say about his big head, they have to come by me.
And I don't play the dozens or believe in standing around with somebody
in my face doing a lot of talking. I much rather just knock you down and
take my chances even if I am a little girl with skinny arms and a squeaky
voice, which is how I got the name Squeaky. And if things get too rough,
I run. And as anybody can tell you, I'm the fastest thing on two feet.

There is no track meet that I don't win the first-place medal. I used 3
to win the twenty-yard dash when I was a little kid in kindergarten.
Nowadays, it's the fifty-yard dash. And tomorrow I'm subject to run the
quarter-meter relay all by myself and come in first, second, and third. The
big kids call me Mercury cause I'm the swiftest thing in the neighborhood. Everybody knows that—except two people who know better, my
father and me. He can beat me to Amsterdam Avenue with me having a
two-fire-hydrant head start and him running with his hands in his
pockets and whistling. But that's private information. Cause can you
imagine some thirty-five-year-old man stuffing himself into PAL shorts to
race little kids? So as far as everyone's concerned, I'm the fastest and that
goes for Gretchen, too, who has put out the tale that she is going to win
the first-place medal this year. Ridiculous. In the second place, she's got
short legs. In the third place, she's got freckles. In the first place, no one
can beat me and that's all there is to it.

I'm standing on the corner admiring the weather and about to take a 4
stroll down Broadway so I can practice my breathing exercises, and I've
got Raymond walking on the inside close to the buildings, cause he's
subject to fits of fantasy and starts thinking he's a circus performer and
that the curb is a tightrope strung high in the air. And sometimes after a
rain he likes to step down off his tightrope right into the gutter and slosh
around getting his shoes and cuffs wet. Then I get hit when I get home.
Or sometimes if you don't watch him he'll dash across traffic to the island
in the middle of Broadway and give the pigeons a fit. Then I have to go
behind him apologizing to all the old people sitting around trying to get
some sun and getting all upset with the pigeons fluttering around them,
scattering their newspapers and upsetting the wax paper lunches in their

laps. So I keep Raymond on the inside of me, and he plays like he's driving a stagecoach which is O.K. by me so long as he doesn't run me over or interrupt my breathing exercises, which I have to do on account of I'm serious about my running, and I don't care who knows it.

5   Now some people like to act like things come easy to them, won't let on that they practice. Not me. I'll high-prance down 34th Street like a rodeo pony to keep my knees strong even if it does get my mother uptight so that she walks ahead like she's not with me, don't know me, is all by herself on a shopping trip, and I am somebody else's crazy child. Now you take Cynthia Procter for instance. She's just the opposite. If there's a test tomorrow, she'll say something like, "Oh, I guess I'll play handball this afternoon and watch television tonight," just to let you know she ain't thinking about the test. Or like last week when she won the spelling bee for the millionth time, "A good thing you got 'receive,' Squeaky, cause I would have got it wrong. I completely forgot about the spelling bee." And she'll clutch the lace on her blouse like it was a narrow escape. Oh, brother. But of course when I pass her house on my early morning trots around the block, she is practicing the scales on the piano over and over and over and over. Then in music class she always lets herself get bumped around so she falls accidently on purpose onto the piano stool and is so surprised to find herself sitting there that she decides just for fun to try out the ole keys. And what do you know—Chopin's waltzes just spring out of her fingertips and she's the most surprised thing in the world. A regular prodigy. I could kill people like that. I stay up all night studying the words for the spelling bee. And you can see me any time of day practicing running. I never walk if I can trot, and shame on Raymond if he can't keep up. But of course he does, cause if he hangs back someone's liable to walk up to him and get smart, or take his allowance from him, or ask him where he got that great big pumpkin head. People are so stupid sometimes.

6   So I'm strolling down Broadway breathing out and breathing in on counts of seven, which is my lucky number, and here comes Gretchen and her sidekicks: Mary Louise, who used to be a friend of mine when she first moved to Harlem from Baltimore and got beat up by everybody till I took up for her on account of her mother and my mother used to sing in the same choir when they were young girls, but people ain't grateful, so now she hangs out with the new girl Gretchen and talks about me like a dog; and Rosie, who is as fat as I am skinny and has a big mouth where Raymond is concerned and is too stupid to know that there is not a big deal of difference between herself and Raymond and that she can't afford to throw stones. So they are steady coming up Broadway and I see right away that it's going to be one of those Dodge City scenes cause the street ain't that big and they're close to the buildings just as we are. First I think I'll step into the candy store and look over the new comics and let them pass. But that's chicken and I've got a reputation to consider. So then I think I'll just walk straight on through them or even over them if necessary. But as they get to me, they slow down. I'm ready to fight, cause

like I said I don't feature a whole lot of chitchat, I much prefer to just knock you down right from the jump and save everybody a lotta precious time.

"You signing up for the May Day races?" smiles Mary Louise, only it's not a smile at all. A dumb question like that doesn't deserve an answer. Besides, there's just me and Gretchen standing there really, so no use wasting my breath talking to shadows. 7

"I don't think you're going to win this time," says Rosie, trying to signify with her hands on her hips all salty, completely forgetting that I have whupped her behind many times for less salt than that. 8

"I always win cause I'm the best," I say straight at Gretchen who is, as far as I'm concerned, the only one talking in this ventriloquist-dummy routine. Gretchen smiles, but it's not a smile, and I'm thinking that girls never really smile at each other because they don't know how and don't want to know how and there's probably no one to teach us how, cause grownup girls don't know either. Then they all look at Raymond who has just brought his mule team to a standstill. And they're about to see what trouble they can get into through him. 9

"What grade you in now, Raymond?" 10

"You got anything to say to my brother, you say it to me, Mary Louise Williams of Raggedy Town, Baltimore." 11

"What are you, his mother?" sasses Rosie. 12

"That's right, Fatso. And the next word out of anybody and I'll be *their* mother too." So they just stand there and Gretchen shifts from one leg to the other and so do they. Then Gretchen puts her hands on her hips and is about to say something with her freckle-face self but doesn't. Then she walks around me looking me up and down but keeps walking up Broadway, and her sidekicks follow her. So me and Raymond smile at each other and he says "Giddyap" to his team and I continue with my breathing exercises, strolling down Broadway toward the ice man on 145th with not a care in the world cause I am Miss Quicksilver herself. 13

I take my time getting to the park on May Day because the track meet is the last thing on the program. The biggest thing on the program is the Maypole dancing, which I can do without, thank you, even if my mother thinks it's a shame I don't take part and act like a girl for a change. You'd think my mother'd be grateful not to have to make me a white organdy dress with a big satin sash and buy me new white baby-doll shoes that can't be taken out of the box till the big day. You'd think she'd be glad her daughter ain't out there prancing around a Maypole getting the new clothes all dirty and sweaty and trying to act like a fairy or a flower or whatever you're supposed to be when you should be trying to be yourself, whatever that is, which is, as far as I am concerned, a poor black girl who really can't afford to buy shoes and a new dress you only wear once a lifetime cause it won't fit next year. 14

I was once a strawberry in a Hansel and Gretel pageant when I was in nursery school and didn't have no better sense than to dance on tiptoe with my arms in a circle over my head doing umbrella steps and being a 15 perfect fool just so my mother and father could come dressed up and clap. You'd think they'd know better than to encourage that kind of nonsense. I am not a strawberry. I do not dance on my toes. I run. That is what I am all about. So I always come late to the May Day program, just in time to get my number pinned on and lay in the grass till they announce the fifty-yard dash.

16   I put Raymond in the little swings, which is a tight squeeze this year and will be impossible next year. Then I look around for Mr. Pearson, who pins the numbers on. I'm really looking for Gretchen if you want to know the truth, but she's not around. The park is jam-packed. Parents in hats and corsages and breast-pocket handkerchiefs peeking up. Kids in white dresses and light blue suits. The parkees unfolding chairs and chasing the rowdy kids from Lenox as if they had no right to be there. The big guys with their caps on backwards, leaning against the fence swirling the basketballs on the tips of their fingers, waiting for all these crazy people to clear out the park so they can play. Most of the kids in my class are carrying bass drums and glockenspiels and flutes. You'd think they'd put in a few bongos or something for real like that.

17   Then here comes Mr. Pearson with his clipboard and his cards and pencils and whistles and safety pins and fifty million other things he's always dropping all over the place with his clumsy self. He sticks out in a crowd because he's on stilts. We used to call him Jack and the Beanstalk to get him mad. But I'm the only one that can outrun him and get away, and I'm too grown for that silliness now.

18   "Well, Squeaky," he says, checking my name off the list and handing me number seven and two pins. And I'm thinking he's got no right to call me Squeaky, if I can't call him Beanstalk.

19   "Hazel Elizabeth Deborah Parker," I correct him and tell him to write it down on his board.

20   "Well, Hazel Elizabeth Deborah Parker, going to give someone else a break this year?" I squint at him real hard to see if he is seriously thinking I should lose the race on purpose just to give someone else a break. "Only six girls running this time," he continues, shaking his head sadly like it's my fault all of New York didn't turn out in sneakers. "That new girl should give you a run for your money." He looks around the park for Gretchen like a periscope in a submarine movie. "Wouldn't it be a nice gesture if you were . . . to ahhh . . ."

21   I give him such a look he couldn't finish putting that idea into words. Grownups got a lot of nerve sometimes. I pin number seven to myself and stomp away, I'm so burnt. And I go straight for the track and stretch out on the grass while the band winds up with "Oh, the Monkey Wrapped His Tail Around the Flagpole," which my teacher calls by some other name. The man on the loudspeaker is calling everyone over to the track and I'm on my back looking at the sky, trying to pretend I'm in the country, but I can't because even grass in the city feels hard as sidewalk, and there's just no pretending you are anywhere but in a "concrete jungle" as my grandfather says.

The twenty-yard dash takes all of two minutes cause most of the little   22
kids don't know no better than to run off the track or run the wrong way
or run smack into the fence and fall down and cry. One little kid, though,
has got the good sense to run straight for the white ribbon up ahead so
he wins. Then the second-graders line up for the thirty-yard dash and I
don't even bother to turn my head to watch cause Raphael Perez always
wins. He wins before he even begins by psyching the runners, telling them
they're going to trip on their shoelaces and fall on their faces or lose their
shorts or something, which he doesn't really have to do since he is very
fast, almost as fast as I am. After that is the forty-yard dash which I use
to run when I was in first grade. Raymond is hollering from the swings
cause he knows I'm about to do my thing cause the man on the loudspeaker has just announced the fifty-yard dash, although he might just as
well be giving a recipe for angel food cake cause you can hardly make out
what he's saying for the static. I get up and slip off my sweat pants and
then I see Gretchen standing at the starting line, kicking her legs out like
a pro. Then as I get into place I see that ole Raymond is on the line on
the other side of the fence, bending down with his fingers on the ground
just like he knew what he was doing. I was going to yell at him but then
I didn't. It burns up your energy to holler.

Every time, just before I take off in a race, I always feel like I'm in a   23
dream, the kind of dream you have when you're sick with fever and feel
all hot and weightless. I dream I'm flying over a sandy beach in the early
morning sun, kissing the leaves of the trees as I fly by. And there's always
the smell of apples, just like in the country when I was little and used to
think I was a choo-choo train, running through the fields of corn and
chugging up the hill to the orchard. And all the time I'm dreaming this,
I get lighter and lighter until I'm flying over the beach again, getting
blown through the sky like a feather that weighs nothing at all. But once
I spread my fingers in the dirt and crouch over the Get on Your Mark, the
dream goes and I am solid again and am telling myself, Squeaky you must
win, you must win, you are the fastest thing in the world, you can even
beat your father up Amsterdam if you really try. And then I feel my
weight coming back just behind my knees then down to my feet then into
the earth and the pistol shot explodes in my blood and I am off and
weightless again, flying past the other runners, my arms pumping up and
down and the whole world is quiet except for the crunch as I zoom over
the gravel of the track. I glance to my left and there is no one. To the
right, a blurred Gretchen, who's got her chin jutting out as if it would
win the race all by itself. And on the other side of the fence is Raymond
with his arms down to his side and the palms tucked up behind him,
running in his very own style, and it's the first time I ever saw that and
I almost stop to watch my brother Raymond on his first run. But the
white ribbon is bouncing toward me and I tear past it, racing into the
distance till my feet with a mind of their own start digging up footfuls
of dirt and brake me short. Then all the kids standing on the side pile on
me, banging me on the back and slapping my head with their May Day

programs, for I have won again and everybody on 151st Street can walk tall for another year.

24 "In first place . . ." the man on the loudspeaker is clear as a bell now, but then he pauses and the loudspeaker starts to whine. Then static. And I lean down to catch my breath and here comes Gretchen walking back, for she's overshot the finish line too, huffing and puffing with her hands on her hips taking it slow, breathing in steady time like a real pro and I sort of like her a little for the first time. "In first place . . ." and then three or four voices get all mixed up on the loudspeaker and I dig my sneaker into the grass and stare at Gretchen who's staring back, we both wondering just who did win. I can hear old Beanstalk arguing with the man on the loudspeaker and then a few others running their mouths about what the stopwatches say. Then I hear Raymond yanking at the fence to call me and I wave to shush him, but he keeps rattling the fence like a gorilla in a cage like in them gorilla movies, but then like a dancer or something he starts climbing hand over hand and remembering how he looked running with his arms down to his side and with the wind pulling his mouth back and his teeth showing and all, it occurred to me that Raymond would make a very fine runner. Doesn't he always keep up with me on my trots? And he surely knows how to breathe in counts of seven cause he's always doing it at the dinner table, which drives my brother George up the wall. And I'm smiling to beat the band cause if I've lost this race, or if me and Gretchen tied, or even if I've won, I can always retire as a runner and begin a whole new career as a coach with Raymond as my champion. After all, with a little more study I can beat Cynthia and her phony self at the spelling bee. And if I bugged my mother, I could get piano lessons and become a star. And I have a big rep as the baddest thing around. And I've got a roomful of ribbons and medals and awards. But what has Raymond got to call his own?

25 So I stand there with my new plans, laughing out loud by this time as Raymond jumps down from the fence and runs over with his teeth showing and his arms down to the side, which no one before him has quite mastered as a running style. And by the time he comes over I'm jumping up and down so glad to see him—my brother Raymond, a great runner in the family tradition. But of course everyone thinks I'm jumping up and down because the men on the loudspeaker have finally gotten themselves together and compared notes and are announcing "In first place—Miss Hazel Elizabeth Deborah Parker." (Dig that.) "In second place—Miss Gretchen P. Lewis." And I look at Gretchen wondering what the "P" stands for. And I smile. Cause she's good, no doubt about it. Maybe she'd like to help me coach Raymond; she obviously is serious about running, as any fool can see. And she nods to congratulate me and then she smiles. And I smile. We stand there with this big smile of respect between us. It's about as real a smile as girls can do for each other, considering we don't practice real smiling every day, you know, cause maybe we too busy being flowers or fairies or straw-

berries instead of something honest and worthy of respect . . . you know
. . . like being people.

❏ **Questions for Discussion**

1. Is the **first person point of view** effective?

2. What is the relationship between Hazel and her brother Raymond? Describe the relationships between Hazel and her father and between Hazel and her mother.

3. Is Hazel bragging or just being honest about her area of expertise, running? Why is practicing important to her?

4. What bothers Hazel about Cynthia Porter? Why?

5. Why does Hazel want Mr. Pearson, who pins on the numbers at the race, to call her Hazel Elizabeth Deborah Parker? What is their relationship? Does Pearson really want Hazel to let Gretchen win the race?

6. Describe the dream Hazel has. Why is it important?

❏ **Suggestions for Exploration and Writing**

1. Looking at Raymond after the race, Hazel has an **epiphany** or awakening. Hazel asks, "But what has Raymond got to call his own?" Discuss Hazel's new aspirations for Raymond, Gretchen, and herself.

2. At various times Bambara emphasizes a genuine smile or a sarcastic smile or the absence of a smile. Reread the last sentence of the story, and write an essay that discusses "real smiling" and the meaning of that last sentence.

GISH JEN (1955–)

Gish Jen, who grew up in New York City, is a second generation Chinese-American fiction writer. Her highly regarded first novel Typical Americans *(1991) highlights the conflict between traditional Chinese values and the American dream of success among Chinese immigrants in New York.*

The Water-Faucet Vision

To protect my sister Mona and me from the pains—or, as they pronounced it, the "pins"—of life, my parents did their fighting in Shanghai dialect, which we didn't understand; and when my father one day pitched a brass vase through the kitchen window, my mother told us he had done it by accident.

2   "By accident?" said Mona.

3   My mother chopped the foot off a mushroom.

4   "By accident?" said Mona. "By *accident?*"

5   Later I tried to explain to her that she shouldn't have persisted like that, but it was hopeless.

6   "What's the matter with throwing things?" She shrugged. "He was *mad.*"

7   That was the difference between Mona and me: fighting was just fighting to her. If she worried about anything, it was only that she might turn out too short to become a ballerina, in which case she was going to be a piano player.

8   I, on the other had, was going to be a martyr. I was in fifth grade then, and the hyperimaginative sort—the kind of girl who grows morbid in Catholic school, who longs to be chopped or frozen to death but then has nightmares about it from which she wakes up screaming and clutching a stuffed bear. It was not a bear that I clutched, though, but a string of three malachite beads that I had found in the marsh by the old aqueduct one day. Apparently once part of a necklace, they were each wonderfully striated and swirled, and slightly humped toward the center, like a jelly fish; so that if I squeezed one, it would slip smoothly away, with a grace that altogether enthralled and—on those dream-harrowed nights—soothed me, soothed me as nothing had before or has since. Not that I've lacked occasion for soothing: though it's been four months since my mother died, there are still nights when sleep stands away from me, stiff as a well-paid sentry. But that is another story. Back then I had my malachite beads, and if I worried them long and patiently enough, I was sure to start feeling better, more awake, even a little special—imagining, as I liked to, that my nightmares were communications from the Almighty Himself, preparation for my painful destiny. Discussing them with Patty Creamer, who had also promised her life to God, I called them "almost visions"; and Patty, her mouth wadded with the three or four sticks of Doublemint she always seemed to have going at once, said, "I bet you'll be doin' miracleth by seventh grade."

9   Miracles. Today Patty laughs to think she ever spent good time stewing on such matters, her attention having long turned to rugs, and artwork, and antique Japanese bureaus—things she believes in.

10   "A good bureau's more than just a bureau," she explained last time we
11   had lunch. "It's a hedge against life. I tell you: if there's one thing I believe, it's that cheap stuff's just money out the window. Nice stuff, on the other hand—now that you can always cash out, if life gets rough. *That* you can count on."

     In fifth grade, though, she counted on different things.

12   "You'll be doing miracles too," I told her, but she shook her shaggy head and looked doleful.

13   "Na' me," she chomped. "Buzzit's okay. The kin' things I like, prayers work okay on."

"Like?"   14

"Like you 'member that dreth I liked?"   15

She meant the yellow one, with the crisscross straps.   16

"Well gueth what."   17

"Your mom got it for you."   18

She smiled. "And I only jutht prayed for it for a week," she said.   19

As for myself, though, I definitely wanted to be able to perform a   20
wonder or two. Miracle-working! It was the carrot of carrots: it kept me
doing my homework, taking the sacraments; it kept me mournfully on
key in music hour, while my classmates hiccuped and squealed their
carefree hearts away. Yet I couldn't have said what I wanted such powers
for, exactly. That is, I thought of them the way one might think of, say,
an ornamental sword—as a kind of collectible which also happened to be
a means of defense.

But then Patty's father walked out on her mother, and for the first time,   21
there was a miracle I wanted to do. I wanted it so much I could see it: Mr.
Creamer made into a spitball; Mr. Creamer shot through a straw into the
sky; Mr. Creamer unrolled and replumped, plop back on Patty's doorstep. I would've cleaned out his mind and given him a shave en route. I
would've given him a box of peanut fudge, tied up with a ribbon, to
present to Patty with a kiss.

But instead all I could do was try to tell her he'd come back.   22

"He will not, he will not!" she sobbed. "He went on a boat to Rio   23
Deniro. To Rio Deniro!"

I tried to offer her a stick of gum, but she wouldn't take it.   24

"He said he would rather look at water than at my mom's fat face. He   25
said he would rather look at water than at me." Now she was really
wailing, and holding her ribs so tightly that she almost seemed to be
hurting herself—so tightly that just looking at her arms wound around
her like snakes made my heart feel squeezed.

I patted her on the arm. A one-winged pigeon waddled by.   26

"He said I wasn't even his kid, he said I came from Uncle Johnny. He   27
said I was garbage, just like my mom and Uncle Johnny. He said I wasn't
even his kid, he said I wasn't his Patty, he said I came from Uncle
Johnny!"

"From your Uncle Johnny?" I said stupidly.   28

"From Uncle Johnny," she cried. "From Uncle Johnny!"   29

"He said that?" I said. Then, wanting to go on, to say *something*, I   30
said, "Oh Patty, don't cry."

She kept crying.   31

I tried again. "Oh Patty, don't cry," I said. Then I said, "Your dad was   32
a jerk anyway."

The pigeon produced a large runny dropping.   33

It was a good twenty minutes before Patty was calm enough for me just   34
to run to the girls' room to get her some toilet paper; and by the time I
came back she was sobbing again, saying "to Rio Deniro, to Rio Deniro"

over and over again, as though the words had stuck in her and couldn't be gotten out. As we had missed the regular bus home and the late bus too, I had to leave her a second time to go call my mother, who was mad only until she heard what had happened. Then she came and picked us up, and bought us each a Fudgsicle.

35   Some days later, Patty and I started a program to work on getting her father home. It was a serious business. We said extra prayers, and lit votive candles; I tied my malachite beads to my uniform belt, fondling them as though they were a rosary, I a nun. We even took to walking about the school halls with our hands folded—a sight so ludicrous that our wheeze of a principal personally took us aside one day.

36   "I must tell you," she said, using her nose as a speaking tube, "that there is really no need for such peee-ity."

37   But we persisted, promising to marry God and praying to every saint we could think of. We gave up gum, then gum and Slim Jims both, then gum and Slim Jims and ice cream—and when even that didn't work, we started on more innovative things. The first was looking at flowers. We held our hands beside our eyes like blinders as we hurried by the violets by the flagpole, the window box full of tulips outside the nurse's office. Next it was looking at boys: Patty gave up angel-eyed Jamie Halloran and I, gymnastic Anthony Rossi. It was hard, but in the end our efforts paid off. Mr. Creamer came back a month later, and though he brought with him nothing but dysentery, he was at least too sick to have all that much to say.

38   Then, in the course of a fight with my father, my mother somehow fell out of their bedroom window.

39   Recently—thinking a mountain vacation might cheer me—I sublet my apartment to a handsome but somber newlywed couple, who turned out to be every bit as responsible as I'd hoped. They cleaned out even the eggshell chips I'd sprinkled around the base of my plants as fertilizer, leaving behind only a shiny silverplate cake server and a list of their hopes and goals for the summer. The list, tacked precariously to the back of the kitchen door, began with a fervent appeal to God to help them get their wedding thank-yous written in three weeks or less. (You could see they had originally written "two weeks" but scratched it out—no miracles being demanded here.) It went on:

40   Please help us, Almighty Father in Heaven Above, to get Ann a teaching job within a half-hour drive of here in a nice neighborhood.

41   Please help us, Almighty Father in Heaven Above, to get John a job doing anything where he won't strain his back and that is within a half-hour drive of here.

42   Please help us, Almighty Father in Heaven Above, to get us a car.

Please help us, A.F. in H.A., to learn French. 43

Please help us, A.F. in H.A., to find seven dinner recipes that cost 44
less than 60 cents a serving and can be made in a half-hour. And
that don't have tomatoes, since You in Your Heavenly Wisdom
made John allergic.

Please help us, A.F. in H.A., to avoid books in this apartment 45
such as You in Your Heavenly Wisdom allowed John, for Your
Heavenly Reasons, to find three nights ago (June 2nd).

Et cetera. In the left-hand margin they kept score of how they had fared 46
with their requests, and it was heartening to see that nearly all of them
were marked "Yes! Praise the Lord" (sometimes shortened to PTL), with
the sole exception of learning French, which was mysteriously marked
"No! PTL to the Highest."

That note touched me. Strange and familiar both, it seemed like it had 47
been written by some cousin of mine—some cousin who had stayed home
to grow up, say, while I went abroad and learned what I had to, though
the learning was painful. This, of course, is just a manner of speaking; in
fact I did my growing up at home, like anybody else.

But the learning *was* painful: I never knew exactly how it happened 48
that my mother went hurtling through the air that night years ago, only
that the wind had been chopping at the house, and that the argument had
started about the state of the roof. Someone had been up to fix it the year
before, but it wasn't a roofer, it was some man my father had insisted
could do just as good a job for a quarter of the price. And maybe he could
have, had he not somehow managed to step through a knot in the wood
under the shingles and break his uninsured ankle. Now the shingles were
coming loose again, and the attic insulation was mildewing besides, and
my father was wanting to sell the house altogether, which he said my
mother had wanted to buy so she could send pictures of it home to her
family in China.

"The Americans have a saying," he said. "They saying, 'You have to 49
keep up with Jones family.' I'm saying if Jones family in Shanghai, you
can send any picture you want, *an-y* picture. Go take picture of those rich
guys' house. You want to act like rich guys, right? Go take picture of
those rich guys' house."

At that point my mother sent Mona and me to wash up, and started 50
speaking Shanghaiese. They argued for some time in the kitchen while we
listened from the top of the stairs, our faces wedged between the bumpy
Spanish scrolls of the wrought iron railing. First my mother ranted, then
my father, then they both ranted at once until finally there was a thump,
followed by a long quiet.

"Do you think they're kissing now?" said Mona. "I bet they're kissing, 51
like this." She pursed her lips like a fish and was about to put them to the
railing when we heard my mother locking the back door. We hightailed

it into bed; my parents creaked up the stairs. Everything at that point seemed fine. Once in their bedroom, though, they started up again, first softly, then louder and louder, until my mother turned on a radio to try to disguise the noise. A door slammed; they began shouting at one another; another door slammed; a shoe or something banged the wall behind Mona's bed.

52   "How're we supposed to *sleep?*" said Mona, sitting up.

53   There was another thud, more yelling in Shanghaiese, and then my mother's voice pierced the wall, in English. "So what you want I should do? Go to work like Theresa Lee?"

54   My father rumbled something back.

55   "You think you're big shot because you have job, right? You're big shot, but you never get promotion, you never get raise. All I do is spend money, right? So what do you do, you tell me. So what do you do!"

56   Something hit the floor so hard that our room shook.

57   "So kill me," screamed my mother. "You know what you are? You are failure. Failure! You are failure!"

58   Then there was a sudden, terrific, bursting crash—and after it, as if on a bungled cue, the serene blare of an a cappella soprano, picking her way down a scale.

59   By the time Mona and I knew to look out the window, a neighbor's pet beagle was already on the scene, sniffing and barking at my mother's body, his tail crazy with excitement; then he was barking at my stunned and trembling father, at the shrieking ambulance, the police, at crying Mona in her bunny-footed pajamas, and at me, barefoot in the cold grass, squeezing her shoulder with one hand and clutching my malachite beads with the other.

60   My mother wasn't dead, only unconscious, the paramedics figured that out right away, but there was blood everywhere, and though they were reassuring about her head wounds as they strapped her to the stretcher, commenting also on how small she was, how delicate, how light, my father kept saying, "I killed her, I killed her" as the ambulance screeched and screeched headlong, forever, to the hospital. I was afraid to touch her, and glad of the metal rail between us, even though its sturdiness made her seem even frailer than she was; I wished she was bigger, somehow, and noticed, with a pang, that the new red slippers we had given her for Mother's Day had been lost somewhere along the way. How much she seemed to be leaving behind as we careened along—still not there, still not there—Mona and Dad and the medic and I taking up the whole ambulance, all the room, so there was no room for anything else; no room even for my mother's real self, the one who should have been pinching the color back to my father's grey face, the one who should have been calming Mona's cowlick—the one who should have been bending over us, to help us to be strong, to help us get through, even as we bent over her.

Then suddenly we were there, the glowing square of the emergency   61
room entrance opening like the gates of heaven; and immediately the talk
of miracles began. Alive, a miracle. No bones broken, a miracle. A
miracle that the hemlocks cushioned her fall, a miracle that they hadn't
been trimmed in a year and a half. It was a miracle that all that blood, the
blood that had seemed that night to be everywhere, was from one shard
of glass, a single shard, can you imagine, and as for the gash in her head,
the scar would be covered by hair. The next day my mother cheerfully
described just how she would part it so that nothing would show at all.

"You're a lucky duck-duck," agreed Mona, helping herself, with a   62
little *pirouette,* to the cherry atop my mother's chocolate pudding.

That wasn't enough for me, though. I was relieved, yes, but what I   63
wanted by then was a real miracle, not for her simply to have survived,
but for the whole thing never to have happened — for my mother's head
never to have had to be shaved and bandaged like that, for her high,
proud forehead never to have been swollen down over her eyes, for her
face and neck and hands never to have been painted so many shades of
blue-black, and violet, and chartreuse. I still want those things — for my
parents not to have had to live with this affair like a prickle bush between
them, for my father to have been able to look my mother in her swollen
eyes and curse the madman, the monster that could have dared do this to
the woman he loved: I wanted to be able to touch my mother without
shuddering, to be able to console my father, to be able to get that crash
out of my head, the sound of that soprano — so many things that I didn't
know how to pray for them, that I wouldn't have known where to start
even if I had the power to work miracles, right there, right then.

A week later, when my mother was home, and her head beginning to   64
bristle with new hairs, I lost my malachite beads. I had been carrying
them in a white cloth pouch that Patty had given me, and was swinging
the pouch on my pinky on my way home from school, when I swung just
a bit too hard, and it went sailing in a long arc through the air,
whooshing like a perfectly thrown basketball through one of the holes of
a nearby sewer. There was no chance of fishing it out: I looked and
looked, crouching on the sticky pavement until the asphalt had crazed the
skin of my hands and knees, but all I could discern was an evil-smelling
musk, glassy and smug and impenetrable.

My loss didn't quite hit me until I was home, but then it produced an   65
agony all out of proportion to my string of pretty beads. I hadn't cried at
all during my mother's accident, and now I was crying all afternoon, all
through dinner, and then after dinner too, crying past the point where I
knew what I was crying for, wishing dimly that I had my beads to hold,
wishing dimly that I could pray but refusing, refusing, I didn't know why,
until I finally fell into an exhausted sleep on the couch, where my parents
left me for the night — glad, no doubt, that one of the more tedious of my
childhood crises seemed to be finally winding off the reel of life, onto the

reel of memory. They covered me, and somehow grew a pillow under my head, and, with uncharacteristic disregard for the living room rug, left some milk and pecan sandies on the coffee table, in case I woke up hungry. Their thoughtfulness was prescient: I did wake up in the early part of the night; and it was then, amid the unfamiliar sounds and shadows of the living room, that I had what I was sure was a true vision.

66   Even now what I saw retains an odd clarity: the requisite strange light flooding the room, first orange, and then a bright yellow-green, then a crackling bright burst like a Roman candle going off near the piano. There was a distinct smell of coffee, and a long silence. The room seemed to be getting colder. Nothing. A creak; the light starting to wane, then waxing again, brilliant pink now. Still nothing. Then, as the pink started to go a little purple, a perfectly normal middle-aged man's voice, speaking something very like pig Latin, told me quietly not to despair, not to despair, my beads would be returned to me.

67   That was all. I sat a moment in the dark, then turned on the light, gobbled down the cookies—and in a happy flash understood I was so good, really, so near to being a saint that my malachite beads would come back through the town water system. All I had to do was turn on all the faucets in the house, which I did, one by one, stealing quietly into the bathroom and kitchen and basement. The old spigot by the washing machine was too gunked up to be coaxed very far open, but that didn't matter. The water didn't have to be full blast, I understood that. Then I gathered together my pillow and blanket and trundled up to my bed to sleep.

68   By the time I woke up in the morning I knew that my beads hadn't shown up, but when I knew it for certain, I was still disappointed; and as if that weren't enough, I had to face my parents and sister, who were all abuzz with the mystery of the faucets. Not knowing what else to do, I, like a puddlebrain, told them the truth. The results were predictably painful.

69   "Callie had a *vision*," Mona told everyone at the bus stop. "A vision with lights, and sinks in it!"

70   Sinks, visions. I got it all day, from my parents, from my classmates, even some sixth and seventh graders. Someone drew a cartoon of me with a halo over my head in one of the girls' room stalls; Anthony Rossi made gurgling noises as he walked on his hands at recess. Only Patty tried not to laugh, though even she was something less than unalloyed understanding.

71   "I don' think miracles are thupposed to happen in *thewers*," she said.

72   Such was the end of my saintly ambitions. It wasn't the end of all holiness; the ideas of purity and goodness still tippled my brain, and over the years I came slowly to grasp of what grit true faith was made. Last night, though, when my father called to say that he couldn't go on living in our old house, that he was going to move to a smaller place, another

place, maybe a condo—he didn't know how, or where—I found myself still wistful for the time religion seemed all I wanted it to be. Back then the world was a place that could be set right: one had only to direct the hand of the Almighty and say, just here, Lord, we hurt here—and here, and here, and here.

❏ Questions for Discussion

1. How does the **narrator,** as a young person, feel about miracles and wonders?

2. What change in Patty is indicated by the following paragraph?

   > Miracles. Today Patty laughs to think she ever spent good time stewing on such matters, her attention having long turned to rugs, and artwork, and antique Japanese bureaus—things she believes in.

3. Why does the story suddenly shift to the religious couple with the prayer list?

4. How would you characterize the prayers of the couple? Are the prayers appropriate?

5. The narrator says of the couple's comment written beside the prayer note:

   > . . . it seemed like it had been written by some cousin of mine . . . who had stayed home to grow up, . . . while I went abroad and learned what I had to, though the learning was painful.

   What does she mean?

6. Why does the narrator not cry over her mother's "accident" but cry over losing her "malachite beads"? Why does the narrator's "water-faucet vision" occur right after her mother's accident?

❏ Suggestions for Exploration and Writing

1. What does the narrator mean by "over the years I came slowly to grasp of what grit true faith was made"? Analyze in detail the nature and/or causes of the change in the narrator's faith. How does her change differ from Patty's?

2. Discuss in detail the nature and causes of a change in your faith or personal quest.

POETRY

Psalm 8, traditionally attributed to David, is one of the 150 poems which make up the book of Psalms in the Old Testament. Often described as a lyrical echo of the first book of Genesis, this psalm celebrates God's creations.

Psalm 8

To the chief Musician upon Gĭ't-tĭth, A Psalm of Dā'-vĭd.

O Lord our Lord, how excellent *is* thy name in all the earth! who hast set thy glory above the heavens.

2 Out of the mouth of babes and sucklings hast thou ordained strength because of thine enemies, that thou mightest still the enemy and the avenger.

3 When I consider thy heavens, the work of thy fingers, the moon and the stars, which thou hast ordained;

4 What is man, that thou art mindful of him? and the son of man, that thou visitest him?

5 For thou hast made him a little lower than the angels, and hast crowned him with glory and honour.

6 Thou madest him to have dominion over the works of thy hands; thou hast put all *things* under his feet:

7 All sheep and oxen, yea, and the beasts of the field;

8 The fowl of the air, and the fish of the sea, *and whatsoever* passeth through the paths of the seas.

9 O Lord our Lord, how excellent *is* thy name in all the earth!

❑ **Questions for Discussion**

1. In what order does the psalmist perceive the wonders of God?

2. What prompts the psalmist's questions? What is the **tone** in the psalm?

3. What vision of humanity and its purpose does the psalmist present? How well has humanity fulfilled that purpose?

JOHN DONNE (1572–1631)

Batter My Heart

Batter my heart, three person'd God; for, you
As yet but knocke, breathe, shine, and seeke to mend;
That I may rise, and stand, o'erthrow mee,'and bend
Your force, to breake, blowe, burn and make me new.
I, like an usurpt towne, to'another due,

5

Labour to'admit you, but Oh, to no end,
Reason your viceroy in mee, mee should defend
But is captiv'd, and proves weake or untrue,
Yet dearely'I love you,'and would be lov'd faine,
But am betroth'd unto your enemie,   10
Divorce mee,'untie, or breake that knot againe,
Take mee to you, imprison mee, for I
Except you'enthrall mee, never shall be free,
Nor ever chast, except you ravish mee.

❏ **Questions for Discussion**

1. What does the strong verb "batter" suggest? What is the speaker asking God to do in this anguished and unorthodox prayer? Why?

2. The first four lines of the **sonnet** are dominated by strong action verbs. What is the effect of these verbs? What is the effect of the **alliterative** *b*s in these lines?

3. Explain the extended **simile** developed in the second quatrain.

4. Explain the **paradoxes** in the last two lines.

❏ **Suggestion for Exploration and Writing**

1. In an analysis, show how **imagery**, sound, **diction**, and **syntax** develop the **tone** of Donne's "Batter my heart."

JOHN MILTON (1608–1674)

John Milton, educated at Cambridge and a master of Greek, Latin, Italian, and Hebrew, isolated himself after graduation from college to read the great books. After writing several controversial pamphlets, including Areopagitica (1644), *an argument for freedom of the press, he served as foreign secretary under Oliver Cromwell, Puritan Lord Protector of England from 1653 to 1658. Milton's* Paradise Lost (1667), *based on the Genesis account of humanity's fall, is regarded as the greatest* epic *poem written in English. Both* Paradise Lost *and* Paradise Regained (1671) *were written during Milton's last years when he was blind and embittered.*

Sonnet 16

When I consider how my light is spent,
  Ere half my days, in this dark world and wide,
  And that one talent which is death to hide,
  Lodged with me useless, though my soul more bent
To serve therewith my maker, and present   5

My true account, lest he returning chide,
Doth God exact day-labour, light denied,
I fondly ask; but Patience to prevent
That murmur, soon replies, God doth not need
10   Either man's work or his own gifts, who best
Bear his mild yoke, they serve him best, his state
Is kingly. Thousands at his bidding speed
And post o'er land and ocean without rest:
They also serve who only stand and wait.

❑ Questions for Discussion

1. To what does Milton refer when he speaks of "that one talent which is death to hide / Lodged with me useless . . ."? Who gave Milton the talent to which he refers?

2. Milton asks, "Does God exact day-labour, light denied?" What does Patience reply?

3. Patience says that man is not going to be judged on his "work" or "gifts." On what is man going to be judged?

4. Explain the last line of the poem.

❑ Suggestions for Exploration and Writing

1. Milton speaks of presenting the "true account" of his life and actions to God. If you had to present the true account of yourself to God or to someone else in authority, what would it be? Why?

2. In an essay, discuss whether you agree with the last line of Milton's poem.

PHILLIS WHEATLEY (1754–1784)

Phillis Wheatley, at age seven, was brought as a slave to Boston and sold to John Wheatley, who later freed her. Phillis Wheatley learned English very quickly and read voraciously in the classics. Her favorite characters were the Greek gods and goddesses. Her poems sought to show that Africans needed the proper environment to flourish.

On Being Brought from Africa to America

'Twas mercy brought me from my pagan land,
Taught my benighted soul to understand
That there's a God, that there's a Savior too:

Once I redemption neither sought nor knew.
Some view our sable race with scornful eye. 5
"Their color is a diabolic dye."
Remember, Christians, Negroes, black as Cain,
May be refined, and join the angelic train.

❏ **Questions for Discussion**

1. Why does Wheatley refer to herself as a "benighted" soul?

2. What are her feelings about being converted to Christianity? Why do you think she has these feelings?

3. Wheatley seems to embrace her new religion. She still, however, thinks there is prejudice against her. What evidence is there to support this contention?

4. What does she caution "Christians" about?

WILLIAM BLAKE (1757–1827)

The Lamb

Little Lamb, who made thee?
  Dost thou know who made thee?
Gave thee life & bid thee feed,
By the stream & o'er the mead;
Gave thee clothing of delight, 5
Softest clothing wooly bright;
Gave thee such a tender voice,
Making all the vales rejoice!
  Little Lamb I'll tell thee,
  Little Lamb I'll tell thee! 10
He is callèd by thy name,
For he calls himself a Lamb:
He is meek & he is mild,
He became a little child:
I a child & thou a lamb, 15
We are callèd by his name.
  Little Lamb God bless thee.
  Little Lamb God bless thee.

❏ **Questions for Discussion**

1. How would you describe the **diction** of this poem? Who is the speaker? Why does Blake use the archaic terms *thee* and *thou*?

2. How does the speaker feel about the Lamb? How do sound, **imagery,** and **diction** develop the **tone?**

3. What particular qualities of the Lamb appeal to the speaker? What does the Lamb **symbolize?**

4. What do the lines "For he calls himself a Lamb," "He became a little child," and "We are calléd by his name" mean?

The Tyger

Tyger! Tyger! burning bright
In the forests of the night,
What immortal hand or eye
Could frame thy fearful symmetry?

5 In what distant deeps or skies
Burnt the fire of thine eyes?
On what wings dare he aspire?
What the hand, dare seize the fire?

And what shoulder, & what art,
10 Could twist the sinews of thy heart?
And when thy heart began to beat,
What dread hand? & what dread feet?

What the hammer? what the chain?
In what furnace was thy brain?
15 What the anvil? what dread grasp
Dare its deadly terrors clasp?

When the stars threw down their spears,
And water'd heaven with their tears,
Did he smile his work to see?
20 Did he who made the Lamb make thee?

Tyger! Tyger! burning bright
In the forests of the night,
What immortal hand or eye
Dare frame thy fearful symmetry?

❏ **Questions for Discussion**

1. What qualities of the tiger are suggested by the phrase "fearful symmetry"?

2. What is Blake alluding to in the lines "When the stars threw down their spears / And watered heaven with their tears"?

3. Can the question "Did he who made the Lamb make thee?" be answered? If so, how? If not, why not?

4. What does the tiger symbolize?

❏ **Suggestion for Exploration and Writing**

1. In an essay, analyze "The Lamb" and "The Tyger" as representing two contrasting but complementary visions of God and of the created world.

WILLIAM WORDSWORTH (1770–1850)

My Heart Leaps Up

My heart leaps up when I behold
  A Rainbow in the sky:
So was it when my life began;
So is it now I am a Man;
So be it when I shall grow old,   5
  Or let me die!
The Child is Father of the Man;
And I could wish my days to be
Bound each to each by natural piety.

❏ **Questions for Discussion**

1. What very familiar figure of speech does the poet use in the first line? What does it suggest about his feeling for nature? Why would he rather die than lose the capacity for this feeling?

2. What does the **paradox** "The Child is Father of the Man" mean? How does this paradox relate to the **sestet** of the sonnet "It Is a Beauteous Evening"?

3. What does the speaker mean by "natural piety"?

It Is a Beauteous Evening

It is a beauteous Evening, calm and free;
The holy time is quiet as a Nun
Breathless with adoration; the broad sun
Is sinking down in its tranquillity;
The gentleness of heaven is on the Sea: 5
Listen! the mighty Being is awake
And doth with his eternal motion make
A sound like thunder—everlastingly.
Dear Child! dear Girl! that walkest with me here,

10   If thou appear'st untouch'd by solemn thought,
Thy nature is not therefore less divine:
Thou liest in Abraham's bosom all the year;
And worshipp'st at the Temple's inner shrine,
God being with thee when we know it not.

❏ Questions for Discussion

1. What contrast does this **sonnet** point out between the speaker and the child he addresses?

2. What kinds of images does Wordsworth use to create the **tone** of the poem? The evening is compared in its quietness to "a Nun / breathless with adoration." What does it mean to be "breathless with adoration"?

3. What does the speaker mean when he says to the child, "Thou liest in Abraham's bosom all the year, / And worshipp'st at the Temple's inner shrine"?

ALFRED, LORD TENNYSON (1809–1892)

Tennyson succeeded Wordsworth as English Poet Laureate. Tennyson's early poems were not acclaimed; however, after the death of a friend caused him to write an extended elegy, In Memoriam *(1853), and Queen Victoria named him a Lord, Tennyson became one of the most popular poets of his day. Among his works are* Maud, and Other Poems *(1855) and* Idylls of the King *(1859), an extended poem about King Arthur.*

Ulysses

It little profits that an idle king,
By this still hearth, among these barren crags,
Match'd with an aged wife, I mete and dole
Unequal laws unto a savage race,
5 That hoard, and sleep, and feed, and know not me.
I cannot rest from travel: I will drink
Life to the lees: all times I have enjoy'd
Greatly, have suffer'd greatly, both with those
That loved me, and alone; on shore, and when
10 Thro' scudding drifts the rainy Hyades
Vext the dim sea: I am become a name;
For always roaming with a hungry heart
Much have I seen and known; cities of men
And manners, climates, councils, governments,
15 Myself not least, but honour'd of them all;

And drunk delight of battle with my peers,
Far on the ringing plains of windy Troy.
I am a part of all that I have met;
Yet all experience is an arch wherethro'
Gleams that untravell'd world, whose margin fades   20
For ever and for ever when I move.
How dull it is to pause, to make an end,
To rust unburnish'd, not to shine in use!
As tho' to breathe were life. Life piled on life
Were all too little, and of one to me   25
Little remains: but every hour is saved
From that eternal silence, something more,
A bringer of new things; and vile it were
For some three suns to store and hoard myself,
And this gray spirit yearning in desire   30
To follow knowledge like a sinking star,
Beyond the utmost bound of human thought.
   This is my son, mine own Telemachus,
To whom I leave the sceptre and the isle—
Well-loved of me, discerning to fulfil   35
This labour, by slow prudence to make mild
A rugged people, and thro' soft degrees
Subdue them to the useful and the good.
Most blameless is he, centred in the sphere
Of common duties, decent not to fail   40
In offices of tenderness, and pay
Meet adoration to my household gods
When I am gone. He works his work, I mine.
   There lies the port; the vessel puffs her sail:
There gloom the dark broad seas. My mariners,   45
Souls that have toil'd, and wrought, and thought with me—
That ever with a frolic welcome took
The thunder and the sunshine, and opposed
Free hearts, free foreheads—you and I are old;
Old age hath yet his honour and his toil;   50
Death closes all: but something ere the end,
Some work of noble note, may yet be done,
Not unbecoming men that strove with Gods.
The lights begin to twinkle from the rocks:
The long day wanes: the slow moon climbs: the deep   55
Moans round with many voices. Come, my friends,
'Tis not too late to seek a newer world.
Push off, and sitting well in order smite
The sounding furrows; for my purpose holds
To sail beyond the sunset, and the baths   60
Of all the western stars, until I die.

It may be that the gulfs will wash us down:
It may be we shall touch the Happy Isles,
And see the great Achilles, whom we knew.
65 Tho' much is taken, much abides; and tho'
We are not now that strength which in old days
Moved earth and heaven; that which we are, we are;
One equal temper of heroic hearts,
Made weak by time and fate, but strong in will
70 To strive, to seek, to find, and not to yield.

❏ Questions for Discussion

1. Why does Ulysses say that he "will drink / Life to the lees"? Why does he still crave the "untraveled world"?

2. Ulysses says he has "enjoyed greatly" and "suffered greatly." Why is the word *greatly* important?

3. Why is Telemachus Ulysses' ideal heir?

❏ Suggestions for Exploration and Writing

1. Write an essay about someone who has the same characteristics and the same yearnings as Ulysses.

2. "Do Not Go Gentle Into That Good Night" by Dylan Thomas has a similar message. Compare the poems' themes.

3. Are you a Ulysses or a Telemachus? Discuss.

GERALD MANLEY HOPKINS (1844–1889)

*Born into a High Anglican family in England, Gerald Manley Hopkins in 1866 converted to Catholicism. Two years later, he entered the Jesuit order and in 1877 was ordained a Jesuit priest. His sometimes anguished poems, which were not published until 1918, reveal a man of strong faith sometimes racked by doubts about the adequacy of his devotion and service. Hopkins developed an experimental metrical system he called **sprung rhythm**, basing his lines on the number of accents rather than the number of syllables.*

God's Grandeur

The world is charged with the grandeur of God.
    It will flame out, like shining from shook foil;
    It gathers to a greatness, like the ooze of oil
Crushed. Why do men then now not reck his rod?
5 Generations have trod, have trod, have trod;

And all is seared with trade; bleared, smeared with toil;
    And wears man's smudge and shares man's smell: the soil
Is bare now, nor can foot feel, being shod.

And for all this, nature is never spent:
    There lives the dearest freshness deep down things;   10
And though the last lights off the black West went
    Oh, morning, at the brown brink eastward, springs—
Because the Holy Ghost over the bent
    World broods with warm breast and with ah! bright
        wings.

❏ **Questions for Discussion**

1. What is the effect of the word *charged* in the first line?

2. What **images** does Hopkins use to characterize the grandeur of God? Where does this grandeur appear?

3. What is the effect of the repetition in line 5?

4. What is Hopkins' answer to the question in line 4? Compare his answer to Wordsworth's lament in "The World Is Too Much with Us."

5. What is the effect of the final image?

Pied Beauty

Glory be to God for dappled things—
    For skies of couple-colour as a brinded cow;
        For rose-moles all in stipple upon trout that swim;
Fresh-firecoal chestnut-falls; finches' wings;
    Landscape plotted and pieced—fold, fallow, and plough;   5
        And áll trádes, their gear and tackle and trim.
All things counter, original, spare, strange;
    Whatever is fickle, freckled (who knows how?)
        With swift, slow; sweet, sour; adazzle, dim;
He fathers-forth whose beauty is past change: 10
                    Praise him.

❏ **Questions for Discussion**

1. What does Hopkins mean by "Pied" and "dappled"? Is he simply referring to coloring? What do his **images** have in common?

2. What does this poem celebrate?

3. Who are the "He" and the "him" of the last two lines?

❏ **Suggestion for Exploration and Writing**

1. Hopkins' poems celebrate the beauty and diversity of God's creation, sensitizing readers to even the apparently dull and ordinary. Compare Hopkins' sense of divine imminence with Annie Dillard's in "Heaven and Earth in Jest"; Wordsworth's in "It Is a Beauteous Evening" and "The World Is Too Much with Us"; or Kinnell's in "Saint Francis and the Sow."

WILLIAM BUTLER YEATS (1865–1939)

The Second Coming

Turning and turning in the widening gyre
The falcon cannot hear the falconer;
Things fall apart; the centre cannot hold;
Mere anarchy is loosed upon the world,
5 The blood-dimmed tide is loosed, and everywhere
The ceremony of innocence is drowned;
The best lack all conviction, while the worst
Are full of passionate intensity.

Surely some revelation is at hand;
10 Surely the Second Coming is at hand.
The Second Coming! Hardly are those words out
When a vast image out of *Spiritus Mundi*
Troubles my sight: somewhere in sands of the desert
A shape with lion body and the head of a man,
15 A gaze blank and pitiless as the sun,
Is moving its slow thighs, while all about it
Reel shadows of the indignant desert birds.
The darkness drops again; but now I know
That twenty centuries of stony sleep
20 Were vexed to nightmare by a rocking cradle,
And what rough beast, its hour come round at last,
Slouches towards Bethlehem to be born?

❏ **Questions for Discussion**

1. In the first eight lines, what does the speaker envision happening to the world?

2. What leads the speaker to conclude that "some revelation is at hand," that "the Second Coming is at hand"?

3. This poem was published in 1921. What events in Ireland and Europe might have led Yeats to conclude that "Things fall apart"?

4. Describe the apocalyptic "beast" Yeats envisions. What are some of the sources of this vision?

5. Yeats' last line invites comparison of his "rough beast" with Jesus Christ. How do they compare? Might this "rough beast" represent a "Second Coming" of Christ in a quite different incarnation?

❏ **Suggestions for Exploration and Writing**

1. Yeats' mystical book *A Vision* develops a cyclical theory of history that informs "The Second Coming." Yeats saw history as a spiraling series of 2000-year cycles each inaugurated by the direct intrusion of the divine into the world. Read Book V of *A Vision* and in a researched paper show how "The Second Coming" exemplifies Yeats' theory of history.

2. Clearly one of the sources for "The Second Coming" is Revelation. Discuss in detail Yeats' use of this source, particularly chapters 4 and 13, in his description of the "rough beast." What conclusions can you draw about Yeats' conception of God?

Sailing to Byzantium

I

That is no country for old men. The young
In one another's arms, birds in the trees
—Those dying generations—at their song,
The salmon-falls, the mackerel-crowded seas,
Fish, flesh, or fowl, commend all summer long   5
Whatever is begotten, born, and dies.
Caught in that sensual music all neglect
Monuments of unageing intellect.

II

An aged man is but a paltry thing,
A tattered coat upon a stick, unless   10
Soul clap its hands and sing, and louder sing
For every tatter in its mortal dress,
Nor is there singing school but studying
Monuments of its own magnificence;
And therefore I have sailed the seas and come   15
To the holy city of Byzantium.

III

O sages standing in God's holy fire
As in the gold mosaic of a wall,
Come from the holy fire, perne in a gyre,
20   And be the singing-masters of my soul.
Consume my heart away; sick with desire
And fastened to a dying animal
It knows not what it is; and gather me
Into the artifice of eternity.

IV

25   Once out of nature I shall never take
My bodily form from any natural thing,
But such a form as Grecian goldsmiths make
Of hammered gold and gold enamelling
To keep a drowsy Emperor awake;
30   Or set upon a golden bough to sing
To lords and ladies of Byzantium
Of what is past, or passing, or to come.

❏ Questions for Discussion

1. What place is the speaker describing in the first stanza? Why is it "no country for old men"? What **images** define this world?

2. What does the "artifice of eternity" suggest about Yeats' conception of life after death?

3. Why would Yeats want to be resurrected as a golden bird?

4. At the beginning of the poem Yeats refers to "whatever is begotten, born, and dies." At the end he imagines himself a golden bird singing "of what is past, or passing, or to come." How do these three-part phrases define the difference between the speaker in his original country and the speaker in Byzantium?

❏ Suggestions for Exploration and Writing

1. Yeats says in *A Vision* that Byzantium represented for him a culture so unified in its religious, cultural, and practical life that an artist spoke for and was heard by the whole people. Read Book V, section IV of *A Vision*, research Byzantium, and write a paper on why Byzantium meant so much to Yeats that he would prefer to spend eternity there.

2. Compare Yeats' bird to Keats' nightingale in "Ode to a Nightingale." How does each bird **symbolize** a means of transcending the physical world?

ROBERT FROST (1874–1963)

After Apple-Picking

My long two-pointed ladder's sticking through a tree
Toward heaven still,
And there's a barrel that I didn't fill
Beside it, and there may be two or three
Apples I didn't pick upon some bough.   5
But I am done with apple-picking now.
Essence of winter sleep is on the night,
The scent of apples: I am drowsing off.
I cannot rub the strangeness from my sight
I got from looking through a pane of glass   10
I skimmed this morning from the drinking trough
And held against the world of hoary grass.
It melted, and I let it fall and break.
But I was well
Upon my way to sleep before it fell,   15
And I could tell
What form my dreaming was about to take.
Magnified apples appear and disappear,
Stem end and blossom end,
And every fleck of russet showing clear.   20
My instep arch not only keeps the ache,
It keeps the pressure of a ladder-round.
I feel the ladder sway as the boughs bend.
And I keep hearing from the cellar bin
The rumbling sound   25
Of load on load of apples coming in.
For I have had too much
Of apple-picking: I am overtired
Of the great harvest I myself desired.
There were ten thousand thousand fruit to touch,   30
Cherish in hand, lift down, and not let fall.
For all
That struck the earth,
No matter if not bruised or spiked with stubble,
Went surely to the cider-apple heap   35
As of no worth.
One can see what will trouble
This sleep of mine, whatever sleep it is.
Were he not gone,
The woodchuck could say whether it's like his   40
Long sleep, as I describe its coming on,
Or just some human sleep.

❏ **Questions for Discussion**

1. What is the significance of Frost's setting up "Toward heaven still" as a separate line?

2. Explain the **symbolism** of the following: the frozen pane of ice, the sleep, the dream, the ladder, and the apples with their varying fates.

Birches

When I see birches bend to left and right
Across the lines of straighter darker trees,
I like to think some boy's been swinging them.
But swinging doesn't bend them down to stay
As ice storms do. Often you must have seen them
Loaded with ice a sunny winter morning
After a rain. They click upon themselves
As the breeze rises, and turn many-colored
As the stir cracks and crazes their enamel.
Soon the sun's warmth makes them shed crystal shells
Shattering and avalanching on the snow crust—
Such heaps of broken glass to sweep away
You'd think the inner dome of heaven had fallen.
They are dragged to the withered bracken by the load,
And they seem not to break; though once they are bowed
So low for long, they never right themselves:
You may see their trunks arching in the woods
Years afterwards, trailing their leaves on the ground
Like girls on hands and knees that throw their hair
Before them over their heads to dry in the sun.
But I was going to say then Truth broke in
With all her matter of fact about the ice storm,
I should prefer to have some boy bend them
As he went out and in to fetch the cows—
Some boy too far from town to learn baseball,
Whose only play was what he found himself,
Summer or winter, and could play alone.
One by one he subdued his father's trees
By riding them down over and over again
Until he took the stiffness out of them,
And not one but hung limp, not one was left
For him to conquer. He learned all there was
To learn about not launching out too soon
And so not carrying the tree away
Clear to the ground. He always kept his poise
To the top branches, climbing carefully

With the same pains you use to fill a cup
Up to the brim, and even above the brim.
Then he flung outward, feet first, with a swish,
Kicking his way down through the air to the ground. 40
So was I once myself a swinger of birches.
And so I dream of going back to be.
It's when I'm weary of considerations,
And life is too much like a pathless wood
Where your face burns and tickles with the cobwebs 45
Broken across it, and one eye is weeping
From a twig's having lashed across it open.
I'd like to get away from earth awhile
And then come back to it and begin over.
May no fate willfully misunderstand me 50
And half grant what I wish and snatch me away
Not to return. Earth's the right place for love:
I don't know where it's likely to go better.
I'd like to go by climbing a birch tree,
And climb black branches up a snow-white trunk 55
Toward heaven, till the tree could bear no more,
But dipped its top and set me down again.
That would be good both going and coming back.
One could do worse than be a swinger of birches.

❏ Questions for Discussion

1. What causes the birch trees to be permanently bent over?
   What would the speaker prefer to think causes the trees to
   bend?

2. Why does Frost italicize the word *Toward* in line 56?

3. What does Frost mean when he says, "One could do worse
   than be a swinger of birches"?

Directive

Back out of all this now too much for us,
Back in a time made simple by the loss
Of detail, burned, dissolved, and broken off
Like graveyard marble sculpture in the weather,
There is a house that is no more a house 5
Upon a farm that is no more a farm
And in a town that is no more a town.
The road there, if you'll let a guide direct you
Who only has at heart your getting lost,
May seem as if it should have been a quarry— 10

Great monolithic knees the former town
Long since gave up pretense of keeping covered.
And there's a story in a book about it:
Besides the wear of iron wagon wheels
15 The ledges show lines ruled southeast-northwest,
The chisel work of an enormous Glacier
That braced his feet against the Arctic Pole.
You must not mind a certain coolness from him
Still said to haunt this side of Panther Mountain.
20 Nor need you mind the serial ordeal
Of being watched from forty cellar holes
As if by eye pairs out of forty firkins.
As for the woods' excitement over you
That sends light rustle rushes to their leaves,
25 Charge that to upstart inexperience.
Where were they all not twenty years ago?
They think too much of having shaded out
A few old pecker-fretted apple trees.
Make yourself up a cheering song of how
30 Someone's road home from work this once was,
Who may be just ahead of you on foot
Or creaking with a buggy load of grain.
The height of the adventure is the height
Of country where two village cultures faded
35 Into each other. Both of them are lost.
And if you're lost enough to find yourself
By now, pull in your ladder road behind you
And put a sign up CLOSED to all but me.
Then make yourself at home. The only field
40 Now left's no bigger than a harness gall.
First there's the children's house of make-believe,
Some shattered dishes underneath a pine,
The playthings in the playhouse of the children.
Weep for what little things could make them glad.
45 Then for the house that is no more a house,
But only a belilaced cellar hole,
Now slowly closing like a dent in dough.
This was no playhouse but a house in earnest.
Your destination and your destiny's
50 A brook that was the water of the house,
Cold as a spring as yet so near its source,
Too lofty and original to rage.
(We know the valley streams that when aroused
Will leave their tatters hung on barb and thorn.)
55 I have kept hidden in the instep arch
Of an old cedar at the waterside

A broken drinking goblet like the Grail
Under a spell so the wrong ones can't find it,
So can't get saved, as Saint Mark says they mustn't.
(I stole the goblet from the children's playhouse.)   60
Here are your waters and your watering place.
Drink and be whole again beyond confusion.

❏ Questions for Discussion

1. Frost begins the poem by inviting the reader to go back to a simpler time and to be guided by one "Who only has at heart your getting lost." Why does Frost want the reader to be lost? Can you think of a Biblical parallel to this suggestion?

2. What does Frost's **narrator,** the guide, mean by "pull in your ladder road behind you" and by his **allusion** to Saint Mark (see Mark 4:10–12 and Matthew 13:10–17)? Why does Frost refer to the brief passage in Mark rather than to the similar longer passage in Matthew?

3. Frost's view of the reaction of nature to human beings is reflected in his description of the "belilaced cellar hole." What does he seem to say about the earth without humanity? Compare this view with that expressed in Walter Van Tilburg Clark's "The Portable Phonograph."

4. Explain the **symbolism** of the brook that is "Cold as a spring as yet so near its source, / Too lofty and original to rage" and the "broken drinking goblet like the Grail." How do they allow the narrator and the reader to "Drink and be whole again beyond confusion"?

❏ Suggestions for Exploration and Writing

1. Write an essay describing a time in your life when you were "weary of considerations / And life [was] too much like a pathless wood." Frost suggests a way of rising above the little problems of life. In your essay explain how you coped with similar problems.

2. Analyze in detail the nature of Frost's quest and questor in "Directive." What kind of person could undergo such a quest? What are the costs and the risks? What are the rewards? Consider allusions to the Grail legend and to the gospels in the New Testament.

3. Using these three Frost poems which present ways to rise above the troubles of life, write an essay discussing either Frost's solutions or the **symbolism** used in the poems.

T. S. ELIOT (1888–1965)

Eliot, born an American and the grandson of a Unitarian minister, changed both his nationality and his religion, becoming a British citizen and a devout Anglican. Eliot's early poems like "The Love Song of J. Alfred Prufrock" and "The Hollow Men" expressed the disenchantment and disillusionment of many people in the early twentieth century. The Waste Land (1922) is considered by many critics to be the ultimate expression of the modern condition. Eliot's conversion to the Anglican faith, however, changed his outlook completely; and his later poems such as "Ash Wednesday" and The Four Quartets (1934–1944) depict human beings' search for a sustaining faith. An ardent admirer of Dante, Eliot learned to read medieval Italian in order to read The Divine Comedy in its original form. The quotation with which Eliot begins "The Love Song of J. Alfred Prufrock" is a statement of Guido da Montefeltro, a sinner in Dante's Inferno, who says that he would not tell Dante his story if he thought that there was any chance that Dante would return to earth to repeat it.

The Love Song of J. Alfred Prufrock

S' io credessi che mia risposta fosse
A persona che mai tornasse al mondo,
Questa fiamma staria senza più scosse.
Ma perciocchè giammai di questo fondo
Non tornò vivo alcum, s' i' odo il vero,
Senza tema d'infamia ti rispondo.

Let us go then, you and I,
When the evening is spread out against the sky
Like a patient etherized upon a table;
Let us go, through certain half-deserted streets,
5 The muttering retreats
Of restless nights in one-night cheap hotels
And sawdust restaurants with oyster-shells:
Streets that follow like a tedious argument
Of insidious intent
10 To lead you to an overwhelming question . . .

Oh, do not ask, "What is it?"
Let us go and make our visit.

In the room the women come and go
Talking of Michelangelo.

The yellow fog that rubs its back upon the window
15   panes,
The yellow smoke that rubs its muzzle on the window
      panes,
Licked its tongue into the corners of the evening,

Lingered upon the pools that stand in drains,
Let fall upon its back the soot that falls from chimneys,
Slipped by the terrace, made a sudden leap,   20
And seeing that it was a soft October night,
Curled once about the house, and fell asleep.

   And indeed there will be time
For the yellow smoke that slides along the street,
Rubbing it back upon the window panes;   25
There will be time, there will be time
To prepare a face to meet the faces that you meet;
There will be time to murder and create,
And time for all the works and days of hands
That lift and drop a question on your plate: 30
Time for you and time for me,
And time yet for a hundred indecisions,
And for a hundred visions and revisions,
Before the taking of a toast and tea.

In the room the women come and go   35
Talking of Michelangelo.

And indeed there will be time
To wonder, "Do I dare?" and, "Do I dare?"—
Time to turn back and descend the stair,
With a bald spot in the middle of my hair—   40
(They will say: "How his hair is growing thin!")
My morning coat, my collar mounting firmly to the chin,
My necktie rich and modest, but asserted by a simple pin—
(They will say: "But how his arms and legs are thin!")
Do I dare   45
Disturb the universe?
In a minute there is time
For decisions and revisions which a minute will reverse.

   For I have known them already, known them all:
Have known the evenings, mornings, afternoons,   50
I have measured out my life with coffee spoons;
I know the voices dying with a dying fall
Beneath the music from a farther room.
   So how should I presume?

   And I have known the eyes already, known them all—   55
The eyes that fix you in a formulated phrase.
And when I am formulated, sprawling on a pin,
When I am pinned and wriggling on the wall,
Then how should I begin
To spit out all the butt-ends of my days and ways?   60
   And how should I presume?

And I have known the arms already, known them all—
Arms that are braceleted and white and bare
(But in the lamplight, downed with light brown hair!)
65   Is it perfume from a dress
         That makes me so digress?
Arms that lie along a table, or wrap about a shawl.
         And should I then presume?
         And how should I begin?

               . . . . . .

70 Shall I say, I have gone at dusk through narrow streets,
And watched the smoke that rises from the pipes
Of lonely men in shirtsleeves, leaning out of windows? . . .
I should have been a pair of ragged claws
Scuttling across the floors of silent seas.

               . . . . . .

75 And the afternoon, the evening, sleeps so peacefully!
Smoothed by long fingers,
Asleep . . . tired . . . or it malingers,
Stretched on the floor, here beside you and me.
Should I, after tea and cakes and ices,
80 Have the strength to force the moment to its crisis?
But though I have wept and fasted, wept and prayed,
Though I have seen my head (grown slightly bald) brought
         in upon a platter,
I am no prophet—and here's no great matter;
I have seen the moment of my greatness flicker,
And I have seen the eternal Footman hold my coat, and
85   snicker,
         And in short, I was afraid.

   And would it have been worth it, after all,
After the cups, the marmalade, the tea,
Among the porcelain, among some talk of you and me,
90 Would it have been worth while
To have bitten off the matter with a smile,
To have squeezed the universe into a ball
To roll it toward some overwhelming question,
To say: "I am Lazarus, come from the dead,
95 Come back to tell you all, I shall tell you all"—
If one, settling a pillow by her head,
         Should say: "That is not what I meant at all;
         That is not it, at all."

   And would it have been worth it, after all,
100 Would it have been worth while,

After the sunsets and the dooryards and the sprinkled
    streets,
After the novels, after the teacups, after the skirts that trail
    along the floor—
And this, and so much more?—
It is impossible to say just what I mean!
But as if a magic lantern threw the nerves in patterns on a
    screen: 105
Would it have been worth while
If one, settling a pillow or throwing off a shawl,
And turning toward the window, should say: "That is not
    it at all,
    That is not what I meant, at all."

      . . . . . .

   No! I am not Prince Hamlet, nor was meant to be;   110
Am an attendant lord, one that will do
To swell a progress, start a scene or two,
Advise the prince: withal, an easy tool,
Deferential, glad to be of use,
Politic, cautious, and meticulous;   115
Full of high sentence, but a bit obtuse;
At times, indeed, almost ridiculous—
Almost, at times, the Fool.

I grow old . . . I grow old . . .
I shall wear the bottoms of my trowsers rolled.   120

   Shall I part my hair behind? Do I dare to eat a peach?
I shall wear white flannel trowsers, and walk upon the
    beach.
I have heard the mermaids singing, each to each.
I do not think that they will sing to me.

I have seen them riding seaward on the waves,   125
Combing the white hair of the waves blown back
When the wind blows the water white and black.

We have lingered in the chambers of the sea
By seagirls wreathed with seaweed red and brown,
Till human voices wake us, and we drown.

❏ Questions for Discussion

1. What does Eliot suggest about Prufrock by beginning the poem
   with a quotation from Dante's *Inferno?*

2. Explain the effect of the description in the opening ten lines.
   What does this description tell you about Prufrock's world?

3. Why must Prufrock "prepare a face to meet the faces that you meet"?

4. Explain the following line: "I have measured out my life with coffee spoons."

5. Why does Prufrock say that he "should have been a pair of ragged claws / Scuttling across the floors of silent seas"? Do you think he could have been more fulfilled as a crab? Why or why not?

6. Explain the pathos of Prufrock's saying, "I have heard the mermaids singing, each to each. / I do not think that they will sing to me." Why is his opinion of himself more pathetic because he has "heard the mermaids sing"?

7. From what do "human voices wake us," and why, then, do "we drown"?

8. What is Prufrock afraid to ask? Why is he afraid to ask it?

❏ **Suggestions for Exploration and Writing**

1. Write an essay using the following thesis statement: J. Alfred Prufrock is the perfect example of the indecisiveness and insecurity of many people in the modern world.

2. In his poem, Eliot alludes to Andrew Marvell's "To His Coy Mistress," thereby inviting comparison between Marvell's speaker and Prufrock. Write an essay in which you contrast these two speakers.

LANGSTON HUGHES (1902–1967)

Harlem

What happens to a dream deferred?

Does it dry up
like a raisin in the sun?
Or fester like a sore—
And then run?
Does it stink like rotten meat?
Or crust and sugar over—
like a syrupy sweet?

Maybe it just sags
like a heavy load.

Or does it explode?

❏ **Questions for Discussion**

1. What does Hughes mean by "a dream deferred"? Why would a dream be deferred?

2. Hughes uses several strong verbs in describing what could happen to a "dream deferred": the dream could "dry up," "fester," "run," "stink," "crust and sugar over," "sag," or "explode." What is your response to these verbs?

3. Why does Hughes never identify the kind of dream he has in mind?

❏ **Suggestion for Exploration and Writing**

1. Discuss what happened to your own unfulfilled or postponed dream.

GALWAY KINNELL (1927–   )

American poet Galway Kinnell has written at least eight books of poems as well as a novel. He has also translated many poems. Most of his poetry, while recognizing the anarchy of the contemporary world and the horrors that confront humanity, is affirmatively Christian, sometimes seeming almost a ritual of prayer, blessing, or praise.

Saint Francis and the Sow

The bud
stands for all things,
even for those things that don't flower,
for everything flowers, from within, of self-blessing;
though sometimes it is necessary   5
to reteach a thing its loveliness,
to put a hand on its brow
of the flower
and retell it in words and in touch
it is lovely   10
until it flowers again from within, of self-blessing;
as Saint Francis
put his hand on the creased forehead
of the sow, and told her in words and in touch
blessings of earth on the sow, and the sow   15
began remembering all down her thick length,
from the earthen snout all the way
through the fodder and slops to the spiritual curl of the tail,
from the hard spininess spiked out from the spine

20

down through the great broken heart
to the sheer blue milken dreaminess spurting and
    shuddering
from the fourteen teats into the fourteen mouths sucking
    and blowing beneath them:
the long, perfect loveliness of sow.

❏ **Questions for Discussion**

1. How does "the bud" symbolize "all things"? What does the speaker mean by "everything flowers, from within"?

2. How does one "reteach a thing its loveliness"?

3. How does Kinnell use line length to emphasize the point and **tone** of his poem?

4. Why does the poet use a sow to exemplify his point?

5. In what sense is the sow "perfect" in its "loveliness"?

6. How would you ordinarily feel about a sow? How does the poem make you feel about one?

❏ **Suggestion for Exploration and Writing**

1. In an essay, demonstrate the "perfect loveliness" of a creature usually thought ugly, obnoxious, or malicious such as a cockroach, a mosquito, a spider, or a garden snake. If necessary, do some background research on the creature in order to demonstrate its special kind of perfection.

JOHN LENNON (1940–1980)
AND PAUL McCARTNEY (1942–)

John Lennon, born in Liverpool, was one of the original Beatles who invaded the United States in the sixties. Gifted with the ability to write the lyrics for many of the Beatles' songs, Lennon later wrote and performed as a solo act. In 1980 he was assassinated outside his apartment building in New York City.

The left-handed guitar player with the Beatles, McCartney collaborated with his fellow musicians to produce many of their songs. After the Beatles broke up, McCartney went on to form his own band, Wings, and to tour the world.

Eleanor Rigby

Ah, look at all the lonely people!
Ah, look at all the lonely people!

Eleanor Rigby picks up the rice in the church
Where a wedding has been.
Lives in a dream.   5
Waits at the window, wearing the face
   that she keeps in a jar by the door.
Who is it for?

All the lonely people,
   where do they all come from?   10
All the lonely people,
   where do they all belong?

Father McKenzie writing the words
   of a sermon that no one will hear—
No one comes near. Look at him   15
   working, darning his socks in the night
   when there's nobody there.

All the lonely people,
   where do they all come from?
All the lonely people,   20
   where do they all belong?

Ah, look at all the lonely people!
Ah, look at all the lonely people!
Eleanor Rigby died in the church and
   was buried along with her name.   25
Nobody came.

Father McKenzie wiping the dirt from
   his hands as he walks from the grave.
No one was saved.

All the lonely people,   30
   where do they all come from?
All the lonely people,
   where do they all belong?

❏ Questions for Discussion

1. What is the "dream" that Eleanor lives?

2. What does the speaker mean by the face "in a jar by the door"?

3. What are the implications of "Eleanor Rigby died in the church and / was buried along with her name"?

4. What causes Father McKenzie's loneliness? Why are the people not saved?

5. What do Eleanor Rigby and Father McKenzie have in common other than loneliness?

❏ **Suggestions for Exploration and Writing**

1. Answer one question that Lennon and McCartney raise. For example, the authors ask where lonely people come from and why people are lonely.

2. Analyze the aspirations of Eleanor Rigby and Father McKenzie. Compare their aspirations with Prufrock's.

3. Contrast the quests of the three people alluded to in the poem: the bride, Eleanor Rigby, and Father McKenzie.

JUDITH ORTIZ COFER (1952–)

Born in Puerto Rico to a teenage mother and a career navy man, Judith Cofer spent part of her childhood in the ghetto of Paterson, New Jersey. There she found the library an oasis for her literary yearnings. Her poems at times reflect the idioms, slang, and substandard English of the ghetto; however, her message is always clear.

Latin Women Pray

Latin women pray
In incense sweet churches
They pray in Spanish to an Anglo God
With a Jewish heritage.
5   And this Great White Father
Imperturbable in his marble pedestal
Looks down upon his brown daughters
Votive candles shining like lust
In his all seeing eyes
10 Unmoved by their persistent prayers.

Yet year after year
Before his image they kneel
Margarita Josefina Maria and Isabel
All fervently hoping
15 That if not omnipotent
At least he be bilingual

❏ **Questions for Discussion**

1. What is Cofer's purpose in referring to God as an Anglo, Jewish "Great White Father"? How is this description related to her line, "Looks down upon his brown daughters"?

2. Why does Cofer say that this God is "Unmoved by their [brown daughters'] persistent prayers"?

3. What is the Latin women's hope? Does the humor distract from the seriousness of their hope?

❏ **Suggestion for Exploration and Writing**

1. The quest for answers to prayers is not new. In an essay, contrast Cofer's hope and Wheatley's prayer in "On Being Brought From Africa to America."

DRAMA

Ancient Greek Drama

Ancient Greek drama was performed in huge outdoor amphitheaters which seated as many as 20,000 spectators on great semicircular stone benches that climbed the slope of a hill. At the bottom center was the skene building, which served both as a dressing room for the actors and as the scenery, most often as the front of a palace or temple. In front of the skene was a circular acting space, the orchestra.

Because of the massive size of such amphitheaters, where many spectators would have been hundreds of feet from the stage, ancient Greek drama emphasizes large, clearly visible, and stylized effects. Actors declaimed their lines through the amplifying mouthpieces of masks and apparently later, in tragedies, wore elevated shoes to enhance their stature. Probably, because of the size of the theaters and the masks, ancient Greek drama relied on bold and dramatic movements rather than on subtle gestures, facial expressions, and asides.

Deriving from the worship of the god Dionysus, Athenian drama was a community celebration. Audiences apparently were quite volatile and deeply involved in the drama. Because almost the only subjects accepted for performance were the Greek myths, the audience already knew the stories behind each play; therefore, Greek drama provided the perfect vehicle for **dramatic irony,** a form of irony made possible by the audience's knowledge of events and relationships of which the characters were often ignorant. In **dramatic irony,** the character's words have a double meaning unknown to the character but known to the audience or to other characters. Apparently, too, the audience had extraordinary attention spans; for on each of the last three days of the Dionysian festival they would sit through five plays—three tragedies, one satyr play, and one comedy.

SOPHOCLES (496?–406 B.C.)

Sophocles, the second of the three great Greek tragedians, wrote at least 120 plays and won first place at the festival of Dionysus twenty-four times. Sophocles' long life spanned the time in history

when the culture of Athens was at its peak. Born to a wealthy
Athenian family, Sophocles was honored both as a producer of
tragedies and as a citizen. He was selected for the highest elective
office as one of the ten generals of Athens and was awarded priest-
hoods for his religious piety. Sophocles won first place in the festival
of Dionysus for the first time in 468 B.C. and was still intellectually
and artistically active until his death at the age of ninety. Three of the
seven extant plays of Sophocles, Oedipus the King, Oedipus at
Colonus, *and* Antigone, *tell the story of the royal family of Thebes.
Aristotle gave* Oedipus the King *the highest praise of any extant
Greek tragedy, and it is often described as the best example of
dramatic irony in literature.*

Oedipus the King

Translated by Thomas Gould

Characters

OEDIPUS:° *The King of Thebes*
PRIEST OF ZEUS: *Leader of the Suppliants*
CREON: *Oedipus's Brother-in-Law*
CHORUS: *a Group of Theban Elders*
CHORAGOS: *Spokesman of the Chorus*
TIRESIAS: *a blind Seer or Prophet*
JOCASTA: *The Queen of Thebes*
MESSENGER: *from Corinth, once a Shepherd*
HERDSMAN: *once a Servant of Laius*
SECOND MESSENGER: *a Servant of Oedipus*

Mutes

SUPPLIANTS: *Thebans seeking Oedipus's help*
ATTENDANTS: *for the Royal Family*
SERVANTS: *to lead Tiresias and Oedipus*
ANTIGONE: *Daughter of Oedipus and
Jocasta*
ISMENE: *Daughter of Oedipus and
Jocasta*

*[The action takes place during the day in front of the royal palace in Thebes.
There are two altars (left and right) on the Proscenium and several steps leading
down to the Orchestra. As the play opens, Thebans of various ages who have
come to beg Oedipus for help are sitting on these steps and in part of the
Orchestra. These suppliants are holding branches of laurel or olive which have
strips of wool° wrapped around them. Oedipus enters from the palace (the
central door of the Skene).]*

Oedipus: The name means "swollen foot." It refers to the mutilation of Oedipus's feet
done by his father, Laius, before the infant was sent to Mount Cithaeron to be put to
death by exposure.   Stage direction *wool:* Branches wrapped with wool are traditional
symbols of prayer or supplication.

PROLOGUE

OEDIPUS.   My children, ancient Cadmus'° newest care,
why have you hurried to those seats, your boughs
wound with the emblems of the suppliant?
The city is weighed down with fragrant smoke,
with hymns to the Healer° and the cries of mourners.
I thought it wrong, my sons, to hear your words
through emissaries, and have come out myself,
I, Oedipus, a name that all men know.

[Oedipus addresses the Priest.]

Old man—for it is fitting that you speak
for all—what is your mood as you entreat me,   10
fear or trust? You may be confident
that I'll do anything. How hard of heart
if an appeal like this did not rouse my pity!
PRIEST.   You, Oedipus, who hold the power here,
you see our several ages, we who sit
before your altars—some not strong enough
to take long flight, some heavy in old age,
the priests, as I of Zeus,° and from our youths
a chosen band. The rest sit with their windings
in the markets, at the twin shrines of Pallas,°   20
and the prophetic embers of Ismēnos.°
Our city, as you see yourself, is tossed
too much, and can no longer lift its head
above the troughs of billows red with death.
It dies in the fruitful flowers of the soil,
it dies in its pastured herds, and in its women's
barren pangs. And the fire-bearing god°
has swooped upon the city, hateful plague,
and he has left the house of Cadmus empty.
Black Hades° is made rich with moans and weeping.   30
Not judging you an equal of the gods,
do I and the children sit here at your hearth,
but as the first of men, in troubled times
and in encounters with divinities.
You came to Cadmus' city and unbound
the tax we had to pay to the harsh singer,°

---

1 *Cadmus:* Oedipus's great great grandfather (although he does not know this) and the founder of Thebes.   5 *Healer:* Apollo, god of prophecy, light, healing, justice, purification, and destruction.   18 *Zeus:* father and king of the gods.   20 *Pallas:* Athena, goddess of wisdom, arts, crafts, and war.   21 *Ismēnos:* a reference to the temple of Apollo near the river Ismēnos in Thebes. Prophecies were made here by "reading" the ashes of the altar fires.   27 *fire-bearing god:* contagious fever viewed as a god.   30 *Black Hades:* refers to both the underworld where the spirits of the dead go and the god of the underworld.   36 *harsh singer:* the Sphinx, a monster with a woman's head, a lion's

did it without a helpful word from us,
with no instruction; with a god's assistance
you raised up our life, so we believe.
Again now Oedipus, our greatest power,   40
we plead with you, as suppliants, all of us,
to find us strength, whether from a god's response,
or learned in some way from another man.
I know that the experienced among men
give counsels that will prosper best of all.
Noblest of men, lift up our land again!
Think also of yourself; since now the land
calls you its Savior for your zeal of old,
oh let us never look back at your rule
as men helped up only to fall again!   50
Do not stumble! Put our land on firm feet!
The bird of omen was auspicious then,
when you brought that luck; be that same man again!
The power is yours; if you will rule our country,
rule over men, not in an empty land.
A towered city or a ship is nothing
if desolate and no man lives within.

OEDIPUS.   Pitiable children, oh I know, I know
the yearnings that have brought you. Yes, I know
that you are sick. And yet, though you are sick,   60
there is not one of you so sick as I.
For your affliction comes to each alone,
for him and no one else, but my soul mourns
for me and for you, too, and for the city.
You do not waken me as from a sleep,
for I have wept, bitterly and long,
tried many paths in the wanderings of thought,
and the single cure I found by careful search
I've acted on: I sent Menoeceus' son,
Creon, brother of my wife, to the Pythian   70
halls of Phoebus,° so that I might learn

---

body, and wings. The "tax" that Oedipus freed Thebes from was the destruction of all
the young men who failed to solve the Sphinx's riddle and were subsequently devoured.
The Sphinx always asked the same riddle: "What goes on four legs in the morning, two
legs at noon, and three legs in the evening, and yet is weakest when supported by the
largest number of feet?" Oedipus discovered the correct answer—man, who crawls in
infancy, walks in his prime, and uses a stick in old age—and thus ended the Sphinx's
reign of terror. The Sphinx destroyed herself when Oedipus answered the riddle. Oedipus's reward for freeing Thebes of the Sphinx was the throne and the hand of the recently widowed Jocasta.   **70–71** *Pythian . . . Phoebus:* The temple of Phoebus Apollo's
oracle or prophet at Delphi.

what I must do or say to save this city.
Already, when I think what day this is,
I wonder anxiously what he is doing.
Too long, more than is right, he's been away.
But when he comes, then I shall be a traitor
if I do not do all that the god reveals.

PRIEST.   Welcome words! But look, those men have signaled
that it is Creon who is now approaching!

OEDIPUS.   Lord Apollo! May he bring Savior Luck,   80
a Luck as brilliant as his eyes are now!

PRIEST.   His news is happy, it appears. He comes,
forehead crowned with thickly berried laurel.°

OEDIPUS.   We'll know, for he is near enough to hear us.

[Enter Creon along one of the Parados.]

Lord, brother in marriage, son of Menoeceus!
What is the god's pronouncement that you bring?

CREON.   It's good. For even troubles, if they chance
to turn out well, I always count as lucky.

OEDIPUS.   But what was the response? You seem to say
I'm not to fear—but not to take heart either.   90

CREON.   If you will hear me with these men present,
I'm ready to report—or go inside.

[Creon moves up the steps toward the palace.]

OEDIPUS.   Speak out to all! The grief that burdens me
concerns these men more than it does my life.

CREON.   Then I shall tell you what I heard from the god.
The task Lord Phoebus sets for us is clear:
drive out pollution sheltered in our land,
and do not shelter what is incurable.

OEDIPUS.   What is our trouble? How shall we cleanse ourselves?

CREON.   We must banish or murder to free ourselves   100
from a murder that blows storms through the city.

OEDIPUS.   What man's bad luck does he accuse in this?

CREON.   My Lord, a king named Laius ruled our land
before you came to steer the city straight.

OEDIPUS.   I know. So I was told—I never saw him.

CREON.   Since he was murdered, you must raise your hand
against the men who killed him with their hands.

OEDIPUS.   Where are they now? And how can we ever find
the track of ancient guilt now hard to read?

CREON.   In our own land, he said. What we pursue,   110
that can be caught; but not what we neglect.

---

83 *laurel:* Creon is wearing a garland of laurel leaves, sacred to Apollo.

OEDIPUS.   Was Laius home, or in the countryside—
or was he murdered in some foreign land?
CREON.   He left to see a sacred rite, he said;
He left, but never came home from his journey.
OEDIPUS.   Did none of his party see it and report—
someone we might profitably question?
CREON.   They were all killed but one, who fled in fear,
and he could tell us only one clear fact.
OEDIPUS.   What fact? One thing could lead us on to more   120
if we could get a small start on our hope.
CREON.   He said that bandits chanced on them and killed him—
with the force of many hands, not one alone.
OEDIPUS.   How could a bandit dare so great an act—
unless this was a plot paid off from here!
CREON.   We thought of that, but when Laius was killed,
we had no one to help us in our troubles.
OEDIPUS.   It was your very kingship that was killed!
What kind of trouble blocked you from a search?
CREON.   The subtle-singing Sphinx asked us to turn   130
from the obscure to what lay at our feet.
OEDIPUS.   Then I shall begin again and make it plain.
It was quite worthy of Phoebus, and worthy of you,
to turn our thoughts back to the murdered man,
and right that you should see me join the battle
for justice to our land and to the god.
Not on behalf of any distant kinships,
it's for myself I will dispel this stain.
Whoever murdered him may also wish
to punish me—and with the selfsame hand.   140
In helping him I also serve myself.
Now quickly, children: up from the altar steps,
and raise the branches of the suppliant!
Let someone go and summon Cadmus' people:
say I'll do anything.

[Exit an Attendant along one of the Parados.]

Our luck will prosper
if the god is with us, or we have already fallen.
PRIEST.   Rise, my children; that for which we came,
he has himself proclaimed he will accomplish.
May Phoebus, who announced this, also come
as Savior and reliever from the plague.   150

[Exit Oedipus and Creon into the Palace. The Priest and the Suppliants exit left and right along the Parados. After a brief pause, the Chorus (including the Choragos) enters the Orchestra from the Parados.]

PARADOS

Strophe 1°

CHORUS.   Voice from Zeus,° sweetly spoken, what are you
that have arrived from golden
Pytho° to our shining
Thebes? I am on the rack, terror
    shakes my soul.
Delian Healer,° summoned by " iē!"
I await in holy dread what obligation, something new
or something back once more with the revolving years,
    you'll bring about for me.
Oh tell me, child of golden Hope,   160
    deathless Response!

Antistrophe 1°

I appeal to you first, daughter of Zeus,
    deathless Athena,
    and to your sister who protects this land,
Artemis,° whose famous throne is the whole circle
    of the marketplace,
and Phoebus, who shoots from afar: iō!
Three-fold defenders against death, appear!
If ever in the past, to stop blind ruin
    sent against the city,   170
you banished utterly the fires of suffering,
    come now again!

Strophe 2

Ah! Ah! Unnumbered are the miseries
I bear. The plague claims all
our comrades. Nor has thought found yet a spear
by which a man shall be protected. What our glorious
earth gives birth to does not grow. Without a birth
from cries of labor
    do the women rise.
One person after another   180
    you may see, like flying birds,
faster than indomitable fire, sped
to the shore of the god that is the sunset.°

151, 162 *Strophe, Antistrophe:* probably refer to the direction in which the Chorus
danced while reciting specific stanzas. Strophe may have indicated dance steps to stage
left, antistrophe to stage right.   151 *Voice from Zeus:* a reference to Apollo's prophecy.
Zeus taught Apollo how to prophesy.   153 *Pytho:* Delphi.   156 *Delian Healer:* Apollo.
165 *Artemis:* goddess of virginity, childbirth, and hunting.   183 *god . . . sunset:* Hades,
god of the underworld.

Antistrophe 2

And with their deaths unnumbered dies the city.
Her children lie unpitied on the ground,
spreading death, unmourned.
Meanwhile young wives, and gray-haired mothers with them,
on the shores of the altars, from this side and that,
suppliants from mournful trouble,
    cry out their grief.   190
A hymn to the Healer shines,
    the flute a mourner's voice.
Against which, golden goddess, daughter of Zeus,
    send lovely Strength.

Strophe 3

Cause raging Ares°—who,
    armed now with no shield of bronze,
burns me, coming on amid loud cries—
to turn his back and run from my land,
with a fair wind behind, to the great
    hall of Amphitritē,°   200
or to the anchorage that welcomes no one,
Thrace's troubled sea!
If night lets something get away at last,
    it comes by day.
Fire-bearing god . . . . . .
    you who dispense the might of lightning,
Zeus! Father! Destroy him with your thunderbolt!

[Enter Oedipus from the palace.]

Antistrophe 3

Lycēan Lord!° From your looped
    bowstring, twisted gold,
I wish indomitable missiles might be scattered   210
and stand forward, our protectors; also fire-bearing
radiance of Artemis, with which
    she darts across the Lycian mountains.
I call the god whose head is bound in gold,
with whom this country shares its name,
Bacchus,° wine-flushed, summoned by "euoi!,"
    Maenads' comrade,
to approach ablaze
    with gleaming . . . . . .
pine, opposed to that god-hated god.   220

---

195 *Ares:* god of war and destruction. **200** *Amphitritē:* the Atlantic Ocean.
208 *Lycēan Lord:* Apollo. **216** *Bacchus:* Dionysus, god of fertility and wine.

EPISODE 1

OEDIPUS.   I hear your prayer. Submit to what I say
and to the labors that the plague demands
and you'll get help and a relief from evils.
I'll make the proclamation, though a stranger
to the report and to the deed. Alone,
had I no key, I would soon lose the track.
Since it was only later that I joined you,
to all the sons of Cadmus I say this:
whoever has clear knowledge of the man
who murdered Laius, son of Labdacus,   230
I command him to reveal it all to me—
nor fear if, to remove the charge, he must
accuse himself: his fate will not be cruel—
he will depart unstumbling into exile.
But if you know another, or a stranger,
to be the one whose hand is guilty, speak:
I shall reward you and remember you.
But if you keep your peace because of fear,
and shield yourself or kin from my command,
hear you what I shall do in that event: 240
I charge all in this land where I have throne
and power, shut out that man—no matter who—
both from your shelter and all spoken words,
nor in your prayers or sacrifices make
him partner, nor allot him lustral° water.
All men shall drive him from their homes: for he
is the pollution that the god-sent Pythian
response has only now revealed to me.
In this way I ally myself in war
with the divinity and the deceased.°   250
And this curse, too, against the one who did it,
whether alone in secrecy, or with others:
may he wear out his life unblest and evil!
I pray this, too: if he is at my hearth
and in my home, and I have knowledge of him,
may the curse pronounced on others come to me.
All this I lay to you to execute,
for my sake, for the god's, and for this land
now ruined, barren, abandoned by the gods.
Even if no god had driven you to it,   260
you ought not to have left this stain uncleansed,
the murdered man a nobleman, a king!
You should have looked! But now, since, as it happens,

---

245 *lustral:* purifying.   **250** *the deceased:* Laius.

It's I who have the power that he had once,
and have his bed, and a wife who shares our seed,
and common bond had we had common children
(had not his hope of offspring had bad luck—
but as it happened, luck lunged at his head);
because of this, as if for my own father,
I'll fight for him, I'll leave no means untried,   270
to catch the one who did it with his hand,
for the son of Labdacus, of Polydōrus,
of Cadmus before him, and of Agēnor.°
This prayer against all those who disobey:
the gods send out no harvest from their soil,
nor children from their wives. Oh, let them die
victims of this plague, or of something worse.
Yet for the rest of us, people of Cadmus,
we the obedient, may Justice, our ally,
and all the gods, be always on our side!   280
CHORAGOS.   I speak because I feel the grip of your curse:
the killer is not I. Nor can I point
to him. The one who set us to this search,
Phoebus, should also name the guilty man.
OEDIPUS.   Quite right, but to compel unwilling gods—
no man has ever had that kind of power.
CHORAGOS.   May I suggest to you a second way?
OEDIPUS.   A second or a third—pass over nothing!
CHORAGOS.   I know of no one who sees more of what
Lord Phoebus sees than Lord Tiresias.   290
My Lord, one might learn brilliantly from him.
OEDIPUS.   Nor is this something I have been slow to do.
At Creon's word I sent an escort—twice now!
I am astonished that he has not come.
CHORAGOS.   The old account is useless. It told us nothing.
OEDIPUS.   But tell it to me. I'll scrutinize all stories.
CHORAGOS.   He is said to have been killed by travelers.
OEDIPUS.   I have heard, but the one who did it no one sees.
CHORAGOS.   If there is any fear in him at all,
he won't stay here once he has heard that curse.   300
OEDIPUS.   He won't fear words: he had no fear when he did it.

*[Enter Tiresias from the right, led by a Servant and two of Oedipus's
Attendants.]*

CHORAGOS.   Look there! There is the man who will convict him!
It's the god's prophet they are leading here,
one gifted with the truth as no one else.

272–273. *Son . . . Agēnor:* refers to Laius by citing his genealogy.

OEDIPUS. Tiresias, master of all omens—
  public and secret, in the sky and on the earth—
  your mind, if not your eyes, sees how the city
  lives with a plague, against which Thebes can find
  no Saviour or protector, Lord, but you.
  For Phoebus, as the attendants surely told you,   310
  returned this answer to us: liberation
  from the disease would never come unless
  we learned without a doubt who murdered Laius—
  put them to death, or sent them into exile.
  Do not begrudge us what you may learn from birds
  or any other prophet's path you know!
  Care for yourself, the city, care for me,
  care for the whole pollution of the dead!
  We're in your hands. To do all that he can
  to help another is man's noblest labor.   320
TIRESIAS. How terrible to understand and get
  no profit from the knowledge! I knew this,
  but I forgot, or I had never come.
OEDIPUS. What's this? You've come with very little zeal.
TIRESIAS. Let me go home! If you will listen to me,
  You will endure your troubles better—and I mine.
OEDIPUS. A strange request, not very kind to the land
  that cared for you—to hold back this oracle!
TIRESIAS. I see your understanding comes to you
  inopportunely. So that won't happen to me . . .   330
OEDIPUS. Oh, by the gods, if you understand about this,
  don't turn away! We're on our knees to you.
TIRESIAS. None of you understands! I'll never bring
  my grief to light—I will not speak of yours.
OEDIPUS. You know and won't declare it! Is your purpose
  to betray us and to destroy this land?
TIRESIAS. I will grieve neither of us. Stop this futile
  cross-examination. I'll tell you nothing!
OEDIPUS. Nothing? You vile traitor! You could provoke
  a stone to anger! You still refuse to tell?   340
  Can nothing soften you, nothing convince you?
TIRESIAS. You blamed anger in me—you haven't seen.
  Can nothing soften you, nothing convince you?
OEDIPUS. Who wouldn't fill with anger, listening
  to words like yours which now disgrace this city?
TIRESIAS. It will come, even if my silence hides it.
OEDIPUS. If it will come, then why won't you declare it?
TIRESIAS. I'd rather say no more. Now if you wish,
  respond to that with all your fiercest anger!
OEDIPUS. Now I am angry enough to come right out   350

with this conjecture: you, I think, helped plot
the deed; you did it—even if your hand
cannot have struck the blow. If you could see,
I should have said the deed was yours alone.

TIRESIAS.   Is that right! Then I charge you to abide
by the decree you have announced: from this day
say no word to either these or me,
for you are the vile polluter of this land!

OEDIPUS.   Aren't you appalled to let a charge like that
come bounding forth? How will you get away?   360

TIRESIAS.   You cannot catch me. I have the strength of truth.

OEDIPUS.   Who taught you this? Not your prophetic craft!

TIRESIAS.   You did. You made me say it. I didn't want to.

OEDIPUS.   Say what? Repeat it so I'll understand.

TIRESIAS.   I made no sense? Or are you trying me?

OEDIPUS.   No sense I understood. Say it again!

TIRESIAS.   I say you are the murderer you seek.

OEDIPUS.   Again that horror! You'll wish you hadn't said that.

TIRESIAS.   Shall I say more, and raise your anger higher?

OEDIPUS.   Anything you like! Your words are powerless.   370

TIRESIAS.   You live, unknowing, with those nearest to you
in the greatest shame. You do not see the evil.

OEDIPUS.   You won't go on like that and never pay!

TIRESIAS.   I can if there is any strength in truth.

OEDIPUS.   In truth, but not in you! You have no strength,
blind in your ears, your reason, and your eyes.

TIRESIAS.   Unhappy man! Those jeers you hurl at me
before long all these men will hurl at you.

OEDIPUS.   You are the child of endless night; it's not
for me or anyone who sees to hurt you.   380

TIRESIAS.   It's not my fate to be struck down by you.
Apollo is enough. That's his concern.

OEDIPUS.   Are these inventions Creon's or your own?

TIRESIAS.   No, your affliction is yourself, not Creon.

OEDIPUS.   Oh success!—in wealth, kingship, artistry,
in any life that wins much admiration—
the envious ill will stored up for you!
to get at my command, a gift I did not
seek, which the city put into my hands,
my loyal Creon, colleague from the start,   390
longs to sneak up in secret and dethrone me.
So he's suborned this fortuneteller—schemer!
deceitful beggar-priest!—who has good eyes
for gains alone, though in his craft he's blind.
Where were your prophet's powers ever proved?

Why, when the dog who chanted verse° was here,
did you not speak and liberate this city?
Her riddle wasn't for a man chancing by
to interpret; prophetic art was needed,
but you had none, it seems—learned from birds   400
or from a god. I came along, yes I,
Oedipus the ignorant, and stopped her—
by using thought, not augury from birds.
And it is I whom you now wish to banish,
so you'll be close to the Creontian throne.
You—and the plot's concocter—will drive out
pollution to your grief: you look quite old
or you would be the victim of that plot!
CHORAGOS.   It seems to us that this man's words were said
in anger, Oedipus, and yours as well.   410
Insight, not angry words, is what we need,
the best solution to the god's response.
TIRESIAS.   You are the king, and yet I am your equal
in my right to speak. In that I too am Lord
for I belong to Loxias,° not you.
I am not Creon's man. He's nothing to me.
Hear this, since you have thrown my blindness at me:
Your eyes can't see the evil to which you've come,
nor where you live, nor who is in your house.
Do you know your parents? Not knowing, you are   420
their enemy, in the underworld and here.
A mother's and a father's double-lashing
terrible-footed curse will soon drive you out.
Now you can see, then you will stare into darkness.
What place will not be harbor to your cry,
or what Cithaeron° not reverberate
when you have heard the bride-song in your palace
to which you sailed? Fair wind to evil harbor!
Nor do you see how many other woes
will level you to yourself and to your children.   430
So, at my message, and at Creon, too,
splatter muck! There will never be a man
ground into wretchedness as you will be.
OEDIPUS.   Am I to listen to such things from him!
May you be damned! Get out of here at once!
Go! Leave my palace! Turn around and go!

[Tiresias begins to move away from Oedipus.]

396 *dog . . . verse:* The Sphinx.   415 *Loxias:* Apollo.   426 *Cithaeron:* reference to the
mountain on which Oedipus was to be exposed as an infant.

TIRESIAS.   I wouldn't have come had you not sent for me.
OEDIPUS.   I did not know you'd talk stupidity,
   or I wouldn't have rushed to bring you to my house.
TIRESIAS.   Stupid I seem to you, yet to your parents   440
   who gave you natural birth I seemed quite shrewd.
OEDIPUS.   Who? Wait! Who is the one who gave me birth?
TIRESIAS.   This day will give you birth,° and ruin too.
OEDIPUS.   What murky, riddling thing you always say!
TIRESIAS.   Don't you surpass us all at finding out?
OEDIPUS.   You sneer at what you'll find has brought me greatness.
TIRESIAS.   And that's the very luck that ruined you.
OEDIPUS.   I wouldn't care, just so I saved the city.
TIRESIAS.   In that case I shall go. Boy, lead the way!
OEDIPUS.   Yes, let him lead you off. Here, underfoot,   450
   you irk me. Gone, you'll cause no further pain.
TIRESIAS.   I'll go when I have said what I was sent for.
   Your face won't scare me. You can't ruin me.
   I say to you, the man whom you have looked for
   as you pronounced your curses, your decrees
   on the bloody death of Laius—he is here!
   A seeming stranger, he shall be shown to be
   a Theban born, though he'll take no delight
   in that solution. Blind, who once could see,
   a beggar who was rich, through foreign lands   460
   he'll go and point before him with a stick.
   To his beloved children, he'll be shown
   a father who is also brother; to the one
   who bore him, son and husband; to his father,
   his seed-fellow and killer. Go in
   and think this out; and if you find I've lied,
   say then I have no prophet's understanding!

[Exit Tiresias, led by a Servant. Oedipus exits into the palace with his Attendants.]

STASIMON 1

Strophe 1

CHORUS.   Who is the man of whom the inspired
      rock of Delphi° said
   he has committed the unspeakable   470
      with blood-stained hands?
   Time for him to ply a foot
   mightier than those of the horses
      of the storm in his escape;

---

443 *give you birth:* that is, identify your parents.   **469** *rock of Delphi:* Apollo's oracle
at Delphi.

upon him mounts and plunges the weaponed
son of Zeus,° with fire and thunderbolts,
and in his train the dreaded goddesses
of Death, who never miss.

Antistrophe 1

The message has just blazed,
 gleaming from the snows   480
of Mount Parnassus: we must track
 everywhere the unseen man.
He wanders, hidden by wild
forests, up through caves
 and rocks, like a bull,
anxious, with an anxious foot, forlorn.
he puts away from him the mantic° words come from earth's
navel,° at its center, yet these live
forever and still hover round him.

Strophe 2

Terribly he troubles me,   490
 the skilled interpreter of birds!°
I can't assent, nor speak against him.
 Both paths are closed to me.
I hover on the wings of doubt,
 not seeing what is here nor what's to come.
What quarrel started in the house of Labdacus°
or in the house of Polybus,°
 either ever in the past
 or now, I never
heard, so that . . . with this fact for my touchstone   500
I could attack the public
 fame of Oedipus, by the side of the Labdaceans
an ally, against the dark assassination.

Antistrophe 2

No, Zeus and Apollo
 understand and know things
mortal; but that another man
 can do more as a prophet than I can—
for that there is no certain test,
 though, skill to skill,
one man might overtake another.   510

---

476 *son of Zeus:* Apollo.   **487** *mantic:* prophetic.   **487–88** *earth's navel:* Delphi.
491 *interpreter of birds:* Tiresias. The Chorus is troubled by his accusations.
496 *house of Labdacus:* the line of Laius.   **497** *Polybus:* Oedipus's foster father.

No, never, not until
    I see the charges proved,
when someone blames him shall I nod assent.
For once, as we all saw, the winged maiden° came
against him: he was seen then to be skilled,
    proved, by that touchstone, dear to the people. So,
never will my mind convict him of the evil.

EPISODE 2

[Enter Creon from the right door of the skene and speaks to the Chorus.]

CREON.   Citizens, I hear that a fearful charge
is made against me by King Oedipus!
I had to come. If, in this crisis,   520
he thinks that he has suffered injury
from anything that I have said or done,
I have no appetite for a long life—
bearing a blame like that! It's no slight blow
the punishment I'd take from what he said:
it's the ultimate hurt to be called traitor
by the city, by you, by my own people!
CHORAGOS.   The thing that forced that accusation out
could have been anger, not the power of thought.
CREON.   But who persuaded him that thoughts of mine   530
had led the prophet into telling lies?
CHORAGOS.   I do not know the thought behind his words.
CREON.   But did he look straight at you? Was his mind right
when he said that I was guilty of this charge?
CHORAGOS.   I have no eyes to see what rulers do.
But here he comes himself out of the house.

[Enter Oedipus from the palace.]

OEDIPUS.   What? You here? And can you really have
the face and daring to approach my house
when you're exposed as its master's murderer
and caught, too, as the robber of my kingship?   540
Did you see cowardice in me, by the gods,
or foolishness, when you began this plot?
Did you suppose that I would not detect
your stealthy moves, or that I'd not fight back?
It's your attempt that's folly, isn't it—
tracking without followers or connections,
kingship which is caught with wealth and numbers?
CREON.   Now wait! Give me as long to answer back!
Judge me for yourself when you have heard me!

---

514 *winged maiden:* The Sphinx.

OEDIPUS. You're eloquent, but I'd be slow to learn 550
   from you, now that I've seen your malice toward me.

CREON. That I deny. Hear what I have to say.

OEDIPUS. Don't you deny it! You are the traitor here!

CREON. If you consider mindless willfulness
   a prized possession, you are not thinking sense.

OEDIPUS. If you think you can wrong a relative
   and get off free, you are not thinking sense.

CREON. Perfectly just, I won't say no. And yet
   what is this injury you say I did you?

OEDIPUS. Did you persuade me, yes or no, to send 560
   someone to bring that solemn prophet here?

CREON. And I still hold to the advice I gave.

OEDIPUS. How many years ago did your King Laius . . .

CREON. Laius! Do what? Now I don't understand.

OEDIPUS. Vanish—victim of a murderous violence?

CREON. That is a long count back into the past.

OEDIPUS. Well, was this seer then practicing his art?

CREON. Yes, skilled and honored just as he is today.

OEDIPUS. Did he, back then, ever refer to me?

CREON. He did not do so in my presence ever. 570

OEDIPUS. You did inquire into the murder then.

CREON. We had to, surely, though we discovered nothing.

OEDIPUS. But the "skilled" one did not say this then? Why not?

CREON. I never talk when I am ignorant.

OEDIPUS. But you're not ignorant of your own part.

CREON. What do you mean? I'll tell you if I know.

OEDIPUS. Just this: if he had not conferred with you
   he'd not have told about my murdering Laius.

CREON. If he said that, you are the one who knows.
   But now it's fair that you should answer me. 580

OEDIPUS. Ask on! You won't convict me as the killer.

CREON. Well then, answer. My sister is your wife?

OEDIPUS. Now there's a statement that I can't deny.

CREON. You two have equal power in this country?

OEDIPUS. She gets from me whatever she desires.

CREON. And I'm a third? The three of us are equals?

OEDIPUS. That's where you're treacherous to your kinship!

CREON. But think about this rationally, as I do.
   First look at this: do you think anyone
   prefers the anxieties of being king 590
   to untroubled sleep—if he has equal power?
   I'm not the kind of man who falls in love
   with kingship. I am content with a king's power.
   And so would any man who's wise and prudent.
   I get all things from you, with no distress;
   as king I would have onerous duties, too.

How could the kingship bring me more delight
than this untroubled power and influence?
I'm not misguided yet to such a point
that profitable honors aren't enough.   600
As it is, all wish me well and all salute;
those begging you for something have me summoned,
for their success depends on that alone.
Why should I lose all this to become king?
A prudent mind is never traitorous.
Treason's a thought I'm not enamored of;
nor could I join a man who acted so.
In proof of this, first go yourself to Pytho°
and ask if I brought back the true response.
Then, if you find I plotted with that portent   610
reader,° don't have me put to death by your vote
only—I'll vote myself for my conviction.
Don't let an unsupported thought convict me!
It's not right mindlessly to take the bad
for good or to suppose the good are traitors.
Rejecting a relation who is loyal
is like rejecting life, our greatest love.
In time you'll know securely without stumbling,
for time alone can prove a just man just,
though you can know a bad man in a day.   620
CHORAGOS.   Well said, to one who's anxious not to fall.
    Swift thinkers, Lord, are never safe from stumbling.
OEDIPUS.   But when a swift and secret plotter moves
    against me, I must make swift counterplot.
    If I lie quiet and await his move,
    he'll have achieved his aims and I'll have missed.
CREON.   You surely cannot mean you want me exiled!
OEDIPUS.   Not exiled, no. Your death is what I want!
CREON.   If you would first define what envy is . . .
OEDIPUS.   Are you still stubborn? Still disobedient?   630
CREON.   I see you cannot think!
OEDIPUS.   For me I can.
CREON.   You should for me as well!
OEDIPUS.   But you're a traitor!
CREON.   What if you're wrong?
OEDIPUS.   Authority must be maintained.
CREON.   Not if the ruler's evil.
OEDIPUS.   Hear that, Thebes!
CREON.   It is my city too, not yours alone!
CHORAGOS.   Please don't, my Lords! Ah, just in time, I see
    Jocasta there, coming from the palace.

---

608 *Pytho:* Delphi.   610–611 *portent reader:* Apollo's oracle or prophet.

With her help you must settle your quarrel.

[Enter Jocasta from the Palace.]

JOCASTA.   Wretched men! What has provoked this ill-
advised dispute? Have you no sense of shame,   640
with Thebes so sick, to stir up private troubles?
Now go inside! And Creon, you go home!
Don't make a general anguish out of nothing!
CREON.   My sister, Oedipus your husband here
sees fit to do one of two hideous things:
to have me banished from the land—or killed!
OEDIPUS.   That's right: I caught him, Lady, plotting harm
against my person—with a malignant science.
CREON.   May my life fail, may I die cursed, if I
did any of the things you said I did!   650
JOCASTA.   Believe his words, for the god's sake, Oedipus,
in deference above all to his oath
to the gods. Also for me, and for these men!

KOMMOS°

Strophe 1

CHORUS.   Consent, with will and mind,
my king, I beg of you!
OEDIPUS.   What do you wish me to surrender?
CHORUS.   Show deference to him who was not feeble in time past
and is now great in the power of his oath!
OEDIPUS.   Do you know what you're asking?
CHORUS.   Yes.
OEDIPUS.   Tell me then.
CHORUS.   Never to cast into dishonored guilt, with an unproved   660
assumption, a kinsman who has bound himself by curse.
OEDIPUS.   Now you must understand, when you ask this,
you ask my death or banishment from the land.

Strophe 2

CHORUS.   No, by the god who is the foremost of all gods,
the Sun! No! Godless,
    friendless, whatever death is worst of all,
let that be my destruction, if this
    thought ever moved me!
But my ill-fated soul
    this dying land   670
wears out—the more if to these older troubles
she adds new troubles from the two of you!

---

654 *Kommos:* a dirge or lament sung by the Chorus and one or more of the chief characters.

OEDIPUS.   Then let him go, though it must mean my death,
or else disgrace and exile from the land.
My pity is moved by your words, not by his—
he'll only have my hate, wherever he goes.
CREON.   You're sullen as you yield; you'll be depressed
when you've passed through this anger. Natures like yours
are hardest on themselves. That's as it should be.
OEDIPUS.   Then won't you go and let me be?
CREON.   I'll go.   680
Though you're unreasonable, they know I'm righteous.

                                                    [Exit Creon.]

Antistrophe 1

CHORUS.   Why are you waiting, Lady?
Conduct him back into the palace!
JOCASTA.   I will, when I have heard what chanced.
CHORUS.   Conjectures—words alone, and nothing based on thought.
But even an injustice can devour a man.
JOCASTA.   Did the words come from both sides?
CHORUS.   Yes.
JOCASTA.   What was said?
CHORUS.   To me it seems enough! enough! the land already
          troubled,   690
that this should rest where it has stopped.
OEDIPUS.   See what you've come to in your honest thought,
in seeking to relax and blunt my heart?

Antistrophe 2

CHORUS.   I have not said this only once, my Lord.
That I had lost my sanity,
          without a path in thinking—
be sure this would be clear
          if I put you away
who, when my cherished land
          wandered crazed   700
with suffering, brought her back on course.
Now, too, be a lucky helmsman!
JOCASTA.   Please, for the god's sake, Lord, explain to me
the reason why you have conceived this wrath?
OEDIPUS.   I honor you, not them,° and I'll explain
to you how Creon has conspired against me.
JOCASTA.   All right, if that will explain how the quarrel started.
OEDIPUS.   He says I am the murderer of Laius!
JOCASTA.   Did he claim knowledge or that someone told him?

705 *them:* the Chorus.

OEDIPUS.   Here's what he did: he sent that vicious seer   710
  so he could keep his own mouth innocent.
JOCASTA.   Ah then, absolve yourself of what he charges!
  Listen to this and you'll agree, no mortal
  is ever given skill in prophecy.
  I'll prove this quickly with one incident.
  It was foretold to Laius—I shall not say
  by Phoebus himself, but by his ministers—
  that when his fate arrived he would be killed
  by a son who would be born to him and me.
  And yet, so it is told, foreign robbers   720
  murdered him, at a place where three roads meet.
  As for the child I bore him, not three days passed
  before he yoked the ball-joints of its feet,°
  then cast it, by others' hands, on a trackless mountain.
  That time Apollo did not make our child
  a patricide, or bring about what Laius
  feared, that he be killed by his own son.
  That's how prophetic words determined things!
  Forget them. The things a god must track
  he will himself painlessly reveal.   730
OEDIPUS.   Just now, as I was listening to you, Lady,
  what a profound distraction seized my mind!
JOCASTA.   What made you turn around so anxiously?
OEDIPUS.   I thought you said that Laius was attacked
  and butchered at a place where three roads meet.
JOCASTA.   That is the story, and it is told so still.
OEDIPUS.   Where is the place where this was done to him?
JOCASTA.   The land's called Phocis, where a two-forked road
  comes in from Delphi and from Daulia.
OEDIPUS.   And how much time has passed since these events?   740
JOCASTA.   Just prior to your presentation here
  as king this news was published to the city.
OEDIPUS.   Oh, Zeus, what have you willed to do to me?
JOCASTA.   Oedipus, what makes your heart so heavy?
OEDIPUS.   No, tell me first of Laius' appearance,
  what peak of youthful vigor he had reached.
JOCASTA.   A tall man, showing his first growth of white.
  He had a figure not unlike your own.
OEDIPUS.   Alas! It seems that in my ignorance
  I laid those fearful curses on myself.   750
JOCASTA.   What is it, Lord? I flinch to see your face.
OEDIPUS.   I'm dreadfully afraid the prophet sees.
  But I'll know better with one more detail.

723 *ball-joints of its feet:* the ankles.

JOCASTA.   I'm frightened too. But ask: I'll answer you.
OEDIPUS.   Was his retinue small, or did he travel
  with a great troop, as would befit a prince?
JOCASTA.   There were just five in all, one a herald.
  There was a carriage, too, bearing Laius.
OEDIPUS.   Alas! Now I see it! But who was it,   760
  Lady, who told you what you know about this?
JOCASTA.   A servant who alone was saved unharmed.
OEDIPUS.   By chance, could he be now in the palace?
JOCASTA.   No, he is not. When he returned and saw
  you had the power of the murdered Laius,
  he touched my hand and begged me formally
  to send him to the fields and to the pastures,
  so he'd be out of sight, far from the city.
  I did. Although a slave, he well deserved
  to win this favor, and indeed far more.
OEDIPUS.   Let's have him called back in immediately.   770
JOCASTA.   That can be done, but why do you desire it?
OEDIPUS.   I fear, Lady, I have already said
  too much. That's why I wish to see him now.
JOCASTA.   Then he shall come; but it is right somehow
  that I, too, Lord, should know what troubles you.
OEDIPUS.   I've gone so deep into the things I feared
  I'll tell you everything. Who has a right
  greater than yours, while I cross through this chance?
  Polybus of Corinth was my father,
  my mother was the Dorian Meropē.   780
  I was first citizen, until this chance
  attacked me—striking enough, to be sure,
  but not worth all the gravity I gave it.
  This: at a feast a man who'd drunk too much
  denied, at the wine, I was my father's son.
  I was depressed and all that day I barely
  held it in. Next day I put the question
  to my mother and father. They were enraged
  at the man who'd let this fiction fly at me.
  I was much cheered by them. And yet it kept   790
  grinding into me. His words kept coming back.
  Without my mother's or my father's knowledge
  I went to Pytho. But Pheobus sent me away
  dishonoring my demand. Instead, other
  wretched horrors he flashed forth in speech.
  He said that I would be my mother's lover,
  show offspring to mankind they could not look at,
  and be his murderer whose seed I am.°

798 *be . . . am:* that is, murder my father.

When I heard this, and ever since, I gauged
the way to Corinth by the stars alone,   800
running to a place where I would never see
the disgrace in the oracle's words come true.
But I soon came to the exact location
where, as you tell of it, the king was killed.
Lady, here is the truth. As I went on,
when I was just approaching those three roads,
a herald and a man like him you spoke of
came on, riding a carriage drawn by colts.
Both the man out front and the old man himself°
tried violently to force me off the road.   810
The driver, when he tried to push me off,
I struck in anger. The old man saw this, watched
me approach, then leaned out and lunged down
with twin prongs° at the middle of my head!
He got more than he gave. Abruptly—struck
once by the staff in this my hand—he tumbled
out, head first, from the middle of the carriage.
And then I killed them all. But if there is
a kinship between Laius and this stranger,
who is more wretched than the man you see?   820
Who was there born more hated by the gods?
For neither citizen nor foreigner
may take me in his home or speak to me.
No, they must drive me off. And it is I
who have pronounced these curses on myself!
I stain the dead man's bed with these my hands,
by which he dies. Is not my nature vile?
Unclean?—if I am banished and even
in exile I may not see my own parents,
or set foot in my homeland, or else be yoked   830
in marriage to my mother, and kill my father,
Polybus, who raised me and gave me birth?
If someone judged a cruel divinity
did this to me, would he not speak the truth?
You pure and awful gods, may I not ever
see that day, may I be swept away
from men before I see so great and so
calamitous a stain fixed on my person!
CHORAGOS.   These things seem fearful to us, Lord, and yet,
      until you hear it from the witness, keep hope!   840
OEDIPUS.   That is the single hope that's left to me,
      to wait for him, that herdsman—until he comes.

---

809 *old man himself:* Laius.   813–814 *lunged . . . prongs:* Laius strikes Oedipus with a
two-pronged horse goad or whip.

JOCASTA.   When he appears, what are you eager for?
OEDIPUS.   Just this: if his account agrees with yours
   then I shall have escaped this misery.
JOCASTA.   But what was it that struck you in my story?
OEDIPUS.   You said he spoke of robbers as the ones
   who killed him. Now: if he continues still
   to speak of many, then I could not have killed him.
   One man and many men just do not jibe.   850
   But if he says one belted man, the doubt
   is gone. The balance tips toward me. I did it.
JOCASTA.   No! He told it as I told you. Be certain.
   He can't reject that and reverse himself.
   The city heard these things, not I alone.
   But even if he swerves from what he said,
   he'll never show that Laius' murder, Lord,
   occurred just as predicted. For Loxias
   expressly said my son was doomed to kill him.
   The boy—poor boy—he never had a chance   860
   to cut him down, for he was cut down first.
   Never again, just for some oracle
   will I shoot frightened glances right and left.
OEDIPUS.   That's full of sense. Nonetheless, send a man
   to bring that farm hand here. Will you do it?
JOCASTA.   I'll send one right away. But let's go in.
   Would I do anything against your wishes?

[Exit Oedipus and Jocasta through the central door into the palace.]

STASIMON 2

Strophe 1

CHORUS. May there accompany me
   the fate to keep a reverential purity in what I say,
   in all I do, for which the laws have been set forth   870
   and walk on high, born to traverse the brightest,
   highest upper air; Olympus° only
   is their father, nor was it
   mortal nature
   that fathered them, and never will
   oblivion lull them into sleep;
   the god in them is great and never ages.

872 *Olympus:* Mount Olympus, home of the gods, treated as a god.

Antistrophe 1

The will to violate, seed of the tyrant,
if it has drunk mindlessly of wealth and power,
without a sense of time or true advantage,   880
mounts to a peak, then
plunges to an abrupt . . . destiny,
where the useful foot
is of no use. But the kind
of struggling that is good for the city
I ask the god never to abolish.
The god is my protector: never will I give that up.

Strophe 2

But if a man proceeds disdainfully
    in deeds of hand or word
and has no fear of Justice   890
    or reverence for shrines of the divinities
(may a bad fate catch him
    for his luckless wantonness!),
if he'll not gain what he gains with justice
and deny himself what is unholy,
or if he clings, in foolishness, to the untouchable
(what man, finally, in such an action, will have strength
enough to fend off passion's arrows from his soul?),
if, I say, this kind of
    deed is held in honor—   900
why should I join the sacred dance?

Antistrophe 2

No longer shall I visit and revere
    Earth's navel,° the untouchable,
nor visit Abae's° temple,
    or Olympia,°
if the prophecies are not matched by events
    for all the world to point to.
No, you who hold the power, if you are rightly called
Zeus the king of all, let this matter not escape you
and your ever-deathless rule,   910
for the prophecies to Laius fade . . .
and men already disregard them;
nor is Apollo anywhere

---

903 *Earth's navel:* Delphi.   904 *Abae:* A town in Phocis where there was another oracle of Apollo.   905 *Olympia:* site of the oracle of Zeus.

glorified with honors.
Religion slips away.

EPISODE 3

[*Enter Jocasta from the palace carrying a branch wound with wool and a jar of incense. She is attended by two women.*]

JOCASTA.   Lords of the realm, the thought has come to me
to visit shrines of the divinities
with suppliant's branch in hand and fragrant smoke.
For Oedipus excites his soul too much
with alarms of all kinds. He will not judge   920
the present by the past, like a man of sense.
He's at the mercy of all terror-mongers.

[*Jocasta approaches the altar on the right and kneels.*]

Since I can do no good by counseling,
Apollo the Lycēan!—you are the closest—
I come a suppliant, with these my vows,
for a cleansing that will not pollute him.
For when we see him shaken we are all
afraid, like people looking at their helmsman.

[*Enter a Messenger along one of the Parados. He sees Jocasta at the altar and then addresses the Chorus*]

MESSENGER.   I would be pleased if you would help me, stranger.
Where is the palace of King Oedipus?   930
Or tell me where he is himself, if you know.

CHORUS. This is his house, stranger. He is within.
This is his wife and mother of his children.

MESSENGER.   May she and her family find prosperity,
if, as you say, her marriage is fulfilled.

JOCASTA.   You also, stranger, for you deserve as much
for your gracious words. But tell me why you've come.
What do you wish? Or what have you to tell us?

MESSENGER.   Good news, my Lady, both for your house and
husband.

JOCASTA.   What is your news? And who has sent you to us?   940

MESSENGER.   I come from Corinth. When you have heard my news
you will rejoice, I'm sure—and grieve perhaps.

JOCASTA.   What is it? How can it have this double power?

MESSENGER.   They will establish him their king, so say
the people of the land of Isthmia.°

JOCASTA.   But is old Polybus not still in power?

MESSENGER.   He's not, for death has clasped him in the tomb.

JOCASTA.   What's this? Has Oedipus' father died?

---

945 *land of Isthmia:* Corinth, which was on an isthmus.

MESSENGER.   If I have lied then I deserve to die.

JOCASTA.   Attendant! Go quickly to your master,   950
and tell him this.

[Exit an Attendant into the palace.]

Oracles of the gods!
Where are you now? The man whom Oedipus
fled long ago, for fear that he should kill him—
he's been destroyed by chance and not by him!

[Enter Oedipus from the palace.]

OEDIPUS.   Darling Jocasta, my beloved wife,
Why have you called me from the palace?

JOCASTA.   First hear what this man has to say. Then see
what the god's grave oracle has come to now!

OEDIPUS.   Where is he from? What is this news he brings me?

JOCASTA.   From Corinth. He brings news about your father: 960
that Polybus is no more! that he is dead!

OEDIPUS.   What's this, old man? I want to hear you say it.

MESSENGER.   If this is what must first be clarified,
please be assured that he is dead and gone.

OEDIPUS.   By treachery or by the touch of sickness?

MESSENGER.   Light pressures tip agéd frames into their sleep.

OEDIPUS.   You mean the poor man died of some disease.

MESSENGER.   And of the length of years that he had tallied.

OEDIPUS.   Aha! Then why should we look to Pytho's vapors,°
or to the birds that scream above our heads?°   970
If we could really take those things for guides,
I would have killed my father. But he's dead!
He is beneath the earth, and here am I,
who never touched a spear. Unless he died
of longing for me and I "killed" him that way!
No, in this case, Polybus, by dying, took
the worthless oracle to Hades with him.

CHORUS.   And wasn't I telling you that just now?

OEDIPUS.   You were indeed. I was misled by fear.

JOCASTA.   You should not care about this anymore.   980

OEDIPUS.   I must care. I must stay clear of my mother's bed.

JOCASTA.   What's there for man to fear? The realm of chance
prevails. True foresight isn't possible.
His life is best who lives without a plan.
This marriage with your mother—don't fear it.
How many times have men in dreams, too, slept

---

969 *Pytho's vapors:* the prophecies of the oracle at Delphi.   **970** *birds . . . heads:* the prophecies derived from interpreting the flights of birds.

with their own mothers! Those who believe such things
mean nothing endure their lives most easily.

OEDIPUS. A fine, bold speech, and you are right, perhaps,
except that my mother is still living, 990
so I must fear her, however well you argue.

JOCASTA. And yet your father's tomb is a great eye.

OEDIPUS. Illuminating, yes. But I still fear the living.

MESSENGER. Who is the woman who inspires this fear?

OEDIPUS. Meropē, Polybus' wife, old man.

MESSENGER. And what is there about her that alarms you?

OEDIPUS. An oracle, god-sent and fearful, stranger.

MESSENGER. Is it permitted that another know?

OEDIPUS. It is. Loxias once said to me
I must have intercourse with my own mother 1000
and take my father's blood with these my hands.
So I have long lived far away from Corinth.
This has indeed brought much good luck, and yet,
to see one's parents' eyes is happiest.

MESSENGER. Was it for this that you have lived in exile?

OEDIPUS. So I'd not be my father's killer, sir.

MESSENGER. Had I not better free you from this fear,
my Lord? That's why I came—to do you service.

OEDIPUS. Indeed, what a reward you'd get for that!

MESSENGER. Indeed, this is the main point of my trip, 1010
to be rewarded when you get back home.

OEDIPUS. I'll never rejoin the givers of my seed!°

MESSENGER. My son, clearly you don't know what you're doing.

OEDIPUS. But how is that, old man? For the gods' sake, tell me!

MESSENGER. If it's because of them you won't go home.

OEDIPUS. I fear that Phoebus will have told the truth.

MESSENGER. Pollution from the ones who gave you seed?

OEDIPUS. That is the thing, old man, I always fear.

MESSENGER. Your fear is groundless. Understand that.

OEDIPUS. Groundless? Not if I was born their son. 1020

MESSENGER. But Polybus is not related to you.

OEDIPUS. Do you mean Polybus was not my father?

MESSENGER. No more than I. We're both the same to you.

OEDIPUS. Same? One who begot me and one who didn't?

MESSENGER. He didn't beget you any more than I did.

OEDIPUS. But then, why did he say I was his son?

MESSENGER. He got you as a gift from my own hands.

OEDIPUS. He loved me so, though from another's hands?

MESSENGER. His former childlessness persuaded him.

OEDIPUS. But had you bought me, or begotten me? 1030

1012 *givers of my seed:* that is, my parents. Oedipus still thinks Merope and Polybus
are his parents.

MESSENGER.   Found you. In the forest hallows of Cithaeron.
OEDIPUS.   What were you doing traveling in that region?
MESSENGER.   I was in charge of flocks which grazed those mountains.
OEDIPUS.   A wanderer who worked the flocks for hire?
MESSENGER.   Ah, but that day I was your savior, son.
OEDIPUS.   From what? What was my trouble when you took me?
MESSENGER.   The ball-joints of your feet might testify.
OEDIPUS.   What's that? What makes you name that ancient trouble?
MESSENGER.   Your feet were pierced and I am your rescuer.
OEDIPUS.   A fearful rebuke those tokens left for me!   1040
MESSENGER.   That was the chance that names you who you are.
OEDIPUS.   By the gods, did my mother or my father do this?
MESSENGER.   That I don't know. He might who gave you to me.
OEDIPUS.   From someone else? You didn't chance on me?
MESSENGER.   Another shepherd handed you to me.
OEDIPUS.   Who was he? Do you know? Will you explain!
MESSENGER.   They called him one of the men of—was it Laius?
OEDIPUS.   The one who once was king here long ago?
MESSENGER.   That is the one! That man was shepherd to him.
OEDIPUS.   And is he still alive so I can see him?   1050
MESSENGER.   But you who live here ought to know that best.
OEDIPUS.   Does any one of you now present know
   about the shepherd whom this man has named?
   Have you seen him in town or in the fields? Speak out!
   The time has come for the discovery!
CHORAGOS.   The man he speaks of, I believe, is the same
   as the field hand you have already asked to see.
   But it's Jocasta who would know this best.
OEDIPUS.   Lady, do you remember the man we just
   now sent for—is that the man he speaks of?   1060
JOCASTA.   What? The man he spoke of? Pay no attention!
   His words are not worth thinking about. It's nothing.
OEDIPUS.   With clues like this within my grasp, give up?
   Fail to solve the mystery of my birth?
JOCASTA.   For the love of the gods, and if you love your life,
   give up this search! My sickness is enough.
OEDIPUS.   Come! Though my mothers for three generations
   were in slavery, you'd not be lowborn!
JOCASTA.   No, listen to me! Please! Don't do this thing!
OEDIPUS.   I will not listen; I will search out the truth.   1070
JOCASTA.   My thinking is for you—it would be best.
OEDIPUS.   This "best" of yours is starting to annoy me.
JOCASTA.   Doomed man! Never find out who you are!
OEDIPUS.   Will someone go and bring that shepherd here?
   Leave her to glory in her wealthy birth!
JOCASTA.   Man of misery! No other name
   shall I address you by, ever again.

[Exit Jocasta into the palace after a long pause.]

CHORAGOS.   Why has your lady left, Oedipus,
  hurled by a savage grief? I am afraid
  disaster will come bursting from this silence.   1080
OEDIPUS.   Let it burst forth! However low this seed
  of mine may be, yet I desire to see it.
  She, perhaps—she has a woman's pride—
  is mortified by my base origins.
  But I who count myself the child of Chance,
  the giver of good, shall never know dishonor.
  She is my mother,° and the months my brothers
  who first marked out my lowness, then my greatness.
  I shall not prove untrue to such a nature
  by giving up the search for my own birth.   1090

STASIMON 3

Strophe

CHORUS.   If I have mantic power
  and excellence in thought,
  by Olympus,
        you shall not, Cithaeron, at tomorrow's
  full moon,
  fail to hear us celebrate you as the countryman
  of Oedipus, his nurse and mother,
  or fail to be the subject of your dance,
        since you have given pleasure
  to our king.   1100
  Phoebus, whom we summon by "iē!,"
  may this be pleasing to you!

Antistrophe

Who was your mother, son?
which of the long-lived nymphs
after lying with Pan,°
        the mountain roaming . . . Or was it a bride
of Loxias?°
For dear to him are all the upland pastures.
Or was it Mount Cyllēnē's Lord,°
or the Bacchic god,°   1110
        dweller of the mountain peaks,
who received you as a joyous find

1087 *She . . . mother:* Chance is my mother.   1105 *Pan:* god of shepherds and wood-
lands, half man and half goat.   1107 *Loxias:* Apollo.   1109 *Mount Cyllēnē's lord:*
Hermes, messenger of the gods.   1110 *Bacchic god:* Dionysus.

from one of the nymphs of Helicon,
the favorite sharers of his sport?

EPISODE 4

OEDIPUS. If someone like myself, who never met him,
may calculate—elders, I think I see
the very herdsman we've been waiting for.
His many years would fit that man's age,
and those who bring him on, if I am right,
are my own men. And yet, in real knowledge,   1120
you can outstrip me, surely: you've seen him.

*[Enter the old Herdsman escorted by two of Oedipus's Attendants.
At first, the Herdsman will not look at Oedipus.]*

CHORAGOS. I know him, yes, a man of the house of Laius,
a trusty herdsman if he ever had one.
OEDIPUS. I ask you first, the stranger come from Corinth:
is this the man you spoke of?
MESSENGER.   That's he you see.
OEDIPUS. Then you, old man. First look at me! Now answer:
did you belong to Laius' household once?
HERDSMAN. I did. Not a purchased slave but raised in the palace.
OEDIPUS. How have you spent your life? What is your work?
HERDSMAN. Most of my life now I have tended sheep.   1130
OEDIPUS. Where is the usual place you stay with them?
HERDSMAN. On Mount Cithaeron. Or in that district.
OEDIPUS. Do you recall observing this man there?
HERDSMAN. Doing what? Which is the man you mean?
OEDIPUS. This man right here. Have you had dealings with him?
HERDSMAN. I can't say right away. I don't remember.
MESSENGER. No wonder, master. I'll bring clear memory
to his ignorance. I'm absolutely sure
he can recall it, the district was Cithaeron,
he with a double flock, and I, with one,   1140
lived close to him, for three entire seasons,
six months long, from spring right to Arcturus.°
Then for the winter I'd drive mine to my fold,
and he'd drive his to Laius' pen again.
Did any of the things I say take place?
HERDSMAN. You speak the truth, though it's from long ago.
MESSENGER. Do you remember giving me, back then,
a boy I was to care for as my own?
HERDSMAN. What are you saying? Why do you ask me that?
MESSENGER. There, sir, is the man who was that boy!   1150
HERDSMAN. Damn you! Shut your mouth! Keep your silence!

1142 *Arcturus:* a star that is first seen in September in the Grecian sky.

OEDIPUS.   Stop! Don't you rebuke his words.
  Your words ask for rebuke far more than his.
HERDSMAN.   But what have I done wrong, most royal master?
OEDIPUS.   Not telling of the boy of whom he asked.
HERDSMAN.   He's ignorant and blundering toward ruin.
OEDIPUS.   Tell it willingly—or under torture.
HERDSMAN.   Oh god! Don't—I am old—don't torture me!
OEDIPUS.   Here! Someone put his hands behind his back!
HERDSMAN.   But why? What else would you find out, poor man?   1160
OEDIPUS.   Did you give him the child he asks about?
HERDSMAN.   I did. I wish that I had died that day!
OEDIPUS.   You'll come to that if you don't speak the truth.
HERDSMAN.   It's if I speak that I shall be destroyed.
OEDIPUS.   I think this fellow struggles for delay.
HERDSMAN.   No, no! I said already that I gave him.
OEDIPUS.   From your own home, or got from someone else?
HERDSMAN.   Not from my own. I got him from another.
OEDIPUS.   Which of these citizens? What sort of house?
HERDSMAN.   Don't—by the gods!—don't, master, ask me more!   1170
OEDIPUS.   It means your death if I must ask again.
HERDSMAN.   One of the children of the house of Laius.
OEDIPUS.   A slave—or born into the family?
HERDSMAN.   I have come to the dreaded thing, and I shall say it.
OEDIPUS.   And I to hearing it, but hear I must.
HERDSMAN.   He was reported to have been—his son.
  Your lady in the house could tell you best.
OEDIPUS.   Because she gave him to you?
HERDSMAN.   Yes, my lord.
OEDIPUS.   What was her purpose?
HERDSMAN.   I was to kill the boy.
OEDIPUS.   The child she bore?
HERDSMAN.   She dreaded prophecies.   1180
HERDSMAN.   What were they?
HERDSMAN.   The word was that he'd kill his parents.
OEDIPUS.   Then why did you give him up to this old man?
HERDSMAN.   In pity, master—so he would take him home,
  to another land. But what he did was save him
  for this supreme disaster. If you are the one
  he speaks of—know your evil birth and fate!
OEDIPUS.   Ah! All of it was destined to be true!
  Oh light, now may I look my last upon you,
  shown monstrous in my birth, in marriage monstrous,
  a murderer monstrous in those I killed.   1190

  [Exit Oedipus, running into the palace.]

STASIMON 4

Strophe 1

CHORUS.   Oh generations of mortal men,
while you are living, I will
            appraise your lives at zero!
What man
comes closer to seizing lasting blessedness
than merely to seize its semblance,
and after living in this semblance, to plunge?
With your example before us,
with your destiny, yours,
            suffering Oedipus, no mortal   1200
can I judge fortunate.

Antistrophe 1

For he,° outranging everybody,
shot his arrow° and became the lord
            of wide prosperity and blessedness,
oh Zeus, after destroying
the virgin with the crooked talons,°
singer of oracles; and against death,
in my land, he arose a tower of defense.
From which time you were called my king
and granted privileges supreme—in mighty   1210
Thebes the ruling lord.

Strophe 2

But now—whose story is more sorrowful than yours?
Who is more intimate with fierce calamities,
with labors, now that your life is altered?
Alas, my Oedipus, whom all men know:
one great harbor°—
one alone sufficed for you,
as son and father,
when you tumbled,° plowman° of the woman's chamber.
How, how could your paternal   1220
            furrows, wretched man,
endure you silently so long.

1202 *he:* Oedipus.   **1203** *shot his arrow:* took his chances; made a guess at the
Sphinx's riddle.   **1206** *virgin . . . talons:* the Sphinx.   **1216** *one great harbor:* meta-
phorical allusion to Jocasta's body.   **1219** *tumbled:* were born and had sex. *plowman:*
Plowing is used here as a sexual metaphor.

Antistrophe 2

Time, all-seeing, surprised you living an unwilled life
and sits from of old in judgment on the marriage, not a marriage,
where the begetter is the begot as well.
Ah, son of Laius . . . ,
would that—oh, would that
I had never seen you!
I wail, my scream climbing beyond itself
from my whole power of voice. To say it straight: 1230
   from you I got new breath—
but I also lulled my eye to sleep.°

EXODOS

[Enter the Second Messenger from the palace.]

SECOND MESSENGER.   You who are first among the citizens,
  what deeds you are about to hear and see!
  What grief you'll carry, if, true to your birth,
  you still respect the house of Labdacus!
  Neither the Ister nor the Phasis river
  could purify this house, such suffering
  does it conceal, or soon must bring to light—
  willed this time, not unwilled. Griefs hurt worst   1240
  which we perceive to be self-chosen ones.
CHORAGOS.   They were sufficient, the things we knew before,
  to make us grieve. What can you add to those?
SECOND MESSENGER.   The thing that's quickest said and quickest
    heard:
  our own, our royal one, Jocasta's dead.
CHORAGOS.   Unhappy queen! What was responsible?
SECOND MESSENGER.   Herself. The bitterest of these events
  is not for you, you were not there to see,
  but yet, exactly as I can recall it,
  you'll hear what happened to that wretched lady.   1250
  She came in anger through the outer hall,
  and then she ran straight to her marriage bed,
  tearing her hair with the fingers of both hands.
  Then, slamming shut the doors when she was in,
  she called to Laius, dead so many years,
  remembering the ancient seed which caused
  his death, leaving the mother to the son
  to breed again an ill-born progeny.
  She mourned the bed where she, alas, bred double—
  husband by husband, children by her child.   1260

1232 *I . . . sleep:* I failed to see the corruption you brought.

From this point on I don't know how she died,
for Oedipus then burst in with a cry,
and did not let us watch her final evil.
Our eyes were fixed on him. Wildly he ran
to each of us, asking for his spear
and for his wife—no wife: where he might find
the double mother-field, his and his children's.
He raved, and some divinity then showed him—
for none of us did so who stood close by.
With a dreadful shout—as if some guide were leading—   1270
he lunged through the double doors; he bent the hollow
bolts from the sockets, burst into the room,
and there we saw her, hanging from above,
entangled in some twisted hanging strands.
He saw, was stricken, and with a wild roar
ripped down the dangling noose. When she, poor woman,
lay on the ground, there came a fearful sight:
he snatched the pins of worked gold from her dress,
with which her clothes were fastened: these he raised
and struck into the ball-joints of his eyes.°   1280
He shouted that they would no longer see
the evils he had suffered or had done,
see in the dark those he should not have seen,
and know no more those he once sought to know.
While chanting this, not once but many times
he raised his hand and struck into his eyes.
Blood from his wounded eyes poured down his chin,
not freed in moistening drops, but all at once
a stormy rain of black blood burst like hail.
These evils, coupling them, making them one,   1290
have broken loose upon both man and wife.
The old prosperity that they had once
was true prosperity, and yet today,
mourning, ruin, death, disgrace, and every
evil you could name—not one is absent.
CHORAGOS.   Has he allowed himself some peace from all this grief?
SECOND MESSENGER.   He shouts that someone slide the bolts and
      show
to all the Cadmeians the patricide,
his mother's—I can't say it, it's unholy—
so he can cast himself out of the land,   1300
not stay and curse his house by his own curse.
He lacks the strength, though, and he needs a guide,

1280 *ball-joints of his eyes:* his eyeballs. Oedipus blinds himself in both eyes at the same time.

for his is a sickness that's too great to bear.
Now you yourself will see: the bolts of the doors
are opening. You are about to see
a vision even one who hates must pity.

[Enter the blinded Oedipus from the palace, led in by a household Servant.]

CHORAGOS.   This suffering sends terror through men's eyes,
terrible beyond any suffering
my eyes have touched. Oh man of pain,
what madness reached you? Which god from far off,   1310
surpassing in range his longest spring,
    struck hard against your god-abandoned fate?
Oh man of pain,
I cannot look upon you—though there's so much
I would ask you, so much to hear,
so much that holds my eyes—
    so awesome the convulsions you send through me.
OEDIPUS.   Ah! Ah! I am a man of misery.
Where am I carried? Pity me! Where
is my voice scattered abroad on wings?   1320
    Divinity, where has your lunge transported me?
CHORAGOS.   To something horrible, not to be heard or seen.

KOMMOS

Strophe 1

OEDIPUS.   Oh, my cloud
of darkness, abominable, unspeakable as it attacks me,
not to be turned away, brought by an evil wind!
Alas!
Again alas! Both enter me at once:
the sting of the prongs,° the memory of evils!
CHORUS.   I do not marvel that in these afflictions
you carry double griefs and double evils.   1330

Antistrophe 1

OEDIPUS.   Ah, friend,
so you at least are there, resolute servant!
Still with a heart to care for me, the blind man.
Oh! Oh!
I know that you are there. I recognize
even inside my darkness, that voice of yours.
CHORUS.   Doer of horror, how did you bear to quench
your vision? What divinity raised your hand?

1328 *prongs:* refers to both the whip that Laius used and the two gold pins Oedipus used to blind himself.

Strophe 2

OEDIPUS. It was Apollo there, Apollo, friends,
   who brought my sorrows, vile sorrows to their perfection,   1340
       these evils that were done to me.
  But the one who struck them with his hand,
    that one was none but I, in wretchedness.
  For why was I to see
  when nothing I could see would bring me joy?
CHORUS. Yes, that is how it was.
OEDIPUS. What could I see, indeed,
  or what enjoy—what greeting
  is there I could hear with pleasure, friends?
  Conduct me out of the land   1350
      as quickly as you can!
  Conduct me out, my friends,
    the man utterly ruined,
  supremely cursed,
    the man who is by gods
  the most detested of all men!
CHORUS. Wretched in disaster and in knowledge:
  oh, I could wish you'd never come to know!

Antistrophe 2

OEDIPUS. May he be destroyed, whoever freed the savage
    shackles
  from my feet when I'd been sent to the wild pasture,   1360
      whoever rescued me from murder
  and became my savior—
    a bitter gift:
  if I had died then,
  I'd not have been such grief to self and kin.
CHORUS. I also would have had it so.
OEDIPUS. I'd not have returned to be my father's
  murderer; I'd not be called by men
  my mother's bridegroom.
  Now I'm without a god,   1370
      child of a polluted parent,
  fellow progenitor with him
    who gave me birth in misery.
  If there's an evil that
    surpasses evils, that
  has fallen to the lot of Oedipus.

CHORAGOS. How can I say that you have counseled well?
  Better not to be than live a blind man.
OEDIPUS. That this was not the best thing I could do—

don't tell me that, or advise me any more!   1380
Should I descend to Hades and endure
to see my father with these eyes? Or see
my poor unhappy mother? For I have done,
to both of these, things too great for hanging.
Or is the sight of children to be yearned for,
to see new shoots that sprouted as these did?
Never, never with these eyes of mine!
Nor city, nor tower, nor holy images
of the divinities! For I, all-wretched,
most nobly raised—as no one else in Thebes—   1390
deprived myself of these when I ordained
that all expel the impious one—god-shown
to be polluted, and the dead king's son!°
Once I exposed this great stain upon me,
could I have looked on these with steady eyes?
No! No! And if there were a way to block
the source of hearing in my ears, I'd gladly
have locked up my pitiable body,
so I'd be blind and deaf. Evils shut out—
that way my mind could live in sweetness.   1400
Alas, Cithaeron,° why did you receive me?
Or when you had me, not killed me instantly?
I'd not have had to show my birth to mankind.
Polybus, Corinth, halls—ancestral,
they told me—how beautiful was your ward,
a scar that held back festering disease!
Evil my nature, evil my origin.
You, three roads, and you, secret ravine,
you oak grove, narrow place of those three paths
that drank my blood° from these my hands, from him   1410
who fathered me, do you remember still
the things I did to you? When I'd come here,
what I then did once more? Oh marriages! Marriages!
You gave us life and when you'd planted us
you sent the same seed up, and then revealed
fathers, brothers, sons, and kinsman's blood,
and brides, and wives, and mothers, all the most
atrocious things that happen to mankind!
One should not name what never should have been.
Somewhere out there, then, quickly, by the gods,   1420

1391–1393 *I . . . son:* Oedipus refers to his own curse against the murderer as well as his sins of patricide and incest. **1401** *Cithaeron:* the mountain on which the infant Oedipus was supposed to be exposed. **1410** *my blood:* that is, the blood of my father, Laius.

cover me up, or murder me, or throw me
to the ocean where you will never see me more!

[Oedipus moves toward the Chorus and they back away from him.]

Come! Don't shrink to touch this wretched man!
Believe me, do not be frightened! I alone
of all mankind can carry these afflictions.

[Enter Creon from the palace with Attendants.]

CHORAGOS.   Tell Creon what you wish for. Just when we need him
he's here. He can act, he can advise you.
He's now the land's sole guardian in your place.

OEDIPUS.   Ah! Are there words that I can speak to him?
What ground for trust can I present? It's proved   1430
that I was false to him in everything.

CREON.   I have not come to mock you, Oedipus,
nor to reproach you for your former falseness.
You men, if you have no respect for sons
of mortals, let your awe for the all-feeding
flames of lordly Hēlius° prevent
your showing unconcealed so great a stain,
abhorred by earth and sacred rain and light.
Escort him quickly back into the house!
If blood kin only see and hear their own   1440
afflictions, we'll have no impious defilement.

OEDIPUS.   By the gods, you've freed me from one terrible fear,
so nobly meeting my unworthiness:
grant me something—not for me; for you!

CREON.   What do you want that you should beg me so?

OEDIPUS.   To drive me from the land at once, to a place
where there will be no man to speak to me!

CREON.   I would have done just that—had I not wished
to ask first of the god what I should do.

OEDIPUS.   His answer was revealed in full—that I,   1450
the patricide, unholy, be destroyed.

CREON.   He said that, but our need is so extreme,
it's best to have sure knowledge what must be done.

OEDIPUS.   You'll ask about a wretched man like me?

CREON.   Is it not time you put your trust in the god?

OEDIPUS.   But I bid you as well, and shall entreat you.
Give her who is within what burial
you will—you'll give your own her proper rites;
but me—do not condemn my fathers' land
to have me dwelling here while I'm alive,   1460
but let me live on mountains—on Cithaeron

1436 *Hēlius:* the sun.

famed as mine, for my mother and my father,
while they yet lived, made it my destined tomb,
and I'll be killed by those who wished my ruin!
And yet I know: no sickness will destroy me,
nothing will: I'd never have been saved
when left to die unless for some dread evil.
Then let my fate continue where it will!
As for my children, Creon, take no pains
for my sons—they're men and they will never lack   1470
the means to live, wherever they may be—
but my two wretched, pitiable girls,
who never ate but at my table, never
were without me—everything that I
would touch, they'd always have a share of it—
please care for them! Above all, let me touch
them with my hands and weep aloud my woes!
Please, my Lord!
Please, noble heart! Touching with my hands,
I'd think I held them as when I could see.   1480

[Enter Antigone and Ismene from the palace with Attendants.]

What's this?
Oh gods! Do I hear, somewhere, my two dear ones
sobbing? Has Creon really pitied me
and sent to me my dearest ones, my children?
Is that it?

CREON.   Yes, I prepared this for you, for I knew
you'd feel this joy, as you have always done.

OEDIPUS.   Good fortune, then, and, for your care, be guarded
far better by divinity than I was!
Where are you, children? Come to me! Come here   1490
to these my hands, hands of your brother, hands
of him who gave you seed, hands that made
these once bright eyes to see now in this fashion.

[Oedipus embraces his daughters.]

He, children, seeing nothing, knowing nothing,
he fathered you where his own seed was plowed.
I weep for you as well, though I can't see you,
imagining your bitter life to come,
the life you will be forced by men to live.
What gatherings of townsmen will you join,
what festivals, without returning home   1500
in tears instead of watching holy rites?
And when you've reached the time for marrying,
where, children, is the man who'll run the risk

of taking on himself the infamy
that will wound you as it did my parents?
What evil is not here? Your father killed
his father, plowed the one who gave him birth,
and from the place where he was sown, from there
he got you, from the place he too was born.
These are the wounds: then who will marry you? 1510
No man, my children. No, it's clear that you
must wither in dry barrenness, unmarried.

[Oedipus addresses Creon.]

Son of Menoeceus! You are the only father
left to them—we two who gave them seed
are both destroyed: watch that they don't become
poor, wanderers, unmarried—they are your kin.
Let not my ruin be their ruin, too!
No, pity them! You see how young they are,
bereft of everyone, except for you.
Consent, kind heart, and touch me with your hand! 1520

[Creon grasps Oedipus's right hand.]

You, children, if you had reached an age of sense,
I would have counseled much. Now, pray you may live
always where it's allowed, finding a life
better than his was, who gave you seed.

CREON. Stop this now. Quiet your weeping. Move away, into
the house.
OEDIPUS. Bitter words, but I obey them.
CREON.   There's an end to all things.
OEDIPUS. I have first this request.
CREON.   I will hear it.
OEDIPUS. Banish me from my homeland.
CREON.   You must ask that of the god.
OEDIPUS. But I am the gods' most hated man!
CREON.   Then you will soon get what you want.
OEDIPUS. Do you consent?
CREON.   I never promise when, as now, I'm ignorant. 1530
OEDIPUS. Then lead me in.
CREON.   Come. But let your hold fall from your children.
OEDIPUS. Do not take them from me, ever!
CREON.   Do not wish to keep all of the power.
You had power, but that power did not follow you through
life.

*[Oedipus's daughters are taken from him and led into the palace by
Attendants. Oedipus is led into the palace by a Servant. Creon and
the other Attendants follow. Only the Chorus remains.]*

CHORUS. People of Thebes, my country, see: here is that
          Oedipus—
    he who "knew" the famous riddle, and attained the highest
          power,
    whom all citizens admired, even envying his luck!
    See the billows of wild troubles which he has entered now!
    Here is the truth of each man's life: we must wait, and see
          his end,
    scrutinize his dying day, and refuse to call him happy
    till he has crossed the border of his life without pain.   1540

          [Exit the Chorus along each of the Parados.]

❏ Questions for Discussion

1. How would you describe the relationship between Oedipus
   and the people of Thebes as the play begins? What kind of
   ruler does Oedipus appear to be?

2. What does Oedipus think of himself? What qualities dominate
   his character? Does he have a tragic flaw? If so, what is it?

3. What is the condition of Thebes as the play begins? Look up
   the myth of the fisher king and explain how it applies to this
   condition.

4. What role does the chorus play? How does its attitude change?

5. Why does Oedipus act so unreasonably toward Tiresias and
   Creon?

6. Why does Oedipus insist on hearing what he must know will
   be horrifying news?

7. At the end, how does Oedipus maintain his position as savior
   and father to his people? What kind of father does he appear
   to be to his daughters? Does he retain nobility and dignity in
   his fall? Explain.

❏ Suggestions for Exploration and Writing

1. Discuss in detail the changing attitudes of the chorus in *Oedipus the King*. Why is the accusation against Oedipus so terrifying to them? What dilemma does it pose for them?

2. Contrast Jocasta's skepticism with Oedipus' insistence on
   knowing the truth. Is he persuaded by her skepticism?

3. Discuss the degree to which Oedipus is triumphant at the end
   of the play. Has his fall ennobled him?

4. Analyze Sophocles' use of image clusters of light and dark and / or of sight and blindness.

5. Discuss in detail the complex familial and communal relationships in Sophocles' play. What light do they shed on the changing nature of American families?

6. Quoting lines from the play to illustrate your points, write an essay discussing the use of **dramatic irony** in *Oedipus the King*.

7. Both Creon and Tiresias act as **dramatic foils** to Oedipus: they emphasize characteristics of Oedipus through marked contrast. In an essay, show how one of these characters is an effective dramatic foil.

MARSHA NORMAN (1947–)

Marsha Norman, born in Louisville, Kentucky, and living now in New York City, won the Pulitzer Prize for 'night, Mother (1983), a play which also won four Tony nominations. Writing about the problems of ordinary people striving to overcome the insignificance of their lives or to break from overbearing parents, Norman also focuses on basic American values and the various dilemmas that cause her characters to search for the meaning of life.

Traveler in the Dark

Characters

STEPHEN, a pale twelve-year-old boy, the son of Glory and Sam. He is a smart boy who speaks quietly and hasn't watched much television or played with many other children. He has an alert, questioning manner, a fierce respect for his father, and a more childlike love for his mother.

SAM, a world-famous surgeon. He is a brilliant loner, a man who has found his problems not quite worthy of his skills in solving them. He can seem preoccupied, impatient and condescending. But he can also be counted on to handle any situation. His sense of humor is what makes you put up with his infuriating personal security.

GLORY, a lovely woman, who takes her responsibilities as a wife and mother quite seriously. She speaks quickly and laughs easily. She is blessed with a rare grace, an elegance of spirit, and nobody understands how on earth she has stayed married to Sam for all these years.

EVERETT, a country preacher, Sam's father. He is a one-time fire-breathing evangelist who now spends his time burying the same people he worked so hard to save. Everett has gotten old, but Sam, in particular, has not noticed this. He is a great favorite with the ladies, has a wizard's command of the language, and a direct, personal relationship to God and the heavenly hosts.

ACT ONE

The play takes place in the overgrown garden of a country preacher's house. There are stone animals, including one large goose, stone benches, a crumbling stone wall and a small pond. Various objects are imbedded in the wall—toys, mainly, but also such household objects as cups and saucers. It is not important that these objects be seen by the audience. In fact, the less impressive this garden appears, the better. It is Sam's connection to the garden that is important, not ours.

Sam comes out the back door onto the porch, then walks down the steps and into the garden. He smiles and nods, happy to see it again. As he walks through the leaves, he kicks a hidden toy, bends over, picks it up and recognizes it as an old toy car of his. He brushes the leaves out of it, then races it up his arm. Then he puts the car back in the wall and walks to the other side of the garden, where he discovers a geode. He picks it up, looks at the upstairs window of the house, then puts the geode back where it was. Now, Sam sees that a section of the wall is completely gone, and with it, apparently, the stone goose. He begins to lift the rocks back into place. Glory opens the back door and calls out.

GLORY: Sam?

SAM: I'm out here. Come. Look.

GLORY: Don't tell me now. Let me guess. *(she looks around)* It's the backyard.

SAM: It's Mother's garden.

GLORY: I'm sorry. *(She walks into the garden)*

SAM: There are all kinds of stone animals, rabbits and things down there, somewhere, and watch where you step. One of those piles of leaves is a pond. *(Now he sees the stone goose buried under a pile of rocks)* Wait a minute. *(He lifts the goose up and puts her in her rightful place on the wall)* There she is. Mother.

GLORY: *(Shakes her head):* Sam . . .

SAM: This place is a mess. Dad never did like this garden. He said Mother should save her knees for church.

GLORY: Sam, I'm worried about Stephen. He doesn't understand.

SAM *(Going to the old tool chest near the porch):* What's there to understand? Mavis is dead.

GLORY: Sam, she was more than your head nurse. Mavis carried a puzzle for Stephen in every purse she owned. She was his friend. He doesn't believe it.

SAM *(As he sweeps the top of the wall with a whisk broom):* He will. He'll be fine. Nobody ever died on him before, that's all. He'll get the hang of it, you'll see.

GLORY: He's upstairs right now going through all your old books.

SAM: That's all right, too. They can't hurt him now. Here, hold this a minute. *(He hands her a stone rabbit, while he cleans out the space in the wall where it belongs)*

GLORY: Stephen needs you to explain this to him, Sam. I try to get him to talk about it, but he won't. You've got to tell him something that will make him feel better.

SAM: Like what? 30

GLORY: If I knew like what, I'd tell him myself.

SAM: What did you say to make *you* feel better?

GLORY: I don't feel better.

SAM: See what I mean?

GLORY *(irritated with him):* But I want to feel better, and so does Stephen.

SAM: There isn't anything to say. Mavis waited too long to have herself checked. I did the operation. She died. Stephen knows all of that already.

GLORY: But he doesn't know what it means. 40

SAM: It doesn't mean anything. It's just . . . bad luck. *(He takes the stone rabbit from her and replaces it in the wall)*

SAM: There. Doesn't that look better?

GLORY *(Giving up for now):* I called your dad. He had another funeral to preach this morning. He'll be here as soon as he can.

SAM: There's no reason for him to come home. We can just meet him at the church.

GLORY: He wants to see you, Sam, and the funeral's not till two o'clock.

Sam resumes his work on the wall.

SAM: Is everybody coming back here or what after the funeral? I know Mavis didn't have any family left here. 50

GLORY: We're all going to Josie Barnett's.

SAM: Josie Barnett is a joke.

GLORY: Mavis loved her.

SAM: Mavis loved Dad.

GLORY: You don't want them all coming here, do you?

SAM: God, no.

GLORY: Well, then . . .

SAM: Is Josie Barnett . . . going to . . . try to . . . sing . . . at the funeral? *(She doesn't answer, so he knows the answer must be yes)* Christ. 60

GLORY: Sam.

SAM: It's just an awful lot to pay for a free meal. *(Still she doesn't answer)* Couldn't we just go to a restaurant?

GLORY: I don't believe you. Can't you let up on these people for one day? One day? Mavis was one of these people, you know, and your dad is one of these people, and I am one of these people. *(She pauses)* And so are you.

SAM: Okay, okay.

STEPHEN *(Calling from inside the house):* Dad?

70 SAM: Out here, Stephen.
GLORY *(To Sam):* Will you try? Will you try to get him to talk about it?
SAM: If he wants to talk, I'll listen. *(Pause)* If that's what you mean.
GLORY: You know what I mean.

> *By now, Stephen is walking up to them, carrying a stack of old nursery rhymes and fairy tales.*

STEPHEN: What a great house! Why didn't we ever come here before?
SAM: It's just easier for Grandpa to visit us, Stephen.
STEPHEN: This garden is terrific! Did you put all these things in the wall?
SAM: No, Stephen, Mother did. *(Smiling at Glory)* It was her way of teaching me not to leave my toys outside.
80 STEPHEN: I found a whole room of books, Dad, way at the top of the house. Like a forest of books growing up out of the floor. Just books and a rocking chair. I've never seen a room like that.
SAM: Those were Mother's books, Stephen.
STEPHEN: The ones I saw were all kids' books. *(Pause)* But where did you sit? Is it your rocking chair or hers?
SAM: Hers.
STEPHEN: They're strange books, Dad. I didn't see a single one I'd ever seen before.
SAM: I know. Your books . . . make sense.
GLORY: I'm sure Grandpa would let you take some of them home if
90 you wanted to.
SAM: Stephen's way too old for those books, aren't you?
GLORY: This a beautiful *Mother Goose.* I can just see her holding you on her lap and reading this to you. *(And she reads)*
Humpty Dumpty sat on a wall.
Humpty Dumpty had a great fall.
All the King's horses and all the King's men,
Couldn't put Humpty together again.
STEPHEN: I don't get it.
SAM *(Laughs):* Good boy.
100 GLORY *(Carefully):* Stephen, it just means, there are some things that once they happen they can't be fixed.
STEPHEN: But how did he get on the wall in the first place? Eggs can't climb.
SAM *(Breaking the bad news):* His . . . mother . . . laid him there.
GLORY: Sam.
STEPHEN: Then how did he fall? Eggs can't walk either.
SAM: She told him he was a man. See? She dressed him up in a little man's suit. He didn't know he could fall. He didn't know he could break. He didn't know he was an egg.
110 STEPHEN: So what happened to him? Did he run all over the sidewalk and people slipped on him or did he dry up in the sun or what?

> *Sam tests a big stone and finds it loose.*

SAM: Something like that.

GLORY *(Not pleased with Sam's answer)*: I'm sure somebody cleaned it up, Stephen.

STEPHEN: But who?

GLORY: Who do you think? *(Pause)* Mom.

SAM: No. I think Mom fell off the wall the day before.

Glory is irritated with Sam, but she does her best not to show it. Sam puts the big stone where it belongs, as Glory turns her attention to Stephen.

GLORY: Now Stephen, the funeral is at two o'clock. But Grandpa's coming home first, and then we'll all go to the church together. He was sorry he couldn't be here to meet us when we got here, but he had another funeral to preach this morning.

STEPHEN: Okay.

GLORY: We'll have to be very careful what we say to Grandpa. Mavis called him every Friday night, you know, told him everything that had gone on at the hospital all week. He loved Mavis more than any of us did, I think. *(Pause)* I know . . . he was disappointed when your dad fell in love with me instead of Mavis. There's nothing he likes better in this world than Mavis and your dad.

STEPHEN: Liked.

GLORY: What?

STEPHEN: Liked better. Nothing he liked better than Mavis and Dad.

GLORY: You don't stop liking people just because they die, Stephen.

SAM: Sometimes you like them better. Harry Truman, for example.

Glory picks up another book and starts to look through it.

STEPHEN: Can we go fishing while we're here? Mavis told me that's what you do in the country. You fish till you're hungry, eat till you're sleepy, then sleep till it's time to wake up and go fishing.

GLORY: I don't know why not.

SAM: We're not going to be here that long, Stephen.

GLORY: Do you want us to tell you what's going to happen at the funeral?

STEPHEN: Am I going to sit by myself?

GLORY: No, you'll sit with us.

STEPHEN: Then no. If I need to stand up or anything, you can just grab me.

Sam gives Glory a "let-him-alone" look, and Glory returns his look, as if to say "this is what I was talking about."

SAM: Stephen, is there anything you want to ask me about any of this?

STEPHEN: Do I have to say anything at the funeral?

SAM: No. And you don't have to listen, either.

Glory doesn't think this is helping Stephen a bit. She tries to interest him in the book she has.

GLORY: Now here's one I like, "The Princess and The Frog." See, Stephen? The princess kisses the frog and he turns into a prince.

Sam makes some move that indicates he has understood her irritation.

150 STEPHEN: You've got the frog colored in, Dad, but you made him all brown.

SAM: That's what color frogs are, Stephen.

STEPHEN: Now how could a frog turn into a prince?

GLORY: It was magic, Stephen. Magic always works.

SAM (*A direct communication to Glory*): Magic had nothing to do with it. The frog *believed* that the beauty could turn him into a prince. One kiss from her and he would be handsome, and play tennis, and mix martinis, and tell jokes at parties, just like all her other boyfriends. (*Pause*) But years later, the prince started to turn, slowly

160 at first, but finally and irreversibly, back into the frog he always was.

STEPHEN: It doesn't say that in this book.

SAM (*Scraping the dirt off some of the toys that have fallen out of the wall*): It doesn't have to. You are born a frog and that is it. It's not so bad, but it is *it*. Frogs should know better, but they don't.

STEPHEN: Then they're not as smart as they think they are.

SAM: Smart isn't magic, Stephen. It's just smart.

GLORY: That is not how the story ends.

SAM (*Quite intense*): It is how the story ends. The princess got old and the frog croaked. (*As Glory stares at him*) Get another book, Stephen.

170 STEPHEN (*Getting what he thinks Sam means*): Go away, Stephen.

SAM: No. Come back. But no more fairy tales. There *are* some good books up there. *Call of the Wild. Lord of the Flies.* Read about Donner Pass.

Stephen jumps down off the wall and goes into the house. There is a moment of silence.

GLORY (*After Stephen has gone*): Is that your idea of help?

SAM: What?

GLORY: You, the frog, married me, the princess, and Humpty Dumpty was a hit-and-run.

SAM: He's old enough to know what happens.

GLORY: Nobody's old enough to know what you think happens.

180 SAM: I refuse to lie to him. He could live a long time *hoping* it will all work out.

GLORY: He could live a long time *having* it all work out, unless you convince him it's impossible and he doesn't even try.

SAM: What do you want me to say?

GLORY: Life is good.

SAM: When?

GLORY: All the time!

SAM: Like today, for example.

GLORY: No, not like today. People don't die every day.

SAM: Oh Glory, I'm afraid they do.

GLORY: Not people you know.

SAM: Oh, I see. It doesn't count if we don't know them.

GLORY: It doesn't hurt if we don't know them.

SAM: It doesn't matter, you mean.

GLORY: No, I don't mean that.

SAM: What *do* you mean?

GLORY: You tell him the wrong things.

SAM: I tell him the truth.

GLORY: And he believes you!

SAM: Well, I can't help that.

GLORY: He's a child!

SAM: I want a divorce.

GLORY: I want this day to be over.

SAM *(After a moment):* I do want a divorce. I want to leave here in the morning and take Stephen with me.

GLORY: You can go for the weekend, Sam, but Stephen has school on Monday.

SAM: Since we're having one funeral anyway, we might as well have the other one and be done with it. When we all wake up, this will *all* be over.

GLORY: What is the matter with you?

Stephen opens the porch door, but they don't hear him. He starts to come down the steps, but then realizes what this conversation is about. He goes back up the steps, climbs quietly over the railing and sits, out of sight, behind a tree.

SAM: I just never stopped to think about it, I guess. It doesn't make sense, this marriage. It never has. Ask your mother.

GLORY: It works well enough, Sam. It calms you down, and it keeps me from getting too comfortable. And no, we don't always agree on things . . .

SAM: We don't ever agree on things.

GLORY: But it's good for Stephen to hear both sides.

SAM: No. It confuses him. I'll tell Dad tonight, and in the morning I'll go over and tell your mother and then I'll get Stephen and go. I'll send you as much money as you need and you can have everything we own. All the houses, all the cars, everything.

GLORY: That's ridiculous.

SAM: Okay, I'll keep the cars.

There is a long silence.

GLORY *(Finally):* You're serious!

SAM: Always have been. *(Then oddly cheerful)* I thought you knew that.

GLORY: You're upset.

SAM: True.

230 GLORY: I mean you're upset about Mavis. You don't think you can work without Mavis. Well, leaving me isn't going to bring Mavis back to you.

SAM: Mavis has nothing to do with this.

GLORY: Nice work, doctor. Quick and clean. You find the tumor and you cut it out. You don't even need your fancy table or your hot-shot team for this surgery, do you? You're so good, you can do it in the backyard.

SAM: Wherever.

GLORY: Look. Let's just get through the funeral, okay? And then if
240 you still feel this way we'll talk about it when we get home.

SAM: I don't want to talk about it. I want to quit. I want to go some-where else. I want to start over.

GLORY: Life doesn't start over. It starts, it goes on for a while, then it stops.

SAM: God that's gloomy.

GLORY: I sound like you!

SAM: No you don't. I would never say *that*. Mavis didn't have to die. There *was* a time she could have done something about it. This is that time for Stephen and me.

250 GLORY: You can't leave me.

SAM: You'll be okay. Move back here if you want. I know your mother has room out there.

glory: Of course I'll be okay. I'm talking about you. Do you have any idea what it takes to live your life?

SAM: I can probably figure it out.

GLORY: I know you can't take care of Stephen.

SAM: Stephen is old enough to take care of himself.

GLORY: Stephen would end up taking care of you. And you're impor-tant, so somebody should do all the things that allow you to work,
260 but it shouldn't be Stephen.

SAM: We'll share it. I'll help him. He'll help me.

GLORY: I think we better wait till we get home to talk about this.

SAM: I think we're talking about it already.

GLORY: The answer is no.

SAM: Yes, well, it wasn't really a question, Glory.

GLORY: I'm going inside.

SAM: I'm not.

GLORY: Fine.

SAM (*Staring at the goose*):

There once was a woman called Nothing-At-All
270 Who rejoiced in a dwelling exceedingly small.
A man stretched his mouth to its utmost extent
And down in a gulp both the house and woman went.

Stephen appears from behind the tree. He is holding a framed photo and another fairy-tale book.

STEPHEN *(Pointing to the photo):* Is this you, Dad?

SAM *(Startled by his presence):* Stephen!

STEPHEN: Is this you in this picture?

SAM *(Staring at the photo):* Yes.

STEPHEN: Who is this with you?

SAM: That's Mother . . . and that's . . . Mavis.

STEPHEN: And it's Halloween I hope.

SAM: Yes.   280

STEPHEN: What were you? I can't tell.

SAM: Elves.

STEPHEN: Did Mavis tell you I lost her cat?

SAM: I gave her that cat.

STEPHEN: I know. I'm sorry, Dad.

SAM: When was this?

STEPHEN: Last Saturday. After the movies we went back to her apartment, and I asked Mavis if I could let Peaches out, only Mavis
   didn't hear me because she went in the bedroom to rest a little bit.
   But Peaches kept crying and scratching at the back door. So I   290
   opened it and she got away. When Mavis woke up, we looked and
   looked, but we couldn't find her anywhere. *(Pause)* I guess Mavis
   didn't tell you because she didn't want you to be mad at me.

SAM: It's all right, Stephen. Cats just . . . go like that.

STEPHEN: Maybe Peaches knew something was wrong.

SAM: Maybe she did. *(Pause)* Stephen, your mother and I were just
   talking—

STEPHEN *(Quickly):* I guess your birthday's going to be pretty lonely
   this year.

SAM *(Pause):* Yes. I guess it will be.   300

STEPHEN: I wouldn't like it if I had the same birthday as somebody. I
   mean, I know there are plenty of people born on the same day as
   me, but—

SAM: People used to ask Mavis where she met me, you know, and
   she'd say, "Oh, at the hospital. In the nursery." And then she'd say,
   "I hadn't been alive two hours when in came Sam Carter screaming
   at me already." *(Pause)* That's a picture I'd like to see, all right.
   Dad and Mavis's dad staring through the glass window looking at
   the two of us side by side in our little beds. One howling boy for
   the preacher, and one rosy-faced dumpling for the custodian at the   310
   church.

STEPHEN: Mavis wasn't fat, Dad.

SAM: No. But I did have the idea that she put on her uniform in the
   morning, and then stepped on an air pump to puff herself up for
   the day.

STEPHEN: I'm not going to like Saturday much either.

SAM: She loved you so much, Stephen. You were the only little boy she had. You were so good to her, you gave her so much.

STEPHEN: All we ever talked about was you, Dad.

320 SAM: Yeah, well, she just loved to talk, Stephen. And I didn't leave her time to learn anything else. *(Pause)* It never occurred to me that she would die, Stephen. It just didn't seem like something she'd do. I'm sorry I didn't warn you, I should have known it, my mother died, didn't she? I guess I just forgot.

STEPHEN: Yeah.

SAM: Well . . .

STEPHEN: Why do people read these books?

SAM: What?

STEPHEN: I know you told me not to read any more, but I was taking
330 it back upstairs and I didn't get this one either.

SAM: Which one?

STEPHEN: I think Sleeping Beauty's father was a fool.

SAM: All right. But don't just say he was a fool. Prove it to me. Build your case.

STEPHEN: He gives a party for his daughter and he invites twelve of the thirteen fairies in the land. Twelve good fairies he invites. He does not invite the thirteenth fairy.

SAM: Because she's a bad fairy, that's right.

STEPHEN: But the bad fairy comes anyway, and now she acts even
340 worse because she wasn't invited. "I have a gift for the little princess," she says. "When she is eighteen, she will prick her finger on a spinning wheel and die."

SAM: That's how it goes, all right.

STEPHEN: It's ridiculous. If you know you have a thirteenth fairy living in your country, and you know what she can do, then how, exactly, can you forget to invite her to a party?

SAM: Well . . .

STEPHEN: How did anybody that dumb get to be king?

SAM: He wasn't dumb. He just forgot.

350 STEPHEN: He forgets there's a bad fairy living there and look what happens. Everybody sleeps for a hundred years, till he wakes up with his kingdom turned into a jungle and some prince upstairs kissing his daughter.

SAM *(Strangely affected by this story)*: He forgot because he didn't want to remember! He didn't want her to come to the party! The *last* person you want at that party is that thirteenth fairy. So you just hope she doesn't show up because you know if she does show up, there isn't a damn thing you can do about it.

STEPHEN *(Reacting to his father's anger)*: It's just a story, Dad.

360 SAM: Yeah, I know. That's why I never let you read them.

STEPHEN: But you read them.

SAM *(Disclaiming all responsibility):* Mother read them to me. *(Almost a confession)* And then, when I learned how, yes, I would read them to her. *(Pause)* Every day when I came home from school, here she'd be, with a glass of milk for me and a pile of things she'd found in the ground that day, like dragons' teeth, witches' fingers and fallen stars. *(Then remembering so clearly)* I would sit, there, where you are, and she would work. And we would sing. Her favorite Mother Goose was page twenty. *(He sings as Stephen is looking for it)*

> We're all in the dumps 370
> For diamonds are trumps
> The kittens have gone to St. Paul's.
> The babies are bit,
> The moon's in a fit
> And the houses are built without walls.

STEPHEN: The houses are built without walls?

SAM: Yes.

STEPHEN: How could they stand up?

SAM *(Suddenly very distant):* She died before I could ask her that, Stephen. 380

STEPHEN: What was she like?

SAM: She was the gingerbread lady. Curly red hair and shiny round eyes and a big checked apron. Fat, pink fingers, a sweet vanilla smell, and all the time in the world. Sing to you, dance with you, write your name on the top of a cake.

STEPHEN: Did she die all of a sudden like Mavis?

SAM: Mother was sick for a long time, Stephen, but sick or not, everybody dies all of a sudden.

STEPHEN: I guess that was pretty hard, too, huh?

SAM: I was awful. I took it, well, like it happened to me instead of to 390 her. I wouldn't eat. I broke things. But now, well, if she hadn't died, I'd be the biggest momma's boy you ever saw.

Everett enters from the side of the house. He walks with some difficulty, but he's keeping his spirits up with an extraordinary act of will.

EVERETT: Samuel!

SAM: Hello, Dad.

They embrace, but it is difficult for them.

SAM *(A bit awkward):* I'm sorry I couldn't save her.

EVERETT *(Pulling away):* You did your best, didn't you?

SAM: Yes.

EVERETT: Well, that's all anybody expects, Sam. *(Shifting his attention to Stephen)* Hello, Stephen. Remember me?

STEPHEN: It's only been a year, Grandpa. 400

Stephen gives him a small hug.

EVERETT: Where's your mother?

STEPHEN: Inside. Want me to go get her?

EVERETT: I'm glad she's here.

SAM: You knew she would come, Dad. *(He helps Everett)* Here. Sit down.

EVERETT: I'm fine. I'm fine. Are you all right?

SAM: I'm fine.

EVERETT: You look tired, Sam.

SAM: I'm not tired, Dad. I'm just grown up.

EVERETT: I miss seeing you, son.

410   SAM: I'm sorry, Dad. They keep me pretty busy these days.

EVERETT: Oh I know. Mavis told me. *(His fatherly pride showing)* She said you could do things nobody else even thought of. She said there were dead people standing in line at the water fountain because of you. She sent me all the clippings. I liked that one about the governor. That was a good picture of you. *(No response from Sam)* Oh how she loved you, son. "Well," she'd say, "we had another miracle today."

Another long silence.

SAM: How was your other funeral? Who was it?

EVERETT *(Glad to have something else to talk about)*: Connie Rich-
420   ards. I told her to come see you when she first got sick, but she wouldn't hear of it. She said you were too famous. You were too far away. *(Sam does not answer)* She felt the same way about God. But I guess she figured she didn't have to get on the bus to go see Him.

Everett reaches down to pat Sam, but he moves away, and Everett goes over to pat Stephen. He just needs to pat somebody, and Stephen is too polite to resist.

STEPHEN: Where did you tell them she went, at the funeral?

SAM: Stephen, Grandpa's sermons are his business. He says what he has to say.

EVERETT: I told them she went to heaven.

STEPHEN: Why did you have to say that?

430   EVERETT *(Ignoring Sam's silencing look)*: Because that's where she went.

STEPHEN *(Doesn't believe this for a minute)*: And that's where she is right now, singing and flying around? It sounds like fairy tales to me.

EVERETT: Oh no, God's heard enough of her singing already. He'll have her light the candles or something.

STEPHEN *(A conspiratorial look at Sam)*: They have candles in heaven? Isn't it too windy for candles?

EVERETT: If God wants a candle to stay lit, it stays lit. What they don't have in heaven is matches. But then, angels don't need matches.

440   They just put their pointer finger up to it, like so, and poof, it's lit.

STEPHEN *(Much simpler, actually childlike)*: How do they do that?

EVERETT *(Sounding more like the wizard he is):* It's because they're
pure spirit now, Stephen. The life in them is like sparks, like fireworks. Oh, they could really light up the sky if they felt like it, but
they don't want to show off, you know. They don't want people
dying down here just to get in on the fun. But now, shooting stars . . .

STEPHEN: Meteors, you mean.

EVERETT: Right. That's somebody new up there. Somebody hasn't
quite figured out how to control themselves. *(Suddenly flinging his
arms out wide)* Pow!   450

STEPHEN: Great!

SAM *(Quietly, but firmly):* Stephen, go find your mother. Tell her
Grandpa's here.

Stephen leaves.

SAM *(After a moment):* That's enough, Dad.

EVERETT: Don't be mad at me, boy. I can't help talking about angels. I
just know so *many* of them, now.

SAM *(Being careful not to get angry):* I don't want you telling Stephen
there's a heaven and a hell, because if you do, I'll have to tell him
who it is who assigns the rooms.

EVERETT: You do want him on the right waiting list, don't you?   460

SAM: I don't want him thinking about it at all. *(Then more calm)* Let's
just say, if there is a hell, if Stephen does go to hell, I'd like for it to
be a surprise.

EVERETT: No grandson of mine is going to hell.

SAM: No grandson of anybody's is going to hell. There is no hell.
There is no heaven. Life is summer camp and death is lights out. It's
all just over, Dad. Time's up. The end. You lose.

EVERETT: Is that what you tell their families at the hospital?

SAM: What is there to say?

EVERETT: There's comfort.   470

SAM: There's all your friends waiting for you? There's your Heavenly
Father with His arms open wide? No, no. I've been straight with
them all along, so I'm not about to get to the end and lie. I do what
I can and then we both just quit.

EVERETT: Mavis would never quit.

SAM: Mavis quit before I did. I briefed the team, I opened her up, but
what did I find? Her bags were packed. She was checking out. She
was going, as you say, home. No, I keep them out of God's hands
as long as possible, so you just keep your sermons to yourself.

EVERETT *(Carefully):* Was Mavis in any pain?   480

SAM: No.

EVERETT: Did she . . . know it was happening?

SAM: No.

EVERETT: So she couldn't give you any . . . message for me.

SAM: No. *(Then trying to concentrate on something else)* But she just bought a new car. I know she'd want you to have it. It has power steering and everything. We drove it down here for you. That's it . . . *(Motioning in that direction)* out in the driveway.

EVERETT: I appreciate the thought, son, but I don't think I could . . . *(Pause)* No. You were right to bring it.

SAM: Glory packed up all her clothes and put them in the trunk. We thought there might be people around here who could use them. Everything else, furniture and everything, was rented. Except her TV, and I took that in for the nurses' lounge. So, it's all done, I think.

EVERETT: That part's done, anyway. *(He notices the picture Stephen brought out before)* Anything I have—of hers, you know—you can have it if you want it. I'd like to keep her letters, but after I die, they'll be yours too, of course, like everything else I have. Do you want this picture?

SAM: Stephen found it.

EVERETT: I always liked this one. *(Hoping Sam will say no)* You don't want it, do you?

SAM: No.

EVERETT: Yes, I guess you have plenty of pictures of the two of you. They're probably all up and down the halls at the hospital.

SAM: Can we talk about something else?

EVERETT: I'm sorry, son. Just all those years of her hanging around you, I think of her as part of the family. Probably thought she'd *be* part of family someday.

SAM: She loved you, Dad, not me.

EVERETT: Oh, she loved you, all right. If it hadn't been for you, she'd be right here, working at County General.

SAM: She was too good for your little hospital.

EVERETT: But not good enough for you.

SAM: We don't have to have this argument anymore, Dad. Mavis is not yours and she's not mine. She's dead.

Stephen enters with a book of illustrated Bible stories.

STEPHEN: Hey, I like this one about the whale. What does it mean? This guy, Jonah, gets swallowed by a whale and then the whale throws him up.

EVERETT: It means you can't run away from God, Stephen.

SAM *(Annoyed that Everett is talking religion again)*: No, Stephen, it means you shouldn't go to sea in too small a boat.

Glory comes out, wearing an apron and drying her hands on a dish towel.

GLORY: Hello, Everett.

They embrace.

EVERETT: Glory Butler, you are still the prettiest girl in ten counties.

GLORY: Are you doing all right, Everett?

EVERETT: Yes I am, thank you.

GLORY *(Remembering how distant this man can be):* I hope you don't have this too often, two funerals in one day.

EVERETT *(Making an effort to talk to her):* Your mother was at the one this morning.

GLORY: How'd she look?

EVERETT: Rich.

GLORY: She does like to show it off, doesn't she?

EVERETT: All she could talk about were her two new fillies—both jumpers, she said. And she's got a new exercise boy. He was . . . there with her today.

GLORY *(A knowing smile):* Was he all dressed up, or was he just driving the car?

EVERETT *(Confirming her worst fears):* All dressed up.

GLORY: She's so funny. When Daddy died, she walked me up to the casket, held my hand and said, "Glory, I'm never going to be lonely again."

Glory laughs and Everett smiles.

EVERETT: I told her you were coming down for Mavis's funeral, but she said she wouldn't bother you here. *(A pause)* Our house always was a little plain for her.

GLORY: I made us some sandwiches. They're on the counter if you want one.

EVERETT: I should eat something I guess. Don't you want one, Sam?

No response from Sam.

GLORY: We'll be there in a minute. *(Pause)* I straightened up your kitchen a little. I hope you don't mind.

EVERETT: No. Just so you put it back the way it was before you leave.

GLORY: Everett, I was just trying to help. I'm sorry.

EVERETT *(Walking toward Stephen):* I know Stephen's hungry, aren't you?

STEPHEN: Grandpa?

EVERETT: What, son?

STEPHEN: If the people in heaven are all spirit, if they don't have any flesh anymore, how does God know who's who?

EVERETT *(Putting his arm around Stephen, and walking him out of the garden):* Spirit's how God tells us apart anyway, Stephen. When we get to heaven, why as far as He's concerned, we haven't changed a bit.

Glory is left alone with Sam. Sam has a pair of snippers from the tool chest and is cutting the weeds that have grown up around the wall.

GLORY: I'm beginning to see the garden now, Sam.

SAM: I don't know why I'm doing this. He'll just let it go again.

GLORY: Did you and Mavis play out here when you were kids?

SAM *(Putting the snippers down)*: Maybe I've done enough.

GLORY: Where did your mother find these animals?

SAM: I don't know.

570 GLORY *(As she picks one up)*: Was she strong enough to carry them? They're very heavy.

SAM: Please. *(Taking it away from her)* Just leave them alone, okay?

GLORY: He won't let me touch anything in the house, and you won't let me touch anything out here. It's just me, I guess, I mean, your mother was . . . allowed to work here, wasn't she? Or maybe it's a museum, or a shrine.

SAM: What's the matter with *you?*

GLORY *(Has to laugh)*: What's the matter with me.

SAM: Did you call your mother?

GLORY: I did, in fact. I told her you were leaving in the morning and
580 taking Stephen with you.

SAM: And what did she say?

GLORY: She said she would see you at the funeral and tell you good-bye.

SAM: So we'll have something to talk about anyway.

GLORY: She said it was another woman. She said you and Mavis were . . .

SAM: . . . having an affair? No.

GLORY: Someone else, then. Do you want to leave me for another woman?

590 SAM: I don't want another woman. I want you to be the woman I want.

GLORY: Can I have a straight answer please.

SAM: We've both had affairs. Haven't we.

GLORY: Well, that's it, I guess.

SAM: It what?

GLORY: The truth.

SAM: That is not the truth. That is just a fact. The truth is what the facts mean.

GLORY: I am so tired of your mind. You would've been so much better off without it.

600 SAM: I would have been nothing without it! With the exception of a mother who died and left me with the preacher, my mind is all I ever had. *(He stops)* Except Stephen.

GLORY *(She shakes her head)*: And your mother and Mavis and me.

SAM: Yes.

GLORY: Did you forget us for a moment?

SAM: No, I didn't forget you. But it *is* getting easier. There's only one of you left.

GLORY: What a lovely thing to say. What a great time we're having here. Such a good reason to come home and such a spirit of love and understanding. Just relax, Glory. This will all blow over in just a little while. He's always like this, but he's not always so much like this.

SAM: I'm not always like this.

GLORY: No. When you're sick, it's worse. When you're tired, it's worse. But the rest of the time you are exactly like this. You just don't notice it, because this is how you always are. Like I said.

SAM: Then why have you stayed with me.

GLORY: I don't know, it's not over yet. Something like that.

SAM: It is over.

GLORY *(Picking up the Sleeping Beauty book):* No, this is just the part where I sleep for a hundred years. Then the prince comes and I wake up.

SAM: Jesus Christ.

GLORY: I'm still here for two reasons. One is that you need me. And I have no idea why you need me but you do. I can feel it. I see it all the time. I don't understand at all, but I have no doubt whatsoever.

SAM: And what is the other reason?

GLORY: The other reason is my business. And I'm not about to tell you when you're threatening to leave me.

SAM: Well, I know it can't be that you're having a good time. You should've married that baseball player.

GLORY: If I had married Jerry Pine, I would've spent half my life at Yankee Stadium, wishing he wouldn't chew tobacco, and hoping he won't spit on national TV. *(A pause)* Maybe I would have a better time without you. I could laugh and travel and give away Mother's money, but you . . . well. . . . This is not a job that just anybody could do, you know, putting up with you.

SAM: So this is your chance. I'm offering you a way out.

GLORY: I want a way in, Sam.

SAM: There isn't any way in. There never was. You never had a chance. I married you to spite my father. *(Pause)* There. Can you hate me now? Can I leave now?

GLORY: I know you loved me.

SAM: Do you?

GLORY: I know you love me now.

He turns to go.

GLORY: Where are you going?

SAM *(After a moment):* I have to find Stephen before Dad turns him into a Christian.

GLORY: Let them alone. You can't change your father and you can't protect Stephen from the entire world. It's one thing to take away the television and give him *Scientific American* instead of *Mother Goose,* but Everett is his grandfather. Let them talk. Stephen can see what there is and decide for himself.

Before Sam can answer, Everett comes back outside alone.

EVERETT: Maybe you two been gone so long you forgot this, but we have a thing out here called respect for the dead.

GLORY: What?

EVERETT: And Glory, if you're going to your mother's, I wish you'd go on and go so we could have our funeral in peace.

GLORY: Everett, I don't know what you're—

660 EVERETT: Don't you realize what you're doing to that little boy?

GLORY: What did he tell you, Everett?

EVERETT: That he's leaving tomorrow with Sam and you're moving in with your mother. Is that right?

GLORY: He hears everything we say, Sam, I've told you that over and over again. Jesus Christ.

SAM: Why shouldn't he know? I'm just sorry I didn't tell him before he heard it through the wall, like that. He wasn't surprised, I'm sure. Divorce is not exactly unknown in the world. Now that he knows the truth, he'll feel better.

670 GLORY *(To Everett):* What did you say?

EVERETT: I didn't know what to say. I said, "Maybe Mom is just lonesome for the country. She'll get tired of it soon enough and be right back home, quick as quick." *(Very strong, as Sam shakes his head)* I said that to make him feel better. I wanted him to feel better.

SAM: And he believed you?

EVERETT: I *saw* him feel a little better, yes.

GLORY: Thank you, Everett. You did the right thing.

SAM: Cover it up, that's right. Put a little Band-Aid on it. It worked with me, didn't it? I have spent my life straightening out the lies

680 people have told him. No, Stephen, there is no Santa Claus. No, Stephen, when you die, you do not go to heaven. No, Stephen, people won't like you better because you're smart, they'll be afraid of you because you're smart. No, Stephen, love is not forever, and God is not good. And tomorrow is not another day. Tomorrow is this day all over again.

EVERETT: Well, wasn't he lucky to have you around.

GLORY: I'd better go find him.

EVERETT: I think that's a good idea.

Glory goes into the house and Everett and Sam are left alone.

SAM: I don't want to hear what you have to say about this, Dad. You

690 don't know what you're talking about, and you're not going to change my mind.

EVERETT: That's as good a confession as I ever heard.

SAM: You never liked Glory in the first place. You should be happy I'm leaving her.

EVERETT: She's a good girl, and she's been a good mother to Stephen. Whatever is the matter between Glory and you . . . is probably you.

SAM: I see.

EVERETT: But it's your boy who'll end up paying for this, Sam.

SAM: Doesn't seem fair, does it? Well, I'm sorry, Stephen, that's just
how God is. Suffer the little children to come unto me, for theirs is   700
the wages of sin.

EVERETT: When somebody dies it makes everything hard, Sam, but
what we all do is try not to make anything worse.

SAM: When somebody dies, you try to make it make a difference,
make it mean something.

EVERETT: Sam, I never thought this marriage would work, you know
that. But we're having a funeral today. Can't you take one day of
your life to think about Mavis? God knows, you took everything
else she had for your own use, but now you're even taking her funeral. *(Pause)* I'm sure she's happy for you to have it, that's just   710
how she was, but it makes me mad, Sam. You make too much
noise, son. You always did. Relax. Grieve.

SAM: No. This marriage was never right, and I want it straight now.

EVERETT: After the funeral, just leave Stephen with me for a few days,
and you and Glory go down to Green River, work this thing out.

SAM: I don't want to work it out. What could we work it out to? Back
to where it was at the beginning? In the beginning was the word,
and the word was *pretend*.

EVERETT: I saw that beginning, same as you, and there wasn't any pretend about it. You were hopeless. You drooled around here for   720
years until Glory called you with that math problem. Here was poor
Mavis practically polishing your shoes to get your attention. But no,
all you wanted was the pretty little rich girl, swimming in her own
private lake out there. But how was she ever going to notice the
preacher's kid? So you took up cross-country, didn't you? And
pretty soon, you could run the ten miles out to her farm, and still
have the breath to stand there and smile.

SAM: Why don't you say what you mean. Divorce is a sin.

EVERETT: Sam, your mother used to say your marriage was like your
favorite shirt. You could wear it day after day, and you could try to   730
keep it clean, but sooner or later it was going to have to go in the
wash. But as soon as it was clean, you could press it fresh, and put
it back on, looking good as new.

SAM: I don't have a favorite shirt. And I don't need advice from you.

EVERETT: What does she say? Does she say "Whatever you want, Sam"?

SAM: She will. Glory will do what Stephen wants. Stephen wants to be
with me.

EVERETT: Stephen will be ready to go home tomorrow morning. Glory
may not have all the answers to his questions, like you do, but she's
home when he gets there.   740

SAM: That's not enough.

EVERETT: If you leave her, you'll lose him.

SAM: Stephen is mine. He always has been.

EVERETT: And you're supposed to be so smart. *(No response)* Maybe you ought to make a list of the things you don't know, just for your own protection, see. *(A pause)* Put this at the top.

SAM: This . . . what?

EVERETT: Boys and their mothers.

SAM: Whatever you say, Dad.

750 EVERETT: This is . . . a subject I took a few lessons in myself, Sam.

Glory comes out onto the porch carrying a cup of coffee for Everett.

GLORY: Sam? Don't you want a sandwich? We should leave in twenty minutes.

SAM: No thanks. I don't want to spoil my dinner.

Stephen runs past her and down the steps.

GLORY: Don't get dirty now, Stephen. Watch where you sit.

Stephen is carrying a Bible he has found inside. Glory follows him into the garden.

STEPHEN: Dad, I found your Bible!

SAM *(Alarmed)*: Glory, where—

STEPHEN *(Still very excited)*: I thought it was Grandpa's, but it's yours!

GLORY *(To Sam)*: In your old bedroom, I think.

STEPHEN *(Showing it to him)*: See? It says Samuel Carter.

760 SAM: The church gives them away, Stephen.

STEPHEN: No, look, Dad! On the next page, it says—

SAM *(To Everett)*: Did you give this to him?

Everett shakes his head no.

STEPHEN: See, it's right here. It says August 27, 1949, Jesus came into my heart.

SAM: Well—

STEPHEN: Only you've got it spelled H-E-R-A-T. Jesus came into your heart before you could even spell it!

SAM: I didn't have any choice, Stephen. Night after night you sit there in the revival and every head is bowed and every eye is closed, and
770 Dad is down there at the altar calling "Oh sinner, come home." And people all around you are saying "Bless me Jesus, save me Lord."

And the first night eight people go down and the second night twenty people go down, and the third night everybody in the whole third grade goes down, and those are the big kids, so I'm impressed. And you look up at Dad and he's looking straight at you, saying "God see my boy, see my own dear child, speak to him, Lord," and I heard it, all right. I couldn't go home if I didn't.

So before I could stop myself, I walked down the aisle, shaking and crying, saying "Here I am, Daddy." I knelt down at the altar,
780 and he put his hand on my head and said "Praise the Lord," and I was saved. And he . . . was relieved. What kind of a preacher are you if you can't save your own child?

EVERETT: I didn't save you. He did.

SAM: Then after the service, we all waited for him in the front pew where he gave us all brand-new Bibles and had us turn to the front page and write down August 27, 1949—

SAM AND STEPHEN: —Jesus came into my heart.

STEPHEN: Did you read this?

EVERETT: He read it straight through before school even started that year.

SAM: I was too young to read, Dad. I just looked at the pictures, Stephen.

EVERETT: He knew hundreds of verses by heart. I'd be reading a verse in a sermon, and I'd look down at him in the front row, and he'd be mouthing the words right along with me.

SAM: Take it easy, Dad.

EVERETT: But I was so proud of you, son!

SAM: I know, but—

EVERETT: Stephen, we had Junior Church one Sunday a month, you know, where only the kids would come, and your dad started preaching there when he was only nine years old. By the time he was twelve, people all over the state had heard about him.

STEPHEN: You never told me you were a preacher, Dad.

EVERETT: That summer, at the revival, I announced in the newspaper that your dad was going to preach the sermon one night, and so many people came that there wasn't enough room for them all in the tent, so we had to open up the sides so people could sit on the grass and see him. He talked about Abraham that night. Abraham and Isaac.

STEPHEN *(Finding the picture in the Bible)*: Here's Abraham right here. *(Walking toward Sam)* But he's killing his little boy.

SAM: That's him all right. God says to Abraham, "If you really love me, you will sacrifice your son. You will build a fire, tie him to the top of it, slit his throat, say a prayer, and burn him up."

STEPHEN: Why?

EVERETT: The Lord was testing Abraham, Stephen.

SAM: The Lord was bored, Stephen. He was just looking for something to do.

EVERETT: Oh no. God had big plans for Abraham. And He had to make sure Abraham was the right man for the job.

STEPHEN: Is this God, here, in the clouds?

SAM: There's a much better picture of Him on page fifty-eight. That's Him in the burning bush.

STEPHEN: And He isn't burned up?

EVERETT: He *is* the fire.

STEPHEN: He is?

EVERETT: God really knows how to get your attention, all right.

SAM: He's lonely, Stephen. He sits and waits for somebody to notice Him, and then, when they don't or when they don't notice Him enough, well, He plays His little tricks, He gives His little tests.

830   EVERETT: He has His reasons for His tests.

SAM: That's what you said when Mother died. God is testing us, son. God has His reasons, only we can't know what they are.

EVERETT: God didn't kill her.

SAM: He just let her die. He took her back. He was only kidding. She wasn't mine. She was His.

GLORY: Stephen, why don't you take the Bible inside. We don't want it to get—

SAM: She died when I was about your age, Stephen. About a month after my preaching triumph. But we didn't call it dying, did we,

840   Dad? We just said God was missing her something awful and she went on back where she belonged, didn't we?

EVERETT: Yes, we did. And I don't know how He got along without her for as long as He did.

STEPHEN: I don't understand. Could God have saved Granny if He wanted to?

EVERETT: Yes, Stephen.

STEPHEN: Then why didn't He?

EVERETT: We do not understand everything that happens, but if we believe He loves us, we don't need to understand. Understanding is

850   His work, not ours.

SAM: That's right. He sets it up, we live through it, and He writes it down. What we think of as life, Stephen, is just God gathering material for another book.

STEPHEN: Was God missing Mavis too?

SAM: Stephen—

EVERETT *(Quickly):* I don't know, Stephen. But I do know He has His mysterious ways of working things out. Your daddy is a doctor today because his mother died when he was so young.

SAM: Jesus Christ.

860   EVERETT: They worked puzzles on her bed right up to the day she died. I'd come in to check on her, and she'd be asleep, but your dad would be reading *Mother Goose* to her like she could hear every word. He worked real hard but he couldn't save her. He was just a boy.

SAM: Jesus God.

EVERETT: But now, every time he goes into that operating room, God gives him another chance. How many people are alive today because of him! Hundreds! Thousands maybe. Praise be to the power and the wisdom of the Almighty God.

SAM: You are a hopeless old fool!

870   GLORY: Sam, you apologize to your father!

SAM: God is not in control.

GLORY: Please, Sam, remember what we're doing here.

SAM: I will not have Stephen walk into that funeral believing God has some reason for this! *(He turns to Stephen)* He's lying to you, Stephen. He lied to me and now he's lying to you and I won't have it! God had nothing to do with Mavis dying. It just happened. It was a goddamn rotten thing to happen, but God didn't do it. No. God is not in control and hasn't been in control for some time. *(He pauses and shifts into the master storyteller he can be)* He lost it . . . over Job. God made a bet with the Devil and lost it all.

Glory shakes her head and wanders off a bit. Sam relaxes a little, now that he has won.

SAM: The Devil said, "Sure Job loves you. Why shouldn't he? He's the richest man on earth. But you take all that away, and he won't pray to you then, no sir."

Well, God just had to find out. So in one afternoon, He killed all his sheep, all his camels, all his oxes and his asses and his daughters and his sons. And Job still prayed. So the next afternoon, God set a fire that burned up his house and everything in it, turned all his friends against him, sat Job down in the ashes and gave him leprosy.

And even then, Job prayed. Job suffered more than any man had ever suffered. As much, in fact, as God had ever suffered. And when God realized that Job could suffer just as well as He could, everything changed. For God saw that He had sinned, but Job loved Him still. And in that moment, God found God, and it was man.

And ever since that time, God has been up there believing in us with all His heart, believing we can do whatever we want, and wondering why, exactly, we do what we do. We must have our reasons, but He can't for the life of Him, figure out what they are.

So He watches, but He can't help us. So He weeps. All God can do now is cry. The oceans, Stephen, are the tears God has cried since Job.

GLORY *(Coming back):* We need to go, Sam.

SAM *(Continuing):* God is not in control. We are. There is no heaven, there is no hell. There is this life, created, in your case, by your mother and me. Life on earth, which we can make better through careful thought and hard work. But *we* make the progress, and *we* make the mistakes. Not God. God has nothing to do with this, so there is no point in believing in Him. He's just another fairy-tale king, as far as I'm concerned. If you want to believe, believe in yourself. In your power, in your mind, in your life. This life. Because that's all there is.

Everett looks at his watch, then straightens his tie.

GLORY *(Coming quickly to be near Stephen):* That's all your father thinks there is, Stephen. But he really doesn't know. Other people . . . *(Her anger is making it hard for her to talk)* find other things. Other people believe other things. And it makes them feel . . . different. Better.

SAM: Well, what can I say after that.

EVERETT *(Standing up):* Maybe you can tell me what to say at this funeral.

SAM: No thanks.

920 EVERETT: I'll say it was an accident, how's that? I'll say it was a stupid mistake that somebody made. And we won't pray, of course, but we will sing. Something like "Moon River," you know, whatever we feel like. It doesn't matter what we do, does it, Sam? It doesn't mean a thing.

SAM: I don't know, Dad. It's your show.

EVERETT: This is no show!

SAM: It is a show and you know it.

EVERETT: Well I'll tell you one thing, boy. My show works.

SAM: Oh, you think so, do you?

930 EVERETT: Yes I do. My show works. It works so well that you—yes, even you—have come home to see it. Haven't you?

SAM (*Brushing off his pants*): We need to take two cars.

GLORY: No we don't.

SAM: I'm not going to the supper. I don't want anybody coming up to me with coleslaw on their plate. I don't have anything to say about it.

GLORY: Stephen, go with your father, then, and I'll take Grandpa.

STEPHEN: Am I going with Dad forever, or just to the funeral?

SAM: I want you to do both those things, Stephen. I want you with me. Some new town, some other place. I'm sorry I didn't tell you

940 myself, but I wanted to—

GLORY: Stephen, do you remember what I told you inside?

STEPHEN: Yes.

GLORY: All right, then.

EVERETT: Let's go, Glory.

GLORY: I'm ready. (*To Sam*) You *are* coming.

SAM: Yes. We're coming.

After Everett and Glory have left, Sam puts on his suit jacket.

SAM: What did she tell you inside?

STEPHEN: She said I shouldn't worry about it. She said you were just upset. She said everything would be all right.

950 SAM: Did she say how it would get that way?

STEPHEN: No.

SAM: She just believes it will.

STEPHEN: That's what she said.

SAM: Funny, huh?

STEPHEN: I don't know.

SAM (*Straightening Stephen's hair*): Well, we can talk about it some more tonight. You're a real smart boy, and you'll just think your way through it. Just like any other problem. And you'll make your decision.

960 STEPHEN: Do I look all right?

SAM: You look good.

STEPHEN: So do you.

SAM: Thanks. Okay. (*Looking at Stephen*) Do we have a handkerchief?

STEPHEN *(Pats his pocket):* Mom gave me some Kleenex.

SAM: Okay, then. Here we go. *(Then quietly)* God help us.

They walk offstage.

ACT TWO

The lights come up, but they are not bright. It is sometime after midnight. Sam wanders into the garden and looks up at the house. There is only one light on, in that little room at the top of the house. Sam whistles the little tune he sang for Stephen in the first act and the light goes out. He sits down on the wall. Stephen opens the back door and walks out. Stephen is wearing his pajamas and a big sweater.

SAM *(As Stephen sits beside him):* Hello, Stephen.

STEPHEN: I waited up for you.

SAM: Yeah. I saw. What time did you get home?

STEPHEN: I don't know. Eight-thirty, something like that.   970

SAM: Is everybody asleep?

STEPHEN: I don't know. They probably think I'm asleep and I'm not, so I probably think they're asleep and they're not. Grandpa was pretty tired. He might be asleep.

SAM: Did you see Granny Butler at the supper?

STEPHEN: She told me I needed a haircut.

SAM: What do *you* think?

STEPHEN: I told her she smelled like bug candles.

SAM: And what did she say to that?

STEPHEN: She said she liked it. She said it kept the bugs away.   980

SAM: So. What time did you get home? *(Then remembering)* Oh, I'm sorry. You already told me that. Let's see. Did you talk to anybody else?

STEPHEN: Not really. This one lady asked me if I ever met Mavis. I said yes and she asked me if I wanted a coke. *(Pause)* But *everybody* was talking to Grandpa, like Mavis was almost his daughter or something.

SAM: She was, in a way. *(Pause)* You know what he did for her? *(Then realizing what he is about to tell)* If I tell you this, you've got to promise me not to let him know you know. I mean, you can't ask him for it.   990

STEPHEN: What is it?

SAM: Well, Mavis's father was the custodian at the church, and her mother worked late, so when she was little, Mavis was always hanging around the church after school. And Dad didn't want her to feel she was any less than me, you know, so . . . *(An odd pause)* Dad sent off for the books, and learned some magic tricks for Mavis. Not big tricks, but . . . making a salt shaker disappear, things like that. And it was their secret, but I found out, of course. Mavis told me. So I went right in and asked him to do it for me, but he said, "What are you talking about? I can't do any magic tricks." But I   1000 badgered him for a solid week until one night at supper, he gave in, picked up the salt shaker and said, "Watch close now."

STEPHEN: Terrific!

SAM: No. Not so terrific. I watched too close, I guess. I saw how it worked and ran around the table to his jacket pocket, reached in and pulled out the salt shaker. I said, "Don't put it in your pocket, Dad. Make it disappear."

STEPHEN: You spoiled it.

SAM: Yes. *(Pause)* Well. What were you reading upstairs?

1010 STEPHEN: Donner Pass.

SAM *(Laughs a little):* Oh yes. The Family Picnic.

STEPHEN: Come on, Dad. Did they really eat each other? Got caught in a blizzard and ate each other?

SAM: That's all they had, Stephen. They had to eat.

STEPHEN: But they died anyway, the Donner Pass people. They ate each other up and it didn't save them.

SAM: They did what they thought they had to do. They didn't know it wouldn't save them. *(Pause)* But the whole trip was like that. Day after day, they'd left things behind, thrown out beds and chests and

1020 tools and toys . . . to make the wagons lighter, so they could travel faster . . . so they could get to Donner Pass.

STEPHEN: If they threw everything out, what did they think they would live on once they got there?

SAM: They thought it was enough just to get there. They thought they were smart enough to figure it out, whatever it was, up the road. It's a pretty standard American idea. All you need is your brain. Then if all you have is your brain, well . . . you can eat it.

STEPHEN: Can we go there sometime? I bet there's a marker, isn't there? Donner Pass Memorial Park or something.

1030 SAM: Sure, Stephen. *(As if reading it)* In memory of the families who died by the side of the road, because the things that would have saved them were too heavy to carry such a long way.

STEPHEN: Didn't anybody tell them what could happen?

SAM: Yeah, probably. But they didn't listen. Other people get caught in blizzards and have to eat their families, not me. I'm smart.

STEPHEN: Not smart enough, huh.

SAM: Nobody is smart *enough.*

STEPHEN: Somebody out there might be. Some spaceman.

SAM: I don't think so, Stephen.

1040 STEPHEN *(A bit disappointed):* Why not?

SAM: See that cloud? Straight across the sky, there?

STEPHEN: Yeah.

SAM: It's not a cloud. It's us. It's the Milky Way. You can't see it in the city, but out here, you can. *(Pause)* The earth spins around the sun, while the sun spins around the center of the Milky Way, while the Milky Way chases Andromeda going like a billion miles an hour. *We're* the spacemen, Stephen.

STEPHEN *(After a moment):* Is there a center of everything?

SAM: The Big Bang Theory says there *was* one, but it blew up.

STEPHEN: Grandpa would say God did it, God lit the fuse.   1050

SAM: Yes. He would.

STEPHEN: Did He? *(Sam doesn't answer)* Is there a God, Dad?

SAM *(Taking Stephen in his arms):* When I am out here, on this wall, in this garden, looking up at the sky, I think, yes, there is something out there. I actually want there to be something out there. I want there to be a God, and I don't want it to be me.

STEPHEN: Are you feeling better, Dad?

SAM: I'm sorry about all this, Stephen. But once we get going. . . . First thing in the morning, we'll put all our things in Mavis's car and take off. Dad doesn't want it he said. So we might as well take it,   1060 don't you think, like she left us a getaway car. When we stop for the night, you can call your mother if you want, and just see if she can guess where we are.

STEPHEN: I don't want to move, Dad.

SAM: You want to stay with your mother, you mean.

STEPHEN: I don't want you to leave us.

SAM: We'll go someplace wonderful. Northern California, maybe, with the ocean out the front door, and the redwoods out the back. And we could get a horse if you want. I always wanted a horse.

STEPHEN: I can't leave, Dad. Mom needs me. She doesn't have any-   1070 body.

SAM: Stephen, your mother has more friends than the Red Cross.

STEPHEN *(Getting up off the wall now):* It's not the same thing. She needs *me.*

SAM: No, you're right. That's true. She does. I need you too, but . . . she said it first, huh?

STEPHEN: Don't you love Mom anymore?

SAM: I guess not.

STEPHEN: What did she do?

SAM: Nothing.   1080

STEPHEN: Did you love her when you married her?

SAM: Yes.

STEPHEN: Did she change?

SAM: No.

STEPHEN: Did you change?

SAM: No, not really.

STEPHEN: So what happened to it?

SAM: Stephen, there will be days when it doesn't matter that you're smart. When it won't help. When your extraordinary mind is of no use whatsoever. When all it will do is tell you how bad things are.   1090

STEPHEN: But you told me to think about it.

SAM: Yes, but . . . *(Struggling here)* You can't think about this the way you would any other problem. You can't just add up the numbers and read the result, because it doesn't work that way. It's like you wanted to open a bottle of beer, but all you had to use was your calculator. It wouldn't work. You need to use something else.

STEPHEN: I would sell the calculator and buy a bottle opener. *(No response from Sam)* I would go next door and borrow a bottle opener.

SAM: I would call upstairs and ask your mother where she hid the bottle opener.

STEPHEN: She didn't hide it. You just didn't look. You never look. You're out of the house for eight hours and you act like we've taken all the stuff out of the cabinets and hidden it away like a treasure hunt. *(Imitating Sam's call)* Glory, where's the peanut butter?

SAM *(Defending himself)*: I just got home. I'm tired. I don't want to go looking. I want the peanut butter.

STEPHEN *(Very angry)*: It's in the basement. It's in a box marked Dad's Old Shoes.

SAM: What does she do? Hold little indoctrination sessions with you?

STEPHEN: I don't want to move, Dad.

SAM: We don't even have to stay in this country, you know. We could go to South America and become river rats. Or how about Africa. Spend the whole day outside.

STEPHEN: So what would I do? Wait outside the hut all day for you to come home?

SAM: You'd go to school.

STEPHEN: I already go to school. And I already sit and wait for you to come home and I already don't like it. I wouldn't like it any better in Africa.

SAM: I'll come home.

STEPHEN: No you won't.

SAM: We'll go fishing.

STEPHEN: No we won't, Dad.

SAM: I love you, Stephen.

STEPHEN: If you could stop loving Mom, you could stop loving me.

SAM: No, Stephen. Your children are not the same as your wife or your husband.

STEPHEN: Your children are an accident.

SAM: Stephen!

STEPHEN: You didn't want any children at all. I wouldn't even be here if it weren't for Mom.

SAM: Did she tell you that?

STEPHEN: No, but it's true, isn't it. Isn't it!

SAM: Yes. But I didn't know I would get you. If I had known it was you, I'd have wanted you. *(No response from Stephen)* I know I've been gone too much and never taken any time off, but I want to change all that. I want to be with you now.

STEPHEN: You don't want to do anything but work and you can't even do that right. What kind of doctor are you if you can't save your own nurse?

Suddenly the back-porch light comes on and Everett steps out.

EVERETT: Stephen? Are you out there?

SAM *(More quiet, but more intense)*: Stephen, I didn't kill Mavis. You
 don't understand.

EVERETT *(Calling again)*: Stephen!

STEPHEN *(To Sam)*: What's there to understand? She's dead.

EVERETT *(To Glory, who is in the kitchen)*: They're outside, Glory.

SAM: Stephen, medicine doesn't always work.

STEPHEN: Then it might as well be magic, Dad.

SAM: Stephen, people die all the time. People have to die sometime.   1150

Everett walks out into the garden.

STEPHEN *(Louder than necessary)*: And it's no big deal, huh.

EVERETT *(Hearing him)*: There you are. We thought we lost you.

SAM *(Sees his father, but keeps talking)*: It's sad, Stephen, but no, it's
 not any big deal.

STEPHEN *(Standing up)*: Well, if it's not any big deal when people die,
 then it's not any big deal when they live, or where they live, so I'm
 living with Mom.

Everett sits down, making Sam even more uncomfortable.

SAM: Stephen, I tried to save her—

STEPHEN *(Jumping up now)*: I'm living with Mom.

SAM: Ask him! He'll tell you. I did everything—   1160

STEPHEN *(Screaming)*: I'm living with Mom.

SAM: Are you listening to me?

STEPHEN: Don't call us! Don't come to see us!

SAM: Stephen!

STEPHEN *(Moving toward the house)*: Don't come get your things!

SAM: What do you want me to say?

STEPHEN: Buy new things!

*Stephen runs out of the garden and up the steps into the house. Sam
 just stands there a minute, then turns to Everett, who is still sitting
 by the wall.*

SAM: If you're looking for Stephen, he went inside.

EVERETT *(After a moment)*: That's good. It's cold out here.

SAM *(Very controlled)*: Then why don't *you* go inside.   1170

EVERETT: And do what?

SAM: And talk to somebody else! *(No response from Everett)* God, for
 example.

EVERETT: I *did* talk to God.

SAM: I'm sure you did.

EVERETT: He told me to come out here and sit with you, and He'd get
 back to me in the morning.

SAM: Did He tell you what to say to me?

EVERETT: No. God's not much good on detail.

SAM: But you have some ideas, I guess.   1180

EVERETT: Are you mad at God or me?

SAM: I'm not sure. I get you confused.

EVERETT: What did I do?

SAM: You let Mother's garden go to hell.

EVERETT: Sam, I'm an old man.

SAM: You didn't deserve her.

EVERETT: Of course I didn't. She was a gift. Like Glory is a gift. Like Stephen is a gift.

SAM: She was nothing to you. Nothing at all. You never paid any attention to her. You spent all your time tending the flock.

EVERETT: I did love your mother, Sam.

SAM: You loved God more.

EVERETT: Of course I did. And she knew I loved God more. She knew I loved *you* more.

SAM: You didn't love me, you loved Mavis. Yes! You even loved Mavis more than Mother. First God, then Mavis, then the ladies in the choir, then the congregation, then the shut-ins, then the sick, then the starving Chinese and the heathen, wherever they are, then me, then Mother.

EVERETT: I'm sorry if it seemed that way.

SAM: It *was* that way!

EVERETT: All right. It *was* that way. She was last on my list. All right. But there was a power in me, like there's a power in you, and I couldn't let anything get in its way.

SAM: Why couldn't you let anything get in its way? What good did it do? I mean, it didn't work, Dad.

EVERETT: I was called to it, Sam. Same as you. And you know your Glory understands what your work means to you. Your mother was exactly that way for me. Of course, I never saved lives the way *you* do, but I *was*—

SAM: We can't save lives. God couldn't save Mother. Medicine couldn't save Mavis. Lives are lost from the start. All you do is promise them another one, and all I do is make this one last longer. But it's *our* victory, not theirs. My work saves *my* life. Or used to. Oh boy. Day after day I've been real proud of myself 'cause I won one more round. Right? Wrong. Death wins. Death always wins.

EVERETT: Not in my book.

SAM: No, not in your book. But I don't believe in your book. I don't, in fact, believe in anything. It has taken me my whole life, Dad, but I have finally arrived. I am free of faith. Glory be. Praise the Lord.

EVERETT (*Almost laughing*): Oh, He's really after you this time, isn't He?

SAM: And He has to shake me to make me listen, doesn't He?

EVERETT: Well, I probably believed that in the old days, but God's not as physical as He used to be.

SAM: That is *not* what you "probably believed" in the old days. That is *exactly* what you said from the pulpit the Sunday after Mother died. You pointed to me, sitting there on the front row of the choir, where everybody in the whole congregation could see me, and you told them the story. "There was my little boy, Samuel, sitting on his dear mother's bed, and he didn't know she was dead, he was just sitting there, reading as loud as he could, as fast as he could, but he was shaking like a young tree in a driving rain. And I walked in and saw that she was dead and put my hands on his shoulders and made him stop shaking and made him stop reading and listen. And I said, 'Son, your mother has gone to her reward.' And he heard me."

Now by this time, they're all crying, the whole church is crying, but you weren't through, were you? You walked over to me and pulled me up out of my seat in the choir and grabbed my hand and held it to your heart and you said to your congregation, "That's what God has to do, sometimes. He has to shake us to make us listen."

EVERETT *(Quite shaken himself):* I didn't mean to talk about it, Sam. Not that Sunday, anyway. I just lost my place in my sermon, somehow. And everything got all blurry, all of a sudden, and all I knew was, I had to keep talking and . . . that was the best I could do, son.

SAM: Yeah, well, do you want to know what God said to me? What I heard when I quit shaking?

EVERETT: Sam, Sam . . .

SAM: I heard God say, and He was almost laughing when He said it— God said, "Sam, Sam, how could you have been so dumb."

EVERETT: I don't know what to say to you, son.

SAM: I don't want you to say anything to me. I want you to leave me alone.

EVERETT: Where am I supposed to go, Sam? This is my house.

SAM: This is Mother's house. Yours is the one with the steeple on the top.

EVERETT: No. That's God's house.

SAM: Then where do you live, Daddy? I mean, when you go home, who opens the door?

EVERETT: Oh, son. *(Pause)* You do.

SAM *(Very cold):* Well I'm awful sorry about that, Dad, but you don't get the boy you want, you get the boy you get.

EVERETT: This hurts me too much now, Sam. You're the only one who. . . . Look, maybe you shouldn't come down here anymore. I'm happy here. My whole life is peaceful here. And I can still pray for you and keep up with you, but well, I'll just see you in the newspapers from now on, okay? Maybe you'll send Stephen to visit me now and then, but I won't come there, and you don't come here, all right?

Sam is suddenly still, and there is a long silence.

SAM: Will Stephen forgive me?

Everett takes a long time here.

1270 EVERETT *(Quietly)*: I don't know. Do you forgive me?

SAM *(Much more quiet)*: I don't know.

EVERETT: Well then, it's hard to say. Some of these things are inherited, I think.

Glory comes out of the house.

GLORY: Everett? Sam? What are you two doing out here?

EVERETT: Oh, you know. Reminiscing.

GLORY: Look Sam. Look what I found. I thought you gave me all your letter sweaters, but you didn't. You kept one for yourself, didn't you.

EVERETT: He couldn't get in the sports banquet without it.

GLORY: I remember that banquet. You were the only member of the
1280 cross-country team.

EVERETT: I remember they served cauliflower. Bless your mother's heart, you were the only athlete who ate it.

GLORY: Everett, you need to put on something warmer if you're going to stay out here.

EVERETT *(Standing)*: Did Stephen go to bed?

GLORY: I made him some warm milk.

EVERETT: I didn't think I had any milk.

GLORY: I made a glass for you, too.

EVERETT: I'll go sit with him, then.
1290 GLORY: Don't you like milk?

EVERETT: I don't know. I'll see. *(He goes into the house)*

GLORY *(Turning to Sam)*: Come on, Sam. Put this sweater on.

Sam takes the sweater finally, and puts it on as he talks.

SAM: I liked that run before school every morning. Out of the house ... down the street. .... Everybody asleep but me and the milkman. I got to feeling real useful, you know, like I was supposed to check out the town before everybody got up. Mile after mile, so far, so good, I'd think. No fires, no stray dogs, and no lights on, so nobody's sick. We did okay. We made it through another night.

GLORY: You were right not to come to the supper, Sam.
1300 SAM: Did they wonder where I was?

GLORY: They're used to your being gone, I think.

SAM: Like you.

GLORY: No. I'm not used to it. But I don't take it personally anymore.

SAM: Like they do.

GLORY: Maybe they do. I don't know.

SAM: They think ... that I think ... that I'm better than they are.

GLORY: You do!

SAM: I know. They're right.

GLORY: And that's why you don't go. You can't stand for them to be
1310 right.

SAM: That's right.

GLORY *(After a moment)*: Well ... you missed some great stories about Mavis.

SAM: I'm sure I did.

GLORY: Your dad told one about you and Mavis, and Timmy some-body—he didn't remember the name—coming back from church camp down at Green River. And you were speeding down the road in that old Volkswagen of hers. And suddenly you saw a policeman coming up behind you and you realized not only were you all three drunk, but you didn't have your driver's license, and you knew you'd never get into medical school with that on your record, so Mavis said, "I'll drive." And you said, "Mavis, we're going seventy miles an hour." And she said, "Move over." 1320

SAM *(Realizing she doesn't know the end of the story):* Is that all he told of it?

GLORY: Is there more?

SAM: We climbed over each other and she got behind the wheel. I told her to slow down, but she told me to shut up. When the police car pulled up beside us, she rolled down the window and yelled to the officer that the accelerator was stuck, and he took one look at the car, and believed her. He made some motions with his hands like she should downshift or kick the accelerator, which she did, then she hit the brake, smiled at him, pulled off the road, got out of the car, and threw up. 1330

GLORY: So she wasn't drunk anymore.

SAM: Right.

GLORY: Smart.

SAM *(With great, unprotected joy):* Yeah. Mavis was as smart as they come.

Pause.

GLORY: Sam, I've been thinking about all of this. 1340

SAM: Yes. It's that kind of night, isn't it.

GLORY: I think you're right. I think I'll go to Mother's for a while. A month maybe. You take Stephen and go, Sam. Back to the city or on a trip, whatever you think is best. I don't want to fight with you now. I'd just like a month to think.

SAM: I see.

GLORY: I didn't bring the right clothes to suit Mother, but she'll take me shopping, I guess. And she's giving a big party next week. People I haven't seen in years. Maybe some of them will have learned something in the meantime. 1350

SAM: Don't count on it.

GLORY: My riding clothes are still out there, so that's good. I'll be able to check out this exercise boy of hers.

SAM: Uh-huh.

GLORY: And I thought maybe Everett might need me. We can go through Mavis's clothes, and I'll help him sort her letters and look at the pictures with him and hear the rest of the stories again. *(Pause)* I'm all packed.

SAM: Glory . . .

1360 GLORY: I just came out here to—

SAM: Will you not leave . . . just yet? Will you sit with me awhile?

GLORY: I will.

SAM (*This is hard for him at first*): When you went to the supper, I drove over to Mavis's house. Where they lived when we were kids, I mean. I don't even know who lives there now. I just parked out front for a while. I always liked that house. Those lilac bushes are still there, remember?

GLORY: Sure I do. All over the place.

SAM: And for one moment, I was sixteen and I had it all to do over

1370 again. And I could forget your hair, and forget your mouth and your smell, and love Mavis. Marry her. Somebody exactly like me. Somebody who believed in hard work, who couldn't wait to be an adult. Somebody who never read "Sleeping Beauty" and never said a prayer except, "God let me stay awake long enough to get everything finished."

GLORY: You were two of a kind all right.

SAM: And in the next moment, the moment after I was sixteen and could forget your hair, I was sixteen and I wanted your hair in my mouth, in my eyes, all over me. I wanted to catch you swimming

1380 naked in your pond. I knew you did it. You told me you did it.

GLORY (*Confessing*): Of course I did. I wanted you to catch me.

SAM: I never had a chance. I hopped over to that pond like every frog in every fairy tale my mother ever read me, and you kissed me, and I believed. I remember that kiss, I can still taste the butterscotch sucker I took out of your mouth to have that kiss, and I'm still dizzy and hot all of a sudden, and I remember loving you. (*Pause*) And I guess that kiss . . . was the last I ever saw of Mavis.

GLORY: Bless her heart, she worshipped you. I knew it, everybody knew it.

1390 SAM: So, once I was in love with you, she had to go to nursing school, didn't she? But she never married, just in case you got hit by a truck or something. (*Glory laughs but knows it's true*) Right. Nursing school was her last chance to get my attention, but it didn't work. I didn't look at her in high school and I haven't looked at her since. Why should I look? I knew she'd be there.

GLORY: Sam . . .

SAM: Mavis was two feet away from me, across the table from me, her whole life, and what did she get from this life with me? Nothing. Invitations to dinner from you. Tennis on Saturday with you. The

1400 four of us at the movies, me sound asleep and Mavis holding the popcorn between you and Stephen. Nothing.

GLORY: Mavis got as much from you as you would let her have. That's all she wanted. You're a genius. People make exceptions. They settle.

SAM: You have done more than settle. You have bet your lives on me. It was worse for Mavis, but it's the same for all of you. None of you had any right to count on me, but you did, and I let you, and now, instead of saving any of you—

GLORY: Is that what you think you're doing in our lives, saving us?

SAM: I want to help you. 1410

GLORY: We're all right down here. We think our little thoughts and we have our silly troubles and we fight our losing battles as bravely as we can. The last thing we need is for you to come in and solve our problems for us. Our problems, Sam, are how we fill up our days.

SAM: It's easier for you in the winter, I guess. Your days are shorter.

GLORY (*A flash of anger*): I don't need you to save me! (*Then recovering*) I just need you to . . . be on my side whenever you can. (*When he doesn't respond, she continues*) See me . . . hear me . . . give me some room, and save me some time. That's all. (*Still no response* 1420 *from Sam*) I've already got a God, Sam. And I see Him all the time, everywhere I go. And He may seem limited and primitive to you, but the dances are fun and the songs are sweet, and every day is a holy day.

SAM: So what is your God doing tonight?

GLORY: I don't know. Maybe He's just . . . watering the grass.

SAM: Okay. I can't save you. But neither do I have the right to destroy you all.

GLORY: I am not destroyed! I'm mad at you because you're acting like this, but I am not destroyed. And if you think you destroyed Mavis 1430 . . . if you're out here feeling sorry for Mavis . . . Mavis had you all day, Sam. Mavis had the best of you! I never had the conversations she had with you. I never sweated with you for twelve hours to work one of your miracles. We—you and I—never held our breath till the dead man sat up, Sam. (*And he doesn't respond*) No, Sam. Don't feel sorry for Mavis. And don't be mad at me. I have been— Stephen and I have been—happy, all these years, to have what was left over when Mavis finished with you.

SAM: So you're happy she's gone.

GLORY (*Horrified*): How can you say that? 1440

SAM: You sounded jealous, that's all.

GLORY: I was jealous. You loved her. But that doesn't—

SAM: No, Glory. I didn't love her. I had every opportunity to, but I didn't.

GLORY: Well . . . I loved her. And I think she loved me. And right now, I'm feeling real lost without her.

SAM: She was jealous of you.

GLORY: What on earth for?

SAM: You've got it all.

GLORY: I've got you, you mean. 1450

SAM: You're a great-looking woman and Stephen adores you, and you
float through everything like you're on a . . . like you were born
wearing a life jacket. *(Pause)* Mavis had to work hard for everything
she ever had, while you . . . well, you . . . just enjoy yourself.

GLORY: Listen, Sam. It's not as easy as it looks.

SAM: Yeah, well, you've had a lot of practice.

GLORY *(In a rage)*: I did not agree to sit here and take the blame for
this. It's not my fault! *(She starts for the house)*

1460 SAM: I didn't love her, I used her. And then . . . when she really
needed me. . . . she was counting on me to see it, Glory, only I
wasn't looking. And I wasn't looking because I didn't want to see it.
Other people die, Glory—not me, not my family, not my friend!

GLORY: None of us were looking, Sam. Three weeks ago, I knew she
looked awful. I told her to get a haircut.

SAM: It's the thirteenth fairy, see. You don't invite her to the party
because you don't want her to come, but she comes anyway, because she lives there, just like you do. But you forgot, didn't you?

GLORY: Sam . . .

SAM: I forgot Mavis was alive and she died.

1470 GLORY: You were trying to save her!

SAM: I was showing off! I could fix it. I could pull her through. I
could make it disappear. She could have lived months. A year
maybe, but no, I have to go in and save her.

GLORY: Even if it was a mistake . . .

SAM: I believed I could save her.

GLORY: Well you couldn't.

SAM: So now I just turn around and believe I couldn't?

GLORY: Yes!

SAM: No! It was the belief that was the problem in the first place! I
1480 believed in everything. I even believed in you—or love, I guess.
Didn't I? Yes. And in God, and fairy tales, and medicine and the
power of my own mind and none of it works!

GLORY: Sam . . . please . . .

SAM: But I want to believe! Stephen wants to believe! He does! I see it!
After everything I've told him, he still wants to believe. But how can
I let him believe when I know what happens, when there is no good
reason for what happens, when there is no reason to believe.

GLORY *(Trying another tack)*: Sam, you've got this all mixed up. You
married me because I'm good for you, and you operated on Mavis
1490 because you were the best one to do it, because she wanted you to
do it, because you wanted to do it.

SAM: No! *(In his own private hell now)* I believed, once again, I believed I might be able to do something and . . . *(Very distant, suddenly)* Mavis believed I could save her and all the faith in the world
wouldn't save her. Won't save any of us. Won't do a thing except
make fools of us. Give us tests we cannot pass. Bring us to our
knees, but not in prayer—in absolute submission to accident, to the

arbitrary assignment of unbearable pain, and the everyday occurrence of meaningless death. Only then can we believe . . . that
dreams, like deadly whirlpools, drown us in their frenzy . . . that
love blazes across a black sky like a comet but never returns . . . and
that time, like a desert wind, blows while I sleep, and erases the
path I walked to here, and erases the path that leads on.

*Sam's anger has been so raw and so violent that he now simply
stands, but we are certain he will not speak for quite a while.*

GLORY (*Without looking up*): Oh, Sam. . . . Oh, sweet baby . . . (*Now
standing up, but not looking at Sam*) I went in to see her, you know
Tuesday morning, and she'd already had her shot, so she was pretty
dopey, but she said, well, she said a lot of things. "Well," she said,
"it looks like Sam's gonna get his hands on me after all."

*She looks to Sam for a response but there is none. As Glory contin-
ues, Sam walks slowly downstage and sits on a rock and buries his
head in his hands.*

GLORY: Anyway, then she said, "Glory . . . Sam might not be able to
fix this, you know. I might not be there for him, this time, when he
needs me . . . I might not be as helpful as I have been. I'll be asleep,
see, that's my excuse. Anyway, if I don't make it . . . I want him to
know what I loved . . . why I loved him. It was only one thing he
did, really. We were ten years old, and Everett had this magic trick
and Sam knew how it worked, and he showed me how it worked.
He knew it wasn't magic, and he knew it didn't always work, and
he wasn't afraid to know. Tell him that's why I loved him. He
wasn't afraid to know." Then she said, "I've caught it from him, I
guess. I'm not afraid either."

*As Glory and Sam remain seated, spent, on the ground, the back
door opens and Stephen comes out.*

STEPHEN: Mom?
GLORY: You need to be in bed, honey.
STEPHEN: Are you going to sleep out here?
GLORY: I don't know.
STEPHEN: Want me to get you a blanket?
GLORY: No thanks, sweetie. I'm going to stand up, just . . . any minute
now.
STEPHEN: What's the matter with Dad?
GLORY: It's just late, honey. He's real tired.
STEPHEN: Why doesn't he say anything?
GLORY: He just needs to be quiet now, Stephen.
STEPHEN (*Walking toward Sam*): Dad?
GLORY: Come over here if you want to keep me warm.

Stephen comes to sit down with Glory and they hug.

STEPHEN: Maybe we should eat again.

GLORY: Anything sound good to you?

STEPHEN: No.

GLORY: Did you and Grandpa have a nice talk?

STEPHEN: He was going to teach me how to play Chinese checkers, but, well . . . he lost his marbles.

GLORY *(Laughing)*: Did you say that or did he?

1540 STEPHEN: I did. He said . . . he couldn't find them. But I thought . . . you could use a joke.

GLORY: Boy, is that the truth. I'd give you a dollar for it . . .

STEPHEN: . . . if you had a dollar.

GLORY: You got it.

STEPHEN: I'll put it on your bill.

GLORY: Done.

STEPHEN: Maybe he's asleep.

GLORY: Who?

STEPHEN: Dad.

1550 GLORY: He might be asleep. But I wouldn't say anything you don't want him to hear.

STEPHEN *(Picking up the geode)*: What's this?

GLORY: I don't know. A rock.

STEPHEN: It's round. Rocks aren't round.

GLORY: I don't know, Stephen. Ask your father.

STEPHEN: You ask him.

GLORY: You're the one who wants to know.

STEPHEN: Maybe it goes in the wall.

Stephen gets up and walks around the garden looking for a place the geode might go. At one point he gets close to Sam, but Glory motions for Stephen to go around him.

1560 STEPHEN: A rock this big ought to be heavier. *(Glory doesn't know how to answer him, so she just smiles and watches)* How did it get so round?

GLORY: I don't know, Stephen.

Everett comes out of the house and takes a couple of steps. He is very reluctant to interrupt this, whatever it is.

EVERETT: I'll say good night, I guess.

GLORY: Good night, Everett.

EVERETT: You can come inside now, if you want. I'm going to bed . . . and there's chairs in here.

GLORY: We're all right, Everett.

EVERETT: Well, then . . .

He looks at Sam, then at Glory, who shakes her head and motions for Everett not to say anything.

STEPHEN: Grandpa, do you know what this rock is?

1570 EVERETT: No, Stephen.

STEPHEN: I found it out here in the garden.

EVERETT: I found a whole drawer full of them upstairs. I brought that one out here to look at one day.

STEPHEN: But whose are they? Where did they come from?

EVERETT: They're Mary's.

STEPHEN: Who's Mary?

EVERETT: Your grandmother. Sam's mother.

GLORY: I saw those dancing pictures upstairs, Everett. If she danced as great as she looked, she was a real catch.

EVERETT *(Pleased to be invited to come talk):* She sure was. And no-   1580
body could understand why she married the preacher except she was having a better time than anybody else and she had to find some way to pay for it.

GLORY: She sounds like me.

EVERETT: If she were alive today, she'd bake you a batch of chocolate chips and eat them every one while they were still hot. Then she'd send you the wax paper she baked them on and write you a note, telling you to let her know the minute you went off your diet.

STEPHEN: And she liked these rocks?

EVERETT: Well, I don't know. I guess so. I didn't even know she had   1590
them till she died. I was looking for a list she made, who she wanted to have her piano, things like that, and I found them. I found a lot of things. I found the world she lived in, a world I knew very little about. I know she loved me, but I don't know why. She must have loved those rocks, but I don't know what they are. *(Now he looks at Sam)* I guess you can be a real big part of somebody else's world without ever understanding the first thing about it. Somebody can give you their life and you'll never know why. Never know what they wanted from you, or if they ever got it. Then when they die, well, knowing so little about these people makes it real   1600
hard to lose them. *(Pause)* I kept meaning to ask Sam about those rocks. I know she'd want him to have them.

SAM *(Finally):* It's not a rock. It's a geode.

STEPHEN *(Running down to him):* You mean with the crystals inside?

SAM: Yes.

STEPHEN: Well, let's open it up and see it? Where's the hammer?

SAM *(Sudden alarm):* No! *(Then more quietly)* Once you crack them . . . She didn't like to crack them.

STEPHEN: Then how do you know what's in there?

SAM: You don't. She said . . . it was better for it to be safe than for   1610
you to know what it was, exactly.

STEPHEN: Dad?

SAM: I'm here, Stephen. *(He sits, but still holds the geode)* I thought I could save Mavis. *(To Stephen)* I thought I could protect you. I can't do any of those things. I don't know what I *can* do. I don't know what to say. I have nothing for you.

STEPHEN *(Pointing to the geode):* I'll take that.

SAM: The geode?

STEPHEN: Yeah.

1620 SAM: It's not mine.

EVERETT: Yes it is.

SAM: It's nothing.

STEPHEN: It's okay. I like it.

SAM: I like it too. When Mother died I gathered them up and put them in that drawer. Yes, you can have it. It's . . . your mystery now.

STEPHEN *(Taking the geode):* Thanks.

There is silence all around.

STEPHEN: Dad?

SAM: Yes.

STEPHEN: Where did she go, Dad?

1630 SAM: Where did Mavis go?

STEPHEN: Yes.

And there is more silence.

SAM: I don't know, Stephen.

STEPHEN: I saw her in the coffin, but it wasn't her.

GLORY *(Gently):* It was her, Stephen.

STEPHEN: I mean, she wasn't there anymore.

SAM: No.

STEPHEN *(Carefully):* Did you see it go, Dad?

SAM: What?

STEPHEN *(Still very careful):* In the operating room? Did you cut her
1640 open and it got out?

And Sam doesn't answer for a moment. His heart is broken, his anger turned to grief and longing. Glory, Everett and Stephen are silent and perfectly still.

SAM: Yes. *(Pause)* I cut her open and it got out. I was standing there over her and . . .

STEPHEN *(Quietly):* What was it like? *(Now very slowly)* Could you feel it or see it or hear it? Was it cold or white or like air maybe or what?

And Sam stands there a moment, searching for the answer, searching for the memory, trying to see it again. Finally, he shakes his head. The words are coming, but he has no idea what they are.

SAM: It was . . . *(And suddenly, the words come from him the way "it" came from Mavis in that moment)* It was forgiveness.

Sam stands there quietly a moment, as a kind of peace seems to come over him, and then over Everett, and then Glory. Stephen, however, doesn't quite understand.

STEPHEN *(Finally):* For what, Dad?

SAM: I don't know, Stephen. For whatever I did. For all those years.

STEPHEN: Did she forgive me for losing her cat?

SAM *(Not directly to Stephen, and not quickly):* Yes, Stephen.

EVERETT *(Quietly):* I wondered what happened to that cat. Every week, on the phone, I had to say hello to that damn cat.

STEPHEN *(To Everett):* I didn't mean to lose Peaches, she just—

GLORY *(Interrupting him, to soothe him):* It's all right, Stephen. I owed Mavis money.

SAM: You? What for?

GLORY *(A bit embarrassed as the story begins):* I had my eyes done. Last March when I told you I came to see Mother, I flew to Chicago and had my eyes done. I didn't want you to know it, so I borrowed that money from Mavis.

SAM: And I never noticed it.

GLORY: No.

SAM *(Inspecting her eyes now):* Nice work. *(Then inspecting more carefully)* Great work.

GLORY: She said we had to preserve your illusions.

SAM: I like it.

GLORY: That's good. It was a lot of money.

EVERETT: It was four thousand dollars.

SAM: I didn't know Mavis had any money.

EVERETT: It was my money.

GLORY: I didn't know that.

EVERETT: I didn't know it was for you.

SAM *(To Everett):* I'll pay you back.

EVERETT: Good.

GLORY: Thank you anyway, Everett.

EVERETT *(After a moment):* I owe you an apology, Glory.

GLORY: What on earth?

EVERETT: I told Mavis your marriage wouldn't last. That your mother was stingy with her money and your looks wouldn't last forever. I told her if she'd just wait, she could have Sam all to herself.

STEPHEN: Why did you do that?

EVERETT: It was . . . an old dream of mine.

SAM: You were wrong.

EVERETT: I know.

GLORY: Well, not completely. Mother *is* cheap.

EVERETT: I'm sorry, Glory.

GLORY: It's all right, Everett. You didn't know.

SAM *(After a moment):* I'm the one who needs to apologize to you, Glory.

GLORY: It's all right, Sam.

SAM: I only wanted to leave because—

GLORY: You don't have to tell me that, Sam.

SAM: I don't know why I wanted to leave you. I can't leave you. But maybe I didn't want to hurt you like I . . . maybe I was afraid I would lose you, too.

GLORY: Sam, it's been a sad, sad day. We're all so lonely for her, we've all . . . said things.

SAM: Yeah, I know, but I said mine on purpose.

GLORY: You were mad.

SAM: That doesn't make it right. I need you. I love you.

1700 GLORY: I know, Sam. I tried to tell you that this afternoon.

SAM: I guess I wasn't listening.

GLORY *(Carefully)*: No, I didn't think you were.

SAM *(Takes his time before he begins)*: Glory, if you could . . . hold on a little longer, I want to be a better man.

GLORY: I can do that, Sam. *(He shakes his head, first out of relief, and then in confusion)* You don't understand, do you. *(He shakes his head no)* I'd explain it to you if I could, or maybe you'll explain it to me in a week or so, or maybe we'll just love each other anyway and never know.

SAM: Please . . . forgive me.

And Glory extends her arms to Sam, and they embrace. And when they break the embrace he sees his father.

1710 SAM: And Dad . . . I'm sorry, Dad.

EVERETT: I'm all right, son.

SAM: No, Dad. I want you to know that I—

EVERETT: I said it's all right, son.

SAM: I love you, Dad.

EVERETT: Yes. I know.

STEPHEN *(After a moment)*: I'm cold. Is anybody else cold? It's cold out here.

And Sam knows they are all waiting for him to speak, to say whether he is finished here.

SAM: Well, maybe . . . we could . . . go in the house. I didn't think I wanted to go in the house, but now—

1720 EVERETT: I haven't changed a thing, Sam.

SAM: Yes, well, *(Smiling at Everett and himself)* that's what I was afraid of.

Glory squeezes his hand or laughs a little at him, and Everett shakes his head, but they are still waiting for Sam to make the next move.

SAM: Dad, if it's all right with Stephen and Glory, we'd like to stay here a few days, if it isn't too much trouble.

STEPHEN: Hey! Great!

EVERETT: What do you mean! You *have* to stay here. You haven't finished cleaning up this garden. And Stephen hasn't read all my books and I know I can't eat all that food we brought home from the supper.

1730 GLORY *(Gathering up something she has brought outside)*: You can't eat all that food because Josie Barnett can't cook. I thought people in the country could cook.

EVERETT *(Now moving toward the house)*: What Josie Barnett can't do is sing. None of these girls can sing a lick. I keep praying I'll go deaf, but then . . . *(Looking to heaven, but aware that he's making a joke)* I ask Him for so much.

Stephen follows Everett's eyes to the heavens and finds the stars.

STEPHEN (*As though they were in the middle of a conversation about stars*): But Dad, what holds the stars up there? Why don't they fall?

And there is a pause, while Sam doesn't explain it.

EVERETT: Sam, what was that other verse, do you remember, that other verse of "Twinkle, Twinkle."   1740

GLORY: I didn't know there was another verse.

EVERETT: Well, maybe it wasn't a real verse, but Sam's mother sure said it all the time.

SAM: No, it was a real verse. I remember reading it. I just don't remember . . .

EVERETT (*Getting it now*):
    As your bright and tiny spark

SAM (*Remembering*): Yes, yes. (*Then repeating*)
    Guides the traveler in the dark
    Though I know not what you are
    Twinkle, twinkle little star.   1750
(*He continues to look at the stars*)

EVERETT: Right. That's it, exactly.

❏ Questions for Discussion
Act One

1. What is the symbolic significance of the setting—an overgrown garden? How does the garden illustrate the relationship between Glory, Sam, Stephen, and Everett?

2. Sam discounts magic and fairy tales. Why? Why is Stephen attracted to them? Why does Stephen talk so much about Sleeping Beauty and the thirteenth fairy? Why did Sam stop reading these stories?

3. What does Sam mean when he tells Glory "I don't want another woman. I want you to be the woman I want"? What does he want her to be?

4. Glory says of Sam, "This is not a job that just anybody could do, you know, putting up with you." Why would Sam be hard to put up with? What does Glory reveal about Sam when she says, "Stephen would end up taking care of you"?

5. Why does Stephen tell his father about losing Mavis' cat Peaches, when the loss is minimal compared to the loss of Mavis?

6. What does Sam mean when he tells his father that Mavis' funeral is "your show"? Why has he come to think of a religious ceremony as a "show"?

7. Sam says he tells Stephen "the truth." What does Sam mean by "the truth"? What different version of "the truth" does Glory

believe? Is it, as Glory says, "good for Stephen to hear both sides"?

Act Two

1. In what sense is Sam trying to protect Stephen "from the entire world," as Glory says? Precisely what is Sam protecting Stephen from?

2. Glory says, "I have been—Stephen and I have been—happy, all these years, to have what was left over when Mavis finished with you." What does she mean?

3. What did Mavis mean when she said she loved Sam because "he wasn't afraid to know"? Is Sam more or less unafraid to know by the end of the play?

❑ **Suggestions for Exploration and Writing**

1. Glory says to Sam, "Do you have any idea what it takes to live your life?" Sam says that he "can probably figure it out." Discuss how these two quotations reveal the character of both Glory and Sam.

2. Choose one of the following quotations and discuss whether you agree or disagree with it:

    "Life doesn't start over. It starts, it goes on for a while, then it stops."

    "Life is summer camp and death is lights out."

    "What we think of as life, Stephen, is just God gathering material for another book."

3. Choose one of the characters and discuss what you think is that person's quest during the first act.

4. What does Sam mean when he says of Mavis, "There was a time when she could have done something about it. This is that time for Stephen and me"? Why does Sam want a divorce?

5. Why does Sam resist loving Glory, accepting fairy tales, and believing in God? What do these actions have in common?

6. Sam says to Stephen, "God is not in control. We are. There is no heaven, there is no hell. There is this life created, in your case, by your mother and me. Life on earth, which we can make better through careful thought and hard work. But we make the progress, and we make the mistakes. Not God. . . . If you want to believe, believe in yourself. In your power, in your mind, in your life." In what ways, late in the play, is Sam forced to question this position?

7. In referring to the pioneers at Donner Pass who were forced to eat the flesh of dead companions to survive, Sam says, "They thought they were smart enough to figure it out, whatever it was, up the road." Then Sam comments, "Nobody is smart enough." In what sense(s) are these pioneers analogous to Sam?

8. As Sam shows Stephen the limits of reason in act II, to what extent is Sam himself becoming aware of reason's limits? What change in himself does Sam reveal by his referring to the geode as Stephen's "mystery" and by his singing the second verse of "Twinkle, twinkle little star"?

9. Sam says to his father that he has "finally arrived," that he is "free of faith," and that his whole life has been an effort to attain such freedom. In what sense has Sam's whole life been an effort to free himself from faith? In what ways has his effort to free himself restricted him?

10. Everett says, "I guess you can be a real big part of somebody else's world without ever understanding the first thing about it." How does this statement apply to the various characters in the play?

CASEBOOK

on Flannery O'Connor

FLANNERY O'CONNOR (1925–1964)

*Flannery O'Connor was a devout Catholic who, in the short time that she lived, wrote two novels and many short stores which vividly portray the incompleteness of human beings without religion. Except for her graduate study at the University of Iowa, O'Connor spent most of her life in Milledgeville, Georgia, where she observed the people and the land which would become the basis for most of her works. Because her characters are far from ordinary and because their fates are often disastrous, O'Connor is frequently described as a Southern **Gothic** writer. Her characters range from unbelievers to women like the grandmother in "A Good Man Is Hard to Find" and Mrs. Turpin in "Revelation," who, in spite of their superficiality and self-centeredness, believe themselves to be good Christians. O'Connor's stories tell of events which cause arrogant and imperceptive people to see more clearly into reality and to begin their quest for truth.*

A Good Man Is Hard to Find

1   The grandmother didn't want to go to Florida. She wanted to visit some of her connections in east Tennessee and she was seizing at every chance to change Bailey's mind. Bailey was the son she lived with, her only boy. He was sitting on the edge of his chair at the table, bent over the orange sports section of the *Journal*. "Now look here, Bailey," she said, "see here, read this," and she stood with one hand on her thin hip and the other rattling the newspaper at his bald head. "Here this fellow that calls himself The Misfit is aloose from the Federal Pen and headed toward Florida and you read here what it says he did to these people. Just you read it. I wouldn't take my children in any direction with a criminal like that aloose in it. I couldn't answer to my conscience if I did."

2   Bailey didn't look up from his reading so she wheeled around then and faced the children's mother, a young woman in slacks, whose face was as broad and innocent as a cabbage and was tied around with a green head-kerchief that had two points on the top like rabbit's ears. She was sitting on the sofa, feeding the baby his apricots out of a jar. "The children have been to Florida before," the old lady said. "You all ought to take them somewhere else for a change so they would see different parts of the world and be broad. They never have been to east Tennessee."

3   The children's mother didn't seem to hear her but the eight-year-old boy, John Wesley, a stocky child with glasses, said, "If you don't want to

go to Florida, why dontcha stay at home?" He and the little girl, June Star, were reading the funny papers on the floor.

"She wouldn't stay at home to be queen for a day," June Star said   4
without raising her yellow head.

"Yes and what would you do if this fellow, The Misfit, caught you?"   5
the grandmother said.

"I'd smack his face," John Wesley said.   6

"She wouldn't stay at home for a million bucks," June Star said.   7
"Afraid she'd miss something. She has to go everywhere we go."

"All right, Miss," the grandmother said. "Just remember that the next   8
time you want me to curl your hair."

June Star said her hair was naturally curly.   9

The next morning the grandmother was the first one in the car, ready to   10
go. She had her big black valise that looked like the head of a hippopot-
amus in one corner, and underneath it she was hiding a basket with Pitty
Sing, the cat, in it. She didn't intend for the cat to be left alone in the house
for three days because he would miss her too much and she was afraid he
might brush against one of the gas burners and accidentally asphyxiate
himself. Her son, Bailey, didn't like to arrive at a motel with a cat.

She sat in the middle of the back seat with John Wesley and June Star   11
on either side of her. Bailey and the children's mother and the baby sat
in front and they left Atlanta at eight forty-five with the mileage on the
car at 55890. The grandmother wrote this down because she thought it
would be interesting to say how many miles they had been when they got
back. It took them twenty minutes to reach the outskirts of the city.

The old lady settled herself comfortably, removing her white cotton   12
gloves and putting them up with her purse on the shelf in front of the
back window. The children's mother still had on slacks and still had her
hair tied up in a green kerchief, but the grandmother had on a navy blue
straw sailor hat with a bunch of white violets on the brim and a navy blue
dress with a small white dot in the print. Her collars and cuffs were white
organdy trimmed with lace and at her neckline she had pinned a purple
spray of cloth violets containing a sachet. In case of an accident, anyone
seeing her dead on the highway would know at once that she was a lady.

She said she thought it was going to be a good day for driving, neither   13
too hot nor too cold, and she cautioned Bailey that the speed limit was
fifty-five miles an hour and that the patrolmen hid themselves behind
billboards and small clumps of trees and sped out after you before you
had a chance to slow down. She pointed out interesting details of the
scenery: Stone Mountain; the blue granite that in some places came up to
both sides of the highway; the brilliant red clay banks slightly streaked
with purple; and the various crops that made rows of green lacework on
the ground. The trees were full of silver-white sunlight and the meanest
of them sparkled. The children were reading comic magazines and their
mother had gone back to sleep.

"Let's go through Georgia fast so we won't have to look at it much,"   14
John Wesley said.

15 "If I were a little boy," said the grandmother, "I wouldn't talk about my native state that way. Tennessee has the mountains and Georgia has the hills."

16 "Tennessee is just a hillbilly dumping ground," John Wesley said, "and Georgia is a lousy state too."

17 "You said it," June Star said.

18 "In my time," said the grandmother, folding her thin veined fingers, "children were more respectful of their native states and their parents and everything else. People did right then. Oh look at the cute little pick-aninny!" she said and pointed to a Negro child standing in the door of a shack. "Wouldn't that make a picture, now?" she asked and they all turned and looked at the little Negro out of the back window. He waved.

19 "He didn't have any britches on," June Star said.

20 "He probably didn't have any," the grandmother explained. "Little niggers in the country don't have things like we do. If I could paint, I'd paint that picture," she said.

21 The children exchanged comic books.

22 The grandmother offered to hold the baby and the children's mother passed him over the front seat to her. She set him on her knee and bounced him and told him about the things they were passing. She rolled her eyes and screwed up her mouth and stuck her leathery thin face into his smooth bland one. Occasionally he gave her a faraway smile. They passed a large cotton field with five or six graves fenced in the middle of it, like a small island. "Look at the graveyard!" the grandmother said, pointing it out. "That was the old family burying ground. That belonged to the plantation."

23 "Where's the plantation?" John Wesley asked.

24 "Gone With the Wind," said the grandmother. "Ha. Ha."

25 When the children finished all the comic books they had brought, they opened the lunch and ate it. The grandmother ate a peanut butter sandwich and an olive and would not let the children throw the box and the paper napkins out the window. When there was nothing else to do they played a game by choosing a cloud and making the other two guess what shape it suggested. John Wesley took one the shape of a cow and June Star guessed a cow and John Wesley said, no, an automobile, and June Star said he didn't play fair, and they began to slap each other over the grandmother.

26 The grandmother said she would tell them a story if they would keep quiet. When she told a story, she rolled her eyes and waved her head and was very dramatic. She said once when she was a maiden lady she had been courted by a Mr. Edgar Atkins Teagarden from Jasper, Georgia. She said he was a very good-looking man and a gentleman and that he brought her a watermelon every Saturday afternoon with his initials cut in it, E. A. T. Well, one Saturday, she said, Mr. Teagarden brought the watermelon and there was nobody at home and he left it on the front porch and returned in his buggy to Jasper, but she never got the water-melon, she said, because a nigger boy ate it when he saw the initials,

E. A. T.! This story tickled John Wesley's funny bone and he giggled and giggled but June Star didn't think it was any good. She said she wouldn't marry a man that just brought her a watermelon on Saturday. The grandmother said she would have done well to marry Mr. Teagarden because he was a gentlemen and had bought Coca-Cola stock when it first came out and that he had died only a few years ago, a very wealthy man.

They stopped at The Tower for barbecued sandwiches. The Tower was   27
a part stucco and part wood filling station and dance hall set in a clearing outside of Timothy. A fat man named Red Sammy Butts ran it and there were signs stuck here and there on the building and for miles up and down the highway saying, TRY RED SAMMY'S FAMOUS BARBECUE. NONE LIKE FAMOUS RED SAMMY'S! RED SAM! THE FAT BOY WITH THE HAPPY LAUGH. A VETERAN! RED SAMMY'S YOUR MAN!

Red Sammy was lying on the bare ground outside The Tower with his   28
head under a truck while a gray monkey about a foot high, chained to a small chinaberry tree, chattered nearby. The monkey sprang back into the tree and got on the highest limb as soon as he saw the children jump out of the car and run toward him.

Inside, The Tower was a long dark room with a counter at one end and   29
tables at the other and dancing space in the middle. They all sat down at a board table next to the nickelodeon and Red Sam's wife, a tall burnt-brown woman with hair and eyes lighter than her skin, came and took their order. The children's mother put a dime in the machine and played "The Tennessee Waltz," and the grandmother said that tune always made her want to dance. She asked Bailey if he would like to dance but he only glared at her. He didn't have a naturally sunny disposition like she did and trips made him nervous. The grandmother's brown eyes were very bright. She swayed her head from side to side and pretended she was dancing in her chair. June Star said play something she could tap to so the children's mother put in another dime and played a fast number and June Star stepped out onto the dance floor and did her tap routine.

"Ain't she cute?" Red Sam's wife said, leaning over the counter.   30
"Would you like to come be my little girl?"

"No I certainly wouldn't," June Star said. "I wouldn't live in a broken-   31
down place like this for a million bucks!" and she ran back to the table.

"Ain't she cute?" the woman repeated, stretching her mouth politely.   32

"Arn't you ashamed?" hissed the grandmother.   33

Red Sam came in and told his wife to quit lounging on the counter and   34
hurry up with these people's order. His khaki trousers reached just to his hip bones and his stomach hung over them like a sack of meal swaying under his shirt. He came over and sat down at a table nearby and let out a combination sigh and yodel. "You can't win," he said. "You can't win," and he wiped his sweating red face off with a gray handkerchief. "These days you don't know who to trust," he said. "Ain't that the truth?"

35 "People are certainly not nice like they used to be," said the grand-mother.

36 "Two fellers come in here last week," Red Sammy said, "driving a Chrysler. It was a old beat-up car but it was a good one and these boys looked all right to me. Said they worked at the mill and you know I let them fellers charge the gas they bought? Now why did I do that?"

37 "Because you're a good man!" the grandmother said at once.

38 "Yes'm, I suppose so," Red Sam said as if he were struck with this answer.

39 His wife brought the orders, carrying the five plates all at once without a tray, two in each hand and one balanced on her arm. "It isn't a soul in this green world of God's that you can trust," she said. "And I don't count nobody out of that, not nobody," she repeated, looking at Red Sammy.

40 "Did you read about that criminal, The Misfit, that's escaped?" asked the grandmother.

41 "I wouldn't be a bit surprised if he didn't attack this place right here," said the woman. "If he hears about it being here, I wouldn't be none surprised to see him. If he hears it's two cent in the cash register, I wouldn't be a tall surprised if he . . ."

42 "That'll do," Red Sam said. "Go bring these people their Co'-Colas," and the woman went off to get the rest of the order.

43 "A good man is hard to find," Red Sammy said. "Everything is getting terrible. I remember the day you could go off and leave your screen door unlatched. Not no more."

44 He and the grandmother discussed better times. The old lady said that in her opinion Europe was entirely to blame for the way things were now. She said the way Europe acted you would think we were made of money and Red Sam said it was no use talking about it, she was exactly right. The children ran outside into the white sunlight and looked at the monkey in the lacy chinaberry tree. He was busy catching fleas on himself and biting each one carefully between his teeth as if it were a delicacy.

45 They drove off again into the hot afternoon. The grandmother took cat naps and woke up every five minutes with her own snoring. Outside of Toombsboro she woke up and recalled an old plantation that she had visited in this neighborhood once when she was a young lady. She said the house had six white columns across the front and that there was an avenue of oaks leading up to it and two little wooden trellis arbors on either side in front where you sat down with your suitor after a stroll in the garden. She recalled exactly which road to turn off to get to it. She knew that Bailey would not be willing to lose any time looking at an old house, but the more she talked about it, the more she wanted to see it once again and find out if the little twin arbors were still standing. "There was a secret panel in this house," she said craftily, not telling the truth but wishing that she were, "and the story went that all the family silver was hidden in it when Sherman came through but it was never found . . ."

"Hey!" John Wesley said. "Let's go see it! We'll find it! We'll poke all the woodwork and find it! Who lives there? Where do you turn off at? Hey, Pop, can't we turn off there?" 46

"We never have seen a house with a secret panel!" June Star shrieked. "Let's go to the house with the secret panel! Hey Pop, can't we go see the house with the secret panel!" 47

"It's not far from here, I know," the grandmother said. "It wouldn't take over twenty minutes." 48

Bailey was looking straight ahead. His jaw was as rigid as a horseshoe. "No," he said. 49

The children began to yell and scream that they wanted to see the house with the secret panel. John Wesley kicked the back of the front seat and June Star hung over her mother's shoulder and whined desperately into her ear that they never had any fun even on their vacation, that they could never do what THEY wanted to do. The baby began to scream and John Wesley kicked the back of the seat so hard that his father could feel the blows in his kidney. 50

"All right!" he shouted and drew the car to a stop at the side of the road. "Will you all shut up? Will you all just shut up for one second? If you don't shut up, we won't go anywhere." 51

"It would be very educational for them," the grandmother murmured. 52

"All right," Bailey said, "but get this: this is the only time we're going to stop for anything like this. This is the one and only time." 53

"The dirt road that you have to turn down is about a mile back," the grandmother directed. "I marked it when we passed." 54

"A dirt road," Bailey groaned. 55

After they had turned around and were headed toward the dirt road, the grandmother recalled other points about the house, the beautiful glass over the front doorway and the candle-lamp in the hall. John Wesley said that the secret panel was probably in the fireplace. 56

"You can't go inside this house," Bailey said. "You don't know who lives there." 57

"While you all talk to the people in front, I'll run around behind and get in a window," John Wesley suggested. 58

"We'll all stay in the car," his mother said. 59

They turned onto the dirt road and the car raced roughly along in a swirl of pink dust. The grandmother recalled the times when there were no paved roads and thirty miles was a day's journey. The dirt road was hilly and there were sudden washes in it and sharp curves on dangerous embankments. All at once they would be on a hill, looking down over the blue tops of trees for miles around, then the next minute, they would be in a red depression with the dust-coated trees looking down on them. 60

"This place had better turn up in a minute," Bailey said, "or I'm going to turn around." 61

The road looked as if no one had traveled on it for months. 62

"It's not much farther," the grandmother said and just as she said it, 63 a horrible thought came to her. The thought was so embarrassing that she turned red in the face and her eyes dilated and her feet jumped up, upsetting her valise in the corner. The instant the valise moved, the newspaper top she had over the basket under it rose with a snarl and Pitty Sing, the cat, sprang onto Bailey's shoulder.

64   The children were thrown to the floor and their mother, clutching the baby, was thrown out the door onto the ground; the old lady was thrown into the front seat. The car turned over once and landed right-side-up in a gulch off the side of the road. Bailey remained in the driver's seat with the cat—gray-striped with a broad white face and an orange nose— clinging to his neck like a caterpillar.

65   As soon as the children saw they could move their arms and legs, they scrambled out of the car, shouting, "We've had an ACCIDENT!" The grandmother was curled up under the dashboard, hoping she was injured so that Bailey's wrath would not come down on her all at once. The horrible thought she had had before the accident was that the house she had remembered so vividly was not in Georgia but in Tennessee.

66   Bailey removed the cat from his neck with both hands and flung it out the window against the side of a pine tree. Then he got out of the car and started looking for the children's mother. She was sitting against the side of the red gutted ditch, holding the screaming baby, but she only had a cut down her face and a broken shoulder. "We've had an ACCIDENT!" the children screamed in a frenzy of delight.

67   "But nobody's killed," June Star said with disappointment as the grandmother limped out of the car, her hat still pinned to her head but the broken front brim standing up at a jaunty angle and the violet spray hanging off the side. They all sat down in the ditch, except the children, to recover from the shock. They were all shaking.

68   "Maybe a car will come along," said the children's mother hoarsely.

69   "I believe I have injured an organ," said the grandmother, pressing her side, but no one answered her. Bailey's teeth were clattering. He had on a yellow sport shirt with bright blue parrots designed in it and his face was as yellow as the shirt. The grandmother decided that she would not mention that the house was in Tennessee.

70   The road was about ten feet above and they could see only the tops of the trees on the other side of it. Behind the ditch they were sitting in there were more woods, tall and dark and deep. In a few minutes they saw a car some distance away on top of a hill, coming slowly as if the occupants were watching them. The grandmother stood up and waved both her arms dramatically to attract their attention. The car continued to come on slowly, disappeared around a bend and appeared again, moving even slower, on top of the hill they had gone over. It was a big black battered hearse-like automobile. There were three men in it.

71   It came to a stop just over them and for some minutes, the driver looked down with a steady expressionless gaze to where they were sitting, and didn't speak. Then he turned his head and muttered something to the other two and they got out. One was a fat boy in black

trousers and a red sweat shirt with a silver stallion embossed on the front of it. He moved around on the right side of them and stood staring, his mouth partly open in a kind of loose grin. The other had on khaki pants and a blue striped coat and a gray hat pulled down very low, hiding most of his face. He came around slowly on the left side. Neither spoke.

The driver got out of the car and stood by the side of it, looking down 72 at them. He was an older man than the other two. His hair was just beginning to gray and he wore silver-rimmed spectacles that gave him a scholarly look. He had a long creased face and didn't have on any shirt or undershirt. He had on blue jeans that were too tight for him and was holding a black hat and a gun. The two boys also had guns.

"We've had an ACCIDENT!" the children screamed. 73

The grandmother had the peculiar feeling that the bespectacled man 74 was someone she knew. His face was as familiar to her as if she had known him all her life but she could not recall who he was. He moved away from the car and began to come down the embankment, placing his feet carefully so that he wouldn't slip. He had on tan and white shoes and no socks, and his ankles were red and thin. "Good afternoon," he said. "I see you all had you a little spill."

"We turned over twice!" said the grandmother. 75

"Oncet," he corrected. "We seen it happen. Try their car and see will 76 it run, Hiram," he said quietly to the boy with the gray hat.

"What you got that gun for?" John Wesley asked. "Whatcha gonna do 77 with that gun?"

"Lady," the man said to the children's mother, "would you mind 78 calling them children to sit down by you? Children make me nervous. I want all you all to sit down right together there where you're at."

"What are you telling US what to do for?" June Star asked. 79

Behind them the line of woods gaped like a dark open mouth. "Come 80 here," said their mother.

"Look here now," Bailey began suddenly, "we're in a predicament! 81 We're in . . ."

The grandmother shrieked. She scrambled to her feet and stood star- 82 ing. "You're The Misfit!" she said. "I recognized you at once!"

"Yes'm," the man said, smiling slightly as if he were pleased in spite of 83 himself to be known, "but it would have been better for all of you, lady, if you hadn't of reckernized me."

Bailey turned his head sharply and said something to his mother that 84 shocked even the children. The old lady began to cry and The Misfit reddened.

"Lady," he said, "don't you get upset. Sometimes a man says things he 85 don't mean. I don't reckon he meant to talk to you thataway."

"You wouldn't shoot a lady, would you?" the grandmother said and 86 removed a clean handkerchief from her cuff and began to slap at her eyes with it.

The Misfit pointed the toe of his shoe into the ground and made a little 87 hole and then covered it up again. "I would hate to have to," he said.

88   "Listen," the grandmother almost screamed, "I know you're a good man. You don't look a bit like you have common blood. I know you must come from nice people!"

89   "Yes ma'am," he said, "finest people in the world." When he smiled he showed a row of strong white teeth. "God never made a finer woman than my mother and my daddy's heart was pure gold," he said. The boy with the red sweat shirt had come around behind them and was standing with his gun at his hip. The Misfit squatted down on the ground. "Watch them children, Bobby Lee," he said. "You know they make me nervous." He looked at the six of them huddled together in front of him and he seemed to be embarrassed as if he couldn't think of anything to say. "Ain't a cloud in the sky," he remarked, looking up at it. "Don't see no sun but don't see no cloud neither."

90   "Yes, it's a beautiful day," said the grandmother. "Listen," she said, "you shouldn't call yourself The Misfit because I know you're a good man at heart. I can just look at you and tell."

91   "Hush!" Bailey yelled. "Hush! Everybody shut up and let me handle this!" He was squatting in the position of a runner about to sprint forward but he didn't move.

92   "I pre-chate that, lady," the Misfit said and drew a little circle in the ground with the butt of his gun.

93   "It'll take a half a hour to fix this here car," Hiram called, looking over the raised hood of it.

94   "Well, first you and Bobby Lee get him and that little boy to step over yonder with you," The Misfit said, pointing to Bailey and John Wesley. "The boys want to ast you something," he said to Bailey. "Would you mind stepping back in them woods there with them?"

95   "Listen," Bailey began, "we're in a terrible predicament! Nobody realizes what this is," and his voice cracked. His eyes were as blue and intense as the parrots in his shirt and he remained perfectly still.

96   The grandmother reached up to adjust her hat brim as if she were going to the woods with him but it came off in her hand. She stood staring at it and after a second she let if fall on the ground. Hiram pulled Bailey up by the arm as if he were assisting an old man. John Wesley caught hold of his father's hand and Bobby Lee followed. They went off toward the woods and just as they reached the dark edge, Bailey turned and supporting himself against a gray naked pine trunk, he shouted, "I'll be back in a minute, Mamma, wait on me!"

97   "Come back this instant!" his mother shrilled but they all disappeared into the woods.

98   "Bailey Boy!" the grandmother called in a tragic voice but she found she was looking at The Misfit squatting on the ground in front of her. "I just know you're a good man," she said desperately. "You're not a bit common!"

99   "Nome, I ain't a good man," The Misfit said after a second as if he had considered her statement carefully, "but I ain't the worst in the world

neither. My daddy said I was a different breed of dog from my brothers and sisters. 'You know,' Daddy said, 'it's some that can live their whole life out without asking about it and it's others has to know why it is, and this boy is one of the latters. He's going to be into everything!' " He put on his black hat and looked up suddenly and then away deep into the woods as if he were embarrassed again. "I'm sorry I don't have on a shirt before you ladies," he said, hunching his shoulders slightly. "We buried our clothes that we had on when we escaped and we're just making do until we can get better. We borrowed these from some folks we met," he explained.

"That's perfectly all right," the grandmother said. "Maybe Bailey has an extra shirt in his suitcase." 100

"I'll look and see terrectly," The Misfit said. 101

"Where are they taking him?" the children's mother screamed. 102

"Daddy was a card himself," The Misfit said. "You couldn't put anything over on him. He never got in trouble with the Authorities though. Just had the knack of handling them." 103

"You could be honest too if you'd only try," said the grandmother. "Think how wonderful it would be to settle down and live a comfortable life and not have to think about somebody chasing you all the time." 104

The Misfit kept scratching in the ground with the butt of his gun as if he were thinking about it. "Yes'm, somebody is always after you," he murmured. 105

The grandmother noticed how thin his shoulder blades were just behind his hat because she was standing up looking down on him. "Do you ever pray?" she asked. 106

He shook his head. All she saw was the black hat wiggle between his shoulder blades. "Nome," he said. 107

There was pistol shot from the woods, followed closely by another. Then silence. The old lady's head jerked around. She could hear the wind move through the tree tops like a long satisfied insuck of breath. "Bailey Boy!" she called. 108

"I was a gospel singer for a while," The Misfit said. "I been most everything. Been in the arm service, both land and sea, at home and abroad, been twict married, been an undertaker, been with the railroads, plowed Mother Earth, been in a tornado, seen a man burnt alive oncet," and he looked up at the children's mother and the little girl who were sitting close together, their faces white and their eyes glassy; "I even seen a woman flogged," he said. 109

"Pray, pray," the grandmother began, "pray, pray . . ." 110

"I never was a bad boy that I remember of," The Misfit said in an almost dreamy voice, "But somewheres along the line I done something wrong and got sent to the penitentiary. I was buried alive," and he looked up and held her attention to him by a steady stare. 111

"That's when you should have started to pray," she said. "What did you do to get sent up to the penitentiary that first time?" 112

113 "Turn to the right, it was a wall," The Misfit said, looking up again at the cloudless sky. "Turn to the left, it was a wall. Look up it was a ceiling, look down it was a floor. I forget what I done, lady. I set there and set there, trying to remember what it was I done and I ain't recalled it to this day. Oncet in a while, I would think it was coming to me, but it never come."

114 "Maybe they put you in by mistake," the old lady said vaguely.

115 "Nome," he said. "It wasn't no mistake. They had the papers on me."

116 "You must have stolen something," she said.

117 The Misfit sneered slightly. "Nobody had nothing I wanted," he said. "It was a head-doctor at the penitentiary said what I had done was kill my daddy but I known that for a lie. My daddy died in nineteen ought nineteen of the epidemic flu and I never had a thing to do with it. He was buried in the Mount Hopewell Baptist churchyard and you can go there and see for yourself."

118 "If you would pray," the old lady said, "Jesus would help you."

119 "That's right," The Misfit said.

120 "Well then, why don't you pray?" she asked trembling with delight suddenly.

121 "I don't want no hep," he said. "I'm doing all right by myself."

122 Bobby Lee and Hiram came ambling back from the woods. Bobby Lee was dragging a yellow shirt with bright blue parrots in it.

123 "Thow me that shirt, Bobby Lee," The Misfit said. The shirt came flying at him and landed on his shoulder and he put it on. The grandmother couldn't name what the shirt reminded her of. "No, lady," The Misfit said while he was buttoning it up, "I found out the crime don't matter. You can do one thing or you can do another, kill a man or take a tire off his car, because sooner or later you're going to forget what it was you done and just be punished for it."

124 The children's mother had begun to make heaving noises as if she couldn't get her breath. "Lady," he asked, "would you and that little girl like to step off yonder with Bobby Lee and Hiram and join your husband?"

125 "Yes, thank you," the mother said faintly. Her left arm dangled helplessly and she was holding the baby, who had gone to sleep, in the other. "Hep that lady up, Hiram," The Misfit said as she struggled to climb out of the ditch, "and Bobby Lee, you hold onto that little girl's hand."

126 "I don't want to hold hands with him," June Star said. "He reminds me of a pig."

127 The fat boy blushed and laughed and caught her by the arm and pulled her off into the woods after Hiram and her mother.

128 Alone with The Misfit, the grandmother found that she had lost her voice. There was not a cloud in the sky nor any sun. There was nothing around her but woods. She wanted to tell him that he must pray. She opened and closed her mouth several times before anything came out.

Finally she found herself saying, "Jesus. Jesus," meaning, Jesus will help you, but the way she was saying it, it sounded as if she might be cursing.

"Yes'm," The Misfit said as if he agreed. "Jesus thown everything off 129 balance. It was the same case with Him as with me except He hadn't committed any crime and they could prove I had committed one because they had the papers on me. Of course," he said, "they never shown me my papers. That's why I sign myself now. I said long ago, you get you a signature and sign everything you do and keep a copy of it. Then you'll know what you done and you can hold up the crime to the punishment and see do they match and in the end you'll have something to prove you ain't been treated right. I call myself The Misfit," he said, "because I can't make what all I done wrong fit what all I gone through in punishment."

There was a piercing scream from the woods, followed closely by a 130 pistol report. "Does it seem right to you, lady, that one is punished a heap and another ain't punished at all?"

"Jesus!" the old lady cried. "You've got good blood! I know you 131 wouldn't shoot a lady! I know you come from nice people! Pray! Jesus, you ought not to shoot a lady. I'll give you all the money I've got!"

"Lady," The Misfit said, looking beyond her far into the woods, "there 132 never was a body that give the undertaker a tip."

There were two more pistol reports and the grandmother raised her 133 head like a parched old turkey hen crying for water and called "Bailey Boy, Bailey Boy!" as if her heart would break.

"Jesus was the only One that ever raised the dead," The Misfit con- 134 tinued, "and He shouldn't have done it. He thown everything off balance. If He did what He said, then it's nothing for you to do but thow away everything and follow Him, and if He didn't, then it's nothing for you to do but enjoy the few minutes you got left the best way you can—by killing somebody or burning down his house or doing some other meanness to him. No pleasure but meanness," he said and his voice had become almost a snarl.

"Maybe He didn't raise the dead," the old lady mumbled, not knowing 135 what she was saying and feeling so dizzy that she sank down in the ditch with her legs twisted under her.

"I wasn't there so I can't say He didn't," The Misfit said. "I wisht I had 136 of been there," he said, hitting the ground with his fist. "It ain't right I wasn't there because if I had of been there I would of known. Listen lady," he said in a high voice, "if I had of been there I would of known and I wouldn't be like I am now." His voice seemed about to crack and the grandmother's head cleared for an instant. She saw the man's face twisted close to her own as if he were going to cry and she murmured, "Why you're one of my babies. You're one of my own children!" she reached out and touched him on the shoulder. The Misfit sprang back as if a snake had bitten him and shot her three times through the chest. Then he put his gun down on the ground and took off his glasses and began to clean them.

137   Hiram and Bobby Lee returned from the woods and stood over the ditch, looking down at the grandmother who half sat and half lay in a puddle of blood with her legs crossed under her like a child's and her face smiling up at the cloudless sky.

138   Without his glasses, The Misfit's eyes were red-rimmed and pale and defenseless-looking. "Take her off and thow her where you thown the others," he said picking up the cat that was rubbing itself against his leg.

139   "She was a talker, wasn't she?" Bobby Lee said, sliding down the ditch with a yodel.

140   "She would of been a good woman," The Misfit said, "if it had been somebody there to shoot her every minute of her life."

141   "Some fun!" Bobby Lee said.

142   "Shut up, Bobby Lee," The Misfit said. "It's no real pleasure in life."

❏ Questions for Discussion

1. How is the end of the story **foreshadowed** in the events that precede it?

2. What is the purpose of the incident at Red Sammy's? What do this incident and the story about Mr. Teagarden reveal about the grandmother?

3. Why does the grandmother tell Red Sammy and the Misfit that they are good men? Does she believe what she says? On what does the grandmother base her moral judgments of people? What does she mean when she says that the Misfit is "'not a bit common'"?

4. Discuss the **symbolism** of the hearse, the woods, and the sky without a sun.

5. Why does the Misfit call himself by that name? What does he resent about Jesus? He says, "'If He did what He said, then it's nothing for you to do but thow away everything and follow Him. . . .'" Does the Misfit's assessment of Christianity here accord with Jesus' gospel?

6. Why does the grandmother say to the Misfit, " 'Why you're one of my babies. You're one of my own children' "? Why does he kill her when she touches him?

7. Explain the Misfit's statement that the grandmother "'would of been a good woman . . . if it had been somebody there to shoot her every minute of her life.'" Do you agree with him?

8. If you knew nothing about his past and had not read the end of the story, how would you judge the Misfit upon meeting him? Does he seem a bloodthirsty killer? How does his treatment of the family compare to the family's treatment of each other? How do you explain the Misfit's murderousness?

Revelation

The doctor's waiting room, which was very small, was almost full   1
when the Turpins entered and Mrs. Turpin, who was very large, made it
look even smaller by her presence. She stood looming at the head of the
magazine table set in the center of it, a living demonstration that the
room was inadequate and ridiculous. Her little bright black eyes took in
all the patients as she sized up the seating situation. There was one vacant
chair and a place on the sofa occupied by a blond child in a dirty blue
romper who should have been told to move over and make room for the
lady. He was five or six, but Mrs. Turpin saw at once that no one was
going to tell him to move over. He was slumped down in the seat, his
arms idle at his sides and his eyes idle in his head; his nose ran unchecked.

Mrs. Turpin put a firm hand on Claud's shoulder and said in a voice   2
that included everyone that wanted to listen, "Claud, you sit in that chair
there," and gave him a push down into the vacant one. Claud was florid
and bald and sturdy, somewhat shorter than Mrs. Turpin, but he sat
down as if he were accustomed to doing what she told him to.

Mrs. Turpin remained standing. The only man in the room besides   3
Claud was a lean stringy old fellow with a rusty hand spread out on each
knee, whose eyes were closed as if he were asleep or dead or pretending
to be so as not to get up and offer her his seat. Her gaze settled agreeably
on a well-dressed gray-haired lady whose eyes met hers and whose
expression said: If that child belonged to me, he would have some
manners and move over—there's plenty of room there for you and him
too.

Claud looked up with a sigh and made as if to rise.   4

"Sit down," Mrs. Turpin said. "You know you're not supposed to   5
stand on that leg. He has an ulcer on his leg," she explained.

Claud lifted his foot onto the magazine table and rolled his trouser leg   6
up to reveal a purple swelling on a plump marble-white calf.

"My!" the pleasant lady said. "How did you do that?"   7

"A cow kicked him," Mrs. Turpin said.   8

"Goodness!" said the lady.   9

Claud rolled his trouser leg down.   10

"Maybe the little boy would move over," the lady suggested, but the   11
child did not stir.

"Somebody will be leaving in a minute," Mrs. Turpin said. She could   12
not understand why a doctor—with as much money as they made
charging five dollars a day just to stick their head in the hospital door and
look at you—couldn't afford a decent-sized waiting room. This one was
hardly bigger than a garage. The table was cluttered with limp-looking
magazines and at one end of it there was a big green glass ash tray full of
cigaret butts and cotton wads with little blood spots on them. If she had
had anything to do with the running of the place, that would have been
emptied every so often. There were no chairs against the wall at the head
of the room. It had a rectangular-shaped panel in it that permitted a view

of the office where the nurse came and went and the secretary listened to the radio. A plastic fern in a gold pot sat in the opening and trailed its fronds down almost to the floor. The radio was softly playing gospel music.

13   Just then the inner door opened and a nurse with the highest stack of yellow hair Mrs. Turpin had ever seen put her face in the crack and called for the next patient. The woman sitting beside Claud grasped the two arms of her chair and hoisted herself up; she pulled her dress free from her legs and lumbered through the door where the nurse had disappeared.

14   Mrs. Turpin eased into the vacant chair, which held her tight as a corset. "I wish I could reduce," she said, and rolled her eyes and gave a comic sigh.

15   "Oh, *you* aren't fat," the stylish lady said.

16   "Ooooo I am too," Mrs. Turpin said. "Claud he eats all he wants to and never weighs over one hundred and seventy-five pounds, but me I just look at something good to eat and I gain some weight," and her stomach and shoulders shook with laughter. "You can eat all you want to, can't you, Claud?" she asked turning to him.

17   Claud only grinned.

18   "Well, as long as you have such a good disposition," the stylish lady said, "I don't think it makes a bit of difference what size you are. You just can't beat a good disposition."

19   Next to her was a fat girl of eighteen or nineteen, scowling into a thick blue book which Mrs. Turpin saw was entitled *Human Development*. The girl raised her head and directed her scowl at Mrs. Turpin as if she did not like her looks. She appeared annoyed that anyone should speak while she tried to read. The poor girl's face was blue with acne and Mrs. Turpin thought how pitiful it was to have a face like that at that age. She gave the girl a friendly smile but the girl only scowled the harder. Mrs. Turpin herself was fat but she always had good skin, and, though she was forty-seven years old, there was not a wrinkle in her face except around her eyes from laughing too much.

20   Next to the ugly girl was the child, still in exactly the same position, and next to him was a thin leathery old woman in a cotton print dress. She and Claud had three sacks of chicken feed in their pump house that was in the same print. She had seen from the first that the child belonged with the old woman. She could tell by the way they sat—kind of vacant and white-trashy, as if they would sit there until Doomsday if nobody called and told them to get up. And at right angles but next to the well-dressed pleasant lady was a lank-faced woman who was certainly the child's mother. She had on a yellow sweat shirt and wine-colored slacks, both gritty-looking, and the rims of her lips were stained with snuff. Her dirty yellow hair was tied behind with a little piece of red paper ribbon. Worse than niggers any day, Mrs. Turpin thought.

21   The gospel hymn playing was, "When I looked up and He looked

down," and Mrs. Turpin, who knew it, supplied the last line mentally, "And wona these days I know I'll we-eara crown."

Without appearing to, Mrs. Turpin always noticed people's feet. The 22 well-dressed lady had on red and grey suede shoes to match her dress. Mrs. Turpin had on her good black patent leather pumps. The ugly girl had on Girl Scout shoes and heavy socks. The old woman had on tennis shoes and the white-trashy mother had on what appeared to be bedroom slippers, black straw with gold braid threaded through them—exactly what you would have expected her to have on.

Sometimes at night when she couldn't go to sleep, Mrs. Turpin would 23 occupy herself with the question of who she would have chosen to be if she couldn't have been herself. If Jesus had said to her before he made her, "There's only two places available for you. You can either be a nigger or white-trash," what would she have said? "Please, Jesus, please," she would have said, "just let me wait until there's another place available," and he would have said, "No, you have to go right now and I have only those two places so make up your mind." She would have wiggled and squirmed and begged and pleaded but it would have been no use and finally she would have said, "All right, make me a nigger then—but that don't mean a trashy one." And he would have made her a neat clean respectable Negro woman, herself but black.

Next to the child's mother was a red-headed youngish woman, reading 24 one of the magazines and working a piece of chewing gum, hell for leather, as Claud would say. Mrs. Turpin could not see the woman's feet. She was not white-trash, just common. Sometimes Mrs. Turpin occupied herself at night naming the classes of people. On the bottom of the heap were most colored people, not the kind she would have been if she had been one, but most of them; then next to them—not above, just away from—were the white-trash; then above them were the homeowners, and above them the home-and-land owners, to which she and Claud belonged. Above she and Claud were people with a lot of money and much bigger houses and much more land. But here the complexity of it would begin to bear in on her, for some of the people with a lot of money were common and ought to be below she and Claud and some of the people who had good blood had lost their money and had to rent and then there were colored people who owned their homes and land as well. There was a colored dentist in town who had two red Lincolns and a swimming pool and a farm with registered white-face cattle on it. Usually by the time she had fallen asleep all the classes of people were moiling and roiling around in her head, and she would dream they were all crammed in together in a box car, being ridden off to be put in a gas oven.

"That's a beautiful clock," she said and nodded to her right. It was a 25 big wall clock, the face encased in a brass sunburst.

"Yes, it's very pretty," the stylish lady said agreeably. "And right on 26 the dot too," she added, glancing at her watch.

The ugly girl beside her cast an eye upward at the clock, smirked, then 27 looked directly at Mrs. Turpin and smirked again. Then she returned her eyes to her book. She was obviously the lady's daughter because, although they didn't look anything alike as to disposition, they both had the same shape of face and the same blue eyes. On the lady they sparkled pleasantly but in the girl's seared face they appeared alternately to smolder and to blaze.

28   What if Jesus had said, "All right, you can be white-trash or a nigger or ugly"!

29   Mrs. Turpin felt an awful pity for the girl, though she thought it was one thing to be ugly and another to act ugly.

30   The woman with the snuff-stained lips turned around in her chair and looked up at the clock. Then she turned back and appeared to look a little to the side of Mrs. Turpin. There was a cast in one of her eyes. "You want to know wher you can get one of themther clocks?" she asked in a loud voice.

31   "No, I already have a nice clock," Mrs. Turpin said. Once somebody like her got a leg in the conversation, she would be all over it.

32   "You can get you one with green stamps," the woman said. "That's most likely wher he got hisn. Save you up enough, you can get you most anythang. I got me some joo'ry."

33   Ought to have got you a wash rag and some soap, Mrs. Turpin thought.

34   "I get contour sheets with mine," the pleasant lady said.

35   The daughter slammed her book shut. She looked straight in front of her, directly through Mrs. Turpin and on through the yellow curtain and the plate glass window which made the wall behind her. The girl's eyes seemed lit all of a sudden with a peculiar light, an unnatural light like night road signs give. Mrs. Turpin turned her head to see if there was anything going on outside that she should see, but she could not see anything. Figures passing cast only a pale shadow through the curtain. There was no reason the girl should single her out for her ugly looks.

36   "Mrs. Finley," the nurse said, cracking the door. The gum-chewing woman got up and passed in front of her and Claud and went into the office. She had on red high-heeled shoes.

37   Directly across the table, the ugly girl's eyes were fixed on Mrs. Turpin as if she had some very special reason for disliking her.

38   "This is wonderful weather, isn't it?" the girl's mother said.

39   "It's good weather for cotton if you can get the niggers to pick it," Mrs. Turpin said, "but niggers don't want to pick cotton any more. You can't get the white folks to pick it and now you can't get the niggers— because they got to be right up there with the white folks."

40   "They gonna *try* anyways," the white-trash woman said, leaning forward.

41   "Do you have one of those cotton-picking machines?" the pleasant lady asked.

42   "No," Mrs. Turpin said, "they leave half the cotton in the field. We don't have much cotton anyway. If you want to make it farming now,

you have to have a little of everything. We got a couple of acres of cotton and a few hogs and chickens and just enough white-face that Claud can look after them himself."

"One thang I don't want," the white-trash woman said, wiping her mouth with the back of her hand. "Hogs. Nasty stinking things, a-gruntin and a-rootin all over the place."

Mrs. Turpin gave her the merest edge of attention. "Our hogs are not dirty and they don't stink," she said. "They're cleaner than some children I've seen. Their feet never touch the ground. We have a pig-parlor—that's where you raise them on concrete," she explained to the pleasant lady, "and Claud scoots them down with the hose every afternoon and washes off the floor." Cleaner by far than that child right there, she thought. Poor nasty little thing. He had not moved except to put the thumb of his dirty hand into his mouth.

The woman turned her face away from Mrs. Turpin. "I know I wouldn't scoot down no hog with no hose," she said to the wall.

You wouldn't have no hog to scoot down, Mrs. Turpin said to herself.

"A-gruntin and a-rootin and a-groanin," the woman muttered.

"We got a little of everything," Mrs. Turpin said to the pleasant lady. "It's no use in having more than you can handle yourself with help like it is. We found enough niggers to pick our cotton this year but Claud he has to go after them and take them home again in the evening. They can't walk that half a mile. No they can't. I tell you," she said and laughed merrily, "I sure am tired of buttering up niggers, but you got to love em if you want em to work for you. When they come in the morning, I run out and I say, 'Hi yawl this morning?' and when Claud drives them off to the field I just wave to beat the band and they just wave back." And she waved her hand rapidly to illustrate.

"Like you read out of the same book," the lady said, showing she understood perfectly.

"Child, yes," Mrs. Turpin said. "And when they come in from the field, I run out with a bucket of icewater. That's the way it's going to be from now on," she said. "You may as well face it."

"One thang I know," the white-trash woman said. "Two thangs I ain't going to do: love no niggers or scoot down no hog with no hose." And she let out a bark of contempt.

The look that Mrs. Turpin and the pleasant lady exchanged indicated they both understood that you had to *have* certain things before you could *know* certain things. But every time Mrs. Turpin exchanged a look with the lady, she was aware that the ugly girl's peculiar eyes were still on her, and she had trouble bringing her attention back to the conversation.

"When you got something," she said, "you got to look after it." And when you ain't got a thing but breath and britches, she added to herself, you can afford to come to town every morning and just sit on the Court House coping and spit.

A grotesque revolving shadow passed across the curtain behind her and was thrown palely on the opposite wall. Then a bicycle clattered down against the outside of the building. The door opened and a colored boy glided in with a tray from the drug store. It had two large red and white paper cups on it with tops on them. He was a tall, very black boy in discolored white pants and a green nylon shirt. He was chewing gum slowly, as if to music. He set the tray down in the office opening next to the fern and stuck his head through to look for the secretary. She was not in there. He rested his arms on the ledge and waited, his narrow bottom stuck out, swaying slowly to the left and right. He raised a hand over his head and scratched the base of his skull.

55   "You see that button there, boy?" Mrs. Turpin said. "You can punch that and she'll come. She's probably in the back somewhere."

56   "Is that right?" the boy said agreeably, as if he had never seen the button before. He leaned to the right and put his finger on it. "She sometime out," he said and twisted around to face his audience, his elbows behind him on the counter. The nurse appeared and he twisted back again. She handed him a dollar and he rooted in his pocket and made the change and counted it out to her. She gave him fifteen cents for a tip and he went out with the empty tray. The heavy door swung to slowly and closed at length with the sound of suction. For a moment no one spoke.

57   "They ought to send all them niggers back to Africa," the white-trash woman said. "That's wher they come from in the first place."

58   "Oh, I couldn't do without my good colored friends," the pleasant lady said.

59   "There's a heap of things worse than a nigger," Mrs. Turpin agreed. "It's all kinds of them just like it's all kinds of us."

60   "Yes, and it takes all kinds to make the world go round," the lady said in her musical voice.

61   As she said it, the raw-complexioned girl snapped her teeth together. Her lower lip turned downwards and inside out, revealing the pale pink inside of her mouth. After a second it rolled back up. It was the ugliest face Mrs. Turpin had ever seen anyone make and for a moment she was certain that the girl had made it at her. She was looking at her as if she had known and disliked her all her life—all of Mrs. Turpin's life, it seemed too, not just all the girl's life. Why, girl, I don't even know you, Mrs. Turpin said silently.

62   She forced her attention back to the discussion. "It wouldn't be practical to send them back to Africa," she said. "They wouldn't want to go. They got it too good here."

63   "Wouldn't be what they wanted—if I had anythang to do with it," the woman said.

64   "It wouldn't be a way in the world you could get all the niggers back over there," Mrs. Turpin said. "They'd be hiding out and lying down and turning sick on you and wailing and hollering and raring and pitching. It wouldn't be a way in the world to get them over there."

"They got over here," the trashy woman said. "Get back like they got over."   65

"It wasn't so many of them then," Mrs. Turpin explained.   66

The woman looked at Mrs. Turpin as if here was an idiot indeed but   67
Mrs. Turpin was not bothered by the look, considering where it came from.

"Nooo," she said, "they're going to stay here where they can go to   68
New York and marry white folks and improve their color. That's what
they all want to do, every one of them, improve their color."

"You know what comes of that, don't you?" Claud asked.   69

"No, Claud, what?" Mrs. Turpin said.   70

Claud's eyes twinkled. "White-faced niggers," he said with never a   71
smile.

Everybody in the office laughed except the white-trash and the ugly   72
girl. The girl gripped the book in her lap with white fingers. The trashy
woman looked around her from face to face as if she thought they were
all idiots. The old woman in the feed sack dress continued to gaze
expressionless across the floor at the high-top shoes of the man opposite
her, the one who had been pretending to be asleep when the Turpins
came in. He was laughing heartily, his hands still spread out on his knees.
The child had fallen to the side and was lying now almost face down in
the old woman's lap.

While they recovered from their laughter, the nasal chorus on the radio   73
kept the room from silence.

> *You go to blank blank*
> *And I'll go to mine*
> *But we'll all blank along*
> *To-geth-ther*
> *And all along the blank*
> *We'll hep each other out*
> *Smile-ling in any kind of*
> *Weath-ther!*

Mrs. Turpin didn't catch every word but she caught enough to agree   74
with the spirit of the song and it turned her thoughts sober. To help
anybody out that needed it was her philosophy of life. She never spared
herself when she found somebody in need, whether they were white or
black, trash or decent. And of all she had to be thankful for, she was most
thankful that this was so. If Jesus had said, "You can be high society and
have all the money you want and be thin and svelte-like, but you can't be
a good woman with it," she would have had to say, "Well don't make me
that then. Make me a good woman and it don't matter what else, how fat
or how ugly or how poor!" Her heart rose. He had not made her a nigger
or white-trash or ugly! He had made her herself and given her a little of
everything. Jesus, thank you! she said. Thank you thank you thank you!
Whenever she counted her blessing she felt as buoyant as if she weighed
one hundred and twenty-five pounds instead of one hundred and eighty.

75 "What's wrong with your little boy?" the pleasant lady asked the white-trashy woman.

76 "He has a ulcer," the woman said proudly. "He ain't give me a minute's peace since he was born. Him and her are just alike," she said, nodding at the old woman, who was running her leathery fingers through the child's pale hair. "Look like I can't get nothing down them two but Co'Cola and candy."

77 That's all you try to get down em, Mrs. Turpin said to herself. Too lazy to light the fire. There was nothing you could tell her about people like them that she didn't know already. And it was not just that they didn't have anything. Because if you gave them everything, in two weeks it would all be broken or filthy or they would have chopped it up for lightwood. She knew all this from her own experience. Help them you must, but help them you couldn't.

78 All at once the ugly girl turned her lips inside out again. Her eyes were fixed like two drills on Mrs. Turpin. This time there was no mistaking that there was something urgent behind them.

79 Girl, Mrs. Turpin exclaimed silently, I haven't done a thing to you! The girl might be confusing her with somebody else. There was no need to sit by and let herself be intimidated. "You must be in college," she said boldly, looking directly at the girl. "I see you reading a book there."

80 The girl continued to stare and pointedly did not answer.

81 Her mother blushed at this rudeness. "The lady asked you a question, Mary Grace," she said under her breath.

82 "I have ears," Mary Grace said.

83 The poor mother blushed again. "Mary Grace goes to Wellesley College," she explained. She twisted one of the buttons on her dress. "In Massachusetts," she added with a grimace. "And in the summer she just keeps right on studying. Just reads all the time, a real book worm. She's done real well at Wellesley; she's taking English and Math and History and Psychology and Social Studies," she rattled on, "and I think it's too much. I think she ought to get out and have fun."

84 The girl looked as if she would like to hurl them all through the plate glass window.

85 "Way up north," Mrs. Turpin murmured and thought, well, it hasn't done much for her manners.

86 "I'd almost rather to have him sick," the white-trash woman said, wrenching the attention back to herself. "He's so mean when he ain't. Look like some children just take natural to meanness. It's some gets bad when they get sick but he was the opposite. Took sick and turned good. He don't give me no trouble now. It's me waitin to see the doctor," she said.

87 If I was going to send anybody back to Africa, Mrs. Turpin thought, it would be your kind, woman. "Yes, indeed," she said aloud, but looking up at the ceiling, "it's a heap of things worse than a nigger." And dirtier than a hog, she added to herself.

88 "I think people with bad dispositions are more to be pitied than anyone on earth," the pleasant lady said in a voice that was decidedly thin.

"I thank the Lord he has blessed me with a good one," Mrs. Turpin   89
said. "The day has never dawned that I couldn't find something to laugh
at."

"Not since she married me anyways," Claud said with a comical   90
straight face.

Everybody laughed except the girl and the white-trash.   91

Mrs. Turpin's stomach shook. "He's such a caution," she said, "that   92
I can't help but laugh at him."

The girl made a loud ugly noise through her teeth.   93

Her mother's mouth grew thin and tight. "I think the worst thing in the   94
world," she said, "is an ungrateful person. To have everything and not
appreciate it. I know a girl," she said, "who has parents who would give
her anything, a little brother who loves her dearly, who is getting a good
education, who wears the best clothes, but who can never say a kind
word to anyone, who never smiles, who just criticizes and complains all
day long."

"Is she too old to paddle?" Claud asked.   95

The girl's face was almost purple.   96

"Yes," the lady said, "I'm afraid there's nothing to do but leave her to   97
her folly. Some day she'll wake up and it'll be too late."

"It never hurt anyone to smile," Mrs. Turpin said. "It just makes you   98
feel better all over."

"Of course," the lady said sadly, "but there are just some people you   99
can't tell anything to. They can't take criticism."

"If it's one thing I am," Mrs. Turpin said with feeling, "it's grateful.   100
When I think who all I could have been besides myself and what all I got,
a little of everything, and a good disposition besides, I just feel like
shouting, 'Thank you, Jesus, for making everything the way it is!' It could
have been different!" For one thing, somebody else could have got Claud.
At the thought of this, she was flooded with gratitude and a terrible pang
of joy ran through her. "Oh thank you, Jesus, Jesus, thank you!" she
cried aloud.

The book struck her directly over her left eye. It struck almost at the   101
same instant that she realized the girl was about to hurl it. Before she
could utter a sound, the raw face came crashing across the table toward
her, howling. The girl's fingers sank like clamps into the soft flesh of her
neck. She heard the mother cry out and Claud shout, "Whoa!" There was
an instant when she was certain that she was about to be in an earthquake.

All at once her vision narrowed and she saw everything as if it were   102
happening in a small room far away, or as if she were looking at it
through the wrong end of a telescope. Claud's face crumpled and fell out
of sight. The nurse ran in, then out, then in again. Then the gangling
figure of the doctor rushed out of the inner door. Magazines flew this way
and that as the table turned over. The girl fell with a thud and Mrs.
Turpin's vision suddenly reversed itself and she saw everything large
instead of small. The eyes of the white-trashy woman were staring hugely

at the floor. There the girl, held down on one side by the nurse and on the other by her mother, was wrenching and turning in their grasp. The doctor was kneeling astride her, trying to hold her arm down. He managed after a second to sink a long needle into it.

103   Mrs. Turpin felt entirely hollow except for her heart which swung from side to side as if it were agitated in a great empty drum of flesh.

104   "Somebody that's not busy call for the ambulance," the doctor said in the offhand voice young doctors adopt for terrible occasions.

105   Mrs. Turpin could not have moved a finger. The old man who had been sitting next to her skipped nimbly into the office and made the call, for the secretary still seemed to be gone.

106   "Claud!" Mrs. Turpin called.

107   He was not in his chair. She knew she must jump up and find him but she felt like some one trying to catch a train in a dream, when everything moves in slow motion and the faster you try to run the slower you go.

108   "Here I am," a suffocated voice, very unlike Claud's, said.

109   He was doubled up in the corner on the floor, pale as paper, holding his leg. She wanted to get up and go to him but she could not move. Instead, her gaze was drawn slowly downward to the churning face on the floor, which she could see over the doctor's shoulder.

110   The girl's eyes stopped rolling and focused on her. They seemed a much lighter blue than before, as if a door that had been tightly closed behind them was now open to admit light and air.

111   Mrs. Turpin's head cleared and her power of motion returned. She leaned forward until she was looking directly into the fierce brilliant eyes. There was no doubt in her mind that the girl did know her, knew her in some intense and personal way, beyond time and place and condition. "What you got to say to me?" she asked hoarsely and held her breath, waiting, as for a revelation.

112   The girl raised her head. Her gaze locked with Mrs. Turpin's. "Go back to hell where you came from, you old wart hog," she whispered. Her voice was low but clear. Her eyes burned for a moment as if she saw with pleasure that her message had struck its target.

113   Mrs. Turpin sank back in her chair.

114   After a moment the girl's eyes closed and she turned her head wearily to the side.

115   The doctor rose and handed the nurse the empty syringe. He leaned over and put both hands for a moment on the mother's shoulders, which were shaking. She was sitting on the floor, her lips pressed together, holding Mary Grace's hand in her lap. The girl's fingers were gripped like a baby's around her thumb. "Go on to the hospital," he said. "I'll call and make the arrangements."

116   "Now let's see that neck," he said in a jovial voice to Mrs. Turpin. He began to inspect her neck with his first two fingers. Two little moon-shaped lines like pink fish bones were indented over her windpipe. There was the beginning of an angry red swelling above her eye. His fingers passed over this also.

"Lea' me be," she said thickly and shook him off. "See about Claud. She kicked him." 117

"I'll see about him in a minute," he said and felt her pulse. He was a thin grey-haired man, given to pleasantries. "Go home and have yourself a vacation the rest of the day," he said and patted her on the shoulder. 118

Quit your pattin me, Mrs. Turpin growled to herself. 119

"And put an ice pack over that eye," he said. Then he went and squatted down beside Claud and looked at his leg. After a moment he pulled him up and Claud limped after him into the office. 120

Until the ambulance came, the only sounds in the room were the tremulous moans of the girl's mother, who continued to sit on the floor. The white-trash woman did not take her eyes off the girl. Mrs. Turpin looked straight ahead at nothing. Presently the ambulance drew up, a long dark shadow, behind the curtain. The attendants came in and set the stretcher down beside the girl and lifted her expertly onto it and carried her out. The nurse helped the mother gather up her things. The shadow of the ambulance moved silently away and the nurse came back to the office. 121

"That ther girl is going to be a lunatic, ain't she?" the white-trash woman asked the nurse, but the nurse kept on to the back and never answered her. 122

"Yes, she's going to be a lunatic," the white-trash woman said to the rest of them. 123

"Po' critter," the old woman murmured. The child's face was still in her lap. His eyes looked idly out over her knees. He had not moved during the disturbance except to draw one leg up under him. 124

"I thank Gawd," the white-trash woman said fervently, "I ain't a lunatic." 125

Claud came limping out and the Turpins went home. 126

As their pick-up truck turned into their own dirt road and made the crest of the hill, Mrs. Turpin gripped the window ledge and looked out suspiciously. The land sloped gracefully down through a field dotted with lavender weeds and at the start of the rise their small yellow frame house, with its little flower beds spread out around it like a fancy apron, sat primly in its accustomed place between two giant hickory trees. She would not have been startled to see a burnt wound between two black-ened chimneys. 127

Neither of them felt like eating so they put on their house clothes and lowered the shade in the bedroom and lay down, Claud with his leg on a pillow and herself with a damp washcloth over her eye. The instant she was flat on her back, the image of a razor-backed hog with warts on its face and horns coming out behind its ears snorted into her head. She moaned, a low quiet moan. 128

"I am not," she said tearfully, "a wart hog. From hell." But the denial had no force. The girl's eyes and her words, even the tone of her voice, low but clear, directed only to her, brooked no repudiation. She had been singled out for the message, though there was trash in the room to whom 129 it might justly have been applied. The full force of this fact struck her only now. There was a woman there who was neglecting her own child but she had been overlooked. The message had been given to Ruby Turpin, a respectable, hard-working, church-going woman. The tears dried. Her eyes began to burn instead with wrath.

130   She rose on her elbow and the washcloth fell into her hand. Claud was lying on his back, snoring. She wanted to tell him what the girl had said. At the same time, she did not wish to put the image of herself as a wart hog from hell into his mind.

131   "Hey, Claud," she muttered and pushed his shoulder.

132   Claud opened one pale baby blue eye.

133   She looked into it warily. He did not think about anything. He just went his way.

134   "Wha, whasit?" he said and closed the eye again.

135   "Nothing," she said. "Does your leg pain you?"

136   "Hurts like hell," Claud said.

137   "It'll quit terreckly," she said and lay back down. In a moment Claud was snoring again. For the rest of the afternoon they lay there. Claud slept. She scowled at the ceiling. Occasionally she raised her fist and made a small stabbing motion over her chest as if she was defending her innocence to invisible guests who were like the comforters of Job, reasonable-seeming but wrong.

138   About five-thirty Claud stirred. "Got to go after those niggers," he sighed, not moving.

139   She was looking straight up as if there were unintelligible handwriting on the ceiling. The protuberance over her eye had turned a greenish-blue. "Listen here," she said.

140   "What?"

141   "Kiss me."

142   Claud leaned over and kissed her loudly on the mouth. He pinched her side and their hands interlocked. Her expression of ferocious concentration did not change. Claud got up, groaning and growling, and limped off. She continued to study the ceiling.

143   She did not get up until she heard the pick-up truck coming back with the Negroes. Then she rose and thrust her feet in her brown oxfords, which she did not bother to lace, and stumped out onto the back porch and got her red plastic bucket. She emptied a tray of ice cubes into it and filled it half full of water and went out into the back yard. Every afternoon after Claud brought the hands in, one of the boys helped him put out hay and the rest waited in the back of the truck until he was ready to take them home. The truck was parked in the shade under one of the hickory trees.

144   "Hi yawl this evening?" Mrs. Turpin asked grimly, appearing with the bucket and the dipper. There were three women and a boy in the truck.

145   "Us doing nicely," the oldest woman said. "Hi you doin?" and her gaze stuck immediately on the dark lump on Mrs. Turpin's forehead.

"You done fell down, ain't you?" she asked in a solicitous voice. The old woman was dark and almost toothless. She had on an old felt hat of Claud's set back on her head. The other two women were younger and lighter and they both had new bright green sun hats. One of them had hers on her head; the other had taken hers off and the boy was grinning beneath it.

Mrs. Turpin set the bucket down on the floor of the truck. "Yawl hep yourselves," she said. She looked around to make sure Claud had gone. "No. I didn't fall down," she said, folding her arms. "It was something worse than that."   146

"Ain't nothing bad happen to you!" the old woman said. She said it as if they all knew that Mrs. Turpin was protected in some special way by Divine Providence. "You just had you a little fall."   147

"We were in town at the doctor's office for where the cow kicked Mr. Turpin," Mrs. Turpin said in a flat tone that indicated they could leave off their foolishness. "And there was this girl there. A big fat girl with her face all broke out. I could look at that girl and tell she was peculiar but I couldn't tell how. And me and her mama were just talking and going along and all of a sudden WHAM! She throws this big book she was reading at me and . . ."   148

"Naw!" the old woman cried out.   149

"And then she jumps over the table and commences to choke me."   150

"Naw!" They all exclaimed, "naw!"   151

"Hi come she do that?" the old woman asked. "What ail her?"   152

Mrs. Turpin only glared in front of her.   153

"Something ail her," the old woman said.   154

"They carried her off in an ambulance," Mrs. Turpin continued, "but before she went she was rolling on the floor and they were trying to hold her down to give her a shot and she said something to me." She paused. "You know what she said to me?"   155

"What she say?" they asked.   156

"She said," Mrs. Turpin began, and stopped, her face very dark and heavy. The sun was getting whiter and whiter, blanching the sky overhead so that the leaves of the hickory tree were black in the face of it. She could not bring forth the words. "Something real ugly," she muttered.   157

"She sho shouldn't said nothing ugly to you," the old woman said. "You so sweet. You the sweetest lady I know."   158

"She pretty too," the one with the hat on said.   159

"And stout," the other one said. "I never knowed no sweeter white lady."   160

"That's the truth befo' Jesus," the old woman said. "Amen! You des as sweet and pretty as you can be."   161

Mrs. Turpin knew just exactly how much Negro flattery was worth and it added to her rage. "She said," she began again and finished this time with a fierce rush of breath, "that I was an old wart hog from hell."   162

There was an astounded silence.   163

164   "Where she at?" the youngest woman cried in a piercing voice.

165   "Lemme see her. I'll kill her!"

166   "I'll kill her with you!" the other one cried.

167   "She b'long in the sylum," the old woman said emphatically. "You the sweetest white lady I know."

168   "She pretty too," the other two said. "Stout as she can be and sweet. Jesus satisfied with her!"

169   "Deed he is," the old woman declared.

170   Idiots! Mrs. Turpin growled to herself. You could never say anything intelligent to a nigger. You could talk at them but not with them. "Yawl ain't drunk your water," she said shortly. "Leave the bucket in the truck when you're finished with it. I got more to do than just stand around and pass the time of day," and she moved off and into the house.

171   She stood for a moment in the middle of the kitchen. The dark protuberance over her eye looked like a miniature tornado cloud which might any moment sweep across the horizon of her brow. Her lower lip protruded dangerously. She squared her massive shoulders. Then she marched into the front of the house and out the side door and started down the road to the pig parlor. She had the look of a woman going single-handed, weaponless, into battle.

172   The sun was a deep yellow now like a harvest moon and was riding westward very fast over the far tree line as if it meant to reach the hogs before she did. The road was rutted and she kicked several good-sized stones out of her path as she strode along. The pig parlor was on a little knoll at the end of a lane that ran off from the side of the barn. It was a square of concrete as large as a small room, with a board fence about four feet high around it. The concrete floor sloped slightly so that the hog wash could drain off into a trench where it was carried to the field for fertilizer. Claud was standing on the outside, on the edge of the concrete, hanging onto the top board, hosing down the floor inside. The hose was connected to the faucet of a water trough nearby.

173   Mrs. Turpin climbed up beside him and glowered down at the hogs inside. There were seven long-snouted bristly shoats in it—tan with liver-colored spots—and an old sow a few weeks off from farrowing. She was lying on her side grunting. The shoats were running about shaking themselves like idiot children, their little slit pig eyes searching the floor for anything left. She had read that pigs were the most intelligent animal. She doubted it. They were supposed to be smarter than dogs. There had even been a pig astronaut. He had performed his assignment perfectly but died of a heart attack afterwards because they left him in his electric suit, sitting upright throughout his examination when naturally a hog should be on all fours.

174   A-grunting and a-rootin and a-groanin.

175   "Gimme that hose," she said, yanking it away from Claud. "Go on and carry them niggers home and then get off that leg."

176   "You look like you might have swallowed a mad dog," Claud ob-

served, but he got down and limped off. He paid no attention to her humors.

Until he was out of earshot, Mrs. Turpin stood on the side of the pen, holding the hose and pointing the stream of water at the hind quarter of any shoat that looked as if it might try to lie down. When he had had time to get over the hill, she turned her head slightly and her wrathful eyes scanned the path. He was nowhere in sight. She turned back again and seemed to gather herself up. Her shoulders rose and she drew in her breath. [177]

"What do you send me a message like that for?" she said in a low fierce voice, barely above a whisper but with the force of a shout in its concentrated fury. "How am I a hog and me both? How am I saved and from hell too?" Her free fist was knotted and with the other she gripped the hose, blindly pointing the stream of water in and out of the eye of the old sow whose outraged squeal she did not hear. [178]

The pig parlor commanded a view of the back pasture where their twenty beef cows were gathered around the hay-bales Claud and the boy had put out. The freshly cut pasture sloped down to the highway. Across it was their cotton field and beyond that a dark green dusty wood which they owned as well. The sun was behind the wood, very red, looking over the paling of trees like a farmer inspecting his own hogs. [179]

"Why me?" she rumbled. "It's no trash around here, black or white, that I haven't given to. And break my back to the bone every day working. And do for the church." [180]

She appeared to be the right size woman to command the arena before her. "How am I a hog?" she demanded. "Exactly how am I like them?" and she jabbed the stream of water at the shoats. "There was plenty of trash there. It didn't have to be me." [181]

"If you like trash better, go get yourself some trash then," she railed. "You could have made me trash. Or a nigger. If trash is what you wanted why didn't you make me trash?" She shook her fist with the hose in it and a watery snake appeared momentarily in the air. "I could quit working and take it easy and be filthy," she growled. "Lounge about the sidewalks all day drinking root beer. Dip snuff and spit in every puddle and have it all over my face. I could be nasty." [182]

"Or you could have made me a nigger. It's too late for me to be a nigger," she said with deep sarcasm, "but I could act like one. Lay down in the middle of the road and stop traffic. Roll on the ground." [183]

In the deepening light everything was taking on a mysterious hue. The pasture was growing a peculiar glassy green and the streak of highway had turned lavender. She braced herself for a final assault and this time her voice rolled out over the pasture. "Go on," she yelled, "call me a hog! Call me a hog again. From hell. Call me a wart hog from hell. Put that bottom rail on top. There'll still be a top and bottom!" [184]

A garbled echo returned to her. [185]

A final surge of fury shook her and she roared, "Who do you think you are?" [186]

187   The color of everything, field and crimson sky, burned for a moment with a transparent intensity. The question carried over the pasture and across the highway and the cotton field and returned to her clearly like an answer from beyond the wood.

188   She opened her mouth but no sound came out of it.

189   A tiny truck, Claud's, appeared on the highway, heading rapidly out of sight. Its gears scraped thinly. It looked like a child's toy. At any moment a bigger truck might smash into it and scatter Claud's and the niggers' brains all over the road.

190   Mrs. Turpin stood there, her gaze fixed on the highway, all her muscles rigid, until in five or six minutes the truck reappeared, returning. She waited until it had had time to turn into their own road. Then like a monumental statue coming to life, she bent her head slowly and gazed, as if through the very heart of the mystery, down into the pig parlor at the hogs. They had settled all in one corner around the old sow who was grunting softly. A red glow suffused them. They appeared to pant with a secret life.

191   Until the sun slipped finally behind the tree line, Mrs. Turpin remained there with her gaze bent to them as if she were absorbing some abysmal life-giving knowledge. At last she lifted her head. There was only a purple streak in the sky, cutting through a field of crimson and leading, like an extension of the highway, into the descending dusk. She raised her hands from the side of the pen in a gesture hieratic and profound. A visionary light settled in her eyes. She saw the streak as a vast swinging bridge extending upward from the earth toward heaven. There were whole companies of white-trash, clean for the first time in their lives, and bands of black niggers in white robes, and battalions of freaks and lunatics shouting and clapping and leaping like frogs. And bringing up the end of the procession was a tribe of people whom she recognized at once as those who, like herself and Claud, had always had a little of everything and the God-given wit to use it right. She leaned forward to observe them closer. They were marching behind the others with great dignity, accountable as they had always been for good order and common sense and respectable behavior. They alone were on key. Yet she could see by their shocked and altered faces that even their virtues were being burned away. She lowered her hands and gripped the rail of the hog pen, her eyes small but fixed unblinkingly on what lay ahead. In a moment the vision faded but she remained where she was, immobile.

192   At length she got down and turned off the faucet and made her slow way on the darkening path to the house. In the woods around her the invisible cricket choruses had struck up, but what she heard were the voices of the souls climbing upward into the starry field and shouting hallelujah.

❏ Questions for Discussion

1. In what ways is the doctor's office a microcosm of Mrs. Turpin's world?

2. By what standards does Mrs. Turpin classify people? Why is she so prejudiced and judgmental? From what does Mrs. Turpin appear to derive her dignity and self-esteem?

3. Why does Mary Grace attack Mrs. Turpin and say to her " 'Go back to hell where you came from, you old wart hog' "? Why is the title of the book Mary Grace throws significant? Which hurt Mrs. Turpin more, the physical attack or the curse? Why does Mrs. Turpin make so much of the girl's "message"?

4. In the final scene, Mrs. Turpin talks to and wrestles with God, asking Him "'Who do you think you are?'" a question as old as Job. What is the **tone** of her question? What answer does she get?

5. In Mrs. Turpin's final vision of heaven, landowning whites like her and her husband are last, behind blacks and less affluent whites. Why? What does "even their virtues were being burned away" mean? Why are "their virtues . . . being burned away"? How is Mrs. Turpin's vision likely to change her life?

The Catholic Novelist in the Protestant South

In the past several years I have gone to speak at a number of Catholic colleges, and I have been pleased to discover that fiction seems to be important to the Catholic student in a way it would not have been twenty, or even ten, years ago. In the past, Catholic imagination in this country has been devoted almost exclusively to practical affairs. Our energies have gone into what has been necessary to sustain existence, and now that our existence is no longer in doubt, we are beginning to realize that an impoverishment of the imagination means an impoverishment of the religious life as well.

I am concerned that future Catholics have a literature. I want them to have a literature that will be undeniably theirs, but which will also be understood and cherished by the rest of our countrymen. A literature of ourselves alone is a contradiction in terms. You may ask, why not simply call this literature Christian? Unfortunately, the word Christian is no longer reliable. It has come to mean anyone with a golden heart. And a golden heart would be a positive interference in the writing of fiction.

I am specifically concerned with fiction because that is what I write. There is a certain embarrassment about being a storyteller in these times when stories are considered not quite as satisfying as statements and statements not quite as satisfying as statistics; but in the long run, a people is known, not by its statements or its statistics, but by the stories it tells. Fiction is the most impure and the most modest and the most human of the arts. It is closest to man in his sin and his suffering and his hope, and it is often rejected by Catholics for the very reasons that make it what it is. It escapes any orthodoxy we might set up for it, because its dignity is an imitation of our own, based like our own on free will, a free will that operates even in the teeth of divine displeasure. I won't go far into the subject of whether such a thing as a Catholic novel is possible or not. I feel that this is a bone which has been picked bare without giving anybody any nourishment. I am simply going to assume that novelists who are deeply Catholic will write novels which you may call Catholic if the Catholic aspects of the novel are what interest you. Such a novel may be characterized in any number of other ways, and perhaps the more ways the better.

4   In American Catholic circles we are long on theories of what Catholic fiction should be, and short on the experience of having any of it. Once when I spoke on this subject at a Catholic university in the South, a gentleman arose and said that the concept *Catholic novel* was a limiting one and that the novelist, like Whitman, should be alien to nothing. All I could say to him was, "Well, I'm alien to a great deal." We are limited human beings, and the novel is a product of our best limitations. We write with the whole personality, and any attempt to circumvent it, whether this be an effort to rise above belief or above background, is going to result in a reduced approach to reality.

5   But I think that in spite of this spotty and suspect sophistication, which you find here and there among us, the American Catholic feels the same way he has always felt toward the novel: he trusts the fictional imagination about as little as he trusts anything. Before it is well on its feet, he is worrying about how to control it. The young Catholic writer, more than any other, is liable to be smothered at the outset by theory. The Catholic press is constantly broken out in a rash of articles on the failure of the Catholic novelist: the Catholic novelist is failing to reflect the virtue of hope, failing to show the Church's interest in social justice, failing to portray our beliefs in a light that will make them desirable to others. He occasionally writes well, but he always writes wrong.

6   We have recently gone through a period of self-criticism on the subject of Catholics and scholarship, which for the most part has taken place on a high level. Our scholarship, or lack of it, has been discussed in relation to what scholarship is in itself, and the discussion—when it has been most valuable—has been conducted by those who are scholars and who know from their own experience what the scholar is and does.

7   But when we talk about the Catholic failure to produce good fiction in this country, we seldom hear from anyone actively engaged in trying to produce it, and the discussion has not yielded any noticeable returns. We hear from editors, schoolteachers, moralists, and housewives; anyone living considers himself an authority on fiction. The novelist, on the other hand, is supposed to be like Mr. Jarrell's pig that didn't know what bacon was. I think, though, that it is occasionally desirable that we look at the novel—even the so-called Catholic novel—from some particular novelist's point of view.

8   Catholic discussions of novels by Catholics are frequently ridiculous because every given circumstance of the writer is ignored except his Faith.

No one taking part in these discussions seems to remember that the eye sees what it has been given to see by concrete circumstances, and the imagination reproduces what, by some related gift, it is able to make live.

I collect articles from the Catholic press on the failures of the Catholic novelist, and recently in one of them I came upon this typical sentence: "Why not a positive novel based on the Church's fight for social justice, or the liturgical revival, or life in a seminary?"

I take it that if seminarians began to write novels about life in the seminary, there would soon be several less seminarians, but we are to assume that anybody who can write at all, and who has the energy to do some research, can give us a novel on this or any needed subject—and can make it positive.

A lot of novels do get written in this way. It is, in fact, the traditional procedure of the hack, and by some accident of God, such a novel might turn out to be a work of art, but the possibility is unlikely.

In this same article, the writer asked this wistful question: "Would it not seem in order now for some of our younger men to explore the possibilities inherent in certain positive factors which make Catholic life and the Catholic position in this country increasingly challenging?"

This attitude, which proceeds from the standpoint of what it would be good to do or have to supply a general need, is totally opposite from the novelist's own approach. No serious novelist "explores possibilities inherent in factors." Conrad wrote that the artist "descends within himself, and in that region of stress and strife, if he be deserving and fortunate, he finds the terms of his appeal."

Where you find the terms of your appeal may have little or nothing to do with what is challenging in the life of the Church at the moment. And this is particularly apparent to the Southern Catholic writer, whose imagination has been molded by life in a region which is traditionally Protestant. The two circumstances that have given character to my own writing have been those of being Southern and being Catholic. This is considered by many to be an unlikely combination, but I have found it to be a most likely one. I think that the South provides the Catholic novelist with some benefits that he usually lacks, and lacks to a conspicuous degree. The Catholic novel can't be categorized by subject matter, but only by what it assumes about human and divine reality. It cannot see man as determined; it cannot see him as totally depraved. It will see him as incomplete in himself, as prone to evil, but as redeemable when his own efforts are assisted by grace. And it will see this grace as working through nature, but as entirely transcending it, so that a door is always open to possibility and the unexpected in the human soul. Its center of meaning will be Christ; its center of destruction will be the devil. No matter how this view of life may be fleshed out, these assumptions form its skeleton.

But you don't write fiction with assumptions. The things we see, hear, smell, and touch affect us long before we believe anything at all, and the

South impresses its image on us from the moment we are able to distinguish one sound from another. By the time we are able to use our imaginations for fiction, we find that our senses have responded irrevocably to a certain reality. This discovery of being bound through the senses to a particular society and a particular history, to particular sounds and a particular idiom, is for the writer the beginning of a recognition that first puts his work into real human perspective for him. What the Southern Catholic writer is apt to find, when he descends within his imagination, is not Catholic life but the life of this region in which he is both native and alien. He discovers that the imagination is not free, but bound.

16   For many young writers, Catholic or other, this is not a pleasant discovery. They feel that the first thing they must do in order to write well is to shake off the clutch of the region. They would like to set their stories in a region whose way of life seems nearer the spirit of what they think they have to say, or better, they would like to eliminate the region altogether and approach the infinite directly. But this is not even a possibility.

17   The fiction writer finds in time, if not at once, that he cannot proceed at all if he cuts himself off from the sights and sounds that have developed a life of their own in his senses. The novelist is concerned with the mystery of personality, and you cannot say much that is significant about this mystery unless the characters you create exist with the marks of a believable society about them. The larger social context is simply left out of much current fiction, but it cannot be left out by the Southern writer. The image of the South, in all its complexity, is so powerful in us that it is a force which has to be encountered and engaged. The writer must wrestle with it, like Jacob with the angel, until he has extracted a blessing. The writing of any novel worth the effort is a kind of personal encounter, an encounter with the circumstances of the particular writer's imagination, with circumstances which are brought to order only in the actual writing.

18   The Catholic novel that fails is usually one in which this kind of engagement is absent. It is a novel which doesn't grapple with any particular culture. It may try to make a culture out of the Church, but this is always a mistake because the Church is not a culture. The Catholic novel that fails is a novel in which there is no sense of place, and in which feeling is, by that much, diminished. Its action occurs in an abstracted setting that could be anywhere or nowhere. This reduces its dimensions drastically and cuts down on those tensions that keep fiction from being facile and slick.

19   The Southern writer's greatest tie with the South is through his ear, which is usually sharp but not too versatile outside his own idiom. With a few exceptions, such as Miss Katherine Anne Porter, he is not too often successfully cosmopolitan in fiction, but the fact is that he doesn't need to be. A distinctive idiom is a powerful instrument for keeping fiction

social. When one Southern character speaks, regardless of his station in life, an echo of all Southern life is heard. This helps to keep Southern fiction from being a fiction of purely private experience.

Alienation was once a diagnosis, but in much of the fiction of our time [20] it has become an ideal. The modern hero is the outsider. His experience is rootless. He can go anywhere. He belongs nowhere. Being alien to nothing, he ends up being alienated from any kind of community based on common tastes and interests. The borders of his country are the sides of his skull.

The South is traditionally hostile to outsiders, except on her own [21] terms. She is traditionally against intruders, foreigners from Chicago or New Jersey, all those who come from afar with moral energy that increases in direct proportion to the distance from home. It is difficult to separate the virtues of this quality from the narrowness which accompanies and colors it for the outside world. It is more difficult still to reconcile the South's instinct to preserve her identity with her equal instinct to fall eager victim to every poisonous breath from Hollywood or Madison Avenue. But good and evil appear to be joined in every culture at the spine, and as far as the creation of a body of fiction is concerned, the social is superior to the purely personal. Somewhere is better than anywhere. And traditional manners, however unbalanced, are better than no manners at all.

The writer whose themes are religious particularly needs a region [22] where these themes find a response in the life of the people. The American Catholic is short on places that reflect his particular religious life and his particular problems. This country isn't exactly cut in his image. Where he does have a place—such as the Midwestern parishes, which serve as J. F. Powers' region, or South Boston, which belongs to Edwin O'Connor— these places lack the significant features that result in a high degree of regional self-consciousness. They have no great geographical extent, they have no particularly significant history, certainly no history of defeat; they have no real peasant class, and no cultural unity of the kind you find in the South. So that no matter what the writer brings to them in the way of talents, they don't bring much to him in the way of exploitable benefits. Where Catholics do abound, they usually blend almost imperceptibly into the general materialistic background. If the Catholic faith were central to life in America, Catholic fiction would fare better, but the Church is not central to this society. The things that bind us together as Catholics are known only to ourselves. A secular society understands us less and less. It becomes more and more difficult in America to make belief believable, but in this the Southern writer has the greatest possible advantage. He lives in the Bible Belt.

It was about 1919 that Mencken called the South the Bible Belt and the [23] Sahara of the Bozarts. Today Southern literature is known around the world, and the South is still the Bible Belt. Sam Jones' grandma read the Bible thirty-seven times on her knees. And the rural and small-town

South, and even a certain level of the city South, is made up of the descendants of old ladies like her. You don't shake off their influence in even several generations.

24 To be great storytellers, we need something to measure ourselves against, and this is what we conspicuously lack in this age. Men judge themselves now by what they find themselves doing. The Catholic has the natural law and the teachings of the Church to guide him, but for the writing of fiction, something more is necessary.

25 For the purposes of fiction, these guides have to exist in a concrete form, known and held sacred by the whole community. They have to exist in the form of stories which affect our image and our judgment of ourselves. Abstractions, formulas, laws will not serve here. We have to have stories in our background. It takes a story to make a story. It takes a story of mythic dimensions, one which belongs to everybody, one in which everybody is able to recognize the hand of God and its descent. In the Protestant South, the Scriptures fill this role.

26 The Hebrew genius for making the absolute concrete has conditioned the Southerner's way of looking at things. That is one of the reasons why the South is a storytelling section. Our response to life is different if we have been taught only a definition of faith than if we have trembled with Abraham as he held the knife over Isaac. Both of these kinds of knowledge are necessary, but in the last four or five centuries, Catholics have overemphasized the abstract and consequently impoverished their imaginations and their capacity for prophetic insight.

27 Nothing will insure the future of Catholic fiction so much as the biblical revival that we see signs of now in Catholic life. The Bible is held sacred in the Church, we hear it read at Mass, bits and pieces of it are exposed to us in the liturgy, but because we are not totally dependent on it, it has not penetrated very far into our consciousness nor conditioned our reactions to experience. Unfortunately, where you find Catholics reading the Bible, you find that it is usually a pursuit of the educated, but in the South the Bible is known by the ignorant as well, and it is always that *mythos* which the poor hold in common that is most valuable to the fiction writer. When the poor hold sacred history in common, they have ties to the universal and the holy, which allows the meaning of their every action to be heightened and seen under the aspect of eternity. The writer who views the world in this light will be very thankful if he has been fortunate enough to have the South for his background, because here belief can still be made believable, even if for the modern mind it cannot be made admirable.

28 Religious enthusiasm is accepted as one of the South's more grotesque features, and it is possible to build upon that acceptance, however little real understanding such acceptance may carry with it. When you write about backwoods prophets, it is very difficult to get across to the modern reader that you take these people seriously, that you are not making fun of them, but that their concerns are your own and, in your judgment,

central to human life. It is almost inconceivable to this reader that such could be the case. It is hard enough for him to suspend his disbelief and accept an anagogical level of action at all, harder still for him to accept its action in an obviously grotesque character. He has the mistaken notion that a concern with grace is a concern with exalted human behavior, that it is a pretentious concern. It is, however, simply a concern with the human reaction to that which, instant by instant, gives life to the soul. It is a concern with a realization that breeds charity and with the charity that breeds action. Often the nature of grace can be made plain only by describing its absence.

The Catholic writer may be immersed in the Bible himself, but if his   29
readers and his characters are not, he does not have the instrument to plumb meaning—and specifically Christian meaning—that he would have if the biblical background were known to all. It is what writer, character, and reader share that makes it possible to write fiction at all.

The circumstances of being a Southerner, of living in a non-Catholic   30
but religious society, furnish the Catholic novelist with some very fine antidotes to his own worst tendencies. We too much enjoy indulging ourselves in the logic that kills, in making categories smaller and smaller, in prescribing attitudes and proscribing subjects. For the Catholic, one result of the Counter-Reformation was a practical overemphasis on the legal and logical and a consequent neglect of the Church's broader tradition. The need for this emphasis has now diminished, and the Church is busy encouraging those biblical and liturgical revivals which should restore Catholic life to its proper fullness. Nevertheless the scars of this legalistic approach are still upon us. Those who are long on logic, definitions, abstractions, and formulas are frequently short on a sense of the concrete, and when they find themselves in an environment where their own principles have only a partial application to society, they are forced, not to abandon the principles but in applying them to a different situation, to come up with fresh reactions.

I often find among Catholics a certain impatience with Southern   31
literature, sometimes a fascinated impatience, but usually a definite feeling that with all the violence and grotesqueries and religious enthusiasm reflected in its fiction, the South—that is, the rural, Protestant, Bible Belt South—is a little beyond the pale of Catholic respect, and that certainly it would be ridiculous to expect the emergence in such soil of anything like a literature inspired by Catholic belief. But for my part, I don't think that this is at all unlikely. There are certain conditions necessary for the emergence of Catholic literature which are found nowhere else in this country in such abundance as in the Protestant South; and I look forward with considerable relish to the day when we are going to have to enlarge our notions about the Catholic novel to include some pretty odd Southern specimens.

It seems to me that the Catholic Southerner's experience of living so   32
intimately with the division of Christendom is an experience that can give

much breath and poignance to the novels he may produce. The Catholic novelist in the South is forced to follow the spirit into strange places and to recognize it in many forms not totally congenial to him. He may feel that the kind of religion that has influenced Southern life has run hand in hand with extreme individualism for so long that there is nothing left of it that he can recognize, but when he penetrates to the human aspiration beneath it, he sees not only what has been lost to the life he observes, but more, the terrible loss to us in the Church of human faith and passion. I think he will feel a good deal more kinship with backwoods prophets and shouting fundamentalists than he will with those politer elements for whom the supernatural is an embarrassment and for whom religion has become a department of sociology or culture or personality development. His interest and sympathy may very well go—as I know my own does— directly to those aspects of Southern life where the religious feeling is most intense and where its outward forms are farthest from the Catholic, and most revealing of a need that only the Church can fill. This is not because, in the felt superiority of orthodoxy, he wishes to subtract one theology from another, but because, descending within himself to find his region, he discovers that it is with these aspects of Southern life that he has a feeling of kinship strong enough to spur him to write.

33 The result of these underground religious affinities will be a strange and, to many, perverse fiction, one which serves no felt need, which gives us no picture of Catholic life, or the religious experiences that are usual with us, but I believe that it will be Catholic fiction. These people in the invisible Church make discoveries that have meaning for us who are better protected from the vicissitudes of our own natures, and who are often too lazy and satisfied to make any discoveries at all. I believe that the Catholic fiction writer is free to find his subject in the invisible Church and that this will be the vocation of many of us brought up in the South. In a literature that tends naturally to extremes, as Southern literature does, we need something to protect us against the merely extreme, the merely personal, the merely grotesque, and here the Catholic, with his older tradition and his ability to resist the dissolution of belief, can make his contribution to Southern literature, but only if he realizes first that he has as much to learn from it as to give it. The Catholic novelist in the South will bolster the South's best traditions, for they are the same as his own. And the South will perhaps lead him to be less timid as a novelist, more respectful of the concrete, more trustful of the blind imagination.

34 The opportunities for the potential Catholic writer in the South are so great as to be intimidating. He lives in a region where there is a thriving literary tradition, and this is always an advantage to the writer, who is initially inspired less by life than by the work of his predecessors. He lives in a region which is struggling, in both good ways and bad, to preserve its identity, and this is an advantage, for his dramatic need is to know manners under stress. He lives in the Bible Belt, where belief can be made believable. He has also here a good view of the modern world. A half-hour's ride in this region will take him from places where the life has a

distinctly Old Testament flavor to places where the life might be considered post-Christian. Yet all these varied situations can be seen in one glance and heard in one conversation.

I think that Catholic novelists in the future will be able to reinforce the 35 vital strength of Southern literature, for they will know that what has given the South her identity are those beliefs and qualities which she has absorbed from the Scriptures and from her own history of defeat and violation: a distrust of the abstract, a sense of human dependence on the grace of God, and a knowledge that evil is not simply a problem to be solved, but a mystery to be endured.

If all that is missing in this scene is the practical influence of the visible 36 Catholic Church, the writer will find that he has to supply the lack, as best he can, out of himself; and he will do this by the way he uses his eyes. If he uses them in the confidence of his Faith, and according to the needs of what he is making, there will be nothing in life too grotesque, or too "un-Catholic," to supply the materials of his work. Certainly in a secular world, he is in a particular position to appreciate and cherish the Protestant South, to remind us of what we have and what we must keep.

❏ Questions for Discussion

1. What advantage does O'Connor say the Southern writer has? In particular, what advantage does she say that the South offers the Catholic writer?

2. O'Connor says, the Catholic novel sees man "as incomplete in himself." Apply this statement to the characters from her stories.

3. According to O'Connor, "[W]hat has given the South her identity are those beliefs and qualities which she has absorbed from the Scriptures and from her own history of defeat and violation: a distrust of the abstract, a sense of human dependence on the grace of God, and a knowledge that evil is not simply a problem to be solved, but a mystery to be endured." How is this statement reflected in the O'Connor stories?

4. Use the last paragraph of this essay to explain the final scenes in each of the short stories.

The Search for Redemption
Flannery O'Connor's Fiction[1]
by Frederick J. Hoffman

The first impression one has of Flannery O'Connor's work is of its extraordinary lucidity; given, that is, what she expects to communicate, she does communicate it with most remarkable clarity and ease. Of

[1] From *The Added Dimension: the Art and Mind of Flannery O'Connor*, ed. Melvin J. Friedman and Lewis A. Lawson (New York: Fordham University Press, 1977), 32–48.

course, one needs to know just what it is; she is concerned with the problem of how a writer, "by indirections, find[s] directions out." She has a reputation for obscurity, for not giving the expected turn to the reader, for not rewarding him for his having taken the trouble to read her.

The best statement she was given of her purpose and method is a talk she gave at the College of Saint Teresa (Winona, Minnesota) in the fall of 1960. Responding to a critic's suggestion that she is probably not a "Catholic novelist" because she doesn't write on "Catholic subjects," she said:

> . . . The Catholic novelist in the South is forced to follow the spirit into strange places and to recognize it in many forms not totally congenial to him. But the fact that the South is the Bible Belt increases rather than decreases his sympathy for what he sees. His interest will in all likelihood go immediately to those aspects of Southern life where the religious feeling is most intense and where its outward forms are farthest from the Catholic. . . .[2]

Her major subjects are the struggle for redemption, the search for Jesus, and the meaning of "prophecy": all of these in an intensely evangelical Protestant South, where the need for Christ is expressed without shyness and where "prophecy" is intimately related to the ways in which men are daily challenged to define themselves.[3] The literary problem raised by this peculiarity of "place" (though it may be located elsewhere as well, as a "need for ceremony," or a desperate desire to "ritualize" life) is neatly described by Miss O'Connor: she must, she says, define in unnaturally emphatic terms what would not otherwise be accepted, or what might be misunderstood. The sentiment (or some emotional reaction) will get in the way. "There is something in us," she said, in the same talk, "as story-tellers and as listeners to stories, that demands the redemptive act, that demands that what falls at least be offered the chance to be restored."[4] But the rituals of any church are not comprehended by a large enough majority of readers; therefore,

---

[2] Flannery O'Connor, "The Role of the Catholic Novelist," *Greyfriar* [Siena Studies in Literature], VII (1964), 8.

[3] See Sister M. Bernetta Quinn, "View from a Rock: The Fiction of Flannery O'Connor and J. F. Powers," *Critique*, II (Fall, 1958), 19–27: ". . . The center of all Catholic fiction is the Redemption. However mean or miserable or degraded human life may seem to the natural gaze, it must never be forgotten that God considered it valuable enough to send His only Son that He might reclaim it . . ." (21). See *A Handbook of Christian Theology* (New York: Meridian Books, 1958), p. 296: "Thus the God who ransoms, redeems, and delivers Israel out of her bondage is the God who, in Christ, pays the price which restores sinful mankind to freedom and new life. In this act of redemption two interrelated theological emphases are dominant: God's *love* by which He takes the initiative, and man's sin which occasions the situation from which God redeems him."

[4] "The Role of the Catholic Novelist," pp. 10–11.

> ... When I write a novel in which the central action is a baptism,
> I know that for the larger percentage of my readers, baptism is a
> meaningless rite: therefore I have to imbue this action with an awe
> and terror which will suggest its awful mystery. . . .[5]

Miss O'Connor writes about intensely religious acts and dilemmas in a
time when people are much divided on the question of what actually
determines a "religious act." Definitions are not easy, and, frequently,
what is being done with the utmost seriousness seems terribly naive, or
simple-minded, to the reader. She must, therefore, force the statement of
it into a pattern of "grotesque" action, which reminds one somewhat of
Franz Kafka,[6] at least in its violation of normal expectations.

We have the phenomenon of a Catholic writer describing a Protestant,
an evangelical, world, to a group of readers who need to be forced or
shocked and/or amused into accepting the validity of religious states. The
spirit of evil abounds, and the premonition of disaster is almost invariably confirmed. Partly, this is because the scene is itself grotesquely
exaggerated (though eminently plausible at the same time); partly it is
because Christian sensibilities have been, not so much blunted as rendered bland and over-simple. The contrast of the fumbling grandmother
and The Misfit, in Miss O'Connor's most famous story, "A Good Man
Is Hard to Find," is a case in point. The grandmother is fully aware of the
expected terror, but she cannot react "violently" to it. She must therefore
use commonplaces to meet a most uncommon situation:

> "If you would pray," the old lady said, "Jesus would help you."
> "That's right," The Misfit said.
> "Well then, why don't you pray?" she asked trembling with
> delight suddenly.
> "I don't want no hep," he said.
> "I'm doing all right by myself."

Another truth about Miss O'Connor's fiction is its preoccupation with
the Christ figure, a use of Him that is scarcely equalled by her contemporaries. The Misfit offers an apparently strange but actually a not
uncommon observation:

> "Jesus was the only One that ever raised the dead, . . . and He
> shouldn't have done it. He thown everything off balance. If He did

---

[5] *Ibid.*, p. 11.

[6] See Melvin J. Friedman, in *Recent American Fiction*, edited by Joseph J. Waldmeir
(Boston: Houghton Mifflin, 1963), p. 241. Friedman also cites Nathanael West, as does
John Hawkes, "Flannery O'Connor's Devil," *Sewanee Review*, LXX (Summer, 1962), 396.
Hawkes mentions an interesting conjunction of influences on himself: ". . . it was Melville's
granddaughter [Eleanor Melville Metcalf], a lady I was privileged to know in Cambridge,
Massachusetts, who first urged me to read the fiction of Flannery O'Connor, and—
further—. . . this experience occurred just at the time I had discovered the short novels of
Nathanael West."

what He said, then it's nothing for you to do but thow away everything and follow Him, and if He didn't, then it's nothing for you to do but enjoy the few minutes you got left the best you can—by killing somebody or burning down his house or doing some other meanness to him. No pleasure but meanness," he said and his voice became almost a snarl.

One of Paul Tillich's most effective statements has to do with the relationship of man to Jesus Christ, in volume two of his most impressive *Systematic Theology*. "Jesus Christ," he says, "combines the individual name with the title, 'the Christ,'" and "Jesus as the Christ is both a historical fact and a subject of believing reception. . . ."[7] Perhaps more important, and in line with his attempt to review theology in existentialist terms, Tillich says: "Son of God becomes the title of the one in whom the essential unity of God and man has appeared under the conditions of existence. The essentially universal becomes existentially unique. . . ."[8]

As all of us know, the crucifixion was historically a defeat for the messianic cause, whose followers wanted Jesus literally to triumph over the Romans and to restore the Jews to power. But it was also, and most importantly, the source of grace; or, as Tillich puts it, "'Christ' became an individual with supernatural powers who, through a voluntary sacrifice, made it possible for God to save those who believe in him. . . ."[9] It is this latter figure whom Miss O'Connor's heroes spend so much energy and time denying; many of them also are on the way to accepting Him.

In almost all of Miss O'Connor's fiction, the central crisis involves a confrontation with Jesus, "the Christ." In the manner of Southern Protestantism, these encounters are quite colloquial and intimate. The "Jesus" on the lips of her characters is someone who hovers very near; with Him, her personalities frequently carry on a personal dialogue. The belief, or the disbelief, in Him is almost immediate. He is "Jesus" made almost entirely human and often limited in theological function. Man often "takes over" from Him, or threatens to do so. The so-called "grotesques" of Flannery O'Connor's fiction are most frequently individual souls, imbued with religious sentiments of various kinds, functioning in the role of the surrogate Christ or challenging Him to prove Himself. Not only for literary strategy, but because such manifestations

---

[7] *Systematic Theology* (Chicago: University of Chicago Press, 1951), vol. II, p. 98. It is interesting that many of Miss O'Connor's characters want to "see a sign": that is, they want Christ's divinity manifested directly. The Misfit is such a one; Hazel Motes of *Wise Blood* struggles against a Christian mission on the grounds that Christ as God has never revealed Himself; Mr. Head and his grandson have a remarkable experience of illumination, when they see the plaster statue of a Negro (in "The Artificial Nigger"); and the young Tarwater of *The Violent Bear It Away* has a "voice" (variously called "stranger," "friend," and "mentor") who tries to deny Jesus because there has been no "sign" of Him.
[8] *Ibid*, p. 110.
[9] *Ibid*, p. 111.

are surreal, Miss O'Connor makes these acts weird demonstrations of human conduct: "irrational" in the sense of their taking issue with a rational view of events. . . .

The figure of Jesus haunts almost all of her characters. They are, half the time, violently opposed to Him (or, in His image, opposed to some elder who has tried to force His necessity upon them), because they cannot see beyond themselves to a transcendent existence. Hazel Motes and Tarwater are both haunted by the rank and stinking corporeality of their elders, whom they have seen dead and—in dream or in reality— been obliged to bury.

These experiences serve to make them resist the compunctions of grace, and turn away from the prospects of redemption. But the alternative is singularly uninviting. Hazel Motes has no success preaching the new church "without Christ," and Tarwater finds his uncle either pathetic or farcical. They react violently at the turn of their journeys: Motes blinds himself in a mixture of the desire for penitence and the will to prove his courage; Tarwater has recourse both to water and fire, from mixed motives of defiance and fear.

This clarity of vision comes in part from Miss O'Connor's having herself had a satisfactory explanation of these religious drives, and therefore being in a position to portray the violent acts of those who possess the drives but are unable to define goals or direct energies toward them. The grotesqueries of her fiction are in effect a consequence of her seeing what she calls "the Manichaean spirit of the times," in which the religious metaphors retain their power but cannot be precisely delineated by persons driven by the necessities they see in them. Violence, in this setting, assumes a religious meaning; it is, in effect, the sparks caused by the clash of religious desire and disbelief.

> The novelist with Christian concerns will find in modern life distortions which are repugnant to him, and his problem will be to make these appear as distortions to an audience which is used to seeing them as natural; and he may well be forced to take ever more violent means to get his vision across to his hostile audience. . . .[10]

The matter becomes extremely delicate, in the light of her other observations: for example, that "Art requires a delicate adjustment of the outer and inner worlds in such a way that, without changing their nature, they can be seen through each other."[11] This remark suggests that the religious metaphors are, above all, psychological realities; that these are dramatized in the desperate struggles her characters have, at one time against but finally in the mood of accepting the Christian demands and rewards. When Miss O'Connor makes the following summary of her

[10] "The Fiction Writer and His Country," in *The Living Novel, a Symposium,* edited by Granville Hicks (New York: Macmillan, 1957), pp. 162–63.
[11] *Ibid,* p. 163.

vision, therefore, she is simply defining the ultimate goals of her characters, whether they have been represented or not in the act of achieving them.

> . . . I see from the standpoint of Christian orthodoxy. This means that for me the meaning of life is centered in our Redemption by Christ and that what I see in the world I see in its relation to that. I don't think that this is a position that can be taken halfway or one that is particularly easy in these times to make transparent in fiction.[12]

Violence and the Grotesque[1]

by Gilbert H. Muller

Miss O'Connor's technical strategy in the application of violence is to show precisely how the destructive impulse brings the horror of man's grotesque state home to him. Because this kind of violence is religiously motivated, it differs considerably from those gratuitous forms of violence in fiction which are used to exploit current tastes. The violence in Miss O'Connor's fiction is real, yet it has a metaphysical dimension arising from man's loss of theological identity. If in terms of effect this violence partakes of exaggeration, sensationalism, and shock, it nevertheless raises problems which treat the moral and religious order of the universe. The author was quick to distinguish violence in the pure grotesque from its presence in other adulterated forms. She objected to the attempts of some critics to place her within the School of Southern Degeneracy, and she asserted that every time she was associated with this gothic beast she "felt like Br'er Rabbit stuck on the tarbaby."[2] She was emphatic in denying that she utilized violence as a gothic contrivance, remarking that gothicism was a degeneracy which was rarely recognized as such. Fictional assessment of violence in ethical and theological terms is one quality which sets the grotesque apart from a gothic aesthetic, since the violence implicit in gothic fiction has little moral foundation: it exists to satisfy itself, and does not serve as a meaningful vision. Conversely, when violence appears in the grotesque, as in the hecatomb which frames "A Good Man is Hard to Find," it is used to suggest the lack of any framework of order in the universe; it reinforces the grotesque by working *against* the ideals of social and moral order to create an alienated perspective. . . .

Acts of violence in Miss O'Connor's fiction illuminate a world of continual spiritual warfare. The Misfit in "A Good Man is Hard to Find"

---

[12] *Ibid*, p. 162.

[1] From *Nightmares and Visions: Flannery O'Connor and the Catholic Grotesque* (Athens: University of Georgia Press, 1972), 72–98.

[2] "Some Aspects of the Grotesque in Southern Fiction," in *Mystery and Manners,* ed. Sally and Robert Fitzgerald (New York: Farrar, Strauss & Giroux, 1969), p. 38.

kills people not because he enjoys murder, but because like Meursault in *L'Etranger* he is powerless to control his impulses when faced with the indifference of the universe. His act of violence is not totally irrational because its manifestation points toward the spiritual disorder of the world. The Misfit therefore is not presented merely as a pathological murderer, but as a crazed latter-day anchorite, wielding a gun instead of a gnarled club. Still he is without grace, and he complicates the grotesque situation of the Bailey family as well as of himself by ignoring the cardinal commandment—"Thou shalt not kill." Slaughter is a part of the natural process, and modern war demonstrates that it is a part of the human process as well. Yet from a Catholic perspective the injunction placed upon man not to kill is a radical one—and one which must be obeyed. In human and theological terms to kill is to lapse into evil.

Ultimately violence in Flannery O'Connor's fiction forces the reader to confront the problem of evil and to seek alternatives to it. Because Miss O'Connor uses violence to shock her characters (and readers), it becomes the most singular expression of sin within her grotesque landscape. Time and again in her stories violence intrudes suddenly upon the familiar and seemingly secure world and turns the landscape into a secular hell. Thus the slow pastoral seduction planned by Hulga in "Good Country People" is disrupted by Manley Pointer's outrages against her body and spirit. Similarly Julian's world in "Everything that Rises Must Converge" suddenly becomes chaotic when violence ruins what previously had been an innocuous, albeit distasteful, bus trip. Obviously violence of this type occupies a crucial position in making the world seem strange, terrifying, and deprived of grace. As Frederick J. Hoffman remarks in what is perhaps the finest book on violence in contemporary literature: "Surprise is an indispensable element of the fact of violence in modern life. A carefully plotted pattern of expected events has always been needed to sustain a customary existence. A sudden break in the routine challenges the fullest energy of man's power of adjustment. Suddenness is a quality of violence. It is a sign of force breaking through the design established to contain it."[3] . . .

The violent figure frequently becomes an extension of the world which he inhabits. His spiritual desolation is reflected in the very landscape through which he moves, for in this landscape images of violence and disorder prevail. Flannery O'Connor pays strict attention to scene, to landscape in disarray, because by being a reflection of the interior self of the character, it assumes a complicity, despite its supposedly inanimate nature, in the bizarre disjunctiveness of the universe. The potentially violent and hostile landscape is a mark of Miss O'Connor's fiction and serves as a vivid image of a worldly Inferno. And of course with the author, a violent landscape is almost by extension a grotesque landscape.

[3] *The Mortal No: Death and the Modern Imagination* (Princeton: Princeton Univ. Press, 1964), p. 292.

In other words the reductive power of violence unleashes essentially grotesque currents of feeling. In "A Good Man is Hard to Find," for instance, the deranged mind of the Misfit, and the secular impulses of a family preordained to destruction, find an objective correlative in images of a distorted and inimical wasteland. The twisted setting in the story mirrors spiritual and moral decay, and the peaceful rhythms usually associated with a family trip are continually undercut by the images of destruction which are juxtaposed against it. Cotton fields with small islands of graves, the dirt road with "sudden washes in it and sharp curves on dangerous embankments," the line of woods which gapes "like a dark open mouth" create a landscape which is menacing and alien. Even the diner which the family stops at for lunch is a precarious structure, lacking any solidarity or harmony, and is presided over by a sadistic monkey which bites fleas between its teeth with delight. Here, and in other stories such as "A Circle in the Fire" (1954) and "A View of the Woods" (1957), the environment impinges upon characters and is potentially violent: physical description consistently works in opposition to people's desire for harmony and order, and it also affords a premonition of disaster.

Flannery O'Connor's technique of description is terse and severe, tending always toward the impressionistic, in which landscape is distilled into primary images which render a picture of a violent physical world. Miss O'Connor, a watercolorist of considerable talent, concentrates upon line and color to evoke locale swiftly; considering the premium which she placed upon the stark outlines of her fiction, any profusion of description would work against her overall narrative intentions, and thus she relied upon the synthetic method of drawing objects in the physical world together to achieve a concentrated effect. Whether describing the countryside or the metropolis, the author is carefully selective and austere, building up a pattern of imagery and frequently counterpointing these images in order to create a charged atmosphere and to make a thematic statement.

The landscapes depicted in Flannery O'Connor's fiction seem to intensify man's propensity for physical, psychological, and spiritual violence. In a world deprived of meaning, in a world which is ruthless and cruel, the only consolation which her characters have is an ability to exploit others through violence. Arson, rape, mutilation, suicide, and murder are some of the extremes of violent behavior that appear in O'Connor's fiction, and what is curious about these manifestations is that characters such as Rufus, Shiftlet, and the Bible salesman actually take pleasure in wanton acts of destruction. This pleasure in violence, a phenomenon which preoccupies many behavioral scientists and such philosophers as Karl Jaspers, deprives men of being, although the malefactors believe mistakenly that it serves to define their lives. As such, violence becomes a manifestation of the demonic, understood in the medieval sense of the word, as a force which obliterates identity and damns human beings.

Even the Misfit, with his debased logic, comprehends a world without meaning, and in such a world, where it is impossible to attach one's loyalties to any overriding ethical or theological position, the only pleasure and consolation for the lack of meaning must come from amoral acts of violence. Unlike the Hemingway protagonist, who attempts to channel violence into such acceptable institutions as war, hunting, and the bullfight, the characters in O'Connor's fiction rarely seek social justification for their destructive acts. If any justification is required, it exists in the universe itself, in a fallen and grotesque world where a perverse Creator forces man to attest to his damnation every moment of his life.

At the root of violence in Miss O'Connor's fiction lies this concept of the depraved and potentially lethal world, in which the destiny of man is seemingly imposed upon him by a vaguely apprehended source. W. M. Frohock in *The Novel of Violence in America* cogently explains the dilemma which faces the violent protagonist: "The hero finds himself in a predicament such that the only possible exit is through infliction of harm on some other human. In the infliction of harm he also finds the way to his own destruction. But still he accepts the way of violence because life, as he sees it, is like that: violence is man's fate." Life—in the existential sense of the word—is like that, even at the most mundane level. . . .

The entire strategy of violence in Flannery O'Connor's stories of the grotesque is to reveal how complicity in destruction carries men away from God, away from that center of mystery which she was constantly trying to define and which Catholics term grace. This is why violent death is the one act of paramount importance in O'Connor's fiction: it serves to define evil in society. The feud violence which exists in "Greenleaf," for example, is clearly delineated not only in terms of class hatreds but also in terms of good and evil. The pervasive aura of violence in this story reveals the corruption of the will and the need of grace. This kind of violence is a form of spiritual punishment, and in "Revelation," "The Lame Shall Enter First," and many other of her tales it is admonitory. Mrs. May obviously disdains the low origins and primitive ways of the Greenleafs as well as their newly acquired success. With their fox-colored eyes and dark crafty faces they seem to be cast in the mold of Faulkner's tenacious Snopes clan. Yet the Greenleafs, as their name implies, are in basic harmony with nature. More importantly Mrs. Greenleaf embraces a variety of worship which is reminiscent of early mystery religions based on vegetation and on earth. Her mortification and ecstasy, which are appalling to Mrs. May, are ways of experiencing the spiritual through nature; moreover, Mrs. Greenleaf thinks in terms of a primitive salvation for mankind. Mrs. May's failure to understand the rituals which Mrs. Greenleaf enacts before her eyes signifies the modern failure to integrate religious mystery with culture. It also explains why Mrs. May's destiny of necessity must be violent, because hers is the fate of the individual who is estranged from the basic forces of the community and from grace.

Another indication of evil in "Greenleaf" is the alienation which exists among the members of the May family. Estrangement within the family is of course one of the most common forms of sublimated violence and overt feuding in Flannery O'Connor's fiction. In "Greenleaf" Mrs. May's two sons loath their mother and hate each other as well. Wesley, the younger of the brothers, bears spiritual kinship to Hulga, Asbury, and other effete intellectuals who are encountered frequently in Miss O'Connor's stories. He is sickly, sardonic, ill-natured, and rude—a vacuous academician consumed by a brutal sense of determinism. Scofield is much coarser than his brother; patterned after Jason Compson, he displays a marked degeneracy in his manners. Both brothers are perversely preoccupied with their mother's death, and this act suggests how individuals can consciously choose to perform or to wish acts of evil. . . .

The ultimate battle is against evil—and against the devil incarnated in concrete forms—in the figure of a Bible salesman, an old man with a peppermint cane, or a friendly figure in a panama hat. In this situation violence becomes a mark of faith. As the noted historian Jacques Ellul has written: "The whole meaning of the violence of love is contained in Paul's word that evil is to be overcome with good (Romans 12:17–21). This is a generalization of the Sermon on the Mount. And it is important for us to understand that this sermon shows what the violence of love is. Paul says, 'Do not let yourself be overcome by evil.' This then is the fight—and not only spiritual, for Paul and the whole Bible are very realistic and see that evil is constantly incarnated."[4]

The violence of love is synonymous with faith, and only this sort of violence is effectual in face of the grotesque. Characters like Thomas in "The Comforts of Home" and Hulga in "Good Country People" fail to recognize the true battle. But others accept it reluctantly, undergo violence and suffering, and rage successfully against the absurd. All O'Connor's protagonists are denied basic needs. A few perceive the grotesque nature of the world; they demand recognition of their own worthiness in this world, sense the futility and frustration arising from this need, and consequently embrace what seemingly is the most lucid course of action —violence. In short, whether we are speaking of the Misfit or of Francis Marion Tarwater, this kind of antagonist revolts against an unsatisfactory state of affairs. He indulges in violence because he wants to see if faith can survive. Flannery O'Connor considers all her characters—

---

[4] *Violence: Reflections from a Christian Perspective* (New York: Seabury, 1969), pp. 172–73. I am indebted to Mr. Ellul for his concept of love as a spiritual force and also for his cogent explanation of the incarnation of spiritual forms. The latter, of course, is standard Catholic doctrine. Miss O'Connor, for instance, in referring to Christ rather than the devil, states: "Christ didn't redeem us by a direct intellectual act, but became incarnate in human form, and he speaks to us now through the mediation of a visible Church. All this may seem a long way from the subject of fiction, but it is not, for the main concern of the fiction writer is with mystery as it is incarnated in human life" *(Mystery and Manners,* p. 176).

and the society they compose—as ruled by this harsh geometry of religion. Against the potential framework of religious order she sets violence and disorder, and then she tries to resolve the ambiguity by forcing her characters into those varieties of extreme situation which test the limits of the grotesque.

The extreme situation reveals the paradoxical nature of violence in O'Connor's fiction. Young Bevel's drowning in "The River," for instance, permits him a unique salvation, as does the drowning of Bishop in *The Violent Bear It Away.* Guizae's crucifixion in "The Displaced Person" is also his sacrifice for a depraved culture. The Misfit's murders reveal the horror of a world without Christ. The flagellation of O. E. Parker, the physical assaults of Manley Pointer, the depravities of Rufus Johnson are all examples of violence operating from the shifting and highly ambiguous perspective, for we see in these stories that the infliction of pain and suffering leads to purification and self-knowledge, either for the victimizer or the victim, or for that curious figure, like the Misfit and Shiftlet, Tarwater and Hazel Motes, who is both victim and victimizer, who initiates violence only to discover that it rebounds upon him. . . .

Revelation of the true kingdom—or, as Miss O'Connor called it, the true country—is a primary concern in her fiction, and it is for this reason that she utilized motifs of violence to get at the incongruous nature of reality and to reveal the vitality of the grotesque as technique and vision. In a paragraph that has become a classic statement on the value of the grotesque one can see how the concept of violence fits into Flannery O'Connor's vision:

> The novelist with Christian concerns will find in modern life distortions which are repugnant to him, and his problem will be to make these appear as distortions to an audience which is used to seeing them as natural; and he may well be forced to take ever more violent means to get his vision across to this hostile audience. When you assume that your audience holds the same beliefs you do, you can relax a little and use more normal ways of talking to it; when you have to assume that it does not, then you have to make your vision apparent by shock—to the hard of hearing you shout, and for the almost-blind you draw large and startling figures.[5]

The world of the grotesque, whether we are talking about O'Connor and Faulkner, Thomas Pynchon and James Purdy, or Vladimir Nabokov and Jorge Borges, is a world of distortions—in character and landscape and also in spirit. Demonic and violent acts therefore are a means whereby we can fix the precise limits of meaning in this alien and mysterious world. At the same time violence becomes a source of hope whereby man can transcend his grotesque condition. As Miss O'Connor has written in reference to "A Good Man Is Hard to Find":

[5] *Mystery and Manners,* pp. 33–34.

We hear many complaints about the prevalence of violence in modern fiction, and it is always assumed that this violence is a bad thing and meant to be an end in itself. With the serious writer, violence is never an end in itself. It is the extreme situation that best reveals what we are essentially, and I believe these are times when writers are most interested in what we are essentially, than in the tenor of our daily lives. Violence is a force which can be used for good or evil, and among the things taken by it is the kingdom of heaven. But regardless of what can be taken by it, the man in the violent situation reveals those qualities least dispensable in his personality, those qualities which are all he will have to take into eternity with him; and since the characters in this story are all on the verge of eternity, it is appropriate to think of what they take with them.[6]

In the broadest sense, to reflect on the grotesque is to reflect upon violence: essentially the modern condition reveals that violence creates a perilous balance between the horrifying and the ludicrous. Flannery O'Connor knew that the grotesque, by descending into the claustral world of violence, of the incongruous and irrational, contains within itself the germ whereby a transcendent order can be discovered: in an ambiguous world you look for absolutes, and when you face the unknown you invariably recognize spiritual mystery. Violence speaks to us about our experience of such a world by revealing the human need for something beyond a purely secular vision.

Grace And Redemption In
"A Good Man Is Hard To Find"
English 102
Eleanor Moyer

Flannery O'Connor's "A Good Man Is Hard To Find" is the story of a family (parents, three children, and the grandmother) on their way to Florida who are killed by an escaped convict and his gang. The main character in the story, the Grandmother, is portrayed by O'Connor as a self-centered, inane busybody. According to Frederick Asals, the Grandmother and many other characters in O'Connor's works, "... are among the least introspective in modern fiction, with minds at once unaware and so absurdly assured that they have refused to acknowledge any deeper self" (93). O'Connor does not show us a demented, evil figure in her depiction of the Grandmother. In fact, in speaking about this character in Mystery & Manners, she tells us that the Grandmother has "a good heart" (110) even though she "is a hypocritical old soul" (111) and that the victory she experiences is one that "we do not allow to someone altogether bad" (111). Even though O'Connor rejects the char-

[6] Ibid., pp. 113–14.

acterization of the demonic for the Grandmother, she and her family are "of the mildly damned—damned not because they are evil, but because they have never seen deeply enough into an experience to be aware that damnation is a possibility or that salvation is an issue" (Martin 134). Using the journey to Florida as the vehicle, O'Connor takes the Grandmother to a destination she has only vaguely imagined and is not prepared for—a violent encounter with reality that will strip away all pretext of superficiality and reveal a moment of grace, the transforming power of redemption.

O'Connor's concern with the presence of sin is portrayed extensively in her works through the use of the grotesque. Wolfgang Kayser's authoritative definition is quoted in Nightmares and Visions:

> THE ESTRANGED WORLD ... Suddenness and surprise are essential elements.... We are so strongly affected and terrified because it is our world which ceases to be reliable, and we feel that we would be unable to live in this changed world. The grotesque instills the fear of life rather than the fear of death. Structurally, it presupposes that the categories which apply to our world view become inapplicable. We have observed the progressive dissolution, ... the fusion of realms which we know to be separated, the abolition of the law of statics, the loss of identity, the distortion of "natural" size and shape, the suspension of the category of objects, the destruction of the personality, and the fragmentation of the historical order.... THE GROTESQUE IS A PLAY WITH THE ABSURD ..., AN ATTEMPT TO INVOKE AND SUBDUE THE DEMONIC ASPECTS OF THE WORLD. (qtd. in Muller 6)

Certainly, the events and characters in "A Good Man Is Hard To Find" would fit this definition: the self-centered but not intrinsically evil grandmother whose salvation is achieved by her being shot to death; the horridly tainted Misfit who mediates Christ's grace; and even the children, John Wesley and June Star, whose obnoxious actions are stilled by a bullet. O'Connor's works are permeated with similar examples of the grotesque whose purpose is to illuminate the horror of evil. Muller describes O'Connor's purpose, stating: "She realized that only a stern intellect, an adamant faith, and an accretion of humor which usually shaded into the grotesque could confront suffering, violence, and evil in this world" (2). O'Connor in Mystery And Manners testifies to her use of the grotesque precisely because her Christian faith makes it so evident. She states:

> ... writers who see by the light of their Christian faith will have, in these times, the sharpest eyes for the grotesque, for the perverse, and for the unacceptable.... Redemption is meaningless unless there is cause for it in the actual life we live, and for the last few centuries there has been operating in our culture the secular belief that there is no such cause. (33)

O'Connor's method of magnifying a character's foibles and self-aggrandizement and/or of exaggerating the action in the plot to the point of the grotesque comes screaming off the page to awaken the modern reader who is so assured that grace is unnecessary because there is no sacred power outside the self to mediate suffering or to protect against the presence of evil.

The Misfit, whose name alone conjurers up the horrors of psychological dementia, is both the focus of evil and the vehicle of grace. The reader first encounters him through hearsay and innuendo. The Grandmother warns, " 'Here this fellow that calls himself The Misfit is aloose from the Federal Pen and headed toward Florida and you read here what it says he did to these people' " (330). Red Sammy's wife declares, " 'I wouldn't be a bit surprised if he didn't attack this place right here ...' " (334). O'Connor heightens our impression of mental instability by a dichotomous description of his appearance that conveys both the wisdom of a sophisticated professor and the horror of a lunatic with a gun:

> The driver got out of the car and stood by the side of it, looking down at them. He was an older man than the other two. His hair was just beginning to gray and he wore silver-rimmed spectacles that gave him a scholarly look. He had a long creased face and didn't have on any shirt or undershirt. He had on blue jeans that were too tight for him and was holding a black hat and gun. The two boys also had guns. (336)

Carter Martin further illuminates the impression of the Misfit created by O'Connor, stating, "... the Misfit is revealed as an outrageous, shocking representative of mankind suffering and protesting against a world of injustice" (229). While he is horrible and perverted, he is not Satan. O'Connor in Mystery and Manners does not "equate the Misfit with the devil" (112). He is as Robert McCown states: " 'a soul blasted by the sin of despair' " (qtd. in Martin 65). It is in this state of emptiness that he is able to perpetrate acts of egregious violence, and it is this emptiness that has theological implications. The Misfit denies his need for God: " 'I don't want no hep. . . . I'm doing all right by myself' " (339). His statement testifies to what O'Connor considers one of the primary evils of this world—individual moral sovereignty. Yet he realizes that it is knowing Christ, having faith in who Christ is, that is the one crucible in life. According to Gilbert Muller: "He indulges in violence because he wants to see if faith can survive" (91). His life, consumed by incarnating evil, is open to some degree to the acceptance of the Christian paradigm. There is then an optimism that the Misfit, according to O'Connor, will become "the prophet he was meant to become" (Mystery 113).

It is the lack of integrity that imbues the Grandmother with the need for grace and redemption. In the opening scene, the Grandmother tries to convince her son to change her vacation plans (which begin the next day) because she wants to travel to east Tennessee instead of Florida.

To enhance her selfish goals, the Grandmother conjures up the dangers to the family of an escaped prisoner and also the need to broaden the experience of the children by taking them to a new place. Yet, despite the futility of her proposal, she is the first one in the car the next morning with her cat Pitty Sing cunningly hidden in a basket. She sets out on the journey satisfied that she has prepared her attire sufficiently to be the one family member who can claim to be "a lady" (331). Her allusions to African-Americans along the way as "pickaninny" (332) and "little niggers" (332) confirm her self-sufficient superiority tinged with racism. Her amusing story of Mr. Edgar Atkins Teagarden is soiled by her declaration that "she would have done well to marry Mr. Teagarden because he was a gentlemen and had bought Coca-Cola stock when it first came out and that he had died only a few years ago, a very wealthy man" (333 emphasis mine). While daydreaming, the Grandmother recalls a plantation she saw in her youth. Knowing that her son Bailey will not want to stop, she garners the support of the children by arousing their curiosity with stories of a " 'secret panel' " (334) hidden in the house. Exasperated by the ensuing melee, Bailey turns the car around to search for the missed turn-off to the plantation, claiming, " '. . . this is the only time we're going to stop for anything like this' " (335). In a brief, throw-away line, O'Connor sets the stage for an encounter with the transcendent.

O'Connor's use of imagery gives the reader sign posts along the way to lead us to this escatological destination along with the Grandmother. The cat is called "Pitty Sing" (331), an almost sarcastic foreshadowing of the impending horror. The journey takes the family past "a large cotton field with five or six graves fenced in the middle of it" (332), an eerie omen which becomes the brunt of the Grandmother's joke. According to Irving Malin in "Flannery O'Connor and the Grotesque," The Tower, a shabby restaurant that offers a brief respite for the family, "is a 'broken-down place' — 'a long dark room' with tables, counter, and little dancing space. Once people went here to find pleasure; now Red Sammy is afraid to leave the door unlatched: he has succumbed to the 'meanness' of the world" (114). As the family continue their journey, they come to the outskirts of Toomsboro, a subtle yet dramatic signal that the climax will soon be at hand. It is here that the family backtracks to the wrong road to meet their fateful destiny.

The Grandmother's willful insistence that they see the Plantation, an ostentatious symbol of exterior pride, drives her to begin a journey that will strip away all pretext of superficiality and lead her to an opportunity for grace and redemption. In her chagrin at realizing she directed the family to the wrong road, she knocks over the cat, who immediately jumps upon Bailey, causing him to drive off the road. Slowly, from the top of a hill, comes a "big black battered hearse-like automobile" (336) that is driven by The Misfit. In an act of impetuous stupidity, the Grandmother blurts out her recognition of the escaped convict, thus placing the family in great jeopardy. From that moment on she tries relentlessly to save her own life. She begins with flattery: " 'I know you're a good man. You don't look a bit like you have common blood. I know you must come from nice people' " (337). After Bailey and John Wesley are killed, she exhorts The Misfit to pray: " 'If you would pray, . . . Jesus would help you' " (339). However, she does not pray herself. After the gang members take the mother, the baby, and June Star into the woods, the Grandmother grovels before The Misfit: " 'Pray, Jesus, you ought not to shoot a lady. I'll give you all the money I've got!' " (340). In her desperation and terror, an epiphany finally dawns: ". . . the grandmother's head cleared for an instant. She saw the man's face twisted close to her own as if he were going to cry, and she murmured, 'Why you're one of my babies. You're one of my own children!' She reached out and touched him on the shoulder" (341). It is this gesture, a touch of mercy and compassion, for which O'Connor offers this explanation: "It would be a gesture that transcended any neat allegory that might have been intended or any pat moral categories a reader could make. It would be a gesture which somehow made contact with mystery" *(Mystery* 111). The Grandmother understands for the first time what she has been prattling about as plea-bargaining material—that he and she are related through the bonds of Christian reality.

With little subtlety, O'Connor culminates the tender moment of the Grandmother's awakening with three bullet holes through her chest. The "shallow, vulgar, selfish" (Martin 134) Grandmother is murdered after finally opening her heart to the movement of grace. Along with many other critics, Claire Katz declares O'Connor's purpose: "to reveal the need for grace in a world grotesque without a transcendent context" (54). Katz goes on to draw this conclusion:

> Again and again she creates a fiction in which a character attempts to live autonomously, to define himself and his values, only to be jarred back to what she calls "reality"—the recognition of helplessness in the face of contingency, and the need for absolute submission to the power of Christ. (55)

It may be somewhat disconcerting but certainly unforgettable to think that the Grandmother's superficial autonomy requires the devastating murders of her whole family before she is drawn into a moment of grace. The idea that the punishment hardly fits the crime catapults the reader into an introspection of his or her own life in ultimate terms. So the reader is drawn along on this journey of salvation. It is not a journey of self-preservation; rather, it is a journey of transcendence into the deepest meaning of reality and humanity.

Works Cited

Asals, Frederick. "The Double." *Flannery O'Connor.* Ed. Harold Bloom. New York: Chelsea House, 1986. 93–109.

Katz, Claire. "Flannery O'Connor's Rage of Vision." <i>American Literature</i> 46 (1974): 54–67.

Malin, Irving. "Flannery O'Connor and the Grotesque." <i>The Added Dimension: The Art and Mind of Flannery O'Connor.</i> Ed. Melvin J. Friedman and Lewis A. Lawson. New York: Fordham UP, 1966. 108–22.

Martin, Carter W. <i>The True Country.</i> Nashville: Vanderbilt UP, 1968.

Muller, Gilbert H. <i>Nightmares and Visions: Flannery O'Connor and The Catholic Grotesque.</i> Athens: U of Georgia P, 1972.

O'Connor, Flannery. "A Good Man Is Hard To Find," <i>Literature: An Introduction to Fiction, Poetry, and Drama.</i> Ed. X. J. Kennedy. 5th ed. New York: Harper Collins, 1991. 330–41.

——. <i>Mystery and Manners.</i> Ed. Sally and Robert Fitzgerald. New York: Farrar, Straus & Giroux, 1961.

❏ Suggestions for Exploration, Research, and Writing

1. In an essay show how the grandmother is responsible for the deaths of her family members.

2. Using the critical essays and at least two characters from the O'Connor stories, discuss what the characters substitute for a belief in God.

3. Compare the grandmother and Mrs. Turpin.

4. O'Connor is especially skillful at using **irony** to portray the problems faced by people who lack a sincere belief in God. Using the critical essays in this casebook and O'Connor's essay, discuss her use of irony in "A Good Man Is Hard to Find" and/or "Revelation."

5. In "The Catholic Novelist in the Protestant South," O'Connor says that a writer's senses respond "to a particular society and a particular history." O'Connor consistently uses the details of her experience to do more than describe. Carefully examine the descriptive passages in the two stories. Then write an essay explaining the functions of the descriptive passages in one or more of the stories: for example, the creation of realism in what some have described as a Gothic world, **symbolism,** or revelation of character.

6. Each of the **protagonists** in the O'Connor stories reaches a point where she realizes her personal inadequacy and helplessness. O'Connor might say that each experiences divine grace. After reading O'Connor's essay and the critical essays in this

casebook, write a researched paper analyzing the nature of divine grace as manifested in O'Connor's fiction.

7. O'Connor has a good eye for the humorously grotesque, seemingly irrelevant details that realistically characterize people. Carefully examine her use of such detail in the stories. Using her essay "The Catholic Writer in the Protestant South" and the critical essays in this casebook, explain how her grotesque descriptions of people express her religious vision.

8. His father said of the Misfit, "'It's some that can live their whole life without asking about it, and it's others has to know why it is, and this boy is one of the latters.'" Compare this Misfit to one or more other questioning misfits such as Mrs. Turpin, Mary Grace, Ozzie Freedman, and/or the narrator of Golding's essay, "Thinking As a Hobby."

9. The Misfit and Mary Grace are violent agents of change in O'Connor's protagonists' lives. Compare them, discussing what each appears to represent in O'Connor's Christian vision.

❏ Suggestions for Writing

1. Several characters in this section think they have all the answers they need about the meaning and purpose of their lives. In an essay, show how these characters are made to see that they, like others, are pilgrims or seekers, that their lives must be a continual quest for meaning.

2. Taking into consideration that the goals of the quest can be defined in a number of ways, choose one essay and one short story and show how they define two different or similar aspects of the quest.

3. Using at least two of the works in this unit, discuss one quest or several quests that seem to be universal.

4. The individual's search for his or her own identity is a major theme in literature. Using two stories and/or plays from this section, write a documented essay on this theme.

5. Using two stories included in this unit, show how complacent people are sometimes forced to seek answers to extremely complex questions about the meaning of life.

6. Write an essay on one of the following topics: quests of the modern individual, religion and the quest, my quest, or my search for identity.

GLOSSARY

Allegory A work in which concrete elements such as characters, objects, or incidents represent abstract qualities. This form of writing is often used to teach religious principles or ethical behavior or to espouse political agendas. Allegories were very popular in the Middle Ages. The play *Everyman* and Dante's *Divine Comedy* are examples. A more modern allegory is George Orwell's *Animal Farm*.

Alliteration Repetition at close intervals of consonant sounds in phrases or lines of poetry: "*b*end / Your force to *b*reake, *b*low, *b*urn, and *m*ake *m*e new."

Allusion An indirect reference to literature, a historical event, a famous person or character, or a work of art.

Anagnorisis In tragedy, the point at which a character reaches recognition, discovery, or self-awareness, the change from ignorance to knowledge.

Analogy Comparison of things otherwise thought to be dissimilar; point-by-point comparison.

Analysis Examination of a subject by separating it or breaking it down into parts.

Anaphora Rhetorical device that repeats a word, phrase, or clause at the beginning of consecutive sentences. For an example, see Elizabeth Barrett Browning's Sonnet 43, lines 7–9.

Antagonist An opposing force or character; that element which opposes or clashes with the main character or **protagonist.**

Apostrophe An address to a real or fictional person or thing.

Aside A dramatic device in which a character delivers a short speech or remark to the audience. This remark usually reveals the speaker's emotions or thoughts; the assumption is that no one except the audience can hear the remark.

Assonance Repetition at close intervals of similar vowel sounds in phrases or in lines of poetry. For example, "I love thee to the d*e*pth, and br*ea*dth and h*ei*ght / My soul can r*ea*ch, when f*ee*ling. . . ."

Beat movement A movement that climaxed in 1956 in San Francisco and New York City and whose members, disgusted by the crass commercialism of society, dropped out, invented their own vocabulary, and experimented with illegal drugs. Beat movement members included writers such as Jack Kerouac, Lawrence Ferlinghetti, Allen Ginsberg, and Norman Mailer.

Blank verse Unrhymed poetry in iambic pentameter (ten syllables with the stress on every second syllable).

Blocking Grouping and arranging action and characters on stage.

Caesura A natural, strong pause within a line of poetry.

Character A person in a work; the personality traits or qualities of that person.

Characterization Development and presentation of the personality of a character, usually through actions, speech, reputation, appearance, and the author's attitude toward this person.

Classification Organization according to a methodical division into groups or clusters; the system of grouping or arranging.

Cliche Expression, idea, or saying that loses its effectiveness through overuse; a platitude; a trite remark.

Climax The moment of greatest excitement, interest, or tension before the resolution of a play or narrative; a turning point.

Comedy A literary work, usually a play, which ends happily and which often includes humor and laughter.

Conflict The opposition between protagonist and antagonist in a play or narrative; the opposition between the protagonist and another force, either within him or her self or without, e.g. between the person and the environment, the person and society, or the person and the cosmic.

Connotation Suggestive, implied, or emotional meaning of a word or phrase.

Consonance Repetition of consonant sounds in a line of verse either at the beginning of or within the words.

Couplet A pair of consecutive rhymed lines in verse. A **closed couplet** has two self-contained, rhymed lines that express a complete thought. An **open couplet** contains two rhymed lines that do not form a complete thought. A **heroic couplet** consists of a closed couplet in iambic pentameter.

Denotation The dictionary, literal, or exact meaning of a word.

Denouement A French term meaning resolution or settlement of loose ends; the untangling of the plot.

Dialect Speech or speech patterns of a particular region, occupational or social group, or culture. Dialect is usually perceived as deviating from "standard" speech.

Dialogue Conversation between at least two **characters.**

Diction An author's choice and arrangement of words and phrases.

Dramatic foil In drama, a character who sets off or intensifies the qualities of another character through a marked contrast.

Dramatic irony Marked difference in knowledge between the audience and a character in the play. The audience understands the meaning of certain words or events which the character does not understand. The most famous example of **dramatic irony** appears in Sophocles' *Oedipus the King.*

Dramatic monologue Poem spoken by one person but addressed to one or more listeners, revealing the speaker's character.

Dynamic Term used to refer to a character that undergoes a change in personality or behavior by the end of the literary work.

Elegy   Lyric poem meditating on or celebrating a death.

Enjambment   The running on of one line of poetry to the next line without end punctuation.

Epic   A long, narrative poem written in a dignified style on a majestic theme, relating the exploits of a national hero.

Epigram   A short, witty poem or saying that makes a satirical point.

Epiphany   In literature, a sudden manifestation or revelation of meaning; an instinctive perception of reality.

Epistolary   Suitable to letters; poetry or fiction composed as a series of letters.

Exposition   The beginning or opening of a play or a story; the introduction of characters, conflicts, and other information important to the reader.

Fable   A short narrative that usually teaches a moral; a short story with an uplifting message; fables often use animals to make a point.

Fiction   An imaginative narrative such as a short story or novel.

Figure of speech   Language not taken literally; image conveyed through nonliteral language such as with a **metaphor** or **simile.**

First person point of view   Narration using *I* or *we*. See unreliable narrator.

Flashback   A break in the chronological presentation of a story to return to the past or to an earlier episode.

Flat character   Character that is not fully developed; the character is often one-dimensional.

Foot   In poetry, a series of stressed and unstressed syllables or heavy and light stresses. The metrical patterns include the following:
Anapest: two unstressed syllables followed by one stressed syllable
Dactyl: a stressed syllable followed by two unstressed syllables
Iamb: an unstressed syllable followed by a stressed syllable
Trochee: a stressed syllable followed by an unstressed syllable
Spondee: two stressed syllables

Foreshadowing   Hints or clues that help to predict a later event.

Genre   Literary type or kind of literature; the four kinds are fiction, drama, poetry, and nonfiction. Genres can be further subdivided, such as nonfiction into the essay or the autobiography and fiction into the novel or the short story.

Gothic   A literary style using a mysterious environment and mood to set the stage for terror and mystery.

Hamartia   The Greek term for the hero's flaw in character or for an error in judgment leading to the hero's downfall.

Hyperbole   Figurative language that uses exaggeration for effect. For example, "It's raining cats and dogs."

Image, Imagery   A mental or visual impression that employs an appeal to one of the five senses.

Imagists   Poets and other artists belonging to a movement that rebelled against Romanticism in the early twentieth century. These artists focused on free verse (unrhymed verse without a metrical pattern) and imagery.

Initiation story A narrative in which a character undergoes some ordeal that leads to maturity.

Irony Contradiction; discrepancy or contrast between what is implied and what is real. **Verbal irony** is the use of words to impart double or opposite meanings. **Situational irony** relates to an event that turns out contrary to what is expected. Also see dramatic irony.

Lyric A short poem expressing the emotions of the writer or singer. In the past, a **lyric** was usually accompanied by the lyre, a musical instrument.

Metaphysical poets A group of seventeenth-century English poets whose works are characterized by incredible and subtle imagery, especially John Donne and Robert Herrick.

Metaphor Figure of speech that uses an implied comparison between two distinctly different things; one term is defined in relationship to another term. For example, life is a cabaret.

Meter The rhythm or beat of verse; a measured pattern of stressed and unstressed syllables. See also **foot**.

Metonymy Figurative language that uses a closely associated attribute to represent the thing itself. For example, the White House often refers to the president of the United States.

Monologue A long speech by a person or character to the audience, to a character not present, or to oneself.

Motivation The reason a character behaves, talks, or becomes what he or she is; the driving force or forces behind a character's actions.

Mystery A narrative whose plot involves the solution of a puzzle or crime and usually creates suspense

Narration A story, fictional or nonfictional; the process of telling a story.

Narrator The teller of a story or novel.

Nonfiction novel A novel that deals with real rather than fictional characters or situations.

Novel A long, fictional prose work with a complex plot.

Octave An eight-line stanza or the first eight lines of a sonnet.

Ode A long lyrical poem addressing or exalting a person or object using a distinguished style and elaborate format.

Omniscient point of view Literally all-knowing point of view whereby the author can recall the thoughts and actions of all characters and can be in several places at once.

Onomatopoeia The use of words that sound like the actions they name: For example, splash or buzz.

Oxymoron A figure of speech which joins two words with contradictory meaning: For example, a heavy lightness or a thunderous silence.

Parable A short story that illustrates a moral or religious lesson.

Paradox A seemingly contradictory or unbelievable statement which upon reflection reveals truth.

Paraphrase Restatement in the writer's or speaker's own words.

Parody A satirical or humorous imitation of another work; a literary work that imitates the style of another work; ridiculing something through imitation.

Personification   Figurative language giving an inanimate object, animal, or abstraction human characteristics: For example, the jungle swallowed him.

Plot   The sequence of events in a narrative. Elements of plot include conflict, complication, climax, and resolution.

Poem   An arrangement of written or spoken words in lines with or without rhyme or meter and typically using figurative language.

Point of view   The perspective from which a story is narrated.

Premise   An assertion serving as the basis for an argument.

Props, property   Furniture or other movable articles in a play. Props do not include costumes, curtains, or background.

Protagonist   The main or central character in fiction or drama.

Pun   Rhetorical device humorously using a word or words with different meanings but with similar sounds; sometimes referred to as a play on words.

Quatrain   A four-line stanza of poetry.

Quintet   A five-line stanza of poetry.

Resolution   See **denouement.**

Rhetorical question   A question that does not require an answer; a question that is asked for effect or to make a point.

Rhyme   In poetry the repetition of sounds at the ends of lines or within lines.

Rhythm   Pattern of stressed and unstressed sounds in poetry.

Round character   A character that is fully developed; a multidimensional character.

Satire   A literary work that ridicules some aspect of society or some human folly or vice.

Satirist   A person who writes satires.

Sestet   The last six lines of a Petrarchan sonnet which rhyme *cde, cde.*

Set   The scenery and properties on the stage.

Setting   The time, place, and physical and cultural environment of a story, play, or poem.

Simile   Figure of speech that compares two distinctly different things using the words *as* or *like.*

Soliloquy   A stylistic technique in which a character voices thoughts aloud to the audience.

Sonnet   A fourteen-line poem in iambic pentameter.

Speaker   The person who speaks a poem.

Sprung rhythm   A highly irregular metrical pattern developed by English poet Gerard Manley Hopkins. A metrical foot may consist either of a single stressed syllable or of a stressed syllable followed by one or more unstressed syllables: for example, "Oh, morning at the brown brink eastward springs—"

Stage directions   Instructions given by the playwright to the stage manager, director, actors, and all others involved in the production of a play.

Static A term used to refer to a stereotypical, simplified character that fails to grow or change in personality or behavior by the end of the work.

Stereotype A fixed or traditional conception of a person, group, or idea held by a number of people without allowing for individuality.

Style The manner in which the author expresses himself or herself. Style includes imagery, symbolism, diction, and sentence structure—the language the author uses.

Symbol An object, person, or action which suggests something else, usually a feeling or abstract quality.

Symbolism The use of symbols in a literary work.

Synecdoche A figure of speech in which the whole stands for a part (e.g., army for a soldier) or a part stands for the whole (e.g., wheels for a car).

Syntax Sentence structure and word order; planned arrangement of words to show relationships.

Terza rima A stanza form utilizing three-line units (tercets) with interlocking rhymes: *aba, bcb, cdc, ded,* and so forth.

Theater of the Absurd Mid-twentieth century drama consisting of absurd, inconsistent, often meaningless situations and conversations which express existentialism or isolation.

Theme Major ideas, moral precepts, or abstract principles underlying a work.

Theme The main idea expressed in a work of literature.

Thesis The central idea of an essay, usually expressed in one sentence in the introduction and then developed in the body paragraphs.

Third person limited Narration of a story in the third person strictly limited to the thoughts and perceptions of a single character.

Tone The attitude of author, speaker, and/or narrator toward the subject or situation of a literary work, for example, ironic, nonchalant, humorous, melancholy, objective, or sarcastic.

Tragedy A play (or other work) showing the protagonist in an internal or external struggle that eventually leads to his downfall or to his ruin; a work in which the protagonist goes from happiness to misery.

Tragic hero or heroine Protagonist in a tragedy who, according to Aristotle, must be basically good but flawed, must be aristocratic, must be believable, and must behave consistently. Modern tragic heroes and heroines do not always fit Aristotle's definition. In particular, they are often working class people.

Unreliable narrator The teller of a story whose narration is biased or limited.

Villanelle A nineteen-line poem made up of five tercets and one quatrain and rhyming aba aba aba aba aba abaa. The first line is repeated in lines 6, 12, and 18; the third line is repeated in lines 9, 15, and 19.

ACKNOWLEDGMENTS

SELECTIONS

Family

"Knoxville: Summer 1915" by James Agee reprinted by permission of Grosset & Dunlap from A DEATH IN THE FAMILY by James Agee, copyright © 1957 by The James Agee Trust, copyright renewed © 1985 by Mia Agee.

"Halfway to Dick and Jane" by Jack Agueros, copyright © 1971 by Doubleday, a division of Bantam Doubleday Dell Publishing Group, Inc. from THE IMMIGRANT EXPERIENCE by Thomas C. Wheeler. Used by permission of Doubleday, a division of Bantam Doubleday Dell Publishing Group, Inc.

"On Going Home" from SLOUCHING TOWARDS BETHLEHEM by Joan Didion. Copyright © 1967, 1968 by Joan Didion. Reprinted by permission of Farrar, Straus & Giroux, Inc.

"Chairman Mao's Good Little Boy" by Liang Heng and Judith Shapiro from SON OF THE REVOLUTION by Liang Heng and Judith Shapiro. Copyright © 1983 by Liang Heng and Judith Shapiro. Reprinted by permission of Alfred A. Knopf, Inc.

"My Oedipus Complex" by Frank O'Connor from COLLECTED STORIES by Frank O'Connor. Copyright 1950, 1951 by Frank O'Connor. Reprinted by permission of Alfred A. Knopf, Inc.

"Why I Live at the P.O." from A CURTAIN OF GREEN AND OTHER STORIES by Eudora Welty. Copyright 1941 and renewed 1969 by Eudora Welty. Reprinted by permission of Harcourt Brace Jovanovich, Inc.

"A Domestic Dilemma" from THE BALLAD OF THE SAD CAFE AND COLLECTED SHORT STORIES by Carson McCullers. Copyright 1936, 1941, 1942, 1950, © 1955 by Carson McCullers. Copyright © renewed 1979 by Floria V. Lasky. Reprinted by permission of Houghton Mifflin Company. All rights reserved.

"A Christmas Memory" by Truman Capote from A CHRISTMAS MEMORY by Truman Capote. Copyright © 1956 by Truman Capote. Reprinted by permission of Random House, Inc. Originally appeared in MADEMOISELLE.

"A Prayer for My Daughter" by W. B. Yeats from THE POEMS OF W. B. YEATS: A NEW EDITION, edited by Richard J. Finneran, pages 188–190. Copyright 1924 by Macmillan Publishing Company, renewed © 1952 by Bertha Georgie Yeats. Reprinted by permission of Macmillan Publishing Company.

"My Papa's Waltz," copyright 1942 by Hearst Magazines, Inc. from THE COLLECTED POEMS OF THEODORE ROETHKE by Theodore Roethke. Used by permission of Doubleday, a division of Bantam Doubleday Dell Publishing Group, Inc.

"There Is No Word for Goodbye" by Mary TallMountain from THE BLUE CLOUD QUARTERLY, Volume 27, Number 1. Copyright © 1981 by Mary TallMountain. Reprinted by permission.

"Nurture," copyright © 1987 Maxine Kumin, from NURTURE by Maxine Kumin. Used by permission of Viking Penguin, a division of Penguin Books USA Inc.

"Daddy" by Sylvia Plath. Copyright © 1963 by Ted Hughes. Reprinted by permission of HarperCollins Publishers and Faber and Faber Limited.

"First Love" by Alicia Suskin Ostriker. Reprinted from GREEN AGE, by Alicia Suskin Ostriker, by permission of the University of Pittsburgh Press. Copyright © 1989 by Alicia Suskin Ostriker.

"Photograph of My Father in His Twenty-Second Year" by Raymond Carver from FIRES: Essays, Poems, Stories. Copyright © 1983 by Raymond Carver. Reprinted by permission of Capra Press.

"Nikki-Rosa" from BLACK FEELING, BLACK TALK, BLACK JUDGMENT by Nikki Giovanni. Copyright © 1968, 1970 by Nikki Giovanni. By permission of William Morrow & Company, Inc.

"The Hongo Store" from YELLOW LIGHT by Garrett Kaoru Hongo. Copyright © 1982 by Garrett Kaoru Hongo. Wesleyan University Press by permission of University Press of New England.

"Fences" by August Wilson from FENCES by August Wilson. Copyright © 1986 by August Wilson. Used by permission of New American Library, a division of Penguin Books USA Inc.

"On Tidy Endings" by Harvey Fierstein from SAFE SEX by Harvey Fierstein. Copyright © 1987 by Harvey Fierstein. Reprinted by permission of Atheneum Publishers, an imprint of Macmillan Publishing Company. This play may not be reproduced in whole or in part without the written permission of the publisher. No performance of any kind, including readings, may be given without permission in writing from the author's agents, William Morris Agency, 1350 Avenue of the Americas, New York, N.Y. 10019.

"Sonny's Blues" from GOING TO MEET THE MAN by James Baldwin. Copyright © 1957 by James Baldwin. Used by permission of Doubleday, a division of Bantam Doubleday Publishing Group, Inc.

"James Baldwin's 'Sonny's Blues': Complicated And Simple" by Donald C. Murray from STUDIES IN SHORT FICTION, Volume 14, Number 4, Fall 1977, pages 353–357. Copyright © 1977 by Newberry College. Reprinted by permission.

" 'Sonny's Blues': James Baldwin's Image of Black Community" by John M. Reilly. Reprinted from NEGRO AMERICAN LITERATURE FORUM, Volume 4, Number 2 (July 1970). Copyright © 1970 Indiana State University. Reprinted by permission.

Men and Women

From "When Grateful Begins to Grate" by Ellen Goodman. Copyright © 1979, The Boston Globe Newspaper Co./Washington Post Writers Group. Reprinted with permission.

"About Men," from THE SOLACE OF OPEN SPACES by Gretel Ehrlich. Copyright © 1985 by Gretel Ehrlich. Used by permission of Viking Penguin, a division of Penguin Books USA Inc.

"Beyond the Cult of Fatherhood" by David Osborne from MS. MAGAZINE, September 1985. Copyright © 1985 by David Osborne. Reprinted by permission of International Creative Management, Inc.

"The Story of an Hour" by Kate Chopin, is taken from *Portraits,* a collection first published by The Women's Press, 1979, 34 Great Sutton Street, London EC1V 0DX.

"Hills Like White Elephants" by Ernest Hemingway from MEN WITHOUT WOMEN by Ernest Hemingway. Copyright 1927 by Charles Scribner's Sons; renewal copyright 1955 by Ernest Hemingway. Reprinted with permission of Charles Scribner's Sons, an imprint of Macmillan Publishing Company.

"The Chrysanthemums," copyright 1937, renewed © 1965 by John Steinbeck, from THE LONG VALLEY by John Steinbeck. Used by permission of Viking Penguin, a division of Penguin Books USA Inc.

"Snapshots of a Wedding" by Bessie Head from THE COLLECTOR OF TREASURES. Reprinted by permission of Heinemann Educational and John Johnson Limited.

"Girl" from AT THE BOTTOM OF THE RIVER by Jamaica Kincaid. Copyright © 1978, 1983 by Jamaica Kincaid. Reprinted by permission of Farrar, Straus & Giroux, Inc.

"What Lips My Lips Have Kissed" by Edna St. Vincent Millay. From COLLECTED POEMS, HarperCollins. Copyright 1923, 1951 by Edna St. Vincent Millay and Norma Millay Ellis. Reprinted by permission of Elizabeth Barnett, literary executor.

"One Perfect Rose," from THE PORTABLE DOROTHY PARKER by Dorothy Parker, Introduction by Brendan Gill. Copyright 1928, renewed © 1956 by Dorothy Parker. Used by permission of Viking Penguin, a division of Penguin Books USA Inc.

"Living in Sin" by Adrienne Rich. Reprinted from THE FACT OF A DOORFRAME, Poems, Selected and New, 1950–1984, by Adrienne Rich, by permission of W. W. Norton & Company, Inc. Copyright © 1984 by Adrienne Rich. Copyright © 1975, 1978 by W. W. Norton & Company, Inc. Copyright © 1981 by Adrienne Rich.

"Metaphors" by Sylvia Plath. Copyright © 1960 by Ted Hughes. From THE COLLECTED POEMS OF SYLVIA PLATH, Edited by Ted Hughes. Reprinted by permission of HarperCollins Publishers and Faber and Faber Limited.

"Breaking Tradition" by Janice Mirikitani from SHEDDING SILENCE, POETRY AND PROSE by Janice Mirikitani. Copyright © 1987 by Janice Mirikitani. Reprinted by permission of Celestial Arts, P.O. Box 7123, Berkeley, CA 94707.

"A Doll's House" by Henrik Ibsen from GHOSTS AND OTHER PLAYS by Henrik Ibsen, translated by Michael Meyer. Copyright © 1966 by Michael Meyer. Reprinted by permission of Harold Ober Associates Incorporated. CAUTION: This play is fully protected in whole, in part, or in any form under the copyright laws of the United States of America, the British Empire including the Dominion of Canada, and all other countries of the Copyright Union, and are subject to royalty. All rights, including motion picture, radio, television, recitation, public reading, are strictly reserved. For professional and amateur rights all inquiries should be addressed to the Author's Agent: Robert A. Freedman Dramatic Agency Inc., 1501 Broadway, New York, N.Y. 10036.

From CATILINE'S DREAM: AN ESSAY ON IBSEN'S PLAYS by James Hurt, pages 102–109. Copyright © 1972 by The Board of Trustees of the University of Illinois. Reprinted by permission of The University of Illinois Press and the author.

From "The Doll House Backlash: Criticism, Feminism and Ibsen" by Joan Templeton from PUBLICATIONS OF THE MODERN LANGUAGE ASSOCIATION, January 1989, pages 37–38. Copyright © 1989 by the Modern Language Association of America. Reprinted by permission of the Modern Language Association of America.

Human Vulnerability

"Heaven and Earth in Jest" from PILGRIM AT TINKER CREEK by Annie Dillard. Copyright © 1974 by Annie Dillard. Reprinted by permission of HarperCollins Publishers.

"So Tsi-fai" by Sophronia Liu. Originally appeared in HURRICANE ALICE, Vol. 2, No. 4 (Fall 1986). Copyright © 1986 by Sophronia Liu. Reprinted by permission of the author.

Reprinted with the permission of Macmillan Publishing Company from KAFFIR BOY by Mark Mathabane. Copyright © 1986 by Mark Mathabane.

"The Grave" from THE LEANING TOWER AND OTHER STORIES by Katherine Anne Porter. Copyright 1944 and renewed 1972 by Katherine Anne Porter. Reprinted by permission of Harcourt Brace Jovanovich, Inc.

"A Rose for Emily" by William Faulkner from COLLECTED STORIES OF WILLIAM FAULKNER by William Faulkner. Copyright 1930 and renewed 1958 by William Faulkner. Reprinted by permission of Random House, Inc.

"A Summer Tragedy" from THE OLD SOUTH AND OTHER STORIES by Arna Bontemps. Reprinted by permission of Harold Ober Associates Incorporated. Copyright 1933 by Arna Bontemps, renewed.

"Death Constant Beyond Love" from COLLECTED STORIES by Gabriel Garcia Marquez. Copyright © 1970 by Gabriel Garcia Marquez. Reprinted by permission of HarperCollins Publishers.

"Where Are You Going, Where Have You Been?" by Joyce Carol Oates from THE WHEEL OF LOVE AND OTHER STORIES. Copyright © 1970 by Joyce Carol Oates. Reprinted by permission of John Hawkins & Associates, Inc.

"Customs of the Country" by Madison Smartt Bell. Copyright © 1988 by Harper's Magazine. All rights reserved. Reprinted from the February issue by special permission.

"I heard a Fly buzz—when I died . ." by Emily Dickinson. Reprinted by permission of the publishers and the Trustees of Amherst College from THE POEMS OF EMILY DICKINSON, Thomas H. Johnson, ed., Cambridge, Mass.: The Belknap Press of Harvard University Press, Copyright © 1951, © 1955, 1979, 1983 by the President and Fellows of Harvard College.

"Because I could not stop for Death . ." by Emily Dickinson. Reprinted by permission of the publishers and the Trustees of Amherst College from THE POEMS OF EMILY DICKINSON, Thomas H. Johnson, ed., Cambridge, Mass.: The Belknap

Press of Harvard University Press, Copyright 1951, © 1955, 1979, 1983 by the President and Fellows of Harvard College.

"My life closed twice before its close; . ." by Emily Dickinson. Reprinted by permission of the Publishers and the Trustees of Amherst College from THE POEMS OF EMILY DICKINSON, Thomas H. Johnson, ed., Cambridge, Mass.: The Belknap Press of Harvard University Press, Copyright 1951, © 1955, 1979, 1983 by the President and Fellows of Harvard College.

"Bells for John Whiteside's Daughter" by John Crowe Ransom from SELECTED POEMS, THIRD EDITION, REVISED AND ENLARGED by John Crowe Ransom. Copyright 1924, 1927 by Alfred A. Knopf, Inc. and renewed 1952, 1955 by John Crowe Ransom. Reprinted by permission of Alfred A. Knopf, Inc.

"Janet Waking" by John Crowe Ransom from SELECTED POEMS, THIRD EDITION, REVISED AND ENLARGED by John Crowe Ransom. Copyright 1924, 1927 by Alfred A. Knopf, Inc. and renewed 1952, 1955 by John Crowe Ransom. Reprinted by permission of Alfred A. Knopf, Inc.

"If We Must Die" by Claude McKay from SELECTED POEMS OF CLAUDE MCKAY, Harcourt Brace, 1981. Reprinted by permission of Archives of Claude McKay, Carl Cowl, Administrator.

"Dulce et Decorum Est" by Wilfred Owen. Wilfred Owen: *Collected Poems of Wilfred Owen*. Copyright © 1963 by Chatto & Windus, Ltd. Reprinted by permission of New Directions Publishing Corporation.

"Incident" from COLOR by Countee Cullen. Copyright 1925 by Harper & Brothers; copyright renewed 1953 by Ida M. Cullen. Reprinted by permission of GRM ASSOCIATES, Inc., Agents for the Estate of Ida M. Cullen.

"Do Not Go Gentle Into That Good Night" by Dylan Thomas. Dylan Thomas: *Poems of Dylan Thomas*. Copyright 1945 by The Trustees for the Copyrights of Dylan Thomas. Reprinted by permission of New Directions Publishing Corporation and David Higham Associates Limited.

"The Death of the Ball Turret Gunner" from THE COMPLETE POEMS by Randall Jarrell. Copyright 1945 and renewal copyright © 1972 by Mrs. Randall Jarrell.

Reprinted by permission of Farrar, Straus & Giroux, Inc.

"On the Subway" by Sharon Olds from THE GOLD CELL by Sharon Olds. Copyright © 1987 by Sharon Olds. Reprinted by permission of Alfred A. Knopf, Inc.

"Othello, the Moor of Venice" from THE COMPLETE WORKS OF SHAKESPEARE, Fourth Edition, edited by David Bevington. Copyright © 1992 by HarperCollins Publishers Inc. Published by HarperCollins College Publishers.

"Design" by Robert Frost from THE POETRY OF ROBERT FROST edited by Edward Connery Lathem. Copyright © 1969 by Henry Holt and Company, Inc. Copyright © 1967, 1970, 1975 by Lesley Frost Ballantine. Reprinted by permission of Henry Holt and Company, Inc.

"Desert Places" by Robert Frost from THE POETRY OF ROBERT FROST edited by Edward Connery Lathem. Copyright © 1969 by Henry Holt and Company, Inc. Copyright © 1967, 1970, 1975 by Lesley Frost Ballantine. Reprinted by permission of Henry Holt and Company, Inc.

"Acquainted with the Night" by Robert Frost from THE POETRY OF ROBERT FROST edited by Edward Connery Lathem. Copyright © 1969 by Henry Holt and Company, Inc. Copyright © 1967, 1970, 1975 by Lesley Frost Ballantine. Reprinted by permission of Henry Holt and Company, Inc.

"Neither Out Far Nor in Deep" by Robert Frost from THE POETRY OF ROBERT FROST edited by Edward Connery Lathem. Copyright © 1969 by Henry Holt and Company, Inc. Copyright © 1967, 1970, 1975 by Lesley Frost Ballantine. Reprinted by permission of Henry Holt and Company, Inc.

"Once by the Pacific" by Robert Frost from THE POETRY OF ROBERT FROST edited by Edward Connery Lathem. Copyright © 1969 by Henry Holt and Company, Inc. Copyright © 1967, 1970, 1975 by Lesley Frost Ballantine. Reprinted by permission of Henry Holt and Company, Inc.

"Home Burial" by Robert Frost from THE POETRY OF ROBERT FROST edited by Edward Connery Lathem. Copyright © 1969 by Henry Holt and Company, Inc. Copyright © 1967, 1970, 1975 by Lesley

Frost Ballantine. Reprinted by permission of Henry Holt and Company, Inc.

"A Servant to Servants" by Robert Frost from THE POETRY OF ROBERT FROST edited by Edward Connery Lathem. Copyright © 1969 by Henry Holt and Company, Inc. Copyright © 1967, 1970, 1975 by Lesley Frost Ballantine. Reprinted by permission of Henry Holt and Company, Inc.

From "Robert Frost and the Darkness of Nature" by Roberts W. French from THE ENGLISH RECORD, Winter 1978. Reprinted by permission.

From "The Hill Wife" by Robert Frost from THE POETRY OF ROBERT FROST edited by Edward Connery Lathem. Copyright © 1969 by Henry Holt and Company, Inc. Copyright © 1967, 1970, 1975 by Lesley Frost Ballantine. Reprinted by permission of Henry Holt and Company, Inc.

From "Storm Fear" by Robert Frost from THE POETRY OF ROBERT FROST edited by Edward Connery Lathem. Copyright © 1969 by Henry Holt and Company, Inc. Copyright © 1967, 1970, 1975 by Lesley Frost Ballantine. Reprinted by permission of Henry Holt and Company, Inc.

From "The Oven Bird" by Robert Frost from THE POETRY OF ROBERT FROST edited by Edward Connery Lathem. Copyright © 1969 by Henry Holt and Company, Inc. Copyright © 1967, 1970, 1975 by Lesley Frost Ballantine. Reprinted by permission of Henry Holt and Company, Inc.

From "Out, Out" by Robert Frost from THE POETRY OF ROBERT FROST edited by Edward Connery Lathem. Copyright © 1969 by Henry Holt and Company, Inc. Copyright © 1967, 1970, 1975 by Lesley Frost Ballantine. Reprinted by permission of Henry Holt and Company, Inc.

From "The Most of It" by Robert Frost from THE POETRY OF ROBERT FROST edited by Edward Connery Lathem. Copyright © 1969 by Henry Holt and Company, Inc. Copyright © 1967, 1970, 1975 by Lesley Frost Ballantine. Reprinted by permission of Henry Holt and Company, Inc.

From " 'My Kind of Fooling': The Decep-

tiveness of Robert Frost" from THE ROBERT FROST HANDBOOK by James L. Potter, pages 47–48, 50–51, 53–61, 64–68, (University Park: The Pennsylvania State University Press, 1980). Copyright © 1980 by The Pennsylvania State University. Reprinted by permission of the publisher.

"It Bids Pretty Fair" by Robert Frost from THE POETRY OF ROBERT FROST edited by Edward Connery Lathem. Copyright © 1969 by Henry Holt and Company, Inc. Copyright © 1967, 1970, 1975 by Lesley Frost Ballantine. Reprinted by permission of Henry Holt and Company, Inc.

"Forgive, O Lord . ." by Robert Frost from THE POETRY OF ROBERT FROST edited by Edward Connery Lathem. Copyright © 1969 by Henry Holt and Company, Inc. Copyright © 1967, 1970, 1975 by Lesley Frost Ballantine. Reprinted by permission of Henry Holt and Company, Inc.

From "The Indispensable Robert Frost" by Donald J. Greiner from CRITICAL ESSAYS ON ROBERT FROST, Edited by Philip L. Gerber. Copyright © 1982 by Philip L. Gerber. Abridged with permission of G. K. Hall, an imprint of Macmillan Publishing Company.

Freedom and Responsibility

"Letter from Birmingham Jail" from WHY WE CAN'T WAIT by Martin Luther King, Jr. Copyright © 1963, 1964 by Martin Luther King, Jr. Reprinted by permission of HarperCollins Publishers.

From I KNOW WHY THE CAGED BIRD SINGS by Maya Angelou. Copyright © 1969 by Maya Angelou. Reprinted by permission of Random House, Inc.

"A Chinese Reporter on Cape Cod," by Guan Keguang from "Freedom of Choice Is Not an Option in China," THE CAPE COD TIMES, March 14, 1987. Copyright © 1987 by Guan Keguang. Reprinted by permission of the author.

"The Man Who Was Almost A Man" from EIGHT MEN by Richard Wright. Copyright © 1987 by the Estate of Richard Wright. Reprinted by permission of Thunder's Mouth Press, Chatto & Windus and Mrs. Ellen Wright.

"Harrison Bergeron" by Kurt Vonnegut,

Art and Language

tion copyright © 1983, 1985 by Alberto Manguel. Reprinted by permission of Farrar, Straus & Giroux, Inc.

"The Kugelmass Episode" by Woody Allen from SIDE EFFECTS by Woody Allen. Copyright © 1977, 1980 by Woody Allen. Reprinted by permission of Random House, Inc.

"Cathedral" by Raymond Carver from CATHEDRAL by Raymond Carver. Copyright © 1981 by Raymond Carver. Reprinted by permission of Alfred A. Knopf, Inc.

"Terence, this is stupid stuff" by A. E. Housman from A SHROPSHIRE LAD—Authorized Edition—from THE COLLECTED POEMS OF A. E. HOUSMAN. Copyright 1939, 1940, © 1965 by Holt, Rinehart and Winston. Copyright © 1967 by Robert E. Symons. Reprinted by permission of Henry Holt and Company, Inc.

"Poetry" by Marianne Moore from COLLECTED POEMS OF MARIANNE MOORE. Copyright 1935 by Marianne Moore, renewed © 1963 by Marianne Moore and T. S. Eliot. Reprinted by permission of Macmillan Publishing Company.

"Ars Poetica," from COLLECTED POEMS 1917–1982 by Archibald MacLeish. Copyright © 1985 by the Estate of Archibald MacLeish. Reprinted by permission of Houghton Mifflin Company. All rights reserved.

"Theme for English B" by Langston Hughes from MONTAGE OF A DREAM DEFERRED by Langston Hughes. Reprinted by permission of Harold Ober Associates Incorporated. Copyright 1951 by Langston Hughes. Copyright renewed 1979 by George Houston Bass.

"Musée des Beaux Arts" by W. H. Auden from W. H. AUDEN: COLLECTED POEMS by W. H. Auden, ed. by Edward Mendelson. Copyright 1940 and renewed 1968 by W. H. Auden. Reprinted by permission of Alfred A. Knopf, Inc.

Lawrence Ferlinghetti: *A Coney Island of the Mind.* Copyright © 1958 by Lawrence Ferlinghetti. "Reprinted by permission of New Directions Publishing Corporation."

"Adam's Task" by John Hollander. Copyright © 1971 by John Hollander. Reprinted by permission.

"The Art of Response" by Audre Lorde from OUR DEAD BEHIND US, POEMS BY AUDRE LORDE. Copyright © 1986 by Audre Lorde. Reprinted by permission of W. W. Norton & Company, Inc.

"beware: do not read this poem" by Ishmael Reed from NEW AND COLLECTED POEMS by Ishmael Reed. Copyright © 1972 by Ishmael Reed. Reprinted by permission of Antheneum Publishers, an imprint of Macmillan Publishing Company and Whitman and Ransom.

"Wadasa Nakamoon, Vietnam Memorial" by Ray Young Bear. Reprinted by permission of the author.

Li-Young Lee. "Persimmons" copyright © 1986 by Li-Young Lee. Reprinted from ROSE by Li-Young Lee with the permission of BOA Editions, Ltd., 92 Park Avenue, Brockport, N.Y. 14420.

"Painting Churches" by Tina Howe. Copyright © 1982 by Tina Howe. Reprinted by permission of Flora Roberts, Inc.

From "Fire and Ice" by Robert Frost from THE POETRY OF ROBERT FROST edited by Edward Connery Lathem. Copyright © 1969 by Henry Holt and Company, Inc. Copyright © 1967, 1970, 1975 by Lesley Frost Ballantine. Reprinted by permission of Henry Holt and Company, Inc.

"There came a Wind like a Bugle . ." by Emily Dickinson. Reprinted by permission of the publishers and the Trustees of Amherst College from THE POEMS OF EMILY DICKINSON, Thomas H. Johnson, ed., Cambridge, Mass.: The Belknap Press of Harvard University Press, Copyright 1951, © 1955, 1979, 1983 by the President and Fellows of Harvard College.

From "I Knew A Woman" by Theodore Roethke from THE COLLECTED POEMS OF THEODORE ROETHKE. Reprinted by permission of Doubleday, a division of Bantam Doubleday Dell Publishing Group, Inc.

From "Le Monocle De Mon Oncle" by Wallace Stevens from COLLECTED POEMS by Wallace Stevens. Copyright 1923 and renewed 1951 by Wallace Stevens. Reprinted by permission of Alfred A. Knopf, Inc.

From "The Sheep Child" by James Dickey from FALLING, MAY DAY SERMON, & OTHER POEMS. Copyright © 1982 by

James Dickey. Wesleyan University Press by permission of University Press of New England.

"Everyday Use" from IN LOVE & TROUBLE: STORIES OF BLACK WOMEN by Alice Walker. Copyright © 1973 by Alice Walker. Reprinted by permission of Harcourt Brace Jovanovich, Inc.

"Nineteen Fifty-five" from YOU CAN'T KEEP A GOOD WOMAN DOWN by Alice Walker. Copyright © 1981 by Alice Walker. Reprinted by permission of Harcourt Brace Jovanovich, Inc.

"In Search of Our Mother's Gardens" from IN SEARCH OF OUR MOTHERS' GARDENS: WOMANIST PROSE by Alice Walker. Copyright © 1974 by Alice Walker. Reprinted by permission of Harcourt Brace Jovanovich, Inc.

"Women" from REVOLUTIONARY PETUNIAS AND OTHER POEMS by Alice Walker. Copyright © 1970 by Alice Walker. Reprinted by permission of Harcourt Brace Jovanovich, Inc.

From FINGERING THE JAGGED GRAIN: TRADITION AND FORM IN RECENT BLACK FICTION by Keith E. Byerman, pages 159–161. Copyright © 1985 by the University of Georgia Press. Reprinted by permission.

From BLACK WOMEN WRITERS by Mari Evans. Copyright © 1983 by Mari Evans. Used by permission of Doubleday, a division of Bantam Doubleday Dell Publishing Group, Inc.

"Patches: Quilts and Community in Alice Walker's 'Everyday Use' " by Houston A. Baker, Jr. and Charlotte Pierce-Baker from THE SOUTHERN REVIEW, Volume 21, Number 3, July 1985, pages 706–720. Copyright © 1985 by Houston A. Baker, Jr. and Charlotte Pierce-Baker. Reprinted by permission.

Quest

"Thinking As a Hobby" by William Golding from "Party of One—Thinking as a Hobby," HOLIDAY MAGAZINE, 1961. Copyright © 1961 by William Golding. Reprinted by permission of Curtis Brown, Ltd.

"Barn Burning" by William Faulkner from COLLECTED STORIES OF WILLIAM FAULKNER by William Faulkner. Copyright 1950 by Random House, Inc. and renewed © 1977 by Jill Faulkner Summers. Reprinted by permission of Random House, Inc.

"The Star" by Arthur C. Clarke. Copyright 1955 by Royal Publications. Reprinted by permission of the author and the author's agents, Scott Meredith Literary Agency, Inc., 845 Third Avenue, New York, N.Y. 10022.

"The Conversion of the Jews" from GOODBYE, COLUMBUS by Philip Roth. Copyright © 1959, © renewed 1987 by Philip Roth. Reprinted by permission of Houghton Mifflin Company. All rights reserved.

"Raymond's Run" by Toni Cade Bambara from GORILLA, MY LOVE by Toni Cade Bambara. Copyright © 1960, 1963, 1964, 1965, 1968, 1970, 1971, 1972 by Toni Cade Bambara. Reprinted by permission of Random House, Inc.

"The Water Faucet Vision" by Gish Jen. Copyright © 1987 by Gish Jen. First published in *Nimrod*. Reprinted by permission of the author.

"The Second Coming" by W. B. Yeats from THE POEMS OF W. B. YEATS: A NEW EDITION, Edited by Richard J. Finneran. Copyright 1924 by Macmillan Publishing Company, renewed © 1952 by Bertha Georgie Yeats. Reprinted by permission of Macmillan Publishing Company.

"Sailing to Byzantium" by W. B. Yeats from THE POEMS OF W. B. YEATS: A NEW EDITION, Edited by Richard J. Finneran. Copyright 1928 by Macmillan Publishing Company, renewed © 1956 by Georgie Yeats. Reprinted by permission of Macmillan Publishing Company.

"After Apple Picking" by Robert Frost from THE POETRY OF ROBERT FROST edited by Edward Connery Lathem. Copyright © 1969 by Henry Holt and Company, Inc. Copyright © 1967, 1970, 1975 by Lesley Frost Ballantine. Reprinted by permission of Henry Holt and Company, Inc.

"Birches" by Robert Frost from THE POETRY OF ROBERT FROST edited by Edward Connery Lathem. Copyright © 1969 by Henry Holt and Company, Inc. Copyright © 1967, 1970, 1975 by Lesley Frost Ballantine. Reprinted by permission of Henry Holt and Company, Inc.

"Directive" by Robert Frost from THE POETRY OF ROBERT FROST edited by Edward Connery Lathem. Copyright © 1969 by Henry Holt and Company, Inc. Copyright © 1967, 1970, 1975 by Lesley Frost Ballantine. Reprinted by permission of Henry Holt and Company, Inc.

"The Love Song of J. Alfred Prufrock" by T. S. Eliot. Reprinted by permission of Faber and Faber Limited.

"Harlem" by Langston Hughes from THE PANTHER AND THE LASH by Langston Hughes. Copyright 1951 by Langston Hughes. Reprinted by permission of Alfred A. Knopf, Inc.

"Saint Francis and the Sow" from MORTAL ACTS, MORTAL WORDS by Galway Kinnell. Copyright © 1980 by Galway Kinnell. Reprinted by permission of Houghton Mifflin Company. All rights reserved.

"ELEANOR RIGBY" Words and Music by JOHN LENNON and PAUL McCARTNEY. © Copyright 1966 by NORTHERN SONGS. All Rights Controlled and Administered by MCA MUSIC PUBLISHING, A Division of MCA INC., New York, NY 10019 under license from NORTHERN SONGS. USED BY PERMISSION. INTERNATIONAL COPYRIGHT SECURED. ALL RIGHTS RESERVED.

"Latin Women Pray" by Judith Ortiz Cofer from TRIPLE CROWN. Copyright © 1987 by Bilingual Press/Editorial Bilingüe (Arizona State University, Tempe, AZ). Reprinted by permission.

"Oedipus the King" by Sophocles, translated by Thomas Gould. Reprinted by permission.

"Traveler in the Dark" by Marsha Norman from FOUR PLAYS MARSHA NORMAN. Copyright © 1984 by Marsha Norman. Reprinted by permission of Theatre Communications Group, Inc.

"A Good Man is Hard to Find" from A GOOD MAN IS HARD TO FIND AND OTHER STORIES by Flannery O'Connor. Copyright 1953 by Flannery O'Connor and renewed 1981 by Mrs. Regina O'Connor. Reprinted by permission of Harcourt Brace Jovanovich, Inc.

"Revelation" from THE COMPLETE STORIES by Flannery O'Connor. Copyright © 1964, 1965 by the Estate of Mary Flannery O'Connor. Reprinted by permission of Farrar, Straus & Giroux, Inc.

"The Catholic Novelist in the Protestant South" from MYSTERY AND MANNERS by Flannery O'Connor, edited by Sally and Robert Fitzgerald. Copyright © 1969 by the Estate of Mary Flannery O'Connor. Reprinted by permission of Farrar, Straus & Giroux, Inc.

From *The Added Dimension: The Art and Mind of Flannery O'Connor,* edd. Melvin J. Friedman and Lewis A. Lawson (New York: Fordham University Press, 1966), pages 32–36 and 45–46. Copyright © 1966, 1977 by Fordham University Press. Reprinted by permission of the publisher.

From NIGHTMARES AND VISIONS: FLANNERY O'CONNOR AND THE CATHOLIC GROTESQUE by Gilbert H. Muller, pages 76–82, 84–87, 88, 90–92 and 97–98. Copyright © 1972 by the University of Georgia Press. Reprinted by permission.

PHOTOGRAPHS

Cover photo by Bob Kolbrener

Page 44: © Henri Cartier-Bresson, Magnum Distribution

Page 238: © Jean Gaumy, Magnum Photos

Page 406: © H. Cartier-Bresson, Magnum

Page 790: © Peter Carmichael, Aspect Picture Library

Page 976: © Graubünden. Foto Heiniger. Photo Researchers, Inc.

INDEX

INSTRUCTOR'S MANUAL

TO ACCOMPANY

LITERATURE AND OURSELVES: A THEMATIC INTRODUCTION FOR READERS AND WRITERS

GLORIA HENDERSON
GORDON COLLEGE

WILLIAM H. DAY
GORDON COLLEGE

SANDRA WALLER
DEKALB COLLEGE

HarperCollinsCollegePublishers

PREFACE

We intend this teacher's manual to serve as a rich and suggestive stimulus to teachers' own ideas for teaching our book. Hence, we have generally avoided prescriptive answers to the questions we ask in the text. If our questions in the text are open-ended enough to stimulate discussion and produce thoughtful essays, it would be presumptuous of us to try to answer them in a few brief comments.

The manual has four parts: an alternate rhetorical table of contents, suggested syllabi, suggestions for teaching writing, and, of course, discussions of each work in the text. The alternate table of contents is intended to help those teachers who want to teach the rhetorical modes. The sample syllabi are intended merely as suggestions for organizing classes. We expect teachers to alter the syllabi to suit their classes. The suggestions for teaching writing contain detailed sample practice exercises.

For our commentaries on the works, we conducted an informal survey of our own English departments to find out what they would use in an instructor's manual. In response to our colleagues' suggestions, we have concentrated on suggesting approaches to works, raising additional questions, and providing background information. Many of the questions and approaches suggested here are reader-oriented, asking students to relate literature to their own experiences.

We have valued inventiveness and usefulness over consistency, providing background on some works while concentrating on student responses to others. Some of the questions are grouped and sequenced while others are not. Believing that the manual should serve as a stimulus for teachers rather than a systematic guide to our book, we have raised far more issues and questions and suggested far more approaches than any teacher could possibly use in a class. We are not prescribing how questions may be used—whether for class discussion, group work, or writing assignments. Moreover, teachers may choose to apply an approach suggested for one work to a different work.

We have endeavored to produce a flexible and useful manual. We hope that teachers will enjoy reading it and that it will help stimulate them to more creative and effective teaching.

Several of our colleagues have been kind enough to share with us classroom techniques and writing assignments that are both innovative and entertaining. In particular, we are indebted to Dr. Susan Ellzey for her suggestions about point of view and imagery in Faulkner's "A Rose for Emily." We are equally indebted to Dr. Rhonda Wilcox for sharing with us Bell's "Customs of the Country" and LeGuin's "The Ones Who Walk Away from Omelas" and for recommending the role-playing exercise in teaching "Customs of the Country." We would also like to thank Landon Coleman for introducing us to Howe's *Painting Churches* and Norman's *Traveler in the Dark* and Dr. Michael Montgomery for suggesting Lee's "Persimmons."

TABLE OF CONTENTS

MEN AND WOMEN

ESSAYS

FICTION

POETRY

FREEDOM AND RESPONSIBILITY

DRAMA

ART AND LANGUAGE

ESSAYS

FICTION

POETRY

QUEST

DRAMA

CASEBOOK STORIES AND ESSAY

RHETORICAL TABLE OF CONTENTS FOR ESSAYS

Personal Narrative

James Agee, "Knoxville: Summer 1915"
Jack Agueros, from "Halfway to Dick and Jane"
Joan Didion, "On Going Home"
Liang Heng and Judith Shapiro, "Chairman Mao's Good Little Boy"
David Osborne, "Beyond the Cult of Fatherhood"
Annie Dillard, "Heaven and Earth in Jest"
Sophronia Liu, "So Tsi-fai"
Mark Mathabane, "The Road to Alexandra" from *Kaffir Boy*
Guan Keguang, "A Chinese Reporter on Cape Cod"
Maya Angelou, from *I Know Why the Caged Bird Sings*
Anne Tyler, "Still Just Writing"
Garrison Keillor, "Attitude"
William Golding, "Thinking As a Hobby"

Exposition

Liang Heng and Judith Shapiro, "Chairman Mao's Good Little Boy"
Virginia Woolf, "Professions for Women"
Gretel Ehrlich, "About Men"
Annie Dillard, "Heaven and Earth in Jest"
Chinua Achebe, "Africa and Her Writers"
Barry Lopez, "Landscape and Narrative"
Alice Walker, "In Search of Our Mothers' Gardens"
Flannery O'Connor, "The Catholic Novelist in the Protestant South"

Comparison-Contrast

Gretel Ehrlich, "About Men"
David Osborne, "Beyond the Cult of Fatherhood"
Guan Keguang, "A Chinese Reporter on Cape Cod"

Argument

Causal Analysis

Classification

Dialogue

WRITING SUPPLEMENT:
SOME USEFUL PRACTICES IN TEACHING WRITING

We use a four-step method of teaching writing that has worked effectively in our classes. This method consists of careful, precisely spelled out assignments, appropriate successful models, repeated practice of writing skills, and thorough marking geared not to justify grading, but to help students learn to write well.

ASSIGNMENTS

Sometimes students come to us asking for help with assignments in other classes. Asked what an assignment requires, a student may respond vaguely, "Just write a ten page research paper on a subject related to the class." In some cases, of course, the student simply has failed to take notes on the assignment or lost the handout specifying it. But in other cases, the teacher has failed to give a clear, specific assignment. Yet the same teacher may complain to the English department about the poor papers he or she receives. We use this example not to criticize teachers in other disciplines who are neither trained to teach writing nor charged with the responsibility of doing so. Rather it is simply to illustrate the necessity for clear, precise assignments.

MODELS

No matter how precise our assignments or how detailed our instructions, students often do not fully understand what is expected of them until they see examples. Either examples of successful student writing or writing done by the teacher for the class may serve as models. These models should be good, but not so good that few if any freshman students can approach their excellence. Nor should they so closely fulfill the assignment that the students are tempted slavishly to imitate their models. The English departments at DeKalb College and Gordon College each regularly produce a book of excellent model essays written by students, *The Polishing Cloth* at DeKalb and *The Gordon Sampler* at Gordon.

PRACTICE

Few of us can do something well on our first attempt. Complex as writing skills are, students should practice them repeatedly. Each stage in writing—brainstorming, organizing, developing, drafting, editing, and proofreading—requires frequent practice. To save grading time, we often assign individual and group practice writing that is later presented to the class.

MARKING

We strive to mark papers carefully and thoroughly, not to justify a grade but to guide the student and help him or her improve. As we read a paper to be marked, we attempt to focus our marking, trying to emphasize a particular weakness and/or strength in each paper and thereby giving students specific skills to practice and reinforcing those skills they have mastered. We do not ignore errors or weaknesses that are outside our focus; rather we try to make our headnote and the bulk of our comments have a consistent direction. If, for example, we find that a student's paper is particularly weak in development, we will mark the usual errors in spelling and grammar, but will emphasize the lack of development in a headnote and marginal notes. We also try to point out one or two examples of specific development, either by marking particularly detailed sentences or by telling the student specifically what he or she might have done to develop the paper more effectively.

NON-TRADITIONAL CLASS STRUCTURES

We have found quite valuable such non-traditional class structures as small groups, pairs, and one-on-one tutorial conferences.

GROUPING

We often ask students to work on assignments in groups of four or five. In dividing a class into groups, it is desirable to group weak students with stronger ones and enthusiastic, assertive learners with quiet, passive ones. If a group repeatedly has trouble getting started, gets off the assignment, or fails to finish its work, we do not hesitate to reorganize it. Group assignments should be clear and precise but open-ended. Groups should also be held accountable either to produce written work or to present to the class the results of their group discussion. Vague assignments and lack of accountability may cause group work to degenerate into bull sessions (not always undesirable). Group work can be effective for practicing brainstorming, organization, and development, and may even help students draft papers.

PAIRS

For some assignments which do not lend themselves to group work, we divide students into pairs. It is best to pair weak students with strong ones. Pairing students works well for editing, proofreading, paraphrasing, and documenting.

4

TUTORIAL CONFERENCES

Often those students who would be reluctant to ask for help benefit most from required conferences with the teacher. We use required one-on-one conferences with students both to help them prepare assignments and to review marked assignments. For example, in helping students prepare a research paper, we might require one conference to review their theses and outlines, a second to discuss their note and bibliography cards, and a third to check their paraphrasing and/or review their rough drafts. These conferences require patience and restraint to guide students in following their own ideas and to refrain from doing too much for them.

SUGGESTIONS FOR IN-CLASS ASSIGNMENTS

The following assignments allow students to practice skills and should follow the teacher's presentation and modeling of the particular skills being practiced.

1. GROUP WORK

a. Practice brainstorming: After dividing the class into groups of four or five, appoint one member of each group to take notes and one member to report to the class the group's findings. Assign to each group a question or a suggestion for exploration. Ask groups to discuss their questions and suggestions in detail and to record their responses. After ten or fifteen minutes ask each group to report to the class a summary of the group's responses.

b. Practice organization or development: Assign to each group a suggestion for writing. Ask each group to produce one or more plans for a paper on the topic assigned, including a thesis and three or four sub-points. After five or ten minutes, have each group report its plan to the class. Then allow fifteen minutes for each student independently to develop a five or six sentence body paragraph on one of the group's sub-points. Encourage students to be specific. Have students within each group share their papers with each member of the group. Encourage students to respond positively to each other's work through smiles, casual praise where appropriate, and comparisons to their own experiences. Discourage negative focus on errors in spelling and grammar. Ask each group to choose its most specific, detailed, successful paragraph to read to the class.

c. Practice development: List on the board or choose from the text several topics which lend themselves to concrete development. Have each student group list details that could develop the topic. If the topic is one that can be developed from personal experience, encourage students to become increasingly specific as they develop their lists. If the topic

5

requires analysis of a work in the text, encourage students to cite specific quotations that develop the topic, then to explain the relevance of each quotation. After fifteen minutes, ask groups to read their lists to the class.

2. PAIRED WORK

a. Practice paraphrasing: After dividing the class into pairs, have students paraphrase a short passage (two or three sentences), then exchange their paraphrases with their partners. Then have students evaluate the paraphrase: explaining in writing how the sentences have been restructured; underlining all words that have not been changed but could and should have been; and circling all words and phrases that distort the meaning of the original. Then have the paired students work together to improve each other's paraphrase.

b. Editing: Have students bring a draft of their next paper to class. After dividing students into pairs, have them exchange, read, edit, and evaluate each others' drafts, following a guide you have prepared for them.

c. Bibliography form: List in scrambled form (e.g. publisher first, followed by title without quotation or underlining, then followed by author's first name, etc.) the information necessary to prepare a bibliography of five works. Have students write the bibliographies, then evaluate each others' bibliographies by comparing them to the models in the text.

3. CLASS RECITATION

a. Practice planning essay test answers: Bring a stop watch to class. Explain to the class that the purpose of this assignment is to train students to respond quickly and efficiently to essay questions without unproductive daydreaming. Tell them that you will read to them an essay question either about a work they have read or about a topic they are all familiar with and that you want them quickly to prepare a simple plan for answering the question. The simple plan should include an abbreviated thesis and a short phrase specifying each of two or three sub-topics for developing that thesis. Tell your students that you will time them, giving them a maximum of five minutes to prepare a plan, and that each should raise his or her hand when finished so that you can indicate how long it took to prepare the plan. Many will surprize both themselves and you by producing competent plans in less than two minutes. After five minutes have elapsed, ask students who finished, particularly the first ones to raise their hands, to read their plans. Students will probably be eager to share their plans; try to avoid calling on students who did not

6

finish as their embarrassment may increase their tension and thereby increase their difficulty in planning papers.

b. Practice specific development: Write on the board two or three very general topics that students can develop concretely such as "Describe the woman at the zoo in Randall Jarrell's poem" or "In response to Agee's 'Knoxville: Summer 1915,' describe a special evening from your childhood." Have each student write two or three sentences specifically developing one of the topics. Give students about ten minutes to write, then have five or six students read what they have written. Ask the class to determine which passage was most specific. Then have students write two or three more sentences making the chosen passage more specific. Encourage students to read their writing aloud.

SAMPLE SYLLABI

1
15 WEEK SEMESTER
INTRODUCTION TO LITERATURE COURSE

This ambitious syllabus, which covers the entire text, is best for experienced teachers working with students who have successfully completed at least one semester of college composition. The syllabus requires six papers, including a major research paper and a final exam. Less experienced teachers or teachers working with less experienced or less capable students should try one of the other, less ambitious syllabi.

Week 1
1 Course introductions
2 "Literature," "Family," Agee, Didion, Capote, Yeats, Hongo, TallMountain, Kumin
3 "Essays," Agueros, Heng & Shapiro, Prodigal Son, Welty

Week 2
1 "Fiction," "Poetry"; McCullers, Plath, Roethke, Ostriker, Carver, Giovanni; assign
       first paper
2 Wilson, "Drama"
3 Wilson, "Writing"; brainstorming and organizing

Week 3
1 Fierstein; practice paragraphs
2 Fierstein, "Sonny's Blues"
3 First paper due; "Men and Women," Shakespeare, Donne, Herrick, Marvell,
       Browning, Millay, Parker

Week 4
1 Assign paper number two; Gilman, Steinbeck, Head, Kincaid
2 Essays, Chopin, Hemingway, Plath, Mirikitani
3 Glaspell, Rich; brainstorming and organizing

Week 5
1 Ibsen
2 Ibsen
3 Ibsen; paper number 2 due

Week 6
1 Faulkner, Mathabane, Oates
2 "Documenting a Research Paper," research skills; Liu, Bontemps, Bell
3 Assign paper number three; Marquez, Dickinson, Robinson, Ransom, Dunbar,
    McKay, Thomas

Week 7
1 Dillard, Porter, Owen, Jarrell, Olds, Frost
2 Shakespeare; brainstorming and organizing
3 Shakespeare

Week 8
1 Shakespeare
2 Paper number three due; Blake, Wordsworth, Jarrell, Sexton, Rich, Ostriker, Mora,
    Harjo, Okita
3 Jefferson, Thoreau, King

Week 9
1 Wright
2 Silko, Vonnegut, Keguang; assign paper number four
3 Soyinka; brainstorming and organizing

Week 10
1 Soyinka
2 Soyinka; paper number four due
3 Lopez, Clark, Allen, Keats, Housman, Moore, Reed

Week 11
1 Tyler, Yourcenar, Keillor
2 Carver, Ferlinghetti, Carroll, Hollander, Lee
3 Achebe, Lorde, Young Bear

Week 12
1 Walker; assign paper number five—research paper
2 Howe
3 Howe, Angelou, Bambara

Week 13
21 O'Connor; brainstorming for research paper
2 O'Connor, Matthew 5, Psalm 8, Milton, Blake, Hopkins, Kinnell, Wordsworth

3 Plato, Golding; researching and organizing

Week 14
1 Roth, Jen, Yeats, Frost, Tennyson, Wheatley
2 Sophocles
3 Sophocles

Week 15
1 Paper number 5—research paper—due
2 Norman
3 Norman

Final exam

2
FIRST QUARTER OF
TWO-QUARTER COMPOSITION SEQUENCE

Week 1
1 Course introduction
2 "Literature," "Family"; Agee, Didion
3 "Essays"; Prodigal Son, Welty
4 "Writing"; writing as process, assign paper #1
5 Writing: brainstorming and freewriting

Week 2
1 Plath, Roethke, Ostriker
2 "Poetry"; Carver, TallMountain, Kumin
3 Writing: organization
4 Write rough draft of paper #1 in class
5 Writing: revising and proofreading

Week 3
1 Write final draft of paper #1 in class
2 Wilson
3 "Drama"; Wilson
4 Wilson
5 Practice writing exercise

Week 4
1 "Men and Women"; Osborne, Ehrlich
2 Goodman, Gilman; assign paper #2
3 Writing: brainstorming and organizing
4 Hemingway, Head
5 Glaspell

Week 5
1 Shakespeare, Donne, Herrick, Marvell, Rich
2 Write rough draft of paper #2
3 Write final draft of paper #2
4 Ibsen
5 Ibsen

Week 6
1 Ibsen
2 Dillard; "Human Vulnerability"
3 Mathabane
4 Marquez; assign paper #3
5 Writing exercise

Week 7
1 Oates
2 Bell
3 Writing: brainstorming and organizing
4 Dickinson, Owen, Thomas, Jarrell, Olds
5 Frost poems

Week 8
1 Paper #3 due
2 "Writing Research Papers"; assign paper #4:
   short, five to seven paragraph research paper based on Ibsen or Frost casebook
3 Writing: brainstorming and organizing
4 Writing: note and bibliography cards
5 Writing exercise

Week 9
1 *Othello*, Act I
2 *Othello*, Act II
3 *Othello*, Act III
4 Paper #4 due: short research paper
5 *Othello*, Acts IV and V

Week 10
1 Writing exercise
2 Brainstorming and organizing
3 Write rough draft of paper #5
4 Write final draft of paper #5
5 Preparation for final exam

Final exam: Paper #6

3
SECOND QUARTER OF
TWO-QUARTER COMPOSITION SEQUENCE

Week 1
1 Indroductions
2 Jefferson
3 Thoreau
4 King
5 Writing: assign first paper; exercise

Week 2
1 Vonnegut
2 LeGuin
3 Brainstorming
4 Organizing
5 Bambara

Week 3
1 Draft paper #1
2 Revise paper #1
3 Silko
4 Soyinka
5 Soyinka

Week 4
1 Soyinka, Jarrell, Mora, Okita; Review of research
2 Walker
3 Walker
4 Brainstorming
5 Organizing

Week 5
1 Achebe
2 Carroll, Keats, Hollander, Lee; Paper #2 due: research optional
3 Keillor, Tyler
4 Allen, Carver
5 Writing exercise

Week 6
1 Brainstorming
2 Howe
3 Howe
4 Draft paper #3
5 Revise paper #3

Week 7
1 Assign research paper; O'Connor
2 O'Connor
3 Writing exercise
4 Brainstorming
5 Plato, Matthew

Week 8
1 Jen, Roth
2 Note taking
3 Donne, Blake, Kinnell
4 Planning conferences on research paper
5 Planning conferences on research paper

Week 9
1 Work on rough drafts in class
2 Sophocles
3 Sophocles
4 Yeats, Frost, Eliot
5 Paper #4 due—major research paper; Yeats, Frost, Eliot

Week 10
1 Clarke
2 Faulkner
3 Writing exercise
4 Review
5 Review

Final exam

FAMILY

ESSAYS

James Agee, "Knoxville: Summer 1915"

Although this essay was published as the prologue, or perhaps, given its musical qualities, as the prelude, to the novel *A Death in the Family,* it was written over a decade earlier than most of the novel and was added by the editors. Readers of the entire novel usually agree with the editors that the essay is the perfect beginning for the book. Given the peaceful mood set in the essay, the date in the title of the essay is especially significant: Agee's father died in 1916.

"Knoxville: Summer 1915" might also be described as a tone poem, for it sets the mood of the novel. A class assignment that should help students to be more aware of the musical and metaphorical effects that Agee creates might start with the second question for discussion. Students could be divided into two groups: one to locate all sound devices such as alliteration, assonance, onomatopoeia, and rhyme and one to locate metaphorical devices--simile, metaphor, personification, oxymoron, synaesthesia. If the class is very large, the groups could be subdivided, with each taking a different device, or the groups could compete to see which finds the most examples of each device.

An interesting discussion or essay on point of view might compare the differing tones created by similar points of view in this essay and in O'Connor's "My Oedipus Complex."

Suggestions for Exploration and Writing, number 1 can lead to excellent class discussions and essays, but it may be difficult for students to comprehend. A good way to start student discussion on this topic might be to ask first "To what extent is a person capable of knowing him or her self?" and second "To what extent can other people ever know an individual?"

Jack Agueros, from "Halfway to Dick and Jane"

This essay is excellent for a discussion of family and friendship, for it has so many implied ideas and has much relevance today, although it was published in 1971. Students might begin by discussing the nature of friendship as opposed to family. Many could point out that some families are dysfunctional, and, therefore, that children turn more and more to others for the togetherness that they crave from a family. Why are families dysfunctional? Why is the lure of the streets more important than life in the house? Agueros does not call the different neighborhood ethnic groups gangs. Are they gangs? Discuss the connotations of friends and gangs. Gangs have increased in many areas. Why do teens and even adults belong to gangs? Are gangs replacing families in the social structure? Note some of the destructive behavior of Agueros and his friends in the essay. Ask students to comment on this behavior.

Agueros says that "the neighborhood had its boundaries." Ask students, "What boundaries does your neighborhood have?" Answers could be physical boundaries such as a certain landmark, intellectual boundaries such as friendship only with those who share a striving for excellence and good grades, or social boundaries such as avoidance of non-Baptists or non-Jews or African Americans. What other types of boundaries exist?

Joan Didion, "On Going Home"

This difficult, but rich and moving essay should appeal to college students whose own perceptions of family and home may very well have changed when they first returned home after going off to college. Many may have experienced a sense of dislocation similar to Didion's. To enhance discussion, it might be useful to divide the class into groups and let them brainstorm about several issues raised by Didion's essay: Have they ever returned home after a long absence to find home radically changed? Have they ever experienced a similar sense of exclusion from their own family? What caused the sense of exclusion? What private languages—methods of communication not understood by outsiders—do their families and groups they belong to use? How do they feel as users of such a language? How do they feel if such languages exclude them? How do older siblings who have left home now relate to the family? How readily do their spouses use private languages and become a part of the family?

Liang Heng and Judith Shapiro, "Chairman Mao's Good Little Boy"

Students may be interested in more background information to further illuminate the relationship between the two authors. Judith Shapiro was the only foreign teacher out of six hundred people in Hunan Province where she worked. The leader of this Province was Deng Ziaoping; the Province was known for its bureaucracy. Also, Mao Zedong had been dead only two years before Liang and Shapiro met. The Chinese people were experiencing the aftershocks of the Cultural Revolution and would have felt disapproval and disdain for both Liang and Shapiro if their relationship had been discovered. When Shapiro confessed to her leader and mentor, officials went to Liang's parents with an

18

image that they hoped would persuade the parents not to approve of the affair: Americans often divorce, and Liang would go to the United States and be abandoned. With this information and the essay in mind, students might be asked to comment on how the two people from two totally different cultures came to be together (other than love). Suggestions might be that one (the Chinese man) wanted to emigrate to the United States or wanted to escape from China's repressive environment.

Following the background discussion, the instructor may want to discuss some of the misconceptions and stereotypes that internationals may have about Americans. For example, students may point out that many Japanese think that Americans are lazy, families are headed primarily by one parent, or Americans are not loyal to each other. Students might want to compare this essay to the ideas presented in Guan Keguang's "A Chinese Reporter on Cape Cod" or to compare the two perspectives (the Chinese child in day care and the Chinese man working as a journalist in the United States).

Another topic for discussion may be the irony of the title in terms of Liang's later relationship and subsequent marriage to an American. Students may comment on the fact that the repressive conditions under which he and others lived did not prevent him from falling in love with an American. Therefore, Liang is no longer Chairman Mao's good little boy. This idea may lead to a writing topic on whether the student is _____'s good little girl or boy.

Or instructors might want students to reflect on childhood remembrances. A good comparison contrast might be chosen from among the following list: Nikki Giovanni's "Nikki-Rosa," Jack Agueros' essay from "Halfway to Dick and Jane," Frank O'Connor's "My Oedipus Complex," and Truman Capote's "A Christmas Memory."

FICTION

Luke, The Parable of the Prodigal Son
Welty, "Why I Live at the P.O."

Many students are probably familiar with Luke's parable, though few are likely to recall its details. The allegorical elements of the parable are simple enough: the son is sinful humanity whom God the Father will love and forgive if only asked. More difficult to comprehend might be the motives of the father (or the Father) and the feelings of the loyal son, who seems justifiably to resent his father's openhearted acceptance of the prodigal.

Welty's story might be seen as a complex variation on the latter issue. Sister is a very complex narrator who would have us believe that, like Luke's stay-at-home son, she remained loyal to the family and that, in fact, she held the family together, in effect serving as the real mother. What she intends as a reasoned explanation for her moving to the post office becomes an inadvertent confession as her petty vindictiveness becomes more and more apparent. She, not the "prodigal" daughter with her unexpected child, disrupts the family with her constant nagging and self-righteousness. Much of the humor of the story arises from the ironic incongruity of Sister's self-justifying tone and her self-condemning revelations.

The difficulty in discussing the story with students is to let them see Sister's character for themselves rather than simply telling them that she is the primary irritant in the family. One might begin by looking at Stella-Rondo's actions, at her presumed guilt, and at her mother's reactions to her return: What, after all, has Stella-Rondo done that provokes Sister's wrathful judgment? Has she in any sense harmed the family or disrupted its members? What are her mother's motives in accepting her and in refusing to consider the questions Sister raises about Stella-Rondo's daughter? What light might the biblical parable of the Prodigal Son shed on her motives and her justification?

You might want to assign Baldwin's "Sonny's Blues" for comparison with the Prodigal Son and Welty's story.

Frank O'Connor, "My Oedipus Complex"

"My Oedipus Complex" is one of several O'Connor stories written from the point of view of a child. O'Connor confessed to having seen an Oedipus complex like his own develop in his son who, according to O'Connor, at the age of eight would willingly have killed his father to marry his mother. Thus when he wrote the story, he had both his own and his son's experiences to draw from.

O'Connor's stories are strongly rooted in his native Ireland, especially in Cork. Students may need help with some of the Irish or British words such as *codded* (made the victim of a hoax), *bloody* (a foul language intensive), and *flaming* (flagrant, glaring). These definitions are taken from the *Oxford English Dictionary*. If students have no previous experience with this dictionary, "My Oedipus Complex" offers a good opportunity for them to learn the advantages of a historical dictionary.

Telling the story from the point of view of an adult recalling a childhood experience has been both popular and successful in modern fiction. Several possibilities for comparison of this point of view are available in the text. Within this unit, students can compare the point of view of "My Oedipus Complex" with that in Capote's "A Christmas Memory." They could also compare it with Porter's "The Grave," Wright's "The Man Who Was Almost a Man," or Faulkner's "Barn Burning."

Question 1 from Questions for Discussion makes a good springboard for essays on irony (definition and exemplification) or on devices which create humor in the story.

Carson McCullers, "A Domestic Dilemma"

The characters in this story, like those in most of Carson McCullers' works, seek to overcome their loneliness and to find a sense of belonging. Like Mick in *The Heart Is a Lonely Hunter*, who incorrectly believes that she is communicating with the deaf mute Singer because he does not answer her, Martin attempts unsuccessfully to communicate with Emily. Like Frankie, who searches for "the we of me" in *The Member of the Wedding*, Emily seeks in vain the sense of belonging and community which she enjoyed in her Alabama home. *The Member of the Wedding* is a short novel and a play, and students might enjoy sharing lines from it with the class. Because both of these novels have been made into movies, the instructor could show part or all of one of the films to the class and ask the class to compare the themes of loneliness and the search for belonging in the story and the movie.

An understanding of the character of Martin is crucial to any interpretation of the story. Ask students to list qualities that Martin exhibits and to prove each quality by matching it with at least one action in the story. Another possibility is to use Question 5 as a springboard to ask students to write a continuation of the story one, five, or ten years later.

For a personal response essay, ask the students to write an essay on "the immense complexity of _____," selecting any concept especially suited to the class (love; hatred; morality; parenting; growing up; resisting peer pressure; selecting a major, a career, a spouse).

A good possibility for a comparison-contrast essay would be to compare the attitudes and consequent behavior of this family with those of the family in "My Oedipus Complex."

21

Truman Capote, "A Christmas Memory"

This beautiful story of a friendship that crosses the generation gap is based on an incident from Capote's childhood. In the *American Short Stories* videotape of "A Christmas Memory," Capote himself narrates the story. After reading the story, students might enjoy telling or writing about their own nontraditional friendships. Another class activity might be to ask students to list the truly unselfish acts of friendship in the story, then list similar acts by their friends.

This story is also an effective vehicle for teaching the use of literary devices in description. Students can be divided into groups to list the uses of onomatopoeia, alliteration, simile, metaphor, and personification and to explain why these devices are effective in the descriptions. Or they might be asked to write descriptions of their own using these devices.

You might ask students to compare Buddy's friend's description of what seeing God will be like and Hopkins' description in "God's Grandeur." Or you might have them compare the friend's description with Mrs. Turpin's vision in O'Connor's "Revelation."

POETRY

William Butler Yeats, "A Prayer for My Daughter"

Yeats' poems are often difficult for students, and this one probably is no exception. One might begin by discussing the highly suggestive image of the still, sleeping child nestled securely in her cradle as the storm howls around her and as her father, in "great gloom," prays for her. One might then ask students to list those qualities the speaker prays his daughter might acquire, then those he prays she not acquire. Then students might discuss in groups the reasons for Yeats' preferences. Why are "beauty overmuch," strong opinions, and "intellectual hatred" undesirable? Why are courtesy and "radical innocence" desirable? How can the soul's "own sweet will [be] heaven's will"? What is the value of "custom" and "ceremony," and how do they relate to the poem's imagery? What is lost when "custom" and "ceremony" are lost?

One might also try to get students to imagine themselves as precisely as possible in the speaker's position and to write their own prose equivalents of the poem, selecting their own images to communicate the concepts of turmoil, of self-defeating zeal, and of serenity. They might also want to consider what part the speaker himself, as father, might have in giving his daughter the serenity he expects the bridegroom to provide through ceremony and custom. It also might be fun to have students write a response to the poem as it might be written by the girl at age eighteen or twenty in a letter to her father. Does she value "custom" and "ceremony" as much as her father does? Does she feel he has provided for her the serenity he demands of her bridegroom?

One might usefully compare Yeats' poem to Head's "Snapshots of a Wedding" and Soyinka's *The Lion and the Jewel*. All three works treat "custom" and "ceremony" with respect. One might consider how much "custom" and "ceremony" might help create the mood of extraordinary serenity and security in Agee's "Knoxville: Summer 1915."

Theodore Roethke, "My Papa's Waltz"

Students usually connect to this short but simple poem. The poem may bring to mind something within their family that is similar to what happens in the poem or the poem may hit a nerve. Students could be asked to respond to the poem by discussing their fathers' negative and or positive characteristics (or the characteristics of whoever reared them). Some may admit that a parent was or is alcoholic or that one parent dominated the other. Some might even discuss abusive homes. Students seem to become very open after reading this poem. From this exchange, instructors can ask the students to respond to the poem in an essay.

Another idea for an essay would be to speculate on what happened to the relationship ten years later. Does the boy become less tolerant of the "whiskey on [his] breath"? Would he still be "clinging" to his father or would he be rebellious? Disillusioned? The students might also want to discuss the relationship from the father's point of view. Would he repeat a similar scene in the kitchen? What about the wife's position in the family? Would her status have changed? Some of these questions might lead to an essay.

One other topic may be to explore father-son relationships through an essay, a short story, this poem or another, and a play. One suggested group would be Liang and Shapiro's "Chairman Mao's Good Little Boy," the parable of the Prodigal Son (or "My Oedipus Complex"), "Photograph of My Father in His Twenty-second Year," and *Fences* or *On Tidy Endings*. Those who wish to go even further can turn the assignment into a research project: they can pick two works and their authors, research the father-son relationship of the authors, and write about the autobiographical nature of the works or about the ways the personal relationships of the authors impacted their work.

If students want to write about broader social issues, the instructor can begin by discussing some of the social pressures on the family and ways that this pressure can be dealt with within the family. Social pressures that students might suggest could include drug abuse (alcohol, prescription drugs, or illegal drugs), criminal behavior, or varieties of sexual behavior that are not accepted by the family members. These social pressures may lead to a discussion of "My Papa's Waltz," "Sonny's Blues," "Nikki-Rosa," and *Fences* or of "My Papa's Waltz," "Nikki-Rosa," and *On Tidy Endings*.

Mary TallMountain, "There Is No Word for Goodbye"

The implications of the poem's title are surprising, even astonishing. Does the Athabascans' lack of a word for goodbye imply that they feel no sense of separation when they are apart? Do they simply not miss the departed person? Is their spiritual sense, their psychic connectedness, so developed that they can sense the presence of people not physically with them? Or do they simply have faith that they will eventually be reunited? One might usefully compare this poem's theme to that of Donne's "A Valediction: forbidding Mourning."

Maxine Kumin, "Nurture"

Kumin's poem, of course, radically extends the idea of family. The poem raises all sorts of questions about the nature of a family. In what sense are pets family members? How well can people of differing cultures blend as a family? How well do families blend when divorcees remarry? How does language bind families together (see also Joan Didion's "On Going Home")?

Sylvia Plath, "Daddy"

This powerful and challenging poem disturbs students and teachers alike. No matter how aware we may be of child abuse, of dysfunctional families, and of the psychological damage many parents inflict on their children, the powerful communication of a woman's undisguised hatred for her father violates our traditional, idealized sense of family. Yet we must recognize that the speaker loves her father as well as fearing and respecting him. One might ask students whether they think the speaker suffered abuse at the hands of the hated father; certainly the poem offers no evidence of physical abuse. If there was no abuse, what accounts for the intensity of the speaker's hatred?

Plath's various images describing the father evoke a stifling, smothering presence, restricting the growth of the young daughter. The memory of that restriction continues to

24

affect the grown woman so that she feels compelled symbolically to exorcise the father, hence the mounting hysteria and ritualized tone of the last few lines. The symbolic, ritualized destruction of the father leaves her free from his haunting presence, free to pursue her own life at last. The imagery and the honesty of the poem might be foreign to us and to our students, but the feeling the poem develops probably is not. To what degree must we all symbolically destroy one or both parents as a part of our growing up and declare psychic independence from them?

Plath's poem might usefully be compared to Roethke's "My Papa's Waltz," where the father's roughness endears him to the son, and to Yeats' "A Prayer for My Daughter." Might the father in Yeats' poem produce such a daughter as the speaker of Plath's? Why or why not? The poem might also be compared to Bell's "Customs of the Country," in which the narrator has lost her child because she abused him, to Roth's "Conversion of the Jews," to Faulkner's "Barn Burning," and even to Soyinka's *The Lion and the Jewel*, where a beautiful young Nigerian girl for a time rejects the traditional male dominance of her community.

Alicia Ostriker, "First Love"

"First Love" is the sixth poem of seven in "A Birthday Suite" published in *Green Age* (1989). The poems in "A Birthday Suite" reveal the tender love of a mother for her daughter through the various stages of the daughter's growth. The first poem, "The Cambridge Afternoon Was Gray," describes the birth of the daughter and the immediate bonding of mother and daughter. The second, "Bitterness," tells of childhood rebellion: The daughter is compared to a bitter, immature apple. The third poem, "Cat," describes the daughter's love for an ugly cat. The fourth, "Design," tells of the flowering of the daughter. In the fifth, "Hair," the mother fondly remembers the scent and feel of brushing and braiding her daughter's hair. The seventh, "Happy Birthday," comes full cycle as the mother telephones her daughter who is about to graduate from college, to celebrate the beginning of a new life for each. In this sixth poem, "First Love," the mother shares with her daughter the agony of the daughter's loss of her first boyfriend.

If the class has both teenagers and parents, several class activities are possible. (1) The instructor can divide the class into groups, being sure that each group has both traditional and nontraditional students. Then each group can share examples of the agony of lost love and techniques of surviving the suffering—from the point of view of the child and of the parent. (2) The groups might be divided into adult groups and teenage groups and asked to give only separate points of view. Another group activity would be to ask students to analyze the similes and metaphors in the poem and to suggest metaphors which illuminate their own experiences. These group exercises can stimulate interchange and understanding and can lead either to personal response essays or to explications of the poem.

Raymond Carver, "Photograph of My Father in His Twenty-second Year"

Carver's moving portrait evokes a man trying to play a role traditionally assigned to his sex, the macho male, but miserably failing. It might be useful to have students try to imagine more precisely those elements of the father's pose that "give him away." What about the father's pose suggests virility? Precisely what look in his eyes and position of his hands detract from his attempt at a virile pose?

Of course, the poem is about the son as well as the father. One might ask what the son has inherited from the father. Does the son share the father's unmanly manner? What are the implications of not knowing where to fish and not holding liquor? Though he cannot thank the father for what the father has not given, what can and does the speaker offer the father in lieu of thanks?

One might usefully compare this poem to Li-Young Lee's quite different tribute to his father in "Persimmons" and to Ehrlich's "About Men" and Osborne's "Beyond the Cult of Fatherhood," two essays about men who break traditional stereotypes.

Nikki Giovanni, "Nikki-Rosa"

This excellent poem shows how a minority culture can be misunderstood. If you have a small class, ask the students to recall one vivid memory. Ask them to freewrite for ten minutes about this recalled experience, using details and appealing to as many senses as possible. Ask for volunteers to read aloud what they have written. Some students may want to develop this freewriting assignment into a full essay.

Those who do not want to write an essay from the freewriting may be interested in contrasting the memories of childhood with the realities. A good question to start discussion would be "What memories have you, as an adult, realized were not as pleasant or happy as remembered?" Some students may want to compare or contrast personal memories with other people's memories of the same event. Students can even interview others who were there to make the contrast lively or the comparison interesting.

Freewriting can elicit other good topics such as the following:
- things that are a "drag"

26

- the innocence of childhood versus the lack of innocence of adulthood
- my secret identity

Garrett Hongo, "The Hongo Store"

You might begin by talking about natural disasters that might strike in your area of the country equal to the danger of the volcano in Hawaii. What precautions might students take? Then a natural progression might be a discussion of what expression of love a family member might use before or during a disaster.

One other natural discussion might result from the poem's language. On one hand, the son is a poet; on the other hand, the father speaks a sort of pidgin English: "'Dees time she no blow!'" and "'I worried she went go for broke already!'" Students might want to explore whether, when there is a gap this large in the language used by father and son, there is also a barrier between the two.

DRAMA

August Wilson, *Fences*

One of the most striking things about this play is the character development: Wilson provides a rich variety of types and individuals. Therefore, a natural beginning point may be a discussion of the protagonist, Troy Maxson. You might begin by asking students what kind of person he is. What is their response to what he does or how he treats others in the play? If the response is negative, why? If positive, why? Can there be both responses to the man? Is he complex or simple, typical or unique? Why are there different responses to him? For example, Cory constantly quarrels with his father, but Lyons seems to get along fairly well with him.

The next character for discussion should be Rose, Troy's wife. When she welcomes Raynelle into her house, is she a saint, a martyr, a Christian? How does she compare to Alberta as a companion and friend to Troy? Is Rose believable?

You might choose to discuss the maturing of the characters. What characters, if any, grow and gain a sense of identity? Does Troy ever gain this growth? What about Cory or Lyons? Ask the students to read "Sonny's Blues" and "Raymond's Run" and to comment on evidence of the characters' growth to maturity.

27

Then ask the students to look at each of the works, including *Fences*, in terms of the African-American experience. Are there any racial or social lessons that are apparent in the stories? An alternate discussion would be to ask the students to compare the three selections in terms of what the narrator, Sonny's brother, says: ". . . what we both were seeking through our separate cab windows was that part of ourselves which had been left behind." Possible ideas would be that Troy Maxson seeks in Alberta the fun-loving side of him that he is missing in his marriage to Rose. In "Raymond's Run," Hazel is seeking the humane, warm side of herself that is missing in her relationship with her brother Raymond and in her relationship with the girls. In her mechanical quest to run and win every race she participates in, Hazel finally has an epiphany about her brother and realizes what she can do to help him and how she can smile at Gretchen and mean it. In "Sonny's Blues" the students may say that the narrator is seeking a bond with his brother, a bond that can help him understand the life Sonny leads and the role music plays in it. This bond may be the part of him that is missing in their familial relationship. Sonny is empty inside because of the perceived suffering that he must experience in order to feel and live his music. The missing part Sonny is seeking is bound up with his brother's failure to understand what Sonny needs.

Another idea is that people sometimes get engulfed by their passion. In *Fences*, Cory's passion is playing football; in "Sonny's Blues," Sonny's passion is his music; in "Raymond's Run," Hazel's is running; in "How Wang-Fo Was Saved," Wang-Fo's is painting. Students may want to compare or contrast the overwhelming passion in any two of the above stories.

Harvey Fierstein, *On Tidy Endings*

Students might be familiar with Harvey Fierstein because of his television roles. He was the voice for the male secretary on *The Simpsons*, a role that he described as the first "openly gay cartoon character," and he played Rebecca's ex-lover on an episode of Cheers entitled "Rebecca's Lover—NOT."

This play is the third in the trilogy of one act plays called *Safe Sex*. The other two plays, *Manny and Jake* and *Safe Sex*, depict conversations between male lovers and are generally described by critics as inferior to *On Tidy Endings*.

A study of this play is an excellent springboard to help students examine the facts and the fallacies about AIDS. Students who have friends, family, or acquaintances who have been victims of this disease may be reluctant to talk about AIDS because of the social stigma attached to it. Some students might be interested in researching the most recent medical knowledge about methods of transmission, progress of the disease, and treatments. Others might like to write essays about the relationships within the play. An instructor might ask the students first to list their honest reactions toward the characters and toward the disease, then to develop essays about the individual characters or about the characters' interrelationships.

One especially effective technique for helping students to discuss AIDS is role playing. Students might be interested in playing the roles within the quadrangle, a variation on the triangle: Collin, the dead man; Marion, his wife; Jim, his son; and Arthur, Collin's "husband." The instructor could ask students to state their feelings in the role as if Collin were alive to hear them; the person in the role of Collin would reply to each of the characters. Students will probably add many dimensions that the instructor may never have imagined. Those with negative views of AIDS and homosexuality may portray the son as embittered about his father's homosexuality; those who feel empathy with Collin may show feelings of sorrow for a life lost or feelings of regret for a son's not knowing more about his father. Students playing the role of Marion may exhibit bitterness or jealousy about a relationship that she believes she deserved but Arthur had.

CASEBOOK STORY

James Baldwin, "Sonny's Blues"

This story appeals to a wide variety of students. It could easily be used in the Art and Language unit because of the theme of communication and the pervasive use of music as a symbol. Students might enjoy comparing the use of music as a means of communication in "Sonny's Blues" with that in Alice Walker's "Nineteen Fifty-five."

A good class activity to help students who are not familiar with jazz is to bring a recording of a jazz improvisation on a melody familiar to the students. If there are music majors or jazz musicians in the class, they can share with the class information about jazz, either recorded or performed live. An excellent paper topic on this story would be a comparison of the two forms of communication—music and speech—or a comparison of the differing forms of musical communication (jazz, blues, whistling, street hymns).

You might also want to divide the class into three groups, giving each group a pair of topics to examine: (1) windows and walls, (2) light and darkness, (3) Sonny and the narrator as parallels to their father and the father's brother. Each group could propose several thesis statements for a comparison. Then individual students can choose from these statements or write their own as a basis for their essays. Because this casebook is short, it is a convenient vehicle for teaching documentation; and all three of these paired topics can be used for short documented essays using one or both of the critical essays.

Further class discussion could stem from asking how the story answers the question "Am I my brother's keeper?" Students could examine both of the brother relationships in the story and show how the mother's account of the father's experience with his brother influences the narrator's behavior toward Sonny. Students might also be asked to draw parallels between "Sonny's Blues" and the Parable of the Prodigal Son.

Students may also use Suggestions for Exploration and Writing numbers 1, 6, and 7 for ideas on documented paper topics. An alternate version of number 6 might be to discuss the two brothers as examples of two different elements of the population of Harlem.

If any of the students are familiar with Harlem today, an interesting comparison-contrast topic could be to discuss changes since Baldwin's time in this multi-racial neighborhood.

MEN AND WOMEN

ESSAYS

Virginia Woolf, "Professions for Women"

Perhaps reading and understanding Woolf's description of "The Angel in the House" will help students to understand the dilemmas faced by Jane in Gilman's "The Yellow Wallpaper," by Minnie Foster in Glaspell's *Trifles*, and by Nora in Ibsen's *A Doll's House*. After the students have carefully examined this description, ask the males in the class to discuss why they would or would not like to be married to The Angel in the House and the females why they would or would not like to be The Angel in the House. Then ask them if The Angel in the House still haunts women today. If so, how? If not, why not? If possible, get a copy of the poem to which Woolf refers, Coventry Patmore's "The Angel in the House," and share it with the class.

This essay presents a good introduction to a variety of topics. Modern stereotypes of men and women could lead to good classification essays. Students could discuss their own experiences resulting from such stereotypes and suggest ways of dispelling or coping with them. Ask students what stereotypes other than sexual they have encountered. This discussion should also be a good exercise in critical thinking; it can help students to see fallacies that are the bases for stereotypes and to question false generalizations used in classifying individuals. If students write classification essays, you might have them exchange readable rough drafts and conduct fallacy hunts. Students who find fallacies in other students' essays should write them on the board without identifying the authors; then the class can identify the fallacies and help to correct them.

Ellen Goodman, "When Grateful Begins to Grate"

The irony of this essay is that even the helpful and sensitive husband unconsciously assumes that certain duties will be performed by his wife and that the wife shares these assumptions. Should a working wife be expected to take charge of household and family management? Is there any reason to assume that women are more capable of such management than men? Why shouldn't men be in charge of certain elements of household management?

To make students aware of just how much more working women do than men, one might have students, perhaps in small groups, list the responsibilities of each of their

31

parents at home. The most striking disparities, of course, are likely to be produced by single parent families, but most students will quickly see that the husband in Goodman's essay is exceptional only because he is far more helpful than the average husband and that most wives, whether working out of the home or not, are likely to work far longer than most husbands. The disparity between women's workloads and men's might make an interesting topic for a comparison-contrast essay.

One might wish to assign this essay with Chopin's "The Story of an Hour," Osborne's "Beyond the Cult of Fatherhood," Ibsen's *A Doll's House*, and Frost's "A Servant to Servants."

Gretel Ehrlich, "About Men"

One might begin a discussion of this amusing essay on the sensitivity of cowboys by asking students what kinds of behavior they expect of cowboys, or even of men in general. The irony of Ehrlich's essay, of course, depends on stereotypical views of both cowboys and men in general as tough and virile. Why, one might ask, do we expect such behavior? To what degree is it natural or genetic? To what degree is it culturally conditioned? How does Ehrlich attack our stereotypes of the tough, macho cowboy?

The undermining of stereotypes in this and the Osborne essay suggests some interesting possibilities for contrast essays. One might ask students to develop an essay contrasting their stereotypes of cowboys (researched perhaps in movies, television programs, or comic books) with the view Ehrlich presents. One might also have students respond by exploring their own confrontations with sexual stereotypes. Discussions of sexual roles might reveal a very petite woman who works as the driver of an eighteen wheeler, eighteen-year-old girls who frequently hunt and fish with their fathers, an eighteen-year-old male baseball player who loves cooking, and a male student who enjoys sewing.

One might usefully assign this essay with the Osborne essay, the Goodman essay, and perhaps even Glaspell's *Trifles*. Would the cowboys in Ehrlich's essay or Osborne, the nurturing father, necessarily be more sensitive husbands than the grating husband of Goodman's essay? Might either be as sensitive to apparently trivial details as the two women in Glaspell's play? One might also compare the men in Ehrlich's essay with those in Hemingway's "Hills Like White Elephants," Browning's two poems, *Othello*, and Soyinka's *The Lion and the Jewel*.

David Osborne, "Beyond the Cult of Fatherhood"

Osborne's essay primarily emphasizes the benefits of the changing role of fatherhood. After students have read the essay, you might separate them into two groups—one male and one female. Ask each group to list the following: the rewards of motherhood, the rewards of fatherhood, the tasks of mothers, the tasks of fathers (perhaps separating these into enjoyable tasks and drudgery). Then ask one student from each group to write the lists side by side on the board for comparison and discussion. You might like next to assign a definition essay, letting each student decide whether to define motherhood or fatherhood.

FICTION

Kate Chopin, "Désirée's Baby"

Although Question 2 asks about the irony of a phrase, students may see other examples of irony in the story. When Désirée's father, because of her having been left on the Valmonde doorstep, asks Armand about the practicality of marrying her, Armand replies that a name does not matter since *his* name is "one of the oldest and proudest in Louisiana." Ironically, he dismisses Désirée because he thinks she has dishonored his name before he discovers that the baby's complexion and race are a result of his own mixed race. It is also ironic that Armand, although reared in France by loving and kind parents until eight years old, treats his "negroes" harshly. Similarly, it is ironic that his father, who loved his mulatto wife dearly, somehow could not convey this loving attitude to their son. Armand rejects his wife Désirée without giving too much thought to the child he has fathered and without any feelings toward the woman whom he had previously loved madly.

Another interesting discussion might be whether opposites attract. Students could be asked to give their opinions and share brief anecdotes to support them. Steer the questions toward a discussion of Armand and Désirée. Are they opposites? Was the marriage doomed from the beginning because of their personalities? Do other character traits also contribute to the breakup? What social factors contribute to marital strife? Students may want to apply some of the answers to marriages or relationships in general.

Another outgrowth of this discussion might be questions of honor: is family honor or name more important than the love between a man and a woman? Does the illusion that Armand has "one of the oldest and proudest [family names] in Louisiana" justify his lying? Armand wants to strike at God or fate by telling Désirée to go without telling her goodbye before she leaves. He feels betrayed by her and by God. Is he justified in feeling betrayed? Is Armand the betrayer at the end? Assemble a panel and ask them to debate these issues.

The concept of betrayal in a relationship could be expanded to include other works in this chapter such as John Steinbeck's "The Chrysanthemums," Robert Browning's "My Last Duchess," Susan Glaspell's *Trifles*, and Henrik Ibsen's *A Doll's House*. Each selection has a different slant on the theme of betrayal, but it might be interesting to note the contrast in who feels betrayed and why.

"The Story of an Hour"

Ask students to discuss the different concepts of freedom in Chopin's story. Louise thinks she is free "body and soul" after she absorbs the news of her husband's death. Yet her freedom is based upon his death. How valid is freedom that is dependent upon someone else's misfortune? Is Brantley free after his wife's death? Students can be asked to read LeGuin's short story "The Ones Who Walk Away from Omelas." This idea of freedom could be applied to marriages or relationships in another way. Does one necessarily give up individuality, i.e., the freedom to be oneself, upon marriage or upon commitment to a relationship? Does personship forbid partnership? What do you think the story is saying about partnerships?

Sometimes students are upset when they realize that Louise is overjoyed that her husband is dead. Ask students to react to her reaction.

Charlotte Perkins Gilman, "The Yellow Wallpaper"

Although this story has an autobiographical basis, students must realize that the story is not straight autobiography but a carefully crafted story. Gilman's illness never progressed as far as the narrator's. Students might enjoy knowing that Gilman mailed a copy of the story to S. Weir Mitchell, the Philadelphia neurologist who recommended the treatment for "hysteria" described in the story, and that he reportedly discontinued the treatment as a result of having read the story.

To emphasize point of view, ask students to rewrite the story from John's point of view or from the point of view of his sister.

34

To see more clearly the extent to which John controls his wife, students should count the number of times that Jane, after giving her opinion, adds "but John says," and then check to see whose opinion results in action.

Students might like to research the treatment of women in the nineteenth century and then discuss the effects of such treatment, using "The Yellow Wallpaper," Chopin's "The Story of an Hour," and/or Ibsen's *A Doll's House*. Class discussions on any of these works could also lead to a comparison of society's expectations of nineteenth-century women with expectations of contemporary women. Students might write essays comparing these roles or expectations or arguing in favor of a particular role for women today.

When "The Yellow Wallpaper" first appeared, it was compared to Poe's Gothic stories. Have students define Gothic and list the Gothic elements of the story such as the "haunted house," the atmosphere of terror, and the chivalric situation of the "damsel in distress" and the hero who attempts to rescue her. (Point out the irony of the husband's fainting.) Then ask students what makes this story more than a simple Gothic tale.

Ernest Hemingway, "Hills Like White Elephants"

The trick in teaching this story is to focus on the nature of the relationship between the man and the woman, not on the abortion. Students must be allowed to discover the truth about the "simple operation" for themselves.

The Questions for Discussion have been carefully arranged to lead students inductively to a discovery of the nature of the operation simultaneously with their growing understanding of the relationship between the man and the woman. One might ask why this man is so insistent on not telling the woman what to do, why he tries to get her to decide to do what he wants. Is he genuinely concerned about her welfare or their relationship? Students might notice that whereas today opposition to abortion is often associated with anti-feminism, in Hemingway's story the chauvinistic and manipulative man clearly supports abortion at least for his lover. In this context, the woman's refusal to have an abortion might be seen as an assertion of her independence from the man. What does the woman's final statement reveal about the change in her relationship to the man? Where and how does the relationship begin to change?

This couple offers opportunities for meaningful comparison to other couples in this unit. One might ask students to compare the man in Hemingway's story to those portrayed in the essays by Osborne and Goodman as well as to the narrators of Herrick's and Marvell's poems. One might also fruitfully compare Hemingway's couple to the couples in Glaspell's *Trifles* and in Ibsen's *A Doll's House*.

John Steinbeck, "The Chrysanthemums"

This story was published in 1937, a time when women were stereotyped as homemakers and growers of flowers, rather than adventurers. Students may want to discuss gender roles. Ask students to make a list of tasks assigned to women and of those assigned to men during the early 1900s. Next, they can make a list of roles in the 1980s and 1990s and compare the list. A lively discussion should follow on whether roles have changed substantially since 1940.

For cultural diversity and gender discussion, have the students read Janice Mirikitani's poem, "Breaking Tradition." Ask them specifically to look at the following lines and relate them to Steinbeck's story:

Discover the lies my mother told me.
The lies that we are small and powerless
    that our possibilities must be compressed
to the size of pearls, displayed only as
passive chokers, charms around our neck.

Students might also look at Jamaica Kincaid's short story "Girl" for the African-American idea of what a female is and/or at Virginia Woolf's "Professions for Women" for the perspective of an actual woman who would have been a contemporary of the character Elisa.

If you wish to continue the discussion of betrayal begun in Kate Chopin's "Désirée's Baby," you could ask the students to write on the following ideas: what would make you feel betrayed in a relationship? Could you get over the betrayal or would it color forever your feelings and the relationship?

Bessie Head, "Snapshots of a Wedding"

Instructors could begin with a general discussion of rituals of marriage in different cultures. For example, students might point out that in the story the bridegroom's maternal aunts enter the yard, sit opposite the bride's maternal aunts, ask questions, and recite the rules. Students may reply that in some households, the father calls the prospective bridegroom in to ask him his plans for the daughter. In some

36

families both the bride's and the groom's parents discuss the wedding plans. Ask the students to relate other rituals. One of them might be that the groom pays only for flowers, but the bride's family pays for everything else. Another is that more and more African Americans are having the usual wedding ceremony first and adding the ritual of jumping the broom at the reception since they have learned that slaves were married by the ceremony of jumping the broom. Asian cultures will have other rituals associated with marriage or courtship. In some cultures, the parents still select the bride for the son or the bridegroom for the daughter.

Essay Question 2 can be expanded into questions about the relationship between gender and education/intelligence. Recent articles in newspapers and in magazines have asked the question of whether girls are smarter than boys. Ask the students to answer this question by secret ballot and to identify the answer only by gender of the respondent. Then tally the results. Are the answers along gender lines? Discuss the results. Next, ask the students whether they think women should have as much education as men. Why or why not? These answers should lead to a discussion of this dilemma: when women show their education or intelligence, they are often considered "haughty [and] arrogant" (as Neo is), yet when men show that they have the same qualities, they are usually considered powerful, masterly, or forthright. Relate these answers to Neo in the story.

You also might want to explore the double standard society has imposed on men and women. For example, Kegoletile's maternal aunts tell Neo to "let him feel free to come and go as he likes," suggesting that he is free to have affairs. Does this freedom to have affairs apply to American men also? If a woman has affairs, how is she judged by society? Read Edna St. Vincent Millay's "What Lips My Lips Have Kissed," and comment on what she says about her lovers.

Jamaica Kincaid, "Girl"

Jamaica Kincaid was born in Antigua; therefore, her directives stem from what she was told to do and not to do. In a culturally diverse class, students might want to discuss differences in what they, as females, have been told or what their sisters or girlfriends have been told. Ask the students to write "Boy." Join all of the sentences with a semicolon as Kincaid does.

As a follow-up to "Boy" or Suggestion 2, divide the class into two groups. Have one group make a list of what males have been told and the other group make a list of what males should have been told. Then have the two groups report the best five from the lists and decide whether the *should*'s ought to be on the *have been* list.

POETRY

Sonnets

This unit presents an excellent opportunity to teach the sonnet form, for it includes both English and Italian sonnets. After teaching students the tradition of the sonnet form, ask them to select two of the love sonnets (Shakespeare, E. B. Browning, Millay) and compare their form, diction, tone, imagery, sound devices, and/or theme.

William Shakespeare, Sonnets 116, 130, 138

Shakespeare's classic definition of love in Sonnet 116 may present special difficulties for students because of its archaic diction. It might be good to begin, then, by simply asking students to define such words and phrases as *impediments, ever-fixed mark*, and *bark*. It might also be helpful to encourage students to paraphrase the poem. You might ask students to compare Shakespeare's definition to other classic definitions of love with which they are familiar such as I Corinthians 13. You might want to ask students how realistic they consider Shakespeare's definition. Is such love genuinely practical or is it an unattainable ideal? If unattainable, is the ideal worth striving for? How practical might such love be as a basis for marriage? Does such love treat the beloved as an inferior, an equal, or a superior? Which, if any, of the characters in the stories and plays and of the people in the essays try to live up to Shakespeare's ideal love?

Students usually find Sonnet 130 more enjoyable and more accessible than Sonnet 116. Sonnet 130 is similar in theme, clearly stating that no matter how physically unappealing his beloved might be, the speaker will continue to love her. He thereby implies that love must depend on more than the merely physical and transitory. You might want to concentrate on the differences in tone between the sonnets. How does the speaker of Sonnet 130 regard the woman he loves? Is his love as pure as the love defined in Sonnet 116? Does he appear to regard his beloved as an inferior, an equal, or a superior?

In discussing Sonnet 138, students might enjoy describing situations (male/female, boss/employee, parent/child) where the participants knowingly lie to each other.

38

Ask the student to explain what a pun is, how it is used in the poem, and how other puns are used in everyday situations to deceive.

John Donne, "A Valediction: forbidding Mourning"

Donne wrote this poem to his wife in 1612 as he prepared to leave home on a journey to continental Europe. According to Izaak Walton, Donne had premonitions of disaster before he left and returned to find that his pregnant wife had lost their child. The calm, reassuring tone of the poem would seem to belie Donne's premonitions. You might ask whom Donne is trying to reassure, his wife or himself? Is the tone of reassurance overstated? How does the carefully controlled versification contribute to the tone? Does it imply that the speaker is trying to control his own feelings as well as his listener's?

As with many poems, while students may feel confused about the poem, they are usually sensitive to its tone. As a brief writing exercise, you might ask students in a paragraph to develop their own extended metaphor for faithfulness. Or you might ask them to write the wife's response.

Robert Herrick, "Corinna's *going a Maying*"

The speaker in Herrick's poem celebrates the beauty of spring, seeing the boundless energy of young couples as a part of nature. You might begin by asking students how the speaker feels about Corinna and about spring. Though they may find parts of the poem difficult, students will almost certainly feel its contagious spirit of joy and energy. How pure are the speaker's motives? What kind of experience is he asking Corinna to share with him? Is he inviting her to join him in lovemaking? In decoration and dancing? In worship? What is the function of the natural imagery? What does the imagery reveal about the speaker's relationship with Corinna? Why, for example, does he describe Corinna's clothes as "foliage" in the second stanza and describe leaves strewn upon her as "gems"? How does the speaker play on religious concepts such as sin, the Ark of the Covenant, prayers (matins), and hymns? You might ask students to describe similarly joyous experiences they have shared with a beloved friend or companion or comparable festivals they have enjoyed.

You will probably have to help students appreciate the precise versification, the use of couplets that seem almost conversational in their rhythms. How does the skillful use of conversational couplets contribute to the theme and tone of the poem, the sense of joyful adoration? How does the versification enhance the religious theme of the poem?

Andrew Marvell, "To His Coy Mistress"

Students have no difficulty understanding the situation and tone of this poem though some may need help fully to appreciate the playful exaggeration of its first stanza. Asked about the speaker's feeling for the listener, some may argue vehemently that his love is genuine while others argue with equal heat that he is simply trying to seduce his listener.

Even if the speaker does love his mistress in the traditional sense, does he respect her as an equal? What is the difference between loving a wife in the traditional sense of possessing her and using a woman as a sexual object? From the perspective of contemporary gender issues, the honorific "mistress" is ironic, and whether the speaker wants to possess his listener only as sexual object or as wife is irrelevant. What in the poem indicates the speaker's desire to possess his listener rather than to love her as an equal? Is he more or less possessive than the speakers of the other love poems in this unit? One might even compare the speaker's attitude to the traditional concept of a husband's possessing his wife with Paul's prescription in Ephesians 5:25 that "husbands love [their] wives, even as Christ also loved the church." It might also be instructive to compare Marvell's poem to Browning's "My Last Duchess," *Othello*, and Oates' "Where Are You Going, Where Have You Been?" How far is Marvell's speaker from the more extreme behavior of Ferrara, Othello, and Arnold Friend?

An interesting writing assignment might be to write a response to Marvell's speaker.

Elizabeth Barrett Browning, Sonnet 43

This beautiful sonnet has been set to lovely but difficult music and is sometimes sung at weddings. Students who are interested in the remarkable love between these two poets might enjoy reading the play *The Barretts of Wimpole Street* or Virginia Woolf's biography of the Brownings' cocker spaniel, *Flush*.

Because the poem is a rich source of poetic devices, it offers a good chance to teach metaphor and sound. Using Suggestion 1, divide students into small groups and ask them to identify all of the examples of these devices. Good class discussions and comparison-contrast essays might be developed by comparing this sonnet with other love sonnets in this unit (see earlier note on sonnets).

Robert Browning, "Porphyria's Lover"
"My Last Duchess"

These two poems by Browning offer a good opportunity to teach the difference between the soliloquy and the dramatic monologue. Interestingly enough, Browning at one time grouped the two poems together under the heading "Madhouse Cells," perhaps because each depicts a man with an obsession. An interesting classroom exercise might be to assign half the class to "My Last Duchess" and half to "Porphyria's Lover." Ask them to explore such topics as (1) the narrators' obsessions, (2) the way each narrator reveals more about himself than about the object of his conversation, (3) the way in which sentence structure in each poem reflects the personality of the narrator. These discussions should lead to a variety of good thesis statements for essays about one poem or for comparisons between the two.

For students interested in more information on "My Last Duchess," a valuable discussion is Loy D. Martin's "The Inside of Time: An Essay on the Dramatic Monologue" in Harold Bloom and Adrienne Munich's *Robert Browning: A Collection of Critical Essays.*

Edna St. Vincent Millay, Sonnet 42

Edna St. Vincent Millay, like Elizabeth Barrett Browning, had a long and happy marriage; however, unlike Browning, Millay had many earlier love affairs during her years of living in poverty as an actress in Greenwich Village. Her memories of these loves are reflected in this sonnet. You might have students explore the similarities in form and differences in mood between this poem and E.B. Browning's Sonnet 43.

Dorothy Parker, "One Perfect Rose"

Ask students to research Dorothy Parker's life to discover some of her witticisms or sharp retorts and to share them with the class. Other students may enjoy rewriting the poem, substituting what they consider the perfect gift. Tell the students to retain Parker's tone.

Adrienne Rich, "Living in Sin"

You might ask students to contrast the two lovers' reactions to the mess of the morning after. In what sense do their responses symbolize their relative positions? What

41

additional responsibilities must the woman assume while the man is free to play at the piano, yawn, and go "out for cigarettes"? In what sense(s) does this poem, in spite of its title, describe a traditional marriage? How does the man in this poem compare to Marvell's speaker and to the man in Goodman's "When Grateful Begins to Grate"? You might ask students to describe the situation from the man's point of view. How might his tone and imagery differ from the woman's?

Sylvia Plath, "Metaphors"

You might discuss the joys, pains, or complaints of pregnancy, asking students for their responses to pregnancies in some of the works in this chapter. For example, examine the father's attitude toward the pregnancy and/or the child in the following stories: "Désirée's Baby," "Snapshots of a Wedding," "The Yellow Wallpaper," and "Hills like White Elephants." What do the fathers have in common? You might also want to branch out into a discussion of women who do not have children. How does being childless affect women? How does society react to childless women? Look at Louise Mallard in "The Story of an Hour," Elisa in "The Chrysanthemums," and Minnie Foster in *Trifles*.

You might also want to discuss abortion. Rather than turn the discussion into a diatribe for or against abortions, form a panel with each student forcefully advocating a method of solving an unwanted pregnancy.

Janice Mirikitani, "Breaking Tradition"

This poem appeals to students. Ask students to list the ways in which they are like or different from their same sex parent or guardian. Then ask the students to write about three generations in their own families, as Mirikitani does, and to explain and describe the differences.

An unusual approach to handling the poem is to have students write an *epistolary essay* to another person (a good friend or an authoritative figure) confessing beliefs or values contrary to those of the recipient of the letter and explaining the reasons for the differences.

DRAMA

Susan Glaspell, *Trifles*

This play is highly teachable because it is accessible to students. In interpreting the play, students quite naturally draw conclusions from symbols, signs, and non-verbal gestures. Nearly all will conclude with the women in the play that Minnie killed her husband because he killed everything she loved. Similarly, most will conclude that the two women are conspiring to conceal evidence from the men. Since neither conclusion is spelled out in the play, one might ask students to elaborate on the basis for their conclusions.

Since the play is short and manageable, it might be good for students to produce in class. Dividing the class into small groups, you might make one group responsible for creating a set design, another for creating props, a third for lighting and other technical effects, a fourth for costuming, a fifth for blocking, and others for interpreting characters' tones of voice, facial features, and gestures. If it is not practical for the class to present the play, each group can present its findings orally to the class. Some may produce drawings, others papers. Alternatively, either let each group produce one long paper or have each person produce a shorter paper on one aspect of the group's assigned task. Several questions may arise within these groups. Why do the men remain ignorant of the evidence that is so obvious to the women and to readers, both male and female? Does the chauvinism of the men in the play contribute to their blindness? How do the women communicate with each other without alerting the men to their findings?

The play raises some interesting moral and legal issues. Why do the women suppress evidence? What might be the legal consequences of their doing so? To what degree are the women morally justified in suppressing evidence about a murder to protect an abused comrade? Should the women have allowed a jury to weigh the validity of Minnie's claims to leniency? Given the nature of legal evidence, what information about Minnie's marriage might have been unavailable to a jury? Considering the setting, how fair might a jury's verdict be? How would the men regard the women's suppression of evidence?

CASEBOOK PLAY

Henrik Ibsen, *A Doll's House*

A Doll's House is significant both as a milestone in the history of drama and as a rich source of discussion about human relations and expectations. An interesting class activity would be to separate the class by gender, then have the males defend Nora's expectations and actions and the females defend Torvald's. Next ask students to write an essay explaining the reasons for the chasm between what these two characters expect and what they actually get.

If you have drama majors or other students who enjoy acting, they can help to make the play come alive by acting roles in key scenes such as the tarantella scene or Nora's final confrontation with Torvald. If not, several excellent film versions are available.

Ibsen's plays are described as problem plays or theater of ideas, yet in his speech to the Norwegian Women's Rights League, he says that he had made no conscious effort to write propaganda. Ask students to define propaganda and to attack or support Ibsen's claim. In the same speech to the Norwegian women, Ibsen states that he writes not about women's rights but about human rights. A class might begin by discussing the concept that no one is free until everyone is free, then discuss the implications of Nora's claims that she is "first and foremost a human being" and that she is not fit to educate her children until she educates herself.

In "On the Poet's Vision," Ibsen says that he has "written on that which only by glimpses and at my best moments I have felt stirring vividly within me as something great and beautiful." Yet he has "also written on the opposite, on that which to introspective contemplation appears as the dregs and sediment of one's own nature." Students might use these statements and others from the speech to develop a documented comparison-contrast essay showing how Ibsen explores both the best and the worst qualities of people in *A Doll's House*.

Students might also be encouraged to develop several comparisons of *A Doll's House* with other works in this text. For example, although "The Yellow Wallpaper" and *A Doll's House* are set in different cultures, they deal with similar situations: husbands who, in the context of their cultural environments, think that they are doing "what is best" for their wives but who underestimate or fail to understand the abilities and desires of their wives. Students might be asked to compare the two situations and to react to the differing ways in which the wives escape. Another interesting possibility would be to compare the repression of Minnie Foster in *Trifles* with that of Nora in *A Doll's House*.

HUMAN VULNERABILITY

ESSAYS

Annie Dillard, "Heaven and Earth in Jest"

Dillard's almost mystical essay might as easily belong in the quest unit as in the unit on human vulnerability. You might begin discussion by asking for students' emotional reactions to the gruesome details Dillard describes. Is the violence of these images necessary or gratuitous? Why? Is the violence of nature a threat to Dillard herself and by extension to the rest of us? Is that violence predictable or explainable? What does the answer suggest about humanity's place in the universe? If, in fact, nature is violent and threatening and if we are all subject to its seemingly whimsical and unpredictable violence, why is the tone of the essay so positive, even joyful?

You might ask students to consider the essay as an extended commentary on the famous opening of William Blake's "Auguries of Innocence":

To see a World in a Grain of Sand
And a Heaven in a Wild Flower
Hold Infinity in the palm of your hand
And Eternity in an hour.

The quality of Dillard's attention to minute natural details results in a powerful sense of divine imminence—a kind of reversal of the journey inward characteristic of both Eastern and Western mystical traditions. You might ask students whether they feel disturbed or comforted by Dillard's essay and why. How do they interpret the presence Dillard vaguely labels "spirit"? How does Dillard develop a sense of that presence? What natural phenomena arouse in your students simultaneous feelings of fear or horror, wonder, and joy? How do they respond to such "pummel[ing]"?

You might usefully assign this essay with and compare it to Blake's "The Tyger," Wordsworth's sonnet "It is a Beauteous Evening," Keats' "Ode to a Nightingale," Psalm 8, Hopkins' "God's Grandeur," Yeats' "Sailing to Byzantium," and/or O'Connor's "Revelation."

Sophronia Liu, "So Tsi-fai"

The young are always curious about death and its meaning. Liu, in her case, wants to know who or what is the arbiter between life and death. Students might want to compare and/or contrast youth's interest in death in the following works: "So Tsi-fai," "The Grave," "The Water-Faucet Vision," *Traveler in the Dark*, and indirectly in "A Christmas Memory."

Liu repeats the phrase, "incorrigible, hopeless, and without hope," in reference to So Tsi-fai. Ask the students whether anyone should be described in this way. If so, why? Form a panel and have the students debate whether these words can be applied to a particular person, group of people, or situation. Some possibilities might be the Somalians after the Americans and United Nations' peacekeeping troops leave, the struggle between the Serbs and Bosnians, black townships in South Africa, the ghettos in inner city America, long-term drug addicts, and religious fanatics.

Although Liu was born in Hong Kong, a British colony, and Liang Heng was born in China, they both write about the school system in their countries. Are the school systems totally different? Compare and/or contrast So Tsi-fai's The Little Flower's School with the day care center in China. Are individual differences celebrated in either system? To what extent do the writers rebel?

Mark Mathabane, "The Road to Alexandra"

It might be helpful to give the class some basic background on South Africa and apartheid. For over three decades South Africa has been ruled by a minority white government representing less than one sixth of the population. Under apartheid, the official system of segregation instituted in 1948 and designed to maintain white minority power and to disenfranchise the black majority, blacks have had virtually no rights. They cannot legally vote, protest in speech or writing against their condition, petition for a redress of grievances, assemble to discuss their plight, or even choose where they live.

Movement of blacks in South Africa is rigidly controlled. Many have been legally confined to government-designated tribal homelands and forbidden to travel out of those homelands without special licensing. Those who work in large cities like Johannesburg must carry special licenses and must live in dismal and crowded slums like Alexandra. Often such workers must leave their families behind in the homelands. Under the so-called pass laws, all people of color must carry identification papers in pass books

48

or risk arrest. During the 1980s yearly arrests for improper papers sometimes exceeded 100,000. "The Road to Alexandra" shows Mathabane's mother's panic when she cannot immediately find her passbook, and a later chapter in *Kaffir Boy* recounts the arrest of Mathabane's father because he is not licensed to live in Alexandra and work in Johannesburg. At least partly as a result of economic pressure from the United States and other countries, the current South African government under President P.W. Botha is working to end apartheid and to expand the rights of South African blacks.

Students will sometimes ask how such a small white minority could maintain such power over a large majority for so long. You might point out that such despotic power has been historically far more common in human societies than has democracy and that arms, armies, and wealth can readily maintain control of a subject population.

In discussing the essay itself, you might want to ask who is responsible for the plight of Mathabane and his family. Apparently, most of the brutal police described in the essay are black. How, then, can the subjection of blacks be blamed on the white minority? To what degree are blacks complicit in their own repression? To what degree are all whites guilty of oppressing the black majority? Does ignorance of the condition of their black neighbors constitute an excuse? Why do whites in South Africa suppress blacks?

You might want to assign this essay with Martin Luther King Jr.'s "Letter from Birmingham City Jail" and Toni Cade Bambara's "Blues Ain't No Mockin Bird." Do these other works suggest similar repression? Who is responsible in these cases? You might ask students to look for and describe evidence of similar conditions in their own communities. Or you might go further and ask students to write a comparison or contrast of their own community to Mathabane's neighborhood.

FICTION

Katherine Anne Porter, "The Grave"

"The Grave" is one of Katherine Anne Porter's most explicated stories. Therefore, it would be a good choice for teaching library research skills. Students could be taught how to locate the earlier explications in *Twentieth Century Short Story Explications* and *Articles on American Literature* and later interpretations in the *Humanities Index* and *MLA International Bibliography*.

As background, students might enjoy knowing that the story is based on an incident in Porter's life but that in the actual incident, Callie (Katherine) told her father about the rabbit and her father beat her brother savagely. Students might also like to know that Miranda Gay and her family are characters in several other Porter stories such as "Old Mortality" and "Pale Horse, Pale Rider." "The Grave" is the last in a sequence of stories about this family entitled "The Old Order." Students working on longer research projects might like to use several of the Miranda stories.

In this initiation story, Porter skillfully blends images of birth and death, but she also shows Miranda's dawning realization of her own femininity and its implications. In addition to asking students to write about their first encounters with death (Suggestion 1), you might ask them to write about any incident which was significant in their own self-realization.

William Faulkner, "A Rose for Emily"

"A Rose for Emily" is often anthologized and often explicated not only because of its excellence but also because it provides examples of many story-telling techniques. In order to illustrate Faulkner's skill in story telling, ask students to rearrange the story in chronological order, then to give their theories about why Faulkner did not write the story in chronological order.

Explain to the students the weaknesses of many surprise endings—when the endings are not foreshadowed in any way or are mere tricks played on the reader because of information withheld. Ask them to prove by listing clues in the story that Faulkner's surprise ending in "A Rose for Emily" is both effective and artistically justified. A good assignment for a comparison-contrast essay might be to have students compare the foreshadowing in this story with that in Flannery O'Connor's "A Good Man Is Hard to Find." For another comparison, see the discussion on Robinson's "Richard Cory."

This story is also especially useful in helping students to see the many facets of good description. Ask them to select descriptive passages which, while conveying vivid sensory detail, also are symbolic or give essential clues about the plot and/or conclusion.

A good class exercise to help students consider to what extent Miss Emily controls her own destiny and to what extent she is controlled (by her father, her cultural environment, Homer Barron, etc.) would be to stage a mock murder trial. The students setting up the prosecution might take the point of view that Miss Emily is a manipulative and arrogant murderess who carefully planned and executed the murder of the man who was about to leave her. The defense might argue that Miss Emily is a victim of circumstances or is not guilty by reason of insanity. Tell students that they must be able to support all of their arguments with examples from the story.

To show how point of view and imagery illuminate interpretation of Emily Grierson (perhaps as a victim or as a sympathetic character), ask students to list all the images that depict her, following the order of the narrator: "fallen monument," grotesque "small fat woman in black," "idol" in window, "slender figure in white," and so on to the end of the story. Then, using the date of 1906 as the death of Colonel Sartoris, ask students to list images in chronological order beginning with the tableau scene—"Emily, a slender figure in white," "A girl with a vague resemblance to those angels in colored church windows—sort of tragic and serene," driving with Homer Barron "in the yellow-wheeled buggy," "lighthouse-keeper's face," and so on. This exercise should help students to realize that images, point of view, and method of narration can control their interpretation of character. By listing events in chronological order, students see Miss Emily as an innocent figure and understand her metamorphosis from a figure in white to a grotesque in black; they see her as a victim of her father, the town, Homer Barron, and her madness.

Arna Bontemps, "A Summer Tragedy"

The language that Bontemps uses is very vivid: "hideous toothless grimace," Jennie's "shrunken voice," her "negligible legs," and Jeff's "dead-leaf appearance." Bontemps also personifies things: Jeff Patton's thoughts "swam, . . . rushed, crossed one another, jostled, collided, retreated, and rushed again." Ask the students to show how Bontemps uses language to create the effect of defeat.

Is the story a tragedy? The instructor should give the students the classical definition of tragedy (or refer them to the entry under *Othello* in the text). Then ask the students if they think the definition is still relevant today. Eventually, bring them around to a modern definition of tragedy, one in which they could use some of Aristotle's characteristics as well as add some of their own. Obviously, Bontemps thinks the story is tragic. Jeff Patton has had a stroke; Jennie, his wife, is nearly blind; they have lost five children in two years; they feel they will never get ahead with their crops that they have to give to Mr. Stevenson; and Jeff feels that he will be "worse off than if he were dead." Yet, the students may argue that the tragedy is not in the conditions of the Pattons' lives but in the act of suicide. Discuss this idea with them. If old age and death are inevitable, why would anyone think the Pattons are tragic figures?

Students may want to debate the pros and cons of suicide. Many of them might want to look at this idea in terms of the Hemlock Society and Jack Kevorkian, the man who uses the suicide machine. Should a man-made machine, medicines, or humans help someone to die?

Gabriel Garcia Marquez, "Death Constant Beyond Love"

You might begin a discussion of Marquez's story by asking students why the people continue to re-elect Sanchez. How does he manipulate voters? In what sense are the people themselves complicit in his corruption and deception? Would your students consider voting for him? Why or why not? What examples can they cite of similar deception and corruption in politicians they may have supported? Have they ever been complicit by silence or tolerance in such corruption and deception? Does willful tolerance of corruption make one morally culpable? You might even consider as a paper topic why students would or would not vote for Sanchez.

Marquez draws his portrait of the corrupt, deceptive, death-denying Sanchez in marked contrast to Marcus Aurelius, the Stoic Roman philosopher-emperor who was honest and incorruptible, who believed in the rule of law and the freedom of the Roman people, and who apparently saw as the highest end of government the happiness of its people. Twice at least Marquez's story clearly alludes to book IV of Marcus Aurelius' *Meditations*. Whereas Sanchez refuses to tell anyone of his impending death "not because of pride but out of shame," Aurelius says:

> Death, like birth, is a mystery of nature. The one is a joining together of the same elements into which the other is dissolving. In any case, it is nothing of which one should be ashamed, for it is not incompatible with the nature of a rational being or the logic of its composition. (IV:5)

Sanchez's speech beginning "'We are here for the purpose of defeating nature,'" which he considers "the opposite of a fatalistic pronouncement by Marcus Aurelius in the fourth book of his *Meditations*," may allude to such Aurelian pronouncements as "'Everything which happens is right'" (IV:10) and "Journey then through this moment of time in accord with nature" (IV:48). After reading to students these quotations from Marcus Aurelius, you might ask them to write a contrast between the philosopher-king and Sanchez. How does Sanchez's usual behavior contrast to Aurelius' philosophy?

After discussing Sanchez as a politician contrasting sharply to the ideal philosopher-king, you might want to examine the moral implications of his behavior. Is

Sanchez wholly without principle? Does he have any compassion at all for his people? Clearly he sees through his own deceptions and sees their tawdriness. Why does he persist in deception? What does his behavior suggest about the nature and place of evil in human personality? Why does he, as a happily married man, begin an affair with Laura? What does he sacrifice in a vain effort to escape or forget his imminent death? In what ways does his obsession with mortality, his acute awareness of his own vulnerability, come to control his life? The question of how impending death changes the behavior of strong-willed, controlling, manipulative people like Sanchez might make another good topic for a paper.

The Meditations of Marcus Aurelius. Trans. G.M.A. Grube. Indianapolis: Bobbs-Merrill, 1963.

Joyce Carol Oates, "Where Are You Going, Where Have You Been?"

This rich and disturbing story can be read in a variety of ways, including the following: as a naturalistic story of a girl's kidnapping by a psychopath, as an exploration of the nature of evil and of its demonic sources, as a dream of wish fulfillment with nightmarish qualities, and as a critique of popular culture. You might begin by asking students how they respond to the story emotionally. Is it frightening, disturbing, encouraging? What do they think will happen to Connie? Expect a variety of answers which may reasonably lead to the conclusion that neither she nor we know what will happen and that uncertainty helps make the story disturbing.

You might follow with questions about how the students respond to Connie. Do they identify with her? Would they have left with Arnold or resisted his seduction? If the latter, how? What makes Connie peculiarly vulnerable to Arnold? What is her home life like? Where does she seek affirmation and identity? How does Arnold seem to fulfill her needs?

At least one student is likely to suggest that Arnold Friend is the devil, or at least a demon. Once the idea is suggested, other students are likely to agree. You might pursue this issue by asking what basis there is for labeling Arnold demonic. Is there physical evidence? Is there psychological and emotional evidence? Arnold's extraordinary insight into Connie and his power over her suggest the supernatural as does his capacity to manipulate her. Does what he wants from her in any way suggest that he might be the devil or the devil's agent? What evidence is there that he is trying to possess her emotionally as well as physically? How might he be said to have raped her in the story itself? What kind of damage has he done to her?

If the story is read as a dream, what does that dream reveal about Connie's needs and values? How might the dream be seen as a symbolic fulfillment of her wishes? What qualities in Arnold Friend are dreamlike, and how does he seem an incarnation of Connie's values and longings? What is the function of Arnold's companion, Ellie?

As a critique of popular culture, the story suggests the seductive dangers of romantic dreams. You might begin by asking your class what kind of music Connie listens to. What kind of world does that music create? How do Connie's friendships, the places where she hangs out, and her activities—in short, the youth culture that defines her—reinforce the effect of this music? How might this culture make young people like Connie vulnerable? How does Arnold exemplify the culture and its dangers?

You might want to compare this story to Marlowe's "To His Coy Mistress," to Walker's "Nineteen Fifty-five," and to "Hills Like White Elephants."

Madison Smartt Bell, "Customs of the Country"

You might want to begin discussion of this heartbreaking story by asking students to play the role of a judge or official asked to rule on Davey's case. Would they award custody to the mother or to the Bakers? Why? Based on the setting of the story, what kind of home could the mother provide for Davey? What kind of home would the Bakers provide? Alternatively, you might want to use role playing, assigning to one or a group of students the role of the mother's lawyer, to another student or group the role of Davey's social worker, to a third the role of the Bakers' attorney, and to a fourth student or group the role of a judge deciding the case. Once the mother's attorney, the Bakers' attorney, and Davey's social worker have presented their cases, the judge should allow rebuttal and cross questioning by each, then open the debate to the class.

In judging the case the students will want to consider, of course, the psychological and emotional condition of Davey's mother. What evidence can they cite that she loves Davey? What does her playing with him at the Bakers' reveal about her relationship to Davey? Why and how did she abuse Davey? She is honest both with the reader and with herself in facing up to her abuse of Davey. Do you admire her for her honesty? Why or why not? Why does she hit Susan's husband with a frying pan? What might this act reveal about her fitness as a mother?

Having analyzed the mother, you might want to ask your students to respond more personally. Can they honestly say that under similar pressure they would not abuse a child? Why or why not? If they insist they would not, precisely what would restrain them? If they think themselves capable of child abuse under such pressures, could they be as honest about it as the narrator of Bell's story? The story creates from its opening sentence a sense of hopeless, futile waiting, as the narrator "just gradually [gets] used to losing [her] child forever." You might ask your students whether they have ever experienced a similar sense of hopelessness. How does the hopelessness of Bell's narrator compare to that of So Tsi-fai?

Finally, students will almost inevitably want to examine the moral implications of Bell's story. What kind of moral environment has the narrator inhabited in her past with her husband? What kind has she chosen in the present? In this apparent moral wasteland, what values does the story affirm? Near the end of the story the narrator says, "There's no forgiveness." What does she mean? Is this a fair assessment of her world and her experience? Who has not forgiven her? Have you forgiven her? Why or why not? Do you approve of her hitting Susan's husband? Why or why not?

You might wish to assign this story with the family unit. Useful comparisons might be made to Wilson's *Fences* and to Fierstein's *On Tidy Endings*. Writing assignments might focus on the story's general tone of hopeless waiting, on whether or not the narrator should get custody of her child, on a contrast between the home the narrator tries to create in her motel-like housing and the home the Bakers have created for Davey, on the values the narrator affirms in spite of the moral wasteland in which she has lived, and on the function in the story of the couple next door.

POETRY

Many of the poems in this section present differing views of death. Dickinson's "I heard a fly buzz" and "Because I could not stop for Death" portray speakers who seem calm about their deaths. Her "My life closed twice" and Ransom's "Bells for John Whiteside's Daughter," on the other hand, reflect pain and anger at the death of another person, and Robinson's "Richard Cory" shows the bewilderment of the townspeople at Cory's suicide. Ransom's "Janet Waking" illustrates what apparently trivial events can teach a child about death just as "I heard a fly buzz" shows the trivial details noticed by one who is dying. In "Do Not Go Gentle into That Good Night," Thomas urges his own father as well as others to fight to delay death. Because of the variety of approaches to the subject, every student should be able to respond either in class discussion or in writing to one or more of these poems.

Emily Dickinson, "I heard a fly buzz"

You might begin discussion of this poem by asking students to list their associations with the word **fly**. Then compile a composite list on the board, asking students to determine which associations are relevant to the poem. You might then ask what the speaker's close attention to the fly reveals about her or his attitude toward death. How does this attitude toward death compare to the attitudes of the speaker in Thomas' "Do Not Go Gentle into That Good Night" and of Sanchez in Marquez's "Death Constant Beyond Love"?

You might ask groups of students to discuss a sequence of personal response questions: How do your students think they would face their own deaths? Would they be as placid as Dickinson's narrator, as resisting as Thomas' speaker, as frightened as Sanchez? What in their experience leads them to respond as they do? Once groups have discussed these questions, you might ask each group to report to the class its various responses.

"Because I could not stop for Death"

In interpreting the symbols in this poem, students may need some help; however, if they are divided into small groups, they often arrive at refreshing and sometimes startling interpretations. You might stimulate reader response to this poem by asking students to select symbols to represent the things they might pass if this journey were their own and to explain the meaning of their symbols.

"My life closed twice"

In "My life closed twice," Dickinson seems to imply that an individual is much more vulnerable to pain in life than in death. Ask students if there are events other than death that might be symbolized by the speaker's saying, "life closed twice." Also ask them to compare the tone of this poem with that of "Because I could not stop for Death" or "I heard a fly buzz," to estimate the age of the speaker in each, and to defend their answers.

Edwin Arlington Robinson, "Richard Cory"

Several good explications of this poem have been published; however, because it is fairly simple to interpret, it helps students develop confidence in their own ability to read poetry perceptively. Help them to determine the identity of the speaker, to pick out

56

symbols of kingship or royalty, and to understand that the tightly controlled form (set stanza form, very regular rhythm, end-stopped lines with all masculine rhymes) may suggest the attempt of the townspeople to impose order and meaning on a situation that is really a puzzle to them.

A comparison of "Richard Cory" and Faulkner's "A Rose for Emily" can shed light on both works and lead to excellent comparison-contrast essays. Ask students to examine similarities in point of view, tone, and conclusion. What false assumptions have the townspeople made? Why are they so fascinated by Richard and Emily? What do the misconceptions of the narrators suggest about our ability to know and understand others who may be famous, rich, powerful, etc.? Are these people more or less vulnerable than others? Why? Why are the narrators so deeply disturbed by their knowledge or lack of knowledge about the fates of Richard and Emily?

Some students may be familiar with Paul Simon's song based on this poem. If you can get a copy or a tape of Simon's song, which adds many details to the original, a comparison of the two can help students realize the value of leaving details to the imagination of the reader. First ask students to theorize about the details of Richard Cory's life which are not in the poem; then let them listen to or read Simon's version to see how it differs both from the original and from their own interpretations.

Paul Laurence Dunbar, "We Wear the Mask"

The wearing of the mask is an important issue since the mask often hides man's vulnerability. Therefore, in addition to the Questions for Discussion and Suggestions for Exploration and Writing, students might want to look at other works in this text that deal with masks people wear. Under "Richard Cory" above, we have suggested that the students would examine how Richard Cory and Emily were vulnerable. Students might go one step further and show what kind of masks these two people wear. Then, they might look at Maya Angelou's refusal to wear a mask for any length of time in the excerpt from *I Know Why the Caged Bird Sings* and discuss masks in all three works.

John Crowe Ransom, "Bells for John Whiteside's Daughter"

In both of Ransom's poems, the form, sound, and phrasing seem to belie the seriousness of the subject. For example, he describes the child as a "little / Lady with rod" who made the geese "scuttle / Goose fashion" and later describes her in her coffin as "Lying so primly propped." Even the speed of the living child reflected in the first two lines is stopped abruptly in that last line. Ask students to discuss the tone of this poem

57

and help them to see that the speaker's anger at the child's death is understated. What are the implications of the bells announcing the child's death? How do the bells suggest that one death affects us all? How might they relate to the bells of which John Donne says, "Never send to know for whom the bell tolls; it tolls for thee" in Meditation 17?

"Janet Waking"

A child's first awareness of death usually results from the loss of a family member. Ask students why Ransom chose such a mundane event as the death of a pet hen for this poem. What do they estimate Janet's age to be? Is the child's refusal to accept the permanence of death unusual? Ask students if they remember what event triggered their first awareness of death and what effect this event has had on the rest of their lives. Phrases such as "sat and put the poison" and "Now the poor comb stood up straight / But Chucky did not" emphasize the incongruity between the actual event and its effect on Janet.

Claude McKay, "If We Must Die"

Ask the students to respond to what Claude McKay says about dying, but fighting back. The speaker suggests that there is no greater glory than dying for a cause. You might ask students to contrast McKay's poem with Wilfred Owen's "Dulce et Decorum Est."

Wilfred Owen, "Dulce et Decorum Est"
Randall Jarrell, "Death of the Ball Turret Gunner"

You will almost certainly want to assign this poem with Randall Jarrell's "Death of the Ball Turret Gunner" and to consider the two poems together. On Jarrell's poem you might want to explain that a ball turret was a bubble-like, glass-enclosed structure mounted to the underbelly of a World War II bomber. Gunners who were hunched in these small turrets fired machine guns at threatening aircraft. These gunners were particularly vulnerable to anti-aircraft fire ("flak").

Since the introduction to poetry in the text analyzes Owen's poem in some detail, you might want to focus class discussion on your students' personal responses to the poems. What are students' expectations about the nature of war? Do they expect war to be honorable, glorious, bloody? How do the two poems address those expectations? What do the poems suggest war does to fighters' attitudes toward each other? If war is so horrible, who is responsible for the horror? How easy is it to fix responsibility? Are those who glorify war morally culpable? Why or why not? How are wars as horrible as those depicted in the two poems justified?

As a writing assignment, you might ask students to imagine and describe in detail the horrors of a particular recent war or military intervention such as Somalia or Desert Storm. Or you might ask them to argue what should be done to a military recruiter who deceives potential recruits by glorifying military service. Students choosing this assignment might cite both Owen's poem and Jarrell's in their arguments.

Ask students to read Young Bear's "Wadasa Nakamoon, Vietnam Memorial." Then ask them to comment on whether memorials help the survivors or relatives of the war dead. If memorials do, in what way? If they do not, why do we have memorials?

Countee Cullen, "Incident"

Countee Cullen's "Incident" might be compared to other works about childhood. Nikki Giovanni in "Nikki-Rosa" remembers her childhood fondly and would want biographers to do so also; Liang in "Chairman Mao's Good Little Boy" at least has recovered from the rigors of Chinese communism; Okita in "In Response to Executive Order 9066" realizes the limits of his lineage and his friendship. Even O'Connor's autobiographical "My Oedipus Complex" shows the fragility of childhood. Ask the students to read each of these works and discuss the bitterness or sweetness in each memory. Or ask students to describe their reactions to an incident from their own childhood and evaluate that incident.

Students can focus on children's points of view in Bell's "Customs of the Country," Wilson's *Fences*, or Fierstein's *On Tidy Endings*. Ask them to choose one incident from each and write about the incident from the child's point of view. For example, in *Fences*, what would Cory remember at the moment he hears news of his father's death? Or in *On Tidy Endings*, what did Jim feel or what were his thoughts when he was told that his father was gay? How will Davey in "Customs of the Country" look back on the incident that landed him in the hospital with a broken leg?

Dylan Thomas, "Do Not Go Gentle into That Good Night"

Ask students to use the four middle stanzas to explain what Thomas means by "wise men," "Good men," "Wild men," and "Grave men." Is he implying that his father is all of these? What are their theories about why a poet advising his father to rage against and resist death would select the tightly controlled form of the villanelle? Can they think of instances in their own experiences in which form (rules of a game, common courtesy, ceremony, etc.) enabled them to express strong emotion without losing control? In what ways does the anger of the speaker differ from or compare to the anger of the speaker in Ransom's "Bells for John Whiteside's Daughter"?

Sharon Olds, "On the Subway"

Students might examine race relations in the United States or, if the class is culturally diverse, in another country such as South Africa, China, Japan, or England. Students might want to focus on some stereotypes that exist in the poem. For example, the speaker says that the black man has the "casual cold look of a mugger." Why does she think of him as a mugger? At another point she says that "he could take [her life] so easily." Why would she make this assumption about him and about her life? Do members of other races automatically think that every black male is a mugger or a murderer? Why?

DRAMA

William Shakespeare, *Othello*

You might want to give students more background on Shakespeare's theater. Among the most useful sources of information about Elizabethan playhouses is the surviving construction contract for the Fortune, a square playhouse whose stage was built in imitation of the round or octagonal Globe playhouse, where many of Shakespeare's plays were first performed. The contract calls for a central yard or pit fifty-five feet square surrounded by three levels of gallery seats twelve feet deep. A stage platform forty-three feet across extended twenty-seven feet into the yard. Even characters in the small inner stage probably were no more than sixty-five feet from the most distant spectator, while characters on the outer edge of the stage platform probably were no farther than thirty-five feet from the most distant spectator and literally within reach of the closest.

Such theaters, then, were extraordinarily intimate. You might ask students what effect such proximity to the play's action might have on them. Certainly the intimacy of Elizabethan theater made practical such Elizabethan conventions as the aside and soliloquy, allowing quite a range of dynamics. It also could make facial expression and subtle gestures important theatrical devices. You might ask students how they would deliver soliloquys such as Iago's at 1.3.384-405, 2.1.287-313, and 2.3.330-356. What changes in volume and tone would they use to avoid monotony? What pauses and breaks would they use to emphasize points in their delivery? What movements, gestures, and facial expressions would they use? In fact, some students might actually be interested in performing a soliloquy for the class, then writing a paper defending the movements, gestures, and facial expressions they use.

Since students often see Shakespeare as high culture unrelated to their own lives and culture, you might also want to emphasize that Shakespeare wrote for an often loud and raucous popular audience more like that at a hockey game, professional wrestling match, or rock concert. A favorite entertainment of Elizabethans was bull and bear baiting, a bloody contest in which pit bull dogs attacked a chained bull or bear until they killed it. This sport was big business, bringing in for the George Steinbrenners and Ted Turners of Shakespeare's day far more money than drama did.

Such an audience demanded the sensational, and in *Othello*, Shakespeare provided it: magnificent costumes, dramatic sword fights and an equally dramatic stabbing, bodies littering the stage, coarse low comedy like the scenes where Iago manipulates Roderigo, and graphic sexual images like Iago's "beast with two backs." References in Phillip Henslowe's *Diary* to purchases of pig's bladders to be filled with red pigment and concealed under costumes suggest, too, that the stage may well have been frequently splattered with blood during performances. Certainly Shakespeare's theater was a theater of spectacle. You might ask students how their parents and neighbors would react to such spectacle in a performance in their community. Would the status of Shakespeare shield the production from criticism? Would local aficionados of Shakespeare declare the performance to be a travesty? How does the violence in *Othello* differ from that in current movies such as *The Texas Chainsaw Massacre* and the interminable *Friday the 13th* sequence? How does it differ from Stephen King's use of violence and gore in his fiction?

Your students will probably need a lot of help just understanding the basics of Shakespeare's play. You might have to read passages to them and pick apart key scenes. Often a skilled reader can help them understand what had been obscure. Many students may misunderstand even basic elements of the plot. Dividing the class into groups and having each group summarize an act in one hundred words or less, then combining the summaries may help enormously. Since this exercise involves the students themselves in such understanding, it is far better than simply explaining the plot to them.

You might also want to explore the racial implications of *Othello*. What evidence is there that Iago is racist? Why does he so detest Othello, the Moor? What current stereotypes of blacks, either represented in Othello's person or expressed by others about him, are apparent in the play? Is there any reason to suppose that Shakespeare shared these stereotypes? Do others, besides Iago, dislike or disapprove of Othello because of his race? If so, why is he allowed such an exalted position as commander in chief? You might want to suggest as a paper topic a comparison between Othello and contemporary black athletes, entertainers, or generals. Or you might ask students to explore in a paper how Othello either represents or defies current stereotypes of black males.

The gender implications of *Othello* are, if anything, even more central to the play than the racial implications. How does Iago feel about women? What is the basis of his animosity toward them? Has Emilia done anything to cause this animosity? Is Othello's initial feeling for Desdemona contaminated by the sexism of his society or does he respect her as his equal? How does Iago use Othello's culturally conditioned sense of honor, his need to treat Desdemona as his exclusive possession? To what degree do men still base their sense of honor on their exclusive possession of women? How might you compare Iago's and Othello's need to possess women exclusively with that of the narrator in Marvell's "To His Coy Mistress," Ferrara in Browning's "My Last Duchess," and Arnold Friend in Oates' "Where Are You Going, Where Have You Been?" You might suggest a paper topic describing the lengths men will go to in order to possess women.

Finally, you might wish to explore with your class *Othello*'s implications about the nature and origin of evil. What evidence is there that Iago is psychotic? Might he, like Arnold Friend, be an incarnation of the devil? How else can you explain his persistent and ingenious malignity, his ability to create incredible anxiety wherever he goes while seeming innocent, his extraordinary sense of timing and ability to appear in just the right (or wrong) place at the best (or worst) time?

CASEBOOK POEMS

Robert Frost

Most students will have studied Robert Frost in their high school courses. However, most high school texts neglect many of Frost's most thought-provoking poems, so the approach to Frost in this casebook may be startling to the students. A good way to introduce the unit might be to use the excellent videotape emphasizing the darker side of Frost's poetry available in the *Voices and Visions* series.

This casebook can lead to documented essays on a variety of subjects and with wide variations in length. For example, students might choose to explicate one poem or to write a longer paper on several. If you wish them to write longer papers, you might suggest topics such as the theme of loneliness in two or more of Frost's poems or the destructive power of nature and/or human nature in two or more poems. You might also like to balance the darker Frost poems with one or more of his poems from the Quest unit.

"Design"

A careful examination of this Italian sonnet can lead to excellent explications because of the abundance of metaphorical and sound devices and because of the easily apparent irony. Ask students why the whiteness is so disturbing to the speaker. To help them understand the irony, ask them to point out incongruities in the poem such as the dimpled baby images to describe the deadly spider or the heal-all that, instead of healing, sets a trap. You might then use the Question for Discussion to help them see that Frost has used even the form of the poem to create irony.

"Desert Places"

Students who are familiar with "Stopping by Woods on a Snowy Evening" should be interested in noting that the similarity of both form and subject in the two poems is pronounced while the tone is dramatically different.

In discussing the symbol of the desert places, you might ask students to think about what frightening desert places they might have within themselves. Then, because most students will not want to reveal very personal details, ask them to meet in small groups to list desert places that might exist within humans and the problems these desert places might cause both for the individuals and for the people around them. Finally, ask students to apply this concept to the problems facing the modern world and to suggest ways to reclaim these desert places.

"Acquainted with the Night"

You might begin a discussion of this poem by asking students to list the references and images in the poem that create the effect of sorrow, loneliness, fear, and perhaps even guilt (rain, darkness, the cry, failure to make eye contact, etc.).

Asking students to explain the difference between the symbol of desert places in the previous poem and the symbol of night in this poem might help them to clarify or to compare the themes of the two poems.

63

"Neither Out Far Nor In Deep"
"Once by the Pacific"

These poems, describing events that involve the land and the sea, are often clearer when studied together. Ask students to theorize about the symbolism of the land and the sea and to explain any differences in the meanings of the symbols in the two poems. They might suggest the land as human and the sea as nonhuman, the land as known and the sea as unknown, the land as safety and the sea as danger, the land as victim and the sea as menace, etc. Then ask them to use these theories to interpret the last four lines of "Neither Out Far Nor In Deep" and the last two lines of "Once by the Pacific." Ask them to explain the difference in tone in the poems: why does one seem much more threatening than the other?

Another exercise that might help students understand the dark side of Frost's poetry is to have them examine all references to night (include "Acquainted with the Night" here also) and explain the implications of the references in each poem. Then ask them to explain the significance of "Put out the light." You might also like to point out the parallel with Othello's words at the death of Desdemona and discuss the implications of each reference.

"Home Burial"

Most students in college classes have been confronted with the death of someone close, either a relative or a friend; fortunately few will have experienced the devastation of losing a child. Ask them to try to imagine the grief of a parent who has lost a first child and to explain the two different reactions of Amy and her husband. They might like to share their suggestions about constructive or comforting ways of dealing with the death of a loved one.

This poem might profitably be compared with some of the works in the Men and Women unit that portray conflicts or differing opinions between husband and wife. For example, a student might write an essay comparing the couple in Gilman's "The Yellow Wallpaper" to Amy and her husband. Another might contrast the man and woman's reactions to the idea of abortion in Hemingway's "Hills Like White Elephants" with Amy and her husband's devastation at the death of a child.

64

"A Servant to Servants"

This poem presents a different form of human vulnerability—the fragility of the human mind. To help students understand this poignant dramatic monologue, you might ask them to list first the clues to the narrator's mental problems and second the examples of the narrator's sense of humor. Ask them why, when the narrator is obviously tired from too much work and too little time, she encourages the listener to stay and visit.

Ask the students to explain the husband's statement that "the best way out is always through" and to compare it to the saying the speaker refers to when she says that her husband's work is "from sun to sun" (but a woman's work is never done) and her later claim that "I shan't catch up in this world, anyway."

A good topic for a comparison-contrast essay would be a study of the narrator, who claims that her mental condition is worsened by the incessant work, and Jane in Gilman's "The Yellow Wallpaper," who is being driven insane by being deprived of any useful activity.

FREEDOM AND RESPONSIBILITY

ESSAYS

Thomas Jefferson, The Declaration of Independence

It would probably be a mistake to assume that students are familiar with this important document. You might wish to begin by having them carefully paraphrase each step in Jefferson's argument. We in this country have accorded the Declaration as well as the Constitution the status of holy writ, have made of it an unquestioned and inviolable secular scripture. It might then be productive to examine the document critically. To what "self-evident" truths does Jefferson refer? What, if anything, makes these truths "self-evident"? Can any truths be "self-evident"? What are "inalienable rights"? Do you agree that the rights listed are indeed inalienable?

What, according to Jefferson, are the purposes of governments? What rights do the governed have if governments fail in these purposes? What kinds of behavior might then be justified by such failure? Which of the offenses listed in the indictment of George III's government apply to American governments today? What have citizens done to change such abuses?

The Suggestion for Exploration and Writing works well for brainstorming in small groups in preparation for papers. You might also ask students to propose a plan for ending government actions they perceive as abusive.

Henry David Thoreau, "Civil Disobedience"

This essay is difficult for students. You will probably want to teach it, along with Dr. King's essay, as a logical and practical extension of the principles embodied in the Declaration of Independence. Here again you might begin by helping students summarize Thoreau's argument, perhaps dividing the class into groups and asking each group to summarize a section of the essay. To what specific government policies or actions does Thoreau object? What action does he take and what are the consequences of that action? Why does he choose to go to jail? How does his time spent in jail affect him? Why?

You might then ask students whether they agree with Thoreau's opening statement: "'That government is best which governs not at all.'" What would be the likely consequences of governments' failure to govern? What would be the condition of your community or state if it had no government? Does Thoreau ultimately advocate the abolition of government?

You might next want to examine Thoreau's concepts of justice, law, and morality. Thoreau maintains that the law perverts justice. How does it do so? Who, according to Thoreau, is responsible for injustice? Under what circumstances does Thoreau advocate breaking the law? To what degree are Thoreau's moral principles Biblical in origin? How might Thoreau respond to Paul's injunction in Romans 13.1 to obey the government? What does he mean when he asks, "Why does it [government] always crucify Christ, and excommunicate Copernicus and Luther, and pronounce Washington and Franklin rebels?"

A variety of personal writing assignments might grow out of your study of Thoreau's essay. You might ask students to write an essay explaining for what beliefs or causes they would willingly go to jail. Or you might ask them in an essay to argue for or against Thoreau's staying in jail. Other students might elaborate in a paper on Thoreau's statement that "If a man is thought-free, fancy-free, imagination-free, . . . unwise rulers or reformers cannot fatally interrupt him." Why does physical incarceration fail significantly to reduce his freedom? Finally, you might ask them to argue for or against Thoreau's quotation from Confucius: "'If a State is governed by reason, poverty and misery are subjects of shame; if a State is not governed by the principles of reason, riches and honors are the subjects of shame.'"

Martin Luther King, Jr., "Letter from Birmingham City Jail"

Some students may think that the letter is dated, but instructors might begin by asking the students to role play a controversial situation involving mutual mistrust between opposing groups. Each group thinks it is right. Some possibilities might be as follows: the police in the Rodney King case versus the black community, David Koresh and the Branch Davidians versus the FBI and the AFT troops, Dr. Gunn versus the pro-life advocates, and Martin Luther King, Jr. versus the white citizens of Birmingham. Once the students have decided on their roles, one way to make the project interesting is to require them to take atypical roles. For example, white students might represent the African-American community, a Hispanic student might play the part of Martin Luther King, Jr., and an Asian student might represent David Koresh. By assuming controversial roles or roles that they do not immediately understand, they will perhaps begin to see another point of view. Next, let them take the assignment home and research the topic.

The instructor can then use the debate format whereby each side has ten minutes to establish its point of view; then each side has ten minutes to rebut the other's arguments. The third group, the students who are not participating in the debate, will be the arbitrators. Their group assignment would be to write up both sides and to come to a consensus about the arguments presented.

Maya Angelou, from *I Know Why the Caged Bird Sings*

If you have students from various cultures, ask them to share some of their coming-of-age rituals and to compare those rituals to the rituals taught in finishing schools. Then you might ask students to compile a newsletter recounting the many rituals described in the class.

In this excerpt, Angelou gets angry because she is called "out of [her] name." You might want to explore with your class the importance of names in defining identity. Some people from different countries Americanize their names when they settle in the United States; others give their children ethnic names to reflect the country of their origin and remind them of their heritage. Many African Americans prefer to give African names to their children. Liang and Shapiro in "Chairman Mao's Good Little Boy" tell about how children are named according to political movements. How liberating or restrictive are names? You might ask students to write a humorous essay on the effect a name can have on personality.

Guan Keguang, "A Chinese Reporter on Cape Cod"

In discussing the excesses of American freedom, Keguang contrasts what he has discovered in America with conditions in China. You might begin with the question of whether Americans have too many choices. First, ask the students whether they have trouble selecting elective courses or choosing a major or a minor. Do they agonize over what movie to see on a Saturday night or what brand of beer to buy? Many students might not want so many choices but might see dictation as a form of tyranny. Students might want to branch out and discuss regional choices, national choices, and international choices.

FICTION

Richard Wright, "The Man Who Was Almost a Man"

This Wright story raises questions about responsibilities that parents, children, employers, and others have toward family and community. For example, students should be able to see the responsibility that the store owner, Mistah Joe, has in selling the gun to a seventeen-year-old boy. You can begin by asking whether Mistah Joe should have sold the gun. Did he have a responsibility to teach Dave how to use the gun?

Does the mother act irresponsibly in giving Dave the two dollars to buy the gun? Some may argue that the mother has no idea that he will act so irresponsibly. Others might point out that the mother who has to take a seventeen-year-old boy's pay from him and dole out money to him must realize that Dave is not a reliable person. Most people would agree that Dave owes money for the dead cow and that his father is right in telling Mr. Hawkins that Dave will pay for the cow. How does Dave's irresponsibility affect his family and community? For example, after Dave leaves town, is his father responsible for the debt? Ask the students to vote on who acts most irresponsibly in the story.

Kurt Vonnegut, Jr., "Harrison Bergeron"

You might begin by dividing the class into groups and asking each group to do two assignments. First, ask them to invent the history that would have led to the situation portrayed in the story. How has an idea that at first glance seems so worthwhile led to such a predicament? Did the people who originated this interpretation of equality have good intentions that went awry? After they have shared their histories with the class, ask each group to predict the future that will follow in the next ten to twenty years for the society portrayed in "Harrison Bergeron" and let them share these ideas as well.

You might ask students, "If you were the Handicapper General, how would you handicap yourself appropriately? Why?" First, have them write their responses; then ask for volunteers to share their responses with the class.

Suggestions for writing other than those elicited by these classroom exercises might include the following:

70

Ask students to write a character sketch of Hazel in which they explain such points as her resemblance to Diana Moon Glampers, her advice to George, and her attitude toward her son;

Ask students to compare the abilities of George and Harrison and then to account for the differences in their behavior.

Ursula K. LeGuin, "The Ones Who Walk Away from Omelas"

This provocative story raises disturbing questions about the cost of our freedom and prosperity. LeGuin has described this parable as the story of a scapegoat. You might want to define the term scapegoat as it appears in the Old Testament (Leviticus 16:20-26). In what sense is the miserable child in Omelas like the Biblical scapegoat? In what sense is it not? If the people of Omelas are rational, why do they react with "anger," "disgust," "outrage," and "impotence" to the child? How does the existence of the child's misery make possible the splendor and happiness of Omelas? In what sense does all human happiness and greatness depend on others' misery? Why would the open presence of the child in Omelas destroy its "prosperity and beauty and delight"?

To what degree does LeGuin's parable describe our own society? Does American prosperity depend on the misery of some Americans? If so, on whose misery does it depend? What are America's ugly, hidden secrets? Are there any in our society who have walked away in the sense of those who walk away from Omelas? How do happy, rational, prosperous people respond to the poor, the weak, the disabled, and the irrational in our society? To what degree are the poor, the weak, the disabled, and the irrational an embarrassment to us? Why do we react negatively to them?

You might ask students to respond to the following quotation in a classification essay on the goods and services of Omelas: "Happiness is based on a just discrimination of what is necessary, what is neither necessary nor destructive, and what is destructive." Or ask them to classify the common goods and services of their community as necessary, neither necessary nor destructive, and destructive.

You might also consider the following writing assignment: many in Omelas feel the child is "too degraded and imbecile to know any real joy." What people in our society are treated similarly? Why? Are they truly incapable of feeling joy?

71

Finally, you might ask students to analyze the premise that the greatness of art depends on the existence of misery and evil, giving examples from works they have read in the course.

Toni Cade Bambara, "Blues Ain't No Mockin Bird"

Students readily see the key conflicts between races and between public and private rights in this story. You might begin by asking students why the grandfather smashes the camera, a seemingly violent action. Probably some students will point out that the government intruders stereotype the Cains according to their preconceptions of poor African-American families and that the intruders are rude and condescending. Precisely how do the filmers stereotype the Cains? Ask your students to cite examples of similar stereotyping from their own experience. How pervasive is such stereotyping? What can such stereotyping do to families? How do the Cains defy both the filmers' stereotypes and the stereotypes your students have encountered? In this regard you might want to compare Bambara's story to some of the works in the family section of the text, particularly Giovanni's "Nikki-Rosa," Wilson's *Fences*, and Fierstein's *On Tidy Endings*.

You might also want to consider the issue of how far government can and should intrude on the privacy of its citizens. Why do the intruders assume that they have a right to film the Cains? How might Jefferson, Thoreau, and/or King have responded to this assumption? To what degree do Americans have a right to privacy? How does such a right reflect the principles embodied in the Declaration of Independence? You might ask students to cite non-fictional examples of government's intruding on the right to privacy. To what degree is Granddaddy Cain morally and legally right when he smashes the camera?

Leslie Marmon Silko, "Lullaby"

This sad and disturbing story portrays a Navajo family's treatment by the Bureau of Indian Affairs and by government social workers. In order to appreciate the story, students might want background information about the Navajos. The Navajos, the largest native American tribe, are descendants of the Apaches. They came from Canada south to New Mexico, Arizona, Colorado, and Utah. The many tribes that formed the Navajos developed into about sixty clans. Clan membership and property rights descended from the mother. However, today members of the clan can inherit from both parents. Navajos were also among the few tribes that practiced *exogamy*: the requirement that one must marry outside the clan.

As they migrated south, Navajos borrowed from other tribes and were quite adaptable. The Spanish settlers had little or no contact with the Navajos, a lack of contact that may be reflected in the way the Spanish men treat Ayah when she goes into the bar. After a period of time as slavers and raiders of villages, the Navajos were eventually subdued by Kit Carson and forced onto a reservation in eastern New Mexico. In 1868, the Navajos signed a peace treaty with the United States government.

During World War II, many Navajos like Jimmy left to go to war, and the United States government encouraged them to move to the cities to work in war industries. As a result, many left the reservation and settled in large cities such as Denver, Los Angeles, Phoenix, and Albuquerque. Since then, the many Navajo tribes have formed the Navajo Nation and live primarily on one large reservation in Arizona or on three smaller ones in New Mexico. Pooling their resources from oil royalties and uranium, they have managed to gain great strides for Dine, Navajo for "The People."

Navajo religious ceremonies stress mental and physical health, and part of the Navajos' religious ritual includes singing. Singers were considered healers and priests; many of the ceremonies called for the singers to practice singing until they were perfect. However, many younger Navajos today, impatient with the amount of time it takes to become a singer/priest, fail to practice the singing. Ask students, after considering the importance of singing to the Navajo, to explain Ayah's motivation in singing the lullaby.

You might ask students to compare Silko's story with Baldwin's "Sonny's Blues" and Young Bear's "Wasada Nakamoon, Vietnam Memorial." How does music heal in these works?

Many Navajos today, especially older Navajos on reservations, speak little or no English because only spoken Navajo was required in the schools. However, since the 1970s the Navajo schools have attempted to teach writing in Navajo to the students and to provide some classes in English. Ask your students how Ayah's inability to read English contributes to her misfortune. Should the Navajos be required to know English if they reside only on the reservation? Should all citizens of the United States be taught English?

POETRY

William Blake, "London"

Students often have difficulty understanding this powerful revolutionary and apocalyptic poem. You might begin by asking what conditions Blake observes that occasion his apocalyptic vision. To what degree are the "mind-forg'd manacles" still oppressing people in contemporary America? What responses to oppression does Blake's speaker foresee? Who are the agents of these responses?

As a devout but unorthodox Christian, Blake combined revolutionary fervor with apocalyptic vision. How does this poem combine the two? We are accustomed to thinking of some governments as oppressive, but Blake implies that the church too is oppressive. How might the church of Blake's day have been oppressive? How is the church oppressive today? To what degree is oppression by the church inconsistent with its mission?

William Wordsworth, "The World Is Too Much with Us"

You might want to ask students what, according to this poem, restricts or limits speaker's freedom. To what degree do similar restrictions limit our freedom today? How do these restrictions relate to the oppression in Blake's poem?

Randall Jarrell, "The Woman at the Washington Zoo"

You might begin by asking students to write a brief character sketch of the woman at the zoo. Ask them to describe her in as much detail as they can imagine, supplying precise details in addition to Jarrell's own. What is she wearing that she describes as "dull null Navy"? What are her hair, walk, facial expression, and gestures like? Who is this woman, and what does she do? What is the source of her entrapment? Why? Where else besides the zoo might you imagine her? Why is the zoo setting particularly appropriate?

You might then ask your students what people they know whom they might compare to Jarrell's speaker. In what ways are these people comparable to the woman at the zoo? What were the situations that made these people feel trapped? To what degree were they responsible for their own entrapment? When and why have your students felt that "the world goes by [their] cage and never sees [them]"?

Anne Sexton, "Ringing the Bells"

After reading this poem aloud to your students to emphasize the tone of monotony, entrapment, and mounting hysteria, you might want to ask students how the speaker appears to feel about the bell therapy session and how helpful it is for the "crazy ladies." If, as the speaker says, the inmates "are no better for it," why does the institution continue such futile exercises as bell therapy? Ask your students to cite comparable examples of futile exercises in mental institutions, prisons, and classrooms. Why do those in charge continue to practice what is ineffective?

Though its setting and tone are different, this poem is very similar in its theme of self-entrapment and boredom to Jarrell's "The Woman at the Washington Zoo," and for that reason, you will probably want to assign them together. In fact, you might ask students to write a paper comparing and contrasting the two speakers. Is the woman at the zoo any better off psychologically than the woman in the mental institution? Does either woman seem to belong in an institution?

Adrienne Rich, "Aunt Jennifer's Tigers"

You might want to assign this poem with "The Woman at the Washington Zoo." Jarrell writes about a woman who feels that she is caged, barred from life. Aunt Jennifer is "mastered by" burdens she has no control over. Both are women who have lost the freedom to be who and what they want to be. Both poems imply that if the women could be free, they would somehow be "prancing, proud and unafraid." Ask the students to discuss what institutions and attitudes weigh women down, preventing them from soaring or being more than they are. How does one balance responsibilities of a job and marriage with personal freedom? Are there similar limits on men's freedom?

Alicia Ostriker, "Watching the Feeder"

This poem about a mother's role after her children are grown and have left home could fit equally well in the unit on family. You might like to have students read it along with the other Ostriker poem, "First Love," so that they can put this poem in the context of a mother's earlier responsibilities. Ask them to list the responsibilities a mother assumes when her children are at home and to explain why losing these responsibilities is both a relief and a source of sorrow: "peaceful but hard." Do fathers face the same dilemma? Why or why not? Since many college classes today have nontraditional students, your class may have students who can share personal experiences that will enrich the poem for younger students. You might also ask younger students if they have seen evidence of similar feelings in their mothers.

Students might like to compare this poem with Millay's Sonnet 42 in which the author describes her life as being like a tree from which the birds have fled. You might want to ask your students why watching birds at the feeder is an appropriate image for the speaker's situation.

To help students appreciate Ostriker's whimsical creativity, ask them to personify the birds with which they are familiar or to describe people they know in terms of the birds they resemble.

Pat Mora, "Immigrants"

You might begin discussing this poem by considering these immigrants' perceptions of Americans. What in American culture do the immigrants choose to imitate? To what degree are immigrants' perceptions of that culture stereotyped? What is the source of their stereotypes? How do media reinforce such stereotypes? Who is usually the victim of such stereotyping? Why do the immigrants suppress their own language, speaking it only in whispers and out of their children's presence? To what degree do immigrants actually seek to imitate a stereotypical impression of America?

Joy Harjo, "The Woman Hanging from the Thirteenth Floor Window"

The Creeks are a mixed group of North American tribes that lived in the Southeast, especially in Georgia and Alabama. Most of the time they lived in maternal clans with annual councils of family and/or related clans. The United States government fought against the Creeks in Alabama during the war of 1812 because the great Creek Chief Tecumseh had an alliance with Great Britain. General Andrew Jackson met the Creeks at Horseshoe Bend and killed over 2,000 of them on March 27, 1814. The treaty signed at Fort Jackson on August 9, 1814, ceded to the United States over twenty million acres. Later, the Creeks were forcibly moved to reservations in Oklahoma.

Knowing the history of the Creeks, readers might want to take another look at the situation in the poem. You might ask your students in what ways the events in the history of Harjo's people might affect the tone of her works. Has life become so unbearable for the woman that death is more valuable than life? Is there such a thing as a living death?

Dwight Okita, "In Response to Executive Order 9066"

You might wish to begin by asking students to consider how they would feel about their own government's forcing them to move out of their homes to an internment camp. What would they probably have to leave behind? What would they miss most? You might then wish to consider the internment policy itself, perhaps supplying more background. All Japanese-Americans, because they were deemed security risks, were forbidden to live in parts of Western states. Most of the Japanese-Americans forced to live in the relocation centers were American citizens. Yet most were interned for nearly two years. Although the government provided food and housing, the camps were crowded and highly restrictive, and overall living conditions were poor. You might want to ask students to suggest the government's reasons for interning Japanese-Americans. What might the internment have done to the interned?

You might ask your students to describe the speaker in the poem. How is she like them? What is the tone of the opening statement, "of course I'll come," and what does it reveal about the speaker? Why does she give the impression of responding to an invitation rather than following orders? Why does she mention hot dogs and chopsticks? To what degree does her doing so make her like the immigrants in Mora's poem? Why does the speaker give Denise tomatoes? How does Denise's missing the speaker relate to the tomatoes' ripening? How do your students respond to Denise? It's easy to blame her, but would they respond any differently? How do most of us respond when something that might humiliate us happens to someone we know?

DRAMA

Wole Soyinka, *The Lion and the Jewel*

Soyinka has said of African drama, including presumably his own, that it might more usefully be compared with epic than with Western drama. Like epic, it celebrates the human hero's victory over cosmic forces that would restrict or destroy humanity (2).

You might explore with your students the concept of Baroka as epic hero. To what degree is the ending of the play a victory for Baroka and also a victory for his culture and people? To what popular culture heroes might he be compared? On the other hand, if we regard Baroka as his culture's epic hero, are we like Sidi being duped by the supreme trickster? Even to raise these questions suggests the complexity of Baroka, at once the wily trickster of much African folklore, the sage who defies the limits of other mortals, the wise prophet propounding his wisdom in traditional proverbs, and the philosopher-king whose solicitude for his people is his greatest concern.

Soyinka also attributes to African drama a far greater cosmic significance, cultural coherence, and social relevance than is characteristic of modern and contemporary Western drama, whose tradition he sees as fragmented. Yeats' comments on Byzantium in *A Vision* (see notes below on "Sailing to Byzantium") seem to define the cultural qualities Soyinka is referring to, where the whole people share a cultural tradition which is an intimate and very significant part of their lives. You might ask students to what degree Soyinka's play defines a culture and places that culture in a cosmic perspective. In what ways is that culture far more coherent than contemporary American culture? What might have been the outcome of the play had Sidi refused to marry Baroka? How might such an action threaten the stability of the village? Many Westerners, although they may reject colonialism, still often think of traditional tribal cultures as "primitive." In what ways does the society depicted in Soyinka's play defy this stereotype? What is complex about the culture of Ilujinle in spite of its rejection of technology? In what ways is it more complex than Western culture as Western culture is presented in the play?

Much traditional African dance and ritual drama was performed in the open clearing at the center of the village. Nothing separated the play space from the audience, which often had a choric function. Masked dancers and clowns, with their mock-threats, often kept the crowds from interfering with performers (Graham-White 36-37). How does this traditional theatrical space figure in Soyinka's play, which was written to be performed in a Western style theater? What are the implications of Soyinka's setting much of his play in this traditional space? You might divide students into groups, asking one group to imagine this setting in detail, another to design costumes for the play, a third to develop the play's elaborate choreography, and a fourth to imagine the setting of the climactic scene in Baroka's lodge.

Works Cited

Graham-White, Anthony. *The Drama of Black Africa*. New York: Samuel French, 1974.

Soyinka, Wole. *Myth, Literature and the African World*. Cambridge: Cambridge UP, 1976.

ART AND LANGUAGE

ESSAYS

Chinua Achebe, "Africa and Her Writers"

This fascinating essay by a distinguished Nigerian writer has profound implications for contemporary Western art. If art is to be an expression of a particular culture or community and if, as Wole Soyinka has suggested, Western art no longer has a recognized tradition on which to draw, what is the purpose of contemporary Western art (37-38)? Has it indeed been cut off from its roots? Which, if any, of the modern or contemporary Western works in this anthology indicate a loss of a common culture? Which of the Western works in this anthology do suggest a common culture? Are contemporary Western equivalents of mbari restricted to popular or local culture?

According to Achebe, art that is vital reflects the community that produced it. To what degree does Achebe's theory suggest that we can respond enthusiastically and appreciatively only to our own community's art? Both Achebe himself and his fellow Nigerian, Wole Soyinka are eclectic in their art, drawing on Western traditions as well as African ones. To what degree is such eclecticism apparent in Achebe's essay? To what degree is it apparent in Soyinka's *The Lion and the Jewel?* To what degree is such eclecticism desirable in art? What might such eclecticism achieve?

Soyinka, Wole. *Myth, Literature and the African World*. Cambridge: Cambridge UP, 1976.

Anne Tyler, "Still Just Writing"

Students react very positively to this essay and to Tyler herself. The tone of the essay gives them a strong sense of its persona. The idea that a writer would have to "[paint] the downstairs hall," take her children to school, prepare those children for summer camp, and take the dog to the vet seems never to have occurred to many of them. They are often delighted by Tyler's sheer humanness. You might begin simply by asking your students what they think of the speaker in the essay. Would they like to meet her and talk to her? What would they like to ask her or tell her? How do they ordinarily think of writers? To what degree does Tyler's essay suggest that they have stereotyped writers? What makes Tyler's persona seem human and real to them? To what degree can this persona be identified with Tyler herself?

You might next begin to explore the sources of Tyler's creative art. From what sources does she draw material for her art? What do your students think her fiction might take as its subject? What tone might it take toward that subject? Based on the short story "Why I Live at the P.O." why do they think Eudora Welty influenced Tyler's writing? What similarities in tone do they see in Tyler's essay and Welty's story?

You might also want to consider Tyler's essay in light of the women's issues raised in Unit 2 and in your discussion of Soyinka's *The Lion and the Jewel.* To what degree does she accept a traditional woman's role and to what degree does her accepting such a role compromise her freedom as a woman and as a writer? As a thoughtful woman and a highly respected writer, how and why can she allow herself to serve her husband as she does? How does she compare to the wife in "When Grateful begins to Grate" and to Virginia Woolf in "Professions for Women"?

Garrison Keillor, "Attitude"

This amusing essay offers an opportunity to explore with your students the non-verbal languages we use almost constantly to define ourselves and our relation to others. What, you might ask, do the various gestures and movements Keillor advocates for his middle-aged ballplayers say about them? What do the gestures he objects to on his team say about the team? Under what circumstances have your students used such a ritualized set of gestures and movements? Why? What were they trying to say or accomplish through these gestures?

You might also want to ask your students to consider sports as art forms. What similarities can they see between a softball game, for example, and a play? Can a game such as softball, football, or soccer reveal character? Is there any sense in which such a game might have a plot? What might be the language of such sports? What might be their theme? What particular plays or stories in this anthology might be most comparable to such games?

Barry Lopez, "Landscape and Narrative"

Since the essay may be difficult for students, you might begin by asking them to summarize Lopez's ideas in a paragraph. You might then have several students read their summaries for the class to discuss. Alternatively, you might ask them to work in groups on producing such summaries. Lopez makes extraordinary, almost religious claims for the art of storytelling. You might, then, ask your students, who may well be skeptical of his claims, to what degree they can accept Lopez's claims for storytelling.

Since Lopez claims for stories a spiritual effect, you might ask students to what degree their own spiritual experience has been enhanced by stories. What kinds of stories have contributed to their spiritual or religious growth? What particular stories have done so? To what degree was their experience of such stories analogous to Lopez's in developing a sense of well-being? What stories among these were non-scriptural or even secular in nature? To what degree can art that has no clearly religious purpose enhance spiritual growth?

FICTION

Walter Van Tilburg Clark, "The Portable Phonograph"

This story offers fine arts majors in the class a chance to share their expertise. You might ask the music majors to bring examples of the music mentioned in the story to share with the class. Ask the students to theorize about the importance of music in their lives. If, as is often the case, students see the relation of music to their lives more clearly than they do the relation of the other arts, you might start the bridge to visual arts with the example of synasthesia ("wet, blue-green notes") or, if they are movie buffs, with film.

The description of the landscape at the beginning of the story graphically portrays the destruction of nature by human beings. Ask students to point out the evidence of the environment's deterioration, then to list ways in which we are now destroying our environment, ways that Clark, writing in 1950, could not have known about. What signs in the story suggest that nature can recover? Are there similar signs today? This exercise could lead to a variety of essay topics about our effects on the environment and our responsibilities for it.

You might ask students to explain how and why Doctor Jenkins' actions are like those of "a prehistoric priest performing a fateful ceremonial rite," and why the young musician thinks that "writing [implies] a greater future than he now [feels] able to consider." You might also ask them to explain the musician's agony. Then ask them to write an essay on the best and the worst qualities of human beings as depicted in "The Portable Phonograph."

Other good essay topics could come from a comparison of the future portrayed in this story with that in Vonnegut's "Harrison Bergeron."

Marguerite Yourcenar, "How Wang-Fo Was Saved"

Wang-Fo leads his life expecting the world to resemble art. You might ask your students whether, in their experience, life resembles or imitates art. If so, how? Though Wang-Fo expects life to resemble art, he paints exactly what he sees despite its squalor and despair. Would your students call him a realist? Would they call him an idealist? Why do they respond as they do? Does Wang-Fo change at the end of the story? How? Why? Why do Wang-Fo and the Emperor clash? Which one is more realistic, which more idealistic? Do realists and idealists always clash? Does the ending vindicate the realist or the idealist?

A follow-up question might be what part art plays in a man's perception of the world. Who defines art? Are MTV videos, graffiti, comics, and tattoos art? Ask your students how much art helps to shape them, others, or the world.

Woody Allen, "The Kugelmass Episode"

You might begin a discussion of this story by asking students if Kugelmass' tendency to look for "magic," a quick fix to his problems or an escape from an ordinary boring life, is characteristic of most human beings. Does such magic usually work? Why or why not? Ask students to define escapist literature and to explain "The Kugelmass Episode" as the ultimate in escapist literature. In what other ways do people escape from their ordinary, sometimes boring lives? You might also ask students whether such escapes can have both good and bad effects. How is Kugelmass' punishment condign?

You might also ask students to write a character sketch of Kugelmass, showing how details about his appearance, elements of his conversation, and his choices of literature reveal his character and/or add to the humor of the story.

The implications of Kugelmass' actually appearing in all copies of one English translation of *Madame Bovary* might be used to encourage any students with a flair for the comic to write their own inserts. You might like to let students in groups propose comic insertions into novels, plays, or short stories with which they are familiar. They might, for example, add a character to Tina Howe's *Painting Churches*, Alice Walker's

"Nineteen Fifty-five," Roth's "Conversion of the Jews," or O'Connor's "A Good Man Is Hard to Find" or "Revelation."

Raymond Carver, "Cathedral"

You might begin by asking the class to respond honestly to questions about their own stereotyping of the disabled. To what degree do your students share the narrator's stereotypical attitudes toward the blind? What other disabled people do they stereotype? How? Why? How do they typically respond to disabled people? You might want to ask students to write an essay comparing or contrasting their own attitudes toward the disabled with the narrator's. Or you might want to ask them to show how the story challenges their stereotypical attitudes toward the disabled.

You might go on to discuss the climax of the story. What do your students feel has happened to the two men? What has brought about the change? To what degree might this story illustrate the transforming and healing power which Lopez claims for art? To what degree does it illustrate Achebe's theory about the power of art to define a community? How good do you suppose the drawing of the cathedral might be? How much does its quality matter?

You might want to compare the use of non-verbal communication in this story to that in Keillor's "Attitude" and Glaspell's *Trifles*. The two men say very little at the end of the story. How, then, do they communicate? To what degree might their non-verbal communication be more profound than speech would be? Precisely what do they communicate to each other non-verbally? What are the implications of the brief and simple comment "'It's really something.'"

POETRY

John Keats,   "Ode to a Nightingale"
"Ode on a Grecian Urn"

Keats' great odes might well be taught as presenting a concept of art and the imagination diametrically opposed to that of Housman's Terence. For Keats, art serves the quasi-religious function of admitting us to a richly satisfying world that transcends change, decay, pain, and evil. You might begin by discussing the tone of longing that opens the first ode. How does the speaker feel? What prompts such feeling? What for

85

your students has occasioned such longing—such a feeling that the material and physical world, beautiful as it sometimes is, is just not enough, not ultimately satisfying?

How do we seek to satisfy this longing? How does art respond to it? To what degree might the stories Lopez discusses in "Landscape and Narrative" satisfy such a longing? To what degree does Keats' ode itself create the satisfying sense of transcendence for which the speaker longs? Can art transport us to a transcendent world? What works of art do so in a satisfying way for your students? How does Keats' view of art differ from an escapist view of art? You might want to consider Plato's Allegory of the Cave and Yeats' "Sailing to Byzantium" in discussing the capacity of art to help us transcend the material world.

Keats' other great ode, similar in theme, raises some additional questions. Why are the boughs, the piper, and the lover all happy? At what point in their lives has the urn pictured them? The temporal arts—narrative, drama, music, dance—do not freeze action as spatial arts do. To what degree can such arts have the same effect of recording and memorializing a moment of greatest intensity? How can they do so?

What does Keats mean by "Heard melodies are sweet, but those unheard / Are sweeter"? Have your students ever produced music, images, or sensations that seemed richer or more satisfying than any actual art? Have your students ever found art that required more of their imaginative participation—a radio play, for example, as opposed to a television drama—more satisfying than art that required no such imaginative participation?

Lewis Carroll, "Jabberwocky"
John Hollander, "Adam's Task"

These two poems go very well together to show the power of nonsense words to convey meaning. Let the students show just how creative they are by writing a narrative essay in which they use nonsense words to tell the story or they use words in different forms. Ask each student to coin a word and use it to communicate with other people in the class.

A. E. Housman, "Terence, This Is Stupid Stuff"

Terence is decidedly stoical; he views art as preparation for disaster. What are the implications of Terence's view of art? What kind of art would meet his standards? Must art be realistic to do so? Must it end unhappily or insist on our unhappiness? If the latter, then how can we account for the comic tone of Housman's poem? Does it meet Terence's criteria? Clearly Terence frowns on the superficial optimism sometimes expressed in art. But how might he feel about such rich comedy as Soyinka's *The Lion and the Jewel*, Howe's *Painting Churches*, Welty's "Why I Live at the P.O.," and Roth's "The Conversion of the Jews"? To what degree does Terence's dismissal of the illusory consolations of malt apply to comedy and melodrama?

How can art prepare its audience for disaster? Can it do so only if it is gloomy, realistic, tragic? What works in this book might help prepare their readers for or warn them against disaster? How might they do so? Aside from serving as symbolic warnings of the difficulties and disasters an audience might face, how else might art prepare its audience for challenges and difficulties? To what degree can comedy, heroic art, tragedy, and even melodrama be regarded as a symbolic triumph over disaster, hence an encouragement to persevere and endure?

Marianne Moore, "Poetry"
Archibald MacLeish, "Ars Poetica"
Lawrence Ferlinghetti, "Constantly Risking Absurdity"

These three poems provide an excellent introduction to poetry. Point out to students that poetry cannot be defined solely in terms of form and that the difficulty of defining poetry is vividly illustrated here: both Moore and MacLeish define poetry in metaphorical terms. Ask students to list from "Poetry" the things that, according to Moore, are not poetry and the things that are. What does Moore mean by saying, "I too dislike it" and adding "one discovers in / it after all, a place for the genuine"? Why must poets rise "above insolence and triviality" to present "imaginary gardens with real toads in them"? Ask your students what "imaginary gardens" and "real toads" mean in the poem.

Next ask them to explain each of the similes and metaphors in "Ars Poetica." In what ways is poetry mute or wordless, "motionless in time"? Each of these similes and metaphors should evoke a picture which in turn evokes a story. Divide the class into three groups and ask them to explain each metaphor or simile and then to invent or recall a story that might explain the image. For example, students might associate the "sleeve-worn stone of casement ledges" with Alfred Noyes' "The Highwayman," or the "empty doorway and a maple leaf" with remembrances of the death of a loved one or the end of a relationship. They might remember the lovers in Robert Browning's "Meeting at Morning" and "Parting at Evening" when reading the "leaning grasses and two lights above the sea." Ask students why MacLeish says that "A poem should be equal to: / Not true" and "should not mean / But be." If poetry evokes all of these feelings, should we even try to explain it? Must we understand the images to enjoy the poem? Will one person respond to the images in the same way as another? What then is the advantage of the metaphor over an explicit statement?

Finally, ask students why Ferlinghetti compares the poet's profession to that of the highwire acrobat. Ask them to list the ways in which the two are similar. Why must the poet be a "super realist"? How does this statement compare to MacLeish's claim that "A poem should not mean / But be"? Ask students to compare Ferlinghetti's statement that the poet must "perceive taut truth" while also capturing beauty to Moore's requirement that the poet present "imaginary gardens with real toads in them." In what way does the poet defy death?

Langston Hughes, "Theme for English B"

You might begin by asking students why being African American makes the assignment to write a theme particularly difficult for the speaker. How are the particular details the speaker uses affected by his racial identity? How does his language—its tone and emphasis—help to define his identity? How highly connotative is the language? Is it angry, defiant, neutral, or angry? You might want to compare Hughes' use of language to define his racial identity with other poets' efforts to do so. Consider the following works for comparison.

Judith Cofer, "Latin Women Pray"
Janet Mirikitani, "Breaking Tradition"
Joy Harjo, "The Woman Hanging from the
        Thirteenth Floor Window"
Garrett Hongo, "The Hongo Store"
Sharon Olds, "On the Subway"

Pat Mora, "Immigrants"
Dwight Okita, "In Response to Executive Order 9066. . ."
Li-Young Lee, "Persimmons"

W. H. Auden, "Musée des Beaux Arts"

The day before discussing this poem, ask one student to get a copy of Breughel's *Fall of Icarus* and another to research the myth of Daedalus and Icarus to expand the brief summary included in the text. · You might remind the students that a major theme in literature is the acquisition of wisdom through suffering and ask them how paintings or other art forms can depict such suffering. If few members of the class have taken art appreciation, you might ask students to bring to class other examples of art that dramatically depict suffering (for example, Michelangelo's *Pieta*, the statue of Laocoon, Picasso's *Guernica*, Rodin's *Gates of Hell*). You might ask the students to share background stories that explain the suffering depicted in the works. Then ask the rest of the class to imagine, based on Auden's theme, what other people were doing while the suffering was endured.

You might also like to ask each student to write an essay using one work of literature in this text to show how a character gained wisdom through suffering.

In order to elicit a more personal response, you might ask students what they were doing when some recent tragedy, natural or man-made, took place and what impact, if any, the tragedy had on them. Did they, like the farmer, simply continue their actions? Did their behavior in any way diminish the significance of the tragedy? Would the outcome of the event have differed in any way if they had become involved? Some students might enjoy writing poems, stories, or plays that show how others gained wisdom through the suffering caused by these tragedies.

Audre Lorde, "The Art of Response"

You might begin a discussion of this poem by asking students to what extent the answer to an open ended question or a subjective question depends on the personality and attitudes of the answerer. Then divide the class into groups of five or six students and ask each group to answer the following:

What question do you believe the people in the poem are answering? Is the meaning of the poem dependent upon our knowledge of the question? Why or why not?

Based on the few details given in the poem, what do you believe to be the personal traits of each of the fifteen responders? What is the significance of each answer? How does your opinion of the responder's personality influence your interpretation of the answer?

If each member of your group could be a responder in the poem, what would your response be? Make responses brief and open-ended like those in the poem.

The wide diversity of answers given to these questions should help students to interpret the poem and should exemplify for them the extent to which poetry can say many things in a concise form.

Ishmael Reed, "beware: do not read this poem"

Ishmael Reed draws the reader into the poem using two very old tricks. First, if you tell a person not to do something, he or she will do it anyway—the title. Next, if you make something exciting enough, that person will want to see what is happening. Why do your students think Reed uses these tricks? What other devices does Reed use? Why does the speaker relate poetry to a mirror? What is Reed saying about the nature of poetry or art? How does art mirror the artist, reader, and society?

Your students might want to discuss other forms of art that mirror society. To what degree do television programs, comics, and graffiti mirror society? How do they do so?

Ray A. Young Bear, "Wadasa Nakamoon, Vietnam Memorial"

The speaker's dilemma is that his song must embody everything that he feels for the Vietnam War and the black rock memorial. The song must show a love for his country yet mixed feelings about America's participation in the war; it must also show the speaker's anger at the senselessness of the war while it honors those who died. Ask your students what other feelings the speaker must incorporate into the song. Then ask them why the speaker expects his song or his art to do so much. What is the social responsibility of art or music? Do concerts, songs, or music of any kind benefit mankind in physical ways? Or is art merely symbolic?

Li-Young Lee, "Persimmons"

This delightful poem suggests many questions about the nature of language. How, for example, can a simple concrete word like persimmons generate such a rich variety of associations? What does the word mean to the speaker? Which is the truer meaning of a word, its dictionary definition or the variety of associations and experience it brings to mind? You might ask your students to write a paper describing the range of experiences and associations brought to mind by a particular concrete word, perhaps another fruit like apple, melon, or tangerine or perhaps a plant like dogwood, oak, or iris. You might use this assignment to practice free writing, or you might wish to assign it for a finished paper.

Another question raised by the poem is the way in which language defines groups, excluding some while including others. How does the teacher use the speaker's confusion of persimmon and precision? Who has a fuller understanding of the word persimmon, the speaker or the teacher? How is language used to define social classes and to exclude people from groups, and how does the poem expose such exclusion? How does the simple word persimmon help to define the speaker's family and culture?

The poem also raises several questions about the nature of art. How is art related to experience? How successful is the poem in making you see the father's painting of the persimmon? How effective does the painting seem? What qualities of persimmons, apparent also in other parts of the poem, does the painting appear to suggest? How could the father have painted the persimmon successfully without seeing it? What, besides the mere appearance of the objects he paints, does the father create in his paintings? How much could the teacher, with a limited experience of persimmons, appreciate the father's painting?

DRAMA

Tina Howe, *Painting Churches*

You might want to begin discussion of this hilarious comedy by asking students to imagine in greater detail the setting of the play. How might the light be handled to give "the room a distinct feeling of unreality"? Of what might this fantastic setting be symbolic? As the scene changes during the course of the play, revealing the progress of the Churches' packing to move, how does the mood of the room change? What do the changes symbolize? What do they suggest about the Churches and about their daughter? In particular, what does the set for the last scene with Mags' covered portrait and the bright red tablecloth in the empty room symbolize? You might ask students to work in groups on these questions. Or you might give students the option of writing on the play's symbolic set.

Each of the three characters is an artist. Even Fanny, who pretends to a practical philistinism, is well informed about art and has produced the rather extraordinary lampshade with the light shining through its portrait of Venice. You might ask students in class discussion, in groups, or in papers to contrast the three characters' attitudes toward art. What part does art play in the life of each? How does each respond to the art of the other? Is Fanny as much of a philistine as her reactions to Gardner's book and Mags' portraits imply? Why does she react so critically to their efforts?

How might her mother's disparagement of her early crayon masterpiece have led Mags to paint portraits? How might her parents' earlier attitudes toward her art lead to Mags' anxiety in the final scene and her incredulous joy at her parents' liking her portrait of them? Finally, Mags' portrait shows Fanny with purple skin and bright orange hair. Why? How could such apparently unreal colors be effective in portraying the couple? How effective is the dialogue itself in giving an impression of the painting?

The Renoir that Fanny recalls is apparently *Dance at Bougival,* which hangs at the Museum of Fine Arts in Boston, though Fanny may have conflated it with *Moulin de la Galette,* which unlike the former painting has a cafe atmosphere and Japanese lanterns. Neither painting features a violinist.

You might want to discuss the dynamics of the Churches' marriage and their relationship to their daughter. Certainly the Churches argue and shout and fight. Fanny constantly disparages Gardner. Why? Why is their marriage happy, even joyful in spite of or even because of this disparagement? Who is dominant in this marriage? It may appear to Mags sometimes that the closeness of her parents almost shuts her out. To what degree do they shut her out, and to what degree is their doing so intentional? Have they in any way neglected her? If so, how? Has she in any way neglected them? If so, how?

Finally, you might ask for students' responses to the ending of the play. What is happening to Gardner? What is the Churches' response to inevitable aging, illness, and death? What does dancing as an art form stress that might be relevant here? What does the Churches' dancing reveal about them here? There is a wonderful episode of the television drama *Northern Exposure* in which Ed gives Ruth Ann a grave site on a high and lonely point in the wilderness for her 80th birthday present. At the end of the program she and Ed literally dance on her grave. If you are familiar with the episode and if some of your students are, you might suggest a paper comparing the endings of the television drama and the play.

CASEBOOK STORIES AND ESSAY

Alice Walker,   "Everyday Use"
                  "Nineteen Fifty-five"
                  "In Search of Our Mothers' Gardens"

You might want to begin this casebook by asking students either in class discussion or in groups to list the pieces that might make up a quilt that Maggie would make. What kinds of materials would she be likely to use? What experiences in her life might be symbolically represented in the quilt? How might her quilt differ from her Aunt Dee's? Could Maggie's mother make a quilt? Why or why not? If she could, what kind of quilt might she make? If she could not, what works of art mentioned in "In Search of Our Mother's Gardens" might she have produced? Similarly, you might ask students to imagine the kinds of experiences that gave rise to Gracie Mae Still's songs. In what kind of place and to what kind of people might she have sung them? Then you might invert the art works, asking what kind of songs Maggie and her mother might sing and what kind of quilt Gracie Mae might make. How does the art of each symbolize her particular experience? How do Aunt Dee's quilt and Gracie Mae's blues songs express the "spirituality" Walker says "is the basis of art"?

You might also want to discuss Maggie's mother and Gracie Mae as matriarchs. How does each serve as protective head of her family? How does each, in spite of difficult circumstances and potential chaos, give order to her life and to the lives of her family without sacrificing spontaneity, warmth, and richness of experience? What does the blunt, direct language of these African-American female narrators say about their values?

Additional topics for research papers on Walker might include the following:

Using research on African-American women as matriarchs, analyze the matriarchal qualities of Walker's women. You might also wish to include Granny from Bambara's "Blues Ain't No Mockin Bird."

Using research on the nature and origin of the blues, analyze Gracie Mae's music.

After researching the housing of rural Southern African Americans, discuss the nature of the cabins Maggie, Gracie Mae, and Granny live in.

Using research on rural Southern African-American dialect, analyze the speech of Walker's women. What does their style of speech reveal about their values?

Research the juke joints Gracie Mae Still might have sung in.

QUEST

ESSAYS

Plato, Allegory of the Cave

This famous allegory from *The Republic* expresses the essence of Plato's philosophy, both his epistemology, or theory of knowledge, and his metaphysics, or theory of the nature of reality. Plato's metaphysics hold that reality adheres neither in the ever-changing physical world nor in the minds of men, but in a world of unchanging forms independent of both. Physical objects and ideas in the minds of people are, to use the metaphor of the cave allegory, mere shadows of the forms, mere ghostly images of reality. An oak tree is merely a pale imitation of the form oak tree, and our ideas of love are merely pale echoes of the noble form love. All forms are derived from the ultimate form, the Good. Moreover, for human beings to attain knowledge of the forms, and particularly to attain knowledge of the Good, they must, through an extraordinary act of will, reject the conventional wisdom and apply careful study and disciplined reasoning to all of their ideas. The true philosopher or lover of wisdom, then, must be willing critically to examine all his or her most cherished assumptions, for "The unexamined life is not worth living."

In Plato's allegory, then, the cave represents the mentally dark world in which most men dwell, the men in the cave represent the masses of mankind, and the sun represents the ultimate form, the Good. Few men have the strength of character to question the conventional wisdom and their cherished assumptions; hence few attain knowledge beyond mere shadows. Those who do attain such knowledge are unlikely to want to return to the world of mere shadows in order to lead and teach the reluctant, ignorant masses. After all, Socrates attempted to instruct the people of Athens and was put to death for his trouble. Hence, we are often forced to choose as leaders, people as ignorant as ourselves because the enlightened refuse to rule.

Platonic realism offers an attractive philosophical middleground between the materialism of some sophists, in which the physical world is seen as ultimate reality, and the idealism of others, where the perceptions and ideas of men are seen as ultimate reality. These two philosophies, which dominated fourth century Athens, dominate our own culture. Plato solves the philosophical dilemma of choosing between materialism, which offers no sense of permanence or direction and no basis for a universal ethics governing human conduct, and idealism, which by emphasizing the perceptions of individual people, can degenerate, and historically often has degenerated, into solipsism.

In a discussion of Plato's seminal allegory, several questions might get students involved. You might begin by searching out the sources of their judgments, asking them to make simple judgments about several popular songs or television shows. What is the worst show on television or the worst song? Why? By comparison to what standard is it worst? Do they have an ideal show or song in mind or do they just compare it to others of its kind?

You might also want to examine the ethical and political implications of Plato's allegory. Why are men so reluctant to question conventional wisdom? What is the result of their failure to do so? What happens to those who do so? You might suggest that students consider Thoreau's "Civil Disobedience," King's "I Have a Dream," and Vonnegut's "Harrison Bergeron" in responding to these questions. You might go on to ask whether religions must suppress questioning, considering Jesus' Sermon on the Mount, Jen's "The Water-Faucet Vision," and Roth's "The Conversion of the Jews."

Finally, you might want to consider to what degree Plato's suggestion that truly wise men often choose not to rule applies to contemporary American politics. To what degree can democracy coexist with a philosopher-politician? Or to what degree is the term philosopher-politician a contradiction?

Matthew 5: from The Sermon on the Mount

Just as the analogy of the cave perhaps best exemplifies Plato's metaphysics, the Sermon on the Mount in Matthew 5–7 perhaps best summarizes the ethical component of Christ's teaching. It may be seen as elaborating the second of the two great commandments Christ used to sum up the Jewish law: love God and love your neighbor. As Christ maintains in saying he has come to fulfill the law rather than to abolish it, his ethics is consistent with Old Testament tradition, which strongly emphasizes taking care of the helpless. You might want to compare Matthew 5 and the law as expounded in the ten commandments (Exodus 20) and in Leviticus 19. To what degree does Jesus' sermon fulfill, extend, and deepen the law?

In spite of its consistency with tradition, Christ's Sermon so extends that tradition as to be almost radically revolutionary. Among the more revolutionary teachings of Jesus are his restrictions on divorce, his profound sympathy for the oppressed, and his essential pacifism in the face of violence. In forbidding men to divorce women except for adultery, does Jesus worsen or improve the condition of women? Would strict adherence to his teaching today help women? Would it help children?

Christ teaches not just unselfishness, but absolute denial of the self. Is it possible for flawed human beings consistently to love their enemies? How is it possible for Christ's followers to do so? How might one feel if one denied oneself as He teaches? To what degree is the absolute denial of self a continuing process rather than an accomplished state?

What would happen if you completely followed Christ's advice to turn the other cheek? What would happen if everyone did? Whom, if anyone, do you know that has consistently turned the other cheek? What if our government and laws operated according to the principles of the Sermon on the Mount? To what degree was the passive disobedience of Martin Luther King, Jr. and the civil rights movement influenced by Jesus' teachings? The civil rights movement did resist authority. Did the movement follow the spirit of Christ's teachings? Was the movement simply a selfish effort at self-liberation or was it more? To what degree should one resist aggression that threatens great numbers with harm? How can one do so and still follow Christ's teachings? Should a follower of Christ have resisted the holocaust, Stalin's oppression in the Soviet Union, apartheid in South Africa, and Serbian aggression in Bosnia?

Perhaps the most revolutionary of Christ's teachings in the Sermon on the Mount is the idea that goodness is a condition or state of being rather than a composite of "good" acts. To what degree is it possible to avoid anger and lust? Did Christ always avoid them? Are such feelings always and completely to be avoided? To what degree do you consider it desirable to avoid them? How might modern psychiatry respond to Christ's teachings on lust and anger?

William Golding, "Thinking As a Hobby"

This classification essay offers an effective way to teach argumentation and critical thinking. After students have read the essay, you might ask them to bring to class advertisements, articles, accounts of comments from radio and television (talk shows are especially rich sources) that exemplify fallacies typical of grade three thinking. Ask them to share their examples with the rest of the class and to explain why they consider their examples to be grade three thinking.

Ask them to classify the characters from some of their favorite television shows according to Golding's three levels of thinking. The paucity of grade one examples might be revealing. You might give the same assignment using world leaders.

Other possibilities for writing topics might include asking students to

•list and explain the qualities and/or abilities that a person must have to be considered a grade one (or three) thinker;

•describe the attributes of a person whom they would consider to be truly educated;

•or describe a real person whom they believe to be a grade one thinker.

Because Golding's essay is an example of a well-organized longer essay with skillful transitions, you might like to use it to show students that longer essays often have subthesis statements that control the individual parts and make the essay clearer to the reader. The essay also illustrates the value of allusions, using the statue of Rodin's *Thinker* as the symbol of a grade one thinker and the *Venus de Milo* to symbolize the complex emotion of love. Ask students what allusions might be used to add depth to essays they are working on and remind them that if the reader does not recognize the allusion, it adds nothing to the content. You might also like to remind them of sources such as the *Oxford Companion to American Literature* and the other Oxford Companions as sources for information about allusions that they do not recognize.

FICTION

William Faulkner, "Barn Burning"

You might begin a discussion of this story by asking students about family goals and ambitions: What are some of the things you and your family have decided are important to you as a family unit? What are your individual goals? Have any of these goals ever come in conflict with those of the other members of your family? If so, which goals and in what way? Ask students what they would do if someone in the family tried to change them, if fathers or mothers tried to make them into carbon copies of themselves as the father does in "Barn Burning"? To what extent is family support necessary in achieving individual goals?

Speculate on what kind of life Colonel Sartoris Snopes will pursue. What is his goal, his quest? Will he be able to reach it? What happens to the rest of the family if one member repudiates what the family seems to represent? You might take a similar approach to the following stories in this unit: "Raymond's Run," "The Conversion of the Jews," and "The Water-Faucet Vision."

Arthur C. Clarke, "The Star"

The quest story in "The Star" is an ironic one: the narrator, an astronomer and a Jesuit priest who has long found comfort in his faith, is seeking not a religious answer but a scientific one. In his quest for scientific knowledge, he finds an answer that challenges his faith. His moral dilemma is obvious in his question "how could that [the destruction of a beautiful and happy civilization] be reconciled with the mercy of God?" You might first ask the students how he answers this question. Then ask them, why, if he has accepted this answer, he is still so deeply disturbed. How would your students answer his questions?

You can help students discover another facet of the irony by asking them to tell the myth of the Phoenix and to explain the irony of Phoenix Nebula as a name for the star system being explored. You might also point out to the students that some critics describe the ironic ending of "The Star" as a "cheap shot" and ask them to support or attack this point of view.

Another topic for possible essays would be to ask students to compare the moral dilemma faced by this Jesuit with that faced by the inhabitants of Omelas in LeGuin's story. You might also ask them to classify the moral dilemmas people today face or to suggest ways to cope with these dilemmas.

The Jesuit priest says, "Everything that they wished to preserve, all the fruit of their genius, they brought here to this distant world in the days before the end, hoping that some other race would find it and that they would not be utterly forgotten." Ask students to write an essay on the following topic: "If you were given the task of selecting what

99

was to be preserved to let future generations or worlds know about our civilization, what would you select? Why? Would you select only the best or would you try to represent all aspects of our culture?"

The form of science fiction represented by this selection should be familiar to most students today, especially because of the Lucas and Spielberg films and the *Star Trek* television series and movies. If the students in your class are familiar with these examples of science fiction or with other works of fantasy, they might enjoy combining their favorite works with this story. For example, they might write a proposal for an episode of *Star Trek* (original, *Next Generation*, or *Deep Space Nine*) in which this Jesuit is a character.

Philip Roth, "The Conversion of the Jews"

After working through the questions in the text, you might want to ask students to apply the story's theme to themselves, perhaps sharing their experience in groups. When have adults suppressed their curiosity about issues important to them? How have your students responded? How desirable is it to take an inherited faith without question? How does one develop one's personal faith?

Toni Cade Bambara, "Raymond's Run"

Hazel Parker is a very practical, no-nonsense person. Ask students to find examples of her no-nonsense attitudes. However, just before she begins a race, she has a dream in which she soars as high as the sky. Ask the students to freewrite for about fifteen minutes on the last daydream they had. If they say they never daydream, have them write about a night dream. Did the dream turn out to be significant? If so, why? Someone once said that if you can picture something, you can accomplish it. For example, in a baseball or softball game, if you can picture hitting the ball over the fence, then you can hit it there. Do you believe this claim? Why or why not?

Gish Jen, "The Water-Faucet Vision"

You might want to begin by discussing Callie's family. Why do her parents fight so violently? How does the family's immigrant status affect their fighting? Why do they try to hide their fighting from the children by speaking in their native Shanghaiese? How effective are their efforts? Based on your students' experiences, how effective are most parents' efforts to hide their fighting?

You might next want to ask how her parents' fights affect Callie and her quest. What is she seeking? Why? Everyone calls it a miracle that Callie's mother does not suffer serious injury when she falls from the window, but Callie wants a different kind of miracle. What kind of miracle is she seeking? Compare her search for a miracle to the prayers of the couple who sublet her apartment. What have the couple's prayers and Callie's quest for a miracle in common? Why do the malachite beads mean so much to her and how do they relate to her quest?

Callie's vision, referred to in the title, is the climax of the story. What is climactic about it? The vision is hilarious to Callie's sister, Mona, and Callie's classmates. How does Callie feel about their laughing at her? Do your students find the vision funny? Why or why not? When have they been mocked for their religious or moral stances? How does the narrator's attitude toward the incident differ from the immediate childhood reaction she recalls? What does the difference in attitude toward the vision reveal about how Callie's religion has changed? Does this change represent growth or loss? Why?

POETRY

Psalm 8

Here the psalmist becomes aware of his own smallness and that of mankind as he ponders the vastness and glories of the heavens. You might begin by asking your students when they have experienced a similar sense of the vastness of the universe. Physicist Stephen W. Hawking has said that the sheer vastness of the universe causes him to doubt the reality of a personal God. You might ask your students to respond to his skepticism. Must the size of the universe and relative insignificance of humanity preclude a creator's taking a personal interest in such minutiae of creation as each of the roughly five billion human beings on earth? Why or why not?

This psalm is traditionally attributed to David. How does the psalm suggest his true greatness? How common is it for rulers and politicians humbly to recognize a power greater than their own? The psalmist declares that God gave people dominion over all the earth and every living thing. What responsibilities does this dominion entail? How effectively have people carried out these responsibilities?

John Donne, "Batter My Heart"

You might want to ask students to consider what kind of experience might have led to such an anguished sonnet. Have they ever experienced similar anguish or a similar sense of alienation from God? A similar desire for God's overwhelming power to transform them? What led to that experience? To what degree is the kind of anguish Donne feels part of a genuine quest for God? Are there Biblical antecedents for such anguish?

John Milton, Sonnet 16: "When I Consider"

In the days of the Roman Republic, the four supreme virtues were pietas, duty or dutiful conduct toward father, country, and the gods; simplicitas, plainness and honesty; gravitas, seriousness; and virtus, manliness or physical courage. In *The Divine Comedy*, Dante pays tribute to the Four Cardinal Virtues of the Christian church: Prudence, Justice, Fortitude, and Temperance. Milton extols Patience as a virtue. Have the students debate what they feel are the four "perfect" virtues. They can divide into four groups with each group choosing one virtue. To prevent repetition, ask the groups to select two or have them announce their choice after five minutes. At the end of the alloted time, the groups will present and argue for the virtue they have selected.

Phillis Wheatley, "On Being Brought from Africa to America"

Why does Wheatley seem to be on the defensive in her poem? Why does she want people to know that she can also be a part of the "angelic train"?

William Blake,   "The Lamb"
"The Tyger"

Taken together, the two poems ask: Did the same God who made the lamb also make the tiger? How can good and evil, innocence and brutality, co-exist? You might ask students why Blake's speaker asks such questions. Then you might ask them to answer the question.

After discussing the questions in Blake's poems, you might ask students to form groups with one task: come up with an equally important, timeless question such as the one Blake posed. Discuss as a group. Then have students write about which is the most important question and why.

William Wordsworth, "My Heart Leaps Up" "It Is a Beauteous Evening"

In discussing "It Is a Beauteous Evening," ask students to examine this line: "God being with thee when we know it not." What evidence is there that God is with the child even though she is unaware of His presence? Both of Wordsworth's poems imply that children are closer to God than adults. Do you agree? Why or why not?

Ask the students to write an essay that discusses what makes their hearts leap up. What are they in awe of?

Alfred, Lord Tennyson, "Ulysses"

You might begin by discussing what Ulysses seeks. What obstacles has he faced? Will his quest ever end? If so, when? If not, why not? What qualities of character does he reveal? Do your students find him admirable? Next you might ask students to compare Ulysses' quest with the quests of others who persevere in spite of obstacles: perhaps Elisa in Steinbeck's "The Chrysanthemums," Ozzie in Roth's "The Conversion of the Jews," Agueros in "Halfway to Dick and Jane," and Milton in "When I consider how my light is spent." You might also ask your students to compare Ulysses' quest to their own quests. What are their most important personal goals? What obstacles might make achieving their goals difficult? How much control do they have over their own quests? What goals do they expect to pursue throughout their lives?

Ulysses says, "that which we are, we are." Ask students to explain what or who they are in terms of what they seek, of their personal quests.

Gerard Manley Hopkins, "God's Grandeur" "Pied Beauty"

You might ask your students how fitting or satisfying these poems seem as responses to Donne's anguished sonnet. In what kinds of things does Hopkins see the

103

greatness, power, and love of God? What does Hopkins see as most satisfying in God's world? How do his sonnets compare to Psalm 8? If, as Hopkins maintains, "the world is charged with the grandeur of God," if God's power is imminent in the world, what other works in the text reveal a sense of that imminent power? Why, if God's grandeur is apparent in the world, do many of us fail to perceive it? To what degree have those forces that prevent our seeing God in the world increased since Hopkins' day? Has man attempted to destroy God's grandeur? If so, in what ways? Is this destruction deliberate? What can be done to preserve the beauty of nature?

William Butler Yeats,　　"The Second Coming" "Sailing to Byzantium"

Some understanding of Yeats' elaborate cosmology and cyclical theory of history can illuminate these poems. The cosmology holds that all things, including human personality and historical periods, represent varied mixes of two opposed forces: the primary is certain, dogmatic, and intolerant, tending toward the autocratic and brutal; the antithetical is tolerant and democratic, tending toward the relativistic, solipsistic, and chaotic.

History consists of cycles lasting roughly 2000 years. Each cycle begins with a violent intrusion of the divine into human affairs, an intrusion that reverses the dominant direction of the preceding cycle. The birth of Christ 2000 years ago introduced antithetical dominance at the beginning of a new cycle. For about 1000 years, the antithetical force, completely dominant at first, became less and less powerful until, about 1000 A.D., it was completely dominated by the primary force. Since that time, the antithetical force has been ascending in power. In our time, as in Christ's, the antithetical is dominant. We are due, then, according to Yeats' theory, a powerful intrusion of the divine to bring about once again the dominance of the primary and to initiate another 2000 year cycle of human history.

For Yeats, Byzantium in about 1000 A.D., when the primary force was dominant, represented the ultimate paradise for any artist. Byzantine civilization was unified in its all-consuming worship of God the Father and Jesus Christ, his son. Every aspect of life was permeated with religious vision. Art, in particular, served an exclusively religious function. As the primary means of religious education, works of art functioned as parts of the great work of art, the cathedral. Each work contributed to the vast harmony of the massive whole, which was dominated by the great dome depicting Christ Pantocrator, Christ as ruler of the universe. All was done for the glory of God.

Of Byzantine civilization, Yeats said in *A Vision*:

> I think that in early Byzantium, maybe never before or since in recorded history, religious, aesthetic, and practical life were one, that architects and artificers—though not, it may be, poets, for language had been the instrument of controversy and must have grown abstract—spoke to the multitude and the few alike. The painter, the mosaic worker, the worker in gold and silver, the illuminator of sacred books, were almost impersonal, almost perhaps without the consciousness of individual design, absorbed in their subject matter and that the vision of a whole people. They could copy out of old Gospel books those pictures that seemed as sacred as the text, and yet weave all into a vast design, the work of many that seemed the work of one, that made building, picture, pattern, metal-work, of rail and lamp, seem but a single image. (280)

"Sailing to Byzantium" focuses on the contrast between the chaos of Ireland and the supreme cultural unity of Byzantium where the artist, intensely absorbed in his art, became a part of a larger whole, of the fervid religious vision of his people that gave the whole of life coherence and purpose.

You might want to read the passage from *A Vision* to your students, then ask what conditions in Ireland might have led Yeats to aspire to be simultaneously a work of art and an artist in Byzantium. Why would he want to be a work of art that produced art? Why would he choose to be a bird? Why an artificial rather than a living bird? Why sing about the conditions he has left?

Ask your students if they have experienced a similar desire for a world that is more coherent and organized, less diverse and chaotic. If so, when? How would they envision their escape to such a world?

In discussing "The Second Coming," you might want to ask your students how they respond to the assertion that "Things fall apart." What feeling does the first section of Yeats' poem evoke in them? Do they ever feel that their own personal world is falling apart, that chaos is taking over? Do they ever think that society is falling apart? What makes them feel that the world is chaotic? How do they respond to this feeling? You might ask whether any of your students have read Chinua Achebe's *Things Fall Apart*. If so, you might have them comment on the appropriateness of Achebe's allusion to Yeats' poem in his title.

In discussing the sources of Yeats' beast you might want to have your students read Revelation 13. Does this beast seem to them a demonic force? Why or why not? How does the theme of Yeats' "The Second Coming" relate to that of Revelation? How does Yeats react to the "revelation" he envisions? How does he seem to feel about the beast? How do your students respond emotionally to the beast? In what sense(s) might it be an emotionally satisfying response to the sense of impending chaos in the first section of the poem? Have your students ever dreamed of God or another mighty force intruding on the world to restore its order? How satisfying was the dream?

Yeats, W. B. *A Vision.* New York: Macmillan, 1937.

Robert Frost,   "After Apple-Picking"
"Birches"
"Directive"

These three poems by Robert Frost, all describing ways to rise above the cares of life, reveal a quite different aspect of his writing from that in the Frost casebook. Frost clearly indicates that the problems hinted at in the poems are not so extreme that they would cause him to want to leave Earth permanently: In both "After Apple-Picking" and "Birches," he emphasizes going toward, not to, heaven.

"After Apple-Picking" has been frequently explicated and is discussed in the essays in the Casebook on Robert Frost as well as in the *Voices and Visions* videotape on Frost. The symbols in the poem have been variously interpreted, and students usually find them fairly easy. To illustrate the lack of rigidity in literary interpretation, you might divide the class into several groups and ask each group to devise a coherent interpretation that explains each of the symbols in Question for Discussion number 2 before sharing the video tape or other interpretations with them.

You might ask them if they see a parallel between "looking through a pane of glass" and "now we see through a glass darkly" (I Corinthians 13:12) and if so, ask them to explain the implications of the reference. Also ask them to explain and interpret the difference between the woodchuck's "Long sleep" and "just some human sleep."

While "After Apple-Picking" is often interpreted as representing the end of a career or of a life, "Birches" is usually seen as describing a brief respite from the smaller problems of life. It also includes some of Frost's most vivid metaphors and similes. One good way to help students interpret the poem and understand Frost's artistry might be to have them list and explain each metaphorical device. Ask them which metaphors or similes primarily help the reader envision the scene ("girls on hands and knees" drying their hair, heaps of broken glass, etc.) and which extend and enrich the meaning of the poem as well (the boy climbing the birch trees, the pathless wood). Why does Frost personify Truth?

Students usually find "Directive" the most difficult of the three poems to interpret. You might develop Question 1 by asking students if they believe that life is simpler in one time or place than in another. For example, was life simpler in ancient Egypt? During the Crusades? During the American Civil War? If so, how? If not, why? What can individuals do to simplify their lives? Why would they want simpler lives? If some students have read Thoreau's *Walden,* ask them to share with the class his reasons for and methods of simplifying his life.

You might ask students to write an essay contrasting this peaceful search to "be whole again beyond confusion," which comes from drinking the waters "too lofty and original to rage," with Mrs. Turpin's vision in O'Connor's "Revelation," a vision which is violently forced upon her. Are the results of her vision any less valid because unsought?

Other possibilities for comparison and contrast might be to contrast the tone, view of life, or metaphorical devices (or even one metaphorical device such as personification) in one of these poems with that of one poem in the Casebook on Robert Frost.

T. S. Eliot, "The Love Song of J. Alfred Prufrock"

Students' first impulse may be to laugh at this ineffectual man who seeks more out of life than the ordinary, who perceives the heroic and the mythic but is afraid to "go for it." However, most students will empathize with Prufrock when they understand him. In order to help them reach this level of understanding, you might lead them through the following questions:

Do you always know what your goals are or do you, like Prufrock, make "a hundred indecisions" followed by "a hundred visions and revisions"? Why do you not always know exactly what you want? Is some indecision inevitable?

Do you sometimes, like Prufrock, hesitate to act in ways that might help you to achieve your goals? Why does Prufrock fail to act? Why do you? What does Prufrock's question "Do I dare / Disturb the universe?" imply about his failure to act and about his opinion of his role in the universe? What does he seem to fear most, in fact, to fear so much that he is willing to settle for spitting out "the butt-ends of [his] days and ways" rather than act? Have you ever failed to act for a similar reason? If so, what was your reason?

Prufrock says that he is not Lord Hamlet but only an "attendant lord." Does his not being the hero or the star excuse him from action? Does your knowledge that you may not always be the leader in an action mean that you need not act?

Is Prufrock's goal as expressed in this poem so lofty as to be unattainable? Is his inaction in this instance probably typical of his whole life? Does your behavior as you seek your day-to-day goals reflect or set a pattern for your actions as you pursue your larger goals?

Does your knowledge that Prufrock sees both the larger possibilities and the higher goals, that he has "heard the mermaids singing" yet says "I do not think that they will sing to me," make him seem more or less tragic to you? Why?

Robert Burns in "To a Louse" asks that we be granted the power to see ourselves as others see. Does Prufrock see himself as others see him? Does this ability or inability help or hinder him? Do you believe that you see yourself as others see you? Does this knowledge or lack of knowledge encourage you to act or discourage you from acting?

This poem is often said to describe the condition of people in the twentieth century. Do you believe our world is peopled by Prufrocks? Why or why not? Can you give examples of modern Prufrocks, either real or fictional? Do we all have some of Prufrock's attributes?

You might like to conclude the discussion of "The Love Song of J. Alfred Prufrock" by reminding students that, unlike Prufrock, Eliot acted on his beliefs and goals, changing his citizenship from the United States to Britain as a protest against the United States' late entry in World War I and becoming a devout member of the Anglican Church.

Langston Hughes, "Harlem"

Ask the students to freewrite for twenty minutes on a dream that did not materialize. Then, without divulging the dream, ask them to tell how it felt to know that the dream did not come true. Did they have some of the same feelings as Hughes has? Ask them to use vivid words and phrases to describe the feelings. At this point the feelings are more important than the dream.

Galway Kinnell, "Saint Francis and the Sow"

In reading this poem, students may find strange the idea of blessing an animal. You might want to begin with some background on St. Francis. An early 13th century monk, Francis of Assisi rejected the wealth of the Church and sought in poverty to follow entirely the way of the gospel, subjecting all things to Christ. He loved all that God had created and felt a particular love for animals.

You might want to discuss the word "self-blessing." What does Kinnell appear to mean by it? How is it possible for a thing or even a person to bless itself? How can the "curl of the [sow's] tail" be "spiritual"? In what sense can the sow be "perfect" in her "loveliness"? In what sense can all beings be regarded as blessed? Compare Psalm 8 and The Sermon on the Mount. How might the requirements of Jesus' Sermon apply to human treatment of animals?

John Lennon and Paul McCartney, "Eleanor Rigby"

If possible, bring a tape of this song to class so that the students who are unfamiliar with it may hear the music along with reading the poem. You might point out to your students that poems set to music are much easier to remember, perhaps because they hear or sing the songs over and over whereas they usually read a poem only once or twice.

An interesting class exercise would be to ask a group of students in the class to write and enact a conversation among Eleanor Rigby, Father McKenzie, and J. Alfred

Prufrock. Then ask the class to write an essay on Suggestion 2 or a comparison of the causes and/or effects of the loneliness of these three people.

Judith Ortiz Cofer, "Latin Women Pray"

Cofer, a Puerto Rican American, often writes of the dual role that women and diverse other groups must play in society. Ask each student to imagine God in his or her own image, then to think of the paradox of the "Anglo God" and the Latin prayers. Would God's being of another race bother your students? In Atlanta, a church called Church of the Black Madonna makes a point of presenting all Biblical characters as African American. Ask students why they think the church does so. What point is Cofer making about institutional religion? Why does she use Latin women?

How important is language in defining ethnic groups? Should English be the official language of the United States? Why was the question of whether it should be the official language on the ballot in some states? Is it fair to ask people of different backgrounds to learn how to speak English? Why cannot ethnic groups have their own communities, their own schools, their own institutions, and their own language? What is the role of language in man's search for meaning in life?

DRAMA

Sophocles, *Oedipus the King*

One activity that students would probably enjoy because it gets everyone involved is a trial. First, have the students choose a judge, twelve members of the jury, the prosecuter, and a defense lawyer. Other students can serve as witnesses for the prosecution and witnesses for the defenses. Charges include killing his father, marrying his mother, and causing the plague on Thebes. The prosecutor and defense attorney can present opening statements, call witnesses, and summarize their cases. Have the jury members put a pebble in one jar for a guilty verdict and in another for an innocent verdict as juries did in Sophocles' Athens. The jury verdict in Athens did not have to be unanimous, so a simple majority will decide the case. The jury foreman might want to review the logic behind the verdict. The rest of the class might critique the trial.

Discuss the role of Tiresias. Ask if a person similar to this soothsayer exists today. For example, some people believe in fortune tellers, palm readers, Tarot card readers, and/or mediums. Others use roots, voodoo, and medicine men to try to control the future. How much faith should people have in these people or devices? What is the difference between a priest or prophet and a soothsayer or fortune teller? Is humanity presumptuous in attempting to know the future? Should Oedipus have discontinued his search for the truth? Why or why not? If he should have discontinued his search, at what point should he have done so? What efforts to find out the future would your students consider unacceptable or immoral? What problems might arise from their knowing the future?

Marsha Norman, *Traveler in the Dark*

Norman's play raises many questions about what people search for. Begin by asking what each character's quest is. For example, is Stephen an average twelve-year-old boy who is asking the average questions that most boys his age might ask? List some of the questions he asks. What about Sam? In the beginning he thinks his religious search is over: he has rejected God in favor of what he thinks is the truth. At the end, is his search over?

You might use Suggestions 2 or 3 as a basis for group work, either assigning to each group one quotation or one character or asking each group to discuss all of the quotations or all of the characters.

Students might choose as an essay topic to write a letter to a parent, asking him or her all the questions that have never been asked in person.

CASEBOOK STORIES AND ESSAY

Flannery O'Connor, "A Good Man Is Hard to Find"
"Revelation"
"The Catholic Novelist in the Protestant South"

This casebook is probably the most challenging of those included in this text. In particular, O'Connor's essay may be difficult for most students. Therefore, you may want to lead class discussion on the major ideas in the essay before asking students to apply them to the stories. On the other hand, because students usually enjoy and respond well to these stories, you might prefer to stimulate interest by starting with the stories and saving the more difficult essay until last.

O'Connor's comments in her letters published in her *Collected Works* (New York: Library of America, 1988) offer a rich and fascinating source of information about her opinions of literature, literary interpretation, and religion. Several of the letters shed light on the stories.

Because "A Good Man Is Hard to Find" and "Revelation" are set in the segregated South of the 1950s, some of the language and content may be offensive to some students. However, class discussion of the situations portrayed in the stories can lead to stimulating and enlightening exchanges. Help the students to understand the context of the stories by examining the prejudice and stereotyping exhibited in the grandmother's comment about the "pickaninny" and in Mrs. Turpin's attitudes toward "white trash" and blacks. If you have older students or students who have heard stories of the 1950s and 1960s, they can help other students to comprehend the effects of such attitudes on individuals living then. Then ask students precisely how these attitudes have changed and whether any of the attitudes still affect people and situations today.

You might also point out to students that neither the grandmother nor Mrs. Turpin fits the archetypal pattern of the questor, that is, neither goes out to seek the Holy Grail like Sir Galahad or the traveler in Frost's "Directive" or to search for truth like Ozzie in "The Conversion of the Jews." However, each finds an answer which changes her vision of life. You might ask students to give Biblical, mythical, or literary examples of people who went on quests. Or ask them to share their own experiences of occasions which exemplified less the advice "Seek and ye shall find" than the sudden and unexpected thrusting of insight (knowledge, inspiration, greatness) upon them.

Obviously the O'Connor stories are strongly informed by her Catholic religion. You might ask the students whether the stories have meaning outside the context of Catholicism or Christianity. You might share with students O'Connor's claim to have no interest in abnormal psychology.

Ask students what O'Connor's conception of a whole person is; then ask them to give their definitions of a whole person. Why do some modern philosophers and theologians describe people today as fragmented? Students who are interested in this subject might be guided to some of the stories and novels of D. H. Lawrence.

When students analyze the stories, basing their interpretations partially on the Muller essay, they may need help in differentiating between the Gothic and the Grotesque. Divide the class into two groups and ask one group to prepare a complete definition of Gothic and the other to prepare a similar definition of Grotesque. Then ask them why and how O'Connor's stories have elements of both.

Additional essay topics for documented essays include the following:

Use the selections in the casebook to explain O'Connor's concept of evil.

According to Muller, the violent landscapes of O'Connor's stories are a reflection of a violent world. Explain and illustrate O'Connor's description of characters and of their world to foreshadow significant events and to reflect the moral condition of the characters.

Use the short stories and the Muller essay to explain O'Connor's unusual combination of the comic and the violent.